`MW00906772`

DICTIONARY

A B C D E F G H I J K L M N O P Q R S T U V W X Y Z

www.dk.com

LONDON, NEW YORK, MUNICH,
MELBOURNE, and DELHI

First American Edition, 1997

Published in the United States by
DK Publishing, Inc.
375 Hudson Street
New York, New York 10014

Published in Great Britain by Dorling Kindersley Limited.

This edition revised by Dorling Kindersley, 2002.

ISBN 0-7894-8502-8

02 03 04 05 10 9 8 7 6 5 4 3 2

Printed and bound in Spain by Artes Gráficas Toledo, S.A.U.
D.L. TO: 249-2002

See our complete product line at www.dk.com

List of abbreviations

a(s)	adjective(s)	fem	feminine	phot	photography
abbr	abbreviation	fig	figurative(ly)	phr v(s)	phrasal verb(s)
adv(s)	adverb(s)	fml	formal	pl	plural
anat	anatomy	geog	geography	polit	politics
ar	archaic	geol	geology	poss	possessive
arch	architecture	geom	geometry	pp	past participle
astron	astronomy	Ger	German	prep	preposition
Aust	Australian	Gk	Greek	pron(s)	pronoun(s)
aut	cars, motoring	gram	grammar	pr p	present participle
aux	auxiliary	her	heraldry	psyc	psychology
avia	aviation	hist	historical	pt	past tense
bio	biology	hort	horticulture	rad	radio
bot	botany	idm	idiom	reflex	reflexive
Brit	British	interj	interjection	Scot	Scottish
cap	capital (initial)	interrog	interrogative	sing	singular
chem	chemistry	It	Italian	sl	slang
coll	colloquial	Lat	Latin	Sp	Spanish
comm	commerce	leg	legal	sup	superlative
comp	comparative	ling	linguistics	telecom	telecommunications
comput	computers	lit	literary	[TM]	Trademark
conj	conjunction	masc	masculine	TV	television
dated	old-fashioned	math	mathematics	US	United States
dem	demonstrative	mech	mechanics	usu	usually
det(s)	determiner(s)	med	medicine	v(s)	verb(s)
dram	drama, theater	met	meteorology		
eccl	ecclesiastical	mil	military		
econ	economics	mus	music		
e.g.	for example	myth	mythology		
elec	electrical, electronics	n(s)	noun(s)		
esp	especially	naut	nautical		

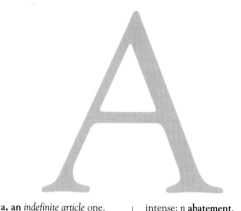

a, an *indefinite article* one.

A1 *a* first-rate.

AA *abbr* Alcoholics Anonymous.

aardvark *n* S African ant-eating mammal.

AB *abbr* Bachelor of Arts.

aback *adv* **be taken aback** be startled.

abacus *n* counting frame with beads strung on parallel wires; *pl* **abacuses**.

abaft *adv, prep* at or toward the stern of ship; behind.

abalone *n* mollusk; shell lined with mother-of-pearl.

abandon *v* **1** desert; forsake **2** give up altogether; *ns* **abandon, -ment** freedom from inhibition; *a* **-ed 1** deserted **2** unrestrained; immoral.

abase *v* humiliate; *n* **abasement**.

abashed *a* ashamed; embarrassed; *n* **abashment**.

abate *v* make or become less intense; *n* **abatement**.

abattoir *n* slaughterhouse.

abbess *n* head of convent or nunnery.

abbey *n* **1** dwelling place of a community of monks or nuns **2** church formerly attached to such a building.

abbot *n* head of abbey or monastery.

abbreviate *v* shorten; *n* **abbreviation**.

ABC[1] *n* **1** the alphabet as learned by children **2** basic facts of a subject.

ABC[2] *abbr* American Broadcasting Company.

abdicate *v* give up (power, position, responsibility); *n* **abdication**.

abdomen *n* belly; *a* **abdominal**.

abduct *v* carry off unlawfully, kidnap; *n* **abduction**.

abeam *adv* at right angle to the length of ship or aircraft.

aberration *n* wandering from natural or fixed course;

mental disorder; *a* **aberrant**.

abet *v* help or take part in (offense); *n* **abettor**.

abeyance *n* temporary suspension.

abhor *v* detest, loathe; *a* **abhorrent**; *n* **abhorrence**.

abide *v* **1** tolerate; endure **2** dwell; remain (*pt, pp* **abode** or **abided**); **abide by** be faithful to; *a* **abiding** lasting.

ability *n* power to do something; skill.

abject *a* miserable, cast down, servile; *adv* **abjectly**; *n* **abjectness**.

abjure *v* renounce on oath; *ns* **abjurer, abjuration**.

ablate *v* remove; vaporize; *n* **ablation** surgical removal.

ablaut *n ling* systematic vowel mutation (e.g., in verb forms *sing, sang, sung*).

ablaze *a* **1** burning fiercely **2** very bright.

able *a* having the power or skill to do a thing; clever; talented; *adv* **ably**; *n* **ability**.

able-bodied *a* strong and fit.

able(-bodied) seaman *n* ordinary trained seaman.

ablution *n* ceremonial washing; **perform one's ablutions** wash oneself.

ABM *abbr* antiballistic missile.

abnegate *v* deny onself; renounce; *n* **abnegation**.

abnormal *a* out of ordinary; deviating from normal; *adv* **-ly**; *n* **-ity**.

aboard *adv* in or on ship, train, airplane, etc.

abode *n* home; dwelling place;

a
b
c
d
e
f
g
h
i
j
k
l
m
n
o
p
q
r
s
t
u
v
w
x
y
z

A

B C D E F G H I J K L M N O P Q R S T U V W X Y Z

pt, pp of **abide.**

abolish *v* do away with, wipe out; *ns* **abolition; abolitionist** one who favors abolition.

A-bomb *n* atomic bomb.

Abominable Snowman *n* yeti.

abominate *v* detest, loathe; *a* **abominable;** *adv* **abominably;** *n* **abomination** object of disgust.

Aboriginal *n* native inhabitant of Australia; *a* relating to the native inhabitants of Australia.

abort *v* **1** (to cause to) miscarry (of a fetus) **2** end prematurely (of a mission or plan); *n* **abortion 1** miscarriage **2** failed project **3** deformed thing; *a* **abortive** unsuccessful.

abound *v* be plentiful, well supplied; *a* **abounding.**

about *prep* **1** concerning; on the subject of **2** around; *adv* **1** nearby; all around **2** nearly; **just about** very nearly; **be about** be going to.

about-face *n* change to opposite direction, opinion, or policy.

above *prep* over; higher than; more than; *adv, a* overhead; *n* **the above,** something mentioned before (in business letters).

aboveboard *a* open and honest.

abracadabra *n* magic formula; spell; gibberish.

abrade *v* rub or wear off; *n, a* **abrasive;** *n* **abrasion** place where skin is scraped off, sore

so caused.

abreast *adv, a* side by side; on a line with.

abridge *v* shorten, condense; *n* **abridg(e)ment.**

abroad *adv* in another country; outdoors; at large.

abrogate *v* repeal; annul; *n* **abrogation.**

abrupt *a* **1** gruff **2** sudden; *adv* **-ly;** *n* **-ness.**

abscess *n* inflamed swelling containing pus.

abscond *v* run away secretly, *esp* to escape law.

abseil *v* make controlled rapid descent of steep rock face by means of rope.

absent *a* not present; inattentive; *v* **absent oneself (from)** stay away; *adv* **absently;** *ns* **absence; absentee** one who is not present, habitually absent; **absenteeism.**

absentminded *n* inattentive; forgetful; *adv* **-ly;** *n* **-ness.**

absinthe *n* wormwood; liqueur flavored with this.

absolute *a* **1** unlimited **2** independent of other factors **3** undiluted; pure; *adv* **absolutely;** *n* **absoluteness.**

absolute pitch *n* ability to identify exact musical pitch.

absolutism *n* (principle of) government with unlimited power.

absolve *v* pronounce free from sin; release from obligation; pardon; *n* **absolution.**

absorb *v* take in; soak up; swallow up; *a* **absorbing**

engrossing; *ns* **absorbent, absorption.**

abstain *v* **1** refrain from (*esp* alcohol or food) **2** refuse to vote; *n* **abstainer;** *a* **abstinent** refraining from food, etc.; *ns* **abstinence** self-denial, **abstention** (case of) not using a right to vote.

abstemious *a* temperate; not given to excess, *esp* in food and drink; *adv* **abstemiously;** *n* **abstemiousness.**

abstract *a* withdrawn from reality; *n* summary; *v* steal; take away; *a* **abstracted** absentminded; *n* **abstraction;** *advs* **abstractedly, abstractly.**

abstruse *a* difficult to understand; obscure; *adv* **-ly;** *n* **-ness.**

absurd *a* unreasonable; ridiculous; *adv* **absurdly;** *ns* **absurdity, absurdness.**

abubble *v* in a state of bubbling or agitation.

abundance *n* plenty; *a* **abundant;** *adv* **abundantly.**

abuse *v* **1** misuse **2** betray trust **3** insult; *ns* **abuse; abusiveness;** *a* **abusive;** *adv* **-ly.**

abut *v* to be adjacent to.

abutter *n* owner of adjacent property.

abysm *n* abyss; *a fig* **abysmal** very bad; *adv* **-ly.**

abyss *n* bottomless pit.

AC *abbr* alternating current.

a/c *abbr* account.

acacia *n* genus of trees.

academy *n* **1** place of higher education **2** society for advancement of learning; n **academician**; a **academic** scholarly; adv **academically**.

Acadia n French-speaking areas of the Atlantic Provinces of Canada.

acanthus n mediterranean herb or a decoration resembling its leaves.

accede v 1 succeed to 2 give consent or support 3 comply with; n **accedence**.

accelerate v increase speed; ns **accelerator** device for increasing speed in machines, etc.; **acceleration**.

accent n stress or emphasis; mark used to indicate sound of vowel; manner of pronunication; v stress; accentuate; n **accentuation**.

accept v receive; take; admit; believe in; agree to; a **-able**; ns **-ability, acceptance**.

access n means of approach; right of entry; v comput retrieve or input (information); a **-ible** easy to reach, approach; ns **-ibility; accession** coming to throne, office.

accessory n additional equipment; a additional.

access time n comput time taken to obtain stored information.

accidence n part of grammar dealing with the variable forms of words.

accident n 1 unexpected events 2 mishap; a **accidental;** adv **-ally**.

accident-prone a liable to accidents more often than most people.

acclaim n loud applause; welcome; approval; v applaud; n **acclamation**; a **acclamatory**.

acclimatize v adapt to a new climate; n **acclimatization**.

acclivity n upward slope of hill.

accolade n 1 light stroke with a sword used in bestowing knighthood 2 any supreme reward.

accommodate n 1 fit 2 lodge 3 help by act of kindness; a **accommodating** obliging; n **accommodation** lodgings.

accompany v 1 go with; escort 2 play music supporting (a soloist); ns **accompanist, accompaniment**.

accomplice n 1 partner in crime 2 confederate.

accomplish v finish; bring to successful conclusion; a **accomplished** 1 finished 2 talented; n **accomplishment**.

accord v 1 be in harmony; agree 2 bestow; a **according** (**according as** conj depending on whether; **according to** prep 1 as stated by 2 following); n **accordance** agreement; adv **accordingly** therefore.

accordion n musical instrument with bellows, keys, and metal reeds.

accost v 1 speak first to.

account n 1 record of money owed or paid 2 record of money or credit transactions 3 report; description 4 credit (**buy something on account**) 5 reason (**on no account** for no reason) 6 consideration (**take into account, take account of**); prep **on account of** because of; v regard; consider; phr v **account for 1** make a detailed record of 2 explain.

accountant n professional person appointed to keep or inspect financial accounts; n **accountancy;** a **accountable** answerable; adv **accountably**.

accoutrements n pl equipment, esp a soldier's.

accredited a officially recognized or having the power to act in a certain capacity.

accretion n 1 growth; increase 2 something added.

accrue v increase, esp interest on invested money.

acculturation n cultural merging or adapting due to extended contact.

accumulate v amass; increase in mass or number; ns **accumulation; accumulator** apparatus for storing electrical or hydraulic energy; a **accumulative**.

accurate a exact in detail; precise; adv **-ly**; ns **accuracy, accurateness**.

accurse v curse; a **accursed** (**accurst**) under a curse; ill-fated; detestable; adv **accursedly**.

accuse v bring charge against; blame; ns **accuser,**

A

B
C
D
E
F
G
H
I
J
K
L
M
N
O
P
Q
R
S
T
U
V
W
X
Y
Z

accusation; *adv* **accusingly**.
accustom *v* make familiar; get used to; *a* **accustomed**.
AC/DC *a* alternating or direct current.
ace *n* **1** single spot on dice or cards **2** highest **3** best.
acephalous *a* headless; having a small head.
acerbate *v* **1** make sour or bitter **2** irritate; *a* **acerbic** sharp; bitter; *n* **acerbity**.
acetate *n* **1** salt of acetic acid **2** any item made with cellulose acetate.
acetic *a* pertaining to vinegar; *n* **a. acid** organic acid giving vinegar characteristic taste.
acetone *n* inflammable liquid used as a solvent.
acetylene *n* inflammable gas formed by the action of water on calcium carbonate.
ache *v* suffer dull, continuous pain, physically or emotionally; *n* dull, continuous pain.
achieve *v* finish; gain; win; *n* **-ment**.
Achilles' heel *n* weakness; vulnerable point.
Achilles' tendon *n* sinew joining the calf muscles to the heel bone.
achromatic *a* colorless.
acid *n* **1** sour substance, as vinegar, usually having corrosive effect **2** *sl* the drug LSD; *a* **1** sour and sharp to taste **2** sharp tempered; *ns* **acidity, acidness**; *adv* **acidly**.
acidosis *n* acid condition of the blood.

acid rain *n* rain polluted by industrial smoke and harmful to crops.
acid test *n* test that shows the real value of something.
acidulous *a* sharp; bitter.
acknowledge *v* admit; recognize as true; indicate receipt of; *n* **acknowledg(e)ment** recognition of; *a* **acknowledgeable**.
acme *n* **1** highest point; summit **2** perfection.
acne *n* pimples; common skin disease.
acolyte *n* **1** priest's attendant **2** any devoted assistant.
aconite *n* **1** poisonous plant with blue or yellow flower **2** drug obtained from such plants.
acorn *n* the fruit of the oak tree.
acorn squash *n* sweet winter squash shaped like an acorn.
acoustic *a* **1** connected with hearing or sound **2** *mus* (of instruments) not electric; *adv* **acoustically**; *n* **acoustics** theory of sound.
acquaint *v* inform; make aware of; *idm* **be acquainted (with)** have some knowledge (of); *ns* **acquaintance 1** slight knowledge **2** person slightly known; **acquaintanceship**.
acquiesce *v* agree passively or tacitly; *n* **acquiescence**; *a* **acquiescent**.
acquire *v* get or gain possession of; *n* **acquisition 1** act of gaining **2** object

gained; *a* **acquisitive** desirous of gain; *n* **acquisitiveness**.
acquit *v* **-quitting, -quitted.** declare not guilty (of offence); *idm* **acquit oneself** behave oneself; *n* **acquittal** release by court.
acre *n* measure of land (4,840 sq. yds.); *n* **acreage** area in acres.
acrid *a* bitter; caustic; *n* **acridity**; *adv* **-ly**.
acrimony *n* bitterness of manner of speech; *a* **acrimonious**; *adv* **-ly**.
acrobat *n* highly skilled gymnast; *n* **acrobatics**; *a* **acrobatic**; *adv* **-ally**.
acronym *n* name or word formed by the initial letters of other words such as NATO, UNICEF, OPEC.
across *adv, prep* **1** on the other side (of) **2** from one side to the other side (of).
across-the-board *a* affecting all members, groups, or types.
acrostic *n* verse or puzzle in which first and/or last letters, reading across and down, make words.
acrylic *n* type of synthetic material.
act *v* **1** do something **2** *dram* perform **3** (of drugs) have effect **4** behave; *phr v* **act up** cause trouble; *n* **1** thing done **2** main section of play or opera **3** item in circus or variety show **4** legislative measure **5** *idm* **put on an act** pretend; *ns* **actor**, *fem* **actress** one who acts (stage, TV or film).

act of God n unforeseeable event, *esp* disaster.

acting n *dram* performing; a functioning temporarily as.

actinium n a radioactive element.

action n 1 act 2 movement 3 effect 4 *dram* main events 5 *sport* exciting play 6 battle 7 lawsuit; a **actionable** giving cause for legal action.

active a in action; quick; lively; *adv* **-ly**; v **activate** make active; set in motion.

activist n one taking active part in politics.

activity n 1 liveliness 2 busy action 3 occupation, *esp* of leisure.

actual a 1 existing 2 real; true; *adv* **-ly** 1 in fact 2 surprisingly; n **actuality** reality.

actualize v make real.

actuary n expert who calculates insurance risks; a **actuarial**.

actuate v 1 cause something to work or begin 2 cause someone to act.

acuity n sharpness of perception.

acumen n ability to judge well.

acupressure n shiatsu massage therapy.

acupuncture n treatment of pain or disease by sticking needles into the patient's body.

acute a 1 sharp 2 severe; agonizing; *adv* **-ly**; n **-ness**.

ad n *coll* advertisement.

AD *abbr* anno Domini (*Lat* =

in the year of the Lord).

adage n old saying; proverb.

adagio a, *adv mus* slow(ly); n slow movement.

adamant a stubbornly determined; *adv* **-ly**; n very hard stone; a **adamantine**.

Adam's apple n *coll* lump at front of throat, prominent in men; thyroid cartilage.

adapt v 1 modify; make fit for new use 2 become adjusted to new circumstances; a **adaptable**; ns **adaptability**; **adaptation**; **adapter** 1 person who adapts (also **adaptor**) 2 device for linking pieces of equipment, *esp* electrical plugs.

ADC *abbr* 1 aide-de-camp 2 analog-digital converter.

ADD *abbr* attention deficit disorder.

add v 1 put something together with something 2 combine numbers and find the sum total 3 say further; ns **addition**; **additive** something added; a **additional**; *adv* **-ly**; *phr vs* add to increase; **add up** 1 calculate sum of 2 make sense; **add up to** 1 amount to 2 indicate.

addendum n *Lat* thing to be added; *pl* **addenda**.

adder n small venomous snake of viper family.

addict n 1 person unable to stop taking drugs, alcohol, etc. 2 person with a passionate interest; a **addicted (to)** 1 dependent

(on) 2 keenly interested (in); n **addiction**; a **addictive** habit-forming.

addled a 1 (of brains) confused 2 (of eggs) rotten.

address n 1 identification of residence or place of work 2 speech to an audience 3 *comput* details about storage location of data; v 1 speak to 2 write on a letter, parcel, etc., details of its destination; n **addressee** person to whom one is writing; *phr v* **address oneself to** turn one's attention to.

adduce v cite as proof.

adenoids n *pl* growths at back of nose, near throat.

adept a expert; n skilled person; expert; *adv* **adeptly**.

adequate a 1 sufficient 2 good enough; *adv* **-ly**; n **adequacy**.

adhere v stick or remain stuck; *phr v* **adhere to** remain loyal to; n **adherence** state of adhering; n **adherent** loyal supporter.

adhesive n (substance) that causes things to be stuck together; n **adhesion** 1 being stuck together 2 loyalty to something.

ad hoc a, *adv Lat* 1 for this purpose 2 not prepared in advance.

adieu *interj*, n goodbye; *pl* **adieus** or **adieux**.

ad infinitum *adv Lat* without limit.

adipose a fatty; n **adiposity**.

adjacent a lying near to; adjoining; *adv* **-ly**.

A
B C D E F G H I J K L M N O P Q R S T U V W X Y Z

adjective n word used to qualify a noun; a **adjectival**.

adjoin v be next to; a **adjoining** neighboring.

adjourn v put off, postpone; n -ment.

adjudge v 1 decide by law 2 grant or award.

adjudicate v judge; pronounce judgment on; act as a judge; ns **adjudicator, adjudication**.

adjunct n thing added, but less important.

adjust v fit; arrange; a -able; n -ment.

ad-lib a, adv Lat unprepared; v improvise.

adman n coll person who works in advertising.

administer v 1 manage 2 dispense; give out; ns **administrator, administration**; a **administrative**.

admirable a worthy of esteem; adv **admirably**.

admiral n high-ranking naval officer.

admire v view with pleasure or respect ns **admirer, admiration**.

admissible a allowable; adv -ibly; n **admissibility**.

admission v 1 being allowed to enter 2 entrance fee 3 acknowledgment of fact; confession.

admit v 1 let in 2 acknowledge; confess; n **admittance** right of entry; adv **admittedly** granted.

admonish v warn; reprove; n **admonition;** a **admonitory**.

ad nauseam adv Lat to a sickening extent; excessively.

ado n fuss; bother; trouble; bustle.

adobe n, a type of brick made from dried clay and straw; structure made from the brick.

adolescence n state of growing up; a, n **adolescent** boy, girl growing up.

adopt v 1 take and bring up as one's own child 2 accept formally; n **adoption;** a **adopted;** n **adoptability**.

adore v worship; regard with lavish affection, love; n **adoration;** a **adorable;** adv -ably.

adorn v beautify; embellish; n **adornment** decoration.

adrenal a near kidney; n **adrenalin** hormone produced by adrenal glands.

adrift a, adv 1 loose on water 2 without purpose.

adroit a dexterous; adv -ly; n -ness.

adulate v admire to excess.

adult a, n grown-up; mature (person).

adulterate v corrupt; make impure; n **adulteration**.

adultery n sexual infidelity in marriage; n **adulterer,** fem **adulteress;** a **adulterous**.

adumbrate v foreshadow; n -ation.

advance v 1 move forward 2 lend money 3 promote; n 1 forward move; progress 2 money paid before due 3 loan 4 increase in amount;

a early; before the due time; idm **in advance** beforehand; idm **make advances** to try to establish a relationship with; a **advanced 1** beyond; intermediate **2** far on in life **3** modern in outlook; n **advancement** promotion.

advantage n favorable condition; a **advantageous;** adv **advantageously**.

advent n coming, esp of Christ; four weeks preceding Christmas; n **Adventism** belief in millennium.

adventitious a accidental; casual.

adventure n exciting incident; hazardous exploit; n **adventurer** one who lives by his wits; a **adventurous;** adv -ly.

adverb n word qualifying verb, adjective, or another adverb; a **adverbial**.

adversary n 1 enemy 2 opponent.

adverse a unfavorable; adv -ly; n **adversity** unfavorable event or circumstances.

advertise v 1 make known publicly 2 praise in order to sell; ns **advertisement** (also coll **ad**), **advertiser, advertising**.

advert to phr v fml mention.

advice n counsel; guidance; information.

advise v give advice to; inform of; n **adviser;** adv **advisedly** expedient; a **advisable, advisory**.

advocate v speak in favor of;

recommend; *n* **1** person who speaks in support **2** defense lawyer; *n* **advocacy** giving of support.

adz *n* curved bladed tool for cutting wood surface.

adzuki bean *n* legume grown in Japan and China whose seeds are grownd into flour.

aegis *n* patronage; protection; auspices.

aeon, eon *n* great age of time; eternity.

aerate *a* expose to air; charge with gas; *n* **aeration**.

aerial *a* of, in, like air; *n* antenna, rod, or wire for receiving or sending electromagnetic waves.

aerobatics *n* spectacular display by aircraft; *a* **aerobatic**.

aerobics *n* system of exercise to increase oxygen in the blood; *a* **aerobic**.

aerodynamics *n* branch of physics dealing with forces exerted by moving air or gases; science of flight; *a* **aerodynamic**; *adv* **-ally**.

aeronaut *n* flyer of balloon or aircraft; *n* **aeronautics** science of air navigation; *as* **aeronautic, aeronautical**.

aerosol *n* (container of) pressurized liquid for releasing as a spray.

aerospace *n* (technology related to) earth's atmosphere and space beyond.

aesthetics *n* study of beauty, *esp* in art; *a* **aesthetic**; *adv -*

ally; *n* **aesthete** one who claims to have a special appreciation of art and beauty.

afar *adv* far away; **from afar** from a great distance.

affable *a* friendly; polite; *adv* **-ably**; *n* **affability**.

affair *n* **1** thing (to be) done **2** event or series of events; **affairs** business matters.

affect *v* act on; influence; work on (feelings); *ns* **affectation** show; **affection** love; *a* **affectionate** (*adv* **-ly**).

affiance *v* betroth.

affidavit *n leg, Lat* written statement made under oath.

affiliate *v* accept persons, societies as members of institution; *n* **affiliation**.

affinity *n* kinship (by marriage); chemical attraction; relations between, implying common origin.

affirm *v* declare positively; confirm; *n* **affirmation**; *n, a* **affirmative**; *adv* **-ly**.

affirmative action *n* positive discrimination.

affix *v* fix; fasten; *n* addition, *esp* to word.

afflict *v* cause to suffer; *a* **afflicted**; *n* **affliction**.

affluence *n* wealth; *a* **affluent**; *adv* **-ly**; *n* **affluent**, tributary stream.

afford *v* **1** have means for **2** supply; furnish; yield.

afforest *v* plant trees on; *n* **-ation**.

affray *n* fight.

affright *n* terror.

affront *v* insult; offend; *n* impudent or defiant act.

afghan *n* knitted or crocheted blanket or shawl.

aficionado *n* enthusiast for a particular activity.

afield *adv* **far afield** far away, *esp* from home.

afire *a, adv* on fire; burning.

aflame *a, adv* in flames; on fire.

afloat *a, adv* floating; in circulation.

aflutter *a* excited; nervous.

afoot *a* **1** on foot **2** happening.

afore-mentioned *a* stated previously.

afraid *a* frightened; timid; feeling fear.

afresh *adv* again; anew; once more.

Afrikaans *n* official language of S Africa.

Afro *a, n* (in a) loose bushy hairstyle, similar to that of some black people.

Afro- *prefix* of Africa.

aff *adv* at or toward the back of a ship.

after *prep* **1** later than **2** following **3** as a result of **4** in pursuit of **5** in the style of **6** despite; *idm* **after all 1** despite everything **2** one must not forget; *conj* **1** later than **2** although; *adv* **1** later **2** behind.

afterbirth *n* placenta and fetal membranes expelled from womb after birth.

afterburner *n* **1** device giving extra thrust to jet engine **2** device to reduce danger of exhaust fumes.

A
B
C
D
E
F
G
H
I
J
K
L
M
N
O
P
Q
R
S
T
U
V
W
X
Y
Z

aftercare n treatment or services offered to a person after medical treatment.

afterglow n 1 glow left after light has faded, (*e.g.*, after sunset) 2 warm and happy feeling after an exciting experience.

aftermath n period following an event.

afternoon n period of day between noon and evening.

aftershave n lotion for use on face after shaving.

aftertaste n flavor lingering after the stimulant is gone.

afterthought n 1 later idea 2 something added later.

afterward adv later on.

again adv 1 once more 2 as before 3 likewise.

against prep close to; opposite; in anticipation of.

agate n semiprecious stone.

age n length of time, thing, or person has existed; historical period; closing years of life; v grow old; a **aged; ageless** timeless.

ageism, agism n discrimination because of age; a, n **ageist, agist.**

agency n place or business providing service; idm **through the agency of** through the action of.

agenda a list of things to be discussed at meeting.

agent n 1 one who acts for person or company 2 natural force.

agent provocateur n Fr person used to tempt criminals or

rebels to act illegally in order to arrest them.

agglomerate v (of volcanic rock) (cause to) form a mass; a, n fused (into a) mass; n **agglomeration.**

agglutinate v glue together; n **-ation.**

aggrandize v make greater in power, rank, or wealth; n **aggrandizement.**

aggravate v 1 make worse 2 annoy; a **aggravating** annoying; n **aggravation.**

aggregate n entire sum; v collect; n **aggregation.**

aggressive a rude; offensive; adv **-ly;** ns **aggression; aggressor.**

aggrieve v hurt; cause distress to; a **aggrieved.**

aghast a struck with horror or amazement.

agile a active; nimble; adv **agilely;** n **agility.**

agism n discrimination on grounds of age.

agitate v disturb; shake violently; stir up unrest; ns **agitation, agitator.**

aglow a, adv glowing; in a glow.

agnostic n one believing that nothing can be known concerning God; n **agnosticism** theory of this belief.

ago adv gone by; in the past.

agog a, adv excited; eagerly anticipating.

agonize v suffer great anxiety; a **agonizing** unbearably painful; a **agonized**

expressing agony.

agony n anguish of mind or body.

agoraphobia n morbid fear of open spaces; a **agoraphobic.**

agrarian a relating to land.

agree v consent (to); settle; concede (that); as **agreed; agreeable** pleasant; adv **agreeably;** n **agreement.**

agribusiness n range of enterprises concerned with processing, distribution, and support of farm products.

agriculture n art and theory of farming; a **agricultural** (adv - **ly).**

agrimony n genus of herbs in the rose family.

agronomy n science of controlling soil for crops.

aground a, adv grounded; beached; stranded (on shore).

ague n fever, as with malaria.

ah interj exclamation of satisfaction, surprise, happiness, pain, etc.

ahead adv 1 in front; in advance 2 forward.

ahoy interj call used in hailing (a ship).

AI abbr artificial intelligence.

aid v help in any way; n 1 support 2 money loan.

aide n assistant.

aide-de-camp n officer assisting a general.

aide-mémoire n Fr document used to aid memory.

AIDS abbr acquired immunodeficiency syndrome.

aikido n Japanese form of self-defense.

ail v be out of health; a **-ing**; n **-ment**.

aileron n flap on airplane wing.

aim v point weapon; direct energy toward; n 1 action of aiming 2 purpose; a **aimless**; adv **-ly**; n **-ness**.

ain't v coll 1 am/is/are not 2 has/have not.

air n 1 gaseous substance around the earth 2 manner 3 tune; pl **airs** affected manner; as **airy, airless**; adv **airily**; n **airing** exposure to air; outing in open air; idms **in the air** a matter of rumor; **on the air** broadcasting; **off the air** not broadcasting; v **air** 1 ventilate 2 dry 3 make known (one's views).

air base n military airport.

airborne a 1 flying 2 moving in the air.

air brake n brake worked by compressed air.

airbrush n device used for spraying paint or ink.

airbus n aircraft making short to medium flights at frequent regular intervals.

air-condition v treat air to ensure purity and even temperature; n **-ing**.

air-cooled a cooled, esp engines, by currents of air.

aircraft n any kind of flying machine.

aircraft carrier n ship designed to carry aircraft.

airfield n place where aircraft land or take off.

air force n airborne branch of armed forces.

air gun n gun discharged by compressed air.

air hostess n stewardess on passenger aircraft.

airily adv in a carefree manner.

air lane n specified route for aircraft.

air letter n sheet of paper that folds and seals to form a cheap lightweight letter to send by air.

airlift n transport of people or supplies, esp to or from a place of difficult access.

airline n company operating aircraft on regular route; **airliner** aircraft used by airline.

air lock n 1 airtight compartment 2 air bubble stopping flow of liquid in pipe.

airmail n mail carried by aircraft.

airman n a member of the crew of an aircraft.

air pocket n current causing aircraft to drop suddenly.

airport n place from which aircraft operate.

air raid n raid by aircraft dropping bombs.

airship n flying machine.

airspace n atmosphere above a country, regarded as its legal property.

airstrip n narrow runway for use by aircraft.

airtight a impermeable to air.

air-to-air a from one aircraft in flight to another.

airway n 1 airline 2 air passage 3 chanel for radio broadcasting.

airworthy a fit or safe to fly; n **airworthiness**.

aisle n passageway between seats or pews.

ajar a partly open.

akimbo adv with hands on hips and elbows bent.

akin a 1 related by blood 2 alike; similar.

alabaster n smooth white stone for making ornaments; a of or like this.

à la carte adv Fr ordering separate items (on a menu).

alack interj expressing dismay, regret, sorrow.

alacrity n speed; briskness; eagerness.

à la mode adv Fr 1 in fashion 2 topped with ice cream.

alarm n 1 call to arms 2 warning of danger; v fill with fear; a **alarming**; adv **-ly**; n **alarmist**.

alas interj expressing dismay, grief, sorrow.

albacore n type of large tuna.

albatross n large seabird of the petrel type.

albeit conj even though; notwithstanding.

albino n person or animal with white skin and hair, and pink eyes due to lack of pigment; pl **albinos**.

album n 1 book of blank pages for stamps, photographs, etc. 2 long-playing record with several tracks.

alchemy n medieval chemistry; n **alchemist**.

alcohol n ethanol, the intoxicating agent in liquor; a **alcoholic**; ns **alcoholism** disease signified by excessive drinking of alcohol; **alcoholic** one so addicted.

alcove n recess in room or garden; artificial bower.

al dente adj cooked to retain firmness.

alderman n senior magistrate in borough or city.

ale n a fermented alcoholic beverage made with malt and hops.

alert a ready in body and mind; n **alertness**.

alfalfa n forage plant.

alfresco adv, a in the open air.

algae n lowly organized group of plant, as seaweed, etc.

algal bloom n sudden excessive growth of algae.

algebra n branch of mathematics using symbols for numbers and quantities; a **algebraic**; adv **-ally**.

algorithm n way of solving problems step by step.

alias adv otherwise; n false name; pl **aliases**.

alibi n proof of being elsewhere when crime was committed; pl **alibis**.

alien a 1 foreign 2 repugnant; n; v **alienate** estrange; ns **alienation; alienist** specialist in mental disease.

alight a lit; v dismount; come to rest.

align v bring into line; n **alignment**.

alike a similar; adv to same degree.

aliment n food; a **alimentary** of food channel in body.

alimentary canal n passage from mouth to anus along which food passes and is digested.

alimony n allowance to wife after legal separation.

alive a living; aware; alert; sensitive; swarming.

alkali n potash; substance neutralizing acid; a **alkaline**.

all a whole of; full number of; total; n everything, everyone; one's whole property; adv entirely; idms **all along** since the start; **all but** almost; **all out** with maximum effort; **all there** sane; quick-thinking; **all up** ended in failure.

Allah n (Muslim name for) God.

all-around a with wide range of skills, esp in sport.

allay v ease; soothe; make more bearable.

all clear n 1 signal of no danger 2 permission to go ahead.

allege v state as fact; a **alleged**; n **allegation**.

allegiance n loyalty.

allegory n story with moral; a **allegorical**.

allegretto n mus fast movement, but slower than allegro; adv at this speed.

allegro n musical composition played in a fast tempo; adj, adv briskly.

Allen wrench n small hexagoanal wrench shaped like an L.

allergy n abnormal sensitiveness to any substance; a **allergic**.

alleviate v lighten; relieve (pain); a **alleviation**.

alley n narrow passage between houses; pl **alleys**.

alliance n treaty between countries.

alligator n reptile of crocodile family.

alliteration n recurrence of same stressed sounds in verse or prose; a **alliterative**.

allocate v grant; assign (to); n **-ation**.

allot v **-lotting, -lotted.** assign as lot; n **allotment** 1 share 2 plot of land.

allow v permit; grant; n **allowance**.

alloy n mixture of two or more metals.

all right a 1 safe 2 acceptable; adv 1 agreed 2 for certain.

allspice n pungent W Indian spice.

all-star a with many famous members.

all-time a surpassing all at any time.

allude v; phr v **allude** refer to; n **allusion**; a **allusive**.

allure v attract; a **alluring**; ns **allure, allurement**.

alluvium n soil deposited by water; a **alluvial**.

ally v combine, join by treaty; n person or state acting in support of another; pl **allies**.

alma mater *n Lat* school or university where one is/was educated.

almanac, *n* calendar of months and days.

almighty *a* omnipotent; *n* **the Almighty** God.

almond *n* kernel of fruit of almond tree.

almoner *n* official distributor of alms.

almost *adv* very nearly; not quite.

alms *n* money given in charity to poor; **almshouse** endowed home for poor and aged people.

aloe *n* desert plant; (**bitter**) **aloes** juice from its leaves.

alone *a, adv* single; apart from others; unsupported.

along *prep* beside whole or part of length of; *adv* lengthwise; **alongside** at side of.

aloof *adv* apart; *a* haughty; *n* **-ness.**

aloud *adv* in an audible voice; loudly.

alp *n* mountain pasture; *a* **alpine;** *n* **alpinist** climber.

alpaca *n* S American llama with soft wool.

alpha *n* first letter of Greek alphabet.

alphabet *n* **1** set of letters used in written language **2** the ABC; *a* **alphabetical;** *adv* **-ly.**

alphanumeric *a* made up of both letters and numbers.

alpine *a* of the mountains, *esp* the Alps.

already *adv* before this; by this time.

also *adv, conj* besides; in addition; as well.

also-ran *n* unsuccessful participant in contest.

altar *n* **1** Communion table **2** slab used for sacrifices.

alter *v* change; *a* **alterable;** *n* **-ation.**

altercation *n fml* angry dispute.

alter ego *n Lat* other self.

alternate *v* occur by turns; *n* **alternating current** electricity reversing direction of flow regularly; *a* **alternate** every second; *adv* **-ly** *a.*

alternative *n* other possible (choice).

alternative medicine *n* forms of treatment offered instead of conventional medicine.

although *conj* even though; notwithstanding.

altitude *n* height above sea level.

alto *n* person with singing voice between soprano and tenor.

altogether *adv* completely; wholly; in the main.

altruism *n* unselfishness; *a* **altruistic;** *n* **altruist.**

alum *n* mineral salt; crystalline substance used as astringent.

aluminum *n* very light white metal.

alumnus *n Lat* graduate of university; *pl* **alumni;** *fem* **alumna;** *pl* **alumnae.**

alveolus *n* small cavity; *a* **alveolate;** *pl* **alveoli.**

always *adv* at all times; invariably.

Alzheimer's disease *n* serious disorder of the brain resulting in premature senility.

am *1st person sing present tense of* BE.

am, AM *abbr* ante meridiem (before noon).

AM *abbr rad* amplitude modulation.

amalgam *n* mixture, *esp* used in dentistry; *v* **amalgamate** unite; *n* **amalgamation.**

amaryllis *n* S African herb known for its large, brightly colored flowers.

amass *v* heap together; pile up.

amateur *n* person following pursuit for love of it, not to make money; *a* **amateurish** not well done.

amaze *v* astound; *n* **-ment** *a* **amazing.**

Amazon *n* legendary female warrior.

ambassador *n* diplomat representing his country at foreign court; *fem* **ambassadress.**

amber *n* hard yellow fossil resin.

ambergris *n* secretion of sperm whale used in making perfume.

ambidextrous *a* able to use both hands equally.

ambient *a* entirely surrounding; *n* **ambience.**

ambiguous *a* not clear in meaning; *adv* **-ly;** *n* **ambiguity.**

ambit *n* full scope; compass; extent.

a
b
c
d
e
f
g
h
i
j
k
l
m
n
o
p
q
r
s
t
u
v
w
x
y
z

A
B
C
D
E
F
G
H
I
J
K
L
M
N
O
P
Q
R
S
T
U
V
W
X
Y
Z

ambition n strong desire for success; a **ambitious**.

ambivalent a undecided; unclear; n **ambivalence**.

amble v move at easy pace, esp horse; walk easily.

ambulance n vehicle for carrying sick and wounded.

ambulatory a connected with walking.

ambush n surprise attack; v waylay.

ameliorate v improve; n **-ation**; a **-ative**.

amen interj "So be it"; n word of assent.

amenable a tractable; submissive; adv **-ably**; n **-ability**.

amend v improve; correct; ns **amendment, amends** reparation.

amenity n desirable feature; pleasantness.

Americana n materials relating to American culture.

amethyst n purple kind of quartz; its color.

amiable a kindly; lovable; adv **-bly**; n **amiability**.

amicable a friendly; adv **-ably**; n **amiability**.

amid prep in middle of; among.

amidships adv in middle of ship.

amigo n Sp friend.

amino acid n any of several organic acids in proteins.

amiss adv wrongly; a faulty.

amity n friendship.

ammeter n meter for measuring ampere units.

ammo n coll ammunition.

ammonia n pungent, colorless gas; a **ammoniac**.

ammonite n type of fossil shell.

ammunition n gunpowder, bullets, shells, etc.

amnesia n loss of memory.

amnesty n pardon given to offenders against state.

amniocentesis n sampling of amniotic fluid to test for abnormality in a developing fetus.

amniotic fluid n fluid surrounding developing fetus.

amoeba, ameba n microscopic one-celled animal.

amok, amuck adv in a frenzy; v **run amok** get out of control.

among, prep in midst of; by joint or mutual action of.

amoral a without morals; n **amorality**.

amorous a prone to love; adv **-ly**.

amorphous a formless.

amortize v pay off a debt gradually.

amount n sum total; quantity; phr v **amount to** add up to.

amour n Fr love affair (usually secret); lover.

amp abbr ampere.

ampere n electric unit of force; n **amperage**.

ampersand n the sign & (meaning "and").

amphetamine n stimulant drug.

amphibian n animal or vehicle able to live or operate on land or in water; a **amphibious**.

amphitheater n arena surrounded by tiered seats.

amphora n Greek or Roman jar; pl **amphorae**.

ample a plenty; large; adv **amply**; n **ampleness**

amplify v **-fying, -fied**. make louder; ns **amplifier, amplification**.

ampoule, ampule n glass tube holding dose of drug.

amputate v cut off part of body; n **amputation**.

amulet n talisman; charm, esp hung round neck.

amuse v provoke mirth or interest; divert; n **-ment**; a **amusing**; adv **-ly**.

an see a.

anabaptist n advocate of adult (re)baptism.

anabolic steroid n synthetic hormone used to promote development of muscle and bone.

anabolism n building up process of metabolism.

anaconda n S American snake of the boa constrictor family.

anchronism n thing or event placed in the wrong context of time.

anagram n word made by rearranging letters in another word; a **anagrammatic**; adv **-ally**.

anal a of the anus.

analets selected excerpts.

analgesia n absence of pain; a **analgesic** pain-killing.

analogy n similarity; a **analogous**; adv **analogically**.

analyze v gram examine

minutely structure of sentence; break down into smallest parts; *a* **analytical;** *adv* **-ly;** *ns* **analysis, analyst.**

anarchy *n* no supreme power in nation; lawlessness; *n* **anarchism** practice of anarchy; *n* **anarchist.**

anathema *n* curse; hateful thing; *v* **-ematize.**

anatomy *n* science of structure of body; *a* **anatomical;** *v* **anatomize** dissect; *n* **anatomist.**

ANC *abbr* African National Congress.

ancestor *n* forebear; *a* **ancestral;** *n* **ancestry** lineage.

anchor *n* **1** mass of iron, securing ships to seabed; **2** broadcaster who coordinates items from different sources; *v* fasten by anchor; *n* **anchorage** place for anchoring.

anchorperson *n* news broadcaster.

anchovy *n* small fish of the herring type.

ancient *a* belonging to distant past; very old.

ancillary *a* subordinate; auxiliary.

and *conj* word joining words, phrases; also; as well as.

andante *adv* (music played) slowly.

andirons *n* fireplace supports for wood.

androgynous *a* with characteristics of male and female.

android *n* robot of human

appearance.

anecdote *n* trivial story of isolated event; *a* **anecdotal.**

anemia *n* lack of red corpuscles in blood; *a* **anemic.**

anemometer *n* gauge for speed and force of wind.

anemone *n* windflower; **sea anemone** small sea creature.

aneroid *a* dry; containing no fluid.

anesthesia *n* insensibility caused by drugs or disease; *ns* **anesthetic; anesthesiologist** one who gives anesthetic.

aneurysm, aneurism *n* blood clot.

anew *adv* again; afresh.

angel *n* celestial being; *a* **angelic.**

angelica *n* herb used in cooking; its candied stalk.

anger *n* wrath; rage; *v* provoke to anger.

angina *n* severe inflammation and spasmodic pain.

angle *v* to fish; *ns* **angling, angler.**

angle *n* space between two lines that meet; corner; *a* **angular.**

Anglican *a* member of the Church of England.

anglicize *v* give English form to (a foreign word).

Anglo- *prefix* of England.

anglophile *n, a* (a person) loving English people and way of life; *n* **anglophilia.**

anglophobe *n, a* (person) hating English people and way of life; *n* **-phobia.**

Anglo-Saxon *n* (language of) inhabitant of England from

5th century until Norman invasion (1066).

angora *n* type of rabbit, cat, or goat; fabric made from this rabbit's or goat's hair.

angostura *n* bitter aromatic bark used as flavoring.

angry *a* **1** full of anger; tempestuous **2** (of a wound or rash) inflamed; *adv* **angrily.**

angst *n* state of acute anxiety about the world, anguish.

angstrom *n* one-billionth of a meter.

anguish *n* acute pain of body or mind.

angular *a* **1** with sharp corners **2** not vertical or horizontal; slanting *n* **angularity.**

animadversion *n* depreciatory reference to.

anima *n* person's true inner self.

animal *n* living creature with power of voluntary motion; *a* of animal nature; sensual.

animate *v* give life to; *a* living; *n* **animation;** *a* **animated** lively; *adv* **-ly.**

animism *n* belief that natural objects have souls.

animosity *n* enmity; hatred.

aniseed *n* aromatic seed used for flavoring.

anisette *n* liqueur made with aniseed.

ankle *n* the joint between foot and leg.

anklet *n* ornament or support for the ankle.

annals *n* yearly chronical of events.

annex v join to; steal; n **annexation**.

annex n supplementary building.

annihilate v destroy utterly; n **annihilation**.

anniversary n yearly celebration of an event.

annotate v make explanatory notes on; n **annotation**.

announce v declare; ns **-ment**, **announcer**.

annoy v vex; irritate; a **-ing**; n **-ance**.

annual a yearly; n plant living for year only; yearly publication of book; adv **annually**.

annuity n fixed sum paid yearly; n **annuitant**.

annul v **-nulling, -nulled.** cancel; nullify; n **-ment**.

annular a ring-shaped.

annunication n announcement, esp of Incarnation made to Virgin Mary; v **annunciate**.

anode n positive electric pole.

anodyne n drug that relieves or soothes pain.

anoint v pour oil on, esp by use of consecrated oil in religious ceremony; n **-ment**; a **anointed**.

anomaly n irregularity; a **anomalous**.

anomie, anomy n immorality resulting in social alienation.

anon adv soon; presently.

anonymous a not named; adv **-ly**; abbr **anon;** n **anonymity**.

anopheles n malaria-carrying mosquito.

anorak n warm, hooded jacket (rain- and windproof).

anorexia n 1 complete loss of appetite for food 2 also **anorexia nervosa** chronic and dangerous form of this; a **anorexic**.

another a 1 additional 2 different; pron one more.

anovulatory adj not ovulating.

answer v give reply to; a **answerable** responsible.

answering machine n machine for answering a telephone and taking messages.

ant n industrious small insect.

antacid n substance that counteracts acid.

antagonist n adversary; opponent; v **antagonize** render hostile; n **antagonism**; a **antagonistic**.

antarctic a belonging to south polar regions.

ante- prefix Lat before.

antecedent a prior to; n pl **-s** line of descent.

antechamber n waiting room outside main room.

antedate v happen earlier than.

antediluvian a 1 of the age before the Flood 2 old-fashioned.

antelope n deerlike animal allied to goat.

antenna n 1 feeler of insect 2 radio aerial; pl **antennae**.

anterior a before; earlier; more to the front.

anthem n sacred words set to music; song of praise.

anthill n pile of dirt dug up by ants while nest-building.

anthology n collection of poems, stories, etc.

anthracite n hard slow-burning smokeless coal.

anthrax n pustular disease attacking animals and human beings.

anthropoid a like a man; n manlike creature.

anthropology n science of man; a **anthropological**; n **anthropologist**.

anthropomorphic a resembling a human being.

anti- prefix Gk 1 against 2 the reverse of (**ant-** before vowel).

antiballistic a against missiles.

antibiotic a destroying growth, esp of bacteria; n such a substance.

antibody n natural antidote to infection produced in blood.

antic n playful, comic gesture; pl **-s** playful or ridiculous behavior.

Antichrist n one hostile to Christ and His teaching.

anticipate v take action in advance; n **anticipation;** a **anticipatory**.

anticlerical a opposed to influence of clergy, esp in political affairs.

anticlimax n disappointing turn to an exciting situation; a **anticlimactic**.

anticonvulsant n agent used to prevent convulsions.

anticyclone n state of high atmospheric pressure,

tending to produce fine weather; *a* **anticyclonic**.

antidemocratic *adj* in opposition to democratic policies.

antidote *n* specific against poison.

antifreeze *n* chemical added to water to prevent it from freezing in winter.

antigen *n* substance causing body to make antibodies.

antihero *n* main character of book or play lacking the traditional virtues of a hero.

antihistamine *n* type of drug used to treat allergies.

antimony *n* brittle silver-white metallic element.

antipasto *n* Italian appetizers.

antipathy *n* dislike; repugnance; *a* **antipathetic**.

antiperspirant *n* substance applied to the body to prevent sweating.

antipodes *n* places on opposite sides of earth.

antiquary, antiquarian *n* one who collects antiques; *a* **antiquated** old-fashioned.

antique *a* old; *n* relic of past age; *ns* **antiquity** remote past; **antiquities** ancient museum pieces.

antirrhinum *n* the snapdragon plant.

anti-Semite *n* hater of Jews; *n* **anti-Semitism**.

antiseptic *n* substance for preventing infection; *n* **antisepsis** method of preventing infection.

antisocial *a* 1 going against the conventions of society 2 avoiding the company of others; unsociable.

antithesis *n* contrast (of ideas); *pl* **antitheses**.

antitoxin *n* substance that neutralizes poison.

antitrust *adj* concening laws that protect commerce from unfair business monopolies

antler *n* a branched horn of deer.

antonym *n* word of opposite meaning to another.

anus *n* opening at lower end of alimentary canal.

anvil *n* block of iron on which blacksmith works.

anxious *a* 1 worried 2 eager to do (something); *adv* **-ly**; *n* **anxiety**.

any *a*, *pron* some; every; *prons* **anybody, anyone, anyway, anywhere**.

aob *abbr* any other business.

aorta *n* main artery of human body; *a* **aortic**.

apace *adv* at a quick pace; swiftly.

apart *adv* separately; aside; *a* separate.

apartheid *n* segregation of races practiced in S. Africa 1948-1992.

apartment *n* room; set of rooms, usually leased.

apathy *n* indifference; *a* **apathetic**.

ape *n* monkey *esp* tailless kind; *v* mimic; *n* **aping**.

aperitif *n* drink taken as an appetizer.

aperture *n* hole; opening, *esp*

that into a camera.

apex *n* tip; top; peak; *pl* **apexes, apices**.

aphasia *n* loss of power of speech.

aphelion *n* point of orbit farthest from the sun.

aphid *n* small insect such as a whitefly that feeds on sap of plants.

aphorism *n* maxim; short pithy saying.

aphrodisiac *a* exciting sexual desire; *n* such a drug.

apiarist *n* beekeeper; **apiary** beehive; **apiculture**.

apical *adj* relating to the tip or peak.

apiece *adv* to or for each; each by itself.

aplomb *n* self-possession.

Apocalypse *n* Book of Revelation; prophetic vision.

Apocrypha *n* noncanonical parts of the Bible.

apocryphal *a* not genuine; fictitious.

apogee *n* point in heavenly body's orbit farthest from earth; culmination.

apology *n* expression of regret; *v* **apologize**; *a* **apologetic**; *adv* **-ally**.

apostle *n* one sent out to preach; reformer; *a* **apostolic**.

apostrophe *n* 1 exclamatory address to person present or absent 2 a mark (') showing omission of letter(s) or the possessive form.

apostrophize *v* (in poem or speech) address or pretend to address.

A B C D E F G H I J K L M N O P Q R S T U V W X Y Z

apothecary *n* old name for druggist, pharmacist.

apotheosis *n* deification of human being.

appall *v* **-palling, -palled.** horrify; *a* **appalling**; *adv* **-ly.**

Appaloosa *n* N American saddle horse, usually spotted.

apparatus *n* equipment; instruments for specific use.

apparent *a* visible; *adv* **apparently** seemingly.

apparition *n* supernatural visual impression; ghost.

appeal *v* seek higher judgment; ask earnestly; attract; *n* act of appealing; *a* **appealing** attractive; *adv* **-ly** earnestly.

appear *v* **1** become visible **2** present oneself; seem; *n* **appearance** bearing; look.

appease *v* soothe; pacify; satisfy; *n* **appeasement.**

appellant *n* one appealing to higher court; *n* **appellation** name or title.

append *v* add; attach; *n* **appendage.**

appendix *n* addition to book; *anat* vermiform appendix tube leading out of cecum; *pl* **appendixes, appendices.**

appendicitis *n* inflammation of vermiform appendix.

apperception *n* self-consciousness.

appertain *v* be appropriate or relate (to).

appetite *n* enjoyment of food; desire; *n* **appetizer** food or drink served before a meal; *a* **appetizing.**

applaud *v* express approval by clapping hands; *n* **applause.**

apple *n* firm, fleshy fruit with seeds.

appliance *n* device; gadget; machine.

appliqué *n* Fr one material cut out and applied to surface of another, as in embroidery.

apply *v* **-plying, -plied. 1** put on; bring into contact **2** administer **3** have relevance; *phr vs* **apply for** request; **apply oneself (to)** devote oneself (to); *a* **applied** put to practical use; *n* **application** act of applying; something applied; close attention; **applicant** person applying; *a* **applicable** relevant, suitable.

appoint *v* fix; ordain; select for office; equip; *n* **-ment 1** act of appointing **2** meeting.

apportion *v* share out; allot; *n* **-ment.**

apposite *a* apt; pointed; *n* **apposition.**

appraise *v* assess price or value of; *ns* **appraisal, appraisement.**

appreciate *v* **1** estimate highly **2** be sensitive to **3** increase value; *n* **-ation**; *a* **-iative** grateful; *adv* **-ly**; *a* **appreciable** noticeable; *adv* **-ably.**

apprehend *v* **1** arrest **2** understand **3** dread; *n* **apprehension**; *a* **apprehensive**; *adv* **-ly.**

apprentice *n* one learning a trade or craft and bound by indentures; *n* **apprenticeship.**

apprise *v* inform.

approach *v* **1** come near **2** make advances to; *n* drawing near; *a* **-able** willing to be consulted.

approbation *n* commendation; approval; *a* **approbatory.**

appropriate *v* take for oneself; filch; *a* suitable to; *adv* **-ly**; *n* **appropriation** funds granted for special purpose.

approve *v* sanction; commend; *n* **approval**; *as* approved, approving; *adv* **approvingly.**

approx *abbr* approximately.

approximate *a* very near; about correct; *v* make or come close to; *adv* **-ly**; *n* **approximation.**

appurtenance *n* adjunct; accessory.

après-ski *n, a* Fr (of or for) leisure time after skiing.

apricot *n* **1** orange-red fruit allied to peach **2** its color.

April *n* fourth month of year.

April Fools' Day *n* April first.

a priori *a, adv* **1** by deductive reasoning **2** formed beforehand.

apron *n* garment to protect clothes; part of theater stage in front of curtain.

apropos *a* appropriate; *adv* with reference to.

apt *a* fit; likely; skilled; *adv* **aptly**; *ns* **aptness; aptitude** fitness; capacity.

Aqua-Lung [TM] *n* underwater breathing apparatus.

aquamarine *n* bluish green stone; color.

aquaplane v ride on board towed by motorboat; n such a board.

aquarium n tank where water plants and fish are kept; pl **aquaria, aquariums.**

Aquarius n 11th sign of the zodiac (the Water-bearer); a, n **Aquarian.**

aquatic a living in water; taking place in or on water.

aquatint n etching process producing print like watercolor; print made by this process.

aqueduct n artificial conduit for water; bridgelike part of a structure supporting conduit.

aqueous a watery.

aquiline a eaglelike; (nose) curved as an eagle's beak.

Arab n member of a group of people who originated in Arabia but now live throughout Middle East and N Africa; a **Arabian;** n **Arabic** language of Arabs.

arabesque n 1 fanciful pattern of leaves, scrolls, etc., in Arabian decoration 2 posture in ballet.

Arabic numeral n any of the numerals 0, 1, 2, 3, 4, 5, 6, 7, 8, 9.

arable a suitable for tilling, cultivation.

arachnid n one of the genus including spiders.

arbiter n person recognized as able to make a decisive judgment.

arbitrage n buying and reselling elsewhere so as to profit from difference of prices in different places.

arbitrary a 1 based on impulse or chance 2 dictatorial; a **arbitrarily;** n **arbitrariness.**

arbitrate v make judgment or settle a dispute between others; ns **arbitrator; arbitration.**

arbor n main support or spindle of machine.

arborist n person caring for welfare of trees.

arc n 1 part of circumference of circle 2 luminous glow made by electricity crossing gap between electrodes; n **arc lamp** lamp that works in this way.

arc welding n welding by means of electrical arc.

arcade n passage with arched roof, lined with stores.

arcane a secret; mysterious.

arch- prefix chief.

arch a coy; prep chief; adv **-ly;** n **-ness.**

arch n curved structure acting as support; curve itself; v build arch over; form an arch.

archaeology n study of prehistoric cultures; a **-ological;** n **-ologist.**

archaic a out of date; adv **-ally.**

archangel n chief angel.

archbishop n chief bishop; n **archbishopric** office of archbishop.

archdeacon n priest next below bishop in rank.

archer n one shooting with bow and arrows; n **archery.**

archetype n prototype; a **archetypal.**

archipelago n sea containing many islands; group of such islands; pl **archipelagoes.**

architecture n art and science of building; a **architectural;** adv **-ly;** n **architect** one who designs buildings.

archives n place where records are kept; records themselves; n **archivist** keeper of archives.

archway n way or passage under an arch.

arctic a of or near region of the N Pole.

ardent a fiery; eager; adv **-ly;** n **ardor.**

arduous a difficult; strenuous; adv **-ly.**

are n 100 sq meters.

area n region; surface measured in square units; scope.

area code n number that identifies a telephone calling area in teh US or Canada.

arena n place of combat or conflict; pl **arenas.**

aren't contracted form of 1 are not 2 am not.

argent n silver; white color in heraldry.

argil n kind of clay used by potters.

argot n slang.

argue v dispute; prove; debate; ns **argument** discussion in which reasons are given; as **arguable, argumentative.**

aria n vocal solo in operas and oratorios.

arid a dry; parched; barren; adv **aridly;** n **aridity.**

a
b
c
d
e
f
g
h
i
j
k
l
m
n
o
p
q
r
s
t
u
v
w
x
y
z

A
B C D E F G H I J K L M N O P Q R S T U V W X Y Z

Aries n first sign of the zodiac (the Ram); a, n **Arian**.

aright adv rightly; without error.

arise v ascend; occur; pt **arose**; pp **arisen**.

aristocracy n ruling class; nobility; n **aristocrat**; a **aristocratic**; adv **-ally**.

arithmetic n science of numbers; n **arithmetician**; a **arithmetical**; adv **-ally**.

arithmetic progression n series of numbers where difference between successive numbers is constant.

ark n flat-bottomed boat; Jewish chest containing Tablets of the Law; coffer.

arm[1] n 1 upper limb of human body 2 anything extending from main body (arm of tree, chair, etc.).

arm[2] n weapon; branch of military forces; v supply with weapons; prepare for battle.

armada n fleet of warships, esp Spanish.

armadillo n S American burrowing mammal.

armament n force equipped for war; pl war equipment.

armchair n chair with armrests.

armistice n truce pending a formal peace treaty.

armlet n cloth band for the arm.

armor n protective covering for the body in battle; protective plating of ship or vehicle; a **armored**; ns **armory; armorer** one who makes or repairs armor.

armorial a relating to heraldic arms.

armpit n hollow under the arm below the shoulder.

arms n pl 1 weapons 2 coat of arms; idm **be up in arms** protest strongly.

army n 1 military force that operates on land 2 large group of people or animals.

arnica n genus of plants; drug used for sprains, etc.

aroma n pleasant smell; a **aromatic** fragrant, spicy.

aromatherapy n the use of scented plant oils in massage; n **aromatherapist**.

arose pt of **arise**.

around prep 1 in a circle around 2 at or to various places within 3 (at) about; approximately; adv 1 here and there 2 somewhere nearby 3 turning in a circle 4 on all sides; phr v **get around** travel widely; idm **have been around** have had experience of the world.

arouse v 1 awaken 2 stimulate; excite; n **arousal**.

arpeggio n notes of a chord played in quick succession.

arr abbr 1 arrival; arrives 2 mus arranged by.

arrack n strong alcoholic drink from rice.

arraign v accuse; indict on criminal charge; n **arraignment** act of indictment.

arrange v put in order; fix; adapt (novel, music); n arrangement.

arrant a unmitigated; out-and-out; adv **arrantly**.

array v 1 dress 2 draw up; n 1 troops 2 impressive display.

arrears n debt not paid; work not done.

arrest v 1 seize by legal authority 2 gain (attention) 3 stop 4 stay (judgment); a **arresting** striking; n **arrest**.

arrive v 1 reach destination 2 achieve fame; n **arrival**.

arrogant a haughty; proud; n **arrogance**; adv **-ly**.

arrogate v claim as one's own; n **arrogation**.

arrow n feathered rod with sharp point shot from bow.

arrowroot n W Indian plant with starchy roots.

arroyo n steep, dry gulch.

arsenal n place where weapons and ammunition are made or stored.

arsenic n metallic poison.

arson n deliberate setting on fire of property.

art n 1 creative skill and its application 2 craft or trade 3 cunning; pl humanities as opposed to sciences.

Art Deco n, a (in) the utilitarian, geometric style of interior design, jewelry, architecture, etc. popular in the 1930s.

arteriosclerosis n disease where hardening of the walls of the arteries impedes circulation of the blood.

artery n blood vessel conveying blood from the

heart; main line of communication; *a* **arterial**.

artesian well *n* well sending up constant supply of water under pressure.

artful *a* cunning; crafty; *adv* **-ly**.

arthritis *n* painful inflammation of joints; *a* **arthritic**.

artichoke *n* plant with edible roots or flower base.

article *n* item; short piece of writing; clause in legal document; in grammar, words *the, a, an; v* bind to trade or profession; *a* **articled**.

articulate *a* 1 formed with joints 2 expressive; having the power of speech; *v* 1 join 2 utter distinctly; *adv* **-ly; ns articulateness** ability to communicate; **articulation**.

artifact *n* any object made by human skill.

artifice *n* ingenuity; trickery.

artificial *a* not natural; *adv* **-ly**; *n* **artificiality** insincerity.

artificial insemination *n* injection of semen into the womb by artificial means to cause conception.

artificial intelligence *n* (study of) capacity for machines to simulate human intelligence.

artificial respiration *n* method of making a person or animal breathe when natural breathing has stopped.

artillery *n* guns of various types; branch of army that uses heavy guns.

artisan *n* skilled manual worker.

artist *n* 1 person who practices any fine art, *esp* painting 2 very skillful worker or performer, *a* **artistic; ** *adv* **-ally**; *n* **artistry**.

artiste *n* professional entertainer, *esp* singer, dancer.

artless *a* naive; sincere; simple.

Art Nouveau *n Fr* late 19th century decorative art style based on curves, with leaf and flower motifs.

artsy-craftsy *a coll* 1 designed to have the look of simple handmade craftware 2 producing such work.

arty *a coll* showing a false enthusiasm for art or adopting a pretentious artistic style.

as *adv, conj* 1 when 2 because 3 equally, in the capacity of 4 in the manner of; like.

ASA *abbr* American Standards Association (of film speeds).

asafetida *n* gum resin with nauseating smell.

asap *abbr* as soon as possible.

asbestos *n* fibrous fireproof mineral substance.

ascend *v* go up; rise to higher rank; slope upward; climb; *ns* **ascent; ascendancy** domination; **ascension**.

ascertain *v* find out; get to know for certain.

ascetic *a* self-denying; austere; *n* hermit; *adv* **-ally**; *n* **asceticism**.

ASCII *abbr comput* American Standard Code for Information Interchange.

ascorbic acid *n* vitamin C.

ascot *n* tie or scarf with broad ends.

ascribe *v* attribute (to); *a* **ascribable**.

aseptic *a* free from pus-forming bacteria; *n* **asepsis**.

asexual *a* 1 without sex 2 having no interest in sex.

ash *n* gray powdery residue of anything burned; *pl* **ashes** cremated human remains; *as* **ashen, ashy**.

ashamed *a* troubled by sense of guilt or shame.

ashore *a, adv* on shore; to shore; on land.

ashtray *n* receptacle for tobacco ash.

Ash Wednesday *n* first day of Lent.

Asian *a, n* native of Asia; *a* **Asiatic**.

aside *adv* on, to, or at one side; apart; *n* phrase spoken in an undertone.

asinine *a* like an ass; stupid; *n* **asininity**.

ask *v* seek answer to; request; invite.

askance *adv* with sideways glance; with suspicion.

askew *a adv* sideways; out of line.

aslant *adv* on the slant; obliquely.

asleep *adv a* 1 into or in a state of sleep 2 numb.

asocial *a* not sociable or friendly.

a b c d e f g h i j k l m n o p q r s t u v w x y z

A

B C D E F G H I J K L M N O P Q R S T U V W X Y Z

asp *n* small poisonous snake.

asparagus *n* plant whose shoots are eaten as a vegetable.

aspect *n* appearance; expression; view; look.

aspen *n* poplar tree with tremulous leaves.

asperity *n* harshness; severity; roughness.

aspersion *n* derogatory, damaging remark.

asphalt *n* bituminous substance for surfacing roads.

asphyxiate *v* cause or undergo suffocation; *ns* **asphyxia, asphyxiation.**

aspic *n* savory jelly.

aspidistra *n* indoor plant with green glossy leaves.

aspirate *n* breathed sound, usually expressed by letter *h*; *v* pronounce with breath; draw off (fluid, etc.) from cavity, by means of **aspirator;** *a* **aspirated.**

aspire *v* seek eagerly; *a* **aspiring;** *n* **aspiration 1** strong desire **2** act of breathing **3** pronunciation of an aspirate.

aspirin *n* drug used for relief of pain.

ass *n* **1** member of horse family **2** stupid person.

assail *v* attack; *a* **assailable;** *n* **assailant.**

assassin *n* treacherous (*usu* political) murderer; *v* **assassinate;** *n* **-ation.**

assault *n* sudden attack; *v* make an assault.

assay *n* testing for characteristics of a substance; *v* test or analyze; *n* **assayer.**

assemble *v* collect; fit together; *ns* **assembler; assembly 1** gathering of persons **2** collection of parts.

assembly line *n* sequence of machines and workers for assembling parts in a factory.

assent *v* agree; concur; *n* compliance, agreement.

assert *v* state strongly; declare; *n* **assertion;** *a* **assertive** aggressively confident; *adv* **-ly.**

assess *v* estimate and fix amount of (fine or tax); estimate value; *a* **assessable;** *ns* **assessment, assessor.**

asset *n* thing of value belonging to person, business, etc.; *pl* all such property.

asset-stripping *n* buying assets from a company in financial difficulties and selling them at a profit.

asseverate *v* state emphatically; *n* **asseveration.**

assiduity *n* diligence; perseverance; *a* **assiduous;** *adv* **-ly;** *n* **-ness.**

assign *v* make over; allot; fix; ascribe; *a* **assignable;** *ns* **assignment** allotted task; **assignee; assignation** secret meeting.

assimilate *v* absorb physically or mentally, make similar; *a* **assimilable;** *n* **assimilation.**

assist *v* help; aid; attend; *ns* **assistant, assistance.**

assize *n* judicial inquest.

associate *v* join; connect; combine; *n* partner; member of a society; *a* linked in function; *n* **association** union of persons for common purposes.

assonance *n* rhyming of vowel sounds; *a* **assonant.**

assort *v* separate into sorts or classes; *a* **assorted;** *n* **assortment** mixed kinds.

assuage *v* soothe; quench; *n* **-ment.**

assume *v* put on; take upon oneself; adopt; *n* **assumption.**

assure *v* make sure; state positively; *a* **assured** confident; *adv* **assuredly** certainly; *n* **assurance** pledge; confidence; insurance.

asterisk *n* symbol (*) used by printers.

asteroid *n* small planet; *a* star-shaped.

asthma *n* chronic or acute condition of the lungs.

astigmatism *n* defect in eye causing faulty vision; *as* **astigmatic;** *adv* **astigmatically.**

astir *a, adv* in motion; in state of excitement.

astonish *v* fill with wonder; amaze; *a* **astonishing;** *adv* **astonishingly;** *n* **astonishment.**

astound *v* strike with amazement or alarm; *a* **astounding;** *adv* **astoundingly.**

astraddle *a, adv* straddling; astride.

astrakhan *n* curly pelt of unborn Astrakhan lamb.

astral *a* of stars; **astral body** ghost.

astray *a, adv* off right path; of mental error; of moral lapse.

astride *adv* with one leg on each side.

astringent *n* drug or other agent causing contraction (of tissues, cut blood vessels); *n* **astringency.**

astro- *prefix* of the stars and outer space.

astrolabe *n* early instrument for measuring altitude of stars, planets, etc., above the horizon.

astrology *n* pseudoscience of prediction of events by stars; *n* **astrologer;** *a* **astrological.**

astronaut *n* traveler in space.

astronomy *n* science of heavenly bodies; *n* **astronomer;** *a* **astronomical 1** of astronomy **2** unusually large in number or quantity.

astrophysics *n* study of physics and chemistry of stars.

astute *a* shrewd; wily; *adv* **astutely;** *n* **astuteness.**

asunder *adv* apart; into parts; *a* separated.

asylum *n* sanctuary; place for care of insane.

asymmetry *n* irregularity; absence of symmetry; *adv* **asymmetrically.**

at *prep* expressing general position in space or time; *idm* **go at it** get busy doing something.

atavism *n* resemblance to remote ancestor; reversion to earlier type; *a* **atavistic.**

ate *pt of* **eat.**

atheism *n* belief that there is no God; *n* **atheist;** *a* **atheistic.**

athirst *a* thirsty; eagerly desiring.

athlete *n* one skilled in physical exercises; *a* **athletic;** *adv* **-ally;** *n* **athletics.**

Atlantic *a* relating to the Atlantic Ocean.

atlas *n* **1** book of maps **2** top vertebra of neck.

atmosphere *n* **1** gaseous envelope surrounding earth or any heavenly body **2** any moral or mental influence; *a* **atmospheric;** *adv* **-ally;** *n* **atmospherics** disturbances in radio reception.

atoll *n* coral island; belt of coral reefs surrounding lagoon.

atom *n* smallest particle of an element; *v* **atomize** reduce to atoms; *ns* **atomization; atomizer** device for changing liquids into fine spray.

atomic *a* pertaining to atoms. Hence: **a. bomb; a. energy; a. reactor; a. warfare; a. weight.**

atomic number *n* number of protons in nucleus of atom.

atomize *v* reduce to fine particles of spray; *n* **atomizer.**

atonal *a mus* without any sense of key; *n* **atonality.**

atone *v* make amends; expiate; *n* **atonement.**

atop *adv, prep* at the top (of).

atrium *n* **1** enclosed court of public building **2** one of two upper chambers of the heart.

atrocious *a* abominable; wicked; evil; *adv* **-ly;** *ns* **-ness; atrocity** brutal deed.

atrophy *n pl* **-atrophies.** wasting away of body; weakening of mental or moral power; *v* **-phying, -phied.** (cause to) waste away; *a* **atrophied.**

atropine *n* poison obtained from belladonna.

attach *v* **1** fasten; affix **2** seize legally; *a* **attached;** *n* **attachment.**

attaché *n Fr* member of diplomatic staff; **attaché-case** small case for carrying documents.

attack *v* **1** assault; assail **2** work on; *n* **attacker.**

attain *v* accomplish; achieve; *a* **attainable;** *ns* **attainment, attainability.**

attainder *n* loss of civil rights through judicial sentence; disgrace; dishonor.

attar *n* perfume distilled from flower petals.

attempt *v* try; endeavor; *n* effort, try.

attend *v* **1** give heed (to) **2** be present **3** escort; *n* **attendance 1** act of being present **2** those present; *a, n* **attendant;** *a* **attentive;** *adv* **-ly;** *ns* **-ness, attention.**

attenuate *v* make thin; *a* **attenuated;** *n* **attenuation.**

attest *v* **1** testify **2** put

a
b
c
d
e
f
g
h
i
j
k
l
m
n
o
p
q
r
s
t
u
v
w
x
y
z

(someone) on oath; *n* **attestation**.

attic *n* small room under roof of house; garret.

attire *v* dress; put robes on; *n* dress; clothing.

attitude *n* posture; disposition; *v* **attitudinize** adopt affected gestures.

attorney *n* lawyer; one acting for another in legal matters; **attorney general** chief legal officer.

attract *v* draw toward; allure; *n* **attraction**; *a* **attractive**; *adv* **-ly**; *n* **-ness**.

attribute *n* characteristic quality of thing or person; *v* ascribe (to); *a* **attributable**; *n* **attribution**.

attrition *n* act of wearing away by friction.

attune *v* **1** bring into harmony **2** help to get used to.

atypical *a* not representative; *adv* **-ly**.

aubergine *n* dark purple color.

auburn *a* reddish- or golden-brown.

auction *n* public sale in which articles are sold to highest bidder; *v* sell by auction; *n* **auctioneer**.

audacious *a* bold; impudent; *adv* **audaciously**; *ns* **audaciousness, audacity**.

audible *a* able to be heard; *adv* **audibly;** *n* **audibility**.

audience *n* **1** assemblance of persons present or looking on **2** interview or formal hearing.

audio *a* of sound signals.

audio- *prefix* of, for, or using sound.

audiometer *n* instrument measuring power of hearing.

audiovisual *a* combining sound and vision.

audit *v* official scrutinizing of accounts; *n* **auditor**.

audition *n* **1** sense of hearing **2** test performance for singer, actor, etc.; *v* conduct such a test.

auditorium *n pl* **-ums, -ia.** building in which an audience gathers.

auditory *a* of the sense of hearing.

au fait *a Fr* well informed.

auger *n* tool for boring holes into wood.

augment *v* cause to increase; *n* **augmentation**.

augur *n* soothsayer; *v* predict; *n* **augury** omen.

August *n* eighth month of the year.

auk *n* type of seabird.

auld lang syne *Scot* traditional expression of friendship and good times long ago.

aunt *n* mother's or father's sister; uncle's wife.

au pair *n Fr* young person, *usu* foreign, living in a family home and helping with housework or care of children.

aura *n* mysterious emanation surrounding living things.

aural *a* of the ear; *adv* **aurally**.

aureola, aureole *n* sun's corona; celestial crown or halo.

auricle *n* external ear of animals; upper chamber of heart; *a* **auricular**.

auricula *n* primroselike flower.

aurora *n* the dawn; **a. borealis** Northern Lights; **a. australis** similar lights in S Polar sky.

auspices *npl* **1** omens **2** patronage; *a* **auspicious** favorable; *adv* **-ly**.

Aussie *n, a coll* Australian.

austere *a* **1** stern **2** ascetic; *adv* **-ly**; *n* **austerity**.

austral *a* of or coming from the south; southerly.

Australasian *a* of Australia, N Zealand, and adjacent islands; native of Australasia.

Austro- *prefix* of Austria.

authentic *a* genuine; reliable; *adv* **-ally**; *n* **authenticity**; *v* **authenticate** prove real or genuine.

author *n* writer of book, play, poem, etc.; originator; *fem* **authoress**; *n* **authorship**.

authoritarian *n, a* (person) expecting complete obedience from others; *n* **authoritarianism**.

authority *n* **1** right to command; natural power **2** expert **3** controlling body; *a* **authoritative**, *adv* **-ly**; *v* **authorize** give authority or approval to.

autism *n* psychological disorder, *esp* in children, where one is unable to relate to or communicate with others; *a, n* **autistic**.

auto- *prefix* **1** self **2** car; motor.

autobiography *n* life of person

written by himself; *a* **autobiographic(al)**; *n* **autobiographer.**

autocrat *n* absolute monarch; *n* **autocracy**; *a* **autocratic**; *adv* **autocratically.**

autoeroticism *n* sexual arousal from one's own body; *a* **autocrotic.**

autograph *n* person's own signature; *v* write one's signature (in); *a* **autographic.**

autogiro, autogyro *n* aircraft designed for vertical ascent and descent by means of horizontal propeller.

autoharmony *n* prefabricated harmony in a musical synthesizer.

autoimmune *a* relating to the body's immune response to its own systems.

automat *n* food dispenser operated by coins in slots.

automate *v* cause to work by automation.

automatic *a* working by itself; behaving mechanically; *adv* **-ally.**

automatic pilot *n* device that automatically maintains an aircraft's course; also called **autopilot.**

automation *n* control of industrial processes by electronic and other means.

automaton *n* machine that performs human actions; *pl* **automatons**; *n* **automatism** mechanical action.

automobile *n* engine-driven passenger vehicle.

autonomy *n* self-government;

as **autonomic, autonomous**; *n* **autonomist** one who supports autonomy.

autopsy *n* examination of dead body by dissection.

autorhythm *n* prefabricated rhythm in a musical synthesizer.

autosuggestion *n* suggestion coming from within oneself.

autumn *n* third season of the year; *a* **autumnal.**

auxiliary *a* helping; additional; supplementary; *n* verb helping to make up tense, mood, etc. of another.

AV *abbr* **1** audiovisual **2** Authorized Version.

avail *v* be of use; benefit; *a* **available** at hand; capable of being used; *n* **availability.**

avalanche *n* mass of snow, ice rushing down a mountain.

avant-garde *a* favoring progressive ideas, *esp* in art and literature; *n* group of people promoting such ideas.

avarice *n* greed; cupidity; *a* **avaricious**; *adv* **-ly.**

avenge *v* inflict retribution for a wrong; take revenge for injury on behalf of someone; *n* **avenger.**

avenue *n* **1** way of approach **2** road bordered by trees **3** wide street in a town.

aver *v* **averring, averred.** affirm.

average *n* mean proportion; *a* mean, ordinary; *v* estimate average of or average rate of.

averse *a* opposed; unwilling; *n* **aversion 1** antipathy; dislike

2 thing or person disliked.

aversion therapy *n* method of curing addiction by instilling unpleasant associations in the mind.

avert *v* turn aside; prevent.

aviary *n* large cage for keeping birds; *n* **aviarist, aviculture.**

aviation *n* art of flying aircraft; everything connected with flying; *v* **aviate** fly an aircraft; *n* **aviator** pilot.

avid *a* eager; greedy; *adv* **avidly**; *n* **avidity.**

avionics *n* science of electronics applied to aviation.

avocado *n pl* **-dos.** pear-shaped tropical fruit.

avocation *n* occupation; minor pursuit; hobby.

avoid *v* shun; keep away from; refrain from; *a* **avoidable**; *adv* **avoidably**; *n* **avoidance.**

avoirdupois *n* **1** system of weights used in US and UK **2** *coll* excessive weight of person.

avow *v* own publicly to; admit openly; *a* **avowed**; *adv* **avowedly** admittedly; *n* **avowal** confession.

avuncular *a* of or like an uncle.

await *v* wait for; expect; be ready for.

awake *v* rouse from sleep or inaction; *pt* **awoke**; *pp* **awoken**; *a* no longer sleeping; vigilant *n* **awakening**; *idm* **a rude awakening** the shattering of an illusion.

a
b
c
d
e
f
g
h
i
j
k
l
m
n
o
p
q
r
s
t
u
v
w
x
y
z

A

B
C
D
E
F
G
H
I
J
K
L
M
N
O
P
Q
R
S
T
U
V
W
X
Y
Z

award *v* grant after due judgment; *n* something awarded after judgment; prize.

aware *a* conscious; cognizant; knowing; *n* **-ness.**

awash *a* just above or level with surface of water.

away *adv* at or to a distance; absent.

awe *n* fear with respect; solemn wonder; *v* fill with awe; *a* **awesome** causing awe.

awe-inspiring *n* causing feelings of awe and wonder.

awestruck *a* filled with awe.

awful *a* appalling; very bad; *adv* **awfully** very.

awhile *adv* for a short time.

awkward *a* **1** clumsy; ungainly **2** difficult to manage; disconcerting **3** ill at ease; embarrassment; *adv* **-ly;** *n* **-ness.**

awl *n* small pointed tool for piercing holes.

awning *n* canvas sheet stretched on framework used as protection from sun.

awoke *pt* **awoken;** *pp of* **awake.**

AWOL *abbr* absent without leave.

awry *a* crooked; twisted; *adv* wrong; askew.

ax, axe *n* chopping tool with wooden handle and iron head.

axiom *n* obvious truth; principle accepted without question; *a* **axiomatic;** *adv* **-ally.**

axis *n* imaginary line about which a body may rotate; real or imaginary line dividing figure into two equal parts; *pl* **axes;** *a* **axial;** *adv* **axially.**

axle *n* rod or bar connecting two wheels and on which wheel revolves.

ay, aye *adv, n ar* **1** always **2** yes.

ayatollah *n* Shiite Muslim religious leader.

azalea *n* flowering shrub of rhododendron family.

azimuth *n* distance of a star in angular degrees from N or S point of meridian; *a* **azimuthal.**

Aztec *n* American Indian people ruling Mexico before Spanish conquest.

azure *a* blue like the sky; *n* the color sky blue.

BA *abbr* Bachelor of Arts.

baa *n* the bleat of a sheep; *v* bleat.

baba *n* sweet rum cake.

babbitt metal *n* alloy of mainly tin and copper used to line verings.

babble *v* **1** talk indistinctly **2** reveal (secrets); *n* **1** foolish talk **2** murmur of stream; *n* **babbler**; *a* **babbling**.

babe *n* baby; inexperienced person.

baboon *n* kind of large ape.

baby *n* young child or animal; infant; *a* **babyish** childish; *n* **babyhood**.

baby boom *n* time of increase in birth rate; **baby boomer** *n* person born in the late 1940s

babushka *n Russ* cotton scarf worn on the head by women.

baby-sit *v* care for children when parents are out; *ns* **baby-sitter, baby-sitting**.

baby grand *n* small piano.

baby's breath *n* plant with small white flowers.

baccalaureate *n* bachelor's degree.

baccarat *n* gambling card game.

bachelor *n* **1** unmarried man **2** holder of degree at a four-year college; *ns* **bachelorette** unmarried girl, **bachelorhood**.

bacillus *n* minute plant organism either harmful or harmless; bacterium; *pl* **bacilli**; *a* **bacilliform**.

back *n* **1** part opposite the front **2** (part of body containing) the spine; *v* **1** move backward **2** support; *a* **1** situated behind **2** of the past **3** overdue; *adv* **1** away from the front **2** in or to an earlier condition **3** in return; *idm* **the back of beyond** isolated place without social or cultural activity; **be on somebody's back** hinder or annoy sb; *phr*

v **back down, back off** yield; *n* **backup 1** support **2** *comput* make a spare copy.

backache *n* lower back pain.

backbiting *n* malicious gossip; *n* **backbiter**.

backbone *n* spine, vertebrae; courage, firmness.

backbreaking *a* exhausting.

backdrop *n* **1** cloth for theatrical background **2** natural background.

backdate *v* make applicable from an earlier date.

backer *n* one who supports another, *esp* with money; one who bets on a horse or sporting event.

backfire *n, v* **1** *aut* (emit) loud explosion due to premature ignition of fuel **2** (of plans) go wrong.

backgammon *n* board game played with checkers and dice.

background *n* part of picture behind main figures **2** person's past history; *n, a* inconspicuous (position).

backhand *n* **1** shot played with back of hand toward opponent **2** side from which such a shot is played; *a* **backhanded 1** played on the backhand **2** (of personal remarks) equivocal.

backing *n* **1** anything used to cover back of object **2** support, aid **3** act of one who backs **4** *mus* accompaniment.

backlash *n* **1** sudden sharp recoil **2** hostile (*esp* political) reaction.

backlog *n* accumulation of unfinished business.

backpack *n* knapsack; *v* hike with backpack; *ns* **backpacker, backpacking**.

backpedal *v* 1 pedal backward 2 reverse in action, policy, or decision.

back projection *n* projection from behind a translucent screen to create an illusion of movement in front.

backseat *n* rear seat; *idm* **take a backseat** accept a less important role; *n* **backseat driver** passenger who tries to tell the driver how to drive.

back-slapping *n, a* jovial and noisy.

backside *n* rear part of person or animal, rump.

backslide *v* relapse into bad habits: *n* **backslider**.

backspace *n, v* (key to) move typewriter carriage back.

backstage *a, adv* 1 behind the stage 2 in private.

backstroke *n* swimming on one's back.

backtalk *n* answering back in an insolent manner.

backtrack *v* 1 go back over same path 2 reverse an earlier action or statement.

backup *n* 1 person or thing that supports or reinforces another 2 accumulation from a stoppage 3 alternative kept in reserve.

backward *adv* toward rear; with back first; *a* 1 turned back 2 retarded mentally 3 shy.

backwash *n* waves caused by passage of vessel.

backwater *n* small creek containing stagnant water; *coll* an isolated place.

backwoods *n* forest region beyond cleared land; *fig* culturally remote.

backyard *n* area behind house.

bacon *n* back and sides of pig, salted and smoked.

bacterium *n* one-celled plant organism; *pl* **bacteria**; *a* **bacterial;** *n* **bacteriology** study of bacteria; *a* **-ological;** *n* **-ologist**.

bad *a* evil; faulty; rotten; ill; *adv* **-ly;** *n* **-ness**.

bad blood *n* resentment.

bad debt *n* debt that cannot be paid.

bade *v pt of* **bid**.

badge *n* emblem of office, token of membership.

badger *n* nocturnal burrowing animal; *v* bait, tease.

bad-off *a* not having enough, *esp* of money; *comp* **worse-off,** *sup* **worst-off**.

badminton *n* game played with shuttlecock and racquets.

bad-mouth *v sl* malign.

baffle *v* confuse; puzzle; *n* plate to divert flow of liquid, gas, or sound waves; *n* **bafflement;** *a* **baffling**.

bag *n* 1 pouch; sack 2 day's take of game; *v* **bagging, bagged.** capture; acquire; *n* **bagful;** *a* **baggy** loosely hanging; *n* **bagginess**.

bagatelle *n* trifle; game where

players roll small metal balls into holes.

bagel *n* hard, ringlike roll.

baggage *n* 1 army equipment 2 luggage.

bagpipes *n pl* musical wind instrument.

baguette *n* long thin loaf of bread made esp. in France.

bail *n* 1 sum paid as security for person's reappearance in court 2 *cricket* one of two small sticks laid across top of wicket; *v* release on bail; **bail (out)** scoop water out; *coll* leave.

bailey *n* outer wall of castle; court enclosed by it.

bailiff *n* sheriff's officer; land agent or steward.

bailiwick *n* 1 district of bailiff's jurisdiction 2 person's area of expertise or authority.

bairn *n esp Scot* child, baby.

bait *n* anything used to lure prey; *v* put bait on; torment; give food to (*esp* horses); *n* **baiting**.

bake *v* cook or harden by means of heat; *ns* **baker; bakery; baking powder** powder used instead of yeast; *n* **baker's dozen** thirteen.

balaclava *n* close-fitting woolen hood, covering ears and neck.

balance *n* 1 weighing instrument 2 equilibrium 3 remainder 4 difference between credit and debit sides of an account 5 regulating mechanism in clock or watch; *v* weigh; be equal in weight to; adjust; be in state of equilibrium; *n* **balance sheet** statement of accounts.

balance of payments *n* difference between money imported and money exported over a given period.

balance beam *n* horizontal beam used for balancing in gymnstics.

balance of power *n* **1** situation where rival powers gain no advantage by making war **2** power of minor political party to influence affairs by alliance with others.

balance of trade *n* difference in value between goods imported and goods exported.

balcony *n* projecting platform outside window protected by railing; tier of seats above circle (in theater).

bald *a* having no natural covering, *esp* of hair; bare; plain; *adv* **baldly;** *n* **baldness.**

bald eagle *n* N American common eagle symbolozing the US.

balderdash *n* rubbish, nonsense.

baldric *n* ornamented belt worn over shoulder to carry sword, bugle, etc.

bale *n* bundle of goods, hay, etc. bound with cord or wire; *v* **1** make into a bale *v* **2** see **bail (out);** *phr v* **bale out** jump from aircraft by parachute in emergency.

baleful *a* evil, malicious; *adv* **-ly;** *n* **-ness.**

balk *n* hindrance; heavy, squared beam; division on billiard table; *v* avoid; hinder; jib *esp* of horse.

ball[1] *n* **1** roundish body of any size **2** bullet or shot; *v* form into a ball; *idm* **on the ball** alert and aware of new ideas; **play ball** cooperate.

ball[2] *n* social gathering for dancing; *n* **ballroom;** *idm* **have a ball** *coll* enjoy oneself.

ballad *n* traditional story in song; simple song.

ballade *n* **1** poem with three eight-lined stanzas and a short conclusion **2** *mus* romantic piece, *usu* for piano.

ballast *n* heavy material placed in ship's hold or balloon, to steady it; *v* steady with ballast.

ball bearings *n* steel balls used to relieve friction on bearings.

ball cock *n* device for regulating level of liquid.

ballerina *n* a female ballet dancer.

ballet *n* action or story expressed by dancing, miming, etc.; **balletomane** ballet lover.

ballistics *n* science of projectiles and means of their propulsion; *a* **ballistic;** *v sl* **go ballistic** go crazy, become irrational.

balloon *n* gas- or hot air-filled bag that rises in air;

inflatable rubber bag; *v* inflate; billow out in wind; *n* **balloonist.**

ballot *n* printed sheet used in voting; act of voting; *v* vote by ballot; *n* **ballot box 1** box for deposit of voting slips **2** system of democratic elections.

ballpark *n* **1** baseball field **2** *coll* approximate range of figures.

ballpoint *n, a* (pen) that dispenses ink by a rollerball.

ballroom *n* large room for dancing.

balm *n* **1** aromatic resin **2** fragrant garden herb **3** healing ointment; *a* **balmy;** *adv* **balmily;** *n* **balminess.**

balmoral *n* shoe, boot; round cap.

baloney, balogna *n* stupid talk; nonsense.

balsa *n* tropical tree whose wood is extremely light.

balsam *n* **1** aromatic resin **2** anything healing, soothing, or restorative.

balsam fir *n* Na American evergreen.

Baltimore oriole *n* orange and black bird.

baluster *n* small post supporting a handrail; *n* **balustrade** set of balusters.

bamboo *n* giant grass with hard, hollow, jointed stem.

bamboozle *v* trick, puzzle, or confuse.

ban *n* prohibition; denunciation; *v* **banning, banned.** forbid; exclude.

a
b
c
d
e
f
g
h
i
j
k
l
m
n
o
p
q
r
s
t
u
v
w
x
y
z

A
B
C
D
E
F
G
H
I
J
K
L
M
N
O
P
Q
R
S
T
U
V
W
X
Y
Z

banal *a* trite, trivial ordinary, *n* **banality**.

banana *n* tropical fruit tree; its fruit; *n* **banana split** rich, sweet dessert with ice cream, syrups, and bananas.

band *n* **1** tie or ligament of any material **2** flat strip applied on another object **3** body of persons united for common purpose, *esp* company of musicians; *v* unite; gather together; tie, fasten with a band.

bandage *n* strip of cloth used to bind up wounds; to apply a bandage to.

bandanna *n* colored handkerchief with design.

B and B *abbr* (place providing) bed and breakfast.

bandbox *n* lightweight box for hats.

bandeau *n* *Fr* **1** band keeping hair in place **2** band inside hat.

bandit *n* outlaw, robber, or brigand.

band saw *n* endless steel saw running over wheels.

bandstand *n* covered platform for band playing outdoors.

bandwagon *n* *idm* **climb/jump on the bandwagon** join in a successful or popular enterprise.

bandy *v* **-dying, -died.** pass to and fro; *idm* **bandy words** quarrel; *a* **bandy-legged** bowlegged.

bane *n* source of evil; curse, ruin; *a* **baneful**; *adv* **-ly**; *n* **-ness**.

bang[1] *n* sudden loud noise; sharp blow; *v* thump; beat, shut noisily; explode.

bang[2] *n* hair cut to form fringe.

bangle *n* ornamental bracelet for arm or ankle.

banish *v* drive into exile; (of mental action) dismiss; *n* **banishment**.

banister *n* rail and supports along a stairway.

banjo *n* *pl* **-jos**, or **-joes.** musical instrument of guitar family.

bank[1] *n* heap or mound of earth; edge of river, etc.; *v* **1** pile up **2** put aircraft at angle when turning.

bank[2] *n* **1** commercial concern engaged in keeping, lending, and exchanging money **2** place where something is stored; *v* deposit money in bank; have an account with bank; *phr v* **bank on** rely on; *ns* **banker, banking**.

bankcard *n* **1** plastic card used at automatic teller machines **2** credit card issued by a bank.

bank holiday *n* weekday when banks are closed.

bank rate *n* minimum interest rate fixed by central banks.

bankroll *n*, *v* (act as somebody's) source of finance.

bankrupt *n*, *a* insolvent person; *v* make bankrupt; *n* **bankruptcy**.

banner *n* flag as symbol of country, regiment, etc.

bannock *n* flat cake made of oatmeal or barley meal.

banns *n* announcement in church of intended marriage.

banquet *n* *Fr* ceremonial or official feast; *n* **banqueter**.

banshee *n* fairy whose wail supposedly warns of death.

bantam *n* **1** breed of small fowl **2** lightweight boxer.

banter *n* good-natured chaff; *v*; *a* **bantering**.

Bantu *n* **1** group of black communities native to central and S Africa **2** languages spoken by them; *a* **Bantu**.

banyan *n* Indian fig tree.

baobab *n* African tree with gourdlike fruit.

baptisia *n* N American legume.

baptism *n* ceremony of admitting person to Christian church by immersing in or sprinkling with water; *v* **baptize** name; *a* **baptismal**; *n* **baptist(e)ry** part of church where baptism is administered; *idm* **baptism of fire 1** first taste of warfare **2** first ordeal of a grueling kind.

Baptist *n*, *a* (member of Protestant church) believing in baptism by full immersion.

bar *n* **1** rod of solid material **2** sandbank at mouth of river **3** rail in courtroom **4** legal profession **5** counter at which alcoholic beverages are sold **6** obstruction **7** musical unit **8** nonmaterial obstacle; *v* fasten with (bar);

rule out; *prep* except; *idm* **bar none** without exception.

barb n backward-curving point on arrow, fishhook, harpoon, etc.; *as* **barbed, barbate**.

barbarian n uncivilized person; *ns* **barbarism, barbarity, barbarousness;** *a* **barbaric;** *adv* **barbarously**.

barbecue n outdoor feast; grid for roasting meat over charcoal fire; *v* cook in such manner.

barbell n weightlifting bar.

barber n one who cuts hair, shaves or trims beards.

babershop n barber's place of business.

barbican n outer defence of castle or fortress.

barbiturates n pl group of drugs used to induce sleep or ease pain; *a* **barbituric**.

bard n poet or minstrel *esp* Celtic; *a* **bardic**.

bare *a* naked; simple; empty; scanty; *v* reveal; *adv* **-ly;** *n* **-ness;** *a* **bare-faced** shameless; *idm* **the bare bones** only the basic essentials.

bargain n 1 agreement; pact 2 something obtained at small price; *v* make agreement; discuss or argue about terms.

barge n broad flat-bottomed boat; state or pleasure boat; *n* **bargee;** *v* force way clumsily.

baritone n, *a* voice ranging between tenor and bass.

barium n heavy white metallic element; **barium meal** n chemical taken internally to

enable the digestive tract to be X-rayed.

bark[1] n outside covering of trees; *v* strip bark from; scrape skin off.

bark,[2] **barque** n three-masted sailing ship; small ship; *ns* **barkentine, barquentine** small bark.

bark[3] n sharp cry or noise made by dog or fox; *v* speak sharply; *n* **barker** person who induces people at a fair or circus to see show.

barley n cereal plant; its seed or grain.

barm n yeast; leaven; *a* **barmy 1** frothy **2** *coll* dim-witted.

bar mitzvah n (ceremony for) Jewish boy of 13, taking on adult religious responsibilities.

barn n building for storing hay, grain, etc.; *ns* **barn dance** lively rustic dance; **barnyard; barn owl**.

barnacle n species of goose; type of shellfish that clings to rocks, ship's bottom, etc.

baro- *prefix* weight, pressure, *esp* of atmosphere.

barometer n instrument for recording atmospheric pressure; *a* **barometric;** *adv* **barometrically;** *ns* **barograph** type of barometer.

baron n lowest rank in peerage; *fem* **baroness;** *n* **barony;** *a* **baronial**.

baronet n lowest hereditary title; *n* **baronetcy**.

baroque *a* grotesque, fantastical; *n* style of music,

architecture, or art.

barrack n (usually *pl*) building in which soldiers live.

barracuda n large edible fierce fish.

barrage n continuous gunfire to cover movement of troops.

barrel n **1** cylindrical vessel or cask with bulging sides; measure of capacity **2** metal tube of gun; *v* pack, stow in barrel; *idm* **over a barrel** helpless; at one's mercy.

barren *a* sterile; bare; bleak; n **-ness**.

barricade n makeshift barrier; *v* block with barricade.

barrier n anything obstructing passage or advance.

barrio n sp Spanish-speaking area or city; *coll* guetto.

barrister n advocate in British courts of law.

barrow[1] n burial mound of earth or stones; tumulus.

barrow,[2] **wheelbarrow** n small wheeled handcart.

bartender n one who serves drinks in a bar.

barter n, *v* trade by exchange of goods.

basal cell n cell in the deepest layer of epidermis

basalt n dark-colored volcanic rock; *a* **basaltic**.

bascule n mechanism working on seesaw principle.

base[1] n **1** bottom; starting point **2** wordstem **3** main ingredient; *as* **basal, basic, baseless;** n **basement** floor below ground level; *idm* **not get to first base** *coll* make an

a b c d e f g h i j k l m n o p q r s t u v w x y z

unsuccessful start; *phr v* **base something on something** use something as a starting point.

base[2] *a* **1** low; mean; vicious; vile **2** (of metal) counterfeit; *n* **-ness;** *adv* **-ly.**

baseball *n* ball game played with two teams of nine players on a diamond-shaped field.

baseboard *n* molding between floor and wall.

baseline *n* line at the back end of a court in sports.

base metal *n* a metal or alloy of comparatively low value and relatively inferior in certain properties.

base rate *n* standard interest rate at a bank.

bases *n pl* of **basis.**

bash *n* a heavy blow; *sl* big party; *v* strike violently.

bashful *a* shy, modest; *adv* **-ly;** *n* **-ness.**

basic *a* fundamental; essential *adv* **-ally,** *n pl* **basics** basic principles.

BASIC (Beginner's All-purpose Symbolic Instruction Code) *n comput* simple programming language.

basil *n* aromatic plant of mint family.

basilica *n* church with double colonnade and apse.

basilisk *n* **1** fabulous lizard whose breath and glance were fatal **2** kind of crested lizard.

basin *n* **1** hollow vessel **2** region drained by river

3 dock; landlocked harbor.

basis *n* base, foundation, or principle; *pl* **bases.**

bask *v* luxuriate in (sun, etc.).

basket *n* **1** container made of woven rushes or canes **2** *banking* group of currencies *ns* **basketwork; basket case** *n sl* badly incapacitated person.

basketball *n* **1** ball game played with two teams of five players on a rectangular court **2** the ball used.

Basque *n* member of people living in W Pyrenees.

bass[1] *n* voice of deep quality; lower part of musical register; *a* low in tone.

bass[2] *n* common perch; **sea-bass** fish like salmon.

basset *n* type of hound with short legs.

bassinette *n* infant's bed.

bassoon *n* woodwind instrument with bass tone.

bast *n* fibrous strips from trees used for mats, ropes.

baste *v* moisten (roasting meat) with melted fat, etc.; tack loosely; thrash; *pr p* **basting.**

bastion *n* projecting part of fortification; bulwark.

bat[1] *n* small nocturnal mammal that flies around.

bat[2] **1** wooden implement used in ball games **2** **batting, batted.** blow; *v* strike with bat; *ns* **batter;** *idm* **not bat an eyelid** be unperturbed.

batch *n* whole product of one baking; set of things of the same kind.

bate *v* diminish; abate; moderate; *a* **bated;** *idm* **with bated breath** too anxious to breathe.

bath *n* act of washing; receptacle to wash in; *pl* place where baths may be taken.

bathe *v* apply water to; swim; *ns* **bather, bathing.**

bathing suit *n* suit for swimming.

bathos *n* fall from sublime to ridiculous; *a* **bathetic.**

bathrobe *n* **1** loose garment worn before and after having a bath **2** dressing gown.

bathroom *n* **1** room with bath **2** lavatory.

bathtub *n* vessel for bathing.

bathysphere *n* large metal sphere used for deep-sea observation.

batik *n* method of dyeing cloth using wax on parts not to be dyed; cloth dyed in this way.

batiste *n* fine cotton muslin.

bat mitzvah *n* (ceremony for) Jewish girl of 13, paralleling the **bar mitzvah.**

baton *n* stick, *esp* of orchestral conductor.

batsman *n* cricket player who bats.

battalion *n* army unit of about 1,000 men.

batten *n* narrow strip of wood; *v* secure with battens.

batten *v* grow fat; *phr v* **batten on** thrive at the expense of.

batter *v* beat heavily with repeated violent blows; *n* **1** mixture of mostly flour, milk, and eggs beaten together **2** baseball player who bats.

battery *n* **1** physical assault **2** artillery unit **3** group of cells for storing electrical energy **4** set of hen coops designed for quick production of eggs.

battle *n* fight between armies, fleets, or aircraft; *v* fight, struggle; *ns* **battlefield** place of battle; **battlefront** place where combat occurs; **battleship** heavily armed and armored warship.

battering ram *n* beam of wood with metal end formerly used in war for breaking down doors and walls.

battle-ax *n* **1** heavy axe used as weapon **2** *coll* hostile, domineering woman.

battlements *n pl* defensive wall(s) of a castle with openings for firing weapons through.

batty *a coll* crazy.

bauble *n* flashy jewelry; trinket; trifle.

baud *n* unit of measure for speed of a signal or data transfer, *esp* in computer modems.

bauxite *n* clay from which aluminum is obtained.

bawd *n* prostitute; procuress *a* **bawdy** lewd *n* **bawdiness**.

bawl *v* shout, cry loudly; *n* loud cry.

bay[1] *n* kind of laurel.

bay[2] *n* **1** inlet of sea **2** division of building **3** recess in a room; **sickbay** sick quarters.

bay[3] *n* deep bark of hound, *esp* in pursuit; *v* howl.

bay[4] *idm* **hold/keep at bay** keep at a safe distance.

bay[5] *n, a* (horse of) reddish brown (color).

bayonet *n* daggerlike blade attached to rifle; *v* wound with bayonet.

bayou *n* arm of a river

bay rum *n* fragrant liquid for cosmetics and medicines.

bay window *n* projecting window area of house.

bazaar *n* **1** Oriental market **2** sale in aid of charity.

bazooka *n* portable antitank gun.

BB *n* small metal shot from an air rifle; *n* **BB gun.**

BC *abbr* before the birth of Christ.

be *v* exist; have quality, feeling, or state; *pt* **was, were;** *pp* **been;** *pr p* **being.**

beach *n* seashore, *esp* if sand; *v* run (a boat) on shore; *ns* **beachcomber** beach-haunting tramp; *n* **beachhead** position established by invading troops.

beach buggy *n* vehicle with large wheels for riding on sand.

beacon *n* signal light or fire on hill, tower, etc.

bead *n* **1** small ball of glass, wood, etc., with hole through it, used to form necklace, rosary **2** small drop of moisture; *as* **beaded; beady** round, bright; *n* **beading**

molded strip of wood, stone, etc., on furniture or wall as decoration.

beadle *n* mace bearer; minor parish or church officer.

beagle *n* small hound used in hunting.

beak *n* bill of bird.

beaker *n* large cup or mug; glass vessel used by chemists.

be-all and end-all *n* only important thing.

beam *n* **1** thick piece of timber; bar of balance **2** shaft of light radio wave **3** extreme breadth of ship; *v* shine, emit, or radiate.

bean *n* leguminous plant; its kidney-shaped seed.

bean sprouts *n pl* edible sprouts from bean.

beanbag *n* **1** small bag of dried beans used for throwing **2** large cushion for use as an informal seat.

bear[1] *n* **1** heavy, clumsy, fur-clad mammal **2** rude, bad-tempered person; *a* **bearish,** *n* **-ness.**

bear[2] *v* **1** support, carry **2** endure **3** bring forth, give birth to; *pt* **bore;** *pp* **borne** (**born** in most contexts relating to birth); *n* **bearer** carrier; *phr vs* **bear down 1** overcome **2** press down hard; **bear down on** approach fast in a hostile manner; **bear on** be relevant to; **bear out** confirm; **bear up** persevere with courage; **bear with** tolerate patiently; *a* **bearable;** *adv* **-ably.**

beard n 1 growth of hair on man's cheeks and chin 2 gills of oyster; v confront face to face, as **bearded, beardless.**

bearing n 1 behavior 2 meaning 3 direction 4 heraldic emblem 5 part of machine where moving parts revolve.

béarnaise sauce n Fr sauce made mainly of egg yolks and butter.

bearskin 1 pelt of bear 2 tall black fur hat worn by guardsmen.

beast n 1 four-footed animal 2 brutal person; a **beastly** brutal; n **beastliness.**

beat v 1 hit repeatedly 2 conquer 3 mark (time) by strokes; 4 pulsate; pt **beat;** pp **beaten;** n 1 blow 2 throb 3 regular route; a **beaten** 1 shaped by beating 2 defeated 3 mixed by beating; idm **beat about the bush** talk indirectly without saying what one means; idm **Beat it!** sl Go away! idm **beat time** mark tempo of music by regular movements.

beater n electrical mixer.

beatify v lit make happy, blessed; a **beatific;** adv **-ally;** n **beatitude** supreme bliss.

beatnik n type of young person in late 1950s who rejected normal social conventions.

beau n boyfriend.

Beaufort scale n number scale indicating wind speeds.

beau geste n Fr gracious gesture.

Beaujolais n red table wine from Beaujolais region of France.

beautician n person who gives beauty treatment.

beauty n 1 loveliness; charm; grace 2 lovely woman; a **beautiful;** v **beautify** make beautiful; n **beauty spot** 1 beautiful place 2 mole or artificial dark spot on a woman's face.

beaver n water-loving rodent; its fur; v work hard.

becalmed a (of a ship) deprived of wind.

became pt of **become.**

because conj prep for the reason that; **because of** on account of.

bechamel n creamy white sauce.

beck n 1 small stream 2 nod, sign of command; idm **at one's beck and call** ready to carry out one's every order or request.

beckon v signal or call by a gesture.

become v **-coming, -came, -come.** come to be; suit; a **becoming** proper, enhancing appearance of; adv **-ly.**

BEd abbr Bachelor of Education.

bed n 1 thing to sleep on 2 piece of ground 3 foundation 4 mineral stratum 5 bottom of sea or river; v **bedding, bedded.** plant out; place on foundations.

bedazzle v enchant.

bedbug n wingless bloodsucking insect found in beds.

bedding n 1 bedclothes and mattress 2 straw or litter for sleeping on 3 foundation 4 geol stratification.

bedfellow n 1 person sharing bed 2 close companion.

bedeck v decorate, adorn.

bedevil v confuse, harass, bewitch; n **bedevilment.**

bedizen v dress in a cheap, gaudy way.

bedlam n lunatic asylum; noisy scene or uproar.

bed of roses n idyllic, carefree state.

Bedouin n sing or pl nomadic Arab(s).

bedpan n container used as toilet by person ill in bed.

bedraggle v drag through mire; a **bedraggled.**

bedridden a confined to bed, esp permanently ill.

bedrock n 1 solid rock 2 basic principles.

bedroll n sleeping blankets rolled up.

bedroom n room where one sleeps.

bedside manner n doctor's way of talking tactfully.

bedsore n raw spot on skin from lying too long in bed.

bedspread n cover for bed, usu decorative.

bedstead n frame of bed on which mattress rests.

bed-wetting n urinating during sleep in bed.

bee n four-winged insect, producing honey; ns **bee-eater** small brightly colored bird; **beehive; beeswax;** idm **a bee in one's bonnet** an obsession; idm **the bee's knees** superior person or thing.

beech n species of tree; its wood.

beef n flesh of ox, cow, considered as food; pl **beeves;** a **beefy** sturdy.

beefcake n sl (photographs of) strong muscular men.

beefsteak n a cut of beef from the hindquarters.

behoove v be necessary for (someone).

beebalm n type of mint favored by bees.

beeline idm **make a beeline for** go directly toward.

been pp of **be.**

beep v, n (make) noise of or as of a car horn.

beer n alcoholic drink make from malted hops, yeast, etc.; a **beery.**

beeswax n wax taken from honeycomb.

beet n edible red vegetable root (**beetroot**); white root used in sugar manufacturing.

beetle[1] n insect with biting mouth parts; heavy wooden mallet.

beetle[2] v overhang; n **beetle brow** heavy projecting brow.

befall v happen to; pt **befell** pp **befallen.**

befit v **befitted.** be worthy of; fitting; a **befitting;** adv

befittingly.

before prep **1** front of **2** preceeding in time, rank; adv in front; sooner; conj rather than; adv, a **beforehand** in advance, ahead of time.

befriend v be a friend to; help.

befuddle v confuse; make hazy.

beg v **begging, begged. 1** entreat **2** live by receiving alms; n **beggar** person who begs; a **beggarly;** idm **beg the question** assume that an answer or proof has been given when it has not; idm **go begging** be unwanted.

beget v **-getting, -get** or **-got.** produce; father; pt **begot, begat;** pp **begotten;** n **begetter.**

begin v **-ginning, -gan, -gun.** commence, start; originate; ns **beginner** novice; **beginning.**

begone interj go away!

begonia n colorful tropical plant.

begrime v soil with dirt or smoke.

begrudge v envy (a person something); be stingy in giving.

beguile v **1** deceive; cheat **2** cheat; amuse; charm; n **beguiler** deceiver, seducer; a **beguiling.**

behalf idm **on behalf of** in the name of.

behave v conduct (oneself); act with decorum; n **behavior** conduct, manners.

behaviorism n belief that all

human action could be related to stimulus and response; n, a **behaviorist.**

behead v cut the head off.

behest n order; command.

behind prep at back of; in support of; inferior to; adv in arrears; idm **run behind** idm be late.

behold v to look at, see; pt, pp **beheld;** n **beholder;** a **beholden** under an obligation.

beige n a (of) light yellowish brown (color).

being n **1** existence **2** human creature **3** essence, nature.

belabor v beat heartily; thrash.

belated a unduly deferred; adv **-ly.**

belay v make fast or secure (a rope).

belch v **1** release wind through mouth **2** pour out under force; n **1** release of wind **2** spurt of flame, smoke, etc.

beleaguer v besiege.

belfry n bell tower.

belie v **-lying, -lied.** give lie to; misrepresent.

believe v accept as true; place trust in; have faith; ns **believer, belief;** as **believable, believing.**

belittle v make little of; disparage; n **-ment.**

bell n **1** hollow cup-shaped object giving musical sound when struck **2** cry of stag in rut; v roar, bellow.

belladonna n deadly nightshade; poisonous drug.

bell-bottoms n pl flared parts.

belle n beautiful young woman.

belles-lettres n pl Fr essays that are purely literary.

bellhop n hotel employee who shows guests to their rooms, carries luggage, etc.

bellicose a warlike; quarrelsome; n **bellicosity**.

belligerent a waging war; aggressive; adv **-ly;** n **belligerence**.

bellow v roar, cry out; n roar of a bull, etc.; any deep cry or shout.

bellows n apparatus for producing drafts of air.

Bell's palsy n paralysis of facial nerve.

bell tower n tower where bell is located.

belly n lower part of body beneath diaphragm, abdomen; v swell out, bulge.

bellyache v grumble frequently, without justification.

belly button n coll navel.

belly dance n erotic type of dance by woman from the Middle East n **belly dancer.**

belly flop n dive that hits water belly first.

belong v be owned; be part or member; n **belongings** possesions.

beloved a, n (one who is) greatly loved.

below prep lower than; a, adv beneath.

belt n 1 band of leather or other fabric worn around waist 2 zone 3 endless band used in driving machinery; v 1 encircle 2 sl thrash; a

belted; idm **below the belt** coll unfair(ly); idm **under one's belt** coll already acquired; **belt out** coll sing or emit very loudly.

beluga n type of sturgeon or its roe; a **beluga caviar.**

belvedere n structure with a beautiful view.

bemoan v lament; grieve for.

bemuse v daze, confuse, stupefy.

bench n long seat, worktable; judge's magistrates' seat in court; coll of judges.

benchmark n 1 mark used by land surveyors 2 standard example for making comparison.

bend n 1 curve 2 type of knot; v twist; turn 1 curve 2 submit; pt, pp **bent;** idm **round the bend** coll insane; n pl **the bends** coll decompression sickness suffered by deep-sea divers who surface too quickly.

beneath adv below; prep underneath.

benediction n blessing; blessing at end of church service.

benefactor n person who gives help or money fem **benefactress;** n **benefaction.**

beneficent a doing good; n **beneficence.**

benefit n favor; profit; v **-fited** or **-fitted.** do or receive good; pt, pp **benefited;** ns **benefaction** good deed; **benefactor;** a **beneficial** useful; improving; adv **-ly;** ns **benefice** church living;

beneficiary one benefiting from will, etc.

benevolence n kindliness; generosity; a **benevolent.**

benighted a 1 overtaken by darkness 2 ignorant.

benign a 1 kindly; gentle; gracious 2 (of diseases) not malignant; adv **- ly** n **benignity.**

benison n blessing.

bent[1] pt, pp of bend idm **bent on** determined on; a 1 distorted 2 sl dishonest.

bent[2] n 1 inclination; aptitude 2 stiff coarse grass.

bentwood a crafted from wood bent into shape.

benumb v make numb.

benzedrine n drug used as stimulant and nasal spray.

benzene n aromatic liquid obtained from coal tar.

benzine n colorless inflammable solvent from petroleum.

bequeath v give or leave by will; n **bequest.**

berate v scold; rebuke.

bereave v to deprive by death; rob fig of immaterial things; pp, pt **bereaved** (but pp **bereft** in fig sense); n **-ment.**

beret n small, soft, flat cap.

berg n iceberg.

bergamot n (oil from) pear-shaped Asian fruit.

beri-beri n disease caused by lack of vitamin B.

Bermuda shorts n pl shorts cut just above the knee.

berry n small fleshy fruit containing seeds but no

stone; a **berried**.

berserk a mad; wild; frenzied.

berth n 1 space for anchoring ship in dock 2 sleeping place on ship or train; v moor a ship; idm give **somebody a wide berth** keep well away from somebody.

beryl n green mineral.

beseech v implore, beg; a **beseeching**; adv -ly; pt, pp **besought**.

beset v -setting, pt -set. surround; assail; a **besetting**.

beside prep at side of; adv, prep **besides** other than; in addition to.

besiege v beset with armed forces; n **besieger**.

besmirch v soil, smear.

besotted a 1 foolish 2 drunk.

bespatter v spatter; **besotted** a 1 foolish 2 drunk.

bespeak v arrange in advance; claim; pt **bespoke**; pp **bespoken**; made to order.

bespectacled a wearing spectacles.

best a, adv (sup of **good, well**) most excellent(ly); v beat (someone); get the better of.

bestial a coarse; brutish; n **bestiality**.

bestir v -stirred. stir up, rouse to action.

best man n bridegroom's attendant.

bestow v give, stow away; n **bestowal**.

bestride v put one's legs on each side of (something); pt **bestrode**; pp **bestridden**.

bet v **betting**. bet or **betted**.

wager; n stake given; n **bettor** one who bets.

beta n second letter of Greek alphabet.

betake v idm **-takes, -taking, -took, -taken. betake oneself to** fml go to.

bete-noire n Fr person or thing one hates most.

bethink oneself v ar remind oneself; think again.

betide v happen to; befall.

betimes adv in good time; early.

betoken v presage.

betray v act falsely toward; reveal secret improperly; ns **betrayal, betrayer**.

betroth v promise, engage in marriage; ns **betrothal, betrothed**.

better a, adv (comp of **good, well**) (in a) superior or improved (way); v, n **betterment**.

between prep, adv separated by.

betwixt prep, adv between.

bevel n 1 sloping edge 2 joiner's tool; v **beveled**. form angle.

beverage n drink (other than water).

bevy n group of girls or women; flock of larks, quails.

bewail v 1 mourn over 2 complain over.

beware v be on one's guard (against).

bewilder v perplex, confuse; as **bewildered, bewildering**; adv -ly; n -ment.

bewitch v cast a spell over; fascinate; a **bewitching**.

beyond prep, adv 1 to or on

the other side (of) 2 exceeding; past the limit of 3 apart from; idm be **beyond somebody** be too hard for somebody to understand.

bezel n stanted surface on a cutting tool or gem.

bi- prefix two.

bialy n flat roll topped with onions.

bias n 1 slant; prejudice 2 tendency; v influence unfairly; pt, pp **bias(s)ed**; pr p **bias(s)sing**; a **biased** prejudiced n **bias binding** strip of material to bind edges.

bib n garment placed under child's chin to protect its clothes; v tipple; n **bibber**.

Bible n sacred book of Jews and Christians; idm **one's bible** authoritative book on any subject; a **biblical**; ns **B.-basher, B.-puncher, B.-thumper** sl over enthusiastic exponent of the Bible.

Bible Belt n area in the south holding to a fervent fundamental belief in the Bible.

bibliography n study of books; list of books on a particular subject; a **bibliographical**; n **bibliographer**.

bibliophile n person who loves or collects books.

bibulous a given to drinking alcoholic drinks.

bicameral a having two legislative chambers.

bicarbonate of soda n baking soda; sodium bicarbonate,

a

b

c

d

e

f

g

h

i

j

k

l

m

n

o

p

q

r

s

t

u

v

w

x

y

z

A
B
C
D
E
F
G
H
I
J
K
L
M
N
O
P
Q
R
S
T
U
V
W
X
Y
Z

used as a medicine or as a raising agent in baking.

bicentenary n a (celebrating) the 200th anniversary.

biceps n muscle with double attachment, *esp* of upper arm.

bicker v quarrel; wrangle; n **bickering**.

bicycle n two-wheeled vehicle propelled by foot pedals; v ride this vehicle.

bid v command, invite; *pt* **bade**; *pp* **bidden**; offer, try; *pt*, *pp* **bid**; n 1 offer to give certain price 2 attempt 3 (in card games) a call *ns* **bidder**, **bidding**.

bide v wait; remain; dwell.

bidet n low bathroom fixture for washing anal area and genitals.

biennial a happening every two years; n plant lasting two years; *adv* **-ly**.

bier n wooden frame on which a coffin is carried.

biff n sharp blow with fist; v strike such a blow.

bifid a divided into two lobes.

bifocals n pl eyeglasses with double lenses to correct both distant and reading vision; a **bifocal**.

bifurcate v divide into two branches.

big a **-gger**, **-ggest.** possessing great size, bulk, etc.

bigamist n one who marries another while still married; n **bigamy**; a **bigamous**; *adv* **-ly**.

big bang n explosion of matter

from which the universe is believed to have originated n **the big bang theory**.

big dipper n *astron* **Great Bear;** *Brit* the Plough.

big end n *aut* end of connecting rod joining crankshaft.

big game n large wild animals, *esp* when hunted.

bighead n *coll* conceited person.

bighearted a generous.

bighorn n N American mountain sheep.

bight n 1 loop in rope 2 a wide bay.

bigot n narrow-minded, intolerant person; a **bigoted**; n **bigotry**.

big shot n very influential person.

big time n *coll* top level in business, *esp* entertainment.

big top n circus tent.

bijou n *Fr* (of house, apartment, etc.) small, elegant.

bigwig n *coll* important person.

bike n, v *coll* bicycle.

bikini n small two-piece bathing suit for women.

bilateral a having two sides; *adv* **-ly**.

bile n 1 secretion of liver, aiding digestion 2 ill humor.

bilious a 1 sick; sickly; 2 yellowish n **-ness**.

bilge n 1 space in ship's bottom into which filth and seawater drain 2 dirt collecting there 3 *coll* stupid talk or writing.

bilingual a of or using two languages.

bilk v cheat, defraud, elude payment of (debt).

bill[1] n 1 bird's beak 2 point of anchor; *idm* **bill and coo** kiss and cuddle.

bill[2] n 1 draft of proposed legislation 2 statement of money due 3 written program of events 4 poster 5 banknote; *idm* **foot the bill** pay the cost.

billabong n *Aust* 1 stagnant backwater pool 2 dry channel or bed of stream.

billboard n large outdoor advertisment.

billet n soldier's quarters; v provide lodgings.

billet-doux n love letter.

billfold n wallet.

billiards n game played with cue and balls on cloth-covered table with pockets.

billion n thousand million.

bill of health n notice of well-being.

billow n large swelling wave; v swell out; a **billowy**, **billowing**.

billy goat n male goat.

bimonthly *adv* every two months.

bin n 1 container for corn, coal, waste, etc. 2 rack for storing wine bottles.

binary a dual; involving two.

bind v 1 tie around; make tight 2 pledge (oneself) 3 fasten sheets of book into cover; *pt*, *pp* **bound;** *ns* **binder** bookbinder; thing that binds;

binding book covering.

bindweed n climbing plant; convolvulus.

binge n spree; drinking bout.

bingo n gambling game with random numbers.

binnacle n box for compass in ship.

binocular a using both eyes at once; n **binoculars** field or opera glasses.

binomial n algebraic expression having two terms.

bio- prefix life.

biochemistry n chemistry of living organisms.

biodegradable a capable of being decomposed by nature.

biography n story of person's life written by somebody else; study of such writings; n **biographer;** a **biographical.**

biology n study of living organisms; n **biologist;** a **biological** adv **-ly.**

bionic a 1 of bionics 2 having superhuman power.

bionics n 1 study of biological functions applicable to development of electronic equipment 2 use of mechanical parts to replace damaged living organs.

biopic n life of a famous person in film.

biopsy n analysis of body tissue and fluid to test for disease.

bioscope n apparatus for projecting motion pictures.

biosphere n the part of the earth's service and atmosphere that supports life.

biotechnology n use of living cells in industry.

bipartisan a representing two parties or sides.

bipartite a in two parts; shared by two parties.

biped n a two-footed animal.

biplane n aircraft with two pairs of wings.

birch n 1 tree with thin, smooth bark; wood of this tree 2 birch rod used for caning; v to flog.

bird n feathered biped that lays eggs.

bird brain n coll stupid person; a **bird-brained.**

birdie n, v golf score (of) one under par; n coll bird.

birdlime n sticky material spread to snare birds.

bird of paradise n songbird of New Guinea with bright plumage.

bird's-eye view n view from above.

biretta n square black cap worn by RC priests.

birth n bearing of offspring; act of being born; parentage; n **birthright** patrimony.

birth control n contraception.

birthday n anniversary of the day one was born.

birthmark n distinguishing mark on skin from birth.

birthrate n number of births over a given period.

birth sign n sign of zodiac under which one is born.

biscuit n thin, crisp bread made of eggs, flour, etc.

bisect v divide into two parts;

a **bisectional;** ns **bisection; bisector** divider of angle into two equal parts.

bisexual a of both sexes; sexually attracted to both sexes.

bishop n clergyman of high rank in Christian church; n **bishopric** his diocese or office.

bismuth n metallic element used as medical drug.

bison n large wild ox, American buffalo.

bistro n Fr small wine shop or restaurant.

bit n 1 small portion; fragment 2 tool for boring 3 metal mouthpiece of bridle 4 comput smallest unit of information; v fit bit in (horse's mouth).

bitch n female dog or wolf, vixen.

bite v 1 use teeth upon 2 act on by friction 3 pierce; pt **bit;** pp **bitten;** pr p biting; a **biting** (adv **-ly**) scathingly; n **bite** 1 nip with teeth 2 wound (by teeth) 3 sting 4 taking of bait; idm **bite off more than one can chew** try something beyond one's ability; idm **bite the bullet** cope with a painful situation; idm **bite the dust** coll 1 fall down dead 2 be defeated.

bit part n dram small speaking part.

bitter a of sharp taste; opposite of sweet; ranking; piercing; adv **-ly;** n **-ness** n **bitter** light beer.

bitters n liquor with bitter

a
b
c
d
e
f
g
h
i
j
k
l
m
n
o
p
q
r
s
t
u
v
w
x
y
z

A
B
C
D
E
F
G
H
I
J
K
L
M
N
O
P
Q
R
S
T
U
V
W
X
Y
Z

vegetable ingredients.

bittern n marsh bird noted for deep, booming cry.

bittersweet n woody nightshade; a fig pleasant but sad.

bitty a made of many bits, without coherence.

bitumen n asphalt; natural mineral pitch; a **bituminous**.

bivalve n mollusk with double-hinged shell, as oyster.

bivouac n temporary rest spot for troops.

bizarre a unusual, odd, fantastic.

blab v reveal secrets; n **blabber** or **blabbermouth** coll indiscreet talkative person.

black n 1 darkest color 2 people of African or Caribbean origins 3 darkness; a 1 somber 2 wicked 3 sullen; v **black, blacken** make black; denigrate; n **-ness;** v **blackball** vote against; ns **blackberry** bramble; **blackbird** song bird; **black humor** grim satire.

black belt n (person of) top grade in judo or karate.

black box n automatic flight recorder in aircraft.

blackcurrant n bush with small edible black berries; fruit of this.

Black Death n 14th century epidemic of bubonic plague.

black economy n unofficial business enterprises that avoid assessment for tax purposes.

blackguard n scoundrel, worthless person; v revile; a **blackguardly**.

blackhead n small black pimple.

black hole n area in outer space from which light or matter cannot escape.

black ice n invisible ice on a road surface.

blackjack n 1 hand weapon type of cosh 2 a card game 3 beer or ale tankard.

blackleg n cheater.

blacklist n list of people in disfavor or due for punishment; v **blacklist**.

black magic n magic invoking the powers of evil.

blackmail n, v 1 attempt to extort money by threatening to reveal a guilty secret 2 use threats to induce someone to act in a certain way; n **blackmailer**.

Black Maria n coll police van for carrying prisoners.

black market n illegal trading of goods; n **black marketeer.**

blackout n failure of electricity; temporary loss of consciousness.

black pepper n condiment from E Indian plant.

black power n movement to promote political power for black people.

black sheep n disreputable member of family.

blacksmith n a smith who forges iron.

black spot n plant disease distinguised by black spots

on leaves.

blackthorn n thorntree, which bears sloes.

black-tie a when dinner jackets should be worn.

black widow n very poisonous type of spider.

bladder n sac in body for holding secreted liquids; any tough, inflated, membraneous bag; n **bladder wrack** seaweed with strings of air capsules.

blade n cutting edge of knife etc; flat of oar; bat, propeller, etc.; long, thin leaf of grass, corn, etc.; a **bladed**.

blame v censure; find fault with; hold responsible; n culpability; a **blameless** adv **-ly**; a **blameworthy**.

blanch v make white; scald; grow pale.

bland a gentle; mild; urbane; n **-ness**.

blandish v flatter; coax; n **-ment**.

blank n empty space; cartridge without shot; a 1 without writing, print expression, or features 2 (of verse) unrhymed 3 (of denial or refusal) total adv **-ly**; idm **draw a blank** get a negative result.

blank check n signed check with the amount left blank 2 authority to make all decisions.

blanket n soft cloth used for bedcover, horse rug, etc.; v cover with (as with blanket); idm **wet blanket** pessimist.

blare v utter loudly, like a

trumpet; *n* harsh noise.

blarney *n* flattery; *v* cajole, speak, coaxingly.

blasé *a Fr* dulled by pleasure, bored, cynical.

blaspheme *v* speak profanely of; talk irreverently; *ns* **blasphemer, blasphemy;** *a* **blasphemous;** *adv* **-ly.**

blast *n* sudden strong gust of wind; explosion; *v* scorch; shatter by explosion; *phr v* **blast off** be launched by firing of rockets; *n* **blastoff.**

blasted *a* 1 ravaged by wind or fire 2 *coll* annoying.

blast furnace *n* furnace for melting iron ore.

blatant *a* noisy, vulgarly obvious; *adv* **blatantly;** *n* **blatancy.**

blather *v* talk foolishly; *n* stupid; foolish talk.

blaze[1] *n* burst of flame or intense light; outburst of rage, etc.; *v* burst into flame; shine brilliantly; *idm* **blaze a trail** act as a pioneer.

blaze[2] *n* mark tree by cutting bark; white mark on face of animal; *v* mark (tree or trail) by cutting bark.

blazer *n* lightweight sports jacket.

blazon *n* coat of arms; *v* paint shield with arms; proclaim widely.

bleach *v* whiten, *esp* of cloth; *n* **bleaching.**

bleachers *n* tiered spectator seats.

bleak *a* bare, desolate; cheerless; *n* **bleakness.**

blear *a* watery, dim; *v* dim, blur; *a* **bleary.**

bleat *n* cry of sheep, goat; *v* cry feebly; *n, a* **bleating.**

bleed *v* draw blood from; extort money from; lose blood; *pt, pp* **bled; bleeding** *a* losing blood; *idm* **bleed somebody dry** take all somebody's money.

bleep *n, v* (emit a) short high-pitched electronic sound, *esp* as a warning signal; *n* **bleeper.**

blemish *n* physical, moral defect; flaw; *v* mar; deface.

blend *v* mix together; *n* mixture; mingling; *pt, pp* **blended.**

bless *v* pronounce benediction; make holy; make happy; *n* **blessing;** *a* **blessed;** *n* **-ness.**

blight *n* disease or insect pest attacking plants; *v* spoil.

blimp *n* 1 small nonrigid airship 2 pompous reactionary 3 *sl* fat person; *a* **blimpish.**

blind *a* 1 sightless 2 lacking foresight 3 reckless 4 closed at one end; *n* 1 window shade 2 artifice; *v* make blind; *adv* **-ly;** *n* **-ness;** *a, n* **blinding;** *v* **blindfold** put something over the eyes of; *idm* **turn a blind eye** pretend not to notice; *idm* **blind somebody with science** impress or confuse somebody by display of specialized knowledge.

blind alley *n* 1 cul-de-sac 2 course of action that seems good but leads nowhere.

blind date *n coll* meeting arranged between two people who have never met, *usu* a man and a woman.

blinders *n pl* small flaps preventing horse from seeing sideways; *a* **blindered** narrow-minded.

blind spot *n* 1 part of retina not sensitive to light 2 area not visible to driver 3 subject on which one is ignorant.

blindworm *n* legless lizard; slow worm.

blink *v* flap eyelids rapidly; flicker; *fig* attempt to evade; *n* wink; twinkle; *idm* **on the blink** not working properly.

blip *n* 1 spot of light on radar screen 2 short, sharp sound.

bliss *n* perfect enjoyment, extreme happiness; *a* **blissful;** *adv* **blissfully;** *n* **blissfulness.**

blister *n* 1 bubblelike swelling full of liquid under the skin 2 swelling on surface of paint; *v* form blisters; *a* **blistering** 1 (of heat) extreme 2 (of criticism) severe.

blithe *a* carefree; *adv* **-ly;** *a* **blithesome.**

blitz *n* sudden attack.

blizzard *n* blinding snowstorm with high wind.

bloat *v* swell *a* **bloated;** *n* **bloater** smoked herring.

blob *n* spot; drop of liquid.

bloc *n* political or national alliance of interests.

block *n* 1 lump of wood 2 mold 3 plate used in

a
b
c
d
e
f
g
h
i
j
k
l
m
n
o
p
q
r
s
t
u
v
w
x
y
z

letterpress printing **4** group of buildings **5** obstruction **6** large quantity; *v* **1** stop **2** shape, *esp* hats; *ns* **blockhead** stupid person; **blockage** obstruction.

blockade *v* stop access by siege; *n* closure of port, etc.

block and tackle *n* device for lifting with pulleys.

blockbuster *n* **1** powerful bomb **2** any successful commercial promotion.

block letters *n* capital letters.

blond(e) *a* fair-colored; *n* person with fair hair and complexion.

blood *n* **1** red fluid circulating through body **2** kinship **3** life itself **4** dashing fellow; *adv* **-ily;** *ns* **-iness; bloodbath** massacre; *as* **bloodless; bloodcurdling** terrifying; **bloodshot** suffused with blood; **bloody 1** bloodstained; murderous **2** *sl Brit taboo* intensifier expressing any positive or negative attitude; *idm* **in cold blood** without emotion.

blood brother *n* man pledged to another like brothers.

blood count *n* (counting of) number of white corpuscles in a blood sample.

bloodhound *n* hunting dog; detective.

bloodletting 1 killing **2** removal of blood for medical reasons.

bloodmobile *n* mobile vehicle for taking blood donations.

blood pressure *n* force of

blood on inner walls of blood vessels.

bloodshed *n* the shedding of blood.

blood sport *n* killing of wildlife for sport.

bloodstock *n* thoroughbred horses.

bloodstone *n* opaque green stone with red flecks.

bloodthirsty *a* ferocious, savage, cruel.

Bloody Mary *n* cocktail of tomato juice with vodka.

bloody murder *idm* **scream bloody murder** protest noisily.

bloom *n* **1** blossom; **2** prime of life **3** thin film on certain fruits; *v* flower; prosper; *a* **blooming 1** flowering **2** *coll Brit* intensifier euphemism for bloody.

bloomers *n pl* short, baggy trousers gathered at the knee for women.

blossom *n* flower; *v* come into bloom.

blot *n* spot; disgrace; *v* **blotted.** stain, smudge, obliterate; *phr v* **blot out** hide; obliterate.

blotter *n* **1** paper for blotting or protecting **2** book for recording events.

blotch *n* discolored patch on skin, etc.; *a* **blotchy.**

blotto *a coll* very drunk.

blouse *n* loose kind of shirt; *usu* for women.

blow *v* produce current or gust of air; expel from lungs into trumpet etc.; *pt* **blew;** *pp* **blown;** *n* **1** blast **2** hard

knock **3** sudden setback; *a* **blown 1** winded **2** putrefying; *idm* **blow one's own trumpet/horn** praise oneself; *idm* **blow one's top/stack** *coll* lose one's temper; *idm* **blow somebody's mind** *sl* give somebody an exhilarating shock; *a* **mind-blowing;** *idm* **blow the whistle on** *coll* expose in order to put an end to (something illicit); *phr vs* **blow over** pass; **blow up 1** fill with air **2** enlarge **3** explode; destroy; be destroyed **4** begin with sudden force **5** reprimand; **blowhole** nostril of whale; breathing hole in ice.

blow-by-blow *a* related in detail chronologically.

blower *n* device that blows currents of air.

blown *pp of* blow.

blowout *n* **1** burst tire **2** melted fuse **3** escape of gas or oil **4** *coll* feast or party.

blowtorch *n* burner for removing old paint.

blubber *n* fat of whales; *v* weep.

bludgeon *n* short, heavy club; *v* strike with this.

blue *n* **1** color of unclouded sky **2** pigment **3** unhappy **4** indecent; *v* make or treat with blue; *idm* **out of the blue** unexpectedly; *n pl* **the blues 1** *coll* mental depression **2** melancholy type of jazz; *a* **bluish;** *ns* **bluebell** wild hyacinth; **blueprint** copy of plan; **bluestocking**

pedantic woman.

blue baby *n* baby with blue skin due to heart defect.

blue-blooded *a* of aristocratic descent.

blue chip *n, a* (industrial share) regarded as safe to invest in.

blue-collar *a* concerned with manual work.

blue-eyed boy *n coll* somebody's favorite who does no wrong.

bluegrass *n* **1** type of N American grass **2** type of country music from Kentucky.

blue jay *n* N American bird.

blue moon *idm* **once in a blue moon** *coll* hardly ever.

blue-sky *a* (of idea) having no practical application.

blue steak *n* rapid stream of words.

blue tit *n* small bird with blue top and yellow breast.

bluff[1] *n* steep headland, bank; *a* **1** having steep perpendicular front **2** hearty; outspoken; *adv* **-ly**.

bluff[2] *v* deceive; *n* deception; *idm* **bluff it out** survive by continued pretense; *idm* **call somebody's bluff** challenge somebody to carry out threat.

bluish *a* fairly blue.

blunder *n* mistake; *v* make such; stumble; flounder; *n* **blunderer;** *a* **blundering;** *adv* **blunderingly**.

blunt *a* having dull edge or point; outspoken; *v* dull edge of; *adv* **bluntly;** *n* **bluntness**.

blur *n, v* **blurred.** smear; blot.

blurb *n* brief description of book's contents.

blurt out *phr v* utter hastily or indiscreetly.

blush *v* grow red; *n* flush; *n, a* **blushing**.

bluster *v* (wind) blow boisterously; rage; scold; *n* noise; empty threats; *n* **blusterer;** *a* **blustery**.

BO *abbr coll* unpleasant body odor.

boa *n* **1** nonpoisonous snake that kills by crushing **2** fur of feather neck wrap.

boar *n* male pig; wild hog.

board *n* **1** plank **2** thick, stiff, compressed paper **3** table **4** official body **5** slab of covered wood or card on which games (chess, etc.) are played; *pl* the stage; *v* provide with meals; *n* **boarder** one who pays for food, lodging; child living at school in term; *idm* **above board** open and honest; *idm* **across the board** involving all members of groups; *idm* **go by the board** be ignored; *idm* **on board** on a ship or aircraft; *coll* part of the group.

boarding school *n* school with living accommodations.

boardroom *n* room for meetings of company directors.

boast *v* praise oneself; claim proudly; *n* **boaster;** *a* **boastful;** *adv* **-ly;** *n* **-ness**.

boat *n* generic term for all water craft; *ns* **boathouse;**

boating; boatswain, bosun ship's officer.

boater *n* hard flat-topped straw hat.

boat hook *n* long pole with hook for pulling boats.

bob *n* **1** quick up-and-down movement; clumsy curtsy **2** short haircut; *v* **bobbed.** move jerkily up and down.

bobbin *n* spool on which thread is wound.

bobble *n* small decorative ball, *usu* woolen, *esp* on a hat.

bobby *n sl Brit* policeman.

bobby pin *n* flat, metal hairpin.

bobby socks, bobby sox *n pl* short socks for girls.

bobcat *n* American lynx, wild cat.

bobolink *n* N American songbird.

bobsled *n* sledge steered by wheel on movable front portion.

bobwhite *n* N American quail.

bode *v* portend; *a* **boding** foretelling.

bodega *n Sp* grocery store.

bodice *n* part of woman's dress above the waist.

bodice ripper *n coll* romantic novel containing sex and violence.

bodkin *n* large-eyed blunt needle.

body *n* **1** physical organism of living creatures **2** corpse **3** main part **4** mass **5** trunk **6** group of people; *v* give shape to; *a* **bodiless;** *a, adv* **bodily**.

body bag *n* zippered bag for transporting human corpse.

a
b
c
d
e
f
g
h
i
j
k
l
m
n
o
p
q
r
s
t
u
v
w
x
y
z

body blow n 1 *boxing* blow to the body 2 severe setback.

bodyguard n person or persons guarding someone.

body language n indication (*usu* subconscious) of one's thoughts and feelings by one's posture and movements.

body snatcher n (formerly) stealer of corpses.

body stocking n close-fitting garment covering body.

body wax n car shampoo containing protective wax.

boffin n *coll* scientific or technical expert.

bog n marsh; swamp; v become stuck in bog, etc.; a **boggy**; *idm* **bogged down** *coll* stuck; unable to progress.

bogey n 1 fearful presence 2 in golf, one stroke above par for a given hole.

boggle v 1 be overwhelmed 2 bungle 3 shrink from; n **boggler**.

bogus a not genuine, sham.

boil¹ v bubble with heat; cook in boiling water; *phr v* **boil down** to be no more than; n **boiler** vessel or tank for heating or boiling.

boil² n inflamed swelling, filled with pus.

boisterous a rough, turbulent; *adv* **boisterously**; n **boisterousness**.

bold a daring; shameless; clear, prominent; *adv* **boldly**; n **boldness**.

bole n trunk or stem of a tree.

bolero n lively Spanish dance; loose, short jacket.

bollard n mooring post for ship at dockside.

bolster n long cushion; v support; a **bolstered**.

bolt n 1 metal rod used to bar door, etc. 2 thunderbolt 3 heavy arrow; v 1 secure with bolt 2 gulp food 3 run away; *idm* **bolt upright** erect and unbending.

bomb n metal shell filled with explosive, etc.; v attack with bombs; n **bomber** bomb-carrying aircraft; failure.

bombard v attack with shells, missiles, words; direct rays from radioactive substance at; ns **bombardment**; **bombardier** artillery NCO.

bombast n pompous, empty, insincere talk; a **bombastic**; *adv* **-ally**.

bombshell n unpleasant shock.

bona fide a *Lat* in good faith.

bonanza n rich vein of ore; unexpected wealth.

bonbon n *Fr* candy.

bond¹ n 1 binding force 2 state of being firmly joined; n **bonding** 3 written promise, *esp* to repay money.

bond² n 1 shackle; 2 covenant; *pl* **bonds** ropes or chains for holding somebody prisoner; v 2 bind 3 store goods until payment of duty; a **bonded** held on bond.

bondage n servitude, slavery; n **bondsman** slave.

bone n substance of which skeleton of vertebrates is made; any part of skeleton; v take out bones; *as* **bony, boneless, bone-dry**; *idm* **cut to the bone** reduce to the bare minimum; *idm* **feel in one's bones** feel instinctively; *idm* **have a bone to pick** have reason to quarrel; *idm* **make no bones (about)** not hesitate (about); *phr v* **bone up on** *coll* find out quickly what needs to be known about.

bonehead n *coll* stupid person.

bonfire n open-air fire for festive occasions, or to burn trash.

bongo n **bongos.** small drum played by hand.

bonhomie n *Fr* hearty friendliness.

bonk v, n *coll* hit (not very hard)

bonkers a *sl* crazy.

bon mot n *Fr* witty saying.

bonnet n head covering.

bonny a handsome; comely; *adv* **bonnily**.

bonsai n dwarf tree or shrub.

bonus n sum paid beyond what is due; premium; *pl* **bonuses**.

boo *interj* used to indicate disapproval, to startle; v make this sound.

boo-boo n 1 mistake 2 minor injury.

boob tube n television.

booby n 1 dunce 2 seabird; ns **booby prize** award for lowest score; **booby trap** device to catch the unwary; practical joke.

book n 1 sheets of paper bound together in cover to form a volume 2 literary composition

3 list of bets in race; *v* reserve in advance; enter in book; *idm* **a closed book** unfamiliar subject; *idm* **by the book** strictly according to the rules; *idm* **throw the book at somebody** remind somebody forcefully of correct procedure; *a* **bookish;** scholarly; *ns* **booklet** small book; **bookkeeper, bookkeeping** keeping of accounts.

book club *n* club selling books cheaply by mail order.

bookend *n* device to stop books from falling over on a shelf.

bookmaker, bookie *n* professional betting man.

bookmark *n* something left inside a book to mark a place.

bookstall *n* stall where books and magazines are sold.

bookworm *n* one devoted to study or reading.

boom *n* **1** long pole keeping bottom of sail extended **2** barrier across harbor **3** hollow roar **4** sudden prosperity; *v* **1** make hollow roar **2** rise in prices, birth rate.

boomerang *n* wooden object returning to thrower.

boom market *n comm* time when shares are rising rapidly in value.

boon *n* blessing; favor.

boondocks *n* **1** backwoods **2** remote rural area.

boor *n* lout; ill-bred person; *a*

boorish; *adv* **-ly;** *n* **-ness.**

boost *v* raise; augment; praise; *n* **booster** device for raising power or voltage.

boot[1] *n* foot and ankle covering; *v* kick; *idm* **give somebody the boot** *coll* dismiss from employment; *v* **boot up** start a computer program.

boot[2] *n* benefit; profit; *v* avail; *a* **bootless;** *adv* **to boot** in addition.

booth *n* temporary stall in market, etc.

bootlegger *n* one engaged in traffic in illicit liquor; *v, a* **bootleg;** *n* **bootlegging.**

booty *n* spoils of war; plunder.

booze *n, v sl* drink; *n* **boozer** one who drinks; *a* **boozy.**

bop, bebop *n, v* dance to pop music.

borage *n* plant used for flavoring.

borax *n* white crystalline salt used as antiseptic, etc.; *a* **boracic.**

bordello *n* brothel.

border *n* **1** edge; frontier **2** flower bed; *v* line; verge (on).

borderline *n, a* (on the) dividing line between two categories.

bore *v* **1** make hole in **2** weary by being dull; *n* **1** hole bored **2** dull person **3** high tidal wave in river; *a, pr p* **boring;** *n* **boredom** state of being bored.

born *v* **be born** come into the world; *a* **born** natural.

born-again *a* converted, *esp* evangelical Christian.

borne *pp of* bear.

boron *n* nonmetallic element used to harden steel.

borough *n* town or city with municipal corporation.

borrow *v* obtain on loan; adopt; use another's material; *ns* **borrower, borrowing.**

bosh *n coll* empty talk; nonsense.

bosom *n* human breast; seat of emotions; *n* **bosom buddy** very close friend.

boss *n* **1** head man; overseer; *v* direct; **bossy** arrogant; *n* **bossiness 2** any projecting part; ornamental stud.

botany *n* science of plant life; *n* **botanist;** *as* **botanic, botanical;** *adv* **-ly;** *v* **botanize.**

botch *v* patch roughly; bungle; *n* clumsy piece of work.

both *a, pron* the two; *conj, adv* as well.

bother *v* worry; feel anxiety; *n* fuss *a* **bothersome.**

bottle *n* glass container for liquids; its contents; *v* put into bottles; *n* **bottler;** *idm* **be on/hit the bottle** drink too much alcohol; *idm* **bottle up** suppress (feelings).

bottleneck *n* narrow passage; condition hindering free circulation.

bottom *n* lowest part of anything; bed of sea, river, lake, etc.; human rump; *a* lowest; *a* **-less;** *idm* **at bottom** basically; *phr v* **bottom out** *comm* reach lowest level

A
B
C
D
E
F
G
H
I
J
K
L
M
N
O
P
Q
R
S
T
U
V
W
X
Y
Z

before recovering.

bottom line n essential fact or factor.

botulism n form of food poisoning.

boudoir n private room for women.

bougainvillaea n climbing shrub with red or purple bracts.

bough n limb of tree.

bought pt, pp of **buy**.

bouillon n clear soup.

boulder n large, rounded mass of rock or stone.

boulevard n broad avenue.

bounce v rebound, as ball, on striking anything; spring; n **bouncer** thrower-out of unruly persons from club; a **bouncing** robust.

bound[1] v move with sudden spring; n leap; spring.

bound[2] pt, pp of **bind**; idm **bound to** certain to; idm **bound up in** busy with.

bound[3] v set limit to, restrict; n that which limits, confines; idm **out of bounds** beyond permitted area; a **boundless** adv **-ly;** n **boundary** something fixing limit, area, etc.

bound[4] a **bound for, -bound** on the way to.

bounty n generous gift; as **bountiful; bounteous** liberal; advs **bountifully, bounteously** plentiful.

bouquet n 1 bunch of flowers 2 aroma of wine.

bourbon n Fr type of whisky.

bourgeois n, a Fr middle-class;

n **bourgeoisie**.

bourn(e) n 1 rivulet 2 limit 3 realm.

bout n 1 spell 2 turn 3 trial; contest.

boutique n small shop selling fashionable clothes.

bovine a 1 pertaining to ox or cow 2 patient; stolid.

bow[1] n inclination of head or body in respect; v make bow 2 submit; yield; defeat; phr v **bow out** resign; phr v **bow to** yield to, n, a (at) front end of ship.

bow[2] n 1 weapon for shooting arrows 2 implement for playing violin, etc. 3 bend; curve; v use bow.

bowels n intestines.

bower n leafy grove.

bowl[1] n hollow dish; drinking cup.

bowl[2] n wooden ball; v roll ball; phr v **bowl over** 1 knock down 2 astound; ns **bowling** game played on **bowling green; bowling alley** indoor area for bowling, etc.; **bowler** one who bowls; hard round felt hat.

bowlegs n pl legs curving outward at the knee a **bowlegged**.

bowman n archer.

bow tie n small tie with double loop.

bow window n curved window.

box[1] n hardwood tree 2 case 3 private compartment in theater 4 sentry's shelter 5 carriage driver's seat 6 ruled-off space; coll **boom**

box (coll) portable radio and tape player; v put in box.

box[2] v strike with fist or hand; n such a blow to head; n **boxer** one who fights with fists as sport (**boxing**).

boxcar n enclosed railroad freight car.

box number n number used for receiving replies to advertisements in newspapers and magazines.

box office n kiosk in movie theater, theater, etc., where tickets are sold.

boy n male child, youth; a **boyish;** n **boyhood**.

boycott v 1 ban 2 stop dealing with.

boyfriend n 1 male sweetheart 2 male friend.

bozo n sl stupid man.

bra n coll brassiere.

brace n 1 support 2 pair 3 device for holding bit; 4 pl dental apparatus for straightening teeth; pl support for trousers; v support; a **bracing** invigorating.

bracelet n wrist band or ornament.

bracken n coarse common fern.

bracket n projecting support; pl symbols [ ] enclosing word, etc.; v join, associate.

brackish a (of water) salty; n **-ness**.

bract n small leaf at base of flower.

brad n thin, flat nail; **bradawl** for tool boring.

brag v **bragging, bragged**.

boast; *n* boast; *n* **braggart** boaster.

Brahman, Brahmin *n* member of highest Hindu caste.

braid *n* plait of hair; band of fabric; *v* plait.

braille *n* system of writing and printing for use by the blind.

brain *n* soft mass of nervous substance within skull; *pl* intelligence; *v* dash out brains of; hit on head; *as* **brainy, brainless;** *n* **brain wave** sudden bright idea; *v* **brain wash** indoctrinate.

brainchild *n* original idea.

brain drain *n* loss of skilled people emigrating to work in other countries.

brainstorm *n* brilliant idea; *n* **brainstorming** way of tackling a problem by rapid interchange of ideas by a group.

braise *v* cook by simmering in closed pan.

brake *n* **1** device for checking wheel's motion **2** thicket **3** kind of wagon; *v* apply brake to, slow down.

bramble *n* prickly shrub, blackberry.

bran *n* husks remaining after grain is ground.

branch *n* limb of tree; any offshoot from main stem; *a* secondary; *v* produce branches; *n*, *a* **branching;** *phr v* **branch out** extend one's range.

brand *n* trademark; identifying mark; particular type of goods; burning stick; *v* mark

with brand.

brandish *v* flourish, wave.

brand-new *a* completely new.

brandy *n* strong spirit distilled from wine.

brash *a* **1** impudently self-assertive **2** loud; *adv* **-ly;** *n* **-ness.**

brass *n* alloy of copper and zinc; *sl* money; effrontery; *as* of brass; *a* **brassy** strident; *n coll* **the brass** high-ranking.

brasserie *n Fr* restaurant for quick meals and drinks.

brass hat *n Brit sl* senior army officer.

brassiere *n Fr* undergarment supporting woman's breasts.

brat *n* uncomplimentary name for a child.

bravado *n* show of boldness or bluster.

brave *a* courageous; fine; *n* N American Indian warrior; *v* face with courage; *adv* **bravely;** *n* **bravery.**

bravo *interj* well done!

brawl *n*, *v* quarrel; fight.

brawn *n* muscle; strength; *a* **brawny** strong.

bray *v* cry, as donkey.

braze *v* cover with brass; join with solder; *a* **brazen** shameless; *v* adopt defiant manner; *adv* **brazenly.**

brazier *n* **1** iron basket for holding hot coals **2** brass-worker.

breach *n* break; violation of law, contract; *v* make an opening in.

bread *n* **1** food made mainly from flour, water, yeast, and

baked **2** food in general **3** livelihood **4** *sl* money; *n* **breadfruit** fruit resembling bread when baked; *idm* **bread and butter** way of earning a living; *a* **bread-and-butter** basic.

breadbasket *n* **1** main grain-producing area **2** stomach.

breadth *n* distance across, width.

breadwinner *n* person supporting family with earnings.

break *v* **1** smash; destroy **2** tame **3** make bankrupt **4** interrupt; *pt* **broke;** *pp* **broken;** *n* **1** breach; fracture **2** interruption **3** lucky change; *a* **breakable;** *idm* **break new ground** begin something new; *idm* **break the back of** do the most difficult part of; *idm* **break the ice** initiate social contact; *idm* **break wind** release air from bowels; *phr v* **break down 1** reduce/be reduced to pieces **2** analyze **3** fail to work **4** lose control of emotions; *idm* **break even** make neither profit nor loss; *phr vs* **break out** start suddenly; **break out in** manifest (visible signs of disease); **break up 1** divide **2** end a relationship **3** collapse.

breakage *n* act of breaking; thing broken.

breakaway *n*, *a* (person or group) deserting main body of an organization.

break-dance n acrobatic style of dance; v perform this.

breaker n wave that breaks near the shore.

break-even a point where income equals spendings.

breakfast n first meal of day.

breakdown n 1 failure to operate 2 nervous collapse 3 statistical analysis.

breakneck a fast and reckless.

breakthrough n important discovery leading to progress.

breakwater n barrier that offers protection from waves.

break-up n 1 violent quarrel 2 end of relationship.

bream n fish of carp family.

breast n bosom; mammary gland; v face boldly; idm **make a clean breast** confess everything; ns **breastplate** armor to cover breast; **breastwork** defensive wall.

breastbone n sternum.

breaststroke n style of swimming using a sideways sweep of both arms simultaneously.

breath n air drawn into or expelled from lungs; slight breeze; fragrance; idm **take one's breath away** astonish one; idm **under one's breath** inaudibly; v **breathe** inhale and exhale air; live; utter gently; blow lightly; idm **breathe down someone's neck** follow someone very closely; idm **breath one's last** die; n **breather** short rest; a **breath-taking** very exciting; ns **breathing**; a **breathless;**

n **-ness**.

breathalyze n measure amount of alcohol drunk by driver; n **breathalyzer** apparatus for this.

breech n hind end of anything; buttocks; pl **breeches** trousers.

breech birth, breech delivery n birth with baby's feet or buttocks emerging first.

breed v bear; offspring; rear; nourish; give rise to; pt, pp **bred**; n strain; kind; ns **breeder; breeding** manners.

breeze n gentle wind; a **breezy** airy; jolly; adv **breezily**.

brethren lit pl of **brother**.

breve n mus note equal in length to four minims.

brevet n promotion without a pay increase.

breviary n book of daily prayers used by Roman Catholics.

brevity n briefness; conciseness.

brew v 1 make beer, tea, etc. 2 contrive 3 be afoot; n act or product of brewing; ns **brewing, brewer, brewery**.

briar, brier n thorny shrub; wild rose; bramble.

bribe n money, favor given to influence person; v influence thus; n **bribery**.

bric-a-brac n curios; knick-knacks.

brick n oblong block of baked clay used in building; v build with bricks; idm **drop a brick** make a gaffe; n **bricklayer**.

brickbat n 1 brick fragment

2 caustic criticism.

brickwork n assembled bricks.

bridal a of a bride or wedding.

bride n newly married woman; **bridegroom** newly married man; **bridesmaid** girl attendant on bride.

bridge1 n card game.

bridge2 n 1 structure allowing access over river, railway, etc. 2 part of ship used by captain and navigating officer 3 wooden strut under strings of violin, etc. 4 upper part of nose; v build bridge over; n **bridge loan** credit for business.

bridgework n partial denture fixed to other teeth.

bridle n head harness of horse; curb; v 1 fit with bridle 2 check 3 show disdain, etc.

bridle path n path for horse riding.

Brie n soft white French cheese.

brief a lasting short time; concise; n synopsis of law case; v give final instructions to; adv **briefly**.

briefcase n flat case for business documents.

briefs n pl short pants or underpants.

brier n 1 thorny shrub 2 tobacco pipe.

brig n two-masted, square-rigged vessel.

brigade n military unit; organized body of people.

brigadier n officer commanding a brigade.

brigand n bandit; outlaw.

brigantine n square-rigged sailing vessel with two masts.

bright a shining; lively; vivid; intelligent; adv **-ly;** adv **-ness;** v **brighten 1** make bright **2** become fine.

brill n flat sea fish similar to turbot.

brilliance n **1** splendor; radiance **2** outstanding talent; a **brilliant;** adv **-ly.**

brim n rim, edge (of cup, hat, etc.); v full to rim; as **brimming, brimful, brimless.**

brimstone n sulfur.

brindle n streaked coloring or an animal with such coloring; **brindled** a light brown color with darker streaks.

brine n salt water used for pickling meat; a **briny.**

bring v cause to come; fetch; carry; cause pt, pp **brought;** phr vs **bring about** cause to happen; **bring forth** give birth; **bring forward 1** introduce; propose **2** put at an ealier time; **bring off** manage successfully; **bring on 1** put on show **2** cause; **bring over/around** convert to another opinion; **bring around/to** restore to consciousness; **bring up 1** rear (children) **2** mention **3** vomit.

brink n edge (of chasm, precipice, etc.).

brinksmanship n art of taking political position as far as safety will allow.

brioche n Fr small light bun made with yeast and eggs.

briquette n Fr small block of compressed coal dust used as fuel.

brisk a lively, energetic, bracing; adv **-ly.**

brisket n joint of beef cut from breast.

brisling n small sardinelike fish.

bristle n short, stiff hair; v **1** stand on end, as bristles **2** show indignation; a **bristly.**

Brit n coll British person.

britches see breeches.

British a of Britain.

Briton n inhabitant of Britain.

brittle a easily broken; n **brittleness.**

broach n boring tool; roasting spit; v pierce (cask); open, begin (a subject).

broad a wide, large; general; coarse; of marked accent; v **broaden** make wider; a **broadminded** tolerant; adv **broadly;** ns **broad bean** large flat edible bean; plant bearing it; **broadcloth** woolen cloth.

broadcast v scatter (seed) widely; spread abroad; transmit (radio, television); pt, pp **broadcast;** n such a transmission.

broadsheet n **1** large sheet printed on one side only **2** broadside.

broadside n **1** naval firing of all guns on one side **2** fierce verbal attack; a sideways.

brocade n stiff silk fabric with raised design.

broccoli n hardy type of cauliflower.

brochure n pamphlet; printed folder.

brogue n **1** stout, rough shoe; **2** accent, esp Irish.

broil n noisy quarrel; v grill on open fire; n **broiler** quickly reared chicken sold ready for broiling; a **broiling** coll very hot.

broke pt of **break;** a coll having no money.

broken pp of **break.**

broken-down a not functioning.

brokenhearted n overcome by grief.

broker n one buying for another on commission; n **brokerage** his commission or business.

bromide n sedative drug.

bronchitis n inflammation of bronchial tubes; a **bronchial.**

bronco n half-tamed horse.

brontosaurus n large herbivorous dinosaur.

bronze n alloy of copper and tin; its color; v make or become bronze; a **bronze** sun-tanned; brozed covered with bronze.

brooch n ornamental clasp or pin.

brood n young of animals, esp birds; v sit on eggs; ponder anxiously; a **broody** inclined to brood.

brook n small stream; v endure, tolerate.

a
b
c
d
e
f
g
h
i
j
k
l
m
n
o
p
q
r
s
t
u
v
w
x
y
z

broom n 1 flowering shrub 2 sweeping brush; n **broomstick**.

broth n thin soup.

brother n 1 son of same parents 2 member of religious order, trade union, etc; pl **brothers, brethren**; a **brotherly**; ns **brotherhood** group united by common interest; **brother-in-law** brother of husband or wife.

brought pt, pp of bring.

brow n 1 eyebrow; forehead 2 top of hill, etc.

browbeat v bully.

brown n color made by mixing black, red, and yellow; a tanned; v make or become brown; **brown study** reverie.

brownie n 1 fairy, elf 2 cap B junior Girl Scout 3 small, square chocolate cake.

brownie point n notional mark of credit for good deed.

browse v feed (as animal) on grass, leaves, etc; glance through book or store.

bruise n injury that discolors flesh; contusion; v inflict this; n **bruiser** big man.

brunch n breakfast and lunch combined.

brunette, brunet n woman with dark brown hair.

brunt n chief stress, strain of attack.

brush n 1 implement for sweeping, painting, brushing hair, etc. 2 tail of fox 3 skirmish 4 small shrubs 5 electrical device 6 light touch; v 1 sweep 2 use brush 3 touch lightly; phr vs **brush up (on)** revive knowledge of; **brush somebody off** ignore the attentions of somebody; ns **brush-off** snub; **brushwood** broken branches or twigs.

brusque a abrupt, curt; n **brusqueness**.

Brussels sprout n (plant with) edible budlike small cabbage.

brute n 1 lower animal 2 cruel person; as **brutal** cruel and violent; adv **-ly** n **-ity**; **brutish**; as of an animal; unrefined; adv **-ly**; n - **ness**.

BS abbr Bachelor of Science.

BTU abbr British Thermal Unit.

bubble n globule of gas, air; plan lacking solidity; v form bubbles; make bubbling sound.

bubble jet printing n fine high-quality printing; **bubble jet printer** machine that produces this.

bubo n suppurating swelling of gland in armpit, groin; a **bubonic (plague)**.

buccaneer n pirate; a **buccaneerish**.

buck n 1 male deer, rabbit, etc. 2 dandy 3 sudden spring 4 sl dollar; v leap suddenly; **buck up** phr v 1 try to improve 2 make more cheerful; n **buckskin** soft leather.

bucket n vessel for carrying water, etc.; pail; scoop in dredger; n **bucketful**.

buckle n 1 clasp with catch for fastening 2 bulge; warp; v fasten with buckle warp; phr v **buckle (down) (to)** begin in earnest.

buckler n shield.

buckram n stiff cotton textile.

buckshot n medium-sized lead shot.

buckskin n skin of a buck.

bucktooth n projecting tooth or teeth.

buckwheat n dark cereal grain.

bucolic a rustic; rural.

bud n growth from which leaf of flower will develop; v **budding, budded.** put forth buds; graft; idm **nip in the bud** stop from developing.

Buddhism n religion based on teachings of Buddha; n, a **buddhist**.

buddy n coll friend; chum.

budge v move position.

budgerigar n small parakeet, lovebird.

budget n estimated financial schedule; v plan spending.

buff n 1 soft leather 2 pale yellow color 3 bare skin; v polish.

buffer n something that protects against or lessens the force of an impact.

buffers n spring-loaded steel pads attached to railway rolling stock and ends of track to cushion impact.

buffalo n **-oes** kind of ox; American bison.

buffet[1] n, v slap; cuff.

buffet[2] n 1 sideboard 2 informal refreshment bar or restaurant.

buffoon n clown; n **buffoonery**.

bug *n* small parasitic insect; *n, v* **bugging, bugged.** (install) hidden device for spying; *a* **bugged.**

bugaboo *n* imaginary fear.

bugbear *n* source of real or fancied fear.

buggy *n* **1** light carriage **2** small motor vehicle **3** also **baby buggy** baby carriage.

bugle *n* **1** kind of small trumpet **2** glass bead; *ns* **bugler, bugle call.**

build *v* **building, built.** construct; *n* form; *ns* **builder, building.**

buildup *n* steady increase .

built-in *a* **1** constructed as part of **2** inherent.

built-up *a* with many buildings.

bulb *n* **1** globular, modified leafbud, *usu* underground; **2** electric lamp; *a* **bulbous.**

bulge *n* rounded swelling; *v* swell; *as* **bulgy, bulging.**

bulgur *n* wheat, often cracked and dried for eating.

bulimia *n* eating disorder in which bouts of overeating are followed by self-induced vomiting.

bulk *n* **1** volume **2** cargo; *idm* **in bulk** in large quantities; *idm* **the bulk of** the larger part of; *a* **bulky** voluminous; *n* **bulkiness.**

bull *n* **1** male of ox family, etc. **2** speculator in rising stock values.

bulldog *n* powerful dog with protruding lower jaw.

bulldozer *n* powerful tractor for moving earth; *v* **bulldoze** overcome opposition by brutal force.

bullet *n* metal ball or missile fired from gun.

bulletin *n* brief official statement.

bullfinch *n* songbird, of which male has pink breast.

bullfrog *n* large frog with loud croak.

bullheaded *a* blindly obstinate.

bullion *n* gold or silver before being coined.

bullish *a* showing promise of success in stock market.

bullock *n* castrated bull.

bull's-eye *n* center of target.

bully *n* **-lies.** overbearing, cruel ruffian; *v* **-lying, -lied,** initimidate.

bully boy *n* thug, *esp* one paid to intimidate people.

bulrush, bullrush *n* large rush of sedge family.

bulwark *n* **1** rampart **2** defense **3** ship's side above deck **4** breakwater.

bum *n* **1** tramp **2** loafer ; *v* beg; *phr v* **bum around** *coll* spend time or travel aimlessly.

bumble *v* speak incoherently; *phr v* **bumble about/along** act in a disorganized way; *a* **bumbling;** *n* **bumbledom** fussy officialdom.

bumblebee *n* large, wild, humming bee.

bump *n* **1** blow; collision **2** swelling due to blow; protuberance; *v* collide with; strike; jolt; *phr vs* **bump off** kill; **bump up** increase; *n*

bumper 1 automobile fender **2** full glass; *a* plentiful; *a* **bumpy 1** covered with bumps **2** giving jolts.

bumpkin *n* country yokel, rustic.

bumptious *a* arrogant; offensively self-assertive; *adv* **-ly;** *n* **-ness.**

bun *n* small cake; small, round bunch of hair.

bunch *n, v* cluster (of things growing or tied together).

bundle *n* number of things tied or rolled together; *v* **1** tie in a bundle **2** hustle (someone) away.

bung *n* cork, wooden stopper *esp* for cask *v* insert bung; *phr v* **bung up** block up.

bungalow *n* one-storied house.

bungle *v* botch; blunder; *n* something botched; confusion; *n* **bungler;** *a* **bungling.**

bunion *n* inflamed swelling, *esp* on big toe.

bunk[1] *n* **1** sleeping berth; **2** trough for feeding livestock.

bunk,[2] **bunkum** *n* empty talk, nonsense.

bunker *n* **1** large bin, *esp* for fuel **2** military dugout **3** hazard on golf course.

bunny *n* (child's word for) rabbit.

Bunsen burner *n* type of gas burner.

bunting *n* **1** small bird allied to finch **2** colored flags used for decoration, *esp* of streets, ships, etc. **3** infant's covering.

a
b
c
d
e
f
g
h
i
j
k
l
m
n
o
p
q
r
s
t
u
v
w
x
y
z

A B C D E F G H I J K L M N O P Q R S T U V W X Y Z

buoy *n* floating object anchored in water to mark channel, rocks, etc.; life-buoy; *v* mark with buoy; *phr v* **buoy up** keep afloat; sustain morally; *a* **buoyant;** *adv* **buoyantly;** *n* **buoyancy.**

burble *v* make gentle gurgling sound; babble.

burden *n* load; something difficult to bear; *v* load; encumber; *a* **-some.**

burdock *n* weed with purple flowers encased by bristles.

bureau *n* **-eaux,** or **-eaus.** *Fr* 1 information office 2 government department.

bureaucracy *n* government by state officials; *n* **bureacrat;** *a* **bureaucratic.**

burgeon *v* to bud.

burger *n coll* = **hamburger.**

burgher *n ar* citizen of a town.

burglar *n* one who breaks into house to steal; *n* **burglary;** *v* **burgle.**

burgundy *n* red or white wine.

burial *n* burying; funeral; *n* **burial ground.**

burlesque *n* derisive imitation; *v* ridicule; *a* mocking.

burly *a* of sturdy build; *n* **burliness.**

burn *v* 1 injure or destroy by fire 2 use as fuel 3 be on fire 4 be consumed by fire 5 yearn; *pt, pp* **burned;** *n* mark caused by heat; *a* **burning;** *n* **burner;** *idm* **burn one's bridges** do something that makes it impossible to turn back; *idm* **burn the candle at both ends** work overtime and risk complete exhaustion.

burnish *v* polish; *n* **burnisher.**

burnous *n* hooded cloak worn by Arabs.

burnout *n* mechanical failure through overheating or exhaustion of fuel.

burn-up *v* have a high fever.

burp *v, n* belch.

burr[1] *n* seed-case covered with hooked spines.

burr[2] *n* 1 low chest of drawers 2 hard stone 3 rough edge or line made by etching tool on metal.

burrow *n* hole scooped in ground by animal, *esp* rabbit, fox, etc.; *v* make hole; dig, search.

bursa *n* sac in the body.

bursar *n* treasurer, *esp* of college; *n* **bursary** grant.

bursitis *n* condition in which a bursa (sac of fluid) becomes inflamed, *esp* in shoulder or elbow.

burst *v* **bursting, burst.** explode; open out; erupt; puncture; *n* explosion; sudden spurt.

bury *v* **burying, buried.** inter; conceal; *n, a* **burial.**

bus[1] *n* large passenger motor vehicle.

bus[2], **busbar** *n comput* group of electrical conductors for carrying data.

bush[1] *n* 1 shrub; thicket 2 wild country; *a* **bushy;** *n* **bushiness.**

bush[2] *n* metal lining for circular hole; *v* fit bush.

bushbaby *n* small African lemur with large eyes.

bushed *a coll* exhausted.

bushel *n* dry measure equal to eight gallons.

bushman *n* African woodsman.

bushwack *v* to blaze a trail through the wilds by cutting plants.

business *n* 1 occupation, profession, trade, etc. 2 affair; *a* **businesslike** efficient; *ns* **businessman, businesswoman, business card, business studies;** *idm* **like nobody's business** very fast or effectively.

busing, bussing *n* transporting schoolchildren to other districts to effect racial equality.

busman's holiday *n* holiday spent doing normal work.

bust *n* upper part of human body; sculpture of such part; *n* **buster;** *a* **bust, busted** *coll* broken; *idm* **go bust** fail; go bankrupt.

bustard *n* large, swift-running bird.

buster way of addressing a man.

bustle *n* noisy movement; *v* move quickly, fussily.

busy *a* **busier, busiest.** at work; fully occupied; *v* **busying, busied.** occupy (oneself); *adv* **busily;** *ns* **busyness; busybody** meddling, officious person; **busy beaver** industrious person.

but *adv* only just; without; *prep* except; *conj* on the contrary;

yet; unless; **all but** almost.

butane n inflammable gaseous compound.

butch a coll vulgar 1 (of women) masculine in appearance and behavior 2 (of men) aggressively masculine.

butcher n 1 tradesman dealing in meat 2 brutal murderer; v kill for food, or indiscriminately.

butcher block n table or surface composed of various laminated wood strips.

butler n head man-servant of a household.

butt n 1 barrel 2 end; stub 3 figure of fun; v 1 align end to end 2 push with head or horns; phr v **butt in** interrupt.

butter n solidified fat obtained from cream by churning; v spread with butter; phr v **butter up** flatter.

buttercup n yellow cup-shaped wild flower.

butterfat n solid fatty part of milk.

butterfingers n person who tends to drop things.

butterfly n 1 four-winged insect, usually brightly colored 2 flighty person; pl **butterflies in stomach** nervousness.

buttermilk n liquid left when butter has been made.

butternut n nut of walnutlike tree.

butterscotch n kind of hard toffee or taffy; flavoring.

buttery n place for storing

wines, liquors, etc.

buttocks n the rump.

button n small flat disk for fastening clothing, etc.; small knob; v fasten with button; idm **buttoned up** 1 fixed 2 inhibited.

buttonhole n 1 slit in lapel 2 worn in this; v detain and force somebody to hear what one has to say.

buttress n support giving extra strength to anything; v support, prop.

buxom a robust, plump, rosy, comely; n **buxomness**.

buy v obtain by paying; bribe; pt, pp **bought**; n **buyer**.

buyer's market n time when low demand leads to low prices.

buy out n giving control of a company by acquiring majority of shares.

buzz n low humming noise, as of bee; v make such sound; murmur; n **buzzer** mechanical device that buzzes; phr v **buzz off** coll go away fast.

buzzword n specialist expression that has become fashionable to use.

buzzard n large, carnivorous bird of prey.

BW abbr biological warfare.

B/W abbr black and white.

by prep 1 near; close to 2 through; over 3 not later than 4 expressing agency; adv 1 at hand 2 aside 3 past; idm **by and by** eventually; idm **by and large** generally;

everything considered.

by- prefix near; secondary; indirect; subsidiary; apart from. *Where the meaning may be deduced easily from the simple word, the compounds are not given here.*

by-and-by adv later.

bye n 1 free entry into next round of contest 2 cricket run scored without the ball touching the bat; interj also **bye-bye** coll goodbye.

bygone a past, gone by; n pl **bygones** the past.

bylaw n local law or regulation.

byline n author's name given at beginning of article.

bypass n 1 route avoiding busy area 2 med alternative passage for blood during surgical operation; v 1 go around 2 avoid consulting sb ns **bypass surgery, bypass valve**.

byplay n action of secondary importance.

by-product n subsidiary product or result.

bystander n one standing near; onlooker.

byte n comput unit of information (= 8 bits).

byway n quiet road or path.

byword n 1 typical example 2 proverb.

Byzantine a 1 of Byzantium 2 of art or architecture of the Byzantine Empire 3 (of politics) complex and inscrutable.

a
b
c
d
e
f
g
h
i
j
k
l
m
n
o
p
q
r
s
t
u
v
w
x
y
z

A
B
C
D
E
F
G
H
I
J
K
L
M
N
O
P
Q
R
S
T
U
V
W
X
Y
Z

cab n **1** taxi **2** driver's shelter on locomotive, truck, or bus **3** elevator car.

cabal n intrigue; secret plot.

cabaret n Fr entertainment in restaurant or nightclub.

cabbage n green edible vegetable.

cabby n coll taxi driver.

cabin n small room on ship, esp for sleeping; hut.

cabin cruiser n motor boat with sleeping berths.

cabinet n **1** case or set of drawers **2** body of legislators governing country.

cable n **1** thick, strong rope or line **2** telephone, telegraph line **3** message sent by cable; v send cable.

cable car n mountain car suspended on cable.

cablegram n telegram sent by underwater wire.

cable television n satellite TV system with multiple channels.

caboodle idm **the whole caboodle** coll a lot; whole.

caboose n **1** ship's galley **2** last car of train for use of crew.

cabriolet n **1** one-horse carriage **2** car with folding top.

cacao n plant from seeds of which cocoa and chocolate are made.

cache n secret store or hiding place.

cachet n Fr mark of excellence, authenticity.

cackle n **1** noise made by hen, goose **2** shrill chatter; v make such noise.

cacophony n harsh discordant sound.

cactus n., pl **-tuses, -ti**. prickly plant with fleshy stem.

CAD abbr computer-aided design.

cad n ill-bred, vulgar person.

cadaverous a looking like corpse; pale, gaunt.

cadenza n mus virtuoso passage for soloist at climax of concerto movement.

caddie, caddy n golfer's attendant.

caddy n small box for tea.

cadence n rhythm in poetry; rise and fall of voice in speaking.

cadet n student training for commissioned rank.

cadge v beg; sponge on others; n **cadger**.

cadmium n white metallic element.

cadre n permanent nucleus of military unit.

café n Fr restaurant serving light meals; n **café society** fashionable society

café au lait n coffee with an equal amount of hot milk.

cafeteria n self-serve restaurant.

caffeine n alkaloid stimulant, obtained from coffee and tea plants.

caftan, kaftan n long, loose robe, as worn by Arabs.

cage n structure for confining animals, etc.; v to confine to cage; a **cagey** wary.

cahoots idm, **in cahoots with** conspiring with.

cairn n **1** pile of stones built as monument, etc. **2** small terrier.

cajole v flatter with ulterior motive; n **cajolery**.

Cajun n **1** Lousiana inhabitant descended from Acadian immigrants **2** food particular to these people.

cake n **1** kind of sweet dough, baked in pan **2** hard mass;

v to form hard mass, as of clay, etc.

CAL *abbr* computer-assisted learning.

calamine *n* pink lotion to soothe sore or itchy skin.

calamity *n* terrible, disastrous event; *a* **calamitous**.

calcareous *a* made of lime.

calcium *n* metallic element, base of lime.

calculate *v* 1 reckon, *esp* by arithmetic 2 fit for particular purpose; *a* **calculating** able to make calculations; scheming; *ns* **calculation, calculator; calculus** branch of mathematics dealing with rates of variation.

calendar *n* almanac; system for setting beginning and end of year; list of official dates.

calender *n* rolling machine for smoothing, polishing paper, etc.; *v* smooth so.

calf[1] *n* young of cow and various other mammals; its leather; *pl* **calves**; *v* **calve** give birth to calf.

calf[2] *n* fleshy back of leg below knee; *pl* **calves**.

calf-love *n* immature infatuation of adolescent.

caliber *n* diameter of bore of gun; quality of mind or character; *v* **calibrate;** *n* **calibration**.

calico *n* cloth made of cotton.

caliope *n* musical instrument with keyboard.

caliper *n* 1 instrument for measuring 2 leg brace.

calisthenics *n* exercises to develop strength and grace.

call *v* 1 name; describe as 2 speak loudly (to); summon 3 visit briefly or regularly 4 telephone 5 rouse; wake 6 convene; *ns* **caller; calling** 1 shouting 2 profession; *phr vs* **call by/in** visit briefly when nearby; **call for** 1 collect 2 require 3 merit; **call off** 1 cancel (event) 2 tell to stop threatening; **call on/upon** 1 visit 2 invite to speak 3 appeal to for help; **call out** 1 shout aloud 2 order to help 3 order to go on strike; *idm* **a close call** narrow escape; *idm* **on call** available for work if needed.

call girl *n* prostitute contactable by telephone.

calligraphy *n* handwriting; beautiful writing; *n* **calligrapher**.

call-in *n* = **phone-in**.

callous *a* hard-hearted; unfeeling; hardened (of skin); *adv* **-ly;** *n* **-ness**.

callow *a* undeveloped; inexperienced.

call-up *n* (order for) recruitment.

callus *n* lump of hard skin.

calm *n* windlessness; stillness; *a* quiet; peaceful; *v* become still, tranquil; *adv* **-ly;** *n* **-ness**.

calorie *n* unit of heat; *esp* in relation to value of food; *a* **calorific** heat-making.

calumet *n* N American Indian pipe used in ceremonies.

calumny *n* false accusation; slander.

calvary *n* place where Jesus was crucified.

calve *v* give birth to calf.

calves *pl of* **calf**.

calypso *n* type of W Indian song.

calyx *n* cup of leaves surrounding flower petals.

CAM *abbr* computer-aided manufacturing.

cam *n* projection on shaft controlling desired movement; *n* **camshaft** device in engine to lift valves.

camaraderie *n* comradeship.

camber *n* slight convexity on road, ship's deck, etc.; curvature of aircraft wing.

cambric *n* fine white linen cloth.

camcorder *n* video camera with recorder.

came *pt of* **come**.

camel *n* large, ruminant, humped animal.

camel hair *n* tan fabric made of camel's hair and wool.

camellia *n* shrub with white, red, or pink flowers.

cameo *n* gem carved in relief on contrasting background.

camera *n* photographic apparatus; *idm* **on camera** live, in front of TV camera; *n* **cameraman**.

camisole *n* woman's sleeveless undergarment.

camomile *n* plant with aromatic flowers, used medicinally.

camouflage *v* disguise appearance of objects, *esp*

a
b
c
d
e
f
g
h
i
j
k
l
m
n
o
p
q
r
s
t
u
v
w
x
y
z

A
B
C
D
E
F
G
H
I
J
K
L
M
N
O
P
Q
R
S
T
U
V
W
X
Y
Z

from enemy; n deception.

camp n 1 temporary shelter for travelers 2 place where tents or huts are erected for troops 3 faction or party; a sl effeminate; too ornate; dandified; v build, lodge in camp; ns **camping, camper;** **camp cot** narrow folding bed; **camp chair** portable folding chair; **campfire** outdoor fire; **camp follower** 1 noncombatant accompanying an army 2 noncommitted hanger-on to a political group.

campaign n 1 series of military operations 2 action to achieve particular purpose; v serve in, organize campaign.

campanile n lofty, detached tower in which bells are rung.

campanologist n one who studies or peals bells; n **campanology.**

camphor n aromatic volatile white substance; a **camphorated** impregnated with camphor.

campus n chief grounds of college, university, school.

can[1] v aux be able, be allowed to; pt **could;** pp **been able.**

can[2] n tin vessel used for holding food for preserving; v preserve in can.

Canada goose n N American wild goose.

canal n 1 artificial waterway 2 duct in living body.

canapé n Fr small savory appetizer on biscuit, toast, etc.

canard n rumor; hoax.

canary n yellow songbird.

canasta n card game similar to rummy.

cancan n high-kicking dance by women in long, petticoated skirts.

cancel v delete; cross out; abolish; suppress; phr v **cancel out** balance each other; n **cancellation.**

cancer n malignant tumor or growth in body; a **cancerous.**

candelabrum n branching ornamental candle holder (pl **candelabra**), also **candelabra** (pl **candelabras**).

candescent a giving off white glow.

candid a frank, honest, outspoken; adv **candidly;** ns **candidness, candor.**

candida n yeastlike parasitic fungus that causes thrush.

candidate n 1 person running for election 2 person taking examination; n **candidacy.**

candle n stick of wax with wick, for giving light; ns **candlelight; candlepower** unit of measure of light; **candlestick** candleholder.

candlepin n slim type of bowling pin.

candor n frankness.

candy n crystallized sugar; v preserve, become encrusted with sugar; a **candied.**

candy striper n teenage volunteer in hospital.

cane n hard stem of bamboo, etc.; walking stick; v beat with stick; n **caning.**

canine a of, related to dog.

canister n box, usually of metal.

canker n 1 ulcerous sore; 2 disease in trees; 3 fig moral corruption; a **cankered** spiteful.

cannabis n 1 hemp 2 drug extracted from this.

canned a put into cans or sealed jars 2 coll recorded in advance.

cannelloni n It pasta tubes with stuffing of meat or vegetable.

cannery n factory where food is canned.

cannibal n human who eats human flesh; n **cannibalism;** v **cannibalize** use (machine product, artifact, etc.) to reassemble in new form; n **-ization;** a **cannibalistic.**

cannoli n Italian pastry filled with sweet cheese, etc.

cannon n 1 large mounted gun 2 stroke in billiards; pl **cannon, cannons;** v make cannon in billiards collide; n **cannonade** discharge of artillery; n **cannon fodder** troops regarded as expendable in war.

cannot v can not.

canny a cautious; shrewd; wary.

canoe n light boat propelled by paddling; pl **canoes;** n **canoeist.**

canola oil n vegetable oil made from pressed canola seeds.

canon n 1 rule, law, esp of church 2 ecclesiastical dignitary 3 list of saints; v

canonize declare officially to have been a saint.

canopy n overhead covering.

can't v coll cannot

cant n 1 insincere speech; 2 jargon; v use cant; adv **canting**.

cant v slope, lean to one side; slant; a **canted**.

cantaloupe n type of melon.

cantankerous a ill-natured; touchy; quarrelsome.

cantata n choral composition.

canteen n 1 restaurant (in factory, school, etc.) 2 camper's water flask.

canter n easy gallop; v ride at such pace.

canticle n chant with biblical text.

cantilever n girder, etc., securely fixed at one end, free-hanging at other; n **cantilever bridge** center part supported by cantilever arms.

canto n chief division of long poem.

canton n state in Swiss Republic.

cantor n synagogue or church singer.

canuck n coll French Canadian.

canvas n strong, coarse cotton, linen, or hempen cloth used for sails or painting pictures on; idm **under canvas** in tents.

canvasback n N American wild duck.

canvass v solicit votes; discuss; n **canvasser** one soliciting votes.

canyon n deep gorge between cliffs.

cap n 1 brimless head covering 2 military headdress; 3 sign of membership of sports team 4 lid; v put cap on.

capable a able; competent; having capacity, power; n **capability**; adv **capably**.

capacity n power of holding, absorbing (material or non-material things); a **capacious** 1 spacious 2 receptive; n **capacitor** elec condensor.

caparison n (formerly) decoration for horses; v adorn.

cape n 1 sleeveless cloak 2 headland; promontory.

caper v skip about; frisk; n leaping about; pl silly pranks.

capillary a hairlike; n very narrow blood vessel.

capital n 1 chief city 2 large-sized letter 3 head of column 4 accumulated wealth; a 1 punishable by death 2 vital 3 excellent 4 leading; adv **-ly**; ns **capitalism** system of individual ownership of wealth; **capitalist**; phr v **capitalize on** take advantage of.

capital gain n profit from the sale of an asset, such as real estate or bonds.

capital punishment n leg punishment by death.

capitation n tax payable by or on each person.

capitol n building used by a legislature, esp Congress.

capitulate v surrender; cease to contend; n **-lation**.

capon n castrated fowl, esp when prepared for table.

cappuccino n Italian coffee made with hot, frothy milk.

caprice n whim; sudden fancy; a **capricious**; n **-ness**.

capsicum n pepper plant with hot-tasting seeds.

capsize v overturn, esp of boats.

capstan n 1 rotating post for winding ship's anchor 2 shaft that winds tape on tape recorder.

capsule n 1 seed container (of plant) 2 part of spaceship in which astronaut travels 3 small, gelatine case containing drug or medicine.

captain n 1 naval or military officer 2 leader of team or side; v act as leader of side or team.

captain's chair n chair with arms and a curved, spoked back.

caption n title of picture, etc.; heading.

captious a fond of finding fault; critical.

captivate n enchant; fascinate; charm; pr p, a **captivating** delightful, alluring.

captive n person held as prisoner; a unable to escape; n **captivity**.

capture v take prisoner; catch; n act of taking; n **captor**.

car n 1 automobile 2 railroad carriage 3 wheeled vehicle; n **car tailgate sale** sale of second-hand goods from car tailgate on a specially leased site.

carafe n bottle, usually glass, for water, wine.

caramel n candy; burned sugar for flavoring.

carapace n shell (of tortoise, crustacean).

carat n measure (of weight of diamonds, etc.; of purity of gold).

caravan n covered vehicle, used as home, by gypsies, vacationers; party of merchants, etc., crossing desert; n **caravanserai** Eastern inn accommodating caravans.

caraway n aromatic seed used for flavoring.

carbide n compound of calcium, producing acetylene gas.

carbine n short rifle used by mounted troops.

carbohydrate n energy-giving food containing sugar or starch.

carbolic a derived from carbon; n **carbolic acid** used as disinfectant.

carbon n nonmetallic element occurring as graphite, diamond, etc.; as **carbonic, carbonaceous** like coal.

carboniferous coal-producing; v **carbonize** impregnate with carbon; n **carbon paper** coated one side with carbon, for duplicating typed or written matter.

carbonated a fizzy; containing carbon dioxide.

carbon dioxide n gas formed by burning of carbon or by breathing of animals.

carbon monoxide n poisonous gas emitted in exhaust fumes of gas engines.

Carborundum [TM] compound of carbon and silicon used for polishing and grinding.

carbuncle n 1 inflamed boil, tumor 2 deep-red gem.

carburetor n device for mixing gas vapor and air, forming explosive mixture, in internal-combustion engines.

carcass n dead body; skeleton or framework (of ship, building).

carcinogen n any substance likely to cause cancer; a **carcinogenic**.

carcinoma n type of cancer.

card¹ v comb wool or cotton; n comb for cleansing wool, etc.

card² n stiff paper; greeting card; playing card; postcard; idm **lay/put one's cards on the table** speak frankly about one's plans; idm **in the cards** quite possible; idm **play one's cards right** adopt the right plan of action.

cardamon n (seed of Indian plant used as) spice.

cardboard n thick paper, often corrigated.

cardiac a concerning heart; n **cardiograph** record of heart action.

cardigan n knitted woolen or cotton jacket.

cardinal a of chief importance; n prince of Roman Catholic Church, next in rank to pope; ns **cardinal numbers** 1, 2, 3, etc.; **cardinal points** north, south, east, west.

care n 1 grief 2 concern 3 charge; v feel anxiety; idm **take care** be careful; phr v **care for** 1 like 2 look after; a **careful** (adv -ly); a **careless** (adv -ly).

careen v expose keel of ship for cleaning or repair.

career n 1 rapid course 2 mode of living 3 occupation; v rush wildly.

carefree a free from anxiety.

caress n mark of affection – kiss, embrace, etc.; v fondle, embrace.

caret n mark (λ) used to show insertion of letter, word.

caretaker n person employed to look after a building.

cargo n freight or load of ship, etc.

caribou n N American reindeer.

caricature n grotesque, laughable drawing or imitation of person; v represent in caricature.

caries n decay, esp of bones, teeth.

carillon n peal or chime of bells; melody played thereon.

carmine n crimson-red color, obtained from cochineal.

carnage n severe slaughter; massacre.

carnal a pertaining to flesh; sensual; adv -ly; n **carnality**.

carnation *n* cultivated variety of clove pink.

carnival *n* organized festivities; revelry.

carnivore *n* flesh-eating mammal; *pl* **carnivora**; *a* **carnivorous** of animals and also some plants.

carob *n* kind of bean used as substitute for chocolate.

carol *n* joyful song, *esp* Christmas hymn; *v* sing.

carom *v* hit and rebound; *n* rebound.

carouse *n* drinking bout; *v* drink deeply; *n* **carousal** noisy drinking bout.

carousel *n* merry-go-round.

carp[1] *n* freshwater fish.

carp[2] *v* find fault unreasonably; *a* **carping** captious.

carpel *n* seed-bearing leaf.

carpenter *n* woodworker in house building, etc.; *n* **carpentry** craft of carpenter.

carpet *n* fabric for covering floor, etc.; *v* cover with carpet.

carpetbagger *n* political opportunist from outside trying to get elected.

car pool *n* group of drivers with shared transportation.

carriage *n* **1** transportation of anything **2** cost of carriage **3** deportment; bearing **4** vehicle.

carrier *n* **1** person or thing that carries **2** one that passes a disease to others **3** = **aircraft carrier**.

carrier pigeon *n* pigeon used to carry messages.

carrion *n* rotten flesh; putrefying animal carcass.

carrot *n* edible reddish orange root; *a* **carroty** reddish, *esp* of hair.

carry *v* **1** transport **2** bear, support weight of anything **3** *mil* capture **4** retain (in memory); *n* range of projectile from gun.

cart *n* two- or four-wheeled vehicle, usually horse-drawn; *v* carry; *ns* **carter; carthorse** strong horse.

carte blanche *n* complete control or authority.

cartel *n* **1** written agreement for exchange of prisoners-of-war **2** agreement between manufacturers, fixing prices, etc.

cartilage *n* strong, elastic tissue; gristle.

cartography *n* art of making maps, charts; *n* **cartographer**.

carton *n* box made of cardboard, corrugated board.

cartoon *n* sketch or design for work of art; topical drawing in newspaper, etc.; *n* **cartoonist**.

cartridge *n* metal case containing charge for gun; *n* **cartridge paper** strong drawing paper.

cartwheel *n* **1** wheel of cart **2** sideways somersault.

carve *v* **1** cut and shape wood, stone, etc.; engrave **2** cut in slices or pieces (meat); *ns* **carving** piece of carved work; *n* **carver 1** person who carves **2 carving knife** long knife

for carving meat.

cascade *n* small waterfall; something resembling this; *v* fall in cascades.

case[1] *n* **1** condition **2** state of affairs **3** grammatical relationship **4** instance **5** lawsuit **6** *med* patient; *idm* **in any case** whatever happens; *idm* **in case of 1** in the event of **2** as a precaution against.

case[2] *n* box; chest; protective covering, wrapping; *v* put in case.

casein *n* main protein of milk; basis of cheese.

case-hardened *n* (of steel) having a toughened surface.

casement *n* window side hung on hinges.

case study *n* extended study of an individual or group.

casework *n* social work, studying family or personal problems.

cash *n* **1** coins and notes **2** any sort of money; *v* exchange for notes and coins; *phr v* **cash in on** profit from (something enjoyed by others); *ns* **cashier** one in charge of cash; **cash register** till.

cash-and-carry *n* shop where goods are paid for in cash and taken away by the customer.

cash card *n* card enabling bank-account holders to get cash from an automaticed teller machine (ATM) at any time.

cash crop *n* crop grown in

a b **c** d e f g h i j k l m n o p q r s t u v w x y z

A B C D E F G H I J K L M N O P Q R S T U V W X Y Z

order to sell.

cashew *n* small, kidney-shaped, edible nut.

cash flow *n* movement of money in business; *idm* **cash-flow problem** lack of funds.

cashier *v* dismiss from the service; deprive of rank.

cashmere *n* soft material woven from goat's hair.

cash register *n* machine in a shop for recording purchases with a drawer for safekeeping of money.

casing *n* protective covering, *as* for machinery.

casino *n* public room with gambling facilities.

cask *n* barrel, mainly used for liquids.

casket *n* **1** small box, plain or ornamented, for jewels, trinkets, etc.; **2** coffin.

casserole *n* fireproof dish for cooking and serving food; food cooked in this way.

cassette *n* **1** plastic or metal container for film or tape **2** cartridge with audio tape.

cassock *n* long vestment, usually black, worn by clergy, etc.

cast *v* **1** throw down, off **2** shed (snakeskin) **3** reckon up (accounts) **4** mold (metal, etc.) **5** hurl **6** assign parts in a play; *pt, pp* **cast;** *idm* **cast an eye over** look quickly over to check; *phr vs* **cast about/around (for)** try to find quickly; **cast aside/away** abandon; **cast off 1** untie a boat **2** finish off a piece of knitting; *n* **1** throw **2** impression taken of something **3** actors in a play; *a* formed by molding metal; *n* **casting** piece of metal shaped by casting.

castanets *n mus* instrument of two wooden shells clicked rapidly together in the hand.

castaway *n* person adrift after a shipwreck.

caste *n* division of Indian society; exclusive social class.

castellated *a* with battlements.

caster, castor *n* small wheel on swivel fixed to leg of chair, etc.

castigate *v* chastise; punish severely; scold bitterly; *n* **castigation**.

casting vote *n* deciding vote when there is a tie.

cast iron *n* hard, brittle type of iron *a* **cast-iron 1** of cast iron **2** tough; unbreakable.

castle *n* fortress; stronghold; piece in chess (rook); *a* **castellated** like a castle, having turrets, etc.

castor oil *n* laxative oil made from seeds of castor-oil plant.

castrate *v* remove testicles; geld; emasculate; expurgate (book, etc.); *n* **castration**.

casual *a* accidental; careless; occasional; *adv* **casually;** *n* **casualty** victim of accident, battle; *pl* **casualties** number killed, wounded in war.

casuistry *n* specious reasoning; application of ethical rules and principles; *n* **casuist**.

CAT *abbr* **1** computer-aided technology **2** computerized axial tomography.

cat *n* **1** small, domesticated, carnivorous quadruped **2** spiteful woman **3** whip with nine lashes; *idm* **a cat-and-dog life** a life full of strife; *idm* **play cat and mouse with** keep in cruel suspense; *idm* **let the cat out of the bag** carelessly reveal a secret; *idm* **the cat's whiskers** the best person, thing; *n* **cat's-eye** semiprecious stone.

catabolism *n* destructive metabolism.

cataclysm *n* violent upheaval, social or physical; *as* **-al, -ic.**

catacomb *n* subterranean cemetery.

catalepsy *n* tracelike state in which the body is rigid; *a* **cataleptic.**

catalog, catalogue *n* list of objects, names, etc., arranged in order; *v* make such list.

catalpa *n* tree with bell-shaped white flowers.

catalyst *n* **1** substance causing chemical change without itself changing **2** person, thing facilitating change.

catalytic converter *n aut* device for converting harmful exhaust fumes into carbon dioxide.

catamaran *n* raft of logs lashed together; twin-hulled sailing boat.

catapult *n* elastic sling fixed on forked stick for shooting pellets, stones; apparatus assisting aircraft to take off, *esp* from ship.

cataract *n* **1** large, high waterfall **2** disease of eye.

catarrh *n* inflammation of mucous membrane, *esp* of nose; *a* **-al**.

catastrophe *n* disaster; sudden irrevocable calamity; *a* **catastrophic**.

catcall *n* jeer.

catch *v* **1** get hold of; seize **2** grasp (of mind) **3** be infected by (disease); become entangled **4** be in time for **5** overtake; *pt, pp* **caught** *n* **1** act of catching; **catch** ball **2** something caught **3** mechanical device to secure lock; *idm* **catch fire** begin burning; *idm* **catch it** be in trouble; *idm* **catch someone's eye** get someone's attention; *phr vs* **catch on 1** understand **2** become fashionable; **catch up 1** make up for lost time **2** draw level with; *idm* **caught up in** deeply involved in; **catcher** one who catches; *as* **catchpenny** worthless; showy; **catchy** attractive; easy to remember (of tune).

catching *a* infectious.

catchment area *n* **1** *geog* area that feeds river, lake, etc., with rainwater **2** area served by a particular school, hospital, etc.

catchphrase *n* widely used saying, *usu* copied from a famous person.

catch-22 *n* bureaucratic regulation giving hope of escape from an intolerable situation, but also containing a clause that makes escape impossible; **catch-22 situation** situation governed by such a regulation.

catchword *n* word or phrase placed to attract attention.

catechize *v* teach by question and answer; examine by searching questions; *n* **catechism** form of instruction, *esp* religious.

categorize *v* divide into classes.

category *n* class; division; mode of grouping; *a* **categorical** absolute; positive.

cater *v* provide food, pleasure for; *n* **caterer**.

cater-cornered *a* diagonal; **diagonally**.

caterpillar *n* **1** larva of butterfly, moth **2** endless belt of plates, on vehicle, used instead of wheels.

caterwaul *v, n* (make) howling voice of a cat.

catfish *n* freshwater fish.

catgut *n* cord from animal intestines used for strings of musical instruments, tennis rackets, etc.

catharsis *n* **1** release of strong emotions, *esp* through drama, art, etc., or by talking **2** *med* emptying of bowels; *pl* **catharses;** *a* **cathartic**.

cathedral *n* chief church of diocese; *a* belonging to, containing such.

catheter *n* tube introduced into one of passages of body, to draw off fluid or to dilate.

cathode *n* negative electrode; **cathode rays** negative discharge.

catholic *a* **1** universal **2** of whole body of Christians **3** of Roman Catholic Church; *ns* **Catholic** a Roman Catholic; **Catholicism**.

catkin *n* furry flower of willow, birch, etc.

catnap *n* short sleep.

catnip *n* plant with scented leaves.

cat-o'-nine-tail *n* tall, spiny marsh plant fashioned into a whip.

cat's paw *n* person used cynically by another; dupe.

CAT scanner *n* type of body scanner used in hospitals using X-rays of cross-sections; CAT scan image made by such.

catsuit *n* close-fitting garment from neck to feet.

catsup, catchup *n* ketchup

cattery *n* home for cats.

cattle *n* bovine animals; human beings (disparaging).

cattle call *n* group audition of actors, dancers, etc.

catty *a* spiteful; *adv* **cattily;** *n* **cattiness**.

catwalk *n* long narrow raised footpath.

Caucasian *n, a* (member) of the white races of mankind.

caucus *n* inner group of people controlling political policy.

a
b
c
d
e
f
g
h
i
j
k
l
m
n
o
p
q
r
s
t
u
v
w
x
y
z

A
B
C
D
E
F
G
H
I
J
K
L
M
N
O
P
Q
R
S
T
U
V
W
X
Y
Z

caudal *a* of the tail.

caught *pt of* **catch**.

cauldron, caldron *n* large metal pot or boiler.

cauliflower *n* white, fleshy, edible flower head, variety of cabbage.

caulk *v* make seam (of ship) watertight, by packing in oakum, tow, and pitch; seal cracks; *n* **caulking, calking**.

cause *n* force producing effect; motive; reason; lawsuit; *v* bring about; effect.

causeway *n* raised path across wet, marshy ground.

caustic *a* **1** corrosive; burning **2** satirical; *n* corrosive substance; *adv* **-ally**.

cauterize *v* sear, burn with hot iron or caustic; *ns* **cautery, cauterization**.

caution *n* carefulness; warning; *v* warn; *a* **cautious;** *n* **-ness;** *a* **cautionary** serving as warning.

cavalcade *n* procession of riders, carriages, etc.

cavalier *n* horseman; *a* careless; thoughtless; *n* **cavalry** horse soldiers.

cave *n* hollow in earth with lateral extension; den; *n* **cavern** deep cave; *a* **cavernous;** *n* **cavity** hole; *phr* *v* **cave in 1** collapse **2** give up; *n* **caveman** primitive man.

caveat *n* *leg* warning.

cavern *n* large cave.

caviar *n* delicacy of salted sturgeon roe.

cavil *v* quibble; raise frivolous objections to.

cavity *n* hole, *esp* in a tooth; *n* **cavity wall** double wall with vertical air space between to give insulation.

cavort *v* prance about noisily.

cavy *n* small rodent, as guinea pig.

caw *n* call of rook, crow; *v* utter such cry.

cayenne *n* ground red pepper.

cayman *n* variety of alligator.

CB radio *abbr* citizens' band radio.

cc *abbr* cubic centimetre(s).

CCTV *abbr* closed circuit television.

CD *abbr* **1** civil defense **2** compact disk.

CD-ROM *n comput* compact disk on which large quantities of information can be stored or viewed.

cease *v* desist from; discontinue; *a* **-less**.

cease-fire *n* truce.

cedar *n* large, coniferous, evergreen tree.

cede *v* **1** yield; surrender **2** grant; admit.

ceiling *n* **1** lining of upper surface of room **2** extreme height attainable by aircraft **3** upper limit of prices, wages, etc.

celandine *n* wild flower, resembling buttercup.

celebrate *v* **1** observe with proper rites **2** do honor to (by ceremony); **3** *coll* have a good time; *ns* **celebrant** priest; **celebration; celebrity** famous person; fame; *a*

celebrated well known.

celerity *n* swiftness, rapidity.

celery *n* vegetable with long, juicy, edible stalks.

celestial *a* pertaining to sky; divine, heavenly.

celibacy *n* unmarried state; abstinence from sexual relations; *n, a* **celibate**.

cell *n* **1** small room, in monastery, prison, etc. **2** biological basic unit **3** compartment in honeycomb **4** component of galvanic battery.

cellar *n* underground part of house; stock of wine; *ns* **coal cellar, wine cellar**.

cello *n mus* stringed instrument of violin type held between the knees; *pl* **cellos;** *n* **cellist**.

cellophane *n* transparent plastic for wrapping.

cell phone *n* mobile telephone used on cellular network.

cellular *a* **1** of living cells **2** porous **3** *telecom* based on communications network; *ns* **c. handset** mobile phone, **c. operator, c. subscriber, c. telephone**.

cellulite *n* type of body fat that causes dimpling of the skin.

celluloid *n* inflammable plastic material.

cellulose *n* carbohydrate cell walls of plants; raw material used in plastics; *v* varnish with nitrocellulose lacquer.

Celsius *a* = **centigrade**.

Celtic *a* of the Celts.

cement *n* **1** powdery substance

that, mixed with water, sets hard **2** liquid adhesive; *v* cover with, join by cement; *fig* unite closely.

cemetery *n* burial ground, other than churchyard.

cenotaph *n* monument raised in memory of one whose body is not therein.

censor *n* **1** one authorized to prevent publication of books, plays, etc. **2** official, *esp* in wartime, empowered to open all written communications and suppress any harmful to safety of nation; *v* subject to censorship; *n* **censorship;** *a* **censorious** disapproving; severely critical.

censure *v* criticize adversely; blame; *n* reproof.

census *n* official periodic counting of population of a state.

cent *n* hundredth part of dollar; **percent** in every hundred.

centaur *n* mythical creature half man, half horse.

centenary *n* hundredth anniversary; *a* celebration of this; *n* **centenarian** one who is 100 years old; **centennial** occurring every 100 years.

center *n* **1** middle point **2** axis **3** point in body on which certain activity depends.

centerboard *n* retractable keel of sailboat.

centerfold *n* (picture filling) center pages of magazine.

center of gravity *n* point of balance.

centi- *prefix a* hundred.

centigrade *a* having 100 equal parts; *esp* **c. thermometer** freezing point 0 and boiling point 100.

centigram *n* measure of weight, hundredth part of a gram.

centimeter *n* measure of length, hundredth part of meter.

centipede *n* long, crawling insect with many feet.

central *a* **1** at the center **2** most important; *adv* **-ly;** *v* **centralize** put under central control; *ns* **-ization, -izationism** policy of central control; *n, a* **-izationist; central heating** *n* heating system from a central boiler through pipes and radiators.

centrifugal *a* moving away from the center; *n* **c. force** tendency for objects to fly outward from circular motion; *n* **centrifuge** machine using this force to separate substances.

centripetal *n* moving toward the center.

centrist *n, a* (person) avoiding political extremes.

centurian *n* Roman officer commanding 100 men.

century *n* **1** 100 years **2** 100 things of same kind, collectively.

ceramic *a* pertaining to pottery; *n pl* **ceramics** art of making pottery, etc., of clay.

cereal *a* pertaining to edible grain; *n* grain itself.

cerebral *a* pertaining to brain;

n **cerebral palsy** disability caused by damage to the brain before or after birth; *n* **cerebration** working of brain.

ceremony *n* act of reverence; public observance of solemn event; *n, a* **ceremonial;** *a* **ceremonious.**

cerise *n, a* pinkish red color.

cert *abbr* **1** certificate **2** *coll* certainty.

certain *a* definite; inevitable; of some amount; unerring; *adv* **-ly;** *ns* **certainty, certitude** mental conviction.

certify *v* **1** assure **2** attest in written document; *a* **certifiable** *esp* of insanity; *n* **certificate** written declaration.

certitude *n* sureness.

cervical *a* of the cervix; *n* **cervical cancer.**

cervix *n., pl.* **cervixes, cervices.** narrow part of womb joined to vagina.

cesarean section *n* surgical operation to deliver baby when normal birth is impossible.

cessation *n* stopping; pause; ceasing.

cesspool *n* cavity in ground, used for draining sewage from house, etc.

CFC *abbr* chlorofluorocarbon.

Chablis *n* dry white Burgundy wine.

chafe *v* **1** rub against **2** become sore from friction **3** become restive.

chaff *n* **1** husk of grain **2** chopped straw **3** teasing.

a
b
c
d
e
f
g
h
i
j
k
l
m
n
o
p
q
r
s
t
u
v
w
x
y
z

chaffer *n* bargain.

chaffinch *n* small, wild, European bird.

chafing dish *n* device for cooking food at the table.

chagrin *n* mortification; disappointment.

chain *n* 1 series of connected metal links 2 connected series of things, visible or nonmaterial; *v* confine; restrain. *Makes many compounds, e.g., c. drive, c. letter, c. reaction.*

chain letter *n* letter sent to several people who are asked to send copies to others in turn, *usu* with a request for money.

chain reaction *n* sequence of events, each leading to further events.

chain-smoke *v* smoke continuously; *n* **chain-smoker**.

chain store *n* one of a group of shops owned by one firm.

chair *n* 1 single seat with back and four legs 2 professorship; seat of authority, etc.; *v* 1 carry person in triumph 2 preside at.

chairperson *n* chairman or chairwoman in charge of a meeting or head of a board of directors.

chaise longue, chaise longe *n* long seat for reclining with single backrest and armrest.

chalet *n* small, wooden, Swiss house; wooden cabin.

chalice *n* 1 drinking cup 2 Communion cup.

chalk *n* soft limestone; crayon; *v* mark with chalk; *a* **chalky**; *phr v* **chalk up** 1 write with chalk 2 record success 3 charge someone's account, *e.g.*, for drinks in a bar.

challenge *n* summons to fight; dispute; objection taken; *v* call in question; summon to fight; *n* **challenger**.

chamber *n* 1 room; apartment 2 body of persons composing legislative assembly; *n pl* 1 lawyer's office 2 lodgings; *n* **chambermaid** housemaid at hotel; *n* **chamber music** music suitable for room or small hall, with few instruments.

chamber pot *n* bedside receptacle for urine.

chameleon *n* small lizard able to change color; *a* inconstant.

chamfer *n* bevel; groove; *v* make bevel, groove.

chamois *n Fr* goatlike animal; *n* **chamois leather** soft pliable leather.

champ[1] *v* (of horses) chew noisily; *idm* **champ at the bit** show signs of impatience and restlessness.

champ[2] *n coll* champion.

champagne *n* French white sparkling wine.

champion *n* upholder of cause; one who excels (in sport, shows or exhibitions); *v* act as champion.

chance *n* 1 opportunity; possibility 2 unforeseen fortune 3 risk; *a* **chancy** hazardous.

chancel *n* east part of Christian church, where altar stands.

chancellor *n* 1 chief judge 2 head of university 3 chief finance minister.

chandelier *n* branched support for lights, hanging from ceiling.

chandler *n* one making, dealing in candles; *n* **ships' chandler** dealer in stores and provisions for ships.

change *v* 1 exchange; alter, substitute 2 interchange (train, etc.) 3 put on different clothes; *n* 1 alteration 2 small money; *as* **-able** variable, fickle; **-less** constant; *n* **changeling** child secretly substituted for another.

channel *n* 1 riverbed; body of water joining two seas; deep passage in shallow water 2 groove 3 that through which liquid flows more 4 *fig* means of communication 5 frequency band for transmission of TV, radio; *v* form, supply through channel.

chant *n* song, sacred hymn; *v* sing; utter in musical monotone; *ns* **chanter** 1 singer 2 pipe of bagpipes, producing notes; **chanty, shanty** sailor's song.

chaos *n* confusion; utter disorder; muddle; *a* **chaotic**.

chap *v.* **chapped.** split, become sore from exposure to cold, etc.; *n* **1** crack in skin **2** *coll* man, boy; a chapped sore.

chapel *n* **1** private church; cathedral antechamber with small altar **2** association of journeymen printers.

chaperon *n* older person accompanying younger one in public or on social occasion; *v* act in this way.

chaplain *n* clergyman attached to institution, armed forces, or private household.

chaplet *n* **1** wreath for the head **2** prayer beads.

chapter *n* **1** main division of book **2** stage in history **3** governing body of cathedral; **chapter house** room where chapter meets, attached to cathedral.

char[1] *v* scorch, burn; *a* **charred**.

char[2] *v* do housework for hourly, daily payment.

char[3] *n* small fish of salmon or trout family.

character *n* **1** mark; symbol; letter **2** essential nature **3** personality (in play, book, etc.) **4** testimonial of ability, habits; *a* **characteristic;** *v* **characterize** describe; *n* **-ization;** *a* **characterless.**

charade *n* form of riddle, when each syllable of word is acted; game using such.

charcoal *n* form of carbon, made from charred wood.

charge *v* **1** load **2** restore electricity to battery **3** cost **4** attack **5** accuse **6** entrust; *n* **1** cost **2** accusation

3 command **4** amount of electricity in battery; *idm* **in charge of** responsible for; *a* **chargeable.**

charge card *n* shopper's credit card.

chargé d'affaires *n Fr* diplomat representing government in absence of ambassador.

charger *n* cavalry horse.

chariot *n* ancient two-wheeled car for fighting, state occasions, racing; *n* **charioteer.**

charisma *n* power to inspire devotion; *a* **charismatic.**

charity *n* love; benevolence (of mind); liberality; *a* **charitable.**

charlatan *n* imposter; quack.

Charleston *n* popular dance of the 1920s.

charley horse *n* cramp or sore muscle, *esp* in leg.

charm *n* magic spell; fascination; small object worn on person; *v* attract; bewitch; enchant; *n* **charmer** fascinating person; *a* **charming.**

charnel, charnel house *n* vault where bodies or bones are stored.

chart *n* map, *esp* for navigational use; graph; *v* make map, graph.

charter *n* document granting rights, etc.; *v* let or hire; *a* **chartered** licensed, privileged; *n* **charter party** contract made between ship owner and skipper.

chartreuse *n* greenish or

yellow color.

charwoman *n* cleaning woman.

chary *a* careful; parsimonious; *n* **chariness;** *adv* **charily.**

chase *v* pursue; drive away; *n* hunting; pursuit; *n* **chaser** drink taken after stronger one.

chase *v* engrave ornamentally.

chasm *n* deep abyss; fissure.

chasse *n ballet* gliding step.

chassis *n* framework, wheels and machinery of motor vehicle; undercarriage of aircraft.

chaste *a* pure; continent; *adv* **chastely;** *n* **chastity.**

chasten *v* punish in order to correct; *a* **chastened** subdued.

chastise *v* punish by beating; *n* **chastisement.**

chasuble *n* loose overgarment worn by priest.

chat *n* easy, informal talk; *v* talk idly; *phr v* **chat up** talk to get better acquainted; *a* **chatty;** *n* **chatter** rapid, trivial talk; *v* talk idly; rattle teeth; *ns* **chatterer, chattering, chatterbox** incessant chatterer.

château *n Fr* castle or large country house; *pl* **-s** *or* **-x.**

chattel *n* movable property; *pl* goods, possessions.

chauffeur *n Fr* driver of automobiles, usually paid.

chauvinism *n* perverted, blind patriotism.

cheap *a* of low price, relative to value; inferior; *adv* **-ly;**

n **-ness;** *v* **cheapen**.

cheapskate *n* miser.

cheat *v* swindle; defraud; practice trickery; *n* swindler; trickster.

check *v* 1 retard; restrain; stop 2 verify; *n* 1 call in chess 2 control 3 ticket (cloakroom) 4 pattern in squares 5 **check** paper form for withdrawing money from bank; *n* **check book;** *ns* **checkmate** final winning move in chess; defeat; **checkout** cashier's counter in supermarket; **checkpoint** place where documents, vehicles, etc., are inspected, *e.g.*, at a border.

checker *n* pattern of squares, as chess board; *v* mark in squares; *a* **checkered** 1 having squares of alternating color 2 with alternating good and bad fortune.

checkerboard *n* board of 64 squares on which the game of checkers is played.

checkup *n* full examination, *esp* medical.

Cheddar *n* firm, smooth, yellow cheese.

cheek *n* 1 side of face below eye 2 impudence; pertness; *v* address rudely; *a* **cheeky**.

cheer *n* 1 state of mind 2 rich food and drink 3 applause; *v* 1 applaud vocally 2 encourage; *a* **cheerful;** *n* **-ness;** *a* **cheery;** *adv* **cheerily; cheerless;** *n* **-ness**.

cheerleader *n* person who leads cheering at sports event.

cheese *n* consolidated milk curd used as food; *ns* **cheesecake** 1 sweet flan with cream cheese 2 *coll* provocative pictures of scantily dressed women.

cheeseburger *n* hamburger topped with melted cheese.

cheesecloth *n* light, thin, cotton fabric.

cheeseparing *n*, *a* miserly.

cheesy *a* cheap, tacky.

cheetah *n* fast-running predator of the cat family with spotted skin.

chef *n* professional cook; chief cook in restaurant.

chef d'oeuvre *n* masterpiece; *pl* **chefs d'oeuvre**.

chemise *n* woman's loose-fitting undergarment or dress.

chemist *n* specialist in chemistry.

chemistry *n* natural science dealing with composition, reaction of substances; *n* **chemist;** *n*, *a* **chemical**.

chemotherapy *n* treatment of disease, *esp* cancer, by use of chemicals.

chenille *n* tufted cord of silk or worsted.

cherish *v* hold dear; take care of; keep in mind.

cheroot *n* kind of cigar, open at both ends.

cherry *n* edible, small-stoned fruit either red, black, or white; tree bearing this fruit; *a* red.

cherub *n* heavenly being, rosy-faced child; beautiful, innocent child; *pl* **cherubim, cherubs;** *a* **cherubic**.

chess *n* game of skill, played with 32 chessmen, on checkered board; *ns* **chessmen, chessboard**.

chest *n* 1 coffer; larger box 2 upper front of body; *idm* **get something off one's chest** make a confession.

chesterfield *n* heavy padded sofa studded with buttons.

chestnut *n* 1 tree bearing nuts (**sweet c.** edible; **horse c.** inedible) 2 reddish brown color 3 old joke.

cheviot *n* sturdy, worsted fabric.

chevron *n* *Fr* V-shaped stripe(s) indicating rank, worn on uniform.

chew *v* masticate; *phr v* **chew over** *coll* think carefully about; *a* **chewy.**

chewing gum *n* flavored substance for chewing, *usu* made of chicle.

Chianti *n* dry red Italian wine.

chic *n* smartness; style; elegance; *a* smart, elegant.

chicane *n* trick; *bridge* hand with no trumps; obstacle in car race; *v* quibble; *n* **chicanery** verbal trickery.

chichi *a* affected in style.

chick *n* 1 newly hatched bird 2 affectionate name for child; *n* **chicken** young bird, *esp* hen; *phr v* **chicken out** refuse to do something out of fear; *n* **chicken feed** 1 food for poultry **2** *coll* paltry amount, *esp* of money; *a* **chicken-hearted** timid; *n* **chicken pox** mild contagious disease, chiefly of children.

chickadee *n* small gray N American bird.

chickpea *n* (Asiatic plant with) yellow pealike seed; its edible seed.

chicory *n* salad vegetable; sometimes dried and roasted with coffe.

chide *v* reprove, scold; *pt* **chid; pp chidden**; *a, n* **chiding**.

chief *n* leader; head; *a* principal; foremost; *adv* **chiefly; n chieftain** head of clan or tribe.

chiffchaff *n* European bird of warbler species.

chiffon *n Fr* thin gauzelike material.

chignon *n Fr* woman's hair worn in a roll or knot at the back.

chihuahua *n* tiny dog with smooth hair.

chilblain *n* painful swelling on feet, hands, or ears, due to cold.

child *n* young human being; *pl* **children; a childish** pertaining to child; foolish; silly; *ns* **childhood** period of life to puberty; **childbirth, childbed** state of giving birth to child; *as* **childless, childlike; n child's play** simple task.

chili *n* (powder from dried) pod of hot red pepper.

chili con carne *n* Mexican meat stew with kidney beans and chilies or chili powder.

chill *n* coldness; illness due to cold; *a* frigid (of manner); discouraging; *v* make or become cold; *as* **chilled, chilly** unwelcoming; *n* **chilliness** coldness of sensation or manner.

chime *n* set of bells; musical sequence produced by such; *phr v* **chime in** break into a conversation.

chimera *n* **1** fabulous monster **2** bogey; fancied horror.

chimney *n* **1** outlet for smoke **2** narrow cleft in rock.

chimpanzee *n* arboreal ape, related to gorilla.

chin *n* part of jaw below mouth.

china *n* fine porcelain ware; *a* made of this.

chinchilla *n* (soft gray fur of) small squirrel-like animal; (similar fur of) rabbit or cat.

chine *n* **1** narrow ravine **2** backbone; *v* to chop backbone (joint of meat).

chink[1] *n* slit; cleft.

chink[2] *n* tinkling, metallic sound; *v* make such sound.

chintz *n* printed cotton fabric, used in upholstery.

chip *n* small piece of substance cut, broken off; *v.* **chipping, chipped.** cut chips off; *idm* **a chip off the old block** just like one's father or mother; *idm* **have a chip on one's shoulder** *coll* maintain a resentful attitude because one feels badly treated in the past; *idm* **when the chips are down** *coll* at a critical moment; *phr v* **chip in;** *coll* **1** interrupt **2** contribute money.

chipmunk *n* small striped squirrel-like mammal.

chipper *a coll* cheerful.

chiropody *n* care of feet; *n* **chiropodist.**

chiropractor *n* person who treats disease by massage and manipulation of joints.

chirp, chirrup *v* utter short piping note (of birds); *n* this sound.

chisel *n* cutting tool, for stone, wood, etc.; *v* to use chisel.

chit[1] *n* short note; memo; *n* **chitchat** gossip.

chit[2] *n* small, slightly built girl.

chivalry *n* **1** body of knights **2** courtesy **3** courage; *a* **chivalrous** having knightly qualities.

chive *n* herb with thin, mildy onion-flavored leaves; *pl* these chopped finely for flavoring food.

chlorine *n* nonmetallic element; poison gas; *ns* **chloral** hypnotic; **chloride** bleaching agent; *v* **chlorinate** purify water.

chlorofluorocarbon *n* compound gas containing chlorine, fluorine, and carbon, used as a refrigerant and a propellant gas in aerosols and believed to be harmful to the ozone layer.

chloroform *n* volatile liquid used as anesthetic; *v* to make insensible with this.

chlorophyll n green coloring matter in plants.

chocaholic n coll person addicted to eating chocolate.

chock n wooden wedge; v make secure, prevent rolling; a, adv **chockful, chockablock** coll packed tight.

chocoholic n person addicted to or very fond of chocolate.

chocolate n candy made from ground cacao beans; drink of this; a dark brown color.

choice n 1 act of choosing 2 something specially selected; a of high excellence.

choir n group of singers, esp in church; chancel; n **chorister** singer; a **choral**.

choke v smother; obstruct; throttle; stifle; phr v **choke back** suppress (bad feelings).

choler n anger; wrath; a **choleric** irascible.

cholera n infectious disease of bile, often fatal.

cholesterol n fatty substance, believed in excess to cause hardening of the arteries.

chomp v chew noisily.

choose v select; prefer; pt **chose**; pp **chosen**.

choosy n fussy; hard to please.

chop v **chopping, chopped**. cut with knife, etc.; make quick blow; n piece of lamb, pork with rib bone; n **chopper** 1 tool for chopping 2 coll helicopter; a **choppy** rough (sea).

chopsticks n pair of sticks designed for taking food to the mouth in Asian countries.

chop suey n Chinese dish of slivers of meat with rice and vegetables.

choral a of a choir; sung by a choir.

chorale n 1 type of hymn 2 group of singers.

chord n blending of notes in harmony.

chore n tedious job of work.

choreography n art of ballet dancing, or arranging dances; n **choreographer**.

chorister n member of choir, esp choirboy.

chortle n, v (utter) loud chuckle of enjoyment.

chorus n group of singers; refrain of song; n **chorale** hymn for congregational use.

chose pt, **chosen** pp of **choose**.

choux pastry n Fr light, thin pastry made with egg.

chow n 1 type of dog with thick fur 2 sl food.

chowder n thick soup of fish, vegetables, or both.

chow mein n Chinese dish served on fried noodles.

christen v 1 make a member of the Christian church by baptism 2 name at official ceremony, esp a ship 3 use for the first time n **christening**.

Christendom n all Christian people in the world.

Christian n followers of Christ; a pertaining to Christians; **C. name**

baptismal name; **C. Science** belief in healing by prayers; ns **Christianity** teaching of Christ.

Christmas, Christmastime/-tide n 1 feast day (December 25) celebrating the nativity of Jesus Christ 2 period of days before and after this..

chromatic a relating to color; mus scale ascending or descending by semitones.

chrome n 1 chromium 2 yellow pigment.

chromium n brittle metallic element, used for plating.

chromosome n tiny rods carrying genes in living cells.

chronic a long-lasting (of disease); sl tedious, bad.

chronic fatigue syndrome n illness characterized by extreme fatigue and muscle weakness.

chronicle n record of events in order of time; v register (events, dates); n **chronicler**.

chronology n table or list of dates; a **chronological** in order of time.

chronometer n watch for measuring time exactly.

chrysalis n., pl. **chrysalises**. sheath enclosing insect larva during resting stage.

chrysanthemum n hardy plant with large flowers in bright colors.

chub n river fish of carp family.

chubby a fat; stumpy; plump; n **chubbiness**.

chuck v throw; phr vs **c. out** eject forcibly; n 1 throw

2 pat (under chin) **3** part of drill holding bit **4** cut of beef from neck.

chuckle *v* laugh softly; *n* low laugh of satisfaction.

chum *n* close friend.

chump *n* **1** block of wood **2** *sl* idiot.

chunk *n* thick piece broken off; *coll* large quantity; *a* **chunky** thick; bulky.

Chunnel *n coll* tunnel under the English Channel.

church *n* **1** place of Christian worship **2** whole body of Christians; clergy; *ns* **churchwarden** officer representing parish; long clay pipe; **churchyard**.

churlish *a* **1** boorish **2** ungracious; selfish; mean.

churn *n* vessel for making butter; *v* shake liquid violently; *phr v* **churn out** *coll* produce in great quantity but not quality.

chute *n* inclined slope for sending down logs, water, any heavy thing.

chutney *n* hot, sweet-tasting pickle or relish.

chutzpah *n coll* nerve; impudence.

CIA *abbr* Central Intelligence Agency.

cicada *n* large grasshopper-like insect.

cicatrice *n Fr* or *Lat* scar; *pl* **cicatrices**.

cider *n* drink made of fermented apple juice.

cigar *n* solid roll of tobacco leaves for smoking.

cigarette *n* finely cut tobacco, rolled in thin paper.

C-in-C *abbr* commander-in-chief.

cinch *n coll* **1** easy task **2** sure thing; *v* pull tight.

cinder *n* remains of burned-out coal; *a* **cindery**.

cine- *prefix* indicating a relationship to cinematography.

cinematography *n* art of producing moving pictures on film; *a* **cinematographic** projecting film.

cinnamon *n* bark of Ceylon laurel, used as spice; *a* of yellowishbrown color.

cipher *n* **1** symbol 0; zero **2** person of no importance **3** monogram **4** secret way of writing.

circa *prep* (of dates) around.

circle *n* **1** perfectly round plane figure **2** group of people united by common interest **3** ring; *v* move around; surround; *n* **circlet** small circular band, *esp* around the head.

circuit *n* **1** distance around **2** path of electric curent; *a* **circuitous** indirect.

circular *a* **1** forming or moving in a circle **2** indirect; *n* letter circulated to many people.

circulate *v* **1** (cause to) move around a closed system **2** move around freely **3** inform by circular letter; *n* **circulation 1** flow through a system **2** passing of money **3** number of people receiving

a publication.

circumcize *v* cut off foreskin; *n* **circumcision**.

circumference *n* boundary of a circle.

circumlocution *n* elaborate way of saying something simple.

circumnavigate *v* sail around.

circumscribe *v* limit; restrict.

circumspect *a* decorous; prudent; cautious.

circumstance *n* event; fact; *pl* financial condition; pomp; *a* **circumstantial** accidental; incidental; indirect.

circumvent *v* outwit; frustrate; *n* **-vention**.

circus *n* **1** entertainment with clowns, animals, etc. **2** round open space in city.

cirrhosis *n* disease of liver.

cirrus *n* high fleecy cloud.

CIS *abbr* Commonwealth of Independent States (territories from former Soviet Union).

cistern *n* **1** water tank **2** natural reservoir.

citadel *n* fortress protecting a town.

cite 1 summon **2** quote an authority; *n* **citation**.

citizen *n* one living in city or town; *n* **-ship**.

citizens band *n* range of radio frequencies usable by the public for private communication.

citron *n* fruit like lemon or lime, less acid; *a* **citric** of acid of lemon, etc.; *n* **citric acid** weak acid found in many fruits, *esp* citrus.

citrus fruit *n pl* citrons, lemons, oranges, etc.

city *n* large-sized town.

civet *n* catlike mammal (*also* **civet cat**); secretion from this animal used in making perfumes.

civic *a* of a city or citizens; *n* **civics** study of rights and responsibilities of citizens; study of government.

civil *a* 1 relating to citizens of same state 2 nonmilitary 3 affable; polite 4 not criminal; *ns* **civility** politeness; **civilian** nonmilitary person; *v* **civilize** bring from barbarism; *n* **civilization;** *a* **civilized.**

civil engineering *n* building of public works.

civil service *n* government departments (except military and legal); people employed there; *n* **civil servant.**

civil war *n* war between citizens of one country.

civvies *n sl* civilian clothes.

cl *abbr* centiliter.

cladding *n* protective covering, *esp* of outside walls.

claim *v* assert; apply for as right; *n* demand for, assertion of just title to something; *n* **claimant.**

clairvoyant *n* person having second sight; *n* **clairvoyance.**

clam *n* edible mollusk; *phr v* **clam up** *coll* refuse to speak.

clambake *n* 1 picnic by the sea 2 informal party.

clamber *v* climb clumsily or laboriously.

clammy *a* moist and cold to touch; sticky; *n* **clamminess.**

clamor *n* loud outcry; noise; *a* **-ous.**

clamp *n* 1 tool for holding things together 2 heap of potatoes, etc., straw covered for winter storage; *v* fasten with clamp; *phr v* **clamp down on** suppress.

clampdown *n* imposing of restrictions.

clan *n* tribe; group of families under chief, having common ancestor; *a* **clannish;** *ns* **-ness; clansman.**

clandestine *a* guiltily secret; surreptitious.

clang *n* loud, metallic ring; *v* make sound; **clangor** repeated ringing; din.

clank *n* sharp metallic sound; *v* to make such sound.

clap *v.* **clapping, clapped.** strike together, with noise; applaud with hands; *n* sharp noise; sudden burst of thunder; *ns* **clapper** tongue of bell.

claptrap empty talk.

claque *n* hired applauders.

claret *n* red wines of Bordeaux.

clarify *v.* **-fying, -fied.** purify; make clear; *ns* **clarification, clarity.**

clarinet *n* woodwind musical instrument.

clarion *n* kind of trumpet; *a* ringing; *ns* **clarionet, clarinet** woodwind instrument.

clash *v* 1 come together suddenly 2 disagree; *n* metallic sound; conflict.

clasp *n* hook, bolt for fastening; *v* fasten; embrace; grasp; *n* **claspknife** pocketknife.

class *n* any division, kind, sort; rank; category; *v* **classify** arrange methodically in classes; *n* **classification;** *a* **classifiable; classless** *a* not having divisions of social class.

class action *n* lawsuit on behalf of a group with a common complaint.

classified *a* (of information) limited to authorized persons.

classic *a* 1 of highest merit 2 of ancient Greek and Roman culture; *n* work of art or literature, regarded as model of excellence; *pl* Greek or Latin language; *a* **classical** possessing excellence *esp* of music.

clatter *n* series of dull, hard noises; rattle; noisy talk; *v* make clatter.

clause *n* short sentence, part of main one; article in treaty, will, contract, etc.

claustrophobia *n* morbid fear of enclosed spaces.

clavichord *n* early predecessor of piano.

clavicle *n* collarbone; *a* **clavicular.**

claw *n* sharp nails or talons of animals and birds; *v* seize, scratch with claws.

clay *n* sticky earth; human body; *a* **clayey;** *n* **clay pigeon** clay disk used in shooting contest.

clean *a* 1 free from dirt 2 pure 3 shapely 4 neat; *v* render clean; *adv* **cleanly; *ns* cleaner, cleanness, cleanliness; *v* cleanse** remove impurity from.

clean-cut *a* neat and presentable; clear in outline.

clean sweep *n* 1 removal of the unnecessary 2 victory.

clear *a* 1 audible 2 bright 3 distinct 4 unimpeded 5 free from doubt 6 transparent; *idm* **in the clear** 1 out of danger 2 known to be innocent 3 with a net profit; *phr vs* **clear off/out** go away; **clear up** 1 elucidate 2 neaten; *adv* **clearly;** *v* make, become clear; acquit; disentangle; *ns* **clearance** 1 act of clearing 2 riddance of surplus stock 3 certificate that ship has discharged port dues 4 clear space between two objects; **clearness; clearing** land cleared of trees; **clearinghouse,** where documents, etc., are sorted; **as clearheaded, clear-sighted** discerning.

cleat *n* small wooden or metal projection used for gripping, as on a football shoe.

cleavage *n* 1 division 2 hollow between a woman's breasts seen above neckline of dress.

cleave *v* split; divide by force; *pt* **clove, cleft;** *pp* **cloven, cleft;** *phr v* **cleave to** 1 stick fast to 2 *fml* remain steadfastly loyal to; *ns* **cleft** split, fissure; **cleaver** chopper.

clef *n* sign of pitch of stave in music.

cleft palate *n* genetic defect of fissure in the roof of the mouth.

clematis *n* climbing, flowering plant.

clemency *n* (of weather) mildness, warmth; *fig* gentleness, leniency; *a* **clement.**

clench *v* make firm; close (fist); set closely together.

clerestory *n* upper rows of windows in church.

clergy *n* body of ordained minister in Christian church; *ns* **clergyman; cleric** any person in Holy Orders; *a* **clerical** of clergy.

clerk *n* official in government corporation service; office subordinate; *a* **clerical** pertaining to office work.

clever *a* intelligent; adroit; dexterous; *adv* **-ly;** *n* **-ness.**

clew *n* ball of yarn.

cliché *n* hackneyed phrase; catchword.

click *v* 1 make slight, sharp sound; 2 *coll* become instantly friendly or popular 3 be understood; *n* thin, rapid, sharp sound.

client *n* customer of professional person or tradesperson; *n* **clientele;** whole body of clients.

cliff *n* steep rock face, *esp* facing sea.

cliffhanger *n* serial story, film, etc., where each episode ends in great suspense.

climacteric *n* critical phase in human life; menopause.

climate *n* weather conditions of a country, etc.; *a* **climatic.**

climax *n* culminating point; point of greatest tension in film, story, etc.; *v* to reach this.

climb *v* ascend by effort; creep up; *n* **climber;** *phr v* **climb down** admit one was wrong.

clinch *v* 1 make fast 2 decide; *n* grip, lock (boxing) 2 *coll* amorous embrace; *n* **clincher** decisive argument.

cling *v* stick to; remain near to; *pt, pp* **clung.**

clinic *n* practical teaching of medicine, surgery; place for medical examination, treatment; *a* **clinical** 1 of the treatment of patients 2 efficient and objective; without feeling (*adv* **-ly** from clinical observation); *n* **clinical thermometer** used to take temperature of patient.

clink *n* slight tinkling sound; *v* make or cause this sound; *n sl* prison.

clinker *n* refuse of coal or coke.

clinker-built *n* (of boats) made with planks overlapping.

clip *v* **clipping, clipped.** cut with shears or scissors.

clip *n* 1 device of metal, plastic, etc., for fastening 2 short extract from film or video; *n* **clipboard** board with clip for holding papers.

clip joint *n sl* nightclub, restaurant, etc., overcharging

A
B
C
D
E
F
G
H
I
J
K
L
M
N
O
P
Q
R
S
T
U
V
W
X
Y
Z

its customers.

clipper *n* fast sailing ship, airliner; *pl* small shears.

clippings *n pl* **1** extracts cut from newspaper **2** ends of hair left after clipping hair or beard.

clique *n Fr* exclusive set; select and snobbish group.

clitoris *n* small erectile part of female genitals.

cloak *n* outer sleeveless garment; disguise; *v* cover; hide; *n* **cloakroom** place where coats, hats, luggage, etc., may be left.

clobber *v* **1** attack violently **2** overwhelm.

cloche *n Fr* bell-shaped protective glass for plants.

clock *n* device for measuring time, not intended for wearing; *idm* **around the clock** day and night; *idm* **turn the clock back** return to old ways and ideas; *idm* **watch the clock** think about the time for finishing work; *idm* **work against the clock** try to complete a job within a given time; *v* **clock in, out** record automatically arrival, departure from work.

clockwise *adv* in the direction of a clock's hands.

clockwork *idm* **like clockwork** smoothly and easily.

clod *n* lump of earth; *fig* stupid person; *n* **clodhopper** oaf.

clog *n* wooden-soled shoe; *v* **clogging, clogged.** hinder, cause to jam.

cloister *n* covered arcade, *esp*

in monastery, college; *v* confine; seclude; *a* **cloistered**.

clone *n* animal or plant produced asexually from the cells of another.

close *a* **1** near **2** dense **3** careful **4** sultry, heavy of (weather); *adv* **-ly;** *n* **-ness;** *idm* **close to home** near to the (unpalatable) truth; *idm* **(sail) close to the wind** operate in a risky, almost illegal way; *a* **close-fisted** mean; *n* **close-up** film shot taken near subject.

close *v* **1** shut; conclude **2** come together; *n* end.

close call *n* narrow escape.

close-cropped *a* (of hair) very short.

closed-circuit television *n* system transmitting within an institution to a limited audience.

closed shop *n* place where employees must join a specified trade union.

close-fisted *a* stingy.

close-hauled *a naut* with sails set for sailing close to the wind.

close-knit, closely knit *a* (of people) united by shared beliefs, interests, etc.

close shave *n* narrow escape.

closet *n* small, private room; cupboard; *a* **closeted** private.

closure *n* closing.

clot *n* coagulated, partially solidified mass, *esp* of blood; *v* **clotting, clotted.** coagulate;

cause to clot.

cloth *n* woven fabric; *pl* **clothes** garments; bedcoverings; **n clothing; clothe** to dress; *pt, pp* **clothed, clad;** *n* **clothier**.

clotheshorse *n* frame on which clothes are hung to dry; *coll* person with love for fashion in clothes.

cloud *n* mass of condensed water vapor in sky; mass of smoke; dust in air; *v* make dark; dim; become cloudy; *as* **cloudy, cloudless, clouded;** *idm* **under a cloud** under suspicion.

cloudburst *n* sudden, heavy downpour of rain.

clout *n* piece of rough cloth; blow, *esp* on head.

clove *n* dried flower bud, used for flavoring.

clove hitch *n* double loop securing rope to a pole.

cloven *pp of* **cleave**.

clover *n* plant, trefoil grown as fodder; *idm coll* **in clover** living in luxury.

cloverleaf *n* highway intersection with links in four directions *pl* **cloverleaves**.

clown *n* jester; buffoon in circus or pantomine; *v* play the fool; *n* **clowning**.

cloy *n* satiate, glut with sweetness or pleasure.

club *n* **1** thick wooden stick **2** stick for golf **3** group of people associated for benefit or pleasure **4** black trefoil on playing card; *v* **clubbing,**

clubbed. beat with club.

club foot n congenitally deformed foot.

cluck n noise made by hen; v make such noise.

clue n guide to solution of mystery, crime; as **clueless** utterly helpless, stupid; **clued in** coll wellinformed.

clump n compact mass; group of trees, plants; clout; v mass together; strike.

clumsy a ungainly; unwieldy; adv **clumsily**; n **clumsiness**.

clung pt, pp of cling.

cluster n bunch; group; v come together; grow in clusters.

clutch v grasp suddenly; n **1** set of eggs hatched at one time **2** device permitting gradual engagement of mechanism; idm **in someone's clutches** under someone's control.

clutter n things left untidily; v make untidy.

cm abbr centimeter.

CNN abbr Cable News Network.

co abbr company.

CO abbr commanding officer.

c/o abbr **1** care of **2** carried over.

coach n railroad car; horse-drawn carriage; instructor; tutor; v tutor; n **coachman**.

coagulate v clot; form moss; curdle; n **coagulation**.

coal n combustible carbonized vegetable matter, used as fuel; v take in, supply with coal; n **coalfield**.

coalesce v unite; intermingle; ns **coalescence, coalition**

alliance, esp political.

coal face n part of coal mine where coal is cut.

coarse a rough; common; crude; gross; adv **-ly**; n **-ness**.

coast n edge of land at seashore; v **1** sail along coast **2** slide down **3** free wheel; idm **the coast is clear** coll one is safe from observation.

coaster n **1** small mat or tray for glasses, bottles, etc. **2** ship that sails along the coast.

coast guard n official employed to enforce maritime law, prevent smuggling, and save lives at sea.

coat n **1** outer garment with sleeves **2** natural covering of animals **3** layer of paint, etc., applied to surface; v cover with coat; n **coat of arms** heraldic device.

coat hanger n shaped piece of wood, wire, or plastic with hook for hanging coats.

coax v persuade by flattery; wheedle; cajole.

coaxial a having a common axis; n **coaxial cable** wire for simultaneous long-distance transmittal and reception for radio or television signals.

cob n **1** thickset, stocky horse **2** male swan **3** building material **4** head of corn.

cobalt n metallic element; a dark blue color.

cobble n round stone; v pave with cobbles; mend roughly; repair shoes; n **cobbler** shoe mender.

COBOL (common business-oriented language) n computer language.

cobra n venomous hooded snake.

cobweb n spider's web, single thread of this.

Coca-Cola [TM] n sweet carbonated drink.

cocaine n drug used as local anesthetic or taken as stimulant.

coccyx n anat small bone at base of spine; pl **coccyxes** or **coccyges**.

cochineal n red dye made from dried insects.

cock[1] n **1** male bird **2** leader **3** stop valve to regulate flow of liquids **4** hammer of gun; v set cock of gun; set, turn up jauntily; n **cockerel** young cock.

cock[2] n pile of hay; v put hay into cocks.

cockade n hat badge, rosette of ribbon.

cock-and-bull story n absurd story, esp one used as an excuse for something.

cockatoo n crested parrot.

cockchafter n large, nocturnal winged beetle.

cocker n small spaniel.

cockeyed a coll **1** crooked **2** squinting **3** impractical.

cockle n edible bivalve; weed; small boat.

Cockney n native of London; London dialect.

cockpit n small space in aircraft for pilot.

cockroach n insect,

a
b
c
d
e
f
g
h
i
j
k
l
m
n
o
p
q
r
s
t
u
v
w
x
y
z

blackbeetle.

cocksure, cocky *a* conceitedly self-confident.

cocktail *n* **1** mixed alcoholic drink **2** mixture of fruits or seafoods **3** *coll* mixture of dangerous substances.

cocoa *n* fine powder made from cacao beans; drink.

coconut *n* tropical palm, with edible nut.

cocoon *n* sheath of silk, silklike thread enclosing chrysalis.

cocopeat *n* fibrous substance obtained from coconuts.

COD *abbr* cash on delivery.

cod *n* large, edible sea fish; *n* **codling** young cod.

coda *n* final passage of a musical movement, following the last formal section.

coddle *v* pamper, cosset.

code *n* **1** cypher used in sending (secret) messages **2** symbols used in computers **3** accepted social customs **4** set of laws; *ns* **codification; coding** translation into code; *v* **codify** put into code or systematic form.

codeine *n* alkaloid narcotic derived from opium.

codex *n* book of ancient texts; *pl* **codices**.

codger *n coll* old man.

codicil *n* addition to will.

codify *v* (of laws, rules) arrange systematically; *n* **codification**.

codpiece *n* bag covering front opening of breeches.

coed *n* female student in mixed college or other school.

coeducation *n* education of boys and girls together; *a* **-ational**.

coefficient *n* joint agent or factor.

coerce *v* constrain; force; *a* **coercive;** *n* **coercion** compulsion.

coeval *a* of same age or date.

coexist *v* exist, live together; *n* **coexistence**.

coffee *n* **1** evergreen shrub; ground roasted coffee beans; drink made from this **2** light brown color.

coffer *n* chest; money-box.

cofferdam *n* enclosure erected in water and pumped dry to allow building or other work to be done safely.

coffin *n* case for dead body.

cog *n* toothlike projection on wheel; *idm coll* **cog in a machine** person playing a small but vital part in a large organization; *n* **cogwheel**.

cogent *a* impelling; urgent; clear, forceful; *n* **cogency**.

cogitate *v* ponder; think deeply; *n* **-ation**.

cognac *n* high-quality French brandy.

cognate *n* related; from common stock; origin.

cognition *n* process of acquiring knowledge; *a* **cognitive**.

cognizance *n* knowledge; fact of being aware; *idm* **take cognizance of** notice; *a*

cognizant.

cognomen *n* appellation; surname.

cognoscenti *n pl It* connoisseurs.

cohabit *n* live together, *esp* as man and wife.

cohere *v* stick together; be consistent; *a* **coherent** intelligible; sticking together; *n* **cohesion** state of union; *a* **cohesive**.

cohort *n* body of troops, army.

coif *n* (formerly) close-fitting cap worn by women.

coiffure *n* arrangement of the hair.

coil *n* **1** series of spiral loops **2** *v* wind in rings, spiral folds.

coin *n* piece of money; *v* mint; invent new word, etc.; *idms* **coin money, coin it (in)** make a lot of money quickly; *ns* **coinage** money of country; **coiner** maker of counterfeit coins.

coincide *v* happen at same time; correspond exactly; *a* **coinciding;** *n* **coincidence**.

coition *n* merging.

coitus *n* sexual intercourse.

coke *n* **1** substance left when gas and tar have been extracted from coal **2** *coll* Coca-Cola **3** *sl* cocaine.

coir *n* fiber from coconut husk, used for making ropes, matting, etc.

cola *n* soft drink containing cola nut extract.

colander *n* strainer used in cooking.

cold *a* **1** without heat

2 unmoved; frigid; n 1 lack of heat 2 acute nasal congestion; *idm* **get cold feet** *coll* lose one's nerve; *idm* **give/get the cold shoulder** rebuff/be rebuffed; *idm* **out in the cold** rejected; isolated. *n* **coldness**; *ns* **c. feet** fear *sl*; **c. shoulder** rebuff; **c. storage** refrigeration.

cold-blooded *a* 1 *bio* with varying blood temperature 2 cruel.

cold comfort *n* little or no consolation.

cold cream *n* skin-cleansing and softening ointment.

coldhearted *a* cruel; indifferent; *adv* **-ly**.

cold storage *n* 1 preservation of food by refrigeration 2 setting aside of a plan or idea until a later date.

cold turkey *n sl* sick feeling of a drug addict when deprived of the drug.

cold war *n* state of continued hostility without military action.

coleslaw *n* salad of shredded cabbage, carrot, etc., with salad dressing.

colic *n* acute pain in abdomen or bowels.

coliseum *n* large stadium.

collaborate *v* work together, *esp* in literature, art; *ns* **-ator, -ation**.

collage *n* picture made by pasting various materials on a flat surface.

collapse *v* fall down or in; fail; *n* 1 break down (of health) 2 falling away; *a* **collapsible** capable of being folded, packed up.

collar *n* band on garment, round neck; *v* capture; *sl* seize hold of; *n* **collarbone** clavicle.

collate *v* 1 compare critically 2 place printed sheets in order; *n* **collation** light repast.

collateral *a* accompanying; from common ancestor; *n* additional security for loan.

colleague *n* associate in work or profession.

collect *v* gather, come together; accumulate; *as* **collected** not distracted; gathered; **collective** viewed as whole; *ns* **collection** group of articles of same nature; **collector**.

collect *n* prayer.

collectible *n* object collected; *a* able to be collected.

collectivism *n* principal of communal control of production, etc.

college *n* institution of higher learning; self-governing body of persons; *a* **collegiate**.

collide *v* crash into; strike forcefully together; *n* **collision**.

collie *n* type of sheepdog.

collier *n* coal miner; coaling ship; *n* **colliery** coal mine.

collocate *v ling* (of words) occur regularly together; *n* **-ation**.

colloquial *a* used in common speech; *n* **colloquy**

conference.

collusion *n* conspiracy (to deceive), *esp* in legal matters; *a* **collusive**.

collywobbles *n coll* 1 stomach pain 2 nervousness.

cologne *n* perfume made of plant oils and alcohol.

colon *n* part of large intestine; punctuation mark (:).

colonel *n* commander of regiment.

colonialism *n* policy of extending national authority over foreign territories; *n* colonialist.

colonic *a* relating to the colon; *n* **colonic irrigation** irrigation of colon for cleansing purposes.

colonnade *n* row of columns.

colony *n* body of people in new country, who remain subject to fatherland; area so settled; group of aliens in city, town, etc.; *ns* **colonist, colonial**; *v* **colonize**; *n* **colonization**.

colophon *n* publisher's device, imprint.

color *n* 1 hue; tint 2 paint; pigment 3 *fig* pretext 4 semblance; *pl* 1 badge, ribbons symbolic of party, school, etc. 2 flag of ship, regiment; *v* 1 paint 2 exaggerate 3 influence 4 blush.

color line *n* legal discrimination between people of different color.

color-blind *a* unable to distinguish certain colors.

A
B
C
D
E
F
G
H
I
J
K
L
M
N
O
P
Q
R
S
T
U
V
W
X
Y
Z

color supplement n free color magazine supplied with (esp Sunday) newspaper.

colossus n huge statue; strikingly large person or thing; a **colossal**.

colt n young male horse.

columbine n flower of buttercup family.

column n vertical pillar or support; vertical division of page; military formation; a **columnar;** n **columnist** journalist.

coma n deep unconsciousness; a **comatose**.

comb n toothed instrument for dressing hair, cleaning wool; cock's crest; v apply comb to.

combat v oppose; fight; n **combatant**.

combine v join together; mix; ns **combination** union; **combine** syndicate.

combine harvester n machine that reaps and threshes grain.

combo n mus small group, esp jazz players.

combustion n process of burning; a **combustible**.

come v **coming, came, come**. move toward; arrive; occur; happen; be derived from; idm **how come?** how did it happen? idm **come what may** whatever happens; phr vs **come about** happen; **come across 1** (of ideas) be received **2** find by chance; **come along 1** appear **2** accompany someone **3** make progress; **come apart** separate; disintegrate; **come**

at attack; **come by 1** pass near **2** acquire; **come down** fall; idm **come down in the world** suffer decline in standard of living; phr vs **come down on** criticize; punish; **come down to** be no more than; **come down with** become sick with; **come forward** offer help or information; **come in** become fashionable; **come in for** be exposed to; **come into** inherit; **come off 1** become detached **2** succeed **3** idm **come off it!** coll expressing disbelief; phr vs **come on** progress; **come out 1** appear **2** be removed **3** go on strike **4** prove to be **5** be clearly reproduced **6** be a debutante **7** sl declare oneself homosexual; **come out against** declare opposition to; **come out with** say unexpectedly; **come over 1** move across **2** pay a visit **3** communicate; **come around/to** regain consciousness; **come around to 1** be converted to **2** eventually find time to; **come up with** devise; produce.

comeback n **1** recovery **2** retort; complaint **3** redress.

comedy n **1** humor **2** light-hearted amusing play; **comedian** comic actor; fem **comedienne**.

comely a attractive;

handsome; n **comeliness**.

comer n all comers anyone who wants to accept a challenge

comet n luminous heavenly body, with gaseous tail.

comeuppance n deserved punishment.

comfit n ar candy containing fruit or nut.

comfort v reassure; console; n well-being; bodily ease; consolation; a **comfortable**.

comfortably off a having adequate money for comfort.

comfy a coll comfortable and cozy.

comic a laughable; funny; n comedian; funny papers or book; a **comical**.

comic strip n sequence of drawings telling a funny incident or story, often in periodicals.

comity n courtesy, urbanity of manners.

comma a punctuation mark (,), separating words, phrases, etc.

command v order; be in authority; n peremptory order; power to control, govern, dominate; ns **commandant, commander, commandment;** v **commandeer;** v appropriate.

command module n control area in a spacecraft.

commando n unit of shock troops; member of such unit.

command performance n special performance for head of state.

commemorate v celebrate

solemnly; *n* -ation; *a* -ative.

commence *v* begin; start; *n* -ment.

commend *v* entrust; praises; *a* **commendable;** *n* **commendation.**

commensurate *a* proportionate; in accordance.

comment *n* remark; annotation; *v* explain; express view; *ns* **commentary** series of critical remarks; **commentator** radio or TV reporter.

commerce *n* dealings; business trading; *a* **commercial;** *v* **commercialize** make business of; *n* -ization.

commie *n, a coll* communist.

commiserate *v* express sympathy; condole; *n* -ation.

commissar *n* head of a Soviet government department.

commissariat *n* department for supplies of food and transport.

commission *n* 1 warrant giving authority, *esp* to officer in armed forces 2 body appointed to hold inquiry 3 authority to act as agent, agent's percentage; *v* authorize; give order for; *idm* **out of commission** 1 not in service 2 out of order; *ns* **commissioner** member of commission; one empowered to act by warrant.

commit *v* -mitting, -mitted. 1 entrust 2 send for trial 3 perpetrate (crime); *ns* **committal, commitment;** *idm*

commit oneself 1 make or decision or promise 2 give a firm opinion.

committee *n* group appointed to consider particular activity.

commode *n* 1 chest of drawers 2 seat to accommodate chamber pot.

commodity *n* article of commerce; useful object.

commodore *n* naval officer; courtesty title (*e.g.,* president of yacht club, etc.).

common *n* tract of public land; *a* 1 shared by two or more 2 usual; ordinary 3 vulgar; *pls* common people of realm; *adv* -ly; *n* **commoner** person not of nobility; *a* **commonplace** ordinary; trite; *n* **commonwealth** democratic state.

common law *n* unwritten law; *a* **common-law.**

common market *n* the EEC (European Economic Community).

common room *n* room that members of a specialized group can use.

commonwealth *n* political unit such as state, nation, etc.

commotion *n* agitation; tumult; upset.

commune[1] *n* 1 smallest unit of local government (*e.g.,* in France) 2 community sharing possessions, living, and working together.

commune[2] *v* share thoughts and feelings; *a* **communal** for

common use; *n* **Holy Communion** sacrament of Eucharist.

communicate *v* 1 impart; transmit; exchange information 2 receive Holy Communion; *a* **communicable;** *n* -ation; *a* **communicative** talkative.

communiqué *n* Fr official communication.

communism *n* extreme form of socialism; *a, n* **communist.**

community *n* body of people sharing locality, religion, etc.; fellowship; **community service** *n* punishment for criminals that involves doing work within the community.

commutator *n* device for altering direction of electric current; *v* **commutate** alter in this way.

commute *v* exchange; travel daily *usu* to place of employment ; *n* **commuter** daily traveler to work.

compact[1] *n* agreement; contract.

compact[2] *a* neatly packed into small space; *n* small case holding face powder.

compact disk *n* recording disc from which sounds are reproduced by laser.

companion *n* comrade, associate; one of matching pair; *a* **companionable;** *n* **companionship.**

companionway *n* staircase on a ship.

company *n* gathering of guests; companionship; group of business associates; group of actors; unit of regiment; ship's crew.

company secretary senior official of business firm who handles legal matters.

compare *v* observe similarity of one thing with another; be like; *as* **comparable**; *adv* **-ably**; **comparative** (*adv* **-ly**) relative; *n* **comparison**.

compartment *n* part divided off by partition, *esp* in railroad car.

compartmentalize *v* separate into distinct categories; *n* **-ization**.

compass *n* boundary; extent; range; instrument showing north and directions from it; *pl* instrument drawing circles.

compassion *n* sympathy; pity; *a* **compassionate**; *adv* **-ly**.

compatible *a* able to coexist; agreeing; *n* **compatibility**.

compatriot *n* countryman.

compel *v* enforce; bring about by force; *a* **compelling** **1** very interesting **2** urgent; *n* **compulsion**.

compendium *n* **1** full information in concise form; *a* **compendious**; **2** box of games.

compensate *v* make amends; reward; make up for; *a* **compensatory**; *n* **compensation**.

compete *v* contend with; vie with; *a* **competitive**; *ns* **competition, competitor**.

competence, competency *n* **1** ability; efficiency

2 sufficiency, *esp* of money; *a* **competent**.

compile *v* collect together from various sources, as a book; *ns* **compiler, compilation**.

complacent *a* self-satisfied; *adv* **-ly**; *ns* **complacence, complancency**.

complain *v* grumble; find fault with; bring charge; *ns* **complaint** expression of discontent; ailment; **complainant** *leg* plaintiff.

complement *n* that which completes; full allowance; *a* **complementary**.

complete *a* entire; finished; *v* make whole; *adv* **-ly**; *ns* **-ness**; *n* **completion**.

complex *a* complicated; involved; *n* psychological obsession; *n* **complexity**.

complexion *n* color, texture of face; disposition.

compliance *n* obedience; *a* **compliant**.

complicate *v* to make difficult, involved; *n* **-ation**.

complicity *n* partnership in crime, etc.

compliment *n* expression of esteem, praise, regard; *v* pay compliment to; *a* **-ary**.

compline *n* last service of the day (Catholic church).

comply *v* **-plying, -plied.** agree; consent; yield.

component *n* constituent part; *a* forming part.

comport *v* **comport oneself** behave oneself; *n* **-ment**.

compose *v* **1** create musical

form, literary work **2** set up type **3** settle; make up; *a* **composed** calm; *ns* **composer** one who composes, *esp* music; **composition; compositor** typesetter; **composure** calmness.

composite *n, a* (thing) made of several elements.

compost *n* mixture of manure, soil, rotten vegetable matter.

compote *n* *Fr* fruit in syrup.

compound *v* mix together; compromise; condone (an offense); *a* not simple; composite; *n* **1** mixture; compound substance **2** enclosure.

compound interest *n* interest on both capital and accumulated interest.

comprehend *v* take in; comprise; understand; *n* **comprehension;** *a* **comprehensive** taking in wide range of objects; *a* **comprehensible**.

compress *v* press together; concentrate; make smaller; *n* wet pad put on inflamed part; *n* **compression**.

comprise *v* include; contain; *pr p* **comprising**.

compromise *v* make concession; incur risk, suspicion; *n* middle course.

compulsion *n* **1** strong urge to do something **2** something that forces action; *a* **compulsive;** *adv* **-ly**.

compulsory *a* required by law or rules; *adv* **compulsorily**.

compunction *n* regret for

wrong done; remorse.

compute v calculate, reckon; n **computation**.

computer n electronic machine for storing, classifying, and reproducing information and relaying instructions; v **computerize;** n **-ization**.

comrade n friend; companion; associate; n **-ship**.

con v **conning, conned.** 1 examine carefully; 2 consideration of opposing evidence; 3 sl swindle.

concave n hollow; curved inwardly; n **concavity**.

conceal v keep secret; hide; n **-ment**.

concede v surrender; admit truth of; allow; n **concession** that which is conceded.

conceit n vanity; a **conceited** holding exaggerated opinion of one's own importance.

conceive v 1 think of; imagine 2 become pregnant; a **conceivable**.

concentrate v direct to single center; increase strength; fix efforts on one point, object; n **concentration**.

concentration camp n prison for political prisoners.

concentric a having common center.

concept n idea; mental picture; a **conceptual;** v **-ualize**.

conception n 1 beginning of pregnancy 2 plan; planning 3 understanding.

concern v relate to; be worried; affect; n business;

affair; a **concerned** interested; anxious; idm **concerned with** connected with; prep **concerning** regarding; about.

concert n 1 harmony; agreement 2 mus entertainment; idm **at concert pitch** in a state of readiness; a **concerted** planned in common; ns **concerto** musical composition for solo instrument with orchestra; **concertina** musical instrument.

concert grand n large piano for concerts.

concertmaster n leader of orchestra.

concession n 1 yielding after argument 2 reduced price; a **concessionary** 3 special permission n **concessionaire** person granted such permission.

conch n large spiral shell.

concierge n resident caretaker.

conciliate v pacify; win over; ns **conciliation, conciliator;** a **conciliatory**.

concise a brief; terse; adv **-ly;** n **-ness**.

conclave n secret, private assembly, esp for election of pope.

conclude v 1 end; finish 2 arrange 3 infer; n **conclusion;** a **conclusive** decisive.

concoct v invent; make up (story, new dish, etc.); n **concoction**.

concomitant a accompanying; simultaneous; adv **-ly;** n **concomitance**.

concord n agreement; harmony; a **-ant;** n **concordance** index (words).

concordat n agreement between the pope and a government.

concourse n crowd; broad open space, esp in airport buildings.

concrescence n growth by accumulation of particles.

concrete n mixture of sand and cement; a 1 of concrete 2 actual; v cover with concrete; adv **concretely**.

concubine n woman living with man, outside lawful wedlock.

concupiscence n sexual desire; lust; a **-scent**.

concur v **-curring, -curred.** agree; coincide; a **concurrent;** n **-rence**.

concuss v shake violently; injure brain by blow on head; n **concussion**.

condemn v 1 censure 2 declare unfit for use 3 find guilty; n **-ation**.

condense v 1 abridge 2 concentrate 3 reduce gas, etc., to liquid; ns **condensation, condenser** device for storing electricity.

condescend v deign; patronize; be affable; a **-ing;** n **condescension**.

condiment n spicy, pungent seasoning for food.

condition n 1 state of being

A
B
C
D
E
F
G
H
I
J
K
L
M
N
O
P
Q
R
S
T
U
V
W
X
Y
Z

2 rank 3 stipulation; *n* determine state or condition; train; make healthy; *a* **conditional** subject to conditions.

condole *v* offer sympathy; grieve with; *n* **condolence**.

condom *n* contraceptive sheath.

condominium *n* block of apartments, each owned by occupier; *coll* **condo**.

condone *v* overlook; find excuses for; *n* **condonation**.

condor *n* large S American vulture.

conduce *v* help; tend to produce; *a* **conducive**.

conduct *v* 1 lead 2 manage 3 transmit (heat, electricity); *idm* **conduct oneself** behave; *n* behavior; *ns* **conductor** 1 guide 2 fare collector on train, etc. 3 director of orchestra 4 substance capable of transmitting (electricity, etc.); **conductivity**.

conduit *n* channel or pipe for conveying fluids or protecting electric cables.

cone *n* 1 solid body with circular base and tapering to apex 2 fruit of conifers 3 storm warning; *a* **conic, conical**.

coney, cony, *n* rabbit; fur made of rabbit skins.

confection *n* candy, preserve; *ns* **confectioner** dealer in candies, cakes, etc.; **confectionery** candies; place where they are made or sold.

confederate *n* accomplice; *v* ally with; *ns* **-ation, confederacy**.

confer *v* **-ferring, -ferred.** grant; discuss; *ns* **-ment** act of bestowing; **conference** meeting to discuss.

confess *v* admit; declare sins orally; *ns* **confession; confessional** priest's box; **confessor** priest hearing confession.

confetti *n* small pieces of colored paper thrown at weddings, etc.

confidant *n* *Fr* person in whom one confides one's private affairs and thoughts; *fem* **confidante**.

confide *v* trust in; tell, as secret; *as* **confident, confidential, confiding** trusting.

confidence *n* 1 trust 2 self-assurance 3 secret; *idm* **in confidence** as a secret; *a* **confidential;** *adv* **-ly**.

confidence trick *n* swindle in which the swindler first gains the victim's confidence; *coll* **con trick.**

configuration *n* 1 figure, form 2 relative aspect of planets.

confine *v* imprison; limit; keep in (bed, house); *n* **-ment** 1 imprisonment 2 childbirth; *a* **confined** undergoing; *n pl* **confines** boundaries.

confirm *v* make firm; ratify; administer confirmation; *n* **confirmation** rite to confirm vows made at baptism; corroboration; *a* **confirmed**

habitual.

confiscate *v* seize; appropriate, *esp* by authority; *n* **-ation**.

conflagration *n* a great fire.

conflict *n* fight; variance; clash (of option); *v* contend; be incompatible.

confluence *n* 1 uniting of streams, etc. 2 crowd; *a* **confluent**.

conform *v* comply; submit; be in agreement; *ns* **-ation,** adaptation; formation; **conformity**.

confound *v* confuse; perplex; dismay.

confounded *a* 1 bewildered 2 damned.

confront *v* bring face to face; meet boldly, in opposition; *n* **-ation**.

Confucian *n*, *a* (follower) of Confucius.

confuse *v* mix up; bewilder; *n* **confusion**.

confute *v* disprove; convict of error; *n* **confutation**.

conga *n* Latin American dance performed in a long line.

congeal *v* freeze, solidify.

congenial *a* having same nature, tastes, etc.; suited to.

congenital *a* born with, *esp* defects, diseases, etc.

conger *n* large salt-water eel.

congest *v* overcrowd; impede flow of; fill to excess; *a* **congested** overcharged (with blood); *n* **congestion**.

conglomerate *v* gather, collect into mass; *n* **-ation** jumble of things.

congratulate *v* wish joy;

express pleasure at; *n* **-ation;**
a **-atory.**

congregate *v* assemble;
n **-ation** gathering of persons,
esp for worship;
a **-ational.**

congress *n* formal assembly;
legislative body; *a*
congressional;
congressman or **-woman**
member of Congress.

congruent *a* 1 of identical
shape 2 congruous; *n* **-ence.**

conical, conic *a* cone-shaped.

conifer *n* cone-bearing tree,
shrub, pine, fir; *a* **coniferous.**

conjecture *v* guess; surmise; *n*
guesswork; *a* **conjectural.**

conjoin *v* unite; combine; *a*
conjoint.

conjugal *a* pertaining to
marriage; between husband
and wife.

conjugate *v* break down verb
into various moods, tenses,
etc.; *n* **-ation.**

conjunction *n* 1 part of
speech, as *and, but;*
2 simultaneous occurrence; *a*
conjunctive done jointly.

conjunctivitis *n* inflammation
of the conjunctiva, the
membrane covering the front
of the eye and the inside of
the eyelid.

conjure *v* 1 ask earnestly
2 perform tricks by sleight-
of-hand; cast spells; *ns*
conjuration solemn spell;
conjurer, -or, conjuring.

conker *n coll* fruit of horse
chestnut; *pl* children's game
with this on string.

conk out *phr v coll* 1 (of
machine) break down 2 (of
person) collapse exhausted
or die.

connate *a* united by birth;
congenital.

connect *v* unite (with); join
together; associate
(mentally); *as* **connective,
connected.**

connection *n* 1 linking;
relationship 2 transfer from
one type of transportation to
another 3 person of
influence to whom one is
related by family, business or
social life; *idm* **in connection
with** regarding.

conning-tower *n* armored
control station on warship,
submarine, etc.

connive *v* acquiesce in wrongdoing of another; *n*
connivance tacit agreement.

connoisseur *n Fr* expert in
artistic matters.

connote *v* imply in addition to
primary meaning; *n*
connotation.

conquer *v* overpower;
subjugate; prevail; *ns*
conqueror, conquest.

consanguinity *n* relationship
by blood; kinship.

conscience *n* sense of right and
wrong; *a* **conscientious**
thorough; *n* **-ness.**

conscience clause *n* clause
allowing conscientious
objector to be exempt on
moral grounds.

conscience money *n* sum paid
to relieve sense of guilt.

conscious *a* in possession of
one's senses; awake; *n* **-ness**
awareness.

conscript *v* enroll by
compulsion for military
service; *n* one so enrolled; *n*
conscription.

consecrate *v* render holy; set
apart as sacred; *n* **-ation**

consecutive *a* following in
regular order; expressing
consequence.

consensus *n* general
agreement.

consent *v* agree to; permit; *n*
acquiescence; permission; *a*
consentient.

consequence *n* outcome;
logical result; importance; *as*
consequent, consequential
pompous; *adv* **consequently**
therefore.

conservatory *n* 1 school of
music, drama 2 greenhouse
joined to main house.

conserve *v* protect; preserve,
esp from change, waste, etc.;
ns **conservancy** board
responsible for preservation
of nature, rivers, trees, etc.;
conservation; conservative
moderate political party; *a*
conservative opposed to
change.

consider *n* 1 think about
2 regard as 3 take into
account; *a* **considering** in
view of; *n* **consideration**
1 thought; reflection
2 concern 3 fact worth
remembering 4 payment; *idm*
take into consideration keep
in mind when judging; *a*

a
b
c
d
e
f
g
h
i
j
k
l
m
n
o
p
q
r
s
t
u
v
w
x
y
z

A B **C** D E F G H I J K L M N O P Q R S T U V W X Y Z

considerate thoughtful for others; careful.

consign v commit; entrust; send goods; ns **consignor, consignee, consignment** goods consigned

consist in phr v be a matter of (doing certain things).

consist of phr v be composed of.

consistent a agreeing with; n **consistence, consistency** degree of density; relevance.

console v comfort; make up for; as **consolable, consolatory**; n **consolation**.

console n **1** ornamental bracket supporting shelf, etc.; **2** large cabinet for radio, TV, etc. **3** control panel, usu for electrical machinery **4** unit for organ keyboard **5** small storage unit in car.

consolidate v make, become solid, firm; combine; n **-ation.**

consommé n Fr clear meat soup.

consonant n letter other than vowel; a agreeing; consistent; n **consonance** harmony, esp of sounds.

consort n **1** husband, wife, esp of monarch **2** ship accompanying another; phr v **consort with** associate with.

consortium n temporary association of (commercial, education, etc.) institutions for a common purpose; pl **-s** or **consortia**.

conspectus n survey.

conspicuous a outstanding; remarkable; plainly visible; n **-ness**.

conspire v plot; join another in secret, usu for unlawful purpose; ns **conspiracy, conspirator**; a **conspiratorial**.

constable n high-ranking officer; warden of fortress; n **constabulary** police force.

constant a **1** continuous; unvarying **2** steadfast; faithful; n math unvarying term, factor; n **constancy** steadfastness.

constellation n group of fixed stars.

consternation n surprise and alarm; dismay.

constipation n inactivity of bowels; v **constipate** make bowels sluggish.

constituent a component; entitled to elect; n essential part; voter in constituency; n **constituency** place represented in legislature; body of voters.

constitute v make into; set up; give form to; n **constitution** structure; natural state of body, mind, etc.; principles of government; a **constitutional** pertaining to constitution; n walk taken for the health; adv **-ly**.

constrain v bring force to bear on person; n **constraint** compulsion; embarrassment.

constrict v contract; compress; cramp; ns **constrictor, constriction**; a **constrictive**.

construct v build; form; put together; ns **constructor, construction;** a **constructive**.

construe v **1** translate **2** analyze grammatically **3** deduce.

consubstantiation n doctrine that after consecration blood and wine become the body and blood of Christ.

consul n official appointed by state, living in foreign country, and protecting nationals and business interests there; a **consular;** ns **consulate, consulship**.

consult v seek advice from; confer with; ns **consultant, consultation;** a **consultative** advisory.

consume v **1** destroy by fire; waste, etc. **2** use up; devour; drink up; ns **consumer** buyer, user of commodity.

consumer credit n credit extended with interest to someone usu for purchase of manufactured goods.

consumer goods n pl goods produced for the general public to buy and use.

consumerism n movement to defend consumer interests.

consummate v complete; finish; a complete, of greatest perfection; n **consummation** completion, esp physical, of marriage.

consumption n **1** using of food or resources **2** amount used **3** tuberculosis (TB); a **consumptive** suffering from TB.

cont *abbr* continued.

contact *n* being in touch; close proximity; *v* get in touch with; *n* **c. lens** lens resting directly on eyeball.

contagion *n* spreading of disease by contact; disease, physical or moral, spread so; *a* **contagious**.

contain *v* hold; compromise; enclose; restrain (oneself); *n* **container** box, jar, etc., holding something.

contaminate *v* pollute; defile; make impure; *n* **-ation** pollution.

contemplate *v* gaze on; consider; intend; meditate; *n* **-ation**; *a* **-ative**.

contemporary *a* living; existing, made at same time; *n* one having same age, or living during same age as another; *a* **contemporaneous**.

contempt *n* act of despising, scorn; **c. of court** disregard for, disobedience to court of law; *as* **-ible** (*adv* **-ibly**), contemptuous (*adv* **-ly**).

contend *v* struggle; fight; assert; *n* **contention** controversy; disputed point; *a* **contentious** quarrelsome.

content *a* satisfied; *n* holding capacity; real meaning; *pl* that which is inside; list of topics in book; *v* satisfy; *n* **-ment** satisfaction; *a* **contented** satisfied, pleased.

contest *v* dispute; fight for; *n* **1** strife **2** competition; *n* **contestant**.

context *n* parts of book, speech, etc., that come immediately before and after passage, words, etc., and that fix meaning.

contiguous *a* touching; adjoining; *n* **contiguity**.

continence *n* self-restraint; *a* **continent** able to control one's elimination functions.

continent *n* one of the great unbroken land areas of Earth; *a* **-al** (*n* inhabitant of Europe).

continental breakfast *n* light morning repast, including coffee and rolls.

continental drift *n geol* theory that continents once belonged to a single land mass and then separated.

continental shelf *n* shallow part of seabed close to continental land mass.

contingency *n* possibility, chance occurrence; *a* **contingent** possible, dependent on; *n* quota, *esp* of troops.

continue *v* go on; persist; prolong; resume; remain; *a* **continual;** *ns* **continuance, continuation** resumption; sequel; *a* **continuous** unceasing; *n* **continuity** unbroken succession.

continuo *n* instrumental accompaniment giving bass part in Baroque music.

continuum *n* thing without breaks or sudden changes; *pl* **-s** *or* **continua**.

contort *v* distort; twist out of

shape; *ns* **contortion, contortionist** acrobat.

contour *n* outline; shape of figure, mountain, etc.

contra- *prefix* **1** against **2** opposite to **3** *mus* of lower pitch.

contraband *n* smuggled goods; illicit trading.

contrabass *n mus* double bass.

contract *n* solemn, binding agreement; *v* **1** enter into agreement **2** become smaller **3** incur **4** catch (disease); *as* **contractual, contracted** shortened; drawn together; *ns* **contraction, contractor** one making contract, *esp* builder.

contradict *v* deny; be opposed to; argue; *a* **contradictory;** *n* **contradiction**.

contralto *n* female voice of deep tone; singer with such a voice.

contraption *n* contrivance; eccentric device.

contrapuntal *a mus* of or involving counterpoint.

contrary *n* exact opposite, of object, fact, quality; *a* different; against; perverse; *advs* **contrarily, contrariwise** conversely; **contrariness** perversity.

contrast *v* compare, show difference; *n* striking difference.

contravene *v* infringe; disobey (law); *n* **contravention**.

contretemps *n* unlucky, embarrassing incident; mishap.

a
b
c
d
e
f
g
h
i
j
k
l
m
n
o
p
q
r
s
t
u
v
w
x
y
z

contribute *v* give to common fund; write for the press; have share in producing result; *ns* **contributor, contribution** donation; *a* **contributory**.

contrite *a* penitent; sorrowful for sin; *n* **contrition** remorse.

contrive *v* 1 invent; devise; scheme 2 manage; *n* **contrivance** device; artful scheme.

control *v* -**trolling, -trolled.** 1 restrain; regulate 2 test 3 command; *n* 1 restraint 2 domination 3 standard for testing; *pl* instruments guiding machine; *a* **controllable;** *n* **controller** person regulating expenditure.

controversy *n* dispute; argument; debate; *a* **controversial** liable to provoke controversy.

contumacy *n* stubborn, perverse resistance; *a* **contumacious**.

contumely *n* 1 contemptuous insolence of speech or manner 2 disgrace.

contusion *n* bruise without breaking skin.

conundrum *n* riddle; difficult problem.

conurbation *n* large urban area formed by expansion of smaller towns close together.

convalesce *v* regain health gradually; *n* **convalescence** state of recovering health; *n, a* **convalescent** (person) recovering from illness; *a* convalescing.

convection *n* transference of heat by liquids or gases; *n* **convector** circulator of warm air.

convene *v* summon; convoke; *ns* **convener** official, who convenes meeting; **convention** 1 formal assembly 2 custom, usage; *a* dictated by convention.

convenient *a* suitable; handy; *n* **convenience** personal comfort; ease.

convenience food *n* food sold ready to eat with minimal preparation, but storable for a time if required.

convenience store *n* small variety store that stays open late.

convent *n* community of monks or nuns; building occupied by community.

converge *v* meet at given point; *a* **convergent;** *n* **convergence, convergency**.

converse *v* talk with someone; *n* **conversation;** *as* -**al** ready to talk; **conversant** familiar with, informed concerning.

converse *a* contrary; opposite; reversed; *n* the opposite.

convert *v* change, transmute a thing; cause to alter religious, moral beliefs; *ns* **convert** one who is converted; **conversion** 1 change of state 2 misappropriation of property; *a* **convertible** capable of being converted; *n* car with top that folds

down; *n* **convertible sofa** coach that folds out into bed.

convex *a* curving outward; reverse of concave; *n* **convexity**.

convey *v* 1 carry 2 impart 3 transmit; *leg* make over by deed; *ns* **conveyance** deed by which title to property is transferred; **conveyancer** lawyer dealing with conveyance of property; **conveyancing** business of such person.

conveyor belt *n* continuous belt for transferring items from one area of factory, airport, etc., to another.

convict *v* prove, find guilty of crime; *ns* **convict** criminal serving sentence of imprisonment; **conviction** act of convicting; assured belief.

convince *v* persuade, arouse belief in, by argument or proof; *a* **convincing** compelling belief.

convivial *a* festive; sociable; *n* **conviviality**.

convoke *n* call together; summon to assemble; *n* **convocation** assembly, *esp* of clergy, university graduates.

convolution *n* spiral fold, coil, whorl; *a* **convoluted**.

convoy *v* escort and protect; *n* **convoy** group of ships, vehicles, etc., being convoyed; protecting force.

convulse *v* agitate violently; cause sudden violent muscular spasms; *a*

convulsive; *n pl* **convulsions** hysterical fits of emotion; spasms.

coo *v* utter soft murmuring sound (of doves); speak softly and caressingly; *n* such sound.

cook *n* one who prepares food for eating; *v* prepare food for tables; *esp* by heat; *idm* **cook the books** falsify the accounts; *idm* **cook somebody's goose** spoil somebody's plans; **cookery** art of cooking; **cookhouse** camp kitchen; **cookware** pots, pans, etc., used in cooking.

cookie *n* 1 small, sweet, baked good 2 *coll* pretty woman.

cool *a* pleasantly cold; *fig* calm; casual; not ardent; *v* make, become cool; *idm* **keep one's cool** remain calm; *ns* **coolness** 1 state of being cool 2 absence of cordiality; **cooler** 1 vessel in which anything is made or kept cool 2 *sl* prison; *adv* **coolly**.

coolant *n* liquid for keeping engine cool.

coomb, combe *n* deep, narrow valley.

coon cat *n* long-haired maine cat.

coop *n* wooden cage or pen for hens; *v* shut up in coop; confine.

cooper *n* one who makes barrels and casks; *n* **cooperage** work, workshop of cooper.

cooperate *v* act together for common aim; *ns* **cooperation** working together; **cooperative** profit sharing concern (*a* working together; helpful).

coopt *v* choose as extra member; *n* **cooption**.

coordinate *a* having equal rank, order, etc.; *v* adjust, cause to harmonize; *n* **coordination**.

coot *n* small black water bird of rail family.

cop *v sl* **copping, copped.** catch; *sl* **cop it** be acquire or steal something, etc.; *phr v* **cop out (of)** *coll* avoid taking responsibility; *n sl* 1 policeman 2 arrest.

cope *n* ceremonial clerical vestment; covering; *n* **coping** protective covering course of wall.

cope *v* handle successfully, contend with efficiently.

copier *n* machine that makes copies.

copious *a* plentiful, abundant, profuse, full; *adv* **copiously**.

cop-out *n coll* evasion through fear.

copper *n* reddish, ductile, malleable metal; washing vessel for clothes; *sl* policeman; *v* cover with copper; *ns* **copper plate** one used for etching, print from this; copybook style of writing.

coppice, copse *n* thicket, wood of small trees.

copra *n* dried, coconut kernels.

copula *n ling* link verb between subject and complement.

copulate *v* join, unite sexually; *n* **-ation;** *a* **copulative**.

copy *n* 1 imitation; reproduction 2 single specimen of book, etc. 3 written material for press 4 example to be copied; *v* **copying, copied.** imitate; follow pattern; **copyright** legal exclusive right to reproduce book, music, work of art, etc.; **copywriter** one who writes text of advertisements.

copybook *n* book for copying model handwriting.

copycat *n coll* person who copies other people's ideas.

coquette *n Fr* female flirt; *a* **coquettish** engagingly enticing; *n* **coquetry**.

coracle *n* light boat made of wicker covered with hide, etc, used in Britain.

coral *n* hard red or white substance made by marine polyps and forms reefs, etc.; *a* made of coral; *a* **coralline** coral (red) in color.

coral snake *n* tropical poisonous snake.

corbel *n* stone or wood support projecting from wall.

cord *n* 1 thick string or thin rope 2 ribbed cloth 3 quantity of stacked cut wood; *v* bind with cord; *n* **cordage** cords or ropes, *esp* rigging of ship.

cordial *a* hearty, friendly, sincere; *n* stimulating, warming drink; *n* **cordiality**.

A
B
C
D
E
F
G
H
I
J
K
L
M
N
O
P
Q
R
S
T
U
V
W
X
Y
Z

cordon n 1 line of troops or police 2 fruit tree pruned to single stem.

cordon bleu a, n Fr (cooking) of highest standard.

cordovan n soft, smooth leathes.

cords n pl coll corduroy trousers.

corduroy n ribbed cotton material, with pile like velvet.

core n 1 innermost, central part 2 seed case of some fruits; idm **to the core** completely; thoroughly; v take out core; n **corer** implement for removing cores.

coreopsis n herb plant with striking flowers.

corespondent n person charged with adultery with petitioner's husband/wife in divorce case.

corgi n breed of small Welsh dog.

coriander n plant with aromatic seeds used as flavoring.

Corinthian a of Corinth; a ornate type of Greek column.

cork n bark of cork oak; piece used as stopper for bottle, etc.; v stop up with a cork; a **corked** (of wine) tasting of decayed cork; ns **corkscrew** tool for extracting corks; **corkage** charge made by innkeepers for serving wine not bought in the house.

corm n solid, fleshy,

underground stem.

cormorant n large seabird.

corn[1] n 1 grain; seed of cereals 2 music or writing that is banal and sentimental; ns **cornbread** cakelike bread made with ground corn; **cornflower** blue-flowered wild plant of cornfields; **cornmeal** finely ground corn; **cornstarch** finely ground flour from corn; **corn syrup** sweet syrup derived from corn.

corn[2] n hardened, thickened skin causing pain, usually on toe.

cornea n transparent protective membrane over front of eyeball; a **corneal**.

corncob n woody core of an ear of corn in which the grains are embedded.

corned beef n processed tinned beef.

cornelian n reddish or white semiprecious stone.

corner n meeting place of two converging lines; hidden remote place; angle formed by meeting walls, sides (of box, etc.); v 1 force into difficult position 2 buy up all available stocks of; a **cornered**; n **cornerstone** fig something indispensable; basis.

cornet n trumpet having valves; cone-shaped wafer holding ice cream.

cornflakes n breakfast cereal of crisp flakes from corn.

cornice n carved molding

around top of building or room.

cornish pasty n small pie with vegetables, esp potato, and meat.

cornrow v braid hair flat to the head in rows resembling corn.

cornucopia n symbolic horn of plenty; fig abundance, overflowing supply.

corny a sl (of jokes, stories) unoriginal; banal.

corolla n cuplike form made by petals of flowers.

corollary n additional inference; result.

corona n luminous circle around heavenly body.

coronary a like a crown; anat relating to arteries supplying heart muscle; **c. thrombosis** formation of clot in coronary artery.

coronation n act or ceremony of crowning a sovereign.

coroner n leg officer holding inquiry as to cause of any unnatural death or into ownership of treasure trove.

coronet n small crown.

corporal[1] n NCO (noncommissioned officer) ranking below sergeant.

corporal[2] a of the human body.

corporation n 1 group of persons regarded as a unit; legally formed business company; civic or municipal authority 2 sl large protruding stomach; a **corporate** relating to corporation.

corporeal n bodily; physical; tangible.

corps n largest tactical military unit; any organized group of persons.

corpse n dead body, usually human.

corpulent a stout; obese; fat; n **corpulence**.

corpus n **corpora**. 1 body 2 principal of estate, fund 3 all extant writings on a subject.

corpuscle n minute body or organism, *esp* red and white constituent particles of blood.

corrade v scrape away, crumble.

corral n fenced enclosure for livestock; v gather as with cattle, etc.

correct v put right; punish; adjust; neutralize; ns **-tion, -ness;** a **-ive.**

correlate v bring into mutual relation; n either of two reciprocally related things; n **-ation;** a **-lative.**

correspond v agree with; be equal to; write letters to; ns **correspondent, correspondence** 1 similarity 2 exchange of letters; a **corresponding.**

corridor n 1 passage in building, railroad car, etc. 2 strip of land (or air route) passing through state to which it does not belong.

corrigible a capable of repair.

corroborate v confirm; make more certain; n

corroboration; a **corroborative.**

corrode v eat into; wear away gradually, *esp* by chemical action; a **corrosive;** n **corrosion.**

corrugate v form wrinkles or folds; bend into ridges; a **-ated;** n **-ation.**

corrupt a rotten, putrid; depraved; bribable; (of texts) not genuine; v make corrupt; pervert; a **-ible;** n **-tion.**

corselet n body armor.

corset n close-fitting undergarment worn for support; stays.

cortège n *Fr* ceremonial procession, *esp* funeral cortège.

cortex n bark; outer covering; *pl* **cortices.**

cortisone n drug used in treatment of rheumatoid arthritis.

corundum n hard mineral used in grinding and polishing.

coruscate v sparkle, scintillate; n **-ation.**

corvine a of crows.

cosigner n person who jointly signs a bank loan.

cosine n sine of complement of angle.

cosmetic n preparation for beautifying hair, complexion, skin; a **cosmetic.**

cosmic a relating to universe and laws governing it; ns **cosmogony** theory of universe and its creation; **cosmography** mapping of universe; **cosmology** science

of universe; **cosmos** n the whole universe; **cosmic rays** shortest electromagnetic rays from outer space.

cosmonaut n astronaut, space traveler.

cosmopolitan n citizen of the world; a of all parts of world; free from national prejudice.

cossack n member of S Russian tribe of horsemen.

cosset v pamper, fondle, pet.

cost n 1 price of purchase 2 expenditure of time, energy, labor; *pl* **costs** expenses; *idm* **at all costs** whatever happens; *idm* **at cost** without making any profit; *idm* **to one's cost** to one's disadvantage; v 1 cause expenditure of 2 cause loss of 3 estimate cost of production; *pt, pp* **cost;** a **costly** expensive; valuable; n **costliness.**

costal a pertaining to ribs or side of body.

costar n famous actor/actress in the same film as another such actor/actress; v appear in this way.

cost-benefit a relating to analysis of cost vs. benefits of operation or business.

cost-effective a profitable enough to justify the investment of capital; *adv* **-ly;** n **-ness.**

costive a constipated; *fig* sluggish.

costume n mode of dress, *esp* if peculiar to nation, period, etc.; theatrical clothes; n

costumier dress-maker;
n **costume jewelry** artificial
jewelry.

cot *n* light bed; swing bed on
ship; child's bed.

cotangent *n* function of angle
in trigonometry.

coterie *n Fr* set, group of
people with similar tastes,
etc.; social clique.

coterminous *a fml* having the
same limit or boundary.

cottage *n* small house, *esp* in
the country; *n* **cottager**
dweller in cottage.

cottage cheese *n* soft cheese
from skimmed milk.

cottage industry *n* small
business where goods are
produced at home or by a
small group of people.

cotter *n* pin fitting into
machinery.

cotton *n* plant; downy
covering of its seeds; thread,
fabric made from this down;
a made of cotton; realize; *idm*
cotton to *coll* take a liking to.

cotton gin *n* machine that
separates parts of cotton
plant.

cottonmouth *n* venomous
snake of southeastern US
swamps (also **water
moccasin**).

cottonseed *n* species of poplar
tree.

cotyledon *n* primary leaf of
seed embryo.

couch *n* sofa, long seat for
reclining on; *v* **1** express
(in words) **2** crouch; lie
down.

couchette *n Fr* train seat
convertible into a bed.

couch potato *n* inactive person
who spends a lot of time
watching television.

cougar *n* puma.

cough *v* expel air noisily,
violently from lungs; *n* act of
coughing, usually caused by
irritation of lungs or throat;
idm **cough up** *coll* pay
reluctantly.

cough drop *n* lozenge sucked
to ease coughing.

could *pt or conditional of* **can.**

coulee *n* small stream.

coulomb *n* unit of measure for
electricity.

coulter *n* cutting tool on plow.

council *n* deliberative or
executive assembly; *n*
council tax tax levied by
local authorities; *n*
councillor, also **counilman**
member of council.

counsel *n* **1** guidance; advice
2 lawyer; *v* advise;
recommend; *n* **counselor**
1 adviser **2** lawyer.

count[1] *v* **1** enumerate
2 reckon total number
3 include **4** possess value; *phr*
v **count on/upon** depend on;
n *leg* each charge in
indictment; act of reckoning;
idm **out for the count** asleep;
unconscious *a* **countless; n**
countdown counting down
to zero in timing firing of
missile; **countinghouse** office
where accounts are kept.

count[2] *n* European title
corresponding to British earl;

fem **countess.**

countenance *n* facial
expression; favor; *v* approve;
tolerate.

counter[1] *n* **1** table in bank,
shop across which money is
paid, goods sold **2** small disc
used in scoring in card or
other games.

counter[2] *a, adv* opposite;
contrary; *v* oppose; *boxing,
fencing* parry; *n* parry.

counter- *prefix makes
compounds meaning* opposite,
retaliatory, neutralizing. *Such
compounds are not given,
where the meaning may be
deduced from the simple word.*

counteract *v* stop or reduce
the effect of.

counterblast *n, v* reply to
criticism in strong terms.

counterclockwise *a* opposite
to the direction of turning
clock hands.

counterfeit *a* forged, spurious;
v imitate with intent to
deceive; *n* **counterfeiter.**

counterfoil *n* part of check,
receipt, etc., kept by issuer as
record.

countermand *v* cancel a
previous order.

counterpane *n* bedspread,
quilt.

counterpart *n* person or thing
exactly resembling another;
duplicate.

counterpoint *n* harmonious,
simultaneous combination of
two or more melodies.

counterpoise *n* weight
balancing another,

equilibrium.

counterproductive *a* achieving opposite of desired effect.

countersign *n* password given in reply to another; *v fig* ratify.

countersink *v* sink head of screw, etc., level with surface of material being used.

countertenor *n mus* adult male alto.

countervailing *a fml* compensating.

countess *n* woman with rank of count or earl; wife of count or earl.

countless *a* innumerable.

country *n* **1** land with definite boundaries, distinctive name, occupied by one nation **2** land of birth **3** rural areas; *a* **countrified** rustic in appearance and manners; *ns* **countryman** one living in country; compatriot; **countryside** rural area.

country-and-western *n* popular style derived from folk music of southern and western states (*also* **country music**).

country cousin *n* person unused to living in a city.

county *n* political division of a state.

coup *n* successful move or gamble.

coup d'état sudden overthrowing of government.

coup de grace *n* finishing touch.

coupé *n Fr* closed two-seater automobile.

couple *n* two objects or persons; leash for two hounds; pair; brace; *v* **1** join; unite; link together **2** (of animals) mate **3** associate (in mind); *ns* **coupling** link connecting railroad cars; **couplet** two lines of rhyming verse.

coupon *n* negotiable ticket, voucher, etc.; entry form for pools, competitions, etc.; voucher exchangeable for goods or a discount on goods.

courage *n* bravery; ability to face danger, pain, etc., without fear; *a* **courageous;** *adv* **-ly;** *n* **-ness.**

courier *n* express messenger; person conducting travelers on tour.

course *n* **1** line followed by moving object **2** passage of time **3** mode of action **4** part of meal served at one time **5** area of land used for racing, golf, etc. **6** channel (water) **7** series of lectures, lessons **8** continuous layer of bricks, etc., at same level in building; *v* hunt, *esp* with greyhounds; *n* **courser** swift horse; *idm* **of course** certainly; *idm* **take its course** develop as normal, as expected.

court *n* **1** open space, paved yard enclosed by buildings or walls **2** space marked out, for playing games like tennis **3** household of sovereign **4** place of justice where trials are held **5** body with judicial powers; *v* woo; seek favor of; *n* **courtier** attendant at royal court; *a* **courtly** elegant, refined; *n* **courtliness; court-martial,** *pl* **court-martials** court of officers trying military or naval offenses; **courtroom, courthouse** room, place where courts of law are held; **courtship** wooing.

courtesy *n* politeness, considerateness, civility; *idm* **by courtesy of 1** with the permission of **2** through the kindness of; *a* **courteous** polite, urbane; *n* **courtesy title** one held by favor, not by right.

courtesan *n* prostitute associating with upperclass men, esp royalty.

couscous *n* semolina dish, served with sauce.

cousin *n* son or daughter of uncle or aunt; any kinsman.

couth *n* sophistication; *a* polished.

cove *n* small sheltered bay or inlet.

coven *n* group of witches.

covenant *n* formal agreement, contract; *v* grant, promise by covenant.

cover *v* **1** place, spread over **2** include **3** shield **4** report on **5** point gun at **6** protect financially, by insurance; conceal; *n* **1** anything that covers **2** individual table setting; *n* **coverlet** counterpane.

A
B
C
D
E
F
G
H
I
J
K
L
M
N
O
P
Q
R
S
T
U
V
W
X
Y
Z

cover charge n fixed charge in a restaurant or club added to cost of actual food.

cover letter n explanatory letter sent, *e.g.*, with a package.

covert n place, *esp* thicket sheltering game; *a* veiled; implied.

cover-up n concealment of illegal activity or a mistake.

covet v **coveting, coveted.** desire ardently, *esp* property of another; *a* **covetous;** n **-ness.**

covey n brood of partridges; set.

cow¹ n adult female of bovine and various other animals.

cow² v frighten; overawe; intimidate.

coward n one lacking courage; *a* **cowardly** fearful; n **cowardice.**

cowbird n small N American blackbird.

cowboy n man, *usu* on horseback, who grazes cattle.

cower v shrink fearfully from; cringe; crouch.

cowl n hooded cloak worn by monk; hood-shaped top for chimney or ventilator; n **cowling** casing around engine.

cowlick n patch of hair growing in opposite direction from other strands.

cowpat n patch of cow dung on the ground.

cowpox n disease of cows, source of vaccine immunizing from smallpox.

cowrie n small shell used as money in parts of S Asia and Africa.

cowslip n wild plant of primrose family.

coxcomb n dandy.

coxswain n one steering boat; (naval) petty officer in charge of ship's boat; v **cox** act as cox.

coy a affecting shyness; demure; n **coyness.**

coyote n N American prairie wolf.

cozen v act deceitfully; beguile.

cozy a warm; snug; comfortable; adv **cozily;** n **coziness.**

cp abbr **1** candlepower **2** compare.

CPR n cardiopulmonary resuscitation, a life-saving techique to restart action of the heart and lungs.

CPU abbr central processing unit.

crab n edible shellfish, with eight legs and two pincers; v find fault with; a **crabbed** bitter; bad-tempered; cramped (handwriting).

crab apple n small, sour, wild apple; wild appletree; its sharp-tasting fruit.

crabby a bad-tempered.

crack n **1** break with sharp noise **2** split partially **3** make sharp noise, (whip, etc.); **4** (of voice) become hoarse **5** make (joke); n **1** fissure **2** sharp blow **3** report of gun; ns **cracker**

firecracker; brittle, thin, breadlike snack ; **crackle** sound of small cracks; **crackling** crisp, browned skin of roast pork; **cracksman** burglar.

crackdown n rigorous campaign to control criminal activity.

cracked a coll insane.

cracker n **1** thin biscuit **2** something that gives off cracking or popping noise.

crackers coll crazy.

crackpot n coll eccentric person.

crack-up n coll **1** disintegration **2** nervous breakdown.

cradle n baby's bed or cot; supported framework; v rock, lay to rest as in cradle; nurse.

craft n **1** cunning **2** manual dexterity **3** members of skilled trade, guild **4** boat; ns **craftsman, craftsmanship;** a **crafty** subtly cunning; adv **craftily.**

crag n rough, steep mass of rock; a **craggy** rugged.

cram v **cramming, crammed.** stuff, pack tightly into; eat greedily; study intensively for exams.

cramp n sudden, painful muscular spasm; tool with tightening screw to hold wood, masonry together; v hamper, confine, restrict **3** idm **cramp one's style** impede one's performance.

crampon n iron spike on climbing boots.

cranberry *n* small red berry, used in cooking.

crane *n* 1 slender wading bird with long neck 2 machine for raising heavy weights; *v* stretch out one's neck.

cranium *n* skull; *a* **cranial**.

crank *n* 1 bar with right-angle bend for turning things 2 eccentricity of manner or thought (person with) 3 fad; *v* wind, turn; start up engine by hand; *a* **cranky** 1 shaky 2 cross 3 crazy; *n* **crankshaft** main shaft of engine.

cranny *n* chink, narrow opening; *a* **crannied**.

crap *n sl* 1 worthless material or words 2 excrement.

crape *n* thin wrinkled black material used for mourning.

crappie *n* small fish.

craps *n* gambling game with dice.

crash *v* 1 fall violently with loud noise 2 *fig* collapse; be ruined 3 (of vehicles) to have collision, smash; *n* loud noise caused by impact or fall; *fig* ruin.

crash dive *v* (of aircraft, submarine) dive suddenly.

crash-land *v avia* land in an emergency, with probable damage; *n* **crash-landing**.

crass *a* grossly obtuse, stupid.

crate *n* wooden or wicker packing case; *v* pack in crate.

crater *n* bowl-shaped hole in ground; mouth of volcano.

cravat *n* necktie.

crave *v* 1 beg; entreat 2 have strong desire for; *n* **craving**

longing.

craven *a* cowardly; fainthearted; *n* coward.

craw *n* bird's crop.

crawl *n* 1 creeping movement 2 stroke in swimming; *v* 1 advance on hands and knees 2 creep 3 *fig* abase oneself.

crayfish, crawfish *n* fresh water edible shellfish like lobster.

crayon *n* stick of charcoal or colored chalk; *v* draw with crayons.

craze *n* popular fashion; exaggerated fondness; *v* become mad; *as* **crazed** insane; marked with surface cracks; **crazy** 1 mentally deranged 2 rickety, shaky (of structure) 3 *coll* madly eager for.

creak *n* grating, squeaking noise; *v* make such sound.

cream *n* 1 fat part of milk 2 best of anything; *v* 1 skim cream from milk 2 form into a creamy consistency; *a* **creamy** like cream; *n* **creamery** place where milk is bottled, butter and cheese are made, or dairy produce is sold; *n* **creamer** 1 small container for serving cream 2 non-dairy cream substitute.

cream of tartar *n* white powder of tartaric acid used in baking powder.

crease *n* wrinkle; ridge made by folding; line marking position of batsman or bowler in cricket; *v* make

creases; become wrinkled.

create *v* make; bring into existence; *sl* make a fuss; *ns* **creator; creature** 1 living being 2 servile dependent; **creation;** *a* **creative;** *n* **-tivity**.

creature comforts *n* things that assist bodily comfort.

crèche *n* public day nursery; Nativity scene.

credence *n* belief.

credentials *n pl* letters of introduction, *esp* of ambassador; testimonials.

credible *a* trustworthy; worthy of belief; *n* **credibility**.

credibility gap *n* difference between what is said and what people believe to be true.

credit *n* 1 belief 2 integrity 3 prestige gained by merit 4 sum in person's bank account; *idm* **on credit** allowing person to have goods for later payment; *idm* **to one's credit** worthily; *v* believe; attribute; place on credit side of account; *a* **-able** adding honour to *adv* **-ably;** *n* **creditor** one to whom money is due.

credit card *n* card that permits buying of goods without cash.

credit union *n* cooperative group that makes loans to its members at low interst rates.

credulous *a* easily deceived; gullible; *adv* **-ly;** *n* **credulity**.

creed *n* set of principles; formally phrased confession

a
b
c
d
e
f
g
h
i
j
k
l
m
n
o
p
q
r
s
t
u
v
w
x
y
z

of faith.

creek n narrow inlet on seacoast; arm of river.

creel n angler's wicker basket.

creep v move stealthily, slowly; crawl; *bot* grow along ground or wall; *fig* squirm with fear; cringe; *pt, pp* **crept;** n **creeper** creeping or climbing plant; a **creepy** eerie; feeling fear; n **creepiness.**

creepy-crawly n *coll* crawling creature, insect, spider.

cremation n burning (corpse) to ashes; v **cremate;** n **crematorium** place where cremation takes place.

crème de menthe n *Fr* peppermint liqueur.

crenellated a having battlements; n **-ation.**

crenulated a wavy.

creole n hybrid of two languages, established as main language of a community; n **Creole** descendant of European settlers in W Indies or southern US.

creosote n oily antiseptic distilled from wood- or coal-tar, used for preserving wood.

crêpe n light wrinkled fabric; n **crêpe-de-chine** fine silk; n **crêpe rubber** washed rubber.

crepe paper n thin, wrinkled paper for decorating and wrapping.

crepitate v crackle, creak, rattle; n **crepitation.**

crept *pt of* **creep.**

crepuscular a of the twilight.

crescendo a, *adv* n gradual increase in loudness, *esp* of music.

crescent n 1 shape of new moon 2 curved row of houses.

cress n various edible pungent leaved plants.

crest n 1 tuft or ridge on animal's head 2 top of mountain, wave, etc. 3 device on coat of arms; a **crestfallen** dejected, disappointed.

cretaceous a chalky.

cretin n idiot, often deformed.

cretonne n *Fr* strong cotton cloth, printed with design.

crevasse n *Fr* deep cleft in glacier.

crevice n small chink, fissure.

crew n ship's aircraft's company; gang (of workmen, people).

crew cut n very short haircut for men.

crewel n twisted yarn for crewelwork or embroidery.

crew neck n plain round neckline, *esp* for pullover.

crib n 1 fodder bin; manger 2 child's bed 3 copy; plagiarism; v **cribbing, cribbed. 1** copy closely 2 confine closely; n **crib death** the sudden death of an infant from no apparent illness

cribbage n card game using pegged scoreboard.

crick n painful spasm of back or neck muscles.

cricket¹ n chirping insect.

cricket² n game played by teams of 11 a side, with wickets, bats, and ball; *idm* **not cricket** *Brit* not fair or honorable.

cried *pt of* **cry.**

cries *3rd sing present of* **cry.**

crime n grave violation of law; any evil act; *mil* offense against regulations; a, n **criminal;** n **criminology** study of crime and criminals.

crimp v press into tiny pleats; curl (hair).

crimson n deep, slightly bluish red color; a of this color; v turn crimson; blush.

cringe v cower; fawn; shrink from.

crinkle v wrinkle; rumple; n undulation.

crinoline n petticoat.

cripple n lame, disabled, or maimed person; v maim; impair.

crisis n decisive movement; turning point, *esp* in illness; time of acute danger or difficulty; *pl* **crises.**

crisp a dry and brittle; curly, *esp* hair; *fig* brisk; bracing; v **crispen** make crispy.

crisscross a, *adv,* v form(ing) a network of lines.

criterion n standard of judgment; test; *pl* **criteria.**

critic n 1 professional reviewer of plays, books, art, etc. 2 fault finder; a **critical 1** relating to crisis; crucial 2 discerning; censorious; v **criticize** pass judgment on; censure; ns **criticism, critique 1** art of criticism

2 critical analysis, (*e.g.*, of writer's work).
croak *v* 1 emit hoarse, dismal cry, as frog, raven 2 grumble 3 *sl* die; *n* sound itself; *a, n* **croaking**.
crochet *n Fr* kind of fancy-work done with small hooked needle; *v* make such work.
crock *n* 1 earthenware pot; broken piece of this 2 old worn-out person, horse; 3 *sl* lot of nonsense; *n* **crockery** domestic china and earthenware articles.
crocodile *n* large amphibious reptile; *n pl* **crocodile tears** insincere show of grief.
crocus *n* **-ses**. small spring-flowering plant.
croft *n* small farm or piece of arable land; *n* **crofter** one who owns and works croft.
croissant *n Fr* flaky crescent-shaped pastry.
cromlech *n* prehistoric structure of flat stone resting on two upright ones.
crone *n* hideous, withered old woman.
crony *n* old friend, close companion.
crook *n* 1 shepherd's staff; long hooked stick 2 *coll* criminal 3 bend; sharp turn; *v* bend sharply; *a* **crooked** 1 bent; winding 2 dishonest 3 deformed; *adv* **-ly; n -ness**.
croon *v* sing softly, sentimentally; *ns* **crooner; crooning**.
crop *n* 1 season's produce or

yield of any cultivated plant 2 pouch in gullet of birds 3 stock of whip 4 closely cut hair; *v* **cropping, cropped.** 1 reap, gather 2 clip hair 3 graze; *idm* **come a cropper** 1 fall 2 fail; *phr* **crop up** occur.
croquet *n* game played on lawn, with mallets, balls and hoops.
croquette *n Fr* fried ball of meat, fish, potato, etc.
crosier, crozier *n* pastoral staff of bishop.
cross *n* 1 upright stake with transverse bar, used for execution; 2 the Cross, on which Christ died; symbol of Christian faith 3 mark made by interesecting lines 4 mixture of breeds; mongrel, hybrid etc 5 affliction; *v* 1 place or lay across 2 traverse 3 interbreed 4 thwart; obstruct; *idm* **cross oneself** make the sign of the cross; *idm* **cross one's mind** occur to one; *phr v* **cross off/out** delete; *a* 1 transverse 2 contrary 3 bad-tempered 4 intersecting; *advs* **crossways, crosswise, crossly**.
cross- *prefix: makes compounds meaning* opposing; crossing; transverse, across. *Such compounds are not given where the meaning may be deduced from the simple word.*
crossbill *n* bird with crossed mandibles.
crossbow *n* small powerful

bow fired from the shoulder by pulling a trigger.
crossbred *a* of mixed breed; *n* **cross-breed**.
crosscheck *v* check again by another method.
cross-country *a* 1 proceeding over fields, through woods, etc., rather than on a road or track 2 from one end of the country to another; *n* sport of **cross-country** running or skiing.
cross-dressing *n* transvestism.
cross-examine *v* interrogate closely.
cross-eyed *a* squinting.
cross-fertilize *v* 1 fertilize a plant with pollen from a different plant 2 stimulate progress in one field of study with ideas from another; *n* **-ization**.
crosspatch *n* cross, peevish person.
crosspiece *n* bar, *usu* horizontal, linking other parts of structure.
cross-reference *n* note referring to another place in a book or article.
crossroads *n* 1 road that crosses another 2 *pl* intersection 3 *pl* decisive point in time.
cross section *n* 1 (image of) surface formed by cutting across, *usu* at right angles 2 representive sample.
cross talk *n* 1 fast witty dialog 2 interference in radio, telephone communication from other voices.

crosswalk n pedestrian crossing area on road.

crossword n puzzle in which words determined from, numbered clues are fit into patterns of horizontal and vertical squares.

crotch n 1 forked stick; 2 fork of tree or branch 3 where legs fork from body.

crotchet n note in music, half time value of minim; a **crotchety** faddy, peevish.

crouch v stoop low; cringe; lie close to ground.

croup n 1 throat disease of children. 2 hindquarters of horse.

croupier n one presiding at gaming table, who rakes in and pays out money.

crouton n cube toasted/fried bread served in soup or on salads.

crow¹ n large black bird of raven family; idm **as the crow flies** in a straight line.

crow² v utter cry of cock; triumph (vocally); pt **crowed, crew** (of birds only); pp **crowed**.

crowbar n heavy iron bar for levering.

crowd n large number of people or things close together; throng; v cram into small place; press forward in mass; phr v **crowd out** exclude for lack of time, space; a **crowded** filled by crowd; too full.

crown n 1 royal headdress 2 wreath worn on head 3 sovereignty; supreme power 4 summit; head 5 top of hat; 6 fig highest achievement; 7 foreign coins; v place crown on; make king; idm **to crown it all** on top of everything else.

crow's feet n pl wrinkles at outer corner of the eye.

crow's nest n lookout platform high up on ship's mast.

crucial a 1 critical; decisive 2 severe.

crucible n melting pot, for use in great heat.

cruciform a in the shape of a cross.

crucify v **-fying, -fied.** 1 put to death by nailing or binding to cross; 2 coll torment; humiliate by ridicule; ns **crucifixion; crucifix** figure of Christ on the Cross.

crude a 1 raw; not prepared for use; in natural state 2 blunt; rude; n **crudity**.

cruel a 1 willing to cause physical or mental pain; pitiless 2 painful; n **cruelty**.

cruet n stoppered containers for condiments.

cruise v travel at leisurely speed, esp ship, car, etc.; n sea voyage for pleasure; n **cruise** ship that cruises; fast warship.

cruise missile n computer-guided missile flying at low altitude.

crumb n very small particle, scrap, esp of bread or cake; v cover with crumbs.

crumble v break into crumbs; decay; disintegrate.

crummy a sl inferior; worthless.

crumpet n thin, unsweetened doughy cake, usually toasted.

crumple v make creases or folds; fall into wrinkles; a **crumpled**.

crunch v chew, crush noisily with teeth; tread heavily on gravel, etc.; n sound made by crunching; idm **the (final) crunch** the final disaster; coll **in a crunch** under tight deadline.

crupper n 1 hindquarters of horse 2 strap passing under tail, holding saddle in place.

crusade n 1 holy war with religious object, esp to free Holy Land 2 campaign against social abuse or evil; n **crusader**.

cruse n small pot or jar for liquids.

crush v compress violently; squeeze, press out of shape; pulverize; fig subdue forcibly; n act of crushing; idm **a crush (on someone)** coll strong but brief adolescent infatuation (with someone).

crust n hard outer part; dry piece of bread; hard covering of anything; v form crust; a **crusty** crustlike; fig harsh, irritable.

crustacean n animal having hard crustlike shell, e.g., lobster, crab, etc.

crutch n staff with crosspiece to go under arm, to help lame to walk; support; crotch.

crux *n* knotty point; important or critical point; puzzle.

cry *n* 1 loud call 2 weep 3 slogan 4 characteristic call of animal; *idm* **a far cry from** quite different from; *v* **crying, cried.** make such sound; announce; weep; *idm* **for crying out loud** *coll expressing protest.*

cryogenics *n* study or use of extremely low temperatures; *a* cryogenic.

crypt *n* underground vault, *esp* of church; *a* **cryptic** secret, mystic.

crypto- *prefix* hidden; *ns* **cryptogram** written cipher; **cryptography** art of cipher writing, decoding.

cryptogam *n* plant reproducing without seed; *a* **-gamous.**

crystal *n* clear, transparent quartz; solidified inorganic substance of geometrical form; fine, hard glassware; *as* **crystalline, crystalloid;** *v* **crystallize** form crystals; become clear; *ns* **crystallization; crystallography** science of structure and formation of crystals.

crystal ball *n* glass sphere used by fortune tellers.

crystal gazing *n* 1 looking into a crystal ball 2 trying to predict future events.

cub *n* young fox, bear, etc; *v* bring forth cubs; *n* **cubbing** hunting of foxcubs.

cubby, cubbyhole *n* snug place; small storage place.

cube *n* 1 regular geometric solid with six equal square faces; anything cube-shaped; 2 *math* third power; *v* calculate cube of; *as* **cubic, cubical.**

cubicle *n* small, enclosed part in larger room, sleeping car, etc.

cubism *n* painting and sculpture style reducing natural forms to geometric shapes; *n* a cubist.

cubit *n* ancient measure of length.

cuckold *n* man whose wife is unfaithful.

cuckoo *n* migratory bird, with characteristic call, that lays eggs in another bird's nest.

cucumber *n* long, fleshy green fruit of plant of gourd family, used in salads.

cud *n* partially digested food brought up by ruminants, to chew at leisure; *idm* **chew the cud** ponder, reflect on.

cuddle *v* hug; nestle; be close to; *n* a hug.

cudgel *n* stout, short thick stick; *v* beat with cudgel.

cue¹ *n* word serving as signal to another to act or speak; *fig* hint, lead.

cue² *n* long tapering rod used in billiards.

cuff¹ *n* wristband of garment; end of sleeve.

cuff² *v* hit with fist or hand; *n* such a blow.

cuisine *n* quality, style of cooking.

cul-de-sac *n* blind alley; passage with one open end.

culinary *a* connected with cooking or the kitchen.

cull *v* 1 gather 2 pluck (flowers) 3 select 4 kill selectively; *n* something picked out.

culminate *phr v* end in; reach its climax in; *n* **-ation.**

culpable *a* worthy of blame; guilty; *n* **culpability.**

culprit *n* one guilty of crime, offender.

cult *n* system of religious belief; devotion to person or cause; fashion.

cultivate *v* till, work land; grow (crops); improve; seek acquaintance of; *ns* **-ation, -ator.**

cultivated *a* educated and wellmannered.

culture *n* rearing of animals, plants; high intellectual development; artificial rearing, *esp* of bacteria; elegance of manners; *as* **cultured** refined; **cultural** pertaining to culture.

culvert *n* channel carrying water under road, etc.

cum *prep* together with.

cumber *v* hinder, hamper; *as* **cumbersome** clumsy, unwieldy; **cumbrous.**

cumin *n* aromatic seed used as flavoring.

cummerbund *n* broad sash around waist.

cumulative *a* increasing in force, value, etc., by successive additions.

cumulus *n* cloud formation of

rounded, heaped-up masses.

cuneiform *a* wedge-shaped, *esp* of form of ancient writing.

cunning *n* skill dexterity; (of mental qualities) slyness; *a* having such qualities; wily; artful; *adv* **-ly.**

cup *n* **1** small drinking vessel with handle **2** contents of cup **3** trophy in shape of cup, usually silver **4** drink made of wine mixed with other ingredients; *ns* **cupful, cupboard** small closet with shelves for china, etc.

Cupid *n* figure of winged boy with bow and arrow, representing love.

cupidity *n* avarice; greed; covetousness.

cupola *n* small dome.

cupreous, cupric, cuprous *a* of, containing or like copper.

cur *n* mongrel dog, *esp* snappy one; low ill-bred fellow.

curable *a* able to be cured.

curacao *n* orange-flavored liqueur.

curate *n* rector's or vicar's assistant; *v* act as curator; *n* **curacy** his office.

curative *n, a* (substance) effecting a cure.

curator *n* person in charge of a museum collection.

curb *n* **1** restricting chain, strap fastened to horse's bit **2** *fig* check; restraint **3** edging of pavement; *v* restrain, subdue.

curd *n* thick substance separated from milk by acid action; *v* **curdle** turn into

curd; coagulate; *fig* **c. the blood** terrify; *a* **curdy.**

cure *v* **1** restore to health; heal **2** preserve (food) by salting; *n* remedy, treatment restoring health.

cure-all *n* cure for anything; panacea.

curet(te) *n* surgical scraper; *n* **curettage** use of this.

curfew *n* regulation requiring all persons to be indoors by stated hour.

curia *n* papal court and government.

curie *n* unit of radioactivity.

curio *n* small, *esp* unusual, collector's item; *pl* **-s.**

curiosity *n* **1** inquisitiveness **2** strange, interesting object; *a* **curious 1** eager to know; prying **2** puzzling **3** rare; *adv* **-ly.**

curl *n* coiled lock of hair; ringlet; spiral or similar shape; *a* **curly;** *v* twist, roll, or press into spirals; play at curling; *n* **curling** game like bowls, played on ice; **curling iron** rod-shaped implement for curling hair.

curlew *n* wading bird of snipe family.

currant *n* small dried grape; edible fruit of various shrubs.

current *a* **1** in general use; **2** up-to-date **3** generally known; *n* **1** flow of body of water, air **2** movement of electricity; *n* **currency** state of being current; money in circulation.

curriculum *n* **-la** *or* **-lums**

course of study at a school, college, etc.

curriculum vitae (cv) *n* (document with) details of one's qualifications and professional experience; **résumé.**

curry[1] *v* **-rying, -ried.** rub down (horse) with comb; dress (leather).

curry[2] *n* **-ries.** highly spiced, hot flavored dish of meat, fish, etc.; *v* make into a curry; *idm* **curry favor with** try to influence by flattery, bribery, etc.; *n* **curry powder** mixture of turmeric and other spices.

curse *v* call down divine wrath or vengeance; swear (at); afflict; *n* words used to curse; profane oath, imprecation; bane; *coll* menstrual period; *a* **cursed** wicked; afflicted by a curse; *n* **cursedness** perversity.

cursive *a* in a flowing style (of handwriting).

cursor *n* mark on a computer screen that shows where you are working.

cursory *a* brief; not careful or detailed.

curt *a* short, abrupt, rudely brief; *n* **curtness;** *v* **curtail** cut short; reduce; *n* **curtailment.**

curtain *n* sheet of material hung to screen window, door, etc.; screen separating stage and audience; anything that screens, covers; *v* cover with a curtain; *idm* **(be) curtains**

for (somebody) (be) the end or a disaster (for somebody).

curtain call *n* reappearance of actor(s) to acknowledge applause at end of play, opera, etc.

curtain-raiser *n* 1 short piece before main play 2 any preliminary event.

curtsy *n* movement of respect, bending, of knees made by women; *v* make such gesture.

curvaceous *a* (of woman) with shapely figure.

curve *n* line of which no part is straight, rounded bend; *v* impart a curve to; *n* **curvature** act of curving, being curved; *a* **curvilinear** bounded by curved lines.

cushion *n* pillow, soft pad to lie, sit, or rest on; any resilient support; lining around inner side of billiard table; *v* protect with cushion.

cushy *a sl* easy; light; profitable.

cusp *n* horn of crescent; *a* **cuspidal** ending in point.

cuspidor *n* spittoon.

custard *n* dessert made of milk, eggs, sugar that is baked or boiled.

custard pie *n* plate of wet sloppy stuff thrown at someone in slapstick comedy.

cute *a* pretty; charming; adorable.

custody *n* safekeeping; guardianship; imprisonment; *n* **custodian** keeper, curator.

custom *n* habit; business patronage; practice; *pls* duties on imports; place where these are collected (*also* **custom house**); *a* **customary** usual; *n* **customer** buyer.

custom-built *n* made to customer's own specifications.

customize *v* adapt to customer's requirements.

cut *v* 1 wound, separate, gash with sharp instrument 2 shape, trim, carve by cutting 3 mow; reap 4 abridge 5 ignore (person) 6 strike sharply 7 intersect; *pt, pp* **cut**; *idm* **cut both ways** have both pros and cons; *idm* **cut corners** sacrifice perfection in interests of speed and economy; *idm* **cut it close** allow the minimum amount of time for sth; *idm* **cut no ice** have no influence; *idm* **cut one's losses** abandon (an enterprise) to avoid further loss; *phr vs* **cut across** 1 take a short route across 2 not correspond to; **cut back** 1 prune 2 reduce; **cut down** 1 fell 2 reduce (*idm* **cut down to size** 1 make humble 2 make more realistic); **cut in** 1 interrupt 2 move too close in front of another vehicle; **cut off** 1 separate 2 disconnect 3 suddenly move off in a new direction 4 deprive of inheritance 5 *sl* kill (*idm* **be cut off in one's prime** die young); *idm* **cut out for** well suited to; *idm* **a cut above** somewhat superior to; *n*

cutting 1 act of cutting 2 thing cut off, *esp* excavation through high ground, for railroad, highway, etc. 3 slip cut from plant; *a* sarcastic; bitter; *a* **cutthroat** merciless; *n* type of razor; fierce ruffian.

cut-and-dried *a* arranged and settled.

cutaneous *a* of skin.

cutaway *n* 1 tailcoat 2 drawing showing internal details, (*e.g.*, of machine) 3 film, TV shot giving view of simultaneous event in a different place.

cutback *n* reduction.

cut glass *n* glass with decorative carved patterns.

cuticle *n* outer layer of skin; skin at base of nails.

cutlass *n* short, broad-bladed sword.

cutler *n* one who makes, mends, sells knives and cutting instruments; *n* **cutlery** such implements.

cutlet *n* small meat chop.

cutoff *n* 1 stopping point 2 device to control flow.

cut-rate *a* cheap.

cutter *n* 1 person who cuts 2 sailing boat 3 small fast boat 4 *esp pl* cutting tool.

cutthroat *a* 1 murderous 2 fiercely competitive; *n* very sharp razor.

cutting edge *a* 1 sharp edge 2 incisiveness of speech or writing 3 key area of technological advance.

cuttle, cuttlefish *n* marine

a
b
c
d
e
f
g
h
i
j
k
l
m
n
o
p
q
r
s
t
u
v
w
x
y
z

mollusk that squirts out inky fluid.

cv *abbr* curriculum vitae.

cyanide *n* prussic acid.

cyanosis *n* blueness of skin.

cybernetics *n* study of automatic communication and control, *esp* in relation to computers.

cyberpunk *n* style of science fiction set in a world of advanced computer technology.

cyberspace *n* the environment through which electronic information and pictures travel when they are sent from one computer to another.

cyclamate *n* artificial sweetener.

cyclamen *n* plant with pink, white, red, or purple flowers and turned-back petals.

cycle *n* **1** period of time during which there is regular orderly series of events **2** great period of time; **3** group of poems, connected with central theme **4** *coll* bicycle; *v* **1** recur in cycles **2** ride bicycle; *a* **cyclic, cyclical; ns cyclist** bicycle rider; **cyclometer** device for measuring distance traveled by wheel.

cyclone *n* rotating winds surrounding regions of low pressure; *a* **cyclonic**.

cyclotron *n* machine for accelerating atomic particles in nuclear research.

cygnet *n* young swan.

cylinder *n* solid or hollow roller-shaped body; piston chamber of engine; *a* **cylindrical**.

cymbal *n* musical percussion instrument, one of two brass plates struck to make clashing sound.

cynic *n* skeptical, mocking person; *a* **cynical sneering;** thinking worst of people; *n* **cynicism** being a cynic.

cynosure *n* center of attraction.

cypress *n* dark evergreen coniferous tree.

Cyrillic alphabet *n* alphabet used in written Russian and some other Slavonic languages.

cyst *n med* abnormal sac containing pus, fluid; *a* **cystic** of bladder; *n* **cystitis** inflammation of the bladder.

cystic fibrosis *n* hereditary disease that affects the respiratory and digestive systems.

cytology *n* study of plant and animal cells.

czar, tsar *n* former emperor of Russia.

DA *abbr* district attorney.

dab *v* **dabbing, dabbed.** touch lightly; *n* **1** slight tap **2** small flat fish.

dabble *v* **1** dip in and out of water **2** engage in halfheartedly (study, etc.); *n* **dabbler.**

dabchick *n* small waterbird.

da capo *a, adv mus* start again from the beginning.

dace *n* small river-fish.

dachshund *n* type of long-bodied, short-legged dog.

Dacron [TM] *n* strong synthetic fabric.

dad, daddy *n* childish word for father.

dadaism *n* art movement based on rejection of traditional values.

daddy longlegs *n* common spider with very long legs.

dado *n* border or panelling on wall of room.

daemon *n* **1** (in Greek myth) demigod **2** spirit that inspires.

daffodil *n* spring-flowering bulb; narcissus.

daft *n* foolish, feeble-minded.

dagger *n* short two-edged blade for stabbing; *idm* **look daggers at** glare at.

daguerreotype *n* early type of photograph.

dahlia *n* bulb type of flowering plant.

Dáil *n* lower house of parliament in Irish Republic.

daily *a, adv* every day; *n* **1** newspaper published on weekdays; *idm* **daily bread 1** daily food **2** *coll* livelihood.

dainty *a* delicate; elegant; refined; *n* delicacy (food); *n* **daintiness.**

dairy *n* place where milk and its products are dealt with or sold; *n* **dairy cattle** cows kept to produce milk; *a* relating to milk.

dais *n* raised platform.

daisy *n* type of common wildflower.

daisy wheel *n, a* (having high-quality printing from) rapidly rotating wheel with choice of typeface.

Dalai Lama *n* Tibetan spiritual leader.

dale *n* valley, *esp* in N England; *n* **dalesman.**

dally *v* **dallying, dallied.** linger; delay; *phr v* **dally with 1** think about **2** flirt with; *n* **dalliance.**

Dalmatian *n* large white dog with black spots.

dam[1] *n* barrier arresting water flow; water so obstructed; *v* **damming, damned.** hold back by dam.

dam[2] *n* mother of animals usually domestic livestock.

damage *n* harm, injury, hurt to persons, property, etc.; *pl* money claimed, or paid as compensation for injury libel, etc.; *v* harm, injure.

damask *n* silk, linen material with pattern woven into it; color of damask rose; rosy-pink; *v* **damascene** decorate metal with inlaid gold or silver.

dame *n* lady; *cap* title of lady member of Order of British Empire.

damn *v* condemn to eternal punishment; curse; *interj* oath; *a, adv* **damned;** *coll* used as intensifier; *idm* **I'll be damned** expressing surprise or frustration; *a* **damnable;** *n* **damnation;** *idm* **in damnation** expressing anger; *idm* **do one's damndest;** *coll*

A
B
C
D
E
F
G
H
I
J
K
L
M
N
O
P
Q
R
S
T
U
V
W
X
Y
Z

do the most one can.

damp n moisture; noxious gas in coal mines; a slightly wet; v make damp; fig discourage; (of plants) to wither off from mildew; v **dampen** become damp; depress; n **damper** anything that discourages; plate in flue to regulate draft.

damp course, damp-proof course n layer of waterproof material preventing rising dampness in a building.

damsel n young girl.

damson n small, purple, very sour plum.

dance v move, leap with rhythmic sequence of steps, usually to music; n social gathering organized for dancing; form of dance; ns **dancer; dancing** art and practice of the dance.

dandelion n common yellow wildflower.

dander idm **get one's dander up** coll make someone angry.

dandle v move (child) up and down in one's arms, on one's knee.

dandruff n small scales of dead skin on scalp, scurf.

dandy n fop; extravagantly fashionable man.

Dane n native of Denmark.

danger n menace; exposure to peril, risk of death; a **dangerous** adv **-ly**.

dangle v hang, sway loosely; show as enticement; idm **keep somebody dangling** keep somebody in suspense.

Danish n, a **1** the language of

Denmark **2** pastry filled with cheese or fruit.

dank a disagreeably damp; n **dankness**.

daphne a flowering shrub.

dapper a neat and trim in appearance.

dapple v mark with spots of different color; a **dappled**, variegated.

dare v **daring, dared.** have courage for; venture to; challenge.

daredevil n, a (person) behaving in a foolishly reckless way.

daren't contracted form of dare not.

daresay idm **I daresay** or **I dare say** probably; it may be true (that).

daring a bold; n audacity.

dark a **1** without light; (of color, complexion) deep in shade **2** secret **3** evil; idm **in the dark** without information; v **darken** make, or become darker; as **darkish; darkling** growing dim; n **darkness**, absence of light.

Dark Ages n period between the end of the Roman Empire and the Renaissance.

dark horse n person whose talents remain hidden.

darkroom n enclosed place for developing and printing film.

darling n dearly loved person; term of endearment.

darn v repair hole with interlacing stitches; n part so mended; n **darning**.

darn interj milder form of damn.

dart n **1** light pointed missile **2** sudden rapid forward movement **3** tapering seam in garment; pl indoor game played with target and small darts; v shoot out or forward quickly, swiftly.

Darwinian a of evolution (as stated by Charles Darwin).

dash v **1** fling with violence **2** rush furiously **3** sprinkle; n **1** rush **2** small quantity (of liquid) **3** short line (-) used to denote a pause; a **dashing** spirited; eager.

dashboard n instrument panel inside car, in front of driver.

dastard n despicable coward; a **dastardly** mean.

DAT abbr digital audio tape.

data bank n comput center with large supply of data.

database n comput large store of data for reference.

data processing n comput operating on data to analyze, solve problems, etc.

data n pl known facts from which conclusion can be drawn; sing datum.

date n **1** particular day in the calendar **2** arrangement to meet **3** person of opposite sex with whom one has a social engagement; idm **out of date 1** old-fashioned **2** no longer valid; idm **to date** until now; idm **up to date 1** modern **2** completed to schedule **3** well informed; phr vs **date from/back to** be applicable from; a **dated**

1 marked with the date **2** old fashioned; *a* **dateless** never becoming dated.

date² *n* sweet, single stoned fruit of date palm.

date palm *n* tree with an edible fruit; *n* date.

dative *n* case of noun or pronoun expressing indirect object.

daub *v* smear; coat; plaster; paint roughly; *n* unskillful painting; smear.

daughter *n* female child or offspring; *a* **daughterly;** *n* **daughter-in-law** son's wife.

daunt *v* inspire with fear, dismay; discourage; *a* **dauntless** intrepid; fearless.

dauphin *n* former title of eldest son of French king.

davenport *n* large sofa.

davit *n* small crane for raising and lowering boats.

Davy Jones's locker *n coll* the bottom of the sea.

daw *n* kind of crow; jackdaw.

dawdle *v* linger; loiter; waste time; *n* **dawdler.**

dawn *v* begin to grow light; *phr v* **dawn on** gradually become evident to; *n* daybreak; *n* **dawning** the dawn; *fig* beginning.

day *n* period between sunrise and sunset; 24 hours; specified day; *pl* epoch, period of time; *idm* **call it a day** (agree to) stop working; *idm* **carry/win the day** be successful; *idm* **make someone's day** make someone happy; *ns* **day care**

daytime care for children, old people; **daybook** for recording daily events; **daybreak** dawn; **daydream** reverie; **daylight** natural light (*idm* **beat/knock/scare the living daylights out of** hit/scare someone very badly); **daytime** hours between sunrise and sunset.

daylight saving time *n* in summer adjusting clocks to make nightfall appear later.

day-to-day *a* **1** everyday **2** one day at a time.

daze *v* stupefy, confuse, usually by blow, shock; *a* **dazed.**

dazzle *v* confuse vision; blind by brilliant light; daze by hope of success.

dB *abbr* decibel.

DBS *abbr* direct broadcasting (by) satellite.

DBX *abbr* Dolby noise reduction.

DC *abbr* **1** *mus* da capo **2** *elec* direct current **3** District of Columbia **4** detective constable.

D-day *n* **1** June 6, 1944, when Allies invaded Normandy **2** any day when an important plan is to be launched.

DD *abbr* direct debit.

DDT *n* type of insecticide that has toxic effects on plant and animal life.

de- *prefix; forms compounds expressing* down, off, away, deficiency, negation. *Where the meaning may be deduced from the simple word, the compounds are not given here.*

deacon *n* ordained person, lower order than priest; *fem* **deaconess** woman appointed to help in church work.

dead *a* no longer living; obsolete (of language); complete; lifeless; extinguished; numbed; *n coll* dead persons; *v* **deaden** reduce force of; muffle; benumb; *a* **deadly** fatal; implacable; *ns* **deadliness.**

deadbeat *a coll* exhausted; *n coll* idle person with no desire for improvement; drop-out.

dead center *n* exact center.

dead duck *n coll* abandoned scheme; one sure to fail.

dead end *n* impasse; *a* **dead-end** without prospects.

dead heat *n* race where two runners reach finish simultaneously.

deadline *n* time limit for finishing a job.

deadlock *n* situation in dispute when neither opposing party will give way, so progress is impossible; *a* **deadlocked.**

deadly nightshade *n* plant with very poisonous black berries (*also* **belladonna**).

dead man's float *n* face-down position for floating.

dead-on *a* exact, correct.

deadpan *a* expressionless; without sign of emotion.

dead reckoning *n* calculation of position without mechanical aids.

dead ringer *n coll* person closely resembling another.

a
b
c
d
e
f
g
h
i
j
k
l
m
n
o
p
q
r
s
t
u
v
w
x
y
z

A
B
C
D
E
F
G
H
I
J
K
L
M
N
O
P
Q
R
S
T
U
V
W
X
Y
Z

dead set *a* positively determined.

dead weight *n* heavy, lifeless mass.

dead wood *n* **1** useless things **2** ineffectual people.

deaf *a* without whole or partial hearing; inattentive; *v* **deafen** make deaf; *n pl* the **deaf** deaf persons; *n* **-ness**; *a* **deafening**; *n* **deaf-mute** person who is deaf and cannot speak.

deal *v* **1** give, hand out **2** distribute, *esp* playing cards; *pt, pp* **dealt;** *phr vs* **deal in 1** buy and sell **2** indulge in; **deal with 1** trade with **2** handle; *n* business transaction; act of dealing cards, etc.; *idm* **a good/great deal** a lot; *ns* **dealer; dealing** trading; *n pl* **dealings (with)** relations (with), *esp* business.

dealership *n* automobile store.

dean *n* head of chapter of cathedral; head of university faculty.

dean's list *n* college honor roll.

dear 1 *a* precious; beloved **2** costly; expensive **3** polite form of address in letter; *n* lovable person; *adv* **dear, dearly,** at high price; *n* **dearness**.

Dear John *n* letter in which woman breaks off relationship with man.

dearth *n* scarcity; want; (*esp* of food) famine.

death *n* end of life; annihilation; state of being dead; *idm* **at death's door** (seeming to be) very ill and about to die; *idm* **do it to death** *coll* play or perform so frequently that people become bored; *idm* **like death warmed over** *coll* looking very ill or tired; *idm* **put to death** execute; *idm* **sick to death (of)** *coll* absolutely fed up with; **on one's deathbed** near death; *a* **deathless,** immortal; *a, adv* **deathly,** like death.

death row *n* place where condemned prisoner awaits execution.

death's head *n* human skull (symbolizing death).

deathwatch beetle *n* beetle whose larva eats wood, causing damage to buildings.

death wish *n* desire for one's own or another's death.

debacle *n* rout; sudden and overwhelming disaster.

debar *v* **-barring, -barred.** prevent; exclude; prohibit.

debark *v* disembark; put, go ashore.

debase *v* lower in value, *esp* of coinage; render base (dignity, morals); *n* **-ment.**

debate *v* discuss; argue; consider; *n* formal public discussion; *a* **debatable** questionable; *n* **debater**.

debauch *v* corrupt; lead astray; seduce; *n* orgy; licentious bout; *ns* **debauchee, debauchery**.

debenture *n* certificate of stock held, bond of company or corporation.

debility *n* weakness, feebleness of health; *v* **debilitate** make weak.

debit *n* entry in account, of sum owing; *v* charge as due.

debit card *n* payment card with which goods are paid for directly from a bank account.

debonair *a* genial; affable; cheerful; sprightly.

debouch *v* come out into a wider space.

debridement *n med* surgical removal of unhealthy tissue; *v* **debride**.

debrief *v* question someone in detail about a mission, task, or enterprise after completion; *n* **debriefing**.

debris *n* broken remains; trash; loose rock fragments.

debt *n* something owed; liability; *n* **debtor**.

debug *v* **1** remove hidden microphones from (*e.g.,* house) **2** identify and remove faults from machine, computer program, etc.

debunk *v* expose as false or exaggerated.

debut *n* first appearance in public; *n fem* **debutante** girl making her debut in society.

dec-, deca- *prefix*, ten, tenfold; *e.g.,* **decameter** ten meters. *Where the meaning may be deduced from the simple word the compounds are not given here.*

decade *n* period of ten years.

decadent *a* deteriorating;

declining in morals; *n*
decadence.

decaffeinate *v* remove caffeine from; **decaffeinated.**

decagon *n* plane figure with ten sides.

decahedron *n* solid with ten faces.

decal *n* picture or design on special paper for transfer to another surface.

decalcify *v* remove lime from, as teeth, bones, etc.

Decalogue *n* Ten Commandments.

decamp *v* 1 break camp 2 run away; abscond.

decant *v* pour off gently, leaving sediment; *n* **decanter** stoppered glass vessel for decanted wine.

decapitate *v* cut off head; behead; *n* **-ation.**

decarbonize *v* remove carbon from; *n* **decarbonization.**

decathlon *n* athletic contest for the best overall result in ten events.

decay *v* 1 rot 2 lose vigor, power, etc.; decline; *n* decomposition; rotting; gradual breaking up; *a* **decayed.**

decease *v* die; *n* death; *n* **deceased** the dead person.

deceive *v* 1 mislead 2 delude oneself 3 cheat; *ns* **deceiver; deceit** act of deceiving; fraud; sham; *a* **deceitful,** misleading; giving false idea; *adv* **-ly;** *n* **-ness.**

decelerate *v* decrease speed; *n* **-ation.**

December *n* twelfth month of year.

decennial *a* 1 ten yearly 2 lasting ten years *n* tenth anniversary.

decent *a* seemly; respectable; modest; *n* **decency.**

decentralize *v* remove from central control; *n* **-ization.**

deception *n* 1 deceiving; being deceived 2 trick *a* **deceptive;** *adv* **-ly.**

deci- *prefix* one-tenth.

decibel *n* unit of measure of loudness of sounds.

decide *v* determine; settle; make up one's mind; *a* **decided** determined; definite; *n* **decision;** *a* **decisive;** *adv* **-ly.**

deciduous *a* (of trees, shrubs, etc.) shedding leaves annually.

decimal *a* based on number ten; *n* decimal fraction; *v* **decimalize** reduce to decimal fractions or system; *n* **-ization** process of converting to decimals.

decimate *v* kill every tenth man or large proportion of anything; *n* **decimation.**

decipher *v* 1 decode 2 make out meaning of; *a* **-able.**

decision *n* 1 conclusion 2 ability to decide *a* decisive; *adv* **-ly;** *n* **-ness.**

decisive *a* 1 determining 2 resolute; *a* decisively.

deck *n* 1 horizontal flooring of ship, bus, etc. 2 pack of cards; *v* 1 cover with deck 2 adorn; decorate.

deck chair *n* folding portable seat for reclining on a beach or patio.

declaim *v* speak or read as to an audience; *n* **declamation;** *a* **declamatory.**

declare *v* 1 state 2 announce formally 3 admit one's interest, liability; *n* **declaration.**

déclassé *a Fr* of inferior social class.

declination *n phys* deviation of compass from true north.

decline *v* 1 slope downward 2 deteriorate 3 refuse 4 give inflections of nouns, etc.; *n* gradual loss of vigor; wasting disease; *ns* **declination** deviation; **declension** act of declining; inflection of nouns, etc.

declivity *n* downward slope.

decoct *v* boil down, extract essence by boiling, *n* **decoction.**

decode *v* translate from cipher or code.

decoke *v aut coll* = **decarbonize.**

décolleté *a Fr* with a low neckline.

decolonize *v* make politically independent; *n* **-ization.**

decommission *v* take out of service or dismantle.

decompose *v* decay; break into constituent parts; *n* **decomposition** state of being decomposed.

decompress *v* reduce air pressure (on); *n* **-ion.**

decongestant *n, a* (medicant) relieving congestion, *e.g.,* of nose, chest.

decontaminate *v* free from contamination; *n* **-ation.**

decor *n Fr* decorative scheme of room, stage set, etc.

decorate *v* adorn by additions; paint, paper a room; invest with badge, medal, etc., showing honor to; *ns* **-ation; -ator** tradesman who paints and papers, rooms, etc.; *a* **-ative.**

decorous *a* seemly; sober; decent; *n* **decorum** propriety.

decortication *n* removal of outer covering, such as bark.

découpage *n* decoration of surfaces with illustrations and several coats of varnish.

decoy *v* lure into danger; *n* thing or person used as a lure or bait.

decrease *v* lessen; grow, make smaller; *n* lessening.

decree *n* decision; formal order; edict; *v* order, command by decree.

decree nisi *n leg Lat* provisional divorce order.

decrepit *a* old; feeble; tottery; *n* **decrepitude.**

decriminalize *v* declare no longer illegal; *n* **-ization.**

decry *v* **decrying, decried.** disparage, cry down.

dedicate *v* devote solemnly; inscribe (book, etc.) to a person; *n* **-ation.**

deduce *v* infer; draw as conclusion from given facts; *n* **deduction** conclusion reached; *a* **deductive** by a deduction.

deduct *v* subtract, take away; *n* **deduction** amount subtracted.

deed *n* **1** action; **2** legal document.

deejay *n* disc jockey, person who plays records.

deem *v* believe; consider; regard.

deep *a* **1** extending far down, in; of, at given depth **2** hard to fathom **3** engrossed (in study, etc.) **4** dark, rich (of color) **5** low-pitched (of sound, etc.) **6** cunning; *n* deep water, sea; *idm* **go off the deep end** *coll* react angrily; *idm* **(get) in (to) deep water** (get) in(to) difficulties; *idm* **thrown in at the deep end** *coll* presented with all possible problems from the start; *v* **deepen;** *ns* **-ness** quality of being deep; **depth** distance from surface; *as* **deep-rooted** firmly fixed; **deep-seated** not superficial; **deep-sixed (something)** discarded it.

deep-freeze *v* freeze (food) quickly to ensure longer preservation; *pt* **deep-froze;** *pp* **deep-frozen;** *n* freezer.

deep-fry *n* fry in deep pan of oil or fat.

deer *n* family of ruminants, with deciduous antlers; *pl* **deer;** *ns* **deerhound; deerstalker; 1** one who hunts deer **2** kind of hat.

deet *n* type of insect repellent.

deface *v* disfigure; mar; obliterate; *n* **-ment.**

de facto *a, adv Lat* in fact (whether legally or not).

defalcation *n* missapropriation of property, funds, etc.; embezzlement.

defame *v* speak evil of; *n* **-ation;** *a* **-atory.**

default *v leg* fail to appear; fail to pay, or act; *n* absence; deficiency; *n* **defaulter; in default of** in absence of.

defeat *v* conquer; frustrate; *n* conquest; frustration; *n* **defeatism** acceptance of defeat; pessimism; *a, n* **-ist.**

defecate *v* remove impurities; void excrement; *n* **defecation.**

defect *n* fault; blemish; shortcoming; *v* desert one's country, duty; *ns* **defector** one who defects; **defection;** *a* **defective** faulty; imperfect.

defend *v* guard; ward off attack; *leg* oppose, fight case; uphold; *ns* **defense; defender;** *a* **defensive** protecting; *n* attitude of defense; *a* **defensible** justified; *n* **-ibility.**

defenestrate *v* throw someone or something out of a window; *n* **-ation.**

defer *v* **-ferring, -ferred.** delay, put off; *n* **-ment.**

defer *v* **-ferring, -ferred.** yield to another's wishes; *n* **deference** respect, consideration for; *a* **deferential.**

defiant *see* **defy.**

deficiency *n* shortage; lack; *a* **deficient** lacking, incomplete in something; *n* **deficit** excess of liabilities over assets.

defile *v* pollute; corrupt; desecrate; *n* **defilement**.

defile *v* march in file; *n* narrow valley or pass.

define *v* 1 show clearly 2 fix limits of 3 state meaning; *as* **definable; definite** exact; clear; certain; **definitive** decisive; *n* **definition** exact description.

definite article *n* the word *the*.

deflate *v* 1 let out air, gas from 2 reduce inflated currency; *n* **-ation; -ationary**.

deflect *v* change course of; deviate; *ns* **deflection; deflector** device causing deflection.

deflower *v ar* deprive (maiden) of virginity.

deforest *v* clear land of trees; *n* **-ation**.

defoliant *n* chemical that destroys leaves; *v* **defoliate**; *n* **-action**.

deform *v* spoil shape, beauty of; disfigure; *ns* **-ation; -ity**.

defraud *v* cheat; swindle; deprive of lawful rights.

defray *v* bear cost of.

defrock *n* banish from priesthood.

defrost *v* remove frost or ice from; unfreeze.

deft *a* skillful; neat; competent; *n* **-ness**.

defunct *a* dead, deceased.

defuse *v* 1 remove fuse; render (bomb, etc.) harmless; 2 make (situation) less dangerous.

defy *v* **-fying, -fied.** challenge; resist; flout; disobey openly; *a*

defiant; insolently disobedient; *n* **defiance**.

degenerate *v* decline from higher to lower state or condition; *a* lower in quality; depraved; *n* degenerate person, thing; *ns* **-ation; degeneracy**.

degrade *v* reduce in rank, status, quality; debase; humiliate; *a* **degraded, degradable;** *n* **degradation** act of degrading; state of misery, squalor.

degree *n* 1 unit of measurement 2 grade in any series 3 extent of progress, skill 4 amount 5 university rank 6 station in life.

degustation *n* act of relishing food.

dehisce *v* split according to nature.

dehumanize *v* 1 make inhumane 2 make mechanical; *n* **-ization**.

dehumidity *v* decrease moisture in air, *usu* by machine.

dehydrate *v* remove water from; *n* **-ration**.

de-ice *v* free from ice; *n* **de-icer**.

deify *v* **-fying, -fied.** look on, worship as god; *n* **deification**.

deign *v* condescend to do; think fit.

deism *n* reasoned belief in God's existence; *n* **deist;** *a* **-istic**.

deity *n* a god or goddess, divinity.

déjà vu *n Fr* 1 sense that a new

event has been experienced before 2 *coll* sense of boredom with familiar situation.

deject *v* depress, dispirit; *a* **dejected;** *n* **dejection**.

de jure *a, adv Lat* by legal right.

delay *v* 1 retard 2 keep back 3 linger; *n* act of delaying; tardiness.

delectable *a* delightful, enjoyable; *n* **delectation** pleasure.

delegate *v* 1 send as representative. 2 entrust with duties, etc.; *n* representative; *ns* **-ation; delegacy** body of delegates.

delete *v* erase; remove; obliterate; *n* **deletion**.

deleterious *a* harmful, injurious.

deliberate *v* 1 discuss; 2 study closely; *a* 1 studied 2 intentional 3 unhurried; *n* **-ation** careful reflection on.

delicatessen *n* shop selling specially imported foods, (*e.g.*, cheese, cooked meats); *coll* **deli**.

delicate *a* 1 sensitive 2 pleasing 3 dainty 4 not robust; finely made 5 easily injured; *n* **delicacy** 1 fineness; refinement 2 weakness (of health) 3 tasty food.

delicious *a* agreable to sense, *esp* taste; delightful.

delight *n* great pleasure; *v* charm; give, take great pleasure; *a* **delighted** very pleased; *a* **delightful** pleasing; fascinating.

A B C D E F G H I J K L M N O P Q R S T U V W X Y Z

delimit v define limits; n **-ation**.

delineate v depict; describe; ns **-ator, -ation**.

delinquent n, a (person) committing illegal acts; n **delinquency**.

deliquesce v become liquid; a **-escent**; n **-escence**.

delirious a 1 subject to delirium 2 coll excited and happy; adv **-ly**; n **delirium** mental disturbance due to illness, esp fever causing wildness of speech.

delirium tremens, DTs n delirium caused by taking too much alcohol.

deliver v 1 set free; hand over 2 utter (sermon, etc.) 3 aim (blow, etc.) 4 assist at childbirth; ns **delivery; deliverer; deliverance** rescue.

dell n small wooded hollow.

delouse v rid of lice.

delphinium n genus of plants, including larkspur.

delta n 1 alluvial land at river mouth 2 Greek letter.

deltoid n shoulder muscle.

delude v deceive; mislead; n **delusion**; a **delusive**.

deluge v inundate; flood; overwhelm; n flood; torrent (of words, etc.); downpour.

deluxe a luxurious.

delve v dig; burrow; fig look deeply into.

demagnetize v deprive of magnetic power.

demagogue, demagog n political agitator.

demand v 1 require 2 ask as by right; n 1 urgent claim 2 need 3 call for specific commodity.

demarcation n boundary line; limit; distinction; v **demarcate**.

demean v behave; conduct oneself.

demean v demean oneself lower, degrade oneself; a **demeaning**.

demeanor n bearing; conduct.

demented a insane; crazy; wild; n **dementia** form of insanity.

demerit n fml fault; defect.

demesne n landed property; estate.

demi- prefix: forms compounds with meaning half, partial. Where the meaning may be deduced from the simple word, the compounds are not given here.

demigod n heroic character.

demijohn n large narrow-necked bottle with wicker covering.

demilitarize v free from military equipment; n **-ization**.

demimonde n any social group not considered to be wholly respectable.

demise v convey by lease; leave as legacy; n 1 conveyance by will, etc. 2 death.

demitasse n small coffee cup.

demo n trial product offered to attract buyers; v **demo**.

demobilize v disband, discharge forces; n **-ization**.

democracy n rule by the people; state so governed; a **-cratic**; n **-crat** supporter of democracy.

démodé a Fr out of style.

demographic a statistics on population; adv **demographically**; n **demography**; adv **demographically**; n **demography**.

demolish v pull down; destroy; break up; n **demolition**.

demon n 1 devil; evil spirit 2 wicked, cruel person; as **demonaic** possessed by demon; **demonic** inspired by demon.

demonetize v deprive currency of value; n **-ization**.

demonstrate v prove by reasoning; show by example; show feelings; as **demonstrable** proved; **-ative** conclusive; showing clearly; ns **-ation** 1 proof 2 exhibition of method 3 expression of force, public feeling; **-ator** one who demonstrates.

demoralize v lower morale of; dishearten, discourage; n **-ization**.

demote v reduce in order, rank, etc.; n **demotion**.

demotic a of the ordinary people; in popular use.

demur v hesitate; raise objections to.

demure a modest; affecting coyness, gravity.

den n lair of wild animals; cage; small room, study.

denationalize *v* remove from state control; *n* **-ization**.

denature *v* alter natural quality of; adulterate.

dendrite *n* branching formation.

dendrogram *n* diagram showing groups with similar characteristics.

denial *n* negation; refusal.

denier *n* **1** unit of weight showing fineness of silk **2** nylon yarn.

denigrate *v* sneer at; defame; *n* **-ation**.

denim *n* coarse cotton, cloth.

denizen *n* inhabitant.

denominate *v* name; designate; *ns* **-ation** name of particular class, religion, etc.; **-ator** divisor in fractions.

denote *v* mark, indicate by sign, symbol; mean.

denouement *n Fr* final situation (in play, book, etc.); climax.

denounce *v* accuse publicly; repudiate (treaty); *n* **denunciation;** *a* **denunciatory**.

dense *a* crowded; thick; compact; *fig* stupid; *ns* **-ness, density,** specific gravity; *fig* stupidity.

dent *n* slight hollow made by blow, etc.; *v* make, mark with dent.

dental *a* pertaining to teeth or dentistry; *a* **dentate** toothed.

dental floss *n* soft thread for cleaning teeth.

dental hygienist *n* person trained to check and clean teeth.

dentifrice *n fml* toothpaste or powder.

dentine, dentin *n* hard substance of tooth beneath enamel coat.

dentist *n* surgeon who cares for teeth; **dentistry** art of dentist; **dentition** teething; **denture(s)** set of false teeth.

denude *v* make bare; strip; *n* **-ation** erosion of soil by natural forces.

denunciation *n* denouncing; being denounced.

deny *v* declare untrue; refuse (request); disown; abstain from; *n* **denial**.

deodorize *v* remove smell from; *ns* **ization; -izer; deodorant**.

deontology *n* branch of ethics dealing with moral duty; *a* **-ological;** *n* **-ologist**.

Deo volente *interj Lat* God willing.

deoxidize *v* remove oxygen from; *n* **-ization**.

depart *v* go away; leave; die; deviate; *ns* **-ment** branch; part; division; **department store** large shop selling variety of goods; *a* **departmental;** *n* **departure** starting out; leaving.

depend *v* **1** hang **2** rely on **3** be contingent on; *a* **dependable** reliable; *ns* **dependent** person relying on another for support; *a* **dependent;** *ns* **dependence; dependency** subordinate territory.

depict *v* describe verbally; represent pictorially.

depilatory *n* substance able to remove hair; *n* **depilation** act of removing hair.

deplete *v* empty out; exhaust; *n* **depletion**.

deplore *v* **1** lament **2** regret **3** disapprove; *a* **deplorable** lamentable; disastrous.

deploy *v* extend; open out (troops, etc.); *n* **deployment**.

deponent *n* one who makes statement on oath; *v* **depone**.

depopulate *v* drive out, destroy population; *n* **depopulation** decline in population.

deport *v* **1** banish **2** expel **3** behave oneself; *ns* **deportee** person deported; **deportation** expulsion from state; **deportment** carriage, behavior.

depose *v* **1** remove from office **2** dethrone **3** testify; *n* **deposition**.

deposit *v* **1** entrust for safekeeping **2** leave (as sediment) **3** set down; *n* **1** sediment **2** money deposited at bank or given as pledge of good faith; *ns* **depositor; depository** place where things are deposited; storehouse.

depot *n* storehouse; regimental headquarters; bus garage; train storage yard.

deprave *v* pervert; corrupt; *n* **depravity** viciousness; moral corruption.

deprecate *v* express disapproval of; *a* **deprecative; -atory;** *n* **-cation**.

A
B
C
D
E
F
G
H
I
J
K
L
M
N
O
P
Q
R
S
T
U
V
W
X
Y
Z

depreciate v 1 lower value of 2 fig disparage 3 lose quality (by wear); n **-ation** reduction in value (by wear and tear); allowance made for this in valuations; a **-atory**.

depredation n plundering; laying waste; n **depredator** one who robs, despoils.

depress n press down; make dejected; weaken; n **depression** 1 concavity 2 despondence 3 low atmospheric pressure 4 slump in trade; a, n **depressant** sedative.

deprive v take away from; dispossess; n **deprivation**.

depth n **depths** degree of deepness; idm **in/out of one's depth** 1 able/unable to touch bottom with head above water 2 able/unable to cope or understand; deepest part or feeling.

depute v appoint as agent, substitute; delegate; ns **deputy** substitute, delegate; **deputation** body of persons acting as deputies; v **deputize** act for another.

derail v leave or cause to leave rails; n **-ment**.

derange v upset; disturb; drive mad; n **-ment** mental disorder.

derby ns 1 annual horse race 2 sport important contest, esp between local teams 3 man's hat with round crown and narrow brim.

deregulate v free from legal control; n **-ation**.

derelict a deserted; worthless; neglected; n thing forsaken; esp ship; n **dereliction** neglect of duty.

deride v mock at; ridicule; n **derision;** a **derisive;** adv **-ly;** a **derisory** mocking, ironical.

de rigueur a required by custom or fashion.

derive v get from; trace origin of; spring from; ns **derivation; derivative;** a **derivative**.

derm, derma n inner layer of skin; as **dermal;** ns **dermatitis** inflammation of skin; **dermatology** study of skin and its diseases; **-ologist**.

dermis n anat layer of skin below surface.

derogate v detract (from); disparage; n **derogation;** a **derogatory** disparaging, taking away merit.

derrick n crane, stationary or movable; latticed tower over oil well.

derring-do n ar heroic deeds.

derringer n short, large-caliber pistol.

dervish n Muslim monk vowed to poverty.

desalinate v remove salt from; n **-ation;** n **desalination plant**.

descale v remove scales from.

descant n song accompanying plainsong; talk at length.

descend v 1 move, come down 2 stoop 3 lower oneself 4 be derived 5 pass by

inheritance; **descend** idm **descended from** have as ancestor(s); n **descendant;** phr v **descend on/upon** 1 visit unexpectedly 2 attack without warning; ns **descendant** offspring.

descent n 1 downward movement 2 downward slope 3 ancestry; family origins.

describe v give account of; depict in words; mark out, trace form or line of; a **descriptive;** n **description** account; kind, species.

descry v **-crying, -cried.** make out; discern.

desecrate v profane; ns **-ation, -ator**.

desegregate v abolish racial segregation in; n **-ation**.

desert v forsake; abandon; mil abscond from service; ns **deserter, desertion**.

desert n barren, uninhabited tract; a uninhabited, lonely.

deserts n pl what is deserved.

deserve v be worthy of; merit; a **deserved;** adv **-ly;** a **deserving** worthy of.

deshabille n partial undress.

desiccate v dry completely; a **desiccated;** n **-ation**.

desideratum n acknowledged want.

design v 1 plan out; intend 2 make, invent, pattern; n 1 purpose, intention 2 decorative pattern; pl **designs;** idm **have designs on** be planning to get or win by unscrupulous means; n **designer** one who makes artistic designs; a **1** made by a notable designer **2** *coll* appearing fashionable; a **designing** artful, scheming.

designate *v* indicate; nominate for office; specify; a nominated but not installed; *n* **-ation** distinctive name.

desire long for; yearn for; request; *n* strong longing; wish, hope; something desired; a **desirable** worth having; *n* **desirability;** a **desirous** wishful.

desist *v* stop, cease.

desk *n* table or other piece of furniture used for reading or writing on.

desktop publishing *n* design and production of publications using a computer.

desolate a waste, dismal; forsaken; lonely, forlorn; *v* lay waste; make lonely, sad.

despair *v* lose hope; *n* hopelessness.

desperado *n dated* dangerous criminal; adventurer; violent ruffian.

desperate a beyond hope; driven to extremity; frantic; *ns* **desperation.**

despise *v* look down on; feel contempt; a **despicable** contemptible; *adv* **-ably** mean.

despite *n* spite; hatred; malice; *prep* in spite of.

despoil *v* plunder; strip of; *n* **despoliation.**

despond *v* lose hope, courage; be dejected; a **despondent;** *n*

despondency.

despot *n* tyrant, oppressor; *n* **despotism** tyranny; a **-ic.**

dessert *n* fruit, sweet served at end of meal.

dessert spoon *n* medium-sized spoon.

destination *n* place where someone or something is going, being sent.

destine *v* determine future of; intend; *n* **destiny** preordained fate.

destined a **1** fated **2** intended.

destitute a extremely poor; lacking; penniless; *n* **destitution.**

destroy *v* ruin; demolish; *n* **destroyer** one that destroys; type of fast warship; *as* **destructible; destructive** ruinous; mischievous; *n* **destruction.**

desultory a rambling; aimless; disconnected.

detach *v* unfasten; disconnect; a **-ed;** separate; impartial; aloof; *n* **-ment 1** separation **2** unconcern **3** number of troops, etc., detached for special duty; a **-able.**

detail *v* deal with item by item; select for duty; *n* small part; item.

detain *v* hinder; withold; retain in custody; *n* **detention** forced delay; keeping in custody.

detainee *n* person detained, *esp* by police.

detect *v* discover; find out; *ns* **detection; detective** police investigator of crime;

detector one who detects; *rad* frequency changer.

détente *n Fr* reduction of international political tension.

detention *n* being kept in a place against will, *esp.* as a pupil in school.

deter *v* **-terring, terred.** hinder; discourage; a, *n* **deterrent.**

detergent a cleansing; *n* cleansing, purifying substance.

deteriorate *v* become worse; depreciate; *n* **-ation.**

determine *v* decide; resolve; set limit to, fix; *as* **determined** resolute; **determinate** fixed; *n* **-ation** resolution.

determinant *n* that which decides or controls result.

determiner *n ling* word that identifies a noun and stands before other adjectives (*e.g.*, *the, this, that*); **determinism** *n* belief that all is decided in life and cannot be changed; *n* **determinist;** a **-istic.**

deterrent *n, a* (thing) that deters.

detest *v* hate, abhor, loathe; a **-able;** *n* **-ation.**

dethrone *v* remove from throne, depose; *n* **-ment.**

detonate *v* explode (bomb, etc.) *ns* **-ator; -ation,** violent explosion.

detour *n* going around; alternative route.

detoxify *v* remove poison from (*also* **detoxificate**); *n* **detoxification.**

detract (from) *v* take away

a
b
c
d
e
f
g
h
i
j
k
l
m
n
o
p
q
r
s
t
u
v
w
x
y
z

from; disparage; n **detraction.**

detrain v get down, alight from train.

detriment n harm; loss; injury; a **-al** damaging.

detritus n rock debris; n **detrition** wearing down by friction.

deuce n 1 die or playing card with two spots 2 score 40-all, in tennis; a **deuced** excessive.

deus ex machina n Lat person whose sudden intervention solves an otherwise insoluble problem.

Deutschmark n main unit of German currency.

devaluate v reduce in value; v devalue; n devaluation.

devalue v reduce in value, esp currency; n **devaluation.**

devastate v lay waste; make desolate; n **-ation.**

develop v grow; unfold; elaborate; cause to appear, esp image on photographic plate; exploit building site; ns **-er; -ment.**

developing country n poor country trying to improve economy and living conditions.

development a **developmental** involved in development; adv **-ly.**

deviance n change from normality a, n **deviant** (person) showing deviance.

deviate v turn aside; diverge; ns **-ator; -ation;** a **devious** rambling; crooked; fig shifty.

device n 1 tool or gadget 2 trick 3 lit special use of

words 4 her emblem; pl idm **leave one to his/her own devices** let someone solve a problem in his/her own way.

devil n spirit of evil, Satan; wicked, evil person; a **devilish** sl very bad; ns **devilry** cruel behavior; **devilment** mischievous prank.

devilfish n large ray or octopus.

devil-may-care a reckless.

devil's advocate n person challenging a proposal or idea simply in order to test its validity.

devil's food cake n chocolate cake usu two layered.

devious a 1 not direct 2 cunningly dishonest; n **-ness.**

devise v 1 invent; contrive; plan 2 leave by will.

devitalize v remove the vitality of; n **devitalization.**

devoid (of) a lacking, without.

devolution n transfer of power to others.

devolve v transfer; delegate; phr v **devolve (up)on** fall upon; leg pass by succession.

devote v set apart, dedicate; addict oneself to; a **devotee** one fervidly devoted; **devotion** strong affection; adherence; pl religious observances; a **devotional.**

devoted a 1 zealous 2 dedicated.

devour v eat voraciously; consume; fig read eagerly, absorb; n **devourer.**

devout a pious; devoted, earnest.

dew n condensed moisture from air, falling on ground; v wet with, or as dew; n **dewiness;** a **dewy;** n **dewpond** ancient artificial pond.

dexterity n adroitness, manual and mental; deftness; manual skill; a **dexterous,** also **dextrous** skillful; quick; a **dexter** on right-hand side; her on spectator's left.

dextrose n starch sugar, glucose.

di- prefix 1 double 2 composed of two atoms.

dia- prefix forms compounds with meaning through, across, apart. Where the meaning may be deduced from the simple word, the compounds are not given here.

diabetes n disease characterised by excess sugar in urine; a, n **diabetic.**

diabolic(al) a devilish, fiendish; sl very bad, unpleasant.

diaconal a of a deacon(ess).

diacritic a distinctive; n mark showing phonetic value.

diadem n fillet, crown.

diagnose v identify disease from symptoms; n **diagnosis;** a **diagnostic.**

diagonal a oblique; n line from corner to corner; adv **-ly.**

diagram n plan, chart; geometric illustration of theorem; a **diagrammatic;** adv **-ally.**

dial *n* **1** face of clock
2 graduated face of gauge,
meter, compass, etc. **3** disk
on automatic telephone; *v*
use telephone.
dialect *n* regional form of
language.
dialectics *n pl* art of logical
discussion and disputation.
dialogue *n* conversation; its
representation in writing, in
drama, books, etc.
dialysis *n med* process for
purifying blood.
diamanté *n, a* (material)
studded with tiny sparkling
stones.
diameter *n* straight line
passing from side to side,
through center of solid or
geometric figure; length of
such line; unit of magnifying
power of lenses; *a*
diametrical opposite;
adv **-ally**.
diamond *n* **1** hard, brilliant,
precious stone of crystalized
carbon **2** suit of cards
3 rhombus; *a* made of, set
with diamonds.
diamond jubilee *n* 60th
anniversary celebration.
diamond wedding *n* 60th
anniversary of marriage.
dianthus *n* genus of plants,
including pinks, etc.
diapason *n* **1** range, compass of
voice, instrument **2** organ
stop.
diaper *n* **1** linen cloth woven
with diamond pattern
2 baby's underpants, often
disposable.

diaphanous *a* transparent,
translucent.
diaphragm *n* **1** muscular wall
between thorax and
abdomen **2** device
controlling transmission of
light, sound, etc. **3** vibrating
disk producing sound waves
4 contraceptive device for
women.
diarrhea *n* excessive, irritable
laxity of bowels.
diary *n* daily record, *esp* of
personal events or thoughts;
book used for keeping such
record; *n* **diarist**.
diaspora *n* exile and dispersal
of Jews to other countries.
diastole *n* dilation of heart
muscle.
diathermy *n* electromedical
treatment with high-
frequency current.
diatonic *a mus* using regular
major or minor scales.
diatribe *n* vituperative attack;
abusive criticism.
dibber, dibble *n* pointed tool
for making holes in ground,
for seeds or plants; *v* **dibble**
use a dibble.
dibs *n sl* claim, as in **(have)
dibs (on something)**.
dice *n pl* (*sing* **die**) **1** cubes
marked on each side (1-6
spots), used in game of
chance **2** small cubes of
meat, vegetables, etc.; *v* **1** to
gamble with dice **2** cut into
small cubes.
dicey *a* not sure about
outcome.
dichotomy *n* division into two

parts; *v* **dichotomize**.
dickens *idm* **catch the dickens**
coll get into trouble.
dicker *v* haggle, bargain,
chaffer.
dickey *n* false shirtfront.
Dictaphone [TM] small
recording machine for
dictating messages.
dictate *v* **1** speak or read aloud
for another to transcribe
2 command **3** prescribe;
impose arbitrarily; *n* order,
command; *ns* **dictation;**
dictator despot, absolute
ruler; **dictatorship;** *a*
dictatorial overbearing,
imperious.
diction *n* choice and use of
word.
dictionary *n* book listing words
alphabetically, with their
meanings, etc.; reference
books with details of subject
arranged alphabetically.
dictum *n* formal statement;
maxim; *pl* **dicta**.
didactic *a* intended to instruct;
dictatorial.
diddle *v* cheat, swindle.
didgeridoo *n* Australian wind
instrument of bamboo.
didn't *contracted form of* did not.
die[1] *v* **dying, died.** expire; cease;
grow weaker; wither; *idm* **be
dying for/to** want urgently;
idm **die hard** resist change;
take long to disappear; *phr vs*
die away fade until no longer
noticeable; **die down** subside;
die off die one by one; **die out**
become extinct; *n* **diehard** one
who resists change to the end.

die[2] *idm* **the die is cast** an irreversible decision has been made.

dieresis *n* sign (¨) placed over second vowel of two, to indicate separate pronunciation.

diesel *a* of oil-burning internal-combustion engine.

diet[1] *n* usual food; planned feeding, for medical reasons; *v* follow prescribed diet, *esp* to lose weight; *a* **dietary**; *n pl* **dietetics** science of diet; *n* **dietitian, dietician** expert in nutrition and dietary requirements.

diet[2] *n* international or parliamentary assembly, conference.

differ *v* disagree; be unlike; quarrel; *n* **difference** disagreement; dissimilarity; remainder left after subtraction; *a* **different** unlike; separate, distinct; *a* **differential** relating to, showing difference in outward circumstances; *n math* having small quantitative differences; **d. gear** one enabling rear wheels to revolve at different speeds, when cornering; *v* **differentiate** discriminate; become different.

differential calculus *n* branch of mathematics concerned with rates of change, etc.

difficult *a* not easy; needing great physical or mental effort; hard to please; *n* **difficulty** obstacle;

objection; *pl* **difficulties** in trouble, *esp* financial.

diffident *a* shy; self-effacing; timid; *n* **diffidence**.

diffract *v* break up light into bands of color or dark and light; *n* **diffraction**.

diffuse *v* scatter, spread around; radiate; *a* **1** not localized **2** verbose; *ns* **diffusion;** act of diffusing; dissemination; **diffuser;** *a* **diffusive** tending to diffuse.

dig *v* digging, dug. **1** turn over and break up (earth) **2** make hole (in earth, sand, etc.) **3** *coll* understand **4** prod; *idm* **dig into one's pocket(s)** provide money reluctantly; *phr vs* **dig in 1** settle securely into a place or activity **2** *coll* begin eating; **dig up 1** unearth **2** reveal **3** invent; *n* **dig 1** act of digging **2** prod **3** gibe; *idm* **get a dig (in) at** tease or criticize.

digest *v* **1** convert food in digestive tract for assimilation into blood **2** summarize, condense **3** absorb mentally; *n* classified summary; magazine containing condensed versions of books, etc.; *as* **digestive; digestible;** *n* **digestion**.

digit *n* **1** any figure 1 to 9 **2** finger or toe; *a* **digital** numerical; *adv* **-ly**; *v* **digitalize** express in digital form.

digital computer *n* computer with data stored in digital

form through electronic circuits.

digital piano *n* keyboard instrument with sound produced artificially by digital electronic means.

digital recording *n* recording made by converting sound into electrical pulses using binary digits.

digitalis *n* genus of plants including foxglove; drug made from foxglove.

dignify *v* do honor to; exalt; ennoble; *n* **dignity** stateliness; serenity; high office, rank; *a* **dignified** stately; serene; *n* **dignitary** holder of high office, *esp* in church.

digoxin *n* poisonous steroid made from foxglove.

digress *v* depart from main subject *esp* in talking, writing, etc.; wander, ramble; *n* **-ion**.

dihedral *a* having two plane faces.

dike *n* ditch; embankment or causeway to prevent flooding.

diktat *n* unreasonable command.

dilapidate *v* fall or allow to fall into disrepair; deteriorate; *a* **dilapidated** fallen into disrepair; (of persons) shabby, down-at-heel; *n* **-ation**.

dilate *v* expand; swell; write, speak at length; *n* **dil(at)ation**.

dilatory *a* causing delay; slow; belated; *n* **dilatoriness**.

dilemma *n* choice of evils; quandary.

dilettante *n It* one with

superficial knowledge of fine arts; *a* unprofessional.

diligent *a* painstaking; industrious; *n* **diligence.**

dill *n* herb of carrot family, used medicinally and for flavoring.

dillydally *v coll* delay.

dilute *v* weaken, thin down fluid by adding another fluid; *a* **diluted;** *n, a* **diluent;** *n* **dilution.**

diluvium *n* deposit left flood or glacier; *as* **diluvial; diluvian.**

dim *a* **dimmer, dimmest. 1** faint; not bright **2** unintelligent; *adv* **-ly;** *n* **-ness;** *v* **dimming, dimmed.** make or become dim *idm* **take a dim view** disapprove.

dime *n* ten-cent coin.

dimension *n* length, breadth, thickness; extent; size; *algebra* number of factors in a term; *a* **dimensional.**

diminish *v* lessen; reduce; *n* **diminution;** *a* **diminutive** tiny.

diminished responsibility *n leg* mental state where one cannot be held fully responsible for actions.

diminishing returns *n* state where more effort or investment leads to reduction in profits.

diminuendo *n mus* gradual decrease in loudness.

diminutive *a* small; familiar.

dimity *n* corded cotton fabric.

dimmer *n* device to vary brightness of light (*also* **d. switch**).

dimple *n* small depression in surface of skin, *esp* of cheek; *v* make dimples.

dimwit *n coll* stupid person; *a* **dimwitted.**

din *n* loud continuous noise; clamour; *v* **dinning, dinned.** make din.

dine *v* take, give dinner to; *phr vs* **dine out** eat away from home; *ns* **dining room; dinette** small dining area near kitchen; **diner** one who dines; dining-car on train; **diner** *n* **1** person dining **2** dining car **3** informal eating establishment.

ding *v* make ringing sound; *n* **dingdong 1** sound of bell **2** *coll* equally balanced, hard-fought fight.

dinghy *n* small boat (*usu* with sails).

dingle *n* dell; small valley.

dingo *n* Australian wild dog.

dingy *a* dull; dirty; shabby; *ns* **dinginess; dinge.**

dining car *n* railroad car with meals served by waiters.

dinky *a coll* small and insignificant.

dinner *n* main meal of the day, eaten in the middle of the day or in the evening.

dinosaur *n* gigantic, extinct reptile.

dint *n* dent, mark; **by dint of** by force of.

diocese *n* district under jurisdiction of bishop; *a* **diocesan.**

diode *n elec* semiconductor coverting alternating to

direct current.

dioxide *n* oxide having two parts of oxygen to one of metal.

dip *v* **dipping, dipped.** put, plunge quickly into liquid; lower and raise rapidly; sink, drop suddenly; *geol* slope down; *v phr v* **dip into** glance at briefly; *n* act of dipping; hollow; *n* **dipper** ladle, etc.; kind of bird.

diphtheria *n* serious, infectious disease of throat.

diphthong *n* two vowel sounds pronounced as one syllable.

diploma *n* document attesting holder's proficiency; one granting honor, privilege; state documents.

diplomacy *n* art of management of international relations; tactful skill in dealing with people, situations, etc.; *n* **diplomat** professional employed in diplomacy; **-matist** tactful person; *a* **-matic;** *adv* **-ally.**

dipolar *a* having two poles; *n* **dipole** type of aerial.

dipsomania *n* morbid and irresistible craving for alcohol.

dipstick *n* marked rod for measuring level of liquid.

dire *a* dreadful; terrible.

direct *v* **1** guide; control **2** address (letter) **3** show way **4** focus (aim) **5** order with authority; *a* straight; frank; without intermediary; *n* **direction 1** guiding **2** command **3** course taken by

moving object; *pls* instruction; *ns* **-ness;**
director one who controls; member of board managing company; **directorate** board of directors; **directory** book listing names and addresses, telephone numbers, etc.

direct deposit *n comm* system of regular payments, often from an employer transferring money directly into a bank account.

direct mail *n* publicity material sent to many people.

directive *n* official order.

direct object *n ling* noun, noun phrase, pronoun, or noun clause following a transitive verb.

direct speech *n* actual words spoken.

dirge *n* lament for dead; mournful song.

dirigible *n* airship capable of being steered; *a* steerable.

dirk *n* short dagger.

dirndl *n* **1** Austrian peasant dress with close bodice and full gathered skirt **2** skirt of this type.

dirt *n* **1** earth; soil **2** filth; grime **3** excrement **4** *coll* obscenity **5** *coll* malicious gossip; *idm* **eat dirt** *coll* accept insults without protest; *idm* **dirt cheap** *coll* very cheap; *a* **dirty 1** not clean **2** causing dirt **3** foul; obscene; indecent **4** unfair **5** (of weather) rough **6** (of color) dingy; *adv* **dirtily** *n* **dirtiness;** *idm* **dirty old man**

coll older man taking unhealthy interest in sex, *esp* in adolescent girls; **dirt track** *n* rough cinder track for motorcycle races.

dirty work *n* **1** unpleasant manual work **2** *coll* illegal or dishonest activity; *idm* **do someone's dirty work** consent to act immorally, illegally on somone else's orders.

dis- *prefix expressing* separation; negation *or* reversal; deprivation; *e.g.,* **disable** make unfit; **disorder** lack of order; **dispossess** deprive of possession. *Where the meaning may be deduced from the simple word, the compounds are not given here.*

disability *n* handicap; incapacity.

disabuse *v* undeceive, free from illusion.

disadvantage *n* unfavorable condition or situation; *as* **disadvantaged; disadvantageous.**

disaffection *n* disloyalty; *a* **disaffected** discontented, seditious.

disaffiliate *a* sever links with; *n* **-ation.**

disagree *v* differ; quarrel; *phr v* **disagree with** (of health) not to suit; *n* **-ment** difference of opinion, dispute; *a* **-able** bad tempered; distasteful; *adv* **-ably.**

disallow *v* refuse to sanction; prohibit.

disappear *v* vanish; *n*

disappearance.

disappoint *v* fail to fulfill the desires or hopes of; *n* **-ment;** *as* **disappointed** (*adv* **-ly**); **disappointing** (*adv* **-ly**).

disapprove (of) *v* show, express unfavorable attitude (to); *a* **disapproving;** *n* disapproval.

disarm *v* deprive of weapons; conciliate; reduce armaments; *n* **disarmament.**

disarrange *v* make untidy.

disarray *v* throw into confusion; disturb.

disaster *n* sudden great misfortune; calamity; *a* **disastrous.**

disavow *v* repudiate; deny belief in; *n* **disavowel.**

disband *v* scatter, disperse; break up (organized body, etc.).

disbar *v* expel from law practice.

disbelief *n* lack of belief; *v* **disbelieve;** *a* disbelieving.

disburse *v* give, pay out, spend money; *n* **disbursement.**

disc *n* cushion of cartilage between vertebrae in spinal column.

discard *v* throw aside as valueless; reject; cast off.

discern *v* make out; distinguish (by senses or with mind); *as* **discerning,** shrewd; discriminating; **discernible** that can be clearly seen; *n* **discernment,** insight; keen judgment.

discharge *v* **1** fire (gun, etc.) **2** emit **3** unload (ship) **4** dismiss **5** release; *n* **1** act of discharging **2** release

3 matter discharged or emitted 4 payment.

disciple n follower, one who learns from another, *esp* one of the twelve Apostles.

discipline n systematic training in obedience, self-control, and orderliness; maintenance of order and control; v control; train mentally, morally, physically; n **disciplinarian** one who enforces strict discipline; a **disciplinary**.

disclaim v repudiate, disown; n **disclaimer**; *leg* renunciation of right, title, etc.

disclose v reveal, bring to light; make known; n **disclosure**, revelation.

disco n 1 party with dancing to recorded pop music 2 club or place where disco dancing occurs 3 type of music for this dancing (*also* **disco music**).

discography n list of recordings on disk.

discolor v alter, change color of; stain; n **discoloration**.

discombobulate v *coll* confuse; a **-d**.

discomfit v disconcert; defeat; n **discomfiture**.

discomfort n 1 lack of comfort 2 embarrassment.

discompose v disturb calmness of, agitate; n **discomposure**.

disconcert v discompose, embarrass.

disconnect v 1 detach 2 deprive of service (*e.g.*, telephone); a **-ed**

1 detached 2 incoherent; n **disconnection**.

disconsolate a forlorn; sad; unhappy.

discord n 1 disagreement; strife 2 harsh sound; a **-ant**; n **-ance**.

discotheque n *Fr* disco.

discount n sum deducted from debt, for prompt or cash settlement; v 1 pay or receive money in advance in payment (for bill of exchange, etc., not yet due) 2 depreciate 3 allow for exaggeration.

discountenance v disapprove; discourage.

discourage v dishearten; advise against; try to prevent; n **-ment**.

discourse n speech; lecture; conversation; v lecture; preach; converse.

discourteous a impolite; *adv* **-ly**.

discover v find out, *esp* something unknown before; ns **discovery**; **discoverer**.

discredit v 1 spoil the good reputation of 2 create doubts about 3 not believe; a **-able** shameful; *adv* **-ably**.

discreet a careful, prudent, circumspect; ns **-ness**.

discrepancy n inconsistency; contradiction; a **discrepant**.

discrete a clearly separate.

discretion n 1 tact 2 ability to judge well; *idm* **at someone's discretion** according to someone's own decision; *idm* **the age/years of discretion**

maturity; a **discretionary** allowing freedom of decision.

discriminate v make a distinction; *idm* **discriminate against/in favor of someone** treat someone worse/better than other people; *as* **discriminating** showing good judgment; **discriminatory** discriminating against; n **discrimination**.

discursive a dealing with wide range of subjects; rambling.

discus n heavy disk thrown in contest of strength.

discuss v debate fully; argue in detail; n **discussion**.

disdain v treat with contempt, scorn; n scorn; aloofness; a **disdainful**.

disease n illness; ailment; a **diseased** suffering from or impaired by disease.

disembark v go, put ashore from ship; n **-ation**.

disembodied a not seeming to belong to a body.

disembody v free from the body.

disembroil v free from entanglement.

disenchant v disillusion; n **-ment**.

disengage v release, set free; a **disengaged** free, at leisure.

disestablish v deprive of established status; n **-ment**.

disfavor n *idm* **fall into disfavor** go out of favor.

disfigure v mar; render unsightly; ns **-ment** defect; blemish; **disfiguration**.

disfranchise v deprive of rights

of citizenship, of right to vote.

disgorge *v* give up; eject from throat.

disgrace *v* bring shame on; dismiss from favor; *n* shame, disrepute; dishonor; *a* **-ful** shameful.

disgruntled *a* displeased; sulky; in bad temper.

disguise *v* change appearance of; conceal identity of; *n* deceptive appearance; misrepresentation.

disgust *n* strong aversion; repugnance; *v* fill with loathing; nauseate; *a* **-ing** repulsive, sickening.

dish *n* shallow vessel with rim, for holding, cooking food; contents of dish; *v* 1 serve in dish 2 *sl* upset, spoil; *idm* **dish out** *coll* give away lavishly; *idm* **dish it out** *sl* attack with words or blows; *phr v* **dish up** *coll* 1 serve up (food) 2 concoct (ideas, etc).

dishcloth *n* cloth used for washing dishes, wiping tables and kitchen surfaces.

dishearten *v* make despondent, depress; *a* **-ing**.

disheveled *a* (of hair) ruffled, untidy; unkempt in appearance.

dishonest *n* not honest; deceitful; *adv* **-ly;** *n* **dishonesty.**

dishonor *n* disgrace; *v* 1 bring disgrace to 2 (of bank) refuse to cash check; *a* **-able;** *adv* **-ably.**

dishwasher *n* person or machine that washes dishes.

dishwater *n* water left from washing dishes.

disillusion *v* make aware of unpleasant truth; *as* **disillusioned, disillusioning;** *n* **-ment.**

disincentive *n* thing that discourages.

disinclined *a* rather unwilling.

disinfect *v* destroy infection; remove harmful germs, etc.; *n* **-ant** substance that disinfects.

disinfest *v* rid of vermin, bugs, etc.

disinformation *n* false information deliberately given to mislead.

disingenuous *a* *fml* pretending to know very little; *adv* **-ly.**

disinherit *v* deprive of right to inherit.

disintegrate *v* split up, resolve into parts, elements; fall to pieces; *n* **-ation.**

disinterested *a* without selfish motives; impartial.

disinvestment *n* selling of investments.

disjoint *v* dismember; separate at joints; *a* **disjointed** dismembered; (of speech, thought) incoherent; disconnected.

disk *n* 1 *comput* disk carrying data 2 round thin object 3 phonograph record; **disk jockey** *sl* radio announcer of program of recorded popular music.

disk drive *n* *comput* device for transferring data between disk and computer memory.

diskette *n* *comput* small disk.

dislocate *v* put out of joint; displace; *fig* disorganize; confuse; *n* **-ation.**

dislodge *v* remove from resting-place; drive out (enemy); *n* **-ment.**

disloyal *a* not loyal; *adv* **-ly;** *n* **disloyalty.**

dismal *a* depressing; gloomy, cheerless.

dismantle *v* strip of equipment, furnishings, etc.; remove (defenses); *n* **dismantling.**

dismay *v* alarm, frighten; *n* apprehension, consternation.

dismember *v* tear limb from limb; divide up; *n* **-ment.**

dismiss *v* 1 send away 2 expel from office 3 banish from mind 4 *leg* reject (case); *n* **dismissal;** *a* **dismissive;** *adv* **-ly.**

dismount *v* 1 get or throw down from saddle 2 remove from mounting.

disobedient *a* not obedient; *adv* **-ly;** *n* **disobedience;** *v* **disobey.**

disoblige *v* refuse to cooperate; *a* disobliging.

disorder *n* lack of order; *a* **-ly** 1 untidy 2 lacking self-control; *n* **-liness.**

disorient *v* take away sense of direction; *n* **-ation.**

disown *v* refuse to acknowledge.

disparage *v* belittle; throw doubt upon; *n* **-ment;** *a* **disparaging;** *adv* **-ly.**

disparate *a* essentially different; unequal; *n* **disparity** inequality; incongruity.

dispassionate *a* calm; unbiased.

dispatch *v* 1 send off 2 kill 3 finish off speedily; *n* 1 sending off 2 official report, message 3 speed.

dispel *v* -**pelling, -pelled.** drive away; cause to vanish.

dispense *v* 1 give out 2 make up medicine 3 grant exemption (from rule, etc.); *phr v* **dispense with** do without; *ns* **dispenser; dispensary** place where medicine is made up; **dispensation** divine decree; *eccles* relaxation of law; *a* **dispensable.**

disperse *v* drive away; scatter; *a* **dispersed;** *ns* **dispersion; dispersal.**

dispirit *v* deject, cast down; discourage; *a* **dispirited.**

displace *v* move out of place; oust; *a* **displaced** out of place; *n* -**ment** displacing; volume of liquid or gas displaced by solid in it.

displaced person *n* refugee.

display *v* show; exhibit; make obvious; *n* parade; showing off; exhibition.

displease *v* annoy; offend; cause dissatisfaction; *n* **displeasure;** anger, indignation.

disposable *a* 1 available 2 to be used once and discarded; *n* article of this kind.

dispose *v* 1 arrange 2 make willing 3 adjust 4 determine; *phr vs* **dispose of** 1 get rid of 2 deal with; **dispose**

someone to make someone willing to; *n* **disposal** removal; *idm* **at one's disposal** available to one for use or for help; *n* **disposition** plan; temperament; ordering.

dispossess *v* deprive of property; *a* -**ed;** *n* **dispossession.**

disproportionate *a* out of proportion; excessive; *n* **disproportion.**

disprove *v* refute; show to be false.

dispute *v* discuss; question validity of; oppose; wrangle; *n* argument; controversy; **beyond d.** finally decided; *n* **disputation** verbal argument.

disqualify *v* make ineligible; debar; incapacitate; *n* **disqualification.**

disquiet *v* make anxious, apprehensive, restless; *n* **disquietude.**

disregard *v* ignore; *n* lack of concern.

disrepair *n* bad condition resulting from negligence.

disreputable *a* of bad repute; *adv* -**ably;** *n* **disrepute.**

disrespect *n* lack of respect; *v* show this; *a* -**ful;** *adv* -**fully.**

disrobe *v* undress; take off official robes.

disrupt *v* upset; cause disorder to; *a* -**ive;** *adv* -**ively;** *n* **disruption.**

dissatisfy *v* fail to satisfy; *a* **dissatisfied;** *n* **dissatisfaction.**

dissect *v* 1 *anat, bot* cut up for examination 2 divide into

pieces 3 criticize in detail; *ns* **dissection; dissector.**

dissemble *v* conceal feelings, motives, etc.; deceive; act hypocritically; *n* -**r.**

disseminate *v* spread abroad; scatter as seed; *ns* -**ation; -or.**

dissension, dissention *n* discord.

dissent *v* disagree; withold assent; *n* **dissenter** nonconformist.

dissertation *n* formal discourse or treatise on selected subject, *usu* submitted for doctorate.

disservice *n* harm or injury.

dissident *a* not in agreement; *n* **dissidence** disagreement.

dissimilar *a* unlike *n* **dissimilarity.**

dissimulate *v* conceal one's feelings; dissemble; *n* **dissimulation.**

dissipate *v* 1 scatter; dispel 2 squander 3 engage in dissolute occupations; *n* **dissipation** 1 dispersion 2 intemperance; extravagance; *a* **dissipated** 1 dispelled 2 debauched.

dissociate *v* separate; sever; repudiate connection with; *n* **dissociation.**

dissoluble *a* able to be dissolved, broken up.

dissolute *a* lax in morals, conduct; debauched; *adv* -**ly;** *n* -**ness.**

dissolve *v* 1 liquefy; melt 2 become faint 3 break up 4 terminate; annul; *a* **dissoluble** capable of being dissolved; *ns* **dissolvent** that

A
B
C
D
E
F
G
H
I
J
K
L
M
N
O
P
Q
R
S
T
U
V
W
X
Y
Z

which dissolves; **dissolution** act or process of dissolving.

dissonant *a* discordant; at variance; *n* **dissonance**.

dissuade *v* persuade against; advise against; *n* **dissuasion**.

dissymmetry *n* lack of symmetry; symmetry in reverse; *a* **dissymmetrical**.

distance *n* 1 space between two things 2 remoteness 3 aloofness; *idm* **go the distance** persevere to the end; *idm* **keep one's distance** 1 remain at a safe distance 2 avoid being too friendly; *idm* **keep someone at a distance** prevent someone from being too friendly; *v* put, keep far away; outstrip; *idm* **distance oneself (from)** avoid being involved (in); *a* **distant** far off; faint; haughty, reserved.

distaste *n* aversion; dislike; *a* **-ful** unpleasant; repellent.

distemper *n* contagious disease of dogs; thick paint used for internal walls; *v* paint with distemper.

distend *v* inflate; become blown out.

distill *v* **-tilling, -tilled.** evaporate liquid and condense it again; refine by this method; trickle; *ns* **distillation; distiller** one who distills, *esp* alcoholic spirit; **distillery** place where distillation is carried on.

distinct *a* 1 separate 2 easily seen; definite; *ns* **distinctness; distinction**

difference; high standing or special quality; mark of favor; *a* **distinctive** characteristic.

distinguish *v* 1 discern; mark difference in 2 make honored; *a* **-ed** famous; celebrated.

distort *v* spoil shape of; misrepresent; *n* **distortion**.

distract *v* 1 divert (thoughts) 2 perplex 3 drive mad; *n* **distraction** 1 amusement 2 madness; *a* **distraught** agitated; driven mad.

distrain *v leg* seize goods to enforce payments; *n* **distraint** legal seizure.

distrait *a* absentminded; preoccupied.

distraught *a* extremely distressed.

distress *n* grief; physical exhaustion; danger; extreme poverty; *v* afflict, cause mental or bodily pain to; *as* **distressed** poor; **distressing** painful.

distribute *v* deal, share out; disperse; *a* **distributive** involving distribution; *ns* **-ution; -uter, -utor** switch distributing electricity in automobile engine.

district *n* region; area; locality.

district attorney *n* government lawyer for a given district, whose main job is prosecuting.

distrust *n* doubt; suspicion; lack of confidence in; *v* feel distrust.

disturb *v* alter normal state, position of; unsettle;

disorder; alarm; *ns* **-ance; -er**.

disunite *v* become, cause to separate; *n* **disunion**.

disused *a* no longer used; *n* **disuse** *idm* **fallen into disuse** disused.

disyllabic *a* having two syllables.

ditch *n* narrow trench cut in earth, used for drainage or defense; *v* 1 make, repair ditches 2 *sl* drive car into ditch; throw away.

dither *v* waver; tremble; hesitate nervously.

ditto *n* the same, as already said or written.

ditto mark *n* mark (") indicating repetition.

ditty *n* short, simple song.

diuretic *a med* causing increase in flow of urine.

diurnal *a* daily; lasting a day; of the day.

diva *n* prima donna.

divan *n* 1 low, backless couch, bed 2 oriental council.

dive *v* plunge, *esp* head first into water; descend suddenly; *phr v* **dive into** become quickly involved in; *n* 1 act of diving 2 *sl* low-class bar; *idm* **take a dive** *coll* deliberately lose a match for dishonest gain; *n* **diver** one who dives; water bird of diving habits.

diverge *v* branch off set course; separate; *n* **divergence; diversion** turning aside or away; alternative route; *a* **divergent**.

diversify *v* make different; give

variety to; *a* **diverse** dissimilar; varied; *ns* **diversification; diversity**.

diversion *n* **1** rerouting of traffic **2** entertainment **3** distraction of attention; *a* **diversionary**.

divert *v* **1** turn aside **2** distract; amuse; *n* **diversion** entertainment; *a* **diverting**.

divertimento *n mus* **-menti**. light chamber suite.

divest *v* deprive (of clothing, of power); *idm* **divest oneself** get rid of.

divide *v* **1** split into two or more parts **2** share out **3** separate for voting (of legislature) **4** find out number of times one number is contained in another; *ns* **dividend 1** number divided by another **2** profit on money invested; share of profits, etc.; *idm* **pay dividends** bring great reward; *pl* **dividers** measuring compasses; *as* **divisible** capable of division; **divisional** pertaining to a division.

divine *a* pertaining to God; godlike; sacred; *n* theologian; priest; *n* **divinity 1** god **2** theology **3** quality of being divine; *v* predict; discover by intuition; *ns* **diviner 1** soothsayer **2** one who finds hidden water, metal; **divining rod** twig used in discovering water.

Divine Office *n* formal prayers led by Roman Catholic priests.

divine right *n* right to power said to be given by God.

division *n* **1** dividing into parts; sharing **2** one such part **3** thing that divides **4** dividing of one number by another **5** disagreement **6** parliamentary voting; *a* **-al**.

divisive *a* causing disagreement; *adv* **-ly;** *n* **-ness**.

divisor *n math* denominator; number dividing another number.

divorce *v* dissolve marriage; separate; *n* legal dissolution of marriage; separation; *n* **divorcee** divorced spouse.

divot *n* small piece of turf.

divulge *v* make known, reveal (secret, etc.); *ns* **divulgement; divulgence**.

Dixie *n* southern states in US.

Dixieland *n* **1** Dixie **2** style of jazz originating from New Orleans.

DIY *abbr* **do-it-yourself**.

dizzy *a* giddy; suffering from vertigo; confused; *v* make dizzy; *n* **dizziness**.

DJ *abbr* disk jockey.

DM *abbr* Deutschmark.

DNA *abbr chem* **deoxyribonucleic acid** (acid carrying genetic information in living cells).

do *v* doing, did, done **1** perform; complete **2** study **3** make **4** be enough **5** *coll* visit as a tourist **6** *coll* swindle **7** *coll* punish; beat; *idm* **do well by** be generous

to; *phr vs* **do away with 1** abolish **2** kill; **do down 1** cheat **2** undermine pride **3** slander; **do for** *coll* **1** clean house for **2** ruin; **do in** *coll* **1** kill **2** exhaust **3** wreck; **do someone out of** cheat someone of; **do over** *sl* attack; beat up; **do up 1** fasten; wrap up **2** make repairs; improvements to; **do with** *idm* **can/could do with** need(s); *idm* **have/be to do with** be connected with; *idm* **what to do with** how to treat or use; *phr v* **do without** manage without; *idm* **do's and dont's** things that must or must not be done.

DOA *abbr* dead on arrival.

dob *abbr* date of birth.

doc *n coll* doctor.

docile *a* tractable; amenable to training and discipline; *n* **docility**.

dock[1] *n* coarse, large-leaved weed.

dock[2] *n* artificial basin where ships are loaded, repaired; *v* enter, put into dock; *ns* **dockyard** series of docks, warehouses, etc.; **docker** dock laborer.

dock[3] *n* enclosure in court, for accused.

dock[4] *v* cut short, *esp* animal's tail; deduct part of.

docket *n* **1** label; ticket **2** list of contents, cases for trial.

Doc Martens [TM] type of ankle boots or shoes with thick soles.

doctor *n* **1** holder of highest

a
b
c
d
e
f
g
h
i
j
k
l
m
n
o
p
q
r
s
t
u
v
w
x
y
z

A
B
C
D
E
F
G
H
I
J
K
L
M
N
O
P
Q
R
S
T
U
V
W
X
Y
Z

degree from a university
2 medical practitioner; v
1 give medical treatment to
2 repair 3 falsify.

doctorate n highest university degree.

doctrine n accepted belief; dogma, *esp* of sect; n **doctrinaire** narrow-minded, obstinate (person) seeking to apply theory, regardless of consequences.

document n written information, evidence; v bring written evidence; n, a **documentary** factual (report, film); n **documentation** documentary proof, evidence.

dodder v move shakily, feebly; totter; n **-er**; a **-ing** infirm; senile.

dodge v 1 swerve from, *esp* pursuit 2 evade by tricking 3 shirk; n 1 act of dodging 2 *coll* trick; ingenious plan; device; n **dodger** trickster; shirker.

dodo n dodos, dodoes. extinct bird, with useless wings.

doe n female of deer, rabbit, hare, etc.

does *3rd sing pres of* do.

doesn't *contracted form of* does not.

doff v take off, *esp* hat, etc.; abandon.

dog n 1 domestic quadruped, related to wolf; 2 male wolf, fox, etc. 3 andiron 4 toothed grip; v. **dogging, dogged.** to follow and watch constantly, to hamper *idm* **dog eat dog**

ruthless competition; *idm* **dog's life** miserable life; *pl* *idm* **go to the dogs** go to ruin; v follow closely; *as* **dogged** obstinate; **doggy** pertaining to dogs.

dog collar n 1 collar for dog 2 *coll* clergyman's stiff white collar.

dog-eared a with corners of pages turned down.

dogfish n small fish related to shark.

doggerel n bad verse.

doggone, doggoned a, adv coll used to express surprise or annoyance.

doggy bag n bag for taking home uneaten food from restaurant.

doghouse n kennel; *idm* **in the doghouse** in disgrace.

dogleg n sharp bend.

dogma n article of belief; body of such theories, etc.; a **dogmatic** relating to dogma; dictatorial; *adv* **-ally;** n **dogmatism**.

do-gooder n *coll* person who tries to do good deeds but is regarded as interfering.

dog paddle, doggie paddle n swimming stroke of quick, short movements.

dogrose n wild hedge rose.

dog tired a *coll* utterly exhausted.

dogwood n flowering tree.

doily n small mat placed on, under dish.

do-it-yourself n doing one's own repairs, decorating, etc., not using professional

workmen.

Dolby [TM] system of noise reduction for recording.

dolcevita n It sweet life, one of pure self-indulgence.

doldrums n pl 1 low spirits; 2 calm seas near equator.

dole n charitable gift; unemployment benefit; v give out sparingly.

doleful a woeful; sad; lugubrious.

doll n child's toy, like human figure; sl sexist woman; n **dolly** child's name for doll.

dollar n unit of coinage in US, Canada, etc.

dollop n big, shapeless lump.

dolmen n prehistoric stone chamber, cromlech.

dolorous a grievous.

dolphin n sea mammal akin to whale, but smaller.

dolt n slow-witted, stupid person; a **doltish** stupid.

domain n land, realm held, ruled over; *fig* sphere of activity or influence.

dome n convex curved roof; cupola; a **domed**.

domestic a 1 pertaining to home or family 2 not foreign 3 (of animals) kept by man; n household servant; v **domesticate** tame animals; ns **-ation; domesticity**.

domicile n usual dwelling place; *as* **domiciliary** of dwelling place; **domiciled** residing.

dominant a 1 most important 2 overpowering; n **dominance**.

dominate *v* **1** have control over **2** tower above; *a* **dominating;** *n* **domination**.

domineer *v* act harshly, arrogantly; tyrannize; bully; *a* **domineering**.

Dominican *n, a* (member) of order of friars of St. Dominic.

dominion *n* supremacy, sovereignty.

domino *n* **dominoes 1** loose cloak with mask **2** small oblong piece of bone, etc. marked with 1-6 dots; game using 28 such pieces.

domino effect *n* sequence of events each resulting in another or others.

don¹ *v* **donning, donned.** put on; assume.

don² *n* **1** Spanish title **2** college professor.

donate *v* give; *ns* **donation** gift; **donor.**

done *pp of* do finished.

Don Juan *n Sp coll* man having reputation for frequent amorous conquests.

donkey *n* ass; *fig* stupid person.

doodle *v* draw, scribble idly; *n* design so made.

doom *n* **1** fate; evil destiny **2** formal judgment; *v* condemn; destine to ruin; *idm* **doom and gloom** despair; *a* **doomed** destined to fail or die; *n* **Doomsday** Day of Judgment.

door *n* hinged, sliding, revolving structure for closing an entrance; *idm* **by the back door** secretly and unofficially; *idm* **shut/close**

the door remove every opportunity; *n* **doorway** means of accessing.

do-or-die *a* recklessly daring.

doorman *n* person who attends to needs of those entering or leaving building such as hotel, apartment house, etc.

doormat *n* **1** mat for wiping dirt from shoes **2** *coll* person who lets others treat him/her with disrespect.

doorstop *n* weight on floor that holds door open.

dopa *n* amino acid.

dope *n* **1** kind of lacquer **2** drug *esp* narcotic **3** *sl* foolish person; *v* treat with dope; drug; *a* **dopey** drugged.

doppelgänger *n Ger* double of another living person.

Doric *a* simplest style of Greek architecture.

dormant *a* inactive; sleeping; hibernating; *n* **dormancy**.

dormer *n* vertical window in sloping roof.

dormitory *n* sleeping room with several beds.

dormouse *n* **dormice** small hibernating rodent, like mouse.

dorsal *a* pertaining to, on, near the back.

dory *n* flat-bottomed rowboat.

dose *a* amount of drug, etc., taken at one time; *v* give medicine to; *n* **dosage**.

dossier *n* set of documents, etc., concerning particular person or subject.

dot¹ *n* small round mark or spot; *idm* **on the dot**

punctually; *v* **dotting, dotted.** mark with a dot or dots; *idm* **dot the i's and cross the t's** complete the final details; *a* **dotted** made of dots; *idm* **sign on the dotted line** make formal written agreement; *a* **dotty** *coll* crazy.

dot² *n* dowry.

dotage *n* senility.

dotard *n* senile person.

dote *v* love blindly; be foolish over.

dot matrix *n* method of printing by pattern of tiny dots.

double *a* twice as much; ambiguous; twofold; *n* **1** thing or person exactly like another **2** twice the amount; *v* make, become double; fold in two; *idm* **on the double 1** running **2** fast; *idm* **double as 1** play another role **2** do another job; *phr vs* **double back** return by the same route; **double up 1** bend at the waist **2** share a room; *adv* **doubly** twice as much; *n pl* **doubles** match for opposing pairs; **doubly** in two ways; twice over.

double agent *n* spy acting for two opposing countries.

double bass *n mus* largest instrument of violin family.

double cross *n, v* swindle; *n* **-er.**

double date *n* two couples going out together.

double-dealer *n* swindler; *n* **double-dealing.**

double-decker *n* **1** bus with

two floors **2** two-layered sandwich.

double-digit *a* involving two-digit numbers.

double Dutch *n coll* jumprope game with two ropes.

double entendre *n* phrase that can have two meanings, one of them sexual.

double feature *n* two films for one price.

double glaze *v* fit window with double glass panel for better heat insulation; *n* **double glazing**.

doubleheader *n* two games played on the same day, one after the other.

double-jointed *a* having very flexible joints.

double play *n* play in baseball in which two players are out at same time.

double standard *n* moral premise that is applied differently to individuals or groups.

double stopping *n mus* playing on two strings together.

double take *n* delayed exaggerated reaction of surprise.

double-talk *n* misleading ambiguous speech.

doublethink *n* ability to accept two contradictory principles or ideas at the same time.

double whammy *n* double portion of something, *esp* troublesome.

doubloom *n* old Spanish gold coin.

doubt *v* be uncertain; waver; suspect; *n* uncertainty; misgiving; lack of belief; *as* **doubtful; doubting;** *adv* **doubtless** assuredly; probably.

douche *n* jet of liquid sprayed onto, into, the body; *v* apply douche to.

dough *n* flour moistened and kneaded; *sl* money; *a* **doughy**.

doughnut *n* small, round or ring-shaped cake cooked in fat.

dour *a* stern; grim; obstinate; *adv* **-ly;** *n* **-ness**.

douse *v* **1** dip in water **2** extinguish (light).

dove *n* bird of pigeon family; symbol of peace; *n* **dovecote** house for doves; *n* **dovetail** joints made with fan-shaped tenons; *v* **dovetail 1** join by dovetails **2** *fig* fit (facts, etc.) together neatly.

dowager *n* widow whose title derives from deceased husband.

dowdy *a* unfashionable; illdressed, shabby; *n* **dowdiness**.

dowel *n* wooden, metal, or plastic peg for joining sheets of wood, metal, or plastic.

dower *n* widow's share of husband's property; dowry; *v* endow.

down¹ fine soft feathers; any fine fluffy substance; *a* **downy** like down.

down² *adv* toward lower position, size, quality, etc.; *prep* from higher to lower position; along; *n idm* **down-and-out** destitute; *idm* **be/go down with** be/fall ill with; *sl* be familiar with; *n*
1 movement downward
2 depressed state of morale
3 hostile attitude; *a, adv* **downward** descending.

downbeat *a* **1** casual **2** pessimistic.

downcast *a* dejected.

downfall *n* collapse; ruin; defeat.

downgrade *v* reduce to lower grade; classify as inferior.

downhearted *a* discouraged.

downhill *idm* **go downhill 1** move down a slope **2** suffer a decline in health or morale.

download *v comput* transfer (data).

down-home *a* relating to common folk, simple life.

down payment *n* first payment of installment payment plan.

downpour *n* sudden heavy fall of rain.

downright *a* **1** frank **2** complete; *adv* absolutely.

downs *n pl* rolling grassy hills.

downsize *v* reduce in numbers, *usu* in business organizations.

downstream *a adv* with the current of a stream.

Down syndrome *n* congenital abnormality causing mental retardation (*also* **mongolism**).

downstage *a, adv* nearer to the audience.

downtime *n comput* time when out of use.

down-to-earth *a* practical; unsophisticated.

downtown *a, adv* to, in the (main business) center.
downtrodden *a* exploited; oppressed.
downturn *n* decline, *esp* economic.
dowry *n* woman's marriage portion.
dowse *v* seek water with divinin grod; *n* **dowser**.
doxology *n* short hymn of praise to God.
doyen *n* senior member of body or profession; *fem* **doyenne**.
doze *v* sleep lightly; be half asleep; *n* light sleep.
dozen *n* set of twelve; **baker's d.** thirteen.
DP *abbr* **1** data processing **2** displaced person.
drab *a* mud-colored; *fig* monotonous.
drachm *n* unit of weight, dram.
drachma *n* unit of Greek currency.
draconian *a* harsh; excessively severe.
draft *n* **1** body of troops for special duty **2** rough sketch, scheme **3** order for payment **4** current of air; *v* **1** send on special duty **2** make draft; *n* **draftsman** one who makes drawings, etc.; *fem* **draftswoman**.
drag *v* **dragging, dragged. 1** pull along **2** sweep with nets, grappling irons, etc. **3** lag behind; move slowly; *idm* **drag one's feet/heels** act slowly and ineffectually on purpose; *phr vs* **drag by** to

pass slowly; **drag in 1** involve unwillingly **2** mention inappropriately; **drag on** continue monotonously; **drag out** prolong needlessly; **drag something out of someone** force someone to say something; **drag up** mention (to someone's embarrassment); *n* **drag 1** something made to be dragged **2** air resistance **3** *sl* boring person or situation **4** *sl* inhaling from a cigarette.
dragée *n* cake decoration, usually a silver ball.
dragnet *n* system for catching a criminal.
dragon *n* fabulous winged reptile, breathing fire.
dragonfly *n* iridescent, long-bodied insect.
dragoon *n* mounted infantryman; *v* enforce rigidly.
drag race *n* race between automobiles.
drain *v* **1** draw off (liquid) gradually **2** exhaust gradually; *n* **1** pipe; ditch; sewer **2** *fig* constant strain (on strength, time, etc.); *idm* **down the drain** wasted; thrown away.
drainage *n* (system for) draining of waste water.
drake *n* male duck.
dram *n* **1** unit of weight; drachm **2** small drink of liquor.
drama *n* play for stage, radio,

TV, etc; *a* **dramatic** pertaining to drama; thrilling, exciting; *adv* **-ally;** *n* **dramatist** playwright; *v* **dramatize 1** make into play, drama **2** exaggerate; *n* **dramatization.**
dramatic irony *n* effect of ambiguous words when audience understand implications unknown to the characters.
dramatics *n* **1** theatrical art **2** exaggerated emotion.
dramatis personae *n pl Lat* characters in a play.
drank *pt of* **drink.**
drape *v* arrange in folds; cover loosely; *n pl* **drapes** curtains; cloth; *n* **draper** dealer in cloth, etc.; **drapery** draper's business, goods, etc.; hangings.
drastic *a* having powerful effect; violent; severe; *adv* **-ally.**
draw *v* **1** drag; haul; pull **2** extract (liquid) **3** inhale **4** obtain (salary, etc.) **5** extend **6** attract **7** sketch with pencil, etc.; *pt* **drew;** *pp* **drawn;** *idm* **draw a blank** be unsuccessful; *idm* **draw blood 1** cause to bleed **2** hurt someone's feelings; *idm* **draw the line (at)** refuse (to go further); *idm* **draw a veil over** tactfully forget; *phr vs* **draw back** be unwilling; **draw in** come to the side of the road; **draw on** (of time) approach; *idm* **draw on someone's**

A
B
C
D
E
F
G
H
I
J
K
L
M
N
O
P
Q
R
S
T
U
V
W
X
Y
Z

experience/knowledge make use of what someone knows; n **1** act of drawing **2** tie at end of game; ns **drawing** art of depicting in pencil, etc.; **drawback** disadvantage; **drawer 1** one who draws **2** lidless, sliding box in table, etc.

drawbridge n defensive lifting bridge over a moat.

drawing room n formal room for entertaining people.

drawl v speak slowly and affectedly; n such manner of speech.

drawn pp of **draw**; a pale and tired.

dray n low, sideless cart used for heavy loads.

dread v feel fear, misgiving; n anxiety, fear; a awesome; **dreadful** terrible; n **dreadnought** battleship.

dreadlocks n pl long curled strands of hair, as worn by Rastafarians.

dream n illusion of senses occurring in sleep; fantasy; idm **a dream of a** coll a beautiful, wonderful; idm **like a dream** very smoothly; without a hitch; v have dreams; idm **would not dream of** would never consider; imagine; phr v **dream up** invent; imagine; pt, pp **dreamed, dreamt;** ns **dreamer, dreaminess;** as **dreamy** vague; **dreamless**.

dreamboat n coll attractive person.

dreary a gloomy; tedious;

dismal; n **dreariness**.

dredge[1] v bring up (mud, etc.) from under water; n type of net, scoop, etc.; n **dredger** ship used for dredging.

dredge[2] v sprinkle with flour, sugar, etc.; n **dredger**.

dregs n pl sediment; fig lowest, most worthless part.

drench v soak thoroughly; give dose of medicine (to animal); n large dose; a, n **drenching** soaking.

dress v **1** put clothes on **2** arrange for display **3** prepare (food) **4** align (troops) **5** apply dressing to (soil, wound, etc.); n frock; formal clothes; ns **dresser 1** one who dresses (actors, etc.) **2** chest of drawers with a mirror **3** kitchen sideboard; **dressing** thing applied (fertilizer, bandage, etc.); a **dressy** stylish, elegant.

dressage n training of horse to make exact movements; performance of these.

dress circle n first tier of seats in theater.

dressing down n reprimand; v wear casual attire.

dressing gown n loose garment worn at home (overnight clothes or underwear).

dress rehearsal n rehearsal in costume before first performance.

drew pt of **draw**.

dribble v trickle; n drop; ns **driblet** small amount.

dribs n **in dribs and drabs** coll in small amounts.

dried pt, pp of **dry**.

drier n **dryer.**

drift n **1** deviation from course **2** something driven by wind, water **3** general meaning; v move aimlessly; ns **drifter** peron who moves frequently to other homes; **drift net** one allowed to float with the tide.

driftwood n wood found floating or washed ashore.

drill[1] n instrument for boring holes; narrow furrow for seeds; v bore hole; sow seed in rows.

drill[2] n regular physical, mental exercise; military training; v perform, cause to perform drill.

drill[3] n coarse cotton twill.

drillmaster n military instructor who uses excessive discipline.

drily = dryly.

drink v **drinking, drank, drunk. 1** swallow liquid **2** fig absorb eagerly **3** take alcoholic liquor; n liquid swallowed; beverage, esp alcoholic; n **drinker;** a **drinkable** fit for drinking.

drip v **dripping, dripped.** trickle, let fall drop by drop; n act of dripping; n **dripping 1** falling in drops **2** fat dripping from roast meat; a **dripping** very wet.

drip-dry v hang up and dry naturally in air.

drive v **1** force into movement **2** set in motion and control (vehicle) **3** go, travel in vehicle **4** advance strongly

5 hit with force (ball, etc.); *idm* **be driving at** be trying to say; *pt* **drove;** *pp* **drive;** *n* **1** strong impulse; energy **2** private road to house **3** ride in vehicle; *n* **driver 1** one who drives **2** golf club; *a* **driving** transmitting force, movement.

drive-in *n* a bank, restaurant, etc., serving people in cars; *a* accommodating people in cars.

drivel *n* talk foolishly; *n* nonsense.

driveway *n* path in front of house.

driving range *n* area for practicing golf drives.

drizzle *v* rain finely; *n* very fine rain.

droll *a* funny; quaint; *n* **drollery**.

dromedary *n* riding camel, having one hump.

drone *n* **1** male honeybee **2** *fig* idler **3** low humming sound; *v* **1** hum **2** speak monotonously.

drool *v* slaver over.

droop *v* sink; hang down limply; wilt; *a* **drooping**.

drop *n* **1** small globule of liquid; minute quantity **2** descent **3** decrease in amount, etc.; *idm* **at the drop of a hat** instantly; on demand; *v* **dropping, dropped. 1** let fall **2** become less **3** give up; abandon **4** let down from vehicle **5** end relationship with **6** leave out of team; *phr vs* **drop**

back/behind go more slowly; **drop in/by/around** pay a brief visit; *phr vs* **drop off 1** go to sleep **2** let down from vehicle; **drop out** choose not to participate; *n pl* **drops** liquid medicine taken a few drops at a time; *n* **droplet** little drop.

drop leaf *n* part of table that can be folded down.

dropout *n* **1** person opting out of conventional society **2** person failing to complete academic course.

dropsy *n* abnormal collection of fluid in tissues, cavities of body; *a* **dropsical**.

drought *n* lack of rain; long period without rain.

drove[1] *pt of* **drive**.

drove[2] *n* moving herd of cattle; *n* **drover** driver of, dealer in cattle.

drown *v* **1** die, kill by suffocation in water **2** *fig* overwhelm **3** muffle (sound); *idm* **drown one's sorrows (in drink)** drink alcohol to console oneself.

drowsy *a* sleepy, lethargic; *adv* **drowsily;** *n* **drowsiness;** *v* **drowse** doze, be half asleep.

drudge *n* overworked servant; *v* work like drudge; *n* **drudgery** hard, wearisome toil.

drug *n* any vegetable, mineral substance used in medicine; *v* **drugging, drugged.** give drug (*esp* narcotic) to; habitually take drugs; *n* **druggist** pharmacist; *n sl*

druggie drug addict.

drugstore *n* pharmacy.

Druid *n* ancient Celtic priest.

drum *n* **1** percussion instrument **2** various hollow cylindrical objects **3** part of ear; *v* **drumming, drummed.** play drum; rap continuously; *phr vs* **drum something into someone** say something repeatedly until it is understood; **drum someone out** dismiss formally with dishonor; **drum up** obtain by sustained effort; *ns* **drummer; drum major** commander of regimental band.

drumstick *n* **1** stick used by drummer **2** lower leg of cooked chicken, turkey, etc.

drunk *a* drinking, drunk. intoxicated; *n* **drunkard** habitual heavy drinker.

drunken *a* intoxicated; *adv* **-ly;** *n* **-ness**.

dry *v* **drying, dried.** remove or lose moisture; *phr v* **dry out 1** remove the wetness from **2** treat, be treated against alcoholism; **dry up 1** end the supply of **2** wither **3** *coll* stop talking; *a* **1** without moisture **2** having low rainfall **3** (*of wine*) not sweet; *adv* **drily, dryly** without emotion; *ns* **dryness; dry dock**.

dryad *n* wood nymph.

dryer *n* machine for removing moisture.

dryly, drily *adv* **1** without emotion **2** ironically.

dryness *n* **1** lack of wetness **2** lack of sweetness **3** lack of

a
b
c
d
e
f
g
h
i
j
k
l
m
n
o
p
q
r
s
t
u
v
w
x
y
z

emotion **4** ironical tone.

dry-clean v clean with chemicals, without washing; ns **dry cleaner, dry cleaning.**

dry-eyed a not moved to tears by sentiment.

dry goods n pl **1** grain, fruit, etc. **2** haberdashery.

dry ice n solid carbon dioxide.

dry rot n (fungus causing) decay of wood into powder.

dry run n coll rehearsal, trial.

DTP abbr desktop publishing.

DTs n coll delirium tremens.

dual a of two; double; twofold; n **duality.**

dub v **1** confer knighthood on **2** (of films, etc.) rerecord sound track, with additions, etc.; n **dubbing.**

dubious a doubtful; n **-ness.**

ducal a of a duke or duchess.

duchess n **1** wife of duke **2** female peer with status of duke.

duchy n land owned by duke or duchess.

duck n **1** flat-billed waterbird **2** heavy cotton fabric; ns **duckling** young duck; **ducky** coll darling.

duck v **1** plunge person, thing into liquid **2** bob down (to avoid blow); n **ducking.**

duckbill n small, egg-laying mammal.

duckpin n type of small bowling pin.

duct n tube for conveying liquid; ventilating flue; as **ductile** malleable; **ductless.**

dud n **1** unsuccessful person, thing **2** bad coin, note; a

useless.

dude n sl **1** city dweller **2** man **3** dandy.

dudgeon n state of sullen resentment, anger.

due a **1** (of money) owing **2** adequate **3** scheduled to arrive; idm **due to** resulting from; adv (of direction) exactly; n something owed, deserved; pls regular fee, levy.

dude n city slicker.

duel n contest (physical or intellectual) between two persons; v fight duel; n **duelist.**

duet n musical work for two performers.

duff v sl mishit, esp in golf.

duffel, duffle n thick woolen cloth; **d. coat** coat made of this fabric.

duffle bag n large cylindrical canvas tote bag.

duffer n stupid, clumsy person.

dug pt, pp of **dig.**

dugout n **1** hollowed out canoe **2** underground shelter.

duke n holder of highest hereditary rank of peerage; fem **duchess;** ns **dukedom; duchy** small state.

dulcet a melodious; sweet-sounding; pleasing.

dulcimer n old, harplike instrument.

dull a **1** stupid; tedious **2** lacking clearness, brightness **3** blunted; **4** overcast; v make, become dull; ns **dullard** oaf; **dullness;** adv **dully.**

duly adv **1** as expected

2 punctually.

dumb a incapable of speech; silent; sl unintelligent; adv **-ly;** n **-ness;** n dumbness.

dumbbell n **1** short bar with a ball at each end for weight-lifting **2** coll stupid person.

dummy n **1** sham object **2** tailor's model; **3** bridge hand exposed on table; a sham; used in pretense.

dummy run n practice attempt, not the real thing.

dump v unload roughly (refuse, etc.); n rubbish heap; place for depositing refuse; depot for ammunition, stores, etc.; pl idm down in **the dumps** sad.

dumper n vehicle used on building sites (also **dump truck**).

dumpling n small piece of boiled suet, dough; a **dumpy** squat and short; n **dumpiness.**

dun[1] a of a dull gray-brown color.

dun[2] v demand persistently for payment of debt.

dunce n dullard; pupil slow to learn.

dunderhead n stupid person.

dune n wind-driven sand hill; n **dune buggy** motor vehicle for use on beach.

dung n excrement of animals; manure.

dungarees n pl overalls of coarse cotton fabric.

dungeon n dark, underground prison cell.

dunk v dip bread, etc., in liquid before eating it.

duo n mus **1** pair of players **2** piece for two; duet.

duodecimal *a* twelfth; reckoned by twelves.

duodenum *n* upper part of small intestine; *a* **duodenal.**

duologue *n* dialogue for two.

dupe *v* deceive; trick; *n* victim of duping.

duplex *a* double; twofold; *v* **duplicate** make double; make exact copy; *n* replica; *ns* **duplication; duplicator** copying machine; **duplicity** double-dealing, deception.

durable *a* long-lasting; *n pl* **durables** goods expected to last; *ns* **durability; duration** length of existence; *prep* **during** throughout; in course of.

duration *idm* **for the duration** while something lasts.

during *prep* **1** in the course of **2** throughout.

durum wheat *n* wheat ground into glutinous starch used in pasta products.

dusk *n* late twilight; *a* **dusky** dark, swarthy.

dust *n* powdery particles (of earth, etc.) suspended in air; *v* remove dust; sprinkle with powder etc.; *phr v* **dust off** start to use again after long disuse; *n* **duster** cloth for wiping away dust; *a* **dusty** (*idm* **a dusty answer** a curt rejection; *idm* **not so dusty** quite good).

dust bowl *n* area suffering from loss of vegetation through drought.

dust jacket *n* protective paper cover of book.

dustpan *n* flat container for collecting dust.

dust-up *n coll* noisy quarrel; brawl.

Dutch *a, n* pertaining to Holland, its people, and language; *idm* **go Dutch (with someone)** share the cost.

Dutch door *n* door that is divided horizontally so either half can be opened separately.

Dutch courage *n coll* courage gained by taking alcohol.

Dutch oven *n* covered pan for cooking slowly.

Dutch uncle *n idm* **talk (to) someone like a Dutch uncle** criticize severely.

duty *n* legal or moral obligation; proper expression of respect; tax on goods; *as* **dutiful** showing respect; **dutiable** liable to customs or other duty.

duvetcover *n* fabric cover for comforter.

dwarf *n* **dwarfs or dwarves.** person, animal or plant much below usual size; *pl* **dwarfs;** *v* make look small, overshadow.

dwell *v* **dwelling, dwelled, or dwelt.** live; reside; *phr v* **dwell on** keep thinking, talking about; *ns* **dweller** inhabitant; **dwelling** abode.

dwindle *v* become smaller, waste away, diminish.

dyad *n* two units considered as one.

dye *v* **dyeing, dyed.** impart color to; tint; change color; *n* substance, coloring matter used for dyeing; *n* **dyer** one whose trade is dyeing.

dyed-in-the-wool *a* unchangeable.

dying *pr p of* **die.**

dynamics *n pl* **1** branch of physics dealing with force as producing changes of motion **2** *pl mus* variations in loudness; *a* **dynamic 1** pertaining to force in motion **2** forceful; vigorous **3** opposed to static; *n* **dynamism.**

dynamite *n* **-mos.** high explosive made with nitroglycerine; *v* blow up with dynamite.

dynamo *n* machine for converting mechanical energy into electrical energy.

dynasty *n* succession of rulers of same family; *n* **dynast** hereditary ruler; *a* **dynastic.**

dysentery *n* disease of large intestine, akin to diarrhea.

dysfunction *n* impaired or ineffective functioning; *a* dysfunctional.

dyslexia *n* pathological inability to spell or read; word-blindness; *as* **dyslectic, dyslexic.**

dyspepsia *n* indigestion; *a* **dyspeptic.**

dysrhythmia *n* abnormal rhythm, *esp* as recorded electrically in heart or brain.

a
b
c
d
e
f
g
h
i
j
k
l
m
n
o
p
q
r
s
t
u
v
w
x
y
z

each *a, pron* every one considered separately; *adv* to or for each one; apiece; *idm* **each way** (of bets) for a win or a place.

eager *a* enthusiastic; impatient to act; *idm* **eager beaver** very enthused, hardworking person; *n* **eagerness** enthusiasm.

eagle *n* large bird of prey; *idm* **eagle eye 1** good eyesight **2** close watchfulness; *n* **eaglet** young eagle.

Eames Chair *n* 1950s swivel wood-and-leather chairs with arms and headrest, designed by Charles Eames

ear[1] *n* **1** organ of hearing **2** sense of tune **3** attention; *idm* **(be) all ears** *coll* (be) listening closely; *idm* **someone's ears are burning** someone not present would be embarrassed if he/she knew what was being said; *idm* **play (it) by ear**

improvise; *idm* **up to one's ears (in)** overwhelmed (with); *idm* **in one ear and out the other** not registering in the mind.

ear[2] *n* spike, cluster of seeds of cereal.

eardrum *n* membrane of inner ear that vibrates in response to sound waves.

earful *idm* **give someone an earful** *coll* reprimand or attack someone with abusive words; fill someone's ears with gossip.

earl *n* rank in peerage below marquis.

earldom title or territory of earl.

earlobe *n* soft lobe of outer ear.

early *a, adv* **1** near start of period of time **2** before the time stated; *idm* **at the earliest** and no sooner.

Early American *a* colonial-style American furniture or architecture.

early bird *n* person who arrives early, gets up early.

earmark *v* note or set aside for a specific purpose.

earn *v* gain by labor, merit, etc.; deserve; *n pl* **earnings** wages; salary *a* **earnings-related** adjusted according to earnings.

earnest *a* sincere; serious; *idm* **in (deadly/real) earnest** with determination; *adv* **-ly;** *n* **-ness.**

earphones *n pl* headphones.

earpiece *n* **1** protective flap on cap **2** part of eyeglasses that hooks over the ear.

earplug *n* small piece of soft material fitting inside the ear, to keep out water, noise, etc.

earring *n* item of jewelery worn on lobe of ear.

earshot *n* **within/out of earshot** within/out of range of audibility.

earsplitting *a* unbearably loud.

earth *n* **1** *cap* planet inhabited by humankind **2** dry land; soil; mold **3** lair of fox, etc.; *v* cover with earth; *as* **earthen** made of baked clay; **earthly** belonging to earth; **earthy** like earth.

earthbound *a* **1** unable to leave the earth's surface **2** lacking in imagination.

earthenware *n* coarse pottery.

earthling *n* inhabitant of earth (in science fiction).

earthquake *n* tremor of earth's surface.

earthshaking, earth-

shattering *a* shocking.
earthwork *n* bank of earth built as fortification.
earthworm *n* burrowing worm.
earwig *n* small insect with pincers at rear.
ease *n* comfort; freedom from pain, trouble, exertion, poverty, etc.; absence of difficulty; *v* relieve pain, anxiety, strain; *adv* **at ease** in relaxed mode; *idm* **ill at ease** awkward; *phr v* **ease off/up** make or become less intense.
easel *n* frame to hold paintings, blackboard, etc.
easement *n* property owner's right to use another's for some limited purpose.
east *n* one of four cardinal points; part of horizon where sun rises; eastern countries; *a* situated in, coming from east; *as* **easterly** from, to east; **eastern** of living in the east; *a adv* **eastward** toward east.
Easter *n* annual festival commemorating Resurrection.
Easter egg *n* decorated egg or egg-shaped confectionery eaten at Easter.
easy *a* not difficult; **easygoing** casual; *idm* **go easy on 1** use economically **2** treat sympathetically; *idm* **on easy street** with plenty of money.
eat *v* **1** partake of food **2** consume **3** corrode; *pt* **ate;** *pp* **eaten;** *idm* **be eaten up (with)** have an intense feeling (of, *usu* negative emotion); *idm* **eat one's**

words admit a bad mistake; *idm* **eat out of someone's hand** do exactly what someone wants without question; *idm* **eat one's heart out** be tortured with jealousy; *a* **eatable;** *ns* **eats** *coll* food; **eatery** restaurant.
eating disorder *n* illness characterized by compulsive dieting or overeating.
eau de cologne *n Fr* scented toilet water.
eau-de-vie *n Fr* brandy made from distilled fruit.
eaves *n pl* projecting edge of roof; *v* **eavesdrop** listen secretly; *n* **eavesdropper.**
ebb *n* going out of tide; *fig* decline; *idm* **at a low ebb** in a poor state; depressed; *v* flow back; diminish; *n* **ebb tide.**
ebony *n* hard, black wood; jet black color.
ebullient *a* boiling; exuberant; *ns* **ebullience** act of boiling over; exuberance; **ebullition;** *fig* sudden outburst.
eccentric *a* **1** odd; unconventional; slightly crazy; **2** *geom* not having same center; *n* **1** odd, slightly mad person **2** device for converting rotary into back-and-forth movement.
ecclesiastic(al) *a* pertaining to church or clergy; *n* clergyman.
echelon *n* arrangement of troops, planes, groups of people, etc., in steplike formation.
echo *n* **1** sounds reflected back

from solid surface **2** imitation; *pl* **echoes;** *v* **-oing, -oed.** reverberate; imitate closely.
echocardiogram *n* visual record of heart functions made by reflection of sound waves; **echocardiography.**
echo sounder *n* device for measuring depth of sea or riverbed, etc.
éclair *n* finger-shaped iced cake filled with cream or custard.
éclat *n Fr* applause; striking success.
eclectic *a* selecting from various sources; not exclusive; *n* philosopher who selects doctrines.
eclipse *n* obscuration of light of sun, moon by another heavenly body; *fig* obscurity; *v* **eclipse** darken.
ecliptic *n* apparent annual path of the sun.
ecocatastrophe *n* widespread destruction of the balance of nature in the environment.
ecology *n* study of relation of living things to the environment *a* **ecological** *n* **ecologist.**
economy *n* management of affairs of household or state; avoidance of waste; *a* **economic(al)** relating to economics; cheap; *n pl* **economics** scientific study of production and distribution of wealth; *n* **economist** expert in economics; *v* **economize** cut down

a
b
c
d
e
f
g
h
i
j
k
l
m
n
o
p
q
r
s
t
u
v
w
x
y
z

expenses.

ecosystem *n* ecological unit with all forms of life that interact within it.

ecru *n a* light brown color.

ecstasy *n* 1 rapture; intense exaltation; 2 *sl* stimulant drug; *a* **ecstatic**.

ectopic pregnancy *n* growth of fertilized egg outside the uterus.

ectoplasm *n* substance said to emanate from body of medium in a spiritualist seance.

ecumenical *a* relating to the universal Christian church or to the matter of Christian unity.

eczema *n* inflammatory disease of skin.

Edam *n* mild-flavored Dutch cheese.

eddy *n* **eddies.** small whirlpool; spiral current of air, etc.; *v* **eddying, eddied.** move in whirls.

edema *n* swelling.

Eden *n* **garden of Eden.** state of innocent bliss (as known by Adam and Eve before their fall from grace).

edge *n* 1 boundary; extreme border 2 cutting side of knife, etc. 3 acrimony; *v* 1 give edge to move little by little, *idm* **have the edge on** be (slightly) superior (to); *idm* **on edge** nervous; *a* **edgy;** *adv* **edgily;** *idm* **take the edge off** soften; reduce the effect of; *adv* **edgeways** sideways; *n* **edging** border.

edger *n* tool for trimming grass next to sidewalk.

edible *a* suitable, wholesome to eat; *n* **edibility**.

edict *n* formal order, decree issued by authority.

edifice *n* large building; *v* **edify** benefit morally; *n* **edification** improvement of mind.

edit *v* prepare for publication, broadcasting; direct policies of editing; *ns* **editor; edition** one of several forms in which a book, etc., is published; total number of copies published at one time; **editorial** leading article; *a* **editorial** of editor; *n* **editorship** position of editor.

educate *v* train, cultivate mind of; instruct; pay for education of; *n* **education;** *as* **educational; educative;** *n* **educator** teacher; **educationalist** expert in educational theory, methods.

educe *v* bring out, elicit.

eel *n* long, snakelike fish.

EEG *abbr* electroencephalograph.

eelgrass *n* marine plant with long, narrow leaves.

eerie, eery *a* strange, uncanny, causing fear; *n* **eeriness**.

efface *v* erase; *reflex* keep oneself in background; *n* **effacement;** *a* **effaceable**.

effect *v* cause; bring about; *n* result; impression (mental or physical); *idm* **in effect** in reality; *idm* **come into effect** come to operation; *idm* **take effect** begin to operate; *pl*

property, goods; *as* **effectual** producing intended effect; **effective** producing result; competent; *adv* **-ly;** *n* **-ness**.

effeminate *a* unmanly; weak; womanish; *n* **effeminacy**.

effervesce *v* 1 bubble up 2 be excited; *n* **effervescence;** *a* **effervescent**.

effete *a* weak, worn out.

efficacy *n* power; effectiveness; *a* **efficacious** having desired effect; *n* **efficiency** confidence; *a* **efficient;** *adv* **-ly**.

efficient *a* acting effectively.

effigy *n* image; representation.

efflorescent *a* blossoming; *n* **efflorescence;** *v* **effloresce**.

effluent *a* flowing out; *n* stream flowing out of lake, etc.; liquid sewage; *ns* **effluvium** exhalation, smell, *esp* tainted; *pl* **effluvia; efflux(ion)** act of flowing out.

effort *n* mental, physical exertion; attempt; *a* **effortless;** *adv* **-ly;** *n* **-ness**.

effrontery *n* impudence, audacity.

effulgent *a* shining, radiant; *n* **effulgence**.

effusion *n* profuse, gushing speech, writing; *a* **effusive** profuse; gushing; *adv* **-ly;** *n* **-ness;** *v* **effuse** pour, gush out.

EFL *abbr* English as a foreign language.

e.g. *abbr Lat* exempli gratia (for example).

egalitarian *n, a* (person)

concerned with social equality; n **-ism**.

egg[1] n oval body, containing embryo, reptile, etc; female cell for producing young; idm **have egg on one's face** appear foolish.

egg[2] v incite, urge.

egg cream n drink made with milk, sparkling water, and flavoring.

eggcup n small cup for serving a boiled egg.

egghead n coll intellectual.

eggnog n drink of eggs, milk, sugar, etc.

eggplant n a purple or white, egg-shaped or elongated vegetable.

eggshell a off-white in color; fragile.

egg timer n timing device for boiling an egg.

ego n conscious awareness of self; ns **egoism** selfishness; **egoist**; a **egoistic(al)**; ns **egotism** self-conceit; **egotist**; a **egotistical** conceited.

ego trip n self-centered activity, esp one that boosts one's sense of importance.

egregious a remarkable, in bad sense; n **egregiousness**.

egress n way out; departure.

egret n a type of heron.

eider n arctic sea duck; n **eiderdown** soft down of eider; conforter stuffed with this.

eight n, pron, det, dets cardinal number, one above seven; n crew of eight-oar boat; as, ns **eighth** ordinal number;

eighth part; **eighteen** eight plus ten; **eighteenth**; **eighty** eight tens; **eightieth**.

either a, pron one of two; adv, conj choice of.

ejaculate v 1 exclaim 2 eject suddenly; n **ejaculation**.

eject v fling out; dispossess; emit; ns **ejection**; **ejector**.

ejection seat n avia seat that ejects pilot clear of plane in emergency.

eke out v add to; spin out; lengthen.

elaborate v work out in detail; a complicated; highly ornamented; ns **elaboration**, **elaborator**.

élan n vigor; enthusiam.

eland n large S African antelope.

elapse v of time pass.

elastic a resuming normal shape after distension; fig adaptable; n fabric having rubber woven in it; n **elasticity** resilience.

elated a very happy; in high spirits; adv **-ly**; n **elation** exaltation; high spirits.

elbow n joint between forearm and upper arm; v push, jostle with elbows.

elbow grease n coll physical hard work, esp polishing, cleaning, etc.

elbow room n coll enough room to operate in.

elder a (comp of OLD) older, senior; as **elderly** growing old; (sup of OLD) **eldest** oldest.

elder n tree having white

flowers and black fruit.

elect v choose, select by vote; a selected, but not yet in office; ns **election**; **elector**; **electorate** body of voters; a **electoral**; v **electioneer** canvass for votes.

Election Day n day designated for electing public officials.

Electra complex n psyc girl's subconscious sexual desire to replace mother in father's affections.

electric chair n method of executing criminal by electrocution.

electricity n form of energy, produced by friction, magnetism, etc.; supply of electrical current, for lighting, etc.; a **electric(al)**; v **electrify** charge with electricity; fig startle; ns **electrification**; **electrician** mechanic who works with electricity.

electro- prefix. Makes compounds with meaning by (or caused by) electricity, e.g., **electrocute** v kill by electricity; n **electroplate** metal articles coated with silver, etc., by electrolysis. Where the meaning may be deduced from the simple word, the compounds are not given here.

electrocardiogram n tracing of electrical activity of the heart; n **electrocardiograph** instrument for doing this (abbr ECG).

electroconvulsive therapy n

a
b
c
d
e
f
g
h
i
j
k
l
m
n
o
p
q
r
s
t
u
v
w
x
y
z

med use of electric shock in treatment of psychic disorder.

electrode *n* either of a pair of conductors of electric current, (*e.g.*, from a battery); terminal.

electroencephalogram *n* tracing of electrical activity in the brain; *n* **electroencephalograph** instrument for doing this (*also* **EEG**).

electrolysis *n* 1 separation of substance into different elements by electric current 2 destruction of hair roots, tumors, etc.; *a* **electrolytic**.

electromagnet *n* iron or steel core with wire wound around that becomes magnetic when electric current is passed through it; *a* **electromagnetic**.

electron *n* particle of matter bearing negative charge, revolving around atom.

electronic *a* related to, operated by movement of electrons, by electric current; *adv* **-ally**.

electronic mail *n* transmission of information and personal messages between computers.

electronics *n* study of behavior of electrons and application of this to technology.

electronic organizer *n* small pocket device in which personal information is stored electronically and displayed on a screen when required.

electron microscope *n* very powerful microscope using electrons in place of light rays.

eleemosynary *a* related to charity.

elegant *a* refined; graceful tasteful; *n* **elegance**.

elegy *n* song of mourning; sad poem; *a* **elegiac** mournful; *v* **elegize**.

element *n* basic constituent; natural, suitable environment; *pl* **the elements** 1 basic facts of subject 2 (inhospitable) weather; *idm* **in/out of one's element** happy/unhappy with one's surroundings or activity; *as* **elemental** relating to elements; **elementary** simple.

elementary school *n* school *usu* covering first six years of education.

elephant *n* very large mammal with trunk and ivory tusks; *a* **elephantine** huge; *n* **elephantiasis** skin and limb disease.

elevate *v* lift, raise up (physically or morally); exalt; *ns* **elevator** 1 person, thing that lifts up 2 grain storehouse.

elevation *n* 1 act of lifting, being lifted 2 height above sea level 3 angle above horizon 4 architect's plan of one side of building.

eleven *n*, *pron*, *det* cardinal number one above ten; team of 11 players; *a*, *det* **eleventh**

ordinal number of 11.

eleventh hour *n* the last possible moment.

ELF *abbr rad* extremely low frequency.

elf *n* small woodland sprite; *fig* mischievous child; *pl* **elves;** *a* **elfin** fairylike; roguish.

elicit *v* bring, draw out (information); obtain.

elide *v* omit in pronunciation.

eligible *a* fit, qualified to be chosen; suitable.

eliminate *v* remove; get rid of; exclude; *n* **elimination**.

elite *n* select body of persons; aristocracy.

elitism *n* discrimination in favor of the elite class.

elixir *n* powerful invigorating remedy.

elk *n* large deer.

ell *n* elbow-type extension, *esp* at right angle on building.

ellipse *n* oval; *a* **elliptic** having sphere of ellipse.

ellipsis *n* omission of word, usually understood, from sentence.

elm *n* kind of deciduous tree; its wood.

elocution *n* art and manner of speaking; voice management; *a* **elocutionary;** *n* **elocutionist** teacher of elocution.

elongate *v* extend; prolong; *n* **elongation**.

elope *v* run away secretly, with lover, sometimes to get married; *n* **elopement**.

eloquence *n* fluency; persuasiveness in speech; *a*

eloquent.

else *adv* besides; instead; otherwise; *adv* **elsewhere** in, to, another place.

ELT *abbr* English language teaching.

elucidate *v* explain, make clear; *n* **elucidation**.

elude *v* dodge, baffle; *n* **elusion**; a **elusive** evasive; difficult to catch, to remember.

elves *pl of* ELF.

em- *prefix* (*see* **en-**).

em *n* unit of measure of type (printing).

emaciate *v* make, become very thin; *n* **emaciation** abnormal thinness.

e-mail *abbr* electronic mail.

emanate *v* issue forth; originate from; *n* **emanation**.

emancipate *v* set free; *n* **-ation** freedom.

emasculate *v* castrate; weaken; *n* **-ation**.

embalm *v* preserve corpse from decay, by use of preservatives; *n* **-ment**.

embankment *n* artificial bank carrying road, railway, etc., or damming water.

embargo *n* order prohibiting movement of ships; official ban on trade, etc.

embark *v* put, go on board ship; *fig* start, engage in; *n* **-ation**.

embarrass *v* hinder; perplex; abash; *n* **-ment**.

embassy *n* 1 staff, official residence, of ambassador 2 deputation 3 mission.

embattled *a* fortified; prepared for battle.

embed *v* **-bedding, bedded.** implant deeply, firmly; *fig* fix deeply.

embellish *v* adorn; improve; *n* **-ment**.

ember *n* (*usu pl*) glowing, smoldering ashes; cinders.

embezzle *v* missappropriate money in trust; *ns* **-ment, embezzler**.

embitter *v* make bitter, worse, discontented.

emblazon *v* adorn with coat-of-arms; extol.

emblem *n* concrete symbol of idea, quality, etc.; badge; *a* **emblematic**.

embody *v* give form to; represent; include; *n* **embodiment**.

embolden *v* become courageous.

embolism *n* *med* blockage of vein/artery by blood clot.

emboss *v* cover with design in relief.

embrace *v* hug, clasp in arms; include; *n* such action.

embroider *v* ornament with needlework; *fig* add fanciful details (to story, etc.); *n* **embroidery**.

embroil *v* involve in quarrel, confusion; *n* **-ment**.

embryo *n* **-bryos.** unborn, not fully developed animal; any rudimentary object, idea, etc.; *pl* **-s;** *idm* **in embryo** undeveloped; *a* **embryonic**; *n* **embryology** study of embryos.

emcee *n* master of ceremonies; director of an event.

emend *v* correct mistake; improve (text); *n* **-ation**.

emerald *n* bright green precious stone; this color.

emerge *v* come out; appear; rise to view; become known, apparent; *n* **emergence;** *a* **emergent**.

emergency *n* unexpected happening, requiring swift action; crisis.

emeritus *n* title given to retired professor, etc.

emery *n* hard variety of corundum, used for grinding, etc.; *n* **emery board** cardboard nail file coated with emery.

emetic *n, a* (medicine) causing vomiting.

emigrate *v* leave one's country to live in another; *ns* **-ation; emigrant**.

eminence *n* distinction, fame; height, high ground; title of cardinal; *a* **eminent** outstanding; famous.

éminence grise *n* *Fr* person who secretly wields great influence.

emit *v* **emitting, emitted.** give out; send out; *ns* **emission; emissary** one sent on mission.

Emmenthaler *n* Swiss cheese similar to Gruyère.

Emmy *n* award for best TV performance/production.

emollient *a* softening, soothing; *n* soothing medicinal substance.

emolument n esp pl salary; profit from employment.

emote v display exaggerated emotion.

emotion n agitation of feelings (joy, fear, hatred, etc.); a -al given to, appealing to, the emotions; adv -ally.

emotive a stimulating emotion.

empathy n ability to identify with another person's feelings; v **empathize**.

emperor n ruler of an empire.

emphasis n stress; emphatic assertion; special importance; v **emphasize**; a **emphatic** positive; stressed; adv -ally.

emphysema n med disease of lungs affecting breathing.

empire n (group of states, under) supreme rule (of an emperor).

empirical a (of knowledge) based on experience and observation, not theory; adv -ly; ns **empiricism, - ist.**

employ v use; give work to; occupy (time); n **employment** work, occupation; use of; **employee; employer.**

emporium n large general store; trading center; pl -s or - ia.

empower v authorize; enable.

empress n 1 female ruler of empire 2 wife of emperor.

empty a -tier, -tiest. containing nothing; unoccupied; pointless, stupid; v **-tying, -tied.** make, become, devoid of contents;

n **emptiness.**

empty-headed a foolish; devoid of common sense.

empyrean n highest heaven; the sky; a **empyreal.**

EMS abbr Emergency Medical Services.

emu n large, flightless, Australian bird.

emulate v try to equal; imitate; n **-ation** rivalry; as **emulative, emulous** eager to imitate.

emulsion n globules of one liquid suspended in another; v **emulsify.**

en- prefix (**em** before labials b, m, p) forms verbs with sense of on, into, put into. Where the meaning may be deduced from the simple word, the compounds are not given here.

en n unit measure of type, half an em (printing).

enable v make able; empower; give means to.

enact v make into law; act a part.

enamel n hard, glossy coating, paint, used to preserve surface; outer coating of tooth; v coat with enamel.

enamored (with) a very fond (of).

en bloc a, adv as a whole.

encamp v settle in camp; pitch tents; n **encampment**

encapsulate n 1 enclose in a capsule 2 summarize.

encase v cover entirely.

encephalitis n inflammation of the brain.

enchant v charm; delight;

captivate; ns **-ment; enchanter;** fem **enchantress.**

enchilada n Mexican dish of tortilla with meat and chili sauce.

encircle v surround; form circle round.

enclave n district surrounded by foreign territory.

enclose v surround completely; insert; n **enclosure** object enclosed.

encode v convert into code.

encomium n speech of praise.

encompass v surround; encircle.

encore n call for repetition (of song, etc.); repetition; v ask for encore.

encounter v meet face to face, in hostility; n meeting.

encounter group n group meeting to increase self-awareness and mutual understanding.

encourage v inspire with courage, hope; further a cause; n **encouragement;** a **encouraging;** adv -ly.

encroach v usurp (rights, etc.); (of sea) advance on; trespass; n **encroachment.**

encrust v form, cover with crust; stud thickly with.

encumber v burden; hinder; n **encumbrance.**

encyclical n papal letter sent to whole Roman Catholic Church.

encyclopedia n book, set of books, of classified information on one or all subjects.

end *n* 1 final limit
2 conclusion 3 cessation
4 death 5 purpose 6 result; *v*
finish; complete; cease; *idm*
in the end finally; *idm* **make
ends meet** cope with
financial problems; *idm* **no
end of** *coll* an unlimited
amount of; *idm* **on end**
1 vertically 2 continuously;
idm **put an end to** terminate;
phr v **end up** finish a journey
or one's life.
endanger *v* put into peril.
endear *v* make, cause to be
dear; *a* **-ing;** *n* **-ment**
affectionate term or word.
endeavor *v* strive; try hard; *n*
vigorous effort.
endemic *a* (*of disease*) regularly
occurring in an area.
endgame *n* last stage of game
of chess.
endive *n* kind of chicory, used
in salads.
endocardium *n* membrane
lining the heart.
endocrine *a, n* (hormone, or
secretion) produced by
ductless glands.
endogenous *a* originating
within an organism.
endometrium *n* lining of
uterus.
endorphin *n* protein in the
brain, released during
exercise and having
analgesic properties.
endorse *v* sanction; ratify;
write (name) on back of
(document, etc.); *n* **-ment.**
endoskeleton *n* animal's
internal skeleton.

endow *v* bestow; provide
permanent income for;
n **-ment.**
endowment policy *n* life
insurance with guaranteed
sum payable to policyholder
on maturity.
endue with *phr v fml* provide
with; endow with.
endure *v* last; remain staunch;
tolerate; *a* **endurable**
bearable; *n* **endurance.**
endways *adv* 1 end to end
2 lengthwise (*also* **endwise**).
enema *n* liquid medicine for
the bowels.
enemy *n* opponent; hostile
person, factor; *a* pertaining
to enemy.
energy *n* power; force; vigor; *a*
energetic; adv **-ally;** *v* **energize**
stimulate.
enervate *v* weaken; *n* **-ation**
weakness.
en famille *adv Fr* with the
family; at home.
enfant terrible *n Fr* person
whose behavior seems
shocking, unconventional.
enfeeble *v* make feeble, weak.
enfilade *v* raking fire from
artillery.
enfold *v fml* embrace; envelop.
enforce *v* demand, insist on;
compel by force; *n* **-ment;**
a **-able.**
enfranchise *v* grant right to
vote; set free; *n* **-ment.**
engage *v* 1 bind by promise,
contract 2 hire 3 interlock
4 occupy 5 join in battle; *idm*
engage in take part in; *a*
engaged 1 occupied; in use

2 promised in marriage;
n **-ment** *esp* betrothal; *a*
engaged.
engender *v* cause; arouse, stir
up.
engine *n* any machine
converting physical force
into mechanical energy; *n*
engineer one skilled in
mechanical science; one in
charge of engine.
engineering *n* practical
application of physics,
chemistry, etc.
English *a, n* relating to
England, the US, or other
areas formerly under British
rule; language, people of
these places.
English muffin *n* thin, round
bread, rolled and toasted.
English sparrow *n* house
sparrow.
engrave *v* cut (lines, etc.)
deeply; *fig* fix firmly; *ns*
engraving print taken from
engraved plate; **engraver.**
engross *v* absorb attention;
n **-ment.**
engulf *v* overwhelm.
enhance *v* add to; heighten;
intensify.
enigma *n* riddle; puzzle;
baffling person; *a* **enigmatic
(al);** *adv* **-ally.**
enjoin *v* insist on; order; give
directions to.
enjoy *v* 1 have pleasure from
2 have the benefit of; *idm*
enjoy one-self be happy;
a **-able;** *adv* **-ably;** *n* **-ment.**
enlarge *v* make, grow larger;
phr v **enlarge upon** explain in

details; n **-ment**.

enlighten v free from ignorance, bias, etc.; make meaning clear; n **-ment**.

enlist v enroll in services; obtain (help, sympathy in a cause, etc.) n **-ment** enrollment, *esp* in services.

enliven v add liveliness to; cheer up.

en masse *adv Fr* as a whole; all together.

enmesh v entangle (as in a net).

enmity n hatred; animosity; hostility.

ennoble v 1 make more dignified 2 raise to mobility.

ennui n boredom; lack of interest.

enormity n atrocious crime; gross offense; a **enormous** huge; vast; *adv* **-ly;** n **-ness**.

enough a as much as necessary; sufficient; n sufficiency; required amount.

en passant *adv Fr* in passing; by the way.

enrage v infuriate; provoke to rage.

enrapture v delight; entrance with joy.

enrich v make rich; add to; n **-ment**.

enroll v **-rolling, -rolled.** record, register (name) on list, etc., *esp* as member; n **-ment**.

en route a on the way.

ensconce v place, conceal safely, snugly.

ensemble n parts considered as whole; *mus* combination of

soloists and chorus.

enshrine v place in shrine; *fig* cherish memory of.

enshroud v cover, hide completely.

ensign n badge of office, etc.; naval, military flag.

ensilage n green fodder stored in silo.

enslave v reduce to slavery; deprive of liberty; n **-ment**.

ensnare v entangle; catch in trap.

ensue v follow; be consequent on.

en suite *adv Fr* (of rooms) forming a unit.

ensure v make safe, secure; guarantee.

ENT *abbr med* ear, nose, and throat.

entail v involve.

entangle v involve; catch (as in net); entrap; n **entanglement**.

entente n friendly understanding, *esp* between nations.

enter v 1 come, go into 2 put in writing 3 enroll 4 pierce 5 join; n **entrance** going, coming in; opening; door; ns **entrant** one who enters, *esp* contest; **entry** way in; item noted down (in book, etc.).

enteric a of, relating to intestines; n typhoid fever; n **enteritis** inflammation of intestines.

enterococcus n genus of bacteria naturally found in intestine.

enterprise n plan, project, *esp*

daring, difficult venture; ability to take initiative; a **enterprising**.

entertain v 1 give, show hospitality to 2 amuse 3 foster (an idea, etc.); ns **-er; -ment** amusement.

enthrall v **-thralling, -thralled.** captivate; absorb; hold spellbound.

enthrone v put on throne.

enthusiasm n zeal; intense admiration; n **enthusiast** one animated by intense zeal; a **enthusiastic;** *adv* **-ally;** v **enthuse** express enthusiasm.

entice v attract; allure; tempt; n **-ment;** a **enticing;** *adv* **-ally**.

entire a whole; complete; perfect; n **entirety**.

entitle v give title to; give right, claim to; n **-ment**.

entity n real thing in itself; being, existence.

entomb v 1 put in tomb 2 imprison underground.

entomology n study of insects; n **entomologist;** a **entomological**.

entourage n surroundings; retainers, associates.

entrails n *pl* internal organs; intestines; viscera.

entrance n place of entry.

entrance v enrapture; carry away with delight.

entrant n person entering race, competition, etc.

entrap v catch; *phr v* **entrap someone (into doing)** entice someone (to do).

entreat *v* beg earnestly; beseech; implore; *n* **entreaty** urgent request.

entrée *n* Fr main dish served in a meal.

entrench *v* establish firmly in position; *n* **-ment.**

entrepreneur *n* 1 person organizing commercial venture, *esp* with risk 2 person acting as intermediary in business for others; *a* **entrepreneurial.**

entropy *n* 1 state of disorder 2 tendency of energy, heat to level out evenly.

entrust *v* give into care of; charge with.

entry *n* 1 act of entering 2 person who enrolls for something.

entwine *v* twist together; wind one round the other.

enumerate *v* count; *ns* **enumeration; enumerator.**

enunciate *v* utter distinctly; proclaim; state formally; *n* **enunciation.**

envelop *v* **enveloping, enveloped.** wrap round; *fig* obscure, conceal; *ns* **-ment; envelope** outer covering, *esp* of paper for enclosing letters, etc.; wrapper.

envenom *v* 1 put poison into 2 fill with hatred.

enviable *a* to be envied; *adv* **-ably.**

envious *n* full of envy; *adv* **-ly.**

environ *v* surround; *pl* **environs** immediate surroundings.

environment *n* conditions of life; surroundings; *a* **-mental; adv -mentally;** *n* **-mentalist** person concerned with protecting, improving the environment; *a* **environmentally friendly** not harmful to the environment.

envisage *v* visualize; contemplate.

envision *v* picture in one's mind.

envoy *n* agent; diplomatic representative.

envy *v* begrudge another's success, possessions, etc.; feel jealous of; *n* covetousness; jealousy; *as* **envious** feeling envy; **enviable** exciting envy.

enzyme *n* chemical ferment; **enzymology** study of science of enzymes; *a* **enzymatic.**

eolith *n* piece of chipped flint from early Stone Age.

eon, aeon *n* long period of time.

ep-, eph-, epi-, *prefix: forms compounds with meaning on, upon, during; e.g.,* **ephemeral** *of short duration;* **epicarp** *outer skin of fruits;* **epitaph** *memorial inscription on tomb. Where the meaning may be deduced from the simple word, the compounds are not given here.*

epaulet, epaulette *n mil* shoulder decoration.

épée *n* Fr thin sharp sword used in fencing; use of this.

ephemeral *a* of short duration; impermanent.

ephemeris *n* tables of perpetual planetary placements, *usu* used in astrology.

epic *n* long, narrative poem; book or film.

epicene *a* having characteristics of both sexes.

epicenter *n* area immediately above origin of earthquake.

epicure *n* person who enjoys good food and drink and has fastidious taste; *a* **epicurean.**

epidemic *a* (of disease) prevalent in one community; *n* such disease.

epidemiology *n* science dealing with all aspects of disease within a population; *n* **-iologist.**

epidermis *n* outer skin.

epidural *n med* anesthetic injected into spine, *esp* to counteract pain during childbirth.

epigean *a* relating to area near the surface of the ground.

epiglottis *n* structure that covers the larynx during swallowing.

epigram *n* brief, pointed, witty saying or poem; *a* **epigrammatic.**

epigraph *n* inscription on stone, etc.

epilepsy *n* nervous disease, attended by fits and unconsciousness; *a, n* **epileptic** arising from, or sufferer from epilepsy.

epilogue *n* concluding lines of play; short speech at end of day.

epinephrine *n* adrenalin; also

used in medicine as heart stimulant.

epiphany n 1 appearance; act of appearing 2 sudden perception or realization; *cap* festival of the manifestation of Christ to the Magi.

episcopal a pertaining to bishop; n **episcopacy** government by body of bishops; n, a *cap* **-ian** member of Episcopal church.

episode n one of series of events; incident in story, etc.; a **episodic**.

epistle n letter, *esp* apostolic.

epitaph n memorial inscribed on tomb.

epithet n descriptive adjective, name, or phrase.

epitome n person or thing that embodies a quality, etc.; v **epitomize** abridge.

e pluribus unum *Lat* out of many, one (motto of the US).

epoch n period of time, era, *esp* of great events; a **epochal** very significant.

epoxy n tough synthetic resin, used in glue.

epsilom n fifth letter of Greek alphabet.

Epsom salts n *pl* white powder with laxative properties.

equable a steady, uniform; unvarying; n **equability**.

equal a of like amount, degree, value, merit; equable; n one having same rank, qualities, etc., as another; v be equal to; n **equality** condition of being equal; v **-ize** make,

become equal; n **-ization**.

equanimity n tranquillity, calmness of mind; composure.

equate v consider as equal; reduce to common standard; n **equation,** *math* statement of equality between known and unknown quantities.

equator n imaginary circle dividing earth into two equal parts; a **equatorial**.

equestrian a pertaining to horses, horseback riding; n horseman; *fem* **equestrienne**.

equi- *prefix* equal(ly).

equidistant a equally distant.

equilateral a having equal sides.

equilibrium n state of perfect balance; n **equilibrist** performer of balancing tricks.

equine a of or like a horse.

equinox n time of year when day and night are of equal length; a **equinoctial**.

equip v **equipping, equipped.** fit out; provide, supply; ns **-ment; equipage** retinue; carriage and horses; requisites.

equipoise n 1 balanced state 2 counterbalance.

equipollent a of equal potency.

equitation n *fml* horseback riding.

equity n 1 fairness; justice 2 correction of severe, unfair law 3 market value; n *pl* **equities** ordinary shares; a **equitable** just, reasonable.

equivalent a equal in value, amount, meaning, etc.

equivocal a ambiguous; doubtful; v **equivocate** use words of doubtful meaning to mislead.

ER *abbr* emergency room.

era n period of time dating from particular point; epoch.

eradicate v root out; destroy; abolish; ns **eradication, eradicator**.

erase v rub out; expunge; ns **eraser; erasure**.

ere *prep, conj lit* before; sooner than.

erect v set upright; raise; build; a upright; ns **erection; erector**.

ergo *adv* therefore.

ergonomic n human engineering.

ergot n fungus disease in cereals; drug from this.

erica n genus of heather plants.

ermine n common weasel; such fur.

erode v eat into; corrode; n **erosion;** a **erosive**.

erogenous a producing sexual desire.

erotic a pertaining to sexual desire, love; n **eroticism** sexual excitement.

erotica n erotic literature or art.

err v go astray; make mistakes; be wrong; *as* **erratic** irregular; wandering; **erroneous** wrong, mistaken; ns **erratum** (*pl* **errata**) mistake in printing, etc.; **error** mistake.

errand n short journey with definite purpose; n **errand**

boy messenger.

errant *a* wandering; roving.

erratic *a* unreliable; unsteady; *adv* **-ally**.

erratum *n* printed error; *pl* **errata**.

erroneous *a* mistaken; incorrect; *adv* **-ly**.

ersatz *n*, *a* substitute.

erst, erstwhile *adv* formerly.

eructate *v* belch; *n* **eructation**.

erudite *a* well read, learned; *n* **erudition** learning.

erupt *v* burst out; become active; *n* **eruption** bursting out, *esp* of volcano.

escalate *v* increase by stages; *n* **escalation**.

escalator *n* moving stairway.

escalope *n Fr* thin slice of meat; cutlet.

escapade *n* daring adventure; prank.

escape *v* get free; issue forth; avoid; elude; *n* evasion; leakage (of gas, etc.); *ns* **escapement** mechanical device; balance wheel of watch, etc.; **escapade**, wild, mischievous prank; **escapism** avoidance of realities by indulging in fantasy or abusing substances.

escape artist *n* person adept at getting out of confinement.

escape velocity *n* minimum speed required for spacecraft to escape earth's gravitational pull.

escapology *n* technique of escape as form of entertainment; *n* **escapologist**.

escarpment *n* steep hillside, inland cliff.

escheat *n* reversion of property to state, in absence of heirs.

eschew *v* shun, avoid.

escort *v* go with, as protector, or as sign of courtesy; *n* person, persons escorting another.

escritoire *n* writing desk or table.

escrow *n* legal contract held by third party until its provisions are fulfilled.

escutcheon *n her* shield bearing coat of arms.

Eskimo *n* member of N American Indian race living in arctic *also* **Inuit**.

ESL *abbr* (the teaching of) English as a second language.

esophagus *n* part of alimentary canal leading from mouth to stomach.

esoteric *a* secret; for initiated only.

ESP *abbr* extrasensory perception.

especial *a* remarkable; principal, particular.

Esperanto *n* artificial, universal language.

espionage *n* spying; use of spies.

esplanade *n* leveled terrace, *esp* promenade along seafront.

espouse *v* marry; support (a cause, etc.); *n* **espousal**.

espresso *n* **-os.** strong black coffee.

esprit de corps *n* group loyalty.

espy *v* **espying, espied.** perceive; catch sight of.

esquire *n* title of respect used on letter, abbreviated to **Esq.**

essay *v* try, attempt; *n* short treatise; attempt; *n* **essayist**.

essence *n* **1** most important quality **2** concentrated extract from plant, etc.; *idm* **in essence** basically; *idm* **of the essence** vitally important; *a* **essential**; *adv* **-ly**.

establish *v* set up; give firm basis to; prove; *n* **establishment** establishing; household; permanent civil, military force; business.

established church *n* official national church.

estate *n* **1** stage, condition of life **2** landed property **3** *leg* possessions.

esteem *v* respect, consider highly; *n* respect.

ester *n chem* compound produced by reaction between alcohol and acid.

esthesis *n* basic sensation.

estimate *v* appraise, calculate value of; form opinion of; *n* computation, in advance, of approximate cost; *ns* **estimation** opinion; esteem; **estimator;** *a* **estimable** worthy of respect.

estrange *v* alienate; hurt feelings of; *n* **estrangement** decrease in affection.

estrogen *n* hormone responsible for female physical characteristics.

estrus *n* phase of sexual receptivity in female; heat.

estrogen *n* female hormone.

A
B
C
D
E
F
G
H
I
J
K
L
M
N
O
P
Q
R
S
T
U
V
W
X
Y
Z

estuary *n* mouth of river, where tide enters.

ETA *abbr* estimated time of arrival.

et al. *abbr coll Lat* **1** et alii (and other people) **2** et alia (and other things).

etc. *abbr* et cetera (and the rest).

etch *v* make designs on metal, by eating away by acid; *ns* **etcher; etching**.

eternal *a* everlasting; increasing; *n* **eternity**.

eternal triangle *n* situation when two people are both in love with the same person of the opposite sex.

ether *n* highly volatile liquid, used as anesthetic; the upper air; hypothetical medium supposed to fill all space; *a* **ethereal** light, airy; spiritual.

ethical *a* moral; *n pl* **ethics** system of morally correct conduct.

ethnic *a* of race; *a* **ethnocentric** having strong prejudice about superiority of one's own race, culture, etc.; *ns* **ethnocentrism, ethnocentricity;** *n* **ethnography** study of races of humanity; *a* **ethnographic;** *n* **ethnology** study of different races; *a* **ethnological;** *adv* **-ly;** *n* **ethnologist**.

ethnic cleansing *n* the mass expulsion or killing of people of certain ethnic groups within an area.

ethos *n fml* characteristic spirit or ideas.

ethyl alcohol *n* drinkable form of alcohol.

etiolated *a* **1** *bot* pale from lack of light **2** weak, pale, and spindly.

etiology *n* study of causes, *esp* of diseases.

etiquette *n* polite conventional procedure, manners.

étude *n Fr* musical composition played for practice.

etymology *n* branch of philology dealing with derivation of words; *a* **etymological;** *ns* **etymologist, etymon** primitive word form.

eucalyptus *n* genus of Australasian trees, yielding pungent, volatile oil.

Eucharist *n* Holy Communion; consecreted elements.

euchre *n* card game.

eugenic *a* promoting breeding of fine, healthy stock; *n pl* **eugenics** this science.

eulogy *n* praise, written or spoken; *v* **eulogize** praise, extol; *a* **eulogistic**.

euphemism *n* mild word used in place of unpleasant one; *a* **euphemistic**.

euphony *n* pleasing sound; *as* **euphonic; euphonious** harmonious; *n* **euphonium** bass saxhorn.

euphoria *n* sense of well-being; *a* **euphoric**.

euphuism *n* artificial, affected literary style.

Eurasian *n* person of mixed European and Asian blood.

eureka *interj* expressing triumph of discovery.

eurhythmics *n pl* art of rhythmical free movement.

Euro- *prefix* of Europe.

Eurodollar *n* US dollar as part of European holding.

European *n, a* (inhabitant) of Europe.

eustachian tube *n* duct leading from pharynx to middle ear.

euthanasia *n* painless death, as administered to avoid suffering by incurable illness.

evacuate *v* make empty; withdraw from; discharge (contents); *ns* **evacuation; evacuee** person removed from danger zone.

evade *v* escape; avoid; shirk; *n* **evasion 1** avoidance **2** excuse for not answering properly; *a* **evasive;** *adv* **-ly;** *n* **-ness**.

evaluate *v* find value of; appraise; *n* **-ation**.

evanesce *v* fade away; vanish; *a* **evanescent** transient; *n* **evanescence**.

evangelic, evangelical *a* of, based on the Gospels; *ns* **evangelism** spreading of the Gospel; **evangelist** one of four writers of Gospels; traveling preacher; *v* **evangelize** preach Gospel to.

evaporate *v* turn into vapor; expel moisture, by heating; *n* **-ation**.

evaporated milk *n* unsweetened, condensed,

canned milk

eve *n* evening or day before festival or event; *ns* **evenfall** dusk; **evensong** evening prayer service.

Eve *n* Biblical: first woman, Adam's wife.

even *a* **1** flat **2** uniform **3** equal **4** balanced **5** divisible by two; *v* **1** make even **2** equalize; *phr v* **even out 1** become level **2** become evenly balanced; *adv* **evenly 1** smoothly **2** equally.

evenhanded *a* fair; impartial.

evening *n* **1** part of day between afternoon and night **2** entertainment at this time of day **3** later part of someone's life.

evening dress *n* formal clothes worn at evening event.

evening primrose *n* herb whose yellow flowers open in evening.

event *n* **1** occurrence; incident **2** race; contest; *idm* **at all events/in any event** in any case; *idm* **in that event** if that happens; *idm* **in the event** as it happened; *idm* **in the event of something** if something happens; *a* **eventful**.

eventual *a* final; *adv* eventually.

eventuality *n* possible event.

eventuate *v fml* turn out.

ever *adv* at any time; in any degree; *adv* **evermore** always.

evergreen *n*, *a* (tree, shrub) with green leaves all year.

everlasting *a* **1** lasting forever

2 continual.

eversion *n* state of being inside out.

every *a* each one of all; **every other** alternate; *ns* **everybody; everyone; everything;** *a* **everyday** usual; *adv* **everywhere**; in all places; *idm* **every which way** scattered everywhere.

evict *v* put out; expel by legal process; *n* **eviction**.

evidence *n* **1** supporting fact(s); testimony **2** sign; indication; *idm* **(be) in evidence** (be) clearly seen.

evident *a* clear; obvious; visible.

evil *a* bad; depraved; ill-omened; *n* evil thing or act; *adv* **evilly**.

evil eye *n* power to harm by a look.

evince *v* show; demonstrate.

eviscerate *v* disembowel.

evoke *v* call forth; cause to appear; *n* **evocation;** *a* **evocative**.

evolve *v* develop, open out gradually, naturally; *n* **evolution** course of development of species; *a* **-ary**.

ewe *n* female sheep.

ewer *n* large water pitcher.

ex-, e-, ef- *prefix: forms compounds with meaning of out from, from, out of. Such words are not given, where the meaning may be deduced from the simple word.*

ex. excl. *abbr* excluding.

exacerbate *v* make worse;

irritate; embitter; *n* **-bation**.

exact *a* absolutely correct, accurate; *v* demand; extort; insist on; *a* **-ing** severe; exhausting; *ns* **-itude; -ness** accuracy.

exaggerate *v* overemphasize; overstate; enlarge; *n* **-ation** overstatement.

exalt *v* raise to higher rank; extol; *n* **exaltation;** elevation; elation.

examine *n* **1** scrutinize **2** investigate **3** question **4** test knowledge of; *ns* **examination; examiner**.

example *n* sample; precedent; model; *idm* **make an example of** single out for reward or punishment to encourage others.

exasperate *v* make angry; aggravate; provoke; *n* **-ation;** *a* **-ating** very annoying.

exc. *abbr* except.

Ex Calibur *n* King Arthur's sword.

ex cathedra *a, adv Lat* (made) with authority.

excavate *v* hollow out; dig out; unearth; *ns* **-ation; -ator**.

exceed *v* go beyond (limit, etc.); surpass; *adv* **exceedingly** extremely.

excel *v* **-celling, -celled.** surpass, rise above; be very good at; *a* **excellent** very good; *ns* **excellence; excellency** title given to ambassadors, etc.

except *v* exclude; object; *prep* omitting; *conj* unless; *n* **-exception** thing excluded;

objection (idm **take exception to** object to; a **-al,** adv **-ally,** a **-able** likely to offend); prep **excepting** excluding.

excerpt n selected passage, extract from book, etc.

excess n amount, sum over normal, usual quantity, etc.; overindulgence; a **-ive** extreme.

exchange v give (something), receive (another thing) in return; interchange; n act of exchanging; place where brokers, merchants transact business; central telephone office; a **-able;** n **-ability.**

excise v cut out; remove cut; away; n **excision.**

excise n duty on goods manufactured, consumed within a country.

excite v rouse up; agitate; stimulate; as **excitable** easily excited; adv **-ly;** n **excitability;** a **exciting** thrilling; n **excitement.**

exclaim v cry out suddenly, loudly; n **exclamation** interjection (of surprise, etc.); **exclamation point** mark of punctuation (!) written after an exclamatory remark; a **exclamatory.**

exclude v shut out; disallow; not include; n **exclusion;** a **exclusive** excluding; snobbish; unsociable; adv **-ly.**

excommunicate v expel from church and deprive of privileges; n **-ation.**

excoriate v flay; graze, abrade skin; n **-ation.**

excrement n waste matter from bowels; dung; v **excrete** discharge waste matter from body; n **excretion;** n, a **excretory** (organ) serving to excrete.

excrescence n abnormal growth on organism.

excruciating a acutely painful; agonizing; adv **-ly.**

exculpate v vindicate; free from blame; n **-ation.**

excursion n journey, esp pleasure trip; digression.

excuse v 1 exonerate 2 overlook (fault, etc.); 3 release from obligation; **excuse oneself** apologize; n apology; pretext; a **excusable.**

execrate v detest; loathe; curse; n **execration;** a **execrable** abominable.

execute v 1 perform; carry out 2 kill 3 complete legal instrument; ns **execution; executioner** one who carries out capital punishment; a **executive** able to put into effect (n one charged with administrative, executive work); n **executor** (fem **executrix**) one appointed to carry out provisions of will.

exemplar n model, example; a **exemplary** worthy, commendable.

exemplify v **-fying, -fied.** serve as example; make official copy of; n **-ification.**

exempt v from duty, obligation; a not liable to; n **exemption.**

exercise n healthy physical activity; mental exertion; use of (rights, etc.); mil maneuvers; v give exercise to; use; train.

exercise bike n stationary exercise machine with pedals.

exert v make an effort; put into action; n **exertion** activity, mental or physical.

exeunt v dram they go out.

ex gratia a Lat payment made as a favor.

exhale v breathe out; evaporate; emit; n **exhalation; exhalant.**

exhaust v drain off; use up; tire out; n waste gas, steam discharged from engine; n **exhaustion** intense fatigue; a **exhaustive** comprehensive; adv **-ly.**

exhibit v show in public; give evidence of; n thing exhibited, esp in museum or as material evidence in court; ns **exhibition** display of works of art, etc.; grant to student; ns **-ism, -ist; exhibitor** one who exhibits, esp in show.

exhilarate v enliven; cheer; raise spirits of; n **-ation.**

exhort v admonish; beg earnestly; n **-ation.**

exhume v disinter; dig up, esp corpse; n **-ation.**

exigent a exacting; pressing; urgent; n **exigence, exigency** urgent need; a **exigible**

capable of being exacted.

exiguous *a* too small; scanty.

exile *n* banishment; one banished; *v* banish; expel.

exist *v* live; be; occur; *n* **-ence**; *a* **-ent**.

existentialism *n philosophy* theory that humans are free agents responsible for their own actions; *a, n* **existentialist**; *a* **existential** 1 relating to existence 2 existentialist; *adv* **existentially**.

exit *n* 1 act of leaving, going out 2 way out; *v* leave stage; go out.

exodus *n* departure, *esp* of many people; *cap* second book of Old Testament.

ex officio *a, adv Lat* by virtue of office (not elected).

exogamy *n* marriage to an outsider.

exonerate *v* free from blame; exculpate; acquit; *n* **-ration**.

exorbitant *a* excessive; immoderate; *n* **exorbitance**.

exorcise *v* expel (evil spirit) by religious means; *ns* **exorcism, -ist**.

exotic *a* foreign; rare, unusual; *n* **exoticism**.

expand *v* spread out; extend; dilate; develop; *phr v* **expand on** explain in more detail; *ns* **expanse** wide, open tract of land; **expansion, -ism, -ist**; *a* **expansive** effusive.

expatiate *v* dilate; enlarge upon.

expatriate *v* banish; quit one's country; *a* **-ated;** *n*

expatriated person; *n* **-ation**.

expect *v* await; anticipate; look for as due, right; *a* **expectant** awaiting; *ns* **expectancy** anxious, eager anticipation; **expectation** that which is expected; future prospects.

expectorate *v* spit; cough up (phlegm, etc.); *n* **-ation**.

expedient *a* suitable; advantageous; convenient; *n* means to an end; device; *n* **expediency** convenience.

expedite *v* hasten, speed up (progress of); dispatch; *n* **expedition** journey for set purpose, *esp* military, exploratory; *as* **expeditionary; expeditious** rapid; prompt.

expel *v* **-pelling, -pelled.** drive out; dismiss; *n* **expulsion**.

expend *v* give out; spend; use up; *ns* **expenditure; expense** *n* cost; disbursement; *idm* **at someone's expense** 1 paid for by someone 2 making mockery of someone; *pl* **expenses** costs incurred; *a* **expensive** costly; **expendable** inessential, of little value.

expense account *n* arrangement for employer to pay all expenses.

experience *n* living through events, emotions, etc.; knowledge, skill, gained by personal practice, observation, etc.; event witnessed, lived through; *v* undergo, meet with; *a* **experienced** skillful,

competent.

experiment *n* trial, undertaken to test theory, discover new facts; *v* make experiments; *a* **-al;** *adv* **-ally**.

expert *a* skilled; dexterous; *n* one having special knowledge; *n* **expertise**.

expiate *v* atone for; make amends for; *n* **-ation**.

expire *v* exhale, die; come to an end; *ns* **expiration; expiry** conclusion.

explain *v* make intelligible; interpret; account for; *n* **explanation;** *as* **explanatory; explanative**.

expletive *a* superfluous; *n* exclamation; oath; obscenity.

explicable *a* able to be explained.

explicate *n* explain.

explicit *a* clearly stated; unequivocal; *adv* **-ly;** *n* **-ness**.

explode *v* burst violently, with loud report; cause to explode.

exploit *n* bold, adventurous deed; *v* make unfair use of; *esp* to one's own benefit; develop resources of; *ns* **-ation; -er**.

explore *v* examine closely; travel in strange region and investigate it; probe; *ns* **exploration; explorer;** *a* **exploratory**.

explosion *n* 1 sudden violent noise 2 sudden increase.

explosive *n, a* (substance) that explodes; *adv* **-ly**.

exponent *n* 1 person explaining a belief, showing

A
B
C
D
E
F
G
H
I
J
K
L
M
N
O
P
Q
R
S
T
U
V
W
X
Y
Z

a skill **2** *math* figure showing how many times a number is to be multiplied by itself; *a* **exponential** resulting from such multiplication.

export *v* sends (goods) abroad for trade; *ns* **exportation; exporter**.

expose *v* lay bare; leave unprotected; display; reveal; *n* **exposure;** *idm* **expose oneself to something** leave oneself unprotected from something.

exposé *n* exposure of wrongdoing.

expository *a* serving to explain ro expound.

exposition *n* **1** setting out; explaining **2** exhibition.

ex post facto *a, adv Lat* acting retrospectively.

expostulate *v* remonstrate; protest against; *n* **-lation**.

expound *v* explain, set forth; *ns* **exponent; exposition** explanation; exhibition; *a* **expository;** *n* **expositor** interpreter.

express 1 *v* make known by speech, visual image, etc. **2** squeeze out; *a* explicit; of special kind; sent, traveling at fast speed; *n* fast delivery, train service; *n* **expression 1** expressing **2** utterance **3** feeling **4** facial aspect; *as* **-ness; expressive;** *adv* **-ly;** *n* **-ness**.

expressionism *n* style of art portraying subjective emotions; *n, a* **expressionist**.

expressway *n* road for high-

speed traffic.

expropriate *v* deprive of possession of; *n* **-ation**.

expulsion *n* act of expelling.

expunge *v* wipe out; erase; delete; *n* **expunction**.

expurgate *v* remove offensive material from text (of books, etc.); *n* **-ation**.

exquisite *a* select; extremely beautiful; tasteful; acutely sensitive.

extant *a* still surviving; still in existence.

extempore *a, adv* without preparation; *as* **extemporaneous; extemporary;** *v* **extemporize** improvise; make up speech, song, etc., on spur of moment.

extend 1 *v* stretch out; expand; prolong **2** offer; bestow **3** last; *n* **extension** stretching out; expansion; addition; *a* **extensive** widespread; comprehensive; *n* **extent** area scope; degree.

extenuate *v* lessen; minimize, *esp* guilt, blame; *n* **extenuation;** *a* **extenuating**.

exterior *a* outside; external; *n* outward appearance.

exterminate *v* wipe out; extirpate; destroy; *ns* **extermination; exterminator**.

external *a* outside; *adv* **-ly;** *v* **externalize** give outward expression to; *pl* **externals** outward appearances.

extinct *a* **1** having died out; no longer existing **2** inactive (of

volcano); *n* **extinction;** *v* **extinguish** quench, stifle; *n* **extinguisher** device for putting out fire.

extirpate *v* root out; destroy; *n* **extirpation** total destruction.

extol *v* **-tolling, -tolled.** laud, praise highly.

extort *v* obtain money by threats; *n* **extortion;** *n, a* **extortionist;** *a* **extortionate** unreasonably expensive.

extra *a* additional; more than usual; *n* something extra.

extra- *prefix: forms compounds with meaning of* outside, beyond. *Where the meaning may be deduced from the simple word the compounds are not given here.*

extract *v* **1** pull, draw out *esp* by force **2** select; distil; *n* thing extracted; *ns* **extraction; extractor**.

extracurricular *a* not part of course of study.

extradition *n* surrender of an alleged criminal, by one nation to another, under treaty; *v* **extradite** give, obtain such surrender.

extramarital *a* (of sexual behavior) outside marriage.

extramural *a* outside walls of; associated with, not taking place within school.

extraneous *a* unrelated to; not essential; foreign.

extraordinary *a* unusual; exceptional; *adv* **-arily**.

extrapolate *v* deduce or guess from known facts or personal observation.

extrasensory perception *n* ability to acquire information not through the physical senses (*also* **ESP**).

extraterrestrial *a* (from) beyond the earth.

extraterritorial *a* outside limits, jurisdiction of country.

extravagant *a* excessive; wasteful; flamboyant; *adv* **-ly;** *n* **extravagance.**

extravaganza *n* elaborate and costly entertainment.

extreme *a* **1** remotest **2** of highest degree **3** severe **4** last; final **5** beyond moderate; *adv* **-ly;** *ns* **extremist** one holding extreme views (in politics); **extremity** end; great distress, danger; *pl* **-ies** hands and feet.

extreme unction *n* sacrament for dying person.

extricate *v* free from; disentangle; **extrication.**

extrinsic *a* not belonging to; from outside; *adv* **-ally.**

extrovert *n* one whose interests are directed outward from self; vigorous personality.

extrude *v* thrust out; expel; *n* **extrusion.**

exuberant *a* full of vitality; overflowing; overabundant.

exude *v* ooze out; discharge through pores; *n* **exudation.**

exult *v* rejoice greatly; trumph; *n* **exultation;** *a* **exultant** jubilant.

eye *n* **1** organ of sight **2** power of observation **3** hole in needle **4** ring for a hook to fit **5** calm spot in center of storm; *idm* **an eye for an eye** retaliation (equal to the offense); *idm* **easy on the eye** good-looking; *idm* **have an eye for** be capable of judging; *idm* **in the eyes of** in the opinion of; *idm* **keep an eye on** watch closely; *idm* **make eyes at** flirt with; *idm* **see eye to eye** understand each other; agree; *idm* **up to one's eyeballs in** *coll* extremely busy with; *idm* **with an eye toward 1** keeping in mind **2** with the intention of; *v* **eyeing or eying, eyed.** look at; stare at; *ns* **eyeball** (*idm* **eyeball to eyeball** *coll* face to face); **eyebrow** ridge of hair above eye; **eyelash** hair fringing eyelid; **eyesore** something offensive to eye; **eyetooth** canine tooth; **eyelet** small hole in material.

eye-catching *a* striking, attractive. **eye contact** *n* attracting someone's gaze by looking into his/her eyes.

eye cup *n* small optic cup for washing or applying medicine to the eyeball.

eyeglasses *n* lenses worn to aid vision.

eyelid *n* skin covering eyeball.

eye-opener *n* thing, event revealing surprising new facts.

eye shadow *n* make-up used on eyelids.

eyesight *n* power of seeing.

eyesore *n* ugly object, *esp* one spoiling landscape.

eyewash *n* *coll* deceptive nonsense.

eyewitness *n* person actually present at event.

eyrie *n* eagle's nest.

a
b
c
d
e
f
g
h
i
j
k
l
m
n
o
p
q
r
s
t
u
v
w
x
y
z

fable *n* short story with moral; myth; fiction; *as* **fabled** legendary; **fabulous** mythical; exaggerated; unbelievable; *adv* **-ly.**

fabric *n* structure, framework; woven cloth; *v* **fabricate** 1 manufacture 2 invent falsely; forge; *n* **fabrication.**

fabulous *a* 1 incredible 2 legendary 3 *coll* wonderful; *adv* **-ly** extremely.

facade *n* front of building; outward appearance.

face *n* 1 front part of head 2 visual expression 3 *coll* make-up 4 top or front surface 5 dignity; prestige 6 effrontery; *idm* **face to face** close up; in direct contact, opposition; *idm* **in the face of** (going) against; in spite of; *idm* **on the face of it** judging by appearances; *idm* **to somebody's face** openly *v* 1 turn toward 2 meet; oppose 3 cover front of; *phr v* **face**

up to 1 meet courageously 2 be realistic about; *a* **faceless** of unknown identity or character.

face card *n* king, queen, and jack in deck of cards.

face-lift *n* plastic surgery to improve face; *fig* (of building) renovation.

face-saver *n* thing that saves somebody from embarrassment; *a* **face-saving.**

facet *n* aspect; side.

facetious *a* not serious; flippant; *adv* **-ly;** *n* **-ness.**

face value *n* (of money) value shown; *idm* **take something at its face value** assume something is what it seems to be.

facial *a* of the face; *n* beauty treatment of face.

facile *a* easily done; fluent; *v* **facilitate** make easier; *n* **facility** 1 ease; dexterity 2 building designated for

specific purpose; *pl* **facilities** 1 helpful opportunities 2 restrooms.

facing *n* decorative or protective lining.

facsimile *n* exact copy.

fact *n* thing known to be true; actual experience; reality; *a* **factual;** *adv* **-ly.**

faction *n* group within a political party *a* **factious** 1 caused by faction 2 quarrelsome.

factious *a* causing trouble.

factor *n* contributory force to a result; agent; *n* **factory** building in which goods are manufactured.

facts of life *n* 1 facts of sexuality 2 true nature of situation.

faculty *n* aptitude; inherent ability; natural or special function (of mind or body); body of teachers; collectively, members of such a division.

fad *n* whim; passing craze; pet notion; *n* **faddiness;** *as* **faddish, faddy.**

fade *v* 1 (cause to) lose color 2 disappear gradually 3 become less audible; *phr vs* **fade away** die;

fade in/out 1 bring slowly into/out of view 2 make more/less clearly audible.

fag end *n* 1 remnant 2 untwisted end of rope.

fagot *n* bundle of sticks for firewood; bundle of steel rods.

Fahrenheit *a* scale of

temperature, having boiling point 212° and freezing point 32°.

fail *v* 1 be unsuccessful 2 let down; disappoint 3 become weak 4 not function properly; *idm* **fail to do** neglect to do; *idm* **without fail** certainly; reliably; *n* **failing** fault, defect; *prep* without.

faille *n* ribbed fabric.

fail-safe *a* designed for extra security in emergency.

failure *n* 1 lack of success 2 person, thing that fails 3 inability.

faint *a* feeble; weak; vague; *v* swoon; *n* fainting fit.

fainthearted *a* cowardly.

fair[1] *n* market for sale of goods, often with sideshows, etc.; trade exhibition.

fair[2] *a* 1 just; impartial; honest 2 quite good; average 3 not dark 4 good-looking 5 favorable; *adv* **-ly** 1 in an honest way 2 rather; *n* **-ness;** *idm* **fair and square** honestly; *idm* **fair enough** all right.

fair game *n* person, thing considered reasonable to mock or take advantage of.

fairground *n* outdoor area where fairs, circuses, etc., are held.

fairway *n* 1 navigation channel 2 *golf* mown part of course between tee and green.

fairy *n* imaginary being with magic powers *ns* **fairyland; f.**

godmother person who helps someone in trouble; **f.-tale** 1 story of magic 2 untrue story; *a* magically wonderful.

fait accompli *n* thing done that cannot be undone.

faith *n* 1 trust 2 strong belief 3 sincerity; *a* **faithful** loyal; reliable *adv* **-ly;** *a* **faithless;** *n* **-ness;** *idm* **break/keep faith (with)** break/keep a promise (to); *n* **f. healing** treatment of disease by prayer.

fake *v* make imitation of something rare, valuable; touch up; counterfeit; *n* sham; fabrication; forgery; *n* **faker.**

fakir *n* Muslim or Hindu monk.

falafel *n* Mideastern fried food made from chick peas and spices.

falcon *n* bird of prey, *esp* female trained in hawking; *ns* **falconer** one who keeps, hunts with, falcons; **falconry** hawking.

fall[1] *v* 1 drop 2 hang loosely 3 become lower 4 occur 5 be killed or wounded 6 be defeated; succumb 7 (of face) become sad 8 enter a specified state; become; *pt* **fell** *pp* **fallen;** *idm* **fall flat** collapse; fail; *idm* **fall foul of** get into trouble with; *idm* **fall short** be inadequate; **fall apart** disintegrate; **fall away** disperse; disappear; **fall back** retreat; **fall back on** use as reserve or support; **fall**

behind fail to keep up; **fall for** 1 be attracted by 2 be deceived by; **fall off** decrease in intensity, quantity, or quality; **fall on** attack; **fall out** 1 quarrel 2 occur; **fall over oneself** make every effort; **fall through** (of plans) fail; **fall to** begin; **fall under** be classified as; *a* **fallen** no longer innocent.

fall[2] *n* 1 act of falling 2 decline 3 distance downward; 4 **The Fall** Bible loss of human innocence; *pl* **falls** waterfall.

fallacy *n* 1 false belief 2 false reasoning; *a* **fallacious;** *adv* **-ly.**

fallible *a* liable to error; *n* **fallibility.**

falling out *n* argument.

falling star *n* shooting star.

fallopian tube *n* tube by which egg passes from ovary to womb.

fall out *n* 1 radio-active dust in air following nuclear explosion 2 effects of this.

fallow[1] *n* land plowed up, left unsown; *a* uncultivated.

fallow[2] *a* of brownish, reddish yellow (of deer).

false *a* 1 wrong; mistaken 2 deceptive 3 disloyal 4 sham; artificial; *ns* **-hood** lie; **-ness** disloyalty; **falsity** quality of being false; *v* **falsify** alter with intent to deceive, misrepresent; *n* **falsification.**

falsetto *n* (use by man of) high-pitched lead voice as of female.

a b c d e f g h i j k l m n o p q r s t u v w x y z

falsies *coll n pl* pads used to make breasts look larger.

falter *v* stumble, be unsteady; stammer; hesitate; *a* **faltering**.

fame *n* renown, reputation; *a* **famed** well known.

familial *a* of the family.

familiar *a* intimate; well known; conversant with; vulgarly cordial; *n* **familiarity; *v* familiarize** accustom someone to something.

family *n* **1** group of people related by blood, marriage **2** one's children **3** people with a common ancestor **4** group of related living things **5** group of related languages; *a* **1** of family members (*ns* **f. gathering; f. planning f. court; f. room; f. tree** genealogical table) **2** suitable for children (*n* **f. entertainment**).

famine *n* acute shortage of food; starvation; *v* **famish** starve.

famous *a* widely known; *adv* **-ly** *coll* extremely well.

fan[1] *n* **1** device causing flow of air; ventilating machine **2** outspread tail feathers of bird; *v* **fanning, fanned.** cause a rush of air with a fan; *v* **fan out** spread like a fan from a center.

fan[2] *n* enthusiastic supporter.

fanatic(al) *a* having violent, unreasoning belief in; *n* zealot; *n* **fanaticism**.

fan belt *n* *aut* belt connecting engine drive to fan for cooling engine.

fancy *n* **1** imagination **2** thing imagined **3** desire **4** small cake; *idm* **take somebody's fancy** attract; *idm* **take a fancy to** become attracted on; *v* **1** like; wish for **2** imagine; *idm* **fancy oneself** have a high opinion of oneself; *n* **fancier** one with special knowledge, *esp* of breeding animals, birds; *as* **fanciful 1** imaginary **2** capricious; **fancy 1** brightly decorated **2** unusual (*n* **f. dress**) **3** extravagant (*n* **f. idea**) **4** specially bred.

fancy-free *a* not committed to any relationship.

fandango *n* **-os.** lively Spanish dance.

fanfare *n* flourish of trumpets.

fang *n* long, pointed tooth; poison tooth of snake.

fan letter *n* letter from an admirer to someone famous.

fanlight *n* small window above main window or door.

fantan *n* card game; Chinese gambling game.

fantasia *n* imaginative composition in free form, *esp* music (*also* **fantasy**).

fantasize *v* have fantasies.

fantasy *a* **1** imagination **2** wild, unrealistic idea **3** fantasia; *a* **fantastic 1** wild and strange **2** impractical **3** *coll* wonderful; *adv* **-ally**.

far *a*, *adv* **1** at a distance **2** very much **3** extreme(ly); *idm* **as far as 1** up to and no farther **2** to the extent that; *idm* **by far/far and away** by a great amount; *idm* **far be it from me to I** certainly would not; *idm* **far from doing** instead of doing; *idm* **so far** until now.

farce *n* ludicrous, boisterous comedy; absurd, futile situation; *a* **farcical**.

fardel *n* burden.

fare *n* sum charged for conveyance of passenger; passenger; food; *v* travel; prosper; feed; get on.

Far East *n* countries of eastern and southern Asia.

farewell *n* leave-taking; *interj* good-bye.

far-fetched *a* unbelievable.

far-flung *a* located at great distances.

far gone *a* almost beyond recovery.

farina *n* flour, meal, ground from corn, nuts, etc.; *a* **farinaceous** mealy.

farm *n* **1** area of land for growing crops and rearing animals **2** house and buildings near this; *ns* **farmer, farming, farmhouse, farmyard; farmhand** farm worker; *phr v* **farm out** delegate; send to be cared for by others.

far-off *a* distant.

far-out *a* *coll* **1** unconventional **2** very good.

far-reaching *a* having extensive influence.

farrier *n* blacksmith who shoes horses.

farrow n litter of pigs; v give birth to pigs.

farsighted a 1 showing awareness of possible future developments (also **far-seeing**) 2 able to see for a long distance.

farther a, adv move distant, esp in space or time.

farthermost adj most distant.

farthest a, adv most distant.

fasces n bundle of rods tied around an ax, representing authority.

fascia, facia n 1 flat strip of wood metal on building 2 part of shipfront, showing name, etc. 3 stripe.

fascinate v enchant, bewitch; subdue by fixed stare; n **fascination**; a **fascinating**.

fascism n extreme right-wing dictatorial political system; n **fascist**.

fashion n style; latest mode, vogue; method; idm **after a fashion** in an inadequate way; v form, shape, make; a **fashionable** modish; adv **-ably**.

fast[1] a 1 firmly fixed; sure 2 rapid 3 (of clock) ahead of actual time 4 dissipated; adv 1 rapidly 2 fixedly; securely; idm **fast asleep**; v **fasten** fix; secure; attach; seize (upon); n **fastness** secure place, stronghold.

fast[2] v abstain from food or some kinds of food; n act of fasting.

fastback n rear of automobile curving downward.

fasten v 1 secure; attach 2 become secured; ns **fastener, fastening**.

fast food n food that can be cooked easily and eaten quickly or taken out.

fast forward n facility on audio or video player for moving quickly ahead.

fastidious a difficult to please; critical; discriminating; n **fastidiousness**.

fast track n route of quick achievement or success.

fat a **fatter, fattest**. 1 plump; obese 2 greasy 3 fertile 4 thick; stumpy; idm **fat chance** coll very little chance; idm **a fat lot of good** coll very little (good); n oily, animal substance; best part; idm **the fat of the land** the finest food and drink; n **fat cat** rich, influential person; v **fatten** (of cattle) make fat for slaughter; a **fatted** fattened; n **fatness**; a **fatty**.

fatal a ending in death; destructive; ns **fatality** calamity; death by accident; **fatalism** doctrine that all events are preordained; a, n **-ist**.

fatback n hog fat usu used in cooking.

fate n supposed power controlling course of all events; destiny; one's lot, condition; evil fate, doom; as **fated** destined; **fateful** fraught with fate; decisive.

father n male parent; forefather; originator; title of respect, esp of priest, etc.; v beget; care for as father; be author of; as **-ly; -less**; ns **fatherhood; f.-in-law** wife's, husband's father; **fatherland** native country.

Father Christmas n Brit old man with red robe and white beard giving presents to children at Christmas (also **Santa Claus**).

father figure n older man who protects and is respected by young people.

Father's Day n third Sunday in June set aside for honoring fathers.

fathom n measure of depth in water, 6 ft.; v take soundings of; understand; a **fathomless** very deep.

fatigue n exhaustion; weariness, of body or mind; weakness in metal after repeated stresses; v weary; weaken; a **-ed.** tired; made to appear old (clothing).

fatten v make fatter.

fatty a 1 like fat; 2 full of fat; n coll fat person.

fatuous a silly; stupid; futile; adv **-ly**; n **-ness**; n **fatuity**.

faucet a tap for drawing liquid from cask, pipe, etc.

fault n 1 defect; error 2 fracture in earth's crust 3 offense; idm **at fault** to blame; idm **find fault (with)** criticize; idm **to a fault** excessively; a **faulty**; adv **-ily**; a **faultless; adv -ly**; n **-ness**.

faun n myth rural deity with

a b c d e f g h i j k l m n o p q r s t u v w x y z

A
B
C
D
E
F
G
H
I
J
K
L
M
N
O
P
Q
R
S
T
U
V
W
X
Y
Z

horns and goat's feet.

fauna *n* all animal life of region or period.

faux pas *n Fr* embarrassing mistake; tactless remark.

favor *n* **1** act of good will **2** partiality **3** rosette; badge; *idm* **in favor of 1** supporting **2** payable to; *idm* **in somebody's favor** to somebody's advantage; *v* **1** approve **2** resemble **3** support; *a* **favorable** propitious; approving; *adv* **-ably;** *n* **favorite** favored person or thing; *a* preferred; most liked; *n* **favoritism** undue partiality.

fawn[1] *n* young deer; *a* pale, grayish brown.

fawn[2] *v* (*of person*) cringe, act servilely toward; (*of dogs, etc.*) show affection by groveling.

fax *n* message sent along a telephone line, then printed on a special machine; *v* send a message in this way; *n* **fax machine.**

faze *v coll* fluster.

FBI *abbr* Federal Bureau of Investigation.

fear *n* dread; anxiety; awe; *idm* **Never fear!** *coll* don't worry; *v* be afraid (of); expect (something bad); *idm* **not much fear of something** something is unlikely to happen; *as* **fearful** apprehensive; awful; **fearsome** horrible; **fearless** courageous.

feasible *a* possible; practicable;

n **feasibility.**

feasibility study *n* preliminary investigation as to whether a project is practicable or not.

feast *n* **1** religious day of rejoicing **2** lavish repast **3** village fete; *idm* **feast one's eyes on** enjoy looking at; *v* give, eat sumptuous banquet.

feat *n* exceptional deed, act of bravery, skill, etc.

feather *n* one of quilled, soft appendages forming plumage of birds; *idm* **feather in one's cap** achievement to be proud of; *v* **1** line, adorn with feathers **2** turn oar; *idm* **feather one's nest** make oneself rich at someone else's expense; *a* **feathery** soft light; *n* **featherweight** very light person, or thing.

featherbedding *n* padding ranks of employees; limiting production.

featherbrained *a* thoughtless and silly.

feature *n* **1** part of face **2** noticeable or prominent part of anything **3** special article in newspaper, etc.; *v* portray; give prominence to; present; *a* **featureless** without anything distinctive.

feature-length *a* (of film) full-length.

febrile *a* feverish.

February *n* second month of year.

fecal *a* relating to feces.

feces *n pl* excrement.

feckless *a* thoughtless, careless, irresponsible.

fecund *a* fruitful; fertile; prolific; *n* **fecundity.**

fed *pt and pp of* **feed.**

federal *a* **1** relating to government that distributes power between central authority and constituent units **2** (cap) of US government; *n* **federate** unite to form federation; *n* **-ation** federal union, society.

fedora *n* soft, felt hat.

fed up *a* bored; dejected; dissatisfied.

fee *n* charge for professional and other services; entrance money for examination, etc.

feeble *a* infirm, weak; ineffectual; frail; *adv* **feebly.**

feed *v* give food to; supply with fuel, material; eat; consume; *pt, pp* **fed;** *n* fodder; material supplied; *ns* **feeder** one who feeds; that which supplies.

feedback *n* **1** information from user back to originator of idea or product **2** *elec* output from (*e.g.*, amplifier) returned as new input.

feeding bottle *n* bottle with small aperture for feeding liquid to babies or small animals.

feel *v* **feeling, felt. 1** explore by touch **2** experience physically or emotionally **3** give specified sensation **4** be affected by **5** be capable of sensation; *idm* **feel like** want; *idm* **feel for** sympathize with; *n* **1** exploration by touch **2** sensation; *idm* **get**

the feel of become used to; *idm* **have a feel for** be appreciative of.

feeler *n* antenna by which insect feels things; *idm* **put out feelers** test people's opinions.

feel-good factor *n* general feeling of optimism among the population of a country.

feeling *n* 1 sensation 2 emotion 3 awareness 4 belief 5 sympathy; *a* showing emotion; *adv* **-ly.**

feet *pl of* **foot.**

feign *v* pretend; assume; simulate.

feint[1] *n* misleading action; pretense.

feint[2] *a* with faintly printed lines.

feisty *a coll* 1 spirited 2 quarrelsome.

feldspar *n* white or red mineral rock (*also* **felspar**).

felicity *n* happiness, bliss; contentment; *a* **felicitous** happy; apt; *v* **felicitate** congratulate; *n* **-ation.**

feline *a* of cats; catlike.

fell[1] *v* 1 *pt of* **fall** 2 cut down.

fell[2] *n* skin, hike; membrane under skin.

fell[3] *a* destructive; *idm* **in one fell swoop** suddenly; devastatingly.

fellow *n* companion; associate; member (of society, governing body of college, etc.).

fellowship *n* 1 companionship 2 society 3 position of fellow in university college.

fellow traveler *n* 1 traveling companion 2 sympathizer with but not member of (*esp* Communist) party.

felony *n* grave crime; more heinous than misdemeanor; *n* **felon** criminal guilty of felony; *a* **felonious.**

felt[1] *n* fabric made of compressed wool; *a* made of felt.

felt[2] *pt of* **feel.**

felt-tip *a, n* (pen) with felt nib.

female *a* 1 of the sex that bears offspring or fruit 2 of women 3 (of mechanical parts) with a hole to accommodate a male part; *n* woman or female animal.

feminine *a* of women; having gender referring to females; *ns* **femininity; feminism** advocacy of complete equality between sexes; *a, n* **-ist.**

femme fatale *n Fr* woman attractive but dangerous to men.

femur *n* thighbone; *a* **femoral.**

fen *n* low, flat, marshy land; *a* **fenny.**

fence *n* 1 hedge; railing; 2 receiver of stolen goods; *idm* **sit on the fence** be noncommital; *v* enclose, protect with fence; fight with sword; avoid direct answer; *ns* **fencer;** swordsman; **fencing** protective fences; art of swordplay.

fend *v* keep, ward off; *phr vs* **fend for** look after; protect; **fend off** ward off; push away;

n **fender** 1 protective frame around fireplace 2 *aut* part of automobile body protecting the wheels 3 rope protecting side of boat or ship.

fender bender *n coll* nonsignificent auto accident.

fennel *n* fragrant herb used in cooking.

feral *a* fatal; gloomy; undomesticated; wild.

ferment *v* undergo chemical process involving effervescence; become excited; *n* substance causing fermentation, (*e.g.*, yeast) tumult, commotion; *n* **-ation** act of fermenting.

fern *n* plant with fronds, feathery or plain; *a* **ferny** abounding in ferns.

ferocious *a* savage, fierce, cruel; *n* **ferocity.**

ferret *n* small, half-tamed animal of weasel family, used for driving rabbits out of holes; *v* hunt with ferret; *fig* search thoroughly.

ferric, ferreous, ferrous *a* of, containing iron; *a* **ferriferous** yielding iron; *n* **ferrite** type of iron ore; **ferro-** *prefix* denoting presence of iron.

Ferris wheel *n* (at amusement park, fairground) big wheel with seats.

ferrule *n* metal cap protecting end of stick, etc.

ferry *v* **-rying, -ried.** convey, cross, over river, channel, etc., *n* **-ies.** boat, raft used for ferrying (*also* **f. boat**); place where ferry is.

fertile *a* fruitful; prolific; abundant; rich in ideas; *n* **fertility;** *v* **fertilize** make fertile; *ns* **-ization, -izer.**

fervent *a* burning, glowing; ardent, intense; *ns* **fervency; fervor;** *a* **fervid** hot; impassioned.

fescue *n* genus of perennial grasses.

festal *a* of feasts.

fester *v* suppurate; putrefy; rankle; *n* ulcer.

festival *n* joyful celebration; series of organized musical, dramatic performances; *a* **festive,** joyous; convivial; *ns* **festivity** gaiety, joyousness; *pl* **festivities** joyful celebration.

festoon *n* chain or garland of flowers, ribbons, etc., hung in loops; *v* decorate with festoons.

fetal position *n* position imitating fetus in womb; on side, with legs drawn up, arms pulled in, head lowered.

fetch *v* **1** go for and bring back **2** be sold for **3** *dated* be the cause of; *a* **fetching** attractive; *adv* **-ly.**

fête *n* festival; fair, *usu* open-air; *v* honor with festivities.

fetid *a* stinking.

fetish *n* object worshiped by savages; object of exaggerated devotion; *n* **fetishism;** *n, a* **-ist.**

fetlock *n* tufted pad at the back of horse's leg, just above hoof.

fetter *n* shackle for feet; *pl*

restraint; *v* put in irons; impede; *a* **fettered** restrained.

fettle *n* condition or state; *v* put in order; repair.

fettucine *n* ribbonlike pasta.

fetus *n* unborn offspring; *a* **fetal.**

feud[1] *n* bitter, long-standing hostility between two persons, clans, etc.

feud[2] *n* land held in return for service to overlord.

feudal *a* pertaining to land held as feud; **f. system** medieval system of land tenure; *n* **-ism.**

fever *n* **1** disorder characterized by high temperature **2** extreme nervous excitement; *a* **feverish;** *adv* **- ly;** *n* **-ness.**

feverfew *n* type of European herb.

fever pitch *n* state of intense excitement or noise.

few *a, n* not many; small number of; *idm* **few and far between** rare.

fey *a* **1** fated to die **2** full of whimsical beliefs, unnatural gaiety.

fez *n* felt cap.

ff. *abbr* **1** following pages **2** *mus* fortissimo.

fiancé *n* betrothed man; *fem* **fiancée.**

fiasco *n* total, utter failure.

fib *n* mild untruth; *v* **fibbing, fibbed.** tell fib; *n* **fibber.**

fiber *n* thread of animal, plant tissue; threadlike substance that can be spun; *a* **fibrous** *ns* **fiberboard** board of

compressed wood fibers; **fiberglass** material from glass fibers and resin for bodywork in cars, boats, etc.; **fiberoptics** transmission of data by infrared signals along thin glass fiber; *a* **fiber-optic.**

fibrillation *n* irregular muscle contractions.

fibrositis *n* inflammation of fibrous tissue, *esp* muscle.

fibula *n* outer bone of lower leg; *a* **fibular.**

fickle *a* changeable; inconstant; *n* **fickleness.**

fiction *n* **1** literature of the imagination **2** untrue statement; *a* **fictional; fictitious;** *v* **-ize.**

fiddle *n* **1** violin **2** *sl* wangle; *idm* **fit as a fiddle** completely healthy; *v* **1** play violin **2** fidget; move restlessly **3** swindle; wangle; *ns* **fiddler, fiddlestick** violin bow; *interj* **fiddlesticks** *dated* nonsense.

fiddlehead *n* edible young fern.

fiddling *a* small and trivial.

fidelity *n* **1** faithfulness **2** exactitude.

fidget *v* move restlessly; be uneasy; fuss; *n* one who fidgets; *pl* nervous restlessness; *a* **fidgety.**

fiducial *a* based on trust, not backed by collateral.

fiduciary *a* of trustee; held in trust.

fie *inter* showing disgust.

field *n* **1** area of *usu* enclosed land for crops or pasture **2** area with specified characteristic **3** area of

military or sporting activity 4
range of operation
5 academic sphere of interest
6 *sport* all competitors 7
comput section of record with
specific information; *idm*
play the field *coll* avoid
committing oneself to one
partner; *idm* **take the field**
mil, *sport* prepare for action;
v 1 deal successfully with
difficult questions 2 *sport*
select (people to play)
3 *cricket* 1 play against the
batting team 2 stop the ball
to prevent scoring of runs; *n*
fielder.
field day *n* 1 day of military
operations 2 day for sport or
outdoor activity (at college);
idm **have a field day** enjoy
period of exciting activity.
field event *n* athletic contest
other than running.
field glasses *n* binoculars.
field test *n* educational visit,
usu with project work.
fieldwork *n* 1 academic work
outside class, laboratory *n*
fieldworker 2 *mil* temporary
fortification.
fiend *n* demon, devil;
excessively evil person; *a*
fiendish, cruel, malevolent.
fierce *a* 1 savage; wild; cruel
2 intense; strong; *n*
fierceness.
fiery *a* 1 of, resembling fire
2 flaming, glowing 3
choleric; spirited; *n* **fieriness**;
adv **fierily**.
fiesta *n* festival, *esp* religious
one in Spanish-speaking

countries.
fife *n* shrill, flutelike
instrument.
fifteen, fifth, fifty *see* **five**.
fifth column *n* group in
country at war helping
enemy secretly.
fifty-fifty *a*, *adv* (shared)
equal(ly) between two.
fig[1] *n* soft, sweet pear-shaped
fruit, with many seeds, eaten
fresh or dried; tree bearing
this.
fig.[2] *abbr* 1 figurative 2 figure.
fight *v* contend against
violently; engage in single
combat; maneuver troops,
etc., in battle; oppose (by
arguments, etc.); *pt, pp*
fought; *phr vs* **fight back** 1
retaliate 2 recover from
losing situation; **fight off**
repel; resist (illness); *ns*
fighter, fighting; *idm* **a
fighting chance** slight but
positive chance of success
with effort; *n* contest;
struggle; *n* **fighter** one who
fights; fast aircraft used for
fighting.
fight song *n* team song used
for inspiration during
athletic activity.
figment *n* fantasy; something
imagined.
figure *n* 1 outer shape; bodily
form *esp* human; appearance
2 statue; ornament
3 diagram 4 numerical
symbol 5 *dancing, skating*
series of movements 6 *gram*
special use of words for effect
7 sum; amount; *v*

1 imagine; depict 2 calculate
3 be conspicuous; *idm* **that
figures** it makes sense; *phr vs*
figure on plan; expect;
figure out calculate; *a*
figurative metaphorical;
symbolic; pictorial; *n*
figurehead 1 figure, bust,
under bowsprit of ship
2 nominal leader.
figure of speech *n* figurative
expression.
figurine *n* statuette.
figwort *n* herbaceous plant in
the snapdragon family.
filament *n* fine thread or fiber;
fine conductor wire in
electric lightbulb, wireless
valve.
filbert *n* type of nut.
filch *v coll* steal, pilfer.
file[1] *n* hard steel tool with
rough surface, for cutting or
smoothing metal, etc.; *v* use
file on; *n* **filing** action of
using file; *pl* particles of
metal removed by filing.
file[2] 1 *n* stiff wire, box or folder
for storing documents 2
collection of documents so
kept for reference; *v* place in
or on file; place on record;
phr vs **file away** classify and
store; **file for** *leg* request
formally.
file[3] *n* line of persons, objects
one behind another; *v*
march, move in file.
file clerk *n* office employee
who works on files.
filet mignon *Fr n* small tender
cut of beef.
filial *a* of, concerning son or

a b c d e f g h i j k l m n o p q r s t u v w x y z

daughter.

filibuster n 1 irregular combatant 2 pirate 3 political obstructionist (also v).

filigree n ornamental work of fine wires.

filing n 1 minute particle of metal filed off, esp pl 2 act of classifying, storing documents; n **f. cabinet**.

fill v 1 make full; occupy completely 2 become full 3 stop up 4 satisfy 5 appoint somebody to (post, office, etc.); phr vs **fill in** 1 complete with details; give information to 2 act in somebody else's place; **fill out** 1 become fatter 2 complete in writing; n full supply; ns **filler** substance for filling holes; **filling** something used to fill cavity in; a **filling** (of food) satisfying.

fillet n 1 headband 2 piece of boneless meat, fish; v slice and remove bones.

filling station n gas/service station.

fillip n exciting or arousing thing.

filly n female foal, young mare.

film n 1 fine, thin skin or layer 2 thin, flexible, sensitized strip or roll used in photography, cinematography 3 motion picture 4 haze; v cover with film; make, direct, produce motion picture; a **filmy** gauzy, delicate; n **filminess**.

film clip n short extract from film.

film maker n one who directs movies.

film noir n Fr dark film, both in characters and setting, usu dealing with crime.

film star n famous film actor/actress.

film strip n length of material with still pictures; to be projected on screen.

filter n 1 cloth, etc., used for straining liquids 2 device eliminating some light or electrical frequencies; v 1 strain liquid; percolate 2 fig leak out; n **filtration**.

filter tip n cigarette with filter for smoke at one end.

filth n 1 nasty, revolting dirt 2 obscenity; a **filthy**; n **filthiness**.

fin n winglike organ by which fish swim; projecting plane on aircraft, etc.

final a at the end; decisive; n last examination, game, or heat of series; ns **finalist** competitor in final of race, game, etc.; **finality, finale** end; concluding movement, number of symphony, opera, etc.

finance n management of (public) money; pl money resources of nation, company, or individual; v supply money for; a **financial**; n **financier**.

finch n small, seed-eating birds.

find v discover for first time; come upon (lost object, person); provide, equip with; return verdict; learn by experience; pt, pp **found**; n thing found; valuable or pleasing discovery; idm **find one's voice** 1 realize one's identity 2 learn how to be independent; idm **be found wanting** prove to be incapable; phr vs **find against** leg give judgment against; **find for** leg give judgment in favor of; ns **finder; finding** esp pl 1 things found by official inquiry 2 leg decision or verdict.

fine[1] n sum exacted as penalty; v punish by fine.

fine[2] a 1 thin; delicate 2 sharp 3 in minute particles 4 refined 5 not raining 6 showy; striking 7 excellent; finished; v 1 refine, purify 2 make thinner; ns **fineness; finery** elaborate dress; **finesse** subtlety; adroitness; cards attempt to take trick with low card while holding higher one (also v).

fine arts n pl painting, sculpture, music, etc.

finery n elaborate attire.

fine-tune v adjust, modify to perfection.

finger n one of five (or four, excluding thumb) members at end of hand; anything finger shaped; v touch with fingers, handle; idm **be all fingers and thumbs** be clumsy with one's hands; idm

have a finger in every pie *coll* be involved in every possible activity; *idm* **keep one's fingers crossed** hope for good luck; *idm* **put one's finger on** identify precisely; *ns* **f.-board** neck of stringed instrument; **f. bowl** bowl for rinsing fingers at table; **fingernail; fingerprint; fingertip** end of finger; **fingering 1** touching with finger **2** indication in music of which fingers to use.

finicky, finicking, finical *a* fussy, overfastidious.

finis *n* end, *esp* of book.

finish *v* **1** bring to an end; complete **2** cease; put an end to **3** kill **4** make perfect; *phr vs* **finish off 1** complete; terminate **2** kill; **finish with 1** have as final item **2** have no further use for **3** end relationship with; *n* end; final appearance; mode of finishing; *a* **finished** accomplished; perfect; *n* **-er.**

finite *a* bounded, having limits.

Finnish *a, n* of Finland.

fir *n* coniferous, evergreen tree of pine family.

fire *n* **1** state of burning; thing burning **2** shooting of weapons **3** passion; *idm* **catch fire** start burning; *idm* **fire away** start asking questions; *idm* **hang fire** make no progress; stagnate; *idm* **open/cease fire** begin/stop shooting; *idm* **on fire** burning; *idm* **under fire**

being shot at; *v* **1** shoot (missile or firearm) **2** dismiss from post **3** inspire; excite **4** bake (pottery) in kiln; *ns* **fire alarm, firearm** gun; **fireball, firebomb; firebrand** *n* **1** piece of burning wood **2** agitator; **firebreak** land cleared to prevent spread of fire; **fire brigade** private body of firefighters; **firebug** arsonist; **firedamp** explosive gas found in coal mine; **f. drill** practice routine for ensuring safe escape from fire; **firefighter, firefighting, fireguard, f. irons, fireman** (*pl* **firemen**); **fireplace; fireplug** hydrant of water for fighting fires; **firepower** power of artillery; **f. station** headquarters of fire fighters; **f.storm; firetrap** dilapidated building; **firewall** *n* wall constructed to prevent spread of fire; **firewood; firework** chemical container emitting bright colored light or exploding when ignited (*pl* **-s 1** display of these **2** violent show of temper **3** brilliant performance, *esp* music).

firefly *n* nocturnal beetle that produces light.

fireplace *n* a recess in a wall of a room for a fire.

fireproof *a* safe against fire; *v* make safe from fire.

fireside *n* area close to fireplace; hearth.

firing line *n* front line of battle; *idm* **in the firing line**

exposed to criticism.

firing squad *n* method of exucution by shooting.

firkin *n* small cask.

firm *a* solid; stable; resolute; steady; not fluctuating; *v* make firm; solidify; *n* partnership; business company.

firmament *n* heaven.

first *a* **1** earliest **2** highest; best **3** principal **4** basic; elementary; *adv* before all else, all others; *n, pron* **1** best person or thing **2** top result; *ns* **f. aid** emergency medical treatment; **firstborn; f. cousin** child of uncle or aunt; **f. floor** ground floor; **f. night** premier of play, opera, etc;

f. person form of pronoun used when speaker refers to himself/herself; **f. strike** attack on enemy before they attack; *as* **f. class, f.hand** (of information) direct from source; **f.-rate** excellent; **f.-string** regularly in team; *adv* **firstly** as first point, argument.

firth *n* estuary; inlet of sea.

fiscal *a* concerned with public revenue; *n* high legal official.

fish *n* cold-blooded vertebrate, with fins, living in water; flesh of fish used as food; *v* **1** catch, or try to catch, fish **2** try to get information; *ns* **fisher;** *ns* **f. farm** place for breeding of fish; **fish fry** *n* picnic, dinner serving fried fish; **fishing; fishmonger**

seller of fish; **fishnet** netlike fabric; **fishwife** *coll* loud, abusive woman; *a* **fishy 1** of fish **2** *coll* dubious; *n* **-iness.**

fish-eye lens *n* wide-angled lens.

fission *n* **1** splitting of atomic nucleus **2** *bio* dividing of cells; *a* **fissile** capable of splitting.

fissure *n* cleft, *esp* in rock.

fist *n* clenched hand; *v* strike with fist.

fistula *n* narrow, winding ulcer.

fit[1] *n* sudden sharp attack of illness; seizure, spasm; passing whim; *idm* **by fits and starts** in an irregular manner; *idm* **have/throw a fit** be deeply shocked, outraged; *a* **fitful** restless; spasmodic; *adv* **-ly.**

fit[2] *a* **1** suitable; competent proper **2** strong; vigorous; *v* **fitting, fitted. 1** suit; be adapted to, of correct size **2** supply; furnish **3** be properly adjusted to; *n* that which fits; adjustment; *v phr* **vs fit in** harmonize; **fit something in** make time, space for something; **fit in (with)** adapt (to); **out fit** equip; *a* **fitted 1** made to size and shape **2** fixed in position; *ns* **fitness** suitability; good body health; **fitting** action of fitting; *pl* furnishings and equipment; *a* **fitting** suitable, proper, seemly.

five *n*, *pron*, *det* cardinal number after four; *as*, *ns*, *dets*

fifth ordinal number; a fifth part; **fifteen** five plus ten; **fifteenth; fifty** five tens; **fiftieth.**

fix *v* make fast **1** stable, secure **2** arrange **3** determine **4** repair **5** gaze steadily at **6** *sl* get even with **7** *sl* bribe or trick; *ns* **fixation** obsession; **fixative** fixing agent; **fixer** person with ability to arrange events by secret influence or dishonest means; **fixity**; immobility, **fixture 1** something fixed in a building **2** *sport* event fixed on a certain date.

fizz *v* hiss; splutter; effervesce; *n sl* champagne; noise of fizzing; *v* **fizzle** splutter weakly; *phr v* **fizzle out** become feeble and ineffective.

fjord *n* long, narrow coastal inlet caused by glaciation.

flab *n coll* flabby, loose flesh.

flabbergast *v* dumbfound; astonish; disconcert.

flabby *a* hanging loosely; limp; flaccid; *n* **flabbiness**.

flaccid *a* limp; weak, without energy; *n* **flaccidity**.

flag[1] *v* **flagging, flagged.** droop; become feeble.

flag[2] *n* name of various kinds of iris.

flag[3] *n* flat paving stone; *n* **flagstone.**

flag[4] *n* sheet of bunting, bearing emblem, etc., attached to mast, etc., used as standard or to signal; *v* signal by flag; *ns* **flag officer**

naval officer entitled to his own flag; **flagship** admiral's ship; **flagstaff** mast pole for flag.

flag day *n* holiday (June 14) for commemorating adoption of first U.S. flag in 1777.

flag-waving *n* noisy expression of patriotic feeling.

flagellate *v* scourge, whip; *n* **-ation.**

flageolet *n* small, flutelike instrument.

flagon *n* vessel for serving wine; large wine bottle.

flagrant *a* scandalous; blatantly evil; *ns* **-ance, -ancy.**

flagship *n* most significant one, as in ship, store, etc.

flail *n* implement for threshing grain by hand.

flair *n* natural aptitude; instinctive discernment.

flak *n* critical remarks.

flake *n* thin, light scale, layer; light, fleecy particle (of snow); *coll* one who is unattentive; *v* come off in flakes; *sl* **flake out** go to sleep; *a* **flaky;** *n* **-iness.**

flambé *a Fr* served with liqueur that has been ignited.

flamboyance *n* ostentation; showiness; exaggeration of speech, manner; *a* **flamboyant 1** showy **2** *arch* having wavelike tracery.

flame *n* **1** burning gas or vapor; jet of fire **2** ardent passion, imagination; *v* emit flames; blaze; flare.

flamenco *n* (music for) lively

Spanish dance.

flaming *a* 1 burning 2 brightly colored, resembling flames.

flamingo *n* scarlet-feathered aquatic bird, with long legs and neck.

flammable *n* easily set on fire.

flan *n* open pie with sweet fillings; custard baked with caramel topping.

flange *n* projecting rim, edge, or rib.

flank *n* part of side of body between hip and ribs; side of hill, building, or body of troops; *v* guard, attack flank; be at side of.

flannel *n* soft, woolen or cotton cloth; *pl* trousers, *esp* casual, sporting; *n* **flannelette** lightweight cotton flannel.

flap *v* **flapping, flapped.** slap lightly; move (wings) up and down; sway; flutter; *n* act of flapping; flat piece of material partly attached and hanging; *n* **flapper** flipper of seal, etc.; *sl dated* young girl; **flapjack** pancake.

flappable *a* able to be easily upset.

flare[1] *n* 1 bright, unsteady flame 2 vivid signal light 3 outburst of anger 4 outward spread, curve; *v* blaze up; spread outward; *a* **flaring** gaudy.

flare[2] *v* be wider at bottom; *n* flare shape.

flare-up *n* outbreak of violent activity.

flash *v* emit sudden, bright light; gleam; pass rapidly by; signal by flashing; *n* 1 sudden brief gleam of light 2 moment; *idm* **in a flash** instantly; *ns* **flashback** episode going back in time; **flashbulb,** device for taking photos in bad light; **flashlight** small, battery-run, handheld light; **flashpoint 1** temperature at which ignition occurs 2 place or situation where violence is likely to break out; *as* **flash, flashy** showy, tawdry.

flasher *n* 1 blinking light 2 exhibitionist.

flask *n* small, flattened pocket container for alcoholic drinks, etc.; wine bottle; small narrow-necked bottle for scientific use.

flat *a* 1 level and smooth; not curved or raised; in a horizontal plane 2 deflated 3 dull; uninteresting; (of pictures) without contrast 4 having lost effervescence 5 *mus* below pitch indicated 6 (of denial) absolute; *idm* **flat out** at full speed; *n Brit* 1 apartment; *ns* 2 flat tire 3 section of stage scenery 4 *usu pl* expanse of level ground 5 flat part of something 6 *mus* sign indicating a semitone lower; *a* **flat-chested** (*usu* of woman) with small breasts; *n* **f. feet** *a* flat-footed; *ns* **flatfish; f. race** race with no jumps; **flat rate** unvarying inclusive price; *adv* 1 *mus*

below pitch 2 at full extent; level with the ground 3 absolutely; *idm* **fall flat on one's face** fail in a humiliating way; *adv* **-ly** absolutely; *n* **-ness;** *v* **flatten** 1 make or become flat 2 overwhelm.

flatcar *n* railroad car without sides or top.

flatter *v* praise insincerely; adulate; represent too favorably; congratulate oneself; *ns* **flatterer; flattery**.

flatulence, flatulency *n* wind, gas in stomach or intestines; *a* **flatulent** caused by, affected with flatulence; *fig* vapid.

flaunt *v* flourish, wave insolently; make display of.

flavor *n* 1 taste (*also* **flavoring**) 2 special characteristic; *v* give taste to; *as* **-ed, -less;** *idm* **flavor of the month** *coll* thing or person now favored.

flaw *n* defect, blemish; crack; *v* crack, make flaw in; *a* **flawless** perfect; irreproachable.

flax *n* herb whose fibers are spun into linen thread, seeds produce linseed oil; *a* of, like flax; pale yellow.

flaxen *a* (of hair) pale yellow.

flay *v* strip off skin; criticize savagely.

flea *n* small, bloodsucking, jumping insect; *idm* **with a flea in one's ear** having been rebuked; *ns* **fleabag** *coll* dirty hotel; **fleabite 1** bite of flea 2 very minor inconvenience; *a*

A B C D E **F** G H I J K L M N O P Q R S T U V W X Y Z

fleabitten scruffy; **f. market** street market for cheap second-hand goods; **f.pit** *coll* dirty old cinema or theater.

fleck *n* spot; freckle; particle; *v* mark with flecks; dapple.

fledgling *n* **1** amateur **2** young bird.

flee *v* run away; avoid; shun; *pt, pp* **fled**.

fleece *n* sheep's wool; *v* swindle, plunder; *a* **fleecy** soft, woolly; resembling, covered with, fleece.

fleet[1] *n* number of warships under one command; number of ships, aircraft, cars owned by one company or person; creek, inlet.

fleet[2] *a* speedy; nimble; swift; *v* move swiftly, silently; *n* **fleetness**; *a* **fleeting** transient; transitory.

flesh *n* **1** soft tissue of body beneath skin, covering bones **2** edible animal tissue; meat **3** pulp of vegetable or fruit **4** animal nature of man; sensuality; *idm* **in the flesh** physically present; in person; *as* **fleshly** carnal; **fleshy** pulpy; plump.

flesh and blood *idm* kin.

fleshpots *n pl* **1** places to indulge bodily pleasures **2** life of self-indulgence.

flew *pt of* **fly**.

flex *v* bend, be bent; *n* flexible, insulated wire; *ns* **flexibility** ability to bend; **flexion** act of bending; inflexion; **flexor** muscle bending joint inward; *a* **flexible** pliant; adaptable;

versatile.

flextime *n* system of variable working hours.

flick *v* tap, flip lightly and jerkily; *n* sharp light blow.

flicker *v* flutter; waver; burn, shine unsteadily; *n* unsteady gleam; or movement.

flier *n* aviator.

flight *n* **1** act of flying; distance flown **2** unit, formation of aircraft **3** volley of arrows **4** series of stairs, steps **5** act of fleeing; *ns* **f. deck, f. path; f. recorder** black box.

flighty *a* giddy; fickle; frivolous; *n* **-iness**.

flimflam *n* deception.

flimsy *a* thin and fragile; weak and paltry.

flinch *v* draw back in pain, fear; wince.

fling *v* throw, hurl; move with haste; lash out; flounce; *pt, pp* **flung**; *ns* **1** throw **2** vigorous dance **3** bout of dissipation; *coll* short love affair.

flint *a* very hard, dark gray quartz; anything hard, obdurate; piece of flint; **flinty** *a* tough; stern.

flintlock *n* old type of gun.

flip *v* **flipping, flipped.** flick; jerk; make smart light tap; *n* **flipper** limb or fin for swimming; *a* **flippant** lacking seriousness; frivolous; *n* **flippancy**.

flip-flop *n* **1** flat, open, rubber sandal **2** electronic circuit switching between two states

3 sudden reversal in point of view.

flip side *n* second side of record; not hit side.

flirt *v* pay amorous attentions without serious intent; *phr v* **flirt with something 1** pretend to be interested in **2** expose oneself to the risk of; *a* **flirtatious**; *adv* **-ly**; *ns* **-ness; flirtation**.

flit *v* **flitting, flitted.** pass lightly, rapidly and quietly; *sl* move house secretly.

float *v* **1** rest, drift on surface of liquid **2** glide through air **3** start; set going; launch (loan, company, etc.); *n* **1** anything that floats, *esp* supporting something else on liquid **2** wheeled motorized platform decorated for parades **3** cork on fishing net **4** sum of cash for running expenses.

flock[1] *n* lock, tuft of wool; wool, cotton fibers used in waste; *a* **flocculent** of, resembling wool or flock.

flock[2] *n* number of animals (*esp* sheep) or birds, as unit; congregation; *v* assemble in large numbers; crowd together.

floe *n* sheet of ice floating on sea.

flog *v* **flogging, flogged.** beat hard; thrash with whip or stick; *idm* **flog a dead horse** *coll* persist in unprofitable activity.

flood *n* inundation; overflow of water in usually dry place;

rising tide; *coll* floodlight; *v* inundate; overflow; overwhelm; *ns* **f.gate** sluice; **f. tide.**

floodlight *n* powerful artificial lighting; *v* illuminate by floodlights; *a* **floodlit.**

floor *n* lower surface of room, etc; story; body of a hall, etc., *idm* **go through the floor** *coll* (or prices) fall below tolerable level; *idm* **take the floor 1** begin dancing **2** speak in public; *v* furnish with floor; knock down; *coll* confound; *ns* **floor** boards, blocks, etc., forming floor; **f. show** cabaret.

floor-through *n* apartment that takes up one whole floor of a building.

floozy *n* woman of loose morals; prostitute.

flop *v* **flopping, flopped.** move limply, heavily; fall clumsily, noisily; *coll* fail utterly; *adv* **floppily;** *n* act, noise of flopping; *coll* fiasco, failure; *a* **floppy** slack; loose, limp; *n* **-iness.**

floppy disk *n comput* plastic disk for storing data.

flora *n* flowers, plants, collectively, of particular areas; classified list of species; *a* **floral** of flowers; *ns* **florescence** season, state of flowering; **floret** small flower; **florist** grower of, dealer in flowers.

florid *a* ruddy.

floss *n* **1** rough silk covering of cocoon; spun silk; **2** fiber for

cleaning between teeth; *a* **flossy.**

flotation *n* starting of a new business company.

flotilla *n Sp* fleet of small ships or boats.

flotsam *n* floating wreckage or goods on the sea.

flounce[1] *v* go, move jerkily, impatiently; *n* such movement.

flounce[2] *n* ornamental strip, frill on garment.

flounder[1] *n* kind of flatfish.

flounder[2] *v* **1** stagger, roll helplessly, *esp* in water, mud; **2** hesitate.

flour *n* finely ground meal, *esp* of wheat; any very fine, soft powder; *v* cover with flour.

flourish *v* thrive; be florid in style, manner; brandish; sound fanfare; *n* act of brandishing anything; fanciful curved line; florid expression; fanfare.

flout *v* show scorn of; mock at; defy.

flow *v* **1** (*of water*) glide along; gush; move along ceaselessly **2** (*of blood*) circulate **3** (*of fabric*) fall in loose folds, or masses **4** (*of food, drink, etc.*) abound; *n* that which flows; rising tide; steady, copious supply.

flow chart *n* diagram showing how stages of a process interconnect (also **flow diagram**).

flower *n* **1** blossom; bloom **2** choicest, prime part; *v* **1** produce blooms **2** reach

highest state of development; *ns* **flower bed** prepared ground for growing flowers; **flower child** hippie; **floweret** small flower; *as* **flowery** abounding in flowers; florid; **flowered** decorated with floral pattern.

flown *pp of* **fly.**

fl. oz. *abbr* fluid ounce(s).

flu *n* influenza.

fluctuate *v* rise and fall; vary; be unstable; *a* **-ating;** *n* **-ation.**

flue *n* tube, pipe, shaft conveying air, smoke, etc.; chimney.

fluent *a* flowing; able to, easily, rapidly; graceful; *n* **fluency.**

fluff *n* soft down, hair; light soft mass of wool, dust; *v* make into fluff; *sl* bungle; *a* **fluffy.**

fluid *n* liquid; gas; not solid; *a* flowing easily; *n* **fluidity.**

fluke[1] *n* flat fish; parasitic worm.

fluke[2] *n* part of anchor; *pl* tail of whale.

fluke *n* lucky stroke, shot; happy chance; *v* make, gain by fluke.

flummox *v* bewilder; abash; disconcert.

flung *pt, pp of* **fling.**

flunk *v* **1** fail **2** mark as failure.

fluor *n* mineral containing fluoride; *ns* **fluorine** non-metallic element; **fluoride** compound of fluorine; **fluoridation.**

fluorescence *n* property possessed by certain

A B C D E F G H I J K L M N O P Q R S T U V W X Y Z

transparent bodies, of emitting light rays of different color from those reflected; *a* **fluorescent**.

fluoride *n* chemical protecting teeth against decay; *v* **fluoridate;** *n* **-ation**.

flurry *n* **1** sudden gust **2** state of agitation of mind.

flush[1] *v* fly, start up suddenly, as when startled; *n* flock of birds put up.

flush[2] *v* **1** flow suddenly, copiously **2** redden **3** cleanse by rush of water **4** elate; exhilarate; *n* **1** rush of water **2** blush; sudden emotion **3** initial vigor; *a* **1** full to brim; level with **2** *sl* having plenty (of money).

flush[3] *n cards* hand of same suit; run of same suit.

fluster *v* **1** muddle; fuss; worry **2** be confused.

flute *n* **1** wind instrument, with side mouthpiece, and holes stopped by keys or fingers **2** narrow groove; *v* make grooves in; *a* **fluted** grooved, *ns* **fluting; flutist** player of flute.

flutter *v* move wings quickly, nervously; quiver; be excited; throb rapidly but feebly; move, wave (flag) quickly; *n* **1** act of fluttering **2** nervousness; **3** *sl* small bet.

fluvial *a* of rivers.

flux *n* **1** flowing state, movement **2** morbid discharge of fluid (from body) **3** substance added to help fusion; *v* fuse (metals)

by melting.

fly[1] *n* two-winged insect; imitation used as fish bait; *idm* **fly in the ointment** nuisance; *idm* **fly on the wall** secret observer; *a* **flyblown** tainted, maggoty; *n* **flycatcher** small bird.

fly[2] *v* **1** move on wings; control, travel in, aircraft **2** be propelled through air **3** flee from **4** flutter;- *idm* **fly in the face of** defy; *pt* **flew;** *pp* **flown** *idm* **fly in the face of** defy.

fly-by-night *a* shady, underhanded; transitory.

flying saucer *n* disk-shaped vehicle, thought to come from outer space.

flyleaf *n* blank page in front or back of book.

flywheel *n* mechanism that equalizes speed of machinery.

FM *abbr* radio frequency modulation.

foal *n* young of horse, ass, etc.; *v* bear (foal).

foam *n* mass of small bubbles, froth, on surface of liquid; *v* form, emit foam; emit thick saliva, or sweat; *as* **-y, -ing**.

fob *n* small pocket for watch, in waistband.

fob off *v* **fobbing, fobbed.** cheat; trick; delude into accepting (worthless article).

focus *n* point at which converging rays of light, heat, waves of sound, meet; center of activity or intensity; *pl* **focuses, foci;** *v* adjust; cause to converge;

concentrate; *a* **focal** pertaining to focus.

fodder *n* dried food for cattle, horses, etc.

foe *n* enemy.

fog *n* thick mass of water vapor, smoke, dust in lower atmosphere; *v* **fogging, fogged.1** cover in fog **2** confuse; *a* **foggy;** *ns* **foghorn** warning for ships in fog; **f. lights** (on car); *a* **fogbound** trapped by fog.

fogy, fogey *n* fussy, slow old-fashioned person.

foible *n* weakness of character; idiosyncrasy.

foie gras *n Fr* liver pâté.

foil[1] *n* **1** thin sheet of metal **2** quick-silver coating behind glass of mirror **3** person, thing enhancing another by contrast.

foil[2] *n* light sword with button on end, used in fencing; *v* baulk; frustrate; repel (attack).

foist *v* palm off; impose fraudulently.

fold[1] *v* bend over back on itself; double up; wrap around; clasp (in arms, etc.); *n* crease made by folding; piece of folded material; hollow in hill; *n* **folder** folded printed circular, paper, etc.; container for documents.

fold[2] *n* enclosure, pen for sheep; *v* enclose in fold.

foliage *n* collectively, leaves of trees, etc.; *a* **foliate** bearing leaves; leaflike.

folio *n* -os. 1 sheet of paper folded once 2 large-size paper; book made of such sheets 3 page number; *v* number pages of book.

folk *n* 1 nation 2 people in general; *ns* **folk dance** traditional dance; **folklore** traditional beliefs, etc.

follicle *n* small sac; seed vessel; cocoon; *a* **follicular**.

follow *v* 1 go, come after 2 go by, along 3 be later than; come (next) after 4 understand 5 arise; be logical, necessary consequence 6 take interest in; monitor 7 obey; be disciple of; *idm* **follow suit** do likewise; *phr v as* **follow through** pursue to the end; **follow up** 1 investigate 2 take further action on; *ns* **follower, f.-through, f.-up;** *a* **following** 1 next 2 (of wind) favourable; *n* group of supporters.

folly *n* 1 foolish act 2 rashness 3 useless, fantastic building.

foment *v* apply hot lotion, poultice to; stir up (trouble, etc.); *n* **fomentation**.

fond *a* loving, affectionate; over-indulgent; *idm* **be fond of** have affection/liking for; *n* **fondness;** *v* **fondle** caress.

font¹ *n* bowl for baptismal holy water, in church.

font² *n* printing type style.

food *n* any substance, *esp* solid, consumed to support life and growth; *idm* **food for thought** something that will stimulate thinking; *ns* **f. chain** sequence of living beings each eating the next as food; **f. poisoning, f. processor, foodstuff, f. value; foodie,** *coll* person obsessed with eating, preparing food.

fool¹ *v* stupid, silly person; dupe; clown; buffoon; *v* 1 act with levity 2 dupe; hoax; *a* **foolish** stupid; absurd; unwise; *n* **foolery** foolish behavior; *as* **foolhardy** rash; foolishly daring (*n* **-iness**); **foolproof** infallible; *n* **foolscap** jester's or dunce's cap.

fool² *n* dish of pureed fruit mixed with whipped cream.

fool's paradise *n* illusory state of happiness that will not last.

foot *n* feet. 1 lowest part of leg below ankle 2 bottom end of sock, stocking 3 base; bottom of something 4 end of bed opposite to head 5 infantry 6 measure of 12 inches 7 metrical unit of verse; *pl* **feet;** *idm* **one foot in the door** advantageous position for further maneuvers; *idm* **put one's foot down** be insistent; *idm* **put one's foot in it** *coll* make a faux pas; *idm* **ten feet tall** very proud and confident; *idm* **foot the bill** pay the cost; **footbridge** bridge for pedestrians; **footfall** sound of walking; **foot fault** *tennis* step over baseline when serving; **foothill** low hill; **foothold** limited secured position for further progress; **footman** uniformed servant; **footpath, footprint, footstep;** *idm* **follow in someone's footsteps** imitate someone's actions; *ns* **footstool, footwear; footwork** agility with one's feet; *v* **footslog** walk or march long distance; *a* **footsore**.

football *n* game played with pointed leather ball on a large field.

footing *n* secured position; **be on a good footing (with)** have a good standing and reputation (with).

footlights *n pl* floor lights at front of stage.

footloose *a* free to move or travel.

footnote *n* note at the bottom of page.

foot-pound *n* work done by force of one pound through distance of one foot.

footsie *n coll* 1 playful touching of feet to arouse sexual interest 2 secret dealings.

fop *n* dandy; vain man; *a* **foppish**.

for *prep* suitable to; because of; toward; in favor of; instead of; during; at price of; in spite of; in search of; *conj* because.

for- *prefix: forms compounds (mostly verbs implying negative action) with meaning of* from,

away, against, *e.g.*, forget,
forbid. *Also contraction of*
fore- (*see later*). *Where the*
meaning may be deduced from
the simple word, the
compounds are not given here.
forage *n* food for horses, cattle;
v search for forage; rummage
around; *ns* **forager**.
forasmuch as *conj* because,
considering that.
foray *n* raid; plundering
incursion; *v* raid; ravage.
forbear *v* refrain, abstain from;
pt **forbore**; *pp* **foreborne**; *n*
forbearance; *a* **forbearing**
patient, lenient.
forbid *v* prohibit; prevent; *pt*
forbade; *pp* **forbidden;** *a*
forbidding threatening;
sinister.
force *n* 1 power; mental, moral
strength 2 compulsion
3 body of troops, police, etc.;
4 violence; *idm* **in force**
operational; *idm* **join forces**
(**with**) unite (with); *v*
1 compel; urge 2 break open
3 cause plants to flower, fruit
before natural season
4 produce by effort; *idm* **force**
somebody's hand make
somebody act before ready to
one's advantage; *as* **forced**;
produced by special effort or
necessity; strained; **forcible**
done by force; convincing;
forceful powerful;
impressive.
force-feed *v* make somebody
eat or drink unwillingly.
force majeure *n Fr* unforeseen
circumstance that excuses

one from keeping a promise
or bargain.
forceps *n* surgical pincers or
tweezers.
ford *n* shallow place in river; *v*
cross by means of ford.
fore[1] *a, adv* before; in front
(of); *comp* **former, further;**
sup **foremost, first, furthest;**
n front, forward part; *idm*
come to the fore become
prominent, well known.
fore[2] *interj* golfer's warning
call.
fore- *prefix* 1 earlier; before,
e.g., **foretell, forewarn**
2 front; leading, *e.g.*,
forecourt, foreman,
forearm.
fore-and-aft *a* along length of
ship.
forearm *n* arm between elbow
and wrist.
forebear *n* ancestor.
forebode *v* prophesy; portend;
n **forboding**, presentiment.
forecast *v* estimate (result)
beforehand; *n* prediction of
future event.
foreclose *v* take away power of
redeeming mortgage; *n*
foreclosure.
forefather *n* ancestor.
forefinger *n* index finger (next
to thumb).
forego *v* foreprecede; *pp*
foregone; *pr p* **foregoing;** *a*
foregone preceding; already
settled.
foregone conclusion *n* certain
outcome.
foreground *n* nearest part of
picture or view; *idm* **in the**

foreground prominent; very
noticeable.
forehand *n, a, tennis* (side)
where player has palm of
hand facing opponent.
forehead *n* part of face
between brow and hairline.
foreign *a* 1 of a country other
than one's own 2 from
outside 3 alien; *idm* **foreign**
to strange, unnatural; *ns* **f.**
affairs; f. exchange (dealing
in) currencies of different
countries; **foreigner** foreign
person of other nationality.
forelock *n* front part of hair.
foreman *n* 1 leading worker
2 leader of jury; *fem*
forewoman.
foremost *a* most distinguished;
first in position, degree,
dignity, etc.
forename *n* first name.
forensic *a* pertaining to
lawcourts; **f. medicine**
medical jurisprudence.
foreplay *n* erotic stimulation
prior to intercourse.
forerunner *n* harbinger;
precursor.
foresee *v* predict; *pt* **foresaw;**
pp **foreseen;** *a* **foreseeable.**
foreshadow *v* presage; indicate
in advance.
foreshore *n* area between
limits of high and low tides.
foresight *n* ability to see and
plan ahead.
foreskin *n* loose skin covering
tip of penis.
forest *n* large tract of land
covered with trees; *ns*
forestry art of managing

forests; **forester 1** one skilled in forestry **2** dweller in forest.

forestall *v* to get ahead of another by anticipation.

forethought *n* prudent thought for future.

forever *adv* always; *n* eternity.

forewarn *v* warn in advance.

forewent *pt of* **forego.**

foreword *n* prefatory comments in book, written by someone other than author.

forfeit *v* lose, as penalty; give up; *n* anything lost as penalty in law or game; *a* confiscated by law; *n* **forfeiture.**

forge *v* **1** soften, shape (metal) by heating **2** imitate deceitfully, counterfeit **3** *fig* hammer out painstakingly; *idm* **forge ahead** progress quickly; *n* smithy; workshop, plant for working red-hot metal; *ns* **forger** counterfeiter; **forgery** fraudulent making or alteration of signature, document, etc.

forget *v* cease to remember; accidentally omit; neglect; *pt* **forgot;** *pp* **forgot, forgotten;** *a* **forgetful** having bad memory; *n* **forget-me-not** marsh plant with small blue flower.

forgive *v* **forgiving, forgave. 1** (offense) pardon **2** (debt); cancel; *n* **forgiveness.**

forgo *v* do without.

fork *n* **1** pronged tool, implement for digging, lifting **2** pronged tool for eating **3** junction of two roads, rivers **4** meeting of bough and trunk of tree; *v* **1** dig, lift, toss with fork **2** divide into branches; bifurcate; *idm* **fork out** *coll* pay reluctantly; *a* **forked** dividing with two or more points or branches.

forklift truck *n* truck with device for lifting heavy weights, crates, etc.

forlorn *a* forsaken; desperate; neglected; **f. hope** very desparate, difficult undertaking; *adv* **forlornly;** *n* **forlornness.**

form *n* **1** shape, visible appearance **2** mode of expression; construction **3** type or kind **4** convention, pattern **5** printed formal document with blank spaces to be filled in with information; *v* **1** shape; create **2** act as **3** develop; educate **4** construct **5** assume shape; *a* **formal** according to rule; orderly; of outward form, lacking reality; stiff; *ns* **formality 1** propriety **2** *esp pl* conventional procedure **3** ceremony, *esp* one without real meaning or use; **formation** forming; structure; *a* **formative** giving form; tending to shape, develop; *a* **formless** shapeless.

formaldehyde *n* colorless chemical compound used mainly as preservative; *n* **formalin** solution of formaldehyde used as antiseptic.

format *n* **1** shape of book **2** general plan of something **3** *comput* arrangement of data; *v comput* **-matting, -matted.** prepare with a format; *a* **formatted.**

formation *n* **1** act or instance of forming **2** thing formed **3** pattern of people or vehicles moving together.

former *a* of earlier time; *n* thing or person referred to first; *adv* **-ly** in the past.

Formica [TM] hard, laminated, heat-resistant plastic sheet.

formidable *a* terrifying; overwhelming; presenting obstacles; huge.

formula *n* **1** set form of words, prescribed for use on particular occasion **2** definition of dogma **3** recipe; prescription **4** method of solving problem; *pl* **formulas, formulae;** *v* **formulate 1** express in formula **2** reduce to definite terms; *n* **formulation.**

forsake *v* abandon; desert; give up; *pt* **forsook;** *pp* **forsaken.**

forswear *v* renounce on oath; perjure onself; *pt* **forswore;** *pp* **forsworn.**

forsythia *n* shrub with bright yellow flowers.

fort *n* fortress; fortified place, stronghold; *idm* **hold down the fort** take care of everything in somebody's

A
B
C
D
E
F
G
H
I
J
K
L
M
N
O
P
Q
R
S
T
U
V
W
X
Y
Z

absence.

forte[1] *n* special ability; strong point.

forte[2] *adv mus* loudly; *adv mus* **fortissimo** very loudly.

forth *adv* forward; onward; *a* **forthcoming** about to appear; *fig* affable; communicative; *adv* **forthwith** at once; immediately.

forthright *a* outspoken; candid.

fortieth *pron, det* ordinal number of 40.

fortify *v* **-fying, -fied**. strengthen; convert into fortress; *n* **fortification** act of strengthening; *pl* defensive works, walls, etc.

fortitude *n* sustained courage, resoluteness in face of pain, danger, etc.

fortnight *n Brit* two weeks; *adv* **fortnightly**.

FORTRAN *n comput* progamming language (mathematics, science, etc.).

fortress *n* fortified place, stronghold.

fortuitous *a* due to chance; accidental; *n* **fortuity**.

fortune *n* 1 chance; luck; lot in life 2 prosperity; wealth; *a* **fortunate** lucky; *ns* **fortune hunter** unscrupulous person, trying to obtain wealth, *esp* by marriage; **fortune-teller** one who predicts one's future.

forty *a, n* four tens; **fortieth**.

forty-five *n* pistol of .45 caliber.

forty winks *n coll* nap.

forum *n Lat* 1 public meeting place 2 tribunal; law court.

forward *a* 1 in front of one 2 *fig* advanced; pert; *adv* toward front; at, in fore part (of ship, etc.); onward (in direction, time); *n sport* one of players in front line; *v* farther; send, mail on farther; dispatch; *n* **-ness** pertness.

forwent *pt of* **forgo**.

fossil *n* petrified remains of prehistoric animal, vegetable organism found preserved in earth or rocks; *fig* antiquated person; *v* **fossilize** petrify; convert into fossil.

foster *v* 1 rear another's child as one's own 2 encourage; cherish; *ns* **foster child** one not related by blood to foster parents; **f. mother; f. father; f. brother**.

foul *a* 1 dirty and disgusting 2 unpleasant 3 evil 4 obscene (*a* **f.-mouthed**) 5 against the rules; *n, v* act against the rules; *v* 1 make dirty 2 become entangled with; *idm* **foul up** *coll* ruin (life, event, etc.) *n* **foul-up**; *n* **f. play** 1 unfair play 2 murder.

found[1] *v* 1 establish; institute 2 endow 3 base; *ns* **foundation** 1 founding 2 substructure of building 3 basis 4 endowed institution 5 **f. garment** corset, girdle; **founder**.

found[2] *v* melt (metal, minerals) and pour into mold; cast; *n* **foundry** place

where founding, casting is carried out.

founder *v* (*of ship*) fill with water and sink; (*of horses*) fall, break down, *esp* through lameness.

fount *n* fountain; *fig* source.

fountain *n* artificial, ornamental jet of water; jet of drinking water; *ns* **f.head** source; origin; **f. pen** one with ink reservoir.

four *n, pron, det* cardinal number next after three; *as, ns, dets* **fourth** a fourth part; ordinal number; **fourteen** four plus ten; **fourteenth**; *ns* **four-in-hand** vehicle with four horses driven by one person; **four-poster** bed with four posts for canopy; **foursome** game, dance for four persons; *a* **foursquare** firm and steady; *n* **four-stroke** type of internal combustion engine.

fourth dimension *n* time.

fourth estate *n* the press.

fowl *n* bird, domestic cock or hen; flesh of birds (as food); *ns* **fowler** hunter of wild birds; **fowling piece** light gun.

fox *n* 1 reddish bushy-tailed animal 2 crafty person; *v* act cunningly; mislead; *ns* **foxglove** plant with long spikes of tubular flowers; **foxhound** hound used for hunting fox; **fox terrier** small terrier formerly used to drive fox from cover; *a* **foxy** cunning; *sl* sexually attractive.

foxhole *n* small pit used for cover in battle.

foxtrot *n* ballroom dance in quadruple time.

foyer *n* large hall, anteroom of theater.

Fr. *abbr* **1** French **2** *eccl* Father.

fr. *abbr* franc(s).

fracas *n* brawl; noisy quarrel.

fraction *n* numerical quantity less or more than integer; small piece; fragment; *a* **-al** insignificant; **-ary** fragmentary.

fractious *a* peevish; fretful; cross.

fracture *n* **1** breaking, *esp* of bone **2** break; crack; *v* break.

fragile *a* easily broken; brittle; frail; *n* **fragility**.

fragment *n* piece broken off; unfinished part; *a* **-ary** incomplete; *n* **-ation** separation into fragments.

fragrant *a* sweet-scented; *n* **fragrance**.

frail *a* fragile; not robust (in health); morally weak; *n* **frailty**.

frame *v* **1** construct; contrive **2** express in words; **3** *coll* cause to appear guilty **4** surround with, serve as, frame; *n* structure; border of wood, etc., around picture setting; wood and glass structure protecting plants, etc.; *idm* **frame of mind** mood; *ns* **framer; frame-up,** false evidence; **framework** substructure, skeleton.

franc *n* French, Belgian, Swiss,

etc., coin, monetary unit.

franchise *n* **1** voting rights of citizen **2** right to sell company's goods or services; *v* grant such a right.

Franciscan *n, a* (friar) of Order of St. Francis.

Franco- *prefix* of France.

Franglais *n* French full of English expressions and words.

frank *a* outspoken; sincere; candid; *ns* signature, mark exempting letter from postal charges; *coll* frankfurter; *v* mark letter so; *adv* **-ly** openly; *n* **-ness** candor.

frankfurter *n* small smoked sausage.

frankincense *n* sweet, pungent gum resin used in incense.

frantic *a* violenty excited, *esp* with rage, grief, pain; frenzied; *adv* **-ally, -ly**.

fraternal *a* pertaining to brother; brotherly; *n* **fraternity 1** brotherhood; **2** brotherliness **3** association of men with common interest **4** male student society; *v* **fraternize** be on friendly terms; *ns* **-ization; fratricide** murder, murderer of brother or sister.

fraud *n* criminal deception, willful dishonesty; impostor; *a* **fraudulent;** *adv* **-ly;** *n* **-ence**.

fraught *a* charged; teeming; full of.

fray[1] *n* noisy fight, brawl; conflict.

fray[2] *v* make, become ragged

(as cloth) by rubbing; wear; ravel edges.

frazzle *v* fray; wear out; exhaust; *n* rags and tatters.

freak *n* abnormal form; monstrosity; whim; caprice; *a* **-ish**.

freckle *n* small brownish spot on skin, caused by sun; *v* mark or become marked with freckles; *a* **freckled**.

free *a* **1** not enslaved, confined, or restricted **2** open; frank **3** independent **4** exempt **5** gratuitous **6** unattached **7** *chem* uncombined; *idm* **free with** generous in giving; *adv* **-ly;** *ns* **freedom; freebie** *coll* free gift; **f. enterprise** system of trade without government control; **freebooter** *n* pirate; **f. fall** falling from plane without parachute open; **f.-for-all** general dispute; *n, a, adv* **freehold** (with) complete ownership of land, building; **f. kick** kick awarded for infringement of rule; *v* **f.lance** (*also* **freelancer**) self-employed independent worker; **freeman** person given the freedom of the city; **Freemason** member of secret society for mutual help; **freemasonry; f. rein** freedom of action; **f. speech; f. thinker, f. thinking, f. trade, f. verse** verse without rhyme, with irregular meter; **freeway** major highway; **f. will;** *as*

freehand drawn without instruments; **free-range** (of eggs) laid under natural conditions; *vs* **free-load** *coll* take advantage of others' generosity; accepting free food, lodging, etc.; *ns* **freeloader; freeway** toll-free highway; **freewheel** 1 cycle without pedaling 2 act casually, irresponsibly.

freeze *v* 1 become ice; 2 congeal with cold 3 refrigerate; chill; keep (wages, interest, etc.) fixed at present level 4 *fig* become rigid 5 *pt* **froze;** *pp* **frozen;** *phr v* **freeze out** prevent from taking part; *ns* **freezer** extracold refrigerator; **freezing point** temperature at which liquids freeze; *a* **frozen** (*food*) preserved by freezing; (assets, etc.) unrealizable.

freight *n* hire of ship for conveyance of goods; any load of goods for transportation, *esp* ship's cargo; *v* hire, load (vessel); *ns* **freighter** cargo vessel; **freightage** charge for transport of goods.

French *n, a* (the language) of France; *pl* people of France; *ns* **F. chalk** chalky marker used mainly in sewing; **F. dressing** salad dressing with oil and vinegar; **F.fries; F. horn** *mus* brass instrument with coiled tube and valves; **F. leave** *coll* unofficial leave; **F. toast** bread dipped in egg and fried; **F.window** glass-

panelee door to garden or balcony.

frenetic *a* very busy, frantic.

frenzy *n* violent excitment; paroxysm of rage, grief, etc.; *a* **frenzied.**

frequency *n* repeated occurrence; *elec* number of cycles per second of alternating current; **high f., medium f., low f.,** *rad* rate of vibration of sound waves.

frequent *a* happening often; numerous; common; *adv* **-ly;** *v* visit habitually.

fresco *n* wall painting on damp plaster.

fresh *a* 1 new; untainted 2 bracing 3 clean 4 inexperienced 5 *sl* impudent 6 (*of food*) not preserved or stale 7 (*of water*) not salt 8 (*of wind*) cool; brisk; *adv* **-ly** with freshness; anew; *n* **-ness;** *v* **freshen** make, become fresh; *ns* **freshnet** freshwater stream flowing into sea; **freshman** undergraduate in the first year.

freshwater *a* of inland (not salinated) water.

fret[1] *v* **fretting, fretted.** harass; vex; worry; *n* worry.

fret[2] *n* 1 complicated, netlike, carved work 2 bar on finger board of stringed instrument; *v* ornament with fret work; *ns* **f.saw** fine-toothed, narrow saw used for fretwork; **f.work** ornamental, lacelike carving on wood.

Freudian *a* pertaining to

Sigmund Freud, psychologist, or his theories; *n* **Freudian slip** error in speech attributed to influence of subconscious thought.

friable *a* crumbly.

friar *n* member of mendicant religious order; *n* **friary** convent of friars.

fricasse *n Fr* dish of meat, cut in pieces, cooked in rich white sauce; *v* cook thus.

fricative *n, a* (consonant) made by air passing through narrow space between teeth, tongue, lips, etc.

friction *n* rubbing; resistance met when surface of body moves across another; *fig* antagonism; *a* **frictional.**

Friday *n* sixth day of week.

fridge *n coll* refrigerator.

friend *n* person for whom one feels affection and respect; companion; helper; associate; member of Society of Friends (Quakers); *as* **-less; -ly** kind, amiable; *ns* **-ship** amity; kindly feeling; **-liness** kind attitude of mind.

frieze *n* 1 kind of coarse woolen cloth 2 ornamental horizontal band in room or building.

frigate *n* light warship; sailing warship.

frigate bird *n* large, aggressive seabird.

fright *n* 1 sudden alarm, fear, terror 2 grotesque, ugly person; *v* **frighten** alarm; terrify; *a* **frightful** shocking;

horrible; *adv* **-ly**; *n* **-ness**.

frigid *a* cold; distant and repellent; devoid of feeling; *adv* **frigidity**.

frill *n* pleated, flounced ornamental trimming on edge of dress, curtains, etc.; *pl* **-s** affected airs; *v* make into, adorn with frills; *a* **frilly**.

fringe *n* **1** ornamental edging of threads, loops, tassels, etc. **2** outer edge; border; limit; *v* adorn with, act as fringe.

fringe benefit *n* benefit from work not part of pay.

Frisbee [TM] saucer-shaped plastic disk for throwing.

frisk *v* gambol, frolic; *coll* search (suspect); *a* **frisky**; *n* **-iness**.

fritter *n* slice of fruit, etc., fried in batter.

fritter *v* waste, dissipate money, time, etc.

frivolous *a* silly; futile; empty-headed; *n* **frivolity** levity.

frizz *v* hiss; splutter (*as bacon being fried*); curl, crisp (hair); *a* **frizzy** curly.

fro *adv* (*only in phrase*) **to and fro** back and forth; up and down.

frock *n* woman's dress; monk's robe; *v* invest as priest.

frock coat *n* (formerly) knee-length coat for men.

frog *n* **1** tailless amphibian, developed from tadpole **2** attachment to belt supporting sword **3** ornamental loop and button on clothes; *ns*

frogman swimmer equipped and trained for underwater operations; **frog spawn** frog's eggs; **frog in the throat** hoarseness.

frolic *a* merry; jovial; *n* merry-making; gaiety; *v* **-icking, -icked.** gambol, play pranks; *a* **frolicsome**.

from *prep* expressing source, distance, divergence, cause; opposite of **to**; not near to.

front *n* **1** forward part **2** battle area, forward line **3** area of land on beach **4** face of building **5** something, person acting as cover for illegal activities **6** forward part of weather change; *v* face; stand opposite to; *idm* **in front of 1** ahead of **2** in the presence of; *idm* **up front** *coll* to be paid in advance; **frontage** width of building or plot at front; *ns* **frontier** boundary between states *pl* **-s** farthest extent; **frontiersman** pioneer of American West; **frontispiece** illustration at front of book; **front line** most advanced position, *a* **f.-line; f. man** *coll* leader of organization in touch with public; **f.-runner** person with best chance of success.

frost *n* **1** particles of frozen moisture on earth's or other surface; air temperature causing this **2** *sl* coolness of manner; *v* affect with frost; make frosted (with sugar icing, etc.); *a* **frosty** freezing;

not genial; hoary; *n* **frostbite** gangrenous injury to tissues, due to exposure to extreme cold; *a* **frostbitten**.

froth *n* light mass of small bubbles; foam; *fig* futile talk; *v* cause to emit froth; *a* **frothy**.

frown *v* wrinkle forehead; seem gloomy, angry; *n* contraction of brows.

frugal *a* **1** sparing; thrifty **2** inexpensive; *n* **-ity**.

fruit *n* **1** edible part of plant containing seed **2** offspring **3** *usu pl* result of effort; reward; *a* **fruitful** successful; *adv* **-ly;** *n* **-ness**; *a* **fruitless** vain; *adv* **-ly;** *n* **-ness**; *ns* **f. bat** tropical fruit-eating bat; **f.cake 1** cake with dried fruit **2** *coll* crazy person; **f. salad** mixture of fruits; *a* **fruity**.

fruition *n* fulfillment; enjoyment.

frump *n* plain, dowdy woman; *a* **-ish**.

frustrate *v* baffle; circumvent; foil; *n* **-ation**.

fry[1] *n* young fishes; **small f. 1** young children **2** insignificant person.

fry[2] *v* **-ying, -ied.** cook, be cooked in hot fat.

frying pan *n* **1** shallow pan for frying; *idm* **out of the frying pan into the fire** *coll* escaping one disaster to land in something even worse.

ft. *abbr* foot.

fuchsia *n* ornamental flowering shrub.

a
b
c
d
e
f
g
h
i
j
k
l
m
n
o
p
q
r
s
t
u
v
w
x
y
z

A B C D E **F** G H I J K L M N O P Q R S T U V W X Y Z

fuddle v make stupid by intoxication; tipple.

fuddy-duddy n, a fussy, old-fashioned (person).

fudge[1] n 1 soft, sugary, chocolate candy 2 nonsense.

fudge[2] v coll 1 perform clumsily 2 evade 3 falsify.

fuel n any material used for burning; v **fueling, fueled.** provide with, take in fuel.

fugitive a fleeing; transient; evanescent; n one fleeing from danger, captivity, etc.

fugue n musical contrapuntal composition with recurring themes.

fulcrum n point on which lever moves.

fulfill v **-filling, -filled.** satisfy; comply with; carry out, perform; n **-ment.**

fulgent a shining; radiant; blazing; n **fulgency.**

full a 1 unable to hold more 2 well fed 3 complete; ample 4 maximum 5 (of sound) resonant 6 (of clothes) hanging loosely 7 plump; v shrink, cleanse, thicken wool; idm **be full of** think only of; as **f.-blooded** genuine; vigorous; **f.-blown** fully developed; **f.-grown** adult; **f.-length, f.-scale, f.-time**; adv **fully**; as **fully fashioned** shaped to fit; **fully fledged 1** with full feathers ready to fly **2** fully trained; ns **fullness; fullback** field sport defender; **f. house 1** capacity audience **2** poker three of one suit and two of

another; **f. moon**; idm **come to a full stop** stop doing, moving altogether.

fuller n tradesman who shrinks, cleanses wool cloth; n **fuller's earth** clay used in fulling.

fulminate v 1 flash; explode; detonate; vapor 2 denounce violently; n highly explosive compound; n **-ation.**

fulsome a excessive.

fumble v grope clumsily with hands; bungle.

fume n 1 esp pl pungent smoke; vapor 2 fig anger; v 1 emit fumes 2 fig fret, be angry; v **fumigate** disinfect by fumes; ns **-ation, -ator.**

fun n mirth; enjoyment; sport; joking; **make f. of** ridicule; **in f.** as joke.

function n 1 normal action, occupation or purpose; duty 2 official task, ceremony 3 large social gathering 4 math quantity whose value is linked to varying value of another; v work; act; a **-al** having special purpose; med affecting function; n **-ary** official.

fund n permanent stock; sum set apart for special purpose; pl **-s** money resources; v convert into, provide, invest in, permanent fund; n **funding** act, process of creating funded debt.

fundament n underlying principle, rule, basis; a **fundamental** basic; essential; adv **-ly**; n basic rule;

principle; ns **-ism, -ist.**

funeral n burial, interment of dead; a relating to funeral; ns **f. director** undertaker; **f. parlor; f. home** undertaker's premises; as **funereal** mournful; dismal; black; **funerary** of, for funeral.

fungus n plant or allied growth reproducing by spores, e.g., mushroom, mildew, etc.; pl **fungi**; a fungoid, fungal; n **fungicide** substance that destroys fungi.

funicular a connected with, worked by rope.

funk n 1 fear 2 coward; v fear; try to avoid, through fear.

funky a coll 1 with simple style 2 fashionable.

funnel n 1 cone-shaped tube for pouring liquids into container 2 smokestack of ship, locomotive; v pour off, as through funnel.

funny a 1 amusing 2 strange; adv **funnily**; ns **funniness; funny bone** elbow; **f. business** coll trickery; **f. farm** mental hospital.

fur n 1 short, soft hair forming animal coat; dressed skin of animal; pl such skins collectively 2 coating; deposit (on tongue, in kettle, etc.) v cover, become coated, with fur, n **furrier** dealer in furs; a **furry** of, like fur.

furbish v polish, clean up; burnish.

furcate a branched; forked.

furious a raging; violent; frenzied; savage; vehement;

ns **-ness, fury.**

furl *v* roll up and bind securely (sail, umbrella).

furlong *n* ⅛ mile, 220 yards.

furnace *n* enclosed chamber of brick, metal in which great heat can be generated.

furnish *v* provide; equip, *esp* house, office, etc., with furniture; *ns* **furnisher** one who sells furniture; **furnishing** act of equipping house; *pl* **-s** furniture, fittings.

furniture *n* movable household equipment.

furor *n* general excitement.

furrow *n* **1** groove made in land by plow **2** deep wrinkle on face, etc.; *v* make furrows.

further *v* forward; promote; *adv* besides; *a, adv* to greater degree, extent; *a, adv* **furthest** to greatest degree, extent; *n* **furtherance** promotion; *adv* **furthermore** besides.

furtive *a* stealthy, secret, sly; *n* **-ness**.

fury *n* **1** extreme anger; rage **2** *cap* avenging, Greek goddess.

furze *n* thick-growing, yellow-flowered, prickly shrub.

fuse *n* **1** device to explode shells, mines, etc. **2** soft wire with low melting point, used as safety device in electric circuits; *v* **1** melt (metal) with heat **2** fit fuse to; *a* **fusible;** *n* **fusion** act of melting, blending; *fig* coalition.

fuselage *n* body of aircraft.

fusel oil *n* mixture of crude alcohols.

fusillade *n* continuous, rapid firing.

fuss *n* nervous, anxious state of mind; needless bustle; *v* worry about; make nervous.

fusspot *n* *coll* fussy person.

fusty *a* old-fashioned; rigid.

futile *a* vain; useless; ineffectual; *n* **futility.**

futon *n* padded type of mattress used on bed or frame.

future *a* happening hereafter; of, connected with time to come; *n* **1** time to come **2** fate **3** tense of verb indicating future; *pl* **-s** *comm* goods or shares for later delivery paid for at today's prices; *ns* **futurity; futurism** nonrepresentational art against tradition; *a* **futuristic.**

fuzz *n* **1** stiff, fluffy hair **2** *sl* police; *a* **fuzzy** fluffy; blurred.

FYI *abbr* for your information.

g. *abbr* gram.

gab *n* chatter; talkativeness; *v* **gabble** utter rapidly and indistinctly; *n* rapid, confused speech; jabbering.

gabardine *n* thin, ribbed woolen fabric; rainproof, coat of this.

gabble *v* speak too fast to be intelligible; *n* such talk.

gable *n* triangular upper part of wall of building enclosed by roof ridges.

gad *v* **gadding, gadded.** wander about aimlessly or seeking pleasure; *n* **gadabout** pleasure seeker.

gadfly *n* very critical person.

gadget *n* ingenious applicance; novel device.

Gaelic *n* Celtic speech, *esp* of Scotland; pertaining to Gaels; *n* **Gael** Scottish, Irish Celt.

gaff *n* **1** spar on top of fore-and-aft sail **2** fraud, trick **3** abuse, criticism.

gaffe *n* blunder; tactlessness.

gaffer *n* aged rustic; foreman.

gag *n* **1** anything thrust into mouth to silence person **2** device for keeping mouth open during operation **3** unscripted remark; *sl* joke; *v* **gagging, gagged. 1** silence by gag **2** put in jokes, remarks not in script **3** retch.

gaga *a coll* senile.

gage *n ar* pledge; symbol of challenge to fight; *v* pledge; stake.

gaggle *n* flock of geese; *v* cackle.

gaiety *n* cheerfulness.

gaily *adv* in a cheerful manner.

gain *v* **1** obtain; secure; win **2** profit **3** improve **4** earn; *n* increase; improvement; *a* **-ful**, yielding gain.

gainsay *v* dispute; contradict; deny; *pt, pp* **gainsaid;** *n* **gainsayer.**

gait *n* manner of walking, running.

gaiter *n* cloth, leather covering for lower leg.

gal *n coll* girl.

gala *n* festivity; fete.

galaxy *n* vast cluster of stars, as Milky Way; *fig* brilliant assembly; *a* **galactic.**

gale *n* strong, violent wind.

galena *n* natural lead sulfide.

gall[1] *n* **1** bile, bitter secretion from liver **2** *fig* bitterness **3** effrontery; *ns* **g.bladder** small bladder, containing bile; **g.stone** hard, stony concretion formed in gallbladder.

gall[2] *n* **1** sore, *esp* on horse, caused by friction **2** growth on tree, *esp* oak, produced by gallfly; *v* make sore by rubbing; irritate.

gallant *a* **1** brave; daring **2** chivalrous; attentive to women; *n* **gallantry.**

galleon *n* old three- or four-decked sailing ship.

gallery *n* **1** upper tier of seats in theater, church, etc. **2** underground passage in mine **3** long, narrow, covered passage, open at one side **4** room, building for showing works of art.

galley *n* **1** low, single-decked ship with sails and oars **2** ship's kitchen **3** tray holding composed type **4** galley proof; *ns* **g. proof** typeset proof before being made up into pages; **g. slave** one condemned to row in galley; drudge.

Gallic *a* of, relating to Gaul;

French; n **Gallicism** French word, idiom used in another language.

gallivant v gad about.

gallon n liquid or dry measure of capacity.

gallop n fastest pace of horse, etc.; quick ride; v move, ride at gallop; fig hurry.

Gallop poll n survey of public opinion.

gallowglass n Irish foot soldier, mercenary.

gallows n wooden structure used for hanging criminals.

gallows humor n jokes about deadly serious situations.

galore adv plentifully; in great abundance.

galosh n protective overshoe worn in wet weather; pl **galoshes**.

galvanism n electricity produced by chemical action; a **galvanic** fig spasmodic; v **galvanize** electrify by galvanism; coat with metal by galvanizing; n **galvanization**.

gam n 1 school of whales 2 sl leg.

gambit n 1 chess opening move, when piece is intentionally sacrificed 2 initial move in action, conversation, etc.

gamble v play games of chance for money stakes; place (money) at stake; fig take risk or chance; n act of gambling; risky chance; n **gambler**.

gambol v frolic.

game[1] n pastime; sporting contest; artful trick; jest; v gamble; a plucky; lame; n **gamester** gambler.

game plan n strategy to reach objective.

game[2] n birds, animals hunted for food, sport; pl **-s** (series of) sporting contests; **gamekeeper** man employed to look after game.

gamesmanship n art of winning by distracting one's opponent without breaking any rules.

gamete n mature sexual reproductive cell that joins with another to from a new organism.

gamin, gamine n Fr 1 street urchin 2 neglected, impertinent child.

gamma n third letter of Greek alphabet; **g. rays** very short electromagnetic waves.

gamma globulin n antibody-rich blood.

gamut n whole range, compass of voice, notes, etc; fig whole extent, scope.

gamy a strong, scented, flavored like game that has been hanging.

gander n 1 male goose 2 sl look.

gang n group; squad; band of criminals; phr v **gang up on** conspire against.

gangland n underworld of professional crime.

gangling a awkwardly tall and thin.

ganglion n 1 nerve center 2 hard, globular swelling,

usually on sinew.

gangplank n movable gangway for boarding, leaving ship.

gangrene n mortification of living tissue, necrosis; a **gangrenous**.

gangster n 1 member of criminal gang; violent, armed criminal.

gangway n passage; road 2 movable bridge from ship to shore 3 way between rows of seats.

gantry n frame structure used for support.

gap n hole, opening, space; interval.

gape v stare in wonder or amazement; open widely.

gar n needlefish.

garage n enclosure for storage or repair of cars; v place car in such an enclosure.

garb n clothing, dress.

garbage n 1 food waste 2 useless information.

garbanzo n type of bean known as a chick pea.

garbled a confused, jumbled.

garçon n Fr waiter.

garden n area of ground for growing flowers, fruit, or vegetables; v cultivate a garden; ns **gardener; gardening; garden center** place where plants, garden tools, etc. are sold.

gargantuan a extremely large.

garish a gaudy; ostentatious.

garland n wreath of flowers, leaves, used as decoration, or sign of victory; v hang, adorn with garlands.

a
b
c
d
e
f
g
h
i
j
k
l
m
n
o
p
q
r
s
t
u
v
w
x
y
z

gargle v wash or soothe sore throat with liquid held there by blowing gently.

gargoyle n often grotesque head carved on waterspout on a church.

garlic n bulbous-rooted plant of onion family, used as flavoring.

garment n article of clothing.

garner v store up; accumulate.

garnet n red semiprecious stone.

garnish v decorate, improve appearance of (esp food); n material for this; n **garniture** ornamentation.

garret n room under roof of house; attic.

garrison n troops defending fortress, town, etc.; v furnish with, act as garrison.

garrotte v execute by strangling; strangle; n instrument used for execution; n -er.

garrulous a talkative; n **garrulity**.

garter n band worn to keep stocking up.

garter snake n small, harmless, stiped snake.

garth n enclosed space; court; yard; garden.

gas n -es or -ses. 1 one of various vaporous substances 2 airlike fluid 3 poisonous vapor used in warfare 4 such vapor used as anesthetic 5 liquid distilled from petroleum; v **gassing, gassed.** use gas upon; sl talk nonsense at length; ns **gasholder;**

gaslight; gasometer; g. mask; g. pedal aut accelerator; **g. station** filling station; **gasworks**; as **gaseous, gassy**; n **gassiness**.

gash n deep cut; slash; v cut deeply.

gasket n 1 rope, cord for securing sail 2 tow; jointing, packing material 3 type of washer.

gasoline n liquid distilled from petroleum for fuel (also **gas**).

gasp v catch breath suddenly, as in surprise or fear; n sudden catching of breath.

gastric a of, relating to stomach; ns **gastritis** inflammation of stomach.

gastroenteritis n inflammation of stomach and bowels.

gastronomy n science of good food; a **gastronomic**; adv -ally.

gate n 1 hinged frame of wood or metal across opening, path, etc. 2 sluice 3 way in or out of place 4 total number of spectators at sporting event 5 total amount paid by these for admission; v **gate-crash** enter uninvited; n -er.

gateleg table n table with folding top and movable legs.

gateway n entrance with gate; idm **gateway to** way of reaching or acquiring something.

gather v 1 bring together; collect 2 acquire 3 infer 4 fester 5 pucker; n **gathering** 1 assembly 2 purulent

swelling; **gathers** small pleats in fabric.

gauche a clumsy; tactless; awkward; n **gaucherie**.

gaucho n S American cowboy.

gaudy a showy; garish; vulgarly fine; n -iness.

gauge n 1 standard of measure (diameter of wire, distance between rails, thickness of sheet metal, etc.) 2 instrument for measuring rainfall, force of wind, speed of current, etc. 3 device for testing size of tools, etc.; v measure; fig estimate.

gaunt a lean and haggard; grim and forbidding.

gauntlet a glove with protective cuff; idm **throw down g.** issue challenge; idm **run the g.** run (as punishment) between two rows of hostile men; fig be exposed to hostile attacks, criticism.

gauss n unit of intensity of magnetic field.

gauze n thin, transparent silk or other fabric; light haze; a **gauzy**.

gavel n judge's, auctioneer's hammer.

gawk v stare at in a stupid way.

gawky a awkward; ungainly; n **gawk** such a person.

gay a 1 dated bright; cheerful 2 homosexual; n homosexual.

gaze v look intently, fixedly.

gazebo n pavilion structure set on a lawn.

gazelle n small, delicately

formed antelope.

gazette *n* newspaper; *v* publish in gazette; *n* **gazetteer** geographical dictionary.

gazpacho *n* cold vegetable soup.

gear *n* **1** apparatus; tools **2** harness **3** mechanism transmitting, regulating, or controlling movement **4** gear ratio **5** *sl* clothes; wheel, cog with teeth; *v* provide with, put in gear; *n* **g. case** case enclosing gear wheels, etc.; **gearing** system of cogwheels, forming gear; **gearshift** mechanism for engating gears; **out of g.** disengaged from gear; *fig* inharmonious.

gecko *n* house lizard.

gee *interj* exclamation of surprise, disappointment, etc.

geek *n* carnival performer; *sl* unattractive person.

geese *pl of* **goose.**

geezer *n* *coll* odd man, *esp* older.

Geiger counter *n* instrument that detects radioactivity.

geisha *n* Japanese singing and dancing girl.

gelatin *n* glutinous substance, obtained by simmering animal tissue, bones, etc.; *a* **gelatinous** like gelatin, jelly.

geld *v* castrate; *n* **gelding** castrated horse.

gelid *a* icy.

gem *n* precious stone, *esp* one cut and polished; *coll* wonderful person, thing; *v* stud, set with gems.

gemini *n* third sign of the zodiac, represented as the twins.

gemsbok *n* large S African gazelle.

gendarme *n* French police officer.

gender *n* **1** classification of nouns, pronouns according to sex **2** sex.

gene *n* carrier of hereditary factor in chromosome.

genealogy *n* line of descent from ancestors; pedigree; study of this; *a* **-logical**; *n* **-logist.**

genera *pl of* **genus.**

general *a* not specific; relating to whole class, group; usual; lacking details; miscellaneous; not specializing; *n* army rank above colonel; *adv* **generally 1** usually **2** by most people **3** without looking at details; *ns* **general election** national election; **g. practitioner** physician who provides everyday medical services; **g. staff** army officers; **g. store** rural variety store; *ns* **generalissimo** supreme commander; **generality** undetailed statement; *v* **generalize** draw general conclusions; *ns* **-ization; generalship** skillful leadership.

generate *v* beget; produce; be cause of; *n* **generation 1** act of generating **2** all persons of approximate same age group **3** all persons in same degree

of descent from common ancestor **4** period of approximate 30 years separating birth of parent and child; *a* **generative**; *n* **generator** apparatus for producing electricity.

generation gap *n* lack of understanding between parents and younger generation.

generic *a* pertaining to genus or class.

generous *a* **1** open-handed; magnanimous **2** abundant **3** (of wine) full bodied; *n* **generosity** quality of being generous; liberality.

genesis *n* origin; mode of production; *pl* **geneses**; *n cap* first book of Bible.

genetics *n* branch of biology dealing with heredity; *a* **genetic.**

genetic engineering *n* artificial change to genetic structure of organism to produce new strain.

genetic fingerprint *n* the genetic information about an individual, used to identify the person or as evidence in court.

genetic marker *n* dominant gene or trait.

genial *a* **1** kindly; amiable; cordial **2** (of climate) mild, warm; *n* **-ity.**

genie *n* Arabian demon or spirit; *pl* **genii.**

genitalia *n pl* reproductive organs; *a* genital.

genius *n* **geniuses 1**

A
B
C
D
E
F
G
H
I
J
K
L
M
N
O
P
Q
R
S
T
U
V
W
X
Y
Z

exceptional intellectual, artistic ability **2** person having such ability **3** natural aptitude **4** guardian spirit.

genocide n deliberate murder of a people.

genotype n species type.

genre n **1** kind; style; species **2** painting of rustic life.

gent n coll gentleman.

genteel a unnaturally polite, elegant or affected (usu sarcastic).

gentian n herb usually having vivid blue flowers.

gentile n person who is not Jewish.

gentle a **1** well-bred **2** mild; serene **3** soft **4** moderate; docile; ns **gentility** gentle breeding; **gentleman** well-bred man; honorable, courteous man; **gentleness** quality of being gentle; kindliness; **gentry** upper-class people, below nobility; **gentleman's agreement** agreement binding by honor (not legally); a **gentlemanly**.

genuflect v bend knee in reverence, etc.; n **genuflection**.

genuine a **1** true; real **2** sincere; adv **-ly**; n **-ness**.

genus n kind; sort; class; species; group of similar species; pl **genera**.

geo- prefix of the earth.

geocentric a having earth as center; seen, measured from center of earth.

geodesic dome n hemispherical structure of polygonal shapes.

geodesy n science of measuring earth and its surface.

geography n **1** science describing earth's physical features, divisions, products, climate, plant and animal life, population, etc. **2** book on geography; n **geographer**; a **geographic(al)**.

geology n science dealing with earth's crust, its history and structure; n **geologist**; a **geologic(al)**; v **geologize** study geology of.

geometry n mathematical science dealing with properties and relations of lines, surfaces, etc.; n **geometrician**; a **geometric(al)**; adv **-ally**.

geophysics n science dealing with earth's physics; a **geophysical**.

geopolitics n study of effects of geographic, economic factors on politics; a **geopolitical**.

geostationary a maintaining the same position above the earth.

geranium n one of genus of flowering plants, as crane's bill; pelargonium (cultivated).

gerbil n small, burrowing rodent often kept as a pet.

geriatrics n pl medical care and treatment of old people; a **geriatric** of old people.

germ n **1** rudimentary form of organism from which new one can develop **2** microbe **3** fig elementary thing; n

germicide substance capable of killing germs.

German n (native, language) of Germany; **G. measles** contagious disease; **German shepherd** large, wolflike dog used in police work and as guide for the blind.

germane a relevant; pertinent; appropriate.

germicide n chemical that kills germs.

germinate v begin, cause, to sprout or develop; n **germination**.

germ warfare n use of harmful bacteria to flight war.

gerontology ns study of old age; **gerontologist**.

gerrymander v falsify facts; manipulate for personal politic advantage.

gerund n verbal noun.

gestapo n Nazi secret police.

gestation n period from conception until birth.

gesticulate v use motions of hands, arms, when speaking, for emphasis; n **gesticulation**.

gesture n **1** movement of limbs, etc. to convey meaning **2** something done for effect.

get v **getting, got. 1** receive; obtain **2** reach; bring to specified state **3** make happen **4** come to the point of doing **5** move **6** induce **7** become **8** understand; phr vs **get around to** find time to; **get at 1** criticize; attack **2** imply; **get away with** avoid being punished for; **get along**

1 progress **2** be friendly; **get by** survive; manage; **get someone down** depress someone; **get down to** start work on; **get off** escape punishment; **get around 1** avoid **2** become known.

getaway n escape.

getup n coll choice of clothes; **g. up** v stand up, arise from bed.

gewgaw n gaudy ornament.

geyser n natural spout of hot water; device for heating domestic water.

ghastly a terrifying; horrible; shocking; pallid.

gherkin n small cucumber used in pickles.

ghetto n Jewish quarter of city, town; any (usu poor) quarter inhabited by one racial or ethnic group.

ghetto blaster n coll large portable radiocassette player.

ghost n spirit; wraith; specter; anything vague, shadowy, ns **g. town** deserted town; **g. writer** person writing material for a well-known person, under whose name it will be published; idm **(not) the ghost of a** (not) the slightest; a **-ly;** n **-liness.**

ghoul n **1** spirit that feeds on corpes **2** person of morbid interests; a **-ish.**

GI n enlisted soldier.

giant n man, animal, or plant of abnormally large size; mythical being of enormous size; fem **giantess;** a huge; a **gigantic** huge, immense.

gibber v talk, chatter incomprehensibly; n **gibberish** incoherent speech; meaningless words.

gibbet n gallows post, used for execution by hanging.

gibbon n small, long-armed ape.

gibbous a convex, bulging; humped; (of moon) between half and full.

gibe v deride; sneer; utter taunts.

giblets n pl edible inner parts of fowl.

giddy a **1** dizzy; have feeling of, cause vertigo **2** flighty; n **giddiness.**

gift n **1** something given; present **2** talent; aptitude **3** act, right of giving; a **gifted** talented.

gift certificate n statement by store, paid for as a gift, allowing recipient to choose merchandise up to a certain amount.

gift wrap v wrap as for presentation; n **g. wrapping.**

gig[1] sl (booking for) performance of pop music.

gig[2] **1** ship's boat **2** two-wheeled carriage.

gigabyte n one billion bytes.

gigantic a enormous.

giggle v laugh in suppressed, nervous way; titter.

gild v coat thinly, with gold; fig embellish; pt **gilded;** pp **gilded, gilt;** a **gilt** gilded; n **gilt** gold leaf or paint.

gilt-edged a (of securities) with fixed, guaranteed interest

rate.

gill[1] n liquid measure, 1/4 pint.

gill[2] n fish's breathing organ; flesh under chin and jaws of man.

gimbals n pl rings and pivot for keeping compass, etc., horizontal.

gimcrack n useless trifle.

gimlet n **1** small tool for boring holes **2** drink with lime juice.

gimmick n sl trick; gadget; device for attracting publicity.

gimp n plaited cord, braid used as trimming.

gimpy a limping or lame.

gin[1] n alcoholic liquor distilled from grain, flavored with juniper berries.

gin[2] n **1** snare; trap **2** kind of crane **3** machine separating seeds from cotton.

ginger n **1** tropical spicy plant **2** sl energy, spirit; a sandy red color; ns **g. ale, g. beer; gingerbread** cake flavored with ginger; **ginger snap** n cookie flavored with ginger; a **gingery 1** of, like ginger **2** reddish **3** fig testy.

gingerly a cautious; adv carefully.

gingham n cotton cloth, often checked or striped.

gingivitis n inflammation of gums.

gin mill n saloon.

gin rummy n two-player card game.

ginseng n root of plant eaten to promote vitality.

giraffe n very tall African

A B C D E F **G** H I J K L M N O P Q R S T U V W X Y Z

ruminant.

gird v **1** encircle with belt, *esp* at waist; put on (belt, etc.); attach to (with belt) **2** prepare oneself for challenge; *pt pp* **girded, girt;** n **girder** large metal or wooden beam.

girl n female child; young unmarried woman; *coll* any young(ish) woman; n **-hood;** a **-ish.**

girth n bellyband of saddle, etc.; circumference.

gist n essence, main points (of speech, etc.).

give v **giving, gave. 1** present; offer **2** pay **3** provide **4** cause; inflict **5** yield **6** utter **7** communicate; *idm* **not give a damn** not care at all; *idm* **give and take** show readiness to compromise; n **give-and-take;** *idm* **give it to somebody 1** attack; criticize **2** admit; **give way (to) 1** yield (to) **2** be superseded (by) **3** fail to control; *phr vs* **give away 1** present **2** sell for no profit **3** betray **4** reveal (secret); **give in** surrender; **give off** emit; **give out 1** distribute **2** be exhausted; fail; **give over** abandon; trust; **give up 1** surrender; abandon **2** treat as lost **3** treat as too difficult; a **given** fixed; n **g. name** first name; *conj* **given (that)** granted (that); *idm* **be given to** have a tendency toward; n **giver.**

givaway n **1** revealing act or remark **2** event where prizes

are awarded.

gizzard n muscular stomach of birds.

glabrous a smooth; hairless.

glacé a *Fr* having glossy finish; glazed.

glaciation n formation of glaciers.

glacier n slowly moving mass of ice in mountain valleys; a **glacial** of ice, glaciers, very cold; *fig* frigid.

glad a happy; joyful; pleased; v **gladden** make glad; cheer; n **-ness; g.-hand** warm welcome; **g. rags** *coll* clothes for special occasion.

glade n opening, clearing in wood, forest.

gladiator n in ancient Rome, professional fighter with sword, etc., in arena.

gladiolus n **gladiola, gladioluses.** plant with spiky flowers.

glamour n mysterious charm; magical illusion; fascination; a **glamorous;** v **glamorize.**

glance n, v (give) quick look; *idm* **at a glance** instantly; *phr* v **glance off** strike at angle and ricochet; a **glancing** hitting at an angle.

gland n organ that secretes substance for use in body and also transforms, excretes; a **glandular;** n **glanders** contagious disease of horses.

glare v **1** emit dazzling light **2** stare angrily; n blinding brightness; a **glaring** dazzling; flagrant.

glasnost n former Soviet policy

of speaking openly.

glass n **1** hard, brittle substance, *usu* transparent, made by fusion of sand, soda, potash, etc. **2** drinking vessel of glass **3** its contents **4** mirror **5** barometer **6** telescope **7** optical lens; *pl* **-es 1** lenses **2** spectacles; ns **g.blower, g.blowing; g.eye, g.ware, glassworks;** a **-y;** *adv* **-ily;** n **-iness.**

glaucoma n disease of the eye.

glaucous a **1** grayish green **2** *bot* with waxy, powdery surface.

glaze v **1** put glass into **2** coat with glassy, glossy substance **3** become glassy; n glasslike surface; vitreous coating for pottery; glossy coating; n **glazier** one who sets glass.

gleam v emit beams of light; reflect light; n beam; transient flash of light.

glean v pick up stray ears of corn, scraps; *fig* gather (facts, etc.); ns **gleaner; gleanings.**

glebe n land held by incumbent of benefice.

glede n bird of prey.

glee n lighthearted mirth; groupsong; a **-ful.**

glee club n chorus formed to sing sheet short songs.

glen n narrow valley, *usu* with woods and stream.

glengary n Scottish woolen cap.

glib a fluent; plausible; smooth-spoken; n **-ness.**

glide v **1** slide, move along smoothly, stealthily **2** fly (aircraft) without use of engine; fly in glider; *n* **1** action, motion of gliding **2** musical slur **3** glancing stroke (cricket); *n* **glider** aircraft without engine.

glim *n* light source.

glimmer *v* flicker, glow faintly; *n* **-ing** fitful dream; *fig* faint idea.

glimpse *a* fleeting view; passing sight; *v* catch glimpse of.

glint *v* flash, reflect light faintly; glitter.

glissade *n* slide, *usu* on feet, down snow or ice slope; sideward glide in dancing.

glisten *v* glitter, shine, sparkle.

glitch *n elec* sudden malfunctioning.

glitter *v* shine, sparkle intermittently; *fig* make brilliant show.

glitterati *n* fashionable, wealthy literary or show-business personalities.

glitz *n* showy glamour; *a* **-y.**

gloat *v* dwell on, exult in silently, with malicious joy.

globe *n* **1** sphere; ball **2** earth; model of earth; *a* **global 1** worldwide; universal **2** covering whole group, overall; *adv* **-ly;** *ns* **globe-trotter** extensive traveler; *v* **g.-trotting;** *n* **global warming** increase in temperature of the earth's atmosphere believed to be caused by the greenhouse effect.

globule *n* drop of liquid; *a* **globular** ball-shaped; *n*

globulin protein constituent of hemoglobin.

glockenspiel *n* instrument of metal bars struck by hammers, giving bell-like notes.

glomerate *v* collect into ball, cluster; *n* **-ation.**

gloom *n* darkness; melancholy; *a* **gloomy 1** dismal; dark **2** pessimistic.

glop *n* tasteless, unappetizing mixture of food.

glory *n* **1** splendor; earthly pomp **2** heavenly bliss; high degree of pride, etc.; *v* take delight in; boast; *v* **glorify** exalt; invest with glory; *n* **-fication;** *a* **glorious** sublime; famous; illustrious.

gloss[1] *n* sheen; polished surface; *v* put gloss on; *phr v* **gloss over** conceal (faults); *a* **glossy.**

gloss[2] *n* marginal note; explanation; *v* comment; explain away; *n* **glossary** explanatory list of words.

glottal stop *n* sound made by closure of glottis followed by release of air, *e.g.*, *little.*

glottis *n* opening of larynx; *a* **glottal.**

glove *n* covering for hand and fingers; *v* provide with gloves; *idm* **hand in g.** very intimate; *ns* **glover** one who sells, makes gloves; **glove compartment** small storage section on dashboard of car; **baseball glove; boxing glove.**

glow *v* **1** be incandescent; emit steady light without flame

2 be hot with emotion **3** be, look warm; *n* incandescence; sense of bodily warmth; ardor; *n* **glowworm** beetle; *a* **glowing.**

glower *v* scowl.

glucose *n* sugar found in fruits.

glue *n* adhesive, *esp* one made from horns, hoofs, etc.; *v* fasten with glue; *idm* **glued to** unable to turn one's attention from.

glum *a* morose; sullen; moody.

glut *v* surfeit; satiate; *n* superabundance.

gluten *n* protein found in wheat flour; *a* **-ous.**

glutinous *a* of nature of glue; adhesive, sticky.

glutton *n* greedy feeder; insatiable enthusiast (for work, etc.); wolverine; *a* **-ous** greedy; *n* **gluttony.**

glycerin(e) *n* sweet, colorless, viscous liquid extracted from fats and oils.

GMT *abbr* Greenwich Mean Time.

gnarl *n* knot on a tree.

gnarled *a* knobby; rugged; weather-beaten.

gnash *v* grind teeth with rage.

gnat *n* small, blood-sucking, winged insect.

gnaw *v* chew, bite steadily at; wear away (by pain, worry, etc.).

gneiss *n* crystalline, banded granitelike rock.

gnome *n* dwarfish goblin.

gnomic *a* (full) of sayings; seemingly profound.

gnosis *n* special mystical

knowledge; *a* **gnostic.**
GNP *abbr* gross national product.
gnu *n* S African antelope; wildebeest.
go *v* **going, went, gone.**
1 move; depart 2 operate; function 3 belong; be appropriate; fit 4 lead to 5 make (noise) 6 become 7 turn out; *idm* **anything goes** anything is acceptable; *phr vs* **go ahead** proceed; **go along with** agree with; **go back on** change one's mind about; **go down** 1 descend 2 be defeated 3 be received; **go by** pass; visit; **go down with** fall ill with; **go for** 1 attack 2 aim at 3 have a liking for 4 be applicable to; **go in for** 1 enter (contest) 2 like 3 practice; **go off** 1 depart 2 explode 3 (of food) turn bad 4 cease to like 5 start ringing, sounding 6 succeed; **go over** 1 check 2 transfer allegiance; **go through** 1 experience 2 succeed 3 search; **go under** fail; become bankrupt; *n* vitality; *idm* **have a go** try; *idm* **make a go of something** make something succeed; *idm* **on the go** very busy.
goad *n* pointed stick for driving cattle; *fig* incentive; *v* urge on; *fig* provoke; incite.
go-ahead *a* forward-looking; *n* permission to begin.
goal *n* 1 score posts in football, etc.; score so made 2 aim; purpose; destination; *ns*

goalkeeper; goaltender; goalie defender of goal; **g. kick; g. line; g.mouth; g.post** one of two posts supporting crossbar to form goal mouth.
goat *n* agile ruminant, often horned and bearded; *n* **goatee** small pointed beard.
gob *n sl* mouth; blob of spittle; *v* **gobble** eat noisily, greedily; make throaty noise (as turkey); *n* **gobbler** male turkey.
gobbledygook *n* jargon; pompous, obscure officialese.
go-between *n* carrier of messages between people who cannot meet directly.
goblet *n* drinking vessel without handles.
goblin *n* malicious ugly sprite.
go-cart *n* small, low vehicle for racing.
god *n* supernatural being with divine powers; object of worship; idol; *cap* the Supreme Creator and Ruler; *fem* **goddess;** *ns* **godfather, -mother, -parent** sponsor at baptism; **godchild** one who is sponsored at baptism; **godhead** godhood, divinity; **godliness** piety; *as* **God-fearing, godly** pious; **godless** wicked; **godforsaken** desolate, depraved.
god-awful *a* very unpleasant.
godsend *n* unexpected blessing; lucky chance.
gofer *n* assistant who runs menial errands.
go-getter *n coll* enterprising

person.
goggle *v* (*of eyes*) bulge; stare stupidly; *n* wide-eyed stare; *n pl* protective glasses; *a* **g.-eyed** having bulging, staring eyes.
go-go *a* 1 energetic 2 of discos, fast music and dancing.
going *n* conditions for travel; *a* thriving; prosperous.
going-over *n coll* 1 inspection 2 beating.
goings-on *n pl* mysterious or undesirable activities.
goiter *n* enlargement of the thyroid gland.
gold *n* 1 yellow precious metal 2 objects, *esp* coins, made of this 3 the color of this; *ns* **goldfish; g. digger** woman interested in a man for his money; **g. leaf** thin sheet of gold; **g. medal, g. medallist, g. mine, g. plate, g. rush, goldsmith; g. standard** economic system with money related to value of gold; *a* **golden** 1 of gold color or appearance 2 valuable; supreme; *ns* **g. age** 1 (mythical) time of universal happiness; prosperity 2 period of artistic, literary excellence; **g. eagle; g. jubilee** 50th anniversary celebration; **g. mean** principle of moderation; **g. rule** vital principle; **g. wedding** 50th wedding anniversary.
goldenrod *n* plant with clusters of yellow flowers.
goldenseal *n* herb in buttercup

family.

golf *n* game in which small, hard ball is struck by clubs into series of holes, on an open course; *v* play golf; *ns* **golfer, golf course, golf links** land laid out for golf; **g. ball** 1 ball for playing golf 2 metal ball with choice of typeface for typewriter; **g. club** 1 stick for hitting golf ball 2 club with grounds and clubhouse for golf players.

golly *interj coll* to express surprise.

gonad *n* reproductive gland.

gondola *n* Venetian canal boat; *n* **gondolier** rower of gondola.

gone *pt of* **go.**

goner *n coll* person doomed to fail or die.

gong *n* 1 metal disk giving resonant note when struck.

goo *n coll* 1 sticky, wet mess 2 sentimentality; *a* **-ey**; *n* **-iness.**

good *a comp* **better;** *sup* **best** 1 right; proper 2 virtuous; pious 3 well-behaved 4 useful; beneficial; valid 5 of positive merit, quality 6 efficient; *idm* **good at** proficient, clever at; *idm* **a good** (+*quantity*) at least; *idm* **a good deal** a lot; *idm* **a good few** several; *idm* **good for somebody** *used in congratulating somebody;* *idm* **for good** forever; *idm* **make good** 1 repair 2 fulfill 3 improve one's ways 4 be a success; *n* 1 what is morally right 2 benefit 3 virtuous people; *pl* 1 wares 2 possessions; *idm* **what's the good (of)?** what's the use of? *ns* **-ness;** **g. afternoon/day/ evening/morning** greeting at time specified; **G. Book** the Bible; **g. faith** sincerity; honesty; **G. Friday** Friday before Easter; **g. humor** cheerfulness (*a* **-ed**); **g. neighborliness; g. offices** help, mediation to someone in difficulty; **G. Samaritan** helper of someone in desperate need; **goodwill** 1 friendship 2 (value estimated for) good reputation of a business firm; **goody** *esp pl* **-ies** 1 tasty thing to eat 2 good person as hero (*e.g.,* in film); *as* **g.-hearted, g.- looking, g.-natured, g.- tempered;** *a, n* **goody-goody** unbearably virtuous.

good-bye *interj, n* farewell.

goodly *a* numerous; abundant.

goof, goofball *n sl* stupid, awkward person; *a* **goofy** silly; stupid; *phr v* **goof** make mistakes; **g. off** *coll* waste time.

goon *n sl* foolish person.

goose *n* **geese.** 1 large, web- footed bird 2 *sl* fool; *ns* **goose bumps** pimply bristling of skin due to cold, fear, etc.; **goose-step** high-stepping way of marching with stiff legs.

gooseberry *n* thorny shrub, with hairy, sweet, edible berries.

gopher *n* burrowing rodent.

gore[1] *n* blood, shed and clotted; *a* **gory.**

gore[2] *n* triangular gusset in garment.

gore[3] *v* pierce with horn or tusk.

gorge *n* 1 deep, narrow valley, ravine 2 throat; *v* eat greedily, in excess; *n* **gorget** throat armor.

gorgeous *a* wonderful; beautiful.

gorgon *n* 1 mythical snake- haired woman 2 terrifying woman.

Gorgonzola *n* Italian blue cheese.

gorilla *n* largest anthropoid ape.

gorse *n* spiny yellow-flowered shrub.

goshawk *n* large, fierce, short- winged hawk.

gosling *n* young goose.

gospel *n* 1 one of four books of New Testament; account of life and teaching of Christ 2 *fig* strongly held principle 3 *coll* absolute truth.

gossamer *n* filmy cobweb threads, floating in air, on bushes and grass; any thin filmy material.

gossip *n* 1 idle talk, *esp* about others; ill-founded rumor 2 busybody; *v* chat casually; spread rumors.

got *pt, pp of* **get.**

Gothic *a* of Goths; *n, a* arch (of) style of pointed arches 2 (of) German black-letter typeface.

A B C D E F **G** H I J K L M N O P Q R S T U V W X Y Z

gotten *pp of* **get.**

gouache *n* opaque watercolor paint mixed with gum; picture painted in gouache.

Gouda *n* type of mild Dutch cheese.

gouge *n* concave chisel for making grooves; *v* cut with gouge; *phr v* **gouge out** dig out with sharp tool.

goulash *n* rich stew of meat and vegetables, seasoned with paprika.

gourd *n* plant of melon, pumpkin class; fleshy fruit of plant; its dried rind used as vessel.

gourmet *n* connoisseur of food and wine; epicure.

gourmand *n* enthusiastic overeater.

gout *n* painful, inflammatory disease of joints, *esp* big toe; *a* **gouty.**

govern *v* 1 direct; control; rule 2 determine; influence 3 restrain 4 *ling* decide (case, etc.); *a* **governable;** *ns* **governor** 1 ruler 2 device regulating speed, etc., of machine; **governess** private woman teacher; **government** ruling of state; ministry, persons responsible for this; political administrative system; *a* **-al.**

gown *n* 1 loose, flowing garment 2 woman's dress 3 academic, official robe.

GP *abbr* general practitioner.

grab *v* **grabbing, grabbed.** 1 seize; grasp suddenly 2 snatch eagerly 3 steal; *phr v*

grab at attempt to seize; *n* action of grabbing; *idm* **up for grabs** *coll* available to anyone to take; *n* **g. bag** bag with small gifts to be drawn.

grabble *v* grope; sprawl.

grace *n* 1 elegant beauty 2 mercy 3 extra time 4 favor; goodwill 5 prayer of thanks for food; *idm* **have the grace** to be polite enough to; *idm* **with good/bad grace** willingly/unwillingly; *a* **graceful** 1 elegant in movement, shape, manner 2 tactful; *adv* **-fully;** *a* **graceless** 1 clumsy; 2 rude; boorish; *adv* **-ly;** *n* **-ness;** *a* **gracious** 1 charming; courteous 2 beneficient; *adv* **-ly;** *n* **-ness;** *v* 1 adorn 2 honor.

grade *n* 1 step 2 degree 3 class; standard; *v* classify; arrange in grades; *ns* **g. crossing** level crossing; **g. school** elementary school; *idm* **make the grade** succeed; *ns* **graduation** arrangement in grades; gradual shading off in color; **gradient** degree of slope; *a* **gradual** coming on by degrees; gentle.

graduate *v* get university degree; mark in degrees, grades; *n* holder of university degree; *n* **graduation.**

graffiti *n pl* writing, drawing on walls and other public places.

graft *n* 1 cutting from one plant attached to grow on the stem of another 2 skin,

bone, etc., transferred to grow elsewhere on the body 3 use of unfair means, *esp* bribery from gaining advantage.

graham *a* made of unsifted whole wheat flour; *n* **graham cracker.**

grail *n* chalice; Holy Grail.

grain *n* 1 small, hard particle 2 hard seed, *esp* of cereals 3 smallest unit of weight 4 texture, direction of fibers (of wood, etc.) 5 natural disposition; *v* give imitation wood graining to; *n* **graining;** *a* **grainy, granular** of, like grains; *idm* **grain of salt** questioning attitude.

gram *n* metric unit of weight.

grammar *n* science dealing with correct use of words, their classes, and structure; book on this; *n* **grammarian;** *a* **grammatic(al)** pertaining to, following rules of, grammar; *n* **grammar school** type of school.

Grammy *n* award for high achievement in music industry.

gramophone *n* phonograph, for reproducing recorded sounds.

gramps *n coll* grandfather.

grampus *n* killer or spouting whale; heavy breather.

granary *n* grain storehouse.

grand *a* 1 big; splendid 2 dignified; important 3 *coll* excellent; delightful 4 chief; *idm* **grand old man** person long and deeply respected; *n*

1 grand piano **2** $1,000; *ns* **grandchild, granddaughter, grandson** child of daughter/son; **grandad/ grandpa** *coll* grandfather; **g. duke; grandfather clock** pendulum clock housed in tall case; **g. finale** ending to performance; **grandma** *coll* grandmother; **g. master** chess champion; **g. opera; grandparent, grandfather, grandmother** parent of father/mother; **g. piano** large piano with horizontal strings; **g. prix** international car race(s); **g. slam** outright victory in all events; **grandstand** tiered seating under cover for spectators; **g. total** final sum.

grand dame *n Fr* elegant older woman.

grandee *n* nobleman.

grandeur *n* imposing greatness.

grandiose *a* imposing; pretentious.

grand jury *n* panel designated to determine if a law has been broken and prosecution should proceed.

grange *n* country house, with farm buildings.

granite *n* very hard, granular, igneous rock.

granny *n coll* grandmother.

granola *n* cereal of dried grain, fruit, nuts, etc.

grant *v* assent to; bestow; concede; *idm* **take for granted 1** assume to be true **2** fail to show due appreciation to/for; *ns* gift;

money given to maintain student; scholarship allowance.

granule *n* small, grainlike particle; *a* **granulous, granular;** *v* **granulate** reduce to particles; roughen surface; *n* **granulation** healing formation of grainlike bodies on wound.

grape *n* fruit of vine; *ns* **g.fruit** large citrus fruit; **g.shot** cluster of small iron balls fired from cannon; **g. sugar** glucose, dextrose; **g. vine** vine on which grapes grow; *idm* **hear on the grapevine** learn from unofficial but well-informed sources.

graph *n* diagram showing relative positions, variations (of quantity, temperature, etc.).

graphic *a* **1** clear; vivid **2** of visual symbols, writing, drawing; *n* **g. equalizer** *elec* device for adjusting selected tonal frequencies; *adv* **-ally 1** clearly **2** using graphs; *n* **graphics 1** drawing by mathematical principles **2** display of information by pictures, etc.

graphology *n* study of handwriting.

graphite *n* form of carbon used in pencils and as lubricant.

grapnel *n* hooked anchor for seizing, mooring ship.

grapple *n* grapnel; close hold, grip; *v* seize tightly; come to grips; *phr v* **grapple with** struggle with.

grappling iron *n* grapnel.

grasp *v* **1** seize, hold firmly; clutch **2** understand; *n* **1** firm hold, grip **2** comprehension **3** reach; *a* **-ing** eager for gain; rapacious.

grass *n* **1** green herbage of fields, lawns, etc. **2** pastureland; *ns* **g.hopper** jumping insect that makes shrill singing noise; **g. roots** *polit* ordinary people; **g. snake; g. widow** woman whose husband is often away from home; *v* sow with grass; *a* **grassy;** *n* **grassiness**.

grate *n* fire bars and framework of fireplace; *n* **grating** open framework of bars.

grate *v* **1** rub, scrape with rough surface **2** grind into small pieces **3** make harsh noise, by rubbing; *fig* annoy, irritate; *n* **grater** kitchen utensil; *a* **grating** rasping; jarring.

grateful *a* thankful; feeling gratitude; *n* **gratefulness**.

gratify *v* **-fying, -fied.** please; satisfy; content; indulge; *ns* **gratification, gratitude** feeling of thankfulness, appreciation.

grating *n* framework of bars across opening allowing passage of air or water, but not larger objects.

gratis *a, adv* free of charge.

gratuitous *a* freely given; unwarranted; *n* **gratuity** gift, *esp* money, for services rendered.

a
b
c
d
e
f
g
h
i
j
k
l
m
n
o
p
q
r
s
t
u
v
w
x
y
z

A
B
C
D
E
F
G
H
I
J
K
L
M
N
O
P
Q
R
S
T
U
V
W
X
Y
Z

grave[1] n hole dug in earth for burial; tomb; ns **gravestone, graveyard**.

grave[2] a weighty, serious, solemn; low pitched; n **gravity**.

gravel n small pebbles, coarse sand; shingle; v surface (path) with gravel; a **-ly** 1 covered with or like gravel 2 (of voice) low and harsh.

gravitate v move by force of gravity; fig be attracted by; n **-tation**.

gravity n 1 force that attracts objects toward one another in space 2 seriousness; importance; phr v **gravitate to/toward** be drawn, attracted to(ward); n **gravitation**; a **-tional**.

gravy[1] n sauce made from juice of roasting meat.

gravy[2] n sl money; n **g. train** easy profit with little effort.

gray a 1 of color between black and white, color of slate, ash, etc. 2 having hair this color; ns **g. area** aspect of situation hard to define, hard to deal with; **greyhound** slim, long-legged dog used for racing; **g. matter 1** brain cells 2 coll intelligence; n gray color; a **grayish**.

grayling n freshwater fish; butterfly.

graze v feed in pastures; n **grazier** one who feeds and fattens cattle.

graze v touch by glancing blow; abrade; n slight abrasion caused by grazing.

grease n soft, melted animal fat; semisolid oil as lubricant; v apply grease to; a **greasy**; ns **greasiness, grease gun** lubricating appliance.

greasepaint n theatrical make-up.

great 1 large; big **2** eminent; important **3** avid **4** coll splendid; ns **great grandparent/grandfather /grandmother/aunt/uncle** parent of grandparent, etc.; **G. Bear** northern constellation (Ursa Major); **great blue heron** large, crested, slate-blue bird; **G. Britain** England, Wales, and Scotland; **greatcoat** military overcoat; **G. Dane** big, powerful, smooth-haired dog; **great horned owl** large, tufted owl; **G. Lakes** five lakes between US and Canada; **G. War** First World War (1914-18); adv **-ly;** n **-ness**.

grebe n freshwater diving bird.

Grecian a of ancient Greece.

greedy a gluttonous; fig covetous; longing for; ns **greed** avarice; **greediness** gluttony.

Greek n native or language of Greece; a **Greek.**

green a 1 of color between blue and yellow, color of grass, leaves, etc. **2** rich in vegetation; n **g. belt** area free from urban development **3** unripe; immature **4** inexperienced; gullible (n **greenhorn**) **5** envious (a

green-eyed, n **g.-eyed monster** jealousy) **6** fertile **7** fresh; vigorous **8** concerned with conservation of environment (n **Greenpeace** nonviolent organization that campaigns actively for protection of nature); idm **(give/get) the green light** (give/get) signal of consent; n **1** green color; green clothing **2** grassy area; pl **-s** green, leavy vegetables; ns **-ness; greenback** banknote; **greenery** vegetation; **greengage** yellowishgreen plum; **greengrocer** seller of fruit, vegetables; **greengrocery** his business; n **greenhouse** building with glass sides and roof for growing plants under protected conditions; **greenhouse effect** gradual warming of earth's atmosphere owing to increased pollution (e.g., buildup of carbon dioxide); **green onion** young onion, scallion; **g.room** room where actors can relax; **green thumb** talent for growing plants; **green wood** chopped wood that has not aged enough to burn well; **greens fee** charge for playing on a golf course; a **greenish**.

greet v salute on meeting; welcome; meet; n **greeting**.

gregarious a living in herds, flocks; sociable; n **-ness**.

gremlin n imaginary creature supposed to be cause of

malfunction in machines.

grenade *a* small bomb thrown by hand.

grenadier *n* (formerly) soldier armed with grenades; (now) member of British infantry regiment.

grenadine *n* thin silk fabric; pomegranate syrup; red dye.

grew *pt of* **grow.**

greyhound *n* slim dog known for speed in racing.

grid *n* **1** grating **2** national network of electricity supply **3** numbered network of squares on map, as reference.

griddle *n* metal plate for baking over fire.

gridiron *n* **1** grill **2** football field.

grief *n* sorrow; distress; woe; *idm* **come to grief** have an accident; fail; *v* **grieve** cause, feel grief; *n* **grievance** cause for complaint; *a* **grievous** distressing; painful.

griffin, griffon, gryphon *n* mythical animal, part eagle, part lion.

grill *n* gridiron; food cooked on this; *v* cook, be cooked on grill; *sl* interrogate closely; *n* **-ing** severe cross-examination; *a* very hot; *n* **grill, g. room** room in restaurant, etc., where grilled food is served.

grille, grill *n* open, metal framework over opening.

grim *a* stern, forbidding; inflexible; cruel.

grimace *n* facial contortion, expressing ridicule, pain,

etc.; *v* make grimaces.

grime *n* soot; ingrained dirt; squalor; *v* soil; begrime; *a* **grimy.**

grin *v* **grinning, grinned.** show teeth in smile, grimace, etc.; *n* broad smile; cruel smile.

grind *v* reduce to small pieces or powder by pressure; wear down; make smooth; sharpen; grate; *pt, pp* **ground;** *n* act of grinding; *sl* hard work; *ns* **grindstone** hard sandstone used for grinding; **grinder.**

grip *v* **gripping, gripped.** clutch, hold firmly; hold interest; *n* **1** grasp **2** mastery **3** handle **4** suitcase; *a* **gripping** thrilling.

gripe *v* cause, feel spasms of pain of colic; *sl* complain; *n* spasm of pain in bowels.

grisly *a* horrifying; gruesome; ghastly.

grist *n* grain for grinding; *idm* **(all) grist to the mill** something useful that can be turned to profit.

gristle *n* cartilage, *esp* in cooked meat.

grit *n* **1** small fragments of stone **2** coarse sand **3** *fig* courage; *pls* coarsely ground oats, etc.; *v* **gritting, gritted. 1** treat surface with grit **2** make grinding sound (with teeth); *v idm* **grit one's teeth** show determination and courage; *a* **gritty;** *n* **grittiness.**

grizzly *a* grayish; *n* **g. bear** large N American bear; *a*

grizzled (of human hair) turning gray.

groan *v* utter deep sound of pain, grief, etc.; be overburdened; (of wood) creak; *n* sound made in groaning; moan.

grocer *n* dealer in dry and canned goods, household items, etc.; *n* **grocery** grocer's trade; *pl* **groceries** goods sold by grocer.

grog *n* alcoholic beverage, *usu* rum, with water; *a* **groggy** unsteady; shaky; weak.

groin *n* **1** depression between thigh and abdomen **2** line made by intersection of two vaults **3** breakwater on beach, to resist tidal erosion; *v* form groin.

groom *n* servant in charge of horses; officer in royal household; bridegroom; *v* tend, care for (horse); keep one's clothes and person neat; *n* **groomsman** best man.

groove *n* narrow channel, furrow, *esp* cut by tool in wood, metal; fixed routine, rut; *v* cut groove in; *idm* **stuck in a groove** fixed in one's habits; *a* **groovy** *dated sl* excellent; modern.

grope *v* **1** feel around blindly, fumble **2** search cautiously **3** touch in an erotic way.

gross *a* **1** fat; coarse **2** obscene **3** flagrant **4** total; not net; *n* **1** the whole **2** twelve dozen; *adv* **-ly;** *n* **-ness.**

grotesque *a* fantastic;

a b c d e f g h i j k l m n o p q r s t u v w x y z

distorted; bizarre; *art* highly decorated with intertwined animal forms and foliage; *n.*

grotto *n* cave; artificial cavern; *pl* **grottoes.**

grouch *n sl* persistent grumbler.

ground *n* **1** surface of earth; area of it **2** soil **3** piece of land for specified use **4** reason; argument **5** area for discussion **6** bottom of sea; *ns* **g. crew, g. floor; g. cloth** waterproof sheet for camping; **g. plan; g. rule** basic rule; **g. stroke** (tennis); **g.swell 1** heavy, slow-moving wave **2** rapid surge of public feeling; **groundwork** work providing for future development; *idm* **get off the ground** make a successful start; *idm* **prepare the ground for** make possible; *idm* **run into the ground** wear out; *v* **1** touch bottom of sea **2** force to stay on the ground **3** connect electrically with the earth; *phr vs* **ground in** give basic instruction in; **ground something on** base something on; *a* **-ed;** *n* **-ing** basic instruction; *a* **groundless** without cause; *adv* **-ly;** *pl* **grounds 1** land round building; land designated for a purpose **2** solid dregs of coffee after brewing.

group *n* collective unit of persons, things; class; number of persons sharing views, interests, etc.; *art*

several figures forming one design; *v* place, form into group.

groupie *n coll* avid fan following pop groups on tour.

group practice *n* group of doctors working as partners.

grouse¹ *n* wild game bird; its edible flesh.

grouse² *v sl* grumble; complain; *n* **grouse.**

grout *n, v* (fill spaces between tiles, etc., with) fine mortar; *v* cover, fill, with grout; *ns* **-er, -ing.**

grove *n* small wood.

grovel *v* **-eling, -eled.** lie flat; *fig* humble oneself.

grow *v* develop; become larger; cultivate; flourish; *pt* **grew;** *pp* **grown;** *phr vs* **grow on** become increasingly attractive to; **grow out of 1** become too big for **2** cease to enjoy; **grow up 1** become adult **2** arise and develop; *a* **grown(-up)** adult; **growing pains** *n* **1** pains in limbs of growing children **2** *fig* problems arising in development of enterprise; *n* **growth** that which has grown or is growing.

growl *v* utter deep rumbling sound of anger; grumble; grouse; *n* make growling sound.

growth *n* **1** process of growing; development **2** increase in economic activity **3** something that has grown **4** abnormal formation on or in the body.

grub *v* **grubbing, grubbed.** dig; uproot; *fig* search arduously; *n* larva of insect; *sl* food; *a* **grubby** dirty.

grudge *v* be reluctant to give or do something; *n* feeling of resentment; *a* **grudging;** *adv* **-ly.**

gruel *n* thin, watery oatmeal; *a* **grueling** exhausting (*n* punishment).

gruesome *a* ghastly; macabre; horrible.

gruff *a* rough; surly; hoarse; *n* **gruffness.**

grumble *v* complain; murmur angrily; rumble; *n* complaint.

grumpy *a* bad-tempered; *adv* **grumpily;** *n* **-iness.**

grungy *a sl* dirty or upkempt.

grunt *v* utter deep, rough, nasal sound; make this sound; *n* deep snort.

Gruyère *n* hard type of Swiss cheese with large holes.

gryphon *n* griffin.

guarantee *n* pledge, promise given that conditions of contract will be carried out; manufacturer's undertaking to make good defects in product; *v* undertake; give guarantee; *ns* **guaranty** surety; undertaking to be responsible for another's debts; **guarantor** one who gives guaranty.

guard *n* **1** protector; sentry **2** state of wariness against danger **3** armed escort **4** rail official in charge of train **5** protective device or part; *v* protect; defend; *idm*

be off/on one's guard be unready/ready to cope with danger; *phr v* **guard against** take care to prevent; forestall; *a* **guarded** 1 protected 2 wary; *adv* **-ly**; *n* **-ness**; *ns* **guardhouse, guardroom** building/room manned by soldiers on guard duty; **guardian** person looking after a child in lieu of parent; **guardianship; guard rail** metal railing or fence installed along highway danger points.

guava *n* tropical tree, having egg-shaped fruit.

gubernatorial *a* of a governor.

guerrilla *n* irregular warfare; one engaged in it.

guerney *n* rolling stretcher.

guernsey *n* breed of tan and white dairy cows.

guess *v* conjecture; form opinion without material evidence; suppose; *ns* **guesstimate** *coll* rough estimate based on a guess; **guesswork** process of guessing.

guest *n* person enjoying another's hospitality; one staying in hotel, etc.

guest house *n* small, private hotel.

guff *n coll* nonsense.

guffaw *n* burst of loud, vulgar laughter.

guide *v* show way; direct; control; advise; *n* one who, that, which, guides; guidebook; one who leads tourists, hunters, etc.; *ns*

guidance 1 leadership 2 help with personal problems; **g.book, g. dog; g.lines** advice on policy; **g.post** sign, marker along the way; *a* **guided** not independent (*ns* **g. missile** rocket controlled by radar; **g. tour**).

guidon *n* small flag.

guild *n* association of people with common trade, profession, or aim; *n* **guildhall** meeting place of guild or corporation.

guilder *n* unit or currency in Netherlands.

guile *n* deceit; wiliness; *as* **-ful, -less**.

guillotine *n* machine for beheading; one for paper cutting; *v* use guillotine.

guilt *n* condition, fact of having committed crime, or sin; culpability; *as* **guilty** having incurred guilt; **guiltless** innocent; *n* **guiltiness**.

guinea fowl *n* domesticated fowl, like pheasant.

guinea pig *n* domestic rodent.

guise *n* disguise; false appearance.

guitar *n* six-stringed musical instrument; *n* **guitarist**.

gulag *n* (formerly) Soviet state labor camp.

gulch *n* deep ravine or torrentbed.

gules *n her* red.

gulf *n* large, deep, inlet of sea; chasm; *fig* impassable gap; *pl* **-s**.

gull *n* 1 web-footed seabird 2 dupe; fool; *v* deceive; cheat; *a* **-ible** credulous, easily duped; *n* **-ibility**.

gullet *n* passage from mouth to stomach.

gully *n* channel worn by water.

gulp *v* swallow noisily; choke back; *n* large mouthful.

gum[1] *n* firm tissue around teeth; *n* **gumboil** abscess in gum.

gum[2] *n* 1 sticky viscid substance exuded by certain trees 2 liquid glue 3 chewing gum; *v* **gumming, gummed.** stick with gum; *a* **gummy**.

gumbo *n* soup made with okra.

gumdrop *n* hard, jellylike candy.

gumshoe *n sl* detective.

gumtree *n* eucalyptus.

gumption *n* shrewdness; common sense; intelligence.

gun *n* tubular weapon from which missiles are fired; any firearm; *phr vs* **gun down** shoot to kill or wound; **gun for** seek chance to attack; *ns* **gunboat diplomacy** negotiation with threat of force; **gunfire** (noise of) shooting; **gunman** armed criminal; **gunner** artilleryman; **gunpoint** *idm* **at gunpoint** with threat of shooting; **gunpowder** explosive powder; **g.running** secret illegal importation of arms; **g.runner** person doing this; **gunshot.**

gung-ho *a coll* thoroughly enthusiastic and loyal.

A B C D E F **G** H I J K L M N O P Q R S T U V W X Y Z

gunk *n sl* stick or gloppy matter.

gunny *n* coarse material used for sacks.

gunwale *n* upper edge of boat's side.

guppy *n* tiny tropical fish.

gurgle *v* flow with, utter, bubbling sound; *n* **gurgling** sound.

guru *n* Hindu spiritual teacher.

gush *v* burst forth; flow out copiously; *coll* talk effusively; *n* violent flow; *fig* effusiveness; *n* **-er** person who gushes; oil well not needing pumps.

gusset *n* triangular section let into garment, to enlarge or strengthen it. **gust** *n* sudden, brief blast of wind, rain, etc.; *fig* brief, outburst of anger, passion, etc.; *a* **gusty**.

gusto *n* relish; zest; enjoyment.

gut *n sing* **1** fine thread made from animal guts, used in surgery, violin strings, etc. **2** narrow passage; *pl* **1** bowels; intestines **2** *coll* courage; stamina; *a sl* **gutted** disappointed, upset *v* **gutting, gutted.** remove guts of; destroy inner contents of (house, etc., *esp* by fire).

gutter *n* **1** narrow trough under eaves to carry rainwater **2** open channel along road **3** *fig* lowest social class; slums; *v* form channels in; *n* **g.snipe 1** ragged child **2** ill-bred person; *v* **g. out** (of candle) burn fitfully; *n* **guttering** system of gutters;

g. urchin street urchins.

guttural *a* pertaining to throat; (of voice) rasping, harsh.

guy[1] *n* rope, wire, chain used to guide, steady, or secure something; *v* steady with guy.

guy[2] *n coll* fellow; man; *v* mock.

guzzle *v* drink, eat greedily and to excess.

gym *n coll* **1** gymnasium **2** gymnastics.

gymkhana *n* athletics display, *esp* equestrian events.

gymnasium *n* hall for physical training and gymnastics; *n pl* **gymnastics** physical exercises, with or without apparatus; *n* **gymnast** one skilled in gymnastics.

gynecology *n* science dealing with functions and diseases of women; *a* **-logical;** *n* **-logist.**

gypsum *n* sulfate of calcium, used for making plaster of Paris.

gyp *v infml* cheat.

gypsy *n cap* **1** member of wandering race of Indian origin **2** their language; Romany; wandering person.

gyrate *v* revolve; whirl around; *n* **-ration;** *a* **-atory** revolving; spinning.

gyrfalcon *n* largest, most powerful of all falcon.

gyrocompass *n* gyroscope with compass attached.

gyroscope *n* flywheel capable of rotating around any axis, used to stabilize ships, aircraft, etc.; *a* **gyroscopic.**

habeas corpus n *leg* writ issued requiring prisoner to be produced in court.

haberdasher n retailer of small articles of dress, sewing thread, pins, etc.; n **-shery.**

habiliments n pl *Fr* clothes, *esp* characteristic of an occupation.

habit n usual behavior; *bio* normal mode of growth; distinctive dress; a **habitual** customary, usual; v **habituate** render familiar with; ns **habitat** natural home of animal; **habitude** usual custom; **habitué** *Fr* regular visitor.

habitable a able to be inhabited; *adv* habitably.

habitant n resident.

habitation n place of abode.

hacienda n estate, *esp* in Spanish-speaking country.

hack[1] v cut roughly; chop; kick shins of; cough harshly; n act of hacking; a trite; routine.

hack[2] **1** n hired horse, *esp* for riding; overworked horse **2** vehicle for hire ; *fig* badlypaid writer; v ride hack; ride at pace of hack; n **hackwork** literary drudgery.

hackamore n type of horse bridle.

hacker n person obtaining illegal entry to computer system and using or altering data stored in it.

hacking cough n hard, dry, persistent cough.

hackles n pl long feathers on cock's neck; hairs on back of animal's neck; *idm* **make somebody's hackles rise/raise somebody's hackles** make somebody very angry.

hackney n medium-sized, ordinary riding horse; carriage for hire.

hackneyed a trite; common.

hacksaw n short saw for cutting metal.

had *pt, pp of* **have.**

haddock n edible salt-water fish, akin to cod.

Hades n abode of dead; underworld.

hadn't *contracted form of* had not.

haft n handle; hilt; v fit haft.

hag n ugly old woman; witch.

haggard a gaunt; having worn, wasted look.

haggis n Scottish culinary dish made from organ meat.

haggle v wrangle over price; dispute terms.

hagiology n study of saints or of their lives; n **hagiographer** writer of saint's life.

haiku n Japanese unrhymed poem of three lines.

hail[1] n small lumps of ice falling like rain; v shower down hail; n **hailstone.**

hail[2] *interj used in greeting;* v greet; accost; **hail from** come from.

hail-fellow-well-met a *coll* friendly and informal.

hair n fine, threadlike growth from skin of animal; mass of such growth on human head; fur of animal; *idm* **let one's hair down** relax; behave in an uninhibited manner; *idm* **not turn a hair** not show any fear, surprise, etc.; *idm* **by a hair's breadth** (of escape, victory) very narrowly; *as* **hair-raising** terrifying; **hairy 1** covered with hair **2** *coll* dangerous; difficult; ns **hairiness, hairdresser** one who cuts, sets, tints hair, *esp*

A B C D E F **H** I J K L M N O P Q R S T U V W X Y Z

women's hair; **hairspring** very fine spring in watch, etc.

haircut n 1 act of cutting hair 2 style in which hair is cut.

hairdo n coll hair style.

hairpiece n small wig covering bald patch.

hairpin curve n sharp, V-shaped corner, esp on steep road.

hairsplitting n fussing about minute unimportant detail.

hairspray n liquid spray to hold hair in place.

hair trigger n very sensitive trigger on gun.

hairy woodpecker n common mid-sized N American woodpecker.

hake n coarse, edible salt-water fish, allied to cod.

halberd n long-handled spiked battle ax.

halcyon n kingfisher; a tranquil, peaceful; **h. days** period of calm weather around winter solstice.

hale a healthy, robust, vigorous, esp of the elderly.

half n one of two equal parts of something; 50%; pl **halves**; a 1 consisting of, equal to half (ns **h. moon, half-dollar**) 2 partial (ns **h. measures, h. truth**); idm **better half** husband/wife; idm **go half-and-half/halves** share equally; idm **go off half-cocked** fail owing to poor preparation; ns **h.back** sport midfield player; **h. brother/sister; h.-life**

time taken for radioactivity of substance to reduce by half; **h.-mast** point halfway up flag mast; **h. nelson** hold in wrestling with opponent's arm bent behind his back; **h.time** short rest midway through sports match; **h.-wit** stupid person; a **h.-witted**; as **h.-baked** inadequate; **h.hearted** lacking in enthusiasm adv -ly; a, adv **h.-price; as h.size; h.-timbered** with wooden framework filled in with brick, stone, plaster; a, adv **h.way** at the midpoint n **h.way house 1** midway position **2** compromise **3** rehabilitation center.

halibut n large, edible, flat salt-water fish.

halitosis n foul breath.

hall n 1 large public room 2 passage, lobby at entrance to building 3 large private house; **hallmark** official mark on gold, silver plate.

hallelujah n, interj praise the Lord!

hallow v make holy; consecrate.

Halloween n October 31, observed by children who dress in costumes and ask for treats.

hallucination n fancied perception by senses of some nonexistent thing; v **hallucinate** affect with hallucinations; a **hallucinatory**.

hallucinogen n drug causing

hallucinations; a **-ic**.

hallway n corridor, passageway.

halo n ring of light around sun, moon, etc.; golden circle, disk around head of figure in picture, symbolizing holiness; pl **haloes**.

halogen n chem any of elements fluorine, chlorine, bromine, astatine forming salts by union with metal n **h. lamp, h. lighting** bright lighting with low energy consumption.

halon n any one of a class of halogenated hydrocarbons, used in fire extinguishers.

halt¹ a lame; v fig hesitate; a **-ing** stumbling; hesitant.

halt² n stoppage of movement; v cause to stop; pause.

halter n style of dress or top with supporting strap around neck, revealing bare back and shoulders.

halvah n Turkish candy made with sesame seeds and honey.

halve v divide in halves; diminish by half; share.

halyard, halliard n rope used for raising sail, flags.

ham n 1 back of thigh 2 thigh of hog, esp smoked and salted 3 amateur radio operator; a **h.-fisted, h.-handed** clumsy; n **hamstring** tendon at back of knee; tendon behind horse's hock; v coll **h. (it up)** overact, exaggerate for humor's sake.

hamburger n patty of ground beef on bread roll.

hamlet n small village.

hammer *n* **1** long-handled tool with heavy head, for driving in nails, working metal, crushing, etc. **2** striking part of gun lock **3** device for striking bell **4** auctioneer's mallet; *idm* **go at it hammer and tongs** argue violently; *idm* **come under the hammer** be sold by auction; *v* strike with, use hammer; knock loudly; *phr v* **hammer out** solve problem by repeated discussion.

hammerhead shark *n* shark with broad, flat nose.

hammertoe *n* medical condition in which first two toes are deformed.

hammock *n* canvas or net bed, slung on cords.

hamper[1] *n* large basket with lid.

hamper[2] *v* hinder; impede; obstruct.

hamster *n* rodent with cheek pouches, often kept as pet.

hamstring *n* cordlike tendon in back of leg; *v* render helpless; *pt, pp* **hamstrung.**

hand *n* **1** end of arm below wrist **2** style of writing **3** pointer on dial, clock, etc. **4** direction; position **5** set of cards held by player; round of cards **6** manual worker **7** assistance **8** measure of four inches; *idm* **at hand** nearby; *idm* **hand in hand 1** holding each other by the hand **2** in collaboration; *idm* **have a hand in** be involved in; *idm* **in hand** being dealt

with; *idm* **on hand** ready; *idm* **off/out of one's hands** not one's responsibility; *idm* **(get) out of hand** (go) out of control; *idm* **at hand** available; *v* pass; give; *idm* **hand it to someone** acknowledge someone's skill, success, courage; *phr vs* **hand down** bequeath; **hand in** deliver; *idm* **hand in one's notice** resign; **hand on** pass; **hand out** issue; *n* **handout 1** something given to a beggar **2** publicity document; *phr vs* **hand over** give possession of, control of; **hand around** distribute; *ns* **handbag** woman's light bag; **handball** ball game; **handbill** small printed notice; **handbook** manual; **handbrake, handcart; handcuffs** chain with rings for holding prisoner by the hands (*v* **handcuff**); *ns* **handful 1** amount that the hand can hold **2** small number **3** *coll* uncontrollable child, animal; **h. grenade, handgun, handhold; hand-me-down** *coll* used clothing passed on to somebody else; **handrail** supportive railing; **handset** telephone receiver; **handshake** right hands of two people gripping in salutation; **handstand** upside-down position supported on hands; **handwriting** (style of) writing by hand (*a* **handwritten**); *as* **h.made;**

h.picked carefully chosen; **h.-to-hand** involving physical contact; **h.-to-mouth** with barely the means to survive; **hands-on** with much personal involvement; *adv* **hands down** without a problem.

handicap *n* disability (physical or mental); disadvantage in time, weight, etc.; race, contest where handicaps are imposed; *v* **-capping, -capped.** impose handicap.

handicraft *n* artistic skill with hands; product of this.

handiwork *n* **1** work needing skill with hands **2** result of somebody's action.

handkerchief *n* small cloth for wiping nose, face, etc.

handle *n* part of tool, utensil, etc., held in hand; *v* **1** touch, feel with hands **2** control; manage **3** deal in *n* **handler** person in control.

handlebars *n pl* bar held by hands for steering bicycle.

handmaid, handmaiden *n* personal female servant.

handsome *a* good-looking; generous; having dignity.

handy *a* **1** useful **2** skillful with the hands **3** accessible; *adv* **handily;** *n* **-iness;** *n* **handyman** person doing minor jobs, repairs.

hang *v* **1** suspend; be suspended **2** fix, attach to wall; *pt, pp* **hung 3** execute by hanging from rope round neck; *pt* **hung,** *pp* **hanged;** *idm* **hang one's head** look

A B C D E F G **H** I J K L M N O P Q R S T U V W X Y Z

ashamed; *phr vs* **hang around** *coll* loiter; **hang back** show reluctance; **hang on** 1 hold on tight 2 wait; **hang in there, hang tough** *coll* persevere; have faith, courage; **hang onto** *coll* keep hold of; **hang out** live; stay; **hang up** 1 suspend 2 end telephone conversation abruptly; **be hung up on/about** be obsessed about; *n* way in which something hangs; *idm* **get the hang of** understand; *a* **h.dog** dejected; guilty; *ns* **hanger** clothes/coathanger; **hanger-on** person hoping to cultivate friendship for personal gain (*pl* **hangers-on**); **h. glider** large kitelike frame for flying without engine; **h. gliding** sport of flying with this; **hanging** execution with rope; **hangman** person doing this; **hangover** 1 sick feeling the day after drinking too much alcohol 2 lasting effect of something; **hang-up** *sl* something causing unusual anxiety.

hangar *n* covered shed, *esp* for aircraft.

hangnail *n* small piece of detached skin around fingernail.

hank *n* skein, coil, length, *esp* measure of yarn.

hanker *phr v* **hanker after/for** desire strongly; *n* **-ing**.

hanky-panky *n* mischief, *usu* sexual.

hansom *n* two-wheeled covered carriage or cab.

Hanukkah *n* annual Jewish festival.

hap *n* chance; *a* **-less** unlucky, wretched; **haphazard** random, accidental.

happen *v* take place; chance; *n* **-ing** occurrence; *sl* fantastic, weird event.

happy *a* cheerful; content; fortunate; *adv* **happily**; *n* **happiness**; *a* **h.-go-lucky** carefree; easygoing.

happy hour *n* time when drinks are sold more cheaply than usual.

hara-kiri, hari-kari *n* Japanese ritual suicide.

harangue *n* vehement speech; *v* harass through speech.

harass *v* worry, vex, annoy by repeated attack; *n* **-ment**.

harbinger *n* forerunner, precursor, herald.

harbor *n* haven, port; shelter; *v* shelter; conceal; lodge.

hard *a* 1 firm; solid 2 difficult 3 strenuous 4 harsh; severe 5 (of water) not lathering well 6 (of drugs) dangerous; addictive 7 (of lines, colors) too emphatic; *adv* intensively; *idm* **hard at it** working hard; *idm* **hard put to** finding great difficulty; *idm* **hard of hearing** rather deaf; *idm* **hard up** *coll* short of money, etc.; *v* **harden** make hard (*phr v* **harden to** make/become less sensitive to); *ns* **-ness**; **hardback** hard-covered book; **hardball**

baseball; **hardboard,** thick fiberboard; **h. cash** coins and notes; **hard cider** fermented apple cider; **h. copy** printed copy; **h. court** asphalt or concrete court; **h. currency** stable currency; **h. disk** *comput* rigid disk with large storage capacity; **h. labor** hard physical work as punishment; **h. landing** landing causing destruction of spacecraft **h. line** unchanging policy; **h.-liner; h. luck** back luck; **h. sell** pressurized method of selling; **hardship** privation; suffering; **hardware** 1 domestic tools, pots and pans 2 *comput* machines 3 weapons; *as* **h.-and-fast** fixed; **h.-bitten** tough; **h.-boiled** 1 boiled till yolk is hard 2 cynical; insensitive; **h.headed** practical; **h.-hitting** ruthless; effective; **h.-nosed** ruthless; **h.-pressed** very busy; **h.-wearing** durable.

hard-core *a* 1 graphic; explicit 2 totally committed.

hardhat *n* 1 worker's helmet 2 working-class conservative.

hare *n* swift rodent, resembling rabbit; *a* **h.brained** rash, flighty; *n* **h.lip** congenital fissure of human upper lip.

harem *n* women's quarters in Muslim house; seraglio.

haricot *n* French bean.

hark *v* listen to; *phr v* **h. back** to revert to (a subject).

harlequin *n* comic character in

pantomime; *a* multicolored; *n* **harlequinade** pantomime scene; buffoonery.

harlot *n* prostitute.

harm *n* physical or moral damage; injury; *idm* **out of harm's way** safe; *v* hurt; injure; *a* **harmful;** *adv* **-ly;** *a* **harmless;** *adv* **-ly;** *n* **-ness.**

harmony *n* concord; agreement; melodious sound, chord; *a* **harmonic** of harmony; *n* one of components of complex musical tone; *n pl* **harmonics** science, art of musical harmony; *a* **harmonious** in harmony; melodious; *n* **harmonica** mouth organ; *v* **harmonize** bring into harmony; reconcile; be in harmony; *n* **-ization; *n* harmonium** small organ.

harness *n* straps, usually leather, and fastenings of horse; any gear resembling this; *v* put into harness; *fig* control, use.

harp *n* musical instrument, with strings plucked by hand; *phr v* **harp on** talk of repeatedly, tediously; *ns* **harpist; harpsichord** forerunner of piano.

harpoon *n* barbed spear with rope attached, for striking whales and large fish; *v* strike with harpoon; *ns* **harpooner, h. gun** one used to fire harpoon.

harpy *n* 1 mythical monster, half woman, half bird 2 cruel merciless person.

harried *a* worried.

harrow *n* spiked frame dragged over ground, to break it up; *v* use harrow; *fig* cause mental distress; *a* **-ing** heartrending.

harsh *a* 1 rough to touch 2 discordant 3 glaring 4 severe.

hart *n* adult male deer; *n* **hartshorn** salvolatile, formerly distilled from hart's antlers; *n* **hart's-tongue** fern with long, narrow leaves.

harvest *n* gathering in of crops; season for this; results of this; *v* gather in; *ns* **h. home** meal given by farmers to farm workers after harvest; **h. moon** full moon nearest to autumn equinox.

has *3rd person sing pres of* **have.**

has-been *n coll* person whose success, popularity are all in the past.

hash *n* 1 dish of chopped cooked meat 2 *coll* mess; muddle 3 hashish; *v* chop up; mismanage.

hash browns *n pl* fried potatoes and onions.

hashish *n* dried hemp, used as narcotic.

hasn't *contracted form of* has not.

hasp *n* metal clasp, or hinged flap for fastening door, etc.

hassle *n coll* 1 difficulty 2 quarrel; *v* 1 harass 2 argue.

hassock *n* tuft of coarse grass; kneeling cushion; low stool.

haste *n* speed; hurry; *v* **hasten** urge on; hurry; move with haste; *a* **hasty;** *adv* **-ily.**

hat *n* head covering, usually with crown and brim; *idm* **keep under one's hat** keep secret; *idm* **take one's hat off to** congratulate; *n* **hatter** one who makes, sells hats; **hatbox** storage box for hat.

hatch[1] *n* trapdoor covering opening (in ship's deck; floor or roof).

hatch[2] *v* incubate; bring forth (young) from shell; emerge from egg.

hatch[3] *v* shade in fine lines (for engraving).

hatchback *n* car with rear door hinged at top.

hatchery *n* place where eggs are hatched.

hatchet *n* small ax; tomahawk; *idm* **bury the hatchet** forget past quarrels; *a* **h.-faced** with sharp, gaunt features; *ns* **h. job** *coll* malicious attack; **h. man** person employed to intimidate opponents, or one to carry out ruthless economies in a business.

hate *v* dislike intensely; detest; *n* loathing; *n* **hatred** profound illwill; *a* **-ful.**

haughty *a* proud; disdainful; arrogant; *n* **-iness.**

haul *v* drag, pull with effort; transport; *naut* alter ship's course; *n* act of hauling; distance hauled; *fig* booty; *ns* **-age** carting, conveying of goods; charge for this; **hauler** carter.

haunch *n* hip, upper thigh, and buttocks; hindquarter.

haunt *v* visit habitually,

a b c d e f g **h** i j k l m n o p q r s t u v w x y z

A B C D E F G **H** I J K L M N O P Q R S T U V W X Y Z

frequent, sometimes as ghost; *n* habitual resort of human or animal.

hausfrau *n Ger* housewife.

haute couture *n Fr* high fashion; companies responsible for this.

haute cuisine *n Fr* high-class cooking.

have *v* 1 possess; own 2 be affected with, subject to; suffer from 3 accept 4 receive 5 experience 6 obtain 7 give birth to; produce 8 *coll* defeat 9 *coll* deceive 10 *used as auxiliary verb in present perfect and past perfect tenses; 3rd sing pres* **has,** *pt, pp* **had;** *idm* **had better (do/not do)** ought to/not to do; *idm* **have done with** finish; *idm* **have had it** *coll* be doomed (to failure, punishment, death); *idm* **have it in for somebody** intend to harass somebody, have vengeance on somebody; *idm* **have it out with** settle by open discussion; *idm* **have to** be obliged to; *idm* **have to do with** deal with; *n* **have-not** poor person.

haven *n* harbor; *fig* refuge; shelter.

haven't *contracted form of* have not.

haversack *n* canvas bag for carrying rations, camping equipment, etc.

havoc *n* devastation; destruction.

haw *n* red fruit of hawthorn; *ns*

hawthorn thorny shrub with white, pink, or red flowers.

haw *v* hesitate in speech; *n* inarticulate sound expressing doubt.

hawk[1] *n* 1 short-winged, long-tailed falcon 2 *polit* person favoring aggressive tactics; *a* **hawkish**.

hawk[2] *v* sell from door to door; *fig* spread around; **hawker** *n* itinerant seller of wares.

hawk[3] *v* clear throat noisily; spit phlegm.

hawk-eyed *a* possessing excellent vision.

hawse *n* part of ship's bows where anchor cables pass through holes.

hawser *n* large rope or small cable.

hay *n* grass mown and dried for fodder; *ns* **haycock** heap of hay; **hayseed** grass seed; **haystack** rick of hay; **hayride** evening ride in hay-filled, horse-drawn wagon or truck; **hayfever** allergic congestion of nose and throat.

haywire *n infml* amiss.

hazard *n* game of chance, played with dice; chance; risk; danger; *v* expose to risk; *a* **hazardous** risky.

haze[1] *n* mist; vapor; *a* **hazy** misty; obscured; vague; confused (mental state).

haze[2] *v* play abusive tricks on.

hazel *n* tree with edible nuts; *a* light brown color.

H-bomb *n* hydrogen bomb.

he *masc nom pron* (*3rd pers sing*) male person, etc., just

referred to; *as prefix* **he-** denotes male animal; *n* **he-man** *coll* virile man.

head *n* 1 part of body housing brain, eyes, mouth, etc. (*ns* **h.ache, h.band, h.dress, h.gear, h.rest**); 2 top or front part (*ns* **headlight, headline**); 3 chief person (*ns* **h.master/mistress/teacher, headman, h. of state**); 4 mind; mental ability 5 individual *n* **h. count;** 6 *elec* part of taperecorder in contact with tape, converting electrical signals into sound 7 froth on top of beer 8 *geog* cape; headland 9 main division of topic (*also* **heading**); *pl* **-s** side of coin showing head of someone; *idm* **above/over one's head** too hard to comprehend; *idm* **bring/come to a head** bring to/reach a vital point; *idm* **go to somebody's head** make somebody overexcited; *idm* **have one's head in the clouds** daydream; *idm* **head and shoulders above** much better than; *idm* **keep one's head** remain calm; *idm* **keep one's head down** avoid danger, distraction; *idm* **head over heels** completely; *idm* **make head or tail of** understand; *idm* **out of one's head** *coll* mad; *v* 1 lead 2 be at front, top of list 3 hit with the head; *phr vs* **head for** go toward; **head off** 1 (cause to) change direction 2 prevent; *ns* **headboard**

board at head of bed; **header 1** act of diving headfirst **2** act of striking ball with head; **h.hunter 1** tribal warrior who collects heads **2** person recruiting senior staff; **headland** promontory; **headphone** listening apparatus *usu pl*; **headquarters** central office; **headset** headphones with microphone; **headship** post of head teacher; **headstand** gymnastic posture with head on ground, supported by hands, and feet up; **h. start** early advantage; **headstone** stone placed at head of grave; **h. waiter** senior waiter of a restaurant; **h.waters** streams at source of river; **headway** progress; **head wind** wind in one's face; *as, advs* **headlong 1** head first **2** in haste; **head-on** with the front part in collision; *as* **headstrong** impetuous; self-willed; **heady** intoxicating.

heal *v* make, become sound or healthy; cure; *n* **health** state of well-being; body condition; *coll* **to your h.** toast drunk wishing one health and prosperity; *ns* **h. farm** place where people go to stay for help with diet, exercise, etc.; **h. food** natural, organic food; *as* **healthful** promoting good health; **healthy** in good health; vigorous; *n* **healthiness**.

heap *n* piled-up mass of things; large number or quantity; *v* amass; form into heap.

hear *v* perceive by ear; listen to; *idm* **won't/wouldn't hear of it** refuse(s) to even consider it; *phr vs* **hear from** get news from; **hear out** listen patiently to; *leg* try as judge; learn; *pt, pp* **heard**; *ns* **hearer, hearing** sense by which sound is perceived; formal, official listening; **hearsay** rumor.

hearken *v* listen attentively.

hearse *n* funeral vehicle for coffin.

heart *n* muscular organ that pumps blood around the body; *fig* seat of human emotions, affection, courage, etc.; core; central part; *n idm* **after one's own heart** exactly as one likes; *idm* **at heart** basically; *idm* **by heart** from memory; *idm* **have a heart** *coll* be merciful, sympathetic; *idm* **have one's heart in one's throat** be terrified; *idm* **no heart for** no appetite for; *idm* **set one's heart on** long for; *idm* **take to heart** feel deeply; *ns* **heartache** sorrow; **h. attack** malfunction of heart; **heartbeat** pumping of heart; **h.break** anguish *as* **h.breaking, h.broken**; **heartburn** indigestion pain; **h. failure**; **heartland** central area; **h.-lung machine** mechanism that maintains circulation during surgery; **h.-searching**

examining of one's conscience; **h.strings** deepest feelings of love, pity; **h.throb** *coll* person arousing strong amorous feeling; *n, a* **h.-to-heart** frank personal (discussion); *v* **hearten**; *v* **hearten** cheer up, encourage; *as* **heartfelt** sincere; **heartfree** not being in love; **heartless** unfeeling, cruel, *adv* **-ly**; *n* **-ness**; *as* **h.rending** deeply moving; **heartwarming** giving great pleasure; **hearty 1** cordial; jovial **2** (of meals) big; *adv* **heartily**; *n* **-iness**.

heartworm *n* canine disease caused by parasite.

hearth *n* place where domestic fire is made; *fig* home.

heat *n* **1** hotness; sensation of warmth **2** *fig* strong emotion **3** period of sexual desire in female mammals **4** eliminating round or course in race or contest; *n, ns* **h. barrier** effect of friction on speed of aircraft; **h. lightning** lightening flashes without thunder; **h. rash**; **h. shield** protective covering on spacecraft; **h.stroke** sunstroke; **h. wave** spell of very hot weather; *n* **-er** machine for heating; *n* **-ing** means of providing heat; *a* **-ed** angry; excited; *adv* **-edly**; *v* make, become hot; *as* **heated** excited, vehement; **heat-resistant** protects against heat.

heath *n* open, shrubby ground;

A B C D E F G **H** I J K L M N O P Q R S T U V W X Y Z

heather.

heathen n one who does not believe in God; barbarous, irreligious person; a unenlightened; savage; a **heathenish** fig barbarous; pagan.

heather n plant of heath family, growing in open areas and on mountains.

heave v lift up; drag along; throw (something heavy); utter (sigh); (of waves) rise up, swell; retch; n effort expended to raise something.

heaven n abode of God; sky; fig state of extreme bliss a **h.-sent** very lucky; timely; a **-ly** of, from heaven sl delightful, beautiful.

heavy a 1 weighty; difficult to lift 2 serious 3 dull; overcast 4 severe 5 clumsy 6 indigestible 7 sad; gloomy; n 1 dram serious or bad character 2 sl big man used as bodyguard; ns **h. breathing** suggestive noises made by anonymous caller on telephone; **h.-duty** a made tough; **h.-handed** a tactless; clumsy; **h.hearted** a full of sorrow or worry; n **h. heartedness**; **h.set** a large-bodied; **h. metal** loud type of pop music; **h. petting** erotic caressing but not sexual intercourse; **h. water** water in which hydrogen is replaced by deuterium; **h.weight 1** heaviest class of boxer **2** very important person; adv **heavily;**

n **-iness.**

hebdomadal a weekly.

Hebrew n language of the Jews.

hecatomb n sacrifice of 100 oxen; fig massacre.

heckle v interrupt public speaker with questions; n **heckler.**

hect-, hecto- prefix hundred.

hectare n (area of) 10,000 square meters.

hectic a exciting; rushed; busy.

hector v bully; browbeat; bluster at.

he'd contraction for **1** he had **2** he would.

hedge n shrubs planted close together as fence or boundary; v **1** enclose with plant, hedge **2** coll refuse to commit oneself; idm **hedge one's bets** protect oneself against loss by backing more than one possibility; ns **hedgehog** small, wild, spiny mammal; **hedger** man who makes, repairs hedges; **hedgerow** wild hedge enclosing field.

hedonism n theory that pleasure is the chief good; n **-ist.**

heebie-jeebies n pl coll uneasiness.

heed v take notice; regard carefully; a **-less** careless; reckless.

hee-haw n sound made by donkey.

heel n hind part of foot; part of shoe, boot supporting this; last part; sl low-down person;

v hit with heel.

heel v tilt to one side, esp of ship; cause to do this; n list.

hefty a weighty; muscular; big and strong.

hegemony n leadership; political control.

heifer n young cow that has not yet calved.

height n vertical dimension; loftiness; culmination; hill; v **-en** make, become higher; augment.

heinous a hateful; atrocious; odious.

heir n one who succeeds to another's rank, property, on the death of the latter; ns **h. apparent** person certain to inherit; **h. presumptive** person who may inherit if no one is born with superior claim; fem **heiress;** n **heirloom** object inherited from ancestors; chattel that goes with real estate.

heist n sl armed robbery.

helical a spiral.

helicon n large tuba.

helicopter n aircraft deriving lift from horizontally rotating rotors.

heliograph n signaling device using reflected rays of sun.

heliport n base for takeoff and landing of helicopters.

heliotrope n plant of borage family, with fragrant purple flowers; a color of flowers; a **-tropic** turning toward sun.

helium n light nonflammable gaseous element.

helix n spiral-shaped form.

hell n abode of damned souls; place, state of intense suffering, misery, cruelty; *fig* gambling den; *idm* **a hell of a** *sl* **1** a dreadful **2** very (*also* **a helluva**); *idm* **like hell** *coll* **1** very fast; very much **2** not at all; *as* **h.-bent** recklessly determined; **hellish** awful; *adv* **-ly;** *n* **-ness;** *ns* **hellion** trouble-making person; **hell's angel** member of leather-clad motorcycle gang.

he'll *contracted form of* he will.

Hellenic *a* Greek.

hello *interj* used in greeting or showing surprise.

helm n steering wheel of ship, tiller; *idm* **at the helm** in control; *n* **-sman** steersman.

helmet n protective covering for head.

help *v* **1** aid; assist **2** serve; supply **1** alleviate; be able; *idm* **(not) be able to help (something)** (not) to avoid (doing something); *n* **-er;** *as* **-ful, -less** powerless; useless; *n* **helpmate,** comrade, partner, *esp* husband or wife.

helter-skelter *adv* in disorderly haste.

hem n edge of cloth turned up and stitched; *v* **hemming, hemmed.** sew thus; confine; *phr v* **hem in** trap; *n* **h.line** lower edge of dress; *n* **hemstitch** decorative stitch.

hem-, hema- hemo- *prefix* of blood.

he-man n extremely strong man.

hematin n pigment found in blood.

hemoglobin n protein substance of red blood corpuscles.

hemophilia n hereditary disease in which blood fails to clot.

hemorrhage n bleeding; *v med* to bleed.

hemorrhoids n *med* inflamed tissue at the anus or rectal area.

hemisphere n half a sphere; half of earth's surface; *a* **-spherical.**

hemlock n plant producing powerful sedative; poison extracted from it.

hemp n plant, fiber of which is used for rope; narcotic drug made from it; *a* **hempen.**

hen n female domestic fowl, or any bird; *a* **henpecked** nagged by wife.

hence *adv* from this; therefore; *advs* **-forth, -forward** from now onward.

henchman n trusty attendant; staunch supporter.

henna n Asian shrub; red dye for hair made from it.

hepatic n pertaining to liver; *n* **hepatitis** inflammation of liver.

hepta- *prefix* seven; *n* **heptagon** plane figure with seven sides; **heptateuch** first seven books of Bible.

her *a object or poss* case of **she;** *pron* **hers** of her; *pron* **herself.**

herald n official who makes public announcements or arranges ceremonies; one charged with care of armorial bearings, etc.; forerunner, harbinger; *v* announce; usher in; *a* **-ic;** *n* **heraldry** study of use of armorial bearings.

herb n plant whose stem dies down annually; one used in medicine or flavoring; *as* **-aceous** dying down in winter; perennial flowering; **-al** of herbs; *ns* **herbage** grass, pasture; **herbalist** dealer in medicinal herbs; **herbarium** collection of preserved plants.

herbicide n substance for killing plants, *esp* weeds.

herculean *a* requiring extraordinary strength, effort, courage, etc.

herd n group, flock of animals, usually of same species, living, feeding together; *fig* rabble; mob; *v* **1** tend (herd) **2** huddle together; *n* **herdsman.**

here *adv* in, toward this place; at this point; *adv* **hereafter** in the future; *n* life after death; *adv* **herewith.**

hereabouts *adv* somewhere near here.

here and now n the present.

hereby *adv fml* by this means.

heredity n passing of body, mental characteristics from parent to child; *a* **hereditary** passing by inheritance or heredity; *n* **hereditament** thing that can be inherited.

herein *adv* in this.

hereinafter *adv leg* in the

following text.

heresy *n* erroneous religious belief; opinion contrary to orthodox one; *n* **heretic** one guilty of religious heresy; *a* **-al**.

herewith *adv* included.

heritage *n* inheritance; characteristic derived from ancestors; *a* **heritable**.

hermaphrodite *n* human being, animal, plant with both male and female characteristics.

hermetic *a* airtight; *adv* **-cally** so as to be perfectly closed.

hermit *n* one living in solitude, for prayer, meditation; *fig* recluse; *n* **-age** cell of hermit.

hermit crab *n* type of crab residing in empty molusk shell.

hernia *n* rupture, *esp* abdominal.

hero *n* **1** one noted for valor, noble qualities **2** chief male character in play, book, etc. **3** demigod; *pl* **heroes**; *fem* **-ine**; *a* **-ic** courageous; larger than life; *adv* **-ally**; *n* **heroic couplet** rhyming pair of iambic pentameters; *n pl* **heroics** bombastic talk, behavior; *ns* **heroism** courage; **hero worship** excessive admiration of someone.

heroin *n* narcotic, habit-forming drug, derived from morphine.

heron *n* long-necked, long-legged wading bird.

herpes *n* skin disease; shingles.

herring *n* edible salt-water fish; *n* **h.bone** pattern of crisscross lines.

herself *reflex or emphatic form of* **she**.

hertz *n* radio unit of frequency.

he's *contracted form of* **1** he is **2** he was.

hesitate *v* pause in doubt; falter; be reluctant; *a* **hesitant** undecided; *ns* **hesitancy, hesitation** indecision; speech · impediment.

heterodox *a* unorthodox.

heterogenous *a* composed of unrelated kinds.

heterosexual *a, n* (person) feeling sexual attraction toward opposite sex.

het up *a coll* excited; upset.

heuristic *a* solving problems by trial and error; *adv* **-ally**.

hex *n* evil spell; *v* **put a hex on**.

hexagon *n* plane figure with six sides; *a* **-al** six-sided.

hexameter *n* verse of six feet.

heyday *n* peak; acme; prime.

hiatus *n* gap; break in continuity; slight pause between two vowels.

hibernate *v* pass winter in torpid state; *ns* **-ation, -ator**.

hibiscus *n* rose mallow; showy flowering plant.

hiccup, hiccough *n* spasm of diaphragm, with closure of glottis; sound made by this; *v* utter this sound.

hick *n* provincial, unsophisticated person.

hickory *n* N American hardwood tree bearing nuts.

hide[1] *n* raw or dressed animal skin; *n sl* **hiding** thrashing; *a* **hidebound** *fig* narrow-minded.

hide[2] *v* **hiding, hid, hidden.** conceal; cover up; keep secret; *ns* **hide-and-seek** game in which players look for one who is hiding; **hideaway** (*also* **hideout**) place of escape from other people.

hideous *a* repulsive; horrible.

hierarchy *n* rank, order, class of sacred persons; any graded system of officials; *a* **hierarchical**.

hieroglyph *n* symbol used in ancient Egyptian picture writing; *fig* secret writing; *a* **hieroglyphic**.

hi-fi *n, a coll* (equipment) for high-fidelity sound reproduction.

higgledy-piggledy *a, adv* completely disordered; jumbled up.

high *a* **1** tall (*n* **h. chair** chair for babies); **2** far above ground (*ns* **h. jump, h. tide, h. water**) **3** raised; elevated (*n* **h. table** table for senior members) **4** near the top **5** exalted **6** chief; most important (*ns* **h. commissioner, h. court, h. priest**) **7** very great (*ns* **h. speed, h. tension, h. treason**) **8** goods (*ns* **h. grade, h. life, h. quality**) **9** raised in pitch (**h. note, h.**

voice) **10** (of meat) tainted
11 *coll* intoxicated; drugged;
idm **high and dry** deserted;
idm **get on one's high horse**
behave in an arrogant way;
idm **on a high note** with
cheerful optimism; *idm* **in
high places** among people of
influence; *n* **1** high point
2 *met* anticyclone **3** state of
excitement; *ns* **highball** drink
of liquor with soda and ice;
h.flier ambitious person; **h.
jinks** *coll* fun and games;
highlands; highlight 1
important detail **2** part
reflecting most light
3 climax (*v* emphasize); **h.
point; h. school** secondary
school; **h. seas** oceans; **h.
spot** *coll* outstanding event;
h. tea early evening meal *usu*
in England; **h. technology**
use of most up-to-date
equipment and processes; *a*
h. tech (*also* **hitech**); **h.-
water mark**
1 mark left by high tide
2 point of greatest
achievement; **highway** main
road; **highwayman**
(formerly) person who robs
travelers; *as* **h.-and-mighty**
arrogant; **h. class** superior;
h.falutin *coll* pretentious; **h.
fidelity** reproducing sound
almost perfectly; **h.-flown**
extravagant; **h.-handed** too
authoritative (*adv* **-ly**;
n **-ness**); **h. minded** with
noble thoughts (*adv* **-ly -
ness**); **h.-rise** multistory; **h.-
spirited** lively; *adv* **highly**

greatly (*a* **h.-strung**
excitable); *n* **highness** title
used in referring to or
addressing members of royal
family.
hijack *v* take over control of
vehicle, *esp* aircraft by force;
stop and rob vehicle; *n*
instance of this; *n* **-er.**
hike *v* walk through country; *n*
walking excursion; *n* **hiker.**
hilarity *n* cheerfulness, mirth,
jollity; *a* **hilarious.**
hill *n* small elevation of earth's
surface; small artificial
mound; *n* **hillock** little hill; *a*
hilly.
hilt *n* handle of sword, dagger;
idm **up to the hilt**
completely.
him *pron* objective case of HE;
pron **himself** emphatic form.
hind *n* female of red deer.
hind, hinder *a* at back,
posterior.
hinder *v* impede; obstruct;
prevent; *n* **hindrance.**
hindmost *a* farthest behind.
hindquarters *n*, *pl* back legs
and rump.
hindsight *n* understanding of
past mistakes.
Hindu *n* Ayran non-Moslem
of N India.
hinge *n* joint on which door,
lid, etc., hangs and turns; *v*
provide hinge; *fig* depend on.
hint *n* indirect suggestion;
brief advice; *v* give hint of;
make hint.
hinterland *n* district behind
coast, or that served by port.
hip *n* **1** projecting part of

upper thigh **2** fruit of briar or
rose; *a* trendy.
hip-hop *n sl* pop culture
started in the 1980s
comprising rap music,
graffite, and break dancing.
hippie, hippy *n* person
rejecting conventions of
society, *esp* in 1960s.
Hippocratic oath *n* oath
relating to ethical practice,
taken by beginning
physicians.
hippodrome *n* arena for
chariot-racing, horse shows,
etc.
hippopotamus *n* large,
ungainly, amphibious
African mammal.
hire *n* payment for services of
person, or use of thing; *v*
engage for wages; pay for
temporary use; *ns* **hireling**
mercenary person.
hirsute *a* hairy.
his *pron*, *a* belonging to him.
Hispanic *a* of Spain, Portugal,
Latin America.
hiss *v* make noise like sound of
prolonged *s*; express
disapproval, scorn by this
sound; *n* **-ing.**
histamine *n* chemical
produced in the body that
can cause allergic reactions.
history *n* systematic record of
past events in existence of
nation, individual, etc.; study
of such events; methodical
account of evolution (of
language, art, etc.); *n*
historian writer of history; *as*
historic famous; epoch-

making; **-ical** based on, recorded in history; *n* **natural h.** zoology; botany.

historiography *n* study of writing of history; *n* **-pher;** *a* **-phic.**

hit *v* **1** strike, knock with blow, missile **2** injure **3** find by design or luck **4** reach target; *pt, pp* **hit;** *idm* **hit it big** have great success; *idm* **hit the hay/sack** go to bed; *idm* **hit the nail on the head** say the right thing; *phr vs* **hit back** retaliate; **hit out at/against** attack vigorously; *n* **1** well-aimed blow **2** popular success; *ns* **hit-and-run 1** type of auto accident where driver at fault doesn't stop **2** baseball play; **h. list** list of people against whom action, *esp* killing, is planned; **h. man** hired assassin; **h. parade** list of best-selling pop songs; *a* **hit-or-miss** casual.

hitch *v* **1** raise with jerk **2** fasten by hook **3** ride free in someone else's car (*also* **hitchike**); *phr v* **hitch up** pull up into place; adjust; *n* **1** temporary problem **2** jerk; lifting movement **3** quick fastening with rope; *a* **hitched** *sl* married.

hi-tech *a* using high technology.

hither *adv lit, ar* to, toward this place; *a* nearer, on this side; *adv* **hitherto** until now, up to this time.

HIV *n* virus in the blood responsible for AIDS; *a* **HIV positive** infected with HIV.

hive *n* box for honeybees to live in; *idm* **hive of industry** busy place; *v* gather, place in hive.

hives *n pl* skin eruption; croup.

HMO *n* health maintenance organization; a health plan providing comprehensive services to subscribers.

hoagie *n* combination sandwich on a long roll (*also* **hoagy**).

hoard *n* secret store; hidden treasure; *v* amass, gather and keep hidden.

hoarding *n* temporary wooden fence.

hoarse *a* husky; rough; harsh; *n* **-ness.**

hoary *a* gray with age; *fig* ancient; grayishwhite.

hoax *n* practical joke; mischievous trick; *v* play practical joke on; *n* **-er.**

hob *n* ledge beside grate for keeping things hot.

hobbit *n* fictional underground creature.

hobble *v* **1** limp, walk clumsily **2** tie two legs (of horse, etc.) together to prevent straying; *n* straps, rope used to hobble animal.

hobby *n* favorite leisure occupation; *n* **h. horse** rocking-horse; *fig* hobby.

hobgoblin *n* mischievous imp; bugaboo.

hobnail *n* large-headed nail for studding boots.

hobnob *v* **-nobbing, -nobbed.** be on familiar terms with.

hobo *n* **hoboes.** tramp; migratory worker.

Hobson's choice *n* situation where no choice is given.

hock[1] *n* joint in middle of hind leg of horse, ox, etc.; *v* hamstring.

hock[2] *v sl* pawn; *idm* **in hock** *sl* **1** pawned **2** in debt **3** in prison.

hockey *n* game played with ball or disk and curved sticks, in field or on ice.

hocus-pocus *n* trickery; conjuror's jargon; nonsense; *v* **hocus** dupe; swindle; stupefy with drugs.

hod *n* small trough on handle for carrying bricks, mortar, etc.

hodge-podge *n* mixture; jumble.

hoe *n* tool for breaking soil, weeding, etc.; *v* **hoeing, hoed.** use hoe.

hog *n* adult male pig, *esp* castrated one; *fig* greedy, filthy person; *n* **hogshead** large cask; liquid measure, 63 gallons.

hogtie *v* **1** tie all four extremities together **2** hamper; thwart.

hogwash *n coll* nonsense.

hoi-polloi *n* common people; the masses.

hoist *v* raise with tackle; heave, lift up; *n*.

hoity-toity *a* haughty.

hold[1] *v* **holding, held. 1** grasp; keep in hand **2** keep in position **3** occupy **4** maintain (opinion)

5 remain fixed **6** enclose; contain **7** restrain **8** be valid **9** detain **10** celebrate; *pt, pp* **held**; *v idm* **hold a candle to** compare with; *idm* **hold court** be the center of attention; *idm* **hold it** stop and wait; *idm* **hold one's own** keep one's position; *idm* **hold water** (of argument, excuse) stand up to testing; be valid; *phr vs* **hold against** oppose; **hold forth** talk pompously at length; **hold off** delay; **hold on 1** wait **2** retain one's grip; persevere; **hold out 1** offer **2** endure **3** last; **hold out for** persevere until one gets; **hold over** postpone; **hold up 1** delay **2** rob with threat of violence (*n* **h.up**); *phr v* **hold with** approve of; *n* **1** grasp **2** manner of holding; *idm* **a hold on/over** means of control, influence; **holder 1** person in possession **2** container; **holding 1** land held by tenant **2** property or shares owned.

hold[2] *n* space below deck, for cargo, in ship.

hole *n* cavity; opening; tear, rent; outlet; den, burrow; *v* make, go into hole.

holiday *n* day, time off from work; time of commemoration; religious festival; *a* festive.

holier-than-thou *a* self-righteous.

holiness *n* **1** state of being holy **2** *cap* title of pope.

holistic *a* related to the whole; *n* **h. medicine** (*also* **alternative medicine**).

hollandaise *n* rich, egg-based sauce.

holler *v* shout.

hollow *n* cavity; depression; hole; small valley; *a* not solid; sunken; echoing; *fig* insincere; *v* make hollow; scoop out.

holly *n* evergreen shrub with glossy, prickly leaves and red berries.

hollyhock *n* tall, flowering plant.

holocaust *n* complete destruction by fire.

hologram *n phot* flat image that appears three-dimensional when lit by laser beam; *n* **holography** science of making holograms; *a* **-phic** *adv*; **-phically**.

holograph *n* document hand-written by signatory; *n* **holography**.

holster *n* leather case for pistol, hung from belt, etc.

holt *n* copse; wooded hill.

holy *a* pertaining to God; sacred, deeply pious; *ns* **H. Ghost** third person of Trinity (*also* **H. Spirit**); **h. of holies** inner sanctum; **H. Week** week leading to Easter; **H. Writ 1** the Bible **2** authoritative writing; *n* **holiness** sanctity; title of pope.

homage *n* declaration of allegiance; *fig* honor, respect, devotion.

home *n* **1** family dwelling place **2** native place **3** place of rest; asylum; *idm* **at home 1** comfortable **2** welcoming visitors; *idm* **bring/come home to one** make/be well understood; *phr vs* **home in on** direct one's aim at; **home onto** be guided automatically toward; *a* pertaining to home or country; *ns* **h.body, h. brew, h.coming; h. front** (wartime activities of) civilians; **h. economics** study of household management; **h. rule** self-government; **h. run** baseball strike enabling batter to complete circuit in one run; **h.stead** house with small farm; **h. truth** unpleasant fact that one has to face up to; **h.work** school assignment to be done outside of class; *adv* at, to home; *as* **h.bound; h.boy; h.-brewed, h.-cured, h.grown, h.made; h.less; homely 1** simple **2** plain looking; **homesick** longing for home; *n* **-ness; homespun** unsophisticated; **homeward** toward home; *adv* **-s.**

homoeopathy *n* treatment of disease, by minute doses of drug, which in healthy person produces symptoms like those of disease itself.

homicide *n* killer, killing of human being; *a* **-idal.**

homily *n* sermon; *fig* tedious lecture.

homing *a* **1** able to find home

A B C D E F G **H** I J K L M N O P Q R S T U V W X Y Z

unaided **2** able to steer automatically to a target or destination.

hominid n human or human-like being.

homo-, homeo- *prefix: forms compounds with meaning* same, same kind. *Where the meaning may be deduced from the simple word, the compounds are not given here.*

homogeneous a belonging to same category; uniform n **homogeneity;** v **homogenize 1** make homogenous **2** treat (milk) to cause blending of cream with the rest.

homograph n word having same spelling as another.

homonym n word having same spelling and sound as another but a different sense.

homophobia n hatred or fear of homosexuals or homosexuality; a **homophobic.**

homophone n word having same sound as another but different spelling.

Homo sapiens n *Lat* the human species.

homosexual a attracted to one's own sex; **-lity.**

honest a straightforward, not criminal, sincere; open frank; n **honesty 1** integrity; trustworthiness **2** garden herb, with transparent seed pods.

honey n sweet, sticky fluid made from nectar by bees; n **honeycomb** mass of hexagonal wax cells, made by bees, to store honey or larvae; v pierce with many holes; riddle; ns **h.dew** sweet deposit on plants; **h.dew melon** melon with sweet greenish flesh; **h.suckle** climbing plant with fragrant flowers; **h.moon** vacation spent alone by newly married couple.

honk n cry of wild goose; similar sound, *esp* of motor horn; v to make this sound.

honky-tonk n, a (of) ragtime piano music.

honor n **1** respect, esteem **2** good reputation; moral dignity, high rank **3** mark of esteem; *pl* **1** distinction in schoolwork **2** face cards; v esteem highly; confer honor on; pay (bill, draft, etc.) when due; *as* **-able, honorary** given, done as honor; giving services without pay; **honorific** conferring, expressing honor; n **honorarium** voluntary payment for services.

hood n **1** soft covering for head and neck **2** cowl **3** covering over automobile engine; v cover with hood; v **hoodwink** deceive.

hoodlum n violent petty criminal.

hoof n horny sheath protecting animal's foot; *pl* **hooves, hoofs**.

hoo-ha n *coll* fuss.

hook n **1** curved piece of metal, wood, plastic, or other substance, for holding, hanging, catching, or pulling something **2** curved cutting implement **3** blow with bent arm in boxing; v **1** grasp, seize, hold, fasten with hook **2** hit ball to striker's left; *idm* **off the hook** freed from danger, difficulty; a **hooked** shaped like a hook; *idm* **hooked (on)** *coll* addicted (to); *idm* **hook line and sinker** totally; ns **h.worm** parasitic worm; *sl* **hooker** prostitute.

hookah n Oriental pipe, in which smoke passes through tube and water bottle.

hook-up n link between electrical circuits, radio or TV stations.

hooky *idm* **play hooky** play truant.

hooligan n noisy, destructive (*usu* young) ruffian.

hoop n circular band of wood, metal, *esp* to bind cask; large ring of wood, bowled along, as toy; v bind with hoop.

hooray *interj expressing delight.*

hoot n **1** cry of owl **2** sound of car horn, etc. **3** cry of derision; v utter hoots; cause to hoot.

Hoover [TM] n vacuum cleaner; v clean with a vacuum cleaner.

hooves *pl of* **hoof.**

hop[1] n plant whose flowers are used in making beer; *pl* dried flower cones; v gather, produce hops; ns **hopping** gathering hops.

hop[2] v **hopping, hopped.** jump

on one leg; advance so; *idm* **hop it** *coll* go away; *idm* **on the hop** unprepared; *n* 1 leap 2 informal dance 3 *coll* short aircraft flight.

hope *n* confident expectation of something desired; likelihood of something desired will happen; thing, person, action that inspires hope; *v* entertain hope; desire and expect; *a* **-ful** (*n* **young h.** promising boy or girl); *a* **-less.**

hopper *n* funnellike device for feeding grain to mill, coal to machine, etc.; self-discharging dredging barge, or rail truck; that which hops; hop picker.

hopscotch *n* children's game of jumping into and across marked squares.

horde *n* band of nomads; destructive gang, rabble.

horehound *n* herb containing bitter juice.

horizon *n* circle bounding visible part of earth's surface; line where earth and sky seem to meet; *fig* limits of interest, mental outlook; *a* -**tal** parallel with horizon; level; *adv* **-ly.**

hormone *n* internal secretion by glands, that stimulates functional activity of organs of body.

hormone replacement therapy *n* hormone treatment for women, *esp* after menopause.

horn *n* 1 one of hard, bony pointed growths on head of cow, etc. 2 substance of horns; various things made of, or like it 3 wind instrument 4 warning device on car, lighthouse, etc.; *as* **-ed** having horns; **horny** hard as horn; *n* **hornpipe** old wind instrument; sailors, dance.

hornbill *n* tropical bird with big, curved beak.

hornblende *n* mineral found in granite and other igneous rocks.

hornet *n* large species of wasp; *idm* **stir up a hornet's nest** provoke trouble.

horn of plenty *n* cornucopia.

horology *n* art of clock making, or measuring time; *n* **horologer** clock- or watchmaker.

horoscope *n* calculation of positions of heavenly bodies at particular moment, *esp* of person's birth, to predict fortune, character, etc.

horrendous *a* terrible, dreadful.

horror *n* terror; disgust; repulsion; its cause; *as* **horrible** causing horror; shocking; terrifying; **horrid** frightful, disgusting; *v* **horrify** excite horror in; *a* **-ific** horrifying.

hors d'oeuvre *n Fr* light savory dish served before meal as appetizer.

horse *n* 1 large four-footed domesticated mammal, used for riding on, or draft 2 stallion 3 cavalry 4 frame with legs, for support 5 vaulting block; *idm* **from the horse's mouth** from the person who knows; *ns* **h. chestnut** tree with inedible shiny brown nuts; **h. laugh** loud coarse laugh; **h.man, h.manship; h.play** rough, noisy play; **h.power** unit of engine power (*also* **hp**); **h.radish** edible root with hot flavor; **h. race; h. sense** common sense; **h.shoe** U-shaped shoe, symbol of good luck; **h.-trading** *coll* clever bargaining; **h.whip** *v* beat with whip; **h.woman;** *a* **horsy** 1 like a horse 2 interested in horses.

hortative, hortatory *a* exhorting; admonitory.

horticulture *n* study of gardening; *a* **-tural;** *n* **-turalist.**

hosanna *interj* Hebrew exclamation of praise.

hose *n* flexible tube for carrying water or other liquids; *pl* **hose** socks, stockings; *ns* **hosiery** underwear, socks, stockings, etc.; shop dealing in this; stockings; **hosier.**

hospice *n* 1 house of rest for travelers, *esp* one kept by monks 2 home for terminally ill or poor.

hospitable *a* welcoming to visitors; *adv* **-ably.**

hospital *n* place where sick and injured are cared for; *v* **-ize** send, admit to hospital; *n* **-ization.**

A
B
C
D
E
F
G
H
I
J
K
L
M
N
O
P
Q
R
S
T
U
V
W
X
Y
Z

hospitality n cheerful, friendly entertainment, feeding, and lodging of guests; a **hospitable** inviting, generous, friendly.

host[1] n one who entertains a guest; hotelkeeper; emcee on TV.

host[2] n army; great number.

hostage n one given or taken as pledge that promises will be kept.

hostel n lodging house for students, workers, young people, etc.

hostess n 1 female host 2 air hostess 3 woman entertaining men at nightclub 4 female emcee on TV.

hostile a unfriendly; warlike; n **hostility** enmity; pl **-ies** acts of war.

hot a 1 of high temperature; feeling, giving heat 2 pungent 3 fig violent 4 lustful 5 coll (of news) exciting and fresh 6 sl (of stolen goods) sought by police 7 angry; ns **h. air** meaningless talk; **h.-air** balloon; **h.bed** place where evil can develop; **h.-cross bun** roll with raisins and icing, often eaten on Good Friday or Easter Sunday; **h. dog** frankfurter in long bread roll; **h.head** n rash person; a hotheaded; **h.-house** greenhouse; **h. line** direct telephone link between heads of state; **h.plate** surface for cooking or for placing hot dishes on table; **h. rod** car rebuilt for speed; **h. seat** (idm **in the h. s.** responsible for making difficult decisions); **h. spot** dangerous place; **h. stuff** coll 1 exciting thing or person 2 skillful person; **h. water** (idm **in h. w.** in trouble); **h.-water bottle** rubber container for warming bed; as **h.-blooded** passionate; **h.-tempered** irascible.

hotel n large, superior inn; n **hotelier**.

hound n dog hunting by scent; v pursue; persecute.

hour n 60 minutes; $\frac{1}{24}$th part of day; fixed point of time; pl regular time of work; adv **hourly** every hour; n **h.glass** sand glass that runs out in one hour.

house n 1 dwelling designed for human habitation 2 hotel, inn, etc. 3 business firm 4 legislative assembly or building used for such 5 family; lineage; v provide house for; harbor; idm **bring the house down** provoke loud laughter or applause; idm **get along like a house on fire** coll have a good relationship; idm **keep house** look after household affairs; idm **keep open house** offer welcome at all times; idm **on the house** coll paid for by manager; ns **h. arrest, h.boat; h.breaker** burglar, **h.breaking; h.coat** woman's informal garment worn at home; **h.hold** people living in a house (**h.hold name/word** well-known name/word); **h.holder** head of household; **h.keeper** person employed to look after house; **h.keeping 1** work of running house **2** money for this; **h. lights** theater auditorium lights; **h.maid** female servant; **h.master, h.mistress** teacher responsible for school house; **h. of cards 1** structure made of playing cards **2** scheme likely to fail and collapse; **H. of Commons** assembly of elected representatives in England and Canada; **H. of Representatives** assembly of elected representatives in US, Australia, New Zealand; **h.-warming** party given by new occupants; **housewife**; as **h.broken** (of animals) trained not to urinate, defecate indoors; **h.-proud** fussy about appearance of home.

housing n 1 living accommodation 2 cover for machinery.

hove pt, pp of **heave**.

hovel n mean dwelling.

hover v 1 (of birds) float motionless in air 2 fig linger; hesitate; n **hovercraft** craft moving along, on cushion of air, over land or water.

how adv in what way; by what means; to what degree; idm **How come?** why?; idm **How do you do?** used as formal greeting.

however *adv* 1 nevertheless 2 in whatever way; to whatever degree 3 by what (possible) means.

howitzer *n* short-barreled canon that fires shells from an angle.

howl *v* utter loud, dismal cry; *n* such cry; *n* **howler** 1 person, animal or thing that howls 2 *sl* stupid mistake.

HP *abbr* horsepower (*also* **hp**).

HQ *abbr* headquarters.

hr., hrs. *abbr* hour(s).

HRT *abbr* hormone replacement therapy.

hub *n* central part of wheel; *fig* center of activity or importance.

hubcap *n* metal cover for center of car wheel.

hubbub *n* uproar; riot.

hubby *n coll* husband.

hubris *n* excessive pride or self-confidence.

huckleberry *n* N American shrub; its fruit.

huckster *n* hawker; peddler; *v* haggle; carry on petty trade.

huddle *v* heap, gather into confused mass; crowd together; *n* such a crowd.

hue *n* color; tint; complexion.

hue and cry *n* loud outcry; angry pursuit.

huff *v* 1 bully; hector 2 take offense; *n* sulkiness; *a* **huffy**; *adv* **-ily**.

hug *v* **hugging, hugged.** embrace warmly; clasp tightly in arms; *fig* keep close to; *n* act of hugging.

huge *a* very great, enormous.

hugger-mugger *n* 1 secrecy 2 disorder; *a, adv* in disorder.

hula *n* Hawaiian dance.

hulk *n* 1 derelict, dismantled ship 2 *fig* clumsy, unwieldy person; *a* **hulking** big and clumsy.

hull *n* 1 body of ship 2 pod, shell of pea; *v* 1 pierce hull of ship 2 remove hull from pea.

hullabaloo *n* uproar; din; clamor.

hum *v* **humming, hummed.** produce low buzzing, droning sound, as bee; utter musical sound with closed lips; *n* continuous low drone.

human *a* pertaining to mankind; associated with man; *adv* **humanly** in human manner; *a* **humane** kind; merciful; *adv* **-ly**; *ns* **humanism** system of thought dealing with human interests; **humanist** 1 student, advocate of humanism 2 classical scholar; **humanity** human race as whole; kindness of heart; *pl* **humanities** classical literary studies; *a, n* **humanitarian** philanthropist; *v* **humanize** make, become human, humane.

humanoid *a* having human characteristics.

humble *a* lowly; meek; modest; not exalted in rank, position; *v* abase; put to shame; *adv* **humbly**.

humbug *n* 1 hoax; nonsense 2 empty, boastful person; *v*

deceive; dupe.

humdinger *n sl* someone or something superb.

humdrum *a* commonplace; dull.

humerus *n* bone of upper arm in man; *a* **humeral** of shoulder.

humid *a* moist; damp; *n* **-idity**; *v* **-ify**.

humidor *n* humid box or chamber, *esp* for smoking materials.

humiliate *v* put to shame; lower pride of; abase; *n* **-ation**.

humility *n* quality of being humble; meekness.

humankind *n* people collectively.

hummingbird *n* minute tropical bird with long beak.

hummus *n Gk* puree of chickpeas, tahini, etc.

hummock *n* knoll; hillock; ridge of ice.

humor *n* 1 mood; state of mind 2 fun; jocular action, saying 3 whim; fancy; *v* indulge moods; act tactfully; *n* **humorist** one who makes jokes; comic writer, artist, or actor; *a* **humorous** laughable, funny; amusing.

hump *n* 1 rounded lump, bulge, or mound 2 *sl* mental depression; *v* carry on back; **-back** person with spinal deformity; *a* **-backed** having hump.

humus *n* decayed organic matter giving fertility to soil.

hunch *n coll* premonition; *v*

a
b
c
d
e
f
g
h
i
j
k
l
m
n
o
p
q
r
s
t
u
v
w
x
y
z

A
B
C
D
E
F
G
H
I
J
K
L
M
N
O
P
Q
R
S
T
U
V
W
X
Y
Z

stoop; draw shoulders up; n **-back** humpback.

hundred n, pron, det cardinal number, ten times ten; a **-th** ordinal number 100th; a, adv **hundredfold**; n **hundredweight** measure of weight = 112 lbs. or ⅟₂₀ ton.

hung pt, pp of **hang**.

hunger n desire for food; exhaustion, emaciation due to lack of food; fig craving; phr v **hunger after /for/** long for; n **h. strike** refusal of all food, as protest; a **hungry** feeling hunger; starving; adv **hungrily**.

hunk n thick piece; sl good-looking, muscular man; a **hunky**.

hunt v pursue (animals), often with hounds in order to kill, or catch; pursue (person); search for, track down; n search; local association of persons with their horses, hounds engaged in hunting; ns **huntsman** man in charge of hounds; **hunter;** fem **huntress**.

hurdle n light wooden framework, as temporary fence or to jump over; n **hurdler** one who runs in hurdle races; **h. race** race in which series of fences or hurdles are leaped.

hurdy-gurdy n small barrel organ.

hurl v throw violently; hurtle; n **-ler**.

hurly-burly n noisy activity.

hurricane n violent wind-

storm of 75 mph or more; tropical cyclone; n **h. lamp** lamp with well-shielded flame.

hurry v **-hurrying, hurried.** move, do quickly; hasten; urge to haste; a **hurried;** adv **-ly**; v,n **h.-scurry** rush.

hurt v cause pain to; injure, distress; damage; pt, pp **hurt**; n harm; wound; pain; a showing, feeling pain or offense; a **-ful**.

hurtle v move violently; dash against; whirl.

husband n married man; v manage thriftily.

husbandry n farming and raising of livestock.

hush v make, become silent, quiet; phr v **hush up** keep secret; n silence; stillness.

husk n dry covering of certain seeds; v strip husk from; a **husky** dry as husk; hoarse; harsh, rasping; adv **huskily;** n **-iness**.

husky n Eskimo sledge dog.

hustings n pl electioneering platform; election proceedings.

hustle v hurry; jostle; urge along roughly; n bustle; hurry; n **hustler** one who gets things done.

hut n shed; small wooden building; hovel; n **-ment** encampment of huts.

hutch n box; bin; chest; boxlike coop for rabbits, etc.

hyacinth bulbous flowering plant.

hybrid n animal or plant

produced by parents of different species; fig anything derived from mixed origins; a cross-bred; v **-ize** cross-fertilize; interbreed; n **-ization**.

hydra n 1 myth many-headed serpent; 2 fig evil that defies destruction 3 freshwater polyp.

hydrangea n shrub with pink, blue, or white flowers.

hydrant n pipe from water main, with attachment for hose.

hydraulic a conveying water; water-powered; n pls science dealing with flow of liquids.

hydr-, hydro- prefix; forms compounds with meaning of water, e.g., **hydroplane** n seaplane. Where the meaning may be deduced from the simple word, such compounds are not given here.

hydrocarbon n organic compound of hydrogen and carbon.

hydrochloric a containing hydrogen and chlorine; n **h. acid**.

hydrodynamics n pl mathematical study of liquids in motion.

hydroelectric a pertaining to electricity generated by water power.

hydrofoil n boat with vanes that lift hull above water to reduce drag and increase speed.

hydrogen n colorless gas combining with oxygen to

form water; **h. bomb** highly destructive atom bomb.

hydrometer n measuring device for density of liquids.

hydrophobia n rabies; abnormal fear of water, *esp* as symptom of this.

hydrotherapy n use of water to treat disease.

hyena n carnivorous, doglike animal with cry like wild laughter.

hygiene n science and principles of maintaining health; cleanliness; a **hygienic**.

hygrometer n instrument for measuring humidity of atmosphere.

hymn n song of praise, *esp* to God; a, n **-al** (book) of hymns.

hype n exaggerated publicity; *phr v* **hype up** publicize in a wildly exaggerated way; a **hyped up 1** overpromoted **2** overstimulated (as if) by drugs.

hyper- *prefix: forms compounds with meaning of* excessive, above; *e.g.,* **hypercritical** a too critical. *Where the meaning may be deduced from the simple word, such compounds are not given here.*

hyperactive n excessively restless; unable to settle down.

hyperbola n curve formed by section of cone when cutting plane makes larger angle with base than side makes.

hyperbole n rhetorical

exaggeration.

hypercritical a overly critical.

hypertension n med **1** abnormally high blood pressure **2** abnormal emotional tension.

hyphen n mark (-) indicating that two words or syllables are connected; a **-ated**.

hypnosis n induction of sleep; artificially induced state resembling deep sleep; a **hypnotic** inducing sleep; v **hypnotize** affect with hypnosis; ns **hypnotism, -ist**.

hypo-, hyph-, hyp- *prefix: forms compounds with meaning of* below, less, under. *Such compounds are not given where the meaning may be deduced from the simple word.*

hypo n solution of hyposulfite used in developing film negatives.

hypoallergenic a (of cosmetics) unlikely to cause an allergic reaction on the skin.

hypocaust n underfloor heating system used by Romans.

hypochondria n morbid obsession with one's health; n **-driac** person with this; a **-driacal**.

hypocrisy n pretending to be better morally than one is; n **-crite**, such a person; a **-critical**.

hypodermic a under the skin; n **h. syringe** one used for giving such injection.

hypotenuse n side of right-

angled triangle opposite the right angle.

hypothermia n very low body temperature, *esp* in old people.

hypothesis n supposition; unproved theory; *pl* **-theses**; a **-thetical**.

hysterectomy n surgical removal of uterus; n **hysterotomy** incision of uterus.

hysteria n extreme emotional excitability and loss of will-power; a **hysteric (al)**; n pl **hysterics** fit of hysteria.

Hz *abbr* hertz.

a
b
c
d
e
f
g
h
i
j
k
l
m
n
o
p
q
r
s
t
u
v
w
x
y
z

I *pron* (1st per sing nom) myself; (*pl* **we**).

iambus *n* metrical foot of one short and one long syllable.

Iberian *a* of Spain and Portugal.

ibis *n* wading bird with long curved bill.

IBM *abbr comput* International Business Machines.

ICBM *abbr* intercontinental ballistic missile.

ice *n* **1** frozen water **2** ice cream; *idm* **break the ice** initiate relations; remove embarrassment; *idm* **keep on ice 1** keep chilled **2** (of ideas) hold in reserve; *idm* **skate on thin ice** take unwise risk; *ns* **i. age** very cold prehistoric era on earth; **i. axe; iceberg** mass of floating ice at sea (*idm* **the tip of the iceberg** only a small part of the problem; **icebox, i.breaker; i. cap** permanently frozen polar region; **i. cream** frozen confection of flavored cream, custard etc; **i. hockey; i. pack** bag of ice for cooling the head or body; **i. pick** tool for breaking ice; **i. rink** artificial sheet of ice for skating, ice hockey, etc.; **i. skate** boot with metal blade for skating on ice (*v* **i.-skate,** *n* **i.-skating**); **i. water**; *as* **i.-blue, i.bound, i.-cold;** *v* **1** make cold with ice **2** cover with sugar icing; *ns* **icicle** long hanging piece of ice formed from dripping water; **icing** (also **frosting**) decorative coating for cake made from icing sugar; *a* **icy;** *adv* **icily;** *n* **iciness**.

ichneumon *n* small Eastern animal, like weasel; *n* **i. fly** parasitic insect.

icon *n* image; sacred portrait; *n* **iconoclast** *fig* one who attacks established customs and beliefs.

icthyology *n* study of fish; *n* **icthyologist**.

I'd *abbr* **1** I had **2** I should **3** I would.

ID *abbr* identification; identity.

id *n psyc* instinctive impulses of the individual.

idea *n* notion; opinion; plan; thought.

ideal *a* **1** visionary **2** of highest standard; *n* supreme perfection; standard of excellence to be copied; *ns* **idealism** practice of seeking perfection in all things; unrealistic attitude to life; **idealist 1** one who believes in idealism **2** impractical person; *v* **idealize** exaggerate good qualities of; *n* **-ization;** idealized view.

idée fixe *n Fr* obsession.

identify *v* show, prove, recognize who/what someone/something is; *n* **i.card;** *idm* **identify with 1** consider someone/something to be connected with **2** sympathize with; *ns* **identification; identikit** artificial portrait of suspected criminal composed from descriptions by witnesses.

identity *n* **1** individuality **2** absolute sameness; *a* **identical** the very same; impossible to distinguish.

ideograph *n* symbolic representation of an object, without naming it; *n* **-graphy** shorthand writing;

symbolic writing.

ideogram n symbol to represent idea (as in Chinese).

ideology n set of political, religious, social ideas; a **-ological** (adv **-ly**); ns **-ologist, -ologue** advocate of particular ideology.

Ides n pl (Roman Calendar) March 15, May 15, July 15, October 15, 13 of other months.

idiocy n stupidity; example of this.

idiom n mode of expression; one peculiar to a language; dialect; a **-atic** character of language; fluent and colloquial.

idiosyncrasy n individual peculiarity of manner, thought, way of speaking, etc.; a **idiosyncratic;** adv **-ally.**

idiot n imbecile; person of defective intellect; n **idiocy;** a **-otic** utterly foolish; senseless; adv **-ically.**

idle a lazy; not functioning; v 1 waste time 2 (of machine) run at low speed; n **-ness;** adv **idly;** n **idler.**

idol n 1 image representing deity 2 false god 3 person, object of extreme devotion; ns **idolater** worshiper of false gods (fem **idolatress**); **idolatry;** a **idolatrous;** v **idolize** make an idol of; love, admire excessively.

idyll n 1 short, simple poem on homely, pastoral subjects 2

romantic incident, usually rural; a **-ic.**

i.e. abbr id est Lat that is.

if conj supposing that; even though; whenever; whether.

iffy a coll uncertain.

igloo n hut of frozen snow blocks.

igneous a fiery; produced by volcanic action.

ignite v set on fire; be kindled; n **ignition** setting on fire; means of firing of explosive gaseous mixture by electric spark.

ignoble a base; degraded; humiliating; shameful; adv **-bly.**

ignominy n dishonor; degradation; public disgrace; a **-minious** shameful; humiliating.

ignorance n lack of education; inexperience; a **ignorant** uninformed; unaware; n **ignoramus** ignorant person.

ignore v disregard; refuse to consider.

iguana n large, crested S American tree lizard.

ilk a Scot same; **of that ilk** 1 of same name, etc. 2 coll of that kind.

ill a 1 physically or mentally sick 2 bad; harmful (ns **i. effects, i. feeling, i. health, i. luck, i. repute, i. will**); n harm; evil; pl **-s** misfortunes; adv (esp prefix forming compound as, vs) badly; wrongly; as **i. -assorted** badly matched; **i.-advised** unwise; **i.-bred, i.-considered, i.-**

defined, i.-fated; i.-gotten dishonestly acquired; **i.-mannered, i.-natured** bad tempered; **i.-omened, i.-timed;** vs **i.-treat** (n **-ment**), **i.-use** (n **i.-usage**).

illegal a unlawful; n **-ity.**

illegible a difficult to read; adv **-ibly;** n **-ibility.**

illegitimate a unlawful; not born in wedlock; n **-timacy.**

illiberal a 1 not generous 2 narrow in attitude or belief.

illicit a prohibited; forbidden.

illiterate a unable to read or write; n **illiteracy.**

illogical a irrational; unsound.

illuminate v make light; adorn with lights; decorate (manuscript) with gold and colors; a **-ating** helpful and revealing; n **-ation;** v **illumine** enlighten.

illusion v deceptive appearance; delusion; n **-ist** conjuror.

illustrate v 1 make clear; explain 2 furnish (book, etc.) with pictures; ns **-ation;** illustrator.

illustrious a famous, distinguished, glorious.

I'm abbr I am.

im- prefix see **in-**

image n 1 visual representation 2 idea, esp popular opinion about a person, company, or commercial product 3 statue or portrait 4 reflection 5 simile 6 counterpart; n **imagery** images; mental pictures.

A
B
C
D
E
F
G
H
I
J
K
L
M
N
O
P
Q
R
S
T
U
V
W
X
Y
Z

imagine v form image, idea in mind; suppose; as **-inative**.

imago n final state of insect, esp of winged one.

imbalance n lack of balance or proportion.

imbecile a mentally deficient; n such a person; n **-ility**.

imbibe v drink in; absorb; drink.

imbue v saturate; dye; phr v fml **imbue (with)** fill (with).

IMF abbr International Monetary Fund.

imitate v copy closely; mimic; n **-tation** act of imitating; copy; counterfeit; a **-tative**; n **-tator**.

immaculate a pure; unsoiled; innocent; n **I. Conception** Roman Catholic belief that the mother of Jesus was born without original sin.

immanent a inherent; ever present.

immaterial a not consisting of matter; spiritual; unimportant.

immature a not adult; unripe; adv **-ly**; n **immaturity**.

immeasurable a vast; incalculable.

immediate a 1 happening now or next; nearest in time 2 nearest in space, in relationship; adv **-ly 1** at once 2 with nothing between; conj as soon as; n **immediacy** nearness; urgency.

immemorial a beyond living memory; very ancient.

immense a very great; vast; sl very good; n **immensity**.

immerse v dip, plunge into liquid; fig engross; n **immersion** (**i. heater** electric water heater).

immigrate v come to foreign country to live; ns **-ation; immigrant** (also a) person settling in foreign country.

imminent a impending; threatening; about to happen; adv **-ently**; n **-ence**.

immobile a not moving; fixed; n **-bility**; v **immobilize** render immobile; n **-ization**.

immoderate a excessive; unrestrained.

immoral a morally wrong; corrupt.

immortal a never dying; everlasting; n **-ity**.

immune a free from; exempt from; resistant to (disease); ns **i. system** function of body to combat disease; **immunity**; v **immunize** (n **-ization**); **immunology** bio study of immunity (a **-logical**, n **-logist**); a **immunosuppressive** bio overriding the immune system (a, n **-essant**).

immure v shut up; enclose; imprison.

immutable a unchangeable.

imp n little devil; mischievous child.

impact n collision; fig strong impression; v press strongly together.

impair v weaken; injure; n **-ment**.

impale v transfix, esp on pointed stake; n **-ment**.

impalpable a that cannot be felt or understood.

impart v transmit; make known; bestow.

impartial a unprejudiced; just; fair; adv **-ly**; n **-ity**.

impassable a not capable of being crossed over.

impasse n deadlock; blind alley.

impassioned a ardent; passionate.

impassive a without emotion; calm; n **-ivity**.

impatient a intolerant of restraint; irritable; restless; adv **-ly**; n **impatience**.

impeach v indict, charge with crime, esp high treason; n **-ment**.

impeccable a faultless; incapable of sin; adv **-ably**; n **-bility**.

impecunious a poor; hard up; n **impecuniosity**.

impede v obstruct; delay; n **impediment**; n pl **impedimenta 1** baggage; equipment **2** encumbrances.

impel v **-pelling, -pelled.** drive forward; urge on; force.

impend v overhang; be about to happen; threaten; a **impending** due.

impenetrable n **1** impassable **2** incomprehensible.

imperative a peremptory; urgent; necessary; n imperative mood.

imperfect a faulty; adv **-ly**; n **-ion** blemish.

imperial a of empire or

emperor; n **1** type of beard **2** paper size; ns **-ism** belief in colonial empire; **-ist.**

imperil v **-illing, -illied.** endanger.

imperious a dominating; dictatorial; haughty.

impersonal a **1** not distinctive **2** automatic; without feelings **3** (*of verb*) without personal subject.

impersonate v pretend to be another; act part of; ns **-ation; -ator.**

impertinent a irrelevant; impudent, insolent; adv **-ly;** n **impertinence.**

imperturbable a calm; not liable to be ruffled; adv **-ably.**

impervious a not allowing entry; fig insensible to; n **-ness.**

impetuous a violent; rash and hasty; impulsive; adv **-ly;** n **impetuosity.**

impetus n momentum; driving force; fig stimulus.

impinge v fall on, against; infringe.

impious a without piety; ungodly; adv **-ly;** n **-ness.**

implacable a inexorable; relentless; n **implacability.**

implant v insert; fig instill (into mind); n something implanted in the body by surgery.

implement n tool; utensil; instrument; v carry into effect; complete; n **-ation.**

implicate v entangle; involve; include; **-tion;** a **implicit 1**

hinted at **2** unquestioning; unquestioned; adv **-ly.**

implore v ask for earnestly; entreat.

imply v **-plying, -plied.** suggest; insinuate.

impolitic a unwise; tactless.

imponderable a, n (thing) the importance of which cannot be assessed.

import v bring in, *esp* goods from abroad; signify, imply; n **1** thing imported **2** consequence; ns **-ation; importer;** a **important 1** distinguished **2** of consequence; essential **3** pompous; adv **-ly;** n **importance.**

importune v pester with troublesome demands; a **importunate** adv **-ly;** n **importunity.**

impose v **1** exact (tax, etc.) **2** foist upon **3** deceive; ns **imposition 1** act of imposing **2** tax **3** deception **4** task given as school punishment; **imposter** deceiver; charlatan; fraudulent person; **imposture; impost 1** tax; duty **2** weight carried by racehorse; a **imposing** impressive.

impossible a not feasible; *coll* insufferable; adv **-ibly;** n **-ibility.**

imposter n person who pretends to be someone else to deceive people.

impotent a powerless; feeble; lacking sexual capacity, *esp* of males; n **impotence.**

impound v **1** confiscate **2** confine; enclose in pound.

impoverish v make poor; weaken; n **-ment.**

imprecation n curse.

impregnable a unassailable; invincible.

impregnate v **1** make pregnant; fertilize **2** saturate; n **-ation.**

impress v stamp; fig affect deeply; fix mark on; n **impression 1** number of copies of book, etc. printed at one time **2** effect produced, *esp* on mind **3** belief; a **-able** easily influenced; ns **impressionism** style of painting giving general effect without detail; **-ist;** a **impressive** making great effect.

impress v compel to serve in army, navy.

imprint v **1** stamp **2** fix in mind; n mark, stamp made by pressure; publisher's, printer's name, etc., in book.

imprison v put in prison; confine; n **-ment.**

impromptu adv, a without preparation; unrehearsed.

improper a **1** incorrect **2** socially unacceptable; indecent; adv **-ly;** n **impropriety.**

improve v make, become better; make good use of; n **-ment.**

improvident a imprudent; wanting foresight; adv **-ly;** n **-dence.**

improvise v compose, do on

a b c d e f g h **i** j k l m n o p q r s t u v w x y z

spur of moment, *esp* with makeshift materials; *n* **-ation**.

impudent *a* insolent; bold; saucy; *adv* **-ly**; *n* **-dence**.

impugn *v* criticize; challenge.

impulse *n* push; sudden inclination to act; stimulus; *n* **impulsion** impetus; *a* **impulsive** rash; acting without thought.

impunity *n* freedom, safety from penalty; *idm* **with impunity** without being penalized.

impure *a* dirty; adulterated; unchaste; *n* **impurity**.

impute *v* ascribe to; credit with; *n* **imputation** reproach; accusation.

in *prep* **1** contained by **2** during **3** into **4** at end of (time) **5** wearing (clothes) **6** showing manner (*e.g.*, **in a hurry**), circumstances (*e.g.*, **in an emergency**), condition (*e.g.*, **in ruins**); *idm* **in all altogether**; *idm* **in that** because; *adv* **1** inside **2** at home **3** included **4** in/into a certain state **5** available; delivered **6** *coll* fashionable; *idm* **be in for** be going to experience; *idm* **be in on** share, participate in; *idm* **be in with** be in favor with; *idm* **have it in for** bear a grudge against; *a* **1** *coll* fashionable **2** belonging to an exclusive group; *n idm* **the ins and outs** complex details.

in- *prefix forming as, advs, ns* (*also* **im-** *before* **b, m** *or* **p** *and*

il-, ir- *before* **l** *and* **r** *respectively*) **1** not **2** lack of **3** opposite of; *e.g.*, *a* **inaccurate** not accurate; *n* **inaccuracy** lack of accuracy; *adv* **illegibly** not legibly; *n* **immodesty** opposite of, lack of modesty. *Such words, if not listed, can have their meaning deduced by removing the prefix; e.g.,* **irregular** (not regular) *and* **irregularity** (lack of regularity) *can be understood by looking up* **regular, regularity.**

inadvertent *a* unintentional; *adv* **-ly**; *n* **inadvertency**.

inalienable *a* that cannot be taken away (*n* **i. right**).

inane *a* senseless; frivolous; *n* **inanity** silly remark.

inasmuch *conj* as seeing that; since.

inaugurate *v* install in office with ceremony; begin, open, *esp* formally; *a* **-al**; *n* **-ation**.

inauspicious *a* ill-omened; unlucky; unfavorable; *adv* **-ly**.

inborn, inbred *a* inherent; natural; *n* **inbreeding** breeding from closely related stocks.

inbuilt *a* forming an inherent part of something.

inc. *abbr* incorporated.

incalculable *a* beyond calculation; unpredictable; uncertain.

incandescent *a* luminous with heat; brilliant; *n* **incandescence;** *v* **incandesce.**

incantation *n* magic spell; charm.

incapacitate *v* render unfit; disable; disqualify; *n* **incapacity.**

incarcerate *v* imprison, confine; *n* **-ation.**

incarnate *a* embodied in human form; personified; *v* give bodily form to; *n* **-ation.**

incendiary *n, a* (one) who maliciously sets property on fire; inflammatory; *n* **incendiarism** arson.

incense[1] *n* fragrant smoke from burning spices, etc.

incense[2] *v* anger, enrage.

incentive *n* stimulus; motive; *a* rousing; inciting.

inception *n* beginning.

incessant *a* constant; unceasing.

inch *n* $\frac{1}{12}$ linear foot; *v* advance by small degrees.

inchoate *a* undeveloped; rudimentary.

incident *n* happening; event; *a* **- al 1** relatively unimportant (*n* **i. music** music played as accompaniment) **2** occurring by chance; *adv* **-ally** by the way; *n* **incidence** fact of affecting; scope of occurrence.

incinerate *v* consume by fire; *ns* **-ation; -ator.**

incipient *a* beginning; in early stages.

incise *v* cut into; carve; *n* **incision; incisor** cutting tooth; *a* **incisive** sharp; *fig* pointed; vigorously clear.

incite *v* inflame; urge; rouse; *n*

-ment.

inclement *a* (*of weather*) cold, severe, rough.

incline *v* 1 slope; lean; bend 2 tend; be disposed; *n* slope; slant; *n* **-ination** 1 slope 2 bow 3 tendency; liking.

include *v* contain; regard as part of whole; *n* **inclusion;** *a* **inclusive.**

incognito *a* passing under assumed name; *n* 1 such a name 2 person adopting it.

incoherent *a* rambling; disconnected; lacking cohesion; *n* **-rence.**

income *n* money received, *esp* annually, from investments, salary, etc. *n* **i. tax.**

incoming *a* coming in; next to take office.

incommode *v* disturb; trouble; *a* **-modious** inconvenient.

incommunicado *adv* not allowed to communicate with anyone.

incomparable *a* too good to be compared; *adv* **-ly.**

incompatible *a* not suited to one another; unable to exist together; *adv* **-ly** *n;* **-bility.**

incongruous *a* inconsistent; unsuitable; *n* **incongruity.**

inconsequential *a* unimportant; irrelevant; *adv* **-ly.**

incontestable *a* that cannot be disputed; *adv* **-ly.**

incontinent *a* unable to control one's bladder; *n* **-ence.**

incontrovertible *a* totally indisputable; *adv* **-ibly.**

inconvenient *a* causing difficulty or discomfort; *adv* **-ly;** *n* **-ence;** *v* **-ence.**

incorporate *v* include; blend; form legal corporation; *n* **-ration.**

incorrigible *a* impossible to correct or improve; *adv* **-ibly;** *n* **-ibility.**

increase *v* 1 grow, become larger; enlarge 2 multiply; *n* enlargement; growth; *adv* **increasingly** more and more.

incredible *a* unbelievable; *coll* remarkable.

incredulous *a* unbelieving; skeptical; *n* **incredulity.**

increment *n* addition; increase.

incriminate *v* accuse; render liable to accusation.

incubate *v* hatch, sit on eggs; *ns* **-ation** *med* period between infection and appearance of symptoms; **-bator** apparatus for artificially hatching eggs, or rearing premature babies.

inculcate *v* implant, impress on mind; *n* **-ation.**

incumbent *a* 1 lying, resting on 2 morally binding; *n* holder of office; *n* **incumbency.**

incur *v* **-curring, -curred.** run into, become liable to (debt, etc.); *n* **-sion** attack; invasion; inroad.

incurable *a* 1 that cannot be cured 2 inveterate.

indebted *a* owing; under obligation; *n* **-ness.**

indecent *a* 1 improper 2

offending against sense of decency, morality; *adv* **-ly;** *n* **indecency.**

indecorous *a* *fml* showing lack of manners, taste; *adv* **-ly;** *n* **indecorum.**

indeed *adv* truly; in fact; certainly.

indefatigable *a* untiring; unremitting; *adv* **-ly.**

indefeasible *a leg* not to be made void, forfeited.

indefensible *a* untenable; inexcusable.

indefinite *a* vague; not precise; *adv* **-ly** for an indefinite period; *a* **indefinable** vague.

indelible *a* not capable of being erased or effaced; *adv* **-ly;** *n* **indelibility.**

indelicate *a* lacking in refinement; embarrassing; *adv* **-ly;** *n* **indelicacy.**

indemnity *n* security from loss, injury, etc.; compensation for loss etc; *v* **indemnify** compensate.

indent *v* 1 notch; carve out 2 make official order for; *n* 1 notch; marginal cut 2 requisition; *ns* **-ation** dent; **indenture** deed, contract drawn up in duplicate, *esp* one binding apprentice to employer.

independent *a* not subordinate; free; financially self-supporting; *adv* **-ly;** *n* one not attached to any political party; *ns* **independence, independency** self-reliance; independent state.

indescribable *a* indefinable;

A B C D E F G H I J K L M N O P Q R S T U V W X Y Z

vague; *adv* **-ly**.

index *n* 1 pointer; indicator 2 forefinger 3 alphabetical list of words, subjects in book 4 *math* exponent; *pl* **indexes** or *math* **indices;** *v* provide with index; enter in index; *n* **i. finger** finger nearest thumb.

Indian *a* of India or N or S American Indians; *ns* **I. club** bottle-shaped object for juggling; **I. corn** maize; **I. ink** thick black ink; **I. summer** warm spell in autumn.

indicate *v* point out; reveal; imply; *ns* **indication** sign; suggestion; **indicator** one who, that indicates; *a* **indicative** 1 *ling* stating facts; asking questions of fact 2 **i. (of)** showing; indicating.

indict *v* accuse formally; *n* **-ment;** *a* **-able**.

indifferent *a* 1 uninterested; callous 2 mediocre 3 impartial; *adv* **-ly;** *n* **indifference**.

indigenous *a* native; not foreign; natural to a country.

indigent *a* needy; destitute; *n* **indigence**.

indigestion *n* dyspepsia; inability to digest food.

indignant *a* feeling, expressing righteous anger; *ns* **indignation; indignity** insult; humiliating treatment.

indigo *n* blue dye got from indigo plant; *a* deep blue.

indirect 1 not straight 2 allusive 3 (*of tax*) imposed on goods, services; *adv* **-ly;** *ns*

i. object *ling* person for whom sth is done, to whom sth is given etc; **i. question, i. speech** report of what is said, not the actual words spoken.

indiscreet *a* not tactful; *adv* **-ly;** *n* **indiscretion** 1 lack of tact 2 indiscreet act or remark.

indiscriminate *a* done at random, without careful thought; *adv* **-ly**.

indisposition *n* 1 slight illness 2 reluctance; *a* **indisposed** 1 unwell 2 averse.

indite *v* write.

individual *n* one particular person, animal, or thing; single person; *a* distinct; characteristic of single person, thing; *adv* **-ly** one by one; *as* **-ist, -istic;** *ns* **-ism, -ist; individuality** personality; individual character.

indoctrinate *v* teach; imbue with particular doctrine; *n* **-ation**.

Indo-European *a* of the family of languages originating in Europe and parts of Asia (*e.g.*, English, French, German, Russian, Greek, Hindi, etc.).

indolent *a* lazy; inactive; *adv* **-ly;** *n* **indolence**.

indomitable *a* unyielding.

indoor *a* pertaining to inside of houses, etc.; domestic; *adv* **indoors**.

indubitable *a* beyond doubt; *adv* **-ably**.

induce *v* persuade; bring about; *n* **-ment** incentive, motive.

induct *v* install formally; *n* **-ion** 1 installation 2 transference of electric force without physical contact; *a* **-ive;** *n* **-or**.

indulge *v* gratify; give way to; pamper; *n* **indulgence** favor; gratification of one's desires; (RC) remission of punishment for sins; *a* **indulgent**.

industrial *a* relating to extraction and refinement of raw materials or production of goods; *ns* **-ism, -ist;** *v* **-ize** (*n* **-ization**); *ns* **i. relations; i. revolution** change in economy from agricultural to industrial basis; *a* **industrious** hard-working; *adv* **-ly;** *n* **industry** 1 hard work 2 manufacturing or production 3 firm that does this.

inebriate *v* intoxicate; *n* **-ation** drunkenness.

inedible *a* not suitable to be eaten.

ineffable *a* unutterable; inexpressibly great.

ineffectual *a* unsatisfactory; futile.

inefficient *a* unable to work properly; *n* **-ency**.

ineligible *a* unqualified; unsuitable; *n* **-ibility**.

ineluctable *a* *fml* inevitable.

inept *a* fatuous; absurd; *n* **-itude**.

inert *a* without power of action; slow; inactive; *ns* -

ness; inertia sluggishness; tendency to resist change (ns **i. reel** reel with tape that resists sudden pull, used for safety belts; **i. selling** mailing of unsolicited goods with demand for payment).

inestimable a not to be estimated; invaluable.

inevitable a unavoidable; certain to happen; adv **-ably;** n **-ability.**

inexorable a relentless.

inexplicable a not able to be explained.

inextricable a impossible to separate, to escape from; adv **-ly.**

infallible a never mistaken; certain; unerring; adv **-ibly;** n **-ibility.**

infamous a disgraceful; notorious; shameful; adv **-ly;** n **infamy.**

infant n very young child; legal minor; ns **infancy; infanticide** murder of child, esp newborn; a **infantile.**

infantry n footsoldiers; n **-man** member of this.

infarction n death of body tissue.

infatuate v make foolish; inspire with extreme passion; a **infatuated** besotted; n **-ation.**

infect v pass disease to; pollute; affect by example; n **-ion;** a **-ious** catching, spreading.

infer v **-ferring, -ferred.** draw conclusions; deduce; n **-ence.**

inferior a lower; of less value, quality; n one lower in rank, etc.; ns **-ity;** i. **complex** psyc lack of self-confidence.

infernal a devilish; fiendish; sl confounded; adv **-ly.**

inferno n **-os** very large fire.

infest v swarm in; overrun; n **-ation.**

infidel n unbeliever; pagan; n **infidelity** (act of) disloyalty.

infield n 1 area inside base lines of baseball field 2 players within infield area; n **-er.**

infighting n discord between members of group.

infiltrate v filter through; permeate; penetrate by stealth; n **-ation.**

infinite a boundless; a **infinitesimal** minute; n **infinity** unlimited time, quality, space, etc.; n ling **infinitive** mood expressing action only, not person, number, etc.

infirm a feeble; physically weak; ns **-ity; infirmary** hospital; sick-quarters.

in flagrante delicto adv leg Lat red-handed.

inflame v set on fire; med make, become red, hot, swollen; fig rouse passion in; a **inflammable** easily set on fire; excitable; ns **-ability;** n **inflammation** morbid condition of redness, swelling, pain; a **inflammatory.**

inflate v 1 swell, distend with air, gas 2 increase (currency) in circulation 3 raise (prices) artificially; as **inflatable, inflated;** n **inflation 1** inflating, being inflated with air, etc. 2 upward trend in costs and prices; a **inflationary.**

inflect v 1 bend, curve inward 2 modify forms of words; n **inflection 1** intonation 2 variation in form of words; a **inflexible** unbending; n **-ibility.**

inflict v cause to undergo; impose; n **infliction** punishment; suffering.

inflorescence n arrangement of flowers on stem; flowering.

inflow n flowing in.

influence v affect; sway; persuade; n effect produced; moral power (over); power of influencing important persons; idm **under the influence** drunk; a **-ential.**

influenza n infectious virus disease.

influx n flowing in, inflow.

info n coll information.

inform v tell; instruct; bring charge against; phr v **inform against/on** report to authorities; ns **informant** giver of information; **informer** one who informs, esp against criminal.

information n facts; knowledge given or obtained (n **i. technology** use of computers for collection, storage, and retrieval of information); a **informative.**

information superhighway n

a b c d e f g h i j k l m n o p q r s t u v w x y z

A B C D E F G H **I** J K L M N O P Q R S T U V W X Y Z

means of transferring information very quickly via an electronic network.

infra *adv* below; farther down, on; **i. dig** *coll* beneath one's dignity; *n* **infrared rays** invisible heat radiation.

infraction *n* infringement of regulation.

infrared *a* rays of spectrum below red.

infrastructure *n* underlying systems and installations that enable an organization or political, social unit to operate.

infrequent *a* rare; unusual; *ns* **infrequence, -quency.**

infringe *v* transgress; disobey; break; *ns* **-ment, infraction** violation; transgression.

infuriate *v* enrage; drive to frenzy; *a* **-ating.**

infuse *v* steep, soak in liquid; *fig* permeate; *n* **infusion** liquid extract so obtained.

ingenious *a* clever at inventing; cleverly made; *n* **ingenuity.**

ingenuous *a* frank; candid; guileless; *adv* **-ly;** *n* **-ness.**

ingestion *n* taking (of food) into stomach.

ingle *n* fire on hearth; *n* **i.nook** chimney corner.

inglorious *a* shameful; *adv* **-ly.**

ingot *n* block of cast metal.

ingrained *a* firmly fixed.

ingrate *n* *fml* ungrateful person.

ingratiate *v* obtain another's good will.

ingredient *n* component; one

part of mixture.

ingress *n* entry; power, right of entry.

in-group *n* group giving preference to members.

inhabit *v* dwell in; occupy; *ns* **-ant; -ation.**

inhale *v* breath in; *n* **inhalation.**

inherent *a* innate; naturally associated with; *adv* **-ly.**

inherit *v* derive from parents, ancestors; succeed as heir; *ns* **-ance** property inherited; **-or** heir, one who inherits.

inhibit *v* restrain; hinder; obstruct; *n* **inhibition** *psyc* unconscious restraint, or suppression of natural urge; *a* **inhibitory.**

in-house *a* within the organization.

inhuman *a* brutally cruel; *n* **inhumanity.**

inhumane *a* unkind; lacking in humanity; *adv* **-ly.**

inimical *a* hostile; unfriendly; antagonistic.

inimitable *a* incapable of being imitated; unrivaled; *adv* **-ably.**

iniquity *n* injustice; wickedness, sin; *a* **iniquitous** unfair, wicked; *ad* **-ly;** *n* **-ness.**

initial *a* occurring at beginning *adv* **-ly;** *n* initial letter; *v* write, mark with, one's initials; *v* **initiate 1** originate **2** admit (to society, etc.); *n* initiated person; *ns* **initiation; initiative** first move; enterprise.

inject *v* introduce, drive in (fluid) by force; fill by this means; *ns* **-ion; -or.**

injunction *n* writ issued to restrain; order; command.

injury *n* **1** harm; hurt; wound **2** moral hurt, insult, etc.; *v* **injure** do harm, hurt to; *a* **injurious.**

injustice *n* wrong; injury; unjust act.

ink *n* colored fluid used for printing and writing; *v* mark with ink; *a* **-y.**

inkjet printer *n* printer in which the characters are produced by tiny jets of ink.

inkling *n* hint; vague idea; suspicion.

inlaid *a* **1** embedded in another substance **2** having with inlaid design.

inland *n* interior of country; *a* away from sea; *adv* in, toward inland.

in-laws *n* relations by marriage other than wife/husband.

inlay *v* decorate by embedding pieces of substance, in contrasting color, in groundwork; *n* inlaid material.

inlet *n* creek; entrance.

in loco parentis *adv* *Lat* acting as parents.

inmate *n* inhabitant; lodger.

in memoriam *adv* in memory of.

inmost *a* deepest; most intimate **inmost** (*also* **innermost**); *sup* of **in.**

inn *n* public house providing lodging, etc., for traveler.

innards *n pl* inside parts (*e.g.*, stomach).

innate *a* native; instinctive; inborn.

inner *a* inside; interior; *comp* of **in**; *n* ring next to bull on target; *ns* **i. city; i. tube** inflatable tube inside outer cover of tyre.

innings *n pl* one round of play in baseball, etc.; *fig* period of active life.

innkeeper *n* landlord, manager of inn.

innocent *a* blameless; guileless; not guilty; simple; *n* guileless child or person; *n* **innocence**.

innocuous *a* harmless; inoffensive.

innovate *v* introduce new methods, changes; *ns* **-ation, -ator;** *as* **-active, -atory**.

innuendo *n* hint; insinuation; *pl* **-does**.

innumerable *a* countless; too many to be counted.

inoculate *v* introduce (disease, etc.) into system, as protection; render immune by infecting with specific germ; *n* **-action**.

inoffensive *a* harmless; giving, causing no offense.

inoperable *a* not suitable for treatment by surgical operation.

inopportune *a* ill-timed; unseasonable.

inordinate *a* excessive; extravagant.

inorganic *a* not result of natural growth; of substances without carbon.

in-patient *n* patient treated in hospital.

input *n* **1** action of putting in **2** (*of ideas, electric power, computer data, etc*) what is put in **3** place on machine where this occurs; *v* **inputing, inputed** *or* **input** *comput* to record data; *n* **i. device**.

inquest *n* legal, judicial inquiry.

inquire *v* ask; *phr v* **inquire into** investigate; *a* **inquiring** showing curiosity, desire for knowledge; *ns* **inquirer; inquiry 1** question **2** investigation.

inquisition *n* **1** searching examination **2** ecclesiastical court for suppression of heresy; *n* **inquisitor;** *as* **inquisitorial; inquisitive** curious; prying.

inroad *n* invasion; incursion; *idm* **make inroads (into) 1** make advance into new area **2** use up substantial amount of.

insane *a* mad; crazy; senseless; *n* **insanity** lunacy; madness.

insanitary *a* unhealthy; filthy.

insatiable *a* that cannot be satisfied; *adv* **-ably**.

inscribe *v* **1** write, engrave on, in **2** dedicate **3** draw (geometric figure within another); *n* **inscription**.

inscrutable *a* enigmatic; impenetrable, mysterious; *adv* **-ably;** *n* **-ability**.

insect *n* invertebrate animal having six legs and

segmented body, usually two or four wings; *n* **insecticide** substance for killing insects; *a* **insectivorous** insect-eating.

insensate *a* unreasoning; inanimate; foolish.

insensible *a* not feeling; unconscious; unaware.

insert *v* set in; introduce; *ns* **insertion; insert** something added, inserted.

in-service *a* (occurring) as part of one's work time.

inset *n* picture, diagram, etc., within the frame of a larger one.

inshore *adv, a* near shore.

inside *a* within; *adv* on the inner side; *n* inner side; *idm* **inside out 1** with the inside part turned outside **2** thoroughly; *ns* **i. story; i. track; insider** *n* person within organization; *ns* **i. trading** illegal dealing in shares by people with inside knowledge of company concerned.

insidious *a* cunning; treacherous; sly.

insight *n* discernment; knowledge.

insignia *n pl* badges of office; distinguishing marks (of honor, etc.).

insinuating *a* ingratiating; *v* **insinuate** hint at; gradually penetrate; *n* **-ation**.

insipid *a* lacking flavor; dull; *n* **-ity**.

insist *v* emphasize; assert; demand urgently; *a* **-ent;**

a
b
c
d
e
f
g
h
i
j
k
l
m
n
o
p
q
r
s
t
u
v
w
x
y
z

A
B
C
D
E
F
G
H
I
J
K
L
M
N
O
P
Q
R
S
T
U
V
W
X
Y
Z

n **-ence.**

in situ *adv Lat* in the original place.

insofar *conj* as far.

insolent *a* insulting; rude; haughty; *n* **-lence.**

insolvent *a* without funds to pay debts; *n* insolvency.

insomnia *a* inability to sleep; sleeplessness.

insomuch *adv* 1 to such a degree 2 inasmuch.

insouciant *a* indifferent; unconcerned; *n* **-ance.**

inspect *v* examine closely, thoroughly; *ns* **inspection; inspector.**

inspire *v* 1 encourage; give stimulus to 2 create a feeling of; *n* inspiration 1 stimulation of ideas 2 someone/something that inspires 3 sudden bright idea; *a* **inspired** brilliant (*n* **i. guess, i. suggestion**).

install *v* 1 place in office formally; establish 2 put in position for use, etc.; *n* **-ation.**

installment *n* 1 one part-payment of debt 2 one part of thing appearing, supplied at intervals.

instance *n* 1 example 2 request; *v* cite; refer to; *a* **instant** 1 urgent; immediate 2 *dated comm* of current month; *n* precise moment; *a* **instantaneous** occurring in and instant; *adv* **instanter** instantly, immediately.

instead *adv* in place of; as alternative to.

instep *n* upper surface of foot in front of ankle.

instigate *v* incite; urge; stir up; *ns* **instigation; instigator.**

instill *v* **-stilling, -stilled.** implant; infuse; *n* **instilation.**

instinct *n* natural aptitude; impulse; intuition; *a* **instinctive;** *adv* **-ly.**

institute *v* set up; found; begin; set going; *n* scientific, social, etc., society; building occupied by such society; *n* **institution** 1 custom 2 organization 3 act of founding; *a* **-al;** *adv* **-ally;** *v* **-alize;** *n* **-alization.**

instruct *v* teach; give orders to; *n* **instruction;** *a* **instructive** informative; *adv* **-ly;** *n* **instructor.**

instrument *n* 1 tool; implement 2 device for producing musical sounds 3 legal document; *a* **instrumental** 1 acting as means, or instrument 2 produced by musical instruments; *adv* **-ly;** *ns* **instrumentality** means; **instrumentation** arrangement of music for particular instruments.

insubordinate *a* rebellious; disobedient; unruly; *n* **insubordination.**

insufficiency *n* inadequacy; lack; *a* **insufficient;** *adv* **-ly.**

insular *a* of, like an island; *fig* narrow-minded; *n* **insularity.**

insulate *v* isolate; prevent passage of electricity by use of nonconducting material;

ns **insulation; insulator.**

insulin *n* extract from animal pancreas, used in treating diabetes, etc.

insult *v* abuse; treat with contempt; *n* affront; insolence; *a* **insulting.**

insuperable *a* not to be overcome or surmounted.

insure *v* 1 enter into contract to secure payment in event of loss of (life, health, etc.) 2 make safe 3 make sure; *ns* **insurance; insurer; insurance policy** written contract of insurance; *a* **insurable.**

insurgent *a* rebellious; *ns* **-ency; insurrection** rebellion.

insurrection *n* armed revolt.

insusceptible *a* not capable of being moved by feeling; unimpressed; *adv* **-ibly;** *n* **-ibility.**

intact *a* untouched; entire; uninjured.

intaglio *n* design carved, engraved on hard surface; jewel carved so (a cameo).

intake *n* 1 what is taken in 2 airshaft in mine 3 (in car) air passage to carburetor 4 body of new recruits, members, etc.

intangible *a* insubstantial; impalpable; vague; *adv* **-ibly;** *n* **-ibility.**

integer *n* anything complete, entire; whole number; *a* **integral** 1 essential 2 whole; complete; *n* **integral calculus** branch of mathematics; *v*

integrate 1 make whole; bring into one body **2** abolish segregation; *a* **integrated** (*n* **i. circuit** very small electronic circuit, *e.g.*, silicon chip); *ns* **-ation** integrating; being integrated; **integrity 1** honesty **2** state of being undivided, unharmed.

integument *n* **1** outer covering; skin **2** rind; shell.

intellect *n* faculty of knowing, reasoning; *a* **-ual** of, exercising intellect; inclined to mental activity (*n* intellectual person; *adv* **-lly**).

intelligence *n* **1** intellect; mental ability; quickness in learning **2** news; information *esp* military, etc.; **i. quotient** number indicating level of intelligence; **intelligent** clever; well informed; *n* **intelligencer** informant; secret agent; *a* **intelligible** clear in meaning; *adv* **-ibly**; *n* **-ibility**; *n* **intelligentsia** cultured, intellectual classes.

intemperate *a* unrestrained; given to excess; *adv* **-ly**; *n* **-erance**.

intend *v* **1** design; destine **2** mean **3** contemplate.

intense *a* **1** excessive; extreme **2** violent **3** ardent; eager; *v* **intensify** increase; deepen; make stronger; *ns* **intensification; intensity** strength; depth; *a* **intensive** thorough; concentrated (*n* **i. care** constant medical attention for patient in critical condition).

intent *a* concentrating; earnest; *n* purpose; motive; *idm* **to all intents and purposes** virtually; *idm* **intent on/upon 1** occupied in **2** intending; *adv* **-ly;** *n* **-ness.**; *ns* **intention** aim; meaning; **-ness;** *a* **intentional.**

inter *v* **-terring, -terred.** bury; *n* **-ment.**

inter- *prefix Lat* among; between; mutual; *forms compounds, e.g.,* **interaction** acting on each other; **interrelation** relation between things, persons. *Such words are not given here where the meaning may be deduced from the simple word.*

interact *v* act upon another; *n* interaction; *a* interactive.

interactive *a* **1** acting on each other **2** *comput* allowing exchange of information between user and machine during program.

inter alia *adv Lat* among other things.

intercede *v* plead for; mediate; *ns* **-cession; -cessor.**

intercept *v* hinder; prevent passage of; *ns* **-ion; -or;** *a* **-ive.**

interchange *v* exchange; alternate with; *n* **1** (act of) interchanging **2** system of linking roads between highways, other main roads; *a* **-able;** *adv* **-ably.**

intercity *a* providing fast transport between cities; *n* **1** such a service **2** such a train,

bus, etc.

intercommunicate *v* communicate with; (*of rooms*) open one into another; *n* **intercom** internal telephone system.

intercontinental ballistic missile *n* long-range missile with *usu* nuclear warhead (*also* **ICBM**).

intercourse *n* mutual dealings, relations.

interdependent *a* mutually dependent; *n* **-ence.**

interdict *n* prohibition; exclusion from sacraments and religious rites; *v* prohibit; restrain; *n* **-diction.**

interest *n* **1** concern; intellectual curiosity **2** advantage; benefit **3** *finance idm* **in somebody's interest** to somebody's advantage; payment made for use of money; *v* rouse, hold attention; concern; *a* **-ing.**

interface *n* point where two systems meet, interconnect, and work together; *v* connect by interface.

interfere *v* meddle; hinder; mediate; *idm* **interfere with 1** hinder **2** cause malfunction by touching; *n* **-ference 1** interfering **2** *rad* extraneous noise.

interferon *n* protein in body that inhibits viruses.

intergalactic *a* between galaxies.

interim *a* temporary; meantime.

interior *a* inner; internal;

inland; n inside; inland.

interject v interrupt by, break in with (word, etc.); n **-jection** exclamation.

interlace v twist together.

interlard v mix in.

interleave v insert blank pages among others in book.

interlock v lock or fit closely together.

interlocutor n person taking part in dialogue; n **-locution**.

interloper n intruder; meddler in another's affairs.

interlude n interval between two acts of play; short entertainment during such interval.

intermediate a in the middle; ns **-mediary; -mediator** mediator.

intermezzo n short piece of music, esp between acts of an opera; pl **-s** or **intermezzi**.

interminable a endless; unduly prolonged.

intermission n interval between acts of play, ballet, etc.; respite; a **-mittent** ceasing at intervals.

intern v confine to specified area; ns graduate or professional student gaining practical experience, as in a hospital; **-ment; internee** person interned.

internal a inner; interior; adv **-ly**; v **-ize**; n **-ization**; n i. **-combustion engine** one driven by explosion of air and fuel in cylinder.

internal medicine n medical branch dealing with diagnosis and nonsurgical treatment of disease.

international a pertaining to relations between nations; n 1 game, match between different countries 2 player taking part in such contest; adv **-ly**; n **-ism; -ist**.

internecine a of conflict within a group; of mutual destruction.

Internet n [TM] wide-reaching computer network offering wealth of information to smaller networks worldwide.

interplay n reciprocal action; interaction.

Interpol n international police organization.

interpolate v insert (spurious matter) in book, etc.; n **-ation** words, etc. added by another author.

interpose v insert; interrupt; intervene; obstruct.

interpret v explain; construe; translate; ns **-er; -ation**.

interregnum n interval between reigns.

interrogate v ask searching questions of; ns **-ation; -ator;** as **-ative;** questioning; **-atory**.

interrupt v break in on; obstruct; cut off continuity of; n **-ruption**.

intersect v cut through; cross each other; n **-section**.

intersperse v scatter among; diversify.

interstice n chink; small opening.

interval n 1 intervening space or time 2 pause; break 3 mus difference of pitch.

intervene v come between; interfere; take part in; n **-vention**.

interview n formal meeting and conversation; one arranged to test suitability of applicant for position, or to obtain views, opinions of a personality; v have interview with; n **interviewer;** n **interviewee** person interviewed.

intestate a not having made a will; n **intestacy**.

intestine n lower part of alimentary canal, bowel; a fig internal; domestic; a **intestinal**.

intimate a 1 inward 2 closely linked 3 familiar; n **-macy**.

intimate v make known; hint; n **-ation** notice.

intimidate v frighten; terrorize; restrain by threats; n **-ation**.

into prep from outside to inside; to place of, condition of, form of.

intone v chant; recite in monotone; n **intonation** modulation of voice; sounding of musical notes.

in toto adv Lat entirely.

intoxicate v make drunk; fig excite greatly; ns **intoxicant** intoxicating liquor; **-ation**.

intransigent a obstinately hostile; uncompromising; n **-ence**.

intravenous a into a vein; adv **-ly**.

intrepid a brave; fearless;

n **-ity.**

intricate *a* involved; entangled; puzzling; *n* **intricacy.**

intrigue *n* secret plot; *v* 1 carry on intrigue 2 interest; *n* **intriguer.**

intrinsic *a* inherent; real; genuine.

intro- *prefix* within; into.

introduce *v* 1 bring into use, notice, etc. 2 make known formally 3 insert; *n* **-duction,** *a* **-ductory** preliminary.

introspection *n* self-analysis; *a* **-spective** dwelling on one's own thoughts.

introvert *n* self-centered, introspective person; *v* direct, cause to turn inward; *n* **-version.**

intrude *v* thrust in; force in uninvited; *ns* **intruder, intrusion;** *a* **intrusive.**

intuit *v fml* sense by intuition; *n* **intuition** (power of) instant understanding without facial evidence or logical reasoning; *a* **intuitive;** *adv* **-ly.**

Inuit *n* Eskimo.

inundate *v* flood; swamp; *fig* overwhelm; *n* **-ation.**

inure *v* accustom; harden.

invade *v* 1 enter with hostile intent 2 *fig* assail 3 encroach on; *ns* **invader; invasion.**

invalid[1] *a* not valid; *n* **-ity;** *v* **-ate.**

invalid[2] *n, a* (person) suffering from ill health, weakness; *v* render infirm; remove from active service.

invaluable *a* priceless; very valuable.

invariable *a* constant; unchanging; *adv* **-ly.**

invective *n* abuse; vituperation.

inveigh *v* attack violently with words.

inveigle *v* delude; lure; entice; *n* **-ment.**

invent *v* originate; contrive for first time; make up; *n* **invention** something that is invented; fabrication; ability to invent; *a* **-ive** originative; resourceful; *n* **-or.**

inventory *n* detailed list of stock, etc.; catalogue.

inverse *a* reversed; contrary; *n* 1 inverted state 2 the opposite; *n* **inversion.**

invert *v* turn upside down; reverse position of; *a* **-ed.**

invertebrate *n* animal without backbone; *a* spineless; *fig* irresolute.

invest *v* 1 use money to earn interest 2 *mil* beseige; *phr vs* **invest in** buy; **invest with** 1 confer (honor) upon 2 deposit money (to earn interest) at; *ns* **investment** 1 act of investing 2 property purchased; **investor.**

investigate *v* inquire into; examine carefully; *ns* **-ation; -ator.**

inveterate *a* persistent; long-established; obstinate; confirmed.

invidious *a* giving offense by injustice; likely to arouse ill-

will; *adv* **-ly;** *n* **-ness.**

invigorate *v* strengthen; refresh.

invincible *a* unconquerable; *adv* **-ibly;** *n* **-ibility.**

inviolable *a* unprofaned; not to be dishonored or violated; *a* **inviolate** strictly preserved; kept sacred; uninjured.

invisible *a* not capable of being seen; *adv* **-ibly;** *n* **-ibility.**

invite *v* 1 ask person to come to social gathering, etc. 2 request 3 attract; provoke; *a* **inviting** attractive (*adv* **-ly**); *n* **invitation** 1 act of inviting 2 request to come 3 provocation.

in vitro *a Lat* in test tube or by artificial means; *n* **i.v. fertilization.**

invoice *n* list of goods sent, with prices; *v* make out invoice.

invoke *v* appeal to; implore; call on; *n* **invocation.**

involuntary *a* unintentional; automatic; instinctive; *adv* **-arily.**

involuted *a* 1 complex 2 coiled in on itself.

involve *v* 1 entangle; complicate 2 implicate; entail 3 imply; *a* **involute** intricate; spirally curved; *n* **-ution.**

inward *adv* 1 towards interior 2 into the mind; *a* 1 internal 2 spiritual; mental; *n pl* entrails; *adv* **-ly** privately.

iodine *n* nonmetallic element used in medicine.

a
b
c
d
e
f
g
h
i
j
k
l
m
n
o
p
q
r
s
t
u
v
w
x
y
z

A
B
C
D
E
F
G
H
I
J
K
L
M
N
O
P
Q
R
S
T
U
V
W
X
Y
Z

iodize *v* treat with iodine.

ion *n* electrically charged atom; *v* **ionize** charge ions with electricity; *n* **-ization**.

ionosphere *n* layers of earth's atmosphere that reflect radio signals.

iota *n* Greek letter *i*; very small part, jot.

IOU *n* signed acknowledgment of debt.

IPA *abbr* International Phonetic Alphabet.

ipecac *n* root of S American plant, used as emetic.

ipso facto *adv Lat* by the fact itself.

IQ *abbr* intelligence quotient.

ir- *prefix see* IN-.

IR *n* information retrieval

IRA *abbr* Irish Republican Army.

Iranian *a, n* (inhabitant) of Iran.

Iraqi *a, n* (inhabitant) of Iraq.

irascible *a* easily provoked to anger; *n* **-ibility**.

irate *a* furiously angry; *adv* **-ly**; *n* **-ness**.

iridescent *a* changing in color, like rainbow; *n* **iridescence**.

iridium *n* hard silvery metallic element.

iris *n* colored part of eye, around pupil; tuberous-rooted plant.

Irish *n, a* (language, inhabitant) of Ireland; *ns* **I. coffee** coffee with cream and whisky; **I. stew** stew of meat, potatoes, and onions.

irk *v* weary; worry; *a* **irksome** tiresome.

iron *n* **1** very hard metallic element; most common metal used for tools, weapons, etc, and the raw material of steel **2** appliance for smoothing, pressing cloth, etc. **3** metal-headed golf club; *n pls* fetters; *idm* **have several irons in the fire** have alternative plans ready; *a* **1** of iron **2** very strong **3** unyielding **4** hard; *v* smooth (clothes) with an iron; *phr v* **iron out** remove (disagreements, problems); *ns* **I. Age** period after Bronze Age; **I. Curtain** frontier between W Europe and Communist countries of E Europe after Second World War; **i. lung** machine to assist breathing; **i. pyrites** fool's gold; *n* **ironing** (**i. board** board for ironing clothes).

irony *n* **1** way of speaking, in which the meaning is the opposite of apparent meaning **2** sarcasm **3** perverseness in a situation occurring in the wrong way or at the wrong time; *n* **dramatic irony ambiguity** in words or fatal course of action, understood by the audience knowing somethingh as yet unknown to the character(s) in the play; *a* **ironic** of irony.

irradiate *v* shine on; illumine; diffuse; *n* **-iation** exposure to therapeutic rays.

irrational *a* without reason or judgment.

irreconcilable *a* **1** that which cannot be brought to an agreement **2** bitterly opposed.

irrefutable *a* indisputable.

irreparable *a* beyond repair; not able to be remedied.

irrespective *a* without regard, reference to; not taking into account.

irrevocable *a* impossible to change later on; *adv* **-ably**.

irrigate *v* water by artificial channels; *n* **-ation**.

irritate *v* **1** annoy; exasperate **2** provoke **3** inflame; make sore; *n* **-ation**; *as* **irritant** causing irritation; **irritable** irascible; easily angered; (*of wounds, etc.*) inflamed; sore; *adv* **-ably**; *n* **-ability**.

irruption *n* invasion; sudden violent incursion.

ISBN *abbr* International Standard Book Number.

Islam *n* Muslim religion of world; *a* **Islamic**.

island *n* **1** piece of land, surrounded by water **2** detached isolated patch, mound; *n* **-er** one who lives on island.

isle *n* island; *n* **islet** small island.

isn't *abbr* is not.

isobar *n* line on map joining places with equal mean atmospheric pressure.

isolate *v* set apart; keep (infected person) away from others; *ns* **-lation; -ationism** policy of avoiding involvement in world politics; **-ationist**.

isomer *n chem* compound with same number of atoms, but arranged differently.

isosceles *a* triangle, having two equal sides.

isotherm *n* line on map joining places of same mean temperature.

isotope *n* atom of element having different atomic weight from other atoms in same element; *as* **-topic**.

issue *n* 1 flowing, coming out 2 publication 3 outlet 4 offspring 5 result 6 problem; *v* 1 go out 2 emit 3 publish 4 be derived from 5 distribute.

isthmus *n* narrow strip of land between two seas, connecting two land areas.

it *pron* 3rd pers. neuter; 1 *referring to inanimate objects* that one 2 *coll* the important thing; *a* **its** belonging to it; *pron* **itself** emphatic form.

IT *abbr* information technology.

Italian *a, n* native or language of Italy.

italic *a* of type, with letters sloping up to right; *n pl* this type, used for emphasis; *v* **italicize** print in italics.

itch *v* 1 feel itch 2 have restless desire; *idm* **be itching** *coll* to be longing to; *idm* **have an itching palm** *coll* be greedy for money; *n* 1 itching feeling 2 strong desire; *a* **itchy**; *ns* **i. feet** *coll* desire to travel; **itchiness**.

it'd *abbr* 1 it would 2 it had.

item *n* single detail in list; piece of news; subsection of agenda etc.; *adv* likewise; *v* **-ize**; *n* **-ization**.

iterate *v* repeat; *n* **-ation**.

itinerant *a* traveling from place to place; wandering; (*of judges, preachers, etc.*) on circuit; *n* **itinerary** route; record of travel; guidebook.

it'll *abbr* it will.

its *poss a* belonging to it.

it's *abbr* it is.

itself *emphatic pron.*

I've *abbr* I have.

IVF *abbr* in vitro fertilization.

ivory *n* hard white substance from tusks of elephants, etc.; **i. black** black pigment made from burned ivory; *i. tower* place where people escape from life's hard realities.

ivy *n* climbing evergreen plant; *a* **I. League** typical of group of older universities in eastern states.

jab *v* **jabbing, jabbed.** poke suddenly, with force; thrust roughly.

jabber *v* speak rapidly, gabble; chatter.

jabot *n* frill, ruffle on bodice, shirtfront.

jacaranda *n* tropical American hardwood tree.

jacinth *n* reddish orange variety of zircon.

jack *n* **1** device for raising load from below **2** *cards* knave **3** *bowls* ball used as mark **4** ship's flag; *prefix* male; large; *phr* v **jack up** raise by jack; *ns* **jackhammer** pneumatic drill; **j.-in-the-box** box with doll that springs up when lid is released; **j.knife** large pocket knife (*v* **jackknife** fold in the middle) **j.-of-all-trades** person of varied skills; **jackpot** maximum prize of money.

jackal *n* wild scavenging animal, allied to a dog.

jackass *n* male ass; *n* **laughing j.** large Australian kingfisher.

jackdaw *n* small kind of crow.

jacket *n* **1** short coat **2** outer casing, covering.

Jack Frost *n* imaginary personification of cold or frosty weather.

jackhammer *n* a rock-drilling tool driven by compressed air.

jackpot *n* pool in poker game; money prize increasing in value until won.

jackrabbit *n* large rabbit of western US.

Jacuzzi [TM] bath with air-jets creating constant bubbles.

jade[1] *n* hard green or white gem stone; color green.

jade[2] *n* **1** wornout horse **2** *sl* disreputable woman; *a* **jaded** tired, wearied.

jag *n* sharp, pointed projection; ragged tear in cloth; *a* **jagged**.

jaguar *n* large carnivorous S American cat.

jai alai *n* a game played on a court with two or four players who hit a ball and try to catch it with a long wicker basket strapped to the wrist.

jail *n* prison; *ns* **jailbait** a girl under the age of consent; **jailbird** *coll* prison inmate or former inmate.

jam *n* **1** fruit preserve **2** crush **3** traffic holdup; *v* **jams, jamming, jammed. 1** block, fill up **2** cease to work *n* **j. session** unrehearsed jazz session; *as* **j.-packed** *coll* very crowded.

jamb *n* side post of door; window frame.

jamboree *n* spree; social gathering; Scout rally.

jangle *v* make harsh, clanging sound; *n* such a sound.

janitor *n* doorkeeper; caretaker.

January *n* first month of year.

Japanese *n* native or language of Japan; *a* **Japanese.**

jape *n* joke.

japonica *n* type of quince tree with red flowers.

jar *n* round glass, earthenware vessel.

jar v **jars, jarring, jarred. 1** be, sound discordant **2** grate upon **3** cause to shake, vibrate; n harsh sound, shock.

jardinière n Fr ornamental trough for plants.

jargon n gibberish; excessively technical language.

jasmine, n fragrant flowering shrub.

jasper n opaque reddish, yellow, or brown quartz.

jaundice n morbid state, characterized by yellow tint of eyes and skin; a **jaundiced** fig jealous; biased.

jaunt n short pleasure trip; v go on jaunt; n **jaunting-car** Irish two-wheeled cart.

jaunty a carefree; sprightly; swaggering; adv **-ily;** n **-iness.**

java n coffee.

javelin n light throwing spear, or shaft.

jaw n two bones, in which teeth are set, and their muscles; pl **-s 1** animal's mouth **2** gripping part of pliers or similar tool; ns **jawbone; jawbreaker 1** word difficult to pronounce **2** hard candy; v sl talk at length; lecture.

jay n noisy, brightly colored bird of crow family.

jaywalk v cross the road without regard for traffic; n **jaywalker.**

jazz n syncopated rhythmical music of black origin; phr v **jazz up** make more lively; a

jazzy with bright colors or vivid patterns.

jealous a envious; grudging; suspicious; distrustful; n **jealousy.**

jeans n twilled cotton fabric; pl trousers, overalls of this cloth.

Jeep [TM] n light, open truck, with four-wheel drive.

jeer v mock, scoff at; n taunt, gibe.

Jehovah n God of Old Testament; n **J.'s Witness** member of fundamentalist sect.

jejune a **1** lacking significance **2** lacking maturity.

jejunum n middle of small intestine.

jell v set; congeal.

Jell-O [TM] n mix for gelatin dessert.

jelly n semisolid, transparent food made with gelatin, any substance of similar consistency; v **jell** turn to jelly; set; sl take definite form; ns **jelly bean** sugar-coated candy in the shape of a bean; **jelly roll** a rolled-up sheet of sponge cake and jelly filling; **j.fish** free floating sea creature; medusa.

jenny n **1** spinning machine **2** female ass.

jeopardy n hazard; peril; danger; v **jeopardize** imperil.

jerboa n small African burrowing rodent; desert rat.

jeremiad n lamentation.

jerk[1] n quick pull; twitch; sudden, sharp movement; v

move with jerk; a **-y;** adv **-ily;** n **-iness.**

jerk[2] n stupid and awkward person.

jeroboam n large wine or champagne bottle holding about three liters.

jerry-built a hastily, flimsily constructed.

jersey n close-fitting knitted sweater; breed of cow.

jest n joke; v make jokes; n **jester** joker.

Jesuit n member of Roman Catholic religious order; a **jesuitical.**

Jesus n the Jewish teacher whose birth, death, and resurrection became the basis for the Christian faith (also **Jesus Christ**).

jet[1] n hard black mineral, used for ornaments, etc.; a **j. black.**

jet[2] n **1** stream, spurt of liquid, gas, forced from small opening **2** nozzle **3** aircraft propelled by jet engine; v **jets, jetting, jetted.** gush, give out in jet; ns **jetfoil** hydrofoil; **j. lag** tiredness after long flight by jet plane; **j. set** rich social group who travel frequently across the world (a, n **j.-setting** n **j.-setter**); n **j. stream** strong winds high up; a **j.-propelled** n **j. propulsion.**

jetsam n things thrown overboard to lighten vessel, and washed ashore.

jettison v throw overboard; fig get rid of; abandon.

a
b
c
d
e
f
g
h
i
j
k
l
m
n
o
p
q
r
s
t
u
v
w
x
y
z

A B C D E F G H I **J** K L M N O P Q R S T U V W X Y Z

jetty n pier, a landing wharf.

Jew n a member or the tribe of Judah; one whose religion is Judaism; *fem* **Jewess; n Jewry** collectively Jews; n **Jew's harp** small musical instrument held in mouth.

jewel n precious stone, gem; ornament set with one; precious object; *ns* **jeweler** dealer in jewels; **jewelry** items worn to ornament the body, as rings, earring, necklaces, etc.

jib n ship's triangular foremost staysail; projecting arm of crane, etc.; v **jibs, jibbing, jibbed.** pull over (sail) to other side; (of horse).

jibe n, v gibe.

jig n 1 lively dance 2 template guiding cutting tool; v **jigs, jigging, jigged.** move jerkily up and down; dance jig.

jigsaw n machine fretsaw for cutting curved, irregular patterns; n **j. puzzle** picture mounted on wood, etc., and cut in irregular pieces, to be reassembled.

jihad n Islamic holy war.

jilt v reject (lover) after encouraging him or her.

jingle n 1 light, ringing, tinkling sound, as of small bells 2 verses with simple catchy words; v make, cause to make this sound.

jingo n warmonger; n **-ism** aggressive patriotism.

jink v move with sudden twists and turns; dodge.

jinx n hoodoo; bringer of bad luck.

jitney n small shuttle bus.

jitters n pl sl extreme nervousness; panic; a **jittery** nervy; jumpy; n **jitterbug 1** one who dances vigorously 2 one who panics easily.

jive n very emotional swing, or jazz music; form of dance; v dance to this style.

job n piece of work; task; employment; matter; affair; *ns* **j. center** office assisting the unemployed to find work; **j. lot** *coll* articles sold together; **job-sharing** dividing fulltime post between two people; v **1** work at piece-rate **2** hire out **3** act as broker; *ns* **jobber 1** wholesaler **2** dealer in stock exchange securities; **jobbery** corrupt practice in public position.

jock n athlete; n **jockstrap** sport garment for protection of man's genitals.

jockey n professional rider in horse racing; v cheat; trick; maneuver.

jocose a facetious; playful; jesting; n **jocosity;** a **jocular** joking; n **-larity.**

jocund a merry; cheerful; n **-ity.**

jodhpurs n pl riding breeches.

jog v **jogs, jogging, jogged.** push; nudge; keep moving steadily; *fig* stimulate memory; n slow steady trot.

joggle v move jerkily; shake slightly.

John n one of the four apostles, credited with authorship of the fourth Gospel.

John Doe n unidentified person or body.

John Hancock n **1** a signer of the Declaration of Independence **2** a signature on a document.

johnnycake n a bread made with cornmeal and sugar.

join v connect; unite; become member of; fasten; *phr v* **j. up** enlist; n place of joining; *ns* **-er** craftsman in wood; **-ery.**

joint n **1** joining place of bones, of pieces of wood, etc. **2** large piece of meat for roasting **3** *sl* bar or nightclub **4** *sl* cigarette with cannabis; *a* shared n **j. venture** enterprise by cooperative management.

joist n one of parallel beams, supporting floor or ceiling.

jojoba n desert shrub with edible seeds that yield liquid wax.

joke n jest; something not meant to be serious; v make jokes; talk jestingly; n **joker** one who jokes; odd card in pack.

jolly a **1** jovial; merry; hearty **2** pleasant; v cajole; persuade by flattery; n **J. Roger** pirate flag with skull and crossbones; *adv coll* very; *ns* **jollity, jollification** merrymaking.

jolt v shake with sudden jerk; jog; n sudden jerk or bump.

Jonah *n* **1** prophet in the Old Testament **2** person thought to bring bad luck to others.

Joneses *idm* **keep up with the Joneses** compete socially by having all the material things one's neighbor has.

jonquil *n* fragrant yellow or white narcissus.

josh *v coll* tease.

joss stick *n* incense.

jostle *v* knock or bump against.

jot *n* trifle; small amount; *v* **jots, jotting, jotted.** make brief written note; *phr v* **jot down** make quick written note of; *n* **jotting** (*usu pl*) brief note.

joule *n* unite of electrical energy.

journal *n* **1** daily record; diary **2** periodical **3** daily newspaper **4** part of axle resting on bearings; *ns* **journalese** newspaper language full of clichés; **journalism** profession of producing, editing, writing in newspapers, etc., **-ist;** *a* **-istic.**

journey *n* act of traveling; distance traveled; *v* travel.

journeyman *n* **1** trained employee **2** reliable but not brilliant worker; *pl* **-men.**

joust *n* encounter between two armed, mounted knights; *v* take part in tournament; tilt.

jovial *a* convivial; cheery; hearty; festive; *n* **-ity.**

jowl *n* lower part of face, jaw; dewlap of cattle.

joy *n* great pleasure, gladness; happiness; cause of this; *n* **j.ride** *coll* car ride taken for fun without owner's permission (*v* take such a ride; *ns* **j.rider, j.riding**); *as* **joyful** (*adv* **-ly,** *n* **-ness**); **joyless** (*adv* **-ly,** *n* **-ness**); **joyous** (*adv* **-ly,** *n* **-ness.**).

joystick *n* control lever of aircraft, or computer.

JP *abbr* justice of the peace.

Jr. *abbr* junior.

jubilation *n* rejoicing; *a* **jubilant** exultant, elated.

jubilee *n* fiftieth anniversary; festive celebration.

Judah *n* biblical name; son of Jacob; ancestor of one of the tribes of Israel.

Judaism *n* Jewish religion, custom.

Judas *n* **1** biblical; apostle who betrayed Jesus **2** traitor.

Judeo-Christian *n* of or having roots in both Judaism and Christianity.

judge *n* official appointment to preside over court of justice; one who decides a dispute; umpire; arbiter; *v* try (case) in law court; form opinion, decide on; estimate worth; *idm* **judge of** person qualified to evaluate; *n* **judgment 1** sentence of court **2** opinion **3** divine retribution (*ns* **j. day, day of j.** day when God will judge the human race) **4** ability to evaluate.

judicature *n* administration of justice; body of judges; judicial system; *as* **judicial** of,

befitting court of law, judge; impartial; **judicious** wise, prudent; *n* **judiciary** body of judges.

judo *n* Japanese system of unarmed combat.

jug *n* **1** vessel with handle and lip or spout, for holding liquids; its contents **2** *sl* prison; *v* stew in jug, *esp* hare.

juggernaut *n* powerful, relentless destructive force.

juggle *v* perform conjuring tricks; *fig* deceive; *ns* **jugglery; juggler.**

jugular *a* of, relating to neck, throat.

juice *n* **1** liquid part of animal or vegetable tissue; **2** *sl* something that supplies power, as gasoline, electricity; *a* **juicy 1** succulent **2** *sl* spicy; suggestive.

ju-jitsu, ju-jutsu *n* judo.

ju-ju *n* W African fetish; charm, taboo.

jukebox *n* automatic coin-operated record player.

julep *n* **1** sweet, soothing, medicated drink **2** iced mint-flavored alcoholic drink.

Julian *a* of Julius Caesar, *esp* of calendar introduced by him.

julienne *v* to slice or cut into long, thin strips.

July *n* seventh month of Gregorian calendar.

jumble *v* mix up, confuse together; *n* disorded heap.

jumbo *a coll* enormous; *n coll* (nickname for) elephant; *n* **j.**

jet very large aircraft.

jump *v* 1 spring into the air by use of leg muscles 2 move suddenly (in specified direction) 3 pass over (obstacle) by jumping 4 react in surprise 5 (of prices, costs, etc.) rise steeply 6 malfunction by moving suddenly out of position 7 attack 8 pass illegally (**j. a barrier**); go out of turn (**j. the gun, the line, the (traffic) lights**); *idm* **jump down someone's throat** *coll* attack someone verbally without waiting for explanations; *idm* **jump bail** fail to appear after being released on bail; *idm* **jump out of one's skin** react with fright; *idm* **jump to it** *coll* be quick; *phr v* **jump at** grab eagerly; *n* 1 act of jumping 2 sharp rise 3 obstacle to cross; *idm* **one jump ahead** able to anticipate rivals and hold an advantage; *ns* **jumper** 1 one who jumps 2 *aut* electric lead for connecting two batteries 3 **jumper**; **jumping** (*n* **j.-off place** starting point); **j.-start** *aut* way of starting car by pushing when battery is flat; **j. suit** garment combining jacket and trousers in one; *as* **jumped-up** upstart; **jumpy** nervous (*n* **-iness.**)

jumper *n* a sleeveless dress usually worn with a shirt or blouse.

jumper cables *n* electrical cables with clamps used for jump starting a battery.

junction *n* joining; place, point of union; station where branches of railway meet.

juncture *n* position of affairs; critical point.

June *n* sixth month of Gregorian calendar.

jungle *n* wild, uncultivated land, with thick undergrowth; *fig* confused, tangled mass.

jungle gym *n* structure with both horizontal and vertical bars, usually for children to play on.

junior *a* younger; of lower status; *n* subordinate; one who is younger; *cap* younger of two men in family with identical names.

junior college *n* education at institution offering a two-year course of studies.

junior high school *n* school *usu* of grades seven through nine (*also* **intermediate school; middle school).**

junior miss *n* a young, usually adolescent girl.

juniper *n* evergreen tree.

junk[1] *n* 1 old rope 2 *sl* useless articles 3 rubbish; *ns* **j. food** snack food that is of little nutritional value; **j. mail** mass-printed, mainly advertising matter sent unsolicited by mail to people's homes; **j. yard** area for storing used items or resalable junk.

junk[2] *n* large flat-bottomed Chinese sailing vessel.

junket *n* 1 milk curdled with rennet 2 *coll* pleasure trip to government official financed with public money.

junkie, junky *n* 1 *sl* heroin addict 2 *coll* any kind of addict (*n* **TV junkie**).

Juno *n* wife of Jupiter Roman goddess of birth, women, marriage.

junoesque *a* of stately or womanly beauty.

junta *n* Spanish or Italian council of state; political faction.

Jupiter *n* supreme Roman god; the largest planet.

Jurassic *a* geological period of Mesozoic era between Triassic and Cretaceous.

jurisdiction *n* authority to administer law; area covered by authority; *a* **juridical** legal; *n* **jurisprudence** science, knowledge of law; *a* **jural** of law; *n* **jurist** law graduate; writer on law.

jury *n* 1 body of persons sworn to return verdict in court of law 2 panel of judges for a contest; *ns* **juror** member of jury; **jury box** enclosed place, in court, for jury to occupy; **jury-rigged** to build a makeshift construction.

just *a, adv* 1 exactly (*e.g.,* **just here, just right, just so**) 2 instantly (*e.g.,* **just coming**) 3 barely; scarcely (*e.g.,* **just about, just missed, just in time, only just**) 4 only (*e.g.,* **just a little, just a minute**); *n* **justice** 1 fairness 2 administration of law **3** punishment for crime **4** judge; magistrate (*n* **j. of the peace**, *also* **JP**); *idm* **do justice to 1** treat fairly **2** show appreciation of the excellence of; *v* **justify 1** prove to be right; vindicate; exonerate *a* **justifiable** (*adv* **-ably**) **2** *printing* space letters to give lines of equal length; *a* **justified** (*n* **j. line**); *n* **justification**.

just-folks *a* unpretentious in manner or bearing.

just-in-time *n* JIT; manufacturing strategy when parts or products are produced or delivered as needed.

jut *v* **juts, jutting, jutted.** project; stick out.

jute *n* fiber of Indian plant, used for rope, canvas etc.

juvenile *a* young; suited to, characteristic of youth; *n* young person; youth; *ns* **j. delinquency** criminal activity by young person; **j. delinquent** such a person; *n* **- ility**.

juxtapose *v* put side by side; *n* **-position**.

A
B
C
D
E
F
G
H
I
J
K
L
M
N
O
P
Q
R
S
T
U
V
W
X
Y
Z

kabab *n* pieces of meat cooked on skewer.

Kabuki *n* Japanese traditional song-and-dance dram, with stylized costumes and plots.

kachina *n* **1** ancestral spirit of SW Native Americans (Hopi, other Pueble Indians) **2** masked impersonator or doll representing a kachina.

kaddish *n* Jewish prayer for mourning the death of a relative.

kaiser *n* German emperor; *n* **k. roll** crusty roll.

kale *n* cabbage with curly leaves, cole.

kaleidoscope *n* tube containing pieces of colored glass and reflectors, showing varying patterns, when tube is moved; *a* **-scopic** ever-changing.

kamikaze *n* (World War II) Japanese suicide pilot (*n* **k. attack**).

kanban *n* card used in manufacturing on assembly lines to indicate that parts or product is needed. *See* **just-in-time.**

kangaroo *n* Australian marsupial with powerful hindlegs; *n* **k. court** *sl* irregular, illegal court; *n* **k. rat** burrowing rodent with large mouth pouches found in estern and southwestern US.

kaolin *n* a powdery clay used in ceramics and medicine for treatment of diarrhea.

kapok *n* soft fiber from silk-cotton tree seeds, used to fill cushions, etc.

kaput *a sl* broken; dead.

karaoke *n* amateur impromptu singing with recorded music.

karate *n* Japanese martial art using hands and feet.

karma *n* fate; destiny; ethical causation.

karoo *n* area of dry flat land in southern Africa.

kart *n* small open motorized vehicle used in racing.

kasha *n* hulled grain from buckwheat.

kashruth *n* kosher, Jewish dietary laws.

katydid *n* large green grasshopper.

kayak *n* Eskimo canoe made of stretched sealskin.

kazoo *n* tubular musical instrument played by humming into a hole covered with a membrane.

kedgeree *n* dish of rice, fish, and chopped, boiled egg.

keel *n* ship's lowest longitudinal timber or plate, on which hull is built; *phr v* **keel over 1** capsize **2** fall over sideways.

keen[1] *a* having a sharp edge, enthusiastic, eager, perceptive.

keen[2] *n* lamenting, wailing cry, usually for a funeral or in grief; *v* wail over; lament.

keep *v* **keeps, keeping, kept. 1** hold; retain **2** preserve; maintain; look after; **3** do (specified action) continuously or repeatedly **4** detain; delay **5** fulfill (promise) **6** (of food) remain fresh; *idm* **keep one's cool/one's head** *coll* stay calm; *idm* **keep someone company** be a companion to someone; *phr vs* **keep back 1** retain **2** not tell about; **keep down** control; **keep in with** stay in favor with; **keep on** continue; **keep on** nag; *n*

1 castle tower; *idm* **for keeps** *coll* forever; *ns* **-er** guard; guardian; **-ing** care; charge; *idm* **in keeping with** consistent with.

keepsake *n* a memento, something given or saved for remembrance.

kefir *n* fermented drink made of cow's milk.

keg *n* small cask.

kelp *n* **1** large brown seaweed, source of iodine **2** source of iodine from kelpashes.

kelvin *n* unit of temperature; **K. scale** international temperature scale.

kempt *a* neat, tidy, well kept.

kennel *n* hut, shelter for dog; *fig* hovel; *pl* boarding, training establishment for dogs; *v* keep, put in kennel.

keno *n* lottery game like bingo with a set of five winning numbers.

Kentucky Derby *n* thoroughbred horserace held in Kentucky the first Saturday in May; the first of three horse races in the Triple Crown.

kept *pt, pp of* **keep.**

keralin *n* protein found in nails, claws etc.

kerchief *n* head covering; scarf.

kernel *n* inner, germinating part of nut, or fruit stone; *fig* essential, vital part.

kerosene *n* flammable oil distilled from petroleum, used for fuel, also as a paint thinner or solvent.

kestrel *n* small migratory falcon or hawk.

ketch *n* small two-masted sailing vessel.

ketchup *n* spicy sauce made from tomatoes, etc.(*also* **catsup, catchup).**

kettle *n* metal vessel with spout and handle, used for boiling water; *idm* **a fine kettle of fish** a messy, unpleasant situation.

kettledrum *n* cauldron-shaped brass or copper drum, having variable musical pitch.

Kewpie [TM] *n* a stylized small doll with a topknot, popular in US during the 1920s and 1930s.

key *n* **1** metal instrument to fasten/unfasten lock, to wind clockwork mechanism, etc. **2** lever, button on typewriter, musical instrument **3** clue; explanation **4** essential factor **5** roughness of prepared surface for repainting; **6** *mus* set of related notes (*n* **k. signature** written symbols indicating key); *idm* **in the same key 1** *mus* **2** (of speech) in similar style or tone; *idm* **in key** harmonizing; *idm* **out of key** discordant; *a* very important (*e.g.,* **k. figure, k. issue, k. speech**); *v* **1** *comput* type **2** prepare surface for painting; *phr vs* **key in** type in; **key up** make anxious (*a* **keyed up** excited); *ns* **keyboard** fingerboard of typewriter, piano,computer, etc. (*n* **k.**

skills ability to type); **keyhole; keynote 1** first note of musical key **2** dominant factor; **keystone** central wedge-shaped stone of arch.

keyhole surgery *n* surgery performed through a very small incision on the body.

kg *abbr* kilogram.

KGB *n* (formerly) Soviet secret police.

khaki *a* dull brownish yellow, earth colored; *n* military uniform.

khan *n* Asian ruler in medieval times.

Khmer *n* Cambodian aboriginal people.

kibbitzer *n infml* person offering unwanted advice.

kibble *v* grind coarsely; *n* animal feed made from coarsely ground grain.

kibbutz *n* Israeli collective farm settlement.

kibosh *n sl* nonsense; *idm* **put the kibosh on** put an end to.

kick *v* **1** strike out with foot **2** recoil **3** resist **4** *sl* give up (harmful habit); *idm* **kick one's heels** be idle; *idm* **kick someone upstairs** give someone an apparent promotion to make him/her less powerful in reality; *idm* **kick the bucket** die; *phr vs* **kick off** *coll* begin; **kick out** dismiss without ceremony; **kick out against** protest strongly about; **kick up** make trouble; *n* **1** act of kicking **2** recoil of gun or motorcycle)

3 *coll* force; *idm* **for kicks** *sl*
for a thrill; *idm* **get/give a
kick** *coll* get/give pleasure; *ns*
k.back *coll* money given for
favors; **k.off** start, *esp* of
football game; *n, v* **k. start**
(method used to) start a
motorcycle.

kid *n* 1 young goat; leather
made of its skin 2 *coll* child;
idm **handle with kid gloves**
deal gently with someone; *v*
kids, kidding, kidded. *sl*
tease; hoax.

kiddy *n* small child.

kiddush *n* Jewish blessing over
wine or bread.

kidnap *v* **kidnaps, kidnapping,
kidnapped.** take someone
away by force and demand a
ransom in exchange for
returning them; *n* **kidnapper;**
n **kidnapping.**

kidney *n* one of a pair of
glandular organs, secreting
urine; *fig* kind; class; *ns* **k.
bean** large red bean; **k.
machine** *med* apparatus to
save life of patient with
diseased kidneys; **k. stone**
calcified obstruction in the
kidneys.

kill *v* 1 cause to die 2 destroy;
neutralize; *idm* **kill time** find
way of making time pass
easily; *idm* **kill two birds
with one stone** take action
that serves two purposes
simultaneously; *n* 1 act of
killing 2 thing killed; *idm* **in
at the kill** present at climax
of struggle; *ns* **killer** (*n* **k.
whale**); **killing** (*idm* **make a**

killing have big success with
stocks and shares); *a coll* very
funny; *adv* **-ly**; *n* **killjoy**
person spoiling pleasure for
others.

kiln *n* furnace, oven.

kilo- *prefix* thousand, as in
kilobyte *comput* 1000 or 1024
bytes; *ns* **kilogram(me)** 1000
grams (*also* **kilo**); **kiloliter**
1000 liters; **kilometer** 1000
meters; **kilowatt** 1000 watts.

kilohertz *n* radio frequency of
1000 cycles per second.

kilt *n* short pleated skirt,
usually tartan; *v* tuck up
(skirt) in pleats; *a* **-ed.**

kilter *n* the usual state or
condition of something; *idm*
out of kilter not working.

kimono *n* loose wide-sleeved
Japanese robe, with sash;
dressing gown in this style.

kin *n* relatives; *a* related by
blood; *a fig* similar;
congenial; *ns* **-ship,
kinsman; -woman.**

kind[1] *n* type; sort; *idm* **a kind
of** *coll* used to express
uncertainty a sort of; *idm* **in
kind** (*of payment*) with goods
(not money); *adv* **kind of** *coll*
rather.

kind[2] *a* friendly; considerate to
others (*also* **kindly**) as
k.hearted (*adv* **-ly**, *n* **-ness**);
ns **kindness, kindliness;** *adv*
kindly; *idm* **take kindly to** be
pleased, willing to accept.

kindergarten *n* first year of
school.

kindle *v* set light to; *fig* excite,
stir up; *n* **kindling** small

sticks to start fire.

kindred *a, n* (people to whom
one is) related; *a* similar; *n* **k.
spirit** person with similar
interests, tastes, ideals.

kinematics *n* science of pure
motion; *a* **kinematic**.

kinescope *n* filmed television
recording

kinetics *n* science of motion in
relation to force; *a* **kinetic**.

king *n* 1 male ruler of nation;
monarch 2 card with picture
of king 3 piece in game of
chess; *a* **kingly** noble, royal;
n **kingdom 1** state ruled by
king; monarchy 2 domain,
sphere, *esp* of nature; heaven
or the next world; *ns* **k. cobra**
very large snake found in
southeast Asia; **k. crab** or
horseshoe crab large crab
found in North Pacific;
k.maker someone who has
influence over choices foe
political office; **k.pin 1**
swivel-pin 2 *fig* chief person;
king post main vertical
support for roof; *a* **k.-size**
extra large.

kingfisher *n* small brilliantly
colored fish-eating bird.

kink *n* twist, bend in rope,
hair, etc.; *fig* eccentricity; *v*
make, put kink in; *a* **kinky**
eccentric; perverted.

kinship *n* relationship.

kinsman *n* relative (*pl* **-men**);
fem **kinswoman** (*pl*
-women).

kiosk *n* open pavilion;
refreshment, newspaper or
other merchandise stall;

telephone booth.

kipper n **1** smoked, salted herring **2** salmon at spawning time; v cure fish by smoking, salting.

kirsch n cherry flavored brandy.

kismet n fate.

kiss v **1** caress with lips **2** *billiards* touch lightly; n act of kissing **3** a **k.-and-tell** *coll* (of story) creating scandal about well-known person and earning large sum of money; ns **k. of death** *coll* cause of certain disaster; **k. of life** form of artificial respiration by breathing into patient's mouth; v **kiss off** dismiss lightly.

kit n **1** small wooden tub **2** equipment **3** outfit; v provide with kit; n **-bag** bag for holding soldier's or traveler's belongings; *phr* v **kit out/up** equip.

kitchen n place where food is cooked; n **k. garden** vegetable garden; **kitchenette** small kitchen.

kite n **1** bird of prey **2** light framework covered with paper, flown in wind; ns **k. balloon** captive observation balloon.

kith and kin n family and relations.

kitsch n trash; inferior, pretentious art.

kitten n young cat; a **-ish** like kitten; playful.

kittiwake n kind of seagull.

kitty n pool of money in some gambling games; jointly held fund.

kiwi n flightless N Zealand bird; *sl* N Zealander.

kiwifruit n oval fruit with green flesh (*also* **Chinese gooseberry**).

Kleenex [TM] n soft paper handkerchief; *sing or pl.*

kleptomania n compulsive impulse to steal; n, a **-maniac**.

klezmer n traditional eastern European Jewish music.

klutz n *sl* idiot.

km *abbr* kilometer.

knack n aptitude; talent; habit; trick.

knapsack n bag carried on back, small rucksack.

knave n rogue; rascal; n **knavery** villainy; a **knavish**.

knead v squeeze and press with hands, *esp* to work bread dough; massage.

knee n **1** joint between upper and lower leg **2** part of trousers covering this; *idm* **bring someone to his/her knees** defeat, humiliate someone; v hit with the knee; *as* **k.-deep; k.-high; k.-jerk** automatic (**k.-jerk reaction**); ns **kneecap** flat bone protecting knee joint.

kneel v rest on knees; *pt, pp* **knelt;** n **kneeler** a cushioned board on which to kneel.

knell n sound of tolling bell; omen of doom.

knew *pt of* know.

knickerbocker n a resident of New York; *pl* loose baggy pants gathered at the knee, also known as knickers.

knickknack n ornament, trinket.

knife n cutting implement with blade set in handle; n **k.-edge 1** cutting edge **2** any sharp edge; *idm* **on a k.-edge** in a critical situation; v cut, stab with knife.

knight n one who receives nonhereditary honor, carrying title Sir; n **-hood;** v create (man) knight; a **-ly**.

knit v **knits, knitting, knitted** or **knit.** make fabric by fastening loops of wool, etc. together with needles (*pt, pp* **knitted**); draw close together, make compact (*pt, pp* **knit**); ns **knitter; knitting** knitted work (**k. needles**); **knitwear**.

knives *pl of* knife.

knob n **1** rounded handle, switch, button, etc. **2** small lump; **knobby** lumpy.

knock v **1** strike **2** collide with **2** *coll* criticize **4** (of car engine) make tapping noise; *phr vs* **knock about/around 1** loiter **2** batter (a **k.-about** boisterous); **knock back** drink quickly; **knock down** reduce (price); **knock off 1** finish work **2** *coll* subtract **3** *sl* steal **4** *sl* kill **5** *coll* finish quickly; **knock out 1** strike unconscious **2** eliminate (n **knockout 1** act of rendering unconscious [[n **k. blow**]] **2** contest in which players are gradually eliminated **3** *coll*

A B C D E F G H I J K L M N O P Q R S T U V W X Y Z

impressive or attractive person); **knock up** *sl* make pregnant; *n* **1** blow **2** tapping noise **3** *coll* slight misfortune; *ns* **-er 1** hinged bar for knocking on door **2** *coll* critic; **-ing;** *a* **k.-kneed.**

knockwurst *n* highly seasoned sausage.

knoll *n* small rounded hill, mound.

knot *n* **1** tightly tied loop of string, rope, etc. **2** *fig* difficulty **3** hard lump where branches joint trunk **4** unit of ship's speed **5** one nautical mile an hour; *ns* **knot garden** flowers or herbs arranged in elaborate designs; **k.hole** hole in tree trunk or a board where a branch or knot has come out; *v* **knots, knotting, knotted.** tie into, make knot; become entangled; *a* **knotty** full of knots; *fig* complicated.

knout *n* whip.

know *v* **1** be aware of, acquainted with **2** understand **3** be informed of **4** recognize; *pt* **knew;** *pp* **known;** *idm* **know apart** be able to distinguish; *idm* **know backward/back to front/inside out** know thoroughly; *idm* **in the know** wellinformed; *ns* **k.-how, k.-it-all;** *a* **knowing;** *adv* **-ly;** *n* **-ness;** *n* **knowledge 1** what is known **2** understanding **3** information; *a* **knowledgeable;** *adv* **-ably.**

knuckle *n* **1** bone at finger joint **2** knee-joint of veal,

pork, etc.; *v* clench hand, showing knuckles; *phr v* **knuckle under** submit; yield; *n* **brass knuckles** metal guard worn on knuckles to add force to blow.

KO *n coll* knockout.

koala *n* small tree-dwelling Australian marsupial with very sharp claws and dense gray fur. Feeds on eucalyptus leaves.

kohlrabi *n* type of cabbage.

Koi *n* Japanese carp raised for their ornamental value.

kola *n* bitter, stimulating extract from kola nut.

kookaburra *n* Australian kingfisher, larger than a crow, whose call sounds like laughter.

kooky *a coll* crazy; eccentric.

Koran *n* sacred book of Muslims.

Korean *a, n* (inhabitant, language) of Korea.

kosher *a* ceremonially fit, pure, clean, as laid down by Jewish law.

kowtow *n* act of bowing, humble situation; *v* bow to; *fig* be servile to.

kraal *n* **1** African fenced village **2** cattle enclosure.

kraut *n* sauerkraut.

Kremlin *n* **1** Russian citadel **2** (seat of) Russian government.

krill *n* tiny crustaceans, food for whales.

Krugerrand *n* S African gold coin.

krummhorn *n* double capped

reed Renaissance instrument.

krypton *n* inert, rare gaseous element, used in electric lights.

kudos *n sl* fame; credit.

kudzu *n* Asian leguminous vine used for erosion control; often found in invasive quantities in southers US.

kumquat *n* small citrus fruit shrub.

kung fu *n* Chinese martial art combining skills of judo and karate.

kvetch *v* to gripe, complain constantly.

kw *abbr* kilowatt.

lab *abbr* laboratory.

label *n* slip of paper, etc., attached to object giving information on it; *v* **labels, labeling, labeled. 1** attach label to **2** *fig* classify as.

labial *a* of lips; sound made by lips.

labile *a* changing; being receptive to change.

labor *n* **1** hard work; task **2** act of childbirth **3** body of workers; *v* **1** work hard; toil **2** (of ship) toss in heavy seas **3** perform with difficulty; *idm* **labor the point** emphasize something unnecessarily; *phr v* **labor under** suffer from; *ns* **-er** manual worker; *a* **-ed** slow; lacking in spontaneity; *a* **l.-intensive** using a lot of manpower; **l.saving** economical of effort; *a* **laborious**, industrious; wearisome.

laboratory *n* scientific establishment for research and experimentation.

Labor Day *n* national holiday (first monday in september) commemorating all worker.

labor-intensive *a* requiring great energy and time.

Labrador *n* large retriever dog.

laburnum *n* tree with pendulous yellow flowers.

labyrinth *n* maze; network of winding paths.

lace *n* **1** patterned netlike fabric **2** string, cord used as fastening, *esp* for shoes; *v* **1** fasten with laces **2** *coll* add liquor to (coffee, etc.); *a* **lacy.**

lacerate *v* tear; mangle; *fig* distress; *n* **laceration.**

lachrymal *a* of tears; *as* **lachrymatory**, causing flow of tears; *lachrymose*, tearful.

lack *n* deficiency; absence; need; *v* be short of; want; *a* **lacking** missing; *idm* **be lacking in** be devoid of, short of; *a* **lackluster** dull; lifeless.

lackadaisical *a* dreamy; affectedly languid.

lackey *n* servile follower.

lackluster *a* dull.

laconic *a* brief; using few words; terse; *adv* **-ally.**

lacquer *n* hard, glossy varnish; *v* paint with this.

lacrosse *n* ball game played with long-handled racquet, or crosse.

lactic, lacteal *a* of milk; *n* **lactation**, secreting of milk; period of suckling.

lactose *n* *chem* form of sugar found in milk.

lacuna *n* **1** gap; hiatus **2** empty space, *esp* in book **3** cavity (in bone or tissue).

lad *n* boy; young man.

ladder *n* climbing device of two poles joined by rungs.

lade *v* load; put cargo into; *pt, pp* **laden** or **laded**; *a* **laden** heavily loaded.

la-de-da *a* feigning refinement.

lading *n* cargo; freight.

ladle *n* long-handled, deep-bowled spoon; *v* serve with ladle.

lady *n* **1** woman of good social standing; **2** *coll* any woman **3** *cap* title of wives of knights, baronets, and peers below rank of duke **4** title of daughters of peers above rank of viscount; *prefix* feminine, female; *ns* **ladybug** small reddish beetle with black spot; **l.-in-waiting** lady's personal servant; **l.-killer** *coll* man who thinks women unable to resist his charm; **ladyship** title of lady; *a* **ladylike.**

ladyfinger *n* small, rectangular cake.

lady's slipper *n* type of N American orchid.

laetrile *n* drug derived from apricot pits, used as medically unproven remedy for cancer.

lag[1] *v* **lags, lagging, lagged.** loiter; walk, move slowly; *n* **laggard** loiterer.

lag[2] *v* wrap boiler, pipes, etc., to conserve heat; *n* lagging.

lager *n* light beer; glass of this.

laggard *n* person lagging behind.

lagoon *n* shallow salt-water channel, enclosed by reef, sandbank, or atoll.

laid *pt, pp of* **lay.**

laid-back *a coll* relaxed; lacking in sense of urgency.

lain *pp of* **lie.**

lair *n* den; resting place, *esp of* wild animals.

laissez-faire *n* policy of noninterference by government, allowing things to take natural course.

laity *n* laypersons.

lake[1] *n* large sheet of water enclosed by land.

lake[2] *n* reddish pigment.

lam *v sl* beat; flog; thrash; *n* **-ming;** *idm* **on the lam** running from the law.

lama *n* Buddhist priest in Tibet; *n* **lamasery** monastery of lamas.

lamb *n* **1** young sheep **2** its

meat **3** *fig* gentle, innocent child, person; *v* give birth to lamb; *a* **lamblike** gentle; *n* **lambkin** very young lamb; term of affection.

lambast(e) *v* attack violently.

lambda *n* 11th letter in Greek alphabet.

lambent *a* **1** twinkling; softly shining **2** *fig* light and witty.

lame *a* **1** disabled, *esp* feet and legs **2** *fig* unconvincing; *n* **l. duck 1** ineffectual person **2** *polit* official whose term of office is nearly over; *v* cripple; *n* **-ness.**

lamé *n Fr* fabric interwoven with metallic threads.

lament *v* bewail; mourn; feel, express deep grief; *n* expression of deep grief; dirge; **-ation;** *a* **-able** deplorable.

lamia *n* female vampire.

lamina *n* thin layer; *pl* **-nae, -nas.**

laminate *v* roll, beat into thin plates; cover with thin sheets (of metal, plastic, etc.); split into layers; *n* thin plate, layer.

lamp *n* any various devices for giving light or therapeutic rays; *ns* **l.black** pigment made from soot; **l.lighter** lighter of street lamp; **l.post** post supporting street lamp; **l. shade.**

lampoon *n* venomous, abusive personal satire; *v* satirize in lampoon.

lamprey *n* eellike fish, with sucker lips.

lanai *n* veranda.

lance *n* long, ceremonial cavalry spear; fish spear; *v* pierce, cut with lance or lancet; *ns* **l. corporal** NCO in army; **lancet** double-edged pointed surgical instrument; **lancer** mounted soldier armed with lance; *pl* kind of quadrille; *a* **lanceolate** lance-shaped.

land *n* **1** dry, solid surface of earth **2** country; nation **3** ground; area; estate; *v* **1** put on shore; disembark **2** set (aircraft) down; **3** catch (fish) **4** succeed in getting (job); *v* **land with** (*esp passive*) saddle with responsibility; *ns* **l.fall** coming to, in sight of land; *n* **l.fill** practice of burying waste in the ground; waste buried in this way; *n* **l.fill site** site where landfill is buried; **l.lady, l.lord** manager or owner of rented accommodation; **l.lubber** person unused to life at sea; **l.mark 1** feature of area easy to recognize and orient oneself by **2** important event; **l.mine** bomb hidden on or under the ground; **l.scape 1** scenery of area **2** picture of this (**l. gardening** planned layout of garden for scenic effect); **l.slide 1** sudden fall of earth, rocks **2** election win by vast majority (*n* **l. victory**); *as* **landed 1** owning land (*n* **l. gentry**) **2** consisting of land (*n* **l. property**); **l.locked** surrounded by land.

landing *n* **1** coming to dry land from air or sea (*ns* **l. craft** flat boat; **l. gear** aircraft undercarriage and wheels; **l. stage** platform for landing passengers or cargo) **2** level area at top of staircase.

lane *n* **1** narrow lane, street **2** regular route for shipping, aircraft **3** marked division on sports track or main road.

lang syne *n*, *adv* the past; in days long gone.

language *n* **1** speech **2** particular form of speech of nation, race, profession, etc. **3** any symbols, gestures expressing meaning; *ns* **l. barrier; l. laboratory** room with audio equipment for individual or group practice in language.

languish *v* become languid; pine; droop from misery, etc.; *a* **languid** weak; spiritless; *adv* **-ly**; *n* **languor** want of interest; lassitude; *a* **-ous**.

langur *n* long-tailed Asian monkey.

lank *a* limp; long and thin; lean; *a* **lanky**.

lanolin *n* refined wool grease.

lantern *n* transparent case for lamp, etc.; lamp room of lighthouse; structure on dome to admit light.

lanyard *n* **1** short cord (for securing whistle or knife) **2** short nautical rope.

lap[1] *n* **1** part between knees and waist of seated person

2 circuit of racetrack; *v* **laps, lapping, lapped. 1** enfold; surround **2** complete, or have lead of, one circuit of racetrack; *n* **l.dog 1** small pet dog **2** person subservient to another.

lap[2] *v* **1** drink by scooping up movement of tongue, as animal **2** splash softly; *phr v* **lap up** listen eagerly to.

lap[3] *n* circuit of racetrack (*n* **l. counter**).

laparoscopy *n med* internal examination of abdomen through narrow tube.

lapel *n* front part of coat folded back to shoulders.

lapidary *n* worker in gems; *a* meticulous in detail.

lapin *n* rabbit.

lapis lazuli *n* semiprecious bright blue stone.

Lapp *n* member of nomadic arctic tribe.

lapse *n* **1** fall; error **2** passing (of time, etc.); *v* fall away; cease to exist.

laptop *n* small personal computer.

larceny *n* stealing; theft.

larch *n* coniferous tree.

lard *n* refined, rendered pig fat; *v* **1** insert strips of fat in meat **2** enrich (style of speech) with; *a* **lardy**.

larder *n* storeroom for food.

large *a* great in size, number; roomy; copious; *idm* **at large** free; *idm* **by and large** in general; *adv* **largely** mainly. *n* **largess, largesse** liberality; gift; *a* **l.hearted** generous;

tolerant.

large intestine *n* part of digestive system consisting of cecum, colon, and rectum.

largo *adv mus* slowly and nobly; *n* such music.

lariat *n* long, noosed string or rope.

lark[1] *n* singing wild bird, skylark.

lark[2] *n* jest; sport; piece of fun; *v* play about; jest.

larva *n* caterpillar, wormlike stage of butterfly, fly, etc.; *pl* **-ae**; *as* **larval, larviform**.

larynx *n* back of throat, containing vocal chords; *n* **laryngitis** inflammation of the larynx.

lasagne *n It* flat rectangular layers of pasta cooked with layers of meat or vegetables, topped with cheese.

lascivious *a* lustful; wanton.

laser *n* device producing intense concentrated light beam; *ns* **l. beam; l. card** plastic card with printed data read by laser; **l. optics, l. technology**.

lash *v* **1** strike with whip **2** *fig* strike violently **3** *fig* scold fiercely **4** fasten, bind tightly; *n* **1** whip **2** eyelash.

lass *n* young girl.

lassitude *n* weariness; weakness.

lasso *n* **-os** or **-oes.** rope with noose; *v* catch with lasso.

last[1] *n* shoemaker's model of foot.

last[2] *a* **1** final **2** previous **3** only remaining; *idm* **have**

a b c d e f g h i j k l m n o p q r s t u v w x y z

A B C D E F G H I J K **L** M N O P Q R S T U V W X Y Z

the last laugh be triumphant in the end; *idm* **on one's/its last legs** nearly dead; worn out; *ns* **l. rites** religious rites for person about to die; **l. straw** problem making total situation beyond endurance; **L. Supper** final meal shared by Jesus and the disciples before his arrest; **l. word** 1 final remark 2 up-to-date example of something; *pron* 1 last person or thing 2 most recent person or thing; *a* **l.-ditch** as a final effort to avoid defeat.

last³ *v* 1 continue; endure 2 suffice (for); *a* **-ing**.

latch *n* fastening for doors and windows; spring lock; *v* fasten with latch; *phr vs* **latch on** *coll* understand; **latch onto** *coll* 1 associate closely with 2 grab the attention, seek out the company of; *n* **latchkey** key to house (**l. child** child whose parents are at work when he/she gets home from school; *pl* **-ren**).

late *a* behindhand; toward end; earlier than present; no longer living; *comp* **later**; *sup* **last, latest**; *adv* (*also* **lately**) recently.

latent *a* hidden; dormant.

lateral *a* at, from side *n* **l. thinking** ability to find original answers to problems by abandoning strictly logical methods, by seeing unusual mental connections; *adv* **-ly** sideways.

latex *n* white, milky juice,

secreted by plants, *esp* rubber tree; *a bot* **lactiferous** bearing latex.

lath *n* thin strip of wood or other material.

lathe *n* machine used in turning wood, metal.

lather *n* 1 froth of soap and water 2 (*of horse*) foamy sweat; *idm* **in a lather** nervously excited; *v* 1 form lather 2 *sl* beat.

Latin *a* of ancient Rome; of languages and races descended from this; *n* member of Latin race **L. America** countries of S and Central America where Spanish or Portuguese is spoken; *a* **-n**.

latitude *n* 1 *geog* distance north and south from equator 2 freedom from restriction; scope 3 *pl* regions; *a* **latitudinal**.

latitudinarian *a* tolerant, *esp* in religious matters.

latrine *n* privy, *esp* in camp, barracks.

latter *a*, *prom* later; second of two; *a* **l.-day** modern; *adv* **-ly** recently.

lattice *n* structure of crisscross laths or metal strips; window with glass crossed by lead strips; *a* **latticed**.

laud *v* praise; extol; *a* **-able** praise-worthy.

laugh *v* utter sounds expressing amusement, joy, scorn; *n* such sound; *as* **laughing**; *ns* **l. gas** nitrous oxide, mild anesthetic; **l. matter; l. stock**

object of ridicule; **laughable** ridiculous; *adv* **-ably**.

launch¹ *v* hurl; fling; initiate; set afloat; *fig* embark on; *phr vs* **launch into** begin boldly; **launch out at** attack physically, verbally; *ns* **-er**.

launch² *n* largest boat carried by warship; large power-driven pleasure boat.

launch pad, launching pad *n* platform for launching rockets.

launder *v* 1 wash and iron (clothes) 2 make source (of stolen money) untraceable by depositing abroad (*n* **-ing**); *ns* **laundress** washerwoman; **laundry** place where linens, etc., are washed; clothes sent there; **laundromat** place where washing machines and dryers can be used for payment of fee.

laureate *n* person crowned with laurels; person honored in a particular field.

laurel *n* evergreen, glossy-leaved shrub; *pl* its leaves; symbol of victory, fame.

lava *n* molten volcanic rock.

lavatory *n* room with sink and toilet.

lave *v* bathe.

lavender *n* shrub with fragrant pale mauve flowers.

lavish *a* profuse; extravagant; abundant; *v* bestow; spend recklessly.

law *n* 1 rule imposed by authority 2 jurisprudence

3 sequence of natural processes in nature **4** sequence of causes and effects; *as* **l.-abiding; lawful** (*adv* **-ly;** *n* **-ness**); **lawless** (*n* **-ness**); *ns* **l.man; l.breaker; l.suit** noncriminal case; **l.yer** attorney at law.

lawn[1] *n Fr* fine linen.

lawn[2] *n* stretch of close-mown grass; *ns* **l. mower, l. tennis** ball game played on grass or hard court.

lax *a* **1** loose **2** slack; careless **3** (*of bowels*) relaxed; *a, n* **-ative** having loosening effect on bowels; *ns* **-ity, -ness** slackness; lack of moral principles.

lay *v* **lays, laying, laid. 1** place horizontally; set in position **2** set out formally **3** deposit **4** produce (egg) **5** settle; *idm* **lay hold of** seize; *idm* **lay low** flatten; knock down; stay out of sight; *idm* **lay waste** devastate; *phr vs* **lay down 1** deposit **2** specify; **lay in** put in store; **lay into** attack; **lay off 1** cease to employ; **2** abandon; **lay on** provide; **lay it on** exaggerate; **lay out 1** set out; arrange (*n* **layout**) **2** knock unconscious; **lay up 1** keep in store **2** confine to bed; *n* act of laying; **layer 1** one of several thicknesses on a surface (*n* **l. cake**) **2** hen that lays eggs; **l. figure** artist's model of human figure; **layman/ -person/-woman** person not a professional expert, not a

priest; **l. reader** lay person entitled to conduct religious services apart from special sacraments.

lay *a* not clerical or professional; *n* ballad, poem; *fig* nonentity.

layaway *n* method of purchase in which item is reserved with down payment, followed by a series of payments.

layette *n* outfit of clothes, etc., for newborn child.

laying on of hands *n* faith healing.

lay of the land *idm* **1** nature, appearance of terrain **2** *fig* state of affairs.

layover *n* stopping point on plane trip, etc.

lazar *n* leper.

laze *v* be idle; rest onself; *a* **lazy** indolent; *n* **laziness.**

lazy Susan *n* circular condiment tray that revolves on table.

lb. *abbr* pound(s) (in weight).

LCD *abbr* liquid crystal display (method of showing figures when electric current through liquid).

LCM *abbr math* lowest common multiple.

LDL *abbr* low-density lipoprotein.

lea *n* meadow, open grassland.

leach *v* draw out by percolating liquid.

lead[1] *n* **1** heavy bluishwhite metal element **2** piece of this used for sounding depth of water; **3** graphite (**l. pencil**);

v cover, space with lead; *as* **leaded** containing lead; **leaden** heavy and dull; **l.- free.**

lead[2] *v* **leads, leading, led.** conduct; guide; act as chief; govern; be ahead; excel; *phr vs* **lead someone on** influence someone to believe or do something wrong; **lead up to** prepare for; *n* **1** guidance **2** extent of advantage in competition **3** first place **4** clue to mystery **5** *elec* wire connecting source of power to appliance; *ns* **l.- in** introduction; **l. time** *comm* time needed to complete; **leader** (**-ship**); *a* **leading** (*n* **l. question** question that implies the answer expected).

leading lady/man *n* actress/actor in film's starring role.

leaf *n* **1** one of lateral growths from plant stem; flat, expanded green organ of photosynthesis **2** thin sheet **3** two pages of book, etc. **4** movable flap of table, etc.; *pl* **leaves;** *phr v* **leaf through** turn the pages quickly; *ns* **leaflet** small printed sheet of paper; *n* **l. mold** compost of rotten leaves; *a* **leafy;** *n* **-iness.**

leaflet *n* **1** division of leaf **2** folded paper *usu* distributed for publicity purposes.

league[1] *n* compact, alliance for mutual protection, etc.; association, group of persons, clubs, etc., with common interest; *idm* **in league with** working in secret with; *v* form alliance, league.

league[2] *n ar* distance of miles.

leak *n* crack, hole through which liquid or gas passes; amount of liquid, gas that leaks; *v* **1** allow liquid, gas, etc., to pass slowly through crack **2** prematurely disclose (news, etc.); *n* **leakage** leaking; gradual escape or loss; *a* **leaky**.

lean[1] *a* thin; containing no fat; *fig* unproductive *n* nonfat part of meat.

lean[2] *v* **1** bend; incline; slope **2** rely on **3** prop against; *idm* **lean over backward** make every possible effort; *phr vs* **lean on** rely on; **lean toward** be in favor of; *n, a* **l.-to** structure built against a wall.

leap *v* spring; jump (*pt, pp* **leaped** *or* **leapt**); *phr v* **leap at** seize eagerly; *n* **1** act of leaping **2** sudden increase; *idm* **by leaps and bounds** very fast; *idm* **a leap in the dark** a risk taken blindly; *ns* **leapfrog** game where players leap over each other in turn (*v* **1** play this game **2** *fig* take turns to go in front); **l. year** year of 366 days occurring every fourth year.

learn *v* acquire knowledge, skill; commit to memory; be taught; find out; *pt, pp* **learned**; *a* **learned** well informed; erudite; *ns* **learner, learning** knowledge acquired

by study.

learning curve *n* curve that measures the increase of performance along with practice.

learning disabled *a* impaired because of learning disorder such as dislexia, etc.

lease *n* contract whereby land, property is rented for stated time by owner to tenant; *v* let, rent by lease; *n* **l.back** (system of) selling property and renting it back from new owner *a* **leasehold** held on lease.

leash *n* **1** chain or strap holding dog **2** set of three dogs so held **3** thong holding hawk; *v* hold by leash; **leash law** ordinance requiring dogs to be on leash outside owner's property.

least *det, pron* the smallest; *idm* **at least 1** not less than **2** in any case; whatever happens; *idm* **(not) in the least** (not) at all; *adv* in the smallest degree; *idm* **not least** especially; in particular.

leather *n* skin of animal prepared by tanning; *as* **leathern** of, like leather; **leathery** tough; *n* **l.back** world's largest sea turtle.

leatherette *a* fake leather.

leave *v* **1** allow, cause to remain **2** go away **3** deposit; *pt, pp* **left**; *phr vs* **leave off 1** cease **2** not wear; **leave out 1** omit **2** leave outside; *n* **1** permission **2** absence from work or duty; allowance of

time for this; *idm* **take leave of** say goodbye to (*n* **l.- taking**); *n* **leavings** leftovers.

leaven *n* **1** yeast **2** *fig* stimulating, spiritual influence; *v* **1** raise with yeast **2** influence.

leaves *pl of* **leaf**.

lecher *n* lustful, sensual person; *n* **-y** inordinate sexual indulgence; *a* **-ous**.

lectern *n* reading desk in church.

lecture *n* instructive discourse; admonishment; *v* deliver lecture; reprove *n* **l. hall, lecturer, lecturing** (*idm* **give someone a (good) lecturing** reprimand someone severely); **lectureship**.

led *pt, pp of* **lead**.

LED *abbr* light emitting diode (luminous semiconductor).

ledge *n* narrow shelf projecting from wall, cliff face, etc.

ledger *n* principal account book of business, etc; flat stone; *n* **l.-line** *mus* additional line above or below stave.

lee *n* side protected from wind; *a* **-ward** on lee side; *n* **-way** leeward drift of ship; *fig* loss of progress.

leech *n* blood-sucking worm; *fig* usurer.

leek *n* vegetable like onion.

leer *v* glance lustfully; slyly; *n* such a look.

leery *a coll* wary; suspicious.

lees *n pl* sediment of wine; dregs.

left[1] *pt, pp of* **leave**.

left² a **1** on the side of the body where the heart is **2** toward this side **3** polit tending to liberal or radical views; n **1** left side **2** polit left wing; as **l.-hand** situated on the left; **l.-handed** using left hand (n **l.-hander**); as **leftist; left-wing** polit.

leftover n **1** food saved from one meal and eaten at another time **2** any extra item or material.

lefty n coll left-handed person.

leg n **1** limb supporting body **2** part of trousers, jeans, etc., covering this **3** support for chair, table, bed, etc. **4** joint of meat **5** stage of journey, of relay race, etc.; idm **a leg up** a boost, helping hand; idm **not have a leg to stand on** have no possible excuse; ns **legroom; l. warmer** woolen garment covering lower part of leg; **legwork** coll work that entails a lot of walking; **leggy** having long legs.

legacy n gift, bequest by will; fig something handed down; n **legatee**.

legal a pertaining to law; lawful; ns **l. aid** subsidized legal representation; **l. tender** forms of money that must legally be accepted in payment; **l. pad** yellow ruled pad of paper, 8 ½ x 14 in.; adv **-ly;** n **legality;** n **legalistic;** v **-ize** make legal; n **-ization**.

legate n ambassador of pope.

legatee n person bequeathed a legacy.

legation n diplomatic body; chief of such body and his staff; his official residence.

legato adv mus smoothly, without breaks.

legend n **1** traditional story, myth **2** inscription, on map or medal; a **-ary** fabulous; mythical.

legerdemain n Fr conjuring trick; sleight of hand.

leggings n pl protective covering for legs.

leghorn n **1** plaited straw **2** breed of domestic fowl.

legible a easily read; adv **-ibly;** n **-ibility**.

legion n unit of ancient Roman infantry; body of troops; multitude; large organized group; a, n **legionary**.

legionnaire's disease n dangerous bacterial lung infection.

legislator n maker of laws; v **legislate** make laws; a **legislative;** n **legislature** legislative body.

legitimate a lawful; justifiable; born in wedlock; v make lawful; n **legitimacy** state of being legitimate; vs **legitimatize, legitimize** to legitimate.

Lego [TM] construction toy of studded, interlocking, colored, plastic bricks and other shapes.

leguminous a pod-bearing (pea, bean, etc); n **legume**.

lei n necklace of flowers.

leisure n freedom from work;

free, unoccupied time; as **-ly** unhurried, deliberate; **leisured** having much leisure.

leisure suit n informal version of suit, including shirt type of jacket.

leitmotif n mus recurring theme; fig recurrent association of ideas.

lemma n auxiliary proposition.

lemming n small, arctic, ratlike animal.

lemur n small, monkeylike animal.

lemon n very acid, pale yellow fruit; its color; ns **lemonade** drink flavored with lemon; **l.grass** tropical herb; **l. sole** flat fish.

lend v **1** grant temporary use of **2** lease out for hire or interest **3** impart; pt, pp **lent;** n **lender**.

length n **1** distance from end to end **2** quality of being long **3** duration in time; extent **4** long piece of something; idm **at length 1** at least **2** extensively; for a long time; idm **go to any/great lengths** be willing to undertake anything; v **lengthen** make longer; adv **lengthways/lengthwise;** a **lengthy;** adv **-thily;** n **-thiness**.

lenient a merciful; tolerant; not severe; ns **lenience, leniency**.

lenitive a, n soothing (drug).

lens n **1** curved disk of glass or transparent plastic that

a
b
c
d
e
f
g
h
i
j
k
l
m
n
o
p
q
r
s
t
u
v
w
x
y
z

magnifies (*e.g.*, **camera lens; contact lens**) 2 part of eye that does this; *n* **l. cap** cover for camera lens.

lent *pt, pp of* **lend**.

Lent *n* period of penance and fasting from Ash Wednesday to Easter; *a* **Lenten**.

lentic *a* relating to still water.

lentil *n* dried seed of leguminous food plant.

lento *a, adv* at slow pace, *esp* as musical direction.

Leo *n* **1** northern constellation **2** fifth sign of zodiac, represented as a lion.

leonine *a* like a lion.

leopard *n* large, spotted carnivore of cat tribe; *fem* **leopardess**.

leotard *n* close-fitting, stretchy garment worn by dancers.

leper *n* sufferer from leprosy; *n* **leprosy** infectious chronic skin disease, also affecting tissues and nerves; *a* **leprous**.

lepidoptera *n pl* insects with four scaly wings, including moths and butterflies.

leprechaun *n* Irish sprite.

lesbian *n, a* female homosexual; *n* **lesbianism** homosexuality between women.

lèse-majesté *n* Fr treason *also* **lese majesty**.

lesion *n* injury; morbid change affecting body functions.

less *a, adv* (*comp* of **little**) not so much; to a lesser degree, amount; *n* smaller amount, quantity; *prep* with deduction of; *v* **lessen** reduce; diminish.

lessee *n* one to whom lease is granted.

lessen *v* reduce.

lesser *a* **1** smaller **2** less important.

lesser celandine *n* N American herb with yellow flowers.

lesson *n* **1** anything learned or taught **2** warning example **3** portion of scripture read in church.

lessor *n* one who grants a lease.

lest *conj* for fear that.

let *v* **1** allow; permit **2** rent out (property); *pt, pp* **let**; *idm* **let alone** and definitely not; *idm* **let go** release; *idm* **let it all hang out** show true feelings; *idm* **let oneself go** behave in an uninhibited way; *idm* **let (someone) know** inform (someone); *phr vs* **let down 1** lower **2** deflate **3** disappoint (*n* **letdown**); **let someone in for** expose someone to (something unpleasant); **let someone in on** share (a secret) with someone; **let off 1** cause to explode **2** release **3** excuse (*n* **let-off**); **let on** tell (secret); **let out 1** reveal **2** utter **3** release **4** conclude (as in school session); **let up** become less intense (*n* **letup**); *n* **1** leasing of property; **2** *tennis* service touching net before landing in court; *n* **letting** renting out.

lethal *a* fatal; deadly.

lethargy *a* abnormal drowsiness; indifference; apathy; *a* **lethargic**.

letter *n* **1** written symbol expressing a sound of speech **2** written message **3** *pl* literary culture; literature; *v* mark with letters; *as* **-ed 1** having education **2** marked with letters; **letter-perfect** correct to the utmost degree; *ns* **l. bomb** bomb inside an envelope; **l.head** printed heading on stationery; stationery with this; **l.press** printing from type.

lettuce *n* plant used for salads.

leukocyte *n* white blood corpuscle.

leukotomy *n* lobotomy.

leukemia *n* malignant disease in which the body produces too many white blood cells.

levee *n* embankment protecting against floods.

level *a* horizontal; even; of same height; equable; *a* **l.-headed** sensible and calm; *n* **1** plane surface **2** usual height **3** moral, intellectual, social standard **4** horizontal passage in mine **5** instrument for testing horizontal plane; *idm* **on the level** honest; *v* **levels, leveling, leveled. 1** make flat **2** bring to same level **3** aim (gun); *phr vs* **level off/out** stop rising; **level with** *coll* speak frankly to; *n* **leveler** person seeking equality.

lever *n* rigid bar (usually

supported at fixed point)
that lifts or moves weight at
one end when power is
brought to bear on the other;
n **-age** action, power of lever;
v use lever.

leveret n young hare.

leviathan n **1** sea monster of
the Bible **2** something very
large or powerful.

Levi's [TM] n denims; blue
jeans.

levitation n power of raising
solid body into air by
nonphysical means; v
levitate cause to do this.

levity n frivolity; facetiousness;
lightness.

levy n **1** collection of tax; sum
thus collected **2** forced
military enlistment; v **levies,
levying, levied**. **1** impose
tax, etc. **2** conscript (troops).

lewd a indecent; obscene;
n **-ness**.

lexical a of words; adv **-ly**.

lexicon n dictionary; ns
lexicography art, process of
making dictionaries;
-grapher.

Lhasa apso n breed of small
dog with long, straight hair.

liable a answerable; legally
responsible; idm **liable to
1** subject to **2** inclined to; n
liability obligation.

liaison n **1** connection
2 cooperation **3** illicit sexual
relationship; v coll **liaise** act
as means of coordination
with; n **l. officer** officer who
acts as link between units,
etc.

liar n untruthful person.

lib abbr liberation.

libation n drink, offering to
gods.

libel n written, printed
statement likely to damage
person's reputation; v **libels,
libeling, libeled**. publish
libel; defame character; a
libelous defamatory; n **-ness**.

liberal a **1** generous **2** tolerant.

liberal arts n college study of
the arts, humanities, natural
and social sciences.

liberate v set free; ns **-ation,
-ator**.

libertarian a, n (person)
believing in freedom of ideas;
n **-ism**.

libertine n debauched,
dissolute man; a dissolute.

liberty n **1** freedom **2** offensive
act or remark; pl privileges,
rights conferred by grant.

libido n sexual desire; a
libidinous.

library n collection of books;
place where books are kept
or may be borrowed; n
librarian.

libretto n words of an opera or
a musical play; pl **libretti** or
-s.

lice pl of **louse**.

license n **1** permission granted
by authority; document
granting it **2** excessive
freedom; dissoluteness;
poetic l. deviation from rules
of his art by writer or artist; v
license grant license to; ns
licensee holder of license;
licentiate one authorized to

practice profession or art.

licentious a dissolute;
immoral.

lichen n flowerless, mosslike
plant growing on trees, rocks,
etc.; a **lichened**.

lick v **1** pass tongue over
2 flicker round **3** sl beat;
defeat; a act of licking; n
licking sl beating, thrashing.

licorice n black, very sweet
substance extracted from
root of plant of same name,
used in medicine and as
candy.

lid n movable cover; eyelid.

lie[1] v recline, be in resting
position; be situated, placed;
pt **lay**; pp **lain**; pr p **lying**; idm
lie low remain hidden; idm
take lying down accept
without protest; n
1 direction **2** way something
lies; phr vs **lie around** be idle;
lie behind be the real
explanation of; ns **lie-down**
siesta; **lie-in** stay in bed later
than usual.

lie[2] v make false statement; pt,
pp **lied**; pr p **lying**; n
deliberate untruth; n **l.
detector** device for
determining whether
someone is telling a lie; ns
white lie justifiable
falsehood; **liar** one who tells
lies.

lief adv glandly.

liege a bound to render feudal
service; n lord; sovereign; n
liegeman vassal, subject.

lien n leg right to hold property
of another until debt is paid.

A B C D E F G H I J K **L** M N O P Q R S T U V W X Y Z

lieu *n Fr* place; **in lieu** instead of.

lieutenant *n* deputy; rank below naval lieutenant commander or army captain.

life *n* 1 animate existence 2 duration of this (**l. imprisonment, l. sentence**) 3 class of living beings (**animal l.**) 4 biography 5 period of usefulness 6 way of living 7 vitality; *pl* **lives**; *idm* **come to life** 1 wake up 2 show enthusiasm; *idm* **take one's life** commit suicide; *idm* **take one's life in one's hands** take dangerous risk; *idm* **take someone's life** kill someone; *n* **l. blood** 1 blood essential for life 2 *fig* thing that gives vitality; **l.boat**; **l. buoy** floating ring for person fallen in water to hold onto; **l. cycle** whole course of development in a living creature; **lifer** *coll* prisoner with life sentence; **l. expectancy**; **l.guard** person employed to ensure safety of swimmers; **l. insurance**; **l. jacket** vest worn to save person from sinking in water; **l.line** 1 rope for saving people's lives 2 *fig* something that enables way of life, organization to survive; **l. preserver**; **l. science** biology, medicine, etc.; **l.pan** length of life; **l.-style**; **l.-support system**; **l.time**; *as* **lifeless** (*adv* **-ly**; *n* **-ness**); **lifelike** looking like the real thing; **lifelong**; **l.-size/-sized**.

lift *v* raise to higher position; take up; (of fog) disperse; *phr v* **lift off** *avia* leave the ground; (*n* **liftoff**); *n* that which lifts.

ligament *n* band of fibrous tissue connecting bones; connecting band; *n* **ligature** anything that binds; thread for tying severed artery; *ling* diphthong.

light[1] *a* 1 not heavy 2 loose 3 friable 4 mild 5 trivial; *adv* in light manner; *idm* **make light** of treat as unimportant; *adv* **-ly**; *n* **-ness**; **l.-headed** dizzy; unable to think clearly; **l.hearted** cheerful; **l.weight** 1 of less than average weight 2 frivolous in attitude (*n* such a person) 3 class in boxing; *v* **lighten**; *n* **-ing**.

light[2] *n* 1 form of energy, acting on optic nerve 2 making vision possible; brightness; source of this 3 knowledge 4 aspect; *idm* **bring/come to light** reveal/be revealed; *idm* **in light of** taking into consideration; *idm* **see the light** understand; *v* 1 set fire to 2 illuminate (*pt, pp* **lighted** *or* **lit**); *phr v* **light up** 1 make or become bright 2 light a cigarette; *ns* **l.bulb**; **lighthouse** tall building with warning light to ships; **l.ship** brightly lit ship moored in location treacherous to other ships; **l.-year** distance traveled by light in one year,

approximate six trillion miles (*idm* **light-years away** *coll* a very long way off); *a* 1 bright 2 pale (*e.g.,* **l. brown**); *v* **lighten** give light to; become brighter; *ns* **lighter** instrument for lighting; boat for unloading goods into; **lighting** system of illumination (**l. circuit**); **lightning** electrical discharge in atmosphere seen as flash in sky; *a* 1 of lightning (*n* **l. rod** wire on house wall for grounding lightning) 2 *fig* very rapid.

ligneous *a* like, made of wood; *n* **lignite** soft, woody brown coal.

like[1] *a* similar; *adv* in same way; *prep* in manner of; *a* **likely** probable (*n* **likelihood**); *a* **like-minded** of similar views; *v* **liken** compare, *n* **likeness** resemblance; portrait; *adv* **likewise** also, moreover.

like[2] *v* be fond of; be attached to; *a* **likeable** agreeable, attractive; *n* **liking**; *idm* **take a liking to** be attracted to.

lilac *n* flowering shrub; pale mauve color.

Lilliputian *a* diminutive.

lilt *v* sing sweetly with spirit; *n* well-marked beat or rhythm in music; swing; *a* **lilting**; *adv* **-ly**.

lily *n* bulbous flowering plant; *as* **l.-livered** cowardly; **l.-white** 1 pure white 2 morally pure.

lima bean *n* bland light green bean.

limb *n* **1** leg or arm; wing **2** bough of tree; *idm* **out on a limb** isolated and unsupported.

limber *a* pliable; supple; *phr v* **limber up** make supple by exercise.

limbo 1 *theology* condition, or region allotted to souls of unbaptized children **2** *fig* place for neglected and forgotten things **3** W Indian dance; *idm* **in limbo** in transition.

limburger *n* strong soft cheese.

lime[1] *n* calcium oxide obtained by burning limestone; sticky substance for catching birds, birdlime; *v* dress, mix, treat with lime; *ns* **limelight** bright white light; *fig* glare of publicity; **limestone** kind of rock, calcium carbonate.

lime[2] *n* kind of tree; its round acid fruit; *ns* **lime juice** sweetened juice of lime used as cordial; **limey** *sl* Briton.

lime[3] *n* linden tree.

limerick *n* nonsense verse of five lines.

limit *n* boundary; *idm* **be the limit** be intolerable; *idm* **off limits** on forbidden territory; *idm* **within limits** to a moderate degree; *as* **limited; limitless** (*adv* **-ly**; *n* **-ness**); *v* restrict; curb; *n* **-ation**; *as* **-able; -ed**.

limn *v lit* paint; depict.

limousine *n* large, closed type of car.

limp[1] *a* flaccid; not firm; *n* **-ness**.

limp[2] *v* walk lamely; *n* lameness.

limpet *n* rock-clinging marine shellfish.

limpid *a lit* clear; transparent; *n* **-ity**.

linchpin *n* metal pin holding wheel onto axle.

linden *n* lime tree with yellow flowers and spade-shaped leaves.

line *n* **1** string; cord **2** very thin threadlike mark, made by pen, etc. **3** wrinkle **4** row **5** people one behind another, *usu* waiting for something **6** mode of action **7** organized system of transportation by road, air, etc. **8** occupation; hobby **9** lineage **10** type of goods **11** channel of telecommunication; *idm* **in line for** eligible for; *v* **1** mark with lines **2** insert lining **3** bring into line; *ns* **lineage** descent; pedigree; *ns* **1. judge** tennis person deciding whether ball has landed in court; **lineament** feature; **lineman** person repairing telephone wires or railroad lines; **1. printer** computer printer; **linesman** sport person who decides if ball has gone out of play; **l.-up 1** people side-by-side standing in line for police identification **2** *sport* all those competing in an event **3** *sport* order of events

planned; **lining** material used to cover inner surface; *a* **linear** of, in lines.

lineal *a* **1** in direct line of descent **2** linear.

linen *n* cloth made of flax; underclothes, bed linens, tablecloths, etc.; *a* made of linen.

liner *n* **1** large passenger ship **2** thing used for lining something (*e.g.*, **garbage can liner**) **3** thing used for making line (*e.g.*, **eyeliner**).

linger *v* **1** delay; loiter **2** be slow to disappear.

lingerie *n* women's underwear.

lingo *n* language or jargon, *esp* foreign.

lingua franca *n* language of communication for people of different nationalities.

lingual *a* **1** of the tongue **2** of languages.

linguini *n* thin, flat pasta in strips.

linguist *n* expert in a language or languages; *a* **-ic**; *adv* **-ically**; *ns* **linguistics** study of nature of language and language acquisition.

liniment *n* embrocation.

link *n* **1** loop, ring of chain **2** unit in communication system **3** connection; *v* join together, as with link; connect; *ns* **linkage**.

links *n* golf course.

linnet *n* songbird of finch family.

linoleum *n* type of floor covering; *n* **linocut** relief engraving on linoleum; print made from this.

A
B
C
D
E
F
G
H
I
J
K
L
M
N
O
P
Q
R
S
T
U
V
W
X
Y
Z

Linotype n [TM] typesetting machine that casts whole line in one piece.

linseed n flaxseed.

lint n 1 soft material for dressing wounds 2 fuzz from yarn, etc.

lintel n horizontal stone or timber bar over doorway or window.

lion n large, powerful carnivore of cat tribe; *fig* celebrity; *fem* **lioness**; *idm* **lion's share** majority; *v* **lionize** treat as celebrity.

lip n 1 one of fleshy flaps of tissue around mouth 2 edge; rim; 3 *coll* impertinence; *idm* **pay lip service to** show support in words but not in deed; *v* **lip-read** decipher speech when deaf by watching speaker's lip movements (*ns* **-er, -ing**); *n* **lipstick** make-up for lips.

lipid n waxy substance in living cells.

liposuction n surgical removal of excess fat from under skin.

liqueur n strong, sweetened, flavored alcoholic liquor.

liquid n substance between solid and gas, fluid; *a* 1 (of sounds) harmonious 2 flowing smoothly; fluid 3 easy to realize as money (*ns* **1. assets, liquidity**); *v* **liquefy** become, make liquid; melt; *n* **liquefaction;** *a* **liquescent**.

liquidate *v* 1 pay (debt) 2 wind up financial affairs and dissolve company 3 *coll*

kill; *ns* **-ation; -ator** official appointed to liquidate business.

liquor n liquid substance, *esp* alcoholic.

lira n unit of currency in Italy and Turkey.

lisle n fine cotton thread or fabric.

lisp *v* speak with imperfect pronunciation of sibilants; *n* speech defect with this tendency.

list n roll, catalog of names, words, etc.; inventory; *v* make, write list.

list n inclination, leaning (of ship, etc.) toward one side; *v* slope; lean.

listeria n bacteria causing food poisoning.

listless *a* languid; apathetic.

listen *v* attend closely so as to hear; *idm* **listen in** 1 listen to radio 2 eavesdrop; *n* **-er.**

litany n prayer with responses from congregation.

liter n metric unit of capacity (about 1 ¼ pints).

literal *a* 1 of letters 2 based on exact words of original; accurate; word for word; *adv* **literally** *coll* absolutely.

literary *a* concerned with literature or writers.

literate *a* educated, able to read and write; *n* educated person; *n* **literacy** ability to read and write.

literati n *pl fml* experts on literature.

literature n writings of country or period; written works on

any subject; *coll* any book or printed matter; *a* **literary** of, learned in literature.

lithe *a* supple; flexible; pliant; *n* **litheness**.

lithium n light metal.

lithography n art of printing copies from designs on prepared stone or metal plates; *ns* **-graph** print so made; **-grapher;** *a* **-graphic.**

litigate *v* contest at law; make subject of lawsuit; *ns* **litigant, litigation;** *a* **litigious** fond of litigation.

litmus n vegetable substance turned red by acids and blue by alkalis; *n* **l. paper.**

litmus test *fig* use of single issue or factor as basis for judgment.

litter n 1 scattered bits of garbage 2 portable couch, stretcher 3 all young born at one time 4 straw, etc., as bedding for animals; *v* 1 make untidy with litter 2 give birth to.

little *a* small; brief; *n* small amount; *adv* slightly.

littoral *a* pertaining to seashore; *n* coastal region.

liturgy n prescribed public worship; *a* **-ical.**

live[1] *v* exist; dwell; subsist; pass one's life; *n* **living** 1 way of life 2 livelihood; maintenance 3 church benefice; *idm* **live it up** have a good time; *phr vs* **live down** bring people to forget (one's errors, misdemeanors, etc.); **live together** live as if married; **live up to** be worthy of; *a* **1** living **2** carrying electric current .

live[2] *a* having life; vital; flaming, glowing; *n* **1. wire 1** wire carrying electric current **2** *coll* lively person **3** not prerecorded (*n* **l. broadcasting**); *a* **lively** (*n* **-iness**); *v* **liven** (**up**) make more lively.

livelong *a* lasting throughout the day.

liver *n* organ secreting bile; *a* **liverish 1** of liver **2** irritable; touchy; *n* **-ness**.

liverwurst *n* liver sausage.

livery *n* **1** uniform of servants **2** food allowance for horses; **3** keeping of horses for hire; **l. stable** one where horses are boarded or hired out.

lives *pl of* **life**.

livestock *n* farm animals.

livid *a* of bluish pale color, as by bruising; *sl* very angry.

living *a* **1** alive **2** active; in use (*e.g.*, **l. language**); *ns* **l. death** terrifying experience; **l. room** main room of house; *n* **living will** document asking that no extraordinary measures betaken to prolong the signer's life in case of terminal illness; *n* **1** livelihood **2** way of life **3** position of clergyman; his income.

lizard *n* four-footed reptile.

llama *n* woolly S American ruminant.

load *n* that which is carried; burden; *elec* amount of energy drawn from source; *v* place burden on, in; charge (gun).

loaf[1] *n* mass of bread of definite size, weight; *pl* **loaves**.

loaf[2] *v* loiter; work lazily; *n* **loafer** lazy person.

Loafer [TM] slip-on casual shoe.

loam *n* rich vegetable soil.

loan *n* something lent; act of lending; money lent; *v* lend.

loath, loth *a* unwilling; *v* **loathe** detest; abhor; *n* **loathing** great disgust, repulsion; *a* **loathsome** disgusting, revolting.

loaves *pl of* **loaf**.

lob *n* high-pitched underhand ball in cricket; high ball in tennis; *v* **lobs, lobbing, lobbed.** bowl, hit shot thus.

lobby *n* hall; anteroom; *v* **lobbies, lobbying, lobbied.** try to influence legislator (to favor particular group, interests, etc.); *n* **-ing** frequent lobby for such purpose; *n* **lobbyist**.

lobe *n* soft, pendulous lower part of ear; rounded projecting part of liver, etc.; *a* **lobed**.

lobelia *n* herbaceous plant.

lobotomy *n med* operation to remove brain tissue.

lobster *n* large, edible, marine crustacean.

lobworm *n* large worm used as fish bait.

local *a* of, in, confined to particular place, region, part of body; *n* person belonging to district; *ns* **locale** scene of event; **locality** position, district; *v* **localize** restrict to particular area; give local character to.

locate *v* discover, set in, particular place or position; *n* **location** position; outdoor set where scenes for film are shot.

loch *n* Scottish lake or arm of sea.

lock[1] *n* tress of hair; tuft of wool.

lock[2] *n* **1** device for closing door, safe, etc., operated by key, combination **2** mechanism for firing gun **3** blockage **4** enclosure on river, canal in which boats can be moved from one level to another; *idm* **lock, stock, and barrel** altogether; *v* **1** close with a lock **2** become fixed, immobile; *phr vs* **lock onto** (of missile) locate and pursue automatically; *n* **locker** lockable small closet (*n* **l. room** changing room); *ns* **l.jaw** tetanus; **l.nut** nut that prevents another from being unscrewed easily; **l.smith** maker, repairer of locks; **l. up** jail where prisoner awaits trial.

locket *n* small metal case for photograph, etc., worn as ornament.

loco *a sl* crazy.

locomotive *a* having power of moving from place to place; *n* steam, diesel, electric engine moving by its own power; n **locomotion** action, power of moving.

locum (tenens) n *Lat* one acting temporarily as deputy, *esp* of doctor or priest.

locus n 1 exact place 2 *math* line tracing path of point through space.

locust n destructive winged insect; n **l. tree** carob tree; **l. bean** its fruit.

locution n mode, style of speech; phrase.

lode n vein of metal ore; **lodestone** n magnet; magnetic iron oxide.

lodge n 1 gatekeeper's house 2 local branch, meeting place of organization v 1 house 2 deposit 3 be embedded 4 lay (accusation, charge against) 5 occupy lodgings; ns **lodging (s)** room(s) rented to lodger; **lodger** one who pays rent for part of another's house; **lodg(e)ment** lodging place; *mil* stable position gained by effort.

loft n attic; room over stable; gallery in church; v hit golf ball high; a **lofty** of great height; *fig* noble; sublime; haughty; adv **-ily**.

log n 1 unhewn piece of timber 2 apparatus for measuring ship's speed 3 daily record of ship's voyage, aircraft flight, etc.; 4 *abbr* logarithm; v **logs, logging, logged.** cut into logs; enter in logbook; *phr v*

log off/out *comput* finish on-line operation; ns **logging** felling, sawing, transporting logs to river; **logger; logbook** daily record of journey;

logjam 1 immovable mass of floating logs 2 *fig* standstill in operations.

loganberry n hybrid fruit, cross between blackberry and raspberry.

logarithm n exponent of power to which invariable number must be raised to produce given number, tabulated for use in calculation.

loggerhead n blockhead; *idm* **at loggerheads** quarrelsome.

logic n art of reasoning; a **-al** of logic; consistent; rational; n **logician**.

logistics n *pl* 1 science of moving and supplying troops 2 skill in maneuvering.

logo n **-os.** design used in emblem for an organization (*also* **logotype**).

logy a heavy; dull.

loin n (meat from) part of body between ribs and hip; n **loincloth** cloth worn to cover this part.

loiter v linger; loaf; delay; n **loiterer**.

loll v 1 sit, lie lazily 2 hang out tongue.

lollipop n 1 hard candy on a stick 2 short piece of popular classical music.

lone a solitary; isolated; a **-ly** feel conscious of solitude; unfrequented; n **-liness**; a **-some**.

loner n *coll* person who does not mix well with other people or who prefers to be alone.

long a having length; protracted; (of series, list, etc.) having many items; ns **l.hand** written script, not typed (*also* adv); **l.johns** long underwear; **l. jump** athletic jumping contest; **l.shoreman** docker; **l. shot** risky attempt; **l. wave** radio using range over 1000m; adv for a long time; *idm* **as/so long as** provided that; *idm* **no longer** no more; as **l.-drawn-out** lengthy; tedious; **l.-life** usable for longer than normal; **l.-range 1** (of forecast) looking far ahead 2 able to reach far away; **l.-standing** existing for a long time already; **l.-suffering** enduring patiently; **l. term** lasting for a long time; **l.-winded** needlessly wordy and boring.

long v desire earnestly; *phr v* **long for** want very much; n **longing** strong desire; a showing such desire; adv **-ly**; yearning; be.

longevity n long life.

longitude n distance in degrees, east or west from given meridian; a **-tudinal** of longitude; lengthwise.

long shot n 1 horse, team etc., with little chance of winning a contest 2 undertaking with little chance of success.

long-winded a speaking at

great length.

loofah *n* fibrous part of tropical gourd, used as sponge.

look *v* 1 use eyes 2 seem to be 3 gaze, stare; *idm* **look as if** seem likely that (*also coll* **look like**); *phr vs* **look after** take care of; **look down on** despise; **look forward to; look into** investigate; **look out** 1 beware 2 search and find among one's belongings *n* **lookout** 1 prospect 2 sentry 3 (bad) luck; **look to** rely on; **look up** 1 raise one's eyes 2 find and visit 3 find by consulting book; **look up to** admire; *n* 1 act of looking; glance 2 facial expression 3 appearance; *pl* **-s** person's appearance; attractiveness; *ns* **l.-alike** one of almost identical appearance; **looker** *coll* attractive female; **looking glass** mirror.

loom[1] *n* weaving apparatus or machine.

loom[2] *v* emerge indistinctly; *fig* appear important and menacing.

loon *n* 1 lout; fool 2 diving bird.

loony *a, n coll* insane (person); *n* **l. bin** *coll* mental hospital.

loop *n* 1 bend in cord, string, etc., made by crossing ends 2 noose 3 railway line branching from main line and rejoining it farther on; *v* form loop; *n* **l. the l.** aerial maneuver in which aircraft describes complete vertical

circle.

loophole *n* 1 means of evasion, or escape 2 small opening in wall, etc.

loose *a* 1 not tied; free from control 2 detached; unattached 3 not constricting; slack 4 vague 5 not compact 6 dissolute; of lax morals 7 having diarrhea; *idm* **at loose ends** with nothing to do; *idm* **tie up the loose ends** complete the last little details; *a* **l.-leaf** having separate sheets of paper (**l.-leaf binder**); *adv* **-ly;** *n* **-ness;** *v* **loosen;** *n* **-ing.**

loot *n, v* plunder.

lop *v* **lops, lopping, lopped.** trim, shorten by chopping (branches, etc.).

lop *v* hang limply; *n* **lop-ear** drooping ear; rabbit with such ears; *a* **lopsided** unevenly balanced.

lope *v* run with long, easy, bounding pace.

loquacious *a* talkative; *n* **loquacity.**

lord *n* 1 ruler; governor; master; owner 2 any peer of realm 3 *cap* God; *idm* **lord it over** dominate; *a* **lordly** magnificent; haughty; *ns* **lordliness, lordship** power of lord; domain; title of peers.

lore *n* knowledge of special kind, often derived from tradition.

lorgnette *n Fr* eyeglasses on handle, opera glass.

loris *n* type of nocturnal lemur.

lose *v* 1 suffer loss 2 get rid of

3 fail to retain, find 4 be bereaved of 5 be defeated; *pt, pp* **lost;** *phr v* **lose out** be at a disadvantage; *n* **loser;** *a* **losing** (*n* **l. battle** struggle one has no chance of winning; **l. streak** sequence of bad luck); *n* **loss** 1 act, result of losing 2 bereavement; *idm* **at a loss** (for words) unable to think of anything to do or say; *idm* **lose one's heart** fall in love; **lose heart** become discouraged.

lost *pt, pp of* **lose;** *n* **l. cause** campaign doomed to failure; **l. property.**

lot *n* 1 quantity 2 fate 3 item of auction; *idm* **a lot** a large quantity; *idm* **one's lot** 1 one's fate 2 *coll* all one is entitled to; *idm* **the lot** all; *idm* **lots of** a large quantity or number of; *idm* **cast/draw lots** decide fate or fortune by chance fall of diee or similar marked object.

lothario *n* seducer of women.

lotion *n* liquid for keeping skin, hair clean, healthy.

lottery *n* gamble; competition in which prizes are allotted by chance drawing of tickets.

lotto *n* game of chance, played as bingo.

lotus *n* kind of water lily.

lotusland *n* utopian places reachable through self-indulgence.

loud *a* 1 producing much sound; noisy 2 boisterous; vulgar; **loudmouth** *coll*

A
B
C
D
E
F
G
H
I
J
K
L
M
N
O
P
Q
R
S
T
U
V
W
X
Y
Z

person who talks too much and without tact; **loudspeaker** equipment that amplifies volume of sound on radio or recording system; *advs* **loud, aloud, loudly;** *n* **-ness**

lounge *v* recline lazily; be idle; *n* **1** room with comfortable seats for guests in home or hotel **2** long couch; *n* **lounger** idler, loafer.

loupe *n* small magnifying glass, used in jewelry profession.

louse *n* parasitic insect; *pl* **lice;** *a* **lousy** having lice; *sl* unpleasant; bad; *idm* **lousy with** *coll* full of; having plenty of.

lout *n* clumsy, mannerless fellow; *a* **loutish.**

louver, louvre *n* window frame with inclined boards or slats for admitting air without rain; ventilating structure resembling this.

love *n* **1** affection **2** charity **3** devotion **4** sexual passion **5** sweetheart **6** *tennis* no score; (formerly) woo with words; *ns* **l. affair; l.bird 1** small green parrot (*pl* **-s** *coll* loving couple); **l. match** marriage of people in love; *v* **1** be fond of; delight in **2** desire passionately, sexually **3** show deep and lasting devotion to; **lover of** enthusiast for; *as* **lovable** (*adv* **-ably;** *n* **-ability; -ableness**); **lovely** (*n* **-iness**); **lovesick** hopelessly in love; *a, n* **loving** (*n* **l. cup** wine

cup passed round and shared at banquet).

loveseat *n* couch or seat that holds only two people.

low[1] *a* **1** not high or tall **2** not intense **3** humble **4** not loud **5** vulgar; mean; sordid **6** depressed **7** inferior in order of merit or importance; *idm* **keep a low profile** contrive not to be conspicuous; *n* **1** low point **2** depression; *ns* **lowdown** *sl* vital information; **lowlands; l. season** less busy part of year; *as* **lowbrow** simple not developed intellectually or aesthetically (*n* such a person); **l.-down** *coll* mean; **l.-key** subdued; **l.-rise; l.- spirited;** *a* **lower 1** less high **2** inferior (*a* **l.-case** not in capitals; *n* **l. class** *a* **l.-class**); *v* **1** make less high **2** bring down **3** reduce; *idm* **lower oneself** humble or disgrace oneself; *a* **lowly;** *n* **-iness.**

low[2] *n* cry of a cow; *v* utter a sound.

low beam *n* short-distance focus of car headlight.

lowboy *n* chest of drawers or dining room sideboard standing only about three feet high.

lowbrow *a* uneducated.

lower *v* be, look threatening (*also* **lour**).

lox *n* salmon cured in brine.

loyal *a* faithful to a cause, person, etc.; upright; honorable; *ns* **loyalty, loyalist.**

lozenge *n* **1** diamond-shaped figure; rhombus **2** small, flat, medicinal tablet.

LP *abbr* long-playing record.

LSD *abbr* lysergic acid diethylamide (dangerous hallucinatory drug) (*also sl* **acid**).

lt. *abbr* lieutenant.

ltd. *abbr* limited.

lubber *n* clumpsy person.

lubricate *n* make slippery, smooth with oil, grease; *ns* **lubrication, lubricant** substance used to reduce friction; **lubricator, lubricity** smoothness.

lucent *a* shining; bright; clear.

lucerne *n* cloverlike plant, used as fodder.

lucid *a* clear; easy to understand; clearheaded; *ns* **lucidity, lucidness.**

luck *n* **1** fate; chance **2** good fortune; *a* **lucky** fortunate; **l. strike** piece of good luck; *adv* **luckily;** *a* **luckless.**

lucrative *a* profitable.

lucre *n* gain, money.

lucubrate *v* work hard, study, *esp* at night; *n* **lucubration** learned writing.

luddite *n* person opposed to new methods or technology.

ludicrous *a* absurd; ridiculous; comical.

lug[1] *n* earlike projection used as handle; *v* **lugs, lugging, lugged.** pull, drag with effort.

lug[2] *n* common worm used as fish bait.

luge *n* small racing sled and the sport; *v* race on a luge.

luggage *n* baggage, trunks, suitcases, etc.

lugubrious *a* mournful woebegone; funereal.

lukewarm *a* tepid; *fig* lacking enthusiasm.

lull *v* 1 soothe; make quiet 2 subside; *n* temporary pause; *n* **lullaby** cradle song; soothing sound.

lumbar *a* of, near loins; *n* **lumbago** rheumatic pain in loins or lower part of spine.

lumber *v* 1 move clumsily, heavily 2 encumber; obstruct; *n* 1 useless odds and ends 2 sawn timber; *n* **l. jack** man who fells and prepares timber for sawmill.

luminary *n* light-giving body, *esp* heavenly; *fig* distinguished, learned person; *n* **luminescence** light emitted at low temperature; *a* **luminous** 1 bright; glowing 2 *fig* clear; *n* **luminosity**.

lump *n* 1 shapeless mass 2 swelling bump; *idm* **lump in the throat** choking sensation caused by strong emotion; *v* throw together in one mass; *idm* **lump it** *sl* put up with it; tolerate, endure it; *phr v* **lump together** treat as one; *n* **l. sum** single amount; *a* **lumpy** *n* **-iness**.

lunar *a* of, relating to moon.

lunatic *a* insane; *n* insane person; *n* **l. fringe** members of (*esp* political) group with eccentric ideas; *n* **lunacy**.

lunch *n* midday meal (*also* luncheon); *ns* **l. meat** cooked preserved meat, *usu* served cold; *v* have lunch.

luncheonette *n* restaurant serving quick, simple food.

lung *n* respiratory organ in vertebrates.

lunge *n* sudden thrust, blow made with weapon; sudden movement of body; plunge; *v* make lunge.

lupin *n* garden plant with long spikes of flowers.

lupine *a* like a wolf.

lupus *n* tuberculous skin disease.

lurch *v* pitch, roll to one side; *n* sudden stagger; *idm* **leave in the lurch** leave in difficult situation.

lure *n* bait used to recall hawk; decoy; *fig* anything that entices; *v* recall (hawk); attract.

lurid *a* 1 ghastly; sensational; crude 2 glaring.

lurk *v* remain hidden; lie in wait.

luscious *a* delicious; excessively sweet.

lush *a* (of grass, etc.) juicy; luxuriant.

lust *n* sexual appetite; *idm* **lust for** feel excessive desire for; *as* **lustful, lusty** vigorous, powerful.

luster *n* 1 gloss; sheen 2 *fig* renown; glory; *a* **lustrous** shining, luminous.

lustration *n* purificatory, expiatory ceremony.

lute *n* stringed musical instrument; *n* **lutanist**.

luxury *n* 1 state, mode of life of great ease and comfort 2 expensive but unnecessary thing; or *a* **luxurious** extravagant; sumptuous; *v* **luxuriate** indulge in luxury; revel in; grow profusely; *a* **luxuriant** abundant; exuberant (*n* **-ance**).

lyceum *n* building with lecture halls, library, etc.

lychee *n* Asiatic fruit with sweet white flesh (*also* **litchi**).

lych-gate *n* gate with roof.

Lycra [TM] stretch material used for making tight-fitting clothes.

lying *v pr p* of **lie**[1], **lie**[2].

lying-in *n* confinement to bed for childbirth.

lymph *n* colorless fluid found in lymphatic vessels; fluid exuding from inflamed tissues; *n pl* vessels in body conveying lymph; *a* **lymphatic** of lymph; *fig* sluggish.

lynch *v* put to death, by mob violence, without trial; *n* **l. law** rapid, summary justice.

lynx *n* fierce wildcat with short tail and tufted ears; *a* **l.-eyed** keen-sighted.

lyre *n* old form of harp.

lyric *n* 1 words for song 2 short emotional poem; *a* **lyric(al)** of poems expressing emotion *adv* **-ly**, *n* **-ism**.

a
b
c
d
e
f
g
h
i
j
k
l
m
n
o
p
q
r
s
t
u
v
w
x
y
z

A B C D E F G H I J K L **M** N O P Q R S T U V W X Y Z

MA *abbr* Master of Arts.

ma *n infml* mother.

ma'am *polite form of address to a woman* (=madam).

macabre *a* gruesome; terrible.

macadam *n* broken stone for road surfacing; *v* pave road with this.

macadamia nut *n* filbertlike nut grown in Hawaii.

macaroni *n* semolina pasta in the shape of slender tubes.

macaroon *n* small sweet cake or cookie made of ground almonds or coconut.

macaw *n* kind of parrot.

mace[1] *n* spice made of dried outer layer of nutmeg.

mace[2] *n* a heavy, often spiked, staff or club used in the Middle Ages.

macerate *v* soften by soaking; become thin through fasting.

Mach *n* ratio of speed of aircraft, etc., to speed of sound.

machete *n Sp* large, heavy chopping knife.

Machiavellian *a* wily.

machine *n* **1** apparatus, contrivance that applies power to perform work, or direct movement **2** organized system to carry out specific functions; *v* print, sew with machine; *ns* **m. gun** gun firing bullets in continuous succession; **m. shop** workshop where product is made to size and assembled for distribution; **m.tool** tool that cuts, shapes: *as* **m.-made; m.-readable** that can be read by a computer; *ns* **machinery** parts of machine; system of machines; **machinist** person who makes, operates machines.

macho *a coll* exaggeratedly masculine; *n* **machismo** quality of being macho.

mackerel *n* type of edible but bony sea-fish.

mackinaw *n* short, heavy woolen coat.

mackintosh, macintosh *n* rubber-coated cloth; raincoat.

macramé *n Fr* craftwork from knotted string.

macro- *prefix* **1** big, prominent **2** large-scale.

macrobiotic *n* restricted diet of whole grains, etc., thought to be extremely healthy.

macrocosm *n* the great world, the universe.

macron *a* symbol placed over a vowel to indicate that the vowel sound is long.

mad *a* **1** insane; irrational **2** angry **3** wildly excited **4** (*of dog*) suffering from rabies; *idm* **mad about** *coll* enthusiastic about; *ns* **madman, madness** insanity; excitement; **madcap** marked by foolishness; *v* **madden** drive mad; infuriate.

mad cow disease *n* informal name for cattle disease.

madam *n* formal mode of addressing women.

made *a* produced, artifically put together.

Madeira *n* amber-colored dessert wine.

madeleine *n* small, buttery shell-shaped cake.

Mademoiselle *n* form of address to young unmarried French girl or woman.

Madonna *n* Virgin Mary; picture, statue of her.

madras *n* brightly colored.

madrigal *n* **1** short lyric

Medieval poem **2** polyphonic vocal piece developed in Renaissance, *usu* having a nonsense-syllable refrain.

maelstrom *n* turbulent or violent whirlpool.

maestro *n* eminent composer, musician or conductor.

Mafia *n* secret criminal society of Sicily or Italy.

magazine *n* **1** storehouse for ammunition, weapons, etc. **2** periodical containing articles, stories, etc. by different authors **3** cartridge chamber of repeating rifle.

magenta *n* purplish-red aniline dye; *a* of this color.

maggot *n* grub, larva *esp* of blow-fly; *a* **maggoty**.

magic *n* feigned superhuman control over natural forces and objects; sorcery **2** unexplained mysterious influence **3** conjuring; *a* **-al** *adv* **-ally**; *n* **magician** conjuror; wizard *a* **magical**; *n* **magician** one skilled in magic; wizard; conjuror.

Magic Marker [TM] *n* ink-filled, felt tipped pen used for marking.

magistrate *n* civil official administering law; *a* **magisterial** of, pertaining to magistrates.

magma *n* molten rock below earth's crust.

Magna Carta *n* document drawn up in 1215 giving the English certain privileges and rights, signed under duress by King John.

magnanimous *a* of generous, noble character; incapable of pettiness, resentment; *n* **magnanimity**.

magnate *n* prominent, influential person, *esp* in finance, industry.

magnesium *n* metallic element; *n* **magnesia** alkaline compound of this used in medicine.

magnet *n* **1** piece of iron with property of attracting other iron objects **2** person or thing with the power to attract others; *a* **magnetic** (**m.field** area influenced by magnetic force; **m.north** Northern pole of axis around which earth rotates; **m. storm** temporary disturbance of the earth's magnetic field, attributed to sunspot activity; **m.tape** tape coated with iron oxide for audio or video recording) *adv* **-ically**; *n* **magnetism**; *v* **magnetize** *n* **magneto** small dynamo with magnet, *esp* one producing ignition spark in internal combustion engine.

magnificent *a* splendid; of surpassing beauty, quality, generosity; *n* **-ficence**.

magnify *v* **magnifies, magnifying, magnified.** cause to appear larger, as with lens; exaggerate; *ns* **magnification; magnifying glass.**

magniloquent *a* speaking pompously; grandiose; *n* **-quence.**

magnitude *n* size; greatness; extent.

magnolia *n* flowering tree.

magnum *n* large wine bottle that holds about one and a half liters.

magpie *n* black and white bird of jay family.

magus *n* **1** Persian priest **2** magician **3** *cap pl* **Magi** traditionally three wise men who brought gifts to the baby Jesus.

Magyar *n* dominant race in Hungary; their language.

maharaja *n* a ruling prince in India, above a raja.

mahatma *n* Indian spiritual adept; one endowed with wisdom and power.

mah-jongg *n* Chinese game.

mahogany *n* reddish brown, fine-grained, tropical hard wood.

Mahomet *n* Mohammad.

maid *n* female servant.

maiden *n* *lit* young unmarried woman, *n* **m. of honor** chief bridesmaid; *a* **1** virginal **2** unused **3** done or experienced for first time; *ns* **maidenhead** virginity; **maidenhood** *a* **maidenly** modest.

mail[1] *n* armor of interlaced metal rings or plates; *a* **mailed** wearing such armor.

mail[2] *n* postal system; letters conveyed at one time; *v* send by post; **mail order** order by mail.

maim *v* cripple; mutilate.

A
B
C
D
E
F
G
H
I
J
K
L
M
N
O
P
Q
R
S
T
U
V
W
X
Y
Z

main *a* chief; most important; leading; *n* **1** principal pipe or cable in water, sewage, electricity, or gas system; *idm* **in the main** mostly; *pl* **mains** source of water, gas, electricity (**m.adaptor** adaptor for certain electrical appliances; **m.supply**); *ns* **mainframe** large computer; **mainland** mass of land not including nearby islands (*also a*); **mainsail** the principal or primary sail on the mainmast; **mainspring** **1** principal spring of watch or clock **2** main motive for action; **mainstay** chief form of support; **mainstream** dominant tendency (**m.jazz**); *vs* **mainline** inject (drug) into vein.

maintain *v* **1** cause to continue **2** keep in good condition **3** support with money **4** assert; *a* **-able**; *n* **maintenance 1** keeping in good condition **2** the act of maintaining.

maisonette *n* Fr small house; part of house used as apartment.

maitre d'hôtel *n* Fr headwaiter (also **maitre d'**).

maize *n* Indian corn.

majesty *n* **1** sovereignty; dignity **2** title of sovereign; *a* **-tic** stately, dignified.

major *a* **1** greater **2** more important **3** elder; *n* **1** person of full age **2** army rank above captain; *ns* **m.general** army officer above

rank of brigadier; **majorette** girl in uniform marching or dancing with band; **majority 1** greater number **2** number of votes by which one party leads in election **3** age at which full civil rights are due; **major-domo** chief steward of household; butler.

make *v* **makes, making, made.** **1** construct; create; produce **2** prepare for use **3** earn; win **4** constitute **5** reach; attain **6** appoint **7** compel **8** estimate; calculate **9** add up to **10** complete; *idm* **make do** manage; *idm* **make good 1** replace **2** be successful; *idm* **make or break** lead to complete success or total failure; *phr vs* **make away/off with** steal; **make out 1** distinguish; understand **2** claim; pretend **3** write (checke) **4** neck, pet; **make over 1** transfer ownership **2** convert; **make up 1** assemble **2** compose; invent **3** apply cosmetics **4** make complete **5** be reconciled; *ns* **m.-believe** imagining; pretending (*also a* imaginary); **m.-up 1** cosmetics **2** combination *a* **m.-shift** improvised (for temporary use); **make-work** *n* busy work, assigned to keep someone occupied.

malachite *n* green mineral used for ornamental purposes.

maladjusted *a* unable to adapt to demands of life or other people.

maladroit *a* clumsy.

malady *n* **-ies.** illness, esp. of the mind or spirit.

malaise *n* Fr slight physical discomfort.

malapropism *n* ridiculous misuse of word.

malaria *n* fever transmitted by mosquito bite.

malcontent *n* discontented person.

male *n* **1** male person: a man or boy; **2** one who produces sperm; *ns* **male chauvinism** assumption by man that he is superior to women; **m. chauvinist** (**pig**) such a man (*also* **MCP**).

malefactor *n* evil-doer.

malevolence *n* illwill.

malformation *n* deformity.

malfunction *v* fail to work properly; *n* such a failure.

malice *n* desire to hurt others; *a* **malicious**; *adv* **-ly**; *n* **-ness**.

malicious *a* spiteful.

malign *v* defame; speak evil of; *a* **malignant 1** filled with ill will **2** (disease) likely to prove fatal; *ns* **malignancy, malignity** spite, malice.

malinger *v* feign illness to escape duty, work, etc.; *n* **malingerer**.

mall *n*, *esp* street or covered area with shops.

mallard *n* common wild duck.

malleable *a* **1** capable of being hammered, pressed into shape **2** amenable; *n* **-ability**.

mallet *n* wooden-headed hammer; polo stick; croquet mallet.

malnourished *a* suffering the effects of poor diet; *n* **-nutrition**.

malodorous *a* smelling bad.

malpractice wrong-doing.

malt *n* dried fermented barley or other grain used in brewing; *n* **malted milk** powder made from dried milk and malted grain; **maltster** maker of malt.

maltreat *v* treat with cruelty; *n* **-ment**.

mama *n*, *coll* mother.

mambo *n* Latin-American dance.

mammal *n* animal which suckles its young; *a* **mammary** pertaining to breast (**m.gland** milk gland).

mammon *n* **1** material wealth **2** greed.

mammoth *n* extinct type of elephant; *a* colossal

man *n* **1** human being **2** adult male person **3** human race **4** piece used in chess, checkers, etc. **5** manservant; (*pl* **men**); *ns* **m.Friday** male assistant; **m.-of-war** armed sailing vessel; *v* **mans, manning, manned.** supply with men for defense, work, etc.; fortify; *ns* **manhole** hole giving access to drains, pipes, etc.; **manikin** dwarf; **manliness; manslaughter** unlawful, unpremeditated homicide; *as* **manful** bold, resolute; **manlike, manly** virile; bold; **mannish** (of woman) like a man.

manage *v* **1** conduct; handle **2** succeed in doing; *a* **manageable** docile; *ns* **management 1** process of managing; administration **2** body of persons managing business; **manager** one who manages; one in charge of business, etc.; (*fem* **-ess**); *as* **managerial, managing**.

mandarin *n* **1** former Chinese high official **2** a form of spoken Chinese used by the court and by officials **3** small, sweet type of orange.

mandate *n* **1** command, commission to follow specified policy, *esp* given by electorate to their representative **2** placing of small country's affairs in care of major power; *as* **mandatory, mandated** entrusted to a mandate.

mandible *n* **1** jawbone **2** either part of bird's beak.

mandolin *n* **1** musical stringed instrument **2** a kitchen tool for slicing, shredding.

mandrill *n* large baboon with blue and red muzzle.

mane *n* long hair on neck of horse, lion, etc.

maneuver *n* **1** strategic movement of troops **2** clever move; *pl* **-s** mock warfare; *v* **1** manage with skilfulness **2** perform maneuvres **maneuvre**; *a* **-verable**.

manganese *n* metallic element.

mange *n* contagious skin disease in animals and humans, caused by a parasitic mite

manger *n* feeding trough in stable, etc.

mangle[1] *v* mutilate, hack, tear.

mangle[2] *n* machine with rollers for pressing laundry, etc.; *v* press in mangle.

mango *n* **-os** or **-oes.** tropical fruit with a firm yellow to red skin, juicy yellow fruit, and large pit; tree bearing it.

manhandle *v* use physical force; handle roughly; move with mechanical aid.

Manhattan *n* **1** central borough of New York City **2** coctail made with bourbon and vermouth.

manhole *n* hole in ground for access to sewers, etc.

mania *n* **1** violent madness **2** *fig* obsession; craze; *a* **manic 1** suffering from mania (*n* **m.-depressive** person prone to sudden extreme mood changes) **2** wildly excited; *n* **maniac** crazy person; *a* **-al**.

manicure *n*, *v* care for hands and nails; *n* **-curist**.

manifest *a* obvious; undoubted; *v* make manifest; *n* list of passengers or of cargo; *ns* **-ation; manifesto** public declaration of policy.

manifold *a* numerous; varied; *n* pipe with several outlets.

manipulate *v* **1** handle; manage skillfully **2** alter fraudulently; *ns* **-ation, -ator;** *a* **-ative**.

manila *n* fibre of the abaca

plant; strong brown paper.

mankind n the human race.

manna n miraculous food of Israelites in wilderness; *fig* spiritual food; gum of Arabian tamarisk.

mannequin n live model or a form employed to display clothes.

manner n way things happen or are done; custom; style; *pl* **-s social behavior;** n **-ism** peculiarity of style; a **-ly** polite.

manor n feudal unit of land; estate, owner or lord of which retains ancient rights over land; n **m.-house** house of lord of manor; a **-ial**.

manpower n **1** people available for work **2** human labor.

manqué a *Fr* unfulfilled.

mansard n roof with two angles of slope.

mansion n large house.

manslaughter n crime of killing without intent.

manta n large triangular fish or ray.

mantel n structure around fireplace; n **mantelshelf**, **mantelpiece** shelf at top of mantel.

mantis n predatory green or brown insect.

mantle n **1** loose sleeveless cloak **2** incandescent mesh covering gas flame **3** *geol* part of earth below crust; *v* cover.

mantra n sacred word or phrase (in Hinduism, Buddhism).

manual *a* of, done with hands; n **1** handbook **2** organ or harpsichord keyboard; n **m. alphabet** finger positions representing the letters of the alphabet, *esp* for deaf people.

manufacture n process of making articles, goods, etc.; *v* produce goods *esp* in large quantities; *fig* fabricate, concoct (story, etc.) n **manufacturer** owner of factory; person, company making goods.

manure n dung, compost used to fertilize land; *v* apply manure to (land).

manuscript *a* written by hand or typed; n handwritten or typed document; draft of book, etc., for printing.

Manx n a Celtic language of the Manx people; *a* of Isle of Man; **M. cat** shorthaired, domestic tailless breed of cat.

many *a* numerous; n large number.

Maori n New Zealand native people; their language.

map n **1** plane representation of earth's surface or part of it **2** chart of heavens; *v* **maps, mapping, mapped.** make map.

maple n deciduous tree; its wood; *ns* **m. sugar** product made from boiling maple syrup; **m. syrup** syrup made from boiling the sap of the maple tree.

mar *v* spoil; ruin.

marabou n large African stork.

maraca n Latin American instrument made of a gourd filled with seeds to make rattling sound.

marathon n long-distance footrace; *fig* endurance competition.

marauder n roving thief; raider; *v* **maraud**.

marble n **1** hard kind of limestone, capable of being highly polished **2** small glass ball used in game; *pl* **-s** child's game; *v* stain with streaks of color.

March n third month of Gregorian calendar.

march *v* walk, proceed in steady rhythmic step, *esp* in military formation; n **1** act of marching **2** distance covered **3** music to accompany march; *idm* **give somebody his/her marching orders** dismiss somebody.

marchioness n wife or widow of marquis.

Mardi Gras n Shrove Tuesday (day before start of Lent); carnival (as in New Orleans) on this day.

mare n female horse; **mares' tails** wispy cirrus clouds.

margarine n manufactured butter substitute.

margin n **1** edge; limit **2** extra amount beyond what is necessary **3** space around printed page; a **marginal 1** of relatively little importance **2** a, n *polit* (seat) capable of being won easily by another candidate at election; *adv*

marginally by a small amount; *v* **marginalize** push aside, away from focus of attention; *n* **-ization**.

marigold *n* plant with yellow-orange flowers.

marijuana *n* leaves of the hemp plant smoked as a drug.

marimba *n* xylophone.

marina *n* harbor for pleasure boats.

marinade *n* sauce for soaking meat, fish before cooking; meat, fish, treated this way; *v* soak in this way (*also* **marinate**).

marine *a* of, connected with sea or shipping; *n* soldier serving on warship; *n* **mariner** seaman, sailor.

marionette *n* Fr puppet moved on strings.

marital *a* of, pertaining to husband, marriage.

maritime *a* 1 connected with, situated near sea 2 having a navy, seacoast, or sea-trade.

marjoram *n* aromatic herb.

mark *n* 1 visible sign; symbol 2 target 3 spot; *idm* **make one's mark** become famous; *idm* **overstep the mark** behave in an unacceptable way; *idm* **up to the mark** fit; well; *idm* **wide of the mark** inaccurate; *v* 1 make mark 2 assign marks to (examination paper, etc.) 3 observe; *idm* **mark time** 1 not move forward 2 wait for something to happen; *phr vs* **mark down/up**

reduce/increase the marks of, the price of; *a* **marked** clear; emphatic (*adv* **-ly**); *ns* **marker** 1 person or thing that marks 2 one who marks a score; **marking; marksman** sharpshooter.

Mark *n* author of second Gospel in New Testament.

market *n* 1 public gathering place for buying and selling 2 demand for goods; *idm* **come onto the market** be offered for sale; *idm* **in the market for** interested in buying; *idm* **play the market** buy and sell stocks and options for profit; *ns* **-er; -ing; mplace** 1 area where market is set up 2 trading activities; **m. research** survey of consumer needs and behavior; **m. value** price that can be asked at given time; *v* buy, sell in, take to market; *a* **-able** saleable; *n* **-ability**.

markup *n* proportion of increase from wholesale to retail price.

marl *n* loose, lime-rich clay soil used as fertilizer.

marlin *n* large game fish.

marmalade *n* jam of fruit and rind usually made of oranges, etc.

marmoset *n* small, bushy-tailed clawed monkey.

marmot *n* bushy-tailed rodent.

maroon *a* dark crimson; *v* abandon on desert island etc; *fig* desert.

marquee *n* Fr large tent *esp*

one used at parties, etc.

marquetry *n* inlaid woodwork.

marquis, marquess *n* title of British nobleman between duke and earl.

marrow *n* 1 soft blood-rich substance inside bones 2 the choicest of foods.

marry *v* **marries, marrying, married.** 1 take as husband or wife 2 join in marriage; *n* **marriage** 1 state of being married 2 *fig* close union; *a* **marriageable**.

Mars *n* 1 Roman god of war 2 fourth planet from the sun.

marsh *n* low-lying water-logged land; *n* **m. -mallow** 1 marsh plant 2 sweet gelatinous confection made from its root; *a* **marshy**.

marshal *n* federal officer; *v* **marshals, marshaling, marshaled.** 1 arrange in position 2 lead with ceremony.

marsupial *n* animal that carries young in pouch, as kangaroo, etc.; *a* pertaining to pouch.

mart *n* 1 trading-center 2 auction room.

marten *n* weasel-like animal, valued for its fur.

martello tower *n* circular fort often connected to a castle wall.

martial *a* suitable for, pertaining to war; warlike *ns* **m. art** fighting sport (*eg* judo, karate) (*usu pl*); **m. law** imposition of military rule (in temporary crisis).

Martian *a, n* (supposed inhabitant) of Mars.

martin *n* species of swallow.

martinet *n* strict, pedantic disciplinarian.

martini *n* mixture of gin or vodka and vermouth.

Martin Luther King Day legal holiday in most states, observed on the third Monday in January.

martyr *n* **1** one who dies rather than give up faith **2** *fig* sufferer (from pain, etc.); *n* **martyrdom** suffering or death of martyr.

marvel *n* something wonderful, amazing; *v* wonder; be surprised; *a* **marvelous** wonderful.

Marxism *n* theories of Karl Marx, basis for Communism; *a, n* **-ist**.

marzipan *n* paste made of ground almonds, sugar, etc.

mascara *n* cosmetic for darkening eyelashes.

masculine *a* **1** relating to males **2** strong; vigorous **3** of **gender denoting males;** *n* **-linity**.

maser *n* *abbrev* microwave amplification by stimulated emission of radiation.

mash *n* soft pulpy mass, warm food given to animals; *v* beat, crush into soft pulp.

mask *n* covering for face; *v* **1** cover with mask **2** *fig* conceal; dissemble *n* **masking tape** sticky tape used by painter to cover areas not to be painted.

masochism *n* sexual perversion, characterized by taking pleasure in physical pain and humiliation; *n* **masochist**.

mason *n* **1** stone worker **2** Freemason; *a* **masonic** of **Freemasonry;** *n* **masonry** **1** trade of mason **2** stonework **3** Freemasonry.

mason jar *n* glass container with a wide opening, used for home canning.

masque *n* verse drama with dance, music, etc. *n* **masquerade** masked ball; *v* be disguised; *fig* assume character of.

Mass *n* celebration of Eucharist *esp* in Roman Catholic church.

mass *n* **1** quantity of matter in one body, lump **2** large amount, number; *pl* the **masses** common people; *idm* **masses of** *coll* lots of; *ns* **m. communications, m. media** way of conveying facts, ideas to wide public (*eg* TV, radio, newspapers); **m. meeting** meeting with very large audience; *v* **m. produce** produce in bulk (*n* **m. production**); *a* **massive** enormous; *adv* **-ly;** *n* **-ness**.

massacre *v* slaughter indiscriminately; *n* killing of helpless persons.

massage *n* remedial treatment consisting of rubbing and kneading affected part; *v* **1** treat with massage **2** *polit* alter (numbers, etc.) to give false impression; *n* **masseur** one who practices massage; *fem* **masseuse**.

massif *n* *Fr* group of mountains forming unit.

mast[1] *n* **1** pole to support ship's rigging, etc, **2** flagpole.

mast[2] *n* nut fruit of beech, oak, chestnut, etc.

mastectomy *n* **-ies.** surgical removal of the breast.

master *n* **1** person having authority; head teacher; head of household **2** owner **3** employer **4** captain of merchantman **5** teacher **6** expert; *ns* **m. key** key to open many different locks; **m. of ceremonies** person making announcements and introductions at big social occasion; *v* **1** overcome **2** acquire knowledge of, skill in; *as* **-ful** imperious; **masterly** showing great talent, skill; **mastermind** clever person, *v* plan and insure success (of difficult operation); *n* **mastery** authority; supremacy.

mastic *n* glue or cement.

masticate *v* chew with teeth; *n* **-ation**.

mastiff *n* large, thickset dog used as guard dogs.

mastitis *n* inflammation of milk duct.

masturbate *v* manual or artificial stimulation one's own genital organs; *n* **-ation**.

mat *n* **1** piece of plaited straw or coconut fiber, etc., for wiping feet on, or covering part of floor **2** small rug **3** tangled hair; *v* **mats, matting, matted** become tangled; *idm* **on the mat** *coll* reprimanded.

mat, matt *a* having dull surface.

matador *n Sp* person who kills bull in bullfight.

match[1] *n* **1** thing exactly like another; person equal to another in quality, power, etc. **2** contest of skill, strength, etc. **3** marriage; eligible person; *v* **1** be equal to in contest **2** pit against in fight, etc. **3** marry **4** correspond; *a* **-less** peerless; unequaled; *n* **-maker** one who arranges marriages.

match[2] *n* **1** small strip of wood, tipped with combustible material **2** fuse for firing gun; *ns* **-wood** small splinters; **-box**.

mate[1] *n, v* checkmate (in chess).

mate[2] *n* **1** comrade **2** husband; wife **3** (*of animals, etc.*) one of pair **4** officer in merchant ship; *v* marry; pair *esp* animals.

material *n* stuff of which thing is made; fabric; cloth; *a* of matter or body; essential; important; *ns* **-ism** theory that matter is the only reality; **-ist** one engrossed in material interests; *a* **-istic**; *v* **materialize** make material; (of spirits, etc.) assume bodily form (*n* **-ization**); *adv* **materially** in relevant way;

essentially.

maternity *n* motherhood; *a* **maternal** related through mother; motherly.

mathematics *n pl* abstract science concerned with properties of and relations between quantities; *a* **-tical**; *n* **mathematician**.

matinée *n Fr* afternoon theatrical or musical performance.

matins *n* morning prayer.

matriarch *n* woman as head of family or household; *n* **-archy** social system where descent is traced through female line.

matri- *prefix* (of) mother.

matricide *n* act of killing one's own mother.

matriculate *v* **1** register as student in university or college; *n* **-ation** act of matriculating.

matrimony *n* marriage; *a* **-monial**.

matrix *n* mold in which a relief surface (as type) is cast; rock, etc. in which gems, stones, etc. are embedded; (*pl* **matrices**).

matron *n* **1** a married woman of maturity and dignity **2** housekeeper, domestic superintendent in institution or boarding school; **3** *lit* married woman; *a* **-ly** dignified; plump.

matter *n* **1** substance of which physical object is made **2** subject of book, discussion etc. **3** affair; reason

4 substance discharged from the body, as pus **5** cause of complaint, trouble; *idm* **a matter of course** taken for granted; **matter of fact** straightforward, plain, unembellished.

matting *n* floor covering of mat.

mattress *n* large cushion placed on bed, above box springs and below bedclothes; similar padding with extra wires built into it.

mature *a* **1** ripe; fully developed **2** prudent; wise; *v* **1** ripen **2** complete **3** (of insurance policy, etc.) become due for payment; *n* **maturity**.

matzo *n* unleavened bread eaten *esp* by Jews at Passover; **m. ball** *n* a small, round dumpling made from matzo meal.

maudlin *a* tearfully sentimental; self-pitying.

maul *v* beat lacerate; handle roughly.

Maundy Thursday *n* Thursday before Easter, commemorates the institution of the Eucharist.

mausoleum *n* large tomb, usually above ground.

mauve *n* pale lilac, violet color; *a* of this color.

maverick *n* **1** person with unorthodox ideas **2** an unbranded range animal, *esp* an orphan calf.

maw *n* stomach, gullet,

A B C D E F G H I J K L **M** N O P Q R S T U V W X Y Z

or open jaws of animal crop of bird.

maxi- *prefix* big, extra large.

maxim *n* rule of conduct; proverb.

maximum *n* greatest size, number, quantity, degree; *a* greatest *a* **maximal;** *v* **maximum size** (*n* **-ization**).

May *n* **1** fifth month of Gregorian calendar **2** hawthorn blossom; **May Day** first day of May (spring festival); *n* **mayfly** ephemeral fly; imitation used in fishing.

may *v aux* expresses permission, possibility, hope; *idm* **may as well** have/has no good reason not to; *idm* **may well** probably will; *pt* **might** (no *pp*); *advs* **maybe** possibly; **mayhap** perhaps.

mayhem *n* **1** willful and permanent disfigurement, crippling, or mutilation of the body **2** intentional, needless damage.

mayonnaise *n* dressing of egg yolk, vegetable oil, and vinegar or lemon juice.

mayor *n* chief officer of city or borough; *a* **-ral;** *ns* **-ality** office, period of office of mayor; **-ress 1** woman holding office of mayor **2** mayor's wife.

maypole *n* flower-topped pole around which people dance on May Day.

maze *n* labyrinth; network of paths, hedges, or lines.

mazurka *n* lively Polish dance in triple measure.

MBA *n* Master of Business Administration; university degree in business management skills.

MC *abbr* **1** master of ceremonies **2** Member of Congress.

MD *abbr* **1** Doctor of Medicine.

ME *abbr* **1** *med* myalagic encephalomyelitis **2** Middle English.

me *pron* objective case of I.

mead *n* alcoholic drink made of fermented honey, malt, and yeast.

meadow *n* grassy field; hayfield.

meadowlark *n* common American songbird.

meager *a* **1** thin; lean **2** scanty; inadequate **3** limited.

meal *n* coarsely ground grain; *as* **mealy, mealymouthed** apt to mince words; devious.

meal *n* eating food; repast.

mean[1] *n* average; midway between two extremes; *ns* **meantime, meanwhile** intervening time.

mean[2] *a* **1** selfish; parsimonious **2** unkind **3** inferior; mediocre **4** *dated* humble; *idm* **no mean something** a considerable something; *adv* **-ly;** *n* **-ness**.

mean[3] *v* **1** have in mind **2** signify **3** intend **4** have meaning; *pt, pp* **meant;** *idm* **be meant to** be supposed to; *idm* **mean business** *coll* be serious in intention; *n* **-ing 1** sense **2** importance;

significance **3** intention; *a* **meaningful;** *adv* **-ly.**

meander *v* wander aimlessly.

means *n pl* **1** method; way **2** agent; cause **3** money; resources; *idm* **by all means** certainly; *idm* **by means of** making use of; *idm* **by no means/not by any means** not at all; *idm* **a means to an end** a way of achieving something important.

measles *n* infectious disease, characterized by red rash and fever; *a* **measly** *coll* parsimonious, small and insignificant.

measure *v* **1** find the size, amount, degree, etc. of something **2** be of a certain size; *idm* **measure up (to)** show the necessary qualities (for); *n* **1** system of measuring **2** unit of measurement **3** degree; amount **4** verse rhythm; rhythmical, musical unit **5** action taken for a purpose; *idm* **for good measure** as an additional item; *idm* **get the measure of** assess somebody's character or capacities; *a* **measured 1** of certain measure **2** careful; steady; *n* **-ment;** *a* **measurable;** *adv* **-ably.**

meat *n* **1** solid food (not drink) **2** flesh of animals used as food; *a* **meaty** *fig* substantial; *n* **m.loaf** ground meat baked in a loaf form.

mecca *n* **1** place that attracts people with a specific interest 2 *cap* spiritual center of Islam, birthplace of Mohammed.

mechanic *a* of machine; *n* skilled, trained worker, *esp* one working with machinery; *pl* **-s** science of motion and force; *a* **-al** concerned with, produced by machines; *fig* acting without thinking; *adv* **-ally.**

mechanism *n* machinery; *n* **mechanization** making; mechanical *esp* change from manpower to machines; *v* **mechanize;** *a* **-ized.**

med *abbr* **1** medical **2** medium **3** medieval **4** *cap* Mediterranean.

medal *a* small metal disk *usu* with inscription used to mark achievement etc.; *ns* **medallion 1** large medal **2** round panel, ornament; **medalist** one who wins medals.

meddle *v* interfere; tamper with; *a* **-some.**

media *n pl* means of mass communication (TV, radio, the press).

median *n, a* middle; average; **medial** in the middle.

mediate *v* intervene as peacemaker; *a* through intermediary, not direct; *ns* **-ation** reconcilement; **-ator.**

medic *n coll* doctor or medical student (*also* **medico.**)

Medicaid *n* government financed medical care.

medical *a* of medicine; of the treatment of illness; *adv* **-ly;**

n assessment of physical health by examination; *ns* **medicament** medicine; **Medicare** *n* government provision of medical care, *esp* for elderly; **medication** (provision of) drugs; *as* **medicated** containing medicinal substance(s); **medicative** of medication.

medicine *n* **1** science of preventing, treating, and curing disease **2** substance taken internally to treat illness; *n* **m.-man** witchdoctor; *a* **medicinal** curative; *adv* **-ly.**

medieval *a* of, belonging to Middle Ages; *n* **-ism** cult, spirit of Middle Ages; *n* **-ist.**

mediocre *a* **1** ordinary; average; of medium quality **2** less than first rate.

meditate *v* contemplate; ponder; *n* **-ation** concentrated thought; solemn contemplation; *a* **-ative.**

Mediterranean *a* of the Mediterranean Sea or the land around it.

medium *n* **1** that which is between extremes **2** agency; channel **3** environment **4** intermediate substance conveying force **5** one who receives messages from spirit world; (*pl* **mediums**); *a* between two extremes.

medley *n* **1** mix up, confused **2** miscellaneous assortment.

meek *a* submissive; mild; humble; *adv* **-ly;** *n* **-ness.**

meerschaun *n* claylike mineral often used to make tobacco pipes.

meet[1] *a* fitting, suitable.

meet[2] *v* **1** encounter; come face to face **2** assemble **3** converge **4** confront **5** satisfy; fullfil (*pt, pp* **met**); *idm* **meet halfway** reach a compromise; *phr v* **meet with 1** be confronted by **2** experience; *n* sporting event, as track and field; *n* **meeting 1** encounter **2** public assembly.

mega- *prefix* **1** very big (*e.g.,* **megadose**) **2** million (*e.g.,* **megaton**).

megabyte *n comput* 2^{20} or 1, 047, 576 bytes (*also* **MB**).

megalith *n* huge prehistoric stone, menhir.

megalomania *n* excessive desire for power over others; *n* **megalomaniac.**

megaphone *n* funnel-shaped device used to increase volume of sound and carry it farther.

melancholy *n* gloom; sadness; dejection; *n* **melancholia** emotional state accompanied by extreme depression; *a* **melancholic.**

mélange *n* mixture.

melanoma *n* cancerous tumor of the skin.

melee, mêlée *n* confused fight, skirmish, *esp* hand-to-hand.

meliorate *v* improve; *n* **melioration** amendment.

melisma *n* musical term for group of notes sung to one

a
b
c
d
e
f
g
h
i
j
k
l
m
n
o
p
q
r
s
t
u
v
w
x
y
z

syllable, syllabic embellishment.

mellow a 1 ripe; well-matured 2 grown gentle through age, experience 3 sl relaxed; v make, become mellow.

melodrama n sensational, high-flown, sentimental play; a **melodramatic**.

melody n tune in music; sweet agreeable sounds; as **melodious** tuneful, musical; **melodic** of melody.

melon n edible gourd with sweet juicy flesh.

melt v 1 make, become liquid by heat; dissolve 2 blend 3 fig make, become tender; phr vs **melt away** disappear; **melt into** become merged with; n **meltdown** melting and leakage of radioactivity from core of nuclear reactor; a **melting** 1 becoming liquid (ns **m. point** temperature at which solid melts; **m. pot** place where people of many nationalities live) 2 tender; affectionate; **molten** of, like melted metal.

member n 1 part, limb of human or animal body 2 single part of complex whole 3 person belonging to group, society, etc.; n **membership** 1 status as member 2 total number of members of club, society, etc.

membrane n thin, supple tissue covering or lining part of organ or body.

memento n **-os** or **-oes.** small item that serves as a reminder of a person, place, etc.

memo n coll see **memorandum**.

memoir n biography; pl **-s** personal experiences and observations.

memorandum n 1 informal record, written reminder 2 informal communication.

Memorial Day n legal holiday in most states on last Monday in May.

memory n ability to remember; recollection of past events, etc.; period of such recollection; n 1 ability to remember 2 period of recollection 3 thing remembered 4 lasting impression of dead or departed person 5 comput place where data are stored; n **memorial** thing commemorating person, event etc; a bringing to mind; v **memorize** commit to memory; a **memorable** noteworthy; remarkable; ns **memorabilia** things that evoke memory; mementos.

men pl of **man**.

menace n threat, impending danger; v threaten.

menagerie n Fr collection of wild animals, esp traveling exhibition.

mend v 1 repair 2 correct; rectify; idm **mend one's ways** behave better; idm **on the mend** recovering from illness; n damaged part that has been repaired, esp of clothes; ns **-er, -ing** n

repaired hole, patch, darn.

mendacious a untruthful; n **mendacity**.

mendicant n beggar; a begging; ns **mendicancy, mendicity**.

menhir n single, rough upright monolith usu prehistoric. See **megalith.**

menial a 1 of household servants 2 servile; mean; n domestic servant.

meningitis n med inflammation of membranes of brain.

meniscus n physics curved surface of liquid in a tube.

menopause n time in life when menstruation ceases.

menorah n symbolic candelabrum used by Jews during Hanukkah.

menses n pl med passing of blood in menstruation.

menstruation n monthly discharge from womb; v **menstruate**; a menstrual.

mensurable a capable of being measured; n **mensuration**.

mental a 1 of, relating to mind 2 sl crazy; ns **m. age** measure of mental ability from the average performance of people at the age specified; n **mentality** mental quality, attitude.

menthol n substance obtained from oil of peppermint.

mention v speak of; refer to; n brief reference.

mentor n counselor; role model; wise, prudent adviser.

menu n list of dishes available or to be served.

meow n sound a cat makes.

Mephistopheles n the devil in Faust legend.

mercantile a connected with trade, commercial.

Mercator's projection n method of depicting the world in maps as rectangular in shape increasing the distance between parallels of latitude from the Equator to the polar regions.

mercenary a working only for payment; eager for gain; n soldier hired by foreign country.

merchant n buyer and seller of goods for profit; ns **m. bank** bank specializing in business and industrial finance; **merchandise** wares; **merchantman** ship bearing goods for trade; **m. marine, m. navy, m. ship, m. shipping**.

mercury n 1 silvery fluid metallic poisonous element; quicksilver 2 cap Roman messenger god 3 cap planet nearest sun; a **mercurial** lively; unpredictable.

mercy n compassion; clemency; leniency shown to offender; **mercy** idm **at the mercy of** having no defense against; as **merciful, merciless**.

mercy killing n act of euthanasia.

mere[1] n lake, pool.

mere[2] a only; simple; nothing but.

merge v lose identity; absorb; fade gradually into; n **merger** absorption of smaller thing by greater; combine (esp of commercial interests).

meridian a Lat/Fr relating to noon; n 1 noon 2 line of longitude passing through poles and cutting Equator at right angles 3 zenith.

meringue n Fr dessert topping of stiffly beaten egg whites mixed with sugar and baked in cool oven.

merino n fine-wooled sheep, very soft cashmerelike wool.

merit n worth; excellence; quality deserving punishment or reward; pl intrinsic rightness or wrongness; v deserve; a **meritorious** praiseworthy.

Merlin n the magician in King Arthur legend.

meritocracy n (system of government by) people with the greatest ability; country with such a system.

mermaid n fantasy creature (half woman, half fish).

merry a joyous; lively; ns **merriment, merry-go-round** carousel with moving wooden animals.

merrymaking n festivities; hilarity; n **merrymaker.**

mesa n flat-topped hill with steep sides.

mesh n one of open spaces in net; pl **meshes 1** network **2** fig snares; traps, v catch in meshes; (of gear wheels) be engaged.

mesmerize v fascinate; completely hold the attention.

meson n type of elementary particle with mass between electron and proton.

Mesozoic a geol of the period lasting from about 225 to 70 million years ago.

mesquite n tree of southwest US.

mess n 1 disarray; disorder 2 difficult position 3 group of persons habitually eating together, esp in armed forces; place for this v 1 eat thus 2 make muddle of; idm **mess about/around** behave in an aimless and irresponsible manner; n **mess-room.**

message n oral or written communication sent to a person; meaning; **messenger** person who delivers a message.

Messiah n expected king and deliverer of the Jews.

metabolism n process of chemical changes in living organism; a **metabolic;** v **metabolize.**

metal n mineral substance that is opaque, ductile, malleable, and capable of conducting heat or electricity; as **metallic** of metal; **metalloid** resembling metal (n substance with some properties of a metal); ns **metallurgy** science and technology of metals; a **-lurgical** n **-lurgist; metalwork** skilled work in metal; product from this;

n **-er**.

metamorphosis *n* transformation; remarkable change; *pl* **metamorphoses**.

metaphor *n* figure of speech in which word or phrase is used to denote something different from its usual meaning; *a* **metaphorical** figurative.

metaphysics *n* branch of philosophical study concerned with nature and causes of being and knowledge; *a* **metaphysical**.

mete *v* (*usu* **mete out**) allot; distribute.

meteor *n* shooting star; *fig* any bright but transient object; *a* **-ic** like meteor; dazzling but brief; *adv* **-ically**; *ns* **meteorite** stony or metallic mass fallen from outer space; **meteorology** science of weather; **-ologist;** *a* **-ological**.

meter[1] *n* mechanical device for measuring quantity, volume, etc.

meter[2] *n* poetical rhythm; group of metrical feet; unit of length in metric system; *as* **metrical** of measurement of poetic meter; **metric** measuring by meters.

methane *n* flammable hydrocarbon gas; marsh gas.

methanol *n* methyl alcohol, a flammable poisonous liquid alcohol.

method *n* mode, manner of procedure; systematic, orderly arrangement; *a* **-ical**

orderly; *adv* **-ically**.

Methodism *n* Protestant denomination founded by John Wesley.

methodology *n* **1** study of methods **2** set of methods; *a* **-ological**.

methyl *n* chemical basis of wood spirit; *n* **methyl alcohol** poisonous alcohol found in organic substances (*also* **wood alcohol**).

meticulous *a* over-careful about details.

métier *n Fr* profession **1** occupation **2** area of expertise.

metric system *n* decimal system of weights and measurements.

metronome *n mus* mechanical device for keeping time.

metropolis *n* capital, chief city of country, state, region.

metropolitan *a* of metropolis; *n* bishop having authority over other bishops of province.

mettle *n* **1** the material or substance of which an object or person is composed **2** rigor and strength of spirit.

mew[1] *n* cry of cat, gull; *v* utter this cry.

mew[2] *v* (of hawk) molt; *v* put (hawk) into cage; *fig* confine, as in cage; *n pl* **mews** stables, originally place where falcons were kept.

mezzanine *n* low-ceilinged story between two higher ones.

mezzo *adv mus* moderately; *n coll* mezzo-soprano; *n*

m.-soprano 1 voice between soprano and contralto **2** singer with such a voice; musical part for this.

mezzotint *n* (print made by) method using metal plate with smooth and rough areas to give light and shade respectively.

mg *abbr* milligram.

MHR *abbr* Member of the House of Representatives.

MHZ *abbr* megahertz.

Michaelmas *n* festival of St. Michael, September 29.

mickey *n* **M.Finn** alcoholic drink laced with drug to induce sleep; **m.mouse** *a coll* trivial; unimportant; corny.

micro- *prefix* **1** very small (*e.g.*, **microorganism**) **2** one millionth (*eg* **microsecond**).

microbe *n* microscopic organism, bacterium, *esp* as cause of disease.

microbiology *n* study of minute living organisms; *a* **-ological;** *n* **-ologist**.

microchip *n* small piece of silicon or similar material; integrated circuit.

microcomputer *n* smallest type of computer.

microcosm *n* **1** little world **2** miniature representation of something larger.

microfiche *n* sheet of microfilm.

microfilm *n* film with minute record of large documents; *v* to take photographs on such film.

micrometer *n* instrument for

measuring very small distances.

microorganism n organism too small to be seen without a microscope.

microphone n instrument converting sound into electrical waves for transmission to a loudspeaker (coll **mike**).

microprocessor n comput central data processing unit.

microscope n instrument that gives enlarged view of extremely small objects; a **microscopic** extremely small; adv **-ally**.

microwave n 1 very short electromagnetic wave 2 oven that cooks food rapidly by use of microwaves (also **microwave oven**).

micturition n med urination.

mid a denoting middle part or position; ns **midday** noon; **midnight** 12 o'clock at night; a, adv **midway** half way.

Midas touch n ability to make money or accumulate riches or luck uncannily.

midden n dunghill; pile of refuse.

middle a equidistant from extremes; halfway; n middle part or point; ns **m.age** period between youth and old age (a **m.-aged**; n **m.-aged spread** coll corpulence that comes in middle age); **M.Ages** period in Europe from about the 6th to the 15th century before the Renaissance; **m.ear** cavity of central part of ear;

M.East countries in Asia west of India (a **M.Eastern**); **middle-of-the-road** supporting policy that appeals to average person and avoids any controversial or extreme position; **middleman** trader, agent between producer and customer; **middle name** 1 name between first name and surname 2 coll (as should be his/her **m.name**) characteristic for which somebody is well known; **m.school** school between primary and upper for pupils usu grades 6-9 or 7-9; **middleweight** boxer of weight between welterweight and heavyweight; **middling** average; mediocre.

midge n tiny flying, biting insect.

midget n dwarf.

midnight n 12 o'clock at night.

midriff n midregion of torso; diaphragm.

midshipman n navy student training to be an officer.

midst prep in middle of; n central part.

midsummer n middle of summer (June 21 or 22); n **Midsummer Day** June 24.

midway a, adv halfway.

midwife n woman who assists women in childbirth; n **midwifery** science, skill of midwife; obstetrics.

midwinter n the winter solstice.

mien n air; bearing.

miff n petty quarrel v offend.

might[1] v aux 1 expressing doubtful possibility 2 pt of MAY; **might have** 1 could have 2 should have; ought to have.

might[2] n power; strength a **mighty**; adv coll very; adv **-ily**.

migraine n recurrent, severe headache with possible vomiting, nausea.

migrate v move from one region to another, esp as certain birds, etc.; a, n **migrant**; n **migration** act of migrating; periodical movement of birds, fish, etc.; body of individuals migrating; a **migratory** having habit of migration; wandering.

mikado n title of emperor of Japan.

mike n coll microphone.

milady n English noblewoman.

milch a giving milk.

mild a 1 gentle; kind; placid 2 temperate 3 not strong in flavor; n **mildness**.

mildew n parasitic fungus growing on plants; mold growing on damp food, paper, etc.; v affect, be affected by mildew.

mile n measure of linear distance, 5,280 ft; ns **mileage** 1 distance traveled 2 cost of travel per mile 3 fig possible amount of use; **m. marker** marker indicating distance in miles from place.

milieu n Fr environment;

A
B
C
D
E
F
G
H
I
J
K
L
M
N
O
P
Q
R
S
T
U
V
W
X
Y
Z

social surroundings; pl -s or -x.

military a of, suitable to or performed by soldiers, or army; n army; a **militant** warlike, combative (n **m.tendency** aggressive element); ns **militancy; militarism** reliance on, enthusiasm for armed strength; **militia** auxiliary infantry force, called out in emergency.

milk n 1 fluid secreted by female mammals to feed their young 2 similar liquid secreted by certain plants; v 1 take milk from 2 (of cow, goat, etc.) give milk 3 extract money, information, etc. from somebody by dishonest means; **m.run** coll regular ordinary journey providing service; **m.shake** sweet milk drink with chocolate or fruit flavor; **milksop** feeble effeminate man; **m.tooth** one of first set (baby teeth) in mammals; as **milk-white, milky;** n **Milky Way 1** luminous belt of stars and nebulae 2 galaxy that our sun and solars system are part of (also **the Galaxy**).

mill n 1 machine for grinding grain; building containing this 2 small machine for grinding pepper, coffee, etc. 3 works, factory for processing cotton, paper etc; v idm **put somebody through/go through the mill**

(cause sb to) undergo difficult or unpleasant experience; phr v **mill about/around** move around aimlessly in a mass of people; ns **miller** person who works in a flour mill; **millrace** current of water driving millwheel; **millstone 1** stone for grinding corn 2 fig burden; **millwheel** large wheel used to drive watermill.

millenium n Lat period of thousand years, esp that of Christ's second Advent; a **millenial.**

millet n small-seeded cereal grass, used as food.

milli- prefix Lat one thousandth (part of weight, measure in metric system), as **milligram** thousandth part of gram; **millimeter** etc.

milliard n Fr billion; 1,000 million.

millibar n unit of pressure of 1000 bars.

milliner n maker, seller of women's hats, ribbons, trimmings, etc.; n **millinery** milliner's business, or articles sold by milliner.

million n, pron, det 1000 thousands; n **millionaire** person possessing a million dollars, etc.; very rich person; fem **-airess**; a, n, pron, det **millionth.**

millipede n Lat wormlike creature with many pairs of legs.

mime n 1 art of

communication by use of gestures and facial expression, esp as entertainment 2 entertainer of this kind; v use this means of communicating; a **mimetic;** n **mimeograph** apparatus for making copies of documents from stencil; v make copies by this method.

mimic v copy, resemble closely; ridicule by imitating speech, action; n one who mimics; n **mimicry.**

mimosa n 1 genus of plants with small, fluffy yellow flowers, and sensitive leaves 2 a drink of orange juice and Champagne.

minaret n tall tower on a mosque from where the call to prayer is cried.

mince v cut, chop in small pieces; speak, behave affectedly; idm **not mince words** speak plainly; n finely chopped meat; n **mincemeat,** mixture of raisins, candied peel, suet, brandy, etc.; **m.pie** small covered pie containing mincemeat.

mind n 1 intellectual faculties 2 memory 3 opinion; thought 4 intention; v 1 pay attention to 2 care for 3 object (to) 4 intend 5 beware of 6 take into account; idm **on one's mind** causing anxiety; idm **out of one's mind** insane; frenzied; as **m.-bending** incredible; **m.- blowing 1** (of drugs) causing

ecstasy, hallucinations, etc.
2 strange and exciting;
m.-boggling *coll* astonishing;
ns **m.reader** person able to
know another person's
thoughts; **m.reading; mind's
eye** imagination; *as* **mindful**
thoughtful; attentive; *adv*
-ly; mindless thoughtless;
stupid; *adv* **-ly;** *n* **-ness.**

mine[1] *n* **1** deep excavation
from which coal, minerals
(except stone) are dug
2 buildings, machinery
connected with this **3** *fig* rich
source of supply
4 tunnel under enemy
position; *v* **1** sink mine
2 extract from mine
3 undermine; *n* **miner.**

mine[2] *n* charge of explosives
detonated in container; *v* lay
mines in sea, on land; *ns*
minefield area where mines
have been laid; **minelayer**
ship laying mines;
minesweeper ship for
clearing minefield.

mineral *n* natural, inorganic
substance found in earth;
anything not animal or
vegetable; anything dug up
by mining; *a* inorganic; *ns*
m.oil petroleum oil used as
laxative; **m.water** water with
mineral salts; **mineralogy**
science of minerals (*n* -
alogist).

Minerva *n* Roman goddess of
wisdom.

minestrone *n* thick soup of
vegetables and pasta.

mingle *v* **1** mix; blend **2** join;
combine.

mini *n* thing smaller than the
usual size.

mini- *prefix* small; short.

miniature *n*, *a* very small
(thing); *v* **miniaturize;** *n*
miniaturist artist who
specializes in small pictures.

miniature golf *n* game played
with a putter on a small
course which has bridges,
tunnels, and other obstacles.

minibus *n* small bus or van.

minicomputer *n* computer
smaller than mainframe.

minim *n mus* halfnote; ¹⁄₆₀th
fluid dram; *a* **minimal** least
possible; *adv* **-ly;** *v* **minimize
1** reduce to smallest possible
amount **2** underestimate;
understate; *n* **minimum**
smallest, least amount,
lowest point possible; *pl*
minima, -mums; *a* least
possible.

mining *n* extracting minerals
from earth.

minion *n* **1** favorite **2**
subordinate; underling .

miniscule *a* very tiny.

minister *n* **1** clergyperson
2 diplomat in charge of state
department; *v* supply; help;
serve; *a* **ministerial;** *n*
ministrant acting as
minister; *n* helper; *n*
ministration service, help.

mink *n* animal of weasel
family; its valuable fur.

minnow *n* tiny fish.

minor *a* less; inferior;
unimportant; *n* person not
legally of age; *n* **minority**

1 state of being a minor
2 smaller number.

Minotaur *n* fabled monster
(half man, half bull).

minster *n* large church;
cathedral.

minstrel *n* medieval singer;
itinerant singer, musician.

mint[1] *n* place where money is
legally coined; *idm* **make a
mint** *coll* earn a great amount
of money; *v* make (money); *a*
in new and perfect
condition.

mint[2] *n* **1** peppermint **2** herb
used to flavor meat, etc.;
a **minty.**

minuend *n* number from
which another is to be
subtracted.

minuet *n* stately dance in
triple meter.

minus *prep*, *a* less; deducted;
subtracted; lacking; *n* minus
sign (–).

minuscule *a* very tiny.

minute[1] *n* **1** ¹⁄₆₀th of hour or
degree **2** moment **3**
memorandum; *n* **m.steak**
thin steak that can be
cooked very quickly; *pl* **-s**
written record of meeting; *v*
record in the minutes.

minute[2] *a* tiny; *adv* **-ly;**
n **-ness; minutiae** small
details.

minyan *n* the amount or
quorum of ten Jews needed
for community worship.

miracle *n* marvel; abnormal
event that cannot be
explained; *n* **m.play** mystery
play from the Middle Ages,

usually based on life of a saint, martyr or on a miraculous happening; *a* **miraculous**.

mirage *n* optical illusion; *fig* misleading delusion.

mire *n* mud; swampy ground; *v* **1** dirty with mud **2** impede, hamper progress.

mirror *n* polished surface that reflects image; *fig* exemplary model; *v* reflect; **m.image** image in which left and right sides are symmetrically reversed.

mirth *n* **1** merriment; gladness **2** hilarity; *a* **mirthful**.

mis-[1] *prefix* **1** *forming ns* bad; wrong; ill (*e.g.*, **misadventure** ill luck; accident; **mischance** bad luck; **misconception** wrong understanding; **misconduct** bad behavior, *esp* sexual; **misfortune, mismatch, misrule**).

mis-[2] *prefix forming ns* lack of (*as* **mistrust** lack of trust; **misunderstanding**).

mis-[3] *prefix forming vs and as* badly; wrongly (*as vs* **misapprehend** understand wrongly (*n* **-hension**); **misappropriate** use wrongly; **misapply, misbehave, miscalculate, miscast; misconceive** understand wrongly (*n* **-conception**); **misconstrue, misdirect, misinform, misjudge, mislead, mismanage, mismatch, misquote, misread, misreport,**

misrepresent, misstate, mistime, misuse; *as* **misguided** mistaken in judgement (*adv* **-ly**); **misshapen** badly formed; **misspent** spent unwisely).

misanthropy *n* hatred of humanity and human society; *ns* **misanthrope, -opist** person who shows this; *a* **-opic;** *adv* **-opically**.

misc *abbr* miscellaneous.

miscarry *v* **1** to experience miscarriage of fetus; **miscarriage** *n* spontaneous end of pregnancy before fetal viability **2** failure (of plan etc); *n* **miscarriage of justice** unjust legal decision.

miscegenation *n* interbreeding of races.

miscellaneous *a* mixed; consisting of various kinds; *n* **miscellany** medley of various kinds.

mischance *n* bad luck.

mischief *n* **1** harm; injury **2** immoral influence **3** troublesome conduct; *a* **mischievous** injurious; causing needless, thoughtless, minor damage; *adv* **-ly;** *n* **-ness**.

misconduct *n* improper or illegal activity.

misconstrue *v* interpret wrongly; *n* **-struction**.

miscreant *n* scoundrel; villain; ruffian.

misdeed *n* immoral act.

misdemeanor *n* misdeed; minor indictable offense.

miser *n Lat* one who hoards

money and lives wretchedly; *a* **-ly** avaricious; *n* **-liness**.

miserable *a* **1** unhappy **2** squalid; wretched **3** scanty **4** pitiable; *n* **misery 1** unhappiness; discomfort **2** squalor.

misfire *v* **1** (of gun) fire badly **2** (of plan) fail.

misfit *n* **1** person not suited to job or social situation **2** badly fitting article of clothing.

misfortune *n* bad luck.

misgiving *n* doubt; mistrust; fear.

mishap *n* accident; bad luck.

mishmash *n coll* confused mixture.

mislay *v* lose temporarily; *pt, pp* **mislaid**.

mislead *v* deceive; lead astray; (*pt, pp* **misled**); *a* **misleading** deceptive.

misnomer *n* wrong name; incorrect description.

misogamy *n* hatred of marriage; *n* **-gamist**.

misogyny *n* hatred of women; *n* **-gynist**.

misplace *v* **1** mislay **2** put in the wrong place.

Miss *n* title of unmarried woman, girl.

miss *v* **1** fail to hit, secure, meet, catch, notice **2** omit **3** feel want of; *phr v* **miss out 1** omit **2** lose an opportunity; *n* failure to hit, secure, etc.; *a* **missing 1** lost; mislaid **2** omitted; *n* **m.link 1** thing needed to complete series **2** animal believed to have existed between apes and early man.

missal *n* book used at mass that contains words and mussic.

missile *n* object thrown or shot (*usu* as rocket or weapon).

mission *n* act of sending or being sent as representative; delegation; vocation; center for missionary or social work; *n* **missionary** one sent on religious mission; *a* of religious missionary.

missive *n* letter.

mist *n* visible water vapor; *a* **misty** covered by mist; dim; obscure.

mistake *v* err in understanding; identify wrongly; be in error; *pt* **mistook;** *pp* **mistaken;** *n* error; fault.

Mister *n* title of address to adult man, written **Mr.**

mistletoe *n* evergreen semiparasitic plant.

mistral *n* cold dry northerly wind of S France.

mistress *n* **1** a man's secret or illicit lover **2** woman with power or control **3** female head of household **4** female teacher.

mistrust *v* not trust; *n* lack of trust; *a* **-ful;** *adv* **-fully.**

mite *n* **1** very small insect **2** anything very small.

miter *n* **1** headdress worn by bishops, etc. **2** angled joint between two pieces of wood; *v* join with miter.

miter box *n* box made with cut-out angles for guiding a handsaw.

mitigate *v* make less severe; alleviate; *n* **-ation.**

mitosis *n* process that takes place within the nucleus of a dividing cell.

mitt *n* **1** glove with finger and thumb ends open **2** baseball, boxing leather glove **3** *pl sl* fists.

mitten *n* handcovering with two areas for thumb and fingers.

mix *v* **1** put together; mingle; blend **2** associate; *n* result of mixing; *a* **mixed 1** of different sorts (*ns* **mixed bag** collection of varied items; **m.economy**) **2** having contradictory elements (*ns* **m. blessing** thing which has bad as well as good in it; **m. metaphor** ludicrous combination of two metaphors) **3** of both sexes (**m. school**); *ns* **mixer 1** person or machine for mixing **2** drink for making cocktails **3** *radio, film, TV* person or device combining two or more inputs into a single output; **4** person in a social role; **mixture 1** combination **2** act of mixing **3** substances mixed; **mix-up** confusion.

mixed grill *n* dish consisting of various meats and vegetables broiled and served together.

ml *abbr* milliliter(s).

Mlle *abbr* Fr Mademoiselle.

mm *abbr* millimeter(s).

Mme *abbr* Fr Madame.

mnemonic *n* (phrase, rhyme, etc.) helping memory.

moa *n* extinct large, flightless bird from New Zealand.

moan *n* low, mournful sound expressing pain, groan; *v* utter moan.

moat *n* defensive trench (*usu* filled with water) around castle, etc.

mob *n* lawless, rough crowd; rabble; excited mass of people; *v* **mobs, mobbing, mobbed.** jostle, attack in mob; crowd hound.

mobile *a* moveable; moving, changing easily; *n* **mobility;** *v* **mobilize** call up (armed forces) for service; gather resources, forces; *n* **-ization.**

mobile home *n* structure on wheels, intended to be a moveable dwelling but often permantly attached to large cinder blocks.

moccasin *n* soft shoe (*usu* deer-skin) of Native Americans.

mocha *n* **1** type of coffee **2** coffee and chocolate flavoring.

mock *v* ridicule; deride; mimic; *fig* delude; *a* sham; imitation; *ns* **mocker; mockery** ridicule; travesty *idm* **make a mockery of** make appear worthless.

mockingbird *n* American bird of thrush family, mimic of other bird calls.

mock-up *n* **1** full-size experimental model **2** lay-out of text, pictures, etc.

before printing.

modal auxiliary *n* verb used in front of other verb to express possibility, obligation, etc. (*as* **can, may, must, shall, will**)

mode *n* method; style; fashion; *a* **modish** fashionable.

model *n* **1** pattern **2** small-scale reproduction **3** mannequin **4** one who poses for artist, etc.; *v* work into shape; act as model, pose.

modem *n* comput device that converts data from separate sources (computer, phone) into compatible form.

moderate *a* not going to extremes; restrained; medium; *v* make, become less extreme or violent; *n* one holding moderate views; *ns* **-ation; -ator 1** arbitrator **2** someone who presides over a meeting, assembly, or discussion.

moderato *adv mus* at moderate speed.

modern *a* of present or recent times; up-to-date; *n* **-ism** movement expressing present day views, methods, etc.; *v* **modernize** make modern; adapt to present-day usage (*n* **-ization**).

modest *a* **1** moderate **2** diffident; humble **3** chaste; *n* **modesty**.

modicum *n* small amount or quantity.

modify *v* qualify; alter slightly; *n* **modification**.

modiste *n* maker of women's clothes.

modulate *v* **1** regulate; adapt; vary **2** inflect (voice, etc.) **3** *mus* change key; *ns* **-ation; -ator**.

module *n* **1** standard part used in construction **2** part of spacecraft that can operate independently **3** unit of study that is assessed independently of other units; *a* **modular** composed of modules.

modus *n* method; style.

modus operandi *n Lat* method of working.

modus vivendi *n Lat* way of coping, of living side by side.

mogul *n* **1** very powerful and wealthy person **2** small hill or bump on a ski run.

mohair *n* fabric made of Angora goat fleece.

moiety *n leg, lit* half-share; part.

moil *v n* labor, to work hard.

moist *a* damp; humid; *v* **moisten**; *n* **moisture** dampness; condensed water vapor.

molar *n* grinding tooth.

molasses *n* thick dark syrup made from raw sugar.

mold[1] *n* furry, fungoid growth caused by dampness; *a* **moldy** musty, decaying; *v* **molder** crumble, decay.

mold[2] *n* **1** pattern, hollow shape, matrix for shaping or casting soft materials **2** *fig* character; *v* give shape to; *n* **molding** modeling;

ornamental strip of wood.

molder *v* decay.

mole[1] *n* **1** small furry animal that lives in underground tunnels **2** spy working within an organization; *ns* **molehill** mound of earth left by mole when digging; **moleskin**.

mole[2] *n* dark-colored permanent spot on skin.

molecule *n* smallest particle of element or compound that can exist without chemical change; *a* **-cular**.

molest *v* trouble; pester; accost illegally.

moll *n sl* **1** girlfriend of gangster.

mollify *v* **1** pacify; appease **2** soften; *n* **mollification**.

mollusk *n* soft-bodied animal usually having hard shell (e.g., snail, oyster).

mollycoddle *v* pamper.

Molotov cocktail *n* homemade bomb made with any flammable liquid in a bottle.

molt *v* shed feathers, fur etc periodically; *n* act or time of moulting; *n* **molting**.

molten *a* (of metal, rock) melted.

molto *adv mus* much; very.

molybdenum *n* metallic element used in alloys.

mom-and-pop *a* of small, owner-operated store or business.

moment *n* **1** brief period of time **2** importance; *a* **momentary** brief; quick **momentous** of great importance; *n* **momentum**

impetus; increasing force.

monad *n* one-celled organism.

monarch *n* sovereign; supreme ruler; *ns* **monarchy** state ruled by monarch; **-ist** supporter of monarchy.

monastery *n* residence of a religious community; *a* **monastic** of monastery; of monks, nuns; *n* **monasticism** monastic life and system.

Monday *n* second day of week.

monetarism *n econ* theory that control of money supply creates stable economy; *n, a* **-ist**.

money *n* 1 coins; paper money; any form of credit usable as payment 2 wealth; *idm* **make money** grow rich; *ns* **m.-bags** *coll* rich person; **m.-box** closed box with slot for keeping money; **m.-changer** person whose job is to change money from one currency to another; **m.-grubber** *coll* person greedy for money and unscrupulous about how to acquire it (*a* **m.-grubbing**); **m.-lender, m.-maker, m.-market; m. supply** money available for spending in given economic system; *a* **moneyed** rich.

mongoose *n* small animal found in India that kills snakes; *pl* **-gooses** or **-geese**.

mongrel *n* animal (*esp* dog) of mixed breed; hybrid; *a* of mixed breeding or origin.

monitor *n* 1 one who warns, advises 2 large lizard 3 heavy gun-boat 4 master screen in TV studio; *v* listen to foreign broadcasts; *a* **monitory**.

monk *n* member of religious order, living under vows of poverty, chastity, etc.

monkey *n* 1 any primate (other than humans or lemurs), *esp* long-tailed 2 *coll* mischievous child; *phr v* **monkey about/around** play the fool; *ns* **m. business** mischievous behaviour; **m.-wrench** 1 wrench with adjustable jaw 2 *fig* something that disrupts (threw a **m. wrench** into the works).

mono- *prefix* single, alone.

mono *a* monophonic; *n coll* monophonic recording.

monochromatic *a* of one color.

monochrome *n* 1 with images in black, white, and shades of gray 2 using shades of one color only.

monocle *n* single eyeglass lens for one eye.

monogamy *n* practice of marrying only one partner at a time.

monoglot *a* able to speak one language only.

monogram *n* single figure made of two or more interwoven initials.

monolingual *a* monoglot.

monolith *n* single block of stone as monument.

monolog, monologue *n* 1 speech by single actor 2 comedy routine by solo comic.

mononucleosis *n* abnormally high levels of circulating white blood cells, causing exhaustion.

monophonic *a* using only one transmission channel.

monopoly *n* exclusive right of trading in specified commodity; *v* **monopolize** engross, enjoy to exclusion of others.

monorail *n* railroad where train runs along single-rail elevated track.

monosodium glutamate *n* chemical compound added to food to improve flavor (*also* **MSG**).

monosyllable word of one syllable; *a* **-syllabic**.

monotheism *n* belief in only one God.

monotone *n* single, unvaried tone; *a* **monotonous** lacking in variety; dully repetitive; *n* **monotony** lack of variety; tediousness.

monotype *n* machine casting type in single letters.

Monsieur *n Fr* form of address to French-speaking man (*pl* **Messieurs**).

Monsignor *n* form of address to senior Roman Catholic priest.

monsoon *n* seasonal wind of Indian Ocean; rainy season in India.

monster *n* 1 person, animal, thing of abnormal shape or huge size 2 abnormally wicked, cruel person; *a*

a
b
c
d
e
f
g
h
i
j
k
l
m
n
o
p
q
r
s
t
u
v
w
x
y
z

1 monstrous; like a monster 2 shocking 3 hideous; n **monstrosity** 1 freak 2 badly made, hideous object.

montage n Fr 1 final selection and arrangement of images in film 2 two or more pictures imposed on single background.

month n one of twelve parts into which year is divided; period of moon's revolution; a **monthly** occurring once a month; n magazine published monthly.

monument n tombstone, building, statue, etc. erected as memorial; a **-al** 1 of, serving as monument 2 massive; enormous.

moo n sound a cow makes.

mood ns a predominant emotion or a particular context; ling form of verb indicating its function.

moon n 1 earth's satellite 2 satellite of another planet; idm **ask for the moon** make an unreasonable request; idm **once in a blue moon** very rarely or never; idm **over the moon** ecstatically happy; phr v **moon about/around** wander aimlessly and gloomily; ns **moonbeam** beam of moonlight; **moonlight** light of the moon (v do a second job as well as regular job, usu undeclared for income tax); **moonshine** 1 moonlight 2 nonsense 3 usu corn liquor distilled illegally; **m.-shot** launch of

spacecraft to the moon; **moonstone** semiprecious stone with milky appearance; a **moonstruck** slightly crazed.

moor n tract of open country, usually hilly and heather-clad; n **m.-hen** water hen.

moor v fasten, secure (ship) by cables, chains etc; n pl **-ings** place where vessel is moored; cables, buoys etc by which it is secured.

moose n large N American deer with large antlers.

mop n bundle of yarn on long handle for washing floors; v **mops, mopping, mopped.** clean, wipe with mop; **mop up** fig round up, defeat.

mope v be low-spirited, depressed.

moped n small low-powered motorbike.

moral a relating to generally accepted ideas of right and wrong; virtuous; of right conduct; n lesson taught by experience, fable; pl **-s** principles of right and wrong conduct; n **m. support** encouragement, n **morality** good moral conduct; virtue; v **moralize** draw moral lesson from, think on moral aspect; n **moralist** teacher of, writer on morals.

morale n mental state, esp regarding courage etc.

morass n swamp, something that traps one.

moratorium n legal authorization to delay or defer payment of debt etc.

morbid a 1 related to disease 2 abnormal; pathological; unwholesome.

mordant a 1 sarcastic 2 corrosive 3 chemical (of dyeing) serving to fix colors.

more a greater in quantity, extent, etc.; comp of **many, much**; adv in addition, to greater degree; adv **moreover** besides.

morel n brown, edible mushroom.

morello n dark red, sour cherry.

mores n pl customs held to be typical of social group.

morganatic a of marriage between royal person and commoner.

morgue n Fr mortuary, storage place for dead people.

moribund a dying; decaying.

Mormon n member of Church of Latter-Day Saints, founded by Joseph Smith.

morn n lit dawn; morning.

morning a first part of day, from dawn until noon; ns **m. dress** clothes for men at formal daytime social occasions, including top hat with morning coat and gray trousers; **m. glory** climbing plant with trumpet-shaped blue flowers; **m. sickness** nausea sometimes experienced during early weeks of pregnancy, esp in morning; **m. star** the planet Venus seen in the eastern sky before dawn.

Morning Prayer n regular

daily service in the Episcopal and Anglican church.

morocco n fine, flexible leather made of goatskin.

moron n 1 mentally deficient person 2 sl fool, stupid person.

morose a surly; sullen; gloomy.

Morpheus n Greek good of sleep, dreams.

morphine n addictive narcotic alkaloid of opium used to relieve pain.

morpho n tropical butterfly with brilliant blue wings.

morphology n 1 bio (study of) form and structure of organisms 2 ling (study of) changing forms of words according to grammatical function; a **-ological;** n **-ologist**.

morris dance n English folk dance for men in costume and bells.

morrow n lit next following day; tomorrow.

Morse code n system of telegraphic signals, consisting of dots and dashes.

morsel n small piece; fragment.

mortal a 1 liable to die 2 causing death 3 implacable; n human being; n **m. sin** sin that leads to damnation unless confessed and atoned for; n **mortality 1** condition of being subject to death 2 deathrate.

mortar n 1 vessel in which substances are pounded

2 short-barrelled cannon 3 cement of lime, sand, water for holding bricks, etc. together; n **mortarboard** square, flat college graduation cap.

mortgage n conveyance of property as security for debt; v convey on mortgage; fig pledge; ns **mortgagee; mortgagor**.

mortician n undertaker.

mortify v 1 discipline by self-denial 2 humiliate 3 become gangrenous; n **mortification**.

mortise, mortice n hole cut in wood, etc. to receive tenon; v join by, make mortise in; n **mortise lock** one embedded in door.

mortuary a of, pertaining to death and burial; n building where corpses are kept before burial.

mosaic n pattern made by fitting together small pieces of colored marble, stone etc.

Moselle n dry white wine from Moselle valley.

mosey v infml stroll.

Moslem, Muslim n Mohammedan; a of, belonging to Mohammedans; Islamic.

mosque n Mohammedan temple for public worship.

mosquito n **-oes** or **-os**. biting gnat.

moss n low-growing tufted plant found on moist surfaces; lichen; a **mossy** covered with moss.

most a greatest in number,

quantity, degree; sup of **many, much;** idm **for the most part** mainly; idm **make the most of** use to the best advantage adv to greatest degree; adv **mostly** generally.

mote n a very small speck.

mot n Fr as **bon mot,** witty saying or remark.

motel n hotel especially designed with adjacent parking.

motet n musical term for polyphonic vocal composition on a sacred text.

moth n night-flying insect, related to butterfly; **clothes m.,** whose larvae feed on wooll, fur, etc.; n **mothball** ball of camphor or naphthalene to dispel moths from clothes; idm **in mothballs** in storage; a **m.-eaten 1** damaged by moths 2 fig shabby.

mother n 1 female parent 2 head of convent, nunnery as Mother Superior; ns **m. country** native land; **m.-in-law** mother of spouse; **m.-of-pearl** iridescent lining of mollusk shells; **m. tongue** native language; **motherhood** state of being mother; a **motherly;** n **-liness**.

Mother Goose n legendary author of nursery rhymes.

Mother's Day n in US, holiday honoring all mothers, observed on the second sunday in May.

Mother Nature n traditionally,

the source, nature personified as a woman.

motif n Fr recurrent theme esp in music; ornamental needlework pattern.

motile a (of organisms) capable of moving spontaneously n motility.

motion n 1 movement 2 proposal put to meeting 3 gesture 4 leg application for ruling; v indicate; makes gesture toward; idm **go through the motions** do in a perfunctory way, without commitment; n **m. picture** cinematic film; a **motionless** (adv **-ly**) a **motionless** at rest; still.

motive n cause; incentive; that which influences behavior or action; v **motivate** impel, induce; n **motivation.**

mot juste n Fr exact word or phrase.

motley a various colors; of mixed ingredients; n multicolored garment esp jester's.

motocross n motorcycle racing over rough ground.

motor n that which imparts movement; machine supplying motive power; engine; v travel or go at a steady pace; ns **motorcade** procession of cars; **m. car** Brit car; **m. cycle** (also **m. bike**) two-wheeled vehicle with engine; **m. cyclist** rider of this; **motoring** driving; **motorist** driver; **m. scooter** small engine-driven vehicle,

usu with two or three wheels.

mottled a mark with spots or blotches.

motto n **-oes** or **-os.** short phrase expressing maxim, rule of conduct, esp on coat-of-arms.

mound n raised heap of earth, stones, etc.; hillock.

mount v 1 climb; ascend 2 get on horseback 3 rise; increase 4 provide frame, setting for (picture, etc.) 5 organize (campaign, exhibition); n 1 that on which thing is mounted; 2 gun-carriage 3 mountain; high hill.

mountain n large, lofty hill; idm **make a mountain out of a molehill** exaggerate the importance e.g., of a problem; n **mountaineer** dweller in, expert climber of mountains; a **mountainous** very high; enormous.

mountain bike n off-road cycle with smaller frame and wider tires.

mountain lion n cougar.

mountebank n charletan; quack.

mourn n lament; grieve for; show sorrow; n **mourner;** a **mournful;** n **mourning** 1 grief esp for death 2 clothes worn as sign of such grief 3 time these are worn.

mouse n small rodent; fig shy person (pl **mice**); v catch, hunt mice; n **mouser** cat good at catching mice; n tool to manipulate cursor on computer.

mousse n 1 frothy dessert 2 foamy hairstyling preparation.

moussaka n esp Middle Eastern ground meat and eggplant casserole.

moustache n hair on upper lip, also **mustache.**

mouth n 1 opening in animal's head by which it eats and utters sounds 2 opening; outlet; aperture; v speak with exaggerated lip and jaw movement; n **mouthpiece** part of pipe, etc. held to or between lips; spokesperson.

move v 1 change position of 2 set into motion 3 affect feelings 4 make formal proposal; phr vs **move on** change to something new; **move out** leave one's accommodation; **move over** make room for somebody else; n 1 movement 2 fig device 3 step 4 change of abode or place of work; a **movable;** n **movement** 1 act, fact, process of moving 2 moving part of mechanism, esp of watch 3 division of musical composition.

movie n coll cinematic film; pl **-s** cinema.

mow v cut down (grass, etc.); fig **m. down** kill indiscriminately; pt **mowed;** pp **mowed, mown**; n **mower** mowing machine, one who mows.

MP abbr 1 Member of Parliament 2 (member of) Military Police.

mpg *abbr* miles per gallon.

mph *abbr* miles per hour.

Mr. *abbr* Mister (form of address to a man).

Mrs. *n* form of address to a married woman.

Ms. *n* form of address to a woman (married or unmarried).

MS *abbr* 1 manuscript 2 multiple sclerosis 3 Master of Science.

MSS *abbr* manuscripts.

much *a* great in quantiy; *n* great deal; *adv* greatly; nearly; *idm* **much as** although; *idm* **(cannot) make much of** (cannot) understand; *idm* **not much of** not a good; *idm* **not much point** no purpose or advantage.

muck *n* 1 filth; dirt 2 manure 3 garbage; *phr vs* **muck about/around** *coll* behave in a silly, inconsiderate way; waste time; **muck up** *coll* 1 make dirty 2 spoil; *ns* **m.-raking** searching for hints of scandal so as to spread malicious rumors; **m.-raker;** *a* **mucky** 1 dirty 2 distasteful.

mucus *n* slimy, viscous secretion of mucous membranes; *a* **mucous** secreting mucus; slimy.

mucilage *n* 1 sticky gelatinous plant secretion 2 glue or adhesive.

mud *n* very wet, moist earth; *ns* **m.-bath** 1 bath in mud for medicinal purposes 2 wet

sloppy conditions, as in sporting events; **mudguard** curved cover above bicycle wheel; **m.-pack** paste applied to face as beauty tonic; *a* **muddy;** *n* **muddiness.**

muddle *v* 1 bewilder; confuse 2 bungle; *n* disorder; mess; confusion; *phr vs* **muddle along** live in a purposeless way; **muddle through** *coll* achieve success in spite of being poorly equipped; *as* **m.-headed** lacking clarity of thought (*n* **-ness**); **muddled, muddling.**

muesli *n* Swiss breakfast food of mixed cereals, nuts, dried fruits, etc.

muff *v sport* miss; bungle; *n* furry tubular covering for hands.

muffin *n* quick bread of egg batter baked in muffin tin.

muffle *v* wrap with covering, for warmth or to deaden sound; *n* **muffler** 1 thick, warm scarf 2 *auto* silencer.

mug *n* 1 drinking cup 2 *sl* face 3 simpleton; *v* **mugs, mugging, mugged.** *sl* rob with violence, in public place; *ns* **mugger; mugging.**

muggy *a* damp; close; oppressive.

mug shot *n sl* photograph.

mugwump *n* person trying to be neutral in politics, an independant.

Muhammadan *a, n* Muslim.

mulberry *n* tree with reddishpurple edible berries.

mulch *n* loose covering of leaves etc. on plants.

mule *n* 1 hybrid between horse and donkey 2 stubborn person 3 spinning machine 4 slip-on shoe with no heal or strap; *n* **muleteer** mule driver; *a* **mulish** obstinate.

mule deer *n* large, long-eared N American deer.

mull *v* 1 heat (wine, etc.) with spices 2 ponder, deliberate over.

mullein *n* tall herb with wooly leaves.

mullet *n* edible seafish.

mulligatawny *n* chicken soup made with curry powder; *also n* **mulligan stew** stew or soup made from any available ingredients.

mullion *n* upright shaft, *usu* of stone, between window panes.

multi- *prefix* many; *as* **multicolored** of many colors; **multifarious** of many kinds; **multilateral** with many participants (*adv* **-ly**); **multimedia** using several types of media; **multiplay** (of CD) providing recording as well as playback facility; **multinational** having offices, manufacturing facilities in many countries (*also n* company of this kind); **multitask** *comput* able to carry out several diverse tasks simultaneously (*n* **-ing**); **multitrack** using tape with two or more

A
B
C
D
E
F
G
H
I
J
K
L
M
N
O
P
Q
R
S
T
U
V
W
X
Y
Z

recording tracks.

multiple *a* having many parts; *n* number that contains another number an exact number of times; *ns* **m. sclerosis** chronic disease of central nervous system resulting in loss of motor control, paralysis (*also* **MS**); **multiplicity** great number; *v* **multiply 1** add (number) to itself specified number of times **2** increase in number **3** breed (*n* **-plication**).

multitude *n* great number; crowd of people; *a* **multidinous** very numerous.

mum¹ *a* silent; *idm* **mum's the word** *coll* keep it secret; *n* chrysanthemum.

mum² *v* mime.

mumble *v* speak indistinctly; mutter.

mumblety-peg *n* game where the players try to throw a jack knife so that the blade sticks into the ground.

mumbo-jumbo *n* meaningless ritual or words.

mummy *n* embalmed body, esp of ancient Egyptian; *v* **mummify;** *a* **mummified**.

mumps *n pl* painful contagious disease, inflammation of parotid and salivary glands.

munch *v* cruch, chew noisily and vigorously.

munchkin *n* small, elflike person.

mundane *a* earthly; worldly; dull.

mung bean *n* leguminous Asian plant or its seeds.

municipal *a* belonging to affairs of boroughs, city, town; *n* **municipality** town, borough, etc. enjoying local government; local authority.

munitions *n pl* military stores.

mural *a* of, on wall; *n* wall-painting.

murder *n* unlawful, intentional homicide; *v* kill thus; *n* **murderer;** *fem* **murderess;** *a* **murderous** intending to murder; deadly.

murk *n* thick darkness; *a* **murky** dark; cloudy.

murmur *v* **1** make low, continuous sound **2** speak in low voice **3** grumble; *n* act, sound of murmuring.

Murphy's law *n coll* fatalistic outlook, as in "anything that can go wrong, will go wrong."

muscat *n* raisin; musky grape; *n* **muscatel** muscat; sweet wine made from it.

muscle *n* animal elastic fibrous tissue, highly contractile, by which movement is effected; *fig* bodily force, strength; *a* **muscular 1** of muscle **2** having well developed strong muscles (*n* **m. dystrophy** long-term illness causing wasting muscle; *a* **muscle-bound** with muscles strained and inelastic through overexercise.

muse *n* **1** one of nine Greek goddesses associated with the arts, sciences, and literature; **2** *fig* **muse** poetic inspiration (*v* ponder; meditate).

museum *n* collection of natural, scientific, historical, or artistic objects; building housing such collection.

mush *n* soft, pulpy mass; *a* **mushy** soft; pulpy.

mushroom *n* quick-growing edible fungus; *v* **1** *fig* grow, expand rapidly; **2** gather mushrooms; *a* of, like mushroom.

music *n* **1** art or method of producing rhythmical, melodious sounds **2** written or printed score of musical composition **3** *fig* pleasing sound; *ns* **m. box** box with mechanism that plays music when lid is opened; **m.-hall** (formerly musical and comic entertainment at) variety theater; **m.-stand** wooden or metal frame to hold printed music for player during performance; *a* **musical; m. chairs** party game in which players compete for chairs to sit on when the music stops.

musk *n* strong scent obtained from male muskdeer; plant with similar scent; *a* **-y; *ns*** **m.deer** small hornless deer; **m.ox** Arctic ox; **m.-rat** N American water rat.

Muslim *n*, *a* (adherent) of religion founded by Mohammad.

muslin *n* plain, woven cotton fabric.

mussel *n* edible bivalve mollusk.

must¹ *n* new unfermented wine.

must[2] *v aux* expressing compulsion, obligation, certainty; *pt* **had to**; no *pp*; *n coll* an essential.

mustache *n* = moustache.

mustang *n* **1** American wild or semiwild prairie horse **2** an officer (as in US Navy) risen from the ranks.

mustard *n* hot, pungent powder made from pounded seeds of mustard plant, used as condiment; *n* **m. gas** poisonous irritant gas.

muster *v* assemble; summon; *n* assembly of troops, etc. for inspection etc.

musty *a* moldy; stale; *n* **-iness**.

mustn't *contraction of* must not.

mutable *a* changeable; *n* **mutation 1** change **2** sudden genetic change.

mutatis mutandis *adv Lat* after making the appropriate changes.

mute *a* dumb; silent; *n* **1** person unable to speak **2** device used to soften tone or reduce sound of musical instrument; *a* **muted** muffled (sound).

mutilate *v* maim; cut off; render imperfect; *n* **mutilation**.

mutiny *n* **-ies.** revolt against authority *esp* in armed forces; *v* **mutinies, mutinying, mutinied.** revolt; *a* **mutinous**; *n* **mutineer**.

mutt *n coll* mongrel dog.

mutter *v* speak indistinctly in low voice; grumble.

mutton *n* flesh of sheep used as food; *ns* **muttonchops** long wide sideburns (*also* **m.-chop whiskers**); **m.-head** *coll* stupid person.

mutual *a* **1** performed by joint action **2** reciprocal **3** common to both.

muu-muu *n* Hawaiian loose, long dress.

muzzle *n* **1** mouth and nose of animal **2** cover for these to prevent biting **3** mouth of gun; *v* **1** put muzzle on **2** impose silence on.

muzzy *a* dazed; vague; fuddled; *n* **-ness**.

MW *abbr* megawatt(s).

my *poss a* belonging to **me**.

mycology *n* biological study of fungi and mushrooms.

myalgic encephalomyelitis *n* viral disease affecting nervous system, with long-lasting effect of fatigue and impaired muscular control (*also* **ME** *or* **post-viral syndrome.**)

mynah, myna *n* Asiatic bird that can be taught to talk.

myopia *n* near-sightedness; *a* **myopic**.

myriad *n* ten thousand; endless number; *a* countless.

myrrh *n* aromatic substance from plants.

myrtle *n* evergreen, flowering shrub.

myself *pron* **1** *emphatic form of* I, ME *reflex form of* I, **me**.

mystery *n* **1** anything secret, unknown, unexplained **2** secret rite **3** obscurity; *a* mysterious; *adv* mysteriously.

mystic *n* having inner, secret meanings; esoteric; *n* one who believes in attainment, through contemplation, of inaccessible truths; *a* **-al**; *n* **-ism**.

mystify *n* puzzle; bewilder; *n* **mystification**.

mystique *n* elusive quality of sth much admired but not properly understood.

myth *n* **1** fictitious story or legend **2** imaginary person or thing; *a* **-ical**; *n* **-ology** collection, body of myths concerning ancient religious belief; *a* **-ological**.

a
b
c
d
e
f
g
h
i
j
k
l
m
n
o
p
q
r
s
t
u
v
w
x
y
z

A B C D E F G H I J K L M **N** O P Q R S T U V W X Y Z

nab *v* **nabs, nabbing, nabbed.** *sl* catch suddenly; arrest.

nabob *n* wealthy or influential person.

nacho *n* tortilla chip with spicy flavoring and topped with cheese.

nacre *n* mother-of-pearl *a* **nacreous.**

nadir *n* point opposite zenith; lowest point.

nag *n* small riding pony; horse.

nag *v* **nags, nagging, nagged.** find fault persistently; scold; *fig* give constant pain.

naiad *n* waternymph.

nail *v* **1** horny sheath at end of fingers and toes **2** talon **3** metal spike for fixing things together; *v* fix, fasten to, with nail; *phr v* **nail down** force to a commitment; *a* **n.-biting** intensely exciting; *n* **n. polish** quick-drying liquid giving hard shiny finish to fingernails, toenails.

naive, naïve *a* Fr **1** natural; ingenuous **2** foolishly simple; *n* **naivete, naivety.**

naked *a* unclothed; nude; exposed; bare; without covering; *n* **-ness.**

name *n* **1** word by which person, thing, idea is known or called **2** lineage; family **3** reputation; *v* call by name; give name to; appoint; identify by name; *idm* **name of the game** essential purpose of activity; *ns* **n. day** feast day of saint after whom one was named; **namesake** person having same name as another; **name-tape** identifying tape sewn onto clothing *v* **n.-drop** refer to well-known people in order to impress others (*ns* **n.-dropper, n.-dropping**) *a* **-less** anonymous; unknown; *adv* **-ly;** that is to say.

nanny *n* child's nurse; **n. goat** female domesticated goat.

nano- *prefix* **1** thousand millionth part of (*eg* **nanometer, nanosecond**) **2** of microscopically small objects and measurements (*eg* **nanotechnology**).

nap¹ *n* downy surface of cloth; *v* **naps, napping, napped.** put, rise nap on.

nap² *n* short sleep; *v* doze; *idm* **be caught napping** be caught unaware.

nape *n* back of the neck.

napkin *n* small cloth or paper used at meals to protect clothes and wipe fingers, lips.

narcosis *n* unconsciousness induced by drugs; *n* **narcotic** drug causing sleep, insensibility; *a* inducing sleep, etc.

narc *n* *sl* government narcotics agent.

narrate *v* relate; tell story of; *ns* **-ation, -ative** story; account; *a* **-ating;** *n* **-ator.**

narrow *a* of small breadth in proportion to length; *v* become, cause to become narrow; *adv* **-ly** closely; only just; *a* **n.-minded** prejudiced, bigoted.

narthex *n* area or vestibule leading into the nave of a cathedral or church.

narwhal *n* Arctic whale.

nasal *a* of or in nose; *n* nasal sound (phonetics).

nasty *a* offensive; dirty; disgusting; disagreeable; *n* **-iness.**

natal *a* of, at, belonging to birth.

natation *n* act of swimming, floating; *as* **natant** floating, as of plants; **natatory** pertaining to swimming.

nation *n* large group of people having common language, culture, etc., and living in one area under one government; *a* **national** of, common to a nation (*n* citizen of a state); *ns* **n. debt** amount owed by country to other countries; **n. park** conservation area under care of the state; **n. service** compulsory military service); *adv* **-ally;** *ns* **nationalism** 1 pride in one's native country 2 political movement for independence (*n* **-ist;** *as* **-ist, -istic**); **nationality** status of belonging to a particular nation; *v* **nationalize** take under government control (*a* **-ized** *n* **-ization**); *a* **nationwide** covering the entire country.

National Guard *n* state military force on call for emergencies.

native *a* 1 belonging to from birth, nationality, tec. 2 of natives, place of origin *n* **native** living thing native to a place.

Native American *n* American Indian.

nativity *n* birth *esp* of Christ.

NATO *abbr* North Atlantic Treaty Organization.

natty *a* *coll* neat and smart in appearance; *adv* **-ily.**

natural *a* 1 arising from the physical world; not artificial (**n. gas**) 2 uncultivated; wild 3 normal (**n. manner**) 4 innate (n. talent) 5 born out of legal marriage (**n. child**); *ns* **n. childbirth** childbirth without use of anesthetic; **n. history** study of plants, animals, etc.; **n. selection** evolutionary process in which the species that are best at adaptation tend to survive; *adv* **-ly** 1 in a natural way 2 of course; *ns* **-ism** style of art, literature that aims at presenting real life (*a* **-istic**); **-ist** person who studies natural history; *v* **naturalize** give officially changed nationality to immigrant; *a* **-ized;** *n* **-ization.**

nature *n* 1 everything not manmade in the world 2 *esp cap* forces controlling events in the physical world 3 character 4 primitive state (*idm* **back to/return to nature**); *idm* **call of nature** *coll* urgent need to defecate/urinate; *idm* **second nature** action that can be performed (as if) by instinct; *ns* **n. trail** marked route through woods, fields for observation of natural phenomena; **naturism** nudism (*a*, *n* **-ist**); **naturopath** expert in treatment of illness by use of herbal remedies, natural dieting and natural healing (*n* **-pathy**; *a* **-pathic**).

naught *n* nothingness; nonexistence; symbol (0).

naughty *a* 1 mischievous; disobedient; badly behaved 2 immoral; *n* **-tiness.**

nausea *n* sickness; disgust; *v* **nauseate** sicken; disgust; *a* **nauseous** causing or feeling nausea; loathsome.

nautical *a* pertaining to ships, sailors, etc.; *n* **n. mile** unit of distance at sea, 6,080 ft.

nautilus *n* mollusk with pearly shell.

naval *a* of, by the navy.

nave *n* central part of church.

navel *n* rounded depression in abdomen, umbilicus.

navigate *v* cause to sail or travel on set course; direct ship or aircraft; *ns* **-ation** act, science of navigating; **-ator** one skilled in science of navigation; *a* **navigable.**

navy *n* *cap* all warships of state; fleet; naval personnel; *n,a* **n.blue** (of) dark blue (color).

nay *n* no.

Nazism *n* National Socialist party led by Hitler in World War II, characterized by totalitarian control and racial supremacy; *n* **neo-Nazi** present-day adherent to Nazi doctrine

NB *abbr Lat* nota bene (note well).

NBC *abbr* National Broadcasting Company.

NCO *abbr* noncommissioned officer, or noncom.

a
b
c
d
e
f
g
h
i
j
k
l
m
n
o
p
q
r
s
t
u
v
w
x
y
z

A B C D E F G H I J K L M **N** O P Q R S T U V W X Y Z

Neanderthal man n Stone Age man.

neapolitan a, n 1 ice cream in different colored, flavored layers 2 cap (inhabitant) of Naples.

near adv close to; not far from; a close in relationship, degree; about to come, happen; v approach; ns **N. East** non-European countries of E Mediterranean; **n.miss** 1 narrow avoidance of collision; narrow escape from bomb, missile 2 failure by very small amount to achieve something; **n.thing** situation so evenly balanced that the outcome is/was unpredictable; idm **(one's) nearest and dearest** (one's) own family; idm **near by** close at hand (a **nearby**); adv **nearly** almost; a **near-sighted** myopic, able to see clearly only close up, short-sighted (n **-ness**).

neat a 1 trim; well-kept; clean and orderly 2 skillful 3 (of utterances) apt 4 (of alcoholic liquor) pure, undiluted; n **neatness**.

nebbish n clumsy or ineffectual person.

nebula n luminous cloudlike area in sky; cluster of stars; a **nebulous** 1 cloudy; misty 2 fig vague; indefinite.

necessary a inevitable; indispensable; requisite; obligatory; n that which is essential or indispensable; n **necessity** 1 compulsion; anything inevitable because of natural law 2 poverty; want; v **necessitate** make necessary; compel; a **necessitous** poor; destitute.

neck n 1 part of body joining head to trunk 2 narrow connecting part 3 isthmus; v sl kiss and cuddle; ns **neckcloth** tie; **necklace** string of jewels, beads, gold chain, etc. worn around neck.

necropolis n large ancient cemetery.

nectar n myth drink of the gods; sugary liquid produced by flowers; ns **nectary** gland that yields nectar; **nectarine** variety of peach with smooth skin.

neé a Fr (fem) born (with the surname).

need n 1 that which is required; necessity 2 poverty; want; as **needful** necessary; **needless** unnecessary; **needy** poor; impoverished.

needle n 1 small sharp instrument with eye to hold thread, for sewing 2 pointed end of hypodermic syringe 3 thin rod of metal, plastic, etc. used in knitting 4 magnetized bar of compass 5 leaf of pine or fir; v coll annoy; goad; ns **needlepoint** fine embroidery of a pattern onto canvas; **-woman** skillful woman sewer; seamstress; **-work** sewing, embroidery.

ne'er-do-well n improvident good-for-nothing.

nefarious a unlawful; wicked.

negate v deny; nullify; n **-ation** contradiction; denial.

negative a 1 expressing denial 2 lacking in positive qualities 3 phot reversing light and dark; n **negative equity** debt that occurs when the value of property falls below the amount of the loan that secured it.

neglect v ignore; pay no heed to; disregard; omit, fail to do; n fact of neglecting or being neglected; a **-ful;** adv **-ly**.

negligee n woman's nightgown or robe.

negligence n heedlessness; lack of care, attention; ns **negligent; negligible** not worth considering.

negotiate v 1 arrange, compromise, settle business matter, by discussion 2 get cash for security 3 discuss terms of peace with 4 surmount (obstacle); a **negotiable;** ns **-iation; -iator**.

negus n a drink of port or sherry mixed with hot water, sweetened, and flavored with nutmeg and lemon.

neigh n whinny of a horse; v make cry of a horse.

neighbor n one who lives next door, or nearby; a **neighboring** adjacent; placed near together; n **neighborhood** (n **n.watch** group of neighbors with mutual arrangement to protect each other against criminal activities); *idm* **in the neighborhood** roughly; *as* **neighboring** nearby; adjacent; **neighborly** friendly (*n* **-iness**).

neither *a, pron* not either; also *adv, conj.*

nelson *n* a wrestling hold.

nemesis *n* cause of one's downfall; enemy.

neo *prefix* new; modern.

neoclassical *a* of any modern style (in art, literature, music, etc.) influenced by classical style.

neolithic *a* of later Stone Age.

neologism *n* **1** new word, phrase **2** act of inventing word.

neon *n* an inert gas occurring in atmosphere; **n.light** glowing light obtained by ionizing gas in tube or bulb.

neonatal *n* of or relating to a newborn.

neophyte *n* new convert; novice; beginner.

nephew *n* brother's, sister's son.

nephritis *n* inflammation of kidneys.

nepotism *n* favoritism toward one's relatives.

neoprene *n* synthetic rubber.

Neptune *n* Roman god of the sea; third largest planet eighth from the sun.

nerd *n sl* inept or clumsy person; idiot; *a* **-ish**.

nerve *n* **1** cord-like fiber, bundle of fibers, carrying sensory and motor impulses from the brain to parts of body **2** courage **3** *coll* impudence (*idm* **what nerve!**) **4** *pl* **-s** nervousness (*idm* **a fit of nerves**); *idm* **get on somebody's nerves** irritate unbearably; *idm* **hit/touch a raw nerve** say something to cause anger, anguish, etc.; *ns* **n.center 1** group of nerve cells **2** control center of organization; **n.gas** gas that paralyses central nervous system with usually fatal effect; *as* **n.-racking** terrifying; causing extreme anxiety; **nervous 1** of the nerves (*ns* **n.breakdown** serious medical condition of acutely depression and exhaustion; **n.system** system of nerves in living creature) **2** tensely excited **3** timid; *adv* **-ly**; *n* **-ness**; **nervy 1** jumpy; easily excited **2** brazen; bold.

nescient *a* not knowing; ignorant; *n* **nescience** agnosticism.

-ness *n suffix* condition or state of.

nest *n* structure built by bird in which it lays eggs and rears young; snug shelter; *v* build, occupy nest; *n* **n.-egg 1** real or dummy egg left in hen's nest to stimulate laying **2** *coll* money saved up.

nestle *v* settle cozily; lie, press closely against.

nestling *n* young bird before it leaves nest.

net *n* **1** meshwork of knotted, woven cord, thread, etc. **2** length of this used to catch anything, or for protection; *v* **nets, netting, netted.** catch in, cover with net; *ns* **netting** string, wire network.

net *n* free of all deductions; remaining after all necessary expenses; *v* yield as clear profit.

nether *a* lower; below.

nethermost *a* lowest.

netherworld *n* underworld, place of the dead.

nettle *n* plant with stinging hairs on leaves and stalks; *v* irritate; annoy.

network *n* **1** meshed structure of wire, cords etc **2** system of intersecting channels of communication (roads, railroads, radio, TV) **3** system of interlinking operations (business, espionage, crime); *v* establish set of contacts; *n* **-ing**.

neuralgia *n* sharp pain along a nerve, esp in the face; *a* **neuralgic.**

neurology *n* study of nerves and nervous disease; *a* **-ological;** *n* **-ologist.**

neurosis *n* **-ses.** mild mental illness that causes irrational fear or worry; *a* **neurotic** abnormally tense, worried, or afraid.

neuter *a* neither masculine nor feminine; *n* **1** noun, pronoun of neuter gender

a b c d e f g h i j k l m **n** o p q r s t u v w x y z

2 animal deprived of sexual organs (*v* castrate or spay).

neutral *a* 1 impartial; not taking either side in dispute, *esp* war; 2 (of gears) disengaged; *n* state or subject of state taking neither side in conflict; *n* **-ity** nonparticipation *esp* in war; *v* **-ize** make, treat as neutral; counteract, make ineffectual; *n* **-ization**.

neutron *n* electrically uncharged atomic particle; *n* **n.bomb** lethal nuclear bomb.

never *adv* not ever; emphatic negative; *adv* **nevertheless** notwithstanding.

new *a* 1 not previously existing 2 recently discovered 3 newly grown, produced; fresh 4 unfamiliar; novel; untried; *as* **n.-born, n.-found;** *ns* **n.blood** new members bringing new ideas, enthusiasm, etc.; **newcomer; n.moon** crescent moon in first days of new quarter; **newspeak** artificial language designed to distort meaning of words; **N.Testament** second part of Bible relating life and teaching of Jesus and his followers; **N.World** western hemisphere; **N.Year** first few days of January; **N.Year's Day** January 1; **N.Year's Eve** December 31; *a* **newfangled** *coll* modern but not easy to adapt to; *adv* **newly** (*n* **newlywed** person just married, *esp pl;*

a **-wedded**) *n* **-ness.**

New Age *a* social movement in late 20th century comprising tenets of Native American and Eastern thought; *mus* soothing, relaxing form of instrumental music.

newel *n* post at bottom or top of stairway.

news *n* information, reports of recent events; tidings; *ns* **n.agency** agency collecting news for media to use; **newscaster** person reading news on radio, TV (*also* **newsreader**); **n.-hound** *coll* over-enthusiastic news reporter; **n.-letter** informal occasional letter to members of club, of organization; **newspaper** daily or weekly printed publication containing news, comment, letters, reviews, etc.; **newsprint** paper on which newspaper is printed; **newsreel** short film on current events; *a* **newsworthy** interesting enough to be reported.

new wave *n* movement away from tradition.

New World *n* the Western hemisphere.

newt *n* small lizardlike amphibian.

next *a, adv* nearest in order, rank time, etc.; *idm* **next to** almost; *adv* **n.door** in adjacent building, house; *idm* **n.door to** close to; *n* **next-of-kin** nearest blood

relative.

nexus *n* link or series of links.

niacin *n* nicotinic acid, a vitamin.

nib *n* split penpoint; point of a quill pen.

nibble *v* 1 bite gently; with small bites 2 *fig* show signs of being attracted by (offer etc); *n* tentative bite.

niblick *n* golf club.

nice *a* 1 fastidious; punctilious 2 pleasing 3 delicate 4 kind, polite; *n* **nicety** accuracy; *pl* **-ies** subtle details.

Nicean Creed *n* Christian statement of belief, used in liturgical worship.

niche *n* small recess in wall; *fig* place, scope suitable for person's work, condition, etc.

nick *n* 1 notch; slit 2 small cut; *idm* **in the nick of time** only just in time; *v* cut notch in.

nickel *n* 1 hard, silver-white metallic element 2 five-cent coin.

nickelodeon *n* electric record player or jukebox.

nickname *n* extra name given in affection or derision.

nicotine *n* oily, poisonous addictive alkaloid in tobacco.

niece *n* brother's, sister's daughter. *See* **nephew.**

nifty *a coll* 1 skillful 2 effective 3 stylish.

niggard *n* covetous, miserly person; *a* **niggardly.**

niggle *v* fret, be fussy over petty details; *a* **niggling** too fussy; small but persistent.

nigh *a, adv, prep, ar* near.

night *n* **1** period from sunset to sunrise **2** darkness; *ns* **n.blindness** inability to see in dark or dim light; **nightcap** drink before bedtime; **nightclub** restaurant with late night entertainment, dancing, etc.; **nightfall** onset of darkness after sunset; **nightgown** garment worn by woman in bed (*also coll* **nightie**); **nightingale** bird with melodious song (often noticed at night); **n.life** entertainments at night **nightmare 1** frightening dream **2** harrowing experience (*a* - **marish**); **nightshade** plant with poisonous berries and bell-shaped flowers; **n.shirt** long loose garment worn in bed by man; **n.watchman** person employed to guard building, construction site, etc. at night; *a, adv* **nightly** (happening) every night.

nihilism *n* systematic rejection of traditional beliefs and moral principles; violent revolutionary beliefs, doctrines etc; anarchism; *n* **-list**.

Nike *n* Greek goddess of victory.

nil *n* nothing.

nimble *a* quick; agile; alert; clever.

nimbostratus *n* low rainy cloud layer *usu* dark and threatening.

nimbus *n* **1** halo **2** rain cloud.

nincompoop *n* fool.

nine *n, pron, det* cardinal number after eight; *idm* **nine day's wonder** short-lived success; *idm* **dressed to the nines** elaborately dressed; *as, ns, prons, dets* **ninth** ordinal number 9th part; **nineteen** nine plus ten; **nineteenth**; **ninety** nine tens; **ninetieth**; *n* **ninepins** a bowling game.

ninny *n* fool.

ninja *n* a person with outstanding ability in Japanese martial arts.

nip *v* **nips, nipping, nipped. 1** pinch sharply with fingers, claws **2** pinch off (buds, leaves, etc.) **3** (*of wind*) cut off; blight; *idm* **nip something in the bud** stop something before it can develop; *n* **1** pinch **2** sharp bite of wind or frost **3** small drink; *a* **nippy 1** quick; active **2** frosty; cold.

nipple *n* **1** small protuberance at center of breast in mammal from which milk flows; **2** artificial rubber or plastic top to baby bottle; **3** metal or plastic device of similar shape that allows for lubrication of machinery.

nisi *conj leg* becoming valid at a certain time unless cause is shown for rescinding it.

nit[1] *n* egg of louse or other parasitic insect; *ns* **nit-picking 1** cleaning hair of nits; **2** concern for little trivial details as a basis for finding fault (*a* showing such concern); **n.-picker**.

nit[2] *n* silly person (*also* **nitwit**).

niter, nitre *n* white salt used in gunpowder

nitrate compound of nitric acid and alkali.

nitrogen colorless gaseous element, forming 78% of the air; *a* **nitric**; *n* **n. acid** powerful corrosive acid.

nitroglycerine *n* explosive liquid.

nitrous oxide *n* colorless, odorless gas used as anesthetic in dentistry. sometimes produces euphoria (laughing gas).

nix *adv* no; a negative.

no *n* refusal; negative word, vote; (*pl* **noes**); *a* not any; *adv* in no respect; none.

no. *abbr* number.

No, Noh *n* classic, stylized Japanese drama.

Noah *n* patriarch in Old Testament who built an ark that survived the Flood.

Nobel prize *n* any of the prizes awarded annually for outstanding achievement in science, literature, or promotion of peace.

noble *a* **1** famous **2** having high ideals; admirable **3** of high rank; *n* person of noble birth; *ns* **nobility** quality of being noble; body of those with hereditary titles; **nobleman** member of nobility; British peer.

noblesse oblige *n Fr* idea of

obligatory, responsible behavior associated with those nobly born or of high social status.

nobody *pron* no person; *n* person of no account.

no-brainer *n sl* something that requires little or no thought.

nocturnal *n* of, in, by night; active at night.

nocturne *n* musical composition dealing with night time, dreams, etc.

nod *v* **nods, nodding, nodded.** bow head slightly, sharply in assent, greeting, etc.; droop head when drowsy; *phr v* **nod off** fall asleep; *n* act of nodding; *idm* (**have a**) **nodding acquaintance** (have) very limited knowledge.

node *n* **1** knot, joint on stem of plant **2** hard swelling on muscle **3** point of intersection; *n* **nodule** small rounded lump; *a* **nodular** of nodes; having nodules.

noel *n* Christmas carol; *cap Fr* Christmas.

no-fly zone *n* area within which no aircraft are permitted to fly.

noise *n* clamor; loud sound; din; *as* **-less; noisy** making much noise; *n* **big noise** *sl* important person.

nomad *n* member of wandering, pastoral tribe; wanderer; *a* **-ic.**

no-man's-land *n* neutral zone between two opposing forces, controlled by neither.

nom de plume *n Fr* writer's assumed name; pen name.

nomenclature *n* system of names or naming used in classifying; terminology.

nominal *a* **1** pertaining to name **2** existing in name only **3** inconsiderable.

nominate *v* name, propose person for post, office; *ns* **-ator; -ation; nominee** person nominated.

nominative *a* in the form used for grammatical subject.

non- *prefix* not; opposite of **1** *forming as;* **nonaligned** not supporting major political power; **noncommissioned** below rank of commissioned officer (*n* **n-officer,** *also* **NCO**); **nonspecific** general; **nonstick** treated to prevent food sticking during cooking; **2** *forming ns;* **nonevent** event that fails to meet expectations; **nonflammable** *a* not burning easily; **non sequitur** statement that does not logically follow what has gone before; **nonsmoker** person who never smokes; **nonstarter 1** competitor that withdraws at the start of a race **2** plan that is seen to be unworkable. *Many other negative compounds are not given here, where the meaning may be deduced from the simple word.*

nonagenerian *n* person aged between 90 and 100.

nonce *n* **for the n.** for the present; once only.

nonchalant *a* indifferent; *n* **nonchalance.**

noncommittal *a* refusal to take sides, neutral **adv -ly.**

nonconformist *n* dissenter.

nondescript *a* not easily classified; vague; indefinite.

none *pron* no one; *adv* in no way.

nonentity *n* unimportant person; nonexistent thing.

nonet *n* composition or combination of nine voices or instruments.

nonetheless *adv* nevertheless.

no-no *n* something forbidden, unacceptable.

nonpareil *n* one without equal; small chocolate disk covered with sugar pellets.

nonplussed, nonplused *a* in state of perplexity, bewilderment; taken aback.

nonsense *n* lack of sense; meaningless words, statement; absurdity; *a* **nonsensical** absurd; ridiculous; *adv* **-ly.**

non sequitur *n Lat* a response that does not logically follow the previous statement.

noodle *n* **1** head, noggin (as use your **n.**) **2** simpleton **3** food made of egg and flour *usu* in ribbon form *v* improvise aimlessly.

nook *n* corner; retreat; hiding-place.

noon *n* midday; twelve o'clock.

no one *pron* nobody, no person.

noose *n* loop of rope with

slipknot, allowing it to be drawn tight.

nope *adv coll* no.

nor *conj* and not.

Nordic *a* pertaining to Germanic races of Europe, *esp* Scandinavian.

norm *n* recognized standard; pattern; type; *a* **-al** average; ordinary; conforming to accepted standard, type; *n* **-ality** *v* **normalize** make normal (*n* **-ization**).

Norman architecture *n* style of Romanesque architecture that appeared around AD 950 in France.

normative *a* prescribing or conforming to a norm.

north *n* cardinal compass point opposite midday sun; northern parts of earth or country generally; *a* to, from, in north; *as* **northern** pertaining to north; **northerly** from, to direction of north; *n* **northerner** inhabitant of northern region of country.

northeaster *n* storm with strong north easterly winds.

northern lights *n* the aurora borealis; shimmering lights that appear in the sky in the northern hemisphere.

nose *n* external organ of smell, used in breathing; any projection like a nose; *idm* **a nose for** an instinctive way of finding; *v* sniff at; *idm* **nose one's way** move cautiously; *phr vs* **nose about/around** *coll* try (stealthily) to satisfy one's

curiosity; **nose out** *coll* discover; *ns* **nosebag** bag of food worn by horse; **nosebleed** instance of spontaneous bleeding from nose; **n.cone** front end of rocket; *v* **nosedive 1** (*of aircraft*) fall suddenly nose first **2** *fig* fall dramatically (*also n* such a fall); **nosegay** small bouquet.

no-see-um *n* very small biting insects.

nosh *n sl* snack; *v sl* to eat.

nostalgia *n* **1** homesickness **2** sentimental, wistful longing for what is past.

nostril *n* one of two external orifices of nose.

nostrum *n* a panacea, medicine made from secret ingredients.

nosy, nosey *a coll* inquisitive.

not *adv* expressing denial, negation, refusal.

notable *a* remarkable; conspicuous; *n* notable person; *adv* **-ably**; *n* **-ability** person of distinction.

notary *n* public official legally entitled to attest, certify deeds, contracts, etc; *v* **notarize** authenticate by notary.

notation *n* system of symbols for representing numbers, musical notes, etc.

notch *n* V-shaped cut, nick; *v* make notches in.

note *n* **1** brief informal letter or memorandum **2** brief comment on textual matter (*e.g.*, footnote) **3** piece of

paper money; printed or written promise of payment **4** single musical sound; symbol for this on paper **5** sign, hint of specified feeling (*e.g.*, **note of anger**); *idm* **of note** famous; *idm* **take note of** pay attention to; *v* **1** observe **2** record in writing; *ns* **notebook** book for making notes; **notepaper** paper for writing letters; *as* **noted** famous; **n.-worthy** of interest and/or importance (*n* **-iness**).

nothing *n* not anything; zero; *adv* not at all.

notice *n* **1** announcement **2** attention **3** dismissal (of employee) **4** written warning; *v* observe; heed; *a* **-able** striking; easily seen; appreciable; *adv* **-ably**.

notify *v* **notifies, notifying, notified.** report; make known; tell officially; *a* **notificable**; *n* **notification**.

notion *n* idea; conception; thought; belief *n* **notional 1** imaginary **2** assumed for the purpose of discussion; theoretical (*adv* **-ly**).

notoriety *n* quality of being well-known in bad sense; *a* **notorious** commonly known in unfavorable sense.

notwithstanding *prep* in spite of; *adv, conj* although.

nougat *n* candy of sugar paste and nuts, fruit, etc.

nought *n* nothing.

noun *n* word used to name person, thing, action, place;

often can be replaced with a pronoun.

nourish *v* feed; sustain with food **2** *fig* foster, encourage; *n* **-ment.**

nova *n* star whose brilliance flares briefly.

nouveau riche *n* person recently wealthy (*pl* **nouveaux riches**).

nouvelle cuisine *n* in French cuisine, food prepared with light sauces and fresh vegetables.

novel[1] *a* new; strange; unfamiliar; *n* **novelty 1** newness **2** newly marketed ornament.

novel[2] *n* fictional prose story in book form; *ns* **-ist** author of novels; **novella** work of fiction longer than short story but shorter and less complex than novel.

November *n* the eleventh month in the Gregorian calendar.

novice *n* **1** inexperienced beginner **2** monk, nun who has not taken vows; *n* **novitiate** period of being a novice; apprenticeship.

now *adv* at present time; *idm* **now and again/then** occasionally; *adv* **nowadays** in these days.

no way *interj, adv sl* certainly not.

nowhere *adv* not in any place; *idm* **nowhere near 1** not at all near **2** nothing like.

nowise *adv* in no way; by no means.

noxious *a* harmful; corrupting; offensive.

nozzle *n* projecting spout.

NSAID *n* acronym for nonsteroidal anti-inflammatory drug like ibuprofen; an aspirin-like substitute.

nth *a* last of an uncountable number; *idm* **to the nth degree** in the extreme.

nuance *n* delicate distinction in color, meaning, feeling, tone of voice, etc.

nubile *a* **1** marriageable (of a girl) **2** sexually attractive.

nuclear *a* **1** of, from an atomic nucleus (*n* **n. energy** energy released by fission or fusion) **2** producing nuclear energy (*ns* **n. fission** splitting of nucleus; **n. fusion** combining of nuclei; **n. reaction, n. reactor**) **3** of atomic weapons (*ns* **n. disarmament, n. deterrent** theory of keeping atomic weapons to discourage potential enemies from attacking; **n. war; n. winter** period of cold and darkness likely to follow atomic war) **4** forming a compact unit (*n* **n. family** parents and children, excluding other relatives).

nucleus *n Lat* **1** central core or kernel **2** *fig* starting point **3** core of atom (*pl* **nuclei**).

nucleic acid *n* complex acid found in all cells (*e.g.*, DNA or RNA).

nude *a* naked; bare; *ns* **nudity, nudism** practice of going

naked for health or religious reasons; **nudist.**

nudge *v* push slightly with elbow; *n* such touch.

nugatory *a* trifling; futile.

nugget *n* **1** small lump of metal, *esp* of natural gold **2** small but valuable piece of information.

nuisance *n* something harmful, offensive, annoying.

nuke *n* **1** *sl* nuclear weapon; *v sl* attack, destroy with this **2** *sl* cook in microwave oven.

null *a* of no effect; void; **null and void** *leg* without legal force; not valid; *n* **nullity;** *v* **nullify** make useless; cancel.

numb *a* deprived of feeling *esp* through cold; *v* make numb; deaden.

number *n* **1** mathematical unit; symbol(s) representing this (*e.g.*, **four-figure number**) **2** countable amount (*e.g.*, **a number of times;** *pl* large numbers of people) **3** issue of periodical **4** item in musical or variety show **5** *ling* category of singular or plural **6** *coll* item (described in admiration); *idm* **have somebody's number** have information to use against somebody; *idm* **somebody's number is up** somebody is about to die; *ns* **n. one 1** most important person **2** oneself.

numeral *a* of, expressing number; *n* graphic symbol of number; *v* **numerate** count (*a* able to calculate; *n* numeracy); ns **numerati** pl coll financial whizz kids; **numeration 1** method or process of numbering **2** expression of numbers in words; **numerator** number above line in a numerical fraction; as **numerical** concerning numbers (adv **-ly**); **numerous** many.

numinous a a spiritual glow, sense of the supernatural.

numismatics n study of coins, metals.

numskull n infml dunce.

nun n member of woman's religious order, living in convent; n **nunnery** community of nuns; convent.

nuncio n diplomatic representative of pope.

nuptial a of, relating to marriage; n pl **-s** wedding ceremony.

nurse n **1** person trained to care for sick or injured **2** woman employed to look after children; v suckle (an infant); act as nurse to; **nurse** n ns **nursemaid** woman employed to look after baby or small child; **nursery 1** room designed for small children (ns **n. rhyme** poem written for small children; **n. school** preschool for children aged **2** to **5**) **2** place for rearing young plants (n **nurseryman** man who grows plants for sale); **nursing** work of a medical nurse; **nursing home** home

where sick or elderly people live and are cared for.

nurture n nourishment; fostering care; training; v rear; educate.

nut[1] n **1** hard-shelled fruit of certain plants **2** sl head; pl sl testicles; idm **a hard nut to crack** a very stubborn person; idm **off one's nut** sl insane; ns **nutcase** sl insane person; **nutcracker** tool for removing hard shell of nut; **nutmeg** hard fragrant seed of Indian tree; this powdered and used as spice; a **nuts** sl insane; n **nutshell** (idm **in a nutshell** to put it concisely); a **nutty 1** containing nuts, nutlike food **2** sl insane.

nut[2] n hollow metal collar with internal thread to fit over bolt or screw; idm **nuts and bolts** basics; skills or facts relating to a job.

nutria n large rodent with lush fur, transplanted from S America, it now breeds relentlessly in parts of the Deep South.

nutrient a nourishing; ns **nutriment** nourishing food that repairs wastage; **nutrition** process of receiving nourishment; as **nutritious, nutritive** nourishing; maintaining growth.

nylon n **1** synthetic plastic material with properties similar to those of silk **2** pl stockings.

nymph n **1** legendary maiden

deity, spirit of woods, hills, rivers, etc.; **2** girl; **3** insect pupa; chrysalis.

nymphet n coll sexually precocious preteen girl.

nymphomania n excessive sexual desire in women; n **-maniac**.

o' *abbr prep* short form of **of**.

oaf *n* clumsy, awkward fellow, clod.

oak *n* type of common tree; oak timber; *a* of oak; *n* **oak apple** fleshy growth on oak caused by gallwasps *a* **oaken** *lit* of oak wood.

oar *n* long pole with flattened blade, used to propel boat; *idm* **put/shove/stick in one's oar/one's oar in** *coll* give unwanted advice; *v* row (*ns* **oarsman, oarswoman**).

oasis *n* fertile place in desert; (*pl* **oases**); *fig* place of refuge or relief.

oat *n pl usu* cereal plant; its seed; *n* **oatmeal**.

oath *n* **1** solemn appeal to God or some sacred thing, as witness to truth of statement **2** curse; profanity.

obdurate *a* stubborn; unpenitent; *n* **obduracy**.

obedience *n* submission to authority; act of obeying.

obedient *a* submissive; willing to obey.

obeisance *n* bow; formal gesture of respect, etc.

obelisk *n* upright, four-sided, tapering stone pillar.

Oberon *n* in medieval folklore the king of the fairies.

obese *a* extremely fat; corpulent; *n* **obesity**.

obey *v* carry out commands of; submit; follow rules of.

obfuscate *v* obscure; bewilder; confuse.

obiter dictum *n* incidental remark (*pl* **obiter dicta**).

obituary *n* notice of death of person, often with short biography.

object[1] *n* **1** material thing **2** aim; purpose **3** *ling* noun, pronoun, noun phrase, noun clause affected by action of transitive verb or following preposition; *idm* **be no object** be no problem; *idm* **(an/the) object of** somebody/something subjected to, likely to arouse (specified feeling or reaction); *n* **object lesson** event that serves as an example or warning; *a* **objective 1** relating to objects **2** existing outside the mind; *n* object, purpose aimed at.

object[2] *v* **1** be opposed to; feel dislike to **2** protest against; *n* **objection;** *a* **-able** liable to objection; offensive; *n* **objector**.

object d' art *n* Fr a curio, piece of art of some value.

objurgate *v* scold; **-tion;** *a* **-atory.**

oblate *a* (of sphere) flattened at both ends.

oblation *n* solemn, religious offering; *n* **oblate** one dedicated to monastic life.

obligato *n usu* elaborate or ornamented background part to a principal tune, often played by a single instrument.

oblige *v* **1** compel by legal, moral force **2** do favor for; *idm* **much obliged** *fml* thank you; *n* **obligation** binding promise, contract, etc.; duty; indebtedness for kindness, favor, etc.; *a* **obligatory** compulsory; necessary; *v* **obligate** bind legally, morally; *a* **obliging** helpful; courteous.

oblique *a* **1** slanting **2** *fig* not straightforward; *n* **obliquity** deviation from straight line.

obliterate *v* blot out; erase;

efface; wipe out; *n* **-ation**.

oblivion *n* forgetfulness; being forgotten; *a* **oblivious** unaware; not realizing.

oblong *n, a* (rectangle) longer than broad.

obloquy *n* reproach; calumny; disgrace.

obnoxious *a* disagreeable; offensive.

oboe *n* double-reed woodwind musical instrument.

obscene *a* indecent; lewd; disgusting; *n* **obscenity**.

obscure *a* **1** dim; indistinct **2** not clear in meaning **3** unimportant; *n* **obscurity 1** darkness **2** ambiguity **3** state of being unknown.

obsequious *a* servilely deferential.

obsequy *n* funeral rite.

observe *v* **1** pay attention to; watch; consider carefully **2** comment; remark; notice; *a* **observant 1** attentive **2** alert; vigilant; *ns* **observance 1** act of observing (laws, etc.) **2** commemoration; **observation 1** act of noticing **2** surveillance; *pl* **-s 1** remarks **2** critical comments on action or event, etc.; **observatory** building with instruments for watching stars, etc.; **observer** one who observes.

obsess *v* haunt, excessively occupy mind; *a* **-ive;** *adv* **-ively** *n* **-iveness**; *n* **obsession** fixed idea; exclusive preoccupation of mind.

obsidian *n* glassy, very hard black volcanic rock.

obsolescence *n* state of becoming obsolete or slowly disappearing through disuse; *a* **obsolescent**.

obsolete *a* disused; out-of-date.

obstacle *n* hindrance; obstruction.

obstacle course *n* athletic training course with ditches hills, walls, etc.

obstetrics *n pl* science and practice of childbirth; *a* **-tric** of childbirth; *n* **-trician** specialist in childbirth.

obstinacy *n* stubborness; persistence.

obstinate *a* stubborn; persistent.

obstreperous *a* noisy; unruly; turbulent.

obstruct *v* block; hinder; impede; *ns* **-ion; -ionism** method of impeding business; **-ionist;** *a* **-ive** causing obstruction.

obtain *v* gain; acquire; be valid; *a* **-able** procurable.

obtrude *v* force upon; thrust out intrude; *n* **obtrusion;** *a* **obtrusive** thrusting; intrusive.

obtuse *a* blunt; (*of persons*) dull, dense; (*of angle*) greater than a right angle.

obverse *n, a* opposite.

obviate *v* get rid of; make unnecessary.

obvious *a* easily seen; clear; lacking subtlety.

ocarina *n* egg-shaped wind instrument with finger holes.

occasion *n* **1** point of time when an event takes place **2** cause; reason **3** special event; *idm* **on occasion** occasionally; *v* give rise to cause; *a* **occasional 1** not all the time **2** composed for special purpose.

Occident *n* the west; Western hemisphere; *a* **occidental**.

occipital *a med* of the back of skull.

occlude *v* close, shut in or out; *n* **occlusion;** *a* **occlusive**.

occult *a* hidden; esoteric; supernatural; *ns* **-ation** eclipse; **-ism** study of supernatural.

occupancy *n* act of taking possession and residing in house, etc.; term of such occupation; *ns* **occupant; occupation 1** possession **2** employment; *a* **occupational; 1** of one's trade, regular employment (*ns* **o. disease, o. hazard**) **2** by physical or mental activity (*ns* **o. therapy, -apist**)

occupy *v* **1** live in, have possession of (house, land, etc.) (*ns* **occupant, occupier**) **2** *mil* take, keep possession of (territory) **3** take up or fill (space or time) **4** keep busy (*a* **occupied**).

occur *v* occurs, occurring, occurred. **1** happen **2** (be found to) exist; *idm* **occur to** come to mind; *n* **occurrence** happening; incident.

ocean *n* the great expanses of

salt water on earth; *pl coll* vast amount; *a* -ic; *ns* -ology, -ography branch of science concerned with oceans (*also* sea).

ocelot *n* small US wildcat.

ocher *n* earthy metallic oxide of iron, used for making yellow-brown pigments.

o'clock *adv* (hour) by the clock.

ocotillo *n* large thorny plant with spreading branches, found in southwest US.

oct-, octa-, octo- *prefix* eight.

octagon *n* plane figure with eight sides.

octave *n* musical interval of eight diatonic notes; group of eight.

octavo *n* size of book or page made from sheets of paper folded or cut into equal eights.

octennial *a* lasting, coming every eight years.

octet, octette *n* group or set of eight musical composition for eight singers or instruments.

October *n* tenth month in the Gregorian calendar (eighth in old Roman calendar).

octogenarian *n* person aged between 80 and 90.

octopus *n* mollusk with eight arms bearing suckers.

ocular *a* of eye or sight; *n* oculist specialist in diseases of eye.

OD *n* Doctor of Optometry; *abbr coll* overdose (*also v coll* take overdose).

odd *a* 1 a number not even; not

divisible by two 2 not part of complete set 3 strange; unusual 4 not regular 5 plus a bit more (*e.g.*, fifty-odd a few more than fifty); *ns* oddball eccentric person (*also a*); oddity 1 strange person, thing 2 strangeness (*also* oddness); odd one out person, thing different from, excluded from rest of group; *adv* oddly 1 strangely 2 surprisingly; *pl n* odds and ends leftover bits, extras, assorted things.

odds *n pl* 1 probability of something happening (odds in favor of/against) 2 (in gambling) ratio between amount of prize money and size of bet.

ode *n* poem in complicated lyrical form.

odometer *n* instrument that measures distance traveled.

odontology *n* study of teeth and their diseases.

odor *n* 1 smell; scent 2 *fig* reputation; *v* odorize perfume; *as* odorous 1 fragrant 2 *coll* bad smelling; odoriferous fragrant.

odyssey *n* long trip, voyage with many adventures; Quest.

Oedipus complex *n psyc* (Freudian theory of) child's subconscious sexual desire for parent of opposite sex and jealousy of the other.

of *prep* 1 belonging to 2 coming from 3 made from 4 containing 5 produced by

6 expressing quantity (half a quart) 7 about; concerning 8 depicting; portraying 9 giving more precise point of reference (*e.g.*, afraid of, aware of, short of).

off¹ *a* 1 unfriendly 2 not fresh 3 not busy (off season) 4 unsatisfactory (off day) 5 cutting off current (off switch).

off² *adv* 1 disconnected; detached 2 (*of fuel or energy supply*) not turned on 3 leaving (just off); 4 gone on vacation (off for a week), on a trip (off to Spain) 5 canceled 6 stressing completion (finished off); *idm* off and on sometimes; *idm* on the off chance in case perhaps; offprint reprint of selected part of publication; offshoot subsidiary branch; offspring child (*pl = sing*); *a* off-putting disconcerting; causing distaste.

off³ *prep* 1 away from 2 down from 3 not far from; *idm* be/go off have/get dislike, no appetite for; *idm* off the cuff impromptu (*a* off-the-cuff); *idm* off the record unofficially (*a* off-the-record); *as* offbeat unconventional (*n mus* beat that is not normally accented); off-color 1 sickly 2 sexually or socially improper; off-limits out of bounds; off-line *comput* not directly linked; not on-line; off-peak of, during less busy period (*also adv*); **off-road vehicle** *n* strong vehicle with four-wheel drive for use on rough ground; *advs* **offshore 1** near land **2** away from land (*a* **offshore**); **off stage** away from view of audience (*a* **offstage**); *as* **off-the-wall** *sl* unexpected and amusing; **off-white** grayish.

offal *n* **1** waste, by-products of a process **2** edible internal organs of animals **3** garbage; waste matter.

offend *v* annoy; do wrong; *ns* **offender; offense** wrongdoing; affront; **offensive 1** position of attack **2** aggression; *a* **offensive 1** unpleasant **2** insulting (*adv* **-ly;** *n* **-nes**) **3** attacking (*n* attack).

offer *v* **1** subject to acceptance or refusal **2** give as sacrifice or sign of worship **3** present for sale at price **4** bid as price for **5** show signs of; *n* **1** bid **2** expression of willingness to do something *esp* to help; *ns* **offering** something offered *esp* sacrifice to God; money donated; **offertory** collection taken in church service.

offhand *a* **1** casual (*adv* **offhand** without reflection) **2** disrespectful.

office *n* **1** duty; function **2** position of trust, authority **3** public, state department **4** building, room where administrative, clerical work is done **5** form of worship; *ns* **officer** one in command in armed forces; one who holds position of trust, authority.

official *n* one holding office *esp* in public organization; *a* having authority; *adv* **-ly;** *ns* **officialdom 1** body of state, public officials **2** bureaucratic attitude **3** red tape; **officialese** pompous, obscure bureaucratic language.

officiate *v* perform duty; preside (at); conduct divine service.

officious *a* meddling; offering uninvited advice; overbearing; *adv* **-ly;** *n* **-ness.**

offing *idm* **in the offing** likely to appear, happen.

offset *n* **1** beginning **2** sideshoot **3** method of printing from rubber roller; *v* compensate for.

offside *a, adv sport* illegally ahead of puck, ball.

offspring *n* child or children; *fig* result.

oft, often *adv* many times; frequently.

ogee *n* an s-shaped molding.

ogle *v* make eyes at; look at amorously; regard greedily.

ogre *n* **1** imaginary, cruel, man-eating giant **2** cruel barbarous person; *a* **ogreish.**

ohm *n* unit of electrical resistance.

oil *n* viscous organic or mineral substance, insoluble in water, and inflammable; *v* lubricate; take oil in as fuel; *ns* **oilcloth** thick waterproof material; **oilfield** area from which mineral oil is extracted; **oilpaint** pigment blended with oil; **oil painting** picture done with oil-based paint; **oil rig** structure to allow drilling of oil from seabed; *pl* clothes from this; **oil slick** area of oil spillage, causing pollution at sea; *a* **oily** like oil; *fig* unctuous.

oink *n* sound a pig or hog makes.

ointment *n* oily substance for healing wounds or softening skin.

okay, OK *adv, a coll* all right; approved; *v coll* sanction; approve; *n coll* agreement; sanction.

okra *n* tall annual plant edible green pods.

old *a* **1** from the remote past **2** having lived, existed for a long time **3** of long standing **4** former; *idm* **any old** *coll emphatic* any; *idm* **any old how** *coll* **1** carelessly; untidily **2** in a poor state of health or morale; *comp* **older, elder;** *sup* **oldest, eldest;** *n* **the old** old people, things; *ns* **old age** late stage in life; **o. boy** former student of school, college etc (**old-boy network** tendency to favor former schoolmates *esp* in business); **o. flame** somebody one was once in love with; **o. guard** group opposing change in organization; **o. hand** expert;

o. maid coll spinster; **o. master** any great classical painter or painting; **o. school** traditional, but now unfashionable way of doing something; **O. Testament** first part of Bible, history of the Jews and their religion; **o. timer 1** old man **2** well established member; **o. wives' tale** old belief that one has doubts about; **O. World** Europe, Asia and Africa (a **old-world** not modern); as **old-fashioned** in style of former times; **out-of-date; olden** lit of the distant past; **old hat** coll out-of-date.

oleaginous a oily, greasy.

oleander n poisonous evergreen shrub.

oleomargarine n edible fat of vegetable oil and skin milk (also **oleo, margarine**).

olfactory a pertaining to sense of smell.

oligarchy n government by small group; n **oligarch** ruler in oligarchy; a **oligarchic.**

olive n evergreen tree; oil-yielding fruit; a yellowish green; n **o.branch** symbol of peace.

Olympiad n period of four years between Olympic Games; as **Olympian 1** athlete **2** godlike; **Olympic, O. Games** modern revival of ancient Grecian athletic meeting.

ombudsman n one officially appointed to investigate and deal with individual complaints against large organizations.

omega n last letter of Greek alphabet.

omelette, omelet n beaten eggs cooked without stirring, then folded in half.

omen n sign, portent of things to come.

ominous a threatening evil.

omission n something left out, not done.

omit v omits, omitting, omitted. leave out; fail to do or include.

omni- prefix Lat all in all.

omnibus n large passenger-carrying road vehicle, on fixed route; a having many uses.

omnipotent a all-powerful; almighty; n **-potence.**

omnipresent a present everywhere; n **-sence.**

omniscient a infinitely wise; all-knowing; n **-science.**

omnivorous a eating all kinds of food; fig assimilating everything.

on¹ a, adv **1** forward; ahead; further **2** in progress **3** illuminated; functioning **4** being worn **5** properly fitted, attached **6** taking place as arranged **7** appearing in public; performing **8** aboard; idm **go on about** coll talk tediously about; idm **on and off** from time to time; idm **on and on** continuously; idm **you're on** coll I accept your challenge.

on² prep **1** touching surface of; covering **2** in close proximity, adjacent to (on the corner) **3** aboard (**on a bus**) **4** giving day, date (**on Friday 13**) **5** about (topic) **6** making habitual use of (**on drugs**), **7** in a (temporary) state (**on call, on duty, on vacation**); idm **on the house** served free (by the establishment).

once adv **1** one time **2** formerly; idm **at once 1** together **2** immediately; idm **once and for all** without change or compromise; idm **once in a while** occasionally; **once more** one more time; conj as soon as; n **once-over** (idm **give the once-over** make a quick inspection.

oncology n medical branch dealing with cancer and tumors; n **oncologist.**

oncoming a approaching.

one det, n **1** lowest cardinal number (1) **2** particular person or thing **3** the same (**at one time, in one try**); idm **at one** in agreement; idm **get it in one** coll guess immediately; idm **one up (on)** with an advantage (over); pron **1** somebody **2** anybody; prons **one another** each other; **oneself** reflex; n **one-armed bandit** slot machine; **one-liner** short joke; **one-night stand 1** play, musical, etc. on tour, performed once only at each place **2** liaison for one night; as **one-sided** unevenly balanced; favoring one side too much; **one-stop** *comm* offering full range of services, facilities as a package; **onetime** former; **one-to-one** 1 exactly corresponding 2 involving only two people (*also adv*); **one-way** moving, allowing movement in one direction only (*ns* **o. street, o. traffic**); *n* **one-upmanship** art of winning psychological advantage over others.

onerous *a* burdensome; weighty; *n* **onerousness.**

ongoing *a* in progress; continuing.

onion *n* strong-smelling vegetable of the lily family.

onionskin *n* lightweight.

on-line *a* connected to, controled by computer (*also adv*).

onlooker *n* spectator.

only *a* single; sole; *adv* solely; exclusively; *conj* except (that); *idm* **if only** expressing frustrated wish; *idm* **only just** 1 barely 2 very recently.

onomatopoeia *n* formation of words by imitation of sounds associated with object named, as cuckoo, hiss.

onrush *n* urgent movement ahead.

onset *n* beginning; attack.

onslaught *n* violent attack.

onstream *a, adv* in or into production.

onto *prep* to and upon.

ontogeny *n* development of an individual organism.

ontology *n* study of the nature of existence (*a* **ontological**).

onus *n* burden; responsibility; mark.

onward *a, adv* forward (in space or time).

onyx *n* variety of agate.

oodles *n pl coll* abundance.

oomph *n coll* 1 energy 2 glamor, charm 3 vitality.

ooze *n* 1 liquid mud; slime *esp* on sea, riverbed 2 slow trickle; *v* exude (liquid); flow slowly out.

op *abbr* 1 *coll* operation 2 *mus* opus.

opal *n* iridescent gemstone; *a* **opalescent.**

opaque *n* not allowing light through; dark; obscure.

op art *n* optical art.

op-ed *n abbr* (opposite editorial) newspaper term for page opposite the editorial page, used for special features.

open *a* 1 not closed 2 not enclosed (**o. country**) 3 without a roof; not covered over (**o. car, o. drain; o. sandwich** sandwich without top slice of bread; **o. wound** injury with broken skin) 4 not buttoned; undone (**o. collar, o. neck, o. shirt**) 5 honest; frank (**o. character**) 6 not hidden (**o. quarrel; o. secret** fact widely known but not so planned) 7 for anyone to visit (**o. house**), to attend (**o. court, o. lecture**), to compete in (**o. race**) 8 undecided (**o. question, o. verdict**); unprejudiced (**o. mind**) 9 (*of position, vacancy*)

available; to be applied for 10 (*of textiles*) loose in texture (**o. weave**) 11 (*of exhibition, public event*) ready for visitors 12 (*of bank account*) ready to use; *idm* **open to** 1 exposed to 2 ready to accept; *as* **o.-air** outdoor; **o.-and-shut** not controversial; easily solved; **o.-cast** (of mining) close to the surface; **o.-door** (of national policy) admitting free trade from other countries; **o.-ended** without limitations imposed beforehand; **o.-handed** generous (*adv* **-ly** *n* **-ness**); **o.-hearted** kind; sincere (*adv* **-ly** *n* **-ness**); **o.-minded** receptive to new ideas (*adv* **-ly** *n* **-ness**); **o.-plan** with few interior walls to divide up living, working space; *ns* **o.-heart surgery** *med* operation on heart with blood circulation maintained mechanically; **o. letter** letter for all to read; **o. season** period of year when fish, game may legally be killed; **o. shop** place of work where union membership is optional; *n* **open space;** outdoors; *idm* **bring out into the open** make known to all; *idm* **in the open** unprotected; *v* 1 unfasten; unlock; uncover 2 make accessible 3 begin; *idm* **open fire** 1 begin shooting 2 *fig* begin asking questions; *phr vs* **open into/onto** give access to; **open out** 1 become wider

A
B
C
D
E
F
G
H
I
J
K
L
M
N
O
P
Q
R
S
T
U
V
W
X
Y
Z

2 develop; **open out 1** become wider 2 develop; **open up 1** unlock 2 make accessible 3 begin business production 4 speak more frankly (*adv* **-ly** *n* **-ness**); *n* **opening 1** gap; hole; breach 2 opportunity; favorable moment 3 job vacancy; *a* first; initial (**o. move**); **opening night** first performance at theatre).

opera *n* drama set to music, sung to orchestral accompaniment; *a* **operatic**; *n* **operetta** short, light opera *n* **o. glasses** small binoculars used by spectator.

operation *n* **1** action **2** plan; project; undertaking **3** act of surgery; *v* **operate 1** work; cause to function **2** perform act of surgery; *a* **operative** working; valid; *n* worker; artisan; *n* **operator** one who works machine.

ophthalmic *a* pertaining to eye; *n* **opthalmology** branch of medicine concerned with eyes *n* **-ologist**.

opinion *n* **1** personal judgment (not necessarily based on facts) **2** public feeling about something **3** professional judgment or advice; *v* **opine** utter opinion; *a* **opinionated** obstinate in beliefs, etc.; dogmatic.

opium *n* narcotic intoxicant and sedative addictive drug obtained from white poppy; *v* **opiate** mix with opium; *n* **1** drug containing opiate

2 *fig* anything that soothes or calms; *a* inducing sleep.

opponent *n* antagonist; rival.

opportune *a* seasonable; suitable; well-timed; *n* **opportunity** lucky chance; favorable occasion or time; *n* **opportunism** policy for taking advantage of circumstances; **-ist.**

oppose *v* place against; withstand; contend against; *n* **opposer**; *a* **opposite 1** in facing position **2** contrary in nature; *as* different as possible (*n* **the o.**, the complete reverse, contrary); *n* **opposition** resistance; political party opposing that in power.

opossum *n* North American marsupial with a long prehensile tail, pointed nose, and gray-white fur.

oppress *v* crush; treat unjustly, cruelly; weigh heavily on, depress; *a* **-ive 1** tyrannical; hard to bear **2** (of weather) heavy; tiring; *ns* **oppression** harshness; tyranny; **oppressor.**

opt (for) *v* choose; decide (in favor of); *phr v* **opt out** choose not to take part.

optic *a* of the eyes or eyesight (*n* **o. nerve**); *pl* **-s** scientific study of vision *esp* in relation to light; *a* **optical** (*ns* **o. character reader** *comput* device that can interpret text by identifying patterns of light and dark, *also* **OCR; o. fiber** thin elongated glass

fiber that transmits light signals; **o. illusion** thing which is misinterpreted by the eye; **optician 1** person who makes prescriptions appropriate glasses, lenses (*also* **ophthalmic o.**) **2** person who makes and sells optical instruments.

optimism *n* habit of looking at brighter side of things; doctrine that good ultimately prevails over evil; *n* **-ist;** *a* **- istic;** *v* **optimize** render as effective as possible (*n* **- ization**); *a* **optimum** best possible; most favorable (*also* **optimal**).

optimum *n* best, most favorable state, condition.

option *n* **1** choice **2** privilege of buying or selling at certain price within specified time; *a* **-al** not obligatory; voluntary.

optometry *n* practice of testing eyes for fitting of eyeglasses or contact lenses.

opulent *a* wealthy; abundant; luxuriant; *n* **-lence.**

opus *n* *Lat* work or composition *esp* in music.

or *conj* introduces alternative; offering choice.

oracle *n* **1** prophecy or answer, divinely inspired, given by ancient Greek, Roman priest **2** place, shrine where answer, often ambiguous, was given; the inspired priest; *a* **oracular** of oracle; ambiguous.

oral *a* **1** *med* of the mouth **2** spoken; not written; *n* test of this kind (*also* **o. test, o.**

examination).

orange *n* large red-gold citrus fruit; tree bearing this; color of fruit *n* **orangeade** orange-flavored soft drink.

orangutan *n* large reddish-colored ape with long arms.

orator *n* eloquent, public speaker; *n* **oration** formal speech; *a* **-ical**; *n* **oratory** 1 eloquence, rhetoric 2 small private chapel.

oratorio *n* musical composition *usu* of sacred nature for solo voices, chorus, and orchestra but whithout scenery or action.

orb *n* 1 sphere; globe 2 ceremonial symbol of royalty; *n* **orbit** 1 path of planet or satellite around another body in space 2 *fig* area of influence; *a* **orbital** 1 of an orbit 2 passing all round outside of city (*n* motorway that does this).

orchard *n* 1 area where fruit trees are planted and cultivated.

orchestra *n* 1 band of musicians playing instrumental music 2 front part of theater where such band plays; *a* **orchestral**; *v* **orchestrate** compose, arrange music for orchestra; *n* **-ration**.

orchid, orchis *n* kind of showy plant with exotic flowers; *a a* light purple color.

ordain *v* 1 admit to holy orders 2 decree; enact, appoint.

ordeal *n* difficult or painful experience.

order *n* 1 relative position in series; sequence 2 tidiness 3 state of calm, discipline 4 command 5 request for goods, service 6 group of monks, etc. 7 *cap* group of people awarded special honor; decoration awarded to them; *idm* **in order** 1 arranged 2 functioning 3 permissible; *idm* **in order that** *conj* expressing purpose so that; *idm* **in order to** expressing purpose so as to; *idm* **on order** due for delivery; *idm* **out of order** 1 not functioning 2 not permissible; *v* 1 command 2 request goods or service 3 arrange in organized way; *phr v* **order about** give series of instructions in a bossy way; *a* **-ly** tidy; law-abiding; *n* **-liness**.

ordinal *a* indicating position in series; *n* such a number (*also* **ordinal number**).

ordinance *n* decree, regulation; religious ceremony.

ordinary *a* normal; usual; average; commonplace; *n* cleric having authority in his or her own right.

ordination *n* ceremony of ordaining clergy.

ordnance *n* artillery; military stores, equipment, material.

ore *n* metal-yielding mineral.

oregano *n* Mediterranean herb used to season food.

organ *n* 1 part of animal or plant performing particular function 2 keyboard wind instrument *also* **pipe organ**); *n* **o. grinder** street musician playing barrel-organ) 3 *fml* organization that serves special purpose (*eg* **o. of government**) 4 *fml* means of communicating views of group (**o. of public opinion**); *a* **organic** 1 of the organs of the body 2 formed by living things, not from artificial chemicals (**o. fertilizer, o. matter, o. soil**) 3 (*of farm produce*) grown without artificial fertilizer or pesticide (**o. food, o. vegetables**) 4 *fig* forming integral part of structure; developing as part of structure (*adv* **-ally**); *ns* **organic chemistry** chemistry of carbon compounds; **organism** 1 living being capable of growth and reproduction 2 system composed of interrelated elements; **organist** player of organ.

organdy *n* thin stiff cotton fabric.

organize *v* arrange, group separate parts into systematic whole; make efficient; unite into society etc; **organization** act of organizing; body of persons having common purpose; **organizer.**

orgasm *n* excitement, peak, paroxysm, *esp* in sexual act.

orgy *n* 1 needless revelry 2 continous round of pleasure *a* **orgiastic**.

oriel *n* projecting bay or recessed

a b c d e f g h i j k l m n **o** p q r s t u v w x y z

A B C D E F G H I J K L M N **O** P Q R S T U V W X Y Z

window.

orient n (usu cap) Far East (esp China, Japan); a, n **-al** (inhabitant) of the Orient; v **orient 1** find sense of direction; steer **2** direct attention and interest of (n **-ation**); ns **orientalist** expert in culture, languages of Orient.

orifice n mouth, outer opening of tube, pipe, etc.

origami n Japanese art of making objects from folded paper.

origin n source; beginning; initial cause; ancestry.

original a **1** earliest **2** new **3** creative; inventive **4** made, done for first time; n that from which copies are made; first pattern, model; eccentric person; ns **o. sin** (Christian belief in) innate wickedness of human beings; n **originality 1** creative faculty **2** novelty, v **originate** bring about; have origin in; n **-ator**.

oriole n yellow and black bird of crow family.

orison n prayer.

ornament n decoration; adornment; trinket; v decorate; embellish; a **-al**; n **-ation**.

ornate a excessively adorned.

ornithology n scientific study of birds; a **-ological**; n **-ologist**.

orphan n child who has lost one or both parents; n **orphanage** institution for care of orphans.

ortho- prefix right, correct.

orthodontics n med branch of dentistry concerned with correcting irregular formation of teeth (a **-tic**; n **-tist**).

orthodox a **1** (of ideas, methods) generally accepted **2** (of people) conventional **3** cap belonging to Eastern group of Christian churches or to strict Jewish sect; n **-doxy 1** orthodox belief **2** state of being orthodox.

orthography n **1** (system of) spelling **2** accepted correct spelling; a **-graphic/ -graphical**; adv **-graphically**.

orthopedics n pl branch of surgery dealing with bone deformities; a **-pedic** pertaining to orthopedics.

Oscar n (statuette presented as) award for best direction, acting, etc. each year; a **o. -nominated** nominated for such an award.

oscillate v swing to and fro; fluctuate between extremes.

osculate v kiss; n **-lation**; a **-atory**.

osier n species of willow, used in basket-making.

osmosis n **1** bio, chem gradual passage of liquid through porous solid matter **2** fig imperceptible process by which ideas or language gradually become absorbed and accepted.

osprey n large hawk, sea eagle.

ossify v **ossifying, ossified**. to become hard (as a bone).

ostensible a apparent; pretended.

ostentation n pretentious show of wealth, etc.; a **ostentatious** given to showing off; pretentious.

osteoarthritis n degeneration of cartilage in the joints, causing pain and stiffness.

osteopathy n treatment of disease by manipulation of bones; n **-path** one who practices osteopathy.

osteoarthritis n degeneration of cartilage in the joints, causing pain and stiffness.

osteology n study of bones, the bony structure.

ostracize v refuse to associate with; banish; n **ostracism** exclusion from social group etc.

ostrich n large, flightless, African bird with plumelike tail feathers.

other a different; additional; not the same; pron other person or thing; adv **otherwise** differently; conj if not.

otherworldy a concerned with spiritual rather than mundane affairs.

otiose a superfluous; unnecessary.

otter n web-footed aquatic mammal.

ottoman n low, padded seat or stool without back; cap a Turkish.

ought v aux expressing obligation, desirability, probability.

Ouija [TM] n lettered and

numbered board used in seances etc.

ounce *n* unit of weight, sixteenth of pound; *fig* small amount.

our *a* belonging to us; *pron* **ours;** *pron* **ourselves** emphatic form of **we.**

oust *v* turn out; expel; eject.

out *adv* **1** not inside **2** not at home **3** away at a distance **4** revealed **5** available; published **6** no longer in power **7** no longer fashionable **8** on strike **9** unconscious **10** not acceptable; not feasible **11** extinguished **12** wrongly calculated **13** *tennis* (of shot) landing on wrong side of court line; *idm* **all out** using every effort; *idm* **out of it** excluded from taking part; *idm* **out to** determined to; *as* **o.-and-o,** thorough; **o.-of -date** no longer fashionable; **o.-of-the way** unusual; *ns* **o. -take** scene in a film or television show that is omitted from the finished product.

out- *prefix* **1** *forming vs* doing better or more; surpassing (*e.g.,* **outclass, outdo** perform better; **outfox, outmaneuver, outsmart, outwit** defeat by cunning; **outgrow** grow too big, old for; **outlast** endure longer than; **outlive** live longer; **outnumber** be more numerous; **outplay** defeat by playing better; **outrank** be of

superior rank to; **outride** ride faster; **outshine** surpass in brilliance; **outstare** manage to hold one's gaze steady longer than; **outstay** stay longer than; **outweigh** be more important than **2** *forming as, ns* isolated (*e.g., n* **outpost**); external (*e.g., a* **outside;** *n* **outpatient**); with sudden effect (*e.g., ns* **outbreak, outburst, outcry**).

outback *n* remote bush country of Australia.

outbreak *n* sudden start (of illness, violence, etc.).

outburst *n* sudden eruption (of emotion).

outcast *n* rejected person.

outclass *v* surpass; excel.

outcome *n* result.

outcrop *n* part of rock stratum coming to surface; *v* to appear; come to surface.

outcry *n* protest.

outdated *a* old-fashioned.

outdoor *a* of the open air; *adv* **-s.**

outer *a* on the outside; farther from the center; *n* **o. space** space beyond earth's atmosphere; *a* **outermost** furthest from the center.

outface *n* **1** outstare **2** overcome with courage.

outfield *n* *sport* players furthest from batter, in baseball.

outfit *n* **1** set of equipment or clothes **2** organization; working group; *v* equip, *esp* with clothes (*n* **outfitter**).

outflank *v* get the better of.

outgoing *a* **1** departing **2** ending term of office **3** extrovert; sociable.

outhouse *n* **1** small building separate from main one **2** privy, outside toilet.

outing *n* excursion.

outlaw *n* fugitive not protected by the law; *v* make an outlaw; ban something by law.

outlay *n* total money invested in enterprise, spent on large or multiple purchases.

outlet *n* **1** way out for liquid, gas, traffic, etc. **2** means of relieving tension or emotion, of releasing energy **3** *comm* shop; trading place.

outline *n* **1** line showing shape or contour **2** statement of main facts, idea; *v* make an outline.

outlook *n* **1** view from a place **2** attitude to life **3** future prospects.

outlying *a* far from center of city, community.

outmoded *a* old-fashioned.

outmost *a* outermost.

output *n* **1** product of physical or mental effort **2** rate of production **3** computer-processed data **4** telecommunications signal.

outrage *n* violation; brutality; violent transgression of law; *v* violate; offend against; *a* **outrageous** disgraceful; *adv* **-ly;** *n* **-ness.**

outré *a* exaggerated; in bad taste.

outrider *n* **1** one who clears the way **2** a mounted attendant.

A B C D E F G H I J K L M N **O** P Q R S T U V W X Y Z

outright *a* 1 unmistakeable (**o. winner**) 2 complete (**o. denial, o. liar**); *also adv.*

outset *n* start.

outside *n* external part; surface; extreme limit; *a* 1 external 2 unconnected 3 unlikely; *adv* out of doors; *prep* on outer side of; apart from; *n* **outsider** 1 person not relating to, not accepted by social group 2 competitor with little chance of success.

outsize *a* unusually large.

outskirts *n pl* outer areas (of city, subject, etc.).

outsourcing *n* practice of contracting work out to companies or individuals.

outspoken *a* frank; not afraid to say what one thinks; *adv -* **ly** *n* **-ness.**

outstanding *n* 1 remarkable 2 excellent; *adv* **-ly.**

outstrip *v* surpass completely.

outward *a* 1 going away (**o.journey**) 2 on the outside (**o. appearances**); visible (**o. sign**); *adv* going away (**o. bound** going away from home; *n* **O. Bound** programs that offer structured outdoor physical adventure for young people); *advs* **-ly** externally.

outwit *v* **outwits, outwitting, outwitted.** deceive or defeat by greater cunning.

outworn *a* no longer useful.

ouzo *n* strong anise-flavored alcoholic beverage from Greece.

oval *a* egg-shaped, elliptical; *n* figure of this shape.

Oval Office *n* oval-shaped room in the White House that serves as the primary office for the US president.

ovary *n* female organ of reproduction; *a* **ovarian.**

ovation *n* enthusiastic welcome or applause.

oven *n* heated metal or brick receptacle, in which food is baked; small kiln, or furnace; *a* **o.-ready** (of food) sold in prepared state ready for baking; *n* **ovenware** heatproof dishes in which food can be baked, roasted.

over *prep* 1 above 2 across; from one side to the other 3 beyond; more than 4 during; throughout 5 by means of 6 because of; *adv* 1 above 2 across 3 finished 4 in excess; *idm* **all over** 1 spread everywhere 2 completely finished; *idm* **over and above** in addition to.

over- *prefix* 1 above (*as* **overarm, overhand, overhead;** *v*, *n* **overhang** (of rock, roof, etc.) project(ion) above) 2 providing cover (*ns* **overall** denim trousers with bib and straps, worn by farmers; **overcoat; overshoes** galoshes) 3 across (*vs* **overfly, overgrow, overlap, overlay, overpass, overrun;** *adv*, *a* **overseas**) 4 indicating superiority (*vs* **overawe** inspire fear or respect in; **overcome, overpower; overshadow** cause to seem inferior;

overthrow, overwhelm conquer completely; *n* **overlord**) 5 beyond limit (*vs* **overbalance** lose equilibrium; **overfill; overrun** exceed scheduled time or budget; **overshoot** pass beyond target; **oversleep; overspill** (of liquid) flow over edge; (of population) spread beyond city (*also n*); **overstep;** *adv* **overboard** over side of ship; *a* **overdue** late) 6 too much (*vs* **overcharge, overcrowd, overdo, overestimate, overload; overplay** exaggerate; **oversell** be too enthusiastic about; **oversimplify, overstate;** *as* **overbearing** dominating; **overblown, overgrown, overjoyed, overladen, overloaded; overmanned** with too many staff; **oversexed; over-subscribed** with too many members or too many orders; **overweening** too arrogant; **overweight; overwrought** too anxious; *adv* **overmuch** too much); **overdraft** *n* money borrowed from bank on current account; amount overdrawn.

overboard *adv* from a vessel into the water; *idm* **go overboard** do too much; show too much enthusiasm.

overdraw *v* draw money beyond the credit in one's account; *a* **-drawn.**

overdrive *n* mechanism giving higher set of gears than usual; *idm* **go into overdrive** 1 use overdrive mechanism **2** work harder than usual.

overhaul *v* **1** check thoroughly and rectify **2** overtake; *n* thorough check.

overhead *a, adv* above one's head; *n, pl* **overheads** *comm* general costs of running business (rent, electricity, wages, etc.)

overhear *v* hear message, conversation intended for others.

overland *adv* by land, rather than water.

overleaf *adv* on reverse side of page.

overlook *v* **1** look out across **2** fail to see; omit by accident **3** ignore; forgive.

overly *adv* too.

overmuch *n* superfluity; *a, adv* excessively(ly).

overnight *adv, a* **1** through, during the night **2** *coll* sudden(ly) (**o. change**).

overpass *n* bridge crossing motorway.

overpower *v* get better of, conquer.

override *v* disregard, nullify, cancel.

oversea(s) *a, adv* over, across sea; abroad; foreign.

overseer *n* foreman, supervisor; *v* **oversee** supervise.

oversight *n* mistake; accidental omission to do something.

overt *a* openly done; apparent.

overtake *v* **1** pass (vehicle ahead) **2** (of misfortune etc)

affect suddenly (*pt* **overtook,** *pp* **overtaken**).

over-the-counter *a* (of medicines) available for purchase without prescription.

over-the -transon *a* unsolicited, unasked for.

overtime *adv* beyond normal working hours; *n* extra work of this kind; money earned from this.

overtone *n* **1** tinge of second color detectable in basic color **2** *mus* harmonic note; *pl* -**s** implication of more than literal meaning in what is said.

overture *n* musical composition played at beginning of opera, etc.; *usu pl* friendly or formal approach.

overturn *v* **1** turn upside-down; upset **2** overthrow (regime) **3** reverse (decision).

overview *n* *fml* survey; short general description.

overwhelm *v* flow, cover over; overpower; engulf; *a* -**ing** irresistible.

oviform *a* egg-shaped.

ovine *a* of, like sheep.

ovoid *a* egg-shaped.

ovulate *a* produce egg(s) from ovary *n* -**ation**.

ovum *n pl* **ova.** female egg-cell; *n* **ovule** unfertilized seed.

owe *v* be indebted to; have to repay; *a* **owing** unpaid; due; *conj* **owing to** as a result of; caused by.

owl *n* night bird of prey; *a*

owlish appearing solemn; *n* **owlet** young owl.

own *v* **1** possess **2** admit; confess; acknowledge; *a* emphasises possession; *ns* **owner** one who possesses; **ownership** possession.

ox *n* castrated adult male of domestic cattle; *pl* **oxen;** *ns* **oxbow** horseshoe bend in river; **oxeye, oxslip** types of flowering plants.

oxblood *a* deep, dull reddish brown color.

oxford *n* **1** low laced shoes **2** soft fabric for shirt material (Oxford cloth).

Oxford movement *n* a High Church development in Anglican churches.

oxide *n* compound of oxygen and another element; *v* **oxidize** unite with oxygen; make, become rusty, or dull; *n* **oxidation.**

oxygen *n* colorless, odorless gas in the atmosphere, essential to life; *prefix* **oxy-** of oxygen; of an oxide.

oxymoron *n* combination of words involving apparent contradiction (*e.g.,* bittersweet).

oyster *n* edible marine bivalve mollusk.

ozone *n* concentrated form of oxygen, with pungent smell; *coll* bracing ocean air; *a* **ozone-friendly** not harmful to the ozone layer; *n* **ozone layer** layer of ozone-rich gases in the earth's atmosphere that absorbs harmful radiation from the sun.

PA *abbr* **1** physician's assistant **2** public address (system) **3** production assistant (film, TV).

pace *n* **1** distance covered by a single step **2** speed (of walking, running, progress, work); *idm* **keep pace with** go as fast as; *idm* **put somebody through his/her paces** give somebody a thorough test of ability, stamina, etc.; *idm* **set the pace** set a speed for others to follow; *v* walk with slow measured steps (across something); *idm* **pace oneself** set oneself a controlled rate of progress; *phr v* **pace out** measure by counting one's strides; *n* **pacemaker 1** person setting speed for others, example for others **2** *med* electrical device implanted to regulate the heart.

pacify *v* **pacifies, pacifying, pacified.** make peaceful; appease; *a* **pacific** peaceable; *ns* **pacification; pacifism** systematic opposition to war, or violence; **-ist** believer in pacifism.

pachyderm *n* thick-skinned elephant, rhinoceros, etc.

pack *n* **1** bundle of things tied together for carrying **2** bag for carrying on back (*also* **backpack**) **3** paper or cardboard container for selling; package **4** set of playing cards **5** group of hunting animals **6** *coll* group of people or things with undesirable characteristic (*e.g.*, **p. of liars, p.of lies**); *v* **1** put things into container(s) for carrying **2** fit tightly into container **3** cover or fill with protective material; *idm* **pack a punch 1** hit hard **2** have a strong effect; *phr vs* **pack in** *coll* **1** abandon (activity) **2** crowd (*e.g.*, spectators) into limited space **3** fit (activities) into short period of time; **pack up** *coll* finish work; *ns* **p.-animal** animal used for carrying goods; **p.-ice** large mass of coagulated icefloes; *a* **packed 1** ready for journey **2** overcrowded; *n* **packer.**

package *n* **1** several things wrapped together; parcel **2** related items offered or sold as a single unit; *v* make into package, *e.g.*, for selling; *ns* **p. deal** set of proposals for collective, not for separate negotiation; **p. vacation/tour** vacation/tour with all costs (travel, food, accommodation, insurance) combined into single fixed price; *n* **packaging 1** act of packing **2** packing material **3** *fig* method of presentation for selling.

packet *n* small package.

pact *n* agreement, compact, deal, covenant.

pad[1] *v* **pads, padding, padded.** go on foot softly; trudge along.

pad[2] *n* **1** piece of soft material to prevent jarring or chafing from movement **2** thick skin under animal's foot **3** *sport* reinforced protection for arms, legs, etc. **4** block of writing-paper sheets **5** *sl* place where one lives, apartment; *v* **1** protect with pad, pads **2** fill with pads to enlarge shape of **3** extend (writing, speech) by adding superfluous material, words; *a* **padded**; *n* **padding.**

paddle *n* short, broad oar used

for propelling a canoe or kayak; *v* propel by paddle; move feet or hands idly in shallow water.

paddock *n* small grass field; enclosure.

paddy, padi *n* field where rice is grown in water.

padlock *n* detachable lock with hinged loop to be hooked through staple, etc.; *v* fasten thus.

padre *n* chaplain in armed forces.

paean *n* song of praise.

paella *n* Spanish dish of rice, saffron, chicken, seafood, etc.

pagan *n*, *a* heathen; barbarian; *n* **-ism**.

page[1] *n* attendant or servant; *v* try to get a person's attention, *esp* by a public address system or transmitter; *ns* **pager** radio apparatus for calling sb by coded signal; **paging** (**p.service**).

page[2] *n* one side of leaf of book; *v* mark page numbers.

pageant *n* splendid, imposing display in costume; series of richly costumed, historical tableaux or scenes; *n* **pageantry** gorgeous display.

paginate *v* number page in book, magazine.

pagoda *n* Oriental temple, tapering pinnacled tower with several stories.

paid *pt, pp* of **pay**; **p.-up member** member who has paid his/her subscription and is a full member.

pail *n* bucket; *n* **pailful**.

pain *n* physical, mental suffering; anguish; *pl* **-s** effort; trouble; *idm* **on/under pain of something** risking (specified penalty); *v* inflict pain on; be source of pain; *as* **painful**; (*adv* **-ly**); **painless** (*adv* **-ly** *n* **-ness**); **painstaking** (*adv* **-ly**); careful, industrious.

painkiller *n* reliever of pain, as an analgesic.

paint *n* coloring matter used to give color to surface; pigment; *v* **1** color; coat; portray with paint **2** *fig* describe vividly; *idm* **paint the town red** go out and enjoy a lively time; *ns* **painter; painting** act of coloring with paint; painted picture, *esp* hand-painted.

pair *n* set of two similar things normally used together; mated couple of animals; *v* arrange in twos; mate; match.

paisley *n* fabric with curved designs and intricate colored abstract patterns.

pajamas *n pl* loose, *usu* two-piece suit for sleep, lounging.

pal *n sl* close friend; *v* spend time (**p. around**).

palace *n* residence of sovereign or bishop; large public hall; *a* **palatial** splendid, sumptuous, spacious; **palatine** with royal privileges.

palaeolithic *a* belonging to earlier Stone Age.

palaeontology *n* scientific study of fossils.

palate *n* roof of mouth; sense of taste; *n, a* **palatable 1** good to taste **2** *fig* acceptable; *adv* **-ably**; *ns* **-ability**.

palatial *a* like, as of a palace; *adv* **-ly**.

palaver *n* conference; idle talk.

pale[1] *a* **1** whitish; wan **2** dimly colored; not bright.

pale[2] *n* enclosure, district, territory with restricted access, egress; *n* **paling** fencing.

palette *n* small board on which colors are mixed; range of colors.

palimony *n* money paid by court order to support former lover.

palindrome *n* word, line, etc., reading same backward and forward.

palisade *n* **1** tall fence **2** series of tall cliffs.

pall[1] *n* **1** cloth spread over coffin **2** *fig* covering of smoke, etc.; *n* **pallbearer** person escorting, carrying coffin.

pall[2] *v* become tedious to.

pallet *n* **1** portable platform used in storage and movement of goods by forklift **2** small, hard straw mattress.

palliate *v* mitigate; relieve without curing; excuse *a, n* **palliative** (giving) temporary relief.

pallid *a* excessively pale; *n* **pallor**.

pall-mall *n* 17th century game resembling croquet.

pallor *n* waxlike paleness.

palm *n* **1** inner surface of hand

A
B
C
D
E
F
G
H
I
J
K
L
M
N
O
P
Q
R
S
T
U
V
W
X
Y
Z

2 tropical tree **3** leaf of this tree as symbol of victory; *v* conceal in palm; transfer by sleight of hand; *ns* **palmistry** fortune-telling from lines on palm of hand; **palmist** fotune-teller; **palm oil** oil from palm tree; *fig* bribe; **Palm Sunday** Sunday before Easter.

palmetto *n* type of low-growing, fan-leaved palm tree.

palomino *n* **-os.** horse of light brown, cream coat.

palpable *a* capable of being felt, touched; obvious; tangible.

palpate *v med* examine by touch.

palpitate *v* beat irregularly; flutter; throb; *n* **palpitation** throbbing; irregular, quickened action of heart.

palsy *n* **1** paralysis **2** muscular condition with tremors.

paltry *a* trifling; petty; insignificant.

pampas *n* grassy plains of S America (**p.grass**).

pamper *v* overindulge; cosset; coddle.

pamphlet *n* short unbound treatise; *usu* on some current topic.

pamphleteer *n* writer of pamphlets.

pan *n* broad, shallow vessel *usu* for cooking; *v* **pans, panning, panned.** wash (gravel, etc.) to extract gold; *phr v* **pan out** result, turn out.

pan-, panto- *prefix* all.

panacea *n* remedy for all ills.

panache *n* ostentation; swagger; dash, verse.

panama *n* hat made from strawlike material.

Pan-American *a* relating to nations of N and S America.

pancake *n* thin flat cake of fried batter; *v* (*of aircraft*) land flatly and abruptly.

panchromatic *a* (*of photographic film*) sensitive to light of all colors.

pancreas *n* gland secreting digestive juices and insulin.

panda *n* large black and white Himalayan bear (giant panda); small reddish bear-cat.

pandemonium *n* complete confusion; wild disorder, uproar.

pandemic *n* disease affecting whole area or community.

pander *n* procurer; go-between; *v* act as pander; *phr v* **pander to** gratify, encourage (unworthy desires, etc.).

Pandora's box *n* situation arousing curiosity and great temptation, but bringing all kinds of trouble.

pane *n* single sheet of glass in window.

panel *n* **1** rectangular piece of material set into surface (of door, dress, etc.) **2** list of persons called for jury service **3** group of persons taking part in discussion, in quiz, or game before audience; *v* **panels, paneling, paneled.**

fit, ornament with panels; *n* **paneling** series of panels.

pang *n* sudden sharp pain *fig* longing, yearning for.

panhandle *n* narrow strip of land; *v coll* accost (passers-by) for money.

Panhellenic *n* relating to Greece, to all Greek's.

panic *n* sudden, excessive, infectious terror, alarm; *as* **p.stricken** terrified; **panicky** *coll* affected by feeling of panic.

pannier *n* basket carried on back or side (of mule, bicycle, etc.).

panorama *n* **1** wide, unbroken view **2** series of scenes, pictures showing historical or other views; *a* **panoramic**.

panpipes *n mus* instrument of reed pipes of different lengths.

pansy *n* wild or garden plant of violet family.

pant *v* gasp for breath; *phr v* **pant for** long intensely for; *n* short, labored breath.

pantaloon *n* **1** a buffoon, foolish old man in pantomime **2** *ar* long tight trousers.

panther *n* leopard.

panties *n pl coll* short close-fitting underpants.

pantograph *n* instrument for reproducing drawing, plan, etc., on larger or smaller scale.

pantomime *n* **1** theatrical performance, often based on legend or fairy tale, *usu* without words **2** wordless.

pantry *n* room where food, plates, etc. are kept.

pants *n pl* **1** trousers; *idm* **with one's pants down** *coll* in a state of embarrassing unreadiness.

pap *n* **1** soft, sloppy food; baby food; mash **2** nipple of breast **3** lacking value, substance.

Papacy *n* office of Pope; papal system; *a* **papal** pertaining to Pope, or Papacy; *a, n* **papist** (adherent) of Papacy; Roman Catholic.

paparazzi *n pl* newspaper photographers or reporters who follow famous people.

papaya *n* tropical tree with fleshy edible fruit (*also* **pawpaw** *or* **custard apple**).

paper *n* **1** substance made from pulped wood fibers, rags, etc., formed into thin sheets for writing, drawing, etc. **2** newspaper **3** report, as for school **4** scholarly study of topic in form of article or lecture; *v* cover with paper; *idm* **on paper** in theory; *ns* **paperback** book with thin cardboard cover; **p. boy/girl** young person delivering newspapers; **p.chase** wend through a daunting bureaucracy; **p.clip** metal clip for holding together several sheets of paper; **p.tiger** person less threatening than he/she tries to appear; **paperweight** heavy object to stop papers from blowing away; **paperwork** writing of reports, letters, memos, etc., in an office.

papier mâché *n Fr* pulped paper mixed with paste and used as modeling material.

papoose *n* Native American baby or young child.

paprika *n* red, capsicum pepper used fresh or dried as a spice.

papyrus *n Gk* sedgelike plant; writing material of this; *pl* **papyri** manuscript written on this.

par *n* equality of value; nominal value (esp of stocks, shares); *fig* normal state of health, etc.; *golf* number of strokes reckoned as perfect score for hole, course; *a* **parity** equality; analogy.

para- (**par-** before vowel or h mute) *prefix* **1** beside; beyond **2** contrary; wrong **3** ancillary to **4** defense against (*e.g.,* **parachute** *abbr* **para** *also used as prefix:* **paratroop, parafoil,** etc.).

parable *n* brief story with moral lesson.

parabola *n* plane curve formed by intersection of cone by plane parallel to cone's side.

parachute *n* umbrella-like apparatus used to retard descent of falling body; *v* leap, fall to earth using parachute; *n* **parachutist.**

parade *n* **1** proud display **2** military review; **3** ground where this takes place **4** promenade; *v* **1** muster; **2** march solemnly past **3** display.

paradigm *n* **1** pattern; model **2** *ling* set of inflections of a word.

paradise *n* Garden of Eden; heaven; place of perfect happiness.

paradox *n* statement or belief apparently absurd or self-contradictory yet true; *a* **-ical.**

paraffin *n* inflammable, waxy hydrocarbon obtained from wood, petroleum, shale, etc.

paragon *n* model of excellence or perfection.

paragraph *n* **1** section in prose writing **2** short, separate news item.

parakeet *n* small, long-tailed domesticated parrot kept as a pet.

paralegal *n* attorney's assistant.

parallel *a* (of lines etc) equidistant in all parts; markedly similar; *n* **1** line equidistant from another; line of latitude **2** comparison; *v* compare; *n* **parallelogram** four-sided plane figure with parallel opposite sides.

paralysis *n* loss of sensation and power of motion in any part of body; (*pl* **-yses**) *v* **paralyze 1** affect with paralysis **2** *fig* check; render inoperative; *n, adj* **paralytic,** paralyzed (person).

paramedic *n* **1** auxiliary employee of medical service (not doctor or nurse) **2** specialist trained in emergency medial care; *a* **-al.**

parameter *n* **1** measurable feature or characteristic **2** *usu pl* limiting factor.

paramilitary *a* (of a force) organized like, but not part of

a
b
c
d
e
f
g
h
i
j
k
l
m
n
o
p
q
r
s
t
u
v
w
x
y
z

an official army.

paramount *a* having supreme authority; preeminent; chief.

paramour *n Fr* illicit lover.

paranoia *n* mental disorder, accompanied by delusions of persecution or of grandeur.

paranormal *a* not explicable by known scientific laws.

parapet *n* low wall; *mil* rampart in front of troops.

paraphernalia *n pl* miscellaneous belongings, accessories, equipment.

paraphrase *n* restatement of any passage; free translation; *v* express in other words.

paraplegic *n* person paralyzed from the waist down.

paraplegia *n* paralysis of lower part of body.

parapsychology *n* study of psychic phenomena.

paraquat very poisonous weed-killer.

parasite *n* useless hanger on; *bio* organism that lives on or within another organism; *a* **parasitic** of, caused by parasite.

parasol *n* sunshade; light umbrella used to protect bearer against sun.

paratroops *n pl* airborne troops landed by parachute; *n* **paratrooper**.

paratyphoid *n* infectious disease resembling typhoid fever.

parboil *v* boil partially.

parcel *n* object, objects wrapped, *esp* in paper, to form single package; piece of land; *idm* **part and parcel of** an essential part of; *v* **parcels, parceling, parceled.** divide into parts; wrap up; *phr vs* **parcel out** share out; **parcel up** wrap as a parcel.

parch *v* make, cause to become excessively dry; scorch.

parcheesi *n* game like backgammon.

parchment *n* animal skin (goat or sheep) treated, prepared for writing on; manuscript, etc., written on this.

pardon *n* forgiveness; excuse; remission of punishment; *v* forgive; grant pardon to; *a* **pardonable.**

pare *v* trim; cut away edge or surface; gradually reduce; *n* **paring** thin slice pared off.

parent *n* father or mother; *a* **parental;** *n* **parentage** ancestry, origin.

parenthesis *n* word, clause, etc. inserted into sentence which is grammatically correct without it; *n pl* **parentheses** brackets () enclosing parenthesis.

par excellence *a Fr* the best of the best, the superior thing.

parish *n* **1** smallest local unit in ecclesiastical administration **2** residents within this area **3** civil divisions in Louisiana; *n* **parishioner** inhabitant of parish.

parity *n* **1** equality **2** *finance* equivalent state of currencies.

park *n* **1** public garden in town **2** area of grass and trees surrounding public building, mansion **3** country area set aside as nature preserve, etc. **4** place where cars, etc., may park; *v* **1** put car, etc. in garage or leave elsewhere **2** *coll* leave object in one place, *usu* temporarily; *n* **parking** act of leaving stationary vehicle (*ns* **p.-meter** machine accepting coins to pay for limited period of roadside parking; **p.-ticket** police citation fining motorist for illegal parking.

parka *n* hooded warm jacket.

Parkinson's disease *n* progressive disease of nervous system causing severe lack of muscular control and immobility.

parlance *n* manner of speaking; words; idiom.

parley *n* conference *esp* between opponents, on peace terms; *v* discuss terms, negotiate.

parliament *n* supreme legislative body of UK; representative law-making body; *a* **parliamentary;** *n* **parliamentarian** one experienced in parliamentary procedure.

parlor *n* **1** (formerly) sitting-room where visitors were received **2** shop that provides specified goods or services (*eg* **beauty-p., ice-cream-p., funeral-p.**); *n* **parlor game** game played in the home, *esp* word game.

parochial *a* pertaining to parish; *fig* narrow-minded.

parody *n* **-dies. 1** mocking imitation of author's style or work **2** bad imitation, travesty; *v* **parodies, parodying, parodied.** make fun of by imitating.

parole *n Fr* word of honor, solemn pledge *esp* given by prisoner released temporarily from prison; *v* release of a prisoner on this.

parquet *n* flooring made of inlaid wooden blocks.

parricide *n* murder or murderer of parent; *v* the act of this.

parrot *n* **1** tropical bird with hooked beak, able to imitate human speech **2** *fig* imitator; *v* repeat unthinkingly.

parse *v* describe (word), analyze (sentence) grammatically.

parsec *n* unit of astronomical distance (approx 3.26 light years).

parsimony *n* undue economy; stinginess; *a* **parsimonious.**

parsley *n* culinary herb.

parsnip *n* plant with edible, cream-colored root often used in soups.

parson *n* rector; vicar; clergyman; *n* **parsonage** house of parson.

part[1] *n* **1** portion; section; component **2** share **3** role (as in play) **4** member of organism; *pl* **-s** area (*e.g.,* **remote parts**); *idm* **look the part** have suitable appearance (for job); *idm*

take somebody's part act in somebody's defense; *ns* **p.of speech** *ling* grammatical category of word; **p.-song** song with musical lines for three or more different voices; *adv* **partly** in part.

part[2] *v* **1** separate; divide **2** go different ways; *idm* **part company (with)** be separated (from); *phr v* **part with** let go; relinquish; *n* **parting 1** departure (*n* **p.shot** final remark or action made when leaving **2** line made where hair is combed in different directions.

partaker *n* participant; one who takes part in; *v* **partake** take share in; *pt* **partook;** *pp* **partaken.**

parterre *n* **1** level space with flowerbeds **2** main floor of theatre, behind orchestra.

parthenogenesis *n bio* reproduction without fertilization by male.

partial *a* **1** forming part of whole **2** biased; *idm* **partial to** fond of; *n* **partiality** bias in favor; fondness.

participate *v* have share in; take part in; partake; *ns* **participant, participation.**

participle *n* verbal adjective, having some functions of verb.

particle *n* **1** very small amount, part **2** minor, indeclinable part of speech.

particolored *a* colored in two or more contrasting hues.

particular *a* **1** distinct;

separate **2** peculiar **3** specific **4** fussy; *n pl* **-s** detailed account; specification; *n* **particularity.**

partisan *n* **1** adherent of party, cause, etc. **2** guerilla fighter *esp* in resistance, revolutionary movement; *a* showing blind devotion.

partition *n* **1** division **2** minor dividing wall in house; *v* divide into parts, sections.

partner *n* **1** member of commercial partnership **2** *golf, tennis, etc.,* one who plays with another, against opponents **3** one who dances with another **4** one person of close couple; *n* **-ship 1** state of being partner **2** association of two or more persons in business, etc.

partridge *n* game bird related to grouse.

parturition *n* act of giving birth.

party *n* **1** group of persons holding same opinions *esp* in politics **2** social gathering, celebration **3** squad of soldiers, etc., **4** *coll* person; *idm* **be (a) party to 1** have knowledge of **2** give support to; *ns* **p.line 1** shared phone line **2** official policy of political party.

PASCAL *n comput* programming language.

Paschal *a* of Passover or Easter.

pas de deux *n Fr* ballet dance for two; *fig* intricate relationship or undertaking.

pass *v* **1** go by or beyond **2**

A
B
C
D
E
F
G
H
I
J
K
L
M
N
O
P
Q
R
S
T
U
V
W
X
Y
Z

(cause to) move in specified direction **3** give (by hand) **4** *sport* give (by throw, kick, etc.) **5** transfer (money, goods) illegally **6** spend (time) **7** reach acceptable standard (in test) **8** examine and find acceptable **9** approve (law, regulation) by voting **10** utter (remark, judgement); **11** be changed (from one state to another); *idm* **let pass** allow; *idm* **pass the buck** declare another else responsible; *idm* **pass the hat** *coll* collect money; *idm* **pass muster** be deemed acceptable; *idm* **pass the time of day (with)** greet and have a conversation (with); *phr vs* **pass away 1** die **2** disappear; **pass by** ignore; **pass for** be accepted as; **pass off 1** take place **2** gradually come to an end (*idm* **pass off as** represent a person or thing falsely as another); **pass on 1** move along **2** die; **pass out 1** faint **2** be demobilized; **pass over** ignore; not select; **pass up** fail to take advantage of; *n* **1** narrow way between mountains **2** permit (for entry, travel, etc.) **3** *fencing* thrust or lunge **4** *cards* no bid; *idm* **make a pass at** try to interest in a flirtatious way; *a* **passable;** *ns* **passer-by; passing 1** going past **2** end; death; *a* **1** going past **2** momentary; brief; *idm* **in passing** incidentally.
passage *n* **1** voyage; crossing **2**

accommodation on ship **3** part of book etc referred to separately **4** means of access; *v* (*of horse*) move, cause to move sideways.
passbook *n* **1** identity document **2** bank account record of transactions.
passé *a Fr* **1** out-of-date **2** past one's best.
passenger *n* one who travels in ship, by car, train etc.
passim *adv Lat* scattered throughout (a text); here and there.
passion *n* **1** strong feeling; enthusiasm **2** sexual desire **3** wrath **4** *cap* suffering and death of Christ **5** oratorio based on Christ's suffering death; *a* **passionate** violent; quick-tempered; intense; ardent; *n* **passion flower** large-flowered climbing plant.
Passion Sunday *n* Sunday before Palm Sunday, fifth Sunday in Lent.
passive *a* **1** inactive; offering no active resistance **2** *ling* of verb form expressing action by which grammatical subject is affected; *n* such a grammatical form (*also* **passive voice**); *n* **p.smoking** inhaling of smoke from other people's cigarettes, etc.; *adv* **-ly;** *ns* **-ness, passivity**.
passkey *n* **1** key given to selected people **2** key to open many locks, skeleton key, master key.
Passover *n* annual Jewish feast

commemorating ancient liberation from Egyptian slavery.
passport *n* official document allowing holder to travel abroad etc.
password *n* secret word, phrase identifying person as entitled to enter (camp, society, etc.); countersign.
past *a* gone by; ended; taking place in past; *n* time gone by; earlier life; *prep* beyond; after; *ns* **p.participle** form of verb that combines with auxiliary verbs to make perfect and passive tenses.
pasta *n It* food from paste of flour, eggs, and water cut into different shapes.
paste *n* **1** soft, slightly moist compound **2** adhesive compound **3** vitreous compound used for artificial gems **4** compound of finely minced food, *esp* meat or fish, for spreading, paté; *v* fasten, affix with glue paste.
pastel *n* crayon made of powdered pigment mixed with gum, or oil; drawing in pastel; *a* delicately colored, pale.
pasteurization *n* sterilization (of milk etc.) by heating; *v* **pasteurize**.
pastiche *n Fr art, lit, mus* **1** work in style of other artist, writer, composer **2** medley.
pastille *n* flavored or medicated lozenge.
pastime *n* recreation; amusement, diversion.

pastor *n* priest; minister; *a* **pastoral 1** of office of pastor **2** connected with shepherds **3** (*of land*) used for pasture.

pastrami *n* seasoned pickled or smoked beef.

pastry *n* **1** sweet baked paste of flour and fat **2** pie, tart, etc. made of this **3** small rich cream-filled cake.

pasture *n* grass for food of cattle; land on which cattle are grazed; *v* graze; *n* **pasturage** cattle-grazing; pasture; *idm* **put out to pasture 1** leave to graze **2** *coll* retire, go into retirement.

pasty *n* small baked pie of meat and potatoes; *a* pale, unhealthy-looking.

pat *n* **1** quick light touch **2** small shaped lump of butter; *v* **pats, patting, patted.** tap (dog, horse, etc.) lightly with hand; *idm* **a pat on the back** (expression) of congratulation; *adv* without hesitation; *idm* **have something down pat** know by heart.

patch *n* **1** piece of material used to cover, repair hole in garment, etc. **2** black spot worn as facial ornament **3** small plot of land; *idm* **a bad patch** a bad period; *v* mend by means of patch; *phr v* **patch up 1** repair temporarily **2** resolve (quarrel, etc.); *a* **patchy** not consistent in quality, etc. *adv* **-ily**; *n* **-iness**; *n* **patchwork 1** needlework of patches of

different colors; quilt **2** *fig* medley; jumble.

pate *n* crown of head.

pâté *n Fr* rich paste of finely minced meat (*esp* liver) or fish.

patella *n Lat med* kneecap.

paten *n* plate, *usu* gold or silver, for holding bread at the Eucharist.

patent *a* **1** obvious; *adv* **-ly** clearly; *n* **p.leather** very glossy *usu* black leather used for handbags, shoes; *n* license granting sole right to make and sell invention; *v* secure patent.

paternal *a* of father, fatherly; *ns* **paternity** fatherhood; **paternalism** policy of controling people by supplying their needs without giving freedom of choice; *a* **-istic.**

paternoster *n* **1** The Lord's Prayer; eleventh bead of rosary **2** word or phrase used for luck.

path *n* **1** way; track; footpath **2** *fig* line of conduct; *n* **p.finder** explorer, discoverer of new route.

pathetic *a* **1** inspiring pity **2** hopelessly ineffectual; feeble in character; affecting emotions; pitiable; *adv* **-ally.**

pathogen *n* organism causing disease.

pathology *n* science of diseases; *a* **pathological** caused by, of nature of disease; morbid; *n* **pathologist.**

pathos *n* that which evokes sympathy, sorrow or pity.

patient *a* **1** enduring provocation or pain **2** persistent; *n* person under medical treatment; *n* **patience 1** endurance without complaint **2** cardgame.

patina *n* **1** greenish film on old copper, bronze **2** fine gloss on old woodwork.

patio *n* paved area close to a house, or courtyard.

pâtisserie *n Fr* (shop selling) cakes and pastries, bakery.

patois *n* local, provincial form of speech, slang.

patriarch *n* father, head of family, clan, etc.; *a* **patriarchal** venerable.

patrician *n* member of ancient Roman nobility; one of noble birth; *a* of noble birth.

patricide *n* murder of one's father.

patrimony *n* property inherited from one's father or ancestors.

patriot *n* one who is devoted to and loyally supports his country; *n* **patriotic** inspired by patriotism; *n* **patriotism** love of one's country.

patrol *v* **patrols, patrolling, patrolled.** walk regularly up and down (in); go the rounds; be on guard duty; *n* **1** small body of groops, police, etc., patroling **2** part of a troop of Boy Girl Scouts.

patron *n* **1** one who encourages and supports social, charitable, or artistic undertaking **2** *fml* regular customer; ns **p.saint** saint regarded as protector of given place, activity or group of people; **patronage** special support; right to distribute jobs, benefits; v **patronize 1** encourage **2** support by being customer **3** treat condescendingly (a **-zing**).

patronym n name derived from father, surname.

patsy n someone easily taken in or fooled.

patten n clog; raised wooden shoe.

patter v **1** run with quick, light steps **2** utter, speak hurriedly; n **1** succession of light taps **2** speech, jargon (of thieves, magicians, comedians, etc.).

pattern n model; shape as guide in constructing anything; sample; design.

patty n **1** small pie **2** round piece of ground meat **3** small flat candy (as peppermint).

paucity n scarceness.

Paul Bunyan n American folkhero of giant stature.

paunch n belly; v remove entrails (of rabbit, etc.).

pauper n destitute person supported by charity or at public expense.

pause n brief stop or rest; v stop for a while; hesitate.

pave v cover surface with flat stones, etc.; idm **pave the way (for)** prepare (for); make possible; ns **pavement** paved walk for pedestrians; **paving 1** act of, material for laying a paved surface **2** flat

smooth rectangular stone (also **paving stone**).

pavilion n **1** large tent **2** building attached to sportsfield **3** summerhouse **4** temporary structure for exhibition, trade show, etc.

paw n foot of quadruped with claws; v scrape with forefoot; handle roughly and unnecessarily.

pawn v deposit article with (pawnbroker); n **1** loan thus raised **2** chess piece **3** someone who is used by someone else; n **pawnbroker** one who lends money at interest on articles pledged.

pawpaw = papaya.

pay v **1** give, exchange money, etc. for goods or services **2** produce profit for **3** discharge (debt) **4** render; offer (**pay heed; pay respects**); idm **pay one's way** not rely on borrowing; idm **pay through the nose** pay too much; phr vs **pay back 1** repay (debt) **2** have revenge on; **pay for 1** pay money for **2** suffer as a result of; **pay off 1** repay (debt) **2** be worthwhile, rewarding **3** pay sb in order to keep silent; **pay out 1** make (big) payment **2** punish **3** unravel; n salary; wages; a **payable** due to be paid (pt, pp **paid**); ns **payee** one to whom payment is made; **payer; payment** amount paid.

pay dirt n **1** earth containing valuable mineral ore **2** fig

useful, highly profitable discovery.

payee n person to whom payment is due.

payload n **1** part of ship's load for which payment is received; passengers and cargo **2** mil explosive power of missile, bomb, etc. **3** amount of equipment and cargo carried by spacecraft.

paymaster n person holding money and in control.

payment n **1** act of paying **2** money paid.

payoff n **1** pay in settlement of debt **2** deserved reward **3** climax of story.

payola n payoff or undercover payment for a commercial favor.

pay phone n public coin-operated phone.

payroll n **1** list of employees **2** company's total expenditure on wages.

PC abbr **1** personal computer **2** politically correct.

PE abbr physical education.

pea n leguminous climbing plant, with edible seeds enclosed in pod; n **peanut** groundnut.

peace n calm; freedom from strife, war; tranquility; as **peaceable** at peace; not quarrelsome; **peaceful** free from war; calm; tranquil.

peach n stonefruit with pink velvety skin; tree bearing this; sl pretty girl; anything very pleasant.

peach v sl inform against.

peafowl *n* bird of pheasant family; **peacock (m)** with brilliantly colored fan-shaped tail, **peahen** (f).

pea jacket *n* short heavy wool coat, often double-breasted.

peak *n* **1** pointed mountain top **2** *fig* highest point **3** projecting part of cap over brow; *v* reach high or highest point; *n* **p.time** TV time when largest number of viewers are watching (*a* **p.-time**); *v* **peaked** having reached one's pinnacle already; *a* **peaked 1** having peak **2** having drawn, emaciated look.

peal *n* loud ringing of bells; set of bells tuned to each other; loud, reverberant sound; *v* ring loudly.

peanut *n* pealike plant with pods that ripen underground (also **groundnut**); *pl* **-s** *coll* very little money.

pear *n* sweet juicy oval fruit; tree bearing this; **prickly pear** type of cactus; its edible fruit.

pearl *n* lustrous concretion found in some mollusks, *esp* oyster, and used as jewel; cultured pearl; mother-of-pearl; *fig* outstandingly fine person or thing; *n* **p.-barley** barley with outer skin rubbed off; *a* **pearly** (*n* **p.gates** *coll* gates of heaven).

peasant *n* country person, rustic; *n* **peasantry** peasants collectively.

peashooter *n* tube or straw for shooting dried peas by blowing.

pea soup *n* **1** thick soup made from dried peas **2** a very thick fog.

peat *n* fibrous, partly decomposed vegetable matter found in bogs; this used for fuel.

pebble *n* small rounded stone; *a* **pebbly.**

pecan *n* N American hicory nut.

peccadillo *n* slight offense; petty crime.

peccary *n* wild US pig.

peck¹ *n* ¼ bushel; *fig* large amount.

peck² *v* **1** strike with beak **2** *coll* kiss hurriedly; *n* **1** blow of beak **2** *coll* quick kiss; *phr v* **peck at** nibble half-heartedly; *n* **1 pecker** something that pecks, *e.g.*, woodpecker **2** *coll* nose; *n* **pecking order** order of importance in hierarchy; **peckish** *a coll* hungry.

pectin *n* gelatinous substance found in some fruits used to bind jelly, jam, candy.

pectoral *a* of, in connection with, worn on the breast.

peculation *n* embezzlement; *v* **peculate** embezzle.

peculiar *a* one's own; individual; unusual; *n* **peculiarity** distinguishing characteristic; eccentricity; oddity; *adv* **-ly** strangely; specially.

pecuniary *a* relating to, connected with money.

pedagogue, pedagog *n* **1** schoolmaster **2** narrow-minded teacher.

pedal *n* **1** lever, operated by foot, for transmitting power or movement **2** lever used by player's foot to modify tone of piano, organ, etc.; *v* **pedals, pedaling, pedaled.** use pedals of organ, etc.; work, drive by pedals.

pedant *n* one who attaches exaggerated importance to minor details; one who makes tiresome display of learning; *a* **pedantic;** *n* **pedantry** tiresome display of learning.

peddle *v* offer goods from house to house; *n* **peddler** itinerant vendor of small wares.

pedestal *n* base of large column or statue.

pedestrian *n* person on foot; walker; *a* going on foot; *fig* prosaic, uninspiring; *v* **-ize** make accessible only to pedestrians; *n* **-ization.**

pediatrics *n* branch of medicine specializing in children; *a* **-tric;** *n* **-trician** children's doctor.

pedicure *n* chiropody; care and treatment of feet.

pedigree *n* genealogy; ancestry; *a* of animals bred from known stock.

pediment *n* gablelike architectural feature.

pedometer *n* instrument recording distance walked.

pee *v coll* urinate; *n coll* **1** urine **2** act of urination.

peek *n* glance with half-closed

eyes.

peel *n* skin of fruit or vegetable; *v* remove any form of covering.

peen *n* sharp or rounded end of hammer head.

peep *v* look hastily, furtively; *n* such a look; *ns* **peeping Tom** voyeur.

peer *v* look closely, gaze fixedly at.

peer *n* person or thing of equal merit, quality, etc.; nobleman; *a* **peerless** unrivaled, without equal; *ns* **peerage** rank of peer; body of peers; *fem* **peeress**.

peeve *v coll* upset; annoy; *as* **peevish** fretful, irritable; **peeved** *coll* annoyed; *n* **peevishness**.

peewee *n* person or thing that is very small.

peg *n* wooden or metal pin, bolt; *v* **pegs, pegging, pegged.** fasten with pegs; fix price etc. by regulations.

Pegasus *n* in Greek mythology, a winged horse.

pejorative *a* disparaging; depreciatory.

Pekingese *n* small Chinese lapdog.

pekoe *n* choice kind of black tea.

pelagic, pelagian *a* of, in, deep sea.

pelican *n* large, fish-eating water bird, with food-storing pouch beneath its beak.

pellagra *n* disease from inadequate diet.

pellet *n* small ball; small shot;

pill.

pellicle *n* thin skin; membrane; *a* **pellicular**.

pell-mell *adv* headlong; confusedly; *n* disordered haste.

pellucid *a* translucent; transparent; *fig* clear; lucid.

pelmet *n* strip of board or cloth concealing curtain rail etc.

pelt[1] *v* throw things at; (*of rain, etc.*) beat down heavily; run quickly.

pelt[2] *n* raw animal skin with fur or wool.

pelvis *n* bony girdle formed by hipbones and sacrum; *a* **pelvic**.

pemmican, pemican *n* Native American dried food made from lean meat, suet, molasses.

pen[1] *n* small enclosure for domestic animals, fowl, etc.; *v* **pens, penning, penned.** put in pen; imprison; *a* **pent** confined; repressed.

pen[2] *n* instrument for writing in ink; *v* write, put on paper; *ns* **p.pal** friend by correspondence; **p.name** pseudonym used by writer (*also* **nom de plume**).

penal *a* connected with punishment, *esp* legal; *n* **p.servitude** imprisonment with hard labor; *n* **penalty** legal punishment; loss, suffering as result of folly, etc.; *sport* disadvantage imposed for breaking rule; *v* **penalize** punish; handicap (of sports).

penance *n* act performed as proof of repentance.

penchant *n* inclination; partiality; liking for.

pencil *n* instrument for writing, etc., consisting of graphite or crayon cased in wood; small brush used by painters; *v* **pencils, penciling, penciled.** draw, write with pencil.

pendant *n* hanging ornament; locket; **pendent** *a* hanging, suspended.

pending *a* not decided, unfinished; *prep* during; awaiting.

pendulous *a* hanging freely; swinging to and fro.

pendulum *n* swinging weight, *esp* one regulating clock mechanism.

penetrate *v* pierce; enter; permeate; *fig* see through; reach mind of; *a* **penetrable; penetrating** piercing; shrill; discerning; *n* **-ation** acute, subtlety of mind.

penguin *n* flightless Antarctic seabird.

penicillin *n* one of anti-infective class of antibiotics, obtained from mold or synthetically derived.

peninsula *n* protuberance of land bordered on three sides by water; *a* **peninsular**.

penis *n* male sex organ.

penitence *n* sorrow for sin; *a* **penitent** having sense of sin; repentant; *n* one who repents of sin; *n* **penitentiary** reformatory; prison.

penknife n small folding pocketknife.

penmanship n the art of handwriting with a pen or pencil.

pennant n tapered, triangular flag (also **pennon**).

penny n copper coin worth one cent; 100th part of one dollar; pl **pennies, pence;** a **penniless** poor, destitute.

pennyroyal n aromatic herb of mint family used in folk medicine.

penology n study of methods of punishment and treatment of criminals.

pension[1] n periodic payment made to retired workers, old people, the aged, etc.; phr v **pension off** dismiss from work with offer of pension; n **-er** person receiving pension.

pension[2] n small private hotel.

pensive a immersed in sad thoughts; wistful; thoughtful.

penta- prefix five.

pentagon n plane figure with five sides; cap Department of Defense building.

pentameter n line of verse with five metrical feet.

Pentateuch n first five books of Moses, Old Testament, the Jewish Torah.

pentathlon n athletic contest comprising five events.

Pentecost n Whitsunday or the seventh Sunday after Easter; Shavuos, Jewish harvest festival.

penthouse n small house or apartment on flat roof of building.

pent up a (of emotion) not expressed.

penult n next to last syllable of word.

penultimate a last but one.

penumbra n partially shaded region round complete shadow esp in eclipse; a **-bral**.

penury n want, destitution; a **penurious** poor; mean.

peon n menial worker, laborer.

peony n shrub with large red, pink, or white flowers.

people n 1 race; nation 2 human beings in general; v populate.

pep n coll vigor; v **peps, pepping, pepped.** coll **pep up** stimulate.

pepper n pungent aromatic spice, made from dried berries of pepper tree; v sprinkle with pepper; pelt with missiles; a **peppery** tasting of pepper; fig irritable; spunky.

peppercorn n dried berry of pepper tree.

peppermint n pungent aromatic herb of mint family.

pep pill n pill containing stimulant drug.

pepsin n liquid in stomach secretion that digests proteins.

per prep by means of; for each; advs **p. annum** each year; **p. capita** per head; **p.cent** per hundred (in percentage); **p. se** in itself.

per- prefix through; completely.

peradventure adv perhaps.

perambulate n walk up and down; walk about.

perambulator n light carriage for child, also coll pram.

perceive v sense; become aware of through senses; apprehend; a **perceptible** that can be perceived; n **perception** faculty of perceiving; immediate awareness; a **perceptive** quick to notice; aware.

percentage n rate, allowance, proportion per hundred.

perch[1] n edible freshwater fish.

perch[2] n rod, branch for birds to roost on; v (of birds) alight, come to rest; sit, balance on high position.

perchance adv perhaps; possibly.

percolate v filter, ooze, drip slowly (through); n **percolation; percolator** coffeepot with filter.

percussion n 1 impact; violent collision 2 musical instruments played by being struck, as drums.

perdition n damnation; ruin.

peregrinate v travel; roam about; n **-ation**.

peregrine falcon n fast bird of prey.

peremptory a imperious; dictatorial; precluding opposition, appeal etc.

perennial a lasting year after year; never failing; n plant lasting more than two years.

perestroika n reform, reconstruction (of Soviet economy and society in 1980s).

A
B
C
D
E
F
G
H
I
J
K
L
M
N
O
P
Q
R
S
T
U
V
W
X
Y
Z

perfect *a* faultless; complete; of highest state of excellence; *n* verbal tense expressing complete action; *v* improve; make highly competent; *n* **perfection** state of being perfect.

perfidy *n* treachery; faithlessness; *a* **perfidious**.

perforate *v* pierce; penetrate; make hole(s) in; *n* **perforation 1** act, result, of perforating **2** holes made in paper to make tearing easy.

perforce *adv* by necessity.

perform *v* **1** accomplish; carry out **2** enact (play) in public **3** play on musical instrument; *ns* **performance; performer** one who performs.

perfume *n* **1** pleasing smell **2** scented liquid applied to body or clothing; *v* impart fragrance to; *ns* **perfumery** place where perfumes are made or sold; **perfumer**.

perfunctory *a* superficial; hasty; indifferent.

perhaps *adv* possibly.

peri- *prefix* round.

perigee *n* point at which orbit of satellite is nearest to Earth.

peril *n* danger; hazard; *a* **perilous** dangerous; risky.

perimeter *n* distance around plane figure; outer edge; boundary.

period *n* **1** interval of time **2** era; epoch **3** phase of menstrual cycle **4** grammatical mark at end of sentence (.); *a* characteristic

of certain period of time (of furniture, dress, etc.); *a* **periodic** recurring at regular intervals (**p. table** list of chemical elements in rising order of atomic weight); *a* **periodical** periodic; *n* magazine published at regular intervals, *e.g.*, weekly.

peripatetic *a* walking about; itinerant.

periphery *n* circumference; outside; outer surface.

periscope *n* apparatus for seeing objects above eyelevel, where direct view is obstructed.

perish *v* die; decay; *a* **perishable** liable to speedy decay; *n pl* goods specially liable to decay; **perished 1** *coll* suffering from exposure to cold **2** (of rubber and fabrics) deteriorated in quality; no longer usable; **perishing 1** unbearably cold **2** *coll* expressing annoyance with.

peritoneum *n anat* membrane lining inner surface of abdomen; *n* **peritonitis** inflammation of peritoneum.

periwinkle *n* **1** trailing blue-flowered plant **2** small edible mollusk.

perjure *v* bear false witness; forswear oneself; *n* **perjury** deliberately false testimony under oath; crime of making false statement under oath.

perk up *v* regain one's health, spirits; *ns* **perkiness**

jauntiness; **perk** *coll* perquisite; *a* **perky** energetic; cheerful.

perm *n* permanent wave (hairstyling).

permafrost *n* permanently frozen subsoil *e.g.*, in Siberia.

permanent *a* continuing without change; lasting; *ns* **permanence** state of being permanent; **permanency** something that is permanent.

permeate *v* pass through; saturate; *a* **permeable** allowing free passage of liquids.

permit *v* **permits, permitting, permitted.** allow; give permission to; tolerate; *n* warrant; license; document giving formal permission; *n* **permission** agree; allow; consent; sanction; *a* **permissible** allowable; **permissive** allowing unusual freedom, *esp* in behavior; *adv* **-ly; *n* -ness.**

permute *v* put in different order; interchange; *n* **permutation**.

pernicious *a* highly injurious; deadly; fatal.

peroration *n* concluding part of a speech.

peroxide *n* compound with maximum proportion of oxygen to other element(s), *esp* **hydrogen p.** colorless liquid used as bleach or antiseptic; *n* **p. blonde** woman who has bleached her hair with this.

perpendicular *a* exactly

upright, vertical; n line at right angles to another line or surface.

perpetrate v commit, be guilty of; ns **perpetration; perpetrator.**

perpetual a everlasting; unceasing; constantly repeated; n **perpetuity (in perpetuity** for ever).

perpetuate v cause to last indefinitely; preserve from oblivion; n **perpetuation.**

perplex v puzzle; make confused; n **perplexity** bewilderment; confusion.

perquisite n profit, monetary or in kind, in addition to regular wages or salary; idm **perk** benefit.

persecute v harass; oppress; treat cruelly, esp for religious or political reasons; ns **persecution,** persecutor.

persevere v persist doggedly, patiently in attaining purpose; n **perseverance** prolonged, steadfast effort.

persiflage n banter.

persimmon n hardwood tree; its edible fruit.

persist v continue in spite of opposition; remain; endure; a **persistent** obstinate; tending to recur; n **persistence** tenacity of purpose; **persistency** obstinacy.

person n 1 human being (pl **people**) 2 individual (pl **persons**) 3 ling category of pronoun or verb, eg **first p.** the one(s) speaking; **second p.** the one(s) spoken to;

third p. any other individual(s); idm **in person** oneself, not somebody acting on one's behalf; **on one's person** being carried with one, where one is; as **personal** 1 by, of, for a person 2 private (**p. letter**) 3 derogatory; impertinent (**p. remark**) 4 of the body (**p. hygiene**) (ns **p. assistant** secretary to manager; **p. column** section in newspaper or magazine for private advertizements; **p. computer** desktop computer, also **PC; p. organizer** 1 looseleaf notebook with diary, addresses, business and personal information, etc. 2 electronic equivalent of this; **p. pronoun** ling pronoun showing person, e.g., I, you, he; a **personable** attractive in appearance and manner; ns **persona** character as seen by other people (**p. grata/non grata** Lat person acceptable or not, esp in diplomacy with foreign powers); **personage** person of importance; **personality** 1 person's qualities and character as a whole 2 (person with) lively or forceful character 3 well-known, usu popular person (n **personality cult** excessive, blind admiration for famous individual, usu entertainer or political leader.

personify v represent as person; typify, embody; n **personification.**

personnel n all members of staff.

perspective n art of depicting three-dimensional objects on plane surface; idm **in perspective** in proper relations.

perspicacious a having keen mental judgement or understanding.

perspicuous a clearly expressed; lucid.

perspire v sweat; exude moisture through pores; n **perspiration.**

persuade v induce to think, believe; n **persuasion** creed; way of thinking; a **persuasive.**

pert a jaunty; lively; flippant.

pertain v belong to; have reference to; concern.

pertinacious a obstinate; tenacious; n **pertinacity** persistance.

pertinent a relevant; to the point.

perturb v disturb; throw into disorder, confusion; n **-ation** agitation of mind; disorder; deviation of planet from true orbit.

peruse v read through; look over; n **perusal.**

pervade v penetrate thoroughly; a **pervasive** (ns **-ness, pervasion**).

pervert v turn, divert from proper use; n apostate; one inclined to perversion; n **perversion;** a **perverse** intractable; self-willed; n **perversity.**

pervious a permeable;

a
b
c
d
e
f
g
h
i
j
k
l
m
n
o
p
q
r
s
t
u
v
w
x
y
z

penetrable.

peso n unit of money in some S and C American countries.

pessimism n tendency to look on dark side of things; doctrine that world is essentially evil; n -**ist**; a - **istic**.

pest n 1 troublesome, vexatious or harmful person, animal or thing 2 garden parasite 3 blight, mildew etc.

pester v worry, plague esp with trivialities.

pesticide n poison to kill pests.

pestilence n fatal infectious, contagious disease; esp bubonic plague; as -**ilent, - ilential**.

pestle n instrument for pounding substances in mortar.

pesto n sauce (for pasta) made form basil, olive oil, garlic, and cheese.

pet[1] n tame animal kept as object of affection; favorite, cherished child; v **pets, petting, petted.** treat as pet; fondle; n **p. name** name for a beloved person.

pet[2] n fit of ill-humor; peevishness; a **pettish** sulky; fretful.

petal n one section of corolla of flowers; a **petaled** having petals.

peter out v coll gradually diminish.

petit a law petty, minor.

petite a (woman) of small, dainty build.

petition n 1 entreaty; urgent request; formal application esp one to sovereign, or court of law 2 list of signatures requesting political action, legislative change; v address petition to; n -**er**.

petrel n small black and gray seabird.

petrify v **petrifies, petrifying, petrified.** turn into stone; fig paralyze with fear, etc.

petrochemical n any chemical derived from natural gas or oil; **p. industry** industry producing this.

petrodollars n pl money surpluses in oil-exporting countries.

petroleum n flammable mineral oil from coal used for fuel, ointments, etc.

petrology n study of origin and structure of rocks; a **petrous** of, like stone.

petticoat n women's underskirt.

pettish a petulant.

petty a trivial; of small worth, scale; n, a **petty bourgeois** member of lower middle class(also **petit b.**); ns **p. cash** money for small payments; **p. officer** naval noncommissioned officer.

petulance n peevishness; irritability; a **petulant**.

petunia n genus of herbs with funnel-shaped purple, dark pink, white, etc. flowers.

pew n 1 fixed bench, used as seat in church, synagogue 2 coll seat, chair.

pewter n alloy of tin and lead; vessel, plate, etc., made of this.

pfennig n German unit of currency $\frac{1}{100}$ of a mark.

PG abbr parental guidance suggested,indicating that filmis suitable for children. **PG-13** abbr indicating film is unsuited for viewers younger than 13 years.

pH n measure of alkalinity or acidity.

phagocyte n white blood corpuscle; leukocyte.

phalanx n 1 body of closely massed soldiers 2 fig resolute group of persons.

phallus n penis; image of it used in some primitive forms of art, religion; a **phallic**.

phantasm n illusion; apparition; n **phantasmagoria** series of optical illusions; a **phantasmagoric**.

phantom n specter; ghost; supernatural or imaginary figure; delusion.

pharaoh n title of kings of ancient Egypt.

pharisee n self-righteous person; idm hyprocrite.

pharmacy n preparation and dispensing of drugs; a **pharmaceutical** of pharmacy; **pharmacology** study of drugs and medicines, n pl science of pharmacy; ns **pharmacopoeia** authoritatve list of drugs and directions for their use and preparation.

pharynx n med cavity at back of nose and mouth opening into larynx n **pharyngitis**

inflammation of this.

phase *n* stage in development; aspect of planet.

phase out *n* gradual termination.

phatic communion *n ling* speech that conveys intent to be sociable without any other message.

PhD *abbr* doctor of philosophy; (person with) higher degree of doctorate.

pheasant *n* gamebird with lond tail and brilliant coloring.

phenobarbital *n* white powder sedative.

phenol *n* carbolic acid.

phenomenon *n* anything perceived by senses; uncommon, remarkable event; *pl* **phenomena**; *a* **phenomenal** relating to phenomena; extraordinary.

pheromone *n bio* chemical secreted by animal, insect to attract others of species.

phil- *prefix* loving; studying.

philander *v* make love insincerely; *n* **philanderer**.

philanthropy *n* love of mankind; goodwill; benevolence; *n* **philanthropist**.

philately *n* stamp-collecting; *n* **philatelist**.

philharmonic *a* devoted to music, symphony orchestra .

philistine *n, a* (person) showing no understanding of, hostile to artistic creation, beauty or culture.

philology *n* study of linguistics.

philosophy *n* **1** theory of knowledge **2** mental balance, calmness in dealing with events, circumstances; *n* **philosopher; (philosopher's stone** (formerly) imaginary substance supposed to transform base metal into gold) *a* **-sophic(al);** *v* **-sophize** indulge in philosophical theories; moralize.

philter *n* magic potion.

phlebitis *n med* inflammation of lining of veins.

phlegm *n* **1** viscid substance secreted by mucous membranes, *esp* in nose and throat **2** apathy; indifference **3** calmness; *a* **-atic** not easily excited; sluggish.

phlox *n* flowering plant.

phobia *n* morbid, irrational fear.

phoenix *n* legendary bird, who burned to ashes then rose alive to live another 500 years; unique thing.

phone *n, v, a coll* telephone; *ns* **p. book** directory of numbers; **phone-in** *TV, radio* broadcast in which listeners at home are invited to give opinions, answer questions by telephone.

phoneme *n ling* single speech sound in given language.

phonetic *a* of, relating to vocal sounds; *n pl* science of vocal sounds.

phono- *prefix Gk* of sounds (*esp* vocal).

phonograph *n* instrument for recording and reproducing sounds on a revolving disc (record) or cylinder.

phonology *n* study of sound changes in a language.

phony *a coll* sham; insincere; bogus; *n coll* insincere person.

phosphorus *n* nonmetallic element emitting glow in the dark; *ns* **phosphate** salt of phosphorus acid **phosphide**, compound of phosphorous; **phosphorescence** property of emitting slight glow in dark, without heat.

photo- *prefix* of light; of photography.

photo *n, v abbr* photograph.

photocopier *n* machine for making multiple photographic copies of documents; *n, v* **photocopy** (make) such a copy.

photoelectric *a* pertaining to effect of light on electrons; *n* **p. cell** device that detects, measures light (*also* **photocell**).

photogenic *a* having qualities that make an attractive photograph; the quality of photographing well (as subject).

photograph *n* picture produced by action of light on sensitized film; *v* take photograph of; *n* **-er;** *a* **-ic** *n* **photography**.

photogravure *n* process of reproducing, by photography, an engraving.

photometer *n* instrument for measuring intensity of light.

photon *n* minute particle of

A B C D E F G H I J K L M N O **P** Q R S T U V W X Y Z

light.

photosensitive *a* affected by action of light.

Photostat [*TM*] apparatus for making photographic copies; fascimile so produced; *v lc* take photostat of.

photosynthesis *n* (in plants) conversion of carbon dioxide and water into food by using energy from sunlight; *v* - **thesize** *a* -**thetic**.

phrasal *a* of a phrase; *n* **p. verb** verb combined with preposition or adverbial particle to give new meaning.

phrase *n* group of words forming part to sentence; striking remark; idiomatic expression; *v* express in words; *ns* **phrasebook** book with useful phrases and expressions to assist conversation in a foreign language; **phraseology** selection of words used.

phrenology *n* theory that one's character, intelligence, etc., can be deduced from shape of skull; study of shape of skull; *n* -**ologist**.

phylum *n* class of plants or animals.

physic *n* medicine; *v* give physic to; *n* **physician** one trained in medical profession, who diagnoses and treats disease, but does not operate.

physical *a* **1** pertaining to matter **2** pertaining to nature and natural features of

universe **3** connected with human or animal body.

physical therapy *n* medical treatment of massage, exercise, etc., for disability or pain.

physics *n* study of properties of matter and energy; *n* **physicist** one skilled in, or student of physics.

physiognomy *n* **1** art of judging character from face **2** general appearance and expression of face **3** *sl* face.

physiology *n* study of functions and vital processes of living beings; *n* **physiologist**.

physiotherapy *n* remedial treatment by massage, heat, exercise etc.; *n* **physiotherapist**.

physique *n* *Fr* physical form, structure; constitution; body.

pi *n* Greek letter π , symbol for ratio of circumference to diameter.

piano *n* keyboard musical instrument with strings struck by hammers; *adv mus* softly; *a, n* soft (passage); *a, adv* **pianissimo** very quiet(ly); *n* **pianist** one who plays the piano.

piazza *n* public square *esp* in Italy.

pica *n* unit used ot measure typographic text; 12 pt size type.

picador *n* *Sp* mounted bullfighter, armed with lance.

picaresque *a* *Fr* (of literature)

concerning adventures of a *usu* likeable rogue.

picayune *a* petty; insignificant.

piccolo *n* small shrill flute.

pick[1] *n* **1** tool with wooden shaft, long curved head pointed at one end and chisel-edge at other **2** flat brittle device of metal or horn for strumming guitar, banjo; *n* **pickax** tool with sharp points and long handle for breaking ground.

pick[2] *n* small thin piece of metal, horn, etc., used for plucking strings of guitar, zither, etc.

pick[3] *v* **1** pluck; gather **2** choose; select **3** open (lock) without key **4** remove unwanted pieces from **5** nibble; *idm* **pick someone's brain** use another's knowledge; *idm* **pick holes** in find fault with; *idm* **pick a fight/quarrel etc with** purposely start a fight/quarrel with; *idm* **pick pocket** steal from a pocket; *phr vs* **pick at** eat without interest, in small quantity; **pick off** shoot one after the other; **pick on 1** select for special attention **2** persecute; victimize; **pick out 1** select **2** distinguish; **pick up 1** take by hand **2** take by transportation **3** acquire or learn informally **4** make a casual acquaintance, *usu* with person of opposite sex **5** resume (activity) after interval **6** recover **7** find by chance; *ns* **p.-me-up** intake of food, drink, or medicine that makes one feel better; *idm* cocktail; **pick-up 1** arm and stylus of record player **2** truck with low open sides; *ns* **pickings** trifles left over; dishonest profits.

pickerel *n* small pike.

picket *n* **1** pointed stake used in fence **2** striker posted outside place of employment to dissuade others from working **3** *mil* patrol on special duty; *v* **1** fence with pickets **2** act as picket in strike.

pickle *n* **1** brine, vinegar, etc., used to preserve food **2** food so preserved **3** *coll* trouble; *v* preserve in pickle; *a sl* **pickled** drunk.

pickpocket *n* thief stealing directly from pockets.

picky *a* fussy.

picnic *n* casual meal eaten out-of-doors; *coll* thing easily done; *v* **picnics, picnicking, picnicked.** go on, take picnic.

Pict *n* member of race formerly inhabiting Scotland.

picture *n* **1** painting; drawing; photograph **2** mental image **3** vivid verbal description **4** *pl* **-s** movies; *v* make picture of; imagine; describe; *a* **pictorial** expressed in pictures; *n* journal, mainly consisting of pictures; *a* **picturesque 1** like, forming striking picture **2** vivid; graphic; *n* **p. gallery** room, building where paintings,

etc., are exhibited.

piddling *a coll* trivial.

pidgin *n* mixture of English and native tongues heard in some Oriental and African countries.

pie¹ *n* magpie; kind of woodpecker; *a* **piebald** marked in black and white blotches.

pie² *n* dish of meat, fruit, etc., covered with pastry and baked; *n* **p. chart** diagram consisting of circle divided into segments to illustrate relative proportions of parts of the whole under study; *a* **pie-eyed** *coll* drunk.

piece *n* **1** bit; part **2** item **3** literary, artistic, or musical composition; *v* put together; join; *idm* **give a piece of one's mind** say bluntly what you think; *idm* **go to pieces** lose self-control; *idm* **of a piece** similar; *idm* **pull to pieces** criticize in every possible way; *idm* **a piece of cake** *coll* very easy to do; *idm* **piece together** recreate; reassemble; *a* **piecemeal** piece by piece.

pièce de résistance *n Fr* **1** best achievement **2** event providing climax to occasion **3** highlight of a meal.

pied *v* of two contrasting colors.

pieplant *n* rhubarb.

pier *n* **1** column, mass of stone, supporting arch, etc. **2** projecting wharf, or landing-place; jetty **3** quay.

pierce *v* make hole in; penetrate; stab; *a* **piercing** keen, sharp, penetrating.

pietà *n It* image or statue of Virgin Mary mourning Christ crucified.

piety *n* devotion to God; dutiful, loyal feelings.

piffle *n sl* trivial; nonsense.

piffling *a coll* worthless; trivial.

pig *n* **1** swine; hog **2** *coll* greedy, selfish person **3** oblong casting of metal; *idm* **pig out** eat excessively; *ns* **p. iron** unrefined form of iron; **p.-swill** waste food fed to pigs; **p.-tail** hair held rubberband *usu* worn aver each ear; *as* **piggish** greedy; stubborn; **pigheaded** stupidly obstinate; *n* **pigsty 1** pen for pigs **2** very dirty room or house.

pigeon *n* wild or domesticated bird of dove species; *as* **p.-toed** with toes pointing inward; *n* **pigeonhole** compartment for papers; *v* **1** store away in a pigeonhole **2** classify in a too-rigid way.

piggyback *a, adv* one person, object on the back of another; *v* double up or carry objects.

pigment *n* substance for coloring, paint, dye; natural color in living tissue.

pigmentation *n* coloration.

pigmy *n* = **pygmy**.

pike *n* **1** large freshwater fish **2** short spear **3** highway.

pilaf, pilaff *n* dish of fragrant rice and spices.

pilchard *n* large-scaled fish of

a
b
c
d
e
f
g
h
i
j
k
l
m
n
o
p
q
r
s
t
u
v
w
x
y
z

A B C D E F G H I J K L M N O **P** Q R S T U V W X Y Z

herring family.

pile[1] *n* pointed beam driven into ground, riverbed, etc.,; *n* **pile driver** machine for driving in piles.

pile[2] *n* heap or mass; large building; *idm* **make a pile** become very rich; *idm* **make one's pile** earn enough to be comfortable for life; *v* heap up; *idm* **pile it on** (thick) *coll* exaggerate; *phr vs* **pile in** enter or begin in a disorderly way; **pile out** come out in a disorderly way; **pile up 1** form, be formed into a pile **2** accumulate **3** (of vehicles) crash into the back of other vehicles that have crashed (*n* **pileup** multiple accident of this kind); **atomic p.** nuclear reactor; *v* heap up; make into pile; stack.

pile[3] *n* nap *esp* of velvet; high standing fibers of cloth.

pilfer *v* steal small quantity; snitch; *n* **-er.**

pilgrim *n* **1** one who visits sacred place, shrine for religious reasons **2** an English colonist settling at Plymouth in 17th century; *n* **-age.**

pill *n* **1** small ball of medicinal drugs, swallowed whole **2** *sl* ball *esp* billiard ball; *n* **p.-box** small box for pills; small round concrete fort.

pillage *v* plunder; rob openly; loot; *n*.

pillar *n* slender supporting column; *idm* **pillar of** supporter of (society, etc.).

pillory *n* framework with holes for neck and wrists, where offenders were secured and exposed to public ridicule; *v* punish by putting in pillory; *fig* expose to public disgrace, scorn, etc.

pillow *n* cushion for head, *esp* in bed; *v* rest on, as on pillow *n* **p.-case** fabric cover for pillow.

pilot *n* **1** one who directs course of vessels *esp* one licensed to navigate into or out of port **2** one qualified to fly aircraft **3** *fig* guide; leader; *v* act as pilot; *a* experimental; preliminary; *ns* **p. light 1** light that indicates apparatus is switched on **2** (*of gas appliance*) small flame that allows main flame to be relit easily.

pimiento *n* large reddish sweet pepper, used for garnish and for making paprika.

pimp *n* *vulgar* man living off earnings of prostitutes.

pimple *n* small pustule on skin; *a* **pimply.**

pimpernel *n* type of primrose.

PIN *abbr banking* personal identification number.

pin[1] *n* **1** short, stiff, pointed wire with head, used for fastening **2** wooden, metal peg or rivet; *v* **pins, pinning, pinned. 1** fasten, attach with pin **2** hold firmly *esp* under weight; **p. down** *fig* bind (person) to; *v* **pin-point** mark precisely.

pin[2] *ns* **pinball** game where

balls are struck, deflected by pins and roll into holes and score points (**p. machine** mechanical version of this); **p.-cushion** (in needlework) soft pad for holding pins ready for use; **p.-money 1** (formerly) allowance for personal needs **2** money earned to cover minor expenses; not a proper living wage; **pinprick 1** pricking with pin **2** *fig* minor inconvenience; **p.-stripe** type of dark cloth with regular pattern of thin stripes (**p. suit** suit made with this); **p.-table** table with pinball; **p.-up 1** photo of *usu* famous person one admires **2** such a person.

pinafore *n* loose sleeveless garment, like an apron.

pince-nez *n* *Fr* eye glasses kept on nose by springclip.

pincers *n pl* **1** gripping tool **2** pair of sharp gripping claws (of some crustaceans).

pinch *v* **1** nip; squeeze **2** *fig* cause to become thin, etc. **3** *coll* steal **4** *sl* arrest; *idm* **pinch and scrape** be drastically economical; *n* **1** painful squeeze, *esp* of skin, with finger and thumb **2** as much as can be taken up between finger and thumb; *idm* **in a pinch** with some difficulty; *a* **pinched 1** (*of face*) drawn; haggard **2** miserable; *n* **p.penny** a miser, stingy person.

pinchbeck *n* zinc and copper

alloy; jewelry of this; *a* sham.

pine *n* **1** evergreen coniferous tree **2** pineapple.

pine *v* **1** languish; waste away through sorrow, etc. **2** long intensely (for).

pineal gland *n* small gland in brain.

pineapple *n* **1** large, cone-shaped edible fruit; plant with spiny leaves bearing this fruit **2** a hand grenade.

ping *v, n* (make) single high-pitched bell-like sound; *n* **pinger** device that makes such sounds as a warning.

Ping-Pong *n* [TM] *coll* table tennis.

pinion *n* **1** feather or wing **2** small cogwheel; *v* bind somebody's arms.

pink *n* **1** garden plant allied to carnation **2** acme; perfection; *a* of pale, delicate reddish color; *idm* **in the pink** *coll* very fit; *idm* **tickled pink** *coll* delighted; *ns* **p.-eye** conjunctivitis; *v* decorate (edge) with zig-zags; *n* **pinking shears** scissors with zig-zag blades.

pinkie *n* little finger or toe.

pinnacle *n* ornamental tapering turret; slender mountain peak; *fig* culminating point.

pins and needles *n* **1** pricking feeling caused by flow of blood after temporary stoppage **2** in a state of nervousness, anticipatory.

pint *n* liquid measure; two cups; half a quart; 1/8th

gallon; *a* **p.-sized** *coll* (of people) small.

pinto *n* piebald horse.

pinto bean *n* mottled kidney bean used as food for humans, animals.

pinwheel *n* windmill-like toy that spins on a stick.

pinyin *n* written form of Chinese using Roman alphabet.

pioneer *n* **1** one who is first in experiments or exploration **2** early settler in new country **3** one of party of troops preceeding army on march and preparing roads etc.; *v* take lead in; be first to introduce.

pious *a* devout; faithful in religious duties.

pip *n* **1** seed in fruit (*eg* **apple pip**) **2** short high-pitched note used as signal; bleep.

pipe *n* **1** long tube conveying water, gas, etc. **2** tube with small bowl at end for smoking tobacco **3** tube-shaped musical wind instruments **4** measure of wine **5** shrill voice, or bird call; *v* **1** play the pipe **2** make sound like pipe **3** convey by pipe **4** make tubular ornamental shapes in icing cake or on clothing; *phr vs* **pipe down** *coll* stop talking; make less noise; **pipe up** *coll* begin suddenly to speak or sing; *ns* **p.dream** unrealistic hope; **pipeline 1** system of connected pipes for conveying oil, gas, etc. **2** *fig*

channel of supply or communication; *idm* **in the pipeline** being prepared, processed, dealt with; to be completed or delivered soon; *ns* **pipe clay** fine white clay; **piper** player on bagpipes; *a* **piped 1** carried by pipes **2** by radio, cable, etc. (**p. music** continuous playing of recorded, not live music); *n* **piping 1** act of playing pipe or making such a sound **2** system of pipes for water, etc.; length of pipe **3** decorative trimming on garment, on cake icing, etc. (*a* high-pitched; *idm* **piping hot** hot to eat or drink).

pipette *n Fr* small graduated tube used in chemistry.

pipkin *n* small earthenware or metal pot with a handle.

pippin *n* name for several varieties of apples.

pip squeak *n coll* insignificant person.

piquant *a* **1** stimulating; lively **2** pleasantly sharp to taste; *n* **piquancy**.

pique *n Fr* resentment; sense of being slighted; *v* wound pride of.

piqué *n* corded cotton, rayon, or silk fabric.

piranha *n* small but dangerous carnivorous freshwater fish from S America.

pirate *n* **1** person illegally plundering vessels on high seas **2** privately owned radio transmitter operating without license **3** one who

a
b
c
d
e
f
g
h
i
j
k
l
m
n
o
p
q
r
s
t
u
v
w
x
y
z

A B C D E F G H I J K L M N O **P** Q R S T U V W X Y Z

infringes another's copyright etc; n **piracy**; a **piratical**.
pirouette n, v Fr rapid turn on toe in dancing.
pistachio n Sp, It edible green nut.
pistol n small firearm held in one hand when fired.
piston n 1 short cylinder within cylindrical vessel, working up and down, used to generate and apply pressure 2 sliding valve in musical instrument; n **p. rod** rod that connects piston to crankshaft.
pit n 1 hole in ground 2 seed in fruit 3 coalmine 4 hollow depression (idm **in the p. of the stomach**) 5 dram area, often sunken, occupied by musicians in front of stage 6 small scar on skin; hollow on surface of something; pl **-s** aut place where racing cars are repaired or serviced during race; idm **be the pits** coll be the worst possible; v make pits in; idm **pit one against another** put one into competition with another; a **pitted** covered with small dents.
pita n flat oval loaf eaten esp in Middle East.
pit-a-pat adv, n (like) succession of light taps, beats.
pitch[1] n thick, dark, resinous substance obtained from coaltar, turpentine, etc.; v coat with this; a **p.-black, p.-dark** very dark.
pitch[2] v 1 set up, erect 2 hurl 3

mus set key 4 (of ship) plunge lengthwise 5 fall headlong; v phr vs **pitch in** 1 join in with energy 2 contribute money; **pitch into** attack violently; a **pitched** (of roof) sloping; n **pitched battle** 1 full battle with troops in formation 2 fig polit full-scale opposition to proposal; n 1 customary position 2 act of throwing 3 cricket area between wickets 4 football, hockey, etc. marked area of play; n
pitchfork fork for lifting hay, etc.
pitchblende n lustrous mineral ore, containing radium, chief source of uranium..
pitcher n 1 large usu earthenware jug 2 baseball player who throws ball at batter.
piteous a arousing pity.
pitfall n unsuspected danger or obstacle.
pith n 1 soft cellular tissue in plant stems and branches 2 fig essential part; a **pithy** 1 of, full of pith 2 fig terse, forceful.
pitiable a to be pitied (adv -**ably**; **pitiful** 1 arousing pity 2 pathetic; contemptible (adv -**ly**); **pitiless** (adv -**ly** n -**ness**).
piton n Fr spike for hammering into rock to support climber.
pittance n meager, inadequate allowance of money.
pitter-patter n, adv (with) sound of tapping or of small footsteps.
pituitary a related to **p. gland**;

p. gland ductless gland at base of brain.
pity n 1 grief, sympathy for suffering of another 2 source of disappointment, regret, etc.; idm **for pity's sake** coll I beg you; idm **more's the pity** coll unfortunately; v **pities, pitying, pitied.** feel pity for; as **piteous** exciting pity; **pitiable** 1 deserving pity 2 deserving contempt; **pitiless** ruthless; hard.
pivot n shaft, fixed point on which something turns; v turn as on pivot; phr v **pivot on** depend on; a **-al** 1 forming pivot 2 of essential importance.
pixel n TV single small element of picture on screen.
pixie, pixy n elf or fairy.
pizza n open pie of flat dough baked with topping of cheese, tomato, olives, etc.
pizzazz n coll sparkle; energy combined with glamor.
pizzeria n restaurant serving mainly pizza.
pl abbr plural.
pacable a forgiving.
placard n public notice or advertisement, esp one displayed on a fence or construction site.
placate v appease; pacify; conciliate; a **placatory**.
place n 1 specific position related to other people, things 2 specific situation in life 3 particular town, village, building, etc. 4 seat 5 unoccupied position 6

position in competition **7** position of importance; *idm* **go places** become famous or successful; *idm* **in the first/second/third place** firstly/secondly/thirdly; *idm* **out of place 1** out of position **2** unsuitable; *idm* **put somebody in his/her place** show somebody that he/she is less clever or important than he/she thinks, put someone down; *idm* **take place** occur; *v* **1** put into a position or situation **2** arrange **3** identify; *n* -**ment.**

placebo *n* -**os** or -**oes.** *med* harmless substance given (as if of medicinal value) to comfort patient.

placenta *n* mass of vascular tissue in womb connecting fetus with mother; afterbirth.

placid *a* calm; serene; unruffled; *n* -**ity.**

plagiarize *v* adopt, reproduce as one's own the work of another; *ns* **plagiarism** act of copying without permission; -**ist.**

plague *n* **1** pestilence; serious epidemic **2** *coll* annoying person or thing; *v* vex; harass; annoy.

plaice *n* edible flatfish, flounder.

plaid *n* woven cloth with tartan pattern, worn as cloak by Scottish Highlanders; *a* **1** tartan **2** cloth with perpendicular woven stripes.

plain *a* **1** clear; obvious **2** easily understood **3** without decoration; simple **4** not beautiful; *n* tract of flat land; *ns* **p. clothes** not in uniform; **p. sailing** straightforward situation, easy to handle; *a* **p.spoken** frank; not discreet about unpleasant facts; *adv* -**ly** *n* -**ness.**

plaint *v* statement of complaint in law court; lament; *n* **plaintiff** one who brings action in court of law; *a* **plaintive** mournful; complaining.

plait *n* **1** flattened fold, pleat **2** braid of three or more strands (of hair etc); *v* weave into plait.

plan *n* **1** drawing, diagram of structure projected on flat surface **2** map of district, etc. **3** mode of action; scheme; *v* **plans, planning, planned. 1** make, draw up plan for **2** think out beforehand.

planchette *n Fr* small triangular or heart-shaped board on casters believed to yield automatic writing.

plane¹ *n* wide-spreading tree with broad leaves.

plane² *n* **1** flat surface **2** carpenter's tool for smoothing wood; *v* use plane; *a* completely flat, level.

plane³ *n* **1** *coll* airplane **2** wing of aircraft; *v* glide in aircraft without use of engine.

planet *n* large solid body orbiting sun or other star; *a* -**ary**; *n* **planetarium** model of solar system; building containing such model.

plank *n* long, flat, broad piece of wood; *n* -**ing.**

plankton *n* microscopic plant and animal organisms drifting in seas, lakes, etc.

plant *n* **1** vegetable organism **2** complete mechanical equipment *esp* for factory **3** *sl* inform, pigeon; *v* **1** put plant, seed, etc. into soil that it may grow **2** fix firmly in position **3** colonize **4** *sl* conceal in another's possession.

plantain *n* **1** low-growing perennial herb **2** species of banana.

plantation *n* **1** collection of growing trees **2** large estate producing cotton, tobacco, sugar, etc. **3** settlement in new area (e.g., Plymouth Plantation).

plaque *n* **1** memorial plate or wall tablet **2** a builup of bacteria on teeth or in veins.

plash *n* gentle splashing sound; *v* dabble in water.

plasma *n* **1** colorless liquid forming part of blood **2** protoplasm.

plaster *n* **1** medical dressing applied to wound, etc. **2** mixture of lime, sand, and water for coating walls, etc.; *ns* **p. cast** protective plaster mold to protect injured limb; **p. of Paris** white paste of gypsum that sets hard when dry; **plasterboard** prepared board for smooth, easy lining of walls and ceilings; *n*

A
B
C
D
E
F
G
H
I
J
K
L
M
N
O
P
Q
R
S
T
U
V
W
X
Y
Z

plasterer; *a* **plastered** *sl* drunk.

plastic *n* 1 any of several synthetic materials produced from heating of chemical compounds, molded in solid blocks, pliable sheets, or threads 2 *coll* credit cards; *a* 1 capable of being molded elastic 2 made of some type of plastic; *ns* **p. bomb** bomb containing plastic explosive; **p. explosive** explosive that can be wrapped round the object to be destroyed; **p. surgery** surgical repair of damaged tissue, or cosmetic improvement of appearance by this.

plate *n* 1 thin sheet of metal or other hard material 2 flat dish for serving or eating food 3 collection of such dishes and cutlery in gold, silver, etc. 4 *geol* section of earth's crust (*also* **tectonic plate**) 5 plastic molded to fit mouth and hold false teeth (*also* **denture**) 6 *phot* sheet of light sensitive glass 7 book illustration from photograph; *idm* **on a table** have something desirous, valuable without effort; *idm* **enough/too much on one's plate** enough/too much to cope with; *v* cover with thin coating of gold, silver, etc.,; *ns* **p. glass** large thick sheets of glass, used for windows etc; **plater; plate-mark** hallmark on gold or silver; mark on engraving left by

pressure of plate.

plateau *n Fr* elevated flat stretch of land.

platelet *n* a tiny flattened disk in blood, aids clotting.

platen *n* plate that presses paper against inked type; typewriter roller.

platform *n* 1 raised floor or stage 2 part of railroad station where passengers enter and leave trains 3 *polit* declared program, policy.

platinum *n chem* grayish white metal used in making jewelry; *n, a* **p. blonde** (woman) with very silvery blonde hair.

platitude *n* commonplace remark; triteness; dullness; *a* **-udinous**.

platonic *a* of, derived from Plato; **p. love** love without sex.

platoon *n* military unit.

platter *n* large flat dish or plate.

platypus *n* duckbilled, egg-laying mammal.

plaudit *n* act of applauding *esp* by clapping; *fig* praise.

plausible *a* seeming fair or reasonable; *adv* **-ibly;** *n* **-ibility**.

play *v* 1 (*of wind, light, etc.*) move capriciously 2 flicker; flutter 3 gamble 4 amuse oneself 5 take part in (game, sport, etc.) 6 perform on musical instrument 7 act part of 8 operate (video, cassette, CD player, etc.); *idm* **play ball** *coll* cooperate; *idm* **play**

for time delay in the hope of gaining an advantage; *idm* **play into somebody's hands** do something that gives another the advantage; *idm* **play it/play things by ear** improvise; operate without advance plan of action; *idm* **something to play with** something to experiment with, make use of; *phr vs* **play along with** *coll* pretend to cooperate with; **play down** make appear less important than it is; **play off** (one against the other) set in opposition (to one another); **play up** cause trouble; **play up to** try to win the favor of; *n* 1 stage performance 2 fun activity, *esp* for children 3 action in sport 4 freedom of movement; *idm* **bring into play** involve in action; make use of; *ns* **p.back** replay of recording; **playboy** rich man living only for pleasure; **playgroup** ongoing social group for very young children; **playhouse** 1 theater 2 small house for children to play in; **p.off** *sport* deciding match, *e.g.*, for teams with equal points; **playpen** enclosure for keeping small child safe; **plaything** 1 toy 2 person badly treated by another or by fate; **playwright** writer of plays; **playing card** one of deck used in card games; **playing field** field designated for team sports; *v* **playact** pretend (*n* **-ing**).

plaza n Sp 1 open square 2 shopping center.

Playbill [TM] n theater program.

plea n 1 urgent request or appeal 2 leg official declaration of guilt or innocence in court of law by or on behalf of defendant; **p.bargaining** practice of admitting guilt in lesser crime to avoid being charged with more serious one; v **plead** argue before court of law; put forward as excuse; entreat.

pleach v (of tree branches) interlace; intertwine.

pleasant a agreeable; affable; pleasing; ns **-ness; pleasantry** jocular remark, jest.

please v be agreeable to; delight; gratify; impress favorably; n **pleasure** 1 enjoyment; satisfaction 2 desire; will; a **pleasurable** giving pleasure.

pleat n three-fold crease in cloth; v form into pleats.

plebeian a of common people.

plebiscite n expression of public opinion by direct ballot of electorate.

pledge n 1 object given as security for repayment of loan, etc. 2 solemn undertaking 3 token 4 toast 5 prospective member; v 1 give as security 2 promise 3 drink toast.

Pleistocene a denoting Ice Age; n geological formation containing greatest number of fossils.

plenary a 1 full; absolute; unlimited 2 representing all sections.

plenipotentiary a, n (ambassador, envoy) having full powers.

plenitude n fullness; completeness.

plenty n prosperity; ample supply; abundance; as **plenteous** plentiful; abundant; **plentiful** ample; present in large quantities; adv **-ly**.

pleonasm n use of more words than necessary to convey meaning; a **pleonastic**.

plethora n 1 superabundance 2 pathological condition due to excess of red blood corpuscles; a **plethoric**.

pleurisy n inflammation of pleura, membraneous covering of lungs.

Plexiglas n [TM] light durable transparent plastic.

pliable a 1 easily bent 2 fig flexible; yielding; a **pliant** flexible; n **pliancy**.

pliers n pl tool for gripping and cutting wire, etc.

plight[1] v **p.one's troth** ar make vow of marriage.

plight[2] n distressing condition; awkward predicament.

plinth n square base to column or pedestal.

Pliocene n, a (geological formation) of the Upper Tertiary period.

plod v **plods, plodding, plodded.** walk laboriously; fig

work conscientiously.

plonk adv, n (with) heavy sound of something dropped; phr v **plonk down** drop, put down with a plonk.

plop adv, n (with) sound of small solid object dropped into water; v 1 **plops, plopping, plopped.** fall, let fall with a plop 2 sit down heavily.

plot n 1 small piece of land 2 conspiracy 3 series of events, etc. forming story of play, novel, etc.; v **plots, plotting, plotted.** conspire; divide into plots of land; make chart, map of; n **plotter** conspirator; one who plots course, etc.

plover n wading bird allied to lapwing.

plow n implement for turning up soil; v 1 furrow 2 sl fail in exam; idm **plow (one's way) through** 1 force a way through physical obstacle 2 fig finish task with much difficulty; phr v **plow back** 1 put back into soil 2 reinvest in business (profits earned from it); ns **plowman (plowman's lunch** bread, cheese, and pickles); **plowshare** blade of plow.

ploy n prank; plan.

pluck v 1 pull, pick off 2 remove feathers (from bird) before cooking 3 sound by pulling and releasing strings (of instrument) with fingertips (**pick**); idm **pluck up courage** find the willpower to overcome fear;

a b c d e f g h i j k l m n o p q r s t u v w x y z

A B C D E F G H I J K L M N O P Q R S T U V W X Y Z

phr vs **pluck at** snatch at; *n* 1 courage 2 act of plucking; *a* **plucky** *adv* **-ily.**

plug *n* 1 piece of rubber, plastic, wood, etc. used to stop up a small hole and prevent leakage 2 device with metal pins to connect electrical appliance with source of current 3 *aut* spark plug 4 *coll* piece of media publicity; *phr v* **plugs, plugging, plugged. plug away (at)** work very hard (at).

plum *n* tree bearing stone fruit with sweet juicy flesh; this fruit; *fig* best of its kind; *idm* **a plummy job** excellent job.

plumage *n* feathers of a bird; *n* **plume** a feather; tuft; *v* dress, preen feathers.

plumb *n* weight, lump of lead on line used to test perpendicular (**p.line** line with weight attached); *adv* absolutely; completely; *v* 1 test using plumb line 2 try to comprehend; *idm* **plumb the depths** reach the lowest point; *ns* **plumber** person who repairs waterpipes, tanks, etc., **-ing** 1 system of waterpipes, etc. 2 work of plumber.

plummet *n* sounding-weight; plumb line; *v* plunge headlong.

plump *a* of rounded form, chubby; *n* **-ness.**

plump *v* 1 fall heavily 2 to make plump; *phr v* **plump for** show strong preference for.

plunder *v* seize by force; loot; despoil; *n* booty; loot.

plunge *v* dive, thrust suddenly into liquid; enter with violence; *n* dive; *idm* **take the plunge** embark on new, doubtful course of action; *n* **plunger** 1 vertically moving part of machine 2 suction cup on stick for clearing blocked pipes; *a* **plunging** (*of neckline*) very low-cut.

pluperfect *n, a* tense expressing action already completed before past point of time.

plural *n, a* (form) denoting more than one; *n* **-ism** holding more than one office at a time.

plurality *n* 1 excess of votes for one candidate in a race 2 majority.

plus *prep* with addition of; *n* symbol (+) denoting addition, positive electric charge.

plush *n* velvetlike fabric with deeper pile.

Pluto *n* planet ninth in distance from sun; Greek god of underworld.

plutocracy *n* government by wealth, or wealthy; state ruled thus; *n* **plutocrat** one whose wealth makes him or her influential.

plutonium *n* artificially produced radioactive element.

pluvial *a* rainy; caused by rain.

ply[1] *n* fold, layer of cloth, wood, etc; strand of wool,

etc.; *n* **plywood** thin, cross-laminated sheets of wood.

ply[2] *v* **plies, plying, plied.** 1 wield 2 work at 3 supply excessively, in pressing manner.

pm, PM *abbr Lat* post meridiem (after noon).

PMS *abbr* premenstrual syndrome.

pneumatic *a* 1 worked by air-pressure 2 air-filled; *n* **p.drill** roadworker's drill run by compressed air.

pneumonia *n med* inflammation of lungs.

PO *abbr* post office.

poach[1] *v* cook eggs, without shell, in boiling water; cook fish.

poach[2] *v* 1 take game or fish illegally 2 encroach on another's sphere of action; *n* **poacher** one who trespasses to take game, etc.

pock *n* pustule on skin; pit, scar left by this.

pocket *n* 1 small bag or pouch in garment for carrying money, etc. 2 small cavity containing mineral ore 3 space where density of air causes aircraft to drop suddenly 4 small hollow; *idm* **in each other's pockets** loyalty exceeding integrity; *idm* **out of pocket** having lost money (as a result of something); *v* 1 put into one's pocket; take as profit 2 accept meekly; *a* meant for putting in pocket; miniature; *ns* **p. book** small notebook;

p. knife small folding knife ; **p. money** allowance for small expenses.

pod *n* long, narrow casing of peas, beans, etc.; group of whales; *v* **pods, podding, podded.** form seedpods; shell (peas, etc.).

podiatry *n* care, treatment of foot; *n* **-trist**.

podium *n* platform for speaker (*pl* **-s** *or* **podia**).

poem *n* literary composition in metrical form, rhymed or unrhymed.

poet *n* writer of poems; *fem* **poetess; poetry** work, art of poet; **p.laureate** official poet appointed by court or government; *as* **-ic** (*ns* **p.justice** misfortune that rightly occurs to wrongdoer; **p.license** freedom of poet to experiment with rules of language, usage, or presentation of the world); **poetical** like poetry; poetic in style or essence (*adv* **-ly**); *n* **poetaster** inferior poet, scribbler of verse.

poignant *a Fr* affecting with feeling of unhappiness; highly pathetic; *adv* **-ly**; *n* **poignancy**.

poinsettia *n* plant with red flowerlike clusters of leaves.

point *n* **1** sharp end of something **2** promontory **3** period at end of sentence **4** unit of scoring **5** particular moment or place **6** detail in argument or statement **7** main idea, purpose **8** sign

preceding decimal (**decimal p.**); *idm* **in point of fact** actually; *idm* **make a point of** take great care to ensure; *idm* **on the point of (doing)** just about to (do); **p.of view** opinion; **p.-to-p.** horse race on level ground; *a*, *adv* **1** fired at close range **2** (*of question or challenge*) direct; without hesitation; *v* **1** raise forefinger (in certain direction) **2** aim **3** sharpen **4** add fresh mortar to gaps between bricks (*n* **-ing**); *phr vs* **point out** draw attention to; **point to 1** indicate **2** suggest; *a* **pointed** tapering; *fig* satiric, critical; *n* **pointer 1** one who, that which points, as hand of clock, etc. **2** indicator **3** dog trained to point muzzle toward bird, game, etc.; *as* **pointless** blunt; purposeless; **point-blank** (of gun) fixed directly at mark; *n* **point-to-point** steeplechase.

pointillism *n* style of painting based on technique of applying minute dots of color.

poise *n* **1** self-possession; calmness **2** equilibrium; balance *v* **1** put in position; keep in balance **2** hover.

poison *n* any substance which when absorbed by living organism will kill or seriously harm it; *ns* **p. ivy, p. cak,** climbing plant causing allergic rash when touched; **p. pen letter** anonymous

letter with malicious threats; *fig* **p. pill** tactics used in business to attempt to avert takeover; *v* **1** administer poison to; kill by poison **2** *fig* corrupt; pervert; *a* **poisonous;** *n* **poisoner**.

poke *v* **1** push, thrust into **2** jab; nudge; *idm* **poke fun at** mock; *idm* **poke one's nose into** interfere with; *phr v* **poke about/around** investigate; *n* **poker** rod for poking fire; card game (*ns* **p.face** solemn expression concealing real feelings.

polar *a* **1** at, near, pertaining to north, south or magnetic poles **2** having positive and negative electricity **3** *fml* (*of opposites*) complete; *n* **polarity;** *v* **polarize** give polarity to; limit vibrations of light to single plane; *fig* give unity of direction to; *ns* **-ization; polar bear** large white Arctic bear.

Polaroid [TM] *n* **1** system of photography giving prints instantly (**P. camera, P. film**) **2** substance that polarizes light, used in making sunglasses.

pole[1] *n* **1** either end of Earth's axis **2** either terminals of electric battery **3** *fig* opposite extreme.

pole[2] *n* long rounded piece of wood; *idm* **poles apart** completely different in character, point of view, etc.; *n* **p. vault** athletic jumping contest over high bar by use of long pole; *v* propel boat by means of pole.

poleax *n* **1** butcher's slaughtering axe **2** short-handle battle-ax with a hook or spike; *v* to strike or attack with poleax, as if with this.

polecat *n* small carnivore related to weasel, a skunk.

polemic *n* attack; *a* controversial; *v* dispute, discussion.

police *n* civil administration for maintaining public order; force of men, women so organized; *v* control; *ns* **policeman/-woman, p.-officer** member of police force; **p. state** country where police wield political power; **p. station** headquarters, precinct of local police.

policy *n* **1** course of action, *esp* of government **2** political ideals of party **3** contract of insurance.

polio *n med* infection of spinal cord often causing permanent paralysis (**poliomyelitis**).

polish *v* **1** make smooth and glossy, *esp* by rubbing **2** *fig* make elegant; refine; *n* **1** smoothness; glossiness **2** substance used for polishing **3** *fig* refinement; *phr vs* **polish off** *coll* finish quickly; **polish up** improve to an acceptable level; *n* **polisher**.

polite *a* well-bred; courteous; refined; *n* **politeness**.

politic *a* **1** prudent; wise **2** cunning **3** opportune; *n pl* art

of government; political affairs, principles, aims, etc. *a*

political of government or administration of state; *ns* **p. asylum** refuge for immigrant wishing to escape oppressive regime in home country; *n* **political correctness** avoidance of language or action that insults or offends racial or social groups; *a* **politically correct; p. economy** science concerned with production, distribution of wealth; **p. prisoner** person imprisoned for opposition to existing political regime; **p. science** study of political institutions and theories (*also* **politics**); **politician** one engaged in party politics; **politicking** political activity aimed at winning votes; **politico** *coll* person of influence on political scene; **politics 1** activity of competing for power **2** science of government; **polity 1** process of government **2** organized state system; *v* **politicize** make political.

polka *n* lively dance; music for this; *n* **p.dot** one of large round dots forming regular pattern on plain fabric.

poll[1] *n* **1** register of electors **2** act of voting at election **3** number of electors voting; *v* **1** vote **2** receive (certain number of votes) **3** survey of opinions; *n* **p.tax** tax charged on each member of

community, not on property or income; **pollster** *coll* person conducting opinion poll.

poll[2] *v* **1** remove top **2** remove horns of (cattle, etc.).

pollen *n* fertilizing powder on flower anther.

pollute *v* make foul; defile; contaminate; *ns* **pollutant** substance that pollutes; **pollution** act or result of polluting.

polo *n* ball game resembling hockey played by two teams of four players on horseback; **waterp.** similar game played by swimmers; *n* **p.neck** (of sweater) with high round turned-over collar.

polonaise *n* **1** slow dance **2** music for this **3** elaborate, fitted overdress with cutaway overshirt.

poltergeist *n* noisy hobgoblin or ghost.

poltroon *n* coward.

poly- *prefix* many; several.

polyandry *n* custom of having more than one husband at same time.

polychromatic *a* many-colored.

polyester *n* synthetic polymers used in making fabric.

polyethylene = **polythene**.

polygamy *n* custom of having more than one wife at same time.

polyglot *a* written in, speaking, made of up, several languages; *n* person able to speak many languages.

polygon n multisided plane figure.

polygraph n device used as lie detector.

polyhedron n multifaceted solid figure.

polymath n person expert in many subjects.

polymer n complex molecule made up of several similar ones; v **-ize**; n **-ization**.

polymorphous a found in many different forms (also **polymorphic**).

polyp n 1 sea anenome or similar creature 2 med kind of growth.

polyphony n music with two or more independent lines of melody played or sung simultaneously; a **-phonic**.

polysyllabic a having many syllables.

polystyrene n thermoplastic material.

polytechnic a pertaining to many arts, crafts and technical sciences; n polytechnic school or institution.

polytheism n belief in more than one deity; a **-istic**.

polythene n tough, flexible plastic material.

polyunsaturated a (of fat, oil) with chemical structure that discourages cholesterol accumulation.

polyurethane n, a resinous plastic polymer.

pomade n scented hair cream.

pomegranate n reddish, many-seeded fruit of African, Asiatic tree.

pommel, pummel n 1 knob of sword-hilt 2 rounded high front part of saddle; v **pommels, pommelling, pommelled.** strike repeatedly; pound with fists.

pomp n splendid display; parade; pageantry; a **pompous** 1 self-important 2 (of speech) florid; bombastic; n **pomposity**.

pompadour n style of hair brushed up high from the forehead.

pom-pom n small, rounded ornamental tuft of ribbon, etc.

poncho n **-os.** S American Sp rectangular blanketlike cloak with hole for head.

pond n small lake or pool of still water.

ponder v consider; think over; muse; cogitate.

ponderous a 1 heavy; unwieldy; massive 2 dull.

pone n unleavened corn bread.

pongee n silk fabric.

pontiff n 1 high priest 2 bishop 3 pope; n **pontificate** dignity or office of bishop; v 1 act as bishop 2 fig speak pompously; a **pontifical**.

pontoon n 1 flat-bottomed boat 2 metal drum supporting temporary bridge.

pony n 1 small horse 2 small glass.

ponytail n hair gathered and fastened at the back of the head.

pooch n coll dog.

poodle n breed of curly haired dog.

pooh interj indicating scorn; v **pooh-pooh** coll reject with scorn.

pool[1] n 1 small body of still water 2 deep place in river where water is slow-flowing.

pool[2] n 1 stakes played for in various games 2 form of billiards 3 common fund 4 commercial combination 5 pl **-s** system for gambling, as in football 6 shared resources v 1 put into common fund; amalgamate.

poop n raised deck at stern of ship.

poor a 1 having little money 2 unfortunate 3 scanty 4 unproductive; of low quality; n **p.relation** person or thing with less prestige or power than the rest; adv **-ly** badly (also a ill); a **poorly** not in good health.

pop[1] n 1 short, explosive sound 2 coll fizzy drink; v **pops, popping, popped.** 1 make such sound 2 put on, into with sudden light movement; vs **p. in** coll visit unexpectedly; **p. off** 1 coll go away, suddenly 2 coll die; idm **pop the question** coll propose marriage; a **pop-eyed** with wide-open eyes.

pop[2] a coll popular; of or producing dance music, jazz, etc.; n coll popular music of the day, esp for young people (also **pop music**); ns **pop art** modern art form based on

A B C D E F G H I J K L M N O P Q R S T U V W X Y Z

ideas from commercial design; **pop group** group of pop musicians.

pop[3] *abbr* population.

popcorn *n* grains of corn heated till they burst.

pope *n* head of Roman Catholic church and bishop of Rome.

popgun *v* toy gun that pops when a cork is fired.

poplar *n* straight, slender, tall tree.

poplin *n* ribbed fabric of silk or cotton and wool.

poppy *n* any plant of genus *Papaver*.

Popsicle [TM] flavored, colored ice frozen on a stick.

populace *n* common people, the masses.

popular *a* of, pertaining to populace liked by, suited to the average person; *n* **popularity** quality of being popular or being generally liked; *v* **popularize** make popular; make familiar to average person.

populate *v* furnish with inhabitants; *n* **population** total number of inhabitants of country, town, etc.; *a* **populous** thickly inhabited.

populist *n*, *a* (person) declaring support for interests of ordinary people (*n* **p. movement**).

porcelain *n* fine, translucent white earthenware; china.

porch *n* projecting, covered area adjoining building entrance with access to doorway.

porcine *a* of, like pigs.

porcupine *n* rodent covered with sharp quills.

pore *n* minute opening *esp* in skin; small interstice between particles of any body; *a* **porous** full of pores; permeable by liquids; *n* **porosity**.

pore *phr v* **pore over** study very closely.

porgy *n* saltwater food fish.

pork *n* pig's flesh as food; *n* **porker 1** pig raised for food **2** one grossly overweight; *a* **porky** fleshy; fat.

porn *n coll* pornography.

pornography *n* indecent, obscene writing, photographs, etc.; *a* **-graphic**.

porous *a* permeable by air, water, etc.; *n* **porousness;** *n* **porosity.**

porpoise *n* blunt-nosed marine mammal, like dolphin.

porridge *n* oatmeal boiled in water or milk; *n* **porringer** small bowl.

port[1] *n* **1** harbor **2** town having harbor **3** *fig* refuge **4** left side of ship **5** gateway **6** opening in side of ship; *idm* **port of call** place to be visited; *v* turn helm of ship to left or port side; *ns* **porthole** round window in side of ship; **portal** large gateway.

port[2] *n* strong, sweet, red wine of Portugal.

port[3] *n*, *comput* point for linking several pieces of equipment.

portable *a* capable of being carried, moved; not fixed; *ns* **portability; portage** carriage; transport; cost of this.

portage *n* **1** overland route between streams **2** act of carrying.

portcullis *n* heavy grating in castle gateway.

portend *v* foretell; presage; *n* **portent** omen *esp* of evil; marvel; *a* **portentous 1** ominous **2** pompous.

porter *n* **1** doorkeeper **2** one employed to carry burden, load **3** kind of dark brown bitter beer.

porterhouse *n* choice cut of beef steak.

portfolio *n* -os. *It* **1** flat case for carrying artworks, papers, etc. **2** State ministerial office **3** list of securities owned.

portico *n* -oes or -os. *It* covered colonnade or walk.

portion *n* **1** part; share **2** one's fate; destiny; *phr v* **portion out** share out.

portly *a* corpulent; stout.

portray *v* depict, describe vividly in words; represent on stage; *ns* **portrait** picture of person; **portraiture** art of portraying; **portrayal** act of portraying.

pose *v* **1** present for consideration **2** place in, assume attitude; *idm* **pose as** pretend to be; *n* **1** held position **2** attitude of mind **3** pretense; *n* **poseur** one who assumes affected attitudes.

posh *a* elegant; luxurious.

posit *v* set out as fact or principle.

position *n* 1 place 2 posture 3 condition 4 situation; employment; *v* place in position; localize.

positive *a* 1 definite 2 convinced 3 absolute 4 real 5 not negative; *n* 1 positive degree 2 photographic print in which light and dark is not reversed 3 *elec* positive pole; anode; *n* **p. discrimination** deliberate favoring of underprivileged social group.

positron *n* positive electron.

posse *n* force of men a sheriff can call out for aid; group of armed men.

possess *v* 1 own 2 dominate; control; *a* **possessed** controlled by evil spirit; *n* **possession** 1 act of possessing 2 ownership 3 thing owned; *n* **possessor**; *a* **possessive** selfishly domineering; indicating possession; *adv* **-ly**; *n* **-ness**; *n* possessive case or pronoun.

possible *a* 1 capable of existing 2 feasible 3 that may or may not happen 4 *coll* tolerable; acceptable; *n* **possibility**.

possum *n* opossum.

post[1] *n* 1 upright stake or pole supporting structure 2 stake marking finishing point of race; *v* fix on post or notice board.

post[2] *n* 1 official collection, transport and delivery of mail 2 letters, parcels, etc. for mailing; **p. office** place for buying stamps, etc.; *v* place in official box for mail; *idm* **keep somebody posted** ensure somebody has up-to-date information; *ns* **postage (p.stamp); postbag** 1 postman's sack 2 total of letters received at one time; **postcard** card for sending message without envelope; **postman/-woman** person employed to deliver mail; **postmark** mark on envelope to show time and place of posting (*also v*); **postmaster/-mistress** manager of post office; *a* **postal**.

post[3] *n* 1 place of duty, *e.g.*, of soldier 2 job; situation of employment; *v* place on duty.

post- *prefix* after; *e.g.*, **postgraduate** *Where the meaning may be deduced from the simple word, such compounds are not given here.*

postdate *n* 1 give a later date to 2 occur at a later date than.

poster *n* large advertising notice in public place; *n* **p. paint** paint with strong bright colors.

posterior *a* situated behind; *n* buttocks; rear part.

posterity *n* descendants; future generations.

postgraduate *a* of studies carried on after college graduation.

posthaste *adv* very quickly.

posthumous *a* after death.

post meridian *a* after midday; of or in afternoon; **pm** or **PM**.

postmodern *a* reaction to modernism.

postmortem *n Lat* 1 medical examination after death 2 *fig* discussion following important event.

postnatal *a* after (giving) birth.

postpone *v* defer; delay; *n* **-ment**.

postscript *n* addition to letter, written after and below signature; **PS, P.S.**

post-traumatic stress *n* condition of recurring stress following a traumatic event.

postulant *n* person preparing to enter religious order.

postulate *v* stipulate; take for granted.

posture *n* attitude; position, carriage of body; *v* assume affected attitude.

posy *n* 1 flower; nosegay 2 brief motto, sentiment.

pot *n* 1 rounded vessel of any material, for holding liquid, etc. 2 flowerpot 3 cooking vessel 4 teapot; *v* 1 put into pot 2 preserve in sealed pot; *ns* **potboiler** artistic or other work done simply to earn money; *n, a* **p. plant** plant that grows in a pot; *a* **potted**; *n* **potting (p. compost, p. shed)**; *pl* **pots** *coll* plenty.

potable *a* drinkable; *n* **potation**.

potash *n* crude potassium carbonate; alkali used in soap and fertilizers; **potash water**

a
b
c
d
e
f
g
h
i
j
k
l
m
n
o
p
q
r
s
t
u
v
w
x
y
z

an aerated water containing potassium bicarbonate.

potassium *n* light metallic alkaline element.

potato *n* **-oes.** cultivated plant with edible tuber.

potbelly *n coll* rounded belly.

potent *a* **1** powerful **2** convincing **3** (*of men*) sexually vigorous; *ns* **potency** power; efficiency; **potential 1** that which has latent power **2** possibility; *a* latent; possible; *n* **potentate** king, ruler.

pothole *n* **1** deep hole in rock, *e.g.,* in limestone (*ns* **potholer** person exploring one of these; **-holing**) **2** hole in road surface.

potion *n* dose of medicine or poison.

potluck *n* whatever is available as food; *idm* **take potluck** accept what comes by chance.

potpourri *n* mixture of dried flower petals, spices, etc; literary, musical medley.

potshot *n coll* quick shot without taking careful aim.

potter *v* dawdle; be busy in desultory manner.

pottery *n* earthenware; art of making it; place where it is made; *n* **potter** one who makes pottery; *n* **potter's wheel** horizontal wheel on which potter turns pots etc.

potty *n sl* toilet.

pouch *n* **1** small bag, sack **2** bag in which marsupials carry young; *a* **pouched** in

form of, provided with pouch.

poult *n* young chicken, turkey, pheasant; *ns* **poulterer** dealer in poultry; **poultry** domestic fowls.

poultice *n* soft mass of hot meal, mustard, etc., applied to inflamed part of body; *v* apply poultice.

pounce *v* swoop down suddenly; leap on; *n* sudden swoop, movement to take something.

pound¹ *n* **1** measure of weight (16 oz avoirdupois, 12 oz troy) **2** British monetary unit, £, (100 p).

pound² *n* enclosure for straying cattle, or dogs.

pound³ *v* **1** reduce to pieces, powder **2** beat; thump **3** run, walk with heavy steps.

pound cake *n* richsweet, butter cake.

pour *v* **1** flow or cause to flow freely; rain heavily; move in continuous stream **2** *fig* emit copiously (words, ideas, etc.).

pout *v* thrust out lips; sulk; look displeased; *n* act of pouting; *n* **-er 1** breed of domestic pigeon **2** one who pouts.

poverty *n* **1** state of being poor **2** unproductiveness; *a* **p.-stricken** very poor.

POW *abbr* prisoner of war.

powder *n* **1** solid reduced to fine, dry particles by grinding **2** drug in this form **3** gunpowder **4** cosmetic powder; *v* sprinkle with

powder; reduce to powder; *ns* **p.-compact** small flat box with face powder and puff; **p.-magazine** store for gunpowder; **p.puff** soft pad for applying face powder; **p.-room** *fml* ladies' toilet; *a* **powdery.**

power *n* **1** capacity, ability to do or act **2** strength **3** energy **4** authority **5** *math* product of number multiplied by itself **6** *optics* magnifying capacity; *idm* **the powers that be** unknown people in power that make decisions; *ns* **p.-boat** fast motor boat for sport; **p.of attorney** *leg* power to make legal decisions for on another's behalf; **p.plant** source of power for factory, etc.; **p.station** electrical generating plant; **p.steering** *aut* system of steering boosted by engine power; *as* **powerful** (*adv* **-ly;** *n* **-ness**); **powerless** (*adv* **-ly;** *n* **-ness**).

powwow *n infml* conference.

pox *n* name for various eruptive diseases, causing pustules on skin, *esp* syphilis.

pp *abbr* past participle.

PR *abbr* personal relations.

practical *a* **1** of, concerning action **2** efficient **3** not theoretic **4** virtual; *n* **p. joke** (*usu* nonverbal) trick played for fun; *adv* **-ly 1** sensibly; **2** almost; *n* **-ity** realistic nature; *pl* **-ities** practical matters; *a* **practicable** able to be done; capable of being used (*n* **-ability**).

practice *n* **1** habitual action **2** exercise of profession **3** clients, patients collectively **4** rules of procedures in court of law; *v* **practice 1** do habitually **2** train, exercise in skill, action, etc. **3** pursue profession; *n* **practitioner** one who carries on profession *esp* medicine.

pragmatic *a* **1** practical, concerned with practical results **2** realistic; *ns* **pragmatism; -ist.**

prairie *n* wide, flat, treeless grassland; *ns* **p. dog** squirrel-like rodent; **p. wolf** coyote.

praise *v* **1** commend highly **2** express approval of, glorify (God); *n* expression of approval; *a* **praiseworthy** commendable; laudable.

praline *n* confection of cooked nuts and sugar.

pram *n abbr* perambulator, baby carriage.

prance *v* **1** move with bounds; swagger **2** (*of horse*) spring from hind legs.

prank *n* mischievous trick, practical joke.

prate *v* chatter; prattle; talk idly.

pratfall *n* pretended clumsy fall.

prattle *v* babble; talk like child; *n* childish talk; *n* **prattler.**

prawn *n* edible, marine crustacean.

pray *v* **1** beg for, ask earnestly **2** offer prayers *esp* to God; *n* **prayer** act of praying to God;

prescribed form of words used; formal petition, request (*n* **p.wheel** drum-shaped box inscribed with prayers used by Tibetan Buddhists).

pre- *prefix* **1** prior to; before (*e.g.*, **preowned, prepaid, prewar**) **2** superior (*e.g.*, **predominant, prevailing**). *Such compounds are not given here where the meaning may be deduced from the simple word.*

preach *v* **1** deliver sermon **2** advocate strongly **3** exhort morally; *n* **-er.**

preamble *n* preface; opening part of speech, etc.

prebend *n* stipend of member of chapter of cathedral; benefice or living in gift of chapter; *n* **-ary** holder of prebend; honorary canon.

precarious *a* **1** uncertain; insecure **2** risky; dangerous; *adv* **-ly.**

precaution *n* careful foresight; measure taken beforehand to guard against danger; *a* **-ary.**

precede *v* come, be before in time, order, rank, etc.; *n* **precedence**; priority derived from birth, official status etc; *n* **precedent 1** something that has happened before, serving as model for future conduct, etc. **2** *leg* previous judicial decision, *esp* as guide for present parallel case.

precept *n* rule of action or conduct; maxim; *n* **preceptor** teacher.

precinct *n* enclosure within outer walls of building *esp* of

cathedral etc; *pl* **-s** environs, neighborhood.

precious *a* **1** of great value **2** beloved **3** affected; overrefined; *adv* **-ly;** *ns* **-ness; preciosity** affectedness.

precipice *n* sheer, perpendicular cliff face; *fig* crisis; *a* **precipitous** sheer, steep.

precipitate *v* **1** throw, hurl down **2** cause (vapor) to fall as rain, snow, etc. **3** cause to be deposited as solid substance; from solution; *a* rash; impetuous; *n* **-tation 1** undue haste **2** that which is precipitated **3** act, process of precipitating.

précis *n Fr* short summary of document; abstract.

precise *a* **1** exactly defined **2** punctilious **3** definite **4** formal; *ns* **precisian** formalist; pedant; **precision** accuracy; exactness.

preclude *v* exclude; prevent; make impracticable.

precocious *a* prematurely developed; *ns* **precocity; -ness.**

precognition *n* advance knowledge, awareness.

pre-Columbian *a* of the period before Columbus' arrival in the Americas.

preconception *n* opinion formed beforehand without actual knowledge.

precursor *n* forerunner; harbinger.

predatory *a* **1** living by

A
B
C
D
E
F
G
H
I
J
K
L
M
N
O
P
Q
R
S
T
U
V
W
X
Y
Z

plunder, robbery **2** (*of animals*) living by preying on others; *n* **predator**.

predecease *v* die before.

predecessor *n* **1** one who precedes another in office, rank, etc. **2** ancestor.

predestine *v* settle beforehand; foreordain; *n* **-tination** belief that life is controlled by divine plan that cannot be changed.

predicament *n* unfortunate or puzzling situation.

predicate *v* declare; affirm; *n* **1** that which is affirmed, denied of something **2** *ling* that which is stated about subject of sentence; *a* **predicative**.

predict *v* foretell; prophesy; *n* **prediction**.

predilection *n* preference; preconceived liking.

predominate *v* be in majority; be chief element or factor in; *a* **predominant**; *adv* **-ly**; *n* **predominance**.

preeminent *a* superior to, excelling all others; *n* **-nence**.

preempt *v* acquire, appropriate by anticipation; *n* **-emption**; *a* **-emptive**.

preen *v* **1** (*of bird*) dress feathers with beak **2** *fig* show off.

prefabricate *v* construct sections (of houses, etc.) for quick assembly; *n* **prefab** *coll* house so made.

preface *n* initial, introductory part of book, speech, etc.; *v*

begin; introduce.

prefatory *a* preliminary; as a preface.

prefect *n* **1** senior pupil in school with authority over others **2** official in ancient Rome **3** *esp cap* head of administrative area, *e.g.*, in France (*n* **prefecture** headquarters of, area under jurisdiction of prefect).

prefer *v* **prefers, preferring, preferred. 1** like better **2** promote; *a* **-able** more to be desired; *a* **-ence 1** favor **2** prior claim; *a* **-ential** giving, receiving preference; *n* **-ment** advancement, promotion.

prefigure *v* be a warning sign of.

prefix *n* **1** word or syllable placed in front of another to create new word **2** word placed before personal name; *v* put as introduction.

pregnant *a* **1** with child; with young **2** *fig* full of meaning, ideas; *n* **pregnancy**.

prehensile *a* adapted for grasping.

prehistoric *a* pertaining to periods before recorded history; *n* **prehistory** prehistoric archaeology.

prejudge *v* judge or decide upon before hearing or enquiry.

prejudice *n* **1** preconceived unreasonable opinion, bias **2** *leg* injury; damage; loss; **without p.** without detraction from any claims or

rights; *v* bias, influence person; *a* **prejudicial** detrimental; causing harm; injury.

prelate *n* church dignatory; *esp* archbishop, bishop.

preliminary *a* introductory; preceding; *n pl* **prelims** something preceding actual event or thing.

prelude *n* introductory act, performance, event; *v* serve, act as prelude to; usher in.

premarital *a* before marriage.

premature *a* happening before normal time; earlier than expected.

premeditated *a* (of crimes) planned in advance.

premeditate *v* plan in advance; *n* **premeditaion.**

premenstrual *a* before menstruation.

premier *a Fr* first in rank, degree etc; principal; *n* prime minister; *n* **premiership**.

première *n Fr* first performance, opening night.

premise *n* **1** assumption, proposition on which inference is based **2** *leg* introductory part of document, *esp* lease **3** *pl* **-s** building; house etc with grounds; *v* **premise** assume.

premium *n* **1** reward; bonus **2** fee paid for insurance **3** *finance* excess of market price over par; *idm* **at a premium** highly valued; difficult to buy; *idm* **put a premium on 1** attach importance to **2** make seem important.

premonition n presentiment; foreboding.

prenatal a occurring before birth.

preoccupy v occupy and engross thoughts to exclusion of other things; n **preoccupation** absent-mindedness; absorption, distraction.

prepare v 1 make ready for use 2 construct 3 teach; train 4 accustom 5 lead up to; n **preparation** 1 act of preparing 2 school work, homework done before lesson; period when this is done (abbr **prep**); a **preparatory** serving to prepare (**p. school** school where students are groomed for college, university).

prepay v pay in advance; pt, pp **prepaid**.

preponderate v exceed in number, importance; n **-derance**.

preposition n part of speech, word placed before noun or pronoun, indicating its relation to another word in sentence; a **prepositional**.

prepossess v influence esp favourably; a **prepossessing** attractive; n **prepossession**.

preposterous a unreasonable; absurd.

preppy n 1 graduate of private preparatory school 2 young person dressed like this.

prerequisite a required in advance; n **prerequisite**.

prerogative n exclusive, peculiar right or privilege.

presage n omen; portent; v foretell; give warning of.

presbyter n Scot church elder, minister; n **presbytery 1** church court **2** priest's house **3** E end of chancel; a, n **Presbyterian** (members) of Church governed by one order of ministers, called presbyters.

preschool n school for children from infancy up till kindergarten.

prescience n foresight; foreknowledge; a **prescient**.

prescribe v 1 ordain; dictate 2 med advise treatment or use of medicine; n **prescription 1** prescribing **2** written directions given by physician **3** medicine prescribed **4** leg uninterrupted possession over long period; a **prescriptive** giving exact rules about something.

preselector n mechanism enabling gear position to be selected before changing into it.

present[1] a existing now, not absent; n present time, tense; a **p.day** modern; n **p.participle** form of verb (ending in **-ing** in English) indicating simultaneous or causal relationship between two verbs; adv **presently** soon; n **presence 1** being present **2** mien **3** nearness (of danger, etc.); n **p. of mind** quick reaction to needs of situation.

present[2] v 1 introduce (person) formally 2 show 3 give, bestow; 4 perform n gift; a **-table** suitable for presentation; wellbred; n **-tation 1** bestowal **2** formal gift **3** introduction esp at court **4** performance.

presentiment n apprehension; foreboding.

preserve v 1 protect, save from injury, harm, etc. 2 prevent (food) from decaying; n 1 that which is preserved, as jam, etc. **2** hunting area preserved for shooting **3** river, etc. preserved for fishing; n **preservation**; n, a **preservative** (substance) that prevents (food, etc.) spillage.

preside v take control at formal meeting; superintend; ns **president** head of republic, society, college, public corporation, etc.; **presidency** office, tenure of president; a **presidential**.

presidium n executive committee of administration in Communist countries.

press v 1 apply weight, force on; squeeze 2 exert pressure; phr vs **press for** ask insistently for; **press on** continue in a determined way; n 1 newspapers 2 people writing for these 3 printing machine 4 apparatus for flattening, compressing, crushing 5 crowded situation; idm **bad/good press** (un)favorable reporting; idm **go to press** begin printing,

A
B
C
D
E
F
G
H
I
J
K
L
M
N
O
P
Q
R
S
T
U
V
W
X
Y
Z

being printed; *ns* **p.box** place for news reporters at sporting event; **p.conference** meeting where important person answers reporters' questions; **p.release** prepared statement for use by media; *idm* **pressed for somethig** short of something; *a* **pressing 1** urgent **2** insistent (*n* act or result of pressing).

pressure *n* **1** act of pressing **2** *fig* compulsion; constraint **3** force exerted on surroundings by solid, liquid, gas; *ns* **p.c ooker** sealed pot in which food cooks quickly under steam pressure; **p.group** organized group that seeks to promote its interests by propaganda, etc.; *v* **pressurize 1** (of aircraft cabin) keep at constant atmospheric pressure **2** persuade forcefully; *n* **- ization.**

prestidigitation *n* sleight of hand; magic.

prestige *n* **1** good repute **2** power to influence; *a* designed to impress; *a* **-gious** highly honoured.

presto *adv, mus* very rapidly; *adv* abruptly, suddenly.

presume *v* **1** take for granted; believe as probable **2** take liberties; *a* **presumable;** probable; *n* **presumption 1** act of presuming **2** probability **3** effrontery; *a* **presumptive** giving reasonable grounds for belief; *a* **presumptuous**

overconfident; arrogant.

presuppose *v* **1** assume to be true **2** imply.

preteen *n, a* child between 10 and 13 years old.

pretend *v* **1** lay false claim to **2** feign **3** imagine oneself as; *ns* **pretender** claimant to throne; **pretense 1** pretext **2** fraud; **pretension** claim; *a* **pretentious** assuming great merit or importance; conceited; snobbish.

preter- *prefix* beyond; more than.

preterite *n, a* (tense) expressing past action.

preternatural *a* beyond what is natural; supernatural.

pretext *n* reason, motive put forward to conceal real one; excuse.

pretty *a* **1** superficially attractive, pleasing, charming **2** considerable *coll* large; *idm* **a pretty penny** *coll* large sum of money; *adv* moderately; considerably; *n* **prettiness** charming personal beauty.

pretzel *n* Ger crisp or chewy salted *usu* knot-shaped slender bread.

prevail *v* **1** triumph **2** be prevalent; be in use; *phr v* **prevail (up)on** persuade; *n* **prevalence** common occurrence; frequency; *a* **prevalent** widely practiced; popular.

prevaricate *v* make evasive answer; quibble; *ns* **prevarication, prevaricator.**

prevent *v* guard against; hinder; stop; *n* **prevention;** *as* **-able, -ative; p.medicine** practice of using healthy diet and exercise to promote health and prevent illness.

preview *n* advance, private showing of pictures, film, etc.

previous *a* **1** prior; preceding **2** *coll* too hasty; *adv* **-ly** before.

prey *n* animal hunted by another, as food; victim; *v* **p.on, upon** kill and eat; oppress; plunder; *n* **bird of p.** bird that kills and eats other birds or animals.

price *n* **1** that which is paid or asked for anything; cost; value **2** betting odds; *v* fix price; value; *idm* **not at any price** expressing refusal not for any reason; *ns* **p.tag 1** ticket indicating price **2** *fig* price demanded; **p.war** competitive reduction of prices by rival companies to attract sales; *as* **priceless 1** very valuable **2** *coll* very amusing; **pricey** *coll* costlier than normal.

prick *v* **1** pierce with sharp pointed object **2** give or experience feeling of this; *idm* **prick up one's ears** start to listen attentively; *n* **1** slight stab of pain on surface of skin **2** mark left by pricking; *n* **prickle** small thorn; *v* tingle as if pricked; *a* **prickly; p. heat** inflammation of sweat glands causing skin irritation; **p. pear** edible fruit of cactus.

pride *n* **1** high opinion of one's merits or achievements **2** self-respect **3** too high an opinion of oneself **4** group of lions; *idm* **one's pride and joy** source of greatest pride; *phr v* **pride oneself on** feel especially proud of.

priest *n* official minister of religion; clergyman; *fem* **-ess;** *n* **priesthood;** *a* **priestly.**

prig *n* conceited, self-satisfied person; *a* **priggish** stuck-up.

prim *a* **1** neat; precise **2** stiffly formal **3** easily shocked.

primacy *n* position of being first; preeminence; *a* **primal** first, original; *a* **prima** first (*p.donna* leading female operatic singer).

prima facie *a, adv Lat leg* based on the apparent facts.

primary *a* **1** main; fundamental **2** earliest; *n* preliminary stage of election at which candidates are selected; *ns* **p. color** any of the colors red, yellow or blue; **p. school** grade, elementary school; *adv* **primarily** mainly.

primate *n* **1** archbishop **2** highest order of mammals, including humans, monkeys, etc.

prime *a* **1** chief; fundamental (**p. cost, p.c oncern, p. importance**) **2** first or best in quality or rank (**p. beef; p. minister**) **3** with all the typical features (**p. example**); *n* the best time of life; *ns* **p. number** any whole number

that has no factors other than itself and 1; **p. time** time of day when the largest number of people watch TV; *v* **1** prepare (*e.g.*, gun for firing, pump for pumping) **2** provide somebody with essential information **3** prepare with primer before painting; *n* **primer 1** protective paint which seals wood etc before other paint is applied **2** container for explosive used to detonate bomb, etc **3** schoolbook used by young children..

primeval *a* of first ages of world; prehistoric.

primitive *a* not elaborate; underdeveloped; old-fashioned; simple.

primogeniture *n leg* system by which title and real estate pass to eldest son on death of father.

primordial *a* of earliest origin; primeval.

primp *v* dress fussily.

primrose *n* wild plant with pale yellow flowers.

prince *n* **1** son of king, queen **2** ruler of royal status; (*fem* **princess**); *ns* **P. Charming** man representing woman's romantic ideal; **p. consort** husband of ruling queen; **P. of Darkness** the Devil; *a* **princely 1** magnificent **2** very generous.

principal *a* main; *n* **1** head (of school, etc.) **2** sum of loan, on which interest is charged; *ns* **p.parts** main parts of verb;

adv **-ly.**

principality *n* country ruled by a prince.

principle *n* **1** basic general truth **2** guiding rule for behavior (*usu pl*) **3** scientific law; *idm* **in principle 1** in theory **2** in general outline; *idm* **on principle** on moral grounds; *a* **principled** morally sound.

print *n* **1** stamp **2** impression **3** printed lettering **4** photographic positive **5** printed fabric; *v* **1** impress **2** reproduce words or pictures on paper, etc. from inked type, plates, etc. **3** obtain positive photograph from **4** stamp with colored design **5** write in letters (not script); *ns* **printer** one engaged in printing; **printing** process, art, style of printing; **printout** *comput* printed record of stored data.

prior *a* earlier; *n* head of religious order or house; *fem* **-ess;** *n* **priory** monastery, nunnery.

prioritize *v* give priority to.

priority *n* superiority; precedence.

prism *n* **1** solid figure whose bases are equal, parallel planes and whose sides are parallelograms **2** transparent triangular prism for refracting light; *a* **-atic** of, like prism.

prison *n* place of captivity; jail; *ns* **prison camp** place of detention for prisoners of

A
B
C
D
E
F
G
H
I
J
K
L
M
N
O
P
Q
R
S
T
U
V
W
X
Y
Z

war; **prisoner 1** captive (**p. of war, pow,** member of armed forces captured by enemy) **2** person in custody.

pristine a **1** original; primitive **2** unspoiled.

prissy a coll fussy; tending to overreact to anything seeming improper; adv **-ly;** n **-ness.**

private a **1** not public; belonging to a particular person or group (**p. performance, p. property**) **2** secret (**p. letter, p. conversation**) **3** not under state control (**p. education, p. industry**) **4** quiet; free from intruders (**p. room, p. corner**) **5** not in any official capacity (**p. visit, p. individual**); n lowest rank of soldier; ns **p. detective** detective paid to work for private individual; **p. enterprise** capitalism; **p. eye** coll detective; **p. parts** genitals; **p. pension** pension for which all contributions are paid by beneficiary, not by an employer; **p. sector** areas of employment not under state control; ns **privacy** state of being undisturbed, free from interference; **privateer** (formerly) pirate; v **privatize** sell (state enterprise) to private ownership (n **-ization**).

privation n want of necessities and comforts of life; hardship.

privet n evergreen shrub, used for garden hedges.

privilege n individual right, advantage; immunity, exemption enjoyed by some; prerogative; v grant privilege to; a **privileged** enjoying privilege; completely confidential.

privy a private; secretly knowing; n toilet; **p.council** body of advisers appointed by sovereign; **p.purse** allowance for sovereign's personal use.

prize n **1** reward given for merit, success in competition **2** thing won in lottery, contest, etc. **3** that which is captured in war, esp vessel; v value, esteem highly; ns **p.fight** boxing match for money prize; **p.money** share of proceeds of sale of war prizes; money given as prize in competition etc.

pro n coll professional.

pro- prefix -at in favor of.

proactive a showing initiative.

pro-am n, a (contest) involving amateur as well as professional contestants.

probable a likely to happen, to be true; n **probability** likelihood; likely event.

probate n proving of will; certified approved copy of will.

probation n **1** (period of) trial to decide if somebody is suitable for job **2** leg system of keeping (esp young) offender out of prison under supervision; n **p.officer**

person appointed to carry out such supervision; a **probationary;** n **probationer** person being given probation.

probe n **1** med instrument for exploring wound, etc. **2** coll investigation **3** exploratory spacecraft; v examine thoroughly.

probity n honesty; integrity.

problem n **1** question set for discussion, or solution **2** difficult situation; a **problematic(al)** doubtful; questionable.

proboscis n **1** elongated flexible snout **2** elephant's trunk **3** elongated mouth-parts of some insects.

proceed v **1** advance; go on; make progress **2** come forth, arise from **3** take legal action; n pl **-s** product; realized profit; ns **procedure 1** mode of action **2** manner of conducting business, esp parliamentary **3** technique; **proceeding** action; pl **-s** record of transactions of society, etc.

process n **1** series of continuous actions and changes **2** method of operation **3** system of manufacture **4** whole course of legal proceedings; idm **in the process of (doing)** actually engaged, involved in (doing); n **procession 1** body of persons marching, riding in formal order **2** act of marching forward **3** progress (*a* -**al**).

processor *n comput* microprocessor.

pro-choice *a* supporting the right to legalized abortion.

proclaim *v* announce, declare officially; make known publicly; *n* **proclamation.**

proclivity *n* inclination; tendency.

proconsul *n* governor of dependency or province, *esp* in ancient Rome; *a* -**ar;** *ns* -**ate, -ship** (period of) office of proconsul.

procrastinate *v* delay; defer; postpone; *ns* -**ation; -ator.**

procreate *v* beget; generate; *n* -**ation.**

proctor *n* university official with disciplinary powers.

procure *v* 1 gain; obtain 2 *leg* act as pimp, pander; *a* **procurable** obtainable; *ns* **procurator** one who manages affairs for another; **procuration; procurement** act of procuring; **procurer** pander, pimp.

prod *n* goad; poke; *v* **prods, prodding, prodded.** poke with pointed instrument; *fig* stir up; incite.

prodigal *a* lavish; open-handed; wasteful; improvident; *n* -**ity** profusion; extravagance.

prodigy *n* 1 extraordinarily gifted person 2 wonder; marvel 3 monstrosity; *a* **prodigious** huge; vast; amazing.

produce *v* 1 bring forward;

bring forth 2 give rise to; make 3 continue 4 yield; *ns* **produce** that which is yielded or made, **producer; product** result of natural growth; anything manufactured; **production** act of producing, manufacturing; that which is produced; *a* **productive** creative; fertile; efficient; *n* **productivity** rate at which something is produced *esp* in industry.

prof *n coll* professor.

profane *a* not sacred; irreverent; pagan; *v* desecrate; *n* **profanity** blasphemous language or behavior.

profess *v* 1 affirm; make public declaration of 2 practice, have as one's business 3 teach as professor; *n* **profession** 1 confession (of faith) 2 occupation requiring training and intellectual ability 3 body of persons following such occupation (*a* -**al** practicing specified profession; engaged in sport or game for money; *n* paid player; *n* -**alism** position (*esp* in sport) of professional as distinguished from amateur); *n* **professor** university teacher of highest rank.

proffer *v* offer.

proficient *a* skilled; expert; *n* **proficiency.**

profile *n* 1 outline of side view of object, *esp* of face 2 short biographical sketch.

profit *n* benefit; financial gain; *v* benefit; *ns* **p. margin** difference between cost of production and selling price; **p. sharing** *comm* practice of giving workers a share in company profits; *a* **profitable** advantageous; lucrative; *n* **profiteer** one who makes exorbitant profits at expense of consumer.

profiterole *n* miniature cream puff *usu* covered with chocolate and served with cream.

profligate *a* dissolute; depraved; recklessly extravagant; *n* **profligacy.**

pro forma done as a matter of form or for the sake of form.

profound *a* deep; very learned; *n* **profundity.**

profuse *a* abundant; prodigal. *n* **profusion.**

progeny *n* children; descendants; *n* **progenitor.**

progesterone *n* hormone that prevents ovulation and prepares uterus for pregnancy.

prognosis *n* -**ses. 1** act of predicting 2 *med* opinion formed as to probable future course and outcome of disease; *a* -**nostic** (*v* -**ate** foretell; predict, warn; *n* -**ation**).

program[1] *v, n comput* (equip with) set of instructons; *a* -**grammable** with facility for programming; *n* -**grammer.**

program[2] *n* 1 printed details of performers, items, etc., in

a
b
c
d
e
f
g
h
i
j
k
l
m
n
o
p
q
r
s
t
u
v
w
x
y
z

A
B
C
D
E
F
G
H
I
J
K
L
M
N
O
P
Q
R
S
T
U
V
W
X
Y
Z

play, concert, broadcast, etc. 2 the performance or broadcast of a program 3 summary of things to be done 4 data for computer; *v* prepare program of work for.

progress *n* 1 advance; forward, onward movement 2 improvement; *v* 1 go forward 2 develop favorably; *n* **progression** 1 act of moving forward 2 *math* series of numbers each of which increase, decrease by regular law 3 *mus* succession of notes, chords; *a* **progressive** 1 progressing 2 advocating reform.

prohibit *v* forbid; prevent; *n* **prohibition** 1 act of forbidding 2 *cap* forbidding by law of supplying and consuming alcoholic drinks; *as* **prohibitive** 1 intended to prevent certain action (*also fml* **prohibitory**) 2 (*of cost*) too high (*adv* **-ly**).

project *n* plan; scheme; *v* 1 throw; propel 2 scheme; plan 3 jut out 4 cast (photographic image, etc.) on screen; *n* **projectile** heavy missile, shell, bullet; **projection** 1 act or result of projecting something 2 thing that sticks out 3 estimate for future based on available facts (*n* **-ist** person working movie projector); *n* **projector** apparatus to project image on screen.

prolapse *n* falling down or out of place.

proletariat *n* lowest class of society; working class, *esp* manual workers; *a* **-arian**.

pro-life *a* opposed to legalized abortion.

proliferate *v* reproduce by budding, or rapid celldivisions; *n* **-ation**.

prolific *a* productive; fertile; fruitful.

prolix *a* lengthy; tedious; verbose; *n* **-ity**.

prologue *n* preface to poem, play, etc.; introductory act or event.

prolong *v* extend, in space or time; *n* **-ation**.

prom *n coll* 1 promenade 2 promenade concert 3 formal dance, *esp* in high school.

promenade *v* stroll for pleasure, exercise; *n* 1 such a walk 2 seaside esplanade (*coll abbr* **prom**); **p. concert** concert where some of audience (**promenaders**) walk about.

prominent *a* 1 standing, jutting out; conspicuous 2 well-known; *n* **-nence**.

promiscuous *a* indiscriminate *esp* in sexual intercourse; *n* **-scuity**.

promise *n* 1 undertaking, assurance to do or not to do something 2 likelihood of success; *v* 1 make promise 2 give cause for hope; *n* **Promised Land** *fig* state of ideal happiness; *as* **promising** likely to develop well or achieve success, etc.; **promissory** containing

promise.

promontory *n* point or headland jutting out into sea.

promote *v* 1 raise, move to higher rank 2 assist in formation of (company, scheme, etc.) 3 publicize; *n* **promotion; promoter**.

prompt *a* done quickly; at right time; immediate; *v* help (actor, etc.) by suggesting forgotten words; *ns* **-er; -itude**.

promulgate *v* 1 put into effect 2 announce publicly; *n* **-ation**.

prone *a* 1 lying face down 2 inclined; liable; *n* **-ness** inclination, tendency.

prong *n* 1 sharp pointed piece of metal; tine of fork 2 point of stag's antler.

pronoun *n* word used in place of noun; *a* **pronominal** of, like pronoun.

pronounce *v* 1 declare, utter solemnly and publicly 2 articulate, utter word, sound 3 give as expert opinion; *a* **pronounced** emphasized; strongly marked; *ns* **-ment** formal declaration; **pronunciation** way in which word, syllable etc is pronounced; articulation.

pronto *adv coll* immediately.

proof *n* 1 act of proving truth of fact, etc.; demonstration 2 test, trial of quality, truth, etc. 3 standard of alcoholic strength 4 trial impression from type, plates, etc.; *v*

proofread read and correct printed proofs (*ns* **-er, -ing**); *a* having standard quality of strength, hardness; *idm* **proof against** strong enough to be impenetrable, unmoved by; *v* make proof against.

prop[1] *n* support; stay; strut; *v* **props, propping, propped.** act as prop; furnish with support.

prop[2] *n dram* any portable article used on stage (*esp pl*).

prop[3] *n coll* propeller.

propaganda *n* act, method of spreading opinions, beliefs to promote a cause; views, doctrines thus spread; *n* **propagandist** zealous supporter of cause, etc.

propagate *v* **1** reproduce; have offspring **2** disseminate **3** cause to multiply by reproduction; *ns* **propagation** act, process of propagating; **propagator 1** one who propagates **2** garden frame used for propagating plants.

propel *v* **propels, propelling, propelled.** drive forward; impel; *ns* **propellant** propelling agent (*e.g.,* explosive for rocket) (*also a, n* **propellent**); **propeller** (*abbr* **prop**) screw of ship or aircraft; **propulsion**; act of driving forward; *a* **propulsive** having power of propelling; *a, n* **propellent** propelling (agent).

propensity *n* inclination; addiction; tendency.

proper *a* **1** suitable **2** peculiar; particular **3** respectable; prim **4** one's own; **p. noun** one denoting particular person or place.

property *n* **1** characteristic; inherent quality, power, etc. **2** that which is owned; possessions (estate, land, goods, money) **4** *pl* objects, costumes used in play, etc (*usu abbr* **props**).

prophet *n* **1** interpreter, teacher, seer; of religious leader, teacher **2** one who foretells the future; *n* **prophecy** prediction, foretelling of future; *v* **prophesy** make predictions; foretell; *a* **prophetic.**

prophylactic *a* guarding against disease or disaster; *n* **1** device having this effect; **2** device to prevent venereal infection, pregnancy *esp* condom; *n* **prophylaxis.**

propinquity *n* nearness, proximity in time, space, relationship.

propitiate *v* appease; conciliate; *n* **propitiation;** *a* **propitious** favorable; fortunate.

proponent *n* supporter; person in favor of something.

proportion *n* **1** part or share **2** comparative relation in size, number, amount, degree **3** harmonious relation of parts in whole **4** symmetry; *pl* **-s** dimensions; *idm* **have something all out of proportion, out of all proportion** attribute too much importance to some aspects of something; *a* **-al** corresponding in amount, size, etc. (**p. representation** *polit* system providing seats for each party in legislative body in proportion to number of votes cast or population) *adv* **-ally; proportionate to** in due proportion to.

propose *v* **1** bring forward, submit for consideration **2** offer marriage **3** intend; *ns* **proposal** plan; offer *esp* of marriage; **proposer; proposition 1** statement expressing considered opinion **2** suggestion **3** bargaining offer or proposal **4** *geom* statement of theorem or problems; *v* make direct proposal, *esp* sexual, to somebody.

propound *v* put forward; offer for consideration.

proprietor *n* owner; *fem* **proprietress; proprietary 1** belonging to owner **2** made, patented, sold under exclusive ownership.

propriety *n* correct behavior; appropriateness; decency.

propulsion *n* act of propelling or driving forward; *a* **-pulsive.**

pro rata *Lat a, adv fml* in proportion.

prorogue *v* **1** defer **2** terminate (session of Parliament) without dissolution; *n* **prorogation.**

pros and cons *n pl* arguments

a
b
c
d
e
f
g
h
i
j
k
l
m
n
o
p
q
r
s
t
u
v
w
x
y
z

A B C D E F G H I J K L M N O **P** Q R S T U V W X Y Z

for and against.

prosaic *a* matter-of-fact; unromantic; dull.

proscenium *n* **1** stage of ancient Greek or Roman Theater **2** part of stage between curtain and orchestra.

proscribe *v* outlaw; denounce and forbid; *n* **proscription**.

prose *n* language, spoken or written without rhyme or meter.

prosecute *v* **1** follow; pursue further **2** start legal proceedings against; *ns* **prosecution; prosecutor** one who prosecutes, *esp* in criminal court.

proselyte *n* convert; *v* **-ytize**.

prosody *n* art of versification; *n* **-odist**.

prospect *n* **1** wide outlook **2** something expected or thought likely **3** possible customer, etc. **4** *pl* **-s** future expectations *esp* financial; *v* inspect, search for *esp* for gold, etc.; *a* **-ive** anticipated; future; *ns* **prospector** one who explores for minerals, etc.; **prospectus** descriptive pamphlet issued by company as stock offering, etc.

prosper *v* **1** excel; succeed financially; flourish **2** be fortunate; *n* **-ity** success; good fortune; *a* **-ous** doing well, rich; thriving.

prostate *n* gland accessory to male generative organs.

prosthesis *n med* artificial replacement for damaged

part of body; *a* **-thetic**.

prostitute *n* person who sells his or her body for sex; *v fig* put to base, dishonorable use; exploit; *n* **-ution**.

prostrate *a* **1** lying flat; prone **2** *fig* crushed; spent; utterly dejected; *v* **1** cast to ground **2** *fig* abase oneself; cringe; *n* **-ation 1** extreme bodily exhaustion **2** extreme depression and distress.

protagonist *n* principal character in play, etc.; lead.

protect *v* keep safe; guard; *ns* **protection 1** protecting; being protected **2** thing that protects **3** paying money to gangsters in return for not having one's business destroyed (*also* **protection racket**); money paid in this way (*also* **protection money**); **protectionism** practice of protecting home trade by taxing imported goods more heavily; *a* **protective** giving, wishing to give protection; *ns* **protector 1** one that protects **2** one appointed as regent; **protectorate 1** rule by protector **2** state as ruled.

protégé *n Fr* person under patronage of another.

protein *n* complex organic compound of numerous amino acids.

pro tem *adv* **pro tempore** for the time being.

protest *v* affirm; raise objection; *n* declaration of objection, disapproval; *ns* **-er, protestation** solemn

affirmation.

Protestant *a* Christian denominations rejecting Roman Catholic and adhering to Reformation principles; *n* member of such church; *ns* **Protestantism**.

proto-, prot- *prefix* first.

protocol *n* **1** diplomatic etiquette **2** first draft agreement for treaty **3** *med* description of treatment plan, etc., in clinical study.

proton *n* positively charged particle in nucleus of atom.

protoplasm *n* basic material of which cells are composed.

prototype *n* original; model; pattern.

protozoan *n* one-celled living creature.

protract *v* lengthen; prolong; draw to scale; *a* **protracted** long and drawn out; tedious; *ns* **protraction; protractor** instrument for measuring angles.

protrude *v* project; stick out; *ns* **protrusion**; *a* **protrusive** thrusting forward.

protuberant *a* bulging out; *n* **protuberance** projection; swelling.

proud *a* **1** feeling or displaying pride **2** arrogant **3** splendid **4** gratified **5** jutting out (*idm* **stand proud** extend above the usual surface level; *idm* **do somebody proud** treat somebody with great generosity.

prove *v* **1** establish truth of **2** turn out to be **3** test quality, accuracy; *a* **proven** proved.

provenance *n* place of origin; source.

provender *n* **1** fodder for cattle **2** *coll* food.

proverb *n* short, pithy, traditional saying; maxim; *a* **-ial** generally known.

provide *v* **1** procure and supply **2** equip **3** furnish with means of support.

providence *n* **1** fate **2** benevolent provision of God **3** foresight **4** thrift.

provident *a* looking ahead; farseeing; thrifty; *a* **-ial** lucky; merciful; beneficial.

province *a* **1** division of country; region **2** sphere of knowledge, thought, action etc; *pl* **-s** any part of country outside capital; *a* **provincial 1** of the provinces **2** countrified; unsophisticated; *n* inhabitant of provinces; country person.

proving ground *n* **1** place for scientific tests **2** *fig* opportunity for testing something new.

provision *n* **1** act of providing, supplying **2** something provided, *esp pl* food **3** *leg* stipulation, condition; *v* supply with food; *a* **provisional** temporary, conditional.

proviso *n* **-os** or **-oes.** condition.

provocation such as to arouse anger, interest (*adv* **-ly**).

provoke *v* give rise to; stir up; make angry; incite; *n*

provocation; *a* **provocative.**

prow *n* front of ship; bow.

prowess *n* **1** bravery; valor **2** skill **3** success.

prowl *v* go about stealthily, furtively, *esp* in search of prey, plunder; *v n* act of prowling; *n* **-er.**

proximity *n* nearness.

proxy *n* **1** authority given to person to act as agent **2** person acting as agent or substitute.

prude *n* excessively prim, proper person; *a* **prudish.**

prudence *n* **1** careful behavior **2** sagacity.

prudent *a* careful; discreet; circumspect; provident; *a* **-ial** showing prudence.

prune *n* dried plum.

prune *v* **1** cut out, shorten unwanted branches (of trees, shrubs, etc.) **2** *fig* shorten by omission.

prurient *a* having morbidly indecent, obscene ideas, etc.; *n* **-ence.**

pruritis *n med* severe itching.

pry *v* **pries, prying, pried. 1** search into; peer, spy, *esp* with unnecessary curiosity **2** break open, as with lever.

PS *abbr* postscript.

psalm *n* sacred song or hymn; *ns* **-ist** composer of psalms; **psalmody** art of singing sacred songs; **psalter** Book of Psalms.

psephology *n* study of elections; *n* **-ologist.**

pseudo- *prefix* false; pretended; seeming. *Such compounds are*

not given where the meaning may be deduced from the simple word.

pseud *n coll* false, pretentious person, *esp* in cultural matters.

pseudonym *n* fictitious name; nom de plume; *a* **-ous**

psittacine *a* pertaining to parrots; *n* **psittacosis** contagious influenza of parrots.

psoriasis *n med* disease causing red, scaly patches on skin.

psych *phr vs* **psych somebody out** *coll* make somebody nervous; beat somebody at sport by this means; **psych up** *coll* prepare mentally (for an ordeal).

psyche *n* human soul or spirit; mentality; mind; *a* **psychedelic** relating to a relaxed, ultraperceptive mental state, or to drugs causing this; *ns* **psychiatry** treatment, cure of mental illness; **psychiatrist** one who practices this.

psychic *a* **1** concerned with phenomena beyond physical, natural laws **2** (seemingly) gifted with supernatural powers **3** relating to communication with the dead *adv* **-ally.**

psycho- *prefix* mental; *ns* **p. analysis** method of treating certain mental disorders; investigation of subconscious mind; **psychoanalyst.**

psychokinesis *n* ability to cause movement of objects

a
b
c
d
e
f
g
h
i
j
k
l
m
n
o
p
q
r
s
t
u
v
w
x
y
z

without touching them.

psychology n branch of science studying mental processes and motives; a **psychological** 1 of or concerning the working of the mind 2 *coll* produced by the mind; imaginary (ns **p. moment** moment most likely to lead to success; **p. warfare** undermining the morale of the enemy by inspiring fear, political doubts, etc.; n **psychologist** one who studies, practices psychology.

psychopath n person with mental disorder that can lead to sudden uncontrollable violence; a **-ic.**

psychosis n chronic mental disorder (pl **-oses**); a **psychotic.**

psychosomatic a physical symptoms, complaint caused by mental disorder.

psychotherapy n psychological treatment of illness without drugs; n **-therapist.**

pt abb 1 point 2 part 3 pint.

PTA abbr parent-teacher association.

pterodactyl n extinct flying reptile.

ptomaine n poisonous alkaloid substance formed by rotten animal or vegetable matter.

pub n *coll* public house; n **p. crawl** visit to many different pubs in one evening.

puberty n the time of first reaching sexual maturity.

pubic a of or close to the private parts (**p. hair**).

public a 1 of the community; not private (**p. building**) 2 not kept secret (**p. knowledge**); n people in general; ns **p.address system** microphones and loudspeakers; **p. company** company selling shares to public (also Brit **public limited company** or **plc**); **p. house** building where alcoholic drinks (and sometimes food) are sold and consumed; **p. relations** 1 work of building public goodwill toward organization, clients, etc. (also **PR;** n **p. relations officer** person engaged in this) 2 relationship between organization and public; **p. school** state-sponsored, tuition-free school; **p. sector** industries owned by the state; **p. spirit** interest in welfare of the community (a **-ed**); **p. works** building and construction carried out by the state; **publication** 1 making available for public to read 2 item printed for general distribution; **publicity** advertizing (**publicist** person responsible for this); v **publicize** make known to public; adv **publicly.**

publicity n state of being generally known; advertisement; notoriety; v **publicize** make known to public, esp by advertisement.

publish v make generally

known; prepare and issue for sale (books, journals etc); ns **-er; publication.**

puce n, a brownish purple color.

puck n black rubber disk used in hockey.

pucker v wrinkle; fall into creases; n crease; fold.

pudding n soft, cooked mixture of flour, milk, eggs etc.; any solid sweet dish.

puddle n 1 shallow muddy pool 2 rough cement lining for ponds, etc.; v 1 make muddy; muddle 2 work a mixture into a dense, impenetrable mass.

pudency n modesty; bashfulness.

pudgy a *coll* short, plump; chubby.

pueblo n village of US Southwestern Indians.

puerile a childish; silly.

puff n 1 short blast of wind, breath, etc. 2 kind of pastry; v blow out, send out in puff; phr vs **puff up** 1 (cause to) swell 2 cause to be out of breath 3 make conceited; ns **p. adder** large poisonous viper; **puffball** fungus with ball-shaped spore case; **p. pastry** light flaky pastry; a **puffy** swollen.

puffin n sea-bird with large parrot-shaped beak.

pug n 1 breed of dog, resembling small bulldog 2 footprint of wild beast; a **pug-nosed** snub-nosed.

pugilist n boxer; a **-ic;** n

pugilism.

pugnacious n fond of fighting; n **pugnacity.**

puke v vomit.

pulchritude n physical beauty.

pull v 1 draw; tug 2 remove by pulling 3 pluck; 4 propel (by rowing); idm **pull a fast one** gain advantage by trickery; idm **pull one's punches** attack without vigor; idm **pull somebody's leg** tease; idm **pull the wool over somebody's eyes** conceal the truth; phr vs **pull off 1** remove 2 achieve; **pull out** withdraw; **pull over** stop (vehicle); **pull through 1** recover 2 survive **pull together** cooperate; **pull up 1** uproot 2 improve; n 1 act of pulling 2 pulling power 3 steep climb 4 power to influence.

pullet n young hen.

pulley n small grooved wheel, carring cord, used to change direction of power.

Pullman [TM] n 1 special railroad luxury coach 2 a large suitcase.

pullover n knitted sweater that goes over wearer's head without fastenings.

pulmonary a of lungs.

pulp n soft, moist vegetable or animal substance; flesh of fruit or vegetable; v reduce to pulp.

pulpit n raised enclosed structure from which clergy delivers sermon.

pulsar n starlike object emitting radio signals.

pulse n 1 throb of blood in arteries, etc. 2 any regular rhythmic vibration or beat; v **pulsate 1** throb; vibrate 2 fig throb with excitement, emotion, etc; n **-ation.**

pulverize v reduce to fine powder, dust, or spray; fig destroy utterly; n **-ation.**

puma n large, carnivorous feline; cougar.

pumice n light, porous volcanic stone.

pummel see **pommel.**

pump n device for raising water, etc., by suction, or for taking out, and putting in air, etc., by piston and handle; v 1 raise 2 compress 3 take out, put in (air, liquids, etc.) 4 fig extract information from.

pumpernickel n Ger dark, coarse rye bread.

pumpkin n round, orange, edible fruit of the gourd family.

pun n play on words; v **puns, punning, punned.** make pun.

punch[1] n 1 blow with fist 2 tool for perforating, stamping 3 force; power; v 1 hit with fist 2 make hole with tool; ns **p. line** climax of joke or anecdote expected to produce laughter; as **p. - drunk 1** stupefied by repeated punching on the head 2 fig dazed; confused.

punch[2] n drink of juice, spiced spirits, or wine.

punctilio n being conscientious about small details; a **punctilious** very exact, particular.

punctual a in good time; prompt; n **-ity.**

punctuate v divide up written or printed words by periods, commas, etc.; ns **-ation** commas, semicolons, etc. in writing to clarify sense.

puncture v make hole in; prick; n small hole made by sharp point.

pundit n 1 learned person 2 one who offers opinions; critic.

pungent a 1 sharp; piercing 2 highly seasoned 3 (of mode of expression) piquant; pointed.

punish v 1 inflict retribution on 2 handle roughly; as **-ing** exhausting; debilitating; **-able,** n **-ment;** a **punitive 1** serving as punishment 2 harsh; severe.

punk n rebel against conventional tastes and ideas; n **punk rock** cacophonous, rebellious rock music; a **punky;** n **-iness.**

punt[1] n flat-bottomed boat with square ends, propelled by long pole thrust against riverbed; v convey, travel in punt.

punt[2] n kick given to football dropped from hands, before it touches ground; v kick thus.

punt[3] v 1 cards lay stake against bank 2 bet, esp on

horse **3** porpel (boat) with pole **4** kick dropped (football) before it hits the ground *fig* improvise; think on one's feet.

puny *a* weak, feeble, undersized.

pup *n coll* puppy.

pupa *n* **-ae** or **-as.** stage between larva and imago; chrysalis of insect; *v* **pupate** become pupa.

pupil *n* **1** person being taught **2** opening of iris in eye.

puppet *n* **1** small jointed figure, moved by strings, wire **2** *fig* person, often political, who is unable to act on his or her own; *ns* **p. -show; puppetry** art of manipulating puppets.

puppy, pup *n* **1** young dog **2** conceited, impudent young man; *p. -love coll* adolescent infatuation.

purchase *v* **1** buy **2** *fig* obtain by effort, etc. **3** move by leverage; *n* **1** that which is bought **2** leverage; *n* **purchaser**.

purdah *n* Muslim or Hindu custom of keeping women hidden from public view; *idm* **go into purdah** hide oneself away; seclude oneself.

pure *a* **1** clean **2** unmixed **3** not tained **4** chaste **5** simple; *adv* **-ly 1** in a chaste manner **2** simply; only; *v* **purify** make pure; *ns* **purification** cleansing, purifying; **purism** strict adherence to correct usage, etc., in language; **-ist;**

purity state of being pure.

purée *n Fr* finely ground solid food; *a* dish made of this; *v* process of changing solid food to this.

purge *v* **1** cleanse; purify **2** *leg* clear of accusation **3** cause evacuation (of bowels) **4** expel unwanted members from political party, armed forces, etc.; *n* that which cleanses; *n, a* **purgative** (medicine) causing evacuation; *n* **purgatory 1** state or place of torment, etc., where souls of dead are purified **2** *fig* any such state or place.

Purim *n* Jewish festival marking deliverance from massacre planned by Haman.

Puritan *n* member of extreme Protestant party in 16th and 17th centuries; one holding very strict religious and moral views; *a* **-ical.**

purl[1] *n* knitting stitch producing ridge; ornamental looped edging to lace, etc.; *v* **1** knit purl stitch **2** edge or border with silver, gold thread, embroidering.

purl[2] *v* flow with gentle murmur; babble.

purloin *v* steal.

purple *n* red-blue color; *a* of this color; *ns* **p. heart** durable purplish wood of leguminous trees; **P. Heart** medal for woundedior killed soldiers.

purport *v* mean to be; seem to signify; *n* significance; bearing.

purpose *n* intention; aim; design; object; *v* intend; *a* **p. -built** made with stated purpose in mind.

purr *v* (*of cats, etc.*) express pleasure by making low vibrating noise; *n* this sound.

purse *n* **1** small bag, pouch for money and other items **2** funds **3** sum of money offered as prize, etc.; *idm* **hold the purse strings** control spending; *v* pucker, wrinkle up (lips); *n* **purser** ship's officer in charge of accounts and passengers' requirements.

pursue *v* **1** follow closely **2** chase **3** follow to desired end **4** continue (speaking); *n* **pursuance** *idm* **in the pursuance of** *fml* while doing; *a* **pursuant** *idm* **pursuant to** *leg* in accordance with; *ns* **pursuer; pursuit 1** chasing after; quest **2** employment; occupation.

purvey *v* provide, supply *esp* provisions; *n* **purveyor**.

purview *n fml* scope; range of operation.

pus *n* yellowish matter produced by suppuration; *a* **purulent** full of, discharging pus; septic; *n* **purulence.**

push *v* **1** use force to move (somebody/something) away from oneself, to another position **2** *fig* urge very strongly **3** *coll* sell (illegal drugs); *idm* **push one's luck** take unwise risk; *phr vs* **push around** order around in a bullying way; **push for** make urgent demands for; **push off** *coll* go away; n **1** act of pushing **2** concerted attack; *idm* **when push comes to shove** if/when the situation becomes urgent; **pusher 1** person that pushes **2** *sl* seller of illegal drugs; **p. -over 1** something easily done **2** person easily persuaded; *as* **pushing, pushy** self-assertive; overambitious.

pusillanimous *a* cowardly; n **pusillanimity**.

pussy n *coll* child's name for cat (also **puss, pussycat**).

pussyfoot *v coll* act timidly, overcautiously.

pussy willow n (tree with) silky gray catkins.

pustule n pimple containing pus; *a* **pustular**.

put *v* **1** place; locate; fix **2** express **3** throw **4** submit for judgment (*pt, pp* **put**); *idm* **not put it past sb** suspect somebody of being capable; *idm* **put it to somebody** challenge somebody to admit or deny something; *idm* **put one's foot in it** make a tactless mistake; *phr vs* **put across** explain (*idm* **put one over on somebody** deceive somebody); **put aside/by** save; **put back** delay; **put down 1** defeat **2** write down **3** humiliate (n **p. -down**); **put something down to** ascribe something to; **put forward** suggest; **put in for** apply for; **put off 1** delay **2**

discourage **3** arouse dislike; **put on 1** increase **2** provide **3** dress oneself in **4** simulate **5** deceive playfully (n **p. -on**); **put out** annoy; inconvenience (*idm* **put oneself out** make a special effort); **put over** explain; demonstrate; **put up 1** erect **2** propose; nominate **3** accommodate **4** provide **5** offer for sale; **put up with** tolerate; *a* **put-upon** exploited; taken advantage of.

putative *a* reputed; supposed; presumed.

putrid *a* decomposed; rotten; *v* **putrefy** make, become putrid; n **putrefaction** process of putrefying rotten, foul-smelling substance; *a* **putrescent** rotting; stinking (n **-ence**).

putsch n sudden move to overthrow government by use of force.

putt *v* **1** strike golf ball gently across green **2** *athletics* throw weight (shot) from shoulder; n distance that ball, weight is putted; n **putter** golfclub used for putting.

putty n **1** soft cement made of linseed oil and clay **2** gem-polishing powder made of tin and lead.

puzzle *v* **1** perplex; baffle **2** try to solve; n **1** difficult problem **2** verbal or mechanical contrivance to test ingenuity.

PVC *abbr* polyvinyl chloride

(form of thermoplastic widely used in domestic articles and industry).

pygmy, pigmy n dwarf; *a* very small, dwarfish.

pylon n tall structure *usu* of steel girders, carrying electric cables, etc.

pyramid n **1** figure with square base and four triangular sides sloping to apex **2** Egyptian tomb of this shape; **p. scheme** form of selling where least commission goes to the one who effects the sale; *a* **-al**.

pyre n pile of wood for burning corpse.

pyrite n common yellow mineral.

Pyrex [TM] heatproof glass ovenware also resistant to chemicals, electricity.

pyrogenic *a* productive of heat or fever.

pyromania n uncontrollable urge to set things on fire; n **-maniac** person suffering from this.

pyrometer n instrument for measuring high temperatures.

pyrotechnics n pl **1** display of fireworks **2** *fig* display of brilliant, ironical oratory.

Pyrrhic *a* **P. victory** one won at enormous and ruinous cost.

python n large nonvenomous snake that crushes its prey.

pyx n vessel in which Host is kept in churches.

A B C D E F G H I J K L M N O P Q R S T U V W X Y Z

QED *abbr Lat* quod erat demonstrandum (which was to be proved), conclusion of formal logical proof in philosophy.

qua *adv* in the capacity of; as.

quack *n* cry of duck; *v* utter such sound.

quack *n* one who pretends to have skill, knowledge *esp* in medicine; charlatan.

quad *n coll* 1 quadrangle 2 quadruplet.

quadrangle *n* 1 four-angled plane figure 2 square or rectangular court with buildings round it; *n* **quadrant** 1 quarter of circle 2 instrument for measuring angles; *n, a* **quadrate** square; *a* **quadratic** (*of equation*) involving square of unknown quantity.

quadraphonic *a* using four sound channels or speakers.

quadrat *n* piece of printer's type-metal used in spacing.

quadrilateral *n, a* (figure) having four sides and four angles.

quadrille *n Fr* dance for four persons; music for this; *a* marked off into rectangles or squares.

quadriplegia *n* paralysis of the body below the neck; *a n* **quadriplegic**.

quadruped *n* four-footed animal.

quadruple *a* fourfold; *v* multiply by four.

quadruplet *n* one of four siblings born of the same pregnancy.

quaff *v* to drink or swallow deeply.

quag, quagmire *n* soft, marshy, quaking ground.

quahog *n* North American clam.

quail *n* small game-bird related to partridge.

quail 1 cower; flinch 2 lose heart.

quaint *a* 1 attractively strange 2 odd; eccentric.

quake *v* shake; tremble; rock from side to side; *n* 1 tremor 2 *coll* earthquake.

Quaker *n* member of Christian group (Society of Friends) opposed to all forms of violence.

quaking aspen *n* northern North American tree with small almost circular leaves

qualify *v* **qualifies, qualifying, qualified.** 1 obtain official qualification by study, etc. 2 limit (by description) 3 become competent; *a* **qualified** 1 having qualifications 2 limited; modified; *n* **qualification** 1 limiting factor 2 act of qualifying 3 proof of having passed examination; *pl* **qualifications** for relevant knowledge and experience for.

quality *n* 1 essential nature or characteristic 2 degree of value 3 high social rank; *a* **qualitative** having to do with quality; *n* **qualitative analysis** chemical identification of components of a substance.

qualm *n* 1 feeling of uneasiness, nausea 2 misgiving; scruple.

quandary n difficult perplexing situation; dilemma.

quantifier n *ling* word or phrase denoting quantity (*e.g.*, some, a few)

quantity n number; amount; extent; specified amount; a **quantitative**.

quantum n *Lat* 1 amount required 2 *physics* minimal unit of energy (*pl* **quant**); ns **q. leap** sudden dramatic advance or breakthrough; **q. theory** *physics* theory that energy exists in units of a discrete size.

quarantine n isolation to prevent spreading of infection; v put, keep in quarantine.

quark n *physics* any of the tiniest elements supposed to be distinguishable in elementary particles.

quarrel n **quarelling, quarelled**. angry dispute; squabble; v disagree; dispute; become estranged; a **-some**.

quarry[1] n one who that which, is hunted or pursued.

quarry[2] n open pit from where stone, sand, etc., is excavated; v dig, excavate from quarry.

quart n quarter of gallon; two pints.

quarter n 1 fourth part 2 area 3 clemency 4 *pl* **-s** lodgings 5 US coin worth 25 cents; v 1 divide into quarters 2 lodge; ns **quarterback** football player who directs, leads team; *fig* leader of strategy, scheme; **quarterdeck** part of ship's upper deck reserved for officers; **q. -final** stage of contest involving eight competitors of whom four will go into the semifinal; **quartering** *her* division of shield or emblem in it; **quartermaster** 1 *army* officer in charge of supplies 2 *navy* petty officer in charge of steering; n **quarter note** *mus* note with time value of ¼ of a whole note; a **quarterly** occurring, due each quarter of year; n periodical published quarterly; ns **quartet(te)** 1 group of four musicians 2 musical composition for four performers; **quarto** size of book with each paper folded four times.

quartz n form of crystalline silica.

quasar n astronomical source of powerful radio energy.

quash v annul; make void; suppress; squash.

quasi a, adv, prefix *Lat* as if; in certain sense; almost; pseudo.

quatercentenary n 400th anniversary.

quatrain n four-line stanza rhymed a b a b.

quaver v 1 tremble; shake; vibrate 2 speak tremulously; n *mus* note, time value of an eighth note; n **-ing** tremulous sound, *esp* made by voice.

quay n a wharf for the loading or unloading of vessels.

queasy a 1 causing, feeling nausea 2 easily shocked; n **-iness**.

queen n 1 wife of king 2 female sovereign 3 playing card 4 most powerful piece in chess 5 fertile female bee, wasp, etc. 6 female cat; n **q. mother** n king's widow; mother of ruling monarch; **the Q.'s English** standard Southern British English; a **queenly** of or like a queen.

queer a 1 odd; strange; suspicious 2 slightly mad 3 unwell.

quell v suppress; stifle; allay; pacify.

quench v 1 extinguish; put out (fire) 2 slake (thirst).

querulous a complaining; whining.

query n question; interrogation mark (?); v question; express doubt about.

quest n search; v search for.

question n 1 act of asking 2 sentence requiring reply 3 point of discussion; v 1 ask question of 2 dispute; *idm* **out of the question** impossible; ns **q. mark** punctuation mark showing end of question; **questionnaire** list of formal questions devised to obtain information, etc.; a **questionable** 1 dubious 2 not completely honest.

queue n *Fr* long braid of hair, line of waiting people or vehicles; v line up, wait in line.

quibble n play on words; v

a
b
c
d
e
f
g
h
i
j
k
l
m
n
o
p
q
r
s
t
u
v
w
x
y
z

A
B
C
D
E
F
G
H
I
J
K
L
M
N
O
P
Q
R
S
T
U
V
W
X
Y
Z

evade point; make puns.

quiche *n* baked custard with egg, cheese, and other savory items in pastry crust, served hot or cold.

quick *a* **1** rapid; keen; brisk; hasty **2** living; *n* sensitive flesh below finger- or toenail; *v* **quicken 1** cause to be quick **2** become faster **3** give life to **4** become living; *ns* **quicklime** unslaked lime **quicksand** very loose, wet, soft sand; **quicksilver** mercury; *as* **quickfire** in rapid succession; **quick-tempered** quick to anger; **quickwitted** reacting quickly.

quickie *n coll* something done very quickly.

quid *n* chew of tobacco.

quid pro quo *n* thing given in return for something.

quiescent *a* still; calm; inactive; passive; *n* **quiescense** inactivity.

quiet *a* **1** peaceful; motionless; serene **2** monotonous; *v* **quiet, quieten** make, become quiet; *ns* **-ness, -ude.**

quietism *n* religious philosophy of calm acceptance *n*, *a* **-ist.**

quietus *n* riddance; final discharge; death.

quill *n* **1** hollow stem of bird's feather **2** long wing feather **3** spine of porcupine **4** object made from these, *e.g.*, a pen.

quilt *n* padded bedcover; *v* stitch pieces of cloth together with padding between *n* **-ing.**

quince *n* pear-shaped fruit with sharp flavor.

quincentenary *n* 500th anniversary.

quincunx *n* certain arrangement of five objects in a square or rectangle.

quinine *n* bitter-tasting drug.

quinquennial *a* occurring once in or lasting five years.

quintal *n* hundred weight, unit of weight equal to 100 kg.

quintessence *n* purest form of some quality; *a* **-ential.**

quintet(te) *n mus* **1** composition for five instruments or voices **2** group of five performers.

quintuplet *n* (*abbr* **quint**) one of five children born of the same pregnancy.

quip *n* **quipping, quipped.** witty remark; clever repartee.

quire *n* twentieth part of ream of paper.

quirk *n* individual trait.

quirt *n* short rawhide whip.

quisling *n* traitor.

quit *a* **quitting, quit.** free, clear, rid of; *v* **1** leave; abandon **2** cease from; give up; retire from; *ns* **quittance** receipt, discharge; **quitter** one who abandons task in face of difficulty, etc.

quitclaim *n* transfer one's interest; release, reling wish legal claim.

quite *adv* **1** to some extent; fairly (**quite good**) **2** completely (**quite right; quite finished**); *det* **quite a/an/the** used as intensifier

(**quite an expert**); *idm* **quite a bit/a few/a lot** a considerable amount; *interj* expressing agreement.

quiver[1] *n* case for holding arrows.

quiver[2] *v* tremble; shake; *n* **-ing.**

quixotic *a* extravagantly generous and chivalrous.

quiz *v* **quizzing, quizzed. 1** question closely **2** stare at inquisitively; *n* game of answering questions, or solving problems, *esp* as public entertainment.

quizzical *a* (*of look, smile*) questioning; with a hint of amused disbelief.

quoin *n* **1** solid exterior angle of building **2** cornerstone **3** wedge used for locking type in form.

quoit *n* ring for throwing at, or over, peg; *pl* **-s** game using this.

quondam *a* former.

Quonset [TM] *n* hut-shaped prefabricated shelter made of metal.

Qur'an *n* variation of Koran, Muslim holy scriptures.

quorate *a* (of meeting) with a quorum of members.

quorum *n* minimum number of members that must be present before meeting may proceed.

quota *n* **1** proportional share; allowance **2** amount of goods allowed to be imported during certain period.

quote *v* **1** repeat or cite

something said, written by
another 2 name price, give
estimate; *n* **q. mark** sign
indicating beginning or end
of quotation.

quoth *v ar, lit* said; spoke.
quotidian *a* daily.
quotient *n* number resulting
from division of one number
by another.

qv *abbr Lat* quod vide
(indicating cross-reference to
be seen).
QWERTY *n* standard
keyboard layout.

a
b
c
d
e
f
g
h
i
j
k
l
m
n
o
p
q
r
s
t
u
v
w
x
y
z

A
B
C
D
E
F
G
H
I
J
K
L
M
N
O
P
Q
R
S
T
U
V
W
X
Y
Z

rabbet *n* groove in woodwork; *v* join by rabbet.

rabbi *n* Jewish religious leader; *a* **rabbinical**.

rabbit *n* **1** burrowing rodent akin to hare **2** the pelt of this **3 Welsh rabbit** (also **rarebit**) **4** pace-setting runner leading foot race.

rabble *n* disorderly, riotous crowd or mob; *a, n* **r.-rousing** stirring up feelings of anger and violence in a mob; *n* **r.-rouser** person doing this.

rabid *a* **1** affected with rabies **2** furious **3** violently fanatical; *n* **rabies** infectious disease of dogs, etc.; distemper.

raccoon *n* small, carnivorous nocturnal mammal.

race[1] *n* **1** contest of speed in running, riding, sailing, etc. **2** strong current of water, *esp* leading to watermill **3** *pl* **-s** horseraces; *v* run, cause to run swiftly; compete in speed (against); *ns* **racer** person, animal, machine that races; **racetrack** course for races; **r.-walking** sport of racing at a fast walk; .

race[2] *n* **1** group of persons descended from same ancestors **2** distinct variety **3** lineage; breed; *ns* **r. relations** relations between different races; **racism 1** belief that one race is superior to others **2** unjust treatment of member(s) of a particular race.

raceme *n* cluster of flowers along stem.

rack *n* **1** framework to hold things (hats, baggage, letters, etc.) **2** medieval instrument of torture **3** *mech* straight bar with teeth on its edge to work with pinion; *idm* **go to rack and ruin** become delapidated; *v* cause great pain or distress to; *idm* **rack** one's brains make hard effort to think.

racket *n* **1** loud noise; din **2** illegal business or way of making money; *n* **racketeer** one who operates illegal business.

racket, racquet *n* bat used in tennis, badminton, etc.

raconteur *n* skilled storyteller.

racquetball *n* game played on enclosed court with rackets and bouncy ball.

racy *a* spirited; piquant; spicy; *n* **raciness**.

radar *n* electronic system for direction finding and observation of distant objects, by reflection of radio waves.

raddled *a* confused.

radial *a* arranged like the spokes of a wheel; *n* outer tire with strengthening cords radial to the wheel hub (also **radial/radial-ply tire**); *adv* **-ly; r. symmetry** *n* having similar parts arranged around a central point.

radian *n geom* angle formed at center of circle by radii drawn from each end of arc with length of one radius.

radiate *v* emit rays of light, heat, etc.; spread from center; *ns* **-ation** emission of rays (of heat, light, etc.) **radiance** brightness; brilliance; *a* **radiant** shining; displaying delight; *n geom* straight line assumed to rotate round fixed point; *n* **radiator 1** that which radiates 2 device for cooling car engine 3 apparatus for heating rooms, etc.

radical *a* 1 of root or origin 2 *polit* advanced; progressive 3 complete; *n* 1 number expressed as root of another 2 politician, person of liberal views.

radicchio *n* red chicory used in salads.

radicle *n* minute root of plant.

radii *pl of* **radius**.

radio- *prefix* of rays; of radium; of radiation.

radio *n* 1 transmission of sounds by electromagnetic waves, without wires 2 receiving apparatus (*also* **receiver**) 3 radio (activity of) the broadcasting industry; *v* send (message) by radio; *ns* **r. astronomy** astronomy using radio telescope; **r. car** cab or car equipped with radio intercom; **r. telephone** telephone using radio waves, not cables; **r. telescope** radio receiver used for tracking movements of bodies in space.

radioactivity *n* spontaneous disintegration and emission of gamma rays, etc.; *a* **radioactive**.

radiocarbon *n* radioactive carbon, whose presence in archaeological or other old material can help determine its age.

radiogram *n* 1 picture made by radiography 2 combined radio and record player.

radiography *n* X-ray photography, *usu* for medical use; *n* **-pher** person qualified to do this.

radiology *n* study of X-rays and their use in medicine; *n* **-ologist** specialist in this.

radiotherapy *n* treatment of disease by radiation; *n* **-therapist**.

radish *n* plant with edible, pungent root.

radium *n* rare, radioactive, metallic element.

radius *n* **radii, radiuses.** 1 straight line from center to circumference of circle 2 shorter bone of forearm.

radix *n* number or quantity taken as basis for calculations.

radon *n* inert gaseous element created by decay of radium.

raffia *n* fiber from leaves of Madagascar palm, used for tying plants, etc.

raffish *a* rakish; disreputable.

raffle *n* sale of article by lottery; *v* dispose of by raffle.

raft[1] *n* flat, buoyant structure of logs, planks, etc.

raft[2] *coll* great amount.

rafter *n* one of pieces of timber supporting roof.

rag[1] *n* shred, tatter of cloth; *pl* -s old clothes; **r. doll** *n* doll made of stuffed cloth; **r. trade** *coll* design, manufacture, selling of clothes; *a* **ragged** 1 jagged; uneven 2 clothed in torn clothes; rough; *ns* **ragamuffin** ragged, dirty person or child;

ragtime strongly syncopated music.

rag[2] *v* **ragging, ragged.** tease good-naturedly; play practical jokes.

raga *n* melodic pattern in Indian music; improvisation based on this.

rage *n* violent anger; frenzy; fury; *v* 1 speak, act with violent anger 2 (*of storm, etc.*) be extremely violent, rough; *idm* **all the rage** *coll* very popular.

raglan *n* of sleeves not set into armhole.

ragout *n* Fr highly seasoned stew of meat and vegetables.

ragtag *a* ragged; motley.

ragweed *n* plant whose pollen causes hay fever.

raid *n* attack, invasion; police search on suspect premises, as low nightclub, etc.; *v* make raid on, into; attack.

rail[1] *n* 1 horizontal wooden or metal bar; *pl* -s system of railroad lines; *v* send by rail; *ns* **railing** *usu pl* fence of wooden or metal rails; **railroad** system of tracks for running of trains; *v coll* 1 force (somebody to do something) 2 use pressure to get proposal accepted quickly.

rail[2] *v* utter complaints against; reproach bitterly; *n* **raillery** good-humored banter.

raiment *n* clothing.

rain *n* condensed vapor of atmosphere falling in drops; *v* fall as rain; *fig* arrive in

A
B
C
D
E
F
G
H
I
J
K
L
M
N
O
P
Q
R
S
T
U
V
W
X
Y
Z

large numbers, in continuous succession; *idm* **come rain or shine** whatever happens; *idm* **right as rain** perfectly all right; completely fit and healthy; *v* fall as rain; *phr vs* **rain down** fall in abundance; **rain down on** (of abuse, etc.) overwhelm; *ns* **rainbow** multicolored arc appearing in sky when sun shines through rain (*a* **r. -colored** multicolored; *n* **r. trout** black spotted trout with reddish stripes); **raincheck** ticket, coupon usable later when event, sale, etc., is postponed (*idm* **take a raincheck** *coll* postpone acceptance of offer or invitation); **rainfall** amount of rain falling on a given area over a given period; **r. forest** tropical wet forest; **r. gauge** instrument for measuring rainfall; *a* **rainy;** *idm* **keep/save for a rainy day** save for an emergency.

raise *n* increase in salary wages; *v* cause to rise; erect; increase amount or value of; evoke; breed, rear; increase in intensity; *idm* **raise Cain** *coll* cause trouble; *idm* **raise the roof** display great anger.

raisin *n* dried grape.

raison d'être *n Fr* reason for existence.

raj *n* (period of) British colonial rule in India.

rajah *n* former title of Indian king or prince.

rake[1] *n* long-handled tool with cross bar set with teeth for gathering hay, leaves, etc., or for breaking, scraping ground; *v* **1** use rake **2** sweep target with fire lengthwise; *phr vs* **rake in** *coll* earn or win quickly, abundantly; **rake up** *coll* collect with some difficulty.

rake[2] *n* dissolute or immoral man; *a* **rakish** dashing; showy.

rake[3] *v* incline backward from perpendicular; *n* (*of ship's mast, stage*) slope.

rally *v* **rallying, rallied. 1** gather together again **2** reform after repulse, etc. **3** recover health, strength, etc. **4** revive; *phr v* **rally round** come to the rescue; *n* **1** act of rallying **2** mass meeting **3** gathering of car drivers, etc., for long competitive drive **4** *tennis* exchange of strokes **5** banter.

RAM *abbr comput* random access memory.

ram *n* **1** adult male sheep **2** device for battering or piercing **3** hydraulic machine; *v* **ramming, rammed. 1** collide forcibly with; crush by repeated blows; crush, cram **2** *fig* instill (ideas, etc.) by persistent effort.

Ramadan *n* ninth month of Muslim year, marked by day-long fasting and feasting after dark.

ramble *v* **1** wander, walk about idly; stroll for pleasure **2** chatter, speak incoherently **3** (*of plants*) grow in long shoots; *n* casual walk; *a* **rambling 1** wandering; poorly organized (**r. speech**) **2** irregularly shaped (**r. mansion**) **3** with long trailing shoots (**r. plant**); *n* **rambler** one who rambles; climbing, trailing plant, *esp* rose.

rambunctious *a* difficult to control or handle; boisterous; *adv* **-ly;** *n* **-ness.**

ramekin *n* small ceramic baking dish.

ramify *v* **ramifying, ramified.** spread, branch out; subdivided; *n* **ramification** branching, subdivision in complex system.

ramjet *n* type of jet engine.

ramp *n* inclined plane joining two level surfaces.

rampage *v* rage, behave turbulently; *n* wild behavior; riot.

rampant *a* **1** flourishing without restraint (**r. disease**) **2** growing too fast and abundantly (**r. weeds**).

rampart *n* defensive mound with parapet; *fig* defense.

ramrod *n* (formerly) stick for ramming charge into muzzle-loading gun.

ramshackle *a* rickety; tumbledown; wornout.

ran *pt of* **run.**

ranch *n* large American cattle farm; *n* **rancher;** *n* **ranch house** one-story, open plan *usu* suburban house.

rancid *a* having offensive smell and taste, *esp* of stale fat or oil; *ns* **-ity**; **-ness**.

rancor *n* deep-rooted hatred, illwill; malice; spite; *a* **rancorous**.

rand *n* S African unit of currency (*pl* **rand**).

R and D *abbr comm* research and development.

random *a* haphazard; made, done by chance; heedless *idm* **at random** in an unplanned way; **r. access** *comput* system allowing information to be stored or retrieved in any order (**r.-access memory**) *comput* memory with this facility, *also* **RAM**); *adv* **-ly**; *n* **-ness**.

randy *a coll* lustful.

range *n* **1** line; row **2** extent; area; scope; sphere **3** distance that can be reached by weapon, vehicle, etc. **4** shooting area **5** cooking stove; *v* **1** place **2** set in rows **3** (*of animals, plants, etc.*) frequent; be found in **4** wander **5** vary within limits; *ns* **r. finder** instrument for measuring distance away of target, etc.; **ranger** forest or park official.

rangy *a* tall and thin; lanky.

rani, ranee, *n* Hindu queen or ruler; wife of rajah.

rank[1] *n* **1** line; row **2** social class, order **3** grade; class **4** *pl* **-s** body of soldiers; *v* take rank; classify; *idm* **rank and file** ordinary members, not leaders.

rank[2] *a* **1** overgrown; coarse **2** rancid **3** flagrant.

rankle *v* fester; *fig* be remembered with bitterness, resentment; cause anger.

ransack *v* **1** hunt for something **2** plunder; pillage.

ransom *n* money, price paid for release of prisoner, or captured goods, etc.; *v* pay ransom for.

rant *v* speak wildly, extravagantly; use violent language; *n* **ranter**.

rap[1] *n* light, smart blow; *idm* **take the rap** *coll* be punished for somebody else's wrongdoing; *v* **rapping, rapped.** tap, strike with quick blow.

rap[2] *v sl* **1** talk rapidly **2** talk rhythmically and continuously to musical accompaniment; *ns* **rapper, rapping.**

rapacious *a* greedy; grasping; avaricious; *n* **rapacity.**

rape[1] *n* plant grown as fodder for sheep; seed of this used as food for birds, and producing oil (**rapeseed oil.**

rape[2] *v* violate; ravish; assault sexually; *n* act of raping; *n* **rapist**.

rapid *a* swift, fast-moving; done quickly; *n usu pl* **-s** swift current in river owing to sudden fall in bed; *a* **r. -fire** in quick succession; *n* **-ity** speed, velocity.

rapier *n* light, thrusting sword.

rapine *n* pillage, plunder.

rapport *n* harmony; sympathetic relationship.

rapt *a* carried away in body or mind; completely absorbed; intent; *n* **rapture** ecstasy; great delight; *a* **rapturous**.

raptor *n* bird of prey; *a* **raptorial** predatory.

rare[1] *a* **1** uncommon; infrequent; exceptional **2** not dense; *adv* **-ly** seldom; *n* **rarity 1** state of being rare **2** rare object or quality.

rare[2] *a* (*of meat*) only slightly cooked.

rarebit *n* **Welsh r.** melted cheese on toast, crackers (also **W. rabbit**).

rarefy *v* **rarefying, rarefied. 1** make rare or thin **2** reduce density of **3** *fig* refine.

raring *a* very eager, as **raring to go.**

rascal *n* **1** rogue; scamp **2** mischievous child (term of affection); *a* **-lly**.

rash[1] *n* skin eruption.

rash[2] *a* impetuous; spoken, done without caution or thought; *n* **-ness**.

rasher *n* thin slice of bacon or ham; portion of same.

rasp *n* **1** coarse file **2** grating sound; *v* **1** file, scrape with rasp **2** grate upon (ear) **3** irritate.

raspberry *n* juicy, bright-red fruit growing on canes; the plant.

Rastafarian *n, a* (member) of Jamaican religious sect (*also* **Rasta**); *n* **-ism**.

rat *n* **1** small, long-tailed rodent, allied to mouse **2** *fig*

a
b
c
d
e
f
g
h
i
j
k
l
m
n
o
p
q
r
s
t
u
v
w
x
y
z

cowardly traitor; *ns* **r. race** competition to succeed in business; **r. trap** *coll* dirty, dilapidated old building; *v* **1 ratting, ratted.** to hunt rats **2** desert a cause, etc. **3** inform against, on; *a* **ratty** *sl* angry; ill-tempered.

ratafia *n* **1** liqueur distilled from almonds, crushed fruit kernels **2** small macaroon.

ratchet *n* set of teeth on bar or wheel, allowing motion in one direction only; *n comm* way of ensuring continual increase in profits.

rate[1] *n* **1** amount, degree measured in relation to something else **2** amount charged.

rate[2] *v* scold; take to task; berate.

rather *adv* **1** sooner; more; slightly; preferably **2** slightly; fairly.

ratify *v* **ratifying, ratified.** confirm; make valid; *n* **ratification.**

rating *n* **1** act of assessing; classification **2** *pl* **-s** order of popularity of TV programs.

ratio *n* **-os** proportion; fixed numerical relations.

ratiocination *n fml* process of logical reasoning.

ration *n* fixed amount or allowance of food, goods; *pl* **-s** daily food allowance; *v* supply with, limit to certain amount.

rational *a* reasonable; sensible; *ns* **-ism** doctrine that reason is only source of knowledge; -

ist; *v* **rationalize** give rational explanation of; *n* **-ization** reorganization of an industry or related group; *n* **rationality** reasonableness.

rationale *n* logical basis or reasoning for something.

rattan *n* species of climbing palm; cane of this.

rattle *v* **1** give out succession of short, sharp sounds **2** move with clatter **3** talk rapidly, briskly **4** *coll* disconcert; confuse; *phr vs* **rattle on** *coll* talk fast without pausing; **rattle through** perform as quickly as possible; *n* **1** this sound **2** device or child's toy, making this sound **3** horny rings on rattlesnake's tail; *n* **rattlesnake** venomous American snake, which can rattle its tail.

raucous *a* hoarse; harsh-sounding.

raunchy *a coll* sexy, slovenly; *adv* **-ily; n -iness.**

ravage *v* **1** devastate by violence **2** plunder; *n pl* **-s** destructive effect.

rave *v* **1** speak wildly in delirium **2** talk enthusiastically about; *n coll* praise; *ns* **r. review** enthusiastic review; **raver** dance party at changing locations; *a* **raving** wild and uncontrolled (*n pl* **-s** wild talk).

ravel *v* **raveling, raveled.** tangle; confuse; fray.

raven *n* large black bird related

to crow; *a* jetblack.

ravenous *a* voracious; famished with hunger.

ravine *n* deep narrow valley or gorge.

ravioli *n pl* Italian dish of small squares of pasta holding seasoned, chopped meat, cheese, etc.

ravish *v* **1** fill with rapture **2** violate; *n* **ravishing** delightful; entrancing.

raw *a* **1** uncooked; in natural state **2** crude **3** sore **4** cold; damp **5** untrained; *n* **r. deal** *coll* unfair treatment; *n* **-ness** *n* **rawhide** untanned hide; *a* **rawboned** thin; gaunt; *idm* **in the raw 1** unprocessed **2** crude; *sl* naked.

ray *n* **1** single beam, shaft of light, heat, etc. **2** any one of group of radiating lines; *v* radiate.

ray *n* flatfish, skate.

rayon *n* artificial silk made from cellulose.

raze *v* obliterate; level with ground; destroy.

razor *n* cutting instrument for shaving.

razz *v* make fun of; mock.

razzmatazz *n coll* noisy excitement, publicity.

RC *abbr* Roman Catholic.

reactive *a* **1** reacting **2** *chem* likely to react.

re, in re *prep* in the matter of; concerning.

re- *prefix* repetition; again; back. *Forms compounds; these are not given where the meaning may be deduced from* *the simple word.*

reach *v* 1 extend 2 touch; take with outstretched hand 3 achieve; *n* 1 act, power of touching 2 range 3 stretch of water, *esp* on river.

react *v* act in response to stimulus; *ns* **reaction** 1 response to stimulus 2 reciprocal action 3 contrary action; **reactionary** one opposed progress and reform; *a* inclined to such action, retrograde.

reactor *n* (*physics*) apparatus for generating heat by nuclear fission; atomic pile.

read *v* 1 see and understand printed, written words, symbols, etc. 2 read and utter 3 (*of thermometer, etc.*) indicate; register; *idm* **read between the lines** understand implied meaning; *idm* **read the riot act** give a strong reprimand; *a* **readable** easy or interesting to read; *ns* **reader** 1 person who reads 2 elementary reading book; **reading** 1 act of reading 2 extract from book 3 interpretation 4 figure shown on measuring gauge; **readership** type or number of regular readers of publication; **r.-only memory** *comput* memory with information that cannot be altered, as by in-putting; **readout** *comput* printed form of data; *pt, pp* **read;** *a* **readable** that can be read; interesting, not tedious; *ns*

readability; reader 1 student, lover of books 2 one who reads manuscripts submitted to publishers 3 one who reads and corrects proofs for press 4 reading book.

ready *a* prepared for use; immediately available; prompt; *ns* **r. money** cash; *a* **r.-made** prepared beforehand; *n* **readiness;** *adv* **readily** easily; willingly; promptly.

reagent *n* substance used to produce chemical change or reaction.

real *a* existing in fact; genuine; actual; *ns* **r. estate** land, property; *a* **r.- time** *comput* that can handle new data and adapt existing data to this very fast; **realism** practical outlook; ability to see things as they are; attempt to depict life, etc., as it actually exists; **-ist;** *a* **-istic;** *n* **reality** state of being real; *v* **realize** 1 become aware of 2 convert into, sell for money; (*ns* **-ization** act of realizing); **realty** *leg* real estate, property.

realm *n* 1 kingdom 2 *fig* sphere; region.

realpolitik *n* realistic policy for promoting national interests.

Realtor *n* [TM] real-estate agent, member of National Association of Realtors.

ream[1] *n* 20 quires of paper, 480 or 500 sheets.

ream[2] *v* 1 bevel out; countersink; *coll* berate, humiliate in anger 2 *naut* open for caulking; *n* **reamer** tool for this.

reap *v* 1 cut and gather (corn, etc.) 2 *fig* obtain as reward, result of action, conduct; *n* **reaper.**

rear[1] *v* 1 raise; lift up 2 bring up; educate 3 (*of horse, etc.*) stand on hind legs.

rear[2] *n* hind apart; part of army behind front line; position of being at back; *idm* **bring up the rear** be the last; *v* **rear-end** *coll* crash into the rear of another vehicle; *ns* **rear admiral** naval officer above captain; **rear guard** body of troops protecting rear of army on march.

rearm *v* arm again; *n* **rearmament.**

reason *n* 1 faculty of thinking logically 2 cause; motive 3 sanity 4 common sense; *adm* **within reason** not beyond reasonable limits; *phr v* **reason with** try to persuade by reasoned argument; *a* **reasonable** 1 fair 2 inexpensive; *adv* **-ably** fairly; *n* **reasoning** logical process; *v* persuade by logical argument.

reassure *v* comfort; give sense of confidence; *n* **-surance;** *a* **-suring.**

rebarbative *a fml* fearsome; harsh.

rebate *n* 1 deduction; discount 2 refund granted after

a
b
c
d
e
f
g
h
i
j
k
l
m
n
o
p
q
r
s
t
u
v
w
x
y
z

purchase 3 rabbet; *v* cut rebate or rabbet in.

rebel *v* **rebelling, rebelled.** revolt; resent control, constraint; take up arms against; *n* one who rebels; *n* **rebellion** organized, open resistance to authority, etc.; *a* **rebellious** 1 taking part in rebellion 2 showing resistance to authority; *adv* **-ly**; *n* **-ness.**

rebore *v* bore through (cylinder) again to regain true shape; *n* act, process of reboring or being rebored.

reborn *a* renewed in morale or religious faith; *idm* born again.

rebound *v* 1 bound, spring back 2 recoil on; *n* act of rebounding; *idm* **on the rebound** 1 when bouncing back 2 when suffering from disillusionment, *esp* in love.

rebuff *n* repulse; snub; check; *v* check; snub; defeat.

rebuke *v* reprove; reprimand; censure for fault; *n* reproof.

rebus *n* riddle or story in which names, syllables, etc., are represented by pictures and letters.

rebut *v* **rebutting, rebutted.** repel, check, *esp* accusations, etc.; refute; *n* **rebuttal.**

recalcitrant *a* refractory; obstinately disobedient; *n* **recalcitrance.**

recall *v* 1 summon, order back 2 remember 3 restore 4 revoke; *n* summons to return.

recant *v* take back; disavow opinions, beliefs, etc.; *n* **-ation.**

recap *v* **recapping, recapped.** *coll* recapitulate; repeat the main points (*also n*).

recapitulate (*coll abbr* recap) *v* summarize; restate briefly; *n* **-lation.**

recede *v* 1 move back 2 slope backward.

receipt *n* 1 written acknowledgment of money, goods received 2 act of receiving or getting 3 recipe 4 *pl* **-s** money earned in trading.

receive *v* 1 take, obtain (something given, sent, offered, etc.) 2 undergo 3 greet; welcome; allow into one's presence; *n* **receiver** 1 person receiving something 2 one receiving stolen goods 3 official appointed to collect money or administer property, *e.g.*, in case of bankruptcy (**receivership** term of office; *idm* **in receivership** under receiver's control) 4 radio receiver 5 earpiece of telephone.

recent *a* new; fresh; modern.

receptacle *n* vessel; container; that which receives or contains.

reception *n* 1 act of receiving 2 formal act of receiving guests, clients, hotel visitors, etc. 3 quality of broadcasting signals received 4 desk in entrance hall of hotel or

business establishment where visitors are received (*also* **r. desk**) 5 area adjacent to this (**r. area**); *ns* **receptionist** person employed to receive hotel guests, patients, etc., and arrange accommodation, appointments, etc.

receptive *a* able, quick to receive, *esp* new ideas, etc.; *adv* **-ly**; *ns* **-ness, receptivity.**

receptor *n* device for receiving signals.

recess *n* 1 cessation, suspension of business 2 alcove 3 secret place; *v* provide a recess; *a* **recessive** *bio* not evident in offspring because of dominant effect of other gene(s).

recession *n* 1 act of receding 2 period of reduction, slackening in industry and trade.

recessional *n* hymn sung at end of church service.

recherché *a* 1 very rare or special 2 affectedly sophisticated.

recidivist *n* one who relapses into crime; *n* **recidivism.**

recipe *n* 1 formula, directions for making, cooking something 2 prescription, *coll* **recipe for disaster** predicts certain failure.

recipient *n, a* (person, thing) that receives.

reciprocal *a* 1 inversely related, opposite 2 felt, done in return; mutual 3 alternating; *v* **reciprocate** 1 exchange mutually 2 alternate 3 move backward and forward; *ns* **-ation; reciprocity.**

recitative *n mus* passage of dialogue or narrative in opera or oratorio, sung in a way that keeps rhythm of natural speech.

recite *v* repeat aloud from memory, *esp* to audience; *ns* **recital** act of reciting; *mus* performance by soloist or small group, or of works of one composer; **recitation** recital of poetry or prose, *usu* from memory.

reckless *a* heedless; careless; rash; incautious.

reckon *v* 1 count; calculate 2 *coll* think; suppose; *phr vs* **reckon on** rely on.

reclaim *v* 1 bring back 2 demand return of 3 reform from vice, etc. 4 recover (land) from sea or waste state; *n* **reclaimable;** *n* **reclamation.**

recline *v* sit, lean backward; rest; repose.

recluse *n* hermit; one who chooses to live alone; *n* **reclusion.**

recognize *v* 1 know again 2 acknowledge; admit to be true, valid; *ns* **recognition; recognizance** 1 obligation to fulfill some condition, undertaken before court 2 sum forfeited if party fails to meet this obligation.

recoil *v* 1 draw back 2 retreat 3 rebound 4 *fig* feel disgust,

horror; *n* rebound, *esp* of gun; backward motion.

recollect *v* recall to mind; remember; *n* **-lection.**

recommend *v* represent as being suitable; advise; entrust to care of; *n* **-ation.**

recompense *v* make equal return for; reward; compensate; *n* that which is given as reward, compensation, etc.

reconcile *v* 1 settle (dispute, quarrel, etc.) 2 bring into logical agreement 3 be resigned to; *ns* **reconciliation** restoration of friendship; act, state of being reconciled; **reconcilement;** *a* **reconciliatory.**

recondite *a* 1 very profound or difficult 2 known by few.

reconnoiter, reconnoitre *v* make preliminary survey (of enemy's position, etc.); explore, examine beforehand; *n* **reconnaissance** act of reconnoitering.

reconstitute *v* restore to usual state; (*e.g.*, dried food by adding water); *n* **-tution.**

record *v* 1 write down for future information 2 store (sound) on disk or magnetic tape for subsequent reproduction; *n* 1 written account, document 2 sound recording, *esp* on vinyl disk (also **LP**) 3 best, finest achievement, *esp* in sport; *idm* **for the record** for the sake of accuracy; *idm* **off the**

record *coll* unofficial(ly); confidentially; *idm* **set the record straight** correct a misunderstanding; *ns* **recorder** 1 wooden or plastic instrument of flute family 2 machine for playing recorded tape (*also* **tape recorder**); **record player** machine for playing recorded music; **recording** 1 act or result of putting onto disk, tape, etc. 2 act of making written record; *a* **recorded** 1 preserved on disk, tape, or cassette; not performed live 2 written down.

recount *v* 1 narrate; relate 2 count again.

recoup *v* compensate; recover; make good (financial losses).

recourse *n* act of seeking help; application for help; *idm* **have recourse to** get help from.

recover *v* get, win back what has been lost; *a* **-able;** *n* **recovery.**

recreate *v* take recreation; *n* **-ation** 1 relaxation 2 amusement; game; sport; pastime; *a* **-al.**

re-create *v* create again, form anew; restore; revive.

recreational vehicle (RV) camper or van fitted for cooking, sleeping used for long-term travel.

recriminate *v* express mutual reproach; make countercharges; *n* **-ation** mutual abuse and reproach.

a
b
c
d
e
f
g
h
i
j
k
l
m
n
o
p
q
r
s
t
u
v
w
x
y
z

recrudesce v break out afresh; n **recrudescence**; a **-escent**.

recruit n newly enlisted member of armed forces; newly enrolled member of society, etc.; v enlist, seek to enlist (new soldiers, members, etc.); n **-ment**.

rectangle n right-angled parallelogram; a **rectangular**.

rectify v **rectifying, rectified**. 1 put right 2 purify 3 adjust 4 refine by distillation; n **rectification** 1 act of rectifying 2 refining 3 conversion of alternating current into direct current; n **rectifier**.

rectilineal, rectilinear a in, consisting of straight lines.

rectitude n moral uprightness; integrity; honesty of purpose.

recto n *Lat* right-hand page.

rector n parish priest; head of certain religious and educational institutions; n **rectory** rector's house.

rectum n **-tums or -ta**. *anat* lowest, terminal part of large intestine; a **rectal**.

recumbent a lying down; reclining; n **recumbence**.

recuperate v 1 recover, regain health, etc. 2 recover from financial losses; n **-ation**.

recur v **recurring, recurred**. 1 happen again 2 return to one's mind 3 *math* be repeated indefinitely; n **recurrence**; a **-rent**.

recusant n, a (one) refusing to obey, conform to laws, etc., *esp* religious matters.

recycle v treat used materials, waste from manufactured articles to make them reusable; a **recyclable** suitable for recycling.

red a 1 of color of blood 2 (*of hair*) reddish-brown or orange 3 *coll usu cap* Communist; n 1 red color 2 *cap coll* Communist; *idm* **in the red** in debt; **r. blood cell** blood cell that carries oxygen to the tissues and that give blood its red color; **r. carpet** ceremonial welcome; **redcoat** British soldier (18th-19th century); **R. Cross** international organization caring for the sick and wounded; **r. eye** 1 cheap whiskey 2 overnight airplane flight; **r. flag** 1 flag warning of danger 2 symbol of Communism or revolution; **r. giant** enormous star cooler than white or yellow star; **r.-green blindness** color blindness in which colors are seen in tones of yellow and blue; **redhead** person with red hair (a **redheaded**); **r. herring** something irrelevant introduced as a distraction; **r. ink** business loss; **r.-letter day** day made memorable by happy event; **r. light** warning light to halt traffic, to call for silence in recording studio, etc.; **redneck** *coll* bigoted, uneducated person; **r.shift** *astron* increase in wavelength indicating that star is moving away from observer; **r. tape** elaborate bureaucratic rules of procedures causing unnecessary delay and inconvenience; **redwood** large conifer with reddish wood; *as* **r.-blooded** full of vigor, patriotic; **r.-handed** (*idm* **catch somebody red-handed** catch somebody doing wrong); **r.-hot** very hot; marked by extreme emotion or violence; v **redden** 1 make red 2 turn red; blush.

redeem v 1 buy back 2 fulfill 3 make amends for 4 ransom 5 (*of God, Christ*) save from damnation; *ns* **redeemer** one who redeems, *esp* **the R.** Jesus Christ; **redemption**; a **redeemable**.

redolent a fragrant; giving out sweet scent; **r. of** *fig* steeped in; reminiscent of; n **redolence**.

redouble v 1 double again 2 make or become more intense.

redoubt n fortified post.

redoubtable a formidable; valiant.

redound *phr vs* **redound on** *fml* recoil on; **redound to** *fml* add to.

redress v put right; make amends for; *idm* **redress the balance** make things equal again; n *fml* reparation; compensation.

reduce v 1 lessen; decrease 2 break down to simpler form 3 cause to grow, try to become, slim **4** bring by force or necessity to some inferior position, state, etc.; *n* **reduction**; *a* **reducing**.

reductio ad absurdum *n Lat* way of disproving something by taking argument to logical but absurd conclusion.

redundant *a* superfluous; unnecessary; *n* **redundancy**.

reduplicate *v fml* double; repeat; *n* **-ation**.

redwood *n* large evergreen of US West.

reed *n* **1** various aquatic or marsh grasses; stem of these **2** vibrating cane or metal strip of some musical instrument; *a* **reedy 1** full of reeds **2** harsh; piping; shrill.

reef *n* **1** part of sail that can be folded up to shorten sail **2** ridge of coral rock just below surface of water **3** lode of auriferous quartz; *v* reduce area (of sail) by taking in reef; *ns* **r. knot** double-knot that does not slip easily; **reefer 1** short close-fitting warm jacket **2** *sl* marijuana cigarette (*also* **joint**).

reek *n* fumes; stench; *v* emit smoke, fumes; smell; stink.

reel *n* **1** small spool or bobbin around which thread fishing line is wound **2** lively Scottish dance; music for it **3** unit of length of film **4** act of staggering; *v* **1** wind on reel **2** stagger sway; *phr v* **reel off** recite rapidly.

reeve *v* pass (rope) through a

hole.

ref *abbr* **1** reference **2** *coll* referee.

refectory *n* room for meals, *esp* in monastery, school, etc.

refer *v* **referring, referred. 1** assign to **2** send to for information **3** allude **4** submit for decision **5** introduce in business; *ns* **reference 1** act of referring **2** testimonial **3** relation; respect; *n* **r. book** book designed for easy retrieval of information; *n* **referendum** submitting of question to electorate.

referee *n* **1** one to whom a thing is referred **2** umpire, *esp* in football (*coll* **ref**); *v* act as umpire.

referent *n* thing to which symbol refers.

refine *v* **1** purify; clarify **2** make, become more elegant; *ns* **refinement 1** act of refining **2** culture **3** fineness of feeling, taste, etc.; **refinery** place where materials are refined or purified.

refit *v* fit new parts in; *n* act or result of doing this.

reflect *v* **1** throw back, emit (light, heat, etc.) **2** reproduce visual image **3** think deeply **4** cast doubt on; *phr v* **reflect (up)on** think deeply about; *idm* **reflect badly/well (up)on** give bad/good impression of; *ns* **reflection** act of reflecting; that which is

reflected (rays of light, heat, etc.); reflected visual image (by mirror, etc.); meditation; *a* **reflective**; *n* **reflector** polished surface that reflects (rays of light, etc.).

reflex *a* directed backward; **r. action** involuntary muscular, nervous reaction to stimulus; **r. angle** angle greater than 180° and less than 360°; *a* **reflexive** *ling* denoting action coming back on agent; **r. pronoun** one referring to subject of sentence.

reflexology *n* use of foot massage to alleviate stress in other parts of body.

reforest *v* replant with forest trees.

reform *v* change; improve condition, by removal of abuses, etc.; *n* improvement; *n* **-er** person initiating social or political change.

reformation *n* amendment; *cap* 16th-century religious revolt against Catholicism.

reformatory *a* corrective institution for young offenders; *a* producing reform.

refract *v* deflect rays or waves from direct course; *n* **refraction**; *a* **-ive**.

refractory *a* **1** unmanageable; stubborn **2** *med* resistant to treatment; hard to cure.

refrain[1] *n* recurring lines, words at end of song, etc.

refrain[2] *v* abstain; forbear; keep oneself from.

A
B
C
D
E
F
G
H
I
J
K
L
M
N
O
P
Q
R
S
T
U
V
W
X
Y
Z

refresh v revive; invigorate; renew; provide with fresh supply; *idm* **refresh somebody's memory** remind somebody of important details; *n* **refresher 1** thing that refreshes **2** further study by qualified person to bring knowledge up to date (*also* **r. course**); *a* **refreshing 1** restoring vitality **2** thirst-quenching **3** new and stimulating; *adv* **-ingly;** *ns* **-ment 1** of refreshing, being refreshed **2** food and drink; *pl* **-ments** snacks.

refried beans n beans that are cooked, fried, mashed, and fried again.

refrigerate v preserve by chilling; keep at very low temperature; *ns* **-ation; refrigerator** machine for cooling, freezing (food, etc.); icebox (*arch*).

refuge n shelter; protection; sanctuary; hiding place; *n* **refugee** one who seeks refuge, *esp* in another country.

refulgent a shining; radiant; *n* **refulgence** brightness; splendor.

refund v repay; restore.

refurbish v renovate.

refuse v decline; reject; (*of horse*) be unwilling to jump; *n* garbage; discarded matter; *n* **refusal 1** act of refusing **2** option.

refute v reject; disprove; *a* **refutable;** *n* **refutation**.

regain v get again.

regal a of, like royalty; *n pl* **regalia** insignia of royalty; insignia, clothes, etc., of a society; formal garb; *adv* **-ly;** *n* **regality**.

regale v **1** feast **2** give great delight to.

regard v **1** gaze at intently **2** consider; esteem; value; *n* **1** look **2** esteem **3** care; attention; *pl* **-s** expression of goodwill; *idm* **with regard to** concerning; *a* **-less** heedless; negligent.

regatta n race for boats, yachts.

regenerate v **1** bring new life to **2** reorganize after decay **3** recreate **4** be reformed morally; *a* **-ative;** *n* **-ation; -ator** device in furnace for saving fuel by heating incoming air.

regent n one who rules during absence, minority, or illness of sovereign; *n* **regency** office or position of regent; *a cap* of, in style prevailing during Regency (*esp* 1810-20 in England and 1715-23 in France).

reggae n popular dance music from the Caribbean.

regicide n killer, killing of king or sovereign.

regime n system, method of government, administration.

regimen n course of treatment *esp* in matters of medicine, diet, exercise, etc.

regiment n military unit; *fig* large quantity; *a* **-al** of regiment; *n pl* uniform of particular regiment.

region n **1** area, district, tract of country **2** area of body; *idm* **in the region on** about; *a* **-al;** *adv* **-ally;** *n pl* **-s** the provinces; *v* **regionalize** organize by regions; *n* **-ization**.

register n **1** official record of names, events, etc. kept for reference **2** range of voice or musical instrument **3** movable plate controlling airflow on stove, heating unit **4** *ling* variety of language (formal/informal, spoken/written, etc.) appropriate to social situation or professional use **5** printing correct alignment; *v* **1** record formally **2** have one's name recorded or checked **3** enroll for something **4** (*of machinery*) give reading or measurement; (*of measurement*) be recorded **5** (*of face*) express **6** be noted or remembered **7** send by registered mail; *a* **registered** sent by special postal service with protection against loss, etc. (*n* **r. mail**).

registered nurse n a trained nurse, licensed after registration.

registrar n one who keeps public records (births, deaths, etc.) or educational records; *n* **registration** act of registering (**r. number** official code for identification of motor vehicle).

registry n place, office where

register is kept; **r.office** local registry for births, marriages, and deaths.

regnant *a* reigning.

regnum *n* kingdom.

regorge *v* 1 vomit 2 swallow again.

regress *n* 1 return; going back 2 relapse; *n* **-ive** falling back; *n* **regression** backward movement.

regret *v* regretting, regretted. be sorry for; remember with grief, sorrow; repent of; *n* grief; repentance; sorrow; *as* **-ful** feeling regret; *adv* **-ly**; **regrettable** to be regretted; *adv* **-ably**.

regroup *v* 1 to form into new groupings 2 to reconsider (a problem).

regular *a* 1 orderly (**r. habits**) 2 normal; according to rule (**r. verb**) 3 habitual (**r. exercise**) 4 symmetrical; even (**r. shape**) 5 unvarying (**r. pattern**) 6 permanent (**r. job**) 7 thorough (**r. check-up**) 8 pleasant (**r. guy**) *n* **regular** visitor, client, etc.; *adv* **-ly**; *n* **regularity**; *v* **regularize** (*n* **-ization**).

regulate *v* 1 put in order 2 control by law, clock, etc. 3 work correctly; *ns* **-ation** act of regulating; rule; order; **regulator** lever of watch, etc.; *a* **regulatory**.

regurgitate *v* flow, gush back; bring up again (swallowed food, etc.); *n* **-ation**.

rehab *n* process of rehabilitation, *esp* from drug or alcohol abuse.

rehabilitate *v* restore normal capacity; reinstate; *n* **-ation**.

rehash *v* 1 rearrange old literary material and produce under new title 2 repeat information.

rehearse *v* perform, practice (play, music, etc.) in private, before public performance; *n* **rehearsal**.

Reich *n* former German state.

reify *v* treat as real, concrete.

reign *n* rule, supreme power of sovereign; period of ruler's reign; *n* **r.of terror** period of violence and murder on a large scale; *v* rule as monarch; be supreme; predominate.

reimburse *v* refund; compensate by payment; *n* **-ment**.

rein *n* leather strap fastened to bit for leading, holding horse; *fig* that which restrains; *v* hold in, control with reins; *idm* **give free rein** allow full play; *idm* **keep a tight rein on** control very strictly.

reincarnation *n* return of soul to life, after death, in fresh form; *v* **reincarnate** cause to be reborn in other form.

reindeer *n* large, domesticated deer of northern Europe.

reinforce *v* 1 *mil* strengthen with additional troops, supplies, etc. 2 strengthen (fabric, etc.) by increasing thickness, etc.; *ns* **-ment**; **reinforced concrete** concrete

strengthened by embedded steel bars.

reinstate *v* restore to former state, position; *n* **reinstatement**.

reiterate *v* repeat many times; *n* **-ation** repetition.

reject *v* discard as imperfect, valueless, useless; refuse to accept; disallow; *n* that which is rejected; *n* **rejection** refusal.

rejoice *v* to make, be glad; feel, express joy; delight.

rejoin *v* 1 join again 2 make answer; *n* **rejoinder** retort; answer to a reply.

rejuvenate *v* renew youth of; become young again; *n* **-ation**.

relapse *v* 1 fall back into former bad state 2 become ill again (*also n*).

relate *v* narrate; *phr v* **relate to** 1 have connection with 2 refer (to) 3 belong to same family as; *phr v* **relate to** 1 connect, be connected with 2 *coll* show sympathy toward; *a* **related** 1 connected 2 of the same kind.

relation *n* 1 connection by blood, marriage; relative 2 connection between things 3 narrative; *n pl* **-s** links between people, groups of people (**international r.; sexual r.**); *n* **relationship** 1 connection 2 friendship or other mutual link between people.

relative *n* member of same

a
b
c
d
e
f
g
h
i
j
k
l
m
n
o
p
q
r
s
t
u
v
w
x
y
z

A
B
C
D
E
F
G
H
I
J
K
L
M
N
O
P
Q
R
S
T
U
V
W
X
Y
Z

family; *a* comparative; not absolute; *idm* **relative to** 1 referring to 2 compared with; *ns* **r. clause** *ling* clause performing adjectival function relating to noun or pronoun; **r. pronoun** *ling* pronoun *who*, *which*, or *that* used to relate relative clause to something in main clause; **relativism** theory that there can be no objective standards of truth (*n*, *a* **-ist**); **relativity 1** fact or state of being relative 2 Einstein's theory based on principle that time and space are inseparable.

relax *n* loosen; slacken; make, become less rigid, tense; unbend; become less severe; *n* **-ation** act of relaxing; slackening of strain, tension, etc.; recreation.

relay *n* **1** team of fresh men, horses, or dogs, etc. replacing tired ones **2** broadcast sent from one station to another; *v* **1** pass on (information) **2** transmit from relay station **3** to lay again; **r. race** race between teams, each member running part of distance and handing baton to next runner.

release *v* give up; free; discharge; *n* **1** liberation **2** formal discharge **3** catch releasing mechanism.

release print *n* the version of a movie distributed for public showings.

relegate *v* send, dismiss to

inferior position; transfer; *n* **-ation**.

relent *v* become less hard, severe, stern or obstinate; give in; *a* **-less** pitiless; inexorable (*adv* **-ly**).

relevant *a* bearing on point at issue; pertinent; applicable; *n* **-ance**.

reliable *a* dependable; trustworthy; *adv* **-ably; ns reliability; reliance on 1** trust in **2** dependence on; *a* **reliant on** dependent on.

relic *n* object surviving from past, *esp* one associated with saint; memento.

relief *n* **1** alleviation of pain, anxiety, etc. **2** help for people in distress (*n* **r. pitcher** in baseball, pitcher who takes the mound after the starting pitcher leaves a game) **3** means of ending, avoiding boredom **4** release from duty **5** person relieving another from spell of duty **6** method of decoration or design that stands out above surface (**r. map** map showing hills, valleys, etc. either by shading or by raised molding); *v* **relieve 1** bring relief to **2** take over duty from **3** lessen (the effect of); *idm* **relieve oneself** *coll* urinate or defecate; *idm* **relieve one's feelings** release emotions by shouting, weeping, violent -action; *phr* *v* **relieve somebody of something 1** take something *esp* burden from somebody **2**

coll rob somebody of something; *a* **relieved** freed of anxiety.

religion *n* belief in and worship of God or gods; *as* **religious 1** pertaining to religion **2** devout, pious **3** person who is devout; monastic, cloistered **4** *fig* conscientious; **religiose** sanctimonious (*n* **-osity**).

reliquary *n* receptacle for religious relics.

relinquish *v* abandon; surrender; let go.

relish *n* **1** enjoyment of food **2** *fig* zest; enthusiasm **3** spicy condiment; *v* enjoy.

relocate *v* move to new place, *esp* of work or residence; *n* **-ation**.

reluctant *a* unwilling, disinclined; difficult to treat; *n* **reluctance**.

rely *phr* *v* **relying, relied.** **rely on** depend on; trust; *a* **reliable** dependable; trustworthy; *ns* **reliability; reliance** ground of trust or confidence; *a* **reliant** confident; trusting.

REM *abbr* rapid eye movement (occurring while dreaming).

remain *v* stay, be left behind; persist; stay, continue in same place; *n pl* **-s** what is left or survives; relics; corpse; *n* **remainder 1** remaining persons or things **2** quantity left after subtraction, division **3** copies of books, etc., unsold in publisher's stock; v offer unsold books, etc., at reduced prices.

remand v send back *esp* into custody.

remark v 1 take notice of; observe 2 utter comment; n observation; comment; a **-able** noticeable; unusual; adv **-ably**.

remedy n **-ies.** 1 substance, treatment which cures disease, etc. 2 action or method tending to mitigate an evil or wrong; v **remedying, remedied.** put right; as **remediable** that can be remedied; **remedial** 1 providing remedy (**r. action**) 2 needing special education (**r. pupil**) 3 provided for pupils requiring support in academics, etc. (**r. class, r. education**).

remember v call to mind; retain in memory; have in mind; n **remembrance** 1 memory 2 keepsake; souvenir.

remex n the wing feather of a bird.

remind v put in mind of, cause to remember; n **reminder** that which reminds.

reminisce v talk, *usu* with enjoyment, about past memories; n **reminiscence** recollection; *pl* **-s** memoirs; a **reminiscent of** tending to remind one of; similar to; evocative of.

remiss a negligent; careless.

remit v **remitting, remitted.** 1 forgo, give up in whole or part 2 send back; transmit; a **remissible;** ns **remission** act of remitting; interval, time during which process is indolent (as disease, cancer); **remittance** sending of money; money sent as payment or allowance.

remnant n 1 remaining fragment 2 short length of fabric.

remodel v renovate.

remonstrate v protest; expostulate, plead, with; n **remonstrance.**

remorse n repentance; regret, as **-ful; -less** ruthless; pitiless; relentless; (adv **-ly;** n **-ness**).

remote a 1 far away 2 aloof; distant; n **r. control** device for controlling machine (as TV), toy (as car), etc. from distance by radio waves.

remove v 1 take, carry (thing) away, off; withdraw 2 erase 3 relieve of office, rank, etc. 4 move from one place to another *esp* residence; *idm* **(at) one remove/two removes from** with a certain degree of distance from.

remunerate v pay; compensate; n **-ation;** a **-ative** profitable.

Renaissance n rebirth; revival; *esp* **the R.** revival of art and learning in 15th and 16th centuries.

renal a of the kidneys.

renascent a reviving; springing into fresh life.

rend v tear apart; split; *fig* cause anguish to; *pt, pp* **rent.**

render v 1 give in return; tender 2 depict by art 3 interpret 4 put on first coat of plaster, etc.; n **-ing** version; interpretation; **rendition** interpretation; performance.

rendezvous n 1 set meeting place 2 popular general resort 3 process of bringing two spacecraft together.

renegade n apostate; deserter; traitor.

renege v break promise.

renew v 1 restore to original condition or state of freshness 2 begin again 3 prolong, extend existence or validity of 4 grow again; n **renewal** revival; restoration; as **-able; -ing** regenerating; quickening.

rennet n preparation (*usu* from membrane of calf's stomach) used to curdle milk, in cheese-making.

renounce v 1 formally give up, disclaim 2 repudiate 3 not to follow suit at cards; n **renunciation.**

renovate v restore to good condition; renew; repair; ns **-ation; -ator** one who renovates.

renown n fame; celebrity; a **-ed** famous.

rent n payment made for use of house, land, etc.; n **r. strike** a refusal, protest by tenants to their rent; v occupy (house, etc.) for payment; rent out; lease; n **rental** apartment, house, etc. available for rent.

A
B
C
D
E
F
G
H
I
J
K
L
M
N
O
P
Q
R
S
T
U
V
W
X
Y
Z

renunciation *n* act of renouncing.

rep *n coll abbr* representative; *n coll abbr* repertory theater.

repair[1] *v* mend; set right; compensate for; *n* act or result of mending; *as* **reparable, repairable;** *n* **reparation** redress, amends.

repair[2] *phr v* **repair to** have recourse to; frequent.

repartée *n Fr* 1 readiness in making witty reply or retort 2 banter, witty clever way with words.

repast *n* meal; feast.

repatriate *v* send back, return to native country; *n* **-iation.**

repay *v* **repaying, repaid.** 1 pay back, refund (money) 2 make return for; reward; *pt, pp* **repaid**; *n* **-ment.**

repeal *v* revoke; abrogate; annul (law, etc.); *n* revocation.

repeat *v* 1 say again, reiterate; recite 2 do again; reproduce 3 recur; *n* **repetition** thing repeated *esp* program or order for goods; *adv* **-edly** over and over again; *n* **repeater** 1 one who or which repeats 2 repeating firearm; *n* **repetition** act of repeating; recital; recitation; *a* **repetitive** tending to repeat.

repel *v* **repelling, repelled.** 1 drive back, spurn 2 rouse dislike, disgust in; *n* **repellence;** *a* **repellent** disgusting; revolting; *n* that which repels (insects, etc.).

repent *v* feel penitence, regret for deed or omission; *a* **repentant;** *n* **repentance.**

repercussion *n* 1 rebound; recoil 2 *fig* indirect effect, consequence *usu pl.*

repertory *n* store; stock; *n* **repertoire** stock of songs, plays that person or company can perform; **repertory theater** theater with permanent company, depending on constant change of plays.

repetition *n* act of repeating; *as* **repetitious; repetitive** containing excessive repetition (*adv* **-ly;** *n* **-ness**).

repine *v* fret; complain; be discontented.

replace *v* put back; supersede; substitute for; *n* **replacement.**

replenish *v* fill up again; restock; *n* **replenishment.**

replete *a* well-filled; sated; gorged; *n* **repletion** surfeit.

replica *n* duplicate, copy of anything; *esp* of work of art, done by the original artist.

reply *v*, **replying, replied.** *n* answer, in speech or writing.

report *v* 1 state formally 2 make official complaint about 3 present oneself for duty or service; *n* 1 objective account 2 rumor (as unsubstantiated r.) 3 sound of an explosion; *n* **reportage** (style of) news reporting on media; *a* **reported** alleged (*n* **r. speech** indirect speech; *adv* **-ly** according to reports); *n* **reporter** journalist.

repose *v* 1 place, rest; 2 eternal sleep, after death; *n* act of reposing; *n* **repository** place where things may be deposited, stored; warehouse.

repossess *v* retake possession of (mortgaged property, leased goods, etc.) when borrower has not kept up payments; *n* **repossession.**

reprehend *v* rebuke; scold; blame; *a* **reprehensible** not good; deserving reproof.

represent *v* 1 depict by painting, etc. 2 symbolize 3 be an example of, the result of 4 act on behalf of 5 act as substitute for; *n* **representation** 1 act of representing, being represented 2 picture or other art form that depicts somebody/something specific(*a* **-al** giving realistic, lifelike image); *a* **representative** 1 typical 2 of elected members (*n* 1 person elected to represent group 2 agent of firm, *esp* as traveling salesman).

repress *v* suppress; put down; curb; check; overcome; *n* **repression** suppression; restraint; *psyc* result of mental conflict; *a* **repressive** cruel and harsh; *adv* **-ly;** *n* **-ness.**

reprieve *v* cancel or defer punishment *esp* death sentence; give respite (to); *n* cancellation or suspension of criminal sentence; respite.

reprimand *v* rebuke, censure

severely; *n* severe reproof.

reprisal *n* retaliation.

reprise *n mus* repeat.

reproach *v* scold; upbraid; charge with some fault; *n* rebuke; thing bringing disgrace, etc.; *idm* **beyond reproach** perfect; *a* **-ful;** (*adv* **-ly**).

reprobate *a*, *n* depraved (person); (one) without honor or principles.

reproduce *v* 1 to procreate, produce young 2 produce afresh 3 repeat 4 present again; *n* **-duction** 1 process of reproducing 2 copy; facsimile; *a* **-ductive** pertaining to, used in, reproduction; fertile.

reprove *v* chide; rebuke; gently disapprove; *n* **reproof.**

reptile *n* cold-blooded, air-breathing, crawling/ slithering vertebrate, as snake, lizard, etc.; *fig* sly, manipulative, cold person; *a* **reptilian**.

republic *n* state having no monarch and governed by representatives elected by people; *a*, *n* **republican** (person) in favor of such a system (*n* **-ism**); *n cap* member of Republican Party.

repudiate *v* reject; disown, disclaim; *n* **-ation.**

repugnant *a* distasteful; offensive; *n* **-ance** dislike; aversion.

repulse *v* 1 drive, beat back 2 *fig* snub; rebuff; *n* **repulsion** aversion; dislike; disgust; *a*

repulsive loathsome; repellent.

repute *n* good or bad name; reputation; *idm* **of repute** of good reputation; *as* **reputable** of good repute; held in esteem; **reputed** considered; believed; thought of as; *n* **reputation** opinion commonly held of person or thing.

request *n* act of asking for something; petition.

requiem *n* dirge; mass for the dead.

require *v* 1 ask, claim as right; command 2 need; want; *n* **-ment** 1 need 2 condition; provision.

requisite *n*, *a* (something) needed, essential.

requisition *n* formal demand or request; *v* demand supply of.

requite *v* 1 reciprocate (love) 2 avenge (injury).

rerun *v*, *n* (broadcast) repeat of film or TV show, or of any planned operation.

reschedule *v* 1 schedule or plan again 2 postpone repayment of loan or interest on it.

rescind *v* cancel; make void; *n* **rescission** act of rescinding.

rescript *n* offical order, reply.

rescue *v* save from danger, injury, etc.; *n* **-er.**

rescue mission *n* 1 effort to save lives, etc. 2 inner-city religious center to aid and convert the needy.

research *n* diligent search and

investigation *esp* with view to gaining new knowledge etc; *n* **-er.**

resection *n* surgery; surgical removal of part of body.

resemble *v* be like; have qualities, features in common with; *n* **resemblance.**

resent *v* feel and show displeasure, irritation at; regard as offensive; *n* **-ment;** *a* **-ful;** *adv* **-fully.**

reserve *v* 1 keep, hold back; keep for specific person or use 2 order in advance; *n* 1 that which is reserved *fig* aloofness; self-restraint 3 part of armed services called only in emergency; *n* **reservation** 1 act of reserving 2 unexpressed doubt 3 tract of land reserved for native residents or for preservation of animals; *a* **reserved** not showing feelings.

reservist *n*, *a* (soldier) serving in reserve force.

reservoir *n* 1 large storage tank or artificial lake for water supply of town, etc. 2 any receptacle holding liquids 3 *fig* reserve supply.

reset *v* 1 set again; 2 change reading (*e.g.,* on clock).

reshuffle *n*, *v* (make) changes in people holding positions of responsibility.

reside *v* dwell in permanently or for long time; *ns* **residence** abode, habitual dwelling; **residency** period of advanced professional training (as in

A B C D E F G H I J K L M N O P Q **R** S T U V W X Y Z

medicine); *a, n* **resident** (one) dwelling permanently in given place; *a* **residential** of part of town etc. mainly of residences.

residue *n* remainder, what is left; *as* **residual, residuary**.

resign *v* give up or back; retire from office, etc.; abandon; *idm* **resign somebody to something** get somebody to accept something; *n* **-ation** 1 act of resigning office, etc. 2 submission to will of God; *a* **resigned** content to endure; uncomplaining.

resilient *a* capable of returning to original shape, state; *n* **resilience** 1 elasticity 2 recuperative power.

resin *n* sticky substance secreted by most plants *esp* pines, firs.

resist *v* withstand; oppose; *n* **resistance** 1 act of resistance 2 organized armed opposition by civilians in occupied country 3 *elec* opposition of conductor to flow of electricity; (**passive r.** nonviolent act done as protest against abuse, etc.); *as* **resistant; resistless** irresistible; with no resistance.

resolute *a* firm; steadfast; determined; *adv* **-ly;** *n* **-ution** 1 firm intention 2 vote or decision of public assembly or legislative body 3 analysis.

resolve *v* 1 separate component parts of 2 make clear 3 decide; firmly intend

4 form by vote or resolution; *n* determination; firmness of purpose; *as* **resolvable** capable of being resolved; *n, a* **resolvent** means of solving problem (as math equation, etc.).

resonant *a* 1 echoing; resounding; sonorous (**r. note, r. voice**) 2 producing prolonged vibration or echo (**r. building, r. cave**); *n* **resonance** 1 quality of being resonant 2 sound caused by vibrations of same wavelength from another body; *v* **resonate** be resonant; *n* **-ator** device that produces or adds resonance.

resorb *v* to draw in again.

resort *phr v* **resort to** have recourse to; frequent; use as means; *n* vacation spot or hotel, *usu* with recreational facilities.

resound *v* 1 ring with prolonged sound; echo 2 be loud and clear; *a* **resounding** 1 loud and clear 2 outstanding (**r. success**) (*adv* **-ly**).

resource *n* inventiveness, skill in adapting thing to one's purpose; *pl* **-s** means of support; stock that can be drawn on; *a* **resourceful**.

respect *v* pay heed to; hold in esteem; treat as binding; *n* 1 attention; esteem 2 special aspect, point; reference; *idm* **with respect to** regarding; concerning; *a* **respectable** estimable; decent; moderate;

passable; *n* **respectability;** *as* **respectful** deferential; **respective** of each individually (*adv* **-ly** taken separately in the order mentioned).

respire *v* breathe; *ns* **respiration; respirator** 1 apparatus worn over mouth and nose to protect lungs from fumes, gas, etc. 2 device to externally support breathing; *a* **respiratory** pertaining to breathing.

respite *n* temporary rest from work, effort, duty, pain, etc.; pause; reprieve.

resplendent *a* gorgeously bright; brilliant; magnificent; splendid; *n* **-ence**.

respond *v* 1 reply, make answer 2 act as result of another's action 3 react *usu* in good sense; *ns* **respondent** one who answers *esp* to lawsuit for divorce; **response** answer; reaction to stimulus; *a* **responsive** sympathetic; readily reacting to stimulus; *adv* **-ly;** *n* **-ness.**

responsible *a* 1 legally, morally answerable for actions, etc.; capable of assuming responsibility 2 of good credit, repute, etc.; *n* **-ibility** moral obligation, liability, duty; charge; state of being answerable.

rest[1] *n* 1 cessation of activity or movement 2 repose 3 support; prop 4 pause; *idm* **put/set someone's mind at**

rest/at ease reassure somebody; *idm* **lay to rest** bury; *v* **1** (let) take repose; stop working for a while **2** lean; support; *idm* **rest assured** be confident; *idm* **rest one's case** *leg* have no further argument to present; *phr vs* **rest on 1** (of gaze) be turned toward **2** (of argument) depend on; **rest with** be the responsibility of; *ns* **r. home** convalescent home, *esp* for aged people; **r.room** *coll* public lavatory; *as* **restful;** *adv* **-ly;** *n* **-ness; restless;** *adv* **-ly;** *n* **-ness.**

rest[2] *n* what is left; residue; others; *v* remain in (specified state or condition).

restaurant *n* place where meals are made, bought, and eaten; *n* **restaurateur** restaurant proprietor, owner.

restitution *n* reparation; act of giving back something that has been taken or lost; *v* **restitute.**

restive *a* restless; fidgety; stubborn; impatient of control; *adv* **-ly;** *n* **-ness.**

restore *v* **1** bring back to former place, state, etc.; reinstate **2** renovate; repair **3** give back; *n* **restoration** act of restoring, *cap* **the R.** return of Charles II to his kingdom; *n, a* **restorative** (medicine, treatment) restoring health, etc.

restrain *v* **1** hold back; control **2** confine legally; *a* **restrained** calm; controlled

(*adv* **-ly**); *n* **restraint 1** control of emotions **2** limitation **3** confinement.

restrict *v* impose limits on; limit by law; *n* **restriction** limitation; law, regulation that restricts; *a* **restrictive 1** prohibiting further negotiation **2** limiting interpretation, application.

result *v* happen, follow as consequence; have as natural effect; *phr v* **result in** end in; *n* consequence; outcome; (in games) final score; *a* **resultant** arising as result.

resume *v* assume, occupy again; begin again; summarize; *n* **résumé** summary, *esp* of job, professional experience; *n* **resumption** starting again; resuming.

resurge *v* rise again; *n* **resurgence;** *a* **resurgent.**

resurrection *n* rising again, *cap* **the R.** rising of Christ from the grave; *v* **resurrect** restore to life; resuscitate.

resuscitate *v* restore to life, consciousness, activity; *n* **-tation.**

retail *n* sale in small quantities to consumer; *a* concerned with such sale; *adv* by retail; *v* sell by retail; repeat (gossip, news, etc.); *ns* **r. politics** campaigning by traditional methods of town meetings, speaking face to face; *n* **-er.**

retain *v* **1** hold back **2** keep control of **3** engage services

of **4** remember; *n* **-er 1** fee to retain lawyer's services **2** dependent, follower.

retaliate *v* pay back in kind; take vengeance; *n* **-iation** return of like for like; reprisals; *a* **-atory.**

retard *v* **1** delay, make slow or late **2** reduce speed or rate; *a* **retarded** slow in physical or mental development; *n* **-ation.**

retch *v* try to vomit, strain as in vomiting.

retention *n* **1** act of retaining **2** memory (**powers of r.**) *a* **retentive** having good memory (*n* **-ness**).

reticent *a* reserved in speech; uncommunicative; secretive; *n* **reticence.**

retina *n* light-sensitive layer of nerve fibers at back of eye.

retinue *n* train of retainers, attendants.

retire *v* withdraw; give up profession, occupation, etc.; go to bed; *a* **retired** private, secluded; having withdrawn from active life, business, etc.; *n* **-ment;** *a* **retiring** shy, unobtrusive.

retool *v* replace tools and machinery.

retort *v* answer sharply; repay in kind; reply with counter-charge; *n* sharp, witty reply; glass vessel with long, bent back used in chemistry, distilling, etc.

retouch *v* touch up; add finishing touches to (photograph, etc.).

a
b
c
d
e
f
g
h
i
j
k
l
m
n
o
p
q
r
s
t
u
v
w
x
y
z

retrace *v* 1 go over again 2 recall; *a* **retraceable**.

retract *v* draw back; disavow, recant; *as* **retractable; retractile** that can be retracted; *ns* **retraction** recantation; **retractor** muscle that draws back; surgical instrument for same.

retread *v* walk over or along again; put new tread on (tire); *n* used tire given new tread.

retreat *v* retire; move, cause to move backward; *n* act of retreating; military signal to retire; secluded, quiet, private contemplative place.

retrench *v* cut down *esp* expenditure; curtail, lessen; *n* **-ment**.

retribution *n* punishment for evil deeds; fitting recompense.

retrieve *v* search for and fetch; regain; make good; atone; *ns* **retrieval; retriever** kind of dog trained to retrieve shot game; *a* **retrievable**.

retro- *prefix* backward in place, time, etc.

retroactive *a* having validity from an earlier date.

retrocession *n* act of yielding, granting back; movement backward; *v* **retrocede** move backward; retire; *a* **-cessive**.

retrofit *v* modify a structure or vehicle.

retroflex *a* 1 bending backward 2 *ling* pronounced with tip of tongue curled back.

retrograde *a* moving, going backward; deteriorating; *n* **retrogression**.

retrogress *v* return to earlier or primitive condition; *a* **retrogressive;** *n* **retrogression**.

retrorocket *n* rocket used to slow down spacecraft or reverse direction.

retrospect *n* mental review of past; *a* **-ive** referring to past; *n* **-ion**.

retsina *n* Greek wine flavored with resin.

return *v* 1 go, come back 2 give, send back 3 reelect to office; *idm* **return a verdict** *leg* (of jury) give verdict; *n* 1 act of returning 2 official report 3 *esp pl* profit 4 ticket for two-way journey (*also* **r. ticket**) 5 ticket for theater, concert, etc., returned before performance for resale; *idm* **many happy returns (of the day)** expressing greetings for a happy birthday; *idm* **in return (for)** in exchange (for).

reunion *n* 1 joining; being joined together again 2 social gathering for family, former associates, friends, etc.

reunite *v* unite after separation.

rev *n coll* revolution (of engine); *v* **revving, revved.** increase speed of engine; *phr v* **rev up** run engine fast to check smoothness of running before engaging gear.

Rev. *abbr* Reverend.

revalue *v* give new higher value to; *n* **-ation**.

revamp *v coll* renew; give a new appearance to.

reveal *v* make known or visible; divulge; *n* **revelation**.

reveille *n mil* awakening signal.

revel *v* **revelling, revelled.** feast; carouse; *phr v* **revel in** enjoy; *n pl* rejoicing; merrymaking; *ns* **reveler; revelry** unrestrained merrymaking.

revelation *n* 1 uncovering of secret 2 surprising fact made known.

revenge *v* avenge; make retaliation for; *n* vindictiveness; vengeance; (sport, cards, etc.) rematch; *a* **-ful;** *adv* **-fully**.

revenue *n* total income, *esp* of state.

revenue stamps *n* a label that shows an appropriate tax has been paid.

reverberate *v* echo, resound; throw back, reflect (sound, etc.); *n* **-ation**.

revere *v* venerate; regard with great or religious respect; *n* **reverence** feeling of awe and admiration; deference; *as* **reverend** worthy to be revered (**R. Mother** mother superior of convent); **reverent, reverential** showing reverence (*adv* **-ly**).

reverie *n* 1 daydream; dreamy contemplation 2 musical composition reflecting this state of mind.

revers *n* lapel; part of garment turned back.

reverse *v* 1 turn upside down 2 cause to go backward 3 cancel; annul; *idm* **reverse charges** make telephone call paid for by recipient; *n* 1 what is contrary, opposite 2 less important side 3 setback; defeat; financial loss; *a* contrary; opposite; *ns* **reversal** act of reversing; state of being reversed; **reversion** *leg* return of estate to grantor or heirs at expiry of grant; *bio* return to ancestral type; *a* **reversionary** *leg* of, pertaining to reversion; *n* **reverse gear** mechanism causing backward motion.

revert *v* pass back legally to grantor; *phr v* **revert to** 1 go back to (former state) 2 refer to again.

revet *v* cover, face (surface) with stone, etc. to strengthen; *n* **-ment** protective covering.

review *v* 1 recall to mind in detail 2 inspect formally, officially 3 write critical notice of book, etc.; *n* 1 revision 2 formal inspection *esp* of troops 3 written criticism of book, etc. 4 periodical with critical articles and discussion of current events; *n* **reviewer**.

revile *v* abuse; bitterly reproach; *n* **reviler**.

revise *v* look over and amend;

n **revision** act of revising; something that has been revised; *n* **-ism** questioning of basic political beliefs, *esp* Marxist (*n*, *a* **-ist**).

revitalize *v* bring new life to.

revive *v* come, bring back to life, consciousness, health, etc.; *ns* **revival** rebirth, *esp* of religious fervor; **revivalist** organizer of, preacher at revival meeting; **revivalism** the spirit of religious revival.

revivify *v* bring back to life.

revoke *v* 1 annul 2 *cards* fail to follow suit, although possible to do so; *a* **revocable;** *n* **revocation** act of revoking *esp leg* repeal, annulment.

revolt *v* 1 rebel 2 disgust; *n* rebellion; *a* **revolting** repulsive; disgusting; *n* **revulsion** marked repugnance.

revolve *v* 1 go around; rotate 2 move, occur in cycles; *phr v* **revolve around** have as main concern; *n* **revolution** 1 complete rotation or turning around 2 complete overthrow of political system; *a* **revolutionary** of, causing, radical change of outlook, methods, etc.; *n* person taking part in revolution; *v* **revolutionize** make fundamental changes in.

revolver *n* pistol with revolving magazine.

revolving charge account *n* a charge account that requires monthly payments and an

interest fee.

revue *n* theatrical entertainment, with songs, sketches, dancing, etc.

revulsion *n* violent feelings, *esp* disgust.

reward *v* repay, recompense for service, conduct, etc.; *n* that which is given in return for goods received, or for return of lost articles etc; *a* **rewarding** satisfying.

rewrite man *n* a journalist who specializes in rewriting.

Reye's syndrome *n* serious encephalopathy of children.

rhapsody *n* 1 highly emotional, enthusiastic utterance 2 emotional musical composition; *idm* **go into rhapsodies** be very enthusiastic; *a* **rhapsodic;** *phr v* **rhapsodize about/over** express eager approval of.

rhea *n* large flightless bird of S. America.

rheostat *n* instrument for regulating value or resistance in electrical circuit.

rhesus *n* small long-tailed monkey; **rhesus factor** *med* substance in blood causing harm to Rhesus-positive fetus or newborn baby if mother is Rhesus-negative (*also* **Rh. factor**).

rhetoric *n* art of oratory; flowery, high-sounding language; *a* **-al** 1 showing rhetoric 2 uttered for effect, not for a response (**r. question**); *adv* **-ally**.

rheumatism *n* name of various

diseases attended with painful inflammation of joints and muscles; *as* **rheumatic** (*n* **r. fever** severe disease that can cause damage to heart, *esp* in children); **rheumatoid** (*n* **r. arthritis** long-term disease causing inflammation of joints).

Rh factor *see* **rhesus factor**.

rhinestone *n* fake diamond stone.

rhino *n coll* rhinoceros.

rhinoceros *n* large, thick-skinned, tropical quadruped, with one or two horns on nose.

rhinoplasty *n* plastic surgery on the nose.

rhizome *n bot* rootlike stem of plants growing underground.

rhodium *n* a white metallic element.

rhododendron *n* evergreen, flowering shrub.

rhombus *n* equilateral parallelogram with two acute and two obtuse angles; *a*, *n* **rhomboid**.

rhubarb *n* perennial garden herb, with thick pink stalks that are cooked and eaten as fruit in pies, etc.; *coll* nonsense; squabble.

rhyme, rime *n* close similarity of sound in words or final syllables, *esp* at ends of lines of verse; *idm* **with no/without rhyme or reason** without sense; *v* make rhymes.

rhythm *n* regular increase and decrease of sounds, movements; pleasant rise and fall *esp* of words, musical sounds; *ns* **r. and blues** popular music based on blues (*also* **R and B**); *a* **-ic, -ical;** *adv* **-ically.**

rib *n* one of bones curving forward from spine and enclosing thorax; curved timber or framework of boat; *n* **r. cage** structure of ribs; *v* **ribbing, ribbed.** furnish with ribs; *coll* tease.

ribald *a* coarse; irreverent; scurrilous; *n* **ribaldry** coarse, indecent joking.

ribbon *n* narrow woven strip of silk, satin, etc.; *fig* long, narrow strip.

riboflavin *n* vitamin B2, found in liver, fish, milk, green vegetables, etc.

ribosome *n* RNA-rich cytoplasmic sites of protein synthesis.

Richter scale *n* scale measuring intensity of seismic activity.

rice *n* grain from grass grown on marshy or flooded ground in tropical climates; seeds of this plant used as food; *n* **r. paper** edible paper used for packing candy, etc.

rich *n* **1** wealthy **2** abundant **3** costly **4** (*of food*) very fatty, sweet, or highly seasoned **5** (*of colors, sound*) full, deep intense; *idm* **that's rich 1** amusing **2** ridiculous; *n* **the r.** wealthy people; *n pl* **riches** wealth; abundance.

rickets *n* deficiency disease of children, marked by deformation of bones; *a* **rickety** suffering from rickets; shaky, tottering.

rickshaw *n* light, two-wheeled, Oriental carriage powered by a person.

ricochet *v* rebound off flat surface; *n* such a movement.

ricotta *n* soft, bland Italian cheese from cow's or sheep's milk.

rid *v* **ridding, ridded.** free, deliver from; clear away; *pt and pp* **rid;** *idm* **be rid of** be free of; *idm* **get rid of** dispose of; *phr v* **rid someone of something** set someone free of something; *n* **riddance** act of getting rid; **good r.** welcome relief from unwelcome, unwanted person or thing.

riddle[1] *n* **1** enigma **2** puzzling question *esp* with pun **3** puzzling thing or person.

riddle[2] *n* large meshed sieve; *v* sift by means of riddle; make many holes in; *phr v* **riddle with 1** pierce with many holes **2** filled with (negative feelings.).

ride *v* **1** go on horseback **2** travel in, be carried by any vehicle **3** (*of ship*) float, lie at anchor; (*pt* **rode;** *pp* **ridden**) *idm* **let things ride** take no action; *idm* **ride high** enjoy success; *idm* **ride roughshod over** treat harshly, with contempt or without sensitivity; *idm* **riding for a**

fall likely to meet with disaster; *phr vs* **ride out** manage to survive; **ride up** (of clothing) work its way up, out of place; *n* **1** journey by vehicle, on horse, or other animal **2** apparatus in fairground for carrying people, *esp* with quick or violent motion **3** session on one of these; *idm* **go along for the ride** be a spectator, not a participant; *idm* **take someone for a ride** cheat someone; *n* **rider 1** one who rides **2** supplementary clause to document or verdict; *as* **riderless; riding** used for riding.

ridge *n* **1** long raised strip **2** elongated summit of mountain, etc. **3** line where two slopes of roof meet **4** elevated part between furrows; *v* form ridges.

ridiculous *a* absurd; preposterous; foolish; *v* **ridicule** make fun of; deride; *n* mockery; derision.

Riesling *n Ger* medium-dry white wine from Germany.

rife *a* prevalent; frequent; common.

riff *n* (in jazz) repeated phrase.

riffle *v* shuffle (cards) by releasing cards from two halves of pack against pressure of thumbs; *phr v* **riffle through** turn pages of (book, etc.) rapidly.

riffraff *n* rabble.

rifle *v* **1** search and rob **2** furnish gun barrel with spiral grooves; *n* type of firearm; *n* **rifling** spiral grooves in gun barrel; plundering.

rift *n* **1** opening; crack; split **2** *fig* serious disagreement between friends, colleagues, etc. *n* **r. valley** steep-sided valley formed by land subsidence.

rig[1] *v* (of ship) equip with spars, ropes, etc.; *phr vs* **rig out** equip with clothes (*n* **r. -out**); **rig up** arrange hastily, *esp* in makeshift way; *n* way ship's masts and sails are arranged; style of dress; *n* **rigging** complete system of ship's ropes, sails, spars, etc.

rig[2] *v* **rigging, rigged.** manipulate dishonestly; arrange by underhand means; *n* dishonest dealing (also **rigging**).

right *a* **1** morally good; just **2** correct **3** on side of body opposite to heart **4** in a healthy state frame of mind **5** proper **6** *coll* absolute; *v* **1** put right **2** set straight or upright; *n* **1** moral goodness; justice **2** moral claim **3** *esp pl* what one is entitled to by law **4** right side **5** political parties opposed to socialism; *idm* **by rights** according to justice; *idm* **within one's rights** with legal justification; *idm* **in one's own right** by one's own authority; *idm* **in the right** morally justified; *ns* **r. angle** *geom* angle of 90°; **r. of way**

1 (right to use) road or path over private land **2** priority over vehicles coming from other directions; *as* **righteous 1** morally good **2** justifiable (*adv* **-ly;** *n* **-ness**); **r.-hand** on the right (*n* **r.- hand man, woman** valued helper); **r.-handed** using the right hand (*n* **rightie** person doing this); **rightist** *polit* of the right (*n* such a person); **r.-minded** with sound principles, views; *adv* **1** toward the right side **2** directly **3** completely **4** correctly **5** certainly; *idm* **right away** immediately; *v* **1** put right **2** set straight; restore to correct position; *adv* **-ly** *n* **-ness**.

rigid *a* **1** stiff; inflexible **2** stern; severe; *adv* **-ly;** *n* **-ity.**

rigmarole *n* long, rambling, incoherent string of words *idm* red tape, bureaucracy.

rigor[1] *n* shivering, with sense of chill; **r. mortis** stiffening of body after death.

rigor[2] *n* severity; inflexibility; austerity; harshness; *a* **rigorous.**

rile *v* make angry; annoy; irritate.

rill *n* small brook.

rim *n* **1** edge; margin; brim **2** outer part of wheel.

rime *n* hoarfrost; crust of snow; *a* **rimy.**

rind *n* **1** peel; bark; crust **2** tough outer layer of orange, cheese, etc.

ring[1] *n* **1** line enclosing round

space **2** flat circular object with large hole in middle **3** hoop of gold, silver, etc. worn on finger **4** area within roped square for boxing, etc. **5** coil; *v* put ring around; put identifying ring or tag on (bird's leg, etc.); *idm* **run rings around somebody** *coll* do things much more efficiently than somebody; *ns* **three-r. binder** binder with metal rings for loose sheets of paper; **r.-leader** leader of group of wrongdoers; **ringlet** loosely hanging curl of hair; **r.master** director of circus performance; **r.-pull** metal ring for opening can; **r.side** area close to boxing ring (*idm* **have a ringside seat** have good view of action); **r.worm** disease causing red patches on skin.

ring² **v 1** cause (bell) to sound **2** (of bell) sound **3** be filled with (ringing) sound; *pt* **rang;** *pp* **rung;** *n* sound of ringing; telephone call; *idm* **ring a bell** remind somebody of something; **ring out** resound loudly; **ring up 1** record (prices) on cash register **2** call by phone **3** raise (curtain in theater); *n* **ringer 1** one who rings, *usu* a bell **2** *coll* one who closely resembles another person.

ring-around-the-rosy *n* a children's circle game featuring a distinctive chant.

ringlet *n* a curl, *esp* of hair.

ringtoss *n* a game in which a ring-shaped disk is thrown onto an upright.

rink *n* **1** sheet of ice for skating or hockey **2** floor for roller skating **3** one of divisions of bowling green.

rinky-dink *a* piddly, poorly constructed.

rinse *v* wash in clean water; *n* act of rinsing; hair dye.

riot *n* **1** disturbance of public peace; tumult **2** *fig* unrestrained profusion; *idm* **run riot** get out of control; *v* take part in riot; *ns* **r. police; rioter; rioting;** *a* **riotous** wild and disorderly (*adv* **-ly** *n* **-ness**).

RIP *abbr Lat requiescat in pace* (rest in peace).

rip *v* **ripping, ripped.** cut; slit; slash, tear with violence; *n* rent, tear; *idm* **let something rip** *coll* take away all restraints; *phr v* **rip off 1** tear off **2** *coll* defraud by overcharging (*n* **r.-off**) **3** *sl* steal; *a* **r.-roaring 1** wild and noisy (*of success*) **2** resounding; *ns* **ripcord** cord to open parachute; **riptide** tide causing violent currents.

ripe *a* **1** ready to harvest as food, etc. **2** fully mature, developed **3** ready for specific use; *v* **ripen** grow, become ripe; mature.

riposte *n Fr* **1** quick return lunge or thrust in fencing **2** *fig* quick retort.

ripple *v* form, flow in, small slight waves; *n* **1** slight wave **2** light, soft sound **3** ruffling of surface.

ripsaw *n* handsaw with coarse, narrow-set teeth.

Rip Van Winkle *n* from Washington Irving, a man who sleeps for 20 years and awakes to discover many changes.

rise *v* **1** ascend; stand up; get up **2** increase in value, price **3** appear above horizon (of sun, moon, etc.); *pt* **rose;** *pp* **risen;** *idm* **rise to the occasion** show oneself capable of success when challenged; *n* **1** increase **2** move toward situation of greater power **3** slope upward; *idm* **give rise to** lead to; *n* **riser** upright face of step, between two treads; person or thing that rises; *n* **rising** uprising; revolt.

risible *a* causing jeering laughter.

risk *n* **1** possibility, likelihood of danger **2** amount covered by insurance; *idm* **at risk** exposed to danger; *idm* **at one's own risk** agreeing to bear the cost of any loss or damage; *v* **1** expose to danger **2** hazard **3** accept the possibility of; *a* **risky** hazardous; *adv* **-ily;** *n* **-iness.**

risotto *n* dish of slowly cooked rice with meat, vegetables, etc.

risqué *a Fr* verging on, tending toward impropriety.

rite *n* solemn act *usu* religious ceremony; *n* **r. of passage** ceremony in some societies marking stage of change (*e.g.,* puberty); *a* **ritual** of rites; *n* system of religious or magical ceremonies; book of prescribed ceremonies; *n* **ritualism** practice of, and insistence on, ritual.

ritzy *a coll* glamorous.

rival *n* one who competes against another for success, favor, etc.; *v* **rivaling, rivaled.** vie with, equal, be comparable to; *n* **rivalry** close approach to equality in merit, etc.; *a* arid competition.

rive *v* split, tear apart; *pt* **rived;** *pp* **riven.**

river *n* large body of water flowing in natural channel to sea; plentiful flow.

rivet *n* bolt or pin for fastening metal plates; *v* **1** fasten with rivets **2** *fig* hold attention of; *n* **riveter;** *a* **riveting** *coll* compelling.

riviera *n* stretch of coast with fashionable resorts.

rivulet *n* small stream, brook.

RNA *abbr chem* ribonucleic acid (acid carrying genetic information in cells).

roach *n* **1** *coll* cockroach **2** *sl* butt of marijuana cigarette.

road *n* **1** track with surface prepared for use by vehicles, *esp* as means of communication between places; highway **2** direction; route **3** *fig* mode, line of action by which aim is attained; *ns* **r.block** barricade across road; **r. hog** reckless or selfish driver; **r.-house**

roadside inn; **roadie** organizer of tour for pop group; **r.-side safety** prevention of road accidents; **r. sense** awareness of dangers on roads and how to avoid accidents; **r. show** entertainment by company on tour; **roadster** open sports car; **roadway** part of road between pavements; **r.- works** (site of) repair or building of road; *a* **roadworthy** in safe enough condition to be driven; *n* **-iness.**

roadrunner *n* a bird of the cuckoo family, native to Mexico and the southwestern US.

roam *v* wander; ramble aimlessly.

roan *n, a* (horse, dog) of bay, sorrel, chestnut mingled with white, gray; of mixed reddish color.

roar *n* loud, deep, resonant sound; bellow; burst of laughter; *v* make such sound.

roast *v* **1** cook in hot oven, bake **2** make, be very hot; *n* roasted meat, chicken, etc.; *n* animal, bird suitable for roasting.

rob *v* **robbing, robbed.** steal; plunder; deprive of unlawfully; *ns* **robber; robbery.**

robber baron *n* a capitalist who makes money through exploitation.

robe *n* long, loose outer garment; (*esp* in *pl*) official,

ceremonial dress; *v* dress; put on robe.

robin *n* small, brown songbird with red breast.

robot *n* **1** automaton man **2** *fig* one who works mechanically with unthinking efficiency *n* **robotics** use of robots in industry.

robust *a* strong; sound; healthy; vigorous; *n* **robustness.**

rock[1] *n* **1** mass of hard mineral matter **2** crag; boulder **3** hard candy; *idm* **on the rocks 1** (*of drink*) with ice cubes **2** (*of marriage etc*) likely to fail *ns* **r. bottom** the lowest point; **r. crystal** pure natural quartz; **r. salt** common salt mined in crystal form; *n* **rockery** mound of earth and rocks, where rock plants are grown; *a* **rocky** full of, made of rocks.

rock[2] *v* sway, move from side to side; shake violently; *idm* **rock the boat** *coll* upset finely balanced situation; *ns* **r. music** rhythmic type of popular music; **r. and roll** early form of rock music; **rocker** curved base of rocking chair, of object that rocks; *idm* **off one's rocker** *coll* insane; **rocking chair** chair with rockers; **rocking horse** wooden horse mounted on rockers as child's toy; *a* **rocky** unsteady.

rockabilly *n* music that features a blend of rock and country.

rocket n 1 projectile driven through space by explosion produced in it 2 large jet-powered missile 3 explosive firework, used for signaling, display, or carrying life-line 4 *coll* reprimand; v 1 rise straight upward 2 *fig* increase sharply (in price, etc.).

rococo a (of furniture, architecture) florid; flamboyantly ornamented in style of 17th and 18th century; n this style.

rod n slender piece of wood; long, light, pole of metal, wood, etc.; wand; cane.

rode *pt of* ride.

rodent a gnawing; n gnawing animal, as rat, rabbit.

rodeo n rounding-up of cattle on ranch; display of skill in rounding up cattle and horsemanship.

roe¹ n small species of deer.

roe² n mass of fish eggs.

roebuck n male roedeer.

Rogation days n three harvest days preceding Ascension Day.

roger *interj* (message) received.

rogue n 1 scoundrel; rascal; criminal; dishonest person 2 mischievous child or person; n rogues' gallery set of pictures of criminals or villains; a roguish arch; mischievous; n roguery.

roister v swagger or carouse; n roisterer.

role n part played by actor; specific function or action *ns* r. model mentor; person

representing ideal to be imitated r.-playing taking part in imaginary situation for practice.

roll v 1 move around and around; turn like wheel 2 (*of ship*) wallow 3 form into ball or cylinder 4 pass roller over something to flatten it 5 wrap around on itself; *phr vs* roll in arrive in large numbers; roll on (*of time*) pass by; roll out 1 unroll 2 (*of pastry*) spread out flat 3 *fig* introduce new product; roll up *coll* arrive; n 1 packet, bundle formed by folding into cylindrical shape 2 small rounded loaf, bun, bread 3 cylindrical mass 4 list of names 5 swaying motion; *ns* r. call calling of names to check absentees; roller 1 long powerful sea wave 2 cylindrical object for smoothing, flattening (*ns* r. coaster amusement park ride with track that rises and falls, twists, and turns sharply; r. skate skate on wheels (v ride on this); r. towel towel in one continuous loop on roller; (a rolling; r. pin cyclindrical object for flattening pastry; *fig* r. stone person with no fixed home, no responsibilities).

rollicking a jolly.

roly-poly a *coll* fat and round.

ROM *abbr comput* read-only memory.

romaine n type of lettuce.

Roman a of Rome; *ns* R.

candle firework that shoots colored balls of flame; R. Catholic member of branch of Christian church headed by the Pope; R. numeral any of the symbols used by Ancient Romans as numbers.

romance n 1 sentimental, adventurous novel 2 happy love affair 3 medieval tale of chivalry 4 glamorous charm, atmosphere; v seduce; invent fanciful stories; exaggerate.

Romance a (of language) derived from Latin.

Romanesque a of architectural style developed from 9th century AD, using rounded arches.

Romansh, Romansch n language spoken in E Switzerland.

romantic a 1 connected with romance 2 (*of literature, etc.*) seeking to rouse personal feelings, expressing sentiment and imaginative episodes, etc. 3 glamorous 4 emotional; n -ism (in literature and art) emphasis on feelings rather than objective realism; v -ize make seem more romantic than in reality.

Romeo n 1 romantic male lover 2 hero of Shakespearean tragedy Romeo and Juliet.

romp v play noisily; *idm* romp home win easily; *phr v* romp through finish easily; n wild, noisy game.

romper n one-piece garment

for baby or small child.

rondo n musical composition with principal theme repeated after each subordinate one.

Roentgen rays n pl X-rays.

rood n crucifix esp one over junction of nave and choir.

roof n -fs outer covering over top of building; **roof of mouth** palate; v put roof on; idm **raise the roof** express loud indignation; ns **r. garden** garden on flat roof; **r. rack** luggage rack on roof of car.

rook¹ n bird of crow family; v cheat, swindle; n **rookery 1** colony of rooks **2** fig crowded tenement building.

rook² n castle piece in chess.

rookie n newly recruited soldier, policeperson, ball player, etc.

room n **1** space **2** separate apartment in a building **3** scope; opportunity; n **r. service** serving of food, drink, etc. in hotel room; n pl **-s** lodgings; a **roomy** large, spacious.

roost n perch for birds at night; v sleep on perch; n **rooster** male chicken.

root n **1** source; origin **2** downward-growing part of plant **3** essential element **4** basic element of word **5** factor of quantity which gives that quantity when multiplied by itself; v implant roots firmly; be firmly established, esp by development of roots; phr vs

root for support enthusiastically; **root out** get rid of; n **r. beer** sweet fizzy drink flavored with roots and herbs; n pl **roots** (one's sense of belonging to) one's place of upbringing; a **rootless** (n - **ness**).

root canal n root part of cavity of tooth; procedure to fill, cover this.

rope n thick cord; idm **give somebody plenty of rope** give somebody freedom of action; idm **know the ropes** have previous experience; v tie with rope; phr vs **rope in 1** bind with rope **2** persuade to take part; **rope off** separate by ropes.

Roquefort n [TM] pungent, blue French cheese of goats' and ewes' milk.

Rorschach test n psyc test based on interpretation of random shapes made by inkblots on paper.

rose n **1** any of genus Rosa; flower of this **2** perforated nozzle **3** pinkish color **4** method of cutting gems; idm **a bed of roses** easy and comfortable; idm **not all roses** not all easy and straightforward; n **rosary 1** rose garden **2** string of beads used by Roman Catholics to count prayers; a **roseate** rose-colored; ns **rosette** rose-shaped bunch of ribbon, etc.; **rosewood** dark-colored fragrant wood used in cabinetmaking; a **rosy 1**

pink; flushed **2** fig favorable; optimistic.

rosemary n evergreen fragrant flowering bush used as herb in cooking, etc.

Rosh Hashana n Jewish New Year.

Rosicrucian n follower of a religious movement focusing on psychic enlightenment.

rosin n distillation of turpentine from pine resin.

roster n list showing rotation of duty, etc.; list of names.

rostrum n platform; pulpit.

rot v rotting, rotted. decompose naturally; n **1** decay **2** fungus disease of timber, plants etc; **3** coll nonsense; a **rotten 4** decomposed **5** coll deplorably bad **6** unwell.

rota n roster; round of duties; tribunal in Catholic Church.

rotary a turning like wheel; v **rotate** revolve around axis; follow regular succession; n **rotation** act of rotating; recurrence; a **rotatory**; ns **Rotary Club** one of international association of business clubs; **Rotarian** member of such; **rotary engine** one turning like wheel.

rote n by rote by heart, from memory.

rotgut n coll cheap strong alcohol.

rotisserie n turning device for roasting meat.

rotor n rotating part of machine, esp of helicopter.

a b c d e f g h i j k l m n o p q **r** s t u v w x y z

A
B
C
D
E
F
G
H
I
J
K
L
M
N
O
P
Q
R
S
T
U
V
W
X
Y
Z

rototiller n rotary cultivator used to lift and turn soil

Rottweiler n large powerful breed of guard dog.

rotund a round; plump; ns **-ity; rotunda** circular building.

rouè n dissolute man.

rouge n 1 red cosmetic used to color cheeks and lips 2 silver polish; v color with rouge.

rough a 1 uneven; not smooth (**r. surface**) 2 stormy; violent (**r. sea; r. weather**) 3 boisterous (**r. play**) 4 unrefined (**r. appearance; r. manners; r. diet**) 5 not precise (**r. calculation; r. estimate; r. figure**) 6 unfair; harsh (**r. justice**); idm **rough and ready** simple; without refinement; adv without comfort or amenities (**live/sleep r.**); n golf areas with unmown grass; idm **rough it** live simple life without comforts; ns **r. -and-tumble** boisterous play or fighting; **diamond in the rough** kind but unrefined person; **roughhouse** brawl; **roughneck** 1 rowdy person 2 oil rig worker; a **r. -hewn** (of wood, stone) cut roughly; v **roughen** make rough; adv **roughly** approximately; n **-ness**.

roughage n coarse fibrous material in food.

roulette n Fr game of chance, played with revolving wheel and ball.

round a 1 spherical; circular; curved 4 approximate 3 plump 4 blunt; outspoken; n 1 circle 2 thing round in shape 3 fixed circuit 4 type of song 5 single shot from rifle 6 series of actions, duties, etc. 7 game (of golf) 8 single bout (in boxing, etc.); ns **r. trip** journey to a place and back; adv converging on central point 2 to a variety of places 3 to a place nearby; v 1 turn, as corner; phr vs **round down** reduce to nearest whole unit or number; **round off** finish; **round up 1** increase to nearest whole number or unit 2 gather together; n **-ness**.

roundabout n 1 merry-go-round 2 (at road junctions) raised circular area around which traffic must follow specified direction; a indirect.

roundelay n song with refrain.

rounders n European children's game similar to baseball.

rouse v wake up; cause to rise; stimulate; excite to action.

roustabout n heavy laborer.

rout n 1 rabble; mob 2 overwhelming defeat; v defeat, put to flight; drag out by force.

route n road; way; mil order to march; n **r. march** long march as part of military training (also v).

routine n customary actions; regular procedure; boringly automatic procedure.

roux n Fr blend of melted fat, flour as base for sauce, gravy, etc.

rove v wander at random; ns **rover** one who wanders.

row¹ n number of things or persons in straight line.

row² v propel (boat) by oars; transport by rowing; n act of rowing; trip in rowing boat.

row³ n disturbance; dispute; quarrel; v quarrel; brawl.

rowboat n a boat designed for rowing.

rowdy a disorderly; noisy; rough; n hooligan.

rowing machine n a piece of exercise equipment that simulates the action of rowing.

rowlock n forked support in boat serving as leverage for oar.

royal a pertaining to, patronized by, king or queen; majestic; n member of the royal family; adv - ly, ns **r. blue** deep rich blue color; **r. jelly** substance with which worker bees nourish queen bee; ns **royalist** supporter of monarchy; **royalty 1** state of being royal 2 royal persons collectively 3 percentage paid to author by publisher 4 payment to owner of land for right to its use 5 or to inventor for use of invention.

rpm abbr revolutions per minute.

repetitive strain or **stress injury** n muscle injury

caused by repetitive work, *esp* keyboarding.

RSI *abbr* repetitive strain injury.

RSVP *abbr Fr répondez s'il vous plaît* (please reply).

rub *v* **rubbing, rubbed. 1** apply friction to **2** abrade, make sore **3** become frayed, worn by friction; *idm* **rub it in** keep referring to fact that causes embarrassment to someone's; *idm* **rub salt in the wound** add further to someone's suffering; *idm* **rub shoulders with** *coll* meet (famous person) socially as if on equal terms; *idm* **rub the wrong way** *coll* cause offense to; *phr vs* **rub down 1** dry by rubbing **2** smooth by rubbing; **rub off** remove, be removed from surface by rubbing; **rub off on** have influence on (through example); *n* **rubbing** impression of relief picture made by laying paper over and rubbing with crayon or charcoal.

rubber[1] *n* **1** elastic substance from sap of rubber tree **2** *coll* condom; *ns* **r. band** loop of rubber for keeping things bundled together (*also* **elastic band**); **r. check** *coll* check that "bounces" (*i.e.*, is refused by bank through lack of money in account); **rubberneck** *coll* **1** tourist **2** inquisitive person; **r. plant** houseplant with large thick leaves; **r. stamp** stamp with

lettering or figures for printing (*v fig* give official approval without questioning anything); *a* **rubbery**.

rubber[2] *n* series of odd number of games; two out of three games won.

rubbish *n* **1** garbage, waste material **2** nonsense; *v coll* discredit; *a* **-y** valueless.

rubble *n* **1** broken, crushed pieces of stone **2** builders' trash.

rubella *n* German measles.

Rubenesque *a* suggestive of the work of the painter Peter Paul Rubens, *esp* pleasingly plump.

rubicund *a* reddish; ruddy.

ruble, rouble *n* Russian coin.

rubric *n* **1** authoritative rule **2** instruction, chapter-heading printed or written distinctively *esp* underlined in red **3** liturgical direction.

ruby *n* deep red, transparent, precious stone; its color; *a* of this color.

rucksack *n* bag, knapsack carried on back.

ruckus *n* rumpus.

rudder *n* steering device at stern of boat or tail of aircraft.

ruddy *a* of fresh, red color; rosy.

rude *a* **1** primitive; rough; crude **2** impolite, ill-mannered; insulting.

rudiment *n* **1** beginning; first principle **2** slight trace; vestige **3** basic elementary facts of subject; *a*

rudimentary in undeveloped, unformed state; vestigial.

rue[1] *n* small, perennial herb with bitter leaves.

rue[2] *v* grieve for; regret; repent of; *a* **rueful** sorry; dejected.

ruff[1] *n* **1** starched frilled collar **2** bird allied to sandpiper *fem* **reeve;** *n* **ruffle** gathered or pleated frill; *v* **1** make uneven, untidy **2** upset; disconcert.

ruff[2] *v* trump at cards; *n* act of trumping.

ruffian *n* rough, violent, lawless person; bully.

rug *n* thick, woolen wrap; coverlet; floor covering *esp* with long pile; *idm* toupee.

rugby *n* English form of football, played with oval ball that may be carried in hands; *also coll* **rugger**.

rugged *a* **1** rough and rocky **2** robust and strong.

ruin *n* state of decay, collapse; destruction; cause of ruin; *pl* **-s** remains of buildings, etc.; *v* **1** reduce to ruins; spoil **2** impoverish; *n* **-ation;** *a* **-ous** tending to cause financial ruin; wasteful; likely to cause destruction.

rule *n* **1** principle, line of conduct **2** government **3** *pl* **-s** regulations of society, game, etc. **4** custom **5** graduated metal or wooden bar for measuring; *idm* **as a rule** normally; *v* **1** govern; give judicial decision **2** draw straight lines; *idm* **rule the**

roost be in charge; *phr v* **rule out 1** regard as impossible **2** render impossible; *n* **r. of thumb** rough type of calculation; *ns* **ruler 1** governor; sovereign **2** instrument of wood, etc., for measuring or drawing straight lines; **ruling** official decision or pronouncement

rum *n* **1** alcoholic spirit distilled from sugar cane **2** general term for liquor (as **demon r.**).

rumba, rhumba *n* dance of Cuban origin; the rhythm of this music.

rumble *v* make low, continuous, rolling noise, as of thunder, or heavy cart, etc.

ruminate *v* chew cud; *fig* mediate, think deeply over, *ns* **-ation** act of chewing cud; *fig* deep thought; **ruminant** animal that chews cud; *a* thoughtful.

rummage *v* grope about; turn over roughly; search thoroughly; *n* **rummage sale** sale of secondhand, cast-off goods at bargain prices.

rummy *n* **1** card game **2** a lush, a drunk.

rumor *n* gossip; hearsay; story; statement without basis.

rump *n* **1** buttocks **2** *fig* last, inferior part.

rumple *v* crease; wrinkle; crush.

rumpus *n* noisy disturbance; confusion.

run *v* **1** travel on foot, more swiftly than walking; flee; compete in race **2** flow **3** melt **4** manage; *pt* **ran**; *phr vs* **run across** meet by chance; **run down 1** knock down with vehicle **2** pursue and catch **3** (of clockwork) lose power and slow down **4** criticize in negative way; **run into** meet by chance; **run off** print or photocopy (multiple copies); **run out 1** leave abruptly **2** (of supply) be used up; **run out of** have none left; **run out on** desert; **run over 1** overflow **2** knock down with vehicle; **run through 1** repeat for practice **2** check over **3** pierce with sword; **run up 1** raise **2** make quickly **3** incur; accumulate (debt); **run up against** be confronted by; *n* **1** act of running **2** continuous sequence **3** animal enclosure **4** unit of score in baseball; *idm* **on the run** trying to escape, *esp* from justice; *idm* **have a run for one's money 1** have satisfaction for what one has paid **2** be in a competitive situation; *ns* **r. -around** *sl* evasive behavior; **runaway** a minor child who has left home; **r.down** *coll* brief report; **r.-in** *coll* **1** time leading to event **2** quarrel; **r.-through 1** review **2** rehearsal; **r.-up** period leading to event; **runway** strip of ground for landing and take-off of aircraft; *as* **runaway 1** having escaped **2**

out of control; **run-down 1** dilapidated **2** in poor health; **runny 1** more liquid than usual **2** producing mucus.

run-in *n* confrontation; quarrel.

runner *n* **1** person who runs **2** smooth or tubular plate making movement of sled, etc., more efficient **3** narrow carpet for stairs, hall, etc. **4** long, fast-growing shoot of plant **5** smuggler; *ns* **r. bean** bean with long edible pod; **r. -up** next one after the winner(s) of contest,

running *n* **1** act or sport of running **2** operation or management of something; *idm* **in/out of the running** having some chance/no chance of success; *a* **1** flowing (**r. water**) **2** continuous (**r. commentary**) **3** performed while running (**r. jump**; *idm* **take a running jump** *coll* blunt expression of refusal to unacceptable proposal) **4** exuding pus (**r. sore**) **5** incurred in operations (**r. costs**); *idm* **in running order** working properly; *adv* in succession; *ns* **r. mate** *polit* partner with whom one hopes to be jointly elected for office; **r. total** total that is continually revised as each new item is added.

rune *n* angular character of Teutonic alphabet; magic sign.

rung[1] *n* crossbar of ladder or

chair.

rung[2] *pt of* **ring.**

runnel *n* gutter; small rivulet.

runt *n* **1** weakest animal *usu* lastborn of litter **2** *sl* small disagreeable person.

rupee *n* Indian coin.

rupture *n* **1** breaking; split **2** hernia; *v* **1** burst; break **2** produce hernia.

rural *a* of country; rustic.

ruse *n* stratagem; trick.

rush[1] *n* aquatic herb, stems of which are used for basket-making etc.

rush[2] *v* move with violent rapidity; take by storm; enter hastily; *n* impetuous forward movement; sudden increase; eagerness to obtain; *n* **r. hour** busiest time of day for commuting, etc.

rushes *n pl cinema* first printing of film.

rusk *n* piece of crisp baked bread or cookie.

russet *a* of reddish brown; *n* this color; homespun fabric; kind of apple.

Russian *n* **1** language of Russia **2** person whose native language is this; *a* of Russia, its culture, people or language; **R. roulette** dangerous game of chance where player fires revolver containing bullet in only one chamber at his own head.

Russo- *prefix* of Russia.

rust *n* **1** reddish brown coating produced on iron, etc. by oxidation **2** disease of plants, caused by fungus.

rustic *a* of country life or people; rural; unsophisticated; *n* **rusticity;** *v* **rusticate** live country life; *n* **rustication.**

rustle *v* **1** emit soft, whispering sound as of dry leaves **2** steal cattle (*n* **rustler**); *phr v* **rustle up** provide *esp* at short notice.

rut *n* wheel track; groove; *idm* **in a rut** leading a boring, meaningless existence; *a* **rutted** full of ruts.

rutabaga *n* yellow turnip.

ruthless *a* pitiless; merciless; cruel.

RV *abbr* recreational vehicle.

rye *n* cereal plant, grain used for fodder and bread; **rye whisky** distilled from rye grains; *n* **rye grass** grass grown for fodder.

A B C D E F G H I J K L M N O P Q R S T U V W X Y Z

Sabbath *n* day of rest and worship, observed by Jews on Saturday and most Christians on Sunday; *ns* **Sabbatarian** strict observer of Sunday; **sabbatical year** one allowed to some university teachers, clergy, as working holiday; *a* **sabbatical** of or like Sabbath.

saber *n* curved cavalry sword; *n* **s.-rattling** trying to intimidate by threat of attack.

sable *n* small Arctic carnivore with valuable dark brown fur; *a* black; dark, gloomy.

sabot *n* **1** wooden shoe, *usu* with strap, worn in Europe **2** missile-carrier in gun barrel, tube that prevents gaseous escape.

sabotage *n* deliberate damage to industrial plant, materials, etc., by strikers or spies; *n* **saboteur**.

sac *n* membraneous pouch in animal or vegetable body.

saccharine *n* very sweet white substance from coal tar; *a fig* too sweet, sentimental.

sacerdotal *a* priestly.

sachet *n* small soft bag for holding handkerchiefs, dried flowers scented powder, etc.

sack[1] *n* **1** large rectangular bag of strong, coarse fabric **2** loose waistless dress **3** base in baseball; *ns* **sackcloth** coarse cloth for making sacks (**s. and ashes** sign of mourning or repentance).

sack[2] *v* destroy (city) in war; *n* act of doing this.

sack[3] *n* dry, white wine.

sacrament *n* **1** one of solemn religious ceremonies of Christian Church *esp* Eucharist **2** any sacred, solemn obligation **3** *cap* bread and wine taken at Catholic Communion.

sacred *a* holy, dedicated to God, a god; set apart; inviolable *n* **s. cow** person or thing felt to be beyond criticism; *n* **-ness**.

sacrifice *n* **1** making offering to God or deity **2** thing offered **3** giving up (something valued) for sake of someone else; *v* offer as sacrifice; give up (something valued); *a* **-ficial**.

sacrilege *n* violation of something sacred; *a* **sacrilegious** profane.

sacristan *n* sexton.

sacristy *n* room in church for keeping ceremonial objects.

sacroiliac *n* joint in lower back.

sacrosanct *a* protected from harm or change by being sacred or very important.

sacrum *n anat* bone at lower end of spine, formed of five fused vertebrae in humans.

sad *a* sorrowful; mournful; lamentable; *v* **sadden** made sad; *n* **sadness**.

saddle *n* **1** rider's seat on horse, bicycle, etc. **2** part of animal's back **3** pass connecting mountain ridges **4** rear part of animal as a roast, including back and both loins; *idm* **in the saddle** in control; *v* put saddle on (horse, etc.); *phr v* **saddle with** burden with (duty, responsibility).

saddler *n* maker of saddles; *n* **saddlery** trade; goods sold by saddler.

sadism *n* **1** perversion marked by cruelty **2** love of inflicting pain; n **sadist** (a -ic)

sadomasochism n (sexual) gratification from inflicting pain on oneself and/or others; n **-ist**.

safari n caravan and equipment for hunting or photographic expedition, *esp* in Africa; ns **s. park** large park where wild animals living in natural habitat can be observed by tourists; **s. jacket** light linen jacket with belt and breast pockets.

safe a 1 free from danger 2 not causing danger 3 not threatened; n strong metal box with lock for keeping valuable objects or documents secure; ns **s. conduct** official protection when traveling; **s.-deposit box** box for storing objects safely *esp* at a bank; **safeguard** means of protection (v protect); adv **safely.**

safe sex n sex in which steps are taken to prevent the spread of sexually transmitted diseases, esp AIDS.

safety n condition of being safe; ns **s. catch** lock to prevent gun from being fired accidentally; **s. glass** glass that does not splinter when broken; **s. match** match which can only be ignited on special material; **s. net 1** net to save people who fall from a height 2 *fig* safeguard; **s. pin 1** pin with protective guard over sharp end **2** pin to prevent premature detonation (of grenade, etc.); **s. valve 1** valve that releases pressure (in machine) if it becomes dangerously high **2** *fig* means of releasing dangerous emotion.

saffron n variety of orange-yellow crocus; dye and flavoring substance from this; a of this color.

sag v **sagging, sagged.** sink, droop downwards in middle; buckle; *fig* become low-spirited; *fig* (of prices) drop in value.

saga n ancient prose epic; long novel or series about family or group; romantic tale of adventure and heroism.

sagacious a shrewd, keenly intelligent; n **sagacity** sound judgement; quality resembling reason in lower animals.

sage a wise; serious; characterized by sagacity; n person of great wisdom.

sage n shrubby aromatic herb, used in cooking.

sagebrush n bushy plant of western US.

sago n edible starchy pith of certain Malayan palms.

sail n 1 piece of canvas, etc. arranged to catch wind, to drive ship *esp* sailing vessel **2** voyage on ship **3** various sail-like objects (*e.g.*, revolving part of windmill, etc.); *idm* **set sail** begin journey at sea; v travel across water; start sea voyage; navigate; ns

sailboard shaped board with sail for windsurfing; **sailcloth** thick canvas for making sails, tents, etc.; **sailing 1** sport of riding, racing in yacht, dinghy, etc. **2** regular voyage on water; (time of) departure for this; **sailor** member of ship's crew (**bad/good s.** person liable/not liable to be seasick.

sailfish n large fish with upright fin.

saint n 1 one recognized and venerated as holy, etc. by Christian Church 2 title of canonized person; a **sainted** venerated, regarded as saint; n **saintliness** piety, holiness of life.

sake n 1 cause 2 benefit 3 purpose; *idm* **for the sake of** in order to please, benefit, obtain.

saké n Japanese wine made from fermented rice, served warm.

salaam n ceremonial bow; Eastern mode of greeting; v make salaam.

salable, saleable a subject to or fit for sale.

salacious a lewd; lecherous; n **salacity**.

salad n 1 dish of raw or cold cooked vegetables or fruit 2 lettuce; n **s. days** age of youth and immaturity.

salamander n small amphibian.

salami n highly seasoned sausage of pork and/or beef,

a b c d e f g h i j k l m n o p q r s t u v w x y z

A
B
C
D
E
F
G
H
I
J
K
L
M
N
O
P
Q
R
S
T
U
V
W
X
Y
Z

either fresh or dried.

salary *n* fixed payment for work made at regular intervals; *a* **salaried**.

sale *n* act of selling; auction; offering of goods for sale *esp* at reduced prices; *ns* **salesperson** one engaged in selling; **salesmanship** business skill of salesman.

salient *a* projecting; prominent; *n* body of troops projecting from main line.

saline *a* consisting of, containing salt; *n* metallic, alkaline salt; *n* **salinity** saltiness.

saliva *n* fluid secreted in mouth to aid digestion; *a* **salivary**.

sallow[1] *n* species of broad-leafed willow.

sallow[2] *a* having sickly, yellow color.

sally *n* 1 quick repartée 2 sudden but brief attack; *phr v* **sallying, sallied. sally forth** set out (on campaign).

salmon *n* large edible silvery fish with pink flesh; *n* **s.-trout** sea trout.

salmonella *n* bacteria causing food poisoning.

salon *n* 1 reception room 2 private reception of people in the arts 3 annual exhibition of pictures 4 public room for specific use (*e.g.*, hairdressing, billiards, etc.).

saloon *n* 1 large reception room 2 main cabin in passenger ship 3 bar serving alcohol.

salsa *n* 1 Latin-American music of jazz, rock, and soul 2 spicy tomato, onion, pepper sauce.

salsify *n* long tapering root vegetable.

salt *n* 1 chemical substance (sodium chloride) used to season and preserve food 2 any of compounds formed by replacing hydrogen of acid, by metal 3 *fig* wit; pungency; *idm* **the salt of the earth** admirable person/people; *idm* **with a pinch of salt** with skepticism; *v* 1 flavor with salt 2 cover (roads) with salt to melt ice; *phr v* **salt away** save (money) secretly, stealthily; *ns* **old s.** sailor; **s.-cellar** small receptacle for salt at table; **s.-lick** 1 place where animals lick salt 2 block of salt for animals.

SALT *abbr* Strategic Arms Limitation Talks.

saltbox *n* wood-frame house with two stories in front, one at back, and elongated rear-sloping roof.

saltpeter *n* *chem* white powder used in making gunpowder, matches, etc.

salubrious *a* healthy; beneficial; promoting health.

salutary *a* wholesome; having good effect.

salute *v* 1 greet, acknowledge by words or customary gesture 2 perform military salute; *n* 1 greeting 2 *mil* formal gesture made by hand to superior; *n* **salutation** act of saluting, usually by spoken or written words.

salvage *n* 1 saving, rescue of ship, cargo, etc., from shipwreck, fire, etc., 2 reward for this act 3 ship, cargo, etc., so saved 4 saving goods from fire etc 5 property so rescued 6 saving and utilization of waste material; *v* save from shipwreck, fire, destruction.

salvation *n* fact or state of being saved; *n* **S. Army** Christian missionary organization.

salve *n* healing, soothing ointment.

salver *n* tray.

salvia *n* herbaceous plant of culinary, medicinal use.

salvo *n* discharge of gunfire, etc.

SAM *n* *abbr* surface-to-air missile.

Samaritan *n* inhabitant of Samaria; helpful, charitable person; *pl* **-s** organization available by telephone to help people in despair.

samba *n* dance of Brazilian origin.

same *a* 1 identical; unchanged 2 aforesaid 3 monotonous; **all the same** after all; nevertheless; *n* **sameness**.

samizdat *n* underground organization in former USSR, publishing literature that had been officially banned.

samosa *n* triangular pastry

snack filled with spicy meat or vegetables (of Indian origin).

samovar n metal urn.

sampan n light, flat-bottomed Chinese river boat.

sample n specimen, example; v test quality of; take sample; n **sampler** piece of embroidery, needlework.

samurai n hereditary warrior class in feudal Japan.

sanatorium n hospital, *esp* one for treatment of tuberculosis; *pl* **-ia** or **-iums**.

sanctify v purify from sin; regard as holy; ns **sanctity** saintliness; inviolability.

sanctimonious a making outward show of piety; *adv* **-ly** n **-ness** hypocritical piety.

sanction n 1 authorization; consent 2 measure taken to compel nation to obey international law 3 justification; v permit; allow; approve.

sanctuary n holy place; place of refuge for fugitives; n **sanctum** any private or inviolate retreat; **sanctum sanctotum** holy of holies.

sand n fine, dry, gritty substance; mass of this found on beaches and in deserts, etc.; *pl* **-s** area of sand or sandbank; ns **sandbag** sand-filled sack used in protecting wall (v **1** protect with these **2** hit with sandbag); **sandbank** shoal of sand in river or sea; **s. bar** sandbank barring estuary or harbor

mouth; **sandpaper** paper coated with abrasive material for smoothing wood, etc. (v rub with this); **sandpiper** wading bird with long thin bill; **sandstone** soft porous type of rock formed from compressed sand; v **sandblast** clean by firing jet of sand at (n **-er** machine for doing this); a **sandy** of sand or color of sand (n **-iness**).

sandal n open shoe consisting of sole secured by straps.

sandalwood n hard, yellowish sweet-scented wood of E Indian tree.

sandman n folklore figure who makes children sleepy.

sandwich n two slices of bread with meat, cheese, or other filling between them; v insert between two other things; squeeze in; ns **s. boards** pair of boards carried on front and back of person to advertise something.

sanforized [TM] a fabrics mechanically preshrunk before fabrication into clothing, etc.

sane a **1** sound in mind; mentally normal **2** sensible; rational, n **sanity**.

sang *pt of* **sing**.

sang-froid n Fr coolness; presence of mind; composure.

sangria n Spanish iced drink of red wine containing fruit juice, sodawater, etc.

sanguine a **1** ruddy; florid **2** hopeful; optimistic; a

sanguinary bloody; bloodthirsty; accompanied by bloodshed; *adv* **-ly** hopefully, confidently.

sanitarium n treatment center for invalids, convalescents.

sanitary a hygienic; having to do with health and cleanliness; n **s. napkin, s. pad** absorbent pad worn during menstruation; v **sanitize 1** make hygienic **2** *fig* censor, make less offensive; n **sanitation 1** public hygiene **2** system of drainage, disposal of sewage, ventilation and pure water supply.

sank *pt of* **sink**.

sans-culotte n Fr extremist revolutionary.

Sanskrit n ancient language of Hindus.

Santa Claus n chubby man with white beard and red clothes believed to distribute toys to children at Christmas.

sap[1] n **1** juice, fluid circulating in plant tissue **2** a fool **3** *fig* vigor; vitality; v **sapping, sapped.** *fig* weaken; drain away strength of.

sap[2] n mil covered trench; v mil construct these; undermine.

sapient a wise; shrewd; knowing; n **sapience**.

sapling n young tree.

saponaceous a containing or like soap, soapy; *fig* unctuous.

Sapphic a of Sappho, Greek poetess; kind of verse.

sapphire n deep blue

a
b
c
d
e
f
g
h
i
j
k
l
m
n
o
p
q
r
s
t
u
v
w
x
y
z

translucent precious stone.

sapsucker n type of woodpecker.

Saracen n Muslim at time of Crusades.

sarcasm n bitter, ironic remark; sneer; mocking taunt, intended to wound; a **sarcastic**.

sard n semi precious stone; variety of chalcedony.

sarcoma n type of malignant tumor.

sarcophagus n stone coffin.

sardine n small fish of herring family, usually preserved in oil; idm **packed like sardines** packed close together.

sardonic a bitter; sneering; insincere.

sardonyx n an onyx with parallel layers of red sard.

sarge n coll sergeant.

sari, saree n wrapped robe worn by women of southern Asia.

sarong n principal garment of Malay people and Pacific islanders.

sarsaparilla n species of smilax; its dried root used medicinally; flavor of birch soda.

sarsen n large block of hard sandstone, as in Stonehenge.

sartorial a pertaining to trade and work of tailor.

SASE abbr self-addressed, stamped envelope.

sash[1] n ornamental scarf worn over shoulder or around waist.

sash[2] n one of two sliding

frames holding glass of window.

sashay v 1 walk with gliding motion 2 strut, stroll in ostentatious, attention-seeking manner.

sassafras n aromatic bark of US tree.

sassy a coll 1 saucy 2 stylish.

sat pt, pp of **sit**.

SAT abbr Scholastic Aptitude Test.

Satan n the Devil; a **satanic(al)** fiendish, malignant, wicked; n **satanism** devil worship (n, a -ist).

satchel n handbag.

sate v satisfy; gratify to the full; glut, surfeit.

sateen n glossy, imitation satin, cotton fabric.

satellite n 1 planet revolving around another 2 projectile in orbit around the earth 3 hanger-on; n **s. dish** concave disk used as aerial for receiving satellite TV; **s. television** TV relayed by satellite to any part of earth.

satiate v 1 satisfy 2 dull, cloy by overindulgence; ns **satiety** feeling of having had too much; **satiation**.

satin n soft silk fabric with glossy surface; n **satinwood** fine, hard yellowish wood used in cabinet-making.

satire n 1 holding up of human follies, vices to ridicule 2 literary work of this nature 3 bitter contempt, directed against hypocrisies of society;

a **satiric(al)**; n **satirist** writer of satires; v **satirize** make object of satire.

satisfy v **satisfying, satisfied.** 1 gratify 2 suffice for 3 comply with, discharge (debt) 4 set doubts at rest; n **satisfaction**; a **satisfactory** (adv -ily).

satori n Zen ideal state of intuitive illumination.

saturate v 1 soak thoroughly 2 chem cause substance to combine completely 3 fig be steeped in, affected by; n **-ation** act, result of saturating (**s. point** stage at which greatest possible amount of something has been absorbed).

saturated fat n fat found in meat and dairy products, thought to be harmful to health in large quantities.

Saturday n seventh day of week.

Saturn n 1 Roman god 2 large planet surrounded by rings; a **saturnine** gloomy, glowering, morose; n **saturnalia** revelry; orgy.

satyr n 1 woodland deity (half beast, half man) 2 lecherous man.

sauce n 1 spiced or flavored liquid used to add to taste of food; gravy 2 coll liquor; impudence; ns **saucepan** cooking pot; **s.-boat** small vessel for serving sauce at table; a **saucy** 1 impertinent 2 (of clothes) jaunty (a -**ily**; n -**iness**).

saucer n shallow dish put

under a cup.

sauerkraut n Ger chopped raw cabbage fermented in brine.

sauna n 1 room heated with brazier to obtain hot dry atmosphere 2 period of relaxation in this, usu followed by ice-cold bath or shower 3 room, cabinet used for this.

saunter v walk slowly; stroll; n leisurely walk.

sausage n minced, seasoned meat packed into skin or thin membrane; n **s. roll** cylinder of pastry baked with sausage meat filling.

sauté a Fr lightly, quickly fried in oil, fat; n a dish thus prepared.

sauternes n light, sweet white French wine.

savage a wild; uncivilized; fierce; cruel; brutal; v bite and worry ferociously; n **savagery**.

savanna, savannah n prairie; extensive grassy treeless plain.

savant n Fr person of learning; scholar.

save v 1 rescue 2 preserve untouched for future use 3 guard against; prevent need of 4 put away (money); idm **save face** avoid embarrassment (a **face-saving**); idm **save one's neck/skin** coll escape from death or serious crisis; idm **save one's breath** not bother to say something which will be ignored; ns **-er** person who

saves money; **saving** amount saved (prep except; n **s. grace** good characteristic that compensates for all the bad ones); n pl **-s** money saved (n **s. bank**).

savior n one who saves, redeems; cap Christ.

savoir faire n ability to know how to behave in any situation.

savor n 1 taste; flavor 2 fig slight trace; v 1 have particular flavor 2 enjoy taste of; phr v **savor of** suggest presence of; a **savory** tasty; appetizing; n light tasty dish, flavor more salt than sweet; **savory** aromatic herb of mint family (summer s., winter s.).

savoy n kind of cabbage with curled leaves.

savvy v sl understand; n common sense.

saw[1] pt of **see**.

saw[2] n maxim; traditional saying.

saw[3] n tool with toothed edge, for cutting wood, etc.; v 1 cut with saw 2 fig make to and fro movement, as of sawing; pt **sawed**; pp **sawn** ns **sawdust** small particles of wood made by sawing; **s.-horse** frame to hold article being sawed; **sawmill** (factory with) machine that saws timber into planks.

sawyer n 1 one who saws, woodsman 2 kind of beetle 3 tree growing in stream bed.

Saxon n, a (member) of Germanic people settling in

Britain from 5th century AD.

saxophone n reeded brass wind instrument with many keys or valves.

say v utter, express in words; state; report; be of opinion; pt, pp **said**; idm **go without saying** be obvious; n expressed opinion; opportunity of stating it; idm **have one's say** (have chance to) express one's view; n **saying** proverb; adage; maxim.

scab n 1 dry crust that forms over wound in healing 2 skin disease 3 plant disease 4 coll worker who crosses union protests to work.

scabbard n sheath for sword or dagger.

scabies n contagious itching skin disease.

scabious n herbaceous plants having round cushionlike mauve flowers.

scabrous a 1 having rough surface 2 difficult, knotty 3 controversial 4 indecent.

scaffold n 1 temporary structure of poles and planks to support workers 2 gallows; n **-ing** collective term for planks and poles used as scaffold, esp by builders.

scalawag n rogue; scamp.

scald v 1 injure tissues with hot liquid, steam 2 heat almost to boiling point; n burn caused by hot liquid, steam, etc.

scale[1] n 1 one of hard, thin

a
b
c
d
e
f
g
h
i
j
k
l
m
n
o
p
q
r
s
t
u
v
w
x
y
z

plates covering fish, reptiles 2 any flaky mineral deposit in boilers, kettles, etc.; v 1 clear scales from 2 flake off.

scale[2] n one of two pans of balance; pl weighing machine; v be weighed.

scale[3] n mus 1 series of graduated notes, esp in octave 2 system of grading by size, rank, amount, degree, etc. 3 ratio of size; v 1 climb up; clamber up 2 increase, reduce according to fixed ratio.

scalene a (of triangle) having unequal sides.

scallion n small green onion.

scallop n edible bivalve mollusk; pl series of curves, like edge of scallop shell, used as ornamental edging; v ornament (dress) with scallops.

scalp n skin and hair on top of head; v strip, cut scalp off.

scalpel n small, slender surgical knife.

scam n coll scheme for swindling people.

scamp n rogue; rascal.

scamper v 1 run about gaily; caper 2 run off hastily.

scampi n pl dish of garlic-flavored large prawns.

scan v **scanning, scanned. 1** look closely at; examine 2 med obtain image(s) of (parts of) body with scanner 3 (of searchlight) pass across several times 4 read quickly to find certain things 5 analyze (verse) metrically 6 (of verse) have metrical pattern; n act of scanning; n **scanner** med apparatus for examining the body by producing images from many angles (ns **body s., head s.**); **scanner** comput device that absorbs graphic, text images and translates them into binary data for storage, retrieval; n **scansion** analysis of metric verse.

scandal n damaging, malicious or idle talk, act, or thing that brings disgrace on reputation; v **-lize** arouse indignation in; shock feelings of; a **-ous;** n **scandalmonger** one who spreads scandal.

scant a small, inadequate in amount; a **-y** insufficient, meager.

scapegoat n one who takes blame, or is punished, for faults of others.

scapula n shoulder blade; pl **-lae, -las;** a **scapular** of scapula; n short cloak worn by monks of certain religious orders.

scar[1] n mark left by wound, burn or sore, after healing; v **scarring, scarred.** mark, heal with scar; a **scarred.**

scar[2] n craggy, precipitous part of mountainside.

scarab n beetle.

scarce a not plentiful; rare; infrequent; uncommon; idm **make oneself scarce** hide away (to avoid trouble); adv **-ly** not quite; only just; n **scarcity** deficiency of supply; rarity.

scare v startle; frighten; n ill-founded alarm; widespread fear; n **scarecrow 1** dummy figure used to scare birds from crops 2 skinny, ragged person.

scarf n long piece of material worn around neck; loose neckerchief; pl **scarves** or **scarfs.**

scarify v **scarifying, scarified. 1** scratch, cut (skin) 2 break, loosen surface (of soil) 3 fig lacerate feelings of; ns **scarification; scarifier** agricultural implement.

scarlet n 1 brilliant, vivid red 2 cloth, clothing of this color; a of this color; ns **s. fever** infectious disease, accompanied by high temperature and red rash; **s. pimpernel** small red flower; **s. woman** prostitute.

scarp n steep slope or face below rampart or hill; escarpment.

scat[1] v coll leave quickly.

scat[2] n improvise wordless jazz singing.

scathe v criticize harshly; a **scatheless** unharmed; uninjured; a **scathing 1** damaging 2 (of remarks, comments, etc.) cutting, bitter.

scatter v 1 sprinkle; spread over 2 be dispersed 3 drive off in disorder; n **scatterbrain** flighty, thoughtless person.

scavenge v 1 feed on dead flesh of other animals 2

search among refuse for usable objects; ns **-enger, -enging**.

scavenger hunt n game where players compete to collect items on a list.

scenario n 1 written outline of action, scenes, etc. for film, play, etc. 2 imagined sequence of coming events.

scene n 1 place of action 2 background for fictional events, as in play, etc. 3 coll outburst of anger, etc. 4 view 5 subdivision of play within an act; idm **behind the scenes** 1 backstage 2 in secret; idm **make a scene** make a great fuss; have an emotional outburst; idm **on the scene** present; idm **set the scene** make everything ready; n **scenery** painted scenes in theater; landscape; woods, hills, etc. collectively as view; a **scenic** theatrical; picturesque; pertaining to natural scenery.

scent v 1 smell 2 track by smell 3 make fragrant; n 1 odor; pleasant smell 2 liquid perfume.

scepter n ornamental rod carried as symbol of sovereignty; a **sceptered** wielding royal power.

schedule n 1 written or printed list 2 tabulated statement 3 timetable; v set out, put into, form of schedule; idm **on schedule** on time; a **scheduled** 1 planned for a certain time 2 regular.

schema n diagram (pl **schemata**); a **schematic** shown by diagrammatic representation (a **-ally**); v **schematize** 1 simplify 2 organize schematically (n **-ization**).

scheme n 1 plan; design; project; enterprise 2 outline; synopsis; v 1 plan as scheme 2 plot dishonestly; intrigue; n **schemer** one who schemes, esp in bad sense.

scherzo n mus lively, playful movement or passage.

schism n division in organized body or society esp in church.

schist n type of crystalline rock.

schizophrenia n psychosis or mental disorder marked by delusions, split personality, etc.; as **schizophrenic**; **schizoid** tending towards schizophrenia.

schlock n infml inferior merchandise; a schlocky.

schmaltz n coll excessive sentimentality in art, music, etc.; a **-y**.

schmuck n coll fool, dupe.

schnapps n strong alcoholic drink.

sciatica n neuralgia in the leg; a **sciatic**.

schlepp v 1 drag, haul 2 move heavily, as burdened.

scholar n 1 learned person 2 holder of scholarship; a **-ly;** n **-liness;** n **scholarship** 1 quality of learned person 2 grant of money to scholar; a **scholastic** 1 of school,

scholars 2 academic (n **-ism**).

school[1] n 1 place of education for children 2 college, university 3 teaching establishment of specified kind (**s. of art**) 4 university department (**law s.**) 5 group of artists, composers, writers sharing common ideas, methods 6 coll experience valued for learning something (**s. of life**); idm **school of hard knocks** learning life's lessons through practical experience; **school of thought** people sharing common ideas; v train; educate; discipline (n **-ing**); ns **schoolmarm** coll domineering woman with old-fashioned ideas; **schoolmaster/-mistress/ -teacher; schoolmate** fellow pupil.

school[2] n large group of fish; group of whales or porpoises.

schooner n 1 fore-and-aft rigged vessel with two or more masts 2 large glass (for beer, etc.).

science n 1 systematized knowledge of natural or physical phenomena; investigation of this; knowledge or skill based on study, experience and practice; ns **s. fiction, scifi** stories of imaginary events set in future, esp involving space or time travel; a **scientific** based on principles and methods of science;

systematic; objective; *n* **scientist** one learned, trained in natural science.

science science *n* religious movement believing in self-awareness and reincarnation, but no supreme being.

scintillate *v* 1 sparkle; twinkle 2 *fig* be witty and brilliant in conversation; *ns* **scintilla** 1 spark 2 *fig* particle; atom; **scintillation** act of sparkling.

scion *n* slip for grafting; young member of family, descendant.

scissors *n pl* 1 cutting instrument of two blades joined together 2 style of high jumping 3 wrestling hold.

sclerosis *n med* hardening of body tissue; disease caused by this.

scoff[1] *n* taunt; expression of contempt, derision; *v* jeer at; mock.

scoff[2] *v coll* eat greedily and quickly.

scold *v* reprove angrily, noisily; find fault with; *n* one who nags, scolds habitually.

sconce *n* 1 metal bracket candlestick on wall 2 electric fixture resembling of candlestick 3 earthwork.

scone *n* small, rich round bread.

scoop *n* 1 article for ladling, dipping, or shoveling 2 tool for hollowing out 3 *sl* unexpected and profitable piece of luck 4 *journalism* exclusive news item; *v* 1 ladle, shovel out 2 hollow out 3 *sl* obtain as profit, before others.

scoot *v coll* run quickly; run away; *n* **scooter** 1 low-powered motorcycle with small wheels 2 child's toy.

scope *n* 1 range of activity 2 extent of view 3 area 4 outlet.

scorch *v* burn superficially (of plants, etc.); dry up; wither; *n* **scorched-earth policy** tactic of devastating one's own land to leave nothing for an invading army.

score *n* 1 notch, mark drawn or scratched 2 reckoning 3 number of points made in game 4 set of 20 persons, or objects 5 *pl* indefinite, large number 6 printed, written copy of orchestral music; *idm* **on that score** as far as that is concerned; *idm* **pay/settle an old score** have revenge; *v* 1 notch 2 cross out 3 record, make points in game 4 *fig* gain advantage; **score out/through** draw line through; delete; *n* **scoreboard** board showing points scored; *n* **scorer** one who keeps or makes score in game.

scorn *n* contempt; disdainful state of mind; *v* feel, show contempt of; treat with derision; *a* **-ful** full of contempt.

scorpion *n* small arachnid with venomous sting in tail and lobsterlike claws.

scot *n* tax; rate; *a* **scot-free** free from payment; unpunished; unhurt.

Scot *n* native of Scotland; *as* **Scotch** contracted form of Scottish (*n* whisky from Scotland; *ns* **S. egg** hard-boiled egg coated with sausage meat; **S. mist** very fine drizzle); **Scottish (S. highlands);** *ns* **Scotland Yard** head office of criminal investigation department in London.

scotch *v* 1 crush, render harmless 2 thwart; hinder; *n* wedge to prevent wheel, etc. from slipping.

scoundrel *n* villain; rogue.

scour *v* 1 clean, polish by friction 2 search thoroughly 3 wash away by rapid flow of water 4 get rid of; free from.

scourge *n* 1 whip; lash 2 affliction; pest; *v* 1 flog; chastise 2 oppress.

scout *n* 1 child enrolled as Boy, Girl Scout 2 soldier sent to reconnôitre 3 person sent out to look for people with talent; *ns* **s. car** armored vehicle; **scouting** activity of being a scout; **scoutmaster** leader of scout group.

scow *n* boat with flat bottom, prow, stern.

scowl *v* frown; look sullen, angry; *n* sullen, angry frown.

scrabble *v* scratch; scramble about; *n* 1 scrawl 2 *cap* [TM] word-building board game.

scrag *n* 1 skinny person 2 bony end of neck of mutton;

a **scraggy** skinny; thin; lean; *v* wring or tackle neck; hang.

scraggly *a* shaggy.

scram *v coll* go away at once.

scramble *v* 1 clamber, climb using arms and legs 2 struggle roughly with 3 cook beaten eggs until set; *n* 1 act of scrambling 2 rough hill climb in motorcycle racing 3 disorderly proceeding.

scrap *n* 1 small detached piece 2 waste material 3 *pl* odds and ends of waste food 4 *coll* fight; *v* **scrapping, scapped.** 1 break up 2 dispose of as useless; *coll* fight; *ns* **s. book** book with blank pages for pasting in press cuttings, etc.; **s. heap** pile of waste material; **s. metal** metal for melting down and re-using; **s. paper** (**scratch paper**) used paper for making notes, etc.

scrape *v* graze, abrade surface with sharp edge; clean thus; scratch *phr vs* **scrape along** 3 *coll* manage with difficulty; **scrape through** pass test with difficulty; **scrape together/up** collect or obtain with difficulty; *n* act, sound of scraping, *coll* awkward predicament; *n* **scraper** instrument for scraping.

scrapple *n* sausagelike food of corn meal, pork, and seasonings.

scratch *v* 1 leave slight mark on skin or surface with claws, or anything pointed 2 *fig* withdraw from game, competition, etc.; *idm*

scratch the surface begin dealing with (problem) without progressing far; *n* 1 wound or mark made by scratching 2 zero, par, in games scored by numerical points; *idm* **up to scratch** satisfactory; *a* arranged at short notice, impromptu.

scratchboard *n* black-coated cardboard with white clay undercoat.

scratch card *n* purchased game ticket on which surface is scratched away to reveal numbers.

scrawl *v* write, draw hastily; scribble; *n* shapeless, scribbling, handwriting, etc.

scrawny *a* thin and lean.

scream *v* utter shrill, piercing cry; laugh wildly and shrilly; *n* shriek, shrill cry.

screech *v* utter shrill harsh cry; *n* scream.

screed *n* 1 shred; strip; border 2 long tedious speech or letter; *v* tear; make a shrill or tearing noise.

screen *n* 1 structure giving shelter from heat, cold, wind, or concealing something 2 large surface on which films, photographic slides, etc. are projected 3 *comput* monitor 4 coarse sieve; *v* 1 shelter, protect with screen 2 conceal 3 project (film, etc.) 4 examine (person) for political motives 5 riddle, sift (*esp* coal) *ns* **screenplay** script for film; **s. test** test of actor's suitability for part in

film.

screw *n* 1 cylindrical piece of metal with spiral groove running around it and used as fastening 2 ship's propeller 3 action of twisting, turning; *idm* **put the screws on** use forceful method to persuade; *v* 1 fasten with screw(s) 2 *fig* extort; *phr vs* **screw off** remove by turning; **screw on** fasten by turning; **screw up** 1 twist (paper, etc.) into a ball 2 fasten with screw(s) 3 distort (one's face) in a grimace 4 *sl* handle badly (*idm* **screw up one's courage** overcome one's fears; *idm* **all screwed up** *coll* mixed up; tense and anxious), *n* **screwdriver** chisel-shaped tool with tip for turning screws.

screwball *a* 1 zany, wacky 2 eccentric comedy.

scribble *v* write carelessly, illegibly; make meaningless marks with crayon, pencil, etc.; *n* something scribbled.

scribe *n* writer; author; *v* mark with scriber; *n* **scriber** tool for marking lines on stone, etc.

scrimmage *n* scuffle; confused struggle.

scrimp *v* make small; be miserly; cut corners; *a* **scrimpy** scanty.

script *n* 1 handwriting 2 text of play, film, etc.

scripture *n* sacred writings; the Bible.

scrod *n* young codfish or

A B C D E F G H I J K L M N O P Q R **S** T U V W X Y Z

haddock.

scroll n 1 roll of parchment or paper 2 ornamental spiral or curved design.

scrooge n miserly person.

scrotum n pouch of skin containing testicles.

scrounge v sl cadge; beg; scavenge; n **scrounger** cadger.

scrub[1] n brushwood; land covered with such; a **scrubby** insignificant; undersized; inferior esp of sports team.

scrub[2] v scrubbing, scrubbed. 1 clean by hard rubbing esp with brush and water 2 sl cancel; n act of scrubbing; ns **scrubbing-brush** hard stiff brush; **scrubber** one who scrubs.

scruff n nape of neck.

scrumptious n coll delicious.

scrunch v 1 crush; crumple 2 chew noisily (n noise of this).

scruple n 1 small weight, 20 grains 2 doubt, hesitation about proposed action 3 conscientious objection; a **scrupulous** punctilious, conscientious; meticulous; n **scrupulousness**.

scrutiny n searching look; careful, official examination (of papers, etc.); v **scrutinize** examine carefully, look into closely.

scuba n self-contained breathing apparatus for divers.

scud v scudding, scudded. move quickly; n type of

missile.

scuff v scratch (shoes) by dragging feet; a **scuffed** (of shoes) roughened, scratched.

scuffle v struggle; push roughly; n confused struggle.

scull n 1 light, small oar 2 a racing shell for one or two persons using sculls; v propel, move (boat) by means of scull(s).

scullery n room near kitchen, where messy kitchen chores and cleaning of pots, etc., is done; ns **scullery-maid; scullion** ar kitchen helper.

sculpture n art of carving or chiselling stone, wood, etc. to form figures in relief or solid; example of this art; v represent by sculpture; n **sculptor** artist who models in clay, carves wood or stone figures.

scum n froth or other floating matter on liquid; waste part of anything; fig lowest, most degraded people; a **scummy**.

scurf n thin flakes of dried skin on scalp; dandruff; a **scurfy**.

scurrilous a coarsely abusive; n **scurrility**.

scurry v run; hurry; scuttle.

scurvy n disease of malnutrition, due to lack of vitamin C; a 1 mean; low; contemptible.

scuttle[1] n basket or receptacle for holding coal, garden produce, etc.

scuttle[2] v run away hurriedly; bolt.

scuttle[3] n covered hole in deck of ship, or in wall, roof etc.; v make holes in ship, to sink it.

scuttlebutt n rumor, gossip.

scythe n tool for mowing, with long curved blade set at right angles to handle; v cut with scythe; mow.

sea n 1 mass of salt water covering much of earth's surface 2 particular named area of this 3 large plane on surface of moon 4 fig large expanse of something; pl **-s** condition of sea as caused by the weather; idm **all at sea** coll confused; ns **s. anemone** sea animal with many tentacles resembling a flower; **seaboard** coastal area of country; **s.-cow** type of marine mammal; **s.-dog** experienced sailor; **seafood** fish and other edible sea creatures; **s. front** area above beach at seaside resort; **seagull** gull; **s.-horse** small fish with horselike head and prehensile tail; **s. legs** ability to walk on moving ship without being seasick; **s. lion** Pacific eared seal; **seaman** sailor, esp one with skill in handling ship; **s. mile** nautical mile; **seaplane** aircraft able to land on the sea; **seascape** picture of sea; **seasickness** nausea from motion of ship; a **seasick; seaside** coast; **s. urchin** small sea creature with prickly shell; **seaweed** any form of plant life growing in the sea;

as **seafaring** traveling by sea (n seafarer); **seaworthy** fit for a sea voyage (n **-iness**).

seal[1] n marine, amphibious fish-eating mammal with flippers; v hunt seals; ns **sealer** ship or man hunting seals; **sealskin** fur of seals.

seal[2] n 1 piece of metal, etc. with engraved design for stamping on wax 2 disk of wax thus stamped as authentication of a document or for security 3 any substance used to fill a crack or gap preventing leakage of gas, air, water, oil, etc. 4 decorative sticker, esp sold in aid of charity; idm **seal of approval** formal approval; idm **set the seal on** 1 finish 2 confirm; make certain; v 1 seal up (document) 2 shut (envelope) 3 close securely (to prevent leakage) 4 coat with protective esp waterproof substance 5 settle (agreement) 6 decide (fate); phr v **seal off** close securely to prevent entry or exit; ns **sealed unit** mechanical part that is sealed to prevent damage from outside; **sealing wax** hard-setting wax for sealing documents or letters.

seam n 1 join between two edges (of cloth, or planks) 2 thin layer; vein; stratum; v join by sewing together; mark with furrows, wrinkles; a **-less**; n **seamstress, sempstress** needlewoman; a

seamy showing rough side of life.

séance n Fr meeting of spiritualists.

sear v dry up; scorch, burn surface of; brand; a **-ing** 1 (of pain) burning 2 fig provoking strong emotion.

search v go through and examine closely; scan; reconnoitre; idm **search me** coll I don't know; idm **search one's conscience/heart** think honestly about one's motives; n act of searching; a **-ing** 1 penetrating (**s. look**) 2 severely testing (**s. question**); ns **searcher** person who searches; **searchlight** powerful beam of light for scanning area in darkness; **s. party** group of people sent to search for missing person.

season n 1 one of four divisions of the year (spring, summer, autumn, winter) 2 period of year associated with specific activity (**planting s.**), with availability of something (**tomato s.**), with more or less of something (**high/low s.**); idm **in season** 1 easily available now 2 (of animal) ready to mate 3 in the most popular vacation months 4 in the period when hunting is permitted (**open season**); idm **out of season** not in season; v 1 give extra flavor to by adding salt, pepper, spice, etc. 2 (of wood) make or become fit

for use by gradual drying out to avoid warping; ns **seasoning** flavoring added to food; **season (ticket)** ticket valid for any number of time uses within a specified period (**weekly/monthly/quarterly/annual s.**); as **seasonable** appropriate for the time of year; **seasonal** varying with the seasons (adv **-ly**); **seasoned** fig with plenty of experience.

seasonal affective disorder n abbr SAD depression related to exposure to sunlight, prevalent in fall, winter.

seat n 1 anything made to sit on 2 right to sit (as in Congress, etc.) 3 way of sitting esp when horse-riding 4 buttocks 5 locality of trouble, disease, etc.; v 1 make sit down 2 provide with seating accommodation.

sebaceous a fatty; **s. glands** sweat glands, or glands of hair follicles.

sec abbr second.

secant n reciprocal of cosine of angle.

secede v withdraw voluntarily from federation, etc.; n **secession** act of seceding.

seclude v shut up, keep apart from others; a **secluded** remote, withdrawn esp of place; n **seclusion**.

second[1] n 1 sixtieth part of one minute 2 coll brief instant of time.

second[2] det 1 2nd (ordinal

number of two); next after first (*also adv, pron*) **2** inferior; *n* **1** helper of boxer **2** second gear (of vehicle) **3** *pl* imperfect goods sold with a reduction; *as* **s. best** not as good as best; **s.-class 1** inferior in quality to first-class **2** (of travel, accommodation) standard class **3** regarded as socially inferior; **s.-hand 1** previously owned, used **2** (of information) obtained indirectly (*also adv*); **s.-rate** of inferior quality; **s.-string** *sport* as substitute for regular player; *ns* **s. childhood** dotage; **s. coming** return of Jesus Christ on Day of Judgment; **s. cousin** (child of) parent's cousin; **s. nature** something done easily through force of habit; **s. sight** ability to foresee the future or know what is happening elsewhere; **s. thought** change of opinion; **s. wind** fresh burst of energy in activity after first onset of tiredness; *v* **s.-guess** *coll* **1** make retrospective criticism of **2** forecast **3** guess better than.

second³ support (proposal or nominee for post); *n* **-er** supporter.

secondary *a* **1** following what is first or primary (**s. education, s. school**) **2** less important than primary (**s. consideration, s. motive**) **3** dependent on, caused by what is primary (**s. infection**); *adv* **-ily.**

secret *a* **1** hidden, meant to be kept from common knowledge **2** mysterious; clandestine **3** remote; secluded; *n* thing kept secret; *n* **secrecy** ability, fidelity in keeping secret; *a* **secretive** unduly reticent; furtive; *n* **secretiveness.**

secretary *n* **1** employee dealing with correspondence, records, and other confidential manners **2** head of state department; *a* **secretarial;** *n* **secretariat** body of secretaries; building occupied by secretarial staff; *n* **s.-bird** long-legged S African bird, resembling heron.

secrete *v* **1** hide, conceal **2** (*of gland, etc.*) collect and distribute material from blood as secretion; *n* **secretion** process of collecting substances from blood for use of body or expulsion as excreta; *a* **secretory** secreting.

sect *n* group holding minority views in religion; religious denomination; *a* **sectarian** characteristic of sect; *n* **sectary** member of sect.

section *n* **1** act of cutting **2** severed part **3** any separate, distinct part of anything **4** smallest military unit **5** drawing of an object cut vertically; *a* **-al.**

sectional *n* piece of furniture

made of modular, multipurpose units.

sector *n* **1** portion of circle enclosed by two radii and arc, which they cut off **2** *mil* part of fortified front or position.

secular *a* **1** worldly; not ecclesiastical **2** age-long; persistent; *v* **secularize** transfer from ecclesiastical to civil ownership or use, etc.; make secular.

secure *a* **1** free from care **2** made safe **3** firm; stable **4** certain; *v* **1** make safe **2** ensure; make certain **3** fasten, firmly **4** get hold of; *n* **security** safety; protection; safeguard; guarantee; *pl* **-s** bonds, title-deeds, stock certificates, etc.; *ns* **s. feature** device that makes theft difficult; **s. system** system of burglar alarm devices for property.

sedan *n* **1** covered chair carried on two poles **2** large closed car.

sedate *a* calm; staid, decorous; *adv* **-ly;** *n* **-ness.**

sedative *a* allaying anxiety; soothing; *n* sedative drug; *n* **sedation** act of administering sedative drug.

sedentary *a* sitting; requiring little bodily exertion.

Seder *n* ceremonial dinner at Jewish Passover.

sedge *n* coarse, perennial, grasslike plants, growing in marshy ground; *n* **s.-warbler** summer migrant bird.

A B C D E F G H I J K L M N O P Q R **S** T U V W X Y Z

sediment *n* matter that settles at bottom of liquid; dregs.

sedition *n* offense against State authority, not amounting to treason; public commotion, riot; *a* **seditious**.

seduce *v* 1 corrupt; lead astray 2 entice sexually 3 charm; entice; *n* **seduction**; *a* **seductive** alluring; attractive; persuasive.

sedulous *a* diligent; assiduous; careful; painstaking; *n* **sedulity**.

see[1] *v* 1 have power of eyesight 2 perceive with the eyes 3 look at 4 understand, comprehend 5 imagine; visualize 6 verify 7 meet 8 interview 9 spend time with 10 experience 11 bear witness to 12 consider possibility; (*pt* **saw**, *pp* **seen**); *idm* (**one must**) **be seeing things** (one must) be suffering from illusions; *idm* **see fit to** decide to; *idm* **see red** become angry; *idm* **see you (around)** *coll* goodbye for now; *idm* **see the light** reach a state of understanding; *idm* (**I'll**) **see you in court** *coll* I'll sue you; *phr vs* **see about** 1 think about 2 deal with; **see off** 1 escort to place of departure 2 chase away; **see out** 1 escort to the exit 2 endure to the end of; **see over/around** inspect (place); **see through** 1 not be deceived by 2 be sure completion of 3 help and support (in difficult

times); **see to** attend to (*idm* **see to it that** ensure that); *conj* **seeing that** because.

see[2] *n* diocese, office, jurisdiction of bishop.

seed *n* 1 fertilized reproductive germs of flowering plants; one grain of this 2 sperm, milt, etc. 3 *fig* offspring 4 seeded player; *idm* **go to seed** 1 (of plant) produce seeds 2 *fig* lose efficiency; become shabby; *v* 1 form seed 2 remove seed 3 arrange tennis or other tournament so that best players, or those of same nationality do not meet in early rounds; *n* **seedling** young plant raised from seed; *a* **seedy** 1 run to seed 2 *coll* shabby 3 *coll* out of sorts.

seek *v* **seeking, sought.** search for; want.

seem *v* look like; give one impression; appear to be; *as* **-ing** ostensible; apparent; **seemly** decent; proper; appropriate.

seen *pp* of **see**.

seep *v* trickle through slowly; percolate; leak *n* **seepage** slow seeping through.

seer *n* prophet, oracle.

seersucker *n* lightweight, puckered, cotton fabric.

seesaw *n* 1 children's play apparatus, plank resting on central support, child sitting on each end, moving up and down alternately 2 any motion as this; *v* move up and down (*also* **teeter-totter**).

seethe *v* boil, bubble up; *fig* be violently agitated.

segment *n* section, portion cut or marked off; *v* divide into parts; *n* **-ation**.

segregate *v* separate from main body; isolate; *n* **-ation**.

seigneur *n Fr* formerly feudal lord.

segue *v* 1 continue smoothly to next section; *n* **seque** smooth transition.

seine *n* kind of fishing net; *cap* river of Paris, France.

seismic *a* pertaining to earthquakes; *ns* **seismograph** instrument for recording earth tremors; **seismology** science of earthquakes.

seize *v* 1 grasp, take by force 2 grasp rapidly with mind; *n* **seizure** 1 forcible taking 2 sudden attack of illness *esp* stroke or fit.

seldom *adv* rarely; not often.

select *v* pick out; choose; *a* chosen; exclusive; fastidious; *a* **selective** having power of selection, able to discriminate; *ns* **selection** act of selecting; collection of samples; **selector; selectivity** ability to discriminate.

selenium *n* nonmetallic element used in photoelectric cells.

self *n* person's own identity and individual character; personality; ego; essential quality, inmost nature of anything; *pl* **selves**.

self- *prefix* expressing reflexive action to, by, for oneself;

a
b
c
d
e
f
g
h
i
j
k
l
m
n
o
p
q
r
s
t
u
v
w
x
y
z

automatic; acting upon agent. *Such compounds are not given here where the meaning may be deduced from the simple word.*

self-addressed *a* addressed for return to sender.

self-absorbed *a* only concerned with one's own interests.

self-assured *a* self-confident.

self-centered *a* preoccupied with one's own affairs or personality.

self-confident *a* sure of oneself and one's ability *adv* **-ly** *n* **- fidence.**

self-conscious *a* easily embarrassed, shy.

self-contained *a* compact or complete within itself; of reserved personality.

self-denial *n* voluntary abstention from pleasures.

self-determination *n* right, power of race, nation to decide on its own form of government.

self-devotion *n* giving up one's time to cause, etc.

self-effacing *a* modest.

self-employed *a* earning money directly from one's own business; not being employed by another.

self-evident *a* clearly so; not needing explanation; *adv* **-ly**.

self-fulfilling *a* happening, likely to happen simply because it has been predicted.

self-image *n* conception of oneself.

self-importance *n* conceited, pompous manner; exaggerated idea of own importance.

self-interest *n* consideration of one's own importance.

self-possessed *a* composed; having presence of mind.

self-reliant *a* independent; *n* **- ance.**

self-respect *n* regard for one's own character, etc.

self-righteous *a* too sure of one's own goodness; *adv* **-ly** *n* **-ness.**

selfsame *a* identical.

self-satisfied *a* conceited.

self-service *a* (*of stores, etc.*) where customers serve themselves.

self-seeking *a* acting only for one's own advantage.

self-styled *a* named, or cited, or titled, by oneself.

self-sufficient *a* able to supply one's needs for existence without outside help; *n* **-ency.**

self-will *n* obstinacy; being headstrong.

sell *v* **1** give, dispose of in return for money **2** be sold **3** deal in **4** persuade people to buy **5** persuade people that something is good; *pt, pp* **sold;** *idm* **be sold on** *coll* be enthusiastic about; *idm* **be sold out (of)** have sold all available; *idm* **sell one's soul** be ready to do anything for money, power, etc.; *idm* **sell down the river** betray

somebody; *idm* **sell short 1** sell at less than true value **2** not recognize the value of **3** deceive; *phr vs* **sell off** dispose of by selling, *esp* at reduced price; **sell out 1** sell one's whole supply **2** be all sold (*n* **sell-out** entertainment for which all tickets are sold) **3** compromise, betray, *esp* for money (*n* **sell-out**); *n coll* deception; poor bargain (*idm* **hard/soft sell** aggressive/discreetly persuasion); *ns* **sell-by date** date marked on perishable product as last acceptable date for selling; **seller** (**seller's market** situation where demand for something is greater than supply, and higher prices can be asked).

selvage *n* edge of cloth woven to prevent fraying.

seltzer *n* carbonated water.

selves *pl of* **self.**

semantics *n pl* branch of linguistic study dealing with development of meaning of words.

semaphore *n* **1** apparatus with two movable arms worked by levers, for signaling **2** signaling by use of person's arms and flags; code used for such signals; *v* signal thus.

semblance *n* appearance; similitude; outward show.

semen *n* spermatic fluid of male animal.

semester *n* school, college, university term of 18 weeks;

two such terms per year.

semi- *prefix* partly, half.

semi *n coll* eighteen-wheel distance-hauling truck.

semibreve *n* whole note.

semicircle *n* halfcircle; *a* **semi-circular.**

semicolon *n* punctuation mark (;).

semiconductor *n* substance that conducts electricity under certain conditions.

semidetached *a* (of house) having another joined to it on one side.

semifinal *n* round before the final.

seminal *a* 1 original; creative 2 of semen.

seminar *n* class for advanced students.

seminary *n* college for clergy.

semiology *n* study of signs and symbols; *a* **-logical** *n* **-logist.**

semiprecious *a* of moderate value.

semiquaver *n* sixteenth note.

Semite *n* member of ancient people of Akkadia, Phoenicia, Hebrews, Arabs; their descendants; *a* **Semitic** pertaining to Semites and their languages.

semitone *n mus* half step.

semolina *n* ground grains of wheat, used in making pasta.

senate *n* 1 ancient Roman legislative assembly 2 *caps* upper legislature of US Congress; academic governing body of university; *n* **senator;** *a* **-torial;** *n* **s. house** building

where senate meets.

send *v* 1 cause to go, be conveyed 2 dispatch 3 *sl* delight, thrill; *pt, pp* **sent; send for** 1 order 2 request to come; **send off** 1 post 2 sport dismiss from field of play (*n* **sending-off**) 3 accompany with good wishes (*n* **send-off** expression of good wishes at start of something); **send up** 1 mock (*n* **send-up**) 2 *coll* send to prison; *n* **sender.**

senescent *a* growing old; *n* **-ence.**

senile *a* showing weakness and decay of mental faculties, due to old age **senile dementia;** *n* mental deterioration in age, resulting in memory loss; *n* **senility.**

senior *a* older, of higher degree, rank, position; *n* older person; superior *n* **s. citizen** person beyond age of retirement; *n* **seniority.**

senna *n* dried leaves of pea-like plant used as laxative.

señor *n* (title of) Spanish man; *fem* **señora** married Spanish woman; **señorita** unmarried Spanish woman, girl.

sensation *n* effect felt by senses; state of excitement; event, person, etc., causing such state of mind; *a* **sensational** arousing, tending to arouse, great interest, curiosity, etc.; *n* **sensationalism** crude, melodramatic presentation of news items *esp* sex and

violence.

sense *n* 1 any of five faculties by which one perceives the world around (sight, hearing, taste, smell, touch) 2 practical wisdom 3 understanding (of something); ability to judge 4 meaning 5 feeling (about something) 6 purpose 7 *pl* ability to think; *idm* **bring/come to one's senses** (cause to) stop acting foolishly; *idm* **make sense** be intelligible; *idm* **make sense (out of)** understand; *idm* **sense of occasion** 1 special atmosphere created by event 2 awareness of how to behave; **sixth sense** ability to know things that one has neither seen nor heard directly; *v* become aware of; feel; detect; *as* **senseless** 1 unconscious 2 foolish; **sensible** 1 conscious 2 wise (*adv* **-ibly**) 3 sensible of aware of; *n* **sensibility** delicate feeling about style, correctness etc (*pl* **-ies** capacity for being shocked easily).

sensitive *a* 1 feeling acutely; keenly perceptive 2 easily distressed 3 reacting quickly to slight changes; *n* **sensitiveness** state of being sensitive; **sensitivity** degree of sensitiveness; *v* **sensitize** *phot* make sensitive to light.

sensor *n* device for detecting presence of heat, sound, smoke, etc.; *a* **sensory** of the

A
B
C
D
E
F
G
H
I
J
K
L
M
N
O
P
Q
R
S
T
U
V
W
X
Y
Z

physical senses.

sensual *a* **1** pertaining to body senses **2** lustful; voluptuous; *ns* **sensuality** proneness to sexual indulgence; **sensualism** sexual indulgence; *a* **sensuous** pertaining to, based on bodily senses.

sent *pt, pp of* **send**.

sentence *n* **1** judgment, decision of court, declaring punishment to be inflicted on criminal **2** combination of words which convey complete meaning; *v* condemn.

sententious *a* full of maxims; uttering trite, pompous expressions.

sentient *a* having sense or feeling.

sentiment *n* **1** tender emotion; tendency to be influenced more by emotion than reason **2** verbal expression of feeling; *a* **sentimental** arising from sentiment rather than logic; foolishly emotional; *ns* **sentimentalist** one affected by or working up sentiment; **sentimentality** tendency to be sentimental; sloppy.

sentinel *n* one who keeps watch; sentry.

sentry *n* armed military guard.

separate *v* divide; cut up, off; come, go apart; part; *a* **1** divided; distinct physically **2** isolated; kept apart; *a* **separable;** *ns* **-ation 1** act, process of separating **2** in law, formal arrangement

when married couple live apart, without divorce; **-ator** that which separates; device for separating cream from milk.

separatism *n* policy of keeping a religious or political group separate and independent; *a, n* **-ist**.

Sephardi *n* **-dim.** European Jews native to Spain, Portugal, later in Western Europe, the Americas, and the Middle East.

sepia *n* dark brown pigment, made from ink of cuttle fish; *a* of this color.

September *n* 9th month of Gregorian calendar.

septennial *a* lasting, occuring every seven years.

septet *n* music for, group of, seven instruments or voices.

septic *a* of, caused by infection or putrefaction; **s. tank** underground tank where sewage is dispersed through action of bacteria; *ns* **sepsis** infection of blood by microorganisms; **septicemia** blood poisoning.

septuagenarian *a* aged between 70 and 80; *n* person so aged.

sepulchre, sepulcher *n* tomb; burial vault; *a* **sepulchral 1** of pertaining to grave, burial or dead; funereal **2** (*of voice, etc.*) deep; hollow; *n* **sepulture** burial.

sequel *n* **1** consequence **2** account, story of later events.

sequent *a* following; *n*

sequence order in which events, objects follow; series; succession **sequential** *a* in sequence; *adv* **-ly**.

sequester *v* set apart; isolate; *v* **sequestrate** confiscate; *leg* take (property) by process of law and divert income to meet claims against owner; *n* **sequestration**.

sequin *n* ornamental disk or spangle; old Venetian gold coin.

sequiteur *n* something that logically follows another; conclusion, consequence.

sequoia *n* large tree of Western US.

serape *n* blanketlike wrap.

seraph *n* one of highest orders of angels; *pl* **seraphim;** *a* **seraphic** angelic.

Serbo-Croatian *n* **1** Slavonic language spoken in Croatia, Bosnia and Herzegovina, Serbia, and Montenegro **2** one whose native language os this.

sere *a* withered.

serenade *n* music sung or played at night (*esp* by lover) beneath lady's window; nocturne; *v* sing serenade to.

serendipity *n* faculty of finding valuable or interesting things by chance.

serene *a* **1** calm; placid **2** unclouded *n* **serenity**.

serf *n* feudal laborer; slave; *n* **serfdom**.

serge *n* hard-wearing, twilled woollen cloth.

sergeant *n* NCO in army;

police officer; **s.-at-arms** ceremonial official.

serial *a* of, forming series; *n* **s. number** identifying number of item in series; *n* story, novel, etc. published in successive installments; *v* **-ize** arrange in series; publish, produce as serial.

serial killer *n* person who commits a series of murders, usu in the same way.

series *n* 1 sequence 2 set; succession 3 linear, end-to-end arrangement.

serif *n* short thin line at top or bottom of letters.

serious *a* 1 solemn; meant in earnest, genuine 2 grave; critical.

sermon *n* discourse on moral and religious subjects forming part of church service; *v* **-ize** preach *esp* tediously.

serpent *n* 1 snake 2 malevolent person 3 obsolete wind instrument.

serrated *a* having notches like teeth of saw; *n* **serration**.

serum *n* watery fluid remaining after coagulation of blood; such fluid prepared by culture for use in inoculation.

serval *n* African wildcat.

servant *n* one employed in domestic service to another.

serve *v* 1 work for; perform duty for 2 wait upon (with food) 3 satisfy 4 undergo (prison sentence) 5 deliver (writ) 6 (*tennis, etc.*) deliver

ball to opponent, by striking it 7 be useful for.

service *n* 1 (performance of) official duty 2 help given 3 *fig* work done by machine 4 public organization or department 5 organized system of transport or communication 6 satisfying of needs of clients; money given in recognition of this 7 maintenance (*eg* of machinery) 8 set of dishes, silverware, etc 9 ceremony of religious worship 10 tennis, squash method of putting ball into play; *ns* **s. area** area near highway with gas station, shop, restaurant, etc.; **s. charge** sum added to basic bill for service; **serviceman/woman** person serving in armed forces; **s. road** minor road alongside main road; **s. station** garage for gasoline and car maintenance; *a* **-able** usable; useful; *ns* **servicing** maintenance; **serving** portion of food.

serviette *n* *Fr* table-napkin.

servile *a* 1 pertaining to slaves, slavery 2 cringing; obsequious; *n* **servility**.

servitude *n* slavery; bondage.

servo-mechanism *n* device controlling larger mechanism.

sesame *n* E Indian annual herb, with seeds yielding oil.

sesquipedalian *a* consisting of very long words.

session *n* 1 formal assembly or

meeting 2 period during which legislative body sits *esp* Congress; continuous series of such meetings.

set *v* **setting, setted.** 1 put; arrange in position 2 cause to be in specified state 3 cause to begin 4 adjust 5 fix 6 establish 7 present (task, problem) to be addressed 8 (cause to) become solid 9 compose music for (words to be sung) 10 (*of sun, moon, etc.*) pass below horizon 11 (*of current, tide*) flow in stated direction; *idm* **be all set** be ready; *idm* **set free** liberate; *phr vs* **set about** 1 begin 2 attack; **set aside** 1 abandon 2 keep, save for later; **set back** 1 place further to the rear 2 delay (*n* **set back**) 3 incur a cost of; **set down** 1 write down 2 let (passenger) get off; **set forth** 1 begin journey 2 *fml* present (in detail); **set in** (of weather, disease) begin and become established; **set off** 1 depart 2 cause to explode 3 initiate 4 make appear better by contrast; **set on** (cause to) attack; **set out** 1 depart 2 arrange in order; **set out to** begin with intention to; **set to** begin eagerly (*n* **set-to** argument or fight); **set up** 1 erect 2 prepare 3 establish; organize (*n* **set up** arrangement; organization) 4 *coll* restore to good health 5 *coll* equip with necessary resources 6 *sl* con or frame; *a*

A B C D E F G H I J K L M N O P Q R S T U V W X Y Z

1 fixed (**s. price**) **2** prescribed (**s. books**) **3** inflexible (**s. attitude**); *idm* **be all set** be quite ready; *idm* **be set on** be determined about; *n* **1** complete group **2** radio or TV receiver **3** arrangement of scenery on stage or for filming **4** *tennis* specified number of games; subdivision of match **5** clique, group identified by social class; *ns* **s. piece** sequence of action executed according to plan; work of art of traditional type; *n* **setting** act, process of setting; background; that in which gems are set.

settee *n* sofa; couch.

setter *n* breed of dog trained to point at game.

settle *n* wooden bench with high back and arms; *v* **1** arrange; establish **2** make firm or quiet **3** decide on **4** endow legally **5** end (dispute) **6** subside **7** pay **8** become clear **9** take up abode; *phr vs* **settle down 1** subside **2** make a home **3** begin to lead a quiet life **4** form a regular pattern of work; **settle for** agree to accept; **settle in** get used to new home, job, etc.; **settle on** agree on; decide on; **settle up** pay what one owes; *a* **settled 1** calm **2** established; *ns* **settlement 1** movement of people to new habitat **2** small, newly built village **3** agreement **4** gift of money **5**

payment of required sum; **settler** colonist.

seven *n, pron, det* cardinal number next above six; *ns, as, dets* **seventh** ordinal number; seventh part; *idm* **(be in) seventh heaven** (be in) state of bliss; **seventeen** seven plus ten; **seventeenth; seventy** seven tens; **seventieth;** *n* **seven-year itch** feeling of restlessness after seven years of marriage.

sever *v* cut off; separate; divide; *n* **severance (s. pay** money paid to dismissed worker.

several *a* **1** separate; distinct **2** more than two; not many; *adv* **-ly** apart from others.

severe *a* **1** harsh; strict **2** rigorous **3** intense **4** austere **5** violent; *n* **severity**.

sevruga *n Russ* gray caviar from roe of Caspian Sea sturgeon.

sew *v* fasten, attach with needle and thread; *pt* **sewed;** *pp* **sewed, sewn** *phr v* **sew up 1** repair by sewing **2** *fig* conclude satisfactorily; *n* **sewing** needlework.

sewage *n* waste matter, excreta, etc. carried away in sewers; *ns* **sewer** underground conduit or drain for carrying off sewage; **sewerage** public drainage.

sex *n* **1** fact or quality of being male or female **2** physiological difference between male and female **3** *coll* sexual intercourse; *ns* **s.**

appeal power of sexual attraction; *n* **sex offender** person who has committed a sexual crime; *n* **sex offence** sexual crime; **s. object** person considered interesting only for sexual attraction; **s. organ** organ of reproduction; *ns* **sexism** discriminatory treatment of one sex by the other (*a* **-ist**); **sexology** study of sexual behavior (*n* **-ologist**); *a* **sexual (s. intercourse** act of intimacy by joining sex organs of male and female) *adv* **-ly;** *n* **-ity;** *a* **sexy**.

sexennial *a* lasting, happening once in, six years.

sexism *n* **1** discrimination, prejudice based on sex, *esp* against women **2** behaviour, mores that foster this discrimination (*a* **sexist**).

sextant *n* astronomical device for determining position.

sextet *n* group of six instruments or players; music for this group.

sexton *n* man employed by church as caretaker, gravedigger, etc.

sextuplet *n* any of six children born of the same pregnancy.

sforzando *a, adv, n mus* (note) played with initial force.

shabby *a* **1** wearing old, worn out clothes **2** well worn **3** worn; squalid **4** shameful; *n* **-iness**.

shack *n* hut; shanty; *phr v* **shack up** *sl* live together as if married.

shackle *n* strong metal link; *pl* -s fetters; chains; *v* fasten with shackles; *fig* hamper.

shad *n* edible marine fish of herring family.

shade *n* 1 partial darkness; shadow 2 depth of color 3 something that gives shelter, protection from light 4 spirit, ghost 5 slight amount, degree; *idm* **put in the shade** outshine; cause to seem inferior; *pl* -s *coll* sunglasses; *idm* **shades of** *coll* a reminder of; *v* 1 darken; screen from light 2 represent light and shade in drawing; *a* **shady** 1 affording, standing in shade 2 *coll* disreputable.

shadow *n* 1 shade cast by person, object in sun's path 2 person who follows another closely or surreptitiously 3 phantom 4 indistinct, imperfect image 5 very slight amount or degree; *v* 1 cast shadow over 2 follow closely, *esp* as detective or bodyguard; *v* **s.** -**box** practice boxing without an opponent (*n* -**ing**); *a* **shadowy** unsubstantial; dim.

shaft *n* 1 handle; stem 2 arrow 3 beam (of light) 4 vertical opening to mine, etc. 5 ventilating channel 6 *pl* -s poles between which horse is harnessed 7 revolving rod transmitting power.

shag[1] *n* 1 long-napped carpet 2 fine-cut tobacco; *a* **shaggy** rough; unkempt (*n* -**iness**); *n*

shaggy-dog story long rambling story with pointless ending.

shag[2] *n* small crested cormorant.

Shah *n* former ruler of Iran.

shake *v* 1 tremble; vibrate 2 totter 3 agitate 4 cause emotional shock to 5 make insecure; (*pt* **shook,** *pp* **shaken**); *idm* **shake hands (with somebody)** grasp somebody's hand in greeting; *idm* **shake (hands) on it** join hands in agreement; *phr vs* **shake down** 1 sleep in improvised bedding 2 settle down 3 *coll* search thoroughly 4 *coll* extort money from (*n* **shakedown** 1 extortion 2 shakeout); **shake off** 1 elude 2 get rid of 3 remove by shaking; **shake out** 1 open out by shaking 2 dispose of unprofitable elements (*n* **shakeout** process of firms going out of business in a recession); **shake up** 1 mix by shaking 2 rouse from apathy 3 reorganize fundamentally (*n* **shake-up**); *ns* **shaker** container for shaking (*e.g.*, cocktail); *pl* **shakes** *coll* shaking of body through fear, disease, etc., (*idm* **in two shakes** very soon; *idm* **no great shakes** not much good); *a* **shaky** insecure; unsteady.

shale *n* clay rock formation, that flakes easily.

shall *v aux* used to denote promise, obligation, intention, command, futurity; *pt* **should**; no *pp.*

shallot *n* kind of onion.

shallow *a* 1 not deep 2 (*of thought, feeling, etc.*) superficial; trivial; *n esp pl* shallow place in body of water.

sham *n* imposture; counterfeit, faked article; imitation; *v* pretend; imitate.

shamble *v* walk with stumbling, shuffling gait.

shambles *n pl* 1 meat market, slaughter house; butcher's stall 2 *fig* place of bloodshed, carnage 3 *coll* confusion, mess.

shame *n* 1 emotion of regret and contrition, caused by guilt, dishonor, etc. 2 disgrace 3 *coll* unfair happening; bad luck; *v* 1 make ashamed 2 bring shame, disgrace on; *as* **shame-faced** ashamed of oneself; **shameful** outrageous; disgraceful; **shameless** 1 impudent; brazen 2 immodest.

shampoo *v* wash (hair) with shampoo; wash carpet, car, etc. with special preparations; *n* special preparation for washing.

shamrock *n* trefoil plant, probably wood-sorrel; national emblem of Ireland.

shandy *n* beer mixed with lemonade or ginger-beer.

shanghai *v* abduct by drugging, intoxicating for service.

shank n 1 lower leg; shin 2 handle; shaft; stem.

shantung n natural Chinese silk.

shanty[1] n small hut; temporary wooden building.

shanty[2], **chanty** n sailor's song.

shantytown n poor residential area consisting of rough improvised huts, tarpaper shacks.

shape n external form or appearance; pattern, mold; v form, fashion; assume shape; as **shapely** well proportioned; **shapeless**.

shard n broken fragment of pottery.

share[1] n 1 portion 2 part played in action 3 one of equal portions into which capital of public company is divided; v give, allot, take a share; n **shareholder**.

share[2] n blade of plow.

sharecropper n farmer paying part of rent in produce; farmer working for self and landowner.

shark n one of large group of carnivorous, voracious sea fishes; fig rapacious, grasping swindler.

sharp a 1 having keen edge, piercing point 2 clearly seen 3 intense 4 shrill 5 alert; brisk 6 dishonest; n mus note raised half note in pitch; v **sharpen** whet edge or point; fig make keen; ns **sharp end** area where most difficulty is found; ns **sharper** one who cheats esp at cards;

sharpness, s. practice methods that are dishonest without being illegal; as **sharp-set** hungry; **sharp-witted** very quick and intelligent; n **sharpshooter** skilled marksman.

shatter v break in fragments; smash; fig cause to crumble.

shave v cut off (hair) with razor; pare; pt **shaved**; pp **shaved, shaven**; n 1 act of shaving 2 fig narrow escape; ns **shaver** 1 one who, that which shaves 2 coll lad; **shaving** thin slice, esp of wood.

Shavian a after, in manner of George Bernard Shaw.

shawl n large square of fabric worn around shoulders, or for wrapping babies in.

she fem nom pron (3rd pers sing) female person, etc. just referred to; a female.

sheaf n bundle of things tied together esp cut wheat, corn stalks; pl **sheaves**.

shear v 1 clip, remove (fleece) from 2 cut off by one stroke; pt **sheared, shore**; pp **shorn, sheared**; n pl **shears** large cutting implement with blades like scissors; n **shearer** one who shears esp sheep.

sheath n 1 close-fitting cover (e.g., for sharp weapon) 2 simple fitted dress; v **sheathe** cover with sheath.

shebang n idm **the whole shebang** coll everything.

shed[1] n wooden hut; outhouse; shelter for cattle, tools, etc.

shed[2] v 1 cast off; emit; molt 2 cause to flow; pt, pp **shed**; idm **shed blood** cause death or injury; idm **shed/cast/throw light on** help to explain.

she'd contracted form of 1 she had 2 she would.

sheen n gloss; luster.

sheep n ruminant mammal with woolly coat and edible flesh; a **sheepish** bashful; **s.-dip** liquid insecticide used to preserve wool and kill vermin.

sheer a 1 clear; unmixed 2 perpendicular (of cliff) 3 (of fabric) transparent; phr v **sheer away/off** turn suddenly in another direction.

sheet n 1 large piece of fabric used to cover bed 2 broad piece of any thin material 3 thin flat piece of paper, metal 4 rope fastened to sail; n **s.-anchor** 1 large emergency anchor 2 fig person, thing which can be relied on; n **sheeting** (material for making) sheets.

sheik, sheikh n Arab chieftain; Muslim title of respect.

shelf n 1 horizontal projecting board on wall, etc. 2 horizontal ledge of rock, etc. 3 reef; pl **shelves**; idm **on the shelf** 1 left aside as no longer useful 2 beyond the age when one is likely to get married; n **s.-life** length of time a product can remain on sale before it deteriorates.

shell *n* **1** hard outer covering of animal or vegetable object **2** explosive projectile **3** framework **4** ruined building with only walls standing; *n idm* **go into/come out of one's shell** behave/stop behaving in a shy, retiring manner; *v* remove shell from (nut, pea, etc.) **2** bombard with shells; *phr v* **shell out** *coll* pay out, *esp* unwillingly; *n* **shellfish** edible marine mollusk or crustacean; *n* **shell shock** functional nervous disorder caused by wartime experience of bursting shells, etc. (*a* **-ed** **1** suffering from this **2** *fig* dazed).

she'll *contracted form of* she will.

shellac *n* colored resin used in varnishes, sealing wax, etc.; *v* coat with shellac.

shelter *n* protection; cover; screen; place of refuge; *v* **1** give, afford cover to; protect **2** seek safety.

shelve *v* **1** put on shelves **2** *fig* postpone; abandon **3** slope gently.

shelves *pl of* shelf.

shelving *n* (structure of) shelves; *a* sloping.

shenanigans *n pl coll* **1** mischief **2** deception.

shepherd *n* one who tends sheep; *fig* minister of religion; **the Good S.** Christ; *fem* **shepherdess;** *n* **shepherd's pie** baked dish of minced meat covered with mashed potato (*also* **cottage pie**).

sherbet *n* frozen fruit-flavored ice dessert *also* **sorbet**.

sherd = **shard**.

sheriff *n* chief officer enforcing law, order in county.

Sherpa *n* member of Tibetan people noted as mountaineers.

sherry *n* type of Spanish wine.

she's *contracted form of* she is.

shiatsu *n* Japanese massage technique using acupuncture pressure points.

shield *n* piece of protective armor carried on arm; that which serves as protection or defense; *v* protect; guard; screen.

shift *v* **1** (cause to) change position **2** remove **3** *coll* move fast; *idm* **shift for oneself** look after oneself; *idm* **shift one's ground** change basis of argument; *n* **1** change in position or direction **2** (period of work allocated to) team of workers interchanging with other teams **3** trick for avoiding a problem **4** woman's straight narrow dress; *ns* **s. key** typewriter key giving access to upper case letters; **s. stick** gear level; *a* **shiftless** lazy (*n* **-ness**); **shifty** evasive, dishonest; furtive.

Shiite *n* Muslim of the Shia branch of Islam.

shill *n* person who poses as a customer to lure others.

shillelagh *n* Irish walking stick.

shilling *n* former British silver coin worth 12 old pence or 5 new (decimal) pence.

shilly-shally *n* indecision; needless delay; *v* hesitate; waver.

shimmer *v* shine with faint light; *n* faint, tremulous light; glimmer.

shimmy *n* **1** nickname for chemise, slip **2** jazz dance, shimmy-shake, where dancers shake bodies from shoulders down.

shin *n* front of lower leg; *v* **shinny shinnying, shinned.** climb, swarm up by using legs and arms.

shindig *n* **1** *coll* noisy party **2** disturbance.

shine *v* **1** emit, reflect light **2** sparkle **3** excel **4** show great intelligence; *pt, pp* **shone;** *n* polish; brilliance; *idm* **take a shine to** *coll* begin to like; *a* **shiny**.

shingle¹ *n* **1** wooden tile for roofing, outside walls, etc. **2** woman's short hairstyle; *v* **1** cover with shingles **2** cut hair in shingle.

shingle² *n* coarse rounded stones, pebbles found on seashore.

shingles *n* acute inflammatory disease of nerve endings.

shinny, shinney *n* type of street hockey.

shin splints *n* painful shins from strenuous activity.

Shinto *n* national religion of Japan.

A B C D E F G H I J K L M N O P Q R **S** T U V W X Y Z

ship n large sea going vessel; v **shipping, shipped. 1** send (goods, etc.) by ship **2** embark, serve in ship; idm **when one's ship comes in** when one becomes rich and successful; v **send by ship; shipper** person sending shipment; **shipping 1** ships **2** transporting by ship; **shipmate** somebody traveling/working on same ship; **shipment** (act of sending) cargo; **shipwreck** destruction of ship by storm, collision, etc. (a **-ed**); **shipwright** builder of ships; **shipyard** place where ships are built; a **shipshape** in good order.

shire n county pl rural counties of England.

shirk v evade, refuse to face (danger, duty, etc.); n **shirker.**

shirr v **1** gather cloth on parallel threads **2** bake eggs.

shirt n sleeved garment, worn under jacket.

shish kebab n pieces of meat cooked on skewers.

shiver v splinter, break in pieces.

shiver v tremble, shake with cold or fear; n shudder, quivering movement; a **shivery** inclined to shiver.

shoal n **1** large mass of fish swimming together **2** submerged sandbank; v **1** form shoal **2** become shallow.

shock¹ n **1** violent jolt,

collision **2** feeling of horror, surprise, disgust, etc. **3** that which causes such feeling **4** discharge of electric current through body **5** upset of nervous system and vital functions of body following accident, operation, etc.; v cause, produce shock; ns **s. absorber** device fitted to vehicle to reduce effects of jolting and vibration; **s. therapy** method of treating mental illness by electric shocks, drugs, etc.; **s. wave 1** air pressure wave in wake of ultrasonic aircraft **2** fig public reaction to spread of bad news; n **shocker** coll sensational novel, film, etc.; a **shocking 1** distressing **2** disgusting (adv **-ly**) **3** coll very bad.

shock² n **1** group, pile of sheaves of corn **2** mass of hair.

shoddy n cheap material; anything made of cheap inferior material; a cheap, insubstantial.

shoe n **1** outer covering for foot **2** metal rim, or plate, nailed to hoof of horse **3** part of brake which presses on rim of wheel; v protect, furnish with shoes; pt, pp **shod;** ns **shoelace** string for securing shoe; **shoestring** idm **on a shoestring** with very little money.

shofar n instrument made from a ram's horn, blown in Jewish religious ceremonies.

shogun n military governor of Japan before the mid-nineteenth century, with power exceeding the emperor's.

shone pt, pp of **shine.**

shoo interj used, esp to animals go away.

shook pt of **shake.**

shoot v **1** move suddenly and rapidly; dart **2** fire (missile) **3** kill or wound with bullet, arrow, etc. **4** project, hurl rapidly **5** take (pictures) with movie or video camera **6** football kick directly toward goal; idm **shoot one's mouth off** coll talk indiscreetly; phr vs **shoot down 1** cause to fall by shooting **2** fig discredit; **shoot up 1** grow rapidly **2** wound by shooting **3** sl inject (drug) into vein; n **1** act of shooting **2** sprout **3** shooting party; a, n **-ing** (ns **s.-gallery** enclosed space where one can practice shooting at targets; **s. star** burning meteor seen as bright streak in sky (also **falling star**).

shop n **1** place where goods are sold **2** workshop **3** fig one's business, etc.; idm **talk shop** discuss one's work on a social occasion; v **shopping, shopped.** visit shops to buy goods; phr v **shop around** compare goods and prices in shops before buying; ns **s. -assistant** person who serves in shop; **s.-floor 1** production area in factory **2** workers; **shopkeeper** owner of small shop; shopper; **shopping 1** act of buying **2** goods bought; **s.-steward** trade union elected representative of workers; *v* **shoplift** steal from shop (*ns* **-er, -ing**).

shore *n* land at edge of sea or lake.

short *a* **1** brief; not tall; scanty **2** concise **3** abrupt **4** deficient; reduced **5** friable; *idm* **short of 1** lacking in; having insufficient supply of **2** failing to reach; *idm* **be short with** be impatient with; *idm* **give short shrift to** pass over quickly without fair consideration; *adv idm* **stop short** stop suddenly; *n* **1** *elec* **short circuit 2** *coll* strong alcoholic drink; *pl* **-s 1** short trousers **2** men's undergarments (as boxers); *as* **s.-haul** (of air flight) over a quite short distance; **s. -lived** not lasting long; **s. -range** covering a short distance or time; **s.-sighted 1** not able to see distant objects clearly **2** not thinking of the future (*adv* **-ly;** *n* **-ness**); **s.-term** for the near future only; *v* **s.-change 1** give back less than the correct amount **2** *fig* treat unfairly; *ns* **shortage** lack; **shortbread** crumbly sweet butter cookie; **s. circuit** *elec* bypassing of normal circuit through faulty insulation or loose connection (*v* **s. -circuit;** *also fig*);

shortcoming failing; **s. cut** quick way; **shortfall** deficit; **shorthand** system for quick writing; **s.list** preliminary selection of applicants from whom an appointment for a post is to be made (*v* select for such a list); **short-term** *a* relating to the immediate future; *n* **short-termism** planning based only on short-term benefits; **s. wave** radio broadcasting on waves of 10–100 m; *adv* **shortly 1** soon **2** briefly.

shot[1] *pt, pp* of **shoot**.

shot[2] *a* fabric woven so as to change color, according to angle of light.

shot[3] *n* **1** small lead pellet in cartridge **2** act of firing **3** noise of this **4** attempt; try **5** *sl* injection, injected dose *esp* of drug; **big s.** important person; **s. in the dark** random guess.

shot put *n* athletic event involving the throwing of a metal ball for distance.

should *modal v* (*pt or conditional of* **shall**) **1** ought to **2** were to **3** 1st person was going to; *neg* **should not** (*contracted form* **shouldn't**).

shoulder *n* **1** part of body to which arm or foreleg is attached **2** strip of land bordering road; *v* put on one's shoulder; *fig* undertake responsibility for; *n* **shoulderblade** shoulder bone.

shout *n* loud outcry; *v* utter

with loud voice.

shove *v, n* push.

shovel *n* broad spade, used for lifting earth, etc.; *v* lift, move with shovel.

show *v* **1** expose to view **2** demonstrate **3** guide **4** exhibit **5** appear; *pt* **showed;** *pp* **shown, showed, shews;** *phr v* **show off 1** show to best effect **2** try to impress others by talk or behavior (*n* **show-off** person who does this); **show up 1** arrive **2** embarrass **3** out do; *n* **1** performance; entertainment **2** display **3** ostentation **4** indication **5** effort; *ns* **s. business** work of people in theater, cinema, etc.; **s.-case** set of shelves in glass case for displaying articles; **s.-down** final settlement of a dispute; **showgirl** young woman who sings and dances in musicals; **s. jumping** sport in which horses are ridden to jump over obstacles; **showing 1** act of showing **2** proof of quality; **showman 1** organizer of public entertainments **2** person skilled in self-promotion (*n* **-ship**); **s.-piece** excellent example of something; *a* **showy** ostentatious; (too) bright, etc., (*adv* **-ily**); make display of one's attainments, abilities, etc.; **s. up** expose, reveal bad side of.

showbiz *n coll* show business.

shower *n* **1** short fall of rain **2** copious discharge (of missiles) **3** device making bath water fall from overhead; *v* **1** fall as shower **2** give out abundantly **3** take shower; *a* **-y** with frequent rain-showers.

shown *pt, pp of* **show**.

shrank *pt of* **shrink**.

shrapnel *n* shell casing filled with bullets or pieces of metal that scatter on bursting; piece of such metal.

shred *n* tattered fragment; strip; *v* **shredding, shredded.** tear into shreds.

shrew *n* **1** virago **2** mouselike carnivorous mammal; *a* **-ish** nagging.

shrewd *a* astute; sharp-witted; piercing; *n* **-ness**.

shriek *v, n* screech; scream.

shrike *n* insect-eating bird of prey.

shrill *a* piercing, high-pitched in tone.

shrimp *n* small edible, long-tailed crustacean; *fig* small person; *v* fish for, catch shrimps.

shrine *n* sacred place, chapel, etc., associated with saint; casket containing holy relics; *fig* something held sacred in memory; *v* **enshrine**.

shrink *v* **1** contract; diminish **2** recoil; retreat; flinch; *pt* **shrank;** *pp* **shrunk, shrunken;** *phr v* **shrink away/back (from) 1** flinch **2** retreat (from); **shrink from doing** be reluctant to do; *n* *coll* psychiatrist or psychoanalyst; *v* **s.-wrap**

wrap in tight-fitting plastic film to exclude air; *ns*

shrinkage act of or degree of shrinking; **shrinking violet** timid, shy person.

shrive *v* absolve; *pt* **shrove;** *pp* **shriven**.

shrivel *v* **shrivelling, shrivelled.** curl, roll up; wither.

shroud *n* cloth wound around corpse; *fig* covering; *pl* ropes from masthead; *v* wrap in shroud; hide, cover, veil.

Shrovetide *n* three days before Lent; **Shrove Tuesday** day before Ash Wednesday.

shrub¹ *n* low-growing bushy, woody plant; *n* **shrubbery** plantation of shrubs.

shrub² *n* drink of sweetened fruitjuice with rum.

shrug *v* **shrugging, shrugged.** lift and draw up shoulders slightly, as sign of doubt, etc.; *phr v* **shrug off** make light of; *n* shrugging.

shrunk(en) *a* contracted; shrivelled; reduced.

shucks *interj coll* expressing regret.

shudder *v* quake, tremble violently; feel aversion, be disgusted at; *n* shuddering.

shuffle *v* **1** move feet without lifting them **2** speak, act evasively **3** mix cards up; *n* shuffling; *n* **shuffler**.

shuffleboard *n* game played on market floor surface.

shun *v* **shunning, shunned.** avoid; keep clear of.

shunt *n* means, device for

redirection, as traffic or blood in body; *v* turn, switch (train) to side line; *fig* push to one side.

shush *interj* hush; requesting silence.

shut *v* close; lock up; imprison; exclude; *pt, pp* **shut;** *n* **shutter 1** hinged window screen **2** device in camera for screening lens.

shut-eye *n coll* sleep.

shut-in *n* person confined by illness to home, hospital, etc.

shutout *n* game in which one team does not score.

shuttle *n* **1** weaver's instrument for carrying weft **2** sliding thread holder in sewing machine; *v* move regularly back and forwards between two places; *ns* **s. diplomacy** international negotiation through diplomats who travel back and forth; **s. service** regular transport service back and forth between two places; **space s.** reusable spacecraft that ferries cargo, personnel from earth to side and back.

shuttle cock *n* feathered, weighted cork, used in badminton.

shy¹ *a* **a shyer, shyest. 1** timid **2** reserved **3** easily frightened; *phr v* **shy away from** turn away in fear; **shy away from** avoid.

shy² *v* **shying, shied.** *coll* fling, throw; *n* act of throwing; *pl* **shies**.

shyster *n coll* unscrupulous person, *esp* lawyer.

Siamese *n pl, a* (people) of Thailand; *ns* **S. cat** cat with short pale brown fur and blue eyes; **S. twin** either of two twins whose bodies are joined at birth.

sibilant *n, a* (consonant) uttered with hissing sound.

sibling *n* brother or sister.

sibyl *n* **1** wise woman; soothsayer **2** witch; *a* **sibylline** oracular.

sic *adv* thus (indicating that previous word is intended as written).

sick *a* **1** ill **2** *fig* (*of humor*) macabre; *idm* **be sick 1** be unwell **2** vomit; *idm* **be sick (to death) of** be angry, fed up, disgusted with; *idm* **feel sick** suffer from nausea; *idm coll* **make somebody sick** disgust somebody; *idm* **sick at heart** very unhappy; *n* **1** vomit **2 the s.** people who are ill; *ns* **s. bay** room for nursing those that are ill; **s. leave** permission to be away from work because of illness; **s. pay** money paid to employee while ill; *v* **sicken 1** become ill **2** disgust (*a* -**ing** *adv* -**ingly**); *a* **sickly 1** often ill **2** unhealthy looking **3** showing or causing distaste (*n* -**iness**); *n* **sickness** illness.

sickle *n* reaping hook; *n* **s.-cell anemia** severe hereditary type of anemia.

side *n* **1** external or internal surface **2** area **3** space that is to right or left **4** edge, margin **5** team **6** group **7** area between ribs and hip in human body **8** line of descent through one parent **9** *sl* arrogance; conceit; *v* support (person, party, etc.); *idm* **on the side** as additional *esp* dishonest activity; *phr v* **side with** support; act or speak in favor of; *ns* **sideboard** cupboard for dishes, glasses, etc. *pl* **sideburns** hair grown in front of man's ears; **s.-car** small passenger cabin attached to motorcycle; **s. effect** secondary effect; **s. issue** not the main issue; **sidekick** *esp coll* companion or assistant, **sidelight 1** small lamp at front of vehicle **2** additional minor fact; **sideline 1** secondary activity **2** secondary line of goods **3** *sport* line marking limit of play (*v* put out of action; *idm* **on the sidelines** not directly involved) **sideshow** amusement stall at fairground or circus; **sideslip** skid; **s.-stroke** swimming stroke performed on one side; **s.-swipe 1** indirect blow **2** *fig* critical remark; **sidewalk** pavement; *as* **sidelong** directed sideways; **sidesplitting** *coll* very funny; *advs* **sidewards** to the side; **sideways** moving or turned towards one side; *vs* **s.-track** divert somebody from his/her purpose.

sidereal *a* relating to, measured by apparent motion of stars.

sidle *v* move, walk sideways in cringing, fawning manner; *phr v* **sidle up** walk nervously toward.

SIDS *abbr* sudden infant death syndrome; crib death.

siege *n* besieging of fort or town.

sienna *n* brownish-yellow earthy pigment.

sierra *n Sp* mountain chain with jagged ridges.

siesta *n Sp* short rest, sleep in early afternoon.

sieve *n* framework of mesh or net for sifting; *v* pass through sieve, sift.

sift *v* pass through sieve or riddle; separate coarse from fine particles; examine carefully; sprinkle; *n* **sifter**.

sigh *v* utter long audible breath; express grief, fatigue etc by this act; **s. for** long for; lament; *n* act, sound of, sighing.

sight *n* **1** faculty of seeing; vision **2** that which is seen **3** device (on gun etc.) for helping vision **4** view; spectacle; *idm* **a sight for sore eyes** somebody/ something one is delighted to see; *idm* **be in sight of** be near to; *idm* **a (damn) sight** (+*comp*) *coll* very much; *idm* **adjust/raise/lower one's sights** be more/less ambitious; *idm* **set one's sights on** aim to have or do; *idm* **take sight** take aim; *v* manage to see (of distant object) (*n* -**ing**); *v* **s.-read**

mus be able to perform at first reading (*ns* **-er, -ing;** *also* **s. sing**); *ns* **s.-seer/seeing** tourist visitor/visiting; *as* **sighted/sightless** able/unable to see.

sign *n* indication, token, symbol which conveys meaning; visible mark; agreed word, gesture expressing meaning; omen; *v* **1** write one's name on **2** ratify **3** indicate by word or gesture; *phr vs* **sign away** formally give up rights, property by signing document; **sign for** acknowledge receipt by signing; **sign in/out** indicate arrival/departure by signing; **sign off 1** end letter with signature **2** stop work **3** end broadcast; **sign on 1** register one's name for activity **2** enlist in armed forces; **sign up** enroll; *ns* **s. language** method of communication by gestures; **signpost** post with signs showing direction, distance (*v* provide with/indicate with signposts).

signal *n* message conveyed to distance; indication, warning of something else; apparatus whereby message is conveyed; *v* **signalling, signalled.** make signal to; send, notify by signals; *a* remarkable; conspicuous (*adv* **-ly**); *ns* **s. box** building with control system for railway points and signals; *v* **signalize**

make conspicuous.

signatory *n* representative of party or state who signs document, treaty, etc.

signature *n* person's name written by same person; **s. tune** one associated with program or performer on radio, etc.

signet *n* small seal.

significant *a* meaningful; noteworthy; suggesting covert meaning; *ns* **significance** import; meaning; **signification** exact meaning or implication.

signify *v* **signifying, signified. 1** mean; imply **2** matter; be of importance.

signor, signore *n* title for Italian man; *fem* **signora** (*married*) **signorina** (*unmarried*).

Sikh *n* member of monotheistic sect in India rejecting idolatry, castes.

silage *n* fodder preserved in silo.

silence *n* absence of noise or sound; refraining from speech; *v* **1** cause to be silent **2** *fig* put to shame; *a* **silent;** *n* **silencer** device for reducing, muffling noise of machinery or firearms.

silhouette *n* **1** portrait in outline or profile, cut from black paper, or painted in solid black, against white background **2** outline, profile, of object seen as dark against light background; *v* show up in outline.

silica *n* hard, white mineral; *n* **silicate** salt of silicic acid; *as* **silicic** pertaining to silica; **siliceous** flinty; *n* **silicon** nonmetallic element, one of principal constituents of earth's surface; *n* **s. chip** microchip of silicon used in making integrated circuit; **Silicon Valley** *fig* area in N California for high-tech and computer development.

silicone *n* one of various compounds of silicon and hydrocarbon, used in lubricants, polishes, etc.

silk *n* fine filament produced by pupae of certain moths; thread, fabric made from this; *as* **silken** made of, like silk; **silky** glossy, fine, soft to touch; *ns* **silkiness; silkworm** silk-producing caterpillar.

sill *n* **1** horizontal block or slab at base of window or door **2** slab of igneous rock between sedimentary layers.

silly *a* foolish; trivial; weak-minded; *n* **s. season** summer period when media have little of importance to report; *n* **silliness**.

silo *n* pit, tower for fodder or grain; *n* **silage** cattle fodder partly fermented and stored.

silt *n* sediment, mud, etc. deposited by water; *v* **silt up** become choked, blocked with silt.

silver *n* **1** white precious metal element **2** objects made of, plated with this **3** coins of silver or similar metal; *a* **1** made of, resembling silver **2** *fig* shining; lustrous **3** (*of sound*) ringing; clear; soft; *v* **s.-coat** coat with silver; *ns* **s. birch** birch with silvery-white bark; **s.-fish** small, flattish wingless insect found *esp* in damp, dark parts of houses; **silversmith** person making or selling articles in silver; **silverware** *n* eating and serving utensils of this or similar-colored metal; **s. wedding** 25th anniversary of wedding; *a* **silvery**.

simian *a* of, like apes.

similar *a* like; resembling; *n* **-ity** likeness; resemblance.

simile *n* figure of speech in which one thing is directly compared to another; often introduced with *like* or *as*.

similitude *n* comparison; likeness; similarity.

simmer *v* **1** boil gently; be just below boiling point **2** *coll* be in condition of suppressed rage or excitement; *n* state of simmering.

simper *v* smile affectedly; smirk; *also n.*

simple *a* **1** clear; intelligible **2** easy **3** austere **4** ingenuous; credulous; foolish **5** not complex or compound; *a* **s.-minded** showing lack of intelligence; *ns* **simpleton** foolish person; **simplicity** quality, state of being simple; *v* **simplify** make less complicated or easier *n* **simplification; simplistic**

treating complex matter as if it were simple (*adv* **-ally**).

simulate *v* imitate; pretend to be, have, or feel; *a* **-ated** artificial; *ns* **-ation** (**s. game** game in which real life activities, relationships are simulated as educational exercise); **-ator** device for simulating real conditions.

simultaneous *a* occurring at same time; *adv* **-ly** *n* **-ness**.

sin *n* **1** transgression of divine law, moral code **2** any offense in general; vice; iniquity; *v* **sinning, sinned.** be sinful; commit sin; *a* **-ful** *n* **sinner**; (*n* **-ness**).

since *adv* from then until now; ago; *prep* after; succeeding; *conj* because; seeing that.

sincere *a* genuine; honest; true; free from deceit or pretence; *n* **sincerity**.

sine *n* trigonometric function that expresses the perpendicular drawn from one extremity of arc to diameter drawn through other extremity; ratio of this perpendicular to radius of circle.

sinecure *n* paid office or work with few or no duties.

sine die *adv leg Lat* without fixed date.

sine qua non *n Lat* essential thing.

sinew *n* **1** tendon **2** *pl* **-s** muscles **3** *fig* (of war) money and material resources; *a* **sinewy** muscular.

sing *v* **1** utter musical notes **2**

(*of birds*) utter melodic natural cries **3** *fig* rejoice; *pt* **sang;** *pp* **sung;** *ns* **singer; singing.**

singe *v* **singeing, singed.** burn superficially; scorch; *n* slight burn.

single *a* **1** one only; not double **2** separate **3** not married **4** for one person; *phr v* **single out** select for special attention; *n coll* record, CD with one song (on each side); *pl* **-s** tennis match between two players; *as* **s.-breasted** (of jacket) with one row of buttons; **s.-handed** unaided (*adv* **-ly**); **s.-minded** with one clear purpose (*adv* **-ly** *n* **-ness**); *n*, *adv* **s. file** in a line one behind the other; *adv* **-ly;** *n* **singleton** something without a pair.

singsong *a* with repeated rising and falling intonation (*n* such speech).

singular *a* **1** of, relating to one person or thing **2** remarkable, unusual, eminent; *adv* **singularly** oddly; outstandingly; *n* **singularity**.

sinister *a* **1** evil; ominous; malevolent **2** *her* on left-hand side.

sink *v* **1** be, become, submerged in liquid **2** subside; become lower (in value, degree, health, etc.) **3** penetrate deeply **4** excavate; *pt* **sank;** *pp* **sunk;** *phr v* **sink in** become fully understood; *a* **-ing** (**s. feeling** *coll* feeling of fear or helplessness; *n* kitchen basin.

Sino- *prefix* Chinese.

sinology *n* study of Chinese language and culture *n* **-ologist**.

sinuous *a* curving, bending; snakelike, undulating; *n* **sinuousity**.

sinus *n med* cavity in tissue or bone, *esp* in facial bone; *n* **sinusitis** inflammation of nasal sinus.

sip *v* **sipping, sipped.** drink in very small quantities; *n* very small mouthful of liquid.

siphon *n* **1** bent tube used for transferring liquid from one level to lower one **2** bottle with tap at top, through which carbonated water is forced by gas pressure; *v* draw off by siphon (*occasionally* **syphon**.)

sir *n* term of respect for man; title of knight or baronet.

sire *n* form of address to monarch; male parent, *esp* of horse, dog; *v* beget, be sire of.

siren *n* **1** mythological sea-nymph **2** *fig* alluring woman **3** loud warning horn or signal.

sirloin *n* upper part of loin of beef.

sirocco *n* hot Mediterranean wind.

sisal *n* fiber of Mexican agave, used for making rope.

sissy *n coll* effeminate male; timid, cowardly person.

sister *n* **1** daughter, woman, born of same parents **2** nun;

a closely related, of same type; *a* **-ly;** *n* **sisterhood** women's club; community of nuns, etc.; **sister-in-law** sister of husband or wife; wife of brother.

sit *v* **1** rest on buttocks or haunches **2** take one's place in assembly **3** pose for portrait **4** fit, hang well **5** (*of birds*) remain on eggs; *pt, pp* **sat;** *idm* **be sitting pretty** *coll* be in a secure position *idm* **sit tight** remain where one is; *phr vs* **sit back** relax and do nothing; **sit in** occupy (premises) in protest (*n* **sit-in**); **sit in for** be a substitute for; **sit in on** be present at; **sit on 1** delay action concerning **2** be a member of; **sit up 1** raise oneself to a sitting position **2** not go to bed until late **3** *fig* suddenly show interest; *n* period of sitting; *ns* **sitdown** form of strike within an institution; **sitter 1** artist's model **2** baby-sitter; **sitting 1** session of parliament, committee, etc. **2** serving of meal **3** period spent in sedentary occupation, *esp* as model for artist, photographer, etc. (*ns* **s. duck** one easy to take advantage of; **s. room** *esp Brit* living-room; **s. tenant** person who occupies rented or leased accommodation).

sitar *n* type of Indian lute.

sitcom *n coll* situation comedy.

site *n* ground; situation; local position; place.

situate(d) *a* placed, having particular site; *n* **situation** place; employment; state of affairs; *n* **s. comedy** television series or program with characters that appear in different comic situations.

six *n, pron, de* cardinal number one above five; *idm* **at sixes and sevens** *coll* confused; *n* **s.-shooter** revolver with six bullet chambers; *a, n, det* **sixth** ordinal number after fifth (**s. sense** facility for knowing things without evidence from any of the five senses; *n* **sixpence** *Brit* silver coin worth six old pennies, two and half decimal pence; *ns, as* **sixteen** six and ten; **sixteenth; sixty** six times ten; **sixtieth**.

size¹ *n* standard measure of length, weight, quantity; magnitude; fixed dimension; *v* arrange according to size; *idm* **cut somebody down to size** make somebody realize he/she is not as good as he/she thought; *phr v* **size up** assess and form opinion of.

size² *n* thin glue used to glaze and stiffen paper, etc.; *v* apply size to.

sizzle *v* make hissing noise; *n* hissing, spluttering sound *esp* in frying.

skate¹ *n* edible flat fish of ray family.

skate² *n* **1** one of pair of steel blades, attached to boot, for gliding over ice **2** roller-

skate; *v* move on skates; *n*
skateboard narrow board on
wheels for standing and
riding on (*ns* **-er, -ing**).
skedaddle *v sl* run away, clear
out; *n* hasty flight.
skeet *n* sport of shooting at
clay targets that simulate
birds (*also* **skeet shooting**)
skein *n* **1** quantity of coiled
and knotted yarn (of cotton,
silk, etc.) **2** flock of wild
geese in flight.
skeleton *n* **1** bony framework
of human or animal body;
such bones preserved in their
natural position **2** *coll* very
thin person **3** outline; draft **4**
framework; *idm* **skeleton in
the cupboard** embarrassing
fact from one's past that one
prefers to keep secret; *ns* **s.
key** key that opens many
different locks; **s. service**
minimal service much
reduced from normal; *a*
skeletal pertaining to,
attached to skeleton.
skeptic *n* one who refuses to
accept statement without
positive proof; agnostic;
doubter; *adv* **skeptically;** *a*
skeptical; *n* **skepticism.**
sketch *n* **1** rough drawing
serving as study for finished
picture **2** rough draft **3** short
play; *v* make sketch of; *a*
sketchy depicted in outline;
unfinished, inadequate.
skew *v* turn aside; swerve or
slant; *fig* present information
in biasel, manipulative
format.

skewer *n* thin pointed pin of
wood or metal for keeping
piece of meat in shape; *v* **1**
pierce or fasten with skewer
2 criticize harshly.
ski *n* long wooden or fiberglass
runner, fastened to foot, for
moving over snow or water; *v*
skiing, skied. use skis for
traveling over snow or water;
n **skier** one who skis; **ski lift**
apparatus for carrying skiers
uphill.
skid *n* drag fixed to wheel, to
reduce speed; *v* **skidding,
skidded.** (of vehicle) slip
sideways out of control *fig*
slip and fall.
skid row *n* rundown, *usu*
urban area frequented by
vagrants.
skiff *n* small rowing, sculling
boat.
skiffle *n* jazz folkmusic; *n* **s.
group** musical group using
improvised instruments.
skill *n* deftness; manual
dexterity; cleverness;
ingenuity; *as* **skilled** skillful;
expert; trained in some
specific trade, etc.; **skillful**
clever, dextrous.
skillet *n* frying pan.
skim *v* **skimming, skimmed. 1**
remove scum, fat, or other
substance from surface of
liquid **2** pass lightly over *fig*
read through (book) rapidly
and perfunctorily; *n* **skim
milk** milk from which fat,
cream have been removed
(*also* **skimmed milk**).
skimp *v* stint; supply in too

small an amount; do
carelessly; *a* **skimpy** meager;
fitting too tightly.
skin *n* outer covering of
anything, as of human or
animal body, fruit, etc.; *v*
skinning, skinned. remove
skin of; *idm* **by the skin of
one's teeth** only just; *n*
skinner dealer in pelts and
hides; *as* **s. deep** superficial;
skinny thin; **s.-tight** very
close fitting; *ns* **s.-flint** miser;
s.-diving underwater
swimming with oxygen tanks
but no diving suit.
skip *v* **skipping, skipped. 1**
leap lightly; gambol **2** jump
on spot, while rope passes
underneath one **3** *coll*
decamp; bolt **4** omit, pass
rapidly over in reading.
skipper *n* captain of ship; *coll*
captain of team; *v* act as
skipper.
skirl *n* shrill, piercing sound of
bagpipes.
skirmish *n* fight between small
groups of soldiers, etc.; *fig*
brief, slight contest or
argument; *v* engage in
skirmish.
skirt *n* **1** woman's garment
hanging below waist **2** flank
of beef **3** outlying part; *v*
border, go around; *n* **-ing**
baseboard running around
bottom of walls of room.
skit *n* light, satirical,
humorous sketch or satire;
a **skittish** playful; lively;
frolicsome.
skitter *v* move rapidly, lightly.

A
B
C
D
E
F
G
H
I
J
K
L
M
N
O
P
Q
R
S
T
U
V
W
X
Y
Z

skittles n game of ninepins.
skulduggery n coll trickery; devious behavior.
skulk v lurk in concealment; sneak away; n **-er**.
skull n bony case containing animal, human brain; n **s. cap** close-fitting cap.
skunk n 1 small, carnivorous N American mammal emitting offensive odor when attacked 2 coll contemptible person.
sky n upper part of earth's atmosphere; fig heaven pl **skies;** v throw, hit (ball) high up; a of color of blue, cloudless sky; ns **s.-diving** sport involving free-fall from aircraft before using parachute (**s.-diver** person doing this); **skylight** window in roof or ceiling; **skyline** line in sky formed by buildings, trees, etc. on horizon; **skyscraper** very tall urban building; as, advs **s.-high** very high; **skyward** upward; vs **skyjack** hijack aircraft; **skylark** play around; frolic; **s.-rocket** (of prices) rise very sharply.
skylark n common bird, noted for its song and soaring flight.
slab n thick, squarish plate or slice.
slack[1] a 1 sluggish; loose; relaxed 2 lazy 3 not busy; n **s. water** period when tide is neither rising nor falling n anything left slack or loose; n pl **slacks** loose sports trousers; v 1 sag 2 be idle, lazy; v **slacken** abate; diminish; reduce (speed).
slack[2], **slag** n dross or refuse of coal or smelted metal.
slag n waste matter from smelting metal from ore.
slain pp of **slay.**
slake v 1 quench; allay 2 mix (lime) with water.
slalom n 1 ski down zig-zag course 2 any similar race, e.g., with canoes.
slam v **slamming, slammed.** shut, close with bang; put down noisily; n loud bang or noise; **grand s.** cards taking of all tricks in one deal.
slander n leg malicious, false spoken statement; v utter such statement; a **-ous;** n **slanderer.**
slang n colloquial word; informal nonstandard vocabulary; argot.
slant v slope; incline from perpendicular; n 1 slope 2 coll point of view; adv **slantwise** obliquely.
slap v **slapping, slapped.** smack, strike smartly with open hand; n such blow; idm **slapbang** coll exactly; as **slapdash** careless and hasty; **slaphappy** carefree and irresponsible; n **slapstick** rough knockabout farce or comedy.
slash v 1 gash; make cuts or slits in; lash violently at 2 reduce (prices) abruptly; n 1 long cut; slit 2 act of slashing.
slat n thin narrow strip of wood or metal a **slatted.**
slate n hard, gray, shale-like rock which splits easily into thin layers; piece of this used for roofing, or writing upon; idm **on the slate** on credit; v 1 cover with slates 2 propose (for office).
slather n large quantity; v 1 slop or smear 2 squander.
slattern n dirty, untidy woman; a **slatternly** unkempt, careless, slovenly, disorderly.
slaughter n 1 butchering of animals for food 2 needless killing (of humans, animals) in large numbers; v 1 kill animals for meat 2 kill needlessly, massacre; n **slaughterhouse** abattoir; place where animals are butchered for market.
slave n 1 one held in bondage to another; drudge 2 one dominated by desire, passion or devoted to cause, principle; v work like slave; ns **s. driver** person who forces one to work hard; **slavery** bondage; serfdom; drudgery; a **slavish** servile; n **slaver** person, ship engaged in slave trade.
slaver see **slobber.**
Slavic a of the Slavs (also **Slavonic).**
slaw n chopped seasoned raw cabbage.
slay v kill (pt slew, pp slain); n **slayer** killer.
sleaze n dishonest or immoral behavior, esp among public figures.

sleazy *a coll* sordid; dirty-looking.

sled, sledge *n* vehicle on runners, for sliding on snow; toboggan; *v* travel, convey by sledge.

sledgehammer *n* heavy hammer with long handle.

sleek *a* glossy; smooth; healthy; prosperous.

sleep *n* **1** natural unconscious state recurring regularly in humans and animals; period during which one sleeps **2** *fig* lethargy **3** *fig* death; *v* **1** slumber; take rest by sleeping **2** *coll* provide beds for; *pt, pp* **slept**; *idm* **lose no sleep over** not worry about; *idm* **put to sleep** euthanize; *v* **1** take rest by sleep **2** provide sleeping accommodation for; *pt, pp* **slept**; *phr vs* **sleep in** remain in bed late in the morning; **sleep off** dispose of (bad effect of something) by sleep; **sleep on something** postpone decision until next day; **sleepover** *n* children's party at which guests stay the night; *n* **sleeper 1** person who sleeps **2** wooden beam supporting railway track **3** someone or something underrated who/that achieves fame, renown **4** child's footed pajama; *a* **sleeping** (*ns* **s. bag** bag for sleeping in, *usu* lined for warmth; **s. car** train car with sleeping accommodation; **s.-pill** drug to make sleep easier; **s. sickness** serious tropical

disease causing great lethargy); *a* **sleepy** (*adv* **-ily;** *n* **-iness**).

sleet *n* mixture of rain and snow falling together; *v* fall as sleet.

sleeve *n* **1** part of garment which covers arm **2** tubular case or cover enclosing smaller tube or rod; decorative outer cover of book, CD, etc.; *idm* **up one's sleeve** in reserve (secretly); *v* furnish with sleeves; *n* **sleeve valve** sliding valve; *as* **sleeved; sleeveless**.

sleigh *n* sled.

sleight *n* dexterity; cunning; **s. of hand** conjuring trick, *esp* by substitution.

slender *a* thin; slight; scanty.

slept *pt, pp* of **sleep**.

sleuth *n* detective; *v* track by scent; *n* **sleuth hound** bloodhound.

slew *pt* of **slay**.

slice *n* **1** flat, thin piece; cross-section **2** wedge-shaped piece **3** spatula for spreading ink, paint **4** slicing stroke, *esp* in ball games; *v* **1** cut in slices **2** hit ball so that it turns away.

slick *a* **1** smooth; sleek **2** *coll* glib; persuasive but not always honest (*adv* **-ly** *n* **-ness**); *v* make smooth or glossy; *n* area of spilled oil floating on water; *n* **slicker 1** slick person, sophisticate **2** raincoat.

slide *v* **1** slip, glide easily, down or off **2** *fig* pass over lightly **3**

propel, push, thrust along slowly; *pt, pp* **slid**; *idm* **let something slide** *coll* let unsatisfactory situation remain or deteriorate even further; *n* **1** act of sliding **2** angled playground toy accessed by ladder (also **sliding pond**) **3** frame of glass or cardboard holding picture for projection, or object to be examined under microscope; *n* **s.-rule** mathematical instrument for rapid calculations; **sliding scale** schedule for raising, lowering taxes, fees, wages, etc. in agreement with fluctuations in cost of living, etc.

slight *a* **1** slim; slender **2** -mild; trivial; *idm* **(not) in the slightest** (not) at all; *v* neglect; disregard; *n* act, utterance of disrepect; humiliation.

slim *a* slender; slight; reverse of stout, thick; *v* make thin; reduce weight by diet, etc.; *adv* **-ly** *n* **-ness;** *n, a* **slimming** reducing one's weight (**s. exercises** exercises to promote this).

slime *n* **1** soft wet dirt; liquid mud **2** moisture secreted by snails, etc.; *a* **slimy 1** like smeared with, slime **2** *fig* fawning; servile.

sling *n* **1** loop of leather, etc. for hurling stones or other missiles **2** strip of cloth supporting injured limb **3** rope, band, etc. for hoisting weights; *v* throw, suspend by

a
b
c
d
e
f
g
h
i
j
k
l
m
n
o
p
q
r
s
t
u
v
w
x
y
z

A
B
C
D
E
F
G
H
I
J
K
L
M
N
O
P
Q
R
S
T
U
V
W
X
Y
Z

sling; *pt, pp* **slung; idm sling
mud at** say damaging or
libelous things about; *phr v*
sling out throw out forcibly;
n **s.-shot** catapult.

slink *v* move furtively,
secretively.

slip *v* **slipping, slipped. 1** slide
2 miss one's footing **3** pass
rapidly **4** to escape memory,
consciousness **5** escape from
6 get speedily into/out of
clothes, etc.; *idm* **let slip 1**
lose (opportunity) **2** make
known by inadvertent
remark; *n* **1** act of slipping **2**
error of judgment **3** moral
lapse **4** loose cover for pillow
5 petticoat **6** cutting for
grafting **7** narrow strip (of
paper, etc.) **8** thin mixture of
clay and water for making
pottery **9** young sole or
plaice **10** space between
piers for vessels; *idm* **slip of a
girl** very small, slim girl; *idm*
give somebody the slip
escape from or elude
somebody; *ns* **s.knot** knot
that slides or comes undone
easily; **s.-on (shoe)** shoe that
slips on easily; **s.over**
garment that slips easily over
the head; **slippage** (degree
of) slipping; **slipped disk**
displacement of cartilage
disk between two vertebrae,
usu causing great pain; **s.-
stream 1** air vacuum that
forms behind fast moving
vehicle **2** air propelled
backward by aircraft engines;
s.-up *coll* mistake; *as* **slippery**

1 smooth and difficult to
keep a firm hold of **2** elusive
(*n* **-iness**); **slipshod** done
without much care and
attention.

slipper *n* soft indoor shoe.

slit *v* **slitting, slit.** cut open,
make incision in; *n* small,
narrow opening; incision.

slither *v* slip and slide slowly
along or down.

sliver *n* small, narrow piece,
cut, torn on anything;
splinter.

slob *n sl* fool, lout, boor.

slobber *v* **1** allow saliva to run
out of mouth; dribble **2** *fig*
show sentimental affection
for; *n* dribbling saliva; *fig*
sentimentality.

sloe *n* bluish-black fruit of
blackthorn; **sloe gin** liqueur
of sloes steeped in gin.

slog *v* **slogging, slogged.** work
hard and persistently; plod
heavily; persevere against
difficulty.

slogan *n* catchword or phrase
used in advertising, etc.

sloop *n* single-masted sailing
vessel; small warship.

slop *v* **slopping, slopped.** spill;
be spilt; overflow; *phr v* **slop
about/around 1** play around
in mud, water, etc. **2** move
about idly, purposelesssly; *n*
pl dirty water, liquid waste;
food waste (garbage) used as
animal feed.

slope *n* inclined direction or
surface; steepness; *v* be, have
inclined (in) surface.

sloppy *a* **1** wet, messy **2**

careless in one's work **3**
maudlin; sentimental; *adv*
-ily; *n* **-iness.**

slosh *v* (*of liquid*) move noisily;
splash; *a* **-ed** *coll* drunk.

slot *n* **1** narrow slit; aperture,
esp for insertion of coins; **2**
niche; *v* **slotting, slotted.**
make slot(s) in; *phr v* **slot
in(to)** fit neatly, closely
(into).

sloth *n* **1** indolence; laziness
2 sluggish S American
mammal; *a* **slothful** lazy;
inactive.

slouch *n* careless, clumsy,
slovenly gait; *v* walk thus;
n **slouch hat** soft hat with
turned down brim.

slough[1] *n* swamp, bog.

slough[2] *n* cast-off skin of
snake; *phr v* **slough off 1** (of
snake) shed skin **2** get rid of
something unwanted.

sloven *n* lazy, dirty and untidy
person; **slovenly** *a* untidy in
appearance; careless;
slipshod; *n* **slovenliness.**

slow *a* **1** moving at low rate of
speed; taking longer than
usual; behind correct time
2 not alert; stupid; inactive;
v reduce speed; *ns* **slowdown**
slackening of pace, speed;
slow motion process of
replaying filmed or
videotaped sequence so
action is slowed down;
-ness; slowpoke person who
acts, moves slowly.

sludge *n* thick, greasy mud;
slush; any slimy deposit.

slue *v* turn around.

slug n 1 land snail with no shell 2 small bullet for airgun, etc. 3 *print* line of type-metal used for spacing; 4 mouthful of alcoholic drink; v **slugging, slugged.** hit hard; slog; a **sluggish** slow; inactive; lazy; (n **-ness**).

sluice n floodgate *coll* brisk wash with water; v 1 provide with sluices 2 *coll* wash down with, splash water over.

slum n dilapidated, squalid street or area, *usu* overcrowded; v **slumming, slummed.** do something considered lower than one's station.

slumber v sleep; *fig* lie dormant; n sleep.

slump n 1 collapsed posture 2 sudden fall in prices, value, etc.; v fall in price, demand; financial depression; *fig* decline in esteem.

slur v **slurring, slurred.** pass lightly over; pronounce indistinctly; *mus* sing, play legato; n act of slurring; stain; stigma.

slurp v drink noisily; n noise caused by this.

slurry n mixture of mud, clay, etc., with water.

slush n liquid, soft mud; melting snow; *coll* sickly sentiment; drivel; n **s. fund** money reserved secretly, often for dishonest use.

sly a cunning; underhand; not frank; artful; *idm* **on the sly** secretly; (*adv* **-ly** n **-ness**).

smack[1] n taste, trace of; suggestion of; *phr* v **smacks of** 1 tastes of; 2 suggests.

smack[2] n smart explosive sound (of lips); crack of whip; slap; v make such sound; *adv* 1 sudden, 2 exactly.

small a 1 little; very young 2 trivial, unimportant; petty; paltry; *ns* **smallness; small arms** revolvers *idm* **feel small** feel ashamed; *idm* **cost a small fortune** *coll* cost a lot of money; n narrow part of back; *ns* **s. arms** revolvers and rifles; **s. change** coins; **s. fry** insignificant; childish; **s.-holding** small plot of agricultural land or farm; **s. hours** *pl* hours after midnight; **smallpox** acute infectious and contagious disease leaving scars on skin; **s. print** detailed terms of a legal contract; **s. screen** *coll* TV; **s. talk** trivial conversation used as a means of socializing; *as* **s.-minded** petty and mean; **s.-scale** limited in size or extent; **s.-time** unimportant; n **smallness.**

smarmy a *coll* ingratiatingly polite; flattering.

smart a 1 sharp; forcible; brisk; alert; clever 2 well-dressed; fashionable; n **s. aleck** *coll* know-all; v 1 feel sore and painful 2 feel hurt, resentful; n sharp pain.

smart card n credit or debit card with built-in

microprocessor to record information on transactions.

smarten v make, give spruce appearance to; a **smartly** fashionably; quickly; n **smartness.**

smash v 1 break to pieces; shatter; hit violently 2 defeat utterly; ruin *esp* financially; n 1 violent shattering 2 bankruptcy; ruin 3 violent collision of vehicles; n **smash hit** *coll* highly popular song, film, etc.; a **smashing** devastating; *coll* outstanding; delightful.

smattering n slight, superficial knowledge of subject.

smear n 1 stain, mark made by contact with oily, greasy substance 2 *coll* malicious rumor; n **Pap s.** screening for cervical cancer, v mark with smear; damage by rumor.

smell v 1 perceive, inhale, emit odor 2 stink 3 *fig* track; discover; *idm* **smell a rat** *coll* suspect something is wrong; n odor; scent; act of smelling; **smelling salts** ammonium carbonate with lavender; *pt pp* **smelled.**

smelt[1] n small edible silvery fish.

smelt[2] v extract metal from ore, by heat.

smidgin n *coll* tiny amount.

smile v 1 curve, part lips in expression of pleasure, amusement 2 *fig* be favorable to; n act of smiling; facial expression showing happiness, affection,

a b c d e f g h i j k l m n o p q r s t u v w x y z

amusement.

smirch v dirty; stain; disgrace.

smirk v smile in affected, smug manner; n conceited; knowing smile.

smite v wound; afflict; affect strongly esp with love, fear; pt **smote**; pp **smitten**.

smith n worker in metal; n **smithy** smith's workshop; forge.

smithereens n idm **in(to) smithereens** in(to) tiny pieces.

smitten pp of **smite**; smitten (with) **1** suddenly in love (with) **2** deeply affected by.

smock n loose outer protective garment, formerly worn by shepherds; v adorn with honeycomb needlework; n **-ing**.

smog n **1** dense mixture of smoke and fog **2** photochemical haze made by auto exhaust and solar ultraviolet rays.

smoke n fine particles, emitted by burning matter; idm **go up in smoke** coll **1** be burned to nothing **2** fail completely; ns **s.-screen 1** smoke used to hide military operation **2** attempt to conceal one's real intentions; **s.-stack** funnel; chimney; v **1** emit smoke **2** inhale and expel smoke from burning tobacco **3** cure (fish, etc.) by exposing to wood smoke; phr v **smoke out** force out of hiding (e.g., by use of smoke); ns **-er, -ing**; a **smoky** (n **-iness**).

smolder v burn slowly without flame.

smooch v coll cuddle and kiss.

smooth a polished; even; level; calm; soothing; unruffled; adv **-ly** n **-ness** v make smooth.

smorgasbord n buffet of assorted dishes.

smote pt of **smite**.

smother v **1** suffocate **2** cover thickly **3** suppress.

smudge n smear; blur; blot; v make smudge.

smug a complacent; self-satisfied; prim; adv **-ly**; n **-ness**.

smuggle v **1** import or export (goods) without payment of customs duties **2** convey secretly; n **smuggler**.

smut n **1** particle of soot, dirt, etc. **2** parasitic fungus **3** obscene talk, writing, etc.; a **-ty**.

snack n light meal eaten quickly; n **snack bar** bar in restaurant where snacks are served; café.

snaffle n light bit for horse; v sl steal, pinch.

snag n **1** tree stump esp in river bed **2** fig unexpected obstacle **3** run or catch in stocking.

snail n shell-bearing, slow-moving mollusk, leaving slimy trail; fig slow-moving person.

snake n scaly limbless reptile, serpent; idm **snake in the grass** false friend a **snaky** of, like snakes; winding; v move like snake; twist; wind.

snap v **snapping, snapped. 1** break suddenly with sharp sound **2** open or close with sharp sound **3** speak sharply in anger; idm **snap to it** coll move quickly into action; idm **snap out of it** coll throw off bad mood; phr v **snap at 1** try to catch in the mouth by snapping one's jaws **2** speak sharply to; **snap up** seize or buy quickly; n **1** act or sound of snapping **2** informal photo (also **s.-shot**) **3** card game; interj showing recognition that two things are identical; a sudden (**s. judgment**); a **snappy 1** hasty **2** impatient; irritable **3** coll stylish (adv **-ily** n **-iness**).

snapdragon n coll antirrhinum.

snapper n tropical fish.

snapshot n spontaneous photograph.

snare n device for catching birds, animals, etc.; n **s. drum** drum with snares, i.e., loose strings that produce rattling effect; v catch in snare; trap.

snarl v growl threateningly; phr v **snarl up** (n facial expression, sound made in snarling; **snarl-up** (n confusion of traffic; traffic jam).

snatch v seize, make quick grab at; n **1** act of snatching **2** a lift in weight-lifting.

snazzy a coll stylishly attractive (adv **-ily** n **-iness**).

sneak v **1** move, creep furtively **2** sl inform against;

n mean, furtive person; informer; *ns* **s. preview** opportunity to view before official public opening or premiere; **s. thief** thief who takes small items without using violence; *a* **sneaky** (*adv* **-ily** *n* **-iness**).

sneaker *n* rubber-soled shoe, *esp* for athletics.

sneer *v* smile, speak scornfully; *n* act of sneering.

sneeze *v* eject air through nostrils with sudden involuntary noise and spasm; *n* **sneezing**.

snicker *v* laugh furtively, slyly; neigh; *n* such sound.

snide *a* implying criticism in an indirect, unpleasant way; sneering.

sniff *v* inhale audibly through nose; *phr vs* **sniff out** *coll* find out (somebody/something secret); **sniff at** express scorn, etc. by sniffing; *n* **-er**.

sniffle *v* sniff repeatedly; *n* **1** slight cold **2** sniffing sound.

snigger *n* unpleasant surreptitious laugh; *v* laugh in this way.

snip *v* **snipping, snipped.** cut, clip with scissors, shears; *n* **1** short, quick cut **2** *sl* profitable bargain; *n* **snippet** small piece.

snipe *n* bird of plover family; *v* shoot at enemy from cover; *n* **sniper**.

snit *n* agitated or irritated state.

snitch *v coll* **1** inform on **2** steal.

snivel *v* **snivelling, snivelled.** whine, whimper peevishly; sniff repeatedly; *n* **snivel**.

snob *n* one who pretends to be better than he or she is; one who puts exaggerated importance on class, wealth, etc.; *n* **snobbery**; *a* **snobbish**.

snood *n* knitted cover for hair.

snooker *n* game combining pool and pyramids played on billiard table.

snoop *v sl* pry; peer into.

snooty *a coll* snobbish; showing a superior unfriendly attitude.

snooze *v* take short, light nap; doze; *n*.

snore *v* breathe heavily, noisily when asleep; *n* act, sound of snoring.

snorkel *n* breathing tube for underwater swimmers; *v* use this.

snort *n* loud noise made by drawing air through nostrils; *v* make this noise.

snot *n sl* mucus from nose.

snot-nosed *a* snooty; annoying, unpleasant.

snout *n* projecting nose of animal.

snow *n* frozen vapor falling as flakes from sky; *v* fall as snow; *idm* **snow under** overwhelm; *ns* **snowdrift** deep mass of snow driven by wind; *a* **snowy** covered with snow; inclined to snow; *n* **snowball** snow pressed into hard ball; something growing bigger; *v* play with snowballs; increase in size

rapidly; *ns* **snowdrop** early spring flower; *n* **snowmobile** vehicle for racing on snow; **snowplow 1** apparatus for clearing snow **2** skier's method of stopping by pointing skis inward; **snowshoe** racquet-shaped frame attached to foot for traveling across snow.

snub *v* **snubbing, snubbed.** rebuff by sneering remark; slight; insult; *n* snubbing; *n* **snub nose** one turned up at end.

snuck *pt, pp of* **sneak**.

snuff *n* powdered tobacco for sniffing up nose; *v* put out (candle); *idm* **snuff it** *coll* die; *phr v* **snuff out 1** extinguish **2** put an end to.

snuffle *n* **1** sniffing noise; *v* **1** make this noise **2** talk through the nose.

snug *a* warm; cozy; trim; *n* **snuggle** nestle, lie close to; cuddle.

so *adv* **1** in such manner; thus **2** to such extent; *conj* **1** therefore **2 so (that)** in order that; *conj* **so as to** in order to; *idm* **or so** approximately; *idm* **so long!** *coll* goodbye; *n* **so-and-so 1** unnamed person **2** annoying person; *a* **so-called** called thus, but without justification.

soak *v* steep; drench; wet thoroughly; *phr v* **soak up** absorb; *n* **1** act of soaking **2** *coll* drunkard; *as* **-ed, -ing** very wet, *n* soaking.

soap *n* compound of fatty acid and base which cleans and washes; *n* **s.box** improvised stand for public speaking; *idm* **get on one's soapbox** express one's opinions like *a* public speaker; **s. opera** serialized drama on radio, TV with melodramatic, sentimental narratives; **soapstone** soft type of stone used for carving; *a* **soapy** (*n* **-iness**.)

soar *v* fly high, effortlessly; *fig* rise to heights of imagination, etc.; *n* **soaring**.

sob *v* **sobbing, sobbed.** weep noisily; catch breath in weeping; *n* sobbing; *n* **sob story** sentimental account evoking sympathy, sadness.

sober *a* **1** temperate; moderate **2** not drunk **3** quiet in color; *v* make, become sober; *n* **sobriety** state of being sober.

sobriquet *n* nickname.

soccer *n coll abbr* game played on field, by teams kicking ball toward goals.

sociable *a* companionable; affable; *n* **-ability**.

social *a* relating to society; gregarious; sociable; *ns* **s. climber** person seeking acceptance by higher social class; **s. democrat** person believing in gradual move toward socialism by democratic means (*n* **s. democracy** this person's theory); **s. science** one of group of subjects dealing with study of society; **s.**

security government program for economic security, social sevices, *esp* for elderly, retired; **s. services** local services dealing with public welfare, health, education, etc.; **s. work** work in giving aid to people in trouble or need (*n* **-er**); *n* **socialite** member of high society.

socialism *n* political movement advocating public ownership of means of production, distribution, and exchange; *n* **-ist** member of socialist party.

socialize *v* **1** mix with other people socially (*n* **-izer**) **2** adapt to society (*n* **-ization**).

society *n* **1** organized community of mutually dependent individuals **2** companionship **3** association; club; group **4** fashionable people collectively.

socioeconomic *a* relating to both social and economic aspects.

sociology *n* social science.

sociopath *n* psychopath.

sock[1] *n* short stocking; inner sole of shoe; *idm* **pull one's socks up** *coll* start to do better; *idm* **sock it to them** *coll* speak forcefully.

sock[2] *v coll* hit; thrash.

socket *n* hollow recess into which something fits.

sod *n* flat piece of turf with roots.

soda *n* any of various sodium compounds; *coll* soda water; *n* **s. fountain** place where soft drinks are served; *n* **soda water** carbonated water.

sodality *n* association.

sodden *a* **1** soaked; saturated **2** *fig* heavy; stupid.

sodium *n* metallic alkaline element *n* **s. bicarbonate** white alkaline salt used in baking powder.

sofa *n* long padded couch with back and arms.

soft *a* **1** not hard; smooth **2** flabby; gentle **3** not loud **4** feeble-minded; (*adv* **-ly;** *n* **-ness**); **s. drink** non-alcoholic carbonated drink; *ns* **s. copy** *comput* information in memory or on screen; **s. currency** *econ* currency not convertible into gold, etc.; **s. landing** spacecraft landing without damage; **s. palate** soft rear part of roof of mouth; **s. pedal** piano pedal for muting sound of notes (*v* **s.-pedal** *coll* make seem of less importance); **s. sell** use gentle persuasion to sell; **s. soap** *coll* flattery (*v*. **s.-soap**); **s. spot** fond feeling; **s. touch** person easy to persuade or deceive; *as* **s.-hearted** kind; easily persuaded to sympathize (*adv* **-ly** *n* **-ness**); **s.-spoken** with gentle voice; *v* **soften** make soft; *phr v* **soften up 1** weaken **2** render unable to resist; *ns* **-ener, -ening**.

softball *n* game similar to

baseball with larger ball pitched underhand.

softie, softy *n* physically weak or sentimental person.

software *n comput* programs that operate computer.

softwood *n* wood from coniferous trees that cuts easily.

soggy *a* soaked with water, sodden.

soigné(e) *a Fr* elegant.

soil[1] *n* surface earth; land; country.

soil[2] *v* make, become dirty; tarnish, sully.

soirée *n Fr* evening party, *esp* with entertainment.

sojourn *v* stay for a time; *n* short visit; *n* **sojourner**.

solace *n* consolation; *v* comfort in distress.

solar *a* pertaining to the sun; *ns* **s. cell** device for converting sunlight into electrical energy; **s. panel** unit composed of several solar cells; *v* **solarize** expose to action of sun; *ns* **solar plexus** network of nerves in pit of stomach; **solar system** system of planets, comets, asteroids, etc. which revolve round the sun.

solarium *n* **1** glass-walled place giving maximum exposure to sunlight **2** bed with lamps for giving artificial suntan (*pl* **-ia** *or* **-iums**).

sold *pt, pp of* **sell**.

solder *n* fusible metal alloy used for joining metal; *v* join

with this; *n* **soldering-iron.**

soldier *n* one enlisted in army; *v* serve as soldier; *n* **soldiery** soldiers collectively.

sole[1] *n* **1** under surface of foot; under part of shoe, etc. **2** edible marine flatfish; *v* (*of shoes, etc.*) fit with (new) sole.

sole[2] *a* one and only; single.

solecism *n* **1** grammatical error **2** social mistake.

solemn *a* serious; formal; grave; deliberate; *n* **solemnity**; *v* **solemnize** perform with legal formalities; make solemn; *n* **-ization.**

sol-fa *n mus* system giving name to each note of scale, applicable to any key (*also* **tonic sol-fa**).

solicit *v* **1** request earnestly **2** accost (person) for immoral purpose; *ns* **-ation**; *n* **solicitor** *Brit* lawyer; *a* **solicitous** eager; anxious; *n* **solicitude** anxiety; concern.

solid *a* **1** not liquid or gaseous **2** compact; not hollow **3** financially sound; *n* solid body of three dimensions; *a* **s. state** *elec* using transistors *n* **solidity**; *v* **solidify** make, become solid; *ns* **solidification; solidarity** unanimity.

solidus *n* **1** ancient Roman gold coin **2** oblique stroke; diagonal.

soliloquy *n* talking to oneself; monologue not addressed to anyone; *v* **soliloquize.**

solipsism *n* theory that one can only have knowledge of oneself (*n* **-ist** *a* **-istic**.)

solitary *a* alone; single; lonely; *n* **solitude** state of being alone; loneliness; *n* **solitaire 1** single gem set on its own **2** card game for one.

solo *n mus* **-os. 1** composition for single instrument or voice **2** *fig* display, performance by one person **3** card game like whist; *n* **soloist**; *a* **solo** alone; unaccompanied.

solstice *n* time of year when earth's orbit makes sun most distant N or S of Equator.

solve *v* work out; answer; *as* **soluble** capable of being dissolved in liquid; **solvable** able to be solved; *ns* **solubility; solution** answer to problem; liquid containing dissolved solid; *a* **solvent** able to pay all debts; *n* substance that dissolves something (*n* **s. abuse** illegal drug abuse); *n* **solvency** ability to pay debts.

somatic *a* of the body.

somber *a* dark, gloomy.

sombrero *n Sp* **-os.** wide-brimmed felt or straw hat.

some *pron* certain number, not specified; *a* unspecified (person, thing, number) *coll* remarkable; great; *n* **somebody**; *adv* **somehow** by means still unknown; *n* **something** thing not clearly defined; *idm* **something of a** rather a; *a* **sometime** formerly; *advs* **sometimes**

A B C D E F G H I J K L M N O P Q R **S** T U V W X Y Z

now and then; occasionally; **somewhat** rather; **somewhere** in unspecified place.

someplace *adv* somewhere.

somersault *v* turn, fall head over heels; *n*.

somnambulist *n* sleepwalker; *n* **-ism.**

somnolent *a* sleepy; drowsy; *n* **-ence.**

son *n* male child; *n* **son-in-law** daughter's husband.

sonar *n* apparatus used in locating underwater objects.

sonata *n* musical composition in several movements; *n* **sonatina** short sonata.

son et lumière *n Fr* outdoor spectacle with music and special flood-lighting to dramatically present the history of a place.

song *n* musical utterance by human voice, or by birds; *idm* **for a song** very cheaply; *idm* **song and dance** *coll* unnecessary fuss; *n* **songster** singer; *esp* singing bird.

sonic *a* of sound; *ns* **s. boom** sound of shock waves set up by aircraft flying through sound barrier.

sonnet *n* short poem of fourteen lines.

sonny *n* friendly way of addressing a young boy.

sonorous *a* deep, resonant.

soon *adv* in short time; early; readily; immediately.

soot *n* black flaky substance produced by burning matter; *a* **sooty;** *v* cover with soot.

soothe *v* appease; comfort; make calm; allay pains, etc.

soothsayer *n* prophet; diviner.

sop *n* **1** bread dipped in liquid **2** *fig* concession; bribe; *a* **soppy** *sl* soft; sloppy; *coll* weakly sentimental; *v* **sop up** absorb (liquid).

sophist *n* plausible reasoner, quibbler; *ns* **sophism** fallacious argument; **sophistry** clever but false argument; *v* **sophisticate** deprive of naturalness; corrupt (*a* **-ated** worldly-wise; artificial; (engine, etc.) having latest refinements, *n* **-ation**).

sophomore *n* second-year university or high-school student; *a* **sophomoric** intellectually immature.

soporific *n, a* (drug) causing sleep.

sopping *a* very wet.

soppy *a see* **sop.**

soprano *n* **-os.** person with highest singing voice; instrument with high register (as **s. saxophone**); musical part for this.

sorbet *n Fr* water-based ices flavored with fruit.

sorcerer *n* wizard, magician; *n* **sorcery** witchcraft; enchantment.

sordid *a* mean; ignoble; squalid; obscene; *n* **-ness.**

sore *a* painful; affronted; grieved; *n* boil; lesion; ulcer; *n* **s.point** painful memory; *adv* **-ly** very greatly; grievously; *n* **-ness.**

sorghum *n* grain grown in tropical countries.

sorority *n* society of female students; sisterhood.

sorrel *n* herb with reddish-brown acrid-tasting leaves; *a* of this color.

sorrow *n* grief; mental pain; regret; *v* grieve, mourn; *a* **-ful.**

sorry *a* **1** regretful; gloomy **2** mean; poor.

sort *a* class; kind; *idm* **out of sorts** *coll* unwell; *idm* **sort of** *coll* rather; *v* arrange, select in groups; *v* put in order; *phr v* **sort out 1** separate from others **2** deal with *n* **sorter.**

sortie *n Fr* sudden attack by besieged troops.

SOS *n abbr* save our souls; international signal of distress.

so-so *a coll* neither good nor bad; mediocre.

sot *n* drunkard; *a* **sottish.**

sotto voce *adv* in an undertone.

soufflé *n Fr* light baked dish made with beaten whites of egg; dish for baking this.

sough *v* rustle or murmur, as the wind; *n* **sough.**

sought *pt, pp of* **seek;** *a* **s.-after** wanted; popular.

soul *n* **1** spiritual, non material part of humans; part thought to be immortal **2** human being **3** quality of decency and sincerity **4** essence (of quality) **5** *coll* **s. music** mid-20th century black American music; *ns* **s. mate**

person with whom one has deep, lifelong understanding; **s.-searching** critical analysis of one's own motives; **soulful** showing deep feeling (*adv -ly*; *n -ness*); **soulless** lacking feeling; without emotion; cruel; impersonal (*adv -ly*; *n -ness*).

sound[1] *n* what is heard; noise; *v* emit, cause to emit noise; seem; *phr v* **sound off** express feelings vigorously; *n* **sound barrier** moment when aircraft's speed equals the speed of sound.

sound[2] *a* **1** healthy; in good condition **2** logical **3** reliable; strong; *adv -ly* thoroughly.

sound[3] *v* measure depth of (water); plunge to bottom; *phr v* **sound out** ascertain views of; test with stethoscope; *n* strait; channel; *n pl* **soundings** depth of water taken with lead; **sound bite** *n* short extract from an interview, eg with a politician quoted in the media; *n* **sounding board** means of testing opinion.

soundtrack *n* band on motion-picture film on which sound is recorded.

soup *n* thick or clear liquid food made from meat or vegetables; *idm* **in the soup** *coll* in trouble; *phr v* **soup up** *coll* increase the power of.

soupçon *n Fr* a little bit.

sour *a* **1** acid; rancid; fermented **2** (*of soil*) poor;

damp **3** morose; *idm* **sour grapes** belittling something out of reach because it is not available; *v* make, become sour; *n -ness*.

source *n* **1** spring **2** starting point; origin.

souse *v* pickle; soak with water; *a* **soused** pickled; *sl* very drunk.

south *n* cardinal point opposite N; region in this direction; *a, adv* towards south; *as* **southerly** towards, coming from south; **southern** pertaining to south; *ns* **sou'wester** waterproof hat.

southpaw *n* left-handed boxer, pitcher.

souvenir *n* keepsake; memento.

sovereign *n* **1** monarch, supreme ruler **2** British gold coin worth £1; *a* supreme; efficacious; effectual; *n* **sovereignty** supreme power or rule.

soviet *n* political unit of former USSR; council of workers, soldiers etc.; **S. Union** former state of Russia and its satellites (1917–1991).

sow[1] *n* fully grown female pig.

sow[2] *v* scatter, cast seed on ground; *pt* **sowed**; *pp* **sown** or **sowed**; *n* **sower**.

soy *n* species of oil-yielding bean; **s. flour** flour made from dried ground soya beans; *n* **soy sauce** dark brown sauce from fermented

soya beans.

spa *n* **1** mineral spring **2** health resort having mineral spring.

space *n* **1** area; distance **2** period of time **3** region beyond earth's atmosphere **4** room; empty place; *v* place at intervals apart; *phr v* **space out** leave plenty of room between; *as* **spaced out** *coll* stupefied (as by drugs); absent-minded; **space cadet** *n* flaky, unfocussed person; *ns* **spacecraft**, **spaceship** vehicle designed for travel outside earth's atmosphere; **spaceman** *coll* astronaut; **s. station** large satellite base from which space research can be carried out; **spacious** extensive, roomy.

spade *n* digging tool with flat blade; playing card of suit of spades; **spade work** preliminary work.

spaghetti *n It* thin macaroni.

span *n* **1** distance between tip of thumb and little finger, when fully extended; approximately 9" **2** full extent **3** space between supports of bridge **4** extreme breadth *esp* of birds or aircraft across wings; *v* **spanning, spanned.** measure with hand; stretch across, over.

spangle *n* small disk of brilliant metal, used as ornament; sequin.

Spaniard *n* Spanish person.

spaniel *n* breed of sporting dog

a
b
c
d
e
f
g
h
i
j
k
l
m
n
o
p
q
r
s
t
u
v
w
x
y
z

with long drooping ears and silky hair.

Spanish n, a (language) of Spain.

spank v slap with open hand; move briskly; n **-ing** series of slaps, as punishment; a brisk, rapid; n **spanker** fast horse; fore-and-aft sail on mizzen mast.

spanner n wrench; tool for tightening or loosening nuts and bolts.

spar[1] n pole used as mast.

spar[2] n kind of crystalline mineral.

spar[3] v **sparring, sparred.** practice boxing blows; box in friendly manner; n **sparring partner** one with whom boxer practises.

spare a 1 meager; lean, thin 2 additional; extra; in reserve; n spare part for machine esp car; v 1 refrain from killing, etc.; show mercy 2 do without; give away.

spare rib n cut of pork ribs.

spark n 1 glowing particle thrown off by burning substance; brief flash of light accompanying electric discharge 2 fig vitality; life; v emit sparks; phr v **spark off** ignite; cause; **spark plug** device for securing electric ignition in internal combustion engine.

sparkle v glitter; effervesce; n brilliance; gaiety, wit; n **sparkler** 1 coll diamond 2 small hand-held firework a **sparkling** 1 scintillating 2

intellectually brilliant 3 (of wine) effervescent.

sparrow n small common brown bird **s.-hawk** small hawk.

sparse a thinly scattered; scanty adv **-ly** n **-ness**.

spartan a austere; hardy; unflinching.

spasm n sudden violent, involuntary muscular contraction; a **spasmodic** jerky; intermittent (adv **-ally**).

spastic a suffering from lack of muscular control, due to congenital brain damage; n person suffering from such damage.

spat n 1 short gaiter 2 brief argument, tiff.

spate n sudden flood of river after rain; fig excessive amount.

spatial a pertaining to space.

spatter v splash drops on; n shower, sprinkling.

spatula n blunt, broad-bladed knife used for mixing paint, and in cooking.

spawn n eggs of fish, frogs, etc.; offspring; v 1 (of fish, etc.) lay eggs 2 fig generate in mass.

spay v remove ovaries of female animal.

speak v 1 utter words; convey meaning 2 give speech, lecture, etc.; converse; pt **spoke**; pp **spoken**; n **speaker** one who delivers, speech, lecture etc; cap presiding officer in House of

Representatives.

speakeasy n place selling liquor, esp place for illegal sale of alcohol (during Prohibition).

spear n long-shafted weapon with pointed head; v pierce, catch with spear.

spearmint n common garden mint.

special a particular; exceptional; not for public, **general use;** for specific purpose; distinctive; ns **s. school** school for handicapped children; n **-ist** one devoted to a particular branch of science, art, or profession; v **-ize** make special; limit; particularize; ns **-ization, speciality** special product, distinctive feature, etc.

specie n coined money.

species n pl **species.** class; group; sort, kind.

specific a 1 characteristic of species 2 definite; 3 med of or for particular disease (n such a remedy; adv **-ally** n **s. gravity** ratio of density of substance to that of water; n pl **-s** particular details; v **specify** state definitely, precisely; n **specification** detailed description or statement.

specimen n representative example or sample; coll odd person.

specious a plausible but deceptive.

speck n small spot, mark; v

speckle mark, be marked with small spots; *a* **speckless** spotless.

specs *n pl sl* **1** spectacles; eyeglasses **2** specifications.

spectacle *n* show; display; *pl* pair of optical lenses in frame; *a* **spectacular** impressive, remarkable; *n* **spectator** onlooker.

specter *n* ghost; apparition; *a* **spectral**.

spectrum *n* series of bands of colored light formed when beam has passed through prism; *pl* **spectra;** *n* **spectroscope** instrument for analyzing spectra.

speculate *v* form theory about; invest in uncertain security; *n* **speculator;** *a* **speculative** given to guessing; risky; *n* **speculation**.

sped *pt, pp of* **speed**.

speech *n* **1** act, faculty of speaking; language **2** formal public discourse; *n* **s. synthesizer** computerized device for generating oral messages in imitation of human speech; *v* **speechify** make long, tedious speeches; *a* **speechless 1** dumb **2** at loss for words.

speed *n* swiftness; velocity; *v* move quickly; drive (vehicle) at high speed; *pt, pp* **sped** or **speeded**; *ns* **s. hump** or **bump** raised surface across width of road causing traffic to move very slowly; **s. limit** maximum legal speed; **s. trap** section of road where

police monitor speed of traffic by radar; *v* **1** (cause to) move quickly **2** exceed speed limit (*n* **-ing**); *phr v* **speed up** go faster; *ns* **speedometer** instrument to show speed of vehicle; **speedway** motorcycle race track; *a* **speedy** rapid; prompt.

speedwell *n* flowering herb related to the snapdragon.

spell[1] *n* **1** magic formula **2** fascination; *as* **spellbinding** fascinating; **spellbound** entranced.

spell[2] *n* bout, short period of activity.

spell[3] *v* say or write letter by letter; *pt, pp* **spelled**; *phr v* **spell out** explain in more detail; *n* **spelling** way in which word is spelled.

spelunker *n* cave explorer; *n* **spelunking.**

spend *v* pay out; expend; wear out, exhaust; *pt, pp* **spent**; *n* **spend-thrift** one who squanders; wasteful person.

sperm *n* **1** male fertilizing fluid (*also* **semen**) **2** single male reproductive cell (*also* **spermatozoon**); *ns* **s. bank** place where supplies of sperm are kept for later use in artificial insemination; **spermicide** substance that kills sperm (*a* **-cidal**); *n* **sperm whale** large whale.

spermaceti *n* white, waxy substance obtained from cetaceans and head of sperm whale.

spew *v* **1** gush out **2** vomit **3** exude or extrude material.

sphere *n* **1** ball; globe **2** scope; range; status; *ns* **spherical**; *n* **spheroid** nearly spherical body.

sphincter *n anat* ring of muscle that contracts to close an orifice (*e.g.,* esophageal sphincter).

Sphinx *n* fabulous human-headed lion; Egyptian statue of this; *fig* inscrutable person.

spice *n* aromatic pungent vegetable seasoning; *fig* that which adds interest or excitement; *a* **spicy**.

spick and span, spic and span *a* bright, fresh, tidy.

spider *n* small eight-legged animal, which spins web to catch prey; *a* **spidery**.

spiel *n coll* long voluble speech intended to create an impression.

spigot *n* **1** plug for stopping air hole in cask **2** faucet.

spike *n* **1** sharp pointed piece of metal, wood, etc. **2** technique of serving ball in volleyball; *pl* **-s** cleats; athlete's running shoes; *v* **1** impale **2** *coll* make (drink) strong by adding alcohol to it **3** prevent (news article) being printed; *a* **spiky** (*n* **-ness**).

spill[1] *v* (*of liquid*) flow, be upset, out of vessel; (*of persons*) fall from vehicle, etc.; *pt, pp* **spilt** or **spilled**; *idm* **spill the beans** *coll* reveal a secret (by accident or

A
B
C
D
E
F
G
H
I
J
K
L
M
N
O
P
Q
R
S
T
U
V
W
X
Y
Z

intentionally); *n* fall.

spill[2] *n* splinter, strip of paper, or wood used as taper.

spin *v* twist (wool, etc. into thread); whirl; (*of spiders, etc.*) exude filament for web; *pt* **spun** (*ar* **span**); *pp* **spun;** *n* act of spinning; twist; whirl; **spin doctor** *n* person who puts a positive slant on events on behalf of a political party or politician; *phr v* **spin out** prolong; *ns* **s.-off** additional indirect benefit; television show developed from previous program, *esp* sitcoms; **spinner; spinning (s.wheel** household machine for spinning wool into thread); *ns* **spinning** act of making web; process of forming thread; **spinneret** silk-spinning organ of silkworm, spider, etc.

spina bifida *n med* fetal malformation of spine which leaves spinal cord partly exposed.

spinach *n* garden vegetable with edible leaves.

spinal *a* of the spine; *n* **s.cord** thick cluster of nerves enclosed within the spine.

spindle *n* rod, axis on which anything rotates; *a* **spindly** long and slender.

spine *n* backbone; thin, sharp thorn, or growth on animal; back of book; *as* **s. chilling** terrifying; **spineless 1** without backbone **2** *fig* weak; cowardly (*adv* **-ly;** *n*

-ness); spiny prickly.

spinet *n Fr* compact upright piano.

spinster *n* unmarried woman.

spire *n* pointed part of steeple.

spiral *a* winding constantly about center, like thread of screw; *n* spiral curve.

spirit *n* **1** person's mind or feelings; soul **2** soul separated from the body (as after death); ghost **3** life force **4** temper; emotion **5** courage **6** liveliness **7** characteristic quality of something **8** intended meaning **9** distilled alcohol for industrial use **10** *usu pl* distilled alcohol as a beverage **11** *pl* **-s** state of morale *n* **s.level** tool used by builder for checking whether surfaces are level; *as* **-ed** lively (*adv* **-ly;** *n* **-ness**); *phr v* **spirit away** remove secretly; *as* **spiritual** pertaining to soul or spirit, not material; **spiritless** listless, apathetic; *ns* **spiritualism** belief that spirits of dead can communicate with living; (*n, a* **-ist**); *a* **spirituous** alcoholic.

spit[1] *n* sharp rod for roasting meat; sandy point projecting into sea; *v* thrust through.

spit[2] *v* **spitting, spat.** eject saliva; *pt, pp* **spat;** *n* saliva; *ns* **spittle** saliva; **spittoon** vessel to spit into.

spite *n* malice; *v* act maliciously toward; *prep* **in spite of** notwithstanding; *a*

spiteful.

spitting image *n* exact likeness.

splash *v* **1** scatter (liquid) on **2** fall in drops on; *phr v* **splash down** (of spacecraft) fall into the sea (*n* **splashdown**); *n* **1** sound of, result of splashing **2** impressive effect; *a* **splashy** flamboyant; showy.

splatter *v* **1** splash noisily **2** cover with splashes.

splay *v* slant; dislocate (joint); *n* slanting edge; *a* **s.-footed** with flat, turned-out feet.

spleen *n* ductless gland in abdomen; *fig* ill humor; *a* **splenetic.**

splendid *a* magnificent; illustrious; *coll* excellent; *n* **splendor** brilliance; magnificence.

splice *v* join by interweaving strands; join (wood) by overlapping; *coll* marry.

splint *n* rigid piece of wood, etc., *esp* when keeping fractured bone in place; *v* support with splint; *n* **splinter** small, sharp broken off piece of wood, glass, etc.; *n* **s.group** group separated from main body; *v* break into fragments.

split *v* **splitting, split. 1** divide lengthways; divide along grain (as wood) **2** divide into parts **3** share; *pt, pp* **split;** *idm* **split hairs** argue over very small differences; *n* cleft, tear (in fabric); *a* **split-level** having rooms on levels a half-story apart.

splotch n blot or stain; a **splotchy.**

splurge n ostentation; v make vulgar display; indulge extravagant impulse.

splutter v spit slightly while speaking; utter indistinctly.

spoil v 1 injure; damage; deteriorate 2 cause (a child, a pet) to become badly behaved, selfish, etc. by over-indulgence; pt, pp **spoiled** or **spoilt**; idm **spoiling for** eager for; n pl **-s 1** booty; stolen goods 2 profits; n **spoil sport** one who prevents others from enjoying themselves.

spoke[1] n radial bar of wheel; n **spokeshave** kind of plane.

spoke[2] pt, **spoken** pp of speak.

spokesperson n person chosen to represent views of group (also **spokesman** pl **-men**, **spokeswoman** pl **-women**).

sponge n 1 marine animal whose fibrous skeleton is used to absorb liquids, or (once dead) for cleaning 2 light cake or pad; v clean with sponge; phr v **sponge off/on somebody** live at somebody's expense (n **sponger**); n **s. cake** very light cake; a **spongy** soft but resilient; having texture of sponge.

sponsor n guarantor; patron; godparent.

spontaneous a (of persons) voluntary; self-acting, or self-originated; n **spontaneity.**

spoof n, v hoax; n amusing untrue copy.

spook n ghost, wraith; v frighten.

spooky a coll ghostly; mysteriously frightening.

spool n reel, bobbin.

spoon n implement consisting of shallow bowl on handle, used in cooking and conveying food to mouth, etc.; v use, lift with, spoon; sl make love; v **s.-feed 1** feed (baby) with spoon 2 fig teach in a way that requires no thinking from pupils.

spoonerism n ridiculous error resulting from accidental exchange of sounds (e.g., 'share of poohs' instead of 'pair of shoes').

spoor n track of wild animal.

sporadic a scattered; occurring in single cases.

spore n minute reproductive organism, of flowerless plant, or as in bacteria.

sport n 1 physical activity, esp outdoor, for exercise or amusement 2 particular form of this; game with set rules 3 fun 4 coll fairminded person with sense of fun; as **sporting 1** relating to sport 2 fond of sport 3 fair and generous (adv **-ly**); **sportive** playful (adv **-ly** n **-ness**); ns **sportscar** low fast car; **sportsman** (pl **-men**; n **-manship** respect for fairness in competing); **sportswoman** (pl **-women**); a **sporty 1** fond of, good at sport 2 attractive to see.

spot n 1 small mark esp if

round; pimple 2 small place; fig moral blemish; idm **hot spot** uncomfortable or dangerous situation; idm **in a tight spot** coll in a difficult situation; idm **put on the spot 1** force to act 2 cause embarrassment; ns **s.check** random check without warning; v **spotting, spotted.** mark with spot; coll see; catch sight of; **spotlight** strong beam of light able to be focused on one spot (v illuminate with spotlight; coll draw attention to); as **spotted** decorated with spots; **spotless 1** without blemish 2 perfectly clean (adv **-ly** n **-ness**); **spotty** with pimples (n **-ness**).

spouse n husband or wife.

spout v gush, pour out; n projecting lip or tube for pouring liquid; gushing jet of liquid, water.

sprain v, n twist or wrench (of muscles, tendons, etc.).

sprat n herringlike fish.

sprawl v lie, be stretched out awkwardly; straggle.

spray[1] n sprig, twig with smaller branches or flowers.

spray[2] n fine droplets of liquid; wind-blown particles of sea-water; atomizer; device for spraying; v squirt, treat, with spray; become spray; n **sprayer** device for spraying.

spread v cover (surface) with; stretch out, extend in all directions; become widely diffused, circulated; pt, pp

A B C D E F G H I J K L M N O P Q R **S** T U V W X Y Z

spread; n 1 extent 2 increase 3 feast; a **s.-eagled** lying with arms and legs stretched wide; n **spreadsheet** *comput* program for displaying rows of figures, *esp* in accounting.

spree n frolic; drinking or spending bout.

sprig n small twig; small nail; scion; a **sprigged** ornamented with spray-like design.

sprightly a lively, brisk; n **sprightliness**.

spring v 1 leap 2 pounce 3 bubble, gush forth 4 sprout up; *pt* **sprang;** *pp* **sprung;** n 1 source; well 2 first season of year 3 recoil 4 piece of coiled resilient metal, etc. 5 leap; *idm* **spring a leak** (of container) begin to let liquid escape; *phr vs* **spring from** originate from; **spring something on somebody** surprise somebody with something; n 1 season after winter 2 natural source of running water 3 coiled or bent length of resilient metal 4 elasticity 5 act of springing; ns **springboard** 1 flexible board used for diving 2 *fig* starting point; **s.onion** small onion eaten raw in salad; **s. roll** small, savory egg roll, eaten as appetizer; **s. tide** strong tide occurring at time of full or new moon; v **s. clean** clean (house etc) very thoroughly; a **springy** elastic; n *cap* **springer** variety of spaniel.

springbok n S African gazelle.

sprinkle v scatter in small drops; strew; ns **sprinkler; sprinkling** small quantity of drops, particles; few scattered people or objects.

sprint v run at full speed for short distance; n such run; n **-er.**

sprite n fairy; elf.

sprocket n projecting tooth on wheel for engaging chain.

sprout v put forth shoots, begin to grow; n young shoot; n *pl* **Brussels sprouts** vegetable like miniature cabbages.

spruce[1] n type of coniferous tree; a smart and neat in dress.

spruce[2] a clean and neat (*adv* **-ly;** n **-ness**); *phr v* **spruce up** make (oneself) clean, neat.

sprung *pp* of **spring.**

spry a nimble, agile; alert; (*adv* **-ly;** n **-ness**).

spud n small spade for digging up weeds, etc.; *sl* potato.

spume n, v foam; froth.

spun *pt, pp* of **spin.**

spunk n 1 *coll* courage 2 *sl* semen.

spur n 1 pricking wheel fixed on rider's heel, for urging on horse 2 pointed projection on rooster's leg 3 projecting ridge or part of mountain range 4 stimulus; *idm* **on the spur of the moment** without forethought; v **spurring, spurred.** prick with spurs; urge; ride hard.

spurious a not genuine; false; sham.

spurn v reject scornfully; repel.

spurt n jet; short vigorous effort, *esp* in race; v gush out suddenly; make sudden brief effort (to increase speed etc).

sputnik n (Russian) satellite.

sputter v make series of spitting noises.

sputum n saliva; spittle.

spy n agent employed to obtain secret information; v **spying, spied.** act as spy; catch sight of; n **spy glass** small hand telescope.

sq *abbr* square.

squab n young pigeon.

squabble n petty quarrel; v quarrel, bicker.

squad n small group of people working together, *esp mil.*

squadron n 1 body of cavalry 2 group of warships.

squalid a foul; dingy; sordid; mean; n **squalor.**

squall n 1 harsh, shrill shriek 2 brief, violent storm; v scream; a **squally** gusty.

squalor n squalid state.

squander v spend, use wastefully.

square n 1 rectangle with sides of equal length 2 open space of similar shape in a town 3 product of number multiplied by itself 4 *coll* very conventional person; a 1 of the shape of a square 2 tidy; arranged straight 3 fair and honest 4 of units used to measure area (*e.g.,* **square miles**) 5 having settled all debts (mutually); v 1 give square shape to 2 divide into squares 3 multiply (number) by itself 4 make even 5 get cooperation of, *esp* by bribery 6 settle debt; *phr v* **square up to** confront (challenging situation) with determination; *ns* **s. dance** dance for four couples; **s. meal** *coll* substantial, hearty meal that satisfies hunger; **s. one** the beginning; **s. rig** way of setting sails on old ships (*a* **s. rigged**); **s. root** factor of a number which, when squared, gives the specified number; *adv* **-ly;** *n* **-ness;** *as* **squared** covered with squares; **squarish** roughly square in shape.

squash *v* crush, press flat; *coll* snub; *n* 1 edible vegetable 2 pulpy mass 3 game for two, played with rackets and soft ball in walled court.

squat *v* **sqatting, squatted.** sit on heels; *a* short and thick; *n* **squatter** illegal settler in unoccupied house or land.

squawk *n* loud, harsh cry; *v* utter such cry.

squeak *v* utter weak, thin cry of fright etc; make high, grating noise, as of unoiled hinge; *n* such noise.

squeal *v* utter shrill prolonged cry; *sl* betray secrets; *n* long shrill cry.

squeamish *a* easily nauseated; oversensitive.

squeegee *n* rubber wiper for cleaning glass surfaces.

squeeze *v* press; wring; extort; extract; *n* act of squeezing.

squelch *v* 1 produce sucking, gurgling sound 2 end abruptly; *n* such a sound.

squib *n* 1 short article; filler 2 small hissing firework.

squid *n* cuttlefish.

squiggle *v* wriggle; squirm; *n* twisty illegible writing.

squint *v* look in different directions with each eye; *n* this eye affliction, strabismus; *coll* glance.

squire *n* county landowner; formerly, attendant on knight; man escorting woman; *v* escort woman.

squirm *v*, *n* wriggle; writhe.

squirrel *n* small bushy-tailed rodent.

squirt *v* eject, be forced out, in jet; *n* jet (of liquid); syringe.

Sr *abbr* Senior.

SS 1 steamship 2 Schutzstaffel (Hitler's secret police force).

ssh *interj* be quiet.

SST *abbr* supersonic transport.

St. *abbr* Saint.

stab *v* **stabbing, stabbed.** pierce with pointed weapon; *n* wound so inflicted; *idm* **have a stab (at)** *coll* make an attempt (at); *idm* **stab in the back** act of betrayal; *a* **stabbing** (of pain) sharp (*n* act of stabbing).

stabilize *v* make stable; restore to equilibrium; *ns* **stabilization, stabilizer** device for keeping ship, aircraft, etc., in equilibrium.

stable *a* firmly fixed; not easily upset; resolute; *n* **stability** steadiness, firmness.

stable *n* building where horses are kept; *v* put in stable.

staccato *a mus* with each note played in sharply detached manner.

stack *n* 1 large heap, *esp* of hay, straw 2 neat pile 3 tall chimney 4 rack with shelves for books; *pl* **-s** *coll* large amount; *v* pile up in orderly way.

stadium *n* **-iums** or **-ia.** open-air arena for athletics, etc.

staff *n* tall pole; organized body of workers; servants of one employer; *mus* five lines on which notes are written (*also* **stave**); *pl* **staffs, staves.**

stag *n* male deer; *a coll* for men only, as **s. party.**

stage *n* 1 raised floor or platform in theater 2 *fig* scene of action 3 fixed stopping place (of bus, etc.) 4 point of development; *ns* **s. coach** (formerly) horse-drawn public vehicle; **s. door** theater back entrance used by actors and staff; **s. fright** nervousness felt when appearing in public; **s. left/right** left/right from actor's point of view; **s. manager** person responsible for arranging stage sets, properties, etc. (*v* **s. manage**); **s. whisper** loud whisper intended for audience to hear; *a* **s.-struck** ambitious to become actor; *v* 1 put (play) on stage 2 cause to happen, *esp* to create effect; *n* **staging** 1 production

a b c d e f g h i j k l m n o p q r **s** t u v w x y z

of drama, opera, etc. **2** scaffolding.

stagger v walk, move unsteadily; reel; shock; prevent from coinciding; n unsteady gait; n pl disease of horses and cattle.

stagnant a **1** (of water) not flowing; stale; unhealthy **2** fig sluggish; not making progress; v **stagnate** be or become stagnant (n **-ation**).

stagy a theatrical; exaggerated; adv **-ily**; n **-iness**.

staid a sedate; sober; steady; n **staidness**.

stain v discolor, impart color deliberately; soil; blemish; n spot, blemish; n **stained glass** colored glass for decorative windows; a **stainless 1** free of stains **2** resistant to rust (n **s.steel**).

stairs n pl series of steps usu in building; ns **staircase, stairway** structure enclosing stairs; flight of stairs; n **stairwell** vertical shaft holding stairs.

stake n **1** pointed stick or post **2** prize **3** money bet **4** financial interest **5** share; idm **at stake** at risk; v bet, risk; mark with posts, etc.; idm **stake a claim** claim ownership; phr v **stake out 1** declare special interest in **2** coll (of police) watch secretly (n **s.-out**).

stalactite n tapering lime formation hanging from roof of cave, etc.; n **stalagmite** similar formation rising from cave floor.

stale a **1** not fresh **2** fig out of practice **3** tired by too much work.

stalemate n **1** chess position in which neither player can win **2** fig deadlock.

stalk[1] v stem of plant.

stalk[2] v walk in stiff, dignified way; pursue (prey, game, etc.) stealthily; ns **stalker**; fig pretext.

stall n **1** division in stable, etc. **2** booth in market for sale of goods **3** front seat in theater, etc. **4** church pew; v unintentionally stop (engine); (of aircraft) lose flying speed.

stallion n uncastrated male horse.

stalwart a strong; brave; unflinching.

stamen n pollen-bearing male organ of flower.

stamina n power of endurance; vigour; vitality.

stammer v speak hesitantly, with repetition of speech sounds; stutter; n this speech defect; n **stammerer**.

stamp v **1** put foot down heavily **2** affix postage stamp **3** impress mark on; phr v **stamp out** fig destroy utterly; n **1** act of stamping **2** imprinted mark, or instrument making it **3** printed, gummed label printed as evidence of postage paid; n **stamping ground** favorite haunt.

stampede n sudden frightened rush, esp of cattle; crowd, etc.; v flee in panic; cause to stampede.

stance n attitude in standing, esp when about to strike ball in golf, etc.

stranch a **1** staunch **2** stop flow, as blood.

stand v **1** be in, move to upright position **2** be on one's feet **3** be in a certain position, condition **4** remain in force **5** endure; tolerate **6** pay for; treat somebody else to; pt, pp **stood**; idm **stand a chance** have some hope or prospect; idm **stand on one's own two feet** be independent; idm **stand to reason** be clear to any sensible person; phr vs **stand back** refrain from taking part; **stand by 1** remain loyal to **2** be ready to act (n **standby** reserve; idm **on standby 1** ready for action **2** waiting for a cancellation (**s. ticket** ticket available if a cancellation occurs) **3** take no part; **stand down 1** resign **2** leg leave witness box; **stand for 1** represent **2** be strongly in favor of; support **3** tolerate; **stand in (for somebody)** be a substitute (for somebody) (n **s.-in**); **stand out 1** be clearly seen **2** be different in quality; **stand up** (of evidence) be convincing; **stand somebody up** fail to keep a date; **stand up for** support; **stand up to** resist; n **standing** a erect;

lasting; *ns* **standpoint** position, repute; point of view; **standstill** complete cessation of progress, etc.

standard *n* flag; fixed rule; quality; approved model; *ns* **s.-bearer 1** person carrying standard **2** leader; **s. of living** level of material comfort and wealth; *v* **-ize** make so as to conform with single standard (*n* **-ization**).

standing *n* **1** rank **2** reputation; *idm* **of long standing** well established; *n* **s. order** order for regular deliveries; **standoffish** *a* unfriendly; *adv* **-ly**; *n* **-ness**.

stank *pt of* **stink**.

stanza *n* group of verse lines.

staphylococcus, staph *n* any of several spherical bacteria, sometimes pathogenic.

staple *n* **1** U-shaped piece of metal with pointed ends, for fastening **2** paper fastener **3** principal commodity **4** chief raw material **5** thread, fiber of wool, cotton; *a* leading, principal; *v* fasten with staple; grade (wool, etc.); *n* **stapler** grader of wool, etc.; machine for wire-stitching paper, etc.

star *n* **1** luminous heavenly body **2** figure, device resembling apparent shape of star **3** popular actor, etc.; leading player; **4** asterisk (*); *ns* **s.chamber** powerful, secret court; **s.-dust** dreamy, romantic fantasy; **s.-gazer 1** *coll* person interested in

astronomy **2** dreamy, unrealistic person (*n* **s.-gazing**); **s. sign** any one of 12 signs of the zodiac; **s. turn** item in entertainment causing greatest attraction; **s.wars** *coll* strategic defense initiative; *as* **s.-crossed** ill-fated; **s. studded** with many famous performers; *v* **starring, starred. 1** play a main role **2** mark with stars; *ns* **stardom** state of being famous; **starfish** (*also* **seastar**) flat star-shaped fish; **starlet** young actress; *a* **starry** full of stars (*a* **s.-eyed** enthusiastic but unrealistic).

starboard *n* right-hand side of ship, looking forward; *a* of, on this side.

starch *n* **1** carbohydrates, main food element in vegetables **2** white soluble powder mixed with water for stiffening linen, etc.; *v* make stiff thus; *a* **starchy** containing starch; stiff, formal.

stare *v* look, gaze at intently, fixedly; *n* prolonged intent look.

stark *a* stiff; rigid; absolute; utter; *adv* absolutely.

starkers *a coll* completely naked.

starling *n* gregarious glossy black bird.

start *v* begin; set going; move with jerk; *n* sudden jerk; beginning; advantage in contest; *n* **-er** signaller for race to start; *idm* **for starters** to begin with.

startle *v* alarm; shock; surprise.

starve *v* die, suffer, from lack of food; suffer from cold; *ns* **starveling** thin, underfed person or thing; **starvation**.

stash *v coll* hide; store away (*also n*).

state *n* **1** condition; rank; position **2** nation and its government; self-governing division of country **3** pomp; *v* **state** express in words; *as* **state-of-the-art** using most modern technology; **stateless** having no citizenship of any country (*n* **-ness**); *ns* **statecraft** skill in handling State affairs; **S. Department** US government department of foreign affairs; **s. room 1** ceremonial reception room **2** cabin for passengers on ship; *a* **stated** previously determined, fixed.

stately *a* dignified; imposing (*n* **-iness**); *n* **s. home** large house or estate, *usu* of historical interest, open to public.

statement *n* **1** formal declaration (oral or written) **2** summary of financial transactions, showing present state of account.

statesman *n* person skilled in management of State affairs; wise leader (*pl* **-men**); *a* **-like** *n* **-ship**.

static *a* stationary; *n* atmospheric interference on radio or TV; **s. electricity** electricity that accumulates in an object; *n pl* **statics**

branch of physics concerned with bodies at rest and balance of forces.

station *n* **1** place, position where thing stops or is placed **2** walk in life; employment; occupation; *v* place in specific spot; *ns* **stationmaster** person in charge of railway station; *n* **s. wagon** elongated car with squared back for families; *a* **-ary** at rest; not moving; not changing.

stationery *n* writing materials, pens, paper, ink, etc.; *n* **stationer** dealer in writing materials.

statistics *n pl* systematic collection and arrangement of numerical facts; study of these; *n* **statistician** one skilled in dealing with statistics; *a* **statistic(al)**.

statue *n* carved or molded figure; *ns* **statuary** statues collectively; **statuette** little statue; *a* **statuesque** having dignity or serenity of stature.

stature *n* **1** bodily height, size **2** prestige, bearing.

status *n* **1** legal or social standing **2** high social position; *ns* **s. quo** present or original state of affairs; **s. symbol** possession believed to show high social standing.

statute *n* law enacted by the legislative branch of government; *a* **statutory** depending on, enacted by statute.

staunch *v* stanch; stop flow (of blood); *a* trustworthy; loyal; *adv* **-ly** *n* **-ness**.

stave *n* curved wooden strip forming part of cask; stanza; *mus* staff; *v pt, pp* **stove** or **staved** *phr vs* **stave in** smash a hole in; **stave off** keep away with a struggle.

stay[1] *v* **1** check **2** remain in place as visitor, etc. **3** last out **4** pause; *idm* **stay put** remain in place; *idm* **stay the course** persevere to the end; *n* rest, visit; *leg* suspension of proceedings, restraint; *n* **staying power** stamina.

stay[2] *n* prop; strut; rope supporting mast, etc.; *pl* corsets; *v* support, sustain.

St. Bernard *n* big powerful dog often used in mountain rescue.

std *abbr* standard.

STD *n abbr* sexually transmitted disease.

stead *n* place; service; **in (one's) stead** in place of; **in good stead** be of good service; *n* **steading** farmstead.

steady *a* firm; regular; sober; reliable; *v* make, become steady; *a* **steadfast** unwavering; resolute; *n* **steadiness**.

steak *n* thick slice of meat *esp* beef, or fish; *n* **s. tartare** highly seasoned raw minced beef.

steal *v* rob; thieve; move furtively, silently; *pt* **stole;** *pp* **stolen;** *idm* **steal the show** attract admiration that should have gone to

somebody else; *n* **stealth** secret, furtive action; *a* **-y**.

steam *n* water vapor; *v* cook, treat with steam; give off steam; move by steam power; *idm* **run out of steam** lose impetus; become exhausted; *idm* **under one's own steam** by one's own effort; *a, ns* **steam engine** one worked or propelled by steam; **steamer** utensil for cooking with steam; steamship; **s.-roller 1** heavy roller for leveling roads **2** *fig* massive force (*v* use forceful means to overcome opposition to proposal); *as* **steamed up** *coll* angry; **steaming 1** very hot **2** *coll* very angry; **steamy 1** full of steam **2** *coll* erotic.

steed *n poetic* horse.

steel *n* iron containing carbon; tool, weapon of steel; *ns* **s. band** Caribbean band of steel drums made from empty oil containers; **s. wool** pad of steel strands used as scourer; *v fig* harden; *a* **steely**.

steep[1] *a* **1** sharply inclined **2** *coll* exorbitant **3** incredible.

steep[2] *v* soak, saturate; *fig* imbue.

steeple *n* tall tapering structure on church; *ns* **steeplechase** cross-country horse race; **steeplejack** man employed to build, repair, clean steeples, tall chimneys, etc.

steer[1] *v* guide, direct course of (car, ship, etc.); aim one's course; *idm* **steer clear (of)** keep well away (from); *ns*

A B C D E F G H I J K L M N O P Q R S T U V W X Y Z

steerage cheapest form of travel by sea; **steering 1** mechanism for controlling direction of travel (**s. wheel**) **2** ability to steer.

steer[2] n young ox, bullock.

stein n mug, as for beer.

stellar a of stars.

stem[1] n **1** stalk; trunk **2** part of word to which inflectional endings are added; *phr v* **stemming, stemmed. stem from** be a result of.

stem[2] v check flow of; resist.

stench n offensive smell.

stencil n thin plate of metal, etc. perforated with design, or letters; pattern, design produced by applying coloring matter through holes of stencil plate; v decorate, make copy of, by using stencil.

stenography n shorthand writing; n **-grapher**.

stentorian a very loud.

step v **stepping, stepped.** lift and set down foot; walk; n **1** act of stepping **2** sound, mark made by foot **3** gait **4** pace **5** procedure **6** stair **7** *fig* degree, stage; *idm* **in/out of step 1** moving one's feet in/out of line with the rest of the group; *idm* **step by step** gradually *idm* **step on it!** *coll* go faster; *idm* **step out of line** fail to conform with accepted behavior; *phr vs* **step aside** make way for somebody else; **step down** resign; **step in** intervene; **step up 1** approach **2** increase; n

stepping-stone 1 stone laid on bed of river to allow walking across **2** *fig* stage in progress towards objective.

stepchild n child of husband or wife by previous marriage; *ns* **stepfather; stepmother**.

steppe n broad, open, treeless plain in Russia.

stereophonic a (*of sound*) giving effect of a live hearing, by sound coming from two speakers.

stereopticon n projector for slides, etc.

stereoscope n optical instrument producing illusion of relief and distance by presenting two different images of same subject, one to each eye.

stereotype n **1** fixed set of ideas or expectations about a certain type of person or thing (*a* **stereotypical;** *adv* **-ly**) **2** metal plate cast from mold of set up type; *a* **-typed 1** repeated without variation **2** printed from stereotype.

sterile a barren; unproductive; *n* **sterility;** *v* **sterilize** make incapable of reproduction; destroy bacteria; *ns* **sterilization** act, process of sterilizing; **sterilizer**.

sterling a **1** in British money; genuine, pure; **2** containing 92.5% silver; *fig* dependable.

stern a severe; strict; *n* **sternness**.

stern n after part of ship; rump of animal.

sternum n *pl* **-nums** or **-na.**

breast bone.

sternum n bone in chest connecting.

steroid n *chem* any one of group of soluble organic compounds having strong effect on development of body.

stertorous a breathing loudly, as with sound of snoring.

stet n direction to printer, on proof, to cancel correction made.

stethoscope n instrument for listening to action of heart or lungs.

stevedore n one who stows and unloads cargo at docks; longshoreman.

stew v cook slowly in closed vessel; n food so cooked; *coll* agitated condition.

steward n **1** salaried manager of large household or estate **2** manager of industrial shop, etc. **3** waiter, attendant on ship's, aircraft's passengers **4** official helping to organize race, meeting, etc.; *fem* **-ess**.

stick[1] v **1** thrust into, stab **2** attach; adhere **3** *coll* bear bravely **4** come to a stop; *pt, pp* **stuck;** *idm* **stick one's neck out** *coll* take a big risk; *idm* **stick to one's guns** refuse to be discouraged; *phr vs* **stick around** linger; **stick by/with** remain loyal to; **stick out** (cause to) protrude (*idm* **stick it out** *coll* persevere); **stick out for** *coll* insist on; **stick to 1** adhere to **2** refuse to change; **stick**

up 1 attach for display (*e.g.*, on a wall) **2** project upward **3** *coll* threaten with gun, etc. (*n* **s.-up** *coll* armed robbery); **stick up for** defend; *ns* **sticker** adhesive label; **stick-in-the-mud** *coll* person without enterprise; one who resists change; *a* **sticky 1** glue-like; adhesive **2** *coll* difficult (*n* **-iness**).

stick *n* slender rod of wood or other substance; *n pl* **the s.** rural area far from any big city.

stickle *v* **1** argue over trivia **2** insist on correctness; *n* **stickler** one who insists on trivial points of procedure.

stiff *a* rigid; not easily moving; thick; formal; difficult; *idm* **stiff upper lip** ability not to show; *v* **stiffen** make, become, stiff; *n* **stiffness**; *a* **stiffnecked** obstinate.

stifle *v* smother, suppress.

stigma *n* **-mas** or **-mata. 1** moral reproach **2** *bot* part of pistil receiving pollen; *v* **stigmatize** mark out (something discreditable); *n* **stigmatism**.

stile *n* steps, rail for climbing hedge or fence; turnstile.

stiletto *n* **-os.** small dagger; small pointed boring instrument; thin high heel of woman's shoe.

still[1] *a* **1** motionless; silent **2** (*of wine*) not sparkling; *v* calm; quieten; *n* **-ness**; *as* **stilly** quiet; **stillborn** born dead; *n* **s. life** picture of inanimate objects.

still[2] *n* apparatus for distilling; *n* **s.-room** store room for liquors, preserves, etc.

stilt *n* (*usu pl*) pole with foot rests, for raising walker above ground; wading bird; *a* **-ed** stiff in manner.

Stilton *n* strong-flavored English cheese with blue veins.

stimulus *n* anything which excites action; incentive; *pl* **stimuli**; *v* **stimulate** rouse up; urge, incite; *n, a* **stimulant** (drink, drug, etc.) producing temporary increase of energy; *n* **stimulation**.

sting *n* sharp, pointed, defensive and offensive organ of insect, reptile, etc.; sharp pain caused by sting; *idm* elaborate con game or ruse designed to entrap, *esp* criminals; *v* thrust sting into; cause, feel sharp pain; *pt, pp* **stung**.

stingy *a* mean; miserly; *n* **stinginess**.

stink *v* give out bad smell; *pt* **stank** or **stunk; pp stunk;** *n* stench; offensive smell.

stint *v* grudge; be stingy with; *n* limitation.

stipend *n* salary, *esp* of clergy; *a* **-iary** salaried.

stipple *v* paint, engrave in dots; *n* this method.

stipulate *v* make conditions in bargain; insist on; *n* **stipulation** proviso.

stir *v* **stirring, stirred.** set in motion; mix around and around with spoon, etc.; arouse, excite; *phr v* **stir up** provoke; *n* mental excitement *esp* public.

stir-crazy *a sl* restless or frantic from confinement.

stir-fry *v* fry quickly while stirring constantly over high heat.

stirrup *v* metal hoop hung by strap from saddle for supporting foot of rider.

stitch *n* **1** movement of needle in sewing; result of such movement **2** sharp pain in side; *idm* **in stitches** laughing uncontrollably; *v* sew.

stoat *n* animal of weasel family.

stock *n* **1** supply **2** goods available for sale **3** cooking liquid saved from food preparation for use in making soup, sauces, etc. **4** farm animals (*also* **livestock**) **5** lineage of family **6** capital of corporation or company **7** thick part of tree trunk or stem of plant **8** sweet-smelling flower; *pl* **-s 1** framework to support ship under repair **2** (formerly) wooden frame in which to place criminals on public display by immobilizing their arms and legs; *idm* **take stock (of)** consider well before making a decision; *v* keep supplies of; *a* **1** constantly available **2** habitually produced **3** commonplace; *ns* **s. car** car modified for use in racing; **S. Exchange, s. market** place for trading in stocks, etc.; **s.-in-trade 1** standard equipment for an occupation **2** *fig* standard behaviour or words of an individual; **s.-taking 1** checking of stock **2** review of progress; *ns* **stockbroker** person trading in stocks and shares on behalf of clients; **stockholder** owner of stocks and shares; **stockman** man looking after livestock; **stockpile** large supply accumulated for future use (*v* accumulate); **stockyard** yard where animals are kept prior to sale or slaughter.

stockade *n* barrier, wooden fence for defense.

stocking *n* close-fitting covering for leg and foot; *n* **s.-stuffer** small gift to put in Christmas stocking.

stocky *a* short, solid in appearance; *n* **-iness**.

stodgy *a* heavy; indigestible; dull.

stogie, stogy *n* inexpensive, long cigars.

stoic *n* person of rigid calm, fortitude; *a* **stoic(al)**, impassive; *n* **stoicism**.

stoke *v* fill with fuel; *idm* **stoke up** *coll* eat plenty; *n* **stoker** person tending furnace; fireman.

stole[1] *pt of* **steal**; *pp* **stolen**.

stole[2] *n* long, narrow wrap of fur, etc. worn about shoulders; narrow strip of cloth or silk worn by priests.

stolid *a* impassive; lacking animation or action; *adv* **-ly;** *n* **-ity.**

stomach *n* **1** sac in abdomen where food is digested; abdomen **2** *fig* liking; wish; *v* **1** eat without falling ill **2** *fig* tolerate; *n* **s. pump** apparatus for emptying stomach quickly; *a* **stomachic** pertaining to stomach; *n* digestive medicine.

stomp *v* walk heavily.

stone *n* **1** fairly small piece of rock **2** gem **3** hard seedcase in certain fruits **4** hard deposits formed in kidneys, bladder, etc. **5** measure of weight, 14 lb; *v* throw stones at; remove stone from fruit; *idm* **stone's throw** a very short distance; *ns* **S. Age** early period of human history when stone tools were used; **stonemason** person who prepares stone for use in building; **stoneware** pottery from clay containing flint; *as* **stone blind/dead/deaf** completely blind/dead/deaf; **stoned** *coll* **1** blind drunk **2** under influence of drugs; **stony 1** full of stones **2** *fig* hard and cruel **2** (of silence) complete (*a* **s. broke** *coll* penniless); *v* **stonewall** cause obstruction and delay without making any positive contribution.

stood *pt, pp of* **stand**.

stooge *n* one who is butt of comedian's jokes; *coll* dupe; butt.

stool *n* **1** backless seat **2** footstool **3** waste evacuated from bowels.

stool pigeon *n coll* person used as decoy or informer by police to trap criminal.

stoop *v* **1** bend forward or down **2** be round-shouldered **3** condescend **4** (*of hawk*) swoop; *phr v* **stoop to (doing something)** lower one's moral standards by (doing something); *n* **1** position of stooping **2** stairway, platform, entry to house or building.

stop *v* **stopping, stopped. 1** cease, cause to cease motion **2** prevent **3** plug, close opening **4** discontinue **5** stay; remain; *n* **1** act of stopping **2** *mus* any device for altering pitch of note **3** peg, block; *idm* **pull out all the stops** *coll* use all one's resources; *ns* **stopgap** temporary substitute; **stopover** short stay in middle of journey; **stoppage** cessation of work; **stopper** plug, *esp* for bottle; **s. watch** with split second start-stop facility for timing races.

store *n* **1** reserve supply, stock **2** warehouse **3** large general shop; *ns* **s.-front** small, street-level store; **s.-house** storage building; **storeroom;** *v* accumulate and keep supplies, etc.; hold storage room for; *ns* **storage** act of storing, being stored.

storied *a* famed in history or in story.

a b c d e f g h i j k l m n o p q r s t u v w x y z

A B C D E F G H I J K L M N O P Q R **S** T U V W X Y Z

stork n large wading bird.

storm n violent atmospheric disturbance; tempest; idm **take by storm 1** overcome by sudden attack **2** fig win enthusiastic approval of; n **s. trooper** Nazi militia man; v assault; fig express rage, scold; a **stormy** tempestuous; passionate.

story¹ n spoken or written narrative; tale; account; coll truth; n **storyteller 1** reciter, writer of stories **2** coll liar.

story² n horizontal division, floor of building.

stoup n basin for holy water.

stout a **1** durable; resolute **2** fat; n strong dark beer; a **stouthearted** lit brave (adv -**ly**; n -**ness**); n **stoutness.**

stove n apparatus for heating and cooking food.

stow v pack away; fill (hold) with goods; phr v **stow away** hide on board ship or plane in hope of having free journey (n **stowaway** person doing this); n **stowage** (room for) stowing.

straddle v spread legs wide; bestride.

straggle v loiter, be apart from main group; a **straggly**; n **straggler.**

straight a **1** not bent or crooked; lit, fig upright **2** in order **3** (of spirits) neat; ns **s. away** straight stretch of road, river, etc.; cards sequence; adv **1** in a straight line **2** directly; idm **go straight** give up life of crime; idm **keep to**

the **straight and narrow** coll lead an honest life; advs **straightaway** immediately; a **straightforward 1** simple **2** frank and honest (adv -**ly**; n -**ness**); v **straighten** make straight or tidy; phr v **straighten out** remove difficulties from.

strain¹ v **1** separate liquids and solids with mesh device **2** make taut **3** overexert; overtax **4** wrench by too sudden effort; n **1** tautness **2** severe physical or mental effort **3** fig tone **4** mus tune; a **strained** showing nervous fatigue, forced.

strain² n breed; stock; ancestry.

strainer n sieve; colander; v filter.

strait a **1** ar narrow; strict; n narrow channel of water between two seas **2** (often pl) difficult position; as **straitened** impoverished, in financial difficulty; **straitlaced** austere, strict; n **straitjacket, straightjacket** heavy canvas coat to confine arms of prisoners, violent patients, etc.

strand¹ n shore; v run aground; leave, be left helpless, destitute.

strand² n single thread of wool, fiber, rope, etc.; lock of hair.

strange a unfamiliar; unusual; foreign; singular; ns -**ness**; -**er** unknown person; foreigner.

strangle v kill by compressing windpipe; throttle; ns

stranglehold powerful control that prevents action; **strangulation** act or result of strangling.

strap n strip of leather or metal for fastening; v **strapping, strapped.** fasten with strap; beat with strap; a **strapping** tall, well-made; n **s.-hanger** standing passenger in train, etc. who holds on to strap.

strata pl of **stratum.**

stratagem n trick, plan for deceiving enemy, opponent; ns **strategy** art of military maneuvring; fig battle of wits; **strategist**; a **strategic(al).**

stratify v arrange in strata; n **stratification.**

stratosphere n upper atmospheric layer beginning approx 6 miles above earth's surface.

stratum n pl **strata 1** geol layer **2** fig social division, class.

straw n dry cut stalks of grain crops; idm **the last straw** new development that makes an already difficult situation quite intolerable; ns **strawberry** plant bearing red sweet juicy fruit (n **s. mark** red birthmark); **s. poll** unofficial survey of public opinion.

stray v wander; lose one's way; a strayed; occasional; n lost animal or child.

streak n **1** long line; stripe **2** (of lightning) flash; v **1** mark with streaks **2** coll rush quickly past (n -**er** person

running naked in public);
a **-y.**

stream *n* body of flowing water
or other liquid; rivulet;
brook; *v* **1** flow, run with
liquid **2** fly out, float on air;
n **streamer** ribbon, flag to fly
in air; party decoration.

streamlined *a* of curved shape,
offering minimum resistance
to water or air.

street *n* road in town or village
with buildings on both sides;
a **street-smart, streetwise**
coll quick-witted enough to
survive in a tough urban
environment.

strength *n* power; intensity;
quality of being strong; force;
idm **on the strength of** on
the basis of; using the
advantage of; *v* **strengthen**
make stronger.

strenuous *a* energetic;
unremitting.

stress *n* **1** strain **2** emphasis **3**
intense pressure **4** *mech* force
exerted on solid body; *v* **1**
emphasize **2** accent **3** subject
to mechanical stress; *as*
stressed out *coll* exhausted
by stress; **stressful** causing
stress (*n* **-ness**).

stretch *v* extend; be elastic;
reach out; exert to utmost;
idm **stretch a point** *coll* make
special concession; *idm*
stretch one's legs exercise by
walking; *n* **stretcher**; **1** light
framework for carrying
disabled person **2** device for
framing artists' canvases.

strew *v* scatter, spread on

surface; *pt* **strewed;** *pp*
strewn or **strewed.**

striated *a* **1** marked in stripes;
2 related to striated muscle;
n **-ation.**

stricken *a* affected by grief,
illness, terror, etc.

strict *a* exact; inflexible; stern;
rigorous; *ns* **strictness;**
stricture 1 *med* contraction
of duct or vessel **2** *fig* severe
criticism.

stride *v* walk with long steps;
cross over with one long
step; *pt* **strode;** *pp* **stridden;** *n*
single step or its length; *idm*
make strides make fast
progress; *idm* **take something
in one's stride** manage a
difficult situation without
any problem.

strident *a* harsh; shrill; grating.

stridulate *v* (*of insects*) make
high-pitched sound by
friction of limbs, etc.; *n*
-lation.

strife *n* conflict; discord.

strike *v* **1** hit; collide; aim,
deliver blow **2** (*of clock*)
sound time **3** affect **4** ignite
5 take down (stage set, tent,
flag, etc.) **6** make (coin,
medal) **7** stop work to
enforce demand; *pt* **struck;**
pp **struck, stricken;** *idm*
strike a balance reach a
compromise; *idm* **strike a
chord** remind somebody of
something; *idm* **strike a note
of** express feeling of; *idm*
strike camp prepare to leave
camp by taking down tents;
idm **strike while the iron is**

hot make use of opportunity;
phr vs **strike off** remove
(person's name) from list;
strike out 1 move in a
determined way (*idm* **strike
out on one's own** *coll* begin
to be independent) **2** in
baseball, put out or be out on
three strikes; **strike up 1**
initiate (friendship) **2** begin
playing (music); *n* **1** refusal
to work **2** attack, *esp* aerial **3**
discovery of mineral deposit,
e.g., oil; *n* **-er;** *a* **-ing 1**
noteworthy **2** attractive to
look at (*adv* **-ly;** *idm* **within
striking distance** nearby); *a*
strikebound affected by
strike; **s.-breaking** refusing to
go on strike (*n* **s.-breaker**); *n*
stoppage of work; *n* **striker**
one who, that which, strikes.

string *n* cord, twine; series of
objects, chain; (*of musical
instrument*) cord of catgut,
wire; *pt, pp* **strung;** *pl* **-s**
(players of) stringed
instruments in orchestra; *idm*
strings attached special
conditions; *v* **1** attach string
to **2** thread onto string **3** tie
with string **4** remove stringy
fibers from (*pt, pp* **strung**);
idm **highly strung** very
sensitive and excitable; *phr
vs* **string along 1** *coll* keep
company for a while **2**
persuade by deception; **string
out; string up** hang; *n* **s.
bean** bean with edible pod;
as **stringed** furnished with
strings; **stringy** fibrous (*n* **-
iness**).

a
b
c
d
e
f
g
h
i
j
k
l
m
n
o
p
q
r
s
t
u
v
w
x
y
z

stringent *a* strict; rigid; binding; *n* **stringency** severity.

strip *v* **stripping, stripped. 1** remove paint, clothing, etc. **2** take away property; *phr v* **strip down** (of machine) remove detachable parts before cleaning, repairing; *n* **1** act of stripping **2** long thin piece (of fabric, wood, etc.) torn off; *ns* **comic s.** comic story in pictures; **s.-tease** type of night-club entertainment where performer undresses slowly in front of spectators (*n* **stripper** person who does this).

stripe *n* narrow mark, band; chevron worn as symbol of military rank.

stripling *n* youth.

strive *v* try earnestly; fight; contend; *n* **-er** one who struggles to improve her/his situation; *pt* **strove** *pp* **striven**.

strobe (light) *n* light that flashes on and off rapidly; *n* **stroboscope** instrument that produces such light (*a* **-scopic**).

strode *pt of* **stride**.

stroke *n* **1** blow **2** line made by single movement of pen, brush, etc. **3** single movement of hands or hand-operated instrument (as in swimming, golf, etc.) **4** rower in stern setting rate **5** sudden cerebrovascular accident; *v* **1** pass hand lightly over, caress **2** row, stroke in boat.

stroll *v* take short leisurely walk; saunter; *n*.

stroller *n* chairlike, often collapsible, carriage in which young children ride.

strong *a* powerful; tough; healthy; affecting senses acutely; *ns* **s. box** secure box for keeping valuables; **stronghold 1** fort **2** *fig* place where specified activity is strongly supported; **s. language** swearing and cursing; **s. point** thing in which one is especially skilled; **s. room** room in bank with strong walls, doors, etc. for storage of valuables; *as* **s.-arm** using pressure, violence; **s.-minded** very determined (*adv* **-ly;** *n* **-ness**).

strontium *n* soft silver-white heavy metal; **strontium 90** dangerous radioactive form of this found in fallout from nuclear explosion.

strop *n* leather strap for putting edge on razor; *v* **stropping, stropped.** apply strop to razor.

strophe *n* one of the units of several lines of which a poem consists (*also* **stanza, verse**).

strove *pt of* **strive**.

struck *pt, pp of* **strike**.

structure *n* **1** formation; construction **2** that which is made up of many parts **3** building; *a* **structural**.

strudel *n Ger* cake of fruit rolled in pastry and baked.

struggle *v* fight; grapple with;

make strenuous effort; move convulsively; *n* contest; violent tussle.

strum *v* **strumming, strummed.** play noisily, idly, or badly on stringed instrument.

strung *pt, pp of* **string**.

strut *n* **1** prop; stay **2** affected, pompous gait; *v* **strutting, strutted.** support with struts; swagger.

strychnine *n* colorless poison.

stub *n* end part, remnant (of cigarette, pencil, etc.); *v* **stubbing, stubbed.** hit one's toe accidentally on something; *phr v* **stub out** extinguish (cigarette); *a* **stubby** short and thick.

stubble *n* short stalks of corn, etc. left after reaping; short growth of hair (as beard).

stubborn *a* resolute; unyielding; obstinate; pig-headed; *n* **-ness**.

stucco *n It* fine plaster for coating walls.

stuck *pt, pp of* **stick**; *a* **stuck-up** conceited.

stud[1] *n* large-headed projecting nail or peg; double headed button for cuff or collar of formal shirt; *v* **studding, studded.** set, decorate with studs.

stud[2] *n* **1** number of horses kept for breeding, hunting, etc. **2** *coll* man regarded as attractive, virile; *n* **s.-farm** place for breeding horses.

student *n* **1** person studying at university, college, evening class, etc. **2** person with specified interest (**student of something**).

studio *n* **1** workroom of artist, photographer, etc. **2** room or premises where films are made or broadcasts transmitted **3** one-room apartment.

study *v* **studying, studied.** learn systematically; analyze; show concern for; *n* **1** subject studied **2** experimental painting, sketch **3** room in which to study; *a* **studied** premeditated.

studious *a* **1** fond of study **2** careful (*adv* **-ly** *n* **-ness**).

stuff *n* **1** substance; material **2** textile fabric **3** *fig* nonsense; *idm* **strut one's stuff** *coll* show what one can do; *v* **1** fill **2** put stuffing inside **3** fill skin of (dead animal for preservation) **4** eat greedily; *phr v* **stuff up** block; *n* **stuffed shirt** *coll* boring, pompous person; *n* **stuffing** filling; savory seasoning used inside bird, meat; *a* **stuffy 1** lacking ventilation **2** *coll* stodgy; too formal.

stultify *v* make a fool of; make ineffectual; *n* **-fication**.

stumble *v* trip up; falter; **s. across, on,** come upon by chance; *n* **stumbling-block** impediment; obstacle.

stump *n* stub; remainder; remnant; *a* **-y** short, thickset.

stun *v* **stunning, stunned. 1** knock senseless **2** shock; amaze; *a* **stunning,** causing

loss of senses; *coll* excellent; very beautiful; (*adv* **-ly**); *n* **stunner** *coll* very attractive person.

stung *pt, pp of* **sting.**

stunk *pp of* **stink.**

stunt[1] *v* **1** *coll* spectacular feat or display, *esp* involving danger **2** sensational newspaper article etc.

stunt[2] *v* check growth of; *a* **stunted** undersized; retarded.

stupefy *v* **stupifying, stupified. 1** make stupid; dull **2** amaze; *n* **stupefaction**.

stupendous *a* astonishing; extra-ordinary; *adv* **-ly**.

stupid *a* slow-witted; dull; lacking intelligence; *adv* **-ly**; *n* **-ity**.

stupor *n* dazed condition; torpor; mental dullness.

sturdy *a* robust; vigorous; well-developed; *n* **-iness**.

sturgeon *n* large fish from which caviar and isinglass are obtained.

stutter *v* speak with hesitation and repetitions; stammer; *n* speech defect.

sty[1] *n* pen for pigs; *fig* filthy place.

sty[2], **stye** *n* inflamed swelling on eyelid.

style *n* **1** manner of doing, expressing **2** deportment **3** sort; variety **4** correct mode of address **5** manner; *v* designate; *idm* **in style** in an elegant way; *a* **stylish** fashionable (*adv* **-ly** *n* **stylist 1** person who aims at good style, *esp* in writing **2** one

who styles clothes, hair, etc.; *v* **stylize** treat in fixed, conventional style (*a* **-ized;** *n* **-ization**).

stylus *n* **-uses. 1** sharp needle fitted to arm of record player, reproducing sound from groove of record **2** sharp instrument for writing, *esp* in ancient times.

stymie *v* puzzle; hinder or obstruct.

styptic *n, a* (preparation) which stops bleeding.

Styrofoam [TM] polystyrene.

suave *a Fr* bland; urbane; affable; *adv* **-ly** *n* **-ness;** *n* **suavity.**

sub- *prefix forming ns, as and vs* **1** under **2** almost **3** smaller than; less than **4** inferior. *A compound may not be listed if the meaning can easily be deduced from the basic word.*

sub *n coll* **1** submarine **2** substitute **3** subscription; *v* **subbing, subbed.** work as substitute (e.g., as teacher).

subaltern *n* commissioned officer in army below rank of captain.

subatomic *a* of particles within an atom.

subconscious *a* not fully realized by mind; *n psyc* individuals part of mind outside personal awareness.

subcontract *v* arrange subsidiary contracts with workers for all or part of a big job for which one has signed the main contract.

subculture *n* (behavior of)

particular group in society.

subcutaneous *a* under the skin.

subdivide *v* divide into smaller units.

subdue *v* **1** overcome **2** soften.

subject *n* **1** thing being considered, discussed; topic **2** branch of learning **3** *ling* (word or phrase referring to) thing or person doing action of verb **4** *med* person being experimented on **5** citizen of a state; *a* **1** under somebody's political control; **subject to 1** exposed to **2** liable to **3** depending on (specified conditions); *v* **1** bring under political control; *phr v* **subject somebody to** cause somebody to undergo; *n* **subjection** act of bringing, or state of being, under control; *a* **subjective 1** existing in the mind; not objective **2** based on personal feeling (*adv* **-ly**; *n* **subjectivity**).

subjoin *v* add later.

sub judice *a Lat leg* not for public comment while being considered in a court of law.

subjugate *v* conquer; force under control; *n* **subjugation**.

subjunctive *n ling* mood of verb expressing wish, possibility; *a* of, in that mood.

sublease, sublet *v* lease or rent to another person or persons property on which one has taken a lease or rental agreement.

sublet *v* let to another, property of which one is tenant.

sublimate *v* **1** refine; purify by heating from solid to vapor and restoring solidity **2** *psych* express undesirable impulses in more socially desirable form; *n* sublimated substance; *n* **-ation** act of sublimation.

sublime *a* majestic; exalted; awe-inspiring; *ns* **sublimity; -ness**.

subliminal *a* at a level where the ordinary senses are not aware; *adv* **-ly**.

submachine gun *n* automatic weapon fired from hip or shoulder.

submarine *a* below surface of sea; *n* ship designed to remain, travel, under water for long period; *n* **submariner** person serving in submarine.

submerge *v* plunge, cause to go, beneath surface of water; *n* **submersion;** *v* **submerse**.

submersible *n, a* (craft) which can be submerged.

submit *v* submitting, submitted. **1** surrender **2** suggest, put forward for consideration, etc.; *n* **submission;** *a* **submissive** resigned, docile.

subnormal *a* **1** below normal **2** inferior in intelligence.

subordinate *a* inferior in rank or importance; dependent upon; *n* **-ation**.

suborn *v* bribe, induce to commit crime; *n* **-er**.

subplot *n* secondary, less important plot (*e.g.*, in play)

subpoena *n leg* writ summoning person to attend court; *v* serve with such writ.

subscribe *v* **1** pay regularly (*e.g.*, contribution to club, payment to magazine) **2 s. to** *fig* be in favor of; *ns* **subscriber; subscription 1** act of subscribing **2** amount of money regularly paid for membership, etc.

subsequent *a* later, following as result; *adv* **-ly** *n* **subsequence**.

subserve *v* promote; assist.

subservient *a* submissive, servile; *n* **subservience; - viency**.

subside *v* settle, sink down; diminish, abate; *n* **subsidence**.

subsidy *n* grant of money by State; *v* **subsidize** give, support by subsidy; *a* **subsidiary** additional; auxiliary; secondary.

subsist *v* sustain life; continue in being; *n* **-tence** means of supporting life.

subsoil *n* level of soil below the surface.

subsonic *a* of less than speed of sound.

substance *n* **1** matter; material **2** essential, most important elements or parts **3** portion of solid **4** considerable wealth; *v* **substantiate** give reality to; prove, establish truth (*n* **-ation** *a* **substantive** having real existence; *ling* expressing existence; *n* noun.

substandard *a* below standard; not good enough.

substation *n* place where electric power is relayed from main power station to other places.

substitute *n* person, thing taking place of another; deputy; *v* put, use in place of another; *n* **-tution.**

substratum *n* underlying layer; basis; *pl* **-ta, -tums.**

subsume *v fml* include; consume.

subterfuge *n* equivocation; means of evasion.

subterranean, -eous *a* situated, existing underground.

subtitle *n* explanatory second title (*v* add subtitle to); *pl* **-s** visual translation of dialogue in foreign film.

subtle *a* **1** elusive **2** discriminating **3** ingenious **4** cunning; *n* **subtlety.**

subtotal *n* part total combining with others to make grand total.

subtract *v* take away; deduct; *n* **subtraction.**

subtropical *a* relating to regions bordering on tropical zones.

suburb *n* outlying part of town or city; *a* **-an.**

suburbia *n* (architecture and lifestyle of) city suburbs.

subvention *n fml* subsidy, endowment.

subvert *v* try to undermine the power of; *a* **subversive;** *adv* **-ly** *ns* **-ness; subversion** act

of subverting.

subway *n* underground passage; underground commuter train.

succeed *v* **1** follow; come after **2** follow (as heir) **3** accomplish purpose; *n* **success** fortunate accomplishment, attainment of desired object, or result; triumph; *a* **successful;** *n* **succession 1** act or right of following in office, rank, etc. **2** series of things, events; *a* **successive** consecutive; *n* **successor** one who follows another in office, etc.; heir.

succinct *a* concisely expressed; terse.

succor *v*, *n* help, comfort, aid in difficulty or distress.

succulent *a* juicy; full of juice, sap; *n* **succulence.**

succumb *v* **1** yield; give way **2** cease to exist.

such *a* of that, of similar kind, degree or quality specified, implied; *a* **suchlike** similar.

suck *v* **1** draw (liquid) into mouth **2** dissolve in mouth; *phr v* **suck up to** *coll* flatter in order to win favor, *n* **sucker 1** organ appliance adhering by suction **2** *sl* gullible person **3** *bot* shoot from subterranean stem.

suckle *v* feed (young) with milk from breast; *n* **suckling** unweaned baby or young animal.

sucrose *n* form of sugar in sugarcane and sugar beet.

suction *n* act of sucking;

creation of partial vacuum causing body to adhere to, or enter, something under atmospheric pressure.

sudden *a* done, occurring unexpectedly; abrupt *adv* **-ly;** *n* **-ness.**

suds *n pl* froth of soap and water, lather.

sue *v* **1** bring, take legal action against **2** beg; plead.

suede *n Fr* leather with napped surface.

suet *n* solid fatty tissue surrounding kidneys, etc. of oxen, sheep, etc.

suffer *v* **1** undergo; withstand **2** be injured; be punished; *ns* **sufferer; sufferance** toleration; *idm* **on sufferance** with reluctant consent.

suffice *v* be enough, adequate; *a* **sufficient;** *n* **sufficiency** adequate supply.

suffix *n* letter or syllable added to end of word.

suffocate *v* deprive of air, stifle; kill by depriving of air; smother; *n* **suffocation.**

suffrage *n* vote, right to vote *esp* at elections; *n* **suffragette** woman who campaigned for right of women to vote in elections.

suffuse *v* (*of fluid, color etc*) spread over, flood, cover; *n* **suffusion.**

sugar *n* **1** sweet, crystalline vegetable substance; **2** *sl* money; *v* sweeten with sugar **3** *fig* flatter; disguise unpleasantness of; *ns* **s.-beet** variety of beetroot yielding sugar; **s.-cane** tall grass from whose juice sugar is obtained; **s. daddy** older man who spoils young person with generous gifts in return for sexual favors; *a* **sugary.**

suggest *v* imply; put forward, present for consideration; *as* **-ible** easy to influence (*n* **-ibility**); **-ive** 1 evoking association of ideas 2 provoking indecent thoughts (*adv* **-ly;** *n* **-ness**); *n* **suggestion** 1 proposal 2 hint 3 *psych* process of persuading somebody to accept an idea, *esp* under hypnosis.

suicide *n* 1 act of killing oneself 2 one who intentionally kills himself/herself; *a* **suicidal.**

suit *n* 1 legal action, lawsuit 2 set of clothes worn together *esp* man's outer clothes 3 one of four sets in pack of playing cards; *v* 1 satisfy 2 match 3 please 4 be convenient; *a* **suited** 1 appropriate 2 compatible; *idm* **suit oneself** do as one wishes; *n* **suiting** material for making suits. *n* **suitcase** portable flat oblong traveling case.

suitable *a* convenient; proper; becoming; *n* **suitability.**

suite *n* Fr 1 band of retainers 2 complete set (as of rooms, furniture, etc.) 3 17th, 18th century musical form.

suitor *n* petitioner; wooer.

sukiyaki *n* Japanese dish of sliced meat and vegetables cooked in soy sauce and sugar.

sulfa drugs *n* antibacterial substances used to treat disease, wounds.

sulfate *n* salt of sulfuric acid.

sulfide *n* compound of sulfur.

sulfur *n* pale yellow, inflammable, non metallic element; *n* **s. dioxide** colorless gas with choking smell; *as* **sulfurous; -ic** (*n* **s. acid** very strong corrosive acid).

sulk *v* resentful and unsociable; *a* **sulky** (*adv* **-ily;** *n* **-iness**); *n pl* **sulks,** sulky mood.

sullen *a* ill-tempered; morose; surly.

sully *v* **sullying, sullied.** stain; defile; tarnish.

sultan *n* Moslem prince or king; *ns* **sultana** 1 sultan's wife 2 kind of date or raisin; **sultanate** (state under) rule of sultan.

sultry *a* 1 (*of weather*) hot and close 2 torrid, passionate; (*adv* **-ily** *n* **-iness**).

sum *n* amount; total; *phr v* **summing, summed. sum up** 1 summarize 2 (*of judge*) review and comment on evidence.

sumac *n* small tree with long pinnate leaves.

summary *a, n* affected, carried out, without delay; brief statement or abridgment of chief points (of document, speech, etc.); *v* **summarize** present briefly and concisely; *n* **summation** reckoning up.

summer *n* warmest season of year; *v* spend summer; *a* **summery;** *ns* **summerhouse** small garden building for sitting in during warm weather; **s. school** short course given during summer vacation period.

summit *n* 1 top; peak 2 *coll* political conference between heads of states.

summon *v* 1 send for 2 *leg* order to attend court 3 *fig* muster (quality in oneself); *phr v* **summon up** evoke, *n* **summons** call; notice to appear before judge or magistrate.

sumptuary *a* relating to expenditure.

sumptuous *a* lavish; splendid; costly; *n* **sumptuousness.**

sun *n* 1 luminous heavenly body round which earth and other planets rotate 2 chief source of light and heat in solar system 3 direct rays of sun; *v* exposed to, bask in, sun's rays; *v* **sunbathe** lie in the sun in order to have a suntan (*ns* **-bather -bathing**) *as* **s.-baked** 1 very sunny 2 hardened by the sun; **s.-drenched** very sunny; *ns* **sunbeam** ray of sunshine; **sundial** device with pointer that shows time by movement of shadow across dial; **sunflower** large flower with yellow petals and edible seeds yielding edible oil; **s.-glasses** spectacles with dark lenses for protecting eyes from strong light **s.-lamp** lamp for giving artificial suntan by ultraviolet rays (*also* **s.-ray lamp**); **sunrise** time when sun rises at start of day; **s. roof** retractable panel in roof of car, etc.; **sunset 1** time when sun sets at end of day **2** view or picture of sky at this time; **sunspot 1** *astrom* dark area on sun's surface **2** *coll* vacation locale where sun usually shines; **sunstroke** illness caused by too much exposure to sun; **s.-tan** browning of skin from exposure to sun (*a* **s.-tanned**); **s.-trap** warm, sunny place sheltered from wind; **s.-worship 1** worship of sun as god **2** *fig coll* (show off) addiction to sunbathing (*n* **s.-worshipper**); *a* **sunless**.

sundae *n* ice cream with crushed fruit, nuts, chocolate syrup, etc.

Sunday *n* first day of week.

sunder *v* put apart; sever.

sundry *a* several, of indefinite number; *n pl* **sundries** unspecified odds and ends.

sup *v* **supping, supped. 1** take by sips **2** eat; take supper.

sung *pp of* **sing**.

sunk *pp of* **sink**.

sunken *a* **1** fallen to the bottom of the sea **2** on a lower level **3** (of cheeks, eyes, etc.) hollow.

super- *prefix; forms compounds with meaning of* above, in excess. *Such words are not given when the meaning may be deduced from the simple word.*

super (*a coll*) marvelous; superb.

superannuate *v* retire; dismiss on account of old age; *a* **-ated 1** too old to work **2** old-fashioned.

superb *a* splendid; magnificent.

supercharge *v* charge, fill to excess; *n* **supercharger** device to increase gas mixture in cylinders of engine; *a* **-ed**.

supercilious *a* disdainful; haughty; *n* **-ness**.

superconductivity *n physics* property of certain metals that allows electricity to be conducted easily at very low temperatures; *n* **superconductor** such a metal.

superego *n psyc* the conscience.

superficial *a* of, on surface; shallow.

superfluous *a* more than necessary; redundant.

superhuman *a* of more than can be expected of ordinary humans.

superimpose *v* put something on top of something so that both can be seen (or heard) together.

superintend *v* direct; control; oversee; supervise; *ns* **-ent** manager; one with executive oversight; **-ence**.

superior *a* **1** higher in position, rank, grade **2** above; *idm* superior to; not affected or biased by; *n* **-ity** (**s. complex** *psyc* aggressively self-satisfied attitude).

superlative *a* of, in highest degree of excellence, or quality; *n ling* superlative degree of adjective or adverb.

superman *n* hypothetical being possessing supreme physical and mental powers.

supermarket *n* large grocery store.

supernatural *a* not explicable by known laws of nature.

supernumerary *n, a* (person, thing) in excess of normal number; extra.

superpower *n* very large, powerful nation.

superscript *n* letter, number, or symbol raised higher on a line of text.

supersede *v* replace; supplant.

supersonic *a* moving faster than speed of sound; of sound waves of too high frequency to be audible to human ear.

superstar *n coll* entertainer, *esp* musician or athlete, with outstanding skill and reputation.

superstition *n* irrational belief in charms, omens, etc.; dread of supernatural; *a* **superstitious**.

superstructure *n* **1** part of building above ground or of ship above main deck **2** institutions arising from an economic system.

a
b
c
d
e
f
g
h
i
j
k
l
m
n
o
p
q
r
s
t
u
v
w
x
y
z

A
B
C
D
E
F
G
H
I
J
K
L
M
N
O
P
Q
R
S
T
U
V
W
X
Y
Z

supervene v happen as consequence, or in addition; n **-vention**.

supervise v oversee; inspect; control; direct; ns **supervisor** (a **-visory**); **supervision**.

superwoman n woman of outstanding physical and mental talents esp one who manages career, family.

supine a lying on back, face up; inactive; n Lat verbal noun.

supper n last meal of day; a **-less**.

supplant v take place of, oust, esp by fraud, craft, etc.

supple a pliant; flexible; docile; amenable n **-ness** adv **supply**.

supplement n 1 something added to fill need 2 separable part of newspaper, etc.; v add to; supply deficiency; a **supplementary** extra; additional.

supplicate v pray for; beg, ask for humbly; ns **-ation** entreaty; **suppliant** petitioner; a beseeching.

supply v supplying, supplied. 1 provide (something to/for somebody) 2 equip (somebody with something); n 1 amount available 2 (system for) providing; idm **in short supply** difficult to obtain; idm **supply and demand** the effect on prices of relating the amount available on the market to the amount needed; pl **supplies** everyday provisions;

n **supplier**.

support v 1 hold, prop up 2 maintain; assist; n act, state of being supported; that which helps, supports; n **-er** 1 person loyal to a team, political party, etc. 2 person devoted to an activity, principle, etc.; as **-able** tolerable; **-ing** giving support (**s. part/role** not a leading role); **-ive** ready to offer encouragement, help (adv **-ly**; n **-ness**).

suppose v 1 assume 2 surmise 3 imagine; imperative used to imply a question what if ? or a suggestion would you like (me/us) to ?; idm **be supposed to** be required, expected to; a **supposed** believed to be (adv **-ly**); conj supposing what if; n **supposition** hypothesis; guess.

suppository n soluble medicinal bolus inserted in rectum or vagina.

suppress v 1 subdue, crush by force 2 prevent publication of; ban; n **-ion** n **-or** 1 person who suppresses 2 device that prevents electrical interference to TV, radio etc.

suppurate v produce pus; n **suppuration**.

supra- prefix above, higher than; beyond.

supranational a going beyond national boundaries n **-ism** n, a **-ist**.

supreme a highest, superior in rank, power, jurisdiction,

etc.; utmost; ns **supremacy** 1 superiority 2 dominance; **-acist** person believing in racial, national superiority of any kind.

surcease n end.

surcharge n extra charge; v demand extra payment.

surd n, a math irrational (root or quantity).

sure a certain; reliable; undoubted; adv, interj coll certainly; willingly; idm **be sure to** coll don't forget to; idm **make sure** 1 verify; be certain 2 guarantee; idm **for sure** certainly; idm **sure enough** as one would expect; as **s.-fire** certain to happen or succeed; **s.-footed** able to walk, climb without fear of falling (n **-ness**); n **surety** 1 one who is responsible for another's good conduct 2 money laid down as pledge of person's good behavior; security.

surf n foam of breaking waves; n **surfboard** board used in sport of surfing; v riding waves for pleasure.

surface n exterior; outside; top; visible side; a superficial; v 1 come to surface of water 2 emerge from hiding; be found after being missing; ns **s. mail** mail sent over land and sea (not by air); **s. tension** property of liquids that they form an apparent film on the surface.

surfeit n excess esp in eating, feeding; satiety; repletion; v overindulge.

surge v (of waves, water) swell; rise powerfully; n sudden rush of electric current in circuit; ns **s. protector** comput electrical device to protect against power surges.

surgeon n doctor who performs operations; n **surgery** treatment of disease and injuries by operation or manipulation; a **surgical**.

surly a sullen; gloomy, churlish; n **surliness**.

surmise v guess; conclude; infer; n conjecture; inference.

surmount v overcome (difficulty); be placed over top of; a **-able**.

surname n hereditary family name usu transmitted in male line.

surpass v go beyond, excel in degree, quality, etc.; a **-ing** excelling all others; matchless.

surplice n loose white vestment worn by clergy, choristers.

surplus n excess quantity; a forming amount over and above what is required.

surprise v come upon unexpectedly; shock; startle; astonish; n astonishment; something unexpected.

surrealism n movement in art or literature that believes in expressing dreamlike effects and irrational fantasies; n, a **-ist**.

surrender v give up under pressure or voluntarily; hand over; submit; n act of surrendering.

surreptitious a stealthy; clandestine; furtive.

surrey n light carriage with two to three seats.

surrogate n substitute; deputy esp of bishop; n **surrogate mother** woman who bears a child for another woman.

surround v encircle; be, come all round; n pl **surroundings** material environment; circumstances.

surtax n additional tax on high incomes.

surveillance n Fr constant watch, observation.

survey v 1 look over; review 2 inspect and assess value of (house, etc.) 3 measure, map (area of land); n record of result of surveying; n **surveyor**.

survive v 1 outlive 2 continue to live or exist; n **survivor** 1 one left alive when others are dead 2 one who does not give in to adversity.

susceptible a highly sensitive; accessible; n **-ibility**.

sushi n Japanese dishes of raw fish seasoned rice, vegetables, etc.

suspect v 1 believe or imagine to be true 2 doubt; mistrust 3 believe guilty; a rousing suspicion; n suspected person.

suspend v hang up; postpone; defer; debar, prohibit temporarily; n pl **suspenders**

device for holding up stockings or socks.

suspense n state of anxious uncertainty; n **suspension** state of being suspended (in various senses) (**s. bridge** bridge hung from cables supported by towers on piers).

suspicion n 1 act of suspecting 2 feeling of doubt, mistrust 3 slight trace; a **suspicious** (adv **-ly**, n **-ness**).

sustain v 1 support; hold up 2 undergo; ns **sustenance** nourishment; maintenance.

suture n 1 act, process of sewing up wound 2 thread, wire used for this 3 anat articulation of bones of skull; v join with suture.

suzerain n Fr feudal law; State with sovereignty over another; n **suzerainty**.

svelte a slender; graceful; willowy.

swab n 1 mop 2 med absorbent pad; v **swabbing, swabbed.** clean; wash out with swab; ns **swab, swabbie** sailor; reprobate.

swaddle v wrap; bundle up; n pl **swaddling-clothes, -bands** strip of cloth formerly wrapped round baby.

swag n sl 1 booty; plunder 2 hanging wreath or festoon.

swagger v strut; show off; bear oneself jauntily; n such gait or manner.

swain n lit country lad; lover; admirer.

swallow[1] n migratory bird with

long, pointed wings and forked tail; *n* **s.-tail** kind of butterfly or humming bird; man's formal dresscoat.

swallow[2] *v* **1** make (food, drink, etc.) pass down gullet **2** put up with (insult) **3** believe implicitly **4** overwhelm; *n* act of swallowing food, etc.

swam *pt of* **swim**.

swamp *n* marsh; bog; *v* cover with water; *fig* overwhelm; *a* **swampy**.

swan *n* large, long-necked aquatic bird; *n* **s.-song 1** fabled song of dying swan **2** *fig* last work, utterance of actor, writer, etc.; *n* **swannery** place where swans are kept.

swank *v coll* behave, talk boastfully; *n* **1** such talk or behavior **2** person who does this; *a* **-y 1** boastful **2** (of clothes, possessions) showy or fashionable.

swap *v* **swapping, swapped.** exchange, barter.

swarm[1] *n* large mass of insects, *esp* cluster of bees with queen; crowd; *v* **1** (*of bees*) leave hive with queen **2** gather in large numbers.

swarm[2] *v* climb (rope, etc.) by clasping with hands and legs.

swarthy *a* dark-complection.

swastika *n* hooked cross, used as a symbol by Nazi Party.

swat *v* **swatting, swatted. 1** crush; squash (insect, etc.) **2** strike ball.

swatch *n* sample of cloth.

swathe *v* cover, wrap with bandage or cloth.

sway *v* swing, cause to swing unsteadily; move; influence; *n* swaying motion; influence; power.

swear *v* **1** promise on oath **2** cause to take an oath **3** curse; *pt* **swore**; *pp* **sworn** *phr vs* **swear by** have great faith in; **swear in** cause to take oath in court or on taking political office.

sweat *n* **1** moisture exuded by pores of skin **2** hard labor inducing this; *idm* **no sweat** *coll* (it causes) no great difficulty; *v* **1** exude sweat **2** (cause to) work hard for low wages **3** suffer great anxiety; *idm* **sweat blood** *coll* work abnormally hard; *idm* **sweat it out** endure (in discomfort) to the end; *ns* **s.-band** strip of material worn to absorb sweat; **s.-shirt** long-sleeved sweater *usu* of cotton; **s.-shop** place where people work hard for low wages; **sweater** thick woollen pullover garment.

Swede *n* **1** native of Sweden.

sweep *v* **1** clean with brush, broom **2** move in stately manner **3** form wide curve **4** drive, move violently away; *pt, pp* **swept**; *idm* **sweep somebody off his/her feet** overwhelm somebody with feelings of love, admiration; *idm* **sweep the board** be completely successful; win all the prizes; *idm* **sweep under the carpet** try to hide (something that causes embarassment); *phr v* **sweep aside** ignore completely; *n* **1** act of sweeping **2** wide curve or curving movement **3** person who cleans chimneys **4** *fig* range **5** *coll* sweepstake; *ns* **sweeper 1** machine for cleaning carpets **2** person who sweeps **3** *football* player giving extra support to defenders; **sweepstake** form of gambling; *a* **sweeping 1** extensive **2** too generalized (*n pl* **-s** collected dust)

sweet *a* **1** tasting like sugar **2** pure **3** fragrant **4** melodious **5** agreeable **6** gentle; *n* dessert; candy; confection; *ns* **sweetbread** thymus or pancreas of calf or lamb served as meat; **s.-briar/brier** wild rose; eglantine; **s.corn** type of corn with sweet grain; **sweetheart** (term of endearment for) person one loves; **sweetmeat** *ar* candy, item of confectionery; **s. pea** climbing plant with colorful, fragant flowers; **s. potato** tropical plant with yellow edible roots; **s. talk** *coll* flattery used to persuade (*v* **s.-talk**); **s. tooth** liking for sweet things; **s.William** biennial plant with clusters of sweet-smelling flowers; *adv* **-ly**; *n* **-ness**; *v* **sweeten 1** make sweet **2** *coll* bribe (*ns* **-er, -ing**).

swell *v* expand; be elated; increase in size; *pt* **swelled;**

pp **swelled** or **swollen;** *n* **1** act of swelling **2** succession of unbroken waves **3** *coll* smartly-dressed person; *a coll* excellent; fine.

swelter *v* suffer discomfort from heat; *a* **-ing.**

swept *pt, pp of* **sweep;** *as* **s.-back 1** with front edge angled backward **2** (of hair) brushed backward.

swerve *v* swing round; deviate from course; deflect; *n.*

swift *a* rapid; quick; speedy; *adv* **-ly;** *n* **-ness;** *n* bird like swallow.

swig *v* **swigging, swigged.** to drink a liquid in large mouthfuls.

swing *v coll* drink *usu* large mouthful (*esp* from bottle); *n* such a mouthful.

swill *v* **1** rinse; wash out with water **2** drink greedily; *n* liquid food for pig.

swim *v* **swimming, swimmed. 1** move through water by motion of limbs, fins, etc. **2** feel dizzy **3** be flooded; *pt* **swam;** *pp* **swum;** *idm* **swim with the tide** copy what others do; *n* spell of swimming; *idm* **in/out of the swim** familiar/unfamiliar with what is happening in the world; *ns* **swimmer; swimming; swimsuit** one-piece costume for swimming; **s.pool** artificial indoor or outdoor pool for swimming; **s.-trunks** men's shorts for swimming); *adv* **swimmingly** *coll* smoothly; pleasantly.

swindle *v* cheat, defraud; *ns* **swindler; swindling.**

swine *n* pig; *coll* unpleasant person; *pl* **swine.**

swing *v* **1** move to and fro, *esp* as suspended body **2** turn on hinge or pivot **3** *coll* be hanged; *pt, pp* **swung;** *idm* **swing into action** begin to act quickly; *n* **1** act of swinging **2** seat for children to swing on for amusement **3** sudden change or reversal **4** type of jazz with strong regular beat, popular in 1930s and 1940s; *idm* **in full swing** operating at its peak; *idm* **get into the swing (of)** *coll* become adapted (to); *ns* **s. bridge** bridge that pivots to allow passage of ships; *n* **swinger** *coll* person with modern, often uninhibited, attitude; *a* **swinging** modern and lively.

swipe *v* strike with powerful blow; *coll* steal.

swirl *v* whirl about; form eddies; *n* such motion.

swish *v* pass, cut through air with hissing sound; move with such sound; *n* swishing sound, or movement.

Swiss *a* of Switzerland; *n* **Swiss cheese** firm pale yellow cheese with many holes.

switch *n* **1** device for interrupting or diverting electrical current in a circuit **2** sudden change **3** substitution **4** slender, flexible twig or rod **5** piece of false hair; *v* **1** change **2** exchange; transfer; *phr vs* **switch off/on 1** turn off/on (electrical device) **2** *coll* cease/begin to show interest; *ns* **switchback** road or track with hairpin turns; **s.-blade** spring-operated folding knife; **switchboard** control center for manual operation of telephone system.

swivel *n* link consisting of ring and shank, allowing two parts to revolve independently; *v* turn on swivel.

swollen *pp of* **swell;** *a* **s.-headed** conceited.

swoon *v, n* (have) faint.

swoop *v* descend steeply through air like hawk; *n* act of swooping; sudden attack.

sword *n* weapon with long sharp blade fixed in hilt; *n* **s.-fish** fish with long, sharp upper jaw **s.-play** fighting with swords; **swordsman** man skilled in using sword (*n* **-manship** this skill).

swore *pt of* **swear.**

sworn *pp of* **swear;** *a* **1** (of statement) made under oath **2** (of friend or enemy) long-established; confirmed by pledge.

swot *v* **swotting, swotted.** *coll Brit* study hard; *n* one who studies hard.

swum *pp of* **swim.**

swung *pt, pp of* **swing.**

sybarite *n* one who is fond of luxurious comfort; *a* **sybaritic.**

a
b
c
d
e
f
g
h
i
j
k
l
m
n
o
p
q
r
s
t
u
v
w
x
y
z

A
B
C
D
E
F
G
H
I
J
K
L
M
N
O
P
Q
R
S
T
U
V
W
X
Y
Z

sycamore n tree related to maple.

sycophant n 1 flatterer 2 parasite; n **sycophancy.**

syllable n division of word, as unit of pronunciation; a **syllabic.**

syllabus n program; list of subjects.

sylph n sprite; a **sylphlike** slender and graceful.

sylvan, silvan a of woods, forests; rustic; rural.

symbiosis n bio condition of living things which depend on each other for survival; a **symbiotic.**

symbol n sign; anything representing or typifying something; a **symbolic;** v **symbolize;** n **symbolism** represented by symbols.

symmetry n balance of arrangement between two sides; a **symmetrical** duly proportioned; harmonious.

sympathy n fellow-feeling; sharing of emotion, interest etc; compassion; a **-pathetic;** v **-pathize.**

symphony n 1 harmony of sounds 2 mus sonata or composition for full orchestra; a **-phonic.**

symposium n meeting or discussion of differing views on a subject.

symptom n outward sign; change in body indicating presence or development of disease; a **-atic.**

synagogue n religious congregation of Jews; Jewish place of worship.

synchro- prefix at the same time; operating together; n

synchromesh aut gearbox system facilitating smooth changing between gears (also a); v **synchronize** 1 make agree in time 2 (cause to) happen at same time (n **-ization**); a **synchronized** (ns **s.swimming** sport where swimmers aim to perform complex movements in complete synchronization.

syncopate v 1 shorten word by omitting medial sound 2 mus begin (note) on normally unaccented beat; n **syncopation.**

syndicate n body of persons, combining for some enterprise.

syndrome n combination of various symptoms of disease.

synod n Church council; convention.

synonym n word with same meaning as another; a **synonymous.**

synopsis n **-opses.** summary; outline.

syntax n ling sentence construction.

synthesis n **-theses.** combination; putting together; a **-thetic** artificial; v **synthesize** make by synthesis; combine into a whole n **-sizer** electronic keyboard instrument with facility for producing and sustaining a variety of instrumental sounds and rhythmic effects.

syphilis n contagious venereal disease; a **-litic.**

syringe n 1 device for injecting, extracting fluids (as the body, etc.) 2 instrument for drawing in liquid by piston and ejecting it in jet; v irrigate, spray.

syrup n thick solution obtained in refining of sugar; a **syrupy.**

system n plan, scheme for organizing, classifying objects; complex whole; a **-atic.**

systemic a affecting entire organism.

systems analysis n analysis of management requirements in a form which can be programmed to a computer; n **s.analyst** specialist in this.

tab n 1 small flap or strip of cloth, paper, etc. attached to larger object 2 restaurant check; idm **keep tabs on** coll keep under observation.

Tabasco [TM] n hot spicy sauce.

tabby n striped cat.

tabernacle n 1 tent of Israelites 2 place of worship 3 small chest on altar to contain host.

table n 1 piece of furniture consisting of flat top supported by legs 2 set of facts, figures, etc., arranged in lines, or columns; idm **turn the tables** reverse situation to one's advantage; ns **t.d'hôte** meal at fixed price; **t.-talk** conversation during meal; **t. tennis** game like tennis played with wooden paddles and hollow plastic ball on table with net (also **ping-pong**); **tablespoon** large spoon for serving food,

eating soup; **tableware** dishes and cutlery; v enter into list, etc.; delay discussion about, etc.

tableau n Fr group of motionless, costumed persons posed to represent known picture, scene, etc.; pl **tableaux**.

tableland n large elevated level region.

tablet n 1 small flat slab (as paper) 2 small flat medicinal pill or sweet.

tabloid n fig small, condensed, sensational newspaper; a concentrated; brief.

taboo n setting apart as supernatural, certain persons or things; ban; restraint; v prohibit, forbid by taboo.

tabor n small drum.

tabulate v arrange (words, figures) in a table; n **-ation**; a **tabular**.

tachometer n device for measuring speed of engine

rotation.

tacit a implied, inferred by silence; a **taciturn** speaking little; n **taciturnity**.

tack n 1 small broad-headed nail 2 long temporary stitch; basting stitch 3 rope fastening corner of sail 4 ship's course 5 fig course of action 6 sl food; v 1 fasten with tacks 2 sew loosely 3 change course obliquely.

tackle n equipment; apparatus for moving, esp raising weights; v grip; grapple with.

tacky a 1 sticky 2 of poor quality.

taco n Mexican tortilla (usu fried) and filled with meat, cheese, lettuce, etc.

tact n skill in dealing with people, situations; natural perception of what is right and fitting; as **tactful**; **tactless** accidentally offensive.

tactic n means of achieving something; pl **-s** mil art of deploying troops, weapons, etc.; a **tactical** 1 of tactics 2 with calculated intent; adv **-ly**; n **tactician** person expert in tactics.

tactile a of, relating to sense of touch; tangible.

tad n small amount or degree.

tadpole n young frog or toad, having gills and tail.

taffeta n Fr stiff lustrous fabric made of cotton, silk, or wool.

taffy n chewy, pulled molasses candy.

tag n 1 projecting flap; end 2

A
B
C
D
E
F
G
H
I
J
K
L
M
N
O
P
Q
R
S
T
U
V
W
X
Y
Z

metal point of shoelace **3** hanging label **4** cliché **5** *coll* nickname, street name; *v* **tags, tagging, tagged.** label; *phr vs* **tag along (with)** *coll* follow closely (behind): **tag on** *coll* add.

tail *n* **1** prolonged extension of animal's spine; anything resembling this; hindmost, rear part of anything **2** *coll* follower; pursuer **3** *pl* -**s** man's tailcoat **4** *pl* reverse side of coin; *v* follow (person) closely; *ns* **t.coat** formal evening dinner jacket; **t. end** very end; **t.gate 1** tail board **2** rear door of hatchback (*v coll* follow closely behind); **t.light** red light at rear of vehicle; **tailpipe** car exhaust pipe; **t.spin** *avia* uncontrolled spiral dive; **t.-wind** wind blowing from behind; *a* -**less**.

tailor *n* one who makes or sells street clothing, *esp* men's; *v* work as tailor; *fig* adapt for special purpose; *a* **t.-made** individually made; precisely made for specific need.

taint *n* stain; trace of decay; disgrace; *v* stain slightly; become infected.

take *v* **1** seize; get possession of **2** accept **3** carry **4** conduct **5** accommodate **6** receive into **7** use (transport) **8** tolerate **9** need (time) **10** imbibe, consume **11** be effective **12** earn **13** record (on film, tape); *pt* **took,** *pp* **taken;** *idm* **take it** presume; *idm* **be**

taken aback be astonished; *idm* **be taken ill** fall ill; *idm* **take it easy** *coll* relax; *idm* **take place** happen; *idm* **take sides** show bias; *phr vs* **take after** look or behave like (parent, etc.); **take apart 1** dismantle **2** *coll* vandalize; **take away 1** subtract **2** remove; **take in 1** provide accommodation for **2** include **3** reduce size of (clothes) **4** deceive **5** understand properly; **take off 1** remove **2** leave unexpectedly **3** leave the ground **4** mimic (*n* **t.off 1** departure of aircraft **2** mimicry; *idm* **take time/a day/week, etc., off** have vacation of stated length) **take on 1** accept a challenge from **2** start to employ **3** accept (work, etc.) **4** *coll* have an emotional outburst; **take out 1** extract **2** escort (socially) **3** obtain by official agreement **4 take-out** prepared food delivered to, carried into home, office, etc. (*a, n* take-out (of) such food); *idm* **take someone out of himself** cause someone to forget worries; *idm* **take it out of someone** exhaust someone; *idm* **take it out/things out on somebody** *coll* make someone else suffer for one's bad feelings; **take over 1** gain control (of) **2** assume responsibility (for) (*n* **t.-over**); **take to 1** like instantly **2** begin doing

regularly **3** escape to (*idm* **take to one's heels** run away); **take up 1** pick up **2** begin to practice or study **3** occupy (time/space) **4** accept (offer) (*n* **t.-up rate** rate at which something is accepted); **take something up with somebody** ask somebody, complain to somebody about something; *ns* **t.-home pay** amount of pay after deduction of taxes, etc.; **taker** person accepting offer or challenge; **takings** money received from selling goods, performing in public, etc.

talc *n* magnesium silicate; *n* **talcum** powdered talc; baby powder.

tale *n* story, account; rumor; narrative.

talent *n* marked aptitude; special faculty; *a* **talented** gifted.

talisman *n* charm, amulet; object regarded as having magic powers.

talk *v* **1** speak; utter in speech **2** converse **3** discuss; *phr vs* **talk down to** speak in a condescending way to; **talk somebody into/out of** persuade somebody to do/not to do; *n* **1** conversation **2** informal lecture **3** words of no special meaning **4** characteristic speech; *idm* **the talk of** subject of gossip for; *pl* -**s** formal discussion *esp* political; *n* -**er;** *as* **talkative** fond of talking (*n* -**ness**);

talking capable of speech (*ns* **t. point** subject of discussion; **t.-to** reprimand).

talk show *n* radio or TV show where guests or members of audience take part in discussion with host or hostess.

tall *a* above average in stature; lofty; *sl* difficult to believe; untrue; *ns* **t. order** *coll* unreasonable request; **t. tale** story difficult to believe.

tallboy *n* high chest of drawers.

tallow *n* melted-down animal fat used in soaps, candles, etc.

tally *n* 1 notched rod to count by 2 system of counting using strokes on paper; *v* **tallies, tallying, tallied.** account by tally; agree, correspond exactly.

tallyho *interj* cry in hunting, on sighting fox.

Talmud *n* written record of Jewish law and tradition.

talon *n* claw.

tamale *n* Mexican dish of cornmeal, meat, peppers, etc., wrapped in corn husks and steamed.

tamarind *n* (fruit or wood of) tropical evergreen tree.

tamarisk *n* evergreen shrub.

tambour *n* 1 bass drum 2 embroidery hoop frame 3 slats of wood joined together to form a sliding cover; *n* **tambourine** small shallow drum fitted with small cymbals on perimeter.

tame *a* 1 not wild 2 subdued 3 *fig* dull; *v* make tame; *n* **tamer**.

Tamil *n* (speaker of) language of S India and Sri Lanka.

tam-o'-shanter *n* Scottish cap with flat crown.

tamp *phr v* **tamp down** pack down tightly.

tamper *v* disturb; *phr v* **tamper with** 1 interfere with 2 alter fraudulently.

tampon *n* internal protection used during menstruation.

tan[1] *n* bark of oak bruised to extract tannic acid; *a* of yellowish brown; *v* **tans, tanning, tanned.** 1 make animal hides into leather 2 make become brown *esp* by exposure to sunlight 3 *coll* flog; *n* **tanner** one who tans; *n* **tannery** place where hides are tanned.

tan[2] *abbr* tangent.

tanager *n* small brightly colored bird.

tandem *n* bicycle for two riders; *idm Lat* **in tandem** (working) in close cooperation.

tandoori *n* food cooked by Indian method in clay oven.

tang *n* 1 projecting spike 2 strong flavor or smell 3 kind of seaweed.

tangent *a* touching, but not intersecting; *n* line touching curve at one point; *n idm* **fly/go off on a tangent** *fig* suddenly change direction; *a* **tangential**.

tangerine *n* small, sweet, thin-skinned orange.

tangible *a* capable of being touched; *fig* clearly defined in mind, practical.

tangle *v* form confused mass, intertwine; **t.with** *coll* come into conflict with; *n* intricate knot; disorder.

tango *n* **-os.** type of S American dance; music for this; *v* dance tango.

tank *n* 1 receptacle for storing liquids, oil, or gas 2 heavy armored vehicle with tracked wheels and guns; *ns* **tanker** ship, truck carrying oil, liquid fuel in bulk; **t. engine** locomotive carrying its own water and fuel.

tankard *n* large beer mug.

tannic *a* of, obtained from tan; *n* **t. acid;** *n* **tannin** astringent substance; tannic acid.

tantalize *v* torment by repeated renewal of hope and disappointment; tease; *n* **tantalus** *cap* 1 mythic king whose attemps to eat, drink were frustrated 2 locked case with contents visible but inaccessible without key.

tantamount *a* equal in value or effect; equivalent.

tantrum *n* fit, outburst of violent temper.

Tao, Taoism *n* 1 unconditional, unknowable guiding principle 2 process of constant change in Nature; religion of Ancient China.

tap[1] *n* 1 device with turning valve or screw for controlling flow of liquid from pipe, cask, etc. **2** instrument for cutting internal screw threads; *idm* **on tap** available for immediate use; *v* **taps, tapping, tapped. 1** fit tap in **2** draw off (liquid) **3** listen in deliberately (to telephone conversation); *ns* **taproot** long tapering root of plant; **tapster** one who draws beer.

tap² *v* strike lightly; *n* light blow; sound of this; *n* **t. dance** dance with special shoes that make rhythm audible; **taps** these shoes.

tape *n* **1** long narrow band of fabric, paper, etc. **2** (spool holding) length of magnetic tape; recording on this; *v* **1** fasten with tape **2** record on tape; *ns* **t. deck** tape recording component of sound system; **t. measure** flexible strip of fabric or metal for measuring lengths; **t. recorder** apparatus for recording on magnetic tape; **tapeworm** parasitic flat worm living in intestine of animals, humans.

taper *n* thin candle; *v* narrow gradually to point at one end.

tapestry *n* fabric with designs hand-worked in wool; *a* **-tried** hung with tapestry.

tapioca *n* starchy food obtained from dried cassava; also a pudding containing this.

tapir *n* tropical swinelike animal.

tappet *n* short rod transmitting motion intermittently.

taps *n* bugle signal sounded for lights-out at night and at military funerals.

tar¹ *n* thick black viscous liquid distilled from coal, etc.; *v* **tars, tarring, tarred.** cover, treat with tar.

tar² *n coll* sailor.

taramasalata *n* Greek appetizer of paste from fish roe.

tarantella *n* rapid Italian dance.

tarantula *n* large venomous spider.

tardy *n* slow; late; reluctant; *adv* **-ily;** *n* **-iness**.

tare *n* weight of unladen goods vehicle; allowance made for this.

target *n* **1** object of attack (military, verbal, etc.) **2** round board marked in circles, to be shot at; butt.

tariff *n* list of duties on imports and exports; list of charges.

tarmac *n* mixture of tar and macadam used as road-surfacing material, *esp* at airports.

tarn *n* small moorland or mountain lake.

tarnish *v* **1** spoil brightness of by exposure to air, etc. **2** *fig* stain; sully; *n* loss of luster.

tarot *n* set of special cards used by fortune-teller.

tarpaulin *n* waterproof canvas treated with tar, plastic, etc.

tarpon *n* large game fish.

tarragon *n* aromatic herb used for flavoring goods.

tarry *v* linger; stay in a place.

tart¹ *a* sour; sharp; acid.

tart² *n* open, or covered fruit pie; *n* **tartlet** small tart.

tartan *n* woolen fabric woven in various colored plaids, each pattern belonging to a Scottish Highland clan.

tartar *n* **1** incrustation forming on teeth **2** deposit formed in wine vats **3** *cap* native of Tartary; Tatar **4** *fig* violent person; *n* **t. sauce** type of mayonnaise with pickles, herbs, etc.; *a* **-ic (t. acid)** acid found in juice of fruit, etc.

task *n* piece, amount of work imposed or undertaken; *idm* **take to task** reprove; *ns* **task force** military, diplomatic, police unit detailed for specific operation; **taskmaster** exacting master; overseer.

tassel *n* knotted bunch of silk or other thread, used as ornament.

taste *v* **1** test, perceive flavor of **2** have particular flavor of; *n* **1** faculty of experiencing flavors on tongue **2** small portion of food or drink **3** discernment; tact; *idm* **a/some taste for 1** tendency toward **2** liking for; *n* **t.bud** cells of tongue sensitive to taste; *as* **tasteful** showing refinement; in good taste; **tasteless** insipid; tactless; **tasty** pleasant to taste; savory.

ta-ta *interj* goodbye.

tatting *n* lacelike trimming of

looped and knotted threads; *v* **tat** make tatting.

tatter *n* rag; torn fragment.

tattle *v* gossip; blame; talk indiscreetly.

tattoo[1] *n* **1** military pageant or spectacle **2** drumbeat or bugle call of recall **3** knocking.

tattoo[2] *v* mark (skin) by pricking and inserting indelible pigments; *n* mark so made.

taunt *v* reproach sarcastically, contemptuously; *n* jeer; gibe.

taupe *n* dark gray, often tinged with purple, brown, yellow, or green.

taut *a* stretched tightly; tense; *a* **-ly;** *n* **-ness;** *v* **tauten** make tight.

tautology *n* unnecessary repetition of same idea in different words; *a* **tautological.**

tavern *n* inn where alcoholic beverages are sold and consumed.

tawdry *a* showy; flashy; ganish; gaudy; *n* **tawdriness.**

tawny *a* of light, brownish yellow color.

tax *n* **1** compulsory duty or levy imposed on income, goods, etc. **2** strain; *v* **1** impose tax on **2** lay heavy burden on; *idm* **tax someone's brains** give someone challenging mental task; *a* **t.-deductible** recognized as an allowance against tax; *ns* **t. haven** country with low tax rate; **t.**

return statement of income for tax authorities; **t. shelter** method of legally avoiding tax on some income; *n* **taxation** act of levying tax; *a* **taxable;** *n* **taxpayer.**

taxi *n* taxicab, car for public hire; *v* **taxies, taxiing** or **taxying, taxied.** (*of aircraft*) travel on ground under own power before takeoff, or after landing; *n* **t. meter** instrument recording fare due for mileage covered; **t. stand** place where taxis wait for customers.

taxidermy *n* art of preparing and stuffing animal skins; *n* **-dermist.**

TB *abbr med* tuberculosis.

T-bone *n* thick steak with T-shaped bone.

tea *n* **1** dried leaves of tea plant, infused to make drink **2** light afternoon meal; *ns* **teabag** paper packet with enough tea leaves for one or two cups of tea; **t.cake** small cake for toasting and serving with butter; **t. chest** large wooden crate for exporting tea; **t. cozy** cover to keep teapot warm; **t. garden 1** tea plantation **2** cafe that serves refreshments outdoors; **t. rose** scented China rose; **t. towel** cloth for drying wet dishes, etc.

teach *v* instruct; train; impart knowledge; *pt, pp* **taught;** *ns* **t.-in** meeting at which knowledge and opinion on subject of interest are

exchanged; **teacher** one who instructs; educator; **teaching 1** job of teacher **2** *esp pl* doctrine of religious leader.

teak *n* East Indian tree with very hard wood.

teal *n* kind of small wild duck; shade of blue-green.

team *n* number of animals harnessed together; number of persons working, acting, playing together; *phr v* **t. up with** *coll* work in harmony; match; *ns* **teamster** truck driver **t.work** combined effort.

teapot *n* container with spout for brewing, serving tea.

tear[1] *n* single drop of saline fluid coming from eye; *as* **tearful** shedding tears; sad; **tearless;** *ns* **teardrop; tear gas** irritant poison gas, causing coughing, abnormal watering of eyes; *n* **t.-jerker** story or film likely to provoke tears.

tear[2] *v* **1** pull apart; be torn; rend **2** rush; *pt* **tore,** *pp* **torn;** *idm* **be torn between** be unable to decide between; *phr vs* **tear down 1** pull down; destroy **2** run fast down **3** *fig* criticize, malign.

tease *v* **1** separate fibers of **2** worry **3** bait; poke fun at; *n* one who torments; *n* **-er** difficult question; *a* **teasing** harassing.

teaspoon *n* small spoon.

technical *a* pertaining to industrial or mechanical arts; peculiar to some specific branch of science or art; not understandable by laypeople; *n* **t. school** school with emphasis on practical subjects; *ns* **-ity** state of being technical; technical term; detail of procedure; **technique** method of execution or performance; skill in methods of special art, etc.; finesse; **technician** one skilled in mechanical art.

Technicolor [*TM*] technique for making color motion pictures.

technocracy *n* **1** control of country's resources by technical experts **2** country where this occurs; *n* **technocrat** scientific expert in favor of technocracy; *a* **-cratic**.

technology *n* science of industrial and mechanical arts; **technologist;** *a* **-ological;** *adv* **-ly**.

tectonic *a* pertaining to art of building; relating to geologic structure of earth; *n pl* **-s** art of functional designing combined with artistic merit.

teddy *n* soft, stuffed toy bear (*also* **t. bear**).

tedium *n* weariness; boredom; *a* **tedious** dull, long, and boring; *adv* **-ly;** *n* **-ness**.

tee *n* small peg off which golf ball is first played at each hole; *phr vs* **tee off** golf drive ball from tee; **tee up** golf place (ball) on tee.

teem *v* rain heavily; *phr v* **teem with** abound with.

teens *n pl* age between 13-19; *n* **teenager** adolescent between 13-19.

teeny-bopper *n sl* young person, *esp* girl following current trends in pop fashion.

teeny (weeny) *a coll* very tiny.

tee shirt *n* cotton knitted garment with short sleeves; *also* **T-shirt**.

teeter *v* move or stand unsteadily.

teeth *pl of* **tooth**.

teethe *v* develop or cut teeth; *n* **-ing** process of (baby) growing teeth (*n* **t. troubles** *fig* problems in early stages of using something).

teetotal *a* of, observing total abstinence from intoxicants; *n* **-(l)er**.

TEFL *abbr* teaching of English as a foreign language.

Teflon [*TM*] substance used on surface of nonstick pans.

tele- *prefix* at or over a distance; from far off.

telecast *v* broadcast on TV.

telecommunications *n pl* communication of messages over distances, *esp* by telephone and radio.

telegraph *n* electrical apparatus for transmitting messages over distance; *n* **t. pole** pole supporting telephone wires; *v* communicate by telegraph; *ns* **-er, -ist;** *a* **-ic;** *ns* **telegraphy** art, process of communicating by telegraph;

telegram message sent by telegraph.

telegraphese *n* written style using as few words as possible.

telekinesis *n* ability to cause objects to move by power of mind.

telemarketing *n* selling, advertising by telephone.

telemeter *n* instrument that takes measurements and sends results by radio; *n* **-metry** collection of information in this way.

teleology *n* belief that all things and events are planned for a purpose; *a* **-logical**.

telepathy *n* thought transference; *a* **-pathic**.

telephone *n* instrument for transmitting conversation over a distance; *v* use, communicate by, telephone *ns* **telephony** telephonic communication; **telephonist** one who works a telephone; *a* **-phonic**.

telephoto *abbr* **telephotography** photograph(ing) of distant objects through magnifying; **t. lens**.

teleprinter *n* machine for handling telex messages.

Teleprompter [*TM*] device used on TV to present script to speaker while he/she looks into the camera.

telescope *n* optical instrument for viewing magnified images of distant objects; *v* close, slide together as parts of telescope; compress forcibly; *a* **telescopic**.

teletext *n* TV system of information presented as written text.

Teletype [TM] teletypewriter; *n* **teletypewriter** telegraphic apparatus with typewriter terminals.

television *n* transmission of visible moving images by electromagnetic waves; viewing of such; object receiving such images; *v* **televise** transmit by television.

Telex [TM] *n* (written message sent by) system of satellite and telephone communication; *v* send (to someone) by telex.

tell *v* **1** narrate; divulge **2** order; command **3** inform; *pt, pp* **told**; *idm* **all told** counting every one; *phr vs* **tell off** reprimand; **tell on 1** have harmful effect on **2** *coll* (*esp* used by children) inform against; *n* **teller**, bank clerk who handles money; *a* **telling** impressive; *n* **telltale** sneak; *a* revealing.

tellurian *a* pertaining to earth; *n* **tellurium** rare, brittle, nonmetallic element; *a* **telluric**.

telly *n Brit coll* television.

temerity *n* rashness; audacity; great boldness.

temp *n coll* person in temporary employment; *v coll* work as a temp.

temper *v* **1** harden (metal, glass, etc.) **2** moderate; knead and moisten clay; *n* **1** degree of hardness (of steel, etc.) **2** frame of mind **3** angry mood.

tempera *n* technique of painting using media containing egg.

temperament *n* natural disposition; emotional mood; *a* **-al** unreliable; unstable; liable to strong changes of mood.

temperate *a* moderate and restrained; (of climate) not extreme; *n* **temperance 1** abstinence, *esp* from alcohol **2** moderation.

temperate zone *n* earth's surface between the tropical zone and the nearest polar circle.

temperature, *n* degree of heat or cold in atmosphere or body; *idm* **have a temperature** be feverish.

tempest *n* violent storm; *fig* violent emotion; *a* **-uous** stormy; violently excited.

template *n* mold, pattern, used as guide in shaping.

temple[1] *n* building, place of worship.

temple[2] *n* flat part of head on either side of forehead.

tempo *n* degree of speed; rate; pace.

temporal *a* **1** pertaining to, limited by time **2** secular; *a* **temporary** lasting short time; not permanent.

temporize *v* try to avoid

making decision; be evasive.

tempt *v* try to persuade *esp* to evil; excite desire in; *ns* **-ter; -tation** act of tempting; attraction; inducement.

ten *n, pron, det* cardinal number next after nine; in digits, 10.

tenable *a* capable of being held, defended; (*of opinions, etc.*) logical.

tenacious *a* holding fast; unyielding; retentive; *n* **tenacity**.

tenant *n* one who holds land or house, etc., on rent or lease; one who rents home, apartment, etc.; *ns* **tenancy; tenantry** body of tenants.

tend[1] *v* take care of; watch over; *n* **tender 1** one who tends **2** small ship in attendance on larger one **3** fuel and water carrier attached to locomotive.

tend[2] *v* have inclination; move in certain direction; *n* **tendency** inclination; bent; trend; *a* **tendentious** not impartial.

tender[1] *v* offer; make estimate; *n* **1** offer made to carry out work, etc., at fixed price **2** money offered in settlement of claim, etc.

tender[2] *a* **1** delicate; sensitive to pain; easily injured **2** kind; loving; *a* **t.-hearted** disposed to show sympathy to others; kind; *ns* **tenderness; tenderfoot** newcomer; novice.

tender[3] *n* **1** container for coal

and water attached to steam locomotive **2** small ship in attendance on larger one.

tenderize *v* make (sinewy meat) more tender.

tenderloin *n* cut of pork, beef between sirloin and ribs.

tendon *n* sinew attaching muscle to bone.

tendril *n* **1** slender coiling stem in climbing plants **2** curl of hair.

tenement *n* house, dwelling divided into separate apartments.

tenet *n* opinion, belief held as true.

tennis *n* game for two or four players, in which ball is struck over net with rackets.

tenon *n* tongue cut on end of piece of wood to fit into mortise; *n* **t.-saw**.

tenor *n* **1** singing voice between baritone and alto; singer with this range; *a* instrument in this range.

tense[1] *n* modification of verb to show time of action.

tense[2] *a* taut; stretched tight; *a* **tensile** capable of being stretched; *n* **tension 1** act, process of stretching, tightening **2** emotional strain **3** *elec* voltage.

tent *n* portable canvas shelter supported by pole(s).

tentacle *n* long, slender, flexible organ of feeling, often with suction pads; feeler.

tentative *a* experimental; provisional.

tenter *n* frame for stretching cloth; **t.hook** hooked nail used in stretching cloth; **on t.hooks** in state of anxiety, suspense.

tenth *a, n, pron, det* ordinal number of ten; next after ninth.

tenuous *a* **1** thin; fine; flimsy **2** too subtle; *n* **tenuity**.

tenure *n* act of, manner of holding land, office, etc.

tepid *a* lukewarm; *fig* showing little interest, etc.

tequila *n* Mexican strong alcoholic drink.

tercentenary *n* three hundredth anniversary.

tergiversation *n* shuffling; evasive conduct; vacillation.

term *n* **1** limit *esp* of time; fixed, limited period **2** period when courts are in session, schools are open, etc. **3** word used in any special art, science **4** *pl* **-s** conditions (of contract etc) **5** *pl* personal relations; *v* designate; call.

terminal *n* **1** (passenger building at) airport or end station of rail, bus line **2** place of connection to electric circuit **3** *comput* apparatus for input to and output from central computer; *a* of, near the end *adv* **-ly**; *n* **t. disease** incurable, fatal illness.

terminate *v* bring, come to an end; *n* **-ation** conclusion; ending.

terminology *n* system of special or technical terms;

a **-ogical**.

terminus *n* **-ni** or **-nuses. 1** station at end of railway line, etc. **2** final point reached.

termite *n* one of order of destructive insects; so-called white ant.

terms *n pl* conditions of agreement or sale; *idm* **come to terms** reach agreement; *idm* **come to terms with** learn to accept; *idm* **(buy/have) on terms** *comm* (buy/have) on credit (with repayment agreement); *idm* **on good/bad/etc. terms (with)** having a good/bad/etc. relationship (with).

tern *n* seabird of gull family.

terpsichorean *a* pertaining to dancing.

terrace *n* raised level platform (of earth, etc.); colonnaded porch, promenade; *v* build up, cut, into form of terrace *a* **terraced** arranged in terraces (*n* **t. house** row house).

terracotta *n It* hard unglazed reddish brown pottery.

terra firma *n Lat* solid, dry land.

terrain *n Fr* tract of land.

terrapin *n* edible fresh-water turtle.

terrarium *n* **1** closed container for growing plants **2** enclosure for animals (*pl* **-s** or **terraria**).

terrestrial *a* earthly; of, living on dry land.

terrazzo *n* mosaic flooring of stone chips and cement.

terrible *a* **1** fearful **2** *coll* very bad; *adv* **-ibly 1** badly **2** *coll* very.

terrier *n* one of several breeds of dogs.

terrific *a* **1** awe-inspiring; enormous **2** *coll* wonderful; excellent; *adv* **-ally** extremely.

terrify *v* fill with terror; *as* **-ified, -ifying.**

territory *n* region; district ruled by state or ruler; *a* **territorial** of territory; *fig* possessive.

terror *n* extreme fear; *v* **terrorize** intimidate with threats of violence; *n, a* **terrorist** (person) using violence for political ends; *n* **-ism.**

terrycloth *n* thick cotton cloth for making towels.

terse *a* concise; curt, abrupt in speech; *n* **terseness.**

tertiary *a* of third rank or order; *n* geological era; *a* **tertian** (fever) recurring every third day.

test *n* method adopted to try or prove knowledge of; critical, searching examination; *idm* **put to the test** test the quality of someone/something; *v* **1** prove the quality, extent, reliability of **2** try by examination; *phr v* **test for** ascertain the presence or absence of (*e.g.*, mineral deposit, disease) by testing; *ns* **t. case** lawsuit which establishes precedent; **t. tube**

small tubular container used in scientific experiments (*n* **t.-tube baby** baby conceived by artificial insemination, *esp* in vitro fertilization); *v* **t.-drive** take vehicle on trial drive before deciding whether to purchase.

testament *n* **1** one of two major divisions of Bible **2** *leg* will; *a* **-ary.**

testate *a* having left a valid will; *ns* **testacy** state of being testate; **testator;** *fem* **testatrix.**

testicle *n* sperm-secreting gland in male animals, typically paired.

testify *v* **testifies, testifying, testified.** bear witness; give evidence; *ns* **testimony** solemn statement; evidence; **testimonial** document setting forth person's character, ability, etc.; tribute given in token of esteem.

testis *n anat* testicle (*pl* **testes**).

testosterone *n* hormone controling development of secondary sex characteristics in males.

testy *a* irritable; irascible.

tetanus *n* lockjaw; violent muscular contraction.

tetchy *a coll* irritable; bad-tempered; *adv* **-ily;** *n* **-iness.**

tête-à-tête *n Fr* private talk, meeting; *a* confidential.

tether *v* fasten, tie up with rope; *n* rope, chain for fastening grazing animal.

tetragon *n* three-dimensional figure with four sides and

four angles.

Teutonic *a* of German language or ancestry.

text *n* **1** original words of author **2** verse, short passage of Scripture **3** main part of book, etc.; *n* **textbook** book used to study a subject; instruction manual (*a* **1** typical **2** exactly as required); *a* **textual** of, based on, text; literal.

textile *a* woven; *n* woven fabric.

texture *n* **1** quality, structure of fabric **2** degree of coarseness, fineness etc as felt by touch.

thalidomide *n* drug formerly used in pregnancy, but now banned due to risk of birth defects.

than *prep* used after compound adjectives and adverbs, before nouns and pronouns; *conj* used after compound adjectives and adverbs before clauses.

thanatology *n* description, study of death and psychological coping strategies.

thank *v* express gratitude to; *n* *pl* **thanks** words of gratitude; *idm* **thanks to** because of; *interj* **t. you** expressing gratitude (*n* such an expression); *as* **thankful** grateful (*adv* **-ly** *n* **-ness**); **thankless** unlikely to bring show of gratitude (*n* **-ness**); *n* **thanksgiving 1** expression of thanks, *esp* to God **2** *cap* national holiday (fourth

A B C D E F G H I J K L M N O P Q R S **T** U V W X Y Z

Thursday in November, US; second Monday in October, Canada) (*also* **T. Day**).

that *dem pron* thing, person just mentioned, or pointed out; more remote thing or person; *pl* **those**; *idm* **that's that** *coll* there is no more to be said; *rel pron* person who, thing which; *dem a* of person, thing just mentioned, etc.; *conj* introduces noun, or adverbial clause.

thatch *v* cover (roof, etc) with reeds, straw, etc.; *n* **thatch, thatching** straw, reeds, etc. used as covering.

thaw *v* **1** (*of snow, etc.*) melt; **2** *fig* become more friendly or genial; *n* **1** melting **2** *fig* detente.

the *definite art* indicating particular person or thing.

theater, theatre *n* **1** place where plays are performed; scene of important events or actions **2** room in hospital where operations are performed **3** drama; dramatic works collectively; *a* **theatrical 1** pertaining to theater **2** showy **3** affected, insincere; *adv* **-ly**; *n* **-ity**.

thee *pron, lit, ar* objective case of **thou**.

theft *n* act of stealing.

their *poss a* of **them**; *poss pron* belonging to them.

theism *n* belief in personal God, transcendent yet imminent; *n* **theist**.

them *pron* objective case of THEY; those persons or

things; *pron* **themselves** emphatic and reflexive form; *idm* **by themselves** (they) alone.

theme *n* **1** recurrent or important idea in speech or writing **2** *mus* brief recurring melody; *n* **t. park** open-air enclosure with entertainments based on a single idea or subject.

then *adv* **1** at that time **2** next **3** that being so; therefore; *n* that time.

thence *adv ar* **1** from that place **2** for that reason; therefore **thenceforth** from that time on (*also* **thenceforward**).

theocracy *n* government by guidance from God; a state so governed; *a* **-cratic**.

theodolite *n* surveying instrument for measuring angles.

theology *n* systematic study of religion and foundations of belief; *a* **theological**; *n* **theologian** student, authority on theology.

theorem *n* proposition to be established by reasoning.

theoretician *n* person developing theory rather than practical aspects of subject; *a* **theoretical** based on theory; speculative (adv **-ly**); *n* **theorist** impractical person; *v* **theorize** form, put forward theories.

theory *n* **1** supposition to explain group of phenomena; underlying principles of body

of facts **2** opinion.

theosophy *n* mystic form of religious thought aiming at direct contact between individual soul and divine principle; *n* **theosophist**.

therapeutic *a* **1** of, for healing **2** promoting better health or mental state; *pl* **-s** branch of medicine concerned with curing disease.

therapy *n* curative treatment; *suffix* as in psychotherapy *n* **therapist**.

there *adv* in that place; *idm* **all there 1** completely sane **2** intelligent; *idm* **there you are 1** used when giving something to somebody **2** used to reassure somebody, to demonstrate something; *idm* **there you go 1** used when giving something to somebody who is going **2** criticizing, *esp* habitual, action or expression one disapproves of; *adv* **thereabouts 1** approximately **2** in that vicinity; **thereafter** *fml* always after that; **thereby** by this means; **therefore** for this reason; **thereof** leg of it, them; **thereupon** *fml* immediately.

therm *n* unit of heat; *a* **thermal** of, by heat; *n* vertical rising hot-air current; *a* **thermic**.

thermion *n* ion emitted by incandescent body; *a* **thermionic**; *n* **t. valve** system of electrodes in glass vacuum.

thermo- *prefix* of, by heat.

thermodynamics *n* branch of science dealing with relation between thermal and mechanical energy.

thermometer *n* instrument for measuring temperature; *a* **thermometric**.

thermonuclear *a* of nuclear fusion reactions at very high temperatures.

thermoplastic *n, a* (substance) that becomes soft and malleable when heated.

Thermos *n* [*TM*] vacuum flask.

thermosetting *a* hardening after being heated and molded.

thermostat *n* device for regulating temperature automatically.

thesaurus *n* treasury of synonyms, antonyms *esp* lexicon of words grouped by meaning.

these *pron pl* of **this**.

thesis *n* proposition; long essay, treatise written for purposes of academic degree; *pl* **theses**.

thespian *a* of acting; *n* actor.

they *pron* third person *pl* nom.

they'd *contracted form of* **1** they had **2** they would.

they'll *contracted form of* they will.

they're *contracted form of* they are.

they've *contracted form of* they have.

thiamine, thiamin *n* Vitamin B_1.

thick *a* **1** of great distance between surfaces **2** (*of liquid*) not flowing easily **3** closely spaced **4** opaque **5** *sl* stupid; *adv* (**-ly**) *idm* **be thick with somebody** *coll* habitually associate with somebody; *idm* **thick and fast** *coll* very frequently; *idm* **thick with** covered, filled with; *idm* **through thick and thin** despite all hardship; *a* **t.-skinned** insensitive to pain or criticism; *v* **-en** *n,* *a* **-ening**; *n* **-ness 1** state of being thick **2** layer; *n* **thicket** dense growth of shrubs, trees; *a* **thick-set** short; broadly built.

thief *n* one who steals; *pl* **thieves**; *v* **thieve** steal; *a* **thievish**.

thigh *n* upper part of leg.

thimble *n* small cap for protecting finger when sewing.

thin *a* reverse of thick; slender; sparse; loosely packed; *v* make, become thin; *n* **t. air** (*idm* **into thin air** completely out of sight and impossible to find); *a* **t.-skinned** easily offended; *adv* **-ly**; *n* **-ness**; *n* **thinner** liquid used to dilute paint.

thine *poss pron lit, ar* 2nd person sing of **thou**.

thing *n* any object, material or immaterial; *idm* **have a thing about** *coll* have strong like or dislike for; *idm* **make a thing of** treat as important; *pl* **-s 1** personal possessions **2** general situation.

think *v* **1** use one's mind; ponder **2** reflect **3** believe; imagine **4** deliberate; *pt, pp* **thought**; *idm* **think better of** decide against; *phr vs* **think out/through** plan in detail; *idm* **think over** consider carefully; **think up** invent; *n* **t. tank** group of experts meeting to advise on national problems.

third *det, pron* ordinal number of three; next after second; *n* third part; *ns* **t. degree** prolonged questioning, *esp* with torture; **t. party** person or body other than those involved in a relationship or contract; **t. person** form of verb or pronoun used for someone other than the speaker/writer or addressee; **T. World** underdeveloped countries; *a* **t.-rate** of poor quality.

thirst *n* **1** craving for liquid **2** *fig* strong desire; *v* suffer thirst; *a* **thirsty**.

thirteen *n, pron, det* cardinal number three and ten; 13 (*n, a, pron, det* **thirteenth** ordinal number 13th).

this *dem a, pron* denotes thing, person near, just mentioned; *pl* **these**.

thistle *n* prickly leaved flowering plant *n* **thistledown** seed-bearing fluff from head of thistle.

thither *adv ar* to, toward that direction, stage, result.

a
b
c
d
e
f
g
h
i
j
k
l
m
n
o
p
q
r
s
t
u
v
w
x
y
z

tho *conj adv* variant of though.

thong *n* narrow strip of leather, strap.

thorax *n* part of body between neck and abdomen; *a* **thoracic.**

thorium *n* gray-white radioactive metallic element.

thorn *n* prickle, spine on plant; *idm* **thorn in one's side** persistent cause of annoyance; *a* **thorny.**

thorough *a* complete, absolute; *a* **thoroughbred** purebred; polished, refined; *n* purebred animal; *n* **thoroughfare** road for public traffic; *a* **thoroughgoing 1** complete **2** conscientious.

those *pron pl* of **that.**

thou *pron lit, ar* second person singular nominative of **you.**

though *conj* in spite of; although; *conj* **as though** as if.

thought *pt, pp* of **think;** *n* **1** idea; impression **2** act of thinking; careful consideration **3** intention **4** regard; *as* **-ful** (*adv* **-ly;** *n* **-ness**); **-less** (*adv* **-ly;** *n* **-ness**).

thousand *n, pron, det* cardinal number, ten hundreds; 1,000; *pl* **-s** a large number *a, n, det* **thousandth** ordinal number 1000th.

thrall *n* **1** slave **2** slavery; bondage; *n* **thralldom.**

thrash 1 beat; flog **2** thresh; *phr v* **thrash out** *fig* clear up (problem, etc.) by discussion.

thread *n* fine cord used for sewing; yarn; spiral groove cut in screw; *v* put thread into (needle etc.); *idm* **thread one's way through** make one's way through patiently in spite of difficulty; *a* **-bare** very worn.

threat *n* statement of intention to injure, punish, etc.; menace; *v* **-en** utter threats; menace (*a* **-ing** foreshadowing disaster, etc).

three *n, pron, det* cardinal number, one more than two; 3; *a* **t-dimensional** with length, width and height (*also* **3-D**); *ns* **t.-legged race** race in which each competitor has one leg tied to leg of partner; **t. R's** reading, writing, and arithmetic; basic educational skills.

thresh *v* separate grain from chaff mechanically or by beating.

threshold *n* stone or plank below door, at entrance to house, etc.; (*fig*) beginning.

threw *pt* of **throw.**

thrice *adv lit, ar* three times.

thrift *n* **1** frugality; economy **2** genus sea plant **3** a savings-and-loan institution; *a* **-y** frugal; *adv* **-ily** *n* **-iness..**

thrill *v* stir emotions of; vibrate, tingle; *n* intense emotional stirring; exciting event; *n* **thriller** book or film of exciting, *usu* crime story *a* **thrilling** exciting.

thrive *v* flourish; grow well; prosper; *pt* **thrived, throve;** *pp* **thriven, thrived.**

throat *n* front part of neck; gullet; windpipe; *a* **throaty** hoarse, guttural.

throb *v* **throbs, throbbing, throbbed.** beat, pulsate strongly; *n* beat, palpitation (of heart, etc.).

throe *n* pang; brief agony; **in the throes of** struggling with, coming to grips with (some difficulty).

thrombosis *n med* clotting of blood in blood vessel.

throne *n* seat of state, *esp* of regent; *v* enthrone.

throng *n* crowd; large number of people; *v* crowd.

throttle *n* **1** valve in engine regulating flow of steam, gas, etc. **2** *coll* throat; *v* **1** reduce flow of steam, etc. **2** strangle.

through *prep* **1** from end to end **2** by means of; **3** across *adv* from end to end; *a* **1** unobstructed **2** *coll* finished **3** going all the way without changes; *adv, prep* **throughout** right through; in every particular; **t. and t.** completely; **be t. with** finish, break with.

throughput *n* quantity of work or material produced in given time.

throughway, thruway *n* wide road carrying fast-moving traffic.

throw *v* **1** hurl; fling **2** dislodge (from saddle) **3** form (pottery) on wheel; *pt* **threw;** *pp* **thrown;** *idm* **throw a fit/tantrum** *coll* have sudden outburst of anger; *idm* **throw one's lot in with** join (*usu* with some misgivings); *idm* **throw one's weight around** behave in a bossy manner; *idm* **throw in the towel** *coll* admit failure or defeat; *phr vs* **throw in** add without extra charge; **throw off 1** escape from **2** resist (illness); **throw open** give free access to; **throw over** end romantic relationship with; throw together *coll* construct hastily; **throw up 1** abandon (job) **2** bring to light **3** *coll* vomit; *n* **1** act of throwing **2** distance thrown; *a* **t.-away 1** expendable **2** (of remark) casual; *n* **t. back** example of regression.

thru *prep adv a* variant of through.

thrum *n* ends of thread of warp on loom after web is cut; loose thread; *pl* waste yarn; *v* **thrums, thrumming, thrummed.** drum, strum, or repeat monotonously.

thrush[1] *n* one of several varieties of songbirds.

thrush[2] *n* fungal infection with candida fungus, *esp* in mouth.

thrust *v* **1** push; lunge; stab with violent action **2** *fig* obtrude oneself; *pt, pp* **thrust**; *n* onset with pointed weapon; lunge.

thud *n* dull, sound as of heavy body or weight falling on ground; *v* **thuds, thudding, thudded.** make such sound.

thug *n* murderous ruffian; robber; *n* **thuggery** *a* **thuggish**.

thumb *n* short thick inner finger of hand; **rule of t.** accepted way of doing something; *idm* **all thumbs** clumsy; *idm* **thumb one's nose at** *coll* show contempt for; *idm* **thumbs up/down** sign of approval/disapproval; *idm* **under someone's thumb** ruled by someone; *idm* **thumb a ride** hitchlike obtain ride from passing motorist; *ns* **t. nail** nail of thumb (**t. sketch** very small portrait); **thumbscrew** former instrument of torture; **t.-tack** pin with large flat head; *v* make dirty (pages of book, etc.) by handling.

thump *v* strike with heavy blow; *n* such blow, or sound of it; *a* **-ing.**

thunder *n* **1** loud rumbling sound following flash of lightning **2** any such noise (as of applause, etc.); *v* **1** emit thunder **2** utter with loud, powerful voice; *ns* **thunderbolt 1** flash of lighting **2** *fig* startling news or event; **thunderclap** single crash of thunder; *as* **thunderstruck** deeply and suddenly shocked; **thundery** oppressive.

Thursday *n* fifth day of week.

thus *adv lit, ar* in this way; accordingly; *idm* **thus far** until this moment or point.

thwack *v, n* whack.

thwart *v* oppose; hinder; obstruct; *n* seat for oarsman in boat.

thy *poss pron lit, ar* of **thee**; *pron* **thyself** emphatic form of **thou**.

thyme *n* pungent, aromatic herb used in cooking.

thyroid *n* large endocrine gland in neck of vertebrates; *a* of thyroid.

tiara *n* **1** jeweled small crown worn by women **2** triple crown of pope.

tibia *n* shin bone; *pl* **-biae**, or **-bias**; *a* **tibial**.

tic *n* convulsive twitching of facial muscles.

tick[1] *n* blood-sucking parasite.

tick[2] *n* outer covering of mattress, pillow, etc.; *n* **ticking** coarse strong material for this.

tick[3] *n* **1** slight clicking, tapping noise, as of clock **2** *Brit* mark (✓) indicating that something has been checked, *esp* for correctness; *v* **1** make sound of tick **2** mark with symbol ✓; *idm* **make somebody tick** *coll* cause somebody to behave as he/she does; *phr vs* **tick off 1** check (items on list) by marking with ✓ **2** reprimand **3** annoy, anger; *n, a* **-ing** (of) sequence of ticks; *n* **t.-tack-toe** written game using Xs and Os.

ticker *n coll* heart; *n* **t.-tape 1** paper from teleprinter **2** such paper thrown in streets to greet well-known person or group (**t.-tape parade**).

ticket *n* 1 marked card or paper entitling holder to admission, travel, view, etc. 2 label; *v* mark with ticket; label.

tickle *v* 1 itch; tingle 2 amuse; please; *n* irritation of superficial nerves; *a* **ticklish** 1 sensitive to tickling 2 difficult to deal with.

tidal wave *n* large, destructive ocean wave caused by earthquake, etc.

tidbit *n* 1 choice morsel 2 small sample 3 *fig* spicy item of news.

tiddlywinks *n* game in which flat circular disks are flipped into a cup.

tide *n* 1 ebb and flow of ocean surface 2 *fig* trend; tendency 3 *ar* period; season; *phr v* **tide over** help through difficult period; *a* **tidal** of, depending on, or regulated by the tide, **tidal flow, tidal power**; *n* **tideland** area alternately covered and exposed by tice; **tideway** tidal part of river or channel affected by tidal current.

tidings *n pl* news.

tidy *a* trim; neat; orderly; *v* **tidies, tidying, tidied.** put in order.

tie *v* 1 fasten with rope, etc. formed into knot 2 (*in games, etc.*) make equal score (*pt, pp* **tied**; *pr p* **tying**); *phr vs* **tie down** 1 restrict 2 force to make a clear statement or decision; **tie in** be connected

with, consistent with; **tie up** 1 bind 2 invest (money) and make it unavailable for immediate use 3 obstruct (work, negotiations, etc.) (*n* **tie-up** 1 link; partnership 2 halt to progress); *n* necktie; connecting piece; moral obligation; equality of scores in contest; *n* **t.-breaker** means of finding winner from contestants with equal scores (*also* **tiebreak**); *v* **t.-dye** make varied patterns on fabric by tying parts together before dying different colors (*n* **-ing**).

tier *n* 1 row; rank 2 several rows placed one above the other.

tiff *n* trifling dispute; passing quarrel.

tiger *n* large, carnivorous Asiatic mammal, having tawny back with black stripes; *fem* **tigress**.

tiger lily *n* flowering plant with orange leaves spotted with black.

tight *a* 1 firm; compact; taut 2 cramped 3 *coll* stingy 4 *sl* drunk; *n pl* close fitting knitted garment covering legs and lower part of body; **tight** *as* **t.-fisted** stingy (*n* **-ness**); **t.-lipped** 1 with lips pressed close together 2 refusing to speak; *ns* **tightrope** rope stretched horizontally for somebody to walk along as acrobatic feat; *sl* **tightwad** stingy person; *v* **tighten** make, become

tighter.

tilde *n* diacritical mark (~) placed over letter.

tile *n* flat cake of baked clay used for roofing; one of finer clay, plastic, etc., for inside use; *v* cover with tiles; *a* **tiled**.

till¹ *prep* up to time of; *conj* to time that.

till² *n* small drawer or box where cash is kept.

till³ *v* cultivate (ground) *n* **tillage** *ar* cultivation of land.

tiller *n* lever to move rudder of boat.

tilt¹ *v* slope; slant; tip; *n* slope; slant.

tilt² *v* take part in medieval contest with lances; *phr v* **tilt at**; attack, criticize; *n* 1 tournament 2 thrust in tilting; **at full t.** with great speed, or force.

timber¹ *n* 1 wood cut and prepared for building 2 trees; *v* furnish with timber; cover with trees; *a* **timbered** built of or with timber *n* **timberline** treeline.

timber² *n* quality of sound of different musical instruments or voices.

timbrel *n* small drum or tambourine.

time *n* 1 concept of past, present and future 2 hour 3 period taken or required for an action 4 period of life or history 5 moment; occasion 6 opportunity 7 experience related to an occasion (good/bad time); *idm* **behind**

the times out-of-date; *idm* **do time** *sl* be in prison; *idm* **in time 1** not too late **2** after some time has passed; *idm* **on time** punctual(ly); *idm* **take one's time** make no attempt to hurry; *as* **t.-and-motion** regarding efficient methods of working; **t.-honored** accepted as good by tradition; **t.-lapse** *phot* running together sequence of still shots giving impression of long process speeded up; **timeworn 1** very old **2** worn or damaged by long use; *ns* **t. bomb** bomb set to explode at given moment; **t. capsule** sealed container with objects and documents to inform people in the future about life in present time; **t. exposure** *phot* (picture taken with) exposure of more than one second; **timekeeper** person recording time taken; **t. lag** period elapsing between two events; **timepiece** watch or clock; **t.-server** person adapting principles to suit occasion, fashion (*a, n* **t.-serving**); **t.-sharing 1** shared access to computer by several users **2** shared ownership or renting of property, with contract allowing limited period of use (*e.g.*, for annual vacation) (*a* **t.-share**); **timetable 1** (list of) times for public transportation **2** (list of) times for lessons, lectures, etc. **3** (plan of) timing for

business operation (*v* plan sequence of events); **t. zone** any one of the earth's zones within which time is standardized for each hour of the day; **timer** device or person that measures time; *a* **timeless 1** never ending **2** unchanging (*adv* **-ly** *n* **-ness**); **timely** well-timed; opportune (*n* **-liness**); *n* **timing** choosing of appropriate moment.

timid *a* shy; easily frightened; *n* **-ity**.

timorous *a* timid; shy apprehensive; *adv* **-ly**; *n* **-ness**.

timothy *n* coarse fodder grass.

timpani *n* kettledrums; *n* **timpanist**.

tin *n* **1** white malleable metal **2** container made of tin or tin-coated iron; *v* **tins, tinning, tinned. 1** coat with tin **2** preserve in tin container; *ns* **tinfoil** thin flexible metallic sheet; *coll* aluminum foil; **t. god** *coll* person with exaggerated sense of self-importance; **t. hat** metal helmet worn by soldiers; *a* **tinny** (*of sound*) shrill; (*of food*) metallic tasting.

tincture *n* **1** tinge, shade of color **2** medicinal solution; *v* tinge; affect slightly.

tinder *n* inflammable material formerly used to catch spark from flint and steel; *n* **t. box 1** (formerly) box holding materials for fire-lighting **2**

fig situation full of danger.

tine *n* prong of fork.

tinge *v* color, flavor slightly; *n* slight trace.

tingle *v* **1** feel prickling or stinging sensation; smart **2** vibrate; *n* such sensation.

tinker *n* mender, *esp* itinerant, of pots and pans; *v* mend, patch *esp* clumsily.

tinkle *v* give out series of light sounds like small bell; cause to do this; *n* this action or sound.

tinnitus *n med* hearing disorder causing ringing sound.

tinsel *n* **1** glittering material made of thin strips of metal, used for decoration **2** anything sham and showy.

tint *v* color; tinge; *v* dye; give color to.

tintinnabulation *n* ringing of bells.

tiny *a* very small; minute.

tip *n* **1** slender or pointed end of anything **2** useful hint **3** gratuity given to waiter, etc., for service **4** private information; **tip** *n idm* **on the tip of one's tongue** momentarily gone from one's memory; *v* **tips, tipping, tipped. 1** tilt; pour; upset **2** lean over; be tilted **3** give tip to; *idm* **tip the balance/scale** be a deciding factor; *phr v* **tip off** *coll* give advance, *esp* secret warning (*n* **t.-off**); *a* **t.-top** *coll* excellent.

tippet *n* scarf.

tipple *v* take strong drink

A B C D E F G H I J K L M N O P Q R S **T** U V W X Y Z

frequently; n **tippler**.

tipster n person giving advice on likely results of (*esp* horse, dog) races.

tipsy a drunk; mildly intoxicated.

tiptoe v **tiptoes, tiptoeing, tiptoed.** walk on toes; walk softly; *fig* continue with caution; aplomb.

tiptop a **1** highest point **2** *coll* first-rate.

tirade n long denunciation or speech.

tire[1] n ring of metal, rubber, etc., on a round wheel.

tire[2] v make or become weary or fatigued; *as* **tired 1** needing rest, sleep **2** lacking in inspiration; *idm* **tired of** having lost patience with; fed up with; *adv* **-ly;** n **-ness;** tiring.

tiresome a **1** annoying **2** tedious; *adv* **-ly;** n **-ness**.

tissue n **1** structural material of body of animals or plants **2** light woven fabric; n **tissue paper** very thin wrapping paper.

tit n **1** any of various small, brightly colored birds **2** *sl* breast; **t. for tat** equivalent given in retaliation, discussion, etc.

titan n person of great strength, intellect.

titanic a **1** huge; gigantic **2** containing titanium.

titanium n rare, gray-colored metallic element.

tithe n tax of the tenth part, *esp* of profit from land,

produce, etc., paid to church.

titillate v tickle; stimulate pleasurably; n **-lation**.

titivate v **1** smarten up oneself **2** adorn; n **-ation**.

title n **1** name, heading of book, picture, etc. **2** appellation of distinction or honor **3** name showing rank, occupation, etc.; a **titled** having title of nobility; n **t.** legal document establishing ownership, *esp* of land, etc.

titmouse n small bird, allied to nuthatch.

titter v laugh quietly; giggle; n such laugh.

tittle-tattle n gossip; *also* v.

titular a having title but no real power.

tizzy n *coll* state of nervous excitement.

T-junction n T-shaped road junction.

TNT *abbr* trinitrotoluene (powerful explosive).

to *prep* **1** toward; as far as **2** expressing comparison, contrast **3** introducing infinitive verb, indirect object; *adv* to, into normal, desired position, etc.; *adv* **to and fro** back and forth.

toad n amphibianlike large frog; ns **toadstool** any fleshy fungus other than mushroom *esp* if poisonous; **toady** servile flatterer; v act thus.

toast v **1** make crisp and brown by heat; warm at fire **2** drink health of; n **1** slice of bread browned by heat **2** proposal to drink health of **3**

person toasted; ns **toaster** appliance for making toast; **toastmaster** announcer of toasts at banquet.

tobacco n plant whose leaves are used for smoking; its prepared and dried leaves; n **tobacconist** one who sells tobacco, etc.

toboggan n sled for sliding down snowy slopes; v **toboggans, tobogganing, tobogganed.** use, slide on toboggan.

toccata n musical composition for keyboard instrument.

tocsin n bell sounded to give alarm.

today n this day; *adv* on this day; at present time.

toddle v **1** walk unsteadily, as small child **2** *coll* stroll; n **toddler** young child just starting to walk.

toddy n hot drink *usu* containing alcohol.

to-do n *coll* brouhaha; fuss and bother.

toe n one of five digits of foot; v touch with toes; *idm* **on one's toes** alert and ready; *idm* **toe the line** conform; obey orders.

toffee n candy made of boiled sugar with butter.

tofu n bean curd.

toga n loose flowing robe of ancient Romans.

together *adv* **1** in company **2** happening at same time, place, etc.; *idm* **together with** as well as; *idm* **get it together** have everything under control; *a sl* well-organized; *n* **-ness**.

toggle *n* short metal or wooden pin fixed through loop (of rope, etc.) to secure it; small wooden bar used instead of button.

togs *n sl* clothes; dress.

toil *n* severe labor; exacting work; *v* work hard; labor; *as* **toilsome** wearying; **toilworn** (of hands, face, etc.) hard and lined.

toilet *n* 1 process, style of dressing 2 bathroom 3 receptacle for bodily waste; *ns* **t. paper** paper for cleaning oneself in a lavatory; **t. roll** roll of toilet paper; **t. water** scented water; dilute form of perfume; **toiletries** articles used for personal cleanliness, etc.

tokay *n* rich sweet wine and its grape.

token *n* symbol; evidence; coin, disk or voucher.

tokenism *n* half-hearted form of positive discrimination to create good impression.

tolerate *v* put up with; *n* **-ation**; *as* **tolerable** fairly good; bearable; **tolerant** forbearing; broadminded; *n* **tolerance**.

toll[1] *n* tax, duty paid for use of road etc.

toll[2] *v* cause (bell) to ring slowly at regular intervals, *esp* at funeral.

tomahawk *n* light hatchet used by Native Americans in war or hunting.

tomato *n* **-oes.** plant with bright red or yellow edible fruit.

tomb *n* grave; vault; *n* **stone** memorial stone on grave.

tomboy *n* romping, athletic, girl.

tomcat *n* male cat.

tome *n* volume; large book.

tomfoolery *n* foolish behavior; silliness.

tommy-gun *n* short-barreled submachine gun.

tommyrot *n sl* nonsense.

tomography *n* X-ray technique used over selected plane of body.

tomorrow *adv* on, during day after this; *n* day after today.

tom-tom *n* primitive African or Oriental drum.

ton *n* 1 measure of weight, 2,000 lb; 2 unit of ship's carrying capacity; *pl* **-s** very large amount (*also adv*). *n* **tonnage** freight-carrying capacity of ship; ships collectively.

tonality *n* 1 (creation of music having) sense of key 2 tonal quality.

tone *n* 1 musical sound 2 pitch of voice 3 shade of color 4 prevailing mood 5 vigor; *v* give tone to *phr vs* **tone down** make less forceful; *as* **tonal** 1 of tone 2 *mus* of tonality; **t.-deaf** unable to distinguish between notes of different musical pitch; *n* **t. poem** *mus* orchestral piece evoking poetic idea, person, legend, etc.

tongs *n pl* hinged or jointed grasping device.

tongue *n* 1 fleshy muscular organ in mouth; chief organ of taste, speech, etc. 2 language; speech 3 anything resembling tongue in shape; *idm* (**with**) **tongue in cheek** insincerely (*a* **t.-in-cheek**) *a* **t.-tied** unable to speak; *n* **mother t.** native language; **t.-twister** phrase difficult to pronounce, *esp* quickly.

tonic *a* (*of tones, sounds*) invigorating; *n* 1 *med* invigorates 2 tonic water 3 *mus* key note; *n* **t. water** carbonated mineral water flavored with quinine.

tonight *n* this night; night after today; *adv* on, during this night.

tonnage *n* cargo capacity of ship, expressed in tons.

tonneau *n* rear passenger seats of automobile.

tonsil *n* oval mass of tissue in throat; *n* **tonsillectomy** surgical removal of tonsils; **tonsillitis** inflammation of tonsils.

tonsorial *a* of barbers.

tonsure *n* shaving of head.

too *adv* 1 in addition 2 excessively; as well; *idm* **only too** very.

took *pt of* **take**.

tool *n* 1 implement; instrument; appliance used in mechanical operations 2 *fig* pawn; puppet; *v* shape, mark with tool.

toot *n* sound of horn or

a
b
c
d
e
f
g
h
i
j
k
l
m
n
o
p
q
r
s
t
u
v
w
x
y
z

trumpet; *v* make this sound.

tooth *n* **1** one of hard bony growths inside jaws of vertebrates used for tearing, chewing **2** various pointed tooth-shaped objects **3** prong **4** cog; *pl* **teeth; tooth** *idm* **tooth and nail** very fiercely; *idm* **set somebody's teeth on edge** (*of sharp taste, sound*) give somebody unpleasant sensation; *idm* **sink one's teeth into** work at in a concentrated way; *as* **toothless** without teeth; **toothsome** *coll* delectable, tasty; **toothy** exposing one's teeth; *ns* **toothbrush, t. gel, t.paste** brush, gel, paste for cleaning teeth; **toothpick** small pointed stick for removing food from between teeth.

top¹ *n* **1** highest part; summit **2** highest rank, degree **3** highest in merit; *idm* **be on top of** be able to cope with; *idm* **get on top of somebody** *coll* outdo somebody; *idm* **on top of the world** *coll* very happy; *idm* **over the top** *coll* excessive; *v* **tops, topping, topped. 1** be higher, better than **2** provide top for; *idm* **top the bill** play leading role; *phr vs* **top off** *coll* finish; replenish; *ns* **t. brass** *coll* high-ranking military officers; **t. dog** person in most powerful position; **t. hat** man's formal tall cylindrical black or gray hat; **topspin** spinning action causing ball to shoot forward as it hits the ground; *as* **t.-flight** of high quality; **t.-notch** *coll* of the best; **t.-secret** highly confidential; *a* **-less** with breasts uncovered.

top² *n* small spinning toy.

topaz *n* semiprecious stone, usually yellowish.

topiary *n* art of cutting living shrubs, trees into shapes of animals, birds, etc.; *n* **-arist**.

topic *n* subject of thought or discussion; *a* **-al 1** of matters of current interest **2** applied to local area; *adv* **topically**.

topography *n* systematic description of place, etc.; detailed features of district; *n* **-grapher**; *a* **-graphical**.

topper *n coll* **1** top hat **2** something that tops another.

topping *n* decoration on top, *esp* garnish on food.

topple *v* fall or tip over; overbalance.

topsail *n* square sail just above chief sail.

topsoil *n* fertile upper soil.

topsy-turvy *a* upset; upside-down.

torch portable flame; *n* **torchlight** light shed by torches.

tore *pt of* **tear**.

toreador *n Sp* bullfighter; matador.

torment *n* suffering; anguish of mind or body; *v* torture; annoy; tease; harass; *n* **-tor**.

tornado *n* **-oes** or **-os.** violent, destructive localized storm; hurricane.

torpedo *n* **-oes.** self-propelled underwater missile used for destroying shipping; **t. fish** electric ray; *v* attack, destroy with torpedo.

torpid *a* sluggish; dull; apathetic; *ns* **-ity** state of being torpid; **torpor** numbness; dullness; inactivity of mind.

torque *n* **1** twisted collar, necklace, or chain **2** *mech* twisting force or movement.

torrent *n* **1** violently rushing flow **2** *fig* rush of words; *a* **-ial** flowing, falling with great violence.

torrid *a* **1** (*of climate*) very hot and dry **2** passionate; **t. zone** that between tropics.

torsion *n* act of twisting; state of being twisted.

torso *n* **-sos. 1** trunk of human body **2** limbless, headless statue.

tort *n leg* injurious, harmful act against which civil action can be brought.

tortilla *n* Mexican flat bread.

tortoise *n* reptile with complete scaly covering for body; *n* **tortoiseshell** mottled brown shell of tortoise, polished and used commercially; *a*.

tortuous *a* **1** twisting; winding **2** (*of mind, aims, etc.*) devious.

torture *n* **1** deliberate infliction of severe pain **2** great mental anguish; *v* subject to torture; *n* **torturer**.

Tory *n, a* (member) of British

Conservative party.

toss v 1 throw up; fling; pitch 2 be flung, thrown; n act of tossing; n **t.-up** uncertain situation.

tot n 1 tiny child 2 small quantity esp of drink; dram, nip.

total n whole amount; complete number; a entire; complete; v **totals, totaling, totaled. 1** add up **2** amount to as whole; n **-ity** entirety.

totalitarian a applied to state run by dictator or single political party, allowing no opposition or other political representation.

totem n tribal symbol or emblem; n **t. pole** post supporting this.

totter v 1 walk unsteadily 2 (of building, etc.) be about to fall.

toucan n large colorful billed S American bird.

touch v 1 put hand on; make physical contact with; reach; 2 move to pity, etc.; n 1 act of touching 2 sense of feeling 3 characteristic method of technique; idm **touch wood** expressing hope of avoiding bad luck; phr vs **touch down** land (n **touchdown,** score in football); **touch off** cause (e.g., violence) to begin; **touch on/upon** mention briefly; **touch up 1** make minor improvements to **2** sl touch in a sexually provocative manner; a **t.-and-go** risky; uncertain; ns **touchstone** something used

to measure integrity, quality; v **t.-type** type without looking at keyboard; a **touchy** easily offended (adv **-ily** n **-iness**).

touché interj Fr acknowledging a hit in fencing or the aptness of a remark.

tough a 1 strong; firm 2 not brittle 3 sturdy 4 ruthless 5 needing effort to chew; n sl hooligan; criminal; ruffianly man; n **toughness;** v **toughen.**

toupee n Fr artificial of hair; wig, usu worn by men.

tour n 1 journey around district 2 excursion 3 series of visits to different places; v make tour; travel; ns **-ist** one who travels for pleasure; **-ism** business of organizing, operating tours, and catering to tourists.

tour de force n Fr highly skillful achievement.

tournament n 1 medieval contest between mounted knights 2 games contest of skill usu for prize, championship.

tourniquet n Fr device or bandage used to stop arterial bleeding.

tousle v make untidy; rumple; ruffle.

tout v importune, pester in order to sell; n one who touts.

tow v pull along (vehicle, etc.) by rope; n act of towing or being towed; idm **in tow** following closely behind.

toward a imminent, at hand; prep **toward** in direction of.

towel n cloth used for drying (skin, china, etc.) after washing; v dry, rub with towel; n **toweling** absorbent cloth for making towels.

tower n 1 tall strong structure often forming part of church or other building 2 fortress; v rise, stand very high; **t. of strength** person that can be relied on for moral support.

town n group of houses and other buildings, larger than village; idm **go to town** behave freely, in an uninhibited way; idm **(out) on the town** (out) enjoying places of entertainment, esp at night; ns **t. clerk** official responsible for records of town or city; **t. crier** person making public announcements; **t. hall** public building, headquarters of local government. n **township** town and surrounding area forming municipality.

towpath n path along bank of river or canal.

toxic a pertaining to, caused by **toxemic** poison; ns **toxemia** blood poisoning; **toxicology** study of poisons and their effects; **toxin** poisonous organic substance.

toy n 1 plaything 2 trifle; bauble; v trifle with; phr v toy **with 1** consider without serious thought **2** handle in an aimless way; n **t. boy**

A B C D E F G H I J K L M N O P Q R S **T** U V W X Y Z

young man with whom older woman has amorous relationship.

trace n **1** one of two straps by which vehicle is drawn by horse **2** visible signs left by anything **3** slight tinge; n **t. element** any chemical element found only in minute quantities in an organism, but essential to its healthy development; v **1** follow course, track of **2** draw, copy exactly *esp* by use of tracing paper; ns **tracer bullet (shell)** one which leaves visible trail; **tracery** intricate decorative pattern of lines; **tracing** traced copy of drawing; **t. paper** thin, transparent paper on which tracings are made.

trachea n -eae. *anat* windpipe.

track n **1** mark, marks left by passing animal, person, vehicle **2** unofficial (rough) path **3** railway line **4** railway platform **5** course for racing **6** rail that supports something moving (*e.g.*, curtains) **7** *mus* any of the sections that make up the contents of a record or CD **8** continuous belt covering wheels of tank, bulldozer, etc.; *idm* **keep/lose track of** manage/not manage to have up-to-date information about; *idm* **make tracks (for)** *coll* leave (for); go on one's way; *idm* **on the right/wrong track** thinking of the right/wrong kind of answer,

solution; v **1** follow the track of **2** (*of camera*) move while filming; *phr vs* **track down** find by tracking, searching; a **-ed** having tracks; ns **t. and field** athletics; **tracker** person tracking wild animals (**t. dog** dog used by police to track down criminal); **t. event** athletic running contest; **tracking** *aut* alignment of car wheels (**t. station** place where movement of satellites, missiles, etc. can be observed by radar, radio); **t. record** past record of achievement; **t. suit** loose-fitting suit worn for confort, warmth when training for sports.

tract n **1** expanse of country **2** *anat* system of related organs.

tract n pamphlet; treatise.

tractable a **1** easily managed **2** docile **3** easily worked.

traction n **1** act, process of drawing along **2** *med* artificial stretching of spine, etc.; ns **t. engine** steam engine for drawing loads along road; **tractor** motor vehicle for drawing plow, etc.

trad n *coll* traditional jazz (*also* **trad jazz**).

trade n **1** commerce; buying and selling **2** those engaged in trade; v traffic; buy and sell; barter; *idm* **do good/bad trade** be successful/ unsuccessful in business; v **1** buy and sell goods **2** barter **3** exchange; *phr vs* **trade in** offer in part exchange for

something new (n **t.-in**); **trade off** something (against something) sacrifice something as compromise in return for something beneficial (n **t.-off**); **trade on** take advantage of; ns **trader, trading; t. gap** difference between value of imports and exports; **t. mark 1** name, symbol, etc, identifying brand of item being sold. **2** *fig* characteristic thing by which one can be identified; **t. name 1** name given by manufacturer to identify brand **2** name by which person, firm is known for business purposes; **t. union** labor organization that protects interests of workers (ns **t. -unionism, -ist**); **t. wind** strong steady wind blowing toward the Equator.

tradition n **1** belief, custom, law, etc., handed down verbally from one generation to another **2** unwritten history; a **-al** (n **-ism;** n, a **-ist;** *adv* **-ly**).

traduce v slander.

traffic n **1** passing to and fro of vehicles, etc. in street **2** body of vehicles using street **3** trade; v trade; *pt, pp* **trafficked;** *pr p* **trafficking;** ns **trafficker** person trading, *esp* in something illicit or immoral; **t. jam** congested state of traffic in which vehicles come to a standstill; **t.-light** light that controls flow of traffic automatically;

t. police officers appointed to monitor illegal parking of vehicles and cite offenders.

tragedy *n* 1 very sad event, calamity *esp* one causing death 2 drama dealing with human misfortunes and sorrows; *a* **tragic** 1 of, like tragedy 2 fatal; disastrous *adv; ns* **tragedian** tragic actor; *fem* **tragedienne; tragicomedy** play with both tragic and comic scenes.

trail *v* 1 drag along ground 2 follow track of; shadow; *n* 1 track or trace 2 rough ill-defined road; *n* **trailer** 1 expert in following trail 2 vehicle towed by another one 3 mobile home 4 advertisement of forthcoming film, etc.

train *v* 1 educate; instruct 2 (*of plants, etc.*) cause to grow in certain way 3 aim (gun) 4 *sport* follow course of physical exercise, diet, etc.; *n* 1 series of cars, etc., drawn by locomotive 2 trailing part of dress hem 3 retinue 4 line of gunpowder to mine, etc.; *ns* **trainee** one who is being trained in certain skill, etc.; **training** 1 process of educating 2 art of preparing (persons for athletic contests, or horses for racing).

traipse *v* walk around aimlessly.

trait *n* characteristic feature.

traitor *n* 1 one who is guilty of treason 2 one who betrays a trust (*fem* **traitress**); *a* **-ous**

treacherous.

trajectory *n* path of missile fired or thrown through air.

tram *n* 1 public vehicle running on rails on road 2 truck used in coalmines; *n* **tramcar.**

trammel *n* 1 kind of fishnet 2 shackle; *pl* **-s** thing that impedes freedom of movement or action; *v* **trammels, trammeling, trammeled.** confine; restrict; hinder.

tramp *v* 1 walk, tread heavily 2 travel as vagabond 3 travel on foot; *n* 1 act of tramping 2 long walk 3 homeless vagrant 4 cargo vessel (also **t. steamer**); *v* **trample** tread under foot.

trampoline *n* frame with sheet of strong fabric stretched by springs where people can jump, bounce, and perform gymnastic; *v* perform on this (*n* **-lining**).

trance *n* 1 state of suspended consciousness 2 ecstasy; rapture.

tranquil *a* calm; serene; peaceful; unruffled; *n* **tranquillity;** *v* **tranquilize** make calm, sedate (*n* **-izer** sedative).

trans- *prefix* across; through; beyond. (*Compounds where the meaning is obvious are not given here*).

transact *v* to carry through; do business (negotiations, etc.); *n* **-ion** piece of business; *pl* proceedings.

transcend *v* rise above; go beyond; surpass; *a* **transcendent** surpassing.

transcendental *a* going beyond normal human knowledge or understanding (**t. meditation** form of meditation with chanted mantra to achieve calm); *n* **-ism;** *n, a* **-ist.**

transcribe *v* copy; write out (notes) in full.

transcript *n* written or printed version of oral speech; *n* **-ion** 1 act of transcribing 2 transcript.

transducer *n* device for converting electrical into mechanical energy.

transept *n* part of cruciform church which crosses main nave.

transfer *v* **transfers, transferring, transferred.** move, convey from one person or place to another; *n* 1 act of transferring; conveyance 2 design, etc. transfered from one surface to another by heat, pressure, etc.; *a* **-able** *n* **-ference.**

transfigure *v* 1 alter appearance of 2 idealize; glorify; *n* **-figuration.**

transfix *v* 1 impale 2 *fig* root to the spot.

transform *v* change shape, character, nature of; *ns* **-ation; -er** mechanical device in electricity for changing voltage of alternating current.

transfuse *v* transfer (blood) from veins of one organism

a b c d e f g h i j k l m n o p q r s t u v w x y z

(*e.g.*, person or animal) to another; *n* **-fusion**.

transgress *v* 1 exceed, violate (law) 2 sin; *ns* **-gression; -gressor**.

transient *a* fleeting; brief; momentary; *n* **transience**.

transistor *n* small electrical device used in place of thermionic valve; small portable radio containing this.

transitory *adv* **-ily;** *n* **-iness**.

transit *n* passage; crossing; *n* **transition** change from one place to another (**a -al**) *as* **-ive** (of verb) requiring direct object; **-ory** not lasting.

translate *v* 1 render into another language 2 transfer (bishop) from one see to another; *ns* **-lator; -lation**.

transliterate *v* render language in script of another alphabet; *n* **-ation**.

translucent *a* letting light pass through.

transmigration *n* (after death) transfer of soul to a different body (human or animal).

transmit *v* **transmits, transmitting, transmitted.** 1 pass on 2 hand down (by heredity, etc.) 3 communicate; *ns* **-mitter** 1 one who transmits 2 apparatus for sending radio waves; **transmission** act of transmitting; that which is transmitted.

transmogrify *v* change appearance in a surprising, *esp* grotesque way; *n* **-ification**.

transmute *n* change into something different (*n* **-mutation**).

transom *n* 1 window above door 2 crosspiece separating door and window.

transonic *a* close to speed of sound, moving 700-780 mph.

transparent *a* 1 permitting passage of light 2 *fig* clear; obvious; *ns* **-ence; -ency** 1 quality of being transparent 2 picture on transparent material, visible when lit from behind.

transpire *v* 1 exhale as vapor 2 become known 3 *coll* happen.

transplant *v* 1 dig up (plant) and replant elsewhere 2 *med* remove (healthy organ, tissue) and graft elsewhere; *n* **-ation**.

transponder *n* radio, radar apparatus sending signal in response to one received.

transport *v* 1 carry, convey from one place to another 2 enrapture; *n* 1 act, method of conveying persons, goods 2 vehicle, ship, etc., so used (also **transportation**).

transpose *v* 1 rearrange; change order of 2 *mus* put into different key; *ns* **transposal; transposition**.

transsexual *n* 1 person who feels he/she belongs to the opposite sex.

transubstantiation *n* change of substance or essence.

transverse *a* set crosswise; at right angles.

transvestism *n* wearing clothes usually associated with opposite sex; *n* **transvestite** person who does this.

trap *n* 1 device for catching, snaring animals, etc.; pitfall 2 two-wheeled carriage 3 device to prevent gas, foul air, etc., escaping; *v* **traps, trapping, trapped.** 1 snare 2 *fig* deceive by cunning; *ns* **t.-door** hinged door in floor, ceiling, etc.; **trapper** one who traps animals for their fur.

trappings *n pl* equipment; ornaments; one's belongings.

trapeze *n* swinging horizontal bar for gymnastic and acrobatic use.

trapezium *n* quadrilateral with no parallel sides, *also* **trapezoid**; *a* **-al**.

trash *n* 1 rubbish; useless matter 2 worthless person; *a* **trashy** cheap; shoddy.

trash can *n* garbage receptacle.

trauma *n* 1 injury 2 emotional injury caused by shock, etc.; *a* **traumatic;** *adv* **-ally;** *v* **traumatize**.

travel *v* **travels, traveling, traveled.** move along; make journey; *n* **t. agent** person who makes travel arrangements and reservations; *n pl* **-s** 1 journeys 2 tour *esp* abroad;. *ns* **traveler** one who travels; one who travels on business, often **commercial t.;** *a* **traveled** worldly, experienced in traveling; n **traveler's check** check issued by bank to client for use abroad.

traveling salesman n person traveling to sell goods for a firm by taking orders.

traverse v 1 pass, lie across 2 swivel; n 1 ledge, etc. crossing rockface horizontally 2 sideways movement (of gun).

travesty n parody; ridiculous distortion; v make, be travesty of.

trawl n open-mouthed fishing net dragged along ocean bottom; v fish with one; n **trawler** fishing vessel using trawl.

tray n flat board, slab of wood, metal, etc., with rim, for carrying things.

treachery n betrayal; perfidy; breach of trust; a **treacherous** disloyal; unreliable; dangerous.

treacle n thick syrup obtained from unrefined sugar, molasses; a **treacly**.

tread v 1 walk; step; set foot on 2 press; crush (e.g., grapes) 3 (+adv) fig speak, act, proceed in specified way; pt **trod,** pp **trodden** or **trod** idm **tread water** remain afloat by moving one's arms and legs; n manner, sound of walking; part of tire in contact with ground; top surface of step; ns **treadle** lever worked by foot; **treadmill** cylinder turned by treading on steps fixed to

rim; exercise equipment for walking running indoors; fig monotonous routine.

treason n violation by subject of allegiance to sovereign or state; as **treasonable; treasonous**.

treasure n valuables; money; riches; v store, regard; as valuable; cherish; ns **treasurer** person in charge of funds of club, society, etc.; **treasury** 1 department of state, collecting and controlling public money and taxation 2 place for storing treasure; **treasure trove** found treasure.

treat v 1 behave toward, use 2 seal with chemically 3 pay expenses of 4 negotiate; n 1 pleasurable event 2 entertaining 3 candy, tasty snack; n **treatment** 1 act, mode of, treating, attempting to cure 2 manner of artistic handling.

treatise n systematic written account of something.

treaty n agreement, contract entered into between states etc.

treble a high pitched; n treble part of voice.

tree n 1 large perennial plant having woody trunk 2 cobbler's last (e.g., shoe tree); **family t.** diagram showing descent from common ancestor; ns **t. fern** large tropical fern with treelike stem; **t. line** line of latitude or height above sea

level beyond which trees will not grow; a **treeless** (n - **ness**).

trefoil n 1 plant whose leaf has three lobes, e.g., clover 2 arch carved three-lobed ornament.

trek v make journey; travel; migrate; n long journey.

trellis n lattice, structure of crossed wooden strips.

tremble v shiver; quake; n tremor; quiver; involuntary shaking.

tremendous a 1 vast; amazing; awe-inspiring 2 coll very exciting; adv **-ly** extremely.

tremolo n quivering effect in playing or singing.

tremor n 1 shaking 2 qualm 3 thrill.

tremulous 1 shaky; trembling 2 timid; fearful.

trench n long opening, furrow, cut or dug in ground; v cut trench or groove.

trench coat n belted raincoat with epaulets.

trenchant a keen; incisive; biting; adv **-ly**; n trenchancy.

trend n 1 course; direction 2 fig general tendency 3 fashion; n **t.-setter** person ahead of fashion; a, n **t.- setting** a idm **trendy** in latest fashions.

trepidation n state of alarm; nervous; flustered.

trespass n 1 go unlawfully on another's land 2 commit an offence; phr v **trespass on** take unfair advantage of; n act of trespassing; offense;

a b c d e f g h i j k l m n o p q r s **t** u v w x y z

A
B
C
D
E
F
G
H
I
J
K
L
M
N
O
P
Q
R
S
T
U
V
W
X
Y
Z

injury; n **trespasser.**

tress n lock of hair; pl hair of head.

trestle n braced framework of wood, steel, etc., for carrying a road over a crevasse; framework of wooden base to support tabletop.

tri- prefix three.

triad n group of three; trinity; mus a chord.

trial n 1 act of trying, testing 2 adversity 3 source of irritation 4 judicial inquiry; idm **stand trial** be tried in court; idm **trial and error** experimental method of solving problem by learning from mistakes.

triangle n figure with three angles; musical instrument; a **triangular.**

triangulation n method of calculating position or distance by use of triangles.

triathlon n athletic contest in running, swimming, and cycling.

tribe n social unit; class; group; a **tribal;** n **tribesman** member of tribe.

tribulation n grief; affliction; mental distress.

tribunal n court of justice; special court of inquiry.

tribune n 1 person who defends other's rights 2 rostrum.

tribute n 1 tax, payment made by one state to another 2 act performed, words uttered as sign of respect, esteem, affection for; a **tributary** 1 paying tribute 2 auxiliary; n stream flowing into larger one.

triceps n large muscle at back of upper arm (pl **triceps**).

trichinosis n food-borne disease from parasitic worm.

trichology n study of hair growth and associated problems; n **-ologist.**

trick n 1 deception; swindle 2 illusion; pranks 3 mannerism 4 cards played in one round; v cheat; deceive; idm **do the trick** achieve one's aim; v **t.-or-treat** (of children) threaten to play tricks on people who will not give a treat (e.g., candy) on Halloween. n **trickery, trickster** a **tricky** shifty; ingenious.

trickle v flow slowly; n thin flow.

tricolor n national flag with three stripes of different colors.

tricycle n three-wheeled cycle.

trident n three-pronged fork.

tried pt, pp of try; a well tested.

triennial a happening every three years.

trier n person who tries.

trifle n 1 small, insignificant thing of no value 2 sweet dish of sponge cake, wine, and whipped cream, etc.; idm **a trifle** coll a little bit; phr v **trifle with** treat casually, without respect; a **trifling** trivial.

trigger n catch which releases spring esp to fire gun; phr v **trigger off** initiate large scale process by small act; a **t.-happy** too eager to use violence.

trigonometry n branch of mathematics dealing with relationship between sides and angles of triangles.

trilateral a having three sides.

trilby n man's soft felt hat.

trill v sing, with vibrating sound; warble; n such singing.

trillion n one million million; pl **-s** enormous quantity; a very large number.

trilogy n series of three connected literary, cinematic, or musical works.

trim v trims, trimming, trimmed. 1 prune 2 decorate (garment, etc.) 3 adjust balance of (ship, aircraft, etc.); a 1 neat; tidy; in good order 2 physically fit (idm **in fighting trim** ready for anything); v, n 1 act of trimming 2 decorative finish (e.g., on car bodywork); n **-ming** decorative addition (pl **-s** 1 pieces trimmed off 2 usual extras).

trimaran n boat with three parallel hulls.

trinity n 1 in Christian dogma, the three divine persons of Godhead 2 state of being threefold.

trinket n bauble; worthless trifle.

trio n **-os.** group of three; music for three voices or instruments.

trip *v* **trips, tripping, tripped.**
1 stumble; make false step 2
skip; dance; *v phr* **trip up**
make a mistake; *n* 1 short
journey 2 act of tripping 3 *sl*
sensations experienced from
taking hallucinatory drug.

tripartite *a* of, in three parts.

tripe *n* 1 stomach of ruminant
animal, prepared as food 2
coll nonsense; rubbish.

triple *a* threefold; *v* increase
threefold; *ns* **t. jump** athletic
contest of hop, stride, and
jump; **triplet** three of a kind,
esp one of three siblings born
together; *as* **triplex** threefold;
triplicate made in three
identical copies; *n* one of
three identical copies.

tripod *n* three-legged stand,
support, etc.

trip wire *n* stretched wire that
activates alarm or other
device when tripped
accidentally.

triptych *n* set of three picture
panels side by side.

trisect *v geom* divide into three
equal parts.

trite *a* banal; commonplace.

Triton *n Gk* 1 minor sea-god 2
lc nucleus of tritium.

triturate *v* grind to powder,
pulverize; *n* **-ation**.

triumph *n* 1 victory; success;
exultation 2 processional
entry of victorious ancient
Roman general; *v* achieve
success; prevail; exult;
as **-al; -ant**.

triumvir *n* member of
triumvirate ruling group of

three such people.

triumvirate *n* 1government by
three joint magistrates 2
office of triumvirate 3
association of three.

trivet *n* 1 tripod, three-legged
stand 2 stand for hot pot or
kettle on table.

trivia *n pl* things of little or no
importance.

trivial *a* 1 of minimal
importance 2 ordinary;
v **-ize**; *n* **-ity**.

troche *n* small tablet of
medicine.

trochee *n* metrical foot of two
syllables, one stressed, one
weak.

trod *pt, pp of* tread.

trodden *pp of* tread.

troglodyte *n* 1 cave dweller 2
common wren 3 *coll* stupid
person.

Trojan *n* 1 inhabitant of Troy
2 person of courage and
endurance.

troll *v* fish by trailing bait *esp*
behind boat; sing cheerfully.

troll *n* fabulous Scandinavian
goblin, giant, or dwarf.

trolley *n* 1 light low cart or
wheeled table, pushed by
hand 2 streetcar on rails 3
metal arm conveying current
from overhead wires to
trolley; **t. car** bus powered by
overhead electric cable.

trombone *n* powerful brass
wind-instrument with sliding
tube; *n* **-bonist** trombone
player.

troop *n* number of people;
subdivision of cavalry

squadron; *pl* soldiers; *v* move
as troop; crowd; *n* **-er** cavalry
soldier.

trope *n* figure of speech.

trophy *n* token of victory;
prize.

tropic *n* one of two parallels of
latitude 23° 28′ N and S of
Equator; *pl* hot regions of
earth between these
parallels; *a* **-al** extremely hot;
growing, occurring in tropics.

trot *v* **trots, trotting, trotted.**
(*of horse, etc.*) move rapidly
but not at gallop; run easily
with short steps; *n* rapid pace
of horse etc; quick walk; *phr*
v **trot out** repeat in an
unoriginal way.

troth *n lit* fidelity; word of
honor.

Trotskyist *a, n* (follower) of
the ideas of Leon Trotsky.

trotter *n* pig's foot.

troubadour *n* French medieval
poet.

trouble *v* 1 disturb; afflict 2
agitate; worry; *n* 1 agitation
2 difficulty 3 disturbance; *ns*
t.-maker person who causes
trouble; **t.-shooter** person
who helps solve mechanical
problems or settle disputes *as*
troublous disturbed;
troublesome annoying;
unruly.

trough *n* 1 long narrow
container for food or water
for animals 2 narrow channel
between waves.

trounce *v* beat; defeat;
censure.

troupe *n Fr* band of actors;

a
b
c
d
e
f
g
h
i
j
k
l
m
n
o
p
q
r
s
t
u
v
w
x
y
z

A
B
C
D
E
F
G
H
I
J
K
L
M
N
O
P
Q
R
S
T
U
V
W
X
Y
Z

touring company.

trouper n **1** performer of long experience **2** one who is patient, steadfast.

trousers n pl two-legged outer garment, enclosing legs from waist to ankles.

trousseau n Fr personal property of a bride (e.g., clothing, linens, etc.).

trout n edible freshwater fish.

trowel n small flat-bladed tool for spreading mortar; small hollow-bladed tool for lifting, planting.

troy n system of weights used for gold, silver, etc.

truant n person who stays away from school, work, etc., without permission; a shirking school or duty **truant;** phr v **play truant** be a truant.

truce n temporary agreement to stop fighting; respite.

truck n motor vehicle for carrying heavy loads; idm **have no truck with** refuse to consider or have dealings with; n **t. farm** farm of vegetables, produce for market; n **trucker.**

truckle v cringe; phr v **truckle to** fawn on; submit to.

truckle-bed n trundle bed; low bed, esp on wheels, which fits under a higher one (also **trundle bed**).

truculent a aggressive; fierce; violent; n **truculence.**

trudge v walk wearily, with effort; n long tedious walk.

true a in accordance with fact;

accurate; genuine; correct; as **t.-blue** totally loyal; **t. life** based on real events and people; ns **t. love** sweetheart; **t. north** north according to earth's axis; ns **truism** statement of something obviously true; adv **truly** really; loyally; sincerely.

truffle n **1** exotic edible fungus, growing below ground **2** small usu rum-flavored chocolate confection.

trump n card of suit temporarily ranking above others; phr v **trump up** coll invent (excuse, accusation); a **trumped up** fabricated; concocted; n **t. card 1** card of suit that is trump **2** fig way of gaining advantage **3** v in cards, take trick with trump.

trumpery n something of no use or value.

trumpet n **1** metal wind instrument **2** funnel-shaped device for directing sound; v sound on trumpet; fig proclaim, announce widely; n **-er** trumpet player.

truncate v cut off; lop off.

truncheon n short thick staff or cudgel, baton of office.

trundle v cause to roll along; move on wheels; n **trundle bed** low bed on casters, usu pushed under another when not in use (also **truckle bed**).

trunk n **1** stem of tree **2** person's body not including head or limbs **3** main body or line (of railroads, telephones,

etc.) **4** large suitcase **5** long flexible snout of elephant, etc.; ns **t. call** Brit long-distance telephone call; **t. line** main line of communication between large towns; **t. road** important main road; pl **trunks** man's swimming shorts.

truss v bind, tie up, tie wings (of fowl, etc.) before cooking; n **1** bundle (of hay, etc.) **2** cluster of blossom **3** surgical support for ruptured organ **4** framework of beams, etc., supporting roof, etc.

trust n **1** confidence; faith **2** group of persons administering fund **3** responsibility **4** property held for another; v have faith in; rely on; **2** on credit; phr v **trust in** fml believe, have faith in; ns **trustee** one legally holding property in trust for another (n **-ship**); **t. fund** money under control of a trust; as **trustful** confiding; **trusting** willing to trust other people; **trustworthy** deserving to be trusted; **trusty 1** fml dependable **2** convict considered trustworthy and granted special privileges.

truth n quality, state of being true; honesty; sincerity a **truthful;** adv **-ly;** n **-ness.**

try v **tries, trying, tried. 1** test; attempt **2** conduct judicial inquiry into **3** purify; refine (metals); phr vs **try on**

1 put on (garment) to examine fit, size, color, etc. **2** behave in an unreasonable way to see if this will be tolerated; **try out** test by experience; *n* attempt; (rugby) touch-down; *as* **tried** proved, reliable; **trying** provoking; painful; wearisome.

tryst *n* appointment, as of lovers, to meet; such a meeting; *v* **tryst** to have such a meeting.

tsar *n* formerly emperor of Russia; *fem* **tsarina** (*also* **czar, czarina**).

tsetse fly *n* African fly that conveys parasite of sleeping sickness.

tsunami *n* large wave caused by undersea earthquake or volcano; tidal wave.

T-shirt casual shirt with short sleeves shaped like T (*also* **tee-shirt**).

T-square *n* ruler shaped like T.

tub *n* **1** wooden vessel, shaped like half barrel; *coll* **2** bath **3** boat used for rowing practice; *v coll* bathe, take bath (**t.-thumper** person doing this).

tuba *n* low-pitched brass wind instrument.

tube *n* long, hollow cylinder; pipe; underground electric railway; *a* **tubular** shaped like tube; *n* **tubing** series of pipes; piece of tube.

tuber *n* swollen part of underground stem; containing buds, *e.g.*, potato; *a* **tuberous** producing, growing from tubers.

tuberculosis *n* infectious disease causing growth of small nodules at affected part, caused by tubercles.

tuberose *n* bulbous garden plant like lily, having spikes of fragrant flowers.

tuck *v* gather up; fold; be folded up; press together; *phr vs* **tuck in/into 1** push end in, so that it is neatly hidden **2** *coll* eat heartily; **tuck up** make comfortable in bed; *ns* stitched fold; *v* **tucker (out)** exhaust, tire out.

Tuesday *n* third day of week.

tuft *n* bunch, bundle *esp* of grass, hair, etc.

tug *v* **tugs, tugging, tugged.** pull violently; *n* **1** act of tugging **2** small boat for towing; **t. of war** contest of strength between two teams pulling in different directions on same rope.

tugboat *n* powerful vessel used for towing.

tuition *n* **1** teaching; instruction **2** fees charged by private schools, colleges, universities, etc., for education.

tulip *n* bulbous plant of lily family; *n* **t.-tree** tree akin to magnolia.

tulle *n Fr* sheer, often stiffened net fabric of nylon, silk, often used in ballet costume.

tumble *v* **1** fall down; stumble **2** turn somersaults **3** upset; *phr vs* **tumble down** collapse (*a* **tumbledown** in ruins); *n* fall; somersault; *ns* **t. drier** machine with rotating drum for drying clothes **tumbler 1** acrobat **2** part of lock moved by key **3** drinking glass without stem or foot.

tumid *a* swollen; enlarged.

tummy *n coll* stomach.

tumor *n* abnormal mass of growing body tissue; *a* **-ous**.

tumult *n* uproar; disturbance; *a* **-uous** noisy; greatly agitated.

tumulus *n* **-li.** ancient burial mound or barrow.

tun *n* large cask for storing, fermenting beer and wine; formerly, measure of liquid: 252 gallons.

tuna fish, tuna *n* large edible ocean fish with dark flesh.

tundra *n* frozen treeless plain, above timberline.

tune *n* **1** air; melody **2** harmony **3** correctness of pitch; *idm* **change one's t.** *fig* speak, act very differently; *idm* **in/out of tune 1** at correct musical pitch **2** in agreement; *idm* **to the tune of 1** using the music of **2** *coll* to the total sum of; *v* adjust to correct pitch; adjust radio, etc., to receive programs on certain wave/length; *phr v* **tune in** turn on radio or adjust controls to particular wavelength; *as* **-ful** melodious; *adv* **-ly;** *n* **-ness;** **-less;** *adv* **-ly;** *n* **-ness;** *n* **tuner 1** person who tunes instrument **2** device for selecting signal of particular frequency.

tungsten *n* grayish white metallic element; wolfram.

tunic *n* military overcoat; loose-belted, knee-length garment.

tuning *n* act of getting in tune; *n* **t. fork** pronged piece of steel that resonates when struck to help check tuning of other instrument(s).

tunnel *n* **1** underground passage *esp* one for cars, trains **2** burrow (of mole, etc.); *n* **t. vision 1** sight defect from which sufferer can only see straight ahead **2** *fig* tendency to see only one aspect of a question; *v* **tunnels, tunneling, tunneled.** make tunnel through.

turban *n* Oriental and Middle Eastern head-covering made by wrapping long strip of cloth around head.

turbid *a* muddy; opaque; *fig* confused, etc.; *adv* **-ly;** *ns* **-ity; -ness.**

turbine *n* motor driven by jets of steam, water, etc., on blades.

turbocharger *n* compressor device that makes internal combustion engine more powerful.

turbojet *n*, *a* (jet engine) using exhaust gas to drive turbine.

turboprop *n* turbojet with turbine-driven propeller.

turbot *n* large edible flat seafish.

turbulent *a* riotous; unruly; disorderly; *n* **-lence.**

tureen *n* deep, covered dish for serving soup.

turf *n* **-fs** or **-ves.** area of earth covered by grass; sod; peat.

turgid *a* swollen; inflated; pompous; *n* **-ity.**

turkey *n* large, domestic edible fowl of pheasant family; *idm* **talk turkey** *coll* speak openly, negotiate seriously.

Turkish *a* pertaining to Turkey, the Turks; *n* **T. bath** steam bath often followed by cold shower, massage, etc.

turmeric *n* aromatic plant of ginger family used as medicine, dye, and condiment.

turmoil *n* agitation; uproar; confusion; tumult.

turn *v* **1** move around an axis; rotate **2** move in different direction **3** reverse; move to reverse side **4** cause to move in specified direction; aim **5** look around **6** curve away **7** (cause to) become **8** fold **9** go sour; *idm* **turn a blind eye/deaf ear** pretend not to see/hear; *idm* **turn a phrase** express cleverly; *idm* **turn one's head** make one conceited; *idm* **turn one's stomach** make one feel sick; *idm* **turn up one's nose at** reject as inferior; *phr vs* **turn down 1** (turn controls to) reduce (heat, volume, etc.) **2** refuse (request); **turn in 1** fold inward **2** *coll* surrender **3** *coll* go to bed **4** hand in; **turn**

off 1 cause to stop operating **2** cause to lose interest, *esp* sexually (*n* **t.-off 1** road branching off main road **2** something boring or disgusting;); **turn on 1** cause to start operating **2** attack without warning **3** depend on **4** *sl* arouse (*n* **t.-on**); **turn out 1** empty **2** extinguish **3** expel **4** happen **5** appear at public event **6** produce (*n* **t.-out 1** number of people attending **2** act of emptying, tidying **3** way of dressing); **turn over 1** move to next page **2** ponder **3** (of engine) idle **4** do trade (*n* **turnover 1** amount of business done or rate of selling **2** changes in staff **3** small pie); **turn up 1** arrive **2** find or be found **3** fold up, *esp* to shorten garment **4** raise in heat, volume, etc., by turning controls; *n* **1** act of turning **2** change of direction **3** rightful time or opportunity **4** move from one period or condition to another **5** attack of illness **6** short theatrical performance; *idm* **give someone a turn** shock someone; *idm* **a good/bad turn** a kind/mean action; *idm* **in turn 1** in rightful order **2** one after the other; *idm* **out of turn 1** before one's proper time **2** in a tactless way; *idm* **(done) to a turn** (cooked) exactly right; *ns* **t. about** change of direction; **turncoat** disloyal person; **turnkey**

jailer (a ready for use and occupation); **turnpike** highway with toll gates; **t.around** time required to complete and return a job; time taken to unload and reload before return journey; **turnstile** revolving gate to control admission, *e.g.*, to sports event; **t.-table** (machine that drives) revolving surface for playing records; *ns* **turner** person working at a lathe; **turning** corner, curve, or branch in road (*n* **t. point** time when important change occurs).

turnip *n* plant with large white globular edible root.

turpentine *n* liquid solvent, distilled from pine resin.

turpitude *n* depravity, infamy.

turquoise *n* semiprecious greenish blue stone; this color.

turret *n* small tower; revolving armored tower for guns in warship tank or aircraft.

turtle *n* marine tortoise; edible species of this; *idm* **turn turtle** (of ship) turn over.

turtledove *n* wild dove.

turtleneck *n* (shirt or sweater with) high close-fitting neck band.

tusk *n* long pointed tooth in some animals, as elephants, etc.; *n* **tusker** animal with fully developed tusks.

tussle *n* scuffle; rough struggle; *v* engage in rough struggle.

tussock *n* clump of grass; tuft.

tut *interj* expressing annoyance or disapproval.

tutelage *n* stage of acting as guardian, or being under guardianship.

tutor *n* teacher, private instructor, *a* **-ial**.

tutti-frutti *n* Italian ice-cream containing small bits of fruit.

tutu *n* **-us** short, full, ballet skirt.

tutu *n* short full skirt worn by ballerina.

tuxedo *n* dinner jacket (also **tux**).

TV *abbr* television.

twaddle *n* empty, foolish talk; nonsense.

twain *a, lit, ar* two; two fathoms deep.

twang *n* **1** nasal speech **2** vibrating metallic sound; *v* pluck strings of musical instrument.

tweak *n, v* nip; pinch.

twee *a* excessively dainty or sentimental.

tweed *a, n* (made from) Scottish woolen cloth *pl* **-s** suit of tweed; tweed clothes; *a* **-y 1** like or made of tweed **2** behaving in a hearty way typifying well-off country people.

tweet *v, n* chirp.

tweezers *n pl* small metal instrument used for plucking, etc.

twelfth *det, pron* ordinal number of twelve; next after eleventh **T.-night** evening, 12 days after Christmas, January 6.

twelve *n, a* cardinal number

one above eleven; 12.

twenty *n, pron, det* cardinal number, twice ten; *a* **twentieth** ordinal number 20th.

twerp *n sl* fool; inept clod.

twice *adv* two times.

twig *n* small branch; shoot.

twilight *n* **1** (fading light at) time after sunset before complete darkness **2** *fig* declining years (of life, career); **t. sleep** state of induced semiunconsciousness; *a* **twilit** lit by twilight.

twill *n* diagonally ribbed fabric; *a* **twilled**.

twin *n* one of two persons, animals born at one birth; *a* **1** double **2** closely connected; resembling; *n* **t. bed** bed for one person; single bed; *v* **1** link, match closely **2** establish special offical relationship between (places in different countries); *ns* **t. set** woman's matching sweater and cardigan; *a* **twinned;** *n* **twinning**.

twine *v* twist, coil around; *n* strong string.

twinge *n* sudden, sharp, shooting pain; pang.

twinkle *v* flash, sparkle intermittently; (*of eyes*) show sudden gleam of mirth; *n* **twinkling** intermittent sparkle; brief moment.

twirl *v* turn or twist quickly; spin around.

twist *v* **1** twine; wind around **2**

A B C D E F G H I J K L M N O P Q R S **T** U V W X Y Z

act dishonestly 3 make, become spiral; *idm* **twist someone's arm** use physical or moral pressure to persuade someone; *idm* **twist someone round one's little finger** be able to get from someone anything one wants; *n* 1 act of twisting 2 spiral 3 bend 4 hand of thread 5 unexpected turn of events; *n* **-er** *coll* 1 swindler 2 tornado 3 difficult puzzle; *a* **twisty** winding.

twit *v* **twits, twitting, twitted.** taunt *n coll* fool.

twitch *v* pluck, pull jerkily; *n* spasmodic movement of body; *a* **-y** showing signs of nervousness; *adv* **-ily;** *n* **-iness;** *n* **twitcher** one who twitches.

twitter *v*, *n* (*of birds*) chirp intermittently; *idm* **all of a twitter** *coll* nervously excited.

twixt *prep lit, ar* between.

two *n*, *pron, det* cardinal number next above one (2); pair; *as* **t.-bit** petty; **t.-faced** insincere; **t.-handed** 1 using two hands 2 needing two people; **t.-way** moving, communicating in both directions; *ns* **twosome** 1 couple 2 game for two; **t.-step** (music for) lively ballroom dance; *v* **t.-time** deceive (*n* **t.-timer**).

tycoon *n coll* magnate; powerful business person.

tyke *n* small child.

tympanum *n* ear drum (*also* **typanic membrane**).

type *n* 1 class; group; kind; variety; example 2 *print* block of wood, metal with letter or symbol on surface 3 set of type; **in t.** set up ready for printing; *v* 1 classify 2 print with typewriter; *vs* **t. cast** (repeatedly) give actor/actress roles of similar character, quality; **t.-set** set for printing (*ns* **t.-setter, -setting**); *ns* **t.-face** style of lettering for printing; **typescript** typed draft of book, etc.; **typewriter** machine with keys to make individual letters and symbols; **typist** person able to type; *a* **t.-written**.

typhoid *n med* infectious enteric fever; *n* **typhus** contagious fever.

typhoon *n* violent whirlwind, hurricane.

typical *a* true to type; characteristic; *v* **typify -fying, -fied.** serve as type or model of.

typography *n* art of style of printing; *n* **typo** error in typography or typing; *a* **typographical;** *n* **typographer**.

tyrant *n* 1 despot; harsh unjust ruler 2 one who rules others cruelly, oppressively; *a* **tyrannical** *v* **tyrannize** rule, exert authority harshly; *n* **tyranny** despotism.

tyro *n* novice.

tzar *n* czar.

ubiquitous *a* present, existing everywhere; *n* **ubiquity**.

udder *n* external milk gland of cow, etc.

U-boat *n* German submarine.

UFO *abbr* unidentified flying object.

ufology *n* study of UFOs.

ugh *interj* expressing disgust, horror.

ugly *a* **1** unpleasant to look at; hideous **2** hostile; threatening; *n* **u. duckling** person who at first seems unattractive, unpromising, but turns out better than expected; *n* **ugliness**.

UHF *abbr rad* ultrahigh frequency.

UK *abbr* United Kingdom (Great Britain and N Ireland).

ukase *n* Russian decree; any aribitrary order.

ukulele *n* small, four-stringed musical instrument, like guitar; *coll* **uke**.

ulcer *n* **1** sore on skin or mucous membrane discharging pus, causing tissue death **2** *fig* corrupting influence; *v* **-ate** (*usu* in *pp* as *a*) infect with ulcer; *n* **-ation**; *a* **-ous**.

ULF *abbr* ultralow frequency.

ullage *n* amount of empty space in container partially filled with liquid.

ulna *n* inner bone of forearm; *pl* **ulnae**; *a* **ulnar**.

ulster *n* long, heavy Irish overcoat.

ulterior *a* **1** later in time **2** lying on farther side **3** (*of motive, etc.*) undisclosed.

ultima *n* last syllable of a word; **ultima ratio** last argument.

ultimate *a* furthest; final; last; fundamental; *n* **ultimatum** final demand, terms offered by person or power; *adv* **ultimo** (*abbr* **ult**) in preceding month.

ultra- *prefix* beyond in space; beyond what is normal; excessively.

ultrahigh frequency *a* (of radio waves) over 300 million Hz.

ultramarine *n* bright blue pigment; *a* of this color.

ultrashort *a rad* of waves below 10 meters.

ultrasonic *a* (*of sounds*) beyond limit of human hearing; *n* **ultrasound**.

ultrasound *n* **1** pressure waves with frequency above 20,000 hertz (Hz) **2** diagnostic treatment using this.

ultraviolet *a* of electromagnetic waves between visible violet and X rays.

ululate *v* howl; screech; wail; *n* **-lation**.

umbelliferous *a* relating to carrot family.

umber *n* brown earthy pigment.

umbilicus *n anat* navel; *a* **-ilical** of, near navel; *n* **u. cord 1** structure joining fetus to placenta **2** tube, cable linking spaceship with astronaut outside.

umbra *n* shaded area, sometimes cone-shaped.

umbrage *n* feeling of resentment or injury; *idm* **take umbrage** be offended.

umbrella *n* **1** folding circular shade or cover, for protection against rain or sun **2** agency, system, or group that coordinates work of other groups in an organization.

umiak n Eskimo canoe-type boat.

umlaut n mark (¨) over vowel to change pronunciation.

umpire n person chosen to judge, decide doubtful point, or enforce rules in game; v act as umpire.

umpteen det, pron coll an indefinite large number of.

UN abbr United Nations (Organization), international organization working for world peace.

un- prefix expressing negation before simple words or reversal of action before verbs. Such words are not given when the meaning may be deduced easily.

unable a not having ability, opportunity, or permission.

unaccountable a inexplicable; not responsible.

unaffected a 1 not touched or influenced 2 not pretentious; simple.

unanimous a being of one mind; agreeing; n **unanimity**.

unassuming a modest; unpresuming.

unattached a 1 not joined 2 not belonging to group 3 not married, engaged, or committed to monogamous relationship.

unavailing a ineffectual; useless.

unaware n ignorant; not noticing; adv **-s** without warning; inadvertently.

unbalance v 1 throw off balance 2 affect the mental stability of; a **-anced** 1 unevenly arranged 2 insane.

unbeknownst to adv without its being known by.

unbelief n lack of (esp religious) faith; n **-liever**; as **lieving** 1 lacking faith 2 skeptical; **-lievable** incredible; adv **-ly**.

unbend v 1 straighten 2 behave less formally; a **-ing** not yielding; stubborn.

unbidden adv 1 uninvited 2 voluntarily.

unblushing a unremorseful; shameless.

unbosom v let oneself share one's personal secrets.

unbowed a fml not defeated.

unbridled a uncontrolled; extravagant.

uncalled-for a not necessary, desirable, or deserved.

uncanny a weird; mysterious.

unceremonious a 1 informal 2 discourteous; adv **-ly**.

uncharitable a (of attitude, comment) unkind; harsh.

uncharted a 1 not marked on map 2 fig unexplored.

uncle n 1 brother of father or mother 2 husband of aunt; n **U. Sam** n coll (people or government of) US.

unconditional a absolute; without reservation.

unconscionable a unscrupulous; excessive.

unconscious a not knowing; involuntary; insensible; n the

subconscious; adv **-ly**; n **-ness**.

unconsidered a 1 spoken thoughtlessly 2 unimportant.

uncouple v separate.

uncouth a awkward; unrefined in manner.

uncover v 1 remove cover from 2 find out (truth).

uncrowned a not officially appointed; **u. king of** person widely recognized as the best.

unction n 1 anointing with oil 2 fig fervor esp religious 3 suavity; gush; **Extreme U.** Christian sacrament given to dying; a **unctuous** 1 greasy; oily 2 fig smug; gushing.

undaunted a bold; intrepid; not frightened.

under prep 1 beneath; below 2 ruled, protected by 3 working for 4 subject to; in the process of 5 less than; idm **under age** less than legal age; idm **under the counter** (of trade) illegally (a **u.-the-counter**); adv 1 below 2 less; idm **down under** coll in Australia, New Zealand, etc.

under- prefix lower; inferior; insufficiently; beneath. Such words are not given when the meaning may be deduced easily.

underact v act with less force than is needed.

underbrush n undergrowth.

undercarriage n wheels on which aircraft lands; framework for these.

undercharge *v* charge too little.

underclothes *n* underwear (also **undergarment, undies**).

undercoat *n* primer; coat of paint applied before top coat.

undercover *a* acting secretly, *esp* as spy.

undercut *v comm* charge less than (competitor).

underdeveloped not fully developed; *n* **u.country** country where economic potential (*e.g.*, in industry) has not been fully exploited.

underdog *n* person regarded as weaker or likely to lose.

undergo *v* experience; *pt* **-went**, *pp* **-gone**.

undergraduate *n* student at college, university not yet awarded degree (*esp* bachelor's degree).

underground *a* below surface of earth; secret; *idm* **go underground** *fig* hide; go into hiding; *n* **1** underground railway **2** secret resistance movement.

undergrowth *n* bushes and other low plants, *esp* growing among trees.

underhand *a* **1** (*of baseball, bowling, tennis*) with arm lower than shoulder **2** sly; (*also* **underhanded**).

underlay *n* material laid under carpet.

underlie *v* be at foundation of.

underline *v* **1** mark (word, etc.) with line underneath **2** *fig* emphasize.

underling *n* subordinate.

undermanned *a* in sufficiently staffed.

undermentioned *a, n* (somebody/something) named below.

undermine *v* wear away by erosion, etc.; *fig* weaken, injure by secret means.

underneath *adv* beneath; below.

undernourished *a* without proper nutrition for good health.

underpants *n pl* garment worn underneath trousers (*also* **underwear**).

underpass *n* tunnel or covered route taking one road under another.

underpin *v* support; *n* **underpinning**.

underplay *v* **1** underact **2** give too little importance to.

underpopulated *a* having fewer people than normal.

underprivileged *a* deniel normal rights or amenities due to poverty etc.

underrate *v* give less value to.

underscore *v* underline; emphasize.

undersea *a* below ocean's surface.

undersell *v* **1** sell too cheaply **2** undervalue.

undersigned *n* person(s) whose signature is at the end of document.

understand *v* **1** comprehend **2** assume; infer **3** learn; be informed of; (*pt, pp* **-stood**); *n* **-ing** comprehension; sympathy; *a* **-able**; *adv* **-ably**.

understate *v* **1** say something is less than it is **2** show strong feeling ironically by less strong expression; *n* **-ment**.

understudy *v* learn part (of actor, etc.) in order to perform in his/her absence, if necessary.

undersubscribed *a* not supported by enough participants.

undertake *v* enter into; promise; pledge oneself; *pt* **-took**; *pp* **-taken**; *n* **undertaker 1** one who undertakes **2** one whose business is to arrange funerals; *n* **-taking** an enterprise; guarantee.

undertone *n* **1** low voice **2** *esp pl* concealed meaning.

undertow *n* undercurrent of wave breaking on shore.

under way *adv* in progress.

underwear *n* clothes worn beneath others.

underworld *n* **1** criminals as social group **2** Hades; place of departed spirits.

underwrite *v* **1** insure shipping **2** undertake to buy, take up shares not brought by public; *n* **-r**.

undesirable *a* unwanted.

undies *n coll* underwear.

undo *v* **1** reverse **2** ruin **3** cancel **4** unfasten; *pt* **undid**; *pp* **undone**; *n* **undoing** cause, source of ruin; unfastening; *a* **undone**

A B C D E F G H I J K L M N O P Q R S T **U** V W X Y Z

1 untied 2 ruined 3 not done.

undoubted *a* acknowledged as certain; *adv* **-ly.**

undress *v* remove clothing.

undue *a* excessive; improper.

undulate *v* rise and fall like waves; *n* **-ation.**

unduly *adv* too much.

undying *a* everlasting.

unearth *v* dig up; discover.

unearthly *a* 1 not of this world; supernatural 2 weird; unreasonable.

uneasy *a* (*of person*) anxious; (*of situation*) worrying; *adv* **-ily;** *ns* **unease, uneasiness** apprehension.

unemployed *a* without a job; *n* **unemployment** state of having no job.

unerring *a* reliably accurate; *adv* **-ily.**

UNESCO *abbr* United Nations Educational Scientific and Cultural Organization.

unexceptionable *a* totally acceptable; beyond criticism.

unfailing *a* 1 constant 2 totally reliable; *adv* **-ly.**

unfazed *a* not worried.

unfeeling *a* insensitive; cruel; *adv* **-ly.**

unfettered *a* free.

unfit *a* not healthy, suitable or capable (*n* **-ness**); *as* **unfitted** unsuited; **unfitting** inappropriate.

unflappable *a* always able to keep calm in a crisis.

unfold *v* 1 open out from folded state 2 be revealed.

unfortunate *a* 1 unlucky 2 regrettable 3 awkward; *adv* **-ly.**

unfounded *a* without justification.

unfrock *v* dismiss from holy orders (*also* **defrock**).

unfurl *v* unfold, as a flag.

ungainly *a* awkward; clumsy.

ungrounded *a* false; unjustified.

ungual *a* relating to hoof or nail.

ungulate *n, a* (animal) that has hoofs.

unhand *v lit* release from hold with hand.

unheard-of *a* very unusual; unprecedented.

unholy *a* 1 wicked 2 *coll* terrible; dreadful; *n* **u. alliance** group of those who are normally opposed to each other for a common evil purpose.

uni- *prefix* one; single.

unicameral *a* with only one legislative chamber.

UNICEF *abbr* United Nations (formerly International) Children's (formerly Emergency) Fund.

unicellular *a* one-celled.

unicorn *n* mythic horse like animal with one horn in middle of forehead.

unicycle *n* pedalled cycle with one wheel.

unifoliate *a* on

uniform *a* not changing; similar in every way; *n* distinctive dress worn by members of organized body;

a **-ed** wearing uniform; *adv* **-ly** evenly; *n* **-ity** sameness.

unify *v* **unifying, unified.** cause to be one, combine; *n* **unification.**

unilateral *a* one-sided; *adv* **-ly;** *n* **-ism;** *n, a* **-ist.**

unimpeachable *a* that cannot be doubted.

union *n* act of uniting or being united; federation; trade union; marriage; *a* of trade union; *ns* **u. card** certification of labor-union membership; **U. Jack** national flag of UK; *v* **-ize** organize into, (cause to) become member of trade union (*n* **-ization**); *n* **ism;** *a, n* **-ist.**

unique *a* having no like or equal; unparalleled; *adv* **-ly;** *n* **-ness.**

unisex *a* suited to both men and women.

unison *n* harmony; concord; *mus* identity of pitch.

unit *n* 1 single complete thing 2 group of people or things forming complete whole 3 least whole number 4 military group (of soldiers, etc.).

unite *v* to join into one; associate; combine; cause to adhere; *n* **unity** state of being unit; agreement of aims, interests, etc.; harmony, amity; *a* **united** joined; in alliance (*ns* **U. Kingdom** *see* **UK**; **U. Nations** *see* **UN**; **U. States** *see* **US**).

univariate *a* relying on only one variable.

universe *n* whole system of created things viewed as whole; the cosmos; *a* **universal** relating to all things or all people; *adv* **-ly**; *n* **-ity**.

universal precautions *n* medical code of practice to prevent transmission of infectious viruses.

Universal Product Code *n* numbers and bar code scanned from product in store.

university *n* institution for higher education, empowered to confer degrees; governing body of such institution.

unkempt *a* of untidy appearance.

unknown *a* not known; *n* **u. quantity 1** *math* unknown number represented by symbols x, y, etc. **2** *fig* somebody/something whose true qualities are yet to be discovered.

Unknown Soldier *n* unnamed combat fatality buried in Arlington National Cemetery; to whom we pay homage as representation of all us soldier.

unleash *v* release from control.

unleaded *a* (of gasoline) free of pollution-causing lead.

unless *conj* if not; except that.

unlettered *a fml* **1** illiterate **2** not well educated.

unloose *v* untie; set loose (*also* unloosen).

unnerve *v* take away (somebody's) confidence; frighten; *a* **unnerving**; *adv* **-ly**.

unnumbered *a* **1** not marked with a number **2** countless.

unplaced *a* **1** not one of the first three in race or contest **2** not accepted **3** having no accommodation.

unprincipled *a* without ethics or principles.

unprintable *a* too offensive to print; obscene.

unqualified *a* **1** with no qualifications **2** absolute.

unravel *v* **1** disentangle **2** solve.

unremitting *a* persistent; *adv* **-ly**.

unrequited *a* (*esp* of love) not reciprocated.

unrest *n* turmoil; state of dissatisfaction; expression of this.

unruly *a* disorderly; ungovernable.

unsavory *a* unappetizing.

unscathed *a* unhurt.

unsightly *a* ugly; *n* **-iness**.

unspeakable *a* too bad to mention; outrageous; *adv* **-ably**.

unstinting *a* given freely; *adv* **-ly**.

unstuck *a* not held by glue; *idm* **come unstuck 1** fall apart **2** *fig coll* fail.

unstudied *a* natural.

until *prep* as far as; up to; *conj* up to time when.

untimely *a* before time; at an unsuitable time; *n* **-iness**.

unto *prep lit, ar* to.

untold *a* **1** not told **2** very great; excessive.

untouchable *a* **1** that cannot be touched, reached, equaled **2** of lowest Hindu caste (*n* such a person).

untoward *a* inconvenient; unlucky; awkward.

untried *a* not proven, untested.

unutterable *a* too great to be put in words; inexpressible; *adv* **-ably**.

unvarnished *a* plain; without embellishment.

unversed in *a* having no skill or experience of.

unwarranted *a* not justified.

unwell *a* ill; not well.

unwieldy *a* too large to be carried or moved easily; too complicated to be managed or controlled easily.

unwind *v* **1** unroll **2** relax.

unwitting *a* unintentional; *adv* **-ly**.

unwritten law *n* custom rather than formal written agreement.

up *adv, prep* **1** to, at higher or better position **2** to, in the north **3** out of bed **4** in phrasal verb denoting finality, completion (**finish up, eat up**) **5** on, at the top (of) **6** at the far end (of); *prep* **up to** as far as; until; *idm* **up against** facing (opposition, difficulty); *idm* **up and about** out of bed and moving; *idm* **up for 1** on trial for **2** being considered for; *idm* **up front** (of money) in advance before delivery; *idm* **be up to 1** be busy doing or planning **2** be capable of **3** be the responsibility of; *idm* **on the up-and-up** making good progress; *as* **up-and-coming** new and promising; **up-market** *comm* of better quality; more expensive; **upscale** high end, up-market.

upbeat *n mus* unaccented beat; *a coll* cheerful.

upbraid *v* censure; reproach; scold.

upbringing *n* way in which a child is educated and disciplined.

upcoming *a* imminent.

update *v* revise; bring up to date; *n* revision.

upend *v* stand, turn upside down.

up-front *a* frank and direct.

upgrade *v* raise status of; put higher price on.

upheaval *n* violent disturbance.

upheld *pt, pp of* **uphold**.

uphill *a* ascending; *fig* difficult.

uphold *v* **upholding, upheld.** support; maintain.

upholster *v* stuff and cover chairs, etc.; *ns* **-sterer** one who repairs, covers chairs, etc. or sells such goods; **-stery** trade of upholsterer; goods supplied by same.

upkeep *n* (cost of) maintenance.

upland *n* (often *pl*) higher ground of region.

uplift *v* lift up, raise *esp* spiritually or culturally.

upon *prep* on.

upper *a* higher; nearer the top; *n* top part of shoe; *n, a* **u.case** capital (letters); *ns* **u. class** privileged class; aristocracy; **u. hand** control; *adv* **u.most** in highest position; on top.

uppercut *n* upward blow to chin.

uppity *a* arrogant, stuck-up .

upright *a* **1** erect **2** *fig* honest; just; *n* upright post, beam, support, etc.

uprising *n* rebellion or revolt.

uproar *n* noisy tumult; clamor; *a* **-ious** noisy, rowdy; *adv* **-ly**; *n* **-ness**.

ups and downs *n* fluctuations in luck.

upset *v* **1** knock, turn over **2** distress, annoy; *n* state of disorder; cause of distress; *coll* quarrel.

upshot *n* result, consequence.

upstairs *a, adv* on, to higher floor; *n* upper floor.

upstanding *a* **1** strong and vigorous **2** honest; marked by integrity; *idm* **be upstanding.**

upstart *n* one who has risen suddenly to high position or wealth, etc.

upsurge *n* sudden increase.

uptake *n* rate of acceptance, absorption; *idm* **quick/slow on the uptake** quick/slow to understand.

uptight *a* anxious and inhibited.

up-to-date *a* **1** modern **2** having all the latest news,

developments.

uptown *a, adv* in, of, or to upper part of town, city, *esp* residential area.

upturn *n* improvement in business or fortune; *a* **-ed** turned upside-down.

upward *a* going higher; *adv* **upward** to higher position; *prep* **upward of** more than; *a* **upwardly mobile** able to, seeking to improve one's economic and social status.

uranium *n* white metallic radioactive element.

Uranus *n* planet seventh in distance from the Sun.

urban *a* pertaining to city or town; *v* **-ize** change from rural to urban condition; *n* **-ization**.

urbane *a* courteous; affable; refined; *n* **urbanity**.

urchin *n* **1** mischievous, roguish boy **2** round, thorny sea creature.

urge *v* **1** drive, push forward **2** exhort insistently; *a* **urgent** requiring immediate attention; highly important; *n* **-ency**.

urial *n* wild sheep with curved horns and tufted chest.

urinary *n* **1** of urine **2** of the organs that secrete urine.

urine *n* fluid secreted by kidneys; *a* **uric** of or from urine; *v* **urinate** pass urine; *n* **urinal** place for urinating, *usu* for men.

urn *n* **1** large, lidded, metal vessel for serving tea or coffee **2** rounded covered

A B C D E F G H I J K L M N O P Q R S T **U** V W X Y Z

vase for ashes of dead.

urology n study of urinary/urogenital system.

us pron objective case of **we**.

US, USA abbr United States of America.

usage n 1 way of using 2 way of speaking 3 custom.

use n 1 act of employing anything 2 advantage; purpose served; utility 3 habit; custom; usage; v 1 employ 2 consume 3 behave toward 4 avail oneself of; idm **make use of** take advantage of; use; idm **of use** useful; idm **put to good use** use profitably; phr v **use up** exhaust supply of; as **usable, useable** fit for use; **used** not new; **used to** familiar with; accustomed to; **useful** of practical use; adv **-ly**; n **-ness; useless**; adv **-ly**; n **-ness**; n **user**; a **u.-friendly** technology designed for easy use by any user).

usher n 1 official in charge of entrance to court, etc. 2 person showing people to seats and maintaining orderly behavior in theater, etc. (fem **-ette** usu in cinema); v escort (somebody) in specified direction; idm **usher in** fig mark beginning of.

USSR abbr (formerly) Union of Soviet Socialist Republics.

usual a commonplace; habitual; adv **usually** generally; as a rule.

usufruct n right to use of and profits from another's property without damage to it or waste.

usurp v take possession of without right or by force; n **usurper**.

usury n lending of money at excessive interest; n **usurer** extortionate money-lender.

utensil n vessel, container for domestic use; any tool or implement for particular purpose.

uterus n womb.

utilitarian a 1 serving material or practical ends 2 based on belief in action that benefits the largest possible number of people (n **-ism**).

utility n 1 usefulness 2 useful thing; pl **utilities** public services, as supplying of water, gas, electricity, etc.; v **utilize** put to use, make profitable use of (n **-ization**).

utmost a most extreme; to greatest, highest degree; n most possible.

Utopia n imaginary state with ideally perfect social and political system; a **utopian** ideally perfect but impracticable.

utter[1] a complete; total; absolute; adv **-ly**.

utter[2] v produce audibly with voice; say; express by word of mouth, or in writing; n **utterance** act of speaking; spoken words.

uttermost a farthest out; n **utmost**.

U-turn n 1 smooth, unbroken turn by vehicle to go in opposite direction 2 politics complete reversal of policy.

uvula a small fleshy lobe of the soft palate.

uxorious a excessively devoted to, submissive to, one's wife.

a
b
c
d
e
f
g
h
i
j
k
l
m
n
o
p
q
r
s
t
u
v
w
x
y
z

vacant *a* empty; unoccupied; *fig* empty-headed; *n* **vacancy** vacant apartment, job; gap.

vacate *v* leave empty; resign; quit; *n* **-ation** act of vacating; fixed holiday period.

vaccinate *v* inoculate with vaccine; *ns* **-ation; vaccine** preparation of virus (*esp* of cowpox) used as inoculation against disease; preparation given to increase immunity against disease.

vacillate *v* waver in mind; hesitate, be undecided; *n* **-lation** indecision, hesitation.

vacuous *a* stupid; empty; expressionless; *adv* **-ly;** *n* **vacuity** lack of ideas, interest, etc.

vacuum *n* **1** space empty or devoid of all matter or content **2** space from which air has been partially exhausted; *a* **v.-packed** enclosed in plastic with air removed; *ns* **v.cleaner** apparatus for removing dirt, etc. by suction; **v. flask Thermos** [TM] vessel with two walls separated by vacuum, used to keep liquids at constant temperature; **v. pump** pump for extracting air or gas.

vagabond *a* wandering; having no fixed abode; *n* tramp, vagrant; *coll* rascal.

vagary *n* caprice; whim; freak.

vagina *n* female genital canal; *a* **vaginal**.

vagrant *a* **1** wandering; nomadic **2** *fig* roving; wayward; *n* tramp; *n* **vagrancy**.

vague *a* **1** indefinite; blurred **2** absentminded **3** not clearly expressed.

vain *a* **1** fruitless; futile **2** conceited; self-satisfied.

vainglorious *a* inordinately proud or boastful; *adv* **-ly;** *n* **-ness**.

valance *n* short curtain above window or around bed, table, shelft, etc.

vale *n* valley.

valediction *n* farewell; *a* **valedictory**; *n* farewell oration.

valence, valency *n chem* combining power of atom or substance.

valentine *n* sweetheart chosen on Valentine's day, February 14; card or gift sent on that day.

valet *n Fr* employee who does personal services for customers; manservant who looks after his master's clothes, etc.; *v* act as valet.

valetudinarian *n*, *a* (person) in poor health; (one) unduly engrossed by state of health.

valiant *a* brave; courageous; heroic; *adv* **-ly**.

valid *a* having legal force; well founded; *n* **-ity** soundness; legal force; *v* **-ate** make valid; *n* **-ation**.

valise *n Fr* small suitcase.

Valium [TM] drug diazepam used as tranquilizer.

Valkyrie *n myth* one of the maidens of Odin, who led the slain to Valhalla.

valley *n* tract of land lying between hills; large river basin.

valor *n* bravery; *a* **-ous**; *adv* **-ously**.

value *n* **1** worth **2** purchasing power **3** precise meaning, force **4** relative proportion of light and dark in picture **5**

duration of note in music; *pl* **-s** principles (**sense of v**. appreciation of what is good or bad); *ns* **v. added tax** tax on increased value at each stage of manufacture of product (*also* **VAT**); **v. judgment** estimate of worth based on personal impression rather than objective facts; *v* estimate worth of; appraise; esteem, rate highly; *a* **valuable** costly; of great worth; very useful; *n usu pl* valuable objects, goods, etc.; *n* **valuation** estimated worth; *a* **valueless**; *n* **valuer**.

valve *n* device that regulates flow of air, liquid, gas, etc. through opening, pipe, etc.; *a* **valvular** of, like, affecting valves.

vamoose *v sl* leave hurriedly.

vamp[1] *n* front upper part of footwear; improvised musical accompaniment; *v mus* improvise.

vamp[2] *n* charming, enticing woman.

vampire *n myth* corpse that revives itself by drinking human blood; *fig* ruthless blackmailer or money-lender; *ns* **vampire bat** American bloodsucking bat.

van *n usu* enclosed small truck, elongated car used for transportation of children, goods, etc.

vanadium *n* rare metallic element used in alloys.

vandal *n* person who willfully damages or destroys objects in art or nature, or items of public or private property; *v* **-ize** damage in this way; *n* **-ism**.

Vandyke *n* short pointy beard.

vane *n* movable device attached to tall structure to indicate wind direction; blade of propellor; sight of quadrant or surveying instrument; web of feather.

vanguard *n* **1** leading part of army or fleet **2** leaders of political, social movement, or fashion.

vanilla *n* kind of orchid; its beans used for flavoring.

vanish *v* disappear; cease to exist; become invisible; *n* **vanishing point** point in perspective drawing where receding parallel lines appear to meet.

vanity *n* conceit; futility; worthlessness.

vanity press *n* publisher who publishes books at the authors' expense.

vanquish *v* conquer; subdue; be victorious; *n* **vanquisher**.

vantage *n* advantage (tennis) first point after deuce; superiority in sport; *v* **v. point** favorable position.

vapid *a* insipid; lifeless; *n* **vapidity**.

vapor *n* substance in gaseous state; steam, mist; *fig* freak of fancy; *v* **vaporize** convert into or pass off in vapor; *a* **vaporous**; *n* **vaporizer** humidifier, atomizer.

variable *a* changing; liable to change; not constant; *n* **1** thing that can be changed, substituted **2** *math* (symbol for) unspecified value; *adv* **-ably**; *n* **-ability**.

variance *n* **at variance (with)** in conflict (with).

variant *a, n* different, alternative (version or form).

variation *n* **1** degree of varying **2** variant **3** one of set of stylistic elaborations on musical, literary theme.

varicose *a* (of veins) abnormally swollen.

varied *a* **1** of different kinds **2** showing change of type.

variegate *v* mark with different colors; *a* **-gated** multicolored; streaked; *n* **-gation**.

variety *n* **1** diversity; varied assortment **2** kind; type; group; *a* **various 1** of several different kinds **2** some **3** *coll* many.

variform *a* found in various forms.

variola *n* smallpox.

varmint *n* **1** undesirable, often venomous, animal **2** undesirable person.

varnish *n* gum or resin dissolved in alcohol, applied to surface to make it shiny; *v* apply varnish to; *phr v* **varnish over** cover up (something inferior, dishonest, etc.).

vary *v* **varying, varied.** change; alter; modify; become different.

vascular *a* containing,

a
b
c
d
e
f
g
h
i
j
k
l
m
n
o
p
q
r
s
t
u
v
w
x
y
z

A
B
C
D
E
F
G
H
I
J
K
L
M
N
O
P
Q
R
S
T
U
V
W
X
Y
Z

concerning vessels conveying fluid in plants and animals, *esp* blood in humans.

vase *n* ornamental container for flowers; similar ornament as architectural feature.

vasectomy *n* surgical division, resection of male vas deferans to induce sterility.

Vaseline [TM] *n* soft petroleum jelly.

vassal *n* feudal tenant; dependant.

vast *a* very extensive; huge; *coll* great; *n* **-ness**; *adv* **-ly** *coll* extremely.

vat *n* large cask or tub.

VAT *abbr* value added tax.

Vatican *n* 1 palace of pope in Italy 2 *fig* papacy; Papal authority, etc.

vaudeville *n* theatrical entertainment consisting of separate acts.

vault¹ *n* 1 arched roof; arched cellar 2 strongroom.

vault² *v* leap, spring over, *esp* with support of hands or pole; *n* such leap or jump.

vaunt *v* boast, brag about.

VCR *abbr* videocassette recorder.

VD *abbr* venereal disease.

VDU *abbr* visual display unit (computer screen).

veal *n* flesh of calf, used for food.

vector *n* 1 animal transmitting parasites 2 *math* magnitude having direction 3 course of aircraft.

veep *n abbr* vice president.

veer *v* shift; change in direction; position; *fig* change (opinion, etc.).

vegan *n* person with strict vegerarian diet; one who neither uses or consumes animal products.

vegeburger, veggie-burger *n* burger of vegetables with no meat.

vegetable *a* pertaining to, concerning, composed of plants or plant life; *n* plant, *esp* edible one; *n* **vegetarian** one who does not eat meat.

vegetate *v* live dull monotonous life; *n* **-ation** plant growth and development; plants collectively.

veg out *v abbr* to vegetate, spend time idly, relax.

vehement *a* passionate; impetuous; *adv* **-ly**; *n* **vehemence**.

vehicle *n* means of conveyance *usu* on wheels; means, medium of expression, etc.; *a* **vehicular**.

veil *n* covering for face or head; *fig* that which conceals; *v* cover with veil; conceal; *a* **-ed 1** covered by veil 2 *fig* with implied meaning.

vein *n* 1 blood vessel conveying blood to heart 2 veinlike marking 3 crack 4 layer or fissure containing metallic ore 5 *fig* mood; disposition; *a* **venous** of veins.

Velcro [TM] *n* fastener of fabric strips that cling when pressed together.

vellum *n* parchment of calfskin used for bookbinding or manuscripts.

velocity *n* speed, rapidity of motion; rate of motion.

velour, velours *n Fr* soft velvety, napped material.

velvet *n* 1 fabric with soft thick pile or nap on one side 2 *fig* soft downy surface; *a* **velvety** like velvet; *n* **velveteen** imitation velvet made of cotton.

venal *a* corruptible; mercenary; influenced by hope of reward; *n* **-ity**.

vend *v* sell; *ns* **vendor; vending machine** automatic selling machine.

vendetta *n* blood feud.

veneer *v* 1 thin layer of fine wood laid over inferior kind 2 *fig* superficial polish concealing defects; *v* cover with veneer.

venerable *a* worthy of deep respect; *v* **venerate** revere; respect; worship; *n* **-ation**.

venereal *a* pertaining, due, to sexual intercourse; *n* **v. disease** (*also* **VD**).

venetian blind *n* one made of horizontal movable slats.

vengeance *n* revenge; infliction of punishment for wrong done; *idm* **with a vengeance** *coll* much more than is normal or desirable; *a* **vengeful** filled with, caused by desire for revenge; *adv* **-ly**; *n* **-ness**.

venial *a* pardonable; trivial.

venison n deer's flesh, as food.

venom n 1 poison secreted by snake, etc. 2 *fig* spite; bitter words; a **-ous** poisonous; spiteful.

venous a 1 of veins 2 (*of blood*) in veins.

vent n slit, hole, outlet; v pour forth; utter; *idm* **give vent to** express openly; *idm* **vent one's anger/feelings**, etc. on find target for one's anger/feelings, etc.

ventilate v 1 supply with fresh air 2 oxygenate, aerate 3 *fig* discuss freely; ns **-ator; -ation.**

ventricle n cavity in organ of body, *esp* main pumping chamber of heart; a **-tricular.**

ventriloquist n one who can speak and throw his or her voice without apparent movement of lips; a **-loquial;** n **-loquism.**

venture n risky course of action; financial speculation; v expose to risk or danger; dare to go, etc.; presume to put forward; n **v. capital** money provided for investment in new business; a **-some;** n **-ness.**

venue n *Fr leg* 1 place fixed for trial 2 *fig* meetingplace.

Venus n 1 Roman goddess of beauty and love 2 planet second nearest to Sun 3 *fig* beautiful woman.

veracious a truthful; true; n **veracity.**

veranda n open portico outside house.

verb n part of speech expression action, existence in present, past, or future; a **-al** pertaining to words; literal; spoken, not written; ns **v. diarrhea** *coll* inability to stop talking; **v. noun** noun derived from verb + -ing; v **-ize** express in words (n **-ization**); advs **-ly** by word of mouth.

verbatim a, adv (recorded, written) in exactly the same words.

verbena n genus of fragrant herbaceous plants.

verbiage n *Fr* use of too many words.

verbose a using too many words; adv **-osely;** n **-osity.**

verdant a green, as of fresh young grass, foliage, etc.; *fig* youthful; n **verdure** green vegetation.

verdict n finding; decision of jury; opinion, judgement.

verdigris n greenish blue deposit formed on copper or brass.

verge n edge; brink; *idm* **on the verge of** very close to; *phr* v **verge on** approach; border on.

verify v **verifying, verified.** prove; confirm; authenticate; a **verifiable;** n **verification.**

verily adv truly; in truth.

verisimilitude n appearance of truth; likelihood.

veritable a real; genuine; true; actual; adv **-ly.**

verify n truth.

vermicelli n *It* thin, stringlike kind of macaroni, thinner than spaghetti.

vermiform a worm-shaped; n **vermicide** preparation for killing worms.

vermilion a, n (of) brilliant red color.

vermin n destructive, harmful animals (*usu* small) collectively; a **-ous** infested with vermin.

vermouth n *Fr* fortified white wine flavored with wormwood, etc.

vernacular a of native, commonly spoken language; n 1 native dialect 2 strong language.

vernal a of spring.

verruca n infectious wart of the foot.

versatile a adaptable; changeable; fickle; manysided; n **versatility.**

verse n 1 subdivision of poem, short division of chapter in the Bible 2 poetry; a **versed (in)** skilled (in); v **versify** tell in verse; compose verses; n **versification.**

version n 1 translation 2 personal account, statement.

verso n *Lat* left hand or reverse of page of book; reverse of coin, medal.

versus prep (abbr **v.**) *Lat* against; in opposition.

vertebra n one of joints of spine; a **-brate** having backbone; n vertebrate animal; pl **-brae;** as **-bral** of vertebrae.

A B C D E F G H I J K L M N O P Q R S T U **V** W X Y Z

vertex n summit; zenith; pl **vertices**; a **vertical**; overhead; perpendicular; adv **-ly**.

vertigo n giddiness; dizziness; a **vertiginous**.

verve n vigor; liveliness of spirit.

very a actual; real; adv exceedingly; absolutely.

vespers n pl evensong; evening worship service.

vespertilian a relating to bats.

vessel n 1 any hollow article or receptacle; ship 2 duct for blood, fluid, sap, etc. of animal or plant body.

vest n sleeveless garment usu worn under jacket; v endow; confer right, power, etc.; phr v **vest in/with somebody** confer (legal right or power) on somebody; idm **have a vested interest (in)** be likely to benefit from; n **vestment** ceremonial garment worn by clergy.

vestal a of Roman goddess Vesta; n **v. virgin** female servant of temple dedicated to Vesta.

vestibule n antechamber; lobby.

vestige n visible trace or mark; rudimentary survival (of organ, etc.); a **vestigial**.

vest-pocket a conveniently small.

vestry n room in church where vestments and Communion vessels are kept and parish meetings are held.

vet n coll abbr of **veteran;**

veterinary (surgeon); v **vetting, vetted.** coll examine critically.

vetch n plant used for forage and soil improvement.

veteran n one with long experience esp in armed services.

veterinary a of, concerned with diseases of animals; n **v.surgeon, veterinarian** one trained to treat sick animals.

veto n **-oes.** Lat constitutional, Presidential right to reject an enactment, or act of administration; absolute prohibition; v **vetoing, vetoed.** forbid; exercise veto against.

vex v irritate; cause worry to; n **-ation** mental distress; worry; a **vexatious; vexed** angry; annoyed (n **vexing question** difficult problem leading to much argument).

VHF abbr rad very high frequency.

via adv by way of; by means of.

viable a capable of maintaining separate existence; practicable; n **viability**.

viaduct n long, high bridge carrying railway, road, etc. over valley.

vial n small glass bottle.

via media n Lat the middle way, road.

viand n article of food; n **viands** dishes of food.

vibes n pl coll 1 vibraphone 2 vibrations; mental effect (on somebody created by

somebody else).

vibrant a 1 throbbing; resonant 2 (of color) bright and exciting 3 (of people) full of vigor; n **vibrancy**.

vibraphone n instrument like xylophone, but with metal bars and electric resonators.

vibrate v move rapidly back and foth; quiver; oscillate; n **-ation**.

vibrato n mus resonance given by singing or playing with slight undulation of pitch.

vibrator n vibrating electrical device esp used in massage.

vicar n clergyman in charge of parish; n **vicarage** house of vicar.

vicarious a acting as substitute; done, felt on behalf of another; adv **-ly**.

vice[1] n defect; fault; wickedness; immoral conduct; depravity.

vice[2] see **vise**.

vice- prefix forms compounds with meaning of second to; in place of. Such compounds are not given where the meaning may be deduced from the simple word.

vice president n officer just under president in rank.

viceroy n one who rules as representative of sovereign; fem **vicereine** wife of viceroy; a **viceregal**; n **viceroyalty**.

vice squad n branch of police force in charge of law enforcement of prostitution, gambling, criminal laws.

vice versa adv Lat conversely.

vicinity n nearness; neighborhood.

vicious a 1 malicious 2 depraved 3 harmful; dangerous; n v. **cycle** cycle of bad events each causing the next to go on recurring; v. **spiral** continuous alternate rise (e.g., in prices and wages, each stimulating the other).

vicissitudes n pl Fr ups and downs of life.

victim n 1 human or animal offered as sacrifice 2 one who suffers through no personal fault; v **victimize** make to suffer, penalize esp unjustly; n **victimization**.

victor n conqueror; winner; n **victory** conquest; act of winning; a **victorious** triumphant; winning.

Victorian a 1 of the time of Queen Victoria (1837-1901) (n person of this time) 2 (of moral attitude) based on principles of self-control, respectability, and thrift.

victual (n usual pl) food; v supply, take in stores, food.

vicuña n S American animal related to the llama, having a fine, soft wool.

video a (for recording, reproducing) televised pictures; n **-os.** 1 videotape recording 2 videocassette 3 machine for recording and replaying this; ns v. **cassette recorder** machine for videoing TV broadcasts (also **video (recorder)**) abbr VCR); v. **clip** short video extract from film, etc.; **videodisk** disk for video recording; **videotape** magnetic tape for recording moving pictures and sound (v record in this way).

vie v **vying, vied.** strive with; rival; content with.

Vienna sausage n small hot dog or frankfurter.

view n 1 act of seeing; sight 2 scene 3 picture, photograph of scenery, etc. 4 opinion; v look at; consider; hold specified opinion; idm **in view of** because of; considering; idm **on view** being exhibited; idm **take a dim/poor view of** regard with strong disapproval; idm **with a view to** with the hope, intention of; ns v.**-finder** part of camera showing area to be photographed; **viewpoint** point of view; opinion; **viewer** 1 one who watches 2 device for looking at photographic slides.

vigil n act of keeping watch (esp on sickbed) or of praying all night; eve of holyday; a **-ant** watchful; alert; adv **-ly;** ns **-ance** watchfulness; **vigilante** member of self-appointed group seeking to prevent crime by unofficial means.

vignette n Fr small delicate illustration in book; fig short, evocative wordsketch.

vigor n strength, potency; vitality; a **-ous** strong; active; forceful; adv **-ly.**

Viking n medieval Scandinavian pirate.

vile a depraved; shameful; atrocious; adv **-ly;** n **-ness;** v **vilify** speak ill of; slander; n **vilification**.

villa n country estate; rural residence of wealthy; country house esp in Italy or south of France.

village n small rural community with cottages, shops, etc.; n **villager.**

villain n scoundrel; a **-ous** wicked; vile; adv **-ly;** n **villainy.**

villein n feudal peasant.

vim n coll energy; vigor.

vinaigrette n Fr 1 salad dressing of oil, vinegar, etc. 2 bottle for smelling-salts.

vindicate v establish truth or merit of; prove innocence of; ns **vindication; vindicator.**

vindictive a revengeful; punitive; adv **-ly** n **-ness.**

vine n climbing plant with tendrils, esp one bearing grapes; ns **-yard** grapevine plantation; **vinery** hot-house for growing grapes.

vinous a of, like wine.

vintage n 1 gathering of grapes for wine-making 2 yield of wine grapes in given year 3 fig date, as criterion of quality; n **vintner** wine merchant.

vinegar n acid liquid from fermented fruit juice, wine, beer, etc.; a **-y** very sour, acid; fig bitter, spiteful.

a
b
c
d
e
f
g
h
i
j
k
l
m
n
o
p
q
r
s
t
u
v
w
x
y
z

A
B
C
D
E
F
G
H
I
J
K
L
M
N
O
P
Q
R
S
T
U
V
W
X
Y
Z

vinyl n any of various tough flexible plastics.

viol n medieval stringed and fretted instrument.

viola¹ n genus of plants including pansy, violet etc.

viola² n stringed instrument slightly larger and lower pitched alto than violin.

violate v desecrate; rape; infringe; ns **-ation** act of, thing that violates; **-ator**.

violent a forcible; boisterous; passionate; using, showing great physical strength; adv **-ly**; n **violence**.

violet n 1 plant of viola species 2 bluish purple color; a of this color.

violin n four-stringed soprano musical instrument; n **-ist** player of violin.

violoncello n cello tenor range, four stringed musical instrument; n **violoncellist.**

VIP abbr very important person.

viper n venomous snake, adder.

viral a of or caused by virus.

virgin n one who has never had sexual intercourse; a 1 being a virgin; chaste 2 (of land) never cultivated; a **virginal** of, like virgin; pure; fresh; unsullied; (n pl **-s** kind of spinet); n **virginity** state of being a virgin.

Virginia creeper n climbing plant with leaves that turn bright red in autumn.

Virginia reel n early American line dance.

viridescence n greenness; verdure; freshness; youthful vitality; a **viridescent**.

virile a manly; potent; n **virility** masculinity; male sexual potency.

virology n study of viruses and diseases caused by them; a **-ological**; n **-ologist**.

virtual a in effect but not in name; adv **-ly** to all intent, and purposes; n **virtual reality** artificial environment created by computer, perceieved as real by user.

virtual reality n environment simulated by computer software in which a user can interact as if it were the real world.

virtue n 1 integrity 2 chastity 3 moral excellence; merit; idm **by virtue of** thanks to; as a result of; a **virtuous** morally good; chaste; adv **-ly**; n **-ness**.

virtuoso n **-sos** or **-si.** one with high degree of technical skill in one of fine arts, esp music; n **-osity**.

virulent a 1 (of disease or poison) powerful and deadly 2 fml bitterly hostile; adv **-ly**; n **virulence**.

virus n **-ses.** one of minute parasitic organisms causing infectious diseases (e.g., common cold, flu, etc.); such a disease.

visa n endorsement on passport; v endorse passport with visa.

vis-à-vis adv, prep Fr opposite,

facing.

viscid a glutinous; sticky; a **viscous** sticky; semifluid; n **viscosity**.

viscose n form of cellulose used in making artificial silk; viscose rayon.

viscount n rank of nobility immediately below earl; fem **-ess**.

viscous a sticky; semifluid but not runny; n **viscosity**.

vise n device with two jaws for holding an object firmly.

visible a perceptible; apparent to the eye; n **-bility 1** state, quality of being visible **2** degree of atmospheric clarity esp in navigation.

vision n 1 sight 2 intuition 3 something seen 4 apparition or phantom; a **-ary** impracticable; unreal; (n impractical idealist).

visit v go to see; call upon socially; inspect; **visit with** coll talk with; n temporary stay; social or professional call; ns **visitor; visitation 1** official, formal visit **2** calamity.

visor n movable front part of helmet or hat.

vista n Sp, It 1 distant view, esp if seen from promontory, through avenue of trees, etc. **2** mental prospect of past events, etc.

visual a of sight; n **v. aid** picture, film, video used as teaching aid; **v. display unit** screen used with computer (abbr **VDU**); adv **-ly**; v **-ize**

form a mental picture of; *n* **-ization**.

vital *a* 1 essential to life 2 lively, animated 3 necessary to some object or purpose; *n* **v. statistics** 1 statistics regarding population changes; **v. signs** signs of life; pulse, respiration, temperature, blood pressure; *n* **vitality** capacity to live; vigor; *v* **-ize** make alive; give animation to.

vitamin *n* organic substances present in food, essential for preventing deficiency diseases.

vitiate *v* destroy force of; taint; *leg* invalidate; *n* **vitiation**.

viticulture *n Lat* cultivation of grapevines.

vitreous *a* pertaining to glass; glassy; transparent; *v* **vitrify** convert, become converted, into glass; *n* **vitrifaction;** *a* **vitriform** glasslike.

vitriol *n* sulfuric acid; *fig* caustic, biting sarcasm; *a* **-lic**.

vituperate *v* abuse loudly; scold violently; *n* **-ation;** *a* **-ative**.

vivacity *n* liveliness; gaiety; sprightliness; *a* **vivacious**.

viva voce *adv Lat* by word of mouth; orally.

vivid *a* 1 (*of color*) brilliant; intense 2 animated; graphic; *adv* **-ly;** *n* **-ness**.

viviparous *a* bringing forth young alive and capable of independent life.

vivisection *n* operating or experimenting on living animals.

vixen *n* female fox; *fig* spiteful woman.

V-neck *n* neckline of dress, sweater, etc. shaped like V; *a* **-ed**.

vocabulary *n* 1 stock of words used by person 2 alphabetical list of words and their meanings.

vocal *a* of voice; uttered by voice; *adv* **-ly;** *v* **-ize;** *n* **-ization;** *n* **-ist** singer; **vocal cords** *n* larynx membranes producing sound by vibration.

vocation *n* 1 profession; occupation 2 divine call to spiritual or religious life; *a* **-al** (*adv* **-ly**).

vociferate *v* shout; bawl, utter loud cries; *n* **-ation;** *a* **vociferous** noisy.

vodka *n* spirit distilled from rye, wheat mash.

vogue *n Fr* prevailing fashion, custom, etc.; popularity.

voice *n* 1 sound produced by organs of speech 2 quality of such sound 3 wish, desire expressed as vote; *v* give utterance to, express; *n* **v.-over** *TV, film* speech of unseen person; *a* **-less** 1 mute 2 without speaking aloud 3 *ling* without vibrating vocal cords (*adv* **-ly;** *n* **-ness**); *n* **voice mail** telephonic, electronic answering system.

void *a* empty; lacking; legally invalid; *n* empty space;

vacuum; *v* excrete from body; nullify.

voile *n Fr* thin cotton, wool, or silk material.

voir dire *n Fr* preliminary check or examination to determine suitability, competence of prospective juror.

volatile *a* evaporating quickly; changeable; lively but unstable; *n* **-tility;** *v* **-tilize** render, become volatile; evaporate.

vol-au-vent *n Fr* light raised savory pie of puff pastry.

volcano *n* **-oes.** mountain formed by eruption of molten lava, ashes, etc. through opening in earth's crust; *a* **volcanic** of, like volcano; *fig* acting with sudden violence.

vole *n* mouselike rodent.

volition *n* act or faculty of willing; choosing.

volley *n* 1 number of missiles thrown or shot at once 2 *fig* torrent of words, etc. 3 (tennis, etc.) striking of ball before it touches ground; *v* fire, hit volley; *n* **v. ball** ball game played over high net.

volt *n* unit of electromotive force; *ns* **-age;** such force measured in units; **-meter** instrument for measuring electromotive force.

volte-face *n Fr* reversal of opinion or direction; about-face.

voluble *a* fluent in speech; talkative; *adv* **-bly;** *n* **-bility**.

volume *n* 1 book 2 mass, bulk,

A B C D E F G H I J K L M N O P Q R S T U V W X Y Z

size in cubic units **3** intensity of sound; *a* **voluminous** bulky; abundant; *adv* **-ly;** *n* **-ness.**

voluntary *a* **1** acting without compulsion **2** made, done freely; **3** given, supported by private donations; *adv* **-ily;** *n* organ music before or after church service.

volunteer *n* one who offers services of own free will; *esp* in armed forces; *v* offer freely.

voluptuous *a* **1** delight in sensual pleasures **2** ripe, sexually attractive; *adv* **-ly;** *n* **-ness;** *n* **voluptuary** one given to luxurious sensual pleasures.

vomit *v* discharge from stomach through mouth; *n* that which has been vomited.

voodoo *n* religion derived from African polytheism and ancestor worship.

voracious *a* greedy; ravenous; *n* **voracity.**

vortex *n* whirlpool; whirling mass; *fig* anything that engulfs; *pl* **vortices;** *a* **vortical.**

votary *n* one vowed to service of a god, devotee of cause, etc.; *fem* **votaress;** *a* **votive** given, offered to fulfill vow.

vote *n* formal expression of one's wish, opinion, etc.; right to vote at elections, etc.; *v* **1** cast vote **2** *coll* suggest; *n* **voter.**

vouch *v; phr v* **vouch for** guarantee; be responsible for;

n **voucher** document confirming fact or authenticity of something; ticket acting as substitute for cash; *v* **vouchsafe** condescend to grant; grant special favor, privilege.

vow *n* solemn pledge, promise, *esp* to God; *v* promise faithfully.

vowel *n* speech sound produced by unhindered passage of breath through mouth; letter representing such sound.

vox populi *n Lat* voice of the poeple, popular opinion.

voyage *n* journey, *esp* long one, by water; *v* travel, make a journey, by water; *n* **voyager.**

voyeur *n Fr* one who derives pleasure from observing others, *usu* secretly; *n* **-ism.**

vs *abbr* versus.

vulcanize *v* treat (rubber) by sulfur, under heat; *ns* **vulcanite** hard substance so made; **vulcanization.**

vulgar *a* **1** (*of person*) uncouth; ill-mannered **2** (*of taste*) unrefined **3** (*of humor*) likely to offend; obscene; *n* **v. fraction** one with numerator above denominator (*also* **simple fraction**); *adv* **-ly;** *ns* **-ism** rude or obscene expression; **-ity** coarseness; lack of refinement; bad taste; *v* **-ize;** *n* **-ization.**

Vulgate *n* 4th century Latin translation of Bible.

vulnerable *a* **1** capable, of being, liable to be, wounded,

attacked, etc. **2** open to criticism **3** easily hurt **4** *bridge* having won one game towards rubber; *n* **-ability.**

vulpine *a* **1** pertaining to foxes **2** sly; crafty.

vulture *n* **1** large carrion-eating bird of prey **2** *fig* rapacious extortioner.

vying *pr, p of* **vie.**

Wac n member of the US Women's Army Corps.

wacky a crazy; zany; n **-iness**.

wad n small pad of fibrous material; compact bundle of paper esp bank notes; v pack, press, etc. with wads; n **wadding** soft material used for stuffing, etc.

waddle v walk heavily with swaying motion, like duck; n this gait.

wade v walk through water, mud, etc.; phr vs **wade in** begin with determination; **wade into** attack with vigor; **wade through** read through (something long and tedious); n **wader** one that wades (pl long waterproof boots).

wadi, wady n dried-up desert watercourse; riverbed; gully.

wafer n **1** light thin biscuit **2** small round disk of special bread eaten at Communion service; a **w.-thin** very thin.

waffle¹ n thin crisp cake of batter.

waffle² v coll talk or write lengthily in a meaningless way; equivocate, vacillate.

waft v carry lightly and smoothly through air or over water; n breath of wind; faint odor, whiff.

wag v **wagging, wagged.** move or shake up and down or from side to side; as of dog's tail; n humorous, joking person; a **waggish** comical, droll; adv **-ly; n -ness**.

wage n payment for work; n **w.-claim** demand by workers for specified increase in wages; **w. freeze** government policy which requires employees not to request wage increases for a specified period; v carry on (war).

wager n, v bet.

waggle v wag; a **waggly**.

wagon n four-wheeled vehicle for heavy loads.

wagtail n small long-tailed bird.

waif n homeless, straying person or animal; fig neglected child.

wail v howl; lament; n cry of grief.

wailing wall n cap **1** remnant wall of ancient temple in Jerusalem; Jewish holy site **2** source of comfort, solace.

wain n Lit wagon or cart; n **wainwright** builder of wagons.

wainscot n wooden paneling on walls of room.

waist n **1** narrow part of body between thorax and hips **2** narrowed middle part of some objects **3** middle part of ship's upper deck; ns **waistband** strip of fabric enclosing waist at top of trousers, skirt etc; **waistcoat** Brit vest; **waistline** measurement around waist; narrow part of garment at the waist.

wait v await; defer action; serve and pass dishes at table; phr v **wait on 1** serve food to **2** act as servant to (idm **wait on somebody hand and foot** be very subservient to); n act of waiting; n **waiter** person serving in restaurant (fem **waitress**); a **waiting** (ns w. **list** list of people waiting their turn; **w. room** room where one waits to be attended to; idm **(play) a waiting game** (use) tactic of

A B C D E F G H I J K L M N O P Q R S T U V **W** X Y Z

delay.

waive *v* relinquish (claim, etc.); forgo; *n* **waiver** legal renunciation.

wake[1] *v* rouse from sleep; stir up, excite; *pt* **woke, waked;** *pp* **waked, woke, woken;** *idm* **wake the dead** cause great disturbance (with noise); *phr v* **wake up to** realize; *v* **waken** wake up; rouse; *as* **wakeful** vigilant (*n* **-ness**) **waking** when one is awake.

wake[2] *n* track left in water by ship; aftermath; *idm* **in the w. of** following as consequence of; close behind.

wake[3] *n* meeting to lament, honor dead person before burial.

Waldorf salad *n* salad of diced apple, celery, nuts, mayonnaise, named for Waldorf-Astoria hotel, New York.

wale *n* vertical rib or cord fabric.

walk *v* travel on foot at moderate pace; cause to go at walk; *n* act of walking; gait; journey on foot *esp* for pleasure, exercise; *idm* **walk of life** job or sphere of activity; *phr vs* **walk into** 1 *coll* obtain (job) easily 2 fall into (trouble, danger, etc.) through lack of vigilance; **walk away/off with** *coll* 1 remove by theft 2 win with ease; **walk on** 1 continue walking 2 go on stage (*n* **w.-on part** *theater* small nonspeaking part; *idm*

walk on air feel happy, carefree; **walk out** 1 leave suddenly without further comment 2 go on strike (*n* **w.-out**); **walk out on** abandon; **walk over** 1 traverse on foot 2 *coll* treat with contempt (*idm* **walk all over** *esp* defeat easily; *n* **walkover** easy victory); *ns* **walkabout** informal walk by famous person among ordinary people; **walker; walkie-talkie** portable radio receiver/transmitter; **walking** (*ns* **w.papers** marching orders; **w.-stick** stick to support person walking); **walkway** passage for walking along.

Walkman [TM] personal stereo with headphones.

wall *n* 1 upright structure of brick, stone, etc. forming part of building or room, or as fence 2 *fig* barrier 3 *bio* outer surface of cell or organ; *idm* **go to the wall** fail; *idm* **go up the wall** *coll* be furious; *idm* **hit the wall** encounter enormous physical, psychological obstacle, frustration; *phr vs* **wall off** separate with wall; **wall up** enclose by walls; *n* **wallpaper** decorative paper for interior walls of house; *v* decorate with this; *as* **walled** having wall(s); **wall-to-wall** covering whole floor area.

wallet *n* small purse for holding money, etc.

wallflower *n* 1 perennial plant

2 *coll* person who has no partners at dance.

wallaby *n* species of small kangaroo.

wallet *n* 1 flat leather case or pocketbook 2 small bag or case for tools.

wall-eyed *a* having eye(s) with whitish iris; squinting.

Walloon *a*, *n* French-speaking Belgian.

wallop *v* beat severely; thrash; *n* **walloping** thrashing; beating; *a coll* of large size.

wallow *v* roll about in water, mud, etc.; *fig* revel in.

Wall Street *n* 1 center of American business world 2 *coll* the American money market.

walnut *n* 1 edible nut with hard ridged shell 2 tree bearing this 3 decorative hardwood used in cabinetry.

walrus *n* large gregarious, marine mammal.

waltz *n* dance in ¾ time, performed by couple; *v* dance waltz; whirl, twirl around; *phr v* **waltz off with** *coll* run away with.

wampum *n* shell beads used by Native Americans as money or decoration.

wan *a* pale; sickly; livid.

wand *n* long, slender rod.

wander *v* 1 roam; ramble; stray 2 be delirious; be absent-minded; *ns* **wanderer; wanderlust** urge to travel.

wane *v* diminish in amount, intensity, power.

wangle *v coll* use irregular

means to obtain something; *n coll* something obtained by guile or dishonesty.

wanna-be *n* one who looks, acts like famous celebrity.

want *v* lack; desire; *n* deficiency; need.

wanton *a* capricious; unchecked; purposeless; dissolute; *v* frolic without restraint.

wapiti *n* N American elk.

war *n* armed conflict between nations; hostility; *v* contend, fight; *ns* **w. clouds** signs that war is imminent; **w. cry 1** something shouted in battle **2** *coll* slogan, *esp* political; **w.-game 1** tactical game with models of troops, weapons, etc. **2** military training exercise; **w.horse 1** (formerly) horse used in battle **2** *fig* seasoned campaigner in war, politics, etc.; **w.-paint 1** body make-up used by Native American warriors **2** *coll* cosmetics; *a* **warlike** martial; bellicose.

warble *v* sing with trills, as bird; *n* **warbler** genus of small wild songbirds.

ward *n* **1** action of watching or guarding **2** minor under care of guardian **3** division of city **4** section of hospital, prison, etc; *pl* ridges, notches in key or lock; *v* guard; *phr v* **ward off** defend oneself against; *ns* **warder** *fem* **wardress** prison officer; **warden** governor; person having authority; **wardrobe** clothes closet;

stock of clothes; **wardroom** naval officers' messroom.

ware[1] *n* articles for sale collectively; manufactured articles *esp* pottery; *pl* **-s** goods; merchandise; *n* **w.-house** storehouse for goods; *v* store; place in warehouse.

ware[2] *v coll* guard against; avoid.

warfare *n* (fighting in) war.

warfarin *n* anticoagulant drug used in human medicine and as rat poison.

warlock *n* wizard; sorcerer.

warlord *n* supreme military commander ruling by force.

warm *a* **1** moderately hot **2** affectionate; ardent **3** (*of color*) suggesting warmth; *v* make, become warm; *idm* **keep somebody's seat warm** reserve seat for somebody (by occupying it); *idm* **make things warm/hot for** punish or reprimand severely; *phr vs* **warm to** begin to like; **warm up 1** make or become warmer **2** prepare for more energetic activity; *as* **w.-blooded 1** having constantly warm body temperature **2** *fig* passionate; **w.-hearted** kind (*n* **-ness**); *n* **warming** (**w. pan** pan formerly filled with hot coals for warming a bed); *n* **warmth 1** mild heat **2** *fig* cordiality **3** anger.

warmonger *n* person that provokes war.

warn *v* caution; admonish; be a signal to; *n* **-ing** notice,

hint of possible danger, consequences, etc.; premonition; notice to terminate employment.

warp *v* twist, distort; become twisted; *n* threads running lengthwise in fabric; rope; distortion in timber caused by contraction.

warpath *n* route taken by Native Americans into battle; *idm* **on the warpath** in fighting mood.

warrant *n* authority; document that authorizes; *v* justify; guarantee; *n* **w. officer** military officer between enlisted and commissioned grades; *n* **warranty** justification; guarantee.

warren *n* ground honeycombed by rabbit burrows.

warrior *n lit* fighter.

warship *n* naval vessel used in war.

wart *n* small hard viral growth on surface of skin; *n* **w.-hog** large wild African pig with tusks.

warts-and-all *a* showing imperfections, defects; unguarded.

wary *a* cautious; prudent; vigilant.

was *1st, 3rd person sing pt of* **be.**

wash *v* **1** clean with water or other liquid **2** wash oneself **3** (of sea, river, etc.) flow over, across, past, against, or cause to move in specified direction; *idm* **(not) wash with somebody** *coll* (not) be accepted as an excuse by somebody; *idm* **wash one's dirty linen (in public)** discuss personal affairs publicly; *idm* **wash one's hands of** refuse to have further interest in or responsibility for; *phr vs* **wash away** (of water) carry elsewhere; **wash down** 1 clean (dirty surface) with water 2 facilitate swallowing of (food, medicine) by drinking; **wash out** 1 (of dirt) be removed by washing 2 clean inside of 3 (*of rain*) cause to be canceled (n **w.-out** *coll* failure); **wash over somebody** *coll* fail to stir somebody emotionally; **wash up** 1 wash oneself 2 wash face and hands 3 (of sea) bring to shore; *n* 1 act of washing 2 load of clothes, etc. (to be) washed 3 waves made by passing boat, etc. 4 painting, thin brushing on of very diluted color; *ns* **w.-basin** bowl for washing hands, etc. (*also* **w.-hand basin; w.bowl**); **washroom** *coll* lavatory; **w.-stand** (formerly) bedroom table with jug and basin for washing; **w.-tub** wooden tub for washing clothes, etc.; *as* **washed-out** 1 faded 2 exhausted; **washed-up** *coll* defeated by failure; *ns* **washing** 1 act of washing 2 clothes, etc. (to be) washed (*ns* **w.-line** line for drying washed clothes; **w.-**

machine/-powder machine/powder for washing clothes; **washerwoman** (formerly) woman who washes clothes, etc.; *a* **washy** 1 pale 2 watery 3 insipid.

wasn't *contracted form of* was not.

wasp *a* **waspish** (*n* **-ness**).

wasp *n* stinging insect; *as* **-ish** spiteful; biting; **w.-waisted** having very slender waist.

WASP *n* American of Caucasian, British ancestry (white Anglo-Saxon Protestant); sometimes used disparagingly.

wassail *n* 1 drinking party 2 warm cider punch.

waste *v* 1 use extravagantly or uselessly 2 devastate 3 cause to shrink 4 lose strength; become emaciated; *a* desolate; useless; *n* 1 desert 2 extravagant, unnecessary expenditure 3 refuse; *phr v* **waste away** become weak and thin; *ns* **w. disposal unit** sink attachment for shredding and washing away waste vegetable matter (*also* **garbage disposal**); **w.-paper** used paper (**w.-paper**) **basket** receptacle for waste paper; **w.-pipe** carrying used water to drain; *n* **wastage** amount lost by waste; loss; *a* **wasteful** extravagant; *ns* **wasteland** 1 barren or desolate area 2 *fig* unproductive situation in life.

watch *v* 1 remain awake and

alert 2 observe; *idm* **watch it/watch one's step** be careful; *phr vs* **watch (out) for** look out for; beware; **watch over** guard and protect; *n* 1 small, portable clock, *usu* worn on wrist (*n* **watchmaker**) 2 act of watching 3 person, group of people employed to watch or protect something (*ns* **w.-dog** 1 dog that guards something 2 *fig* person or group acting to protect people's rights; **watchman** person employed to protect property); *a* **watchful** vigilant; observant; *ns* **watcher** observer; **watchword** slogan expressing principles and beliefs.

wastrel *n* 1 spendthrift 2 idler.

water *n* 1 transparent, tasteless liquid that descends as precipitation and is major constituent of all livng matter 2 body of water (sea, river, lake, etc.) 3 liquid secretion of animal body, *e.g.*, urine 4 quality (of diamond, sapphire, etc.); *pl* **-s** 1 sea, river, lake (**coastal/inland w.**) 2 amniotic fluid surrounding fetus in womb; *idm* **(not) hold water** (not) be credible or logical; *idm* **make/pass water** urinate; *v* 1 pour water on (plants, land) 2 supply with drinking water 3 produce tears or saliva; *phr v* **water down** 1 dilute 2 reduce strength of; *ns* **w.**

bed bed with water-filled mattress; **w. closet** lavatory (*abbr* WC); **w. lily** floating pond plant with large round leaves; **w. pistol** toy gun that squirts water; **w. polo** ball game with goal posts for two competing teams of swimmers; **w. softener** device or chemical for softening hard water; **w. table** underground water level; **w. wings** pair of floats to help people learning to swim; *a* **watery.**

watercolor *n* (picture painted with) paint made to be mixed with water.

watercourse *n* (channel of) stream, river, etc.

watercress *n* strong-flavoured cress grown in water.

watered silk *n* glossy silk fabric with wavy markings.

waterfall *n* cascade of water.

waterfront *n* harbor side.

waterhole *n* pool at which animals drink.

watering *n* act of pouring on or supplying water; *a* exuding tears, saliva; *ns* **w. can** vessel for sprinkling water on plants; **w. hole 1** waterhole **2** bar; **w. place 1** spa **2** waterhole.

waterlogged *a* saturated, soaked with water.

Waterloo *n* scene of Napoleon's defeat in 1815; *idm* **meet one's Waterloo** be finally defeated.

watermark *n* faint design in paper.

watermelon *n* **1** large round oblong fruit with hard rind, *usu* red or pink flesh, and many seeds **2** African gourd vine, bearing these.

water moccasin *n* cottonmouth snake

waterproof *a, n* (garment) proof against water.

watershed *n* **1** *geog* ridge of high land on either side of which streams and rivers flow in opposite directions **2** *fig* moment of important change in life or career.

waterspout *n* **1** pipe, duct, opening that carries water **2** funnel-shaped column of water drawn up from ocean, lake by strong winds.

water supply *n* source(s) of water for region, community, area.

watertight *a* tightly fitting to totally exclude water; *fig* flawless, unassailable.

waterworks *n pl* **1** place where public water supply is controlled **2** *coll* person's urinary system; *idm* **turn on the waterworks** *coll* weep intentionally.

watt *n* unit of electrical power.

wattle *n* **1** fencing of woven poles, twigs, and wicker **2** fleshy lobe on neck of turkey **3** Australian acacia.

wave *v* **1** move to and fro in air; undulate **2** greet by raising and moving hand **3** (*of hair*) arrange in undulations; *phr v* **wave aside** reject without consideration;

n **1** act of, gesture of waving **2** swelling ridge on surface of water **3** (*of specified activity*) sudden, temporary increase **4** form of each vibration of light, sound, etc. **5** curve of line of hair; *ns* **waveband** *rad* specified range of wavelengths; **wavelength** *rad* **1** distance between two waves **2** signal using particular frequency (*idm* **on the same wavelength** having a mutual understanding); **wavelet** ripple; *a* **wavy.**

waver *v* fluctuate; hesitate; yield, give way.

wax[1] *v* increase in size (chiefly of moon).

wax[2] *n* solid insoluble substance, nongreasy and melting at low temperature, used for candles, models, sealing, etc.; secretion of ear, bees; *a* **waxy;** *n* **waxwork** wax model of person (*pl* exhibition of wax models of famous people), *also* **w. museum; waxbill, waxwing** kinds of small birds.

waxed paper *n* paper coated with wax for wrapping food, etc.

way *n* **1** road; path; track **2** direction **3** distance **4** manner **5** means; method **6** point of view; respect; *pl* **-s** habits; customs; *idm* **by the way** incidentally; *idm* **by way of 1** going past, through **2** as a form of; *idm* **get in the way (of)** impede; *idm* **get into the way of** acquire habit of; *idm* **get/have one's own way** do or get what one wants irrespective of other considerations; *idm* **give way** collapse; *idm* **give way (to)** 1 yield (to) 2 wait for (other traffic to go first) 3 be superseded (by); *idm* **go out of one's way** make a special effort; *idm* **have a way with** have pleasant, persuasive personality; *idm* **make one's way** progress; *idm* **make way (for)** 1 allow to pass 2 give scope to; *idm* **no way** *coll interj* expressing strong denial or refusal; *idm* **out of the way** conveniently absent (*a* **out-of-the-way** unusual) *idm* **under way** 1 moving 2 happening; *a* **w.-out** *coll* bizarre; unorthodox; *n* **wayside** side of road or path; *n* **wayfarer** traveler; *v* **wayward** perverse, wilful; *n* **waybill** list of passengers and goods.

we *pron* 1st *pers pl nom* of I.

weak *a* lacking strength; frail; irresolute; insipid; faint; *a* **w.-kneed** feeble; cowardly; *a* **weakly** not robust; *v* **weaken** make, become weaker; *ns* **weakling** person or animal lacking strength; **weakness**.

weal[1] *n* mark left on flesh by blow from lash, etc.

weal[2] *n* well-being; welfare.

wealth *n* abundance; profusion; riches; *a* **wealthy** rich; *n* **wealthiness**.

wean *v* accustom to food other than mother's milk; to detach from dependence on; *phr v* **wean somebody (away) from** help somebody to gradually give up someone/something.

weapon *n* any object used for attack or defense.

wear *v* 1 to be clothed in; bear 2 diminish 3 be reduced by use 4 withstand usage 5 *coll* tolerate; *pt* **wore**; *pp* **worn**; *phr vs* **wear down** weaken; **wear off** become less intense, less effective; **wear on** (of time) pass slowly, tediously; **wear out** 1 exhaust 2 make or become unserviceable; *n* 1 act of wearing 2 clothes 3 damage from usage 4 lasting quality.

weary *a* 1 tired 2 bored by; tedious; *v* 1 tire 2 become bored by; *a* **-ily**; *n* **-iness**; *a* **wearisome** tiresome; tedious.

weasel *n* carnivorous animal resembling ferret; *phr v* **weasel out (of)** *coll* avoid fulfilling duty or promise.

weather *n* general atmospheric conditions; *v* 1 expose to action of weather, season 2 show effect of such exposure 3 come safely through; *idm* **under the weather** slightly ill or depressed; *ns* **w.-board(ing)** board(s) on outside wall or door to protect house from wind and rain; **weathercock** weathervane shaped like rooster; **w. forecast** description of expected weather; **weatherman -**

woman *coll* weather forecaster; meteorologist; **w.-ship/-station** ship/station for monitoring weather; **w.-vane** device on top of building indicating wind direction; *as* **w.-beaten** having rough, sunburned skin; showing effects of exposure; *as* **w.-bound** restrained (at port, indoors) by inclement weather; **weatherproof** able to withstand, keep out wind and rain (*n* **-ing** material that serves this purpose).

weave *v* form (threads) into web or fabric by intertwining; braid; wind in and out; *pt* **wove**; *pp* **woven**; *ns* **weaver**; **weaving** act of doing this; fabric so made.

web *n* 1 something woven; net; web spun by spider 2 membrane between digits of aquatic bird, frog, etc.; *as* **webbed** having skin between toes to assist swimming; **w.-footed** with webbed feet; *n* **webbing** strong woven fabric used to make straps, etc.

wed *v* **wedding, wedded.** 1 marry 2 *fig* unite.

we'd *contracted form of* 1 we had 2 we would.

wedding *n* marriage ceremony; **w. ring** ring worn as sign of being married.

wedge *n* V-shaped piece of wood, metal, etc.; *v* make, become firm with wedge; split with wedge; fix immovably.

Wedgwood n [TM] fine earthenware; **W. blue** soft powdery blue.

wedlock n fml state of being married; idm **born out of wedlock** born to unmarried parents.

Wednesday n fourth day of week.

wee a very small; tiny.

weed n wild plant esp one which tends to choke cultivated ones; v free (ground) from weeds; phr v **weed out** select for rejection; n **w.-killer** chemical for killing weeds; a **weedy 1** full of weeds **2** lanky.

week n period of seven days esp from Sunday to Saturday; ns **weekday** any day except Sunday; **weekend** from Friday or Saturday until Monday; a, adv **weekly** once a week.

ween v ar suppose, imagine.

weep v shed tears; (of trees, etc.) droop gracefully; pt, pp **wept**.

weevil n small beetle harmful to corn, etc.

weft n threads interlacing with warp.

weigh v phr vs **weigh down** burden; **weigh in 1** be weighed before contest or race **2** coll join in (discussion, argument, fight); **weigh up** consider (by balancing facts, arguments).

weight n **1** heaviness of something **2** something heavy **3** piece of metal used as standard for weighing other things **4** importance; idm **a weight off one's mind** a cause of anxiety removed; ns **w.-lifting** contest in lifting heavy weights (**w.-lifter** person doing this); **w.-watcher** person trying to lose weight by dieting, etc. as **weightless** (n **-ness**); **weighty 1** heavy **2** serious.

weir n **1** fence, enclosure set in waterway for fishing; **2** dam in stream, river to divert flow.

weird a eerie; uncanny; adv **-ly**; n **-ness**; n **weirdo** coll odd, eccentric person.

welcome a causing gladness; free to use or enjoy; n cordial greeting on arrival; v greet.

weld v **1** unite (hot metal) by fusion or pressure **2** fig unite; n **welder**.

welfare n **1** well-being; comfort, health, and happiness **2** social care for well-being of individuals, families, etc. (ns **w. work; w. worker**); **3** money paid by government to those in need; n **w. state** (country with) system of social, medical, financial, etc. help for those in need.

well[1] a **1** in good health **2** favorable **3** satisfactory; comp **better**, sup **best**; adv **1** in a good way **2** skillfully **3** thoroughly **4** easily; idm **as well 1** also **2** equally well (prep **as well as** in addition to); as **w.-adjusted** at ease in society; **w.-advised** sensible; **w.-appointed** well-equipped; **w.-connected** related to or friendly with influential people; **w.-done 1** thoroughly cooked **2** praise for good job; **w.-heeled** rich; **w.-lined** coll full of money or food; **w.-off 1** rich **2** fortunate; **w.-oiled** coll drunk; **w.-rounded 1** pleasantly plump **2** mature and pleasant **3** (of education) wide-ranging; **w.-to-do** rich.

well[2] n **1** shaft sunk to obtain water or oil **2** natural spring **3** elevator shaft; deep enclosed space in building; n **w.-spring** (constant) source; v spring; gush.

wellingtons n pl knee-high waterproof boots.

Welsh a of Wales, its people or language; n **W. rabbit (rarebit)** toasted cheese poured over crackers, toast.

welt n **1** strip fixed to shoe to strengthen seam between sole and upper **2** ribbed edging to top of sock, etc. **3** weal; v **1** provide with welt **2** coll thrash.

welter v wallow; tumble; n tumult; disorder.

welterweight n **1** boxer weighing between 135 and 147 lb **2** extra weight carried by racehorse.

weltschmerz n often cap **1** apathy; intellectual depression **2** sentimental, sad mood.

a
b
c
d
e
f
g
h
i
j
k
l
m
n
o
p
q
r
s
t
u
v
w
x
y
z

wen *n* small cyst.

wench *n* young woman.

wend *v* **w. one's way** proceed slowly on journey.

went *pt of* **go**.

wept *pt, pp of* **weep**.

were *pt of* **be**.

we're *contracted form of* we are.

werewolf *n myth* person changed into wolf.

west *n* **1** direction of setting Sun **2** one of four points of compass **3** *usu cap* capitalist as opposed to Communist countries; America and Europe as opposed to Asia; *a* pertaining to the west; situated in or facing west; *idm* **go west** *dated coll* seek one's fortune; lost; *as* **westerly; western** (*n* film of cowboy life; *v* **-ize** adapt to lifestyle of US and Europe; *n* **-ization**); **westward** towards the west; *n, a* **W Indian** of W Indies.

wet *a* **wetter, wettest.** **1** covered, saturated, moistened with liquid **2** rainy; *v* **wetting, wetted.** make wet; *n* moisture; rain; *ns* **w. blanket** *coll* spoilsport; *ns* **w. nurse** woman employed to feed another's baby (*v* cosset); **w. suit** rubberized body garment to keep swimmer, kayaker warm.

wetlands *n* swamps, tidal flats, where soil contains much moisture; refuge for wild fowl, etc.

we've *contracted form of we* have.

whack *v* hit, slap sharply, noisily *esp* with stick; *n* such blow; *coll* due share; *a* **-ing** *coll* huge (*n* beating).

whale *n* huge aquatic mammal; *idm* **have a whale of a time** *coll* enjoy oneself a lot; *ns* **whalebone** thin, horny substance growing in upper jaw of some whales; **whaler** person, ship engaged in hunting whales; *v* **whale** hunt whales; *n* **whaling**.

wham *n coll* (sound of) heavy blow; *v* **whammed, whamming** hit violently.

whammy *n* curse; spell yielding bad luck.

wharf *n* berth where ships tie up, load and unload; *ns* **-age** dues for use of wharf; **-inger** wharf owner or manager.

what *pron* that, those which; which thing? *a* which? of which kind? how much, how great; *idm* **what with** because of.

what(so)ever *pron, a* anything at all; no matter which; emphatic form of **what**.

whatnot *n* shelved display case for ornaments, etc.

wheal *n* swelling, as from insect bite.

wheat *n* grain plant; edible grain, ground into flour; *ns* **wheat germ** part of wheat kernel rich in vitamins; **whole w.** brown flour from wheat; *a* **wheaten** made from wheat.

wheedle *v* coax; cajole.

wheel *n* circular frame with spokes or solid disk, revolving round axle; *v* **1** move on wheels **2** cause (line of people) to turn as on pivot; *idm* **wheel and deal** *coll* negotiate in cunning, unscrupulous way (*n* **wheeler-dealer**); *ns* **wheelbarrow** small one-wheeled cart; **wheelbase** distance between front and rear wheels; **wheelchair** mobile chair for transporting those who cannot walk; **w. clamp** device for immobilizing illegally parked car; **wheelhouse** enclosed space on deck for housing helmsman, wheel, compass, etc.; **wheelwright** one who makes and repairs wheels and wheeled vehicles.

wheelie *n coll* stunt of riding bike, motorcycle with front wheel raised.

wheeze *v* breathe with audible friction; *n* noisy breathing; *a* **wheezy**.

whelk *n* edible marine mollusk.

whelm *v* **1** engulf **2** overwhelm.

whelp *n* puppy; cub of lion, tiger, etc.; ill-bred youth; *v* bring forth young (*esp* animals).

when *adv* at what time? how soon? *conj* on the occasion that; at the time that; *adv, conj* **whenever** as soon as; as often as.

whence *adv, conj* from where.

where *adv, conj* to, at, or in which place or part? *adv* **whereabouts** in what place? *n* locality; situation; *conj* **whereas** in view of the fact that; but on the contrary; while; *advs* **wherever 1** in, to, at, any place **2** no matter where **wherefore** why?; for which reason.

whereby *a fml* by means of which.

whereupon *conj* (immediately) after which.

wherewithal *n* resources; money needed.

whet *v* **whetting, whetted.** sharpen; stimulate, excite (appetite, curiosity) *n* **whetstone** stone for sharpening knives, etc.

whether *pron ar* which of two; *conj* expressing doubt, alternative possibility.

whey *n* watery part of milk separated from curds.

which *a* what person or thing? *pron* the thing(s) that; what person, thing?

whichever *det, pron* **1** the one which **2** no matter which.

whiff *v* puff; emit slight unpleasant smell; inhale odor; strike out; *n* **1** puff; breath; slight gust **2** scent, flavor.

while *n* space of time; period; *conj* as long as; during; *phr v* **while away** pass (time) idly; *conj* **whilst** while.

whim, whimsy *n* passing fancy; impulse; caprice; *a*

whimsical capricious; quaint; *n* **whimsicality**.

whimper *n* feeble, fretful cry; *v* cry thus.

whine *n* high-pitched noise (in motors) or long, drawn-out thin wail; *v* cry or emit this.

whinny *v* (*of horse*) neigh gently; *n* such sound.

whip *v* **whipping, whipped. 1** strike with lash **2** whisk (eggs, cream) **3** *coll* defeat, overcome **4** move fast and suddenly; *n* lash attached to handle; *phr v* **whip up 1** stir up (feelings) **2** quickly enlist (support); *ns* **whipcord 1** thin strong cord **2** ribbed cloth; **whiplash 1** blow from whip **2** sudden violent jerk to head and neck as in road accident; **whippersnapper** impudent person; small, impudent boy; **whipping boy** scapegoat.

whippet *n* small, swift, slender racing dog.

whippoorwill *n* nocturnal US bird.

whir(r) *v* **whirring, whirred.** revolve, move with rapid buzzing sound; *n* this sound.

whirl *v* rotate; spin rapidly on axis; *n* **1** rapid rotation **2** bewilderment; *idm* **give something a whirl** *coll* try something; *idm* **in a whirl** bewildered; *ns* **whirligig** top; spinning toy; merry-go-round; **-pool** rapid circular eddy; **-wind** column of rapidly rotating air.

whisk *v* **1** sweep lightly, briskly **2** twitch; beat lightly; *phr v* **whisk off** carry away suddenly; *n* **1** light, stiff brush **2** kitchen instrument for beating eggs, etc.

whisker *n* one of long bristles growing from side of animal's mouth; *pl* **-s** hair growing on man's face.

whiskey, whisky *n* alcoholic liquor distilled from malted grain *esp* barley.

whisper *v* speak in low voice; *fig* tell as secret; *n* such speech.

whist *n* card game for two pairs of players.

whistle *v* **1** produce shrill piping sound from wind instrument or through pursed lips **2** (*of bird, missile, etc.*) make shrill sound **3** summon by whistle; *n* **1** shrill, piercing sound **2** device, instrument producing such sound; *n* **w.-stop** brief visit by politician in election campaign (**w.-stop tour**); *n* **whistler**.

whit *n* particle; bit.

white *a* **1** colorless **2** of color of unstained snow **3** of fair complexion; Caucasian **4** *fig* honorable, sincere; *n* **1** white pigment **2** egg white **3** caucasians; *pl* **-s** white sports clothes, *esp* for tennis; *ns* **w. ant** termite; **w. corpuscle** leukocyte; blood cell that fights infection; **w. dwarf** hot, dense star; **w.**

A
B
C
D
E
F
G
H
I
J
K
L
M
N
O
P
Q
R
S
T
U
V
W
X
Y
Z

elephant something useless; **w. flag** sign of surrender; **w. heat** temperature at and above which metal glows white (*a* **w.-hot**); **w. hope** *coll* person expected to be sure of success; **W. House** official residence in Washington, DC, of US President; **w. knight** *coll* person, organization that saves business company from takeover by investing money in it; **w. lie** trivial lie, *esp* one that avoids hurt to somebody; **w. noise** ambient background noise; jumbled noise made up of many frequencies; **w. paper** Government paper on policy; **w. spirit** form of petroleum used as paint solvent or cleaner; *as* **w.-collar** of office work; working in an office; **w.-tie** (of social occasion) when men wear tails and white bow ties; *v* **whiten** make, become white; *n* **-ness;** *a* **whitish.**

whitewash *n* **1** white liquid for wall decor **2** *fig* attempt to conceal fault or error; *v* **1** cover with whitewash **2** try to make (something bad) seem good.

whither *adv* to what place? to any place that.

whitlow *n* inflammation of finger or toe.

Whitsunday *n* seventh Sunday after Easter.

whittle *v* **1** shape, pare (wood)

with knife **2** *fig* reduce gradually.

whiz, whizz *n* buzzing sound; *v* **whizzing, whizzed.** move very quickly; make buzzing sound; *n* **w. kid** brilliant person; one who very quickly becomes successful.

who *pron* (*obj* **whom** *poss* **whose**) which or what person? that person who; *pron* **who(so)ever** anyone (at all) who.

WHO *abbr* World Health Organization.

whoa *interj* used to stop horse moving.

whodunit *a coll* detective story.

whoever *pron* **1** no matter who **2** anyone at all.

whole *a* **1** intact **2** entire; complete; *n* complete sum, amount; entirety; *adv* **wholly;** *idm* **on the whole** mostly; generally; *idm* **go the whole hog** *coll* do something to the limit, *esp* for pleasure; *as* **w.-hearted** without doubt or restraint; unqualified (*adv* **-ly;** *n* **-ness**); *ns* **w. note** *mus* note equal to four counts in ¾ time; equal to full ¾ measure; equal to two half notes; **w. number** *math* number without fraction; integer; *n, a* **wholemeal** (of) flour made from whole unrefined grain of wheat, etc.; *as* **wholesale 1** of selling goods in bulk to retailers (*also adv; n* **wholesaler**) **2** *fig* complete; **wholesome 1** (*of food*) good for health **2** (*of people*)

looking healthy and morally sound.

whom *pron fml* object form of **who.**

whoop *n* loud cry or yell; noise peculiar to whooping cough; *v* utter such sound; *idm* **whoop it up** *coll* have a good time; *ns* **whooping cough** pertussis; infectious respiratory disease *esp* of children; **whoopee** *coll* merrymaking.

whoops *interj* used after mistake or clumsy action.

whoosh *n* noise of rushing wind, etc.

whop *v* **whopping, whopped.** beat severely; **whopper** *n coll* **1** big thing **2** big lie; *a* **whopping** *coll* big.

whore *n* prostitute.

whorl *n* circular group of petals, leaves, etc.; single coil of spiral.

whose *det, pron* of who; of which.

whosoever = **whoever.**

why *adv* for what reason? because of which; *interj* expressing surprise; *n* cause of reason for something; *idm* **whys and wherefores** explanations.

wick *n* length of thread in candle or oil lamp, which burns until wax or oil is consumed.

wicked *a* **1** evil; vicious; depraved **2** *coll* mischievous; *n* **wickedness.**

wicker *n, a* made of interwoven osiers, etc.; *a, n*

wickerwork (made of) woven wickers.

wicket n **1** small gate or door in larger one **2** set of three cricket stumps and bails **3** arch, hoop in croquet.

wide a broad; far-reaching; spacious; vast; of extensive scope, range; n ball bowled past wicket out of reach of batsman; idm **wide of the mark** badly mistaken; as **w.-eyed 1** with eyes wide open **2** gullible; **w.-open** without restrictions or limits; **w.-ranging** extending in many directions; **widespread** extended over a large area; v **widen** (n **-ing**).

widgeon n freshwater duck.

widget n gadget; unnamed object used in business hypotheses.

widow n woman who outlives her husband; masc **-er**; v make widow of.

width n distance from side to side.

wield v handle; make use of (implement, weapon, etc.) control.

wiener n small sausage; frankfurter.

wife n married woman; pl **wives; a wifely.**

Wiffleball n baseball-like game with hollow, plastic, perforated ball; n **Wiffle** [TM] this ball.

wig n artificial hair for head; a **wigged.**

wigged-out a sl out of touch with the real world; crazy.

wiggle v move quickly from side to side; wriggle.

wigway v signal in code with flags.

wigwam n Native American rough hut.

wild a **1 w. animal** not domesticated **2 w. plant** uncultivated **3** uncivilized (**w. tribe**) **4** uncontrolled (**w. behavior**) **5** stormy (**w. night**) **6** irrational (**w. guess**); idm **beyond one's wildest dreams** better than one could ever have hoped; idm **run wild** go out of control; ns the **w.** natural habitat (pl **-s** remote area); **wild card 1** card usable as equal in value to others **2** fig secret advantage, e.g., in business; **wildfowl** game bird(s); **w.-goose chase** useless search; a **wildcat** reckless (**w. scheme; w. strike** unofficial strike); adv **-ly;** n **-ness.**

wildebeest n large African gnu (pl same or **-s**).

wilderness a desert; desolate expanse of land, water; idm **in(to) the wilderness** out of active, esp political, life.

wildfire n **1** sweeping, destructive braze, esp in rural area, forest, etc. **2** phosphorescent light; idm **like wildfire** very rapidly.

wildlife n animals living in nature.

wile n (usu pl) ruse, cunning stratagem; a **wily** crafty; artful.

will[1] v aux forms moods and tenses expressing future, intention, resolve, etc.; pt **would.**

will[2] n **1** faculty of deciding what one will do; volition **2** wish **3** document making disposition of property after death; idm **at will** at any time one wishes; idm **with a will** with enthusiasm; v **1** wish **2** leave as bequest; a **willing** ready, eager to help (adv **-ly;** n **-ness**).

willful a stubborn; capricious; premeditated; n **wilfulness.**

willies n pl coll nervous feeling.

will-o-the-wisp n **1** phosphorescent light over marshy ground **2** fig elusive person or thing.

willow n genus of trees, yielding osiers; this wood; n **w. pattern** traditional blue and white oriental-style design, esp for china (also a); a **willowy** slender; graceful.

willy-nilly adv whether one will or not; haphazard.

wilt v (of plants) fade; droop; wither.

wily a full of wiles; cunning (n **-iness**).

wimp n coll weak, ineffectual person; a **-ish;** n **-ness.**

win v **winning, won. 1** gain, achieve by effort **2** obtain as prize **3** prevail; pt, pp **won** phr v **win over** gain favor of by persuasion; n victory, success esp in contest.

wince v shrink away; flinch; n involuntary recoil.

a
b
c
d
e
f
g
h
i
j
k
l
m
n
o
p
q
r
s
t
u
v
w
x
y
z

winch n machine for hoisting, windlass; crank used as handle.

wind[1] n 1 air in rapid motion 2 breath 3 flatulence; *idm* **break wind** expel air from bowels; *idm* **get wind of** hear about by chance; *idm* **in the wind** likely to happen soon; *idm* **take the wind out of somebody's sails** *coll* make unable to act or speak with confidence; *ns* **w.-break** line of trees, etc. giving shelter from the wind; **w.-breaker** anorak; **windfall 1** fruit blown off tree 2 *fig* piece of unexpected good fortune; **w. instrument** *mus* instrument played by blowing (brass, woodwind); **wind-jammer** large sailing vessel; **wind -mill** mill, water-pump driven by force of wind; **windshield** front window of vehicle (**w. wiper** rotating arm with rubber blade that keeps windshield clear of rain, etc.); **w.-sock** canvas tube blown from mast to show wind direction; **windsurfer 1** flat board with keel and sail 2 person using this (v **windsurf;** n **windsurfing**); **w. tunnel** tunnel along which air is forced at speed to test aircraft; a **w.-swept 1** exposed to strong wind 2 (of hair) untidy; n, a, adv **windward** (of, on, to) the side from which the wind blows; a **windy 1** bringing much wind 2 exposed to wind.

wind[2] v 1 turn, meander 2 tighten (watch spring) by turning 3 make into ball 4 twine; *pt, pp* **wound;** *phr vs* **wind down 1** lower by winding 2 (*of machinery*) go slow and stop 3 *coll* relax after stress, etc.; **wind up** finished 2 *coll* arrive finally 3 *coll* tease or provoke n **windlass** apparatus for hoisting or hauling.

window n opening in wall, roof, vehicle, etc. to admit light, air, etc. *usu* filled by glass panes; *ns* **w.-dressing** art of arranging goods in store windows; *fig* attractive presentation; **w.-sill** ledge under window.

Windows [TM] n computer operating system with which several programs that can be run simultaneously using different parts of the screen.

wine n fermented grape juice; v entertain (person) to wine; drink wine.

winery n place that makes wine.

wing n 1 limb by which bird, insect, etc. flies 2 projecting part of aircraft's structure by which it is supported in air 3 side, flank 4 side projection from building etc.; v 1 fly (over or through) 2 wound in wing 3 *fig* disable *idm* **take wing 1** fly away 2 become active; *idm* **under the wing of** protected, helped by; *pl* **-s**

theater hidden area at sides of stage (*idm* **in the wings 1** waiting to enter 2 *fig* ready to become involved); *ns* **w. chair** high-backed chair with projecting arms; **w.-nut** nut with flanges for easier turning with finger and thumb; **w.-span** distance between tips of wings; *as* **-ed; -less.**

wingding n lively, lavish, extravagant party.

wink v open and close eye rapidly; blink with one eye; *phr v* **wink at** *coll* connive at; n act of winking.

winkle n edible shellfish, periwinkle.

winner n 1 person who wins 2 winning stroke or move, **winning** a 1 bringing victory 2 pleasantly persuasive; *adv* **-ly;** n pl **-s** money won.

winner's circle n area where winning horses, jockeys meet press, fans after race.

winnow v separate grain from husks by fanning; *fig* sort out good from bad.

wino n **-os.** *coll* alcoholic, *esp* wine drinker.

winsome a engaging; attractive; charming.

winter n coldest season of year; v spend winter in; tend animals, plants during winter; a **wintry 1** of, like winter; cold; snowy 2 *fig* frigid.

wintergreen n creeping aromatic shrub.

winterize v prepare for cold

weather.

wipe *v* clean, dry by rubbing with cloth, etc.; *idm* **wipe the floor with** *coll* defeat utterly; humiliate; *idm* **wipe the slate (clean)** *coll* forget all past debts or offenses; *phr vs* **wipe off 1** clean by wiping **2** *coll fig* remove; **wipe out** eliminate; *n* **wiper**.

wire *n* **1** fine-drawn slender flexible thread of metal **2** *coll* telegram; *idm* **get one's wires crossed** *coll* have misunderstanding with somebody; *v* **1** fasten with wire **2** equip or connect with electric wiring **3** telegraph; *a* **w.-haired** having short, stiff hair; *ns* **w. tapping** using secret connection to overhear somebody's telephone conversations; **wiring** connection or system of wires; *a* **wiry** like wire; tough and flexible (*n* **-iness**).

wireless *n* transmission of sound by electromagnetic waves; *coll* radio; *a* pertaining to radio or broadcasting.

wire service *n* news agency serving subscribers via satellite, wire communications.

wise[1] *a* **1** prudent; sagacious **2** having knowledge, intelligence; *idm* **be/get wise to** *coll* be/become aware of (something important); *phr v* **wise up** *coll* (be) inform(ed); *n* **w. guy** *coll* person who gives impression of being very knowledgeable *coll*

gangster; *ns* **wisdom** sagacity, sound judgement; **w. tooth** one cut during adult years.

wise[2] *n* way; manner; fashion.

wiseacre *n* conceited sassy person.

wisecrack *n coll* smart remark; joke; witticism.

wisenheimer *n* smart aleck.

wish *v* have desire; long for; *n* desire; expression of desire, *esp* order, request; *phr v* **wish somebody/something on somebody** *coll* pass somebody/something (unwanted) on to somebody; *n* **w. fulfillment** *psyc* means of gratifying subconscious desire in fact or through fantasy; *a* **wishful** expressing desire or hope (**w. thinking** belief based on unrealistic desire); *n* **wishbone** forked breast bone of chicken, turkey, etc., often split by pulling between two people, of whom recipient of larger piece may make a secret wish.

wishy-washy *a coll* weak; insipid; *n* **-iness**.

wisp *n* small bunch of straw, etc.; thin, straggly lock of hair.

wisteria *n* climbing perennial plant with blue flowers.

wistful *a* yearning; sadly pensive.

wit *n* **1** ability to express something with clever, humorous words **2** person able to do this **3** *esp pl* mental capacity; quick

understanding; *idm* **at wit's end** at a loss; too desperate and anxious to know what to do next; *idm* **have keep one's wits about one** be alert and ready to act; *idm* **to wit** *leg, lit* that is; *as* **witless** foolish; **witty** cleverly amusing; *n* **witticism** witty remark; *a, adv* **wittingly** knowingly; deliberately.

witch *n* sorceress; hag; crone; *ns* **witchcraft** magic **w. doctor** professional worker in magic, medicine in primitive tribe; **witchery** fascination; **w.-hunt 1** hunt to destroy witches **2** *fig* campaign to persecute those with unorthodox views on morality, politics etc.

witch hazel *n* N American shrub whose bark yields astringent medicinal substance.

with *prep* against; in company of; beside; possessed of; by means of; *adv* **withal** besides, moreover.

withdraw *v* **1** draw, take back **2** retire; not take part; *pt* - **drew** *pp* **-drawn**.

wither *v* fade; decay; grow feebler; *fig* snub; *a* **-ing** severe; contemptuous (**w. look**); *adv* **-ly**.

withhold *v* keep back; refuse to bestow; *pt, pp* **-held**.

withholding tax *n* money deducted (from wages, etc.) as advance payment on income tax.

within *prep, adv* in, inside; *adv*

a b c d e f g h i j k l m n o p q r s t u v w x y z

A B C D E F G H I J K L M N O P Q R S T U V **W** X Y Z

without outside; *prep* lacking.

without *prep* **1** lacking **2** beyond; *adv* **1** outside; outwarly **2** lacking.

withstand *v* resist; *pt, pp* **-stood**.

witless *a* foolish; *n* **-ness**.

witness *n* **1** testimony; corroboration; **2** one who gives evidence; person or thing furnishing proof; *v* see; attest; testify **n w. box** area in court where witness sits, stands (*also* **w. stand**).

witticism *n* witty remark.

wizard *n* **1** sorcerer; magician **2** *fig* expert; ingenious person.

wizened *a* shriveled; dried up.

wobble *v* move, sway unsteadily; *n* oscillation; unsteady movement.

woe *n* cause of sorrow; misfortune; *as* **woebegone** mournful; doleful; **woeful** sorrowful; pitiful (*adv* **-ly**).

wok *n* deep curved pan used in Chinese cuisine.

woke *pt*, **woken** *pp* of **wake**.

wold *n* expanse of high open country.

wolf *n* **1** large wild carnivorous animal of dog family **2** man who pursues women mainly for sex; *pl* **wolves**; *idm* **wolf in sheep's clothing** person seemingly innocent but having secret evil intentions; *ns* **w. cub 1** young wolf **2** junior Boy Scout; **wolfhound** large hunting dog; *n, v* **w. whistle** (give) loud whistle

to seek attention of attractive female.

wolverine *n* small carnivorous animal; its fur.

woman *n* adult human female; female sex; *pl* **women;** *ns* **-hood** condition of being a woman; **-kind** women in general; *as* **-ly** having good qualities of woman; **-ish** effeminate *v* **-ize** (of man) have affairs with many different women (*ns* **-izer; -izing**).

womb *n* uterus; female organ in which embryo develops.

wombat *n* small bearlike Australian wild animal.

won *pt, pp* of **win**.

wonder *n* **1** prodigy; marvel **2** emotion, feeling of awe, excited by marvelous object, person etc; *v* be amazed; be curious about; *as* **-ful** amazing; marvelous (*adv* **-ly**); **wondrous** inspiring wonder (*adv* **-ly**); *n* **wonderment 1** astonishment **2** deep admiration.

wonder bread [TM] *n* soft, *usu* white mass-produced sliced sandwich bread.

wonk *n* *coll* nerd; egghead.

wont *a* accustomed; *n* usual practice.

won't *contracted form of* will not.

woo *v* court, seek to win love of; *n* **-er** suitor.

wood *n* tract of tree-covered land; solid substance of trees; timber; *idm* **out of the wood(s)** *coll* free from

danger, problems; *as* **-ed** covered with trees; **wooden 1** made of wood **2** *fig* stiff; inhibited; **woody 1** wooded **2** like wood, *a, n* **woodland**.

woodcock *n* woodland game bird with long straight beak.

woodcut *n* engraving on wood block; print from this.

woodlouse *n* small insect (*pl* **woodlice**).

woodpecker *n* bird that pecks holes in trees.

woodsman *n* forester.

woodwind *n* musical instruments *usu* made of wood and played by being blown.

woodwork *n* carpentry; wooden part of structure.

woof[1] *n, interj, v coll* (sound of dog's) bark.

woof[2] *n* threads crossing warp in woven fabric.

woofer *n* speaker, *usu* large, reproducing primarily low-frequency sounds.

wool *n* fleece, coat of sheep, angora goat, alpaca, etc.; *n, a* **woollen** (cloth) made of wool; *n, a* **woolly** (garment, jersey) made of wool; (*n* **-iness; w.-headed** not thinking clearly); *n* **w.-gathering** letting the mind wander instead of concentrating.

woozy *a coll* **1** dizzy, *e.g.,* from drinking alcohol **2** mentally confused; *adv* **-ily;** *n* **-iness**.

word *n* **1** simplest element of speech; unit of language serving as name of object, etc. **2** brief speech; message; promise; *v* express in words; *idm* **have words (with)** quarrel (with); *idm* **(not) in so many words** (not) using exactly these words but implying them; *idm* **put words into somebody's mouth** *coll* **1** tell somebody what to say **2** claim falsely that somebody said something; *idm* **word for word** using exactly the same words; *n* **w. processor** computerized keyboard with programs and VDU for editing text, etc.; *v* **w.-process** type, edit in this way (*n* **-ing**); *a* **wordy** verbose (*adv* **-ily** *n* **-iness**).

work *n* **1** bodily, intellectual labor **2** occupation **3** product of labor or artistic activity; *pl* **-s 1** factory **2** mechanism **3** *coll* everything; *idm* **all in a day's work** nothing abnormal; easy to cope with; *idm* **have one's work cut out** find it difficult in the time available; *idm* **give somebody the works 1** give somebody full treatment **2** tell somebody everything **3** treat somebody harshly; *v* **1** do one's job **2** do activity needing effort **3** (make) function **4** produce (effect) **5** manipulate **6** gradually move or turn to specified position or condition; *phr vs* **work off** reduce by working; **work out 1** calculate **2** develop **3** decide **4** *coll* do physical

exercise (*n* **w.-out**); **work up 1** develop by stages **2** arouse **3** make nervous, excited; *a* **-able** able to be arranged, achieved, used; *n* **-er**.

workaday *a* ordinary; routine.

workaholic *n* person unhealthily obsessed with work.

workbench *n* table where mechanic, artisan, etc. works.

workbook *n* supplementary schoolbook with practice exercises.

work force *n* total number of workers.

work camp *n* **1** prison camp; punitive detention **2** temporary volunteer work encampment.

workhorse *n* **1** useful machine **2** somebody doing routine jobs.

workhouse *n* penal institution for minor offenders.

working *n* functioning; way in which process works; excavated area of mine *pl* **-s** way in which something operates; *idm* **in (full) working order** functioning properly; *a* **1** of, at, for work **2** used at, spent in work; *ns* **w. capital** money used for running costs of business; **w. class** proletariat (*a* **w.-class**); **w. knowledge** sufficient practical knowledge to put to some use; **w. party 1** group appointed to investigate and report on special area of concern **2** group of manual

workers.

workload *n* amount of work expected from machine or employee in specified time.

workman, worker *n* manual laborer; *a* **-like** of or like a good workman; *n* **-ship** (result of) skillful working.

workout *n* concentrated spell of physical exercise.

workshop *n* **1** room or building where goods are made or repaired **2** group meeting where members exchange ideas and develop skills, methods, projects, etc.

work station *n* **1** work area for one person, often with computer **2** small powerful computer.

world *n* **1** the universe **2** the Earth **3** humanity **4** category of specified living creatures **5** sphere of human activity; *idm* **a world of difference** a great deal of difference; *idm* **be/mean the world to** *coll* be very precious to; *idm* **do the world of good** *coll* benefit greatly; *idm* **for all the world as if/like** *coll* just as if/like; *idm* **out of this world** *coll* wonderful; *idm* **worlds apart** *coll* totally different; *as* **w.-class** among the best in the world; **w.-famous** well-known everywhere; **w.-weary** tired of life; **w.-wide** found, happening in all parts of the world (*also adv*); *ns* **w.-beater** somebody/ something better than all others; **w. power** powerful nation; **w. view 1**

A
B
C
D
E
F
G
H
I
J
K
L
M
N
O
P
Q
R
S
T
U
V
W
X
Y
Z

attitude to life 2 philosophy; **w. war** calamitous war involving many major countries; *a* **worldly 1** experienced in the ways of society 2 regarding human affairs as more important than religious life; materialistic (*n* **-iness; w.- wise** shrewd in handling of human affairs).

World Series *n* contest for athletic championship, *esp* in baseball leagues in US.

world wide web *n* body of data stored in computers worldwide, accessible using the Internet.

worm *n* 1 long invertebrate; earthworm; grub; maggot 2 spiral thread of screw 3 *fig* weak, obsequious person; *v* wriggle, edge along slowly; *idm* **worm one's way into** gain (affection, trust) by flattery, etc., *usu* in order to deceive; *phr v* **worm out** extract (secret information) by cunning questions; *n* **worm's-eye view** view from below, from inferior position; *a* **w. -eaten 1** full of worm holes 2 *fig* old.

wormwood *n* aromatic bitter herb; *fig* bitterness.

worn *pt, pp of* **wear**; *a* 1 much used 2 threadbare (**w.-out 1** exhausted 2 too worn to be usable any longer.

worrisome *a* 1 anxious 2 causing anxiety; *adv* **-ly**.

worry *v* **worrying, worried. 1** (cause to) be anxious 2

pester; harass; *n* 1 anxiety 2 cause of this; *as* **worried** (*adv* **-ly**); **worrying** (*adv* **-ly**).

worse *a comp of* **bad**; *v* **worsen** make, grow worse; deteriorate.

worship *v* **worshipping, worshipped.** revere, adore as God; idolize; adore; *a* **-ful;** *n* **worshipper**.

worst *a sup of* **bad**.

worsted *a, n* (made of) woollen yarn.

wort *n* liquid from malt used in beer-making.

worth *a* having specified value; deserving of; *n* merit; material value; *idm* **for all one's worth** with maximum effort; *idm* **for what it's worth** although it's probably not of much value; *idm* **be worth it 1** be of use 2 be of the value claimed; *idm* **worth one's salt** competent; *idm* **worth while** profitable; *as* **- less** (*n* **-ness**); **-while** sufficiently rewarding.

worthy *a* 1 virtuous 2 deserving; *n* eminent person; *adv* **-ily;** *n* **-iness**.

would *pt of* **will**; *a* **w.-be** aspiring (*usu* in vain).

wouldn't contracted form of would not.

wound[1] *n* cut, hole or tear in skin or tissue of body; *v* inflict such injury on; hurt (feelings of).

wound[2] *pt, pp of* **wind**; *a* **w.-up** intensely excited or anxious.

wove *pt,* **woven** *pp of* **weave**.

wow[1] *interj* expressing surprise;

n coll great success; *v sl* impress.

wow[2] *n mus* distortion in reproduced sound, variation in pitch from irregularity in playing speed of tape or disk.

wpm *abbr* words per minute.

wrack *n* ruin.

wrangle *v* 1 quarrel; dispute angrily 2 herd, care for horses, cattle; *n* noisy quarrel; *n* **wrangler 1** one who argues thus 2 one who works with horses, cattle, etc. 3 one who rides in rodeos, exhibitions.

wrap *v* **wrapping, wrapped.** fold around; cover (person, thing) in (folding material or garment); *phr v* **wrap up 1** put on warm clothes 2 complete (task, agreement) 3 make obscure (by using difficult words) (*idm* **wrapped up in** *coll* engrossed in); *n* garment covering woman's shoulders; *idm* **under wraps** *coll* being kept secret; *ns* **wrapper** protective outer covering (*esp* for goods on sale or sent by mail); **wrapping** material, used to cover or wrap something (**w. paper** paper for wrapping parcel or gift)

wrath *n* anger; *a* **-ful;** *adv* **-ly;** *n* **-ness**.

wreak *v* give vent to (anger, etc.); exact (vengeance).

wreath *n* circle of intertwined leaves or flowers; garland; wisp of smoke; *v* **wreathe** twist, wind into wreath;

surround; wind round.

wreck n destruction esp of ship by wind and waves; ship fast on rocks; ruin; broken remains of structure; v cause wreck of; ns **-age; -er** one who engineers wreck.

wren n species of small songbird.

wrench n **1** violent twist **2** adjustable tool to turn nuts **3** fig grief felt at separation; v twist; seize forcibly.

wrest v tear away, take by force.

wrestle v grapple with and try to throw opponent; fig strive with (difficulties, etc.); n **wrestler**.

wretch n miserable unfortunate person; a **-ed** miserable, unhappy; squalid; adv **-ly;** n **-ness**.

wriggle n squirming, twisting movement; v move thus.

wright n worker who builds.

wring v twist; squeeze out moisture; pt, pp **wrung;** idm **wringing wet** very wet; n **-er** machine for wringing clothes.

wrinkle n **1** small crease, fold esp of skin **2** coll small, unexpected problem; v make wrinkles in; pucker; a **-kly**.

wrist n joint between forearm and hand.

wrist band n part of sleeve covering wrist.

wrist shot n ice hockey play with puck pushing against stick blade, then snapping forward.

writ n leg document issued in sovereign's name giving instructions to do or refrain from doing, something.

write v **1** mark paper, etc. with symbols representing words or sounds **2** compose (letter for sending; work for publication, etc.) **3** complete (check) in words and figures with signature; pt **wrote,** pp **written;** phr vs **write down** record in writing; **write off** acknowledge as irretrievable or irreparable (n **w. -off**) **2** treat (debt) as no longer existing; **write off (for)** send written request (for); **write out** write in full; **write up** give full written account of (n **w. -up** report or review); ns **writer; writing 1** act of writing (a of or for writing) **2** written symbols; handwriting **3** form of written expression (pl literary works).

writhe v twist, contort body about (in pain, etc.); be distorted.

written pp of **write**.

wrong a **1** wicked **2** incorrect **3** mistaken in opinion, etc. **4** unsuitable; idm **go wrong 1** miscalculate; make errors **2** stop functioning properly **3** become difficult, troublesome; n **1** that which is wrong **2** harmful act; idm **in the wrong** responsible for error; blameworthy; v do wrong to; ns **-doer; -doing;** v **w. -foot** esp sport put at disadvantage by change of

tactics; a **wrongful** unjust or illegal; adv **-ly;** n **-ness; w.-headed** obstinately holding mistaken opinion; misguided; adv **-ly;** n **-ness**.

wrote pt of **write**.

wrought a worked; **w. iron** iron hammered, beaten into shape.

wrung pt, pp of **wring**.

wry a **1** twisted **2** fig ironical; expressing distaste; adv **-ly;** n **-ness;** n **wryneck** bird related to woodpecker; a **wry-necked** with deformed, twisted neck.

wunderkind n child prodigy; one who succeeds quickly in a competitive area.

a
b
c
d
e
f
g
h
i
j
k
l
m
n
o
p
q
r
s
t
u
v
w
x
y
z

A
B
C
D
E
F
G
H
I
J
K
L
M
N
O
P
Q
R
S
T
U
V
W
X
Y
Z

X, x *n math* unknown quantity; *fig* any person, anything unknown.

Xanadu *n* exotic, unusual place.

xanthic *a* yellow.

xanthan gum *n* thickening agent used in prepared foods and pharmaceuticals.

X chromosome *n* the set chromosome with female characteristics.

xen-, xeno- *prefix* relating to hospitality; external, foreign.

xenogenesis *n* offspring that differ markedly from either parent.

xenon *n* inert, heavy gas present in air.

xenophile *n* someone attracted to anything foreign, *e.g.*, people, culture, languages, etc.

xenophobia *n* irrational hatred or fear of foreigners, strangers.

X-er *n* member of Generation X.

xer(o)- *prefix* dry; dryness.

Xerography *n* [TM] dry photocopying process.

xerophilous *a* able to thrive in conditions of drought; *n* **xerophyte** drought-loving plant.

Xerox [TM] **1** dry process for making multiple photocopies **2** photocopy thus made; *v* produce photocopy by this method; *n* **X. machine**.

XL *abbr* extra long or extra large.

Xmas *n coll* Christmas.

X-rated *a* (*of film, video*) classified as unsuitable for young people under 18 years of age; *n* **X-rating**.

X-ray *n* **1** *usu pl* electromagnetic short-wave radiation capable of penetrating matter **2** photograph taken with this **3** medical examination by this method; *v* take such a

photograph or examine by this method.

xylem *n* woody tissue of plants.

xyl(o)- *prefix* wood, pertaining to wood.

xylograph *n* woodengraving; *n* **-grapher**; *a* **-graphic**.

xyloid *a* of, like wood.

xylophone *n* musical percussion instrument of graduated wooden bars that vibrate when struck.

yacht n light sailing vessel used for racing or pleasure-cruising; n **-sman** owner or sailor of yacht.

yahoo n coarse ignorant person.

yak, yack¹ v sl talk noisily and continuously on trivial matters (*also* **yak**); n sl chat; ns **-ing**; **yackety-yack** sl incessant chatter (*also* **yakkety-yak**).

yak² n long-haired ox of Central Asia.

yam n fleshy edible root of tropical climbing plant; sweet potato.

yammer v coll talk incessantly in complaining manner; n **-ing.**

yang n (in Chinese philosophy) active male principle; of heat, light, dryness.

yank v coll pull sharply, jerk; n sharp tug.

Yankee n (also **Yank**) inhabitant of New England states; coll American.

yap n bark of small dog; v **yapping, yapped.** yelp, bark; coll chatter.

yard¹ n unit of length, 36 in; long spar supporting sail; n **yardstick** yard measure; fig standard of comparison.

yard² n **1** enclosed space, often paved, adjoining building **2** enclosure for some specific purpose.

yarmulke n skullcap worn by Jews, esp for prayer.

yarn n continuous thread of twisted fibers (of wool, cotton, etc.); coll tale, chat; v tell a yarn; talk at length.

yarrow n white-flowered perennial herb.

yashmak n veil worn by Muslim women.

yaw v deviate; n deviation.

yawl n small sailboat.

yawn v **1** open mouth widely and inhale involuntarily **2** fig open wide; gape; n act of yawning esp arising from boredom, sleepiness.

Y chromosome n sex chromosome of male cells.

yea interj, n yes; affirmative statement.

yeah adv sl yes.

year n period of time taken by Earth to revolve once round Sun; unit of time, 365¼ days; n **y.book** book of information revised each year; a **y.long** lasting all year; n **yearling** animal one year old; a **yearly** every year; adv annually.

yearn v desire earnestly; feel tender longing toward; n **yearning.**

yeast n fungoid substance used as ferment in brewing, bread-making, etc.; a **yeasty** frothy, fermenting.

yell v cry loudly and sharply; n loud piercing cry.

yellow a **1** of color between green and orange in spectrum **2** similar to color of gold, lemons, etc. **3** sl cowardly; n this color; ns **y. fever** serious infectious tropical disease; **y.hammer** yellow feathered bird; **y.jacket** vicious ground wasp with yellow; **Y. Pages** telephone directory arranged under categories of business, etc.; **y. press, y. journalism** newspapers trading on sensationalism; v turn yellow, esp with age; as **-ed; -ing.**

yelp v give short sharp bark of pain or anger; n such cry.

A
B
C
D
E
F
G
H
I
J
K
L
M
N
O
P
Q
R
S
T
U
V
W
X
Y
Z

yen n 1 Japanese currency 2 idm intense desire, urge.

yeoman n hist small landowner cultivating his own land; **y. service** effective assistance; n **yeomanry** yeomen collectively; territorial volunteer cavalry force recruited mainly from country districts.

yes interj expressing affirmation, consent; is that so? n **yes-man** one who always agrees with his leader's opinions.

yesterday n day before today; pl -s past times, former days.

yesteryear n lit recent past.

yet adv until now; now; besides; conj nevertheless, but still; idm **as yet** so far; until now.

yeti n hairy humanoid creature believed to live in Himalayan mountains (also **Abominable Snowman**).

yew n evergreen coniferous tree; its wood.

Yiddish n mixed dialect of German, Hebrew, and Slavonic, spoken by Jews in Europe, America, Israel, etc.

yield v 1 produce, return as food 2 bring in (as financial return) 3 concede; give up; 4 be amenable (to treatment); n amount produced; result, profit, return; a **-ing 1** flexible 2 easily persuaded.

yin n (in Chinese philosophy) inactive female principle, of dark, cold, and wet.

yip v bark sharply.

yippee interj shout of delight.

YMCA abbr Young Men's Christian Association.

yodel v yodeling, yodeled. warble, changing rapidly from natural voice to falsetto; n wordless song or cry in this style.

yoga n Hindu system of relaxation, exercise, and meditation, controlling the body and mind; n **yogi** one who practices yoga.

yogurt, yoghurt n thick milk preparation, fermented by bacterial action.

yoke n 1 crosspiece shaped to fit necks of draft animals, to which plow, etc., may be attached 2 part of garment cut to fit shoulders 3 fig authority; dominion; v harness with yoke; fig unite.

yokel n countryman; rustic.

yolk n yellow central part of egg.

Yom Kippur n Jewish holiday (Day of Atonement) marked with fasting and prayer.

yon a lit that, those over there; a ar **yonder** over there; adv in that direction.

yore n time past.

Yorkshire pudding n baked batter eaten with roast beef.

you pron 2nd pers sing, pl) 1 person(s) lately spoken to 2 one, anyone.

you'd contracted form of 1 you had 2 you would.

you'll contracted form of you will.

you're contracted form of you

are.

young a in early stages of life; not yet old; immature; inexperienced; n offspring; n **-ster** child esp boy.

your a belonging to you; pron **yours** poss of you idm **yours truly 1** formally polite phrase for ending letter 2 coll myself; pron **yourself** emphatic form of you (pl **yourselves**) idm (**all**) **by yourself 1** alone 2 unaided; idm (**keep/have** etc) **to yourself** (keep/have) as exclusively for you or as a secret.

youth n early life; state of being young; young person; young people; a **-ful;** n **-ness.**

you've contracted form of you have.

yowl v, n (make) loud wailing cry.

yo-yo toy consisting of double disk with groove between that runs up and down on a string.

yucca n tall plant with white bell-like flowers.

yuck interj sl expressing disgust; a **-y** sl disgusting (also **yukky**).

Yule n Christmas season or festival; **Yuletide** Christmas time.

yuppie, yuppy n coll ambitious young person in well-paid professional or business job; a typical of such people and their lifestyle.

YWCA abbr Young Women's Christian Association.

zabaglione n It rich creamy sauce of egg yolk, sugar, and sweet wine, usu served over fruit for dessert.

zaftig a Y plump, well-rounded womanly figure.

zany a wacky, crazy; adv **-ly;** n **-ness;** n 1 clown 2 idiot, fool.

zap v **zapping, zapped.** coll 1 move suddenly with great force 2 attack with destructive force.

zapper n electric device that kills insects; constant TV channel changer.

zeal n enthusiastic; earnest; adv **-ly;** n **-ness;** a **zealous** full of zeal; n **zealot** fanatic.

zebra n striped African quadruped.

Zen a, n (of) Buddhist sect seeking truth through meditation.

zenith n point of heavens directly overhead; fig highest point, climax; acme.

zephyr n 1 west wind; 2 lit gentle breeze 3 very thin fine woolen fabric.

zeppelin n German dirigible airship used in World War I.

zero n 1 figure 0 2 starting point in scale of measurement 3 fig lowest point; phr v **zero in on** 1 aim (missile, etc.) at 2 fig direct one's attention to; n **z.-hour** exact time at which important operation (esp mil) is due to begin.

zest n 1 keenness; gusto; ardor 2 relish; flavoring; a **-ful;** adv **-ly.**

Zeus n Greek king of the god.

zigzag n line having repeated sharp bends in alternate directions; shaped as the letter "z"; a forming zigzag; adv with such course; v **zigzagging, zigzagged.** move in such course.

zilch n sl zero; nothing.

zillion det, n, pron extremely large number.

zimmer frame [TM] n metal walking frame.

zinc n bluish white metallic element.

zing n 1 sharp singing sound 2 excitement.

zinnia n annual plant of aster family.

Zion n hill in Jerusalem; fig City of Jerusalem; religious system of Jews; Christianity; n **Zionism** political and military movement which established independent Jewish state of Israel.

zip n 1 device for fastening with two rows of interlocking teeth, opened by sliding grip 2 **zipper** light whizzing sound 3 coll energy, vigor; v **zipping, zipped.** fasten with zipper; ns **Zip code** numerical code used to sort mail; a **zippy** coll fast.

zircon n transparent mineral used as gem.

zit n sl pimple.

zither n flat, stringed musical instrument.

ziti n short tubular pasta.

zodiac n imaginary belt in heavens, divided into twelve sections or signs, within which moon, sun, and chief planets have their paths; a **-al.**

zombie n 1 supernatural power in revived corpse in voodoo belief 2 coll one who acts mechanically, without feeling or intelligence; as **-ish, -like.**

A
B
C
D
E
F
G
H
I
J
K
L
M
N
O
P
Q
R
S
T
U
V
W
X
Y

zone *n* belt, band; one of five horizontal regions of earth differentiated by climate; specified area, region; *a* **zonal;** *n* **zoning** designated areas of town, etc.

zonked *a sl* **1** exhausted **2** drunk, drugged.

zoo *n* park where wild animals are kept and exhibited.

zoolite *n* fossil animal.

zoology *n* scientific study of animals; *n* **-logist;** *a* **-logical** of, for zoology (*n* **z.gardens** or **zoo** place where wild animals are exhibited), *ns* **zoo-dynamics** animal physiology; **zoogeography** study of distribution of animals on surface of earth.

zoom *v* **1** compel aircraft to ascend rapidly at sharp angle **2** *fig* rise sharply in price; *n* **zoom** zooming; *n* **z. lens** camera lens allowing quick focus change, making distant subject suddenly seem much closer.

zoonosis *n* disease that can be transmitted from animals to humans.

zoophyte *n* plantlike invertebrate animal, *e.g.*, sponge.

zucchini *n sing* or *pl* green summer squash.

Zulu *n* member, language of Bantu people of S Africa.

zwieback *n* crisp, twice-baked bread.

zydeco *n* Cajun dance music that combines blues and Louisiana two-step.

zygote *n* fertilized ovum.